T0190143

Lecture Notes in Computer Science 12896

More information about this subseries at http://www.springer.com/series/7409

Denis Dennehy · Anastasia Griva ·
Nancy Pouloudi · Yogesh K. Dwivedi ·
Ilias Pappas · Matti Mäntymäki (Eds.)

Responsible AI and Analytics for an Ethical and Inclusive Digitized Society

20th IFIP WG 6.11 Conference on e-Business, e-Services and e-Society, I3E 2021
Galway, Ireland, September 1–3, 2021
Proceedings

Springer

Editors
Denis Dennehy
National University of Ireland, Galway
Galway, Ireland

Nancy Pouloudi
Athens University of Economics
and Business
Athens, Greece

Ilias Pappas
University of Agder
Kristiansand, Norway

Norwegian University of Science
and Technology
Trondheim, Norway

Anastasia Griva
National University of Ireland, Galway
Galway, Ireland

Yogesh K. Dwivedi
Swansea University
Swansea, UK

Symbiosis Institute of Business Management
Pune
Pune, India

Matti Mäntymäki
University of Turku
Turku, Finland

ISSN 0302-9743 ISSN 1611-3349 (electronic)
Lecture Notes in Computer Science
ISBN 978-3-030-85446-1 ISBN 978-3-030-85447-8 (eBook)
https://doi.org/10.1007/978-3-030-85447-8

LNCS Sublibrary: SL3 – Information Systems and Applications, incl. Internet/Web, and HCI

This Springer imprint is published by the registered company Springer Nature Switzerland AG
The registered company address is: Gewerbestrasse 11, 6330 Cham, Switzerland

Preface

This book presents the proceedings of the 20th International Federation of Information Processing (IFIP) Conference on e-Business, e-Services, and e-Society (I3E), which was hosted in Galway, Ireland, 1–3 September 2021. The annual I3E conference is a core part of Working Group 6.11, which aims to organize and promote exchange of information and co-operation related to all aspects of e-business, e-services, and e-society (the three Es). The I3E conference series is truly interdisciplinary and welcomes contributions from both academics and practitioners alike.

The central theme of the 2021 conference was Responsible AI and Analytics for an Ethical and Inclusive Digitized Society although, in line with the inclusive nature of the I3E series, all papers related to e-Business, e-Services, and e-Society were welcome. Digital technologies (e.g., AI, Blockchain, Big Data Analytics), and ICT in general, create opportunities and unintended or negative consequences for individuals and society (Gupta et al., 2021; Majchrzak et al., 2016). These opportunities and consequences have not been evenly distributed. Therefore, the aim of the conference was to bring together a community for the advancement of knowledge regarding the adoption, use, impact, and value of digital technologies across e-business, e-services, and e-society.

Despite the many personal, economic, and societal benefits offered by AI and analytics (Dennehy, 2020; Pappas et al., 2018), their use raises a variety of ethical concerns that need to be addressed in order to create a "good AI society" (Fossa Wamba et al., 2021). Ethics permeates the entire analytics process, from what data to use, to how to represent the extracted knowledge and exploit the insights to create economic and social value. Ethical concerns (e.g., illegitimate surveillance, invasion of privacy, unemployment, malicious use, etc.) are frequently used to portray AI and other digital technologies as a danger to humanity. For example, digital exclusion is part of the overall challenge of exclusion, a growing phenomenon which carries with it a series of deteriorations in life paths (e.g., poor lifelong earnings and an increased risk of marginalization). There are many who are currently excluded for reasons of low income and education, location, culture, trust and confidence levels or various disabilities. These concerns warrant the attention of the academic community to ensure the information society is built on a foundation in which integrity and rigor for good science will promote quality systems, and good ethics will promote good professional practice (Calzarossa et al., 2009). Hence, in order to be able to practice in an ethical manner, professionals must see vistas beyond technology (Stoodley et al., 2010).

At the same time, we acknowledge that AI and other digital technologies can offer transformational power across sectors, namely, public (Alshahrani et al., 2021), private (Mikalef and Gupta, 2021), and not-for-profit (Dennehy et al., 2021), ranging from enhanced business operations and supply chains (Cadden et al., 2021) to reinventing business models (Duan et al., 2019) to decision-making (Paschen et al., 2020) to changing the nature of work (Schwartz et al., 2019) to enhanced human capabilities (e.g., AI-enabled recruiting) (Dwivedi et al., 2021).

The Call for Papers solicited submissions in two main categories: full research papers and short research-in-progress papers. Each submission was reviewed by at least two knowledgeable academics in the field, in a double-blind process. The 2021 conference received submissions from more than 33 countries across the world, including China, Mexico, India, Pakistan, Japan, Kenya, Ghana, Morocco, South Africa, Finland, Sweden, Norway, Greece, the Netherlands, the UK, Papua New Guinea, Canada, and the USA to name a few. The best papers were selected for inclusion in a special issue of Information Systems Frontiers or their authors were given the opportunity to enhance the manuscript for fast-track review and publication in International Journal of Information Management and Journal of Decision Systems. The final set of 57 full papers and 8 short papers submitted to I3E 2021 and appearing in these proceedings were clustered into twelve groups, each of which are outlined below.

Part I encapsulates a core theme of the conference, with nine manuscripts that address the adoption and diffusion of AI for digital transformation and public good.

Part II contains five manuscripts relating to AI and analytics for decision making.

Part III continues the core theme of the conference, drawing together seven manuscripts related AI philosophy, ethics, and governance.

Part IV complements the previous clusters, with five manuscripts related to privacy and transparency in a digitized society.

Part V captures five manuscripts focused on digitally enabled sustainable organizations and societies.

Part VI dovetails with the theme of the previous cluster, with five manuscripts that address digital technologies and organizational capabilities.

Part VII consists of four manuscripts that investigate the role of AI and analytics in digitizing supply chains.

Part VIII contains five manuscripts that address customer behavior and e-business.

Part IX is made up of four manuscripts that examine the opportunities afforded by blockchain technology.

Part X consists of three manuscripts that explore the growing use of AI and analytics in the context of information systems development.

Part XI draws together eight manuscripts that explore social media analytics in a variety of contexts.

Part XII is the final cluster of these proceedings, with five manuscripts focused on AI and analytics in the context of teaching and learning.

In addition to the above papers, we were delighted to welcome Professor Katina Michael, Professor H. Raghav Rao, and Professor Dinesh Kumar as our keynote speakers.

Katina Michael has recently moved to Arizona State University, holding a joint appointment in the School for the Future of Innovation in Society and the School of Computing, Informatics, and Decision Systems Engineering. She is also the director of the Centre for Engineering, Policy, and Society. Katina Michael is also affiliated with the School of Computing and Information Technology at the University of Wollongong. Until recently she was the Associate Dean – International, in the Faculty of Engineering and Information Sciences. Katina was formerly the long-standing IEEE

Technology and Society Magazine editor-in-chief (2012–2017), and is presently an IEEE Consumer Electronics Magazine senior editor. Since 2008 she has been a board member of the Australian Privacy Foundation, and was formerly the Vice-Chair. Her research focuses on the socio-ethical implications of emerging technologies. She has written and edited six books, guest edited numerous special issue journals on themes related to radio-frequency identification (RFID) tags, supply chain management, location-based services, innovation, and surveillance/uberveillance. In 2017, Katina was awarded the prestigious Brian M. O'Connell Award for Distinguished Service to the IEEE Society on the Social Implications of Technology (IEEESSIT).

H. Raghav Rao was named the AT&T Distinguished Chair in Infrastructure Assurance and Security at The University of Texas at San Antonio College of Business in January 2016. He also holds a courtesy appointment as full professor in the UTSA Department of Computer Science. Prior to working at UTSA, H. R. Rao was the SUNY Distinguished Service Professor at the University at Buffalo. He graduated from Krannert Graduate School of Management at Purdue University. His interests are in the areas of management information systems, decision support systems, e-business, emergency response management systems, and information assurance. He has chaired sessions at international conferences and presented numerous papers. He also has co-edited four books, including Information Assurance Security and Privacy Services and Information Assurance in Financial Services. He has authored or co-authored more than 200 technical papers, of which more than 125 are published in archival journals. H. R. Rao was the inaugural recipient of The Bright Internet Award for his contributions to the information systems discipline by KMIS, the Korea Society of Management Information Systems. In 2018, H. R. Rao was awarded the International Federation for Information Processing (IFIP) Outstanding Service Award for significant service contributions to the field of information systems and information systems security. In November 2016, H. R. Rao received the prestigious Information Systems Society Distinguished Fellow Award (Class of 2016) for outstanding intellectual contributions to the information systems discipline. Rao's work has received best paper and best paper runner up awards at ISR, AMCIS, and ICIS. He has received funding for his research from the National Science Foundation, the Department of Defense, and the Canadian Embassy. He also received the Fulbright fellowship in 2004. Rao is a past chair of IFIP WG 8.11/11.13, the working group for Information Systems Security Research. He is co-editor-in-chief of Information Systems Frontiers, advisory editor of Decision Support Systems, associate editor of ACM TMIS, and senior editor at MIS Quarterly.

U Dinesh Kumar is a professor in decision sciences area and also the chairperson of DCAL at the Indian Institute of Management, Bangalore (IIMB). Dinesh Kumar holds a Ph.D. in Mathematics from IIT Bombay and has over two decades of teaching and consulting experience. He has been recognized as one of the top 10 most prominent analytics academicians in India for his extensive research in big data analytics. He has spearheaded the analytics education industry in India. IIMB was one of the first education institutes in the country to offer a regular long-duration certification program on Business Analytics & Intelligence (BAI) in the year 2010. U. Dinesh Kumar is also the Programme Director of the Big Data Analytics certification program. He has published several research articles in reputed academic journals such as the European Journal of

Operational Research, Annals of Operations Research, the International Journal of Production Economics, The Journal of Operational Research Society, Computers and Operations Research, IEEE Transactions on Reliability, and the International Journal of Reliability, Quality and Safety Engineering. He has also published more than 30 case studies on business analytics and machine learning algorithms based on Indian and multinational organizations at Harvard Business Publishing. He has authored 3 books and his most recent book titled "Business Analytics - The Science of Data Driven Decision Making" has been recommended by the All India Council for Technical Education (AICTE). He is the Founder-President of the Analytics Society of India (ASI). U. Dinesh Kumar regularly conducts corporate training programs in analytics and has trained many professionals in the field of analytics in the last 11 years. He has provided analytics consulting services to organizations such as Boston Consulting Group, GE Healthcare, General Motors, Hindustan Aeronautics Limited, Indian Army, TVS Motors, Wipro, and so on. He has conducted in-house training programs on analytics for several organizations including Accenture, Aditya Birla Group, Allianz Benelux, Ashok Leyland, Bank of America, CISCO, Fidelity, Honeywell, and ITC Infotech.

The conference schedule included the IFIP 6.11 Committee Meeting (day 1), live traditional Irish Sean-nós (old style) dancing (day 1), virtual coffee house meet ups (days 1-3), Dr. John Oredo chaired a panel discussion with renowned academics and practitioners on the topic of ethical AI (day 2), Best Paper award (day 2), and the conference concluded with a closing ceremony that included a presentation about I3E 2022 (day 3). Supplementary to the conference was a one-day doctoral symposium that involved presentations from 10 Ph.D. candidates and discussions with the symposium committee.

The success of the 20th IFIP I3E conference was a result of the enormous effort of numerous people and organizations. Firstly, this conference was only made possible by the continued support of WG 6.11 for this conference series and for selecting Galway to host I3E 2021, and for this we are extremely grateful. We are privileged to have received so many good quality submissions from authors across the globe and the biggest thank you must go to them for choosing I3E 2021 as the outlet for their current research. We are indebted to the Program Committee who generously gave up their time to provide constructive reviews and facilitate enhancement of the manuscripts submitted. Finally, we extend our sincere gratitude to everyone involved in organizing the conference, to our esteemed keynote speakers, and to Springer LNCS as the publisher of these proceedings, which we hope will be of use for continued development of research related to the three Es and social media in particular.

References

Cadden, T., Dennehy, D., Mantymaki, M., Treacy, R.: Understanding the influential and mediating role of cultural enablers of AI integration to supply chain. Int. J. Prod. Res. (2021)

Calzarossa, M. C., De Lotto, I., Rogerson, S.: Ethics and information systems—guest editors' introduction. Inf. Syst. Front. **12**(4), 357–359 (2010)

Dennehy, D., Oredo, J., Spanaki, K., Despoudi, S., Fitzgibbon, M.: Supply chain resilience in mindful humanitarian aid organizations: the role of big data analytics. Int. J. Oper. Prod. Manag. (2021)

Dennehy, D.: Ireland after the pandemic: utilising AI to kick-start a sustainable economic recovery. Cutter Bus. Technol. J. **33**(11), 22–27 (2020)

Dwivedi, Y.K., et al.: Artificial intelligence (AI): multidisciplinary perspectives on emerging challenges, opportunities, and agenda for research, practice and policy. Int. J. Inf. Manag. **57**, 101994 (2021)

Gupta, M., Parra, C., Dennehy, D.: Questioning racial and gender bias in AI recommendations: do individual-level cultural values matter? Inf. Syst. Front. 1–17 (2021)

Wamba, S.F., Bawack, R.E., Guthrie, C., Queiroz, M.M., Carillo, K.D.A.: Are we preparing for a good AI society? A bibliometric review and research agenda. Technol. Forecast. Soc. Change **164**, 120482 (2021)

Mikalef, P., Gupta, M.: Artificial intelligence capability: conceptualization, measurement calibration, and empirical study on its impact on organizational creativity and firm performance. Inf. Manag. **58**(3), 103434 (2021)

Pappas, I.O., Mikalef, P., Giannakos, M.N., Krogstie, J., Lekakos, G.: Big data and business analytics ecosystems: paving the way towards digital transformation and sustainable societies. Inf. Syst. e-Bus. Manag. **16**(3), 479–491 (2018)

Paschen, J., Wilson, M., Ferreira, J.J.: Collaborative intelligence: how human and artificial intelligence create value along the B2B sales funnel. Bus. Horiz. **63**(3), 403– 414 (2020)

Stoodley, I., Bruce, C., Edwards, S.: Expanding ethical vistas of IT professionals. Inf. Syst. Front. **12**(4), 379–387 (2010)

Majchrzak, A., Markus, M.L., Wareham, J.: Designing for digital transformation: lessons for information systems research from the study of ICT and societal challenges. MIS Q. **40**(2), 267–277 (2016)

September 2021

Denis Dennehy
Anastasia Griva
Nancy Pouloudi
Yogesh K. Dwivedi
Ilias Pappas
Matti Mäntymäki

Organization

Conference Chairs

Denis Dennehy	National University of Ireland Galway, Ireland
Anastasia Griva	National University of Ireland Galway, Ireland

Conference Co-chairs

Yogesh K. Dwivedi	Swansea University, UK
Matti Mäntymäki	University of Turku, Finland
Ilias Pappas	University of Agder and NTNU, Norway
Nancy Pouloudi	Athens University of Economics and Business, Greece

Program Co-chairs and Co-editors of Conference Proceedings

Denis Dennehy	National University of Ireland Galway, Ireland
Anastasia Griva	National University of Ireland Galway, Ireland
Nancy Pouloudi	Athens University of Economics and Business, Greece
Yogesh K. Dwivedi	Swansea University, UK
Matti Mäntymäki	University of Turku, Finland
Ilias Pappas	University of Agder and NTNU, Norway

I3E 2021 Keynote Speakers

Katina Michael	Arizona State University, USA
H. Raghav Rao	The University of Texas San Antonio, USA
Dinesh Kumar	Indian Institute of Management Bangalore, India

Doctoral Consortium Co-chairs

Kieran Conboy	National University of Ireland Galway, Ireland
Nancy Pouloudi	Athens University of Economics and Business, Greece
Cleopatra Bardaki	Harokopio University, Greece

I3E 2021 Program Committee

Aishvarya	Indian Institute of Management Bangalore, India
Ali Tarhini	Sultan Qaboos Univeristy, Oman
Ali Intezari Harsini	University of Queensland, Australia
Alta Van der Merwe	University of Pretoria, South Africa
Amit Anand Tiwari	Indian Institute of Management Rohtak, India
Andreas D. Landmark	SINTEF, Norway

Angeliki Karagiannaki	Athens University of Economics and Business, Greece
Antoine Harfouche	Université Paris Dauphine, France
Aparna Gonibeed	Manchester Metropolitan University, UK
Ariana Polyviou	University of Nicosia, Cyprus
Arif Wibisono	Institut Teknologi Sepuluh Nopember (ITS) Surabaya, Indonesia
Arisa Shollo	Copenhagen Business School, Denmark
Arpan Kar	Indian Institute of Technology Delhi, India
Bernard Quinio	Université Paris Nanterre, France
Brenda Scholtz	Nelson Mandela University, South Africa
Brendan Keegan	Manchester Metropolitan University, UK
Caleb Amankwaa Kumi	Kwame Nkrumah University of Science and Technology, Ghana
Carina De Villiers	University of Pretoria, South Africa
Cathal Doyle	Victoria University of Wellington, New Zealand
Chris Barry	National University of Ireland Galway, Ireland
Christian Janiesch	Julius-Maximilians-Universität Würzburg, Germany
Christoph Peters	University of Saint Gallen, Switzerland
Christos Douligeris	University of Piraeus, Greece
Cleopatra Bardaki	Harokopio University, Greece
Conn Smyth	National University of Ireland Galway, Ireland
Corné Van Staden	UNISA, South Africa
Cristina Paupini	Oslo Metropolitan University, Norway
David Asamoah	Kwame Nkrumah University of Science and Technology, Ghana
Davit Marikyan	Newcastle University, UK
Debora Jeske	University College Cork, Ireland
Devinder Bahadur Thapa	University of Agder, Norway
Dimitris Papakiriakopoulos	University of West Attica, Greece
Dimosthenis Kotsopoulos	Athens University of Economics and Business, Greece
Dinara Davlembayeva	Newcastle University, UK
Djamal Benslimane	Claude Bernard University Lyon 1, France
Dora Trachana	Athens University of Economics and Business, Greece
Douglas Parry	Stellenbosch University, South Africa
Sandip Mukhopadhyay	Institute of Management Technology, India
Parijat Upadhyay	IMT Nagpur, India
Edward Bernroider	Vienna University of Economics and Business, Austria
Efpraxia D. Zamani	University of Sheffield, UK
Ekaterina Glebova	University of Paris-Saclay, France
Eleftherios Manousakis	Athens University of Economics and Business, Greece
Elena Parmiggiani	Norwegian University of Science and Technology, Norway
Eleni Zampou	Athens University of Economics and Business, Greece
Elias Polytarchos	Athens University of Economics and Business, Greece
Elli Diakanastasi	Athens University of Economics and Business, Greece

Emanuele Gabriel Margherita	University of Tuscia, Italy
Fred Creedon	Munster Technological University, Ireland
Georgios Zois	Athens University of Economics and Business, Greece
Gustavo Velasco-Hernandez	Munster Technological University, Ireland
Hafiz Imtiaz Ahmad	Higher Colleges of Technology, UAE
Hanlie Smuts	University of Pretoria, South Africa
Hans Weigand	Tilburg University, The Netherlands
Hans-Dieter Zimmermann	Eastern Switzerland University of Applied Sciences, Switzerland
Hassan Dennaoui	University of Balamand, Lebanon
Hiroshi Yoshiura	The University of Electro-Communications, Japan
Hongxiu Li	Tampere University, Finland
Hugo Lotriet	University of South Africa, South Africa
Jamil Arida	Saint Joseph University, Lebanon
Jan H. Kroeze	UNISA, South Africa
Janis Gogan	Bentley University, Massachusetts, USA
Jari Veijalainen	University of Jyvaskyla, Finland
Jaspreet Kaur	Georgia State University, USA
Jean-Paul Van Belle	University of Cape Town, South Africa
Jennifer Ferreira	Victoria University of Wellington, New Zealand
Jenny Eriksson Lundström	Uppsala University, Sweden
John Oredo	University of Nairobi, Kenya
John Barry	Munster Technological University, Ireland
Joseph Walsh	Munster Technological University, Ireland
Katina Michael	Arizona State University, USA
Katja Bley	TU Dresden, Germany
Khalid Benali	Université de Lorraine, France
Konstantina Spanaki	Loughborough University, UK
Laleh Kasraian	De Montfort University, UK
Lisa Seymour	University of Cape Town, South Africa
Lynette Barnard	Nelson Mandela University, South Africa
Machdel Matthee	University of Pretoria, South Africa
Manas Paul	Institute of Management Technology, India
Manjul Gupta	Florida International University, Miami, USA
Markus Zimmer	University of Turku, Finland
Michael Lang	National University of Ireland Galway, Ireland
Mohammad Merhi	Indiana University South Bend, USA
Morteza Namvar	University of Queensland, Australia
Nandini Seth	Indian Institute of Management Bangalore, India
Natasha Evers	Trinity College Dublin, Ireland
Niki Panteli	Royal Holloway University of London, UK
Ola Ogunbodede	Newcastle University, UK
Omotolani Olowosule	Loughborough University, UK
Muhammad Ovais Ahmad	Karlstad University, Sweden
Paidi O'Reilly	Cork University Business School, Ireland

Pat Doody	Munster Technological University, Ireland
Patrick Mikalef	Norwegian University of Science and Technology, Norway
Peter Saba	EMLV Business School Paris, France
Pieter Toussaint	Norwegian University of Science and Technology, Norway
Polyxeni Vassilakopoulou	University of Agder, Norway
Rakhi Tripathi	FORE School of Management, India
Randsome Bawack	Toulouse Business School, France
Rennie Naidoo	University of Pretoria, South Africa
Rob Gleasure	Copenhagen Business School, Denmark
Rogier Van de Wetering	Open University, The Netherlands
Rónán Kennedy	National University of Ireland Galway, Ireland
Saad Alshahrani	University of Tabuk, South Arabia
Sachin Modgil	International Management Institute, Kolkata
Samrat Gupta	Indian Institute of Management Ahmedabad, India
Samuli Laato	University of Turku, Finland
Sarah Sabbaghan	London South Bank University, UK
Savvas Papagiannidis	Newcastle University, UK
Shang Gao	Örebro University, Sweden
Sobah Abbas Petersen	Norwegian University of Science and Technology, Norway
Sofia Papavlasopoulou	Norwegian University of Science and Technology, Norway
Stavros Lounis	Athens University of Economics and Business, Greece
Stephen McCarthy	Cork University Business School, Ireland
Stratos Baloutsos	Athens University of Economics and Business, Greece
Sunet Eybers	University of South Africa, South Africa
Sven Laumer	Otto-Friedrich-University Bamberg, Germany
Tania Prinsloo	University of Pretoria, South Africa
Tendani Mawela	University of Pretoria, South Africa
Trevor Cadden	University of Ulster, UK
Umair Ul Hassan	Maynooth University, Ireland
Vasiliki Chronaki	Athens University of Economics and Business, Greece
Vasiliki Koniakou	University of Turku, Finland
Vasilis Stavrou	Athens University of Economics and Business, Greece
Vigneswara Ilavarasan	Indian Institute of Technology Delhi, India
Vincent Dutot	Ipag Business School, France
Yashoda Karki	University of South-Eastern Norway
Ying Tueanrat	Newcastle University, UK

Contents

Adopting AI for Digital Transformation and Public Good

Affordances in Human-Chatbot Interaction: A Review of the Literature 3
Morten Johan Mygland, Morten Schibbye, Ilias O. Pappas, and Polyxeni Vassilakopoulou

AI in the Workplace: Exploring Chatbot Use and Users' Emotions 18
Lorentsa Gkinko and Amany Elbanna

Chatbots at Work: A Taxonomy of the Use of Chatbots in the Workplace . . . 29
Lorentsa Gkinko and Amany Elbanna

A Process Model of Artificial Intelligence Implementation Leading to Proper Decision Making. 40
Mohammad I. Merhi

AI: Opportunities and Challenges - The Optimal Exploitation of (Telecom) Corporate Data 47
Polyxeni Palaiogeorgou, Christos A. Gizelis, Antonios Misargopoulos, Filippos Nikolopoulos-Gkamatsis, Michalis Kefalogiannis, and Antonis M. Christonasis

Electronic Procurement Practices in the Public Sector: The Case of an Inter-organizational Information System in Ghana. 60
Michael Nartey Agbeko, John Effah, and Richard Boateng

Adopting Artificial Intelligence in the Saudi Arabian Public Sector: Preliminary Findings 71
Albandari Alshahrani, Denis Dennehy, and Matti Mäntymäki

Achieving Digital-Driven Patient Agility in the Era of Big Data 82
Rogier van de Wetering

Responsible Machine Learning Pilot Test Projects: A Medical Coding Case Study. 94
Samantha Champagnie and Janis L. Gogan

AI and Analytics Decision Making

Wise Data-Driven Decision-Making 109
Morteza Namvar and Ali Intezari

Data-Driven Collaborative Human-AI Decision Making 120
Gregoris Mentzas, Katerina Lepenioti, Alexandros Bousdekis, and Dimitris Apostolou

Always Trust the Advice of AI in Difficulties? Perceptions Around AI in Decision Making 132
Amit Kumar Kushwaha, Ruchika Pharswan, and Arpan Kumar Kar

Big Data Analytics Affordances for Social Innovation: A Theoretical Framework 144
Ilias O. Pappas and Devinder Thapa

COVID-19 Discrepancies Rising from Population Density Political Polarization Exacerbates Policy Gap 150
Mouwafac Sidaoui, Nicholas Abrams, and Abhishruti Adhikari

AI Philosophy, Ethics and Governance

Ethics and AI Issues: Old Container with New Wine? 161
Fred Niederman and Elizabeth White Baker

Governing Artificial Intelligence and Algorithmic Decision Making: Human Rights and Beyond 173
Vasiliki Koniakou

Analysing AI via Husserl and Kuhn How a Phenomenological Approach to Artificial Intelligence Imposes a Paradigm Shift 185
Daire Boyle

The Ethical Implications of Lawtech 198
Rónán Kennedy

Deploying AI Governance Practices: A Revelatory Case Study 208
Emmanouil Papagiannidis, Ida Merete Enholm, Chirstian Dremel, Patrick Mikalef, and John Krogstie

Towards Ecosystems for Responsible AI: Expectations on Sociotechnical Systems, Agendas, and Networks in EU Documents 220
Matti Minkkinen, Markus Philipp Zimmer, and Matti Mäntymäki

Ethics in AI: A Software Developmental and Philosophical Perspective 233
Tanay Chowdhury and John Oredo

Privacy and Transparency in a Digitised Society

Stop Ordering Machine Learning Algorithms by Their Explainability! An Empirical Investigation of the Tradeoff Between Performance and Explainability 245
Jonas Wanner, Lukas-Valentin Herm, Kai Heinrich, and Christian Janiesch

Gender Bias in AI: Implications for Managerial Practices. 259
Ayesha Nadeem, Olivera Marjanovic, and Babak Abedin

A Systematic Review of Fairness in Artificial Intelligence Algorithms 271
Khensani Xivuri and Hossana Twinomurinzi

Is Downloading This App Consistent with My Values?: Conceptualizing a Value-Centered Privacy Assistant 285
Sarah E. Carter

Operationalization of a Glass Box Through Visualization: Applied to a Data Driven Profiling Approach 292
Niels Netten, Arjen Suijker, Mortaza S. Bargh, and Sunil Choenni

Digital Enabled Sustainable Organisations and Societies

Artificial Intelligence and the Evolution of Managerial Skills: An Exploratory Study 307
Laurent Giraud, Ali Zaher, Selena Hernandez, and Akram Al Ariss

The Diffusion of Innovation Experience: Leveraging the Human Factor to Improve Technological Adoption Within an Organisation. 318
Gustav du Plessis and Hanlie Smuts

Exploring the Link Between Digitalization and Sustainable Development: Research Agendas. 330
Yashoda Karki and Devinder Thapa

Research Trends, Theories and Concepts on the Utilization of Digital Platforms in Agriculture: A Scoping Review 342
Abraham Kuuku Sam and Sara Saartjie Grobbelaar

The Impact of Industry 4.0 on the Business Models of Small and Medium Enterprises: A Systematic Literature Review. 356
Abdul Qadir Soondka and Hanlie Smuts

Digital Technologies and Organisational Capabilities

BIM as a Boundary Object in Construction Projects: A Knowledge-as-PracticePerspective 371
Jing Wang, Pamela Y. Abbott, and Efpraxia D. Zamani

Understanding How Enterprise Architecture Contributes to Organizational Alignment 383
Hong Guo, Jingyue Li, Shang Gao, and Darja Smite

How EA-Driven Dynamic Capabilities Enable Agility: The Mediating Role of Digital Project Benefits 397
Rogier van de Wetering

ICT-Based Inter-organisational Knowledge Exchange: A Narrative Literature Review Approach 411
Yuzhen Zhu, Efpraxia D. Zamani, Jorge Tiago Martins, and Ana Cristina Vasconcelos

Industry 4.0 and Organisations: Key Organisational Capabilities 423
Stefan Smuts, Alta van der Merwe, and Hanlie Smuts

Digitised Supply Chains

How Does IOS-Enabled Business Intelligence Enhance Supply Chain Performance? 441
Caleb Amankwaa Kumi, David Asamoah, and Benjamin Agyei-Owusu

A Review of AI in the Supply Chain Industry: Preliminary Findings 454
Conn Smyth, Denis Dennehy, and Samuel Fosso-Wamba

Dynamic Capability Theory as a Lens to Investigate Big Data Analytics and Supply Chain Agility 467
Trevor Cadden, Guangming Cao, Raymond Treacy, Ying Yang, and George Onofrei

The Effect of Data Driven Culture on Customer Development and Firm Performance: The Role of Supply Chain Information Sharing and Supply Chain Information Quality 481
Benjamin Agyei-Owusu, Mawuli Kobla Amedofu, David Asamoah, and Caleb Amankwaa Kumi

Customer Behavior and E-business

The Use of Elaboration Likelihood Model in eWOM Research: Literature Review and Weight-Analysis 495
Elvira Ismagilova, Yogesh K. Dwivedi, and Nripendra Rana

Explaining the Network of Factors that Influence the Timing of and Decision to Upgrade Enterprise Systems 506
Candice Petersen and Lisa F. Seymour

An Overview of the Application of Sentiment Analysis in Quality Function Deployment 519
Blessed Sarema and Stephen Matope

Cash is King, Isn't It? Payment Preferences and Switching Intentions of German Customers 532
Matthias Murawski, Serena Scomparin, and Markus Bick

Mining Segmentation Patterns Using e-Commerce Retail Data: An Experience Report 545
Anastasia Griva and Denis Dennehy

Blockchain

Blockchain in a Business Model: Exploring Benefits and Risks 555
Davit Marikyan, Savvas Papagiannidis, Omer Rana, and Rajiv Ranjan

Key Characteristics to Create Optimized Blockchain Consensus Algorithms 567
J. Leo and M. J. Hattingh

A Systematic Literature Review of Blockchain Consensus Protocols 580
Sikho Luzipo and Aurona Gerber

Blockchain's Impact on Consumer's Perspective in the Luxury Fashion Industry: A Position Paper 596
Jean Noonan and Patrick Doran

Information Systems Development

Digital Transformation of Software Development: Implications for the Future of Work 609
Samuli Laato, Matti Mäntymäki, Teemu Birkstedt, A. K. M. Najmul Islam, and Sami Hyrynsalmi

Business Analytics Continuance in Software Development Projects – A Preliminary Analysis 622
Muhammad Ovais Ahmad, Iftikhar Ahmad, and Iqra Sadaf Khan

Artificial Intelligence (AI) Capabilities, Trust and Open Source Software Team Performance 629
Babu Veeresh Thummadi

Social Media and Analytics

Modeling Malicious Behaviors and Fake News Dissemination on Social Networks 643
Kento Yoshikawa, Masatsugu Ichino, and Hiroshi Yoshiura

Developing Machine Learning Model for Predicting Social Media Induced Fake News 656
David Langley, Caoimhe Reidy, Mark Towey, Manisha, and Denis Dennehy

A Deep Multi-modal Neural Network for the Identification of Hate Speech from Social Media 670
Gunjan Kumar, Jyoti Prakash Singh, and Abhinav Kumar

Influencer is the New Recommender: Insights for Enhancing Social Recommender Systems 681
Ransome Epie Bawack and Emilie Bonhoure

Impact of COVID-19 Pandemic on E-participation of Fans in Sports Events 692
Vishal Mehra, Pooja Sarin, Prabhsimran Singh, Ravinder Singh Sawhney, and Arpan Kumar Kar

Investigating the Dynamics of Polarization in Online Discourse During COVID-19 Pandemic. 704
Samrat Gupta, Gaurav Jain, and Amit Anand Tiwari

Ecosystem of Social Media Listening Practices for Crisis Management 710
Lucia Castro Herrera, Tim A. Majchrzak, and Devinder Thapa

#SDG13: Understanding Citizens Perspective Regarding Climate Change on Twitter 723
Prabhsimran Singh, Surleen Kaur, Yogesh K. Dwivedi, Sandeep Sharma, and Ravinder Singh Sawhney

Teaching and Learning

A Multi-level Analysis of Mistrust/Trust Formation in Algorithmic Grading 737
Stephen Jackson and Niki Panteli

Computational Numeracy (CN) for Under-Prepared, Novice Programming Students 744
Carla Coetzee and Machdel Matthee

Using Data Analytics to Detect Possible Collusion in a Multiple Choice Quiz Test 757
Michael Lang

Perceptions of Students for a Gamification Approach: Cities Skylines as a Pedagogical Tool in Urban Planning Education 763
Tayyeb Ahmed Khan and Xin Zhao

Social Exclusion in Gamified Information Systems 774
Arthur E. van der Poll, Izak van Zyl, and Jan H. Kroeze

Correction to: Responsible AI and Analytics for an Ethical and Inclusive Digitized Society C1
Denis Dennehy, Anastasia Griva, Nancy Pouloudi, Yogesh K. Dwivedi, Ilias Pappas, and Matti Mäntymäki

Author Index 787

Adopting AI for Digital Transformation and Public Good

Affordances in Human-Chatbot Interaction: A Review of the Literature

Morten Johan Mygland[1], Morten Schibbye[1], Ilias O. Pappas[1,2(✉)], and Polyxeni Vassilakopoulou[1]

[1] Department of Information Systems, University of Agder, Universitetsveien 25, 4630 Kristiansand, Norway
{mortjm14,morten.schibbye,ilias.pappas,polyxenv}@uia.no
[2] Department of Computer Science, Norwegian University of Science and Technology, Sem Saelandsvei 9, 7491 Trondheim, Norway

Abstract. The present study advances our understanding of human-AI interactions, by identifying and analyzing chatbot affordances in prior research. The results of this review consolidate research findings on chatbots' affordances, which must be taken into consideration when chatbot-based services are designed and deployed. Specifically, the review of state-of-the-art literature led to the identification of nine high level affordances: Human Like Conversing, Assistance Provision, Facilitation, Distilling Information, Enriching Information, Context Identification, Personalization, Fostering Familiarity and Ensuring Privacy. Our contribution is twofold. First, we map the chatbot affordances identified in prior research and group them in higher-level, overarching affordances through a thematic analysis. Furthermore, we identify areas for future research providing a foundation for researchers aiming to engage with the research area.

Keywords: Chatbots · Human-Chatbot interaction · Human-AI interaction · Affordances · Review

1 Introduction

Chatbots, or conversational agents, are increasingly being used in various contexts to handle large volumes of inquiries from customers [1], to automate mundane tasks internally in organizations [2], or for the delivery of public services, with a focus on citizen inquiries and information [3]. They use natural language to interact and communicate with different users, allowing 'rich' and expressive digital interactions convincingly simulating how a human would behave in a conversation [4]. Chatbots not only automate communication tasks replacing humans but also, provide opportunities for developing new types of services through synergies between humans and digital agents [5]. Since the early chatbot developments back in the 1960s, chatbots have significantly improved leveraging advancements in machine learning (ML), natural language processing (NLP) [6], natural language understanding (NLU) [1], natural language generation (NLG) [7], and other artificial intelligence techniques. By 2024, chatbots are projected to facilitate

Published by Springer Nature Switzerland AG 2021
D. Dennehy et al. (Eds.): I3E 2021, LNCS 12896, pp. 3–17, 2021.
https://doi.org/10.1007/978-3-030-85447-8_1

142 billion US dollars of retail enabled by the advances in NLU capabilities that allow to significantly increase chatbot effectiveness [8].

There is an increase in implementing chatbots in online service encounters. Many companies communicate with their end users through chatbots, on either their own website or via social media [9]. Typically, chatbots are introduced to reduce or eliminate the waiting time customers spend on phone or email-inquiries or reduce the workload of chat employees [1]. Chatbots have proven to be very useful for addressing demand surges handling inquiries that correspond to the capacity of multiple human agents. This has been especially useful during the major crisis caused by the Covid-19 pandemic [10]. Recent studies discuss the required characteristics of chatbots along with the pitfalls that must be avoided [11, 12], while offering suggestions for further advancements in chatbot technologies through innovations such as sentiment-adaptive responses for increased empathy [13]. There is extensive research on chatbot features, nevertheless, for the design and deployment of chatbot-based services it is important to leverage insights that go beyond chatbots' capabilities. Service design relies on insights for the emergent relations between users and chatbots and especially the synergetic relationships that make possible human-AI hybridization in service offerings [14].

To better understand and explain the complex relations between humans and AI, we take an affordance theory perspective [15], as it can help conceptualize what action possibilities chatbots afford to their users. Affordances are "possibilities for goal-oriented action afforded to specified user groups by technical objects" [16]. Taking into account the vast increase of chatbot implementations across industries, it is critical to explore the action possibilities offered by chatbots helping to advance research and practice from the traditional uses of chatbots for task substitution (AI substitutes humans by chatbots responding to user inquiries) towards the combination of chatbots with human agents in new types of task assemblages.

The present study identifies, analyses, and integrates empirical research on chatbot affordances across different contexts. We performed a systematic literature review covering empirical studies done in the last five years in this research area. The research question is as follows: What affordances of chatbots are identified in prior literature? Our contribution is twofold. First, we map the chatbot affordances identified in prior research and group them in higher-level, overarching affordances through a thematic analysis. The results of this review offer important information on chatbots' affordances, which can inform the design of chatbot-based services. Furthermore, we identify areas for future research providing a foundation for researchers aiming to engage with this research area.

The remainder of the paper is organized as follows. First, we present the method used for selecting and analyzing the articles for this review. Then, we present the findings and the groupings of affordances. We continue by discussing the implication these findings have for further research, before we end with overall concluding remarks.

2 Research Method

In this systematic literature review we followed the process as described by Kitchenham [17] who presents a structured approach comprising three main steps: a) planning the review, where a detailed protocol containing specific search terms and inclusion/exclusion criteria is developed, b) conducting the review, where the selection, appraisal and synthesis of prior published research is performed and c) reporting the review, where the write-up is prepared. We used these steps as our methodological framework. Further, we implemented key principles offered by Webster and Watson [18] for the article analysis. Following these principles, we identified key concepts and created a concept-centric matrix that provides an overview of the literature reviewed.

To identify and select research articles to be reviewed, we used the terms "Chatbot AND affordance", "Conversational-agent AND affordance", "Chat-agent AND affordance". We searched for these combinations in the abstract, title and keywords of published articles. Moreover, we performed backward and forward searches to review relevant citations. While the main search was performed in Scopus, we used Google Scholar for our backward and forward searches.

Inclusion and exclusion criteria were established to reduce selection bias, guarantee the quality of the papers selected and increase the validity of our review. Peer-reviewed, empirical papers, written in English, published in the last five years were included. Conceptual papers that lacked empirical evidence, reviews, papers that did not have an author, all duplicate, and papers not in English were excluded. The initial search yielded 67 articles in total. The next step was to read the titles and abstracts of the articles identified checking their relevance to the research question. For this step the exclusion criteria were used. After this step, 48 papers were shortlisted. Finally, the full text of the shortlisted papers was assessed for relevance leading to 9 papers being included in the review. Figure 1 provides an overview of the selection process and Table 1 presents the list of articles included in the final review corpus.

Fig. 1. The literature selection process.

Table 1. Final article corpus

#	References
1	Barnett, A., Savic, M., Pienaar, K., Carter, A., Warren, N., Sandral, E., & Lubman, D. I. (2020). Enacting 'more-than-human' care: Clients' and counsellors' views on the multiple affordances of chatbots in alcohol and other drug counselling. International Journal of Drug Policy, 102910
2	Knote, R., Janson, A., Söllner, M., & Leimeister, J. M. (2020). Value Co-Creation in Smart Services: A Functional Affordances Perspective on Smart Personal Assistants. Journal of the Association for Information Systems, 78

(*continued*)

Table 1. *(continued)*

#	References
3	Lippert, A., Gatewood, J., Cai, Z., & Graesser, A. C. (2019). Using an Adaptive Intelligent Tutoring System to Promote Learning Affordances for Adults with Low Literacy Skills. Adaptive Instructional Systems. HCII 2019. Lecture Notes in Computer Science, 11597, 327–339
4	Lunberry, D., & Liebenau, J. (2020). Human or Machine? A Study of Anthropomorphism Through an Affordance Lens. Digital Transformation and Human Behavior. Lecture Notes in Information Systems and Organisation, 37, 201–215
5	Meske, C., Amojo, I., & Thapa, D. (2020). Understanding the Affordances of Conversational Agents in Mental Mobile Health Services. ICIS 2020 Proceedings
6	Moussawi, S. (2018). User Experiences with Personal Intelligent Agents: A Sensory, Physical, Functional and Cognitive Affordances View. SIGMIS-CPR'18: Proceedings of the 2018 ACM SIGMIS Conference on Computers and People Research, 86–92
7	Stoeckli, E., Dremel, C., Uebernickel, F., & Brenner, W. (2020, 06). How affordances of chatbots cross the chasm between social and traditional enterprise systems. Electron Markets, 30, 369–403
8	Stoeckli, E., Uebernickel, F., & Brenner, W. (2018). Exploring Affordances of Slack Integrations and Their Actualization Within Enterprises – Towards an Understanding of How Chatbots Create Value. Hawaii International Conference on System Sciences (HICSS)
9	Waizenegger, L., Seeber, I., Dawson, G., & Desouza, K. (2020). Conversational agents-exploring generative mechanisms and second-hand effects of actualized technology affordances. In Proceedings of the 53rd Hawaii international conference on system sciences

The full texts of the papers identified were analyzed. All the different chatbot affordances identified in the papers were listed. We then performed a thematic analysis grouping together affordances in higher level affordances. The outcome of this analysis is presented in the next section.

3 Results

This section presents the literature review results. Prior research has investigated the action possibilities provided by chatbots in different contexts. Across these different contexts, 91 different affordances have been identified and grouped in nine categories.

Affordances Related to Human-Like Conversing

Chatbots provide to users action possibilities for engaging in conversations. They represent a shift in how people interact with software applications. They can produce human-like message content allowing users to communicate with computers using natural language. Due to advancements in natural language processing and interpretation and progress in conversational modelling the flow of conversation with chatbots is becoming smoother than ever. Chatbots can infer users' intent, synthesize answers responding to users in natural language and retain the conversation context to answer follow-up questions. Table 2 provides an overview of the affordances related to human-like conversing in the literature reviewed.

Table 2. Affordances related to human-like conversing

Related affordances identified in the literature	
Capture, storage and renderings of voice recordings	Lunberry and Liebenau [19]
Mimicry of human-like conversation methods	
Mimicry of human-like conversational elements	
Presentation of human-like message content	
Fostering team cohesion	Stoeckli, Dremel [2]
Enforcing discipline and compliance	
Socializing	Waizenegger, Seeber [20]
Mitigating boredom	
Simulating a human-like interaction	
Depending on the degree of anthropomorphism of virtual anthropomorphic advisors, they afford users to establish positive emotions (such as empathy) to increase users' satisfaction during and after value co-creation in a U-shaped manner	
Through their anthropomorphic design, virtual anthropomorphic advisors help users overcome information disclosure barriers in value co-creation	
Hands-free and eyes-free use	Moussawi [21]
Communication	Lippert, Gatewood [22]

Affordances Related to Assistance Provision

Chatbots are commonly used to assist employees of organizations or external audiences (customers, patients, or citizens in general in the context of public services) in their everyday transactions. They can carry out a range of assistive tasks such as setting and getting reminders and notifications, invoking software functionality, or accessing relevant information. The chatbot assistance capabilities provide to users interesting

Table 3. Affordances related to assistance provision

Related affordances identified in the literature	
Receiving status notifications and updates	Stoeckli, Dremel [2]
Receiving real-time information	
Receiving metrics and key performance indicators	
Setting and getting reminders	
Setting and getting nudges/triggers to action	
Having messages processed and replaced	
Increasing visibility and ambient awareness	
Relieving employees from application switching	
Relieving employees from repetitive work	
Receiving status notifications and updates	Stoeckli, Uebernickel [23]
Receiving real-time information	
Receiving metrics and key performance indicators	
Getting reminded	
Getting nudges	
Getting a nudge to action and resolve it	
Invoking functionality	
Invoking functionality and making invocation visible	
Instantaneous solving of fact-based questions	Waizenegger, Seeber [20]
Executing tasks	
Help-seeking for personal issues	
Relief from mundane tasks	
Self-servicing	
Different affordances according to their unique combinations of material properties that influence value co-creation in smart services	Knote, Janson [24]
Afford users to spend more cognitive load on the actual value-creating task rather than on interacting with the system	
Afford users to identify the technical object as an expert in a certain domain	
Speedy assistance	Moussawi [21]
Usefulness	
Access relevant information	Meske, Amojo [25]
Engage with application	

(*continued*)

Table 3. (*continued*)

Related affordances identified in the literature	
Minimising human error and maximising expertise	Barnett, Savic [26]

novel action possibilities, they can offload some of their everyday tasks to these smart agents and they can get smart support for their exchanges with service providers. Table 3 provides an overview of the affordances related to assistance provision in the literature reviewed.

Affordances Related to Facilitation

Chatbots can offer facilitation in the relationship between users and organizations. They provide users action possibilities for querying information or invoking functionalities from third party systems without engaging directly with the third parties. They can unify access across multiple systems offering external integration. Overall, chatbots can reduce the effort required for different tasks through their facilitation. Table 4 provides an overview of the affordances related to facilitation in the literature reviewed.

Table 4. Affordances related to facilitation

Related affordances identified in the literature	
Capturing data in third party systems	Stoeckli, Dremel [2]
Querying information from third-party systems	
Invoking functions from third-party systems and make this invocation visible	
Unifying access to third-party systems	
Building rapid prototypes (F)	
General activity assistants afford smart service stakeholders to co-create value through external integration, and, thus, shape affordances accordingly in a reciprocal and dynamic manner	Knote, Janson [24]
Contact relevant institutions	Meske, Amojo [25]

Affordances Related to Distilling Information

Chatbots provide users with action possibilities related to distilling information. For instance, they aggregate information, they facilitate users' understanding of large information amounts and they can even help users reflect on the information they provide for their own mood or mental state. Table 5 provides an overview of the affordances related to distilling information in the literature reviewed.

Table 5. Affordances related to distilling information

Related affordances identified in the literature	
Receiving aggregated information	Stoeckli, Uebernickel [23]
Ensuring information flow through uncoupling	Stoeckli, Dremel [2]
Receiving aggregated information	
Afford users to effectively access and better understand large amounts of potentially consecutive information necessary for information-intensive value co-creation in a particular domain of interest	Knote, Janson [24]
Reflect own mood/mental state	Meske, Amojo [25]

Affordances Related to Enriching Information

Chatbots can enrich the information provided. For instance, they can enrich information visually or with additional text. This way, they can accelerate communication making it possible to connect more effectively. AI-enabled information enrichment makes chatbots more helpful as assistants in everyday tasks. Table 6 provides an overview of the affordances related to assistance provision in the literature reviewed.

Table 6. Affordances related to enriching information

Related affordances identified in the literature	
Having messages processed and enriched with additional information	Stoeckli, Dremel [2]
Having messages processed and visually enriched with user interface elements	
Voice facilitators afford the facility to complement or replace interaction modes other than voice in value co-creation with respect to specific user needs	Knote, Janson [24]
Voice facilitators afford the facility to complement other smart services through external integration that enable/shape new value co-creation possibilities	
General activity assistants rely on continuous adaptation in affordance actualization processes through crowd data integration to improve value co-creation	

Affordances Related to Context Identification

Chatbots can provide context to what users are talking about or looking for. Hence, they can identify problem-specific information, provide feedback as reaction and orient ongoing conversations. Related affordances are presented in Table 7.

Table 7. Affordances related to context identification

Related affordances identified in the literature	
Consolidating information flow	Stoeckli, Dremel [2]
Facilitating feedback as reaction and discussions	
Separating organizational units	
Capturing data	Stoeckli, Uebernickel [23]
Querying information	
Having messages processed and replaced	
Afford users to explore a wide range of value co-creation possibilities for different purposes within their ecosystem	Knote, Janson [24]
Identify problem specific information	Meske, Amojo [25]
Access to other affordances	
Identify relevant institutions	
Identify others with similar problems	
Identify problem specific information	

Affordances Related to Personalization

Chatbots contribute to the provision of personalized experiences. They are able to adapt interactions to their users providing tailored responses, adjusting their tone and style. Personalization means that the chat becomes more appealing to the user. As chatbots learn from interactions further they continually improve personalization. Related affordances found in the papers reviewed are presented in Table 8.

Table 8. Affordances related to personalization

Related affordances identified in the literature	
Personal assistance	Waizenegger, Seeber [20]
SPAs provide different affordances for specified users or user groups, which in turn influences value co-creation in smart services	Knote, Janson [24]
Personalization and learning from interactions	Moussawi [21]
Interactivity	Lippert, Gatewood [22]
Adaptivity	
Feedback	
Choice	
Nonlinear access	

(*continued*)

Table 8. (*continued*)

Related affordances identified in the literature	
Linked representations	
Open-ended learner input	

Affordances Related to Fostering Familiarity

The use of chatbots requires little prior experience as practically everybody is familiar with chat applications nowadays. Users are increasingly familiar with messaging and chatbots allow them to express their needs directly through a familiar interaction mode. The familiarity with the channel allows also tensions to emerge, user satisfaction can be followed by disappointment when expectations are not fulfilled. Related affordances found in the papers reviewed are presented in Table 9.

Table 9. Affordances related to fostering familiarity

Related affordances identified in the literature	
Emerging tensions: satisfaction and disappointment	Moussawi [21]
Emotional connection	
Familiarity and potential improvement	

Affordances Related to Ensuring Privacy

Chatbots employ privacy preserving approaches and may also act as gatekeepers for access to different functions. Chats may require the disclosure of key information about users so, it is important to ensure privacy in conversations. Related affordances found in the papers reviewed are presented in Table 10.

Table 10. Affordances related to ensuring privacy

Related affordances identified in the literature	
Adding gatekeepers that validate access to function of third-party systems	Stoeckli, Dremel [2]
Adding gatekeeper Stoeckli, Dremel [2]	Stoeckli, Uebernickel [23]
Leveraging anonymity	Waizenegger, Seeber [20]

(*continued*)

Table 10. (*continued*)

Related affordances identified in the literature	
If the user is aware that the data-driven active observer collects context and usage data, information disclosure barriers (such as privacy and trust concerns) will negatively influence value co-creation in smart services	Knote, Janson [24]

4 Discussion and Conclusions

The present study advances our understanding of human-AI interactions, by identifying and analyzing the affordances of chatbots through a systematic review of the state-of-the-art literature in the area. By conducting a thematic analysis, we present 9 higher level affordances that capture the variety of action possibilities that chatbots afford to their users. Table 11 provides a concise overview of the papers reviewed in the form of a concept matrix.

The results show that the literature covers the two key perspectives regarding the users of chatbots. These are: 1) the customers' perspective, including a large variety of audiences, such as consumers, patients, and service seeking citizens, and 2) the employee's perspective, including employees that seek interorganizational collaboration but also employees that simply aim to improve their efficiency in day-to-day tasks. Furthermore, prior research covers both text and voice based chatbots. The mapping of these affordances enables the better understanding of the complex interrelations between humans and AI enabled services, towards the creation of human-AI hybrids [14]. This is particularly interesting for the design and deployment of novel types of services.

The most commonly researched affordances for chatbots are *human-like conversing* and *assistance provision*. These two, form the basis of conventional human-chatbot interactions. Our study shifts attention beyond the conventional human chatbot interaction by pointing to 7 additional affordances. Specifically, the *facilitation* affordance indicates that there are significant opportunities for digital intermediation by chatbots in service provision. Such intermediation can pave the way towards the creation of one stop services, where the chatbots provide a gateway to multiple systems in an easy and seamless manner. Furthermore, the *distilling* and *enriching information* affordances create prospects for more synergies between chatbots and human service agents. For instance, chatbots can enrich the content of short messages drafted quickly by agents, increasing their efficiency allowing them to serve a greater number of customers. Furthermore, the *personalization* affordance is especially interesting as it can enable private and public organizations to revolutionize customer experience. Personalization may be achieved through implementation of authentication functionalities, that are widely used in other contexts. User authentication allows chatbots to access customers' personal and case-related data.

The findings reveal 3 affordances that need to be further researched aiming to more mature and reliable chatbot implementations through the use of emerging technologies. These are the *context identification*, *familiarity* and *privacy* affordances. Identifying context is critical in any service provision. For example, if the chatbot is aware that an

Table 11. Concept matrix

Article	User		Means of communication		Affordance								
	Customer	Employee	Text	Voice	Human Like Conversing	Assistance Provision	Facilitation	Distilling Information	Enriching Information	Context Identification	Personalisation	Fostering familiarity	Ensuring privacy
Stoeckli, Dremel [2]		X	X		X	X	X	X	X	X			X
Stoeckli, Uebernickel [23]		X	X			X		X		X			X
Waizenegger, Seeber [20]	X	X	X	X	X	X					X		X
Knote, Janson [24]	X		X	X	X	X	X	X	X	X	X		X
Moussawi [21]	X			X	X	X					X	X	
Meske, Amojo [25]	X		X			X	X	X		X			
Lunberry and Liebenau [19]	X			X	X								
Lippert, Gatewood [22]	X		X		X						X		
Barnett, Savic [26]	X		X			X							

inquiry relates to private or business purposes, it may provide the appropriate type of information in a faster way requiring less iterations. However, identifying the context in a human-chatbot interaction requires access to information that is not always available (e.g., due to privacy issues) or because the chatbot is not advanced enough to ask the right questions, as a human agent would do when interacting with a customer. Regarding familiarity, although the findings show that only one paper has explicitly examined related affordances, the general chatbot literature suggests that creating chatbots with high empathy that are able to mimic emotional responses remains a challenge [13]. Privacy is by itself a very complex and sensitive issue, thus creating challenges for chatbot development, as for example in cases where access to personal data is required for service provision.

The current work can contribute to research on AI and autonomous agents in the context of citizen and worker behavior towards successful digital transformation [27, 28]. Overall, we find that the studies reviewed, explored different chatbot characteristics and related action possibilities afforded to users. Nevertheless, we find little engagement with aspects that are critical for the actualization of affordances such as digital literacy and the elimination of digital inequalities [29] and the responsiveness of structures and processes at the organizational level. A clearer focus on relevant users' and organizational aspects could be helpful for service designers and those who define digital channel strategies in organizations. Affordances create potential, it is important to have in place the necessary conditions for goal-oriented actions [16]. In conclusion, we call for further research on affordances related to context identification, familiarity and privacy and on the different facilitating conditions for the actualization of chatbot affordances in different contexts.

References

1. Nuruzzaman, M., Hussain, O.K.: IntelliBot: a dialogue-based chatbot for the insurance industry. Knowl-Based Syst. **196**, 105810 (2020)
2. Stoeckli, E., Dremel, C., Uebernickel, F., Brenner, W.: How affordances of chatbots cross the chasm between social and traditional enterprise systems. Electron. Markets **30**(2), 369–403 (2020)
3. Mehr, H., Harvard Ash Center Technology & Democracy Fellow: Artificial Intelligence for Citizen Services and Government. Ash Center for Democratic Governance and Innovation, Harvard Kennedy School, August 2017, pp. 1–12 (2017)
4. Androutsopoulou, A., et al.: Transforming the communication between citizens and government through AI-guided chatbots. Gov. Inf. Q. **36**(2), 358–367 (2019)
5. Vassilakopoulou, P., Pappas, I.O.: Streamlining chatbot – chat employee interaction: an exploratory study. In: Information and Communication Technologies in Organizations and Society (ICTO 2020). Springer (2020)
6. Poser, M., Singh, S., Bittner, E.: Hybrid Service Recovery: Design for Seamless Inquiry Handovers between Conversational Agents and Human Service Agents. ScholarSpace (2021)
7. Gatt, A., Krahmer, E.: Survey of the State of the Art in natural language generation: core tasks, applications and evaluation. J. Artif. Intell. Res. **61**, 65–170 (2018)
8. Juniper Research: Chatbots: Vendor Opportunities & Market Forecasts 2020–2024 (2020)
9. Feine, J., Morana, S., Gnewuch, U.: Measuring Service Encounter Satisfaction with Customer Service Chatbots Using Sentiment Analysis. AIS eLibrary (2019)

10. National Association of State Chief Information Officers (NASCIO): Chat with us: How States are Using Chatbots to Respond to the Demands of COVID-19 (2020). https://www.nascio.org/wp-content/uploads/2020/06/NASCIO_ChatbotsRespondtoCOVID-19.pdf.
11. Amershi, S., et al.: Guidelines for human-AI interaction. In: Proceedings of the 2019 CHI Conference on Human Factors in Computing Systems. ACM, New York (2019)
12. Følstad, A., Nordheim, C.B., Bjørkli, C.A.: What makes users trust a chatbot for customer service? An exploratory interview study. In: Bodrunova, S.S. (ed.) INSCI 2018. LNCS, vol. 11193, pp. 194–208. Springer, Cham (2018). https://doi.org/10.1007/978-3-030-01437-7_16
13. Diederich, S., et al.: Emulating empathetic behavior in online service encounters with sentiment-adaptive responses: insights from an experiment with a conversational agent (2019)
14. Rai, A., Constantinides, P., Sarker, S.: Editor's comments: next-generation digital platforms: toward human–AI hybrids. MIS Q. **43**(1), iii–x (2019)
15. Gibson, J.J.: The theory of affordances. In: Perceiving, Acting and Knowing, pp. 67–82. Lawrence Erlbaum Associates, Mahwah (1977)
16. Markus, M.L., Silver, M.S.: A foundation for the study of IT effects: a new look at DeSanctis and Poole's concepts of structural features and spirit. J. Assoc. Inf. Syst. **9**(10), 5 (2008)
17. Kitchenham, B.: Procedures for Performing Systematic Reviews. Keele University Technical Report, UK, 2004, TR/SE-0401, pp. 1–26 (2004)
18. Webster, J., Watson, R.T.: Analyzing the past to prepare for the future: writing a literature review. MIS Q. xiii–xxiii (2002)
19. Lunberry, D., Liebenau, J.: Human or machine? a study of anthropomorphism through an affordance lens. In: Metallo, C., Ferrara, M., Lazazzara, A., Za, S. (eds.) Digital Transformation and Human Behavior. LNISO, vol. 37, pp. 201–215. Springer, Cham (2021). https://doi.org/10.1007/978-3-030-47539-0_15
20. Waizenegger, L., et al.: Conversational agents - exploring generative mechanisms and second-hand effects of actualized technology affordances. In: Hawaii International Conference on System Sciences (HICSS), p. 10 (2020)
21. Moussawi, S.: User experiences with personal intelligent agents: a sensory, physical, functional and cognitive affordances view. In: Proceedings of the 2018 ACM SIGMIS Conference on Computers and People Research, Buffalo-Niagara Falls, pp. 86–92. Association for Computing Machinery (2018)
22. Lippert, A., Gatewood, J., Cai, Z., Graesser, A.C.: Using an adaptive intelligent tutoring system to promote learning affordances for adults with low literacy skills. In: Sottilare, R.A., Schwarz, J. (eds.) HCII 2019. LNCS, vol. 11597, pp. 327–339. Springer, Cham (2019). https://doi.org/10.1007/978-3-030-22341-0_26
23. Stoeckli, E., Uebernickel, F., Brenner, W.: Exploring affordances of slack integrations and their actualization within enterprises – towards an understanding of how chatbots create value. In: Hawaii International Conference on System Sciences (HICSS), p. 10 (2018)
24. Knote, R., et al.: Value co-creation in smart services: a functional affordances perspective on smart personal assistants. J. Assoc. Inf. Syst. **22**, 78 (2020)
25. Meske, C., Amojo, I., Thapa, D.: Understanding the affordances of conversational agents in mental mobile health services. In: ICIS 2020 Proceedings (2020)
26. Barnett, A., et al.: Enacting 'more-than-human' care: clients' and counsellors' views on the multiple affordances of chatbots in alcohol and other drug counselling. Int. J. Drug Policy 102910 (2020)
27. Pappas, I.O., Mikalef, P., Giannakos, M.N., Krogstie, J., Lekakos, G.: Big data and business analytics ecosystems: paving the way towards digital transformation and sustainable societies. IseB **16**(3), 479–491 (2018)

28. Pappas, I.O., et al.: Social innovation and social entrepreneurship through big data: developing a research agenda. In: 11th Mediterranean Conference on Information Systems (MCIS), Genoa, Italy (2017)
29. Vassilakopoulou, P., Hustad, E.: Bridging digital divides: a literature review and research agenda for information systems research. Inf. Syst. Front. (2021). https://doi.org/10.1007/s10796-020-10096-3

AI in the Workplace: Exploring Chatbot Use and Users' Emotions

Lorentsa Gkinko(✉) and Amany Elbanna(✉)

Royal Holloway University of London, Egham TW20 0EX, UK
Lorentsa.Gkinko.2015@live.rhul.ac.uk, Amany.Elbanna@rhul.ac.uk

Abstract. The adoption of Artificial Intelligence (AI) applications in organisations is growing rapidly. In this study, we focus on Chatbots as one type of AI applications in the workplace. Chatbots differ from traditional organisational ICTs in many aspects including machine learning and exhibiting social presence. These characteristics motivate us to explore the role of emotions on chatbot use in the workplace. Following a case study approach and collecting rich qualitative data, the research identifies the different emotions involved in chatbot use in the workplace and their effect on employees' use behaviour. The findings surprisingly highlight that excitement, hope and playfulness in addition to empathy towards the chatbot offset the negative emotions of frustration experienced when getting wrong results and propel users to continue their use. The social presence of the chatbot and its potential to learn infuses a more tolerant forgiving user behaviour towards the chatbot. The study theoretically contributes to the understanding of chatbot adoption and use in organisations and informs research into the adoption, use and design of this new class of technology. Further research is encouraged to take the findings of this study and test them on a large sample of employees.

Keywords: Chatbots · Artificial Intelligence · Emotions · Emotions at work · Digital workplace · Technology adoption · AI adoption · Future of work · Chatbot use

1 Introduction

The use of AI in organisations is increasing exponentially [1, 2]. Chatbots present a class of new technology that relies on Artificial Intelligence (AI), Natural Language Processing (NLP) and Machine Learning (ML) [3, 4] to provide human-like conversational agents. The adoption of chatbots in the workplace is growing, which is motivated not only by the efficiency and cost reduction potential but also by the possibility of projecting a contemporary office that appeals more to modern workers and digital native generations while they enter the workplace [5] and to improve employee experience and satisfaction [6]. In a recent survey by Gartner, CIOs identified chatbots as the main AI-based application used in enterprises and its adoption is expected to soar, where 70% of white-collar workers are expected to interact with conversational platforms on a daily basis by 2022 [5]. This trend has been accelerated as a result of the Covid-19 pandemic

Published by Springer Nature Switzerland AG 2021
D. Dennehy et al. (Eds.): I3E 2021, LNCS 12896, pp. 18–28, 2021.
https://doi.org/10.1007/978-3-030-85447-8_2

and the associated forced home office work and social distancing measures. Despite its growth and potentials, research into the integration of this new class of technology into the workplace is in its infancy. Indeed, little is understood regarding their use and impact on employees' experience.

As chatbots exhibit conversational abilities with natural language processing, "it is important to understand the emotional, relational and psychological outcomes that chatbots covey to the user through their communication" [7]. Emotions have been associated with information systems use in organisations. Research shows that the successful use of organisational systems is impacted by users' emotions [8]. Beaudry and Pinsonneault [8] argue that excitement and happiness are positively related to organisational IT use while anxiety is negatively related to it. Evidence from the fields of management, marketing and information systems finds that emotions and feelings play an important role in job satisfaction, decision-making behaviour and technology adoption and "can even have more explanatory power" on behaviour than cognition [9, 10]. Hence, understanding emotions in chatbots adoption and use is vital and can inform technology design, management and use.

Against this backdrop, this research questions: What are the types of emotions involved in chatbot use in the workplace and what role they play in its adoption and use? To answer the research questions, we conducted an in-depth qualitative study in a large organisation that implemented a chatbot for the exclusive use of its employees. Through inductive research processes and benefitting from Beaudry and Pinsonneault's framework [8] and Richins' emotions inventory [11], the findings identify the different emotions associated with chatbots' use in the workplace. They highlight that excitement, hope and playfulness, in addition to empathy towards the chatbot, offset the negative emotions of frustration experienced when getting wrong results and propel users to continue their use. The social presence of the chatbot and its potential to learn infuses a more tolerant forgiving user behaviour towards the chatbot. This research contributes to the nascent literature on AI and chatbots adoption and use in organisations. It draws the attention to the role played by emotions and their impact on chatbot adoption and use and informs research in this domain. Further research can take the findings of this study and quantitatively test them on a large sample of chatbot users in the workplace.

Following the introduction, this paper is structured as follows: Sect. 2 presents a brief literature review on chatbots and their emotional aspects. Section 3 introduces the theoretical framework on emotions and technology adoption, followed by the outline of the research methodology including the case description and data collection in Sect. 4. Section 5 presents the research findings in terms of the key emotional aspects upon which users interact with the chatbots. The paper closes with a discussion of key insights from the study (Sect. 6) and the conclusion (Sect. 7).

2 Literature Review

Chatbots refer to any software application that engage in a dialog with a human by using natural language [12]. They are conversational agents that typically have a natural language interface which allows users to explore data and services either via text or voice [9]. The natural language interface component is a distinct characteristic of chatbots and provides them a human-like conversational capability. In general, there are three types of chatbots, namely, chatbots without embodiment, virtually embodied avatars and physically embodied robots [13]. The ability of chatbots to interact with users through the use of natural language is a unique characteristic that distinguish this class of technology from other software [14].

As an AI-based technology, chatbots use machine learning and artificial intelligence methods to imitate human-like behaviours and provide a task-oriented framework [15]. The chatbot architecture comprises of a language model and computational algorithms [16]. Hence, chatbots consistently learn from their users and the ways they interact with them. Therefore, understanding their use is of paramount importance. The chatbot design consists of two fundamental components: the form and the function [17]. The function of a product, which is dominated by principles from engineering, refers to product specifications and standard architectures. It focuses on the utilitarian aspect through addressing the practical needs of users, such as being able to communicate with an agent in natural language, whereas the form of a product refers to the individual design components. It represents the aesthetic component and can be interpreted as a user's perception of non-utilitarian aspects. Moreover, a form feature that has attracted a lot of attention in chatbots is the anthropomorphic presentation. Apart from the human-like visual cues of chatbots, the language is a major aspect as it might be enriched by emotional semantics or expression of emotions [17].

3 Theory of Emotions in Technology Adoption and Use

3.1 Emotions and Feelings

Much has been done on the cognitive side of technology adoption and use, while the affect side has received less attention despite its importance. Studies of technology adoption embracing emotions have mostly focused on the negative affect such as computer anxiety [18–20]. According to Venkatesh [21] the emotional aspect of technology usage could be captured through the construct of computer anxiety [21]. Furthermore, people establish judgments and feelings about any technology. These judgments and feelings are essential factors in the adoption of new technologies. To improve our understanding of the motivation of people to adopt and use new technologies, a fundamental step is to understand the influence of emotions and feelings [18].

Emotions and feelings have been used to measure affect. However, these two terms are distinct. Emotions have been defined as a mental state of readiness that occurs from cognitive appraisals of events or thoughts [22]. As such, emotions influence behaviours or changes in action readiness [8]. On the other side, feelings are different in the sense that they lack the evaluative, cognitive and motivational components which are distinctive of emotions [23]. In addition, moods are low intensity mental states which have a longer duration than emotions and lack intentional capacity and action tendencies [24].

3.2 Triggers and Appraisals of Emotions

Laros and Steenkamp [25] distinguished between negative and positive emotions. A narrower distinction between different emotions has been introduced by Richins [11] within the consumption context, who developed the "Consumption emotions set" (CES). This set of descriptors represents the range of emotions consumers most frequently experience in consumption situations [11]. Furthermore, Beaudry and Pinsonneault [8] developed a framework that classifies emotions based on two appraisals. The primary appraisal is goal achievement which is the opportunity/threat to the personal goals [26]. The secondary appraisal is the degree of certainty users feel about the outcome [26]. Accordingly, they suggest four distinct types of emotions: achievement, challenge, loss and deterrence emotions as presented in Fig. 1.

Achievement emotions are triggered from the appraisal of an event with positive outcome and high degree of certainty over its consequences. This category of emotions includes happiness, satisfaction, joy and pleasure. Challenge emotions are also caused by the appraisal of an event as being an opportunity over which individuals feel they have some control. These emotions might evoke excitement, hope, anticipation, playfulness and flow. On the other side, loss emotions reflect the perception of an IT event as a threat and the perception of a lack of control over its consequences. This category of emotions includes anger, dissatisfaction and frustration. Similarly, another class of emotions that perceives IT as a threat is the deterrence emotions however, with some degree of control over its consequences. Emotions such as worry, fear and distress are included in this category [8].

Since this paper aims to understand the types of emotions involved in chatbot use in the workplace we adopt Beaudry's and Pinsonneault's [8] emotion framework that classifies emotions and concentrates on how they are related to the usage of a new IT system [8]. Richins [11] has provided an inventory of emotions that complements Beaudry and Pinsonneault [8]. Based on these two studies, and informed by our analysis, we introduce the framework in Fig. 1 as a guidance for the reader and not to represent the order of the research process.

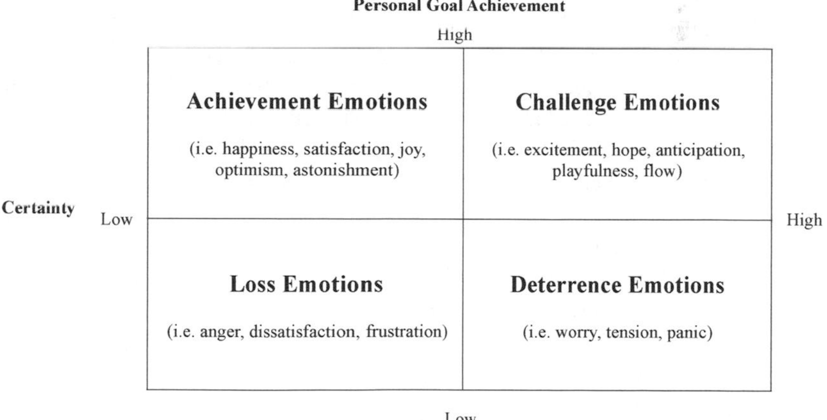

Fig. 1. Classification of emotions, adapted from Beaudry and Pinsonneault [8].

4 Methodology

4.1 Case Description

Omilia (a pseudonym) is a global organisation that has developed an internal chatbot for its employees to provide IT services. The main reason for the creation of the chatbot was initially to reduce cost and later evolved to provide seamless work experience to their employees. The chatbot provides employees with a wide range of IT-related information and support of the kind typically held and done by traditional IT helpdesk. One of the objectives of implementing the chatbot was to enable the users to be self-sufficient. The chatbot was developed based on the Microsoft Bot Framework utilizing the Azure Cloud Services. The implementation of the cognitive services of the chatbot was initially challenging for the project team, however, soon, they mastered it and expanded the functionalities of the chatbot. The utilization of the cognitive services helps the chatbot to continuously learn based on users' input. Nevertheless, the team implemented supervised learning to be able to review and approve the suggestions they receive from the cognitive services.

4.2 Data Collection

In terms of data collection, we gained access to the development team and users in December 2019 and continued with data collection till September 2020 as part of a wider research programme investigating chatbots' use in the workplace. Data collection took place in two rounds and the third is planned. Data collection consisted of interviews and document reviews. We conducted 28 semi-structured interviews with users and developers. The first round of interviews included the product owner and professionals from the development team. The focus of these interviews was on understanding organisational objectives behind the creation of the chatbot and its development approach and use within the organisation. In the second round of interviews, which took place from the beginning of July until the end of September 2020, we conducted 24 interviews with users. Participants were randomly selected from different teams, who agreed to participate in the study. The interviews addressed themes relevant to the research topic, including people's experiences and emotions on their use of the chatbot in their daily work. The interviews were semi-structured and conversational in nature, addressing participants' experience of using the chatbot in their day-to-day activities at work. Interviews lasted between 20 min to 1 h. Each participant was interviewed over a conference line, due to Covid-19 lockdown and travel restrictions. All interviews were transcribed verbatim. In addition to the interviews, data was also collected from different organisational documents and internal links. Moreover, observations of use took place and the users shared screen shots with the researcher. All the data and the organisation's name have been anonymized to maintain confidentiality.

4.3 Data Analysis

This study is part of a wider research programme on chatbots' use in organisations. We performed inductive analysis in coding, followed by themes development [27]. "The primary purpose of the inductive approach is to allow the research findings to emerge from the frequent, dominant or significant themes inherent in the raw data" without the enforcement of any structured theory upfront [28]. This approach is suitable for the exploratory nature of the study and considering the novelty of chatbots adoption in the workplace [29]. The data analysis initially focused on the participants' perceptions and experiences with the chatbot. During the data analysis, emotions emerged as a key concept that influenced the adoption and use of the chatbot in the organisation. Hence, the data was coded to identify different types of emotions. In doing so, we benefited from Beaudry and Pinsonneault's [8] classification and Richins' [11] inventory of emotions. While Beaudry and Pinsonneault's [8] study focused on four emotions, namely, happiness, excitement, anger and anxiety in IT use, we complemented it with emotions of 'hope' and 'anticipation' from Richins' as they were emerging from our data [11]. Throughout the analysis, we did not force the data into categories. This allowed for the emotion of empathy to emerge from the data as a new emotion associated to chatbot use.

5 Research Findings

The findings show that users experience different emotions in their chatbot use. These emotions are not discrete, and one user could experience a mixture of emotions. The following sections present the emotions experienced by chatbot users in their workplace.

5.1 Achievement Emotions

Achievement emotions result from the appraisal of an upcoming event that generates primarily from users' perception that new ICT offers them opportunities to achieve their personal goals. It includes emotions such as happiness, satisfaction, joy, and pleasure [8]. For example, the interviewees expressed their view of the chatbot as useful. This perspective is illustrated below:

> *"I just wrote 'software' and then it gave me the* ***options****, like 'do you want to request a software', 'do you want to review an order' and all that. So, it was* ***quite handy****, very useful. For all these cases I just went to the chatbot because it's quite handy, especially for ticket creation. […] it gives you all the possible options* ***quite nicely****." Interviewee 5*

Achievement emotion was also expressed even when the chatbot did not provide the required information, but it offered to assist in generating a request to the helpdesk from where the user can get support. This reference to the helpdesk was perceived as useful in assisting with the process and influenced positive emotions towards the chatbot use. A user eloquently expresses this view in the following quote:

> *"It didn't give me the information I wanted, but what I did* ***like*** *when it got to the end and* ***it couldn't help me, it said 'do you want to open a ticket?'*** *that aspect was very useful because that is really what I wanted to do in the first place." Interviewee 12*

5.2 Challenge Emotions

Emotions from this class are triggered by the appraisal of an event as being an opportunity likely to result in positive consequences and over which users feel they have some control. This category includes the feelings of excitement, hope, anticipation and playfulness [8]. Challenge emotions were evident in the data. In this regard, we found that users were excited to use the chatbot due to its novelty and their curiosity to try it. The following quote expresses this view:

> *"I just knew that it was kind of AI and because it was an AI,* ***I just wanted to try it*** *out, because we didn't have anything like that before and that was what actually drove me to just use the chatbot." Interviewee 5*

Users find the chatbot as a potential opportunity that is likely to result in positive consequences now or in the future. The characteristic of chatbots as learning agents brings about users' anticipation that it will improve based on their continuous use. This is despite delayed or mistaken results of the chatbot. The following quote shows this anticipation and hope from users which is driving their continuous use:

> *"Well, I think it's fine. I mean, it's I think it's just a matter of time before it gets* ***smarter and better****. I mean* ***the more training it has it would definitely get better****." Interviewee 10*

Users are also hopeful that the chatbot with their learning capability will improve based on acquiring more users. Hence, as good citizens, users find their continuous use to be a contribution to the chatbot future improvement. The following quote presents an example of this view:

> *"****If less people are using it****, I don't see how the robot can learn." Interviewee 6*

5.3 Loss Emotions

Loss emotions are negative emotions such as anger, dissatisfaction and frustration. According to Beaudry and Pinsonneault [8], these emotions are stemmed from user perception of lack of control. However, in the case of chatbot, while users exhibit frustration of its use, they surprisingly find different excuses for its faulty results. The following is a representative quote that shows that users experience lack of goal achievement and less control over results. However, they continue to use the chatbot, despite their frustration, annoyance and the fact that they find excuses for it, based on its characteristic as an "intelligent agent", that is here to help. The following quote encapsulates this view:

> *"Not upset, maybe just a little* ***bit frustrated****...,* ***it tries to help you so it's not its fault****, but yeah. It's not upsetting, it's just a little* ***bit annoying*** *sometimes." Interviewee 5*

While users get frustrated from the use of the chatbot, they sometimes blame the complexity of the task as a satisfying reason for its confused results. In this case, they revert to a human to help them with their queries. It is intriguing that users refer to their colleagues, in this case, as "humans" and not as "colleagues", nor they mention their names or use their job title. This is illustrated in the following quote:

"So, that way it is good and the only problem for me it's that you know, sometimes, it doesn't understand you and then it becomes ***frustrating****. [...] Yes, when it's a complicated issue maybe it's better, because the chatbot doesn't solve every issue so it's good to have the* ***human*** *aspect as well." Interviewee 9*

5.4 Deterrence Emotions

Deterrence emotions are perceived when the IT event was considered as a threat to personal goal achievement and the users feel that they have some control over the expected consequences. Emotions such as anxiety, worry, fear, and distress could be experienced in this situation [8]. Sometimes users show their panic and tension over the use of the chatbot. However, for some users, this frustration and panic, triggered by the chatbot use, deterred them from trying it again. The following quote depicts this perspective:

"The chatbot was first saying 'is it maybe one of these issues'? I said 'No'. Next, 'Is it maybe one of these issues'? 'No'. Ok, let's create a ticket together. And then you create a ticket and then the bot was also asking additional questions and then I didn't understand anymore, I don't know, it's like, ***fed up*** *with." Interviewee 11*

Furthermore, users express their tension which is based on their expectations by saying that they stopped using it after their first attempt:

"Once I realised it didn't answer my question as I expected, I ***stopped using it****. Because one negative experience, I think for such cases it prevents you for using it further." Interviewee 14*

5.5 Empathy Emotions

In addition to the four categories of emotions, the data analysis revealed a new category of emotions: empathy towards the chatbot. A number of users expressed sorrow towards the chatbot when it did not return correct answers. This made them more forgiving for its mistakes. The following quote from one of the users summarises this view:

"I'm not mad at the bot, I just ***feel sorry for the bot****." Interviewee 5*

Besides, employees avoided blaming the chatbot for faulty results. They were tolerant to mistakes as they felt they are part of the interaction into which they enter the chatbot and they play an active role in the conversation. The following quote encapsulates this view:

"I mean, I have no frustration, but I thought ***maybe I was not typing*** *the right way that it could give the information." Interviewee 8*

6 Discussion

With the proliferation of innovative technologies, the workplace of the future becomes a digitally enhanced workplace [30]. This study focuses on the use of chatbots by employees in organisational setting. It aims to answer the research question of what the emotional aspects of chatbot use are. The research provides an inductive exploratory analysis based on Beaudry and Pinsonneault's [8] classification of IT-related emotions complemented by the emotions inventory developed by Richins [11].

The findings identify a range of emotions involved in a chatbot used by employees. They highlight that chatbots trigger emotions of achievement, challenge, loss, deterrence and empathy. The conversational characteristic of the chatbot infuses a feeling of flow where users enjoy the interaction with it. Flow characterises the subjective human-computer collaboration as playful and exploratory. The concept of flow indicates the extent to which the user perceives a sense of control while gaining optimal and enjoyable experiences [31].

Our findings extend Beaudry and Pinsonneault's [8] framework to include the emotion of empathy, as a new category of emotions. We theorise that this emotional reaction could be stemmed from the social presence of the chatbot and its characteristic as a conversational agent. We also find that emotions towards the chatbot were mixed. A user could experience more than one category of emotions, when using the same chatbot under study. Further exploration of this aspect is needed.

The study mainly contributes to the literature on technology adoption and use, by examining the actual use of technology and by exploring the emotional aspects of chatbot use in its organisational setting. In highlighting the different emotional aspects of chatbot use and identifying the emotion of empathy, the research extends the IT-related emotions framework to include the category of empathy. Multiple studies showed that humans react to artificial entities with social cues such as use of natural language, and interactivity, by showing social reactions and behaviour due to the humanlike characteristics of CAs [32].

This study contributes to the understanding of chatbots as a new class of technology based on AI. As an AI technology, Chatbots are learning agents; this characteristic triggers different emotions for the users including joy, excitement, frustration and tension. Also, as chatbots rely on Machine Learning and Natural Language Processing, they create a new class of interactive technology for corporate users beyond the typical passive corporate systems they are familiar with and used to. This new technology is different from other corporate systems in that it is not passive, but it engages users on a voluntary basis. Hence, users are curious, excited and playful in their use. They are always hopeful, expect improvement, and they want to contribute to its learning as they anticipate the future advancement of it. In addition, users feel they should be part of a critical mass of chatbot learning and contribute to its development by acting as chatbot trainers.

7 Conclusion

In summary, the study emphasises the collaboration between users and chatbots, by revealing how users feel about this partnership and their attempts on defining its future advancement by their use. Consideration of this individualisation of chatbots provides useful direction for managers seeking to connect these components as they manage new technologies. It provides researchers and designers with knowledge about how users adopt and engage emotionally with chatbots in their work.

References

1. Elbanna, A.: Sociotechnical approaches in the era of data science and AI: a research agenda. In: Proceedings of the 6th International Workshop on Sociotechnical Perspective in IS Development (STPIS 2020), CEUR-WS, Grenoble, France, 8–9 June, pp. 4–6 (2020)
2. Elbanna, A., Dwivedi, Y., Bunker, D., Wastell, D.: The search for smartness in working, living and organising: beyond the 'Technomagic.' Inf. Syst. Front. **22**(2), 275–280 (2020)
3. Gkinko, L., Elbanna, A.: Chatbots at work: an employees' perspective. In: The Future of Digital Work: The Challenge of Inequality IFIP Joint Working Conference, Hyderabad, India, 10–11 December 2020, pp. 53–58 (2020)
4. Gkinko, L., Elbanna, A.: The creation of chatbots at work: an organizational perspective. In: AI@Work. ai.reshapingwork.net, Amsterdam, 5–6 March 2020 (2020)
5. Goasduff, L.: Chatbots Will Appeal to Modern Workers. https://www.gartner.com/smarterwithgartner/chatbots-will-appeal-to-modern-workers/. Accessed 17 Mar 2021
6. Panetta, K.: Gartner Top 10 Strategic Predictions for 2021 and Beyond. https://www.gartner.com/smarterwithgartner/gartner-top-10-strategic-predictions-for-2021-and-beyond/. Accessed 17 Mar 2021
7. De Cicco, R., De Silva, S.C., Alparone, F.R.: Millennials' attitude toward chatbots: an experimental study in a social relationship perspective. Int. J. Retail Distrib. Manag. **48**, 1213–1233 (2020)
8. Beaudry, A., Pinsonneault, A.: The other side of acceptance: studying the direct and indirect effects of emotions on information technology use. MIS Q. Manag. Inf. Syst. **34**, 689–710 (2010)
9. Brandtzaeg, P.B., Følstad, A.: Why people use chatbots. In: Kompatsiaris, I., et al. (eds.) INSCI 2017. LNCS, vol. 10673, pp. 377–392. Springer, Cham (2017). https://doi.org/10.1007/978-3-319-70284-1_30
10. White, C.J.: The impact of emotions on service quality, satisfaction, and positive word-of-mouth intentions over time. J. Mark. Manag. **26**, 381–394 (2010)
11. Richins, M.L.: Measuring emotions in the consumption experience. J. Consum. Res. **24**, 127–146 (1997)
12. Dale, R.: The return of the chatbots. Nat. Lang. Eng. **22**, 811–817 (2019)
13. Van Pinxteren, M.M.E., Pluymaekers, M., Lemmink, J.G.A.M.: Human-like communication in conversational agents: a literature review and research agenda. J. Serv. Manag. **31**, 203–225 (2020)
14. Seeger, A.-M., Pfeiffer, J., Heinzl, A.: When do we need a human? Anthropomorphic design and trustworthiness of conversational agents. In: SIGHCI 2017 Proceedings, pp. 1–6 (2017)
15. Vaidyam, A.N., Wisniewski, H., David Halamka, J., Kashavan, M.S., Blake Torous, J., Torous, J.: Chatbots and conversational agents in mental health. Can. J. Psychiatry **64**, 456–464 (2019)
16. Shawar, B.A., Atwell, E.: Chatbots: are they really useful? LDV-Forum **22**, 29–49 (2007)
17. Rietz, T., Benke, I., Maedche, A.: The impact of anthropomorphic and functional chatbot design features in enterprise collaboration systems on user acceptance. In: Proceedings of the 14th International Conference on Wirtschaftsinformatik, Siegen, Germany, pp. 1656–1670 (2019)

18. Perlusz, S.: Emotions and technology acceptance: development and validation of a technology affect scale. In: IEEE International Engineering Management Conference, pp. 845–847 (2004)
19. McGrath, K.: Affection not affliction: the role of emotions in information systems and organizational change. Inf. Organ. **16**, 277–303 (2006)
20. Sarabadani, J., Compeau, D., Carter, M.: An investigation of IT users' emotional responses to technostress creators. In: Proceedings of the 53rd Hawaii International Conference on System Sciences, pp. 6113–6122 (2020)
21. Venkatesh, V.: Determinants of perceived ease of use: integrating control, intrinsic motivation, and emotion into the technology acceptance model. Inf. Syst. Res. **11**, 342–365 (2000)
22. Bagozzi, R.P., Gopinath, M., Nyer, P.U.: The role of emotions in marketing. J. Acad. Mark. Sci. **27**, 184–206 (1999)
23. Christodoulides, G., Michaelidou, N., Siamagka, N.T.: A typology of internet users based on comparative affective states: evidence from eight countries. Eur. J. Mark. **47**, 153–173 (2013)
24. Stam, K.R., Stanton, J.M.: Events, emotions, and technology: examining acceptance of workplace technology changes. Inf. Technol. People **23**, 23–53 (2010)
25. Laros, F.J.M., Steenkamp, J.B.E.M.: Emotions in consumer behavior: a hierarchical approach. J. Bus. Res. **58**, 1437–1445 (2005)
26. Davis, F.D., Bagozzi, R.P., Warshaw, P.R.: Extrinsic and intrinsic motivation to use computers in the workplace. J. Appl. Soc. Psychol. **22**, 1111–1132 (1992)
27. Boyatzis, R.: Transforming Qualitative Information: Thematic Analysis and Code Development. Sage, Thousand Oaks (1998)
28. Thomas, D.R.: A general inductive approach for analyzing qualitative evaluation data. Am. J. Eval. **27**, 237–246 (2006)
29. Gioia, D.A., Corley, K.G., Hamilton, A.L.: Seeking qualitative rigor in inductive research: notes on the Gioia methodology. Organ. Res. Methods **16**, 15–31 (2013)
30. Meyer von Wolff, R., Hobert, S., Schumann, M.: How may I help you? – State of the Art and open research questions for chatbots at the digital workplace. In: Proceedings of the 52nd Hawaii International Conference on System Sciences (HICSS 2019), pp. 95–104 (2019)
31. Webster, J., Trevino, L.K., Ryan, L.: The dimensionality and correlates of flow in human-computer interactions. Comput. Human Behav. **9**, 411–426 (1993)
32. Poser, M., Bittner, E.A.C.: Hybrid teamwork: consideration of teamwork concepts to reach naturalistic interaction between humans and conversational agents. In: WI2020 Zentrale Tracks, pp. 83–98 (2020)

Chatbots at Work: A Taxonomy of the Use of Chatbots in the Workplace

Lorentsa Gkinko(✉) and Amany Elbanna(✉)

Royal Holloway University of London, Egham TW20 0EX, UK
Lorentsa.Gkinko.2015@live.rhul.ac.uk, Amany.Elbanna@rhul.ac.uk

Abstract. The adoption of Artificial Intelligence (AI) applications in organisations is growing rapidly. In this study, we focus on chatbots as one type of AI applications in organisations. As an AI-enabled application, Chatbots learn from their use patterns. Therefore, the ways users adopt and use chatbots will have significant impact on the future evolvement of this technology. This study examines the use of chatbots in the workplace. It questions how employees use chatbots in the workplace. It adopts an inductive approach to examine the use of the same chatbot in the same organisation. The findings highlight the existence of different patterns of use. Based on the inductive analysis of data, we develop a taxonomy of chatbot users. The taxonomy offers four types of users based on two prominent criteria. The study presents a key step in understanding chatbot use in the workplace that could pave the way for future research.

Keywords: Chatbots · Future of work · Artificial Intelligence · AI adoption · AI use · Smart organisation · Smart technology · Technology appropriation · Taxonomy

1 Introduction

The growth of Artificial Intelligence (AI) use and popularity in organisations is continuing apace. A recent report shows that 85% of the surveyed organisations are either evaluating or using AI [1]. AI technology is an umbrella term that covers Robotics, Natural Language Processing, Machine Learning among other smart capabilities [2, 3].

Chatbots are widely used by organisations to externally serve customers in many service domains and are recently used by organisations to internally serve its employees. In the customer service context, chatbots promise to create a fast, convenient, and cost-effective channel for communicating with customers [4]. In the workplace context, chatbots are implemented to enhance the productivity of the employees through assisting them in information retrieval tasks [5]. It has been also argued that chatbot use in the workplace could reduce stress and information overload and provide employees with valuable assistance [6, 7]. The increasing use of chatbots in the workplace presents a significant development in the digitalisation of the workplace [8], that has consequences for organisations and employees. However, integrating such digital innovations into the

D. Dennehy et al. (Eds.): I3E 2021, LNCS 12896, pp. 29–39, 2021.
https://doi.org/10.1007/978-3-030-85447-8_3

workplace has received little attention despite its importance as a key area in workplace transformation that drives efficiency [9, 10].

While the use of chatbots in the workplace is increasing, limited research is available in the applications of chatbots in employee support services. As chatbots are AI-enabled applications, they consistently learn from use patterns and the ways users interact with them. Therefore, understanding how employees interact with this technology and how they use it is of particular importance. This study contributes to closing this research gap by exploring the use of chatbots in the workplace from the employees' perspective. It aims to answer the research question of: how employees use chatbots in the workplace?

To answer the research question, we conduct an inductive qualitative research to examine the use of a chatbot in a large international organisation. Data analysis shows that employees use chatbots in different ways. Accordingly, we develop an inductive taxonomy to categorise users based on their patterns of use. This research contributes to the very thin literature on chatbots and AI adoption in the workplace. By building a taxonomy of users in relation to chatbot use, it lays the foundation for further work and theory building in this domain [11, 12].

Following the introduction, the paper is organised into six sections. Section 2 presents the concept of Technology Appropriation a brief literature review on chatbots in the workplace. Section 3 provides the research methods including the case description, data collection and taxonomy development method. Section 4 presents the research findings in terms of the key themes upon which users were organised into four types. Section 5 discusses the findings while Sect. 6 presents the conclusions, limitations and future research.

2 Literature Review

2.1 Technology Appropriation

The concept of Technology Appropriation explains the transformation process of a technology as it is envisaged by its designer (technology-as-designed) into technology as it is being used (technology-in-use). It studies the cycle of the usage after the initial adoption, thus complementing existing technology adoption, use and implementation research [13]. The core focus of research adopting the Technology Appropriation concept is that users make technology their own, in a process of adaptation, by which both the technology and individuals and/or collective practices are transformed [14]. It involves the adaptations, the practices and skills that users initiate of the novel technology [14]. It is recognised that there are multiple views on appropriation: organisational, technical and personal [13]. However, following the inductive analysis, this paper embarks on classifying the different use patterns and how users appropriate chatbots in the workplace, it concentrates on the behavioural outcome of the individual users. While many existing Technology Appropriation models draw on social science principles to consider appropriation by groups, Carroll's [15] proposed an individual-based model of Technology Appropriation that focuses on the interplay between an individual and a technology. We adopt this model of Technology Appropriation [15] that focuses on the concept of appropriation from an individual user perspective.

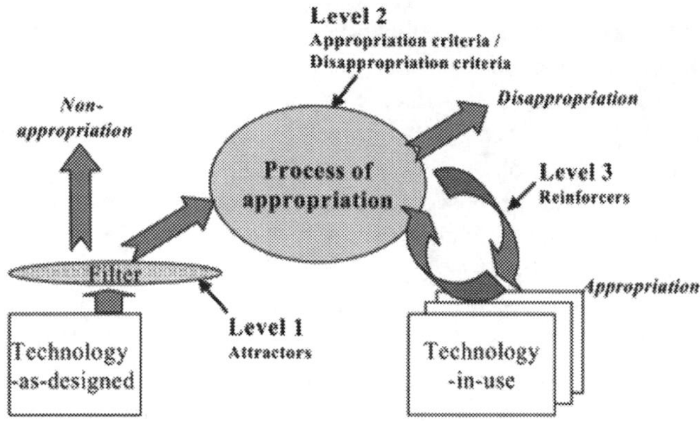

Fig. 1. The model of technology appropriation adopted from Carroll et al. [20]

Carroll et al. [16] suggest that users evaluate a technology at three levels which reflects different degrees of familiarity with the technology as shown in Fig. 1:

Level 1: At this level, initial judgements are made with the users' first encounter with a new technology. The outcome of this encounter is the decision to non-appropriation, where users are not interested in this technology, or to the adoption, where the appropriation process begins.
Level 2: Through the process of appropriation users explore the technology in depth. The outcome of this process is either the appropriation, where the users take possession of its capabilities in order to satisfy their needs, or the disappropriation, where users, at some stage during the appropriation process, choose not to persist with the technology.
Level 3: The technology is appropriated and integrated into users' everyday practices based on the long-term use of the technology. However, changes in users' evaluation of the technology may lead to disappropriation [15].

The individual model of Technology Appropriation maintains that the use of technology is strongly influenced by users' understandings of the capabilities of the technology [17]. Users adapt by changing their practices and situations of use to fit in with the technology, in both intended and unintended ways [15]. Consequently, they might not use it in ways that were initially expected by the developers [17].

2.2 Chatbots' Use in the Workplace

The use of chatbots has been studied from a human computer interaction (HCI) perspective and in marketing from a customer service perspective. However, there is little understanding of chatbots use in the workplace and how employees use this AI-enabled technology. From a HCI perspective, chatbots' design features could provide social cues to users. For example, human-like function/appearance, language style, personality, the degree of interactivity and assumed agency could trigger social responses and influence users' perception and behaviour [18, 19]. These 'social cues' can substantially affect users' perception and as a result impact the adoption and use of these systems

[18]. Moreover, the social presence of chatbots technologies is believed to influence the development of social and emotional bonds with this intelligent system [20].

Schmitt [21] distinguished five strategic experiential modules of creating different types of customer experiences: sensory experience (Sense), affective experience (Feel), cognitive experience (Think), physical experience (Act) and experience defined by social identity (Relate). Hoyer [22] proposed that AI-enabled technology, including chatbots, create experiential value and identified three dimensions of this experiential value involving cognitive, sensory/emotional, and social. Cognitive value is the experiential value that consumers receive as a result of processing the information and decision-making and is closely tied to the analytical features of AI technologies [22]. Sensory/emotional value comprises the value consumers get from sensory stimulation and emotional attachment, which results from the sensory and affective features of the AI technologies. The sensory/emotional value of chatbots consists of making intelligence tangible, making them a true human companion. It is recognised that anthropomorphisation falls in this category and increases this type of value [22].

3 Research Methods

3.1 Research Site and Data Collection

Omilia (a pseudonym) is a large international organisation that has recently developed an internal chatbot for its employees to support them in IT related issues as a virtual IT help desk. We gained access to the development team and users since December 2019 as part of a wide ongoing research project. We also had access to the different documents and internal links. We conducted 28 semi-structured interviews with users and developers in two rounds. The first round of interviews included the product owner and professionals from the development team. The focus of these interviews was on understanding the initial purpose of the creation of the chatbot and how the development cycle works. In the second round of interviews, which took place from the beginning of July until the end of September 2020, we conducted 24 interviews with users aged between mid-twenties to 50s with a University degree; they were randomly selected from different teams across the IT department, who agreed to participate in the study. These interviews broadly explored people's experiences and use of the chatbot in their daily work. The interviews lasted between 20 min to 1 h. Each participant was interviewed over a video/audio conferencing line. All interviews were recorded following participants' consent and transcribed verbatim. All the data that were collected from the interviews and the organisation's name have been anonymized for the purposes of confidentiality.

3.2 Taxonomy Development

We adopted an inductive approach to data analysis [23, 24]. Our analysis highlighted the existence of different patterns of use among users. We therefore embarked in the categorization of these patterns in a taxonomy. There is a variety of ways to present taxonomies and the literature does not recommend how a taxonomy should be presented [25]. However, once we observed in the data the existence of different pattern of use, we adopted Nickerson's et al. [11] recommendation on developing taxonomy through empirical inductive approach – which is strongly rooted on Bailey's [26]. This involves inductive analysis to extract patterns, dimensions and characteristics upon which a taxonomy is constructed. The characteristics of a useful taxonomy include being concise, robust, comprehensive, extendible and explanatory [11]. The analysis proceeded in three steps. In the first step, an inductive coding was performed on the raw data [24]. The second step, two broad themes were users differed were identified. The two themes that emerged were: Interaction and Perception which served as the basis of the classification. In the third step, data was re-analysed based on these two themes which led to the emergence and identification of four types of users as shown in Fig. 2:

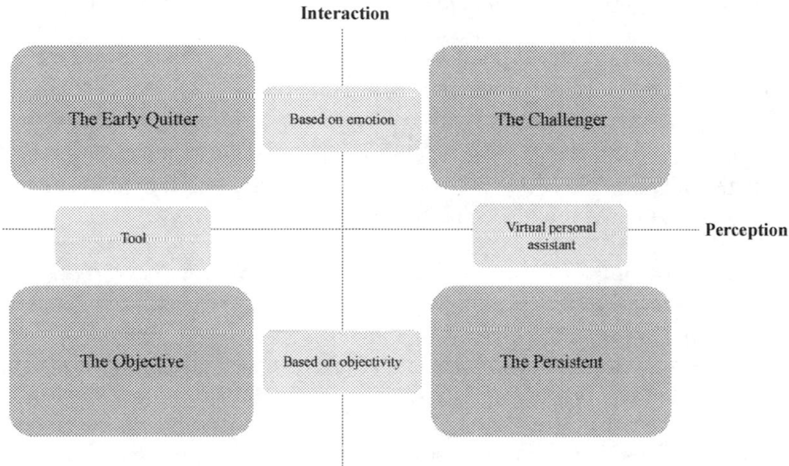

Fig. 2. User classification based on the two themes: interaction and perception

4 Research Findings

4.1 Key Themes

Through data analysis, two main themes related to users' appropriation of chatbots were identified using an iterative process and later used to create the taxonomy. The first theme that emerged from the analysis of data is the employees' perception towards the chatbot. The perception ranges from considering the chatbot just as other applications for information retrieval to considering it as a human-like assistant and a colleague.

The second theme that arose from data is related to the interaction with the chatbot. The interaction ranges from emotional to functional based. The following section presents how these two themes provided the base for further analysis that resulted in the taxonomy building.

4.2 A Taxonomy of Chatbot Users

Based on the two identified themes mentioned above, four distinct types of chatbot users in an organisation were identified. Each type comprises a unique combination of dimensions related to the above-mentioned themes [11, 26]. The four types of chatbot users are: 'The Early Quitter', 'The Challenger', 'The Objective' and 'The Persistent' as explained in the following sections.

The Early Quitter. The Early Quitter represents the category of users who perceive the chatbot as a machine, as another additional tool to support their daily work and interact based on emotions. The following quote encapsulates this view.

"If you ask me right now, I see it simply as a search engine." Interviewee 22

In terms of interaction, this type of user tends to act based on emotion as they have a biased opinion about the chatbot which is based on their previous encounter with such an application in a different setting. Furthermore, this type of user gets easily frustrated in cases where the chatbot is not responding as they would assume, and they assign the dysfunctionality to the chatbot without thinking of the possibility to change their language pattern. This view was succinctly summarised as follows:

"Because in your daily life you are also confronted with these bots, right? So, if you go on an internet page and then you see some kind of smart robot on a certain web page 'can I help you?', you know it's just a robot, you never get anything out of it. But I typed some questions and what I could recall is that it never really gave me the answer I was looking for." Interviewee 11

The Challenger. This type of users finds the chatbot to be an assistant and interact based on emotions. They embrace the chatbot and experiment with its use. They try to find different ways to use the chatbot so that it could assist them in daily activities. This type of users is interested in the technology and tries to experiment with the chatbot, to test it, evaluate it and find its limits.

In terms of perception, the Challenger considers the chatbot not only as a mere tool, but also as a personal virtual assistant. For example, Interviewee 19 mentions:

"I really try to imagine the chatbot as my personal virtual assistant." Interviewee 19

In addition, in terms of interaction, these users express, and act based on emotions, due to the enthusiasm towards technology they emanate. Interviewee 6 shares this notion:

"The chatbot also needs to learn. I guess it asks me at the end 'was this helpful or how did I find it', and when I tell him no, I feel bad for the bot." Interviewee 6

The Objective. The Objective represents the category of users who perceive the chatbot as a machine, as another additional tool to support their daily work and also hold a functional view of the chatbot. For example, Interviewee 9 refers to the functionality of the chatbot as a machine that needs to be trained and compares its performance to human interaction:

"If the bot can be trained in a way that it's giving better results, more efficient results, then it's fine otherwise it's better to talk to a person." Interviewee 9

In terms of interaction, this type of user tends to act based on their logical analysis of chatbot functions and capability. For example, Interviewee 23 gives a rationale behind the interaction with the chatbot in terms of its capability:

"So, to be able to trust the chatbot, I would personally also like to understand and see what information sources it covers. So how much can I really trust, how deep does the chatbot go into the different pages. So, I would need to first understand how detailed its searches are and how widespread it is looking to be able to trust it." Interviewee 23

The Objective type of users will continue to use the chatbot for as long as it is functioning to their expectations. They will discontinue its use once its usability weakens.

The Persistent. This type of users sees the chatbot as a personal assistant and interact with it based on its functions and capabilities. The element that differentiates the Persistent from the Objective type, is the former's perception of the chatbot as an assistant, having a human cue as well as their continued use of the chatbot by rephrasing their question. As below, Interviewee 16 expresses their perception of the chatbot as communicating with a person:

"I always chat as if I am chatting to a person, it's not like I am searching for anything." Interviewee 16

In terms of interaction, they act based on objective and functional understanding that is driven by emotions. Interviewee 5 provides a justification behind the chatbot interaction:

"So, that's better than the human interaction because it is actually giving you the links and pages and everything that you need. So that way, it is more helpful when you really want information about something." Interviewee 5

5 Discussion

The use of AI in organisations is growing. This study focuses on the use of chatbots as one type of AI. It aims to answer the research question of: how employees use chatbots in the workplace? To do so, it adopted an inductive qualitative approach to examine a chatbot use in an organisation. The findings show that employees vary in their appropriation of the chatbot at work and the way they perceive it. In this study, we categorised the differences under two themes namely: perception of the chatbot (tool or assistant), and basis of interaction (based on emotion or objective and function). Accordingly, four types of users were identified.

Regarding perceptions, the study finds that users either perceive the chatbot as a mere tool or as an assistant. Both 'The Early Quitter' and 'The Objective' types of users perceive it as a machine that supports their daily activities, while 'The Challenger' and

'The Persistent' perceive it as an intelligent tool or a person (Fig. 3). Consequently, the latter type recognises it as a personal virtual assistant and a viable replacement of a colleague. Hence, they continue with its use and act as chatbot trainers due to their tendency to experiment. Figure 3 provides a review of the identified types in light of Carrol's et al. [20] appropriation framework. It shows that the perception of the chatbot as an assistant that is integrated into the users' practices reinforces its appropriation.

In terms of interaction, the study finds two types of interaction namely logical and emotional. The 'Objective' and the 'Persistent' interact with the chatbot based on logic while the 'Early Quitter' and the 'Challenger' interact with it based on emotions. However, the logic in the interaction does not translate into persistent use unless the user also perceives the chatbot as an assistant. Hence, the 'Persistent' type of user rarely quits and tries to use the chatbot until some answer is found. They interact based on logic and do not express any emotion towards the chatbot. In contrast, as the findings demonstrate, the 'Early Quitter', who is interacting based on emotion, considers the chatbot as a tool and has a limited view about the chatbot's capabilities. When faced with an irrelevant answer, the 'Early Quitter' exhibits negative emotions and becomes more frustrated. As a result, this dissatisfaction leads to the non-appropriation of the chatbot during the initial encounter with the technology, which is represented by the Level 1 in the appropriation process (Fig. 3). However, the Objectives also consider the chatbot as a tool, but they are based on logic. Additionally, they continue to appropriate the chatbot for as long as it is functioning to their expectations, explore the chatbot in depth and disappropriate it once its usability weakens, which is represented by the Level 2 in the appropriation process (Fig. 3).

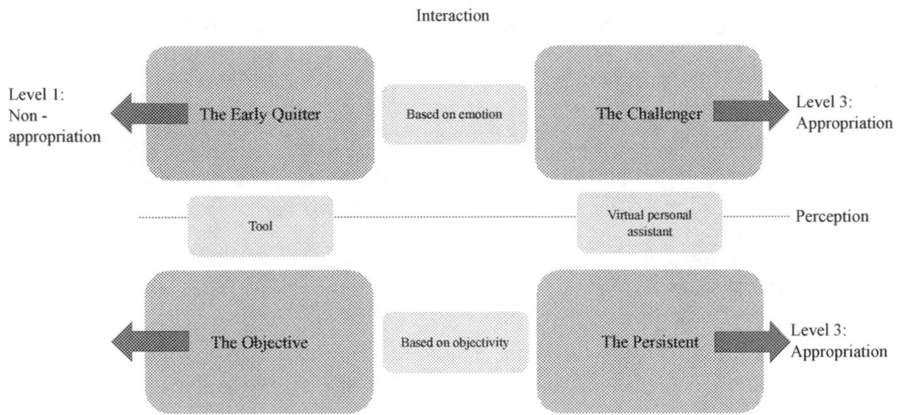

Fig. 3. Users' taxonomy and appropriation levels

The study contributes to the emerging literature on chatbot use through providing a case study of their use in an organisational setting. In highlighting the different types of chatbot use, the study draws the attention that AI-based technology might not bring about homogeneous use. Accordingly, training AI and chatbots in organisational settings might be impacted by the different patterns of use. In building a taxonomy of users, this study provides a vital base to research on chatbot use and training. In evaluating the proposed taxonomy, we found that it meets both the criteria of mutual exclusion and exhaustion [27]. As none of the types of users has two different characteristics in a dimension, the developed taxonomy provides mutual exclusive classification. As each user type has one of the characteristics in a dimension, the taxonomy also provides collective exhaustive classification. As a consequence, each user type has exactly one of the characteristics in each dimension, interaction based on emotion with shared responsibility or logic with non-shared responsibility, perception as a tool or virtual personal assistant, as shown in Fig. 3.

6 Conclusions, Limitations and Further Research

In short, this study focuses on employees' perspectives on using chatbots at work and contributes to the existing literature of AI adoption and use in organisations by proposing a taxonomy of chatbot users. The taxonomy presented here facilitates a more deeply nuanced understanding of the use of chatbots by the employees in a process of appropriation in an organisational setting. Ultimately, the findings show that specific types of users are more enamoured of appropriating the chatbot than others and the characteristics of these types of users have been presented based on the two themes identified: Perception: tool/virtual personal assistant, Interaction: based on emotion/logic, shared/non-shared responsibility. Therefore, the 'Challenger' and the 'Persistent' user type can have a greater influence on the advancement and training of AI applications by use.

The taxonomy developed by this study is based on the examination of chatbots, future research could extend it to other AI applications. Understanding the use of AI applications in practice is particularly important in this new type of technology since it plays a substantial role in the learning and advancement of such applications [28, 29]. The taxonomy reveals heterogeneity in the employees' characteristics on how they use AI applications and what they expect from them. Ultimately, the findings show that specific types of users can have a greater impact on the learning of AI applications, thus helping designers and researchers in the advancement of such applications while creating value and efficiency for the organisation. The results of this study could be further strengthened by examining the use of chatbots in multiple organizations. Moreover, additional interviews would allow to evaluate if participants demographic data such as gender and experience could further explain the criteria of this classification. The results of this study emerged from the qualitative data inductively, to create the different chatbot user types and did not originate from the theory. Future studies could test the user types and further validate them to a population with sampling techniques.

References

1. Magoulas, R., Swoyer, S.: AI Adoption in the Enterprise 2020. https://www.oreilly.com/radar/ai-adoption-in-the-enterprise-2020/. Accessed 17 Mar 2021
2. Elbanna, A.: Sociotechnical approaches in the era of data science and AI: a research agenda. In: Proceedings of the 6th International Workshop on Sociotechnical Perspective in IS Development (STPIS 2020), CEUR-WS, Grenoble, France, 8–9 June, pp. 4–6 (2020)
3. Elbanna, A., Dwivedi, Y., Bunker, D., Wastell, D.: The search for smartness in working, living and organising: beyond the 'Technomagic.' Inf. Syst. Front. **22**(2), 275–280 (2020)

4. Gnewuch, U., Morana, S., Maedche, A.: Towards designing cooperative and social conversational agents for customer service. In: ICIS 2017: Transforming Society with Digital Innovation (2018)
5. Brandtzaeg, P.B., Følstad, A.: Why people use chatbots. In: Kompatsiaris, I., et al. (eds.) INSCI 2017. LNCS, vol. 10673, pp. 377–392. Springer, Cham (2017). https://doi.org/10.1007/978-3-319-70284-1_30
6. Kimani, E., Rowan, K., McDuff, D., Czerwinski, M., Mark, G.: A conversational agent in support of productivity and wellbeing at work. In: 2019 8th International Conference on Affective Computing and Intelligent Interaction (ACII), pp. 332–338. IEEE (2019)
7. Meyer von Wolff, R., Hobert, S., Schumann, M.: How may I help you? – State of the Art and open research questions for chatbots at the digital workplace. In: Proceedings of the 52nd Hawaii International Conference on System Sciences (HICSS 2019), pp. 95–104 (2019)
8. Yoo, Y., Boland, R.J., Lyytinen, K., Majchrzak, A.: Organizing for innovation in the digitized world. Organ. Sci. **23**, 1398–1408 (2012)
9. Larivière, B., et al.: "Service Encounter 2.0": an investigation into the roles of technology, employees and customers. J. Bus. Res. **79**, 238–246 (2017)
10. Barrett, M., Oborn, E., Orlikowski, W.J., Yates, J.: Reconfiguring boundary relations: robotic innovations in pharmacy work. Organ. Sci. **23**, 1448–1466 (2012)
11. Nickerson, R.C., Varshney, U., Muntermann, J.: A method for taxonomy development and its application in information systems. Eur. J. Inf. Syst. **22**, 336–359 (2013)
12. Szopinski, D., Schoormann, T., Kundisch, D.: Because your taxonomy is worth it: towards a framework for taxonomy evaluation. In: 27th European Conference on Information Systems - Information Systems for a Sharing Society, ECIS 2019 (2020)
13. Rahim, N.Z.A., Alias, R.A., Carroll, J.: Multiple perspectives technology appropriation: analysis of open source software implementation failure. In: PACIS 2010 - 14th Pacific Asia Conference on Information Systems (2010)
14. Riemer, K., Johnston, R.B.: Place-making: a phenomenological theory of technology appropriation. In: International Conference on Information Systems, ICIS 2012, pp. 3106–3124 (2012)
15. Carroll, J., Howard, S., Peck, J., Murphy, J.: From adoption to use: the process of appropriating a mobile phone. Australas. J. Inf. Syst. **10**, 38–48 (2003)
16. Carroll, J., Howard, S., Vetere, F., Peck, J., Murphy, J.: Just what do the youth of today want? Technology appropriation by young people. In: Proceedings of the Annual Hawaii International Conference on System Sciences, pp. 1777–1785. IEEE Computer Society (2002)
17. Orlikowski, W.J.: Using technology and constituting structures: a practice lens for studying technology in organizations. Organ. Sci. **11**, 404–428 (2000)
18. Gnewuch, U., Morana, S., Adam, M., Maedche, A.: Faster is not always better: understanding the effect of dynamic response delays in human-chatbot interaction. In: 26th European Conference on Information Systems: Beyond Digitization - Facets of Socio-Technical Change, ECIS 2018 (2018)
19. Nass, C., Moon, Y.: Machines and mindlessness: social responses to computers. J. Soc. Issues **56**, 81–103 (2000)
20. Rietz, T., Benke, I., Maedche, A.: The impact of anthropomorphic and functional chatbot design features in enterprise collaboration systems on user acceptance. In: Proceedings of the 14th International Conference on Wirtschaftsinformatik, Siegen, Germany, pp. 1656–1670 (2019)
21. Schmitt, B.: Experiential marketing. J. Mark. Manag. **15**, 53–67 (1999)
22. Hoyer, W.D., Kroschke, M., Schmitt, B., Kraume, K., Shankar, V.: Transforming the customer experience through new technologies. J. Interact. Mark. **51**, 57–71 (2020)

23. Gioia, D.A., Corley, K.G., Hamilton, A.L.: Seeking qualitative rigor in inductive research: notes on the Gioia methodology. Organ. Res. Methods **16**, 15–31 (2013). https://doi.org/10.1177/1094428112452151
24. Thomas, D.R.: A general inductive approach for analyzing qualitative evaluation data. Am. J. Eval. **27**, 237–246 (2006)
25. Land, L., Smith, S., Pang, V.: Building a taxonomy for cybercrimes. In: Proceedings - Pacific Asia Conference on Information Systems, PACIS 2013 (2013)
26. Bailey, K.D.: Typologies and Taxonomies: An Introduction to Classification Techniques. Sage, Thousand Oaks (1994)
27. Følstad, A., Skjuve, M., Brandtzaeg, P.B.: Different chatbots for different purposes: towards a typology of chatbots to understand interaction design. In: Bodrunova, S.S., et al. (eds.) INSCI 2018. LNCS, vol. 11551, pp. 145–156. Springer, Cham (2019). https://doi.org/10.1007/978-3-030-17705-8_13
28. Gkinko, L., Elbanna, A.: Chatbots at work: an employees' perspective. In: The Future of Digital Work: The Challenge of Inequality IFIP Joint Working Conference, Hyderabad, India, 10–11 December 2020, pp. 53–58 (2020)
29. Gkinko, L., Elbanna, A.: The creation of chatbots at work: an organizational perspective. In: AI@Work. ai.reshapingwork.net, Amsterdam, 5–6 March 2020 (2020)

A Process Model of Artificial Intelligence Implementation Leading to Proper Decision Making

Mohammad I. Merhi(✉)

Department of Decision Sciences, Judd Leighton School of Business and Economics, Indiana University South Bend, South Bend, IN, USA
mmerhi@iusb.edu

Abstract. This study aims to fill a gap in the literature by identifying and extracting critical success factors that impact the success of AI implementation. The factors are then categorized and presented in a process model that demonstrates the sequence of the factors and the interrelationships among them. The model is composed of three stages: pre-implementation, implementation, and post-implementation. The implementation is composed of three categories organization, process, and technology. Each of these categories contains several critical factors. The model presented helps both researchers and practitioners. Details, discussion, and future research opportunities are discussed in the paper.

Keywords: Artificial intelligence implementation · Decision making · Data intelligence · Analytics

1 Introduction

The adoption and implementation of Artificial Intelligence (AI) is rapidly growing across global businesses [1–3]. According to Gartner's 2019 CIO Agenda survey, 48% of global CIOs planned on implementing AI systems by 2020 [4]. It is forecasted that AI will grow into a $118.6 billion industry by 2025 [5]. AI is defined as systems that mimic cognitive functions/tasks, such as learning, speech and problem solving, that are associated and performed by humans within the workplace and society in general [6]. AI offers multitude of benefits to businesses such as reducing costs, eliminating human errors, being able to work 24/7, improving customer experience, enhancing productivity and operational efficiency, and streamlining and accelerating decision-making to make the proper decisions [5, 7]. One can perhaps argue that the last one on decision-making is the most important applications in AI since decisions impact all other areas in any business. AI systems can be used to either support the human decision makers or replace them [8].

The benefits of AI for decision making have been praised by many researchers and practitioners because AI is believed to be able to help organizational decision makers

Published by Springer Nature Switzerland AG 2021
D. Dennehy et al. (Eds.): I3E 2021, LNCS 12896, pp. 40–46, 2021.
https://doi.org/10.1007/978-3-030-85447-8_4

to reach better decisions, to enhance employees' analytic and decision-making abilities, and to intensify creativity e.g., [9, 10]. At the same time, researchers and practitioners admit that without a successful implementation of AI systems, organizations cannot achieve the desired outcomes including the correct and proposer decisions. For this reason, researchers in recent papers called for research that examine the critical factors affecting AI's success in decision making [6, 9]. This research satisfies the calls and attempts to answer the following research questions: What are the critical factors that will significantly affect AI's success for decision making?

The extant literature on successful AI implementation lacks comprehensive studies that combine the critical success factors. A model that demonstrates the process to achieve success in AI implementation is also missing. To our best knowledge and based on the search we conducted, there exist two peer-reviewed academic studies [11, 12], two peer-reviewed practitioners' studies [13, 14], and four practitioners reports [2, 4, 15, 16] on AI implementation. None of these papers present a comprehensive model since their aim was not to present such a model. In this paper, we intend to fill this gap in the literature by:

- Identifying and extracting the significant factors from previous studies,
- Explaining how these factors impact successful AI implementation and decision making, and
- Presenting a comprehensive model that includes the critical factors.

We argue that a successful implementation of AI needs to pass through three major stages: pre-implementation, implementation, and post-implementation. Each of these stages has different critical factors. The first stage includes planning, budget, analysis, etc. The second stage includes critical factors that have been found to be important in literature. In this study, we categorize these factors to three categories: organization, process, and technology. The last and final stage is the outcome desired including proper decisions.

The presented model is a holistic, flexible, and dynamic framework expected to help both researchers and practitioners. Practitioners will find in this study a powerful means for identifying fundamental factors that can lead to smooth AI implementation and success. This model is flexible in that it can be used in different sized organizations: large, medium, or small; and countries: emerging or developed. Different organizations have different resources and cultures; depending on its use, this model can function as an integrated tool with all the factors, or with just a few of them. For researchers, the framework presented can be used as a foundation. To our best knowledge, no study has yet presented a taxonomy model on AI's success for decision making. Future research can empirically assess this model and/or add other critical factors that may influence AI's success for decision making.

2 Background and Literature Review

As mentioned earlier, the extant literature lacks a comprehensive study that examine the success factors of AI for decision making. To collect the factors that act as barriers or those that lead to successful implementation of AI, we searched three main databases, Business Source Complete, IEEE Xplore, and Emerald Insight. We only found two peer-reviewed academic studies and two peer-reviewed practitioners' studies on AI implementation. We also searched for AI practitioners reports in Google.com and found four reports. We briefly mention the factors indicated by these previous peer-reviewed articles and practitioners reports.

Of the two peer-reviewed journal articles, [11] suggested that lack of benefits visibility, integration complexity, and cost of AI are barriers to the success of AI. [12] indicated that resistance, ethics issues, low data quality, insufficient quantity of data, and responsibility and accountability are critical factors leading to success or failure of AI.

After interviewing more than 3000 business executives, managers, and analysts from organizations around the world, [13] found that top management, security and confidentiality, lack of technical expertise, lack of benefits visibility, and IT infrastructure play an important role in the success or failure of AI. [14] identified nine critical factors that can challenge the success of AI. These factors are organizational structure, security and confidentiality, lack of technical expertise, integration complexity, ethics issues, data governance issues, low data quality, responsibility and accountability, and high cost of AI.

[15] advised that security and confidentiality, IT infrastructure, insufficient quantity of data, and high cost of AI are important factors leading to success of AI. In their report, [2] indicated that organizational structure, lack of technical expertise, lack of benefits visibility, resistance, integration complexity, IT infrastructure, ambiguous strategic vision, low data quality, insufficient quantity of data, and project champion as critical factors to AI success. In a report published by Gartner after interviewing CEOs of different organizations, [4] mentioned twelve critical factors to AI. These factors are top management support, security and confidentiality, lack of technical expertise, lack of benefits visibility, resistance, integration complexity, ambiguous strategic vision, data governance issues, low data quality, insufficient quantity of data, responsibility and accountability, and selection of vendors. Recently, [16] suggested that lack of technical expertise, resistance, ambiguous strategic vision, and ethical issues are barriers to AI success.

3 Proposed Model and Taxonomy

The research framework introduced in this paper classifies the factors of successful AI implementation into three phases. An illustration of the AI Process Model is depicted in Fig. 1.

3.1 Pre-implementation

The first is the pre-implementation, in which decision makers choose to go with the project or not. Every project, including AI systems implementation, should start by defining the goals to be achieved, the available resources, the timeline, the required budget, the scope of the project, the systems to be implemented, the vendors, and the possible methods needed to accomplish these goals. This step serves as the blueprint of the project and helps motivate the stakeholders to commit to the project and work harder towards achieve its goals.

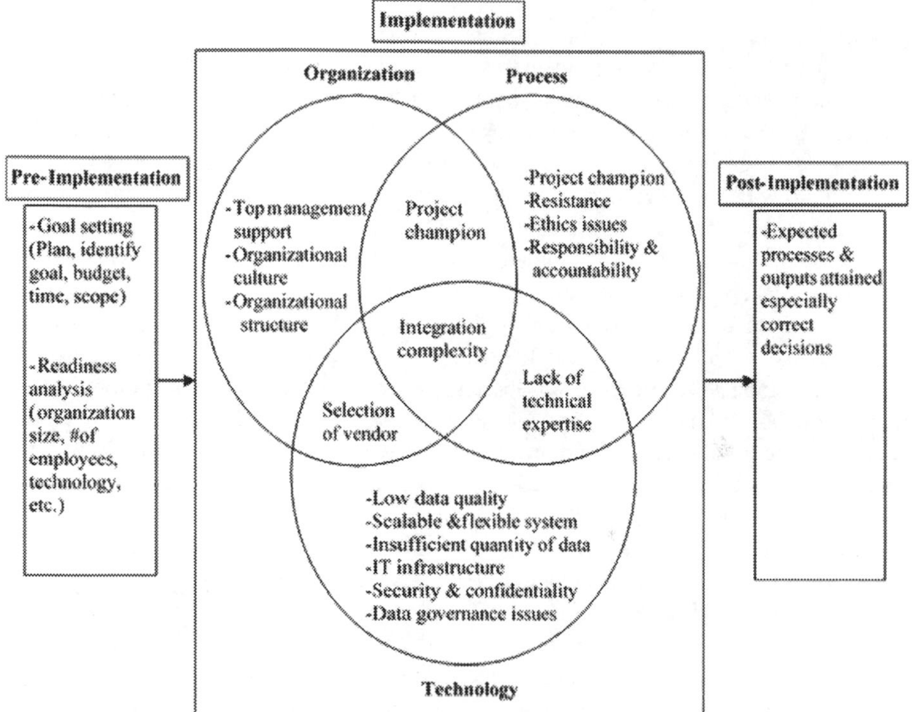

Fig. 1. A process model of AI success leading to proper decisions.

3.2 Implementation

The second stage – the implementation – is made up of three subcategories: organization, process, and technology. These categories are interrelated because AI implementation is a very complex process that touches different sections of the organizations. Factors under the category organization are top management, organizational culture, and organizational structure. Researchers and practitioners have validated the importance of top management on the success of IS and considered it to be a very critical factor leading to successful implementation of high cost and strategic value IS (e.g. [17, 18]). AI systems are like any other strategic IS and thus require top management support.

Organization's culture can be defined as the values, social ideals, and beliefs that employees of an organization share [19]. Because AI impacts all the decisions taken in an organization, it, thus, have an influence on the organizational culture and structure since the processes that are set inside the organization will change after the implementation of these systems. In their interviews with business executives, managers, and analysts, [13] found that the changes of culture and structure caused by AI are daunting.

Factors under the "process" category deal mostly with the employees inside the organization. Employees are the backbone of any organization. They are the ones who use the technology, make decisions, and advance the organizations. Factors that are under this category are: resistance, ethics issues, and responsibility and accountability. AI systems introduce new processes and methods, causing changes in social and technical environments that can lead to confusion and inefficiency in the organization. The changes caused by the implementation of the new systems usually generate users' resistance because employees generally prefer the status-quo and avoid the changes. Employees' resistance to change has been found to be a major factor in many IS project failures [20, 21].

Technology factors are those related to the systems such as data quality and quantity, IT infrastructure, data security and governance issues. [22] emphasize that the data intelligence system's technical framework should be scalable and flexible with respect to additional data sources, attributes, and dimensions. AI are systems depend on data and technology. Data accuracy and reliability should be top priorities in the implementation of AI systems because they can lead to failure. AI systems rely on data and the quality of these data impact the output/result. Unreliable, incorrect, and poor data input impact the functionalities of the systems and lead to incorrect decisions. At the same time, these data need to be highly secured and protected to prevent misuse, fraud, or breaches. All stakeholders must feel confident that their private information will not be lost, sold, or otherwise, misused.

From the taxonomy model presented above, one can see that the three major categories are not separated. Conversely, these categories are interrelated. For instance, a project champion supervises the factors of both organization and process categories. A "champion project manager," who is a person that possesses managerial competencies in personal, technical, and business-oriented, is the one who sets all these objectives and leads the project. Without a strong managerial leader, the project will most likely fail. Also, having a technical expertise is necessary to link the technology to the process categories. Employees need to have the technical expertise necessary to use AI systems. If not, these employees need to be trained. An organization also need to select a vendor that can meet the criteria set by the management and that can have a good relationship with. Finally, three categories are linked by integration. AI systems depend on data collected from multiple databases that must be integrated. Also, outputs of AI systems impact all departments of an organization.

3.3 Post-implementation

Once the factors presented above are done correctly, the successful implementation (goal of the project) will be achieved. A successful implementation should lead to success in decision making and help organizations achieve competitive advantage and all desired outcomes of AI.

4 Discussion and Conclusion

Organizations across the globe of all sizes and sectors are interested in implementing AI systems. The enormous amount of produced data has also proliferated the need for intelligence systems. AI and data intelligence systems convert the collected data and transform them to knowledge and information that help enhancing decision making. AI systems also make decision by themselves. Studies on the implementation of AI systems in are scarce as discussed earlier and there are calls for studies that examine this area. This paper fills a gap in the literature by identifying and extracting the most critical factors that were found to influence the implementation of AI and presenting them in a process model. To our best knowledge, no study has yet combined the factors and presented them in a taxonomy model.

This paper is expected to help both practitioners and researchers. The model presented helps practitioners in identifying fundamental factors that can lead to success of AI implementation. This model demonstrates how the factors are interrelated. For researchers, the framework presented can be used as a foundation. Future research can empirically assess this model and/or add other critical factors that may influence AI's success for decision making. For instance, the factors presented in the model can be evaluated and assessed using the analytical hierarchy process, a quantitative method of decision-making, to evaluate the importance of the factors presented in the study based on data collected from experts. Such studies can help both researchers and practitioners to understand the importance of the factors presented here.

5 Limitations and Future Research

This study has several limitations. First, the research model includes several factors and sub-factors that are the most critical factors; however, as mentioned, there may exist other factors that influence the implementation of artificial intelligence. We call for future research to investigate and find other critical success factors that may impact the implementation of artificial intelligence.

Factors that are specific for specific countries such as national culture factors, corruption, legal systems, etc. can be added to the list of factors identified in this study. Nations that suffer from high levels of corruption tend to face more resistance to IT-related projects because data analytics and intelligence systems fight the corrupt people and stop their business. Also, different nations have different levels of advancements, sizes, as well as resource capabilities. Another potential area for research is by collecting secondary or primary data on the factors included in the study and empirically examine the relationships help improving and enriching the body of knowledge.

Lastly, AI and data intelligence are evolving and changing drastically which means that new factors may become more important in the coming years. Thus, we call for future research to investigate the importance of new factors that may influence the implementation of AI systems as these phenomena evolve.

References

1. Borges, A.F., Laurindo, F.J., Spínola, M.M., Gonçalves, R.F., Mattos, C.A.: The strategic use of artificial intelligence in the digital era: systematic literature review and future research directions. Int. J. Info. Manage. 102225 (2021)

2. Chui, M., Malhotra, S.: AI adoption advances, but foundational barriers remain (2018). https://www.mckinsey.com/featured-insights/artificial-intelligence/ai-adoption-advances-but-foundational-barriers-remain. Accessed 15 Dec 2020
3. Nishant, R., Kennedy, M., Corbett, J.: Artificial intelligence for sustainability: challenges, opportunities, and a research agenda. Int. J. Info. Manage. **53**, 102104 (2020)
4. Goasduff, L.: 3 barriers to AI adoption. Gartner (2019). https://www.gartner.com/smarterwithgartner/3-barriers-to-ai-adoption/. Accessed 10 Dec 2020
5. Ideamotive. Implementing artificial intelligence in your business (2020). https://www.ideamotive.co/ai-developers/guide#introduction-to-ai-and-machine-learning. Accessed 2 Jan 2021
6. Dwivedi, Y.K., et al.: Artificial Intelligence (AI): multidisciplinary perspectives on emerging challenges, opportunities, and agenda for research, practice and policy. Int. J. Info. Manage. 101994 (2019)
7. Davenport, T.H., Ronanki, R.: Artificial Intelligence for the real world (2018). https://hbr.org/2018/01/artificial-intelligence-for-the-real-world. Accessed 02 Jan 2021
8. Edwards, J.S., Duan, Y., Robins, P.C.: An analysis of expert systems for business decision making at different levels and in different roles. Eur. J. Inf. Syst. **9**(1), 36–46 (2000)
9. Duan, Y., Edwards, J.S., Dwivedi, Y.K.: Artificial intelligence for decision making in the era of big data–evolution, challenges and research agenda. Int. J. Info. Manage. 48, 63–71 (2019)
10. Wilson, H.J., Daugherty, P.R.: Collaborative intelligence: humans and AI are joining forces. Harv. Bus. Rev. **96**(4), 114–123 (2018)
11. Bergstein, B.: Can AI pass the smell test? MIT Technol. Rev. **122**(2), 82–86 (2019)
12. Faraj, S., Pachidi, S., Sayegh, K.: Working and organizing in the age of the learning algorithm. Inf. Organ. **28**(1), 62–70 (2018)
13. Ransbotham, S., Kiron, D., Gerbert, P., Reeves, M.: Reshaping business with artificial intelligence: closing the gap between ambition and action. MIT Sloan Management Review, 59(1), n/a-0 (2017)
14. Wirtz, B.W., Weyerer, J.C., Geyer, C.: Artificial intelligence and the public sector—applications and challenges. Int. J. Public Adm. **42**(7), 596–615 (2019)
15. Broda, E.: The most difficult part about AI/Machine learning occurs after the model is created (2019). Towards Data Science. https://towardsdatascience.com/the-most-difficult-part-about-ai-machine-learning-occurs-after-the-model-is-created-b585480c6918. Accessed 1 Dec 2020
16. Marr, B.: The 4 biggest barriers to AI adoption every business needs to tackle (2020). https://bernardmarr.com/default.asp?contentID=1826. Accessed 20 Dec 2020
17. Merhi, M.I., Koong, K.: A process model leading to successful implementation of electronic health record systems. Int. J. Electron. Healthc. 8(2/3/4), 185–201 (2015)
18. Merhi, M.I., Bregu, K.: Effective and efficient usage of big data analytics in public sector. Transforming Government People Process Policy **14**(4), 605–622 (2020)
19. Yeung, A.K., Brockbank, J.W., Ulrich, D.O.: Organizational culture and human resource practices: an empirical assessment. Res. Organ. Chang. Dev. **5**, 59–81 (1991)
20. Merhi, M.I., Ahluwalia, P.: Top management can lower resistance toward information security compliance. In: Proceedings of International Conference on Information Systems, Fort Worth, Texas (2015)
21. Merhi, M.I., Ahluwalia, P.: Examining the impact of deterrence factors and norms on resistance to information systems security. Comput. Hum. Behav. **92**, 37–46 (2019)
22. Yeoh, W., Koronios, A.: Critical success factors for business intelligence systems. J. Comput. Info. Syst. **50**(3), 23–32 (2010)

AI: Opportunities and Challenges - The Optimal Exploitation of (Telecom) Corporate Data

Polyxeni Palaiogeorgou, Christos A. Gizelis(✉), Antonios Misargopoulos, Filippos Nikolopoulos-Gkamatsis, Michalis Kefalogiannis, and Antonis M. Christonasis

Hellenic Telecommunications Organization S.A., 99 Kifissias Avenue, Athens, Greece
{ppaleogeor,amisargopo,fnikolop,mkefalogiannis,achriston}@ote.gr,
cgkizelis@cosmote.gr
http://www.ote.gr

Abstract. This paper introduces the Telecommunication's Industry approach to adopt Artificial Intelligence mechanisms into daily tasks and operations, in order to accelerate digital transformation. The scope of this paper is to analyze and explore the opportunities and the challenges that are raised for telecommunications organizations by exploiting vast amounts of data they own or handle. The opportunities and challenges that are created by AI technologies are presented through several Use Cases, that IT Innovation Center of OTE Group is investigating, and create the baseline towards digital transformation and the engagement in future markets. However, as depicted in this paper, although the numerous opportunities, telecoms in this AI journey face many challenges that they need to overcome. This work in progress is under the DataPorts project that is funded by the European Union's Horizon 2020 Research and Innovation Programme under grant agreement No. 871493.

Keywords: AI · Big data · Services · Telecommunications · Digital transformation

1 Introduction

Nowadays, Artificial Intelligence (AI) is the main driving force behind Digital Transformation. AI is the engine to lead this transformation and the data is the fuel to power this engine. AI algorithms and models need vast amounts of data they can rely on to produce valid results; therefore, a hand-in-hand relation is created between AI and Data. Telecoms have a plethora of available data from multiple sources such as, customer data, network, mobility tracking, billing, sales, etc. The correlation of such datasets, as well as the combination of them with external publicly available data (or other types of data that may not be publicly available), may potentially create great value for solving problems and serving

Published by Springer Nature Switzerland AG 2021
D. Dennehy et al. (Eds.): I3E 2021, LNCS 12896, pp. 47–59, 2021.
https://doi.org/10.1007/978-3-030-85447-8_5

future needs. Since it is a new field of operations and since until now such data availability and correlation wasn't possible for many different reasons, the value or what needs data can fulfil may be uncertain yet. Today, Europe is considered a weak player in the data-driven market, trying to catch up to US and Asia. The volume of data that will be produced globally is expected to reach 175 zettabytes in 2025 and Europe is aiming to position itself and become a leader in this area [1].

Open data in Greece can generate an additional 3.2 bn euros GDP and approximately 12 bn euros in cumulative benefits within 5 years. That led researchers and other related entities in Greece, to be highly involved in order to benefit from these numbers. Telecom operators own rich sources of data that should be utilized by other sectors Use Cases as well, that will could create opportunities for new services. Incumbent telecoms often face difficulties exploiting the data they own or handle through AI-based mechanisms. In most cases it is due to the complexity of the corporate environment but also due to the lack of prioritization or digital transformation maturity. According to Tata Consultancy Services Global Trend Study [2] AI is expected to have a dramatic impact on organizations. AI functionality [3] is becoming a standard feature instead of a special capability in existing software products. Hence, the AI adoption time by the organizations will become minimum. Artificial Intelligence (AI) has come to be a great enabler for businesses on the way to their digital transformation and the number of enterprises adopting AI has increased by 270% over the past 4 years (and tripled in the past year alone!), according to Gartner [4].

In the following sections an overview of the relation between the Telecom industry and the adoption of AI-based solutions is presented, as well as the opportunities and the challenges that exist in the Telecommunications sector. Moreover, several AI-related Use Cases are presented and analyzed.

2 Related Work

At Telcos, text services have reduced by around 75%, followed by voice services and the average revenue per user as stated in [5]. This result signifies that Telecoms are being affected by digital disruption. Towards this direction, several telecommunications service providers have started implementing AI Use Case in the form of AI services. Some of these services aim to transition Network Operation Centers (NOCs), where human administrators manage the telecommunications network, to Service Operation Centers (SOCs), where analytics and AI deliver automation. Telefónica, for instance, has launched pilot SOCs in several markets. Other telecommunications service providers are adopting AI in different ways. AT&T, for example, is researching how to use AI algorithms to enable drones to inspect and repair base stations. SK Telecom in South Korea is using machine learning to analyze network traffic to detect abnormalities and enhance network operations. Hong Kong telecom PCCW is testing AI-powered tools to forecast growth in network capacity and predict network failures [4].

MIT Sloan Management Review [6] predicted that 58% of all organizations foresee modifications to their business models due to AI within five years. AI-powered mechanisms are used to extract business insights from vast amounts of data from multiple data sources they own or handle. These insights are the enablers for better customer experience and process optimization towards a positive impact on companies' revenues. Telecoms worldwide invest or develop internally AI-based solutions. Deutsche Telekom has developed a chatbot that helps the company offer 24/7 assistance to customers in Austria. Tinka, the chatbot, can process about 80% of the customer requests. Globe Telecom uses ML to enhance the Omni-channel customer experience. Using predictive models based on their data sources makes decisions faster and more target specific. Telefonica uses a platform for a new customer relationship model exploiting personal data, while Nokia ML platform is used for network management purposes that improve planning and predicts service fluctuations in advance [7].

However, although AI may surpass humans in many areas it is considered impossible for computers to emulate human abilities. AI can either protect or damage people depending on how it is used and while AI technologies, remain neutral, it is on humans to determine the purposes of how AI will be used [8]. In the following sections, opportunities and challenges that emerge in the Telecommunications sector are presented in some depth. The need for transformation will force to be adopted and resolved by the industry in the upcoming period.

3 Opportunities

We have encountered many opportunities for AI adoption within the organization and many of them were tested and evaluated. These optimizations according to Deloitte [9], give several major advantages of the adoption of AI in enterprises, including, enhancing existing products and creating new ones, increasing the efficiency of internal processes, decision making based on processed data, optimizing external operations, as well as, optimizing resource allocation by taking off routine tasks from the employees.

3.1 Network Management Optimization

AI will benefit network monitoring and network management for organizations. The demand for more automated processes and tasks is because of the ability to identify complex network operational problems and provide diagnostics in a very short time. In addition, AI is the process of network monitoring that is also known as AIOps (Artificial Intelligence for Operations) [10]. AIOps are capable to reduce the time-critical troubleshooting and process analysis and create an opportunity to network units to deal with network planning issues. Hence, AI can also be applied to enhance the awareness and the accuracy improving the network capacity in a cost-effective manner. The use of AI may be a valuable tool for logs analysis but also an alerting mechanism for an AI-assisted, real-time, centralized network management, which can handle multiple anomalies, including node or link failures, degradation, congestion, and overload.

3.2 Customer Centricity

Telecoms, nowadays owning and handling vast amounts of data related to their customer's services, billing information, traffic analysis, using AI are now able to provide personalized services and recommendations to targeted consented customers. An offer very appealing to the customers. The early use of AI-based applications/services related to customer support, has resulted in the ability for organizations to reduce costs and improve their customers' retention and therefore increase revenues through their customer satisfaction. Customer requests could be handled using AI technologies without a customer agent's involvement: hence, the most important benefit is ensuring expertise of them and the so-called boring jobs to truly require assistance. A survey conducted by Tata Consultancy Services depicted that 32% of major companies around the world are currently using AI customer service technologies. It is the second most common use of AI after IT-related services [11], and according to IDC [12], AI is the game changer technology across customer-facing industries, that has the power to elevate customer experience using virtual assistants, product recommendations, or visual searches. Moreover, AI as a tool for biometrics is used as a mechanism for authentication, identification and access control, or as call classification and routing at a call center. Combining the power of AI with the capabilities of human support agents gives companies the ability to provide the high level of service their customers expect and deserve.

3.3 AI for Hardware Monitoring

AI-driven predictive analytics are helping Telecoms to provide better services by utilizing data, sophisticated algorithms and machine learning techniques to predict results based on historical data. By this Telecoms can use data-driven insights to monitor the infrastructure, anticipate failure based on patterns given by internal and external datasets (e.g., weather data), and proactively fix problems with communications hardware, such as Base Stations, power lines, data center servers, and even set-top boxes in customers' homes. In the short term, network automation and intelligence will enable better root cause analysis and prediction of issues, while in the long term, these technologies will underpin more strategic goals, such as creating new customer experiences and dealing efficiently with emerging business needs.

3.4 Process Automation

AI is indented to free up employees for more value-added activities, aiming to enable employees to perform more efficiently, to enhance existing processes, to adapt quickly and eventually to improve business results. The most obvious and common use of AI when it comes to processes and operations is the automation of tasks. This implies to the use of 'robotic process automation' (RPA) technologies. RPA is considered the easiest form of AI to implement since it operates across multiple back-end systems. It is not a new form of AI but lately, it is adopted by more and more organizations.

3.5 Management Support

Prior to the resurgence of AI and its eventual commercial application, executives have had to rely on inconsistent and incomplete data. With AI, they have data-based models and simulations to rely on. Today's AI systems are trained based on substantial amounts of data. This is augmented intelligence in action, which eventually provides executives with sophisticated models as basis for their decision-making. AI models can analyze vast amounts of data and therefore provide critical insights to management and business owners as well as make critical decisions for businesses autonomously. AI exploitation can provide extremely helpful forecasts and predictions. Reasonably, it is undoubtedly better than relying only on experience, or intuition and hypothetical scenarios. Humans now play the role of the final processor, relying on accurate figures and insights.

3.6 New Products and Services

Since people are able of consuming products and obtaining services using the internet, a widespread usage of AI has played a major role in that. AI creates an opportunity for organizations only if they pursue the right Use Cases, build analytics capability and finally embed the analytics in the day-to-day processes. It is perfectly understood that the more data it is consumed the greater insights AI can provide, especially in Telecoms where, a plethora of data from many different sources exist. As a result of AI, services can be more personalized and could match real customers' needs. The AI-driven mechanisms used to analyze corporate data create an opportunity for better exploitation towards the monetization of those data and set up a new revenue stream for the organizations. However, in order to achieve monetization of data there are several prerequisites that should be met. AI may be applied only on proper/accurate datasets, otherwise, the results may end up disastrous for the organization.

4 Challenges

Despite the numerous potential benefits of AI technologies for Telecoms, there still exist several challenges in the successful adoption of it. AI technology is still in its infancy, and this creates different challenges for Telecoms that aim to break into AI. One of the main problems many data owners face is the quality of the data. So, before the presentation of the identified challenges it seems reasonable to demonstrate the below figure. A process that could be followed in order a data owner to prepare and exploit data toward AI-based service creation is depicted in Fig. 1. This presents the stages that not only a Telecom organization, but also, any other industry that owns vast amounts of data should follow, in order to benefit from the power given by data.

Fig. 1. Data exploitation process

4.1 From Data to Business Value

In the State of Data Culture Report by Alation[13], several challenges were identified as important by companies in their AI transformation. Alation performed a quantitative research study among 300 Data and Analytics leaders. The study identified eight major challenges in using data to drive business value. More specifically, lack of analytical skills among employees emerged as the top challenge in 42% of the responses. Data democratization, the fact that not everyone can access data on their own, also ties for the first place at 42% of the responses. Closely related comes the challenge of organizational silos, the fact that data is not shared among different groups, at 41% of the responses. As in many Telecom Operators, OTE is addressing this issue by reskilling and training its employees. Additionally, IT Innovation Center forms cross functional teams and onboards experts from other units on all AI-related PoCs.

4.2 Lack of Technology Maturity

Due to the relative infancy of AI technology, perhaps the biggest obstacle for AI adoption for Telecoms is lack of technology maturity. With the number of commercial AI solutions growing every day, it is hard to identify the best solution for your company's individual needs. As an Innovation Team, we have faced the challenge of constantly evaluating the potential value of external AI solutions and collaborations with innovative partners. Moreover, according to McKinsey [14], one of the challenges to Supervised Machine Learning is the need for large amounts of human effort to label training data. In addition, the large amounts of data required for Deep Learning may be challenging to collect or may even not be available.

4.3 Lack of Expertise

Another barrier for the adoption of AI in Telecoms is lack of AI expertise. Companies have only recently started investing in AI talent. In addition, people specializing in AI and Data Analytics are in short supply. Currently, the demand for such talent certainly exceeds supply. This alone is a challenge and a threat that Telecoms must deal with in order to keep their competitive advantage. They need to provide career incentives and proper growth opportunities to attract data scientists and data analytics experts.

4.4 AI Ethics and Trust

An ethical perspective of AI is the ability of algorithms and models to optimize tasks by learning from large available amounts of data without any human intervention. Another important consideration that has to do with the explain-ability of AI algorithms and possible algorithmic bias. Regarding AI and trust, according to Accenture [15], several risks arise in this context. These include unethical or even illegal use of insights, amplifying biases that stem from issues of social and economic justice, and using data for purposes to which its original disclosers have not given their consent. Moreover, risks of AI adoption also include lack of transparency, biased algorithms, unclear liability for actions and decisions taken, loss of control, loss of privacy, the great influence of big data-driven AI companies like Facebook and Google, impact in the labor market, and the emergence of deep fake videos and fake news, among others. Thus, organizations should carefully consider the ethics behind the data collection, manipulation, and use.

4.5 Data Security and Privacy

A risk that Telecoms should mitigate has to do with how they handle security and privacy issues related to their data. For instance, as stated by SAS in [16], especially in Europe, General Data Protection Regulation (GDPR) in many cases restricts or, at least, complicates the process of personal data in the context of Analytics and AI. This is another challenge that European Telecoms must overcome. GDPR may eventually help create the trust that is necessary for AI acceptance by consumers and governments as we continue to progress toward a fully regulated data market. According to Accenture [15], AI risks that are left unchecked can severely damage the consumer trust in a brand. Interestingly, digital trust is difficult to build but easy to lose.

4.6 Data Infrastructure

For enterprises to transition from proofs of concept to deployed AI, existing data infrastructure and data management should be reconfigured. Machine learning systems require large amounts of data to function meaningfully, and it is not uncommon that the data needs to be in real-time, streaming format. Typically, most enterprise application systems are not set up this way. In contrast, AI adoption requires a highly flexible technology stack that can support big data volumes and cloud-native solutions. This also brings in additional costs related to the storage of large amounts of data and machines with the capability to process it. Moreover, another challenge related to data infrastructure is the scalability of models in production. Moving a model to production and having it scale to large amounts of data is a challenge that enterprises must overcome before they reap the real benefits of AI [16].

4.7 AI in the Change Management Process

In order AI to move to production and influence or automate day-to-day decisions, it should also convince C-executives about the positive Return on Investment (ROI). The business owners of a final product should stay in close contact with the people that are building the AI solutions, since relatively inexpensive proofs of concept get the green light but never make it to production when the associated costs of such a move are increased. AI requires a transformation in the mindset of enterprises not only technologically but also from a business point of view. A solution could be the involvement of outsourced experts that have already adopted AI in their enterprises and can help with the transition through the learnings they have acquired [17]. This cultural transformation is one that many Telecoms have started and should continue investing in the future.

5 Use Cases

Since the opportunities and challenges of the adaptation of AI technologies have been thoroughly presented in the sections above, the next logical step is to demonstrate the Use Cases that we are experimenting with, in order to evaluate AI technologies and measure potential benefits. Table 1 presents those Use Cases and illustrates their connection with the opportunities and challenges as we have previously identified.

Table 1. Use Cases mapping

Use cases	Oportunities	Common challenge
Chatbot & NLP	Customer centricity	Lack of analytical skills
Robotics	Process automation Customer & employee centricity	Security & privacy
Sentiment analysis	Customer & employee centricity	Lack of technology maturity
Machine vision	AI monitoring	Lack of expertise
Sales forecasting	Decision support New products & services	Ethics & trust
Predictive maintenance (Network/customer)	Operational support Optimization AI monitoring	Infrastructure

The potential for AI to drive revenue and profit growth is enormous. Marketing, customer service, and sales were identified as the top three functions where AI can realize its full potential according to a survey of more than one thousand executives by Forbes [18]. One of the biggest goals is to incorporate AI solutions in the daily operations of the company with a slow but certain and steady growth in the upcoming years. Of course, similar Use Cases have already been and will continue being experimented and tested within our organization, since there is efficient support and documentation that AI and Big Data Analytics projects bring financial and operational gain [19].

5.1 Chatbot and NLP

Today's natural language processing systems can analyze unlimited amounts of text-based data in a consistent and unbiased manner. They can understand concepts within complex contexts and decipher ambiguities of language to extract key facts and relationships [20]. Given the huge quantity of unstructured data that is produced every day this form of automation has become critical to analyzing text-based data efficiently. The basic concept here is the creation of chatbots that takes advantage of NLP systems in an interactive layout. Telecoms are among those that adopted chatbots at early stages. This innovative trend offered value to the customers as well as to the employees. Conversational AI chatbots in Telecom industry can reduce the waiting time of internal and external customers to a few seconds. Especially for external customers, apart from operating in simple and repetitive customer demands, chatbots can redirect complex cases enquires to appropriate departments on complex cases. Through chatbots a customer support center can operate effectively and minimize costs, while at the same time can allow agents to focus on their selling campaigns.

5.2 Robotics

The next AI area that it is believed that will be a future trend of Telecoms is the area of robotics applications. The adoption of their communication skills and the fast-operating tasks will make them an ideal assistant to Shop agents. Physical stores of the future will either be digital or at least have a high volume of digital flavor. Not far from now, humanoid robots will assist Shop agents in their tasks to interact and serve customers. Tasks that until now are difficult or even time consuming will be carried out by humanoid robots. Humanoid robots are being tested and used to enhance customer experience and engagement. Such robots can capture emotional cues from people and adapt their behavior appropriately [21]. Leading organizations should be planning on using intelligent robots to inform customers about their offerings in an interesting way, ensuring increased engagement.

5.3 Sentiment Analysis

Sentiment analysis is extremely important because it helps businesses quickly understand the overall opinions of their customers. By automatically sorting the sentiment behind reviews, social media conversations, and more, you can make faster and more accurate decisions. In today's Big Data environment and especially in Telecoms there is quite often a data overload issue created by customer feedback. Reasonably, it seems rather impossible for individuals to analyze the data manually without any sort of error or bias [22]. Thus, sentiment analysis could be used in order to sort/filter the data at scale by providing answers into what the most important issues are. Furthermore, by using a centralized sentiment analysis system, companies can apply the same criteria to all their data and minimize bias caused by subjectivity and opinions that are influenced by personal experiences and beliefs. Sentiment analysis can be used by companies to gain insights about how customers feel about certain topics, the company in general and finally it enables them to detect urgent issues or crisis in real time before they spiral out of control. By doing so, Telecoms can automatically organize incoming support queries (verbal and textual) by topic and urgency in order to route them to the correct person or department. This application also increases efficiency and ensures that customers are not left waiting for support and as a result decreases churn rate.

5.4 Machine Vision

Due to the existing covid-19 pandemic, several actions were forced to be adopted by large organizations. AI through Machine Vision mechanisms came to assist on issues such as the social distancing between the employees, as a mechanism to count people in a meeting room or even in stores. The fact that the exploitation of such Use Cases demonstrated a rapid volume of usage due to the pandemic, most definitely does not mean that their usage is limited to the existing situation. Evidence that supports the above statement can be found in multiple types of Organizations and Markets. The brightest example is Amazon [23] which has more than 25 autonomous stores scattered across the United States. One of the benefits from the implementation of computer vision in Telecom's retail stores is Stock visibility [24] (the awareness of what is basically happening at the Shop). The camera system intertwined with AI technology can detect all kinds of fraudulent attempts. It is also worth mentioning the stock visibility in the context of stock replenishment. The camera system can record deficiencies in specific products and inform the management in real time.

5.5 Sales Forecasting

Nowadays, where data availability, artificial intelligence (AI) and machine learning (ML) technologies are at their peak [25], accurate forecasts can most certainly become reality. Next to generic demand drivers like expected revenue, sales, and transactions, retailers would want to know the estimated foot fall, call centers the number of calls to expect and warehouse the number of orders. In addition, demand forecasting can form the foundation on which businesses can execute their supply chain systems, from procurement and inventory and warehouse management to distribution management [26]. Companies that utilize demand forecasting, can easily find themselves getting ahead of competition and assess their own performance. Improvement in supply chain efficiency is probably the most essential reason to use demand forecasting in operations management. Given the forecast of the level of sales and when they will occur, management can better schedule the procurement, warehousing, and shipping. This even enables management to plan scheduled maintenance shutdowns and most importantly to have adequate materials and labor on hand throughout the year. The need for such models became even more important during the pandemic. It is of vital importance that customers can purchase the products that they want, when they want them, and without delays.

5.6 Predictive Maintenance (Network/Customer)

Predictive maintenance is a technique that collects, analyzes, and utilizes data from various manufacturing sources like machines, sensors, switches, etc. It applies intelligent algorithms to the data to anticipate equipment failure before it happens [27]. In the Telecom industry insights on internal data to generate cost optimization in maintenance, analyze extra streams of revenue and their potential, and establish comparative advantage against competition is of essential value. An efficient AI-based alerting notification solution can be introduced in order to preserve the high QoS provided as a contractual requirement conforming to customer Service Level Agreement (SLA). Advanced ML techniques could be used in business context exploiting big data analytics or prediction capabilities. To do this, Petabytes (PBs) of data streams in real-time coming from core network backbone, log files from back-end infrastructure monitoring applications, anonymized subscribers' Call Detail Records (CDRs), etc. in daily basis in conjunction with a vast amount of historical data proceed to predictions on potential service degradation based on probabilistic models and ML techniques. A predictive maintenance example in research is the Typhon H2020 project [28] where its architectural components were deployed by using Telecom data. The project strives to anticipate equipment failures to allow for in advance scheduling of corrective actions, thereby preventing unexpected equipment downtime and improving customer service quality. By that, it enables proactive scheduling of corrective work, and thus prevents unexpected failures.

5.7 Research Collaborations

An industry that owns and handles vast amounts of data like mobility, sales, demographic, and traffic data, should search for the right methods and services to benefit from. A common and successful approach is through participation of research and innovation projects and partnerships to benefit from third parties' expertise in certain fields. For example, on the seaport transformation journey, the Telecommunication industry (also actively involved in ICT services) can have a significant role and perhaps become a key player towards the transformation success. Telecom holds the backbone of the data-driven environment [29,30] through its networks. DataPorts H2020 project [31] is such an example, where OTE offers anonymized mobility data to be used for seaport related analytic services and by that enhance the offered analytic services to the ecosystem.

6 Conclusions

Undoubtably, AI is in our daily routines and is an integral part of our work environments. Therefore, it is a reality and not a trend idea. AI is a tool for large organizations to leverage their assets and begin their digital transformation journey. A continuous journey that besides the numerous opportunities, there are many challenges and risks needed to be overcome. The digital transformation will emerge if the entire organization clearly plans the next steps and use AI as the technology that will push the organization forward. As it has been stated above, several beneficial use cases have already been implemented. It may be pointed out and verified by OTE as a Telecom Operator that more complex applications, such as traffic management and 5G related issues, are being considered for the foreseen future [32]. Thus the intention of large organizations should be to form and to establish innovation teams with data science and AI engineering capabilities. However, most organizations strive hard to match existing business problems/ needs with AI initiatives. What is needed is to set a concrete strategy, to on-board personnel with AI-related skillsets and in parallel to follow an AI lifecycle that fits properly with the organizations' business needs, otherwise the results might prove harmful for the organization. As in every case, there are considerations and risks that should be considered. Since the adoption of AI is today's reality, the legal and regulatory environment should be clearly understood, especially when data contains private or sensitive information. Regarding offering data service offering, entering a new area always demands careful business approaches. Since this contains data sharing, trust should also be considered, not only from a technological perspective but also from an ethical. The benefits of AI solutions in today's organizations have become more evident than ever, and many of them have already drive their digital transformation journeys.

Acknowledgements. This work does not necessarily reflect company's implementation plans as use cases mentioned later in this paper are in a proof-of-Concept phase.

References

1. European Commission Homepage. https://ec.europa.eu/info/sites/info/files/commission-white-paper-artificial-intelligence-feb2020_en.pdf
2. TCS Report. https://www.tcs.com/content/dam/tcs/pdf/Industries/global-trend-studies/ai/TCS-GTS-how-13-global-industries-use-artificial-intelligence.pdf
3. TechRepublic Homepage. www.techrepublic.com/google-amp/article/is-the-ai-software-market-headed-for-150-billion-or-closer-to-37-billion/
4. Gartner Research Homepage. https://www.gartner.com/en/newsroom/press-releases/2019-01-21-gartner-survey-shows-37-percent-of-organizations-have
5. Dachyar, M., Zagloel, T.Y.M., Saragih, L.R.: Enterprise architecture breakthrough for telecommunications transformation: a reconciliation model to solve bankruptcy. Heliyon **6**(10), e05273 (2020). https://doi.org/10.1016/j.heliyon.2020.e05273
6. TheMatic Homepage. https://getthematic.com/insights/sentiment-analysis/
7. MITSLoan Management Review. https://sloanreview.mit.edu/projects/artificial-intelligence-in-business-gets-real/

8. Feijóo, C., Kwonc, Y.: AI impacts on economy and society: latest developments, open issues and new policy measures. Telecommun. Policy **44**(6), 101987 (2020). https://doi.org/10.1016/j.telpol.2020.101987
9. Deloitte Homepage. https://www2.deloitte.com/content/dam/insights/us/articles/4780_State-of-AI-in-the-enterprise/DI_State-of-AI-in-the-enterprise-2nd-ed.pdf
10. Gartner Research Homepage. https://www.gartner.com/smarterwithgartner/how-to-get-started-with-aiops/
11. TCS Homepage. https://www.tcs.com/artificial-intelligence-to-have-dramatic-impact-on-business-by-2020
12. Techsee Homepage. https://techsee.me/blog/ai-customer-service/
13. Alation Homepage. https://go.alation.com/hubfs/Resources_Assets/alation-state-of-data-culture-report-q4-2020.pdf
14. McKinsey & Company Homepage. https://www.mckinsey.com/featured-insights/artificial-intelligence/the-promise-and-challenge-of-the-age-of-artificial-intelligence
15. Accenture Homepage. https://www.accenture.com/_acnmedia/pdf-22/accenture-data-ethics-pov-web.pdf
16. SAS Homepage. https://www.sas.com/en_id/insights/articles/data-management/gdpr-and-ai-friends-foes-or-something-in-between-.html#/
17. SearchEnterpriseAI Homepage. https://searchenterpriseai.techtarget.com/feature/Ignoring-infrastructure-leads-to-major-challenges-for-AI-adoption
18. Forbes Homepage. https://www.forbes.com/sites/forbesinsights/2020/05/08/realizing-the-growth-potential-of-ai/?sh=685de17d33f3
19. Kastouni, M.Z., Lahcen, A.A.: Big data analytics in telecommunications: governance, architecture and use cases. J. King Saud Univ. - Comput. Inf. Sci. (2020). https://doi.org/10.1016/j.jksuci.2020.11.024. ISSN 1319–1578
20. Linguamatics Homepage. https://www.linguamatics.com/what-text-mining-text-analytics-and-natural-language-processing
21. RobotLAB Homepage. https://www.robotlab.com/blog/introducing-robotics-in-interactive-marketing
22. MonkeyLearn Homepage. https://monkeylearn.com/sentiment-analysis
23. Amazon Web Services Homepage. https://aws.amazon.com/blogs/industries/seeing-dollar-signs-ways-to-leverage-computer-vision-in-retail-stores
24. FutureMind Homepage. https://www.futuremind.com/blog/use-cases-computer-vision-retail
25. Gartner Research Homepage. https://blogs.gartner.com/smarterwithgartner/files/2019/08/CTMKT_736691_Hype_Cycle_for_AI_2019.png
26. TCS Homepage. https://www.tcs.com/blogs/how-ml-can-take-demand-forecasting-to-next-level-in-supply-chain
27. Readitquik Homepage. https://www.readitquik.com/articles/data/using-ai-for-predictive-maintenance/
28. TYPHON Horizon 2020 Project. https://www.typhon-project.org
29. Gizelis, C.-A., Mavroeidakos, T., Marinakis, A., Litke, A., Moulos, V.: Towards a smart port: the role of the telecom industry. In: Maglogiannis, I., Iliadis, L., Pimenidis, E. (eds.) AIAI 2020. IAICT, vol. 585, pp. 128–139. Springer, Cham (2020). https://doi.org/10.1007/978-3-030-49190-1_12
30. Bonneau, V.: Data monetization: opportunities beyond OTT: finance, retail, telecom and connected objects. Commun. Strateg. **97**, 123 (2015)
31. DataPorts Horizon 2020 Project. http://dataports-project.eu
32. Balmer, R.E., Levin, S.L., Schmidt, S.: Artificial intelligence applications in telecommunications and other network industries. Telecommun. Policy **44**(6), 101977 (2020). https://doi.org/10.1016/j.telpol.2020.101977

Electronic Procurement Practices in the Public Sector: The Case of an Inter-organizational Information System in Ghana

Michael Nartey Agbeko(✉), John Effah, and Richard Boateng

Department of Operations and Management Information Systems, University of Ghana Business School, Accra, Ghana
mnagbeko@st.ug.edu.gh

Abstract. The importance of inter-organizational information systems (IOISs) to contemporary organizations has been demonstrated in research and practice. However, the effects of IOISs use on procurement practices in the public sector are less understood. The practice lens theory is drawn upon in this study to understand IOIS effects on procurement activities in the public sector of Ghana, a developing country context. The findings show the effects as: (1) successful online tendering processes; (2) unsuccessful online procurement execution processes; and (3) continuing use of paper-based document exchanges. The paper discusses how the effects resulted in a partial online procurement system and the failure to realize the desired benefits. It also discusses the constraints of a full-scale e-procurement platform deployment and use in developing country public sector and how they can be addressed.

Keywords: Inter-organizational information systems · Public sector · E-Procurement · Practice lens theory · Interpretive case study · Ghana

1 Introduction

The purpose of this study is to understand the effects of inter-organizational information systems (IOISs) use in public sector procurement practices. IOISs are ICT infrastructure that enables interactions between actors in different organizations [1]. Governments around the world pursue e-government initiatives to digitalize operations and improve effectiveness and efficiency [2]. One of such initiatives is electronic procurement (e-procurement) [3].

Within the public sector, e-procurement refers to the use of integrated web-based IOISs for government purchasing processes [4, 5]. E-procurement enables government institutions to conduct online public tenders and reach out to potential bidders [6]. In the public sector, e-procurement is noted to be one of the means to reduce corruption [6, 7].

Information systems (IS) research on IOISs in the public sector has focused on knowledge sharing and data synchronization [8, 9]. However, studies aiming at the effects of IOISs on procurement practices in the public sector are limited. Thus, this

Published by Springer Nature Switzerland AG 2021
D. Dennehy et al. (Eds.): I3E 2021, LNCS 12896, pp. 60–70, 2021.
https://doi.org/10.1007/978-3-030-85447-8_6

study is a novel attempt to extend the literature on IOISs to the area of e-procurement in the public sector. The research question we address is how does the use of IOISs influence procurement practices in the public sector?

Accordingly, we employ the practice lens theory [10] as analytical lens and qualitative interpretive case study [11] as the methodology to gain rich insight into the use of an IOIS for procurement activities in the public sector of Ghana, a developing country in Africa. Ghana was chosen because it has recently migrated its public sector procurement activities from offline to IOISs to improve operational processes and service delivery.

The rest of the paper is structured as follows. Section 2 reviews literature on IOISs and public sector e-procurement. Section 3 presents the practice lens as the theoretical foundation. Section 4 presents the methodology. Section 5 reports the empirical findings. Section 6 provides a practice lens analysis of the empirical findings. Section 7 discusses the research findings while Section 8 concludes the paper with its contribution.

2 Inter-organizational Information Systems and Public Sector E-Procurement

IOISs are central to business ecosystems and for communication between suppliers and buyers of goods and services [12]. The advantages that IOISs offer have motivated existing firms to move towards web-based business models [13]. Thus, actors in business ecosystems use IOISs to enable exchange of information on goods and services. A crucial characteristic of IOISs is the provision of digital affordances [12]. Digital affordance denotes what an individual or organization with a particular purpose can do with a technology [12, 13]. IOISs thus provide digital affordances to consumers and suppliers by offering them the technological infrastructure for easy communication [14].

In practice, some e-procurement systems provide information only (e-announcement), while others facilitate transactions [5]. The benefits of an e-procurement platform to adopting organizations include efficient procurement processes, cost reduction, improved internal services, and improved purchasing functions [6]. Specifically in the public sector, e-procurement systems offer additional benefits such as enhanced transparency, reduced corruption, and access to foreign and SME bidders [4].

In general, e-procurement practice in the public sector is more complicated than in the private sector [4]. It adheres to rigid regulations, depends on political decisions, and involves a variety of goods or services [15]. Transparency is one of the basic requirements in public sector e-procurement, and it usually involves a variety of stakeholders with different and often conflicting agendas [15]. Consequently, institutionalizing and using such systems become very challenging and more complex [3, 15].

Despite the insights from existing studies on IOISs and e-procurement, they fail to unearth knowledge on the relationship between IOIS use and procurement activities in the public sector. Thus, it is important to understand how procurement practices are influenced by IOISs use in the public sector.

3 Theoretical Foundation

The guiding lens for this study is the practice lens theory [10]. This study employs the practice lens theory to understand the effects of IOIS on procurement practices in the public sector. The basic concepts of the theory are facilities, norms, interpretive schemes, technology-in-practice, and ongoing situated use of technology.

Facilities refer to resources needed to accomplish work, n*orms* are rules that define the organizationally sanctioned way of executing work and *interpretive schemes* signify reflected knowledge of the work done [16]. *Technology-in- practice* denotes the specific interaction with technology repeatedly enacted in everyday situated activities [17]. *Ongoing situated use of technology* portrays a revised version of the technology-in-practice through repeated use as experienced differently by users at different times and circumstances [10].

The fundamental principle of the theory is enactment. Enactment is the reconstitution of technology-in-practice [10, 17]. Constant enactment of a technology-in-practice tends to reinforce it, so that it becomes standardized and repeated [10]. Enactment may occur in one of two forms: *reinforcement,* where actors enact essentially the same structures with no noticeable changes; or *transformation,* where actors enact changed structures with the changes ranging from incremental to substantial [10, 18].

The practice lens theory has been employed severally in IS research in recent years (e.g., use of technology in work places [19, 20], smart systems services [21], strategizing ICT practices [22]). However, the application of the theory in e-procurement studies IOISs studies is less hence its use in this study. The rationale for using it is that the principle and concepts are useful to understand the effects of IOISs use on online procurement services in the public sector.

4 Research Setting and Methodology

As part of a larger research project, this study was conducted as an interpretive qualitative case study [11] in Ghana. The study focuses on the effects of the use of an IOIS initiative aimed at transforming public sector procurement practices from physical to digital processes. The Ghana Electronic Procurement Systems (GHANEPS) is the IOIS and the Public Procurement Authority (PPA) is the government institution in charge of its implementation and use. GHANEPS interconnect the information systems of PPA, the Registrar General's Department (RGD), the Social Security and National Insurance Trust (SSNIT), the Ghana Revenue Authority (GRA) and the Ghana Integrated Financial Management Information System (GIFMIS).

4.1 Methodology

Interpretive case study was employed to understand how the use of IOISs shapes procurement practices in the public sector. Interpretive case study was used because it falls in line with the view that reality and the knowledge are socially constructed between researchers and respondents. The motivation for choosing qualitative interpretive case study approach is based on the understanding that the research phenomenon and its context can be understood through the meanings that participants assign to them.

4.2 Data Collection

We collected data from multiple sources, including interviews, observations, documents, and media news perusal. This approach is in conformity with interpretive research where many data sources can be used by a researcher. Interviews were conducted between 1st August, 2020 and 31st January, 2021. We used purposive sampling and snowballing to identify the various stakeholder-groups and interviewees. In all, 21 respondents were interviewed at their own convenience with sessions recorded upon gaining consent. Interviews were semi-structured [23, 24], lasted between 30 and 45 min, and transcribed. Table 1 shows the user-groups, interviewees, and number of interviews carried out.

Table 1. Stakeholder Groups, Interviewees and No. of Interviews

Stakeholder Groups	Interviewees	No. of Interviews
Central Government	Senior Government Official	1
Regulator (PPA)	Deputy CEO	1
	Head of MIS	2
	IT Officer	2
Public Agencies	Head of Agency	2
	Head of Procurement Unit	2
	Tender Coordinator	3
	Tender Evaluation Member	2
Suppler Organizations	Head of Organization	2
	Head of Procurement Department	2
	Staff of Procurement Department	2
Total		21

4.3 Data Analysis

We conducted data analysis by reading and re-reading all the data gathered from the interview transcripts, documents and field notes to derive logical meanings. In doing so, we sought to gain broad understanding of how the data gathered made sense towards the research question and the research purpose. Then, we iteratively compared the data with emerging findings for verification and confirmation. Where necessary, we followed up with interviewees to verify the emerging findings according to the principles of the hermeneutic circle [25].

5 Empirical Findings

Public procurement plays a significant role in national development. In view of this, the Government of Ghana passed the Public Procurement Act (Act 663) in 2003 to regulate procurement activities at all levels of government. Before 2019, procurement practices were carried out through physical interactions. However, from 2019, a digital transformation of these practices was initiated through the implementation of GHANEPS. The sections below describe procurement practices before GHANEPS and its use.

5.1 Procurement Practices Before GHANEPS

Procurement activities before GHANEPS involved invitation to tender, submission of tender, tender evaluation, and award of contract. At the time, a public agency would invite tenders by publishing in the procurement bulletin and/or at least two national newspapers. In the case of international competitive tendering, the invitation was published in an international newspaper, a technical or professional journal, or relevant trade publication. The public agency physically provided tender documents to potential suppliers in accordance with the procedures and requirements specified in the procurement Act.

Potential suppliers were allowed four weeks for national competitive tendering or at least six weeks in the case of international competitive tendering for submission of tenders. Tenders were formulated in English and physically submitted at a place and time fixed by the public agency. Public agencies could extend the deadline for submission of tenders before its expiration. Notice of the extension was communicated by fax, e-mail or any other expedited written means of communication to suppliers to whom tender documents had been given.

Tenders were physically opened and evaluated when the time specified in their documents as deadline for the submission or extension is due. A supplier who had submitted a tender or their representative was permitted to be physically present at the opening. During the examination of tenders, a supplier could be asked for clarification of its tender in order to assist in the examination, evaluation, and comparison of tenders.

Award of contract involved acceptance of the tender by the public agency and the signing of a procurement agreement with a successful supplier. A contract came into force on the commencement date indicated therein. A public agency could select the next successful tender if a supplier whose tender had been accepted failed to execute the tender within 30 days, unless otherwise stated. A head of a public agency during one of the interviews noted that:

> *"Before a contract is signed, a public agency must ensure that the service provider meets all statutory requirements. The challenge here is that the verification of statutory requirement is cumbersome. This is due to the lack of interconnectivity between the information systems of statutory bodies in the country."*

5.2 Use of GHANEPS

GHANEPS is a web-based, collaborative IOIS that offers a secure and dynamic environment for carrying out procurement of all categories, complexity or value. It is expected to be used by all public agencies and the general population. GHANEPS was designed to support online procurement practices and procedures such as tender invitation, preparation, submission, and evaluation. It also supports advanced procurement procedures such as contract awarding, catalogue creation and management, framework agreements, auctions and payments, and asset disposal.

Public agencies are required to register on GHANEPS before they can invite and issue tenders. The head of the procurement unit (HPU) of a public agency initiates the invitation process on GHANEPS by creating a workspace per tender. The HPU then uploads a procurement plan onto the workspace and associates other users with the tender. The users associated with tenders are procurement officers (POs), tender opening panel (TOP) members, and tender evaluation panel (TEP) members of which one is the chairperson (TEPC). The associated PO uploads all documents for the tender, after which the HPU defines the workflow and evaluation criteria for the tender. The HPU then creates and publishes tender notices on GHANEPS and/or send them via emails to registered suppliers.

A supplier needs to register with PPA to bid for and submit tenders. Apart from the information systems of the RGD, SSNIT, and GRA, GHANEPS was supposed to interconnect with the Payment and SMS Gateways for effective delivery of services. The interconnections of these systems are needed for the necessary background checks on the supplier to be done. While the information system of the RGD enables PPA to verify if a supplier has been registered and incorporated as a business entity in Ghana, that of SSNIT helps to check if the supplier pays employee contributions. The information system of GRA helps to check whether a supplier has paid all relevant taxes and that of Payment Gateway is to enable the payment of procurement processing charges to PPA and public agencies to pay suppliers for executed contract.

If a supplier is interested in a particular tender, its associated documents are downloaded. After downloading the documents, the supplier then creates and submits a bid for the tender on GHANEPS. During an interview, an IT officer at PPA noted that:

> *"Apart from the SMS gateway which GHANEPS has successfully connected to for the sending of emails, it is unable to connect to the information systems of other public institutions and service providers which it is required to link up with. This is because the owners of the systems such as SSNIT, Registrar General and Ghana Revenue Authority are unwilling to connect them to GHANEPS due to security reasons. This means that some tendering processes involving third party organizations are still done manually"*

Tender evaluation is digitally performed on GHANEPS by the TEP. Members of the TEP with conflicts of interest are not allowed to evaluate tenders. Evaluation of a submitted bid is performed when TEP members unlock bided documents and assess them. TEP members unlock bids by clicking on the unlock-bid button on the evaluation page of GHANEPS. Documents on the unlocked bids then appears on the assessment page of GHANEPS. A TEP member then assesses the unlocked bid by reading through the documents and inputting the result and other observations on the assessment page. Evaluation is finalized when the TEPC using GHANEPS generate a report that consists of summed up results of each TEP member on each submitted bid in ascending order.

The evaluation report is then approved by the TEP and head of the public agency (HPO) on GHANEPS.

After the approval of the tender evaluation report, the PO announces the results on GHANEPS, by SMS, and email to bidders. The HPO then awards a contract to the bidder with the highest evaluation result by uploading contract documents on GHANEPS. The bidder who wins the contract receives SMS message from GHANEPS about the uploaded contract documents, digitally signs it, and uploads it back on GHANEPS. Lack of necessary ICT gadgets, high cost of internet data, slow and unstable internet connectivity, high ICT illiteracy rate among service providers are some challenges that users complain about when using GHANEPS.

6 Analysis

The empirical findings raise a number of interesting issues for analysis and discussion. However, in line with the research question and the practice lens theory, this section focuses on the technology-in-practice and ongoing situated use before and after the IOIS for procurement.

6.1 Technology-in-Practice and Ongoing Situated Use Before E-Procurement IOIS

The empirical findings suggest the existence of some form of technology-in-practice before the e-procurement IOIS. The pre e-procurement technology-in-practice included: paper based forms; physical tender documents, procurement plans and related records; physical signature; telephone communication and emails, and the procurement act (Act 603). The use of these technology-in-practice elements before the adoption of GHANEPS constrained effective delivery of procurement services in the public sector. This led to challenges such as frustration on the part of the organizations that access procurement services, bureaucracy and unprofessional attitude of procurement officers in public agencies, delay in document processing, and corruption. The findings also suggest that invitation of tenders, submission of tenders, tender evaluation, and contract awarding were the main procurement activities to be routinely carried out i.e. ongoing situated use before GHANEPS and these activities were physically performed.

6.2 Technology-in-Practice and Ongoing Situated Use After E-Procurement IOIS

GHANEPS is the main facility needed to ensure effective offering of procurement services in the public sector. It was designed to migrate all procurement activities online, thus removing the use of physical paper and signature, as well as reducing physical contact between stakeholders. Attestation, tender notification, tender submission, contract awarding, cataloging, auctioning, and project management are the practices (i.e. norms) routinely performed through the IOIS. GHANEPS connects third-party information systems such as RGD, SSNIT, GRA, Payment Gateway, and SMS Gateway for these activities to be successfully carried out. These third-party systems, GHANEPS, and the norms were to ensure the following interpretive schemes (i.e. benefits): improve public procurement integrity; reduce corruption and procurement malpractices; enhance regulator and public entities decision making capabilities; increase compliance to procurement laws and regulations; and shortened procurement processes and cycles.

These interpretive schemes are however constrained by lack of necessary ICT gadgets, high cost of internet data, slow and unstable internet connectivity, and high ICT illiteracy rate among staff of supplier organizations. This has made GHANEPS a partial online system offering basic electronic procurement practices such as tender invitation, submission, evaluation, contract awarding, as well as SMS messaging. However, advance procurement practices such as project management, attestation, management of framework agreements, auctions and payments, and asset disposal are still offered offline.

7 Discussion

GHANEPS was intended to enable the offering of all public sector procurement practices online. The empirical findings however show that this agenda was not entirely achieved. This is because GHANEPS could not interconnect with some third-party systems needed to efficiently carry out procurement activities online. This is due to the unwillingness of the management of some of the institutions to allow interconnection between GHANEPS and their information systems because of security reasons. Effective collaboration between information systems of different organizations has been found to be one of the main benefits of IOISs [4, 9]. Nevertheless, such interconnectivities are usually associated with high security risks due to interactions between customer devices, organizations' back-end infrastructure and other third-party information systems [9]. The lack of interconnectivity between GHANEPS and related third-party systems in the public sector leads to the offering of basic electronic procurement practices such as tender invitation, submission, evaluation, contract awarding as well as SMS messaging. Advanced electronic procurement practices such as attestation, cataloging, and project management are not carried out on GHANEPS.

Other factors also shape the non-effective use of GHANEPS. These factors include: lack of necessary ICT gadgets; high cost of internet data; slow and unstable internet connectivity; and high illiteracy rate among suppliers. Public agencies and suppliers need computers to connect and use the functionalities on GHANEPS. However, due to the lack of these devices, users from these agencies and supplier organizations are unable to connect, access, and use the platform satisfactorily.

Additionally, the high cost of internet data and the slow and unstable internet connectivity discourage stakeholders from the using GHANEPS. Third-party systems need to be always available and connected to GHANEPS for effective use. However, it is sometimes difficult to access the interconnected third-party systems through GHANEPS, even in Accra, the capital city due to unstable internet. Also, the internet is not available in most of rural Ghana, thus making it difficult for users in the remote parts of the country to access and use GHANEPS and its third-party systems. Challenges with internet connectivity are identified as one of the constraints of IOIS adoption [26, 27].

Moreover, Ghana has a large segment of her population being illiterate, particularly in ICT. Employees of small scale setups and suppliers are largely ICT illiterates. Thus, they are mostly unable to use ICT devices. Those who can use ICT devices sometimes find it difficult to understand some of the functionalities on GHANEPS. This discourages them to connect and use GHANEPS and its third-party systems. Thus, lack of IT expertise and infrastructure, technology competence, technology integration, technology readiness, unresolved technical issues, and web functionalities misunderstandings are key technological factors identified by prior research as inhibiting the effective use of IOISs [27, 28].

Finally, this study suggests that neither reinforcement nor transformation, outcomes of the enactment has been achieved as a result of the ongoing situated use of GHANEPS. Thus, enactment of technology in practice has not been realized in the case of GHANEPS making it a partial online IOIS.

8 Conclusion

The purpose of this study was to understand how the use of e-procurement IOIS influences procurement practices in the public sector. By applying the practice lens theory to analyze IOIS use in e-procurement practices, our work, in a novel way, contributes to IOIS research in the public sector in general and e-procurement utilization in particular. The findings show that though IOISs are promising means for effective collaboration between actors in public sector procurement, it was not entirely so in this case. The analysis demonstrates that the effects of using e-procurement IOIS on procurement practices in the public sector include the offering of basic procurement activities to the detriment of advanced procurement practices, and persistence use of physical documents, signature, contacts, and disjointed third-party systems. As a result, the e-procurement IOIS has become a partial instead of a full online platform. This is attributed to constraining factors in the environment such as lack of ICT devices, high cost of internet data, slow and unstable internet connectivity, and high ICT illiteracy rate among staff of supplier organizations. Accordingly, to derive intended benefits, attention should be paid not only to enablers, but also to constraints that shape the use of IOISs for procurement in the public sector.

This study contributes to research, practice and policy. For research, the study reveals the emergent structures that enable and/or constrain the link between e-procurement practices and IOISs usage (i.e. technology in practice) in the public sector. By identifying these structures, the study extends existing knowledge in IOISs use in the public sector in developing countries. For practice, the study shows that managers of government institutions should not only be interested in implementing digital infrastructures such as GHANEPS but should be equally concerned with how the use of such infrastructures can affect procurement in the public sector. For policy the study calls on governments, particularly in developing countries to create the right structures (i.e. institutional environment and frameworks, and provision of appropriate technological infrastructure) to support IOISs use in the public sector. The study is limited by its single country focus. However, with the principles of interpretive study, the findings are applicable to developing countries with similar context. Future research can look at the creation of public value via e-procurement platform use.

References

1. Schultze, U., Hiltz, S.R., Nardi, B.: Using synthetic worlds for work and learning. Commun. Assoc. Info. Syst. **22**, 351–370 (2007)
2. Effah, J.: Virtual platforms for government services in covid-19 and beyond: a sociomaterial case study of passport service in Ghana. In: International Working Conference on Transfer and Diffusion of IT, pp. 150–161. **IFIP**, Tiruchirappalli (2020)
3. Tiwana, A.: Platform Ecosystems: Aligning Architecture, Governance, and Strategy. Kaufmann Publishers Inc., San Francisco (2014)
4. Ahmad, T., Aljafari, R., Venkatesh, V.: The government of Jamaica's electronic procurement system: experiences and lessons learned. Internet Res. **29**(6), 1–18 (2019)
5. Vaidya, K., Campbell, J.: Multidisciplinary approach to defining public E-Procurement and evaluating its impact on procurement efficiency. Info. Syst. Front. **18**, 333–348 (2016)
6. Wahid, F., Sein, M.K.: Steering institutionalization through institutional work: the case of an eprocurement system in Indonesian local government. In: 47th Hawaii International Conference on System Science, Hawaii, pp. 4264–4274 (2014)
7. Seo, D., Tan, C.-W., Warman, G.: Vendor satisfaction of E-Government procurement systems in developing countries: an empirical research in Indonesia. Info. Technol. Develop. **24**(3), 554–581 (2018)
8. Mohungoo, I., Brown, I., Kabanda, S.: A systematic review of implementation challenges in public E-Procurement. In: Hattingh, M., Matthee, M., Smuts, H., Pappas, I., Dwivedi, Y.K., Mäntymäki, M. (eds.) I3E 2020. LNCS, vol. 12067, pp. 46–58. Springer, Cham (2020). https://doi.org/10.1007/978-3-030-45002-1_5
9. Al-Busaidi, K.A., Olfman, L.: Knowledge sharing through inter-organizational knowledge sharing systems. J. Info. Knowl. Manage. Syst. **47**(1), 110–136 (2017)
10. Corbiere, F.D., Rowe, F.: From ideal data synchronization to hybrid forms of interconnections: architectures, processes, and data. J. Assoc. Info. Syst. **14**(10), 550–584 (2013)
11. Orlikowski, W.J.: Using technology and constituting structures: a practice lens for studying technology in organizations. Organ. Sci. **11**(4), 404–428 (2000)
12. Walsham, G.: Interpretive case studies in is research: nature and method. Euro. J. Info. Syst. **4**(2), 74–81 (1995)
13. Parker, G., Van Alstyne, M., Jiang, X.: Platform ecosystems: how developers invert the firm. MIS Q. **41**(1), 255–266 (2016)
14. Asadullah, A., Faik, I., Kankanhalli, A.: Evolution mechanisms for digital platforms: a review and analysis across platform types. In: 39th International Conference on Information Systems, ICIS, San Francisco, pp. 1–9 (2018)
15. Hein, A., Setzke, D.S., Hermes, S., Weking, J.: The influence of digital affordances and generativity on digital platform leadership. In: 40th International Conference on Information Systems, **ICIS**, Munich, pp. 1–10 (2019)
16. Orlikowski, W.J.: Knowing in practice: enacting a collective capability in distributed organizing. Organ. Sci. **13**(3), 249–273 (2002)
17. Boudreau, M.C., Robey, D.: Enacting integrated information technology: a human agency perspective. Organ. Sci. **16**(1), 3–18 (2005)
18. Giddens, A.: The Constitution of Society: Outline of the Theory of Structure. University of California Press, Berkeley (1984)
19. Orlikowski, W.J.: Sociomaterial practices: exploring technology at work. Organ. Stud. **28**(9), 1435–1448 (2007)
20. Wessel, L., et al.: Configuration in smart service systems: a practice-based inquiry. Info. Syst. J. **29**, 1256–1292 (2019)

21. Kwayu, S., Lal, B., Abubakre, M.: Enhancing organisational competitiveness via social media - a strategy as practice perspective. Info. Syst. Front. **20**, 439–456 (2018)
22. Sergeeva, A., Huysman, M., Soekijad, M., Hooff, B.V.: Through the eyes of others: how onlookers shape the use of technology at work. MIS Q. **41**(4), 1153–1178 (2017)
23. Myers, M.D.: Qualitative research in information systems. MIS Q. **21**(2), 241–242 (1997)
24. Myers, M.D.: Qualitative Research in Business and Management. Sage, Thousand Oaks (2013)
25. Klein, H., Myers, M.: A set of principles for conducting and evaluating interpretive field studies in information systems. MIS Q. **23**(1), 67–93 (1999)
26. Webb, P.C., P.: Demystifying a hermeneutic approach to IS research. Australasian J. Info. Syst. **13**(2), 31–48 (2006)
27. Kreuzer, S., Krönung, J., Bernius, S.: Dismantling the environmental context - the role of environmental characteristics in the organizational adoption of open standard-based inter-organizational information systems. In: 22nd European Conference on Information Systems, ECIS, Tel Aviv, Isreal, pp. 1–16 (2014)
28. Lairet, G., Rowe, F., Geffroy, B.: Understanding the undesirable effects of using interorganizational systems and integrated information systems: case studies among supply chain partners. In: 24th European Conference on Information Systems, **ECIS**, İstanbul, Turkey, pp. 1–16 (2016)

Adopting Artificial Intelligence in the Saudi Arabian Public Sector: Preliminary Findings

Albandari Alshahrani[1(✉)], Denis Dennehy[1], and Matti Mäntymäki[2]

[1] National University of Ireland Galway, Galway, Ireland
{a.alshahrani2,denis.dennehy}@nuigalway.ie
[2] University of Turku, Turku, Finland
matti.mantymaki@utu.fi

Abstract. Artificial Intelligence (AI) has received significant attention in recent years, with claims of unlimited potential across sectors and industries. Despite the media hype about AI, there is limited understanding of how governments can utilize AI for the delivery of value to citizens and what are the barriers and trade-offs that need to be addressed to lead to value realization. AI has the potential to bring transformative benefits to society, but first we need to understand the current state of play in the public sector through an appropriate theoretical lens. We adopt the attention-based view of the organization to identify key challenges in terms of organizational attention. This study draws on a single case study in Saudi Arabia to identify key challenges associated with the adoption of AI.

Keywords: Artificial Intelligence · Data · Big data · Public sector · AI adoption · Saudi Arabia

1 Introduction

AI has been claimed to convey significant transformative potential across sectors. Global spending on AI is predicted to be nearly $98 Billion in 2023, more than double what was spent in 2019 (International Data Corporation), and by 2025, nearly a quarter (24%) of global GDP will come from AI technologies (World Economic Forum). AI technologies have the potential to significantly change how we live and work, as Google CEO Sundar Pichai recently stated "*AI is one of the most important things humanity is working on. It is more profound than electricity or fire*" [8]. In the words of the late Stephen Hawking: "*AI could be the biggest event in the history of our civilization. Or the worst! We just don't know*". For example, the power of IBM Watson in a cancer diagnosis and Google DeepMind in a military sphere [9–11].

Simply put, AI can be described as a set of techniques used to simulate human cognitive processes such as learning, inference, and self-correction human-like tasks [1, 2]. AI is attributed as being the catalyst of the so-called Fourth Industrial Revolution [3]. AI as a concept is not new, as it can be traced back to 1956 but since then it experienced cycles of silence known as AI winter [5]. Despite its long history, there is still no universal standardized definition [4]. AI aims to improve computer capability in four broad domains,

Published by Springer Nature Switzerland AG 2021
D. Dennehy et al. (Eds.): I3E 2021, LNCS 12896, pp. 71–81, 2021.
https://doi.org/10.1007/978-3-030-85447-8_7

namely, natural language processing (NLP), knowledge representation (KR), automated reasoning (AR), and machine learning (ML) [6, 7]. AI can also be used in general tasks such as fraud detection [12, 13], robotic process automation (RPA) [14], chatbots being used as an interactive model with citizens [15], and use in new drug discovery [16–19].

Despite the popularity of AI there is a scarcity of rigorous studies that focus on AI adoption in the real world, specifically within the public sector [20–22]. Furthermore, there is a need to advance understanding of AI, by considering the mixed views regarding AI applications and providing empirically based insights [20, 23, 24]. Arguably, AI in the public sector has a different area of implementation with diverse opportunities and challenges, where the decision-making context is heavily influenced by policies, effects on society and commerce, and the wider environmental characteristics are continuously changing [21, 25, 26,].

To this end, the aim of this study is *"to explore the challenges of AI adoption in the public sector of Saudi Arabia"*.

We draw on the attention-based view (ABV) of the organisation as the theoretical lens through which to study AI adoption in Saudi Arabia as it encompasses the noticing, encoding, interpreting, and focusing of time and effort by organizational decision-makers to address challenges and seize opportunities.

The remainder of this paper is structured as follows. First, we provide context to this study by reviewing extant literature on AI in the public sector and Saudi Arabia. Then the research methodology and data collection methods are discussed. Next, key findings and discussion are presented. The paper ends with conclusion, limitations, and future research.

2 Related Literature

2.1 AI in the Public Sector

The reported opportunities of AI in the public sector include increased productivity and performance, less human errors and lower costs, by removing administrative duties and better resource allocation [12, 14, 27–29]. There are also claims that AI impact many rules-based activities and repetitive, while also creating more than 133 million new jobs by 2022 [30, 31].

In the context of AI adaption budget, AI technology spending in Europe for 2019 has increased 49% over the 2018 figure to reach $5.2 billion [32]. By 2030, AI may lend 20% of GDP in China by 2030 [33]. The value of Saudi Arabia's data and AI economy is currently estimated at 4–5.3 billion USD, and there is an opportunity to generate additional revenues and savings of over 10.6 billion USD using these insights to help guide government decisions. It is expected to contribute an estimated 14 percent growth to its GDP by 2030, "the equivalent of an additional 15.7 trillion USD". [34–36]. Furthermore, the importance of data for artificial intelligence (AI), such as the importance of water for plants. As Clive Hamby stated that "*Data is the new oil*" [36]. Some studies argue about AI ability to interpret and learn from external data to obtain useful outcomes in a dynamic way. The success of AI in delivering outstanding performance for specific tasks, such as robotic vehicles, flexible scheduling, etc. relies on big data availability. AI and big data are now apparently inseparable [37, 38].

Along similar lines, recently, the importance of AI and Data can be shown when it comes to deal with the COVID-19 pandemic. For example, an AI-based model of HealthMap used as a tracking model at Boston Children's Hospital (USA). It alarmed the first sign earlier than a scientist warning at the Program for Monitoring Emerging Diseases (PMED). Moreover, a prognostic prediction model was developed using Algorithmic Machine learning at Tongji Hospital in Wuhan, China. It predicts the death-rate risk of an infected person and how accurate s/he is affected by COVID-19 (with 80% accuracy). [39, 40].

Despite the raised level of AI adoption advantages within many areas in term of efficiency, improved productivity and reliability, and a big bright picture, these technologies are not welcoming globally when it is deal with work displacement [41], as well as it raises ethical concerns connected to data bias, governance, safety, privacy, and data ownership [42]. The adoption of AI technology in the public sector creates a demanding challenge that likely remains a shortcoming within the next years [27, 43, 44]. AI and Data regulations and ethics are another global concern [45, 46]. Nevertheless, there is still humble knowledge about the types of AI applications' contribution for governments and how to bridge the gap between citizens' satisfactions and government abilities considering AI within the capabilities of arising challenges [47].

2.2 AI Adoption in Saudi Arabia

The government of Saudi Arabia launched the Vision 2030 initiative in 2016 with specific goals and development directions to diversify its economy. Driven by this vision to ensure the nation can reduce its dependency on oil [6, 48]. One plan covers investing and developing in AI technology and its assimilation into a new mega-city called "*Neom*" [6, 49]. Recent developments have seen Saudi Arabia become increasingly interested in the AI revolution. For instance, in September 2019, King Salman Bin Abdulaziz gave a decree to set up a "National Authority for Data and Artificial Intelligence". There are currently several AI-related technologies available, but none have explanations of their challenges in Saudi Arabia, particularly from the viewpoint of leadership.

In line with AI and Data opportunity, Saudi Data and AI Authority (SADAIA)[1] in partnership with the Ministry of Health, launched two common applications called Tawakkalna, "توكلنا" and Tabaud "تباعد" in response to Covid-19. Both applications use Machine learning algorithms and citizens/foreigner's data to manage virus spreading. Tabaud uses in tracking and predicting affected areas [50, 51]. Despite AI contribution to the COVID-19 outbreak, it is used to help the vaccination process. For instance, Tawakkalna application has been used in vaccination organizing where it helps to identify automatic alerts to determine where the closed vaccination center is and generate e-pass to those who are already vaccinated to let them free public moving [50]. Another example indicating the importance of AI to Saudi Arabia's economic development, the Global Artificial Intelligence Summit 2020 was held in Riyadh in Oct 2020 [6]. And then Saudi government announced the Line, it is a proposed smart city project where it is in Neom

[1] The Saudi Data and Artificial Intelligence Authority (SDAIA) was set up by a Royal Decree in August 2019.

under construction; it seeks to integrate robotics and AI seamlessly into every aspect of citizens' lives [52].

3 Methodology

This exploratory work embraces the most widely recognized methods for data gathering used in qualitative research, interview study. It involves professionals responsible for the adoption of AI technology in the public sector of Saudi Arabia. The case study method was selected because it is suited to explore experiences and views on specific issues [53–55]. The case was chosen for two key reasons that are pertinent to this study. First, this case is considered an exemplar case of a public sector organisation adopting AI technology in Saudi Arabia at different stages, which provided rich awareness of the challenges encountered. Second, a member of the research team had direct access to the case, as they are a citizen of Saudi Arabia, and their doctoral research is funded by the Saudi Arabian government.

The case studied is a public university established in 1998. It is one of the top universities in Saudi Arabia, with more than 70,000 students. This university has earmarked AI & Data department responsible for coordinating the adoption AI to automate more than 137 tasks such as evaluating student performance, student performance prediction, learning outcomes, predicting students learning style, a recommendation system for students, and more [56]. This University classified as F9. Education in OECD Classification where the sectors are categorized by function of government [57].

To select individuals that are representative of the population in the case studied, we employed 'snowball sampling' [58, 59]. Five key decision-makers (see Table 1) were interviewed as they had extensive experience with AI hold PhD qualifications in data science.

Table 1. Interviewee profile

Code	Job title	Years of experience
R1	Director of Centre for AI	16
R2	Vice Dean of IT	9
R3	Academic staff in IT	11
R4	E-learning department and IT project	7
R5	Project manager and data scientist	7

The interviews were conducted remotely using online meeting tools (e.g., Zoom, Microsoft Teams, and Google Meeting). The duration of interviews ranged between 40 and 60 min. Semi-structured interviews were used to obtain rich insights to the context of the three cases studies and the emergent challenges. Interviews were recorded and transcribed, some in Arabic Language and then translated to English. Notes were taken during the interviews. For the purpose of research rigour and anoymonity, a code (e.g., R1) was assigned to each interviewee.

Analyzes of the data was guided by the Gioia method [cf. 63] as this method can extract novel insights by carefully investigating how different actors of an organizational process experience events (i.e., adoption of AI). The Gioia method also facilitates 'research rigor' [*ibid*] as it enables inductive researchers to use systematic, conceptual, and analytical discipline, that can lead to findings that are credible.

4 Analysis and Findings

Analyzes of the data was guided by the Gioia method as it facilitates 'research rigor' [63], by enabling researchers to use systematic, conceptual, and analytical discipline, that can lead to findings that are credible. The key findings that emerged from the interviews are presented in the remainder of this section.

Theme 1: Fear of AI

Fear of failure: A number of employees have the ability and capability to learn and master new experiences. However, to adapt to a complex technology like AI, most university staff fear failure. This was explained by one of the managers in the department when he commenced that:

> *"The employees in some departments have passion about AI, but they fear failure".* ***R4***

Losing Jobs*:** Job security is the main challenge factor for employees who work ***routine jobs. They are not aware of AI, which uses as assisting tools not to replace their jobs. One of the respondents said:

> *"Many employees are influenced by the media about AI danger and the uncertainty of the future when using AI".* ***R3***

Theme 2: Administrative Challenges

Understanding the Significance of Data and AI Technology: At the administrative level, some managers are not aware of AI and Data's importance to ease the decision-making process. One of the interviewers mentioned this in his statement:

> *"There are some decision-makers who are still stuck working on a traditional way. They don't want technological intervention or any innovations to interrupt the ongoing processes. It is difficult to deal with them or convince them of the benefits of the technology in facilitating work".* ***R5***

Department Collaboration: At the administrative level with the same organization, they have a conflict where different colleges, departments, and sections have a different system. Some departments do not integrate with some initiatives launched AI center. They do not share data, *"There is no administrative incorporation with each other, as each* *department has a different system"……….."No one wants to take the responsibility to share data, as we still do not have any regulation or rules to manage this"*. ***R3.***

Theme 3: Issues with Data

Data Digitalization: Digital transformation will also contribute to achieving sustainable development goals. There is a massive amount of data at the university still saved and stored handily way, one of the E-learning Department and IT project team reported:

> *"We have a huge number of documents still stored in a traditional way, paper-based stores. It takes years to Digitalize it"*. ***R4***

Big Data: Dealing with big data is a significant challenge facing organizations. Big data management and engineering require efforts to handle data size, variety, and processing methods. It also demands a suitable infrastructure and tools and needs advanced technology to store, clean, update and analysis, etc. the Dean of Information Technology reported:

> *"We have a large volume of data,75K students, and each student has dedicated data. In addition, university's materials, employees' databases, etc. This huge number needs to be managed efficiently also need a well technological infrastructure must be established to manage it"*. ***R5***

Lack of Data Specialist: Data expert can be someone who has the capability to deal with data warehouse tools as well as an individual or group of specialists to build, clean, engineering, and preparing data for AI algorithmic models. Specialization and expertise are other important aspect of implementing AI technology in the public sector. Some organizations called them data scientists where other data engineers. In Saudi Arabia, this skill is absent, especially for someone with relevant skills to support and promote AI development.

"To build a solid infrastructure, we need manpower, such as database administrators, data scientist, data engineer, we need a real data scientist who has a good experience, not those who attended three months online course". ***R5.***

Data Governance: One of the problems that is almost repeatedly mentioned by most of the interviewees was Data governance, policies, and guidelines. In the use of AI, we are in circle one of Data accessibility and regulations. The Director of the Centre for AI stated:

"We don't have ethical regulations for using AI and its consumed Data specifically here in the university, and you could use that as the novelty of your research". ***R1.***

Furthermore, another informant shared a similar view saying *"There are many legislations for the uses of technology in the university such as not inappropriately using personal data also not disclosing them, but currently, there is no governance and legislation for artificial intelligence and its structured data"*. ***R2.***

A summary of the preliminary findings is provided in Table 2.

Table 2. Challenges to AI adoption.

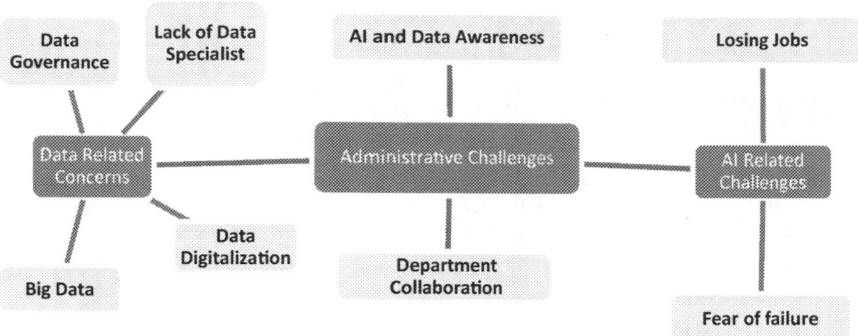

5 Discussion and Implications

Within the scope of our literature research, the scientific contribution to this study is inspired by its usefulness and originality. First, the most significant contribution of this research is addressing eight main challenges of AI adoption and Data in the context of public sector organizations in Saudi Arabia. Second, by providing an empirical review of the existing adaption plan and concerns related to AI and Data as Interdependence phases. Further, the insights achieved from this study offer implications in AI and data opportunities and challenges which helps decision-makers in the public sector to consider when adopting AI technologies.

Implications for Research: As our research develops upon existing AI adoption literature in a public sector, it contributes to the original knowledge [60, 61]. This research helps develop and implement AI adoption and placement policies that can contribute to embedding AI-based capabilities within and throughout the organization, leading to both business and social value to be generated by the specific AI technology. An implication for public sector leaders and key decision-makers is the need. Besides, research on AI adoption still lacks in the public sector, and its outcomes need to be regulated.

Implications for Practice: Based on the convincing evidence currently available, our research seems fair to suggest practical insights. First, it delivers a first overview step of the challenges associated with adopting AI in the public sector in Saudi Arabia. An implication for public sector associations targeting at development of AI-based public services is the need to review the organizational readiness [62]. This includes considerations of social and technical aspects. Second, despite the potential benefits of AI in the public sector, one of the AI adoption challenges that key decision-makers should consider as fundamental issues are data-related challenges that should not be set aside. As examples of these obstacles, data availability, quality, confidentiality, ethics, and integrity. There will be additional costly effort associated with collecting, storing, and sharing AI technology-derived large data sets. This cost can be related to the budget or extra space and management requirements for data storage, cleaning, integrating, readiness, validation, and infrastructure tools. Although, if the data are not accessible, AI adoption is a waste of effort and might fail.

6 Conclusion and Future Work

In this study, we focused on the challenges of AI in the context of a public sector organization in Saudi Arabia. As with all research, however, we acknowledge this study has two limitations, which also offer directions for future research. First, the collection and analysis of the data from a single case study limits generalisability of the findings. Future research could focus on multiple case studies of public sector organizations in Saudie Arabia or other countries. Despite this limitation, this paper provides a starting point to study the adoption of AI in the context of public sector organizations in Saudi Arabia.

To conclude, adopting AI requires consideration of not just its technical characteristics, but to take into consideration the context of its intended use and the readiness of the organization as a whole. Concluding, public sector organizations need to continually learn how to balance the social and technical aspects of AI as both can directly and indirectly have a positive or negative impact on people internal and external to the organization.

References

1. Pomerol, J.-C.: Artificial intelligence and human decision making. Eur. J. Oper. Res. **99**(1), 3–25 (1997)
2. Mikalef, P., Fjørtoft, S.O., Torvatn, H.Y.: Artificial intelligence in the public sector: a study of challenges and opportunities for norwegian municipalities. In: Pappas, I.O., Mikalef, P., Dwivedi, Y.K., Jaccheri, L., Krogstie, J., Mäntymäki, M. (eds.) I3E 2019. LNCS, vol. 11701, pp. 267–277. Springer, Cham (2019). https://doi.org/10.1007/978-3-030-29374-1_22
3. Brynjolfsson, E., McAfee, A.: The Second Machine Age: Work, Progress, and Prosperity in a Time of Brilliant Technologies. WW Norton & Company, New York (2014)
4. Grosz, B.J., et al.: Artificial intelligence and life in 2030: One hundred years study on artificial intelligence. Stanford University (2016)
5. Hendler, J.: Avoiding another AI winter. IEEE Ann. Hist. Comput. **23**(02), 2–4 (2008)
6. Hassan, O.: Artificial intelligence, neom and Saudi Arabia's economic diversification from oil and gas. Polit. Q. **91**(1), 222–227 (2020)
7. Advani, V.: What is Artificial Intelligence? How does AI work, Types and Future of it? https://www.mygreatlearning.com/blog/what-is-artificial-intelligence/. Accessed 31 Mar 2021
8. Clifford, C.: Google CEO: AI is more important than fire or electricity, CNBC. https://www.cnbc.com/2018/02/01/google-ceo-sundar-pichai-ai-is-more-important-than-fire-electricity.html (2018). Accessed 25 Mar 2021
9. Bole, U., Popovič, A., Žabkar, J., Papa, G., Jaklič, J.: A case analysis of embryonic data mining success. Int. J. Inf. Manage. **35**(2), 253–259 (2015)
10. Duan, Y., Edwards, J.S., Dwivedi, Y.K.: Artificial intelligence for decision making in the era of Big Data – evolution, challenges and research agenda. Int. J. Inf. Manage. **48**, 63–67 (2019)
11. Jarrahi, M.H.: Artificial intelligence and the future of work: human-AI symbiosis in organisational decision making. Bus. Horiz. **61**(4), 577–586 (2018)

12. Agrawal, A., Gans, J., Goldfarb, A.: How AI will Change the Way we Make Decisions. Harvard Business Press, Boston (2017)
13. Herrera, J.L.L., Figueroa, H.V.R., Ramírez, E.J.R.: Deep fraud. a fraud intention recognition framework in public transport context using a deep-learning approach. In: 2018 International Conference on Electronics, Communications and Computers, pp. 118–125. IEEE (2018)
14. Davenport, T.H., Ronanki, R.: Artificial intelligence for the real world. Harvard Bus. Rev. **96**(1), 108–116 (2018)
15. Park, D.: A study on conversational public administration service of the chatbot based on artificial intelligence. J. Korea Multimedia Soc. **20**, 1347–1356 (2017)
16. Coldeway, D.: AI and big data won't work miracles in the fight against coronavirus. Techcrunch, 26 March 2020
17. Fleming, N.: Computer-calculated compounds: researchers are deploying artificial intelligence to discover drugs. Nature **557**, S55–S57 (2018)
18. Segler, M., Preuss, M., Waller, M.: Planning chemical syntheses with deep neural networks and symbolic AI. Nature **555**, 604–610 (2018)
19. Smith, S.: 6 things we learned about artificial intelligence in drug discovery from 330 scientists. BenchSci Blog, 19 September 2018
20. Mikalef, P., Boura, M., Lekakos, G., Krogstie, J.: Big data analytics and firm performance: findings from a mixed-method approach. J. Bus. Res. **98**, 261–276 (2019)
21. Wilson, H.J., Daugherty, P.R.: Collaborative intelligence: humans and AI are joining forces. Harvard Bus. Rev. **96**(4), 114–123 (2018)
22. Cellan-Jones, R.: Stephen Hawking warns artificial intelligence could end mankind (2014). https://www.bbc.co.uk/news/technology-30290540. Accessed 11 Mar 2021
23. Grandhi, B., Patwa, N., Saleem, K.: Data driven marketing for growth and profitability. In: 10th Annual Conference of the EuroMed Academy of Business (2017)
24. Reis, J., Santo, P.E., Melão, N.: Artificial intelligence in government services: a systematic literature review. In: New Knowledge in Information Systems and Technologies, pp. 241–252 (2019)
25. Russek. S., Norvig, P.: Artificial Intelligence A Modern Approach, vol. 53, no. 9., 2nd edn. (2019)
26. Mikhaylov, S., Esteve, M., Campion, A.: Artificial intelligence for the public sector: opportunities and challenges of cross-sector collaboration. Philos. Trans. R. Soc. Lond. Ser. A Math. Phys. Eng. Sci. **376**(2128), 20170357 (2018)
27. Thierer, A., Castillo O'Sullivan, A., Russel, R.: Artificial intelligence and public policy. Mercatus Center - George Mason University (2017). https://www.mercatus.org/publications/artificial-intelligence-public-policy. Accessed 28 Mar 2021
28. Zheng, Y., Yu, H., Cui, L., Miao, C., Leung, C., Yang, Q.: SmartHS: an AI platform for improving government service provision. Association for the Advancement of Artificial Intelligence, 22 January 2018
29. Eggers, W.D., Schatsky, D., Viechnicki, P.: AI-augmented government. Using cognitive technologies to redesign public sector work. Deloitte Center for Government Insights, pp. 1–24 (2017)
30. Dwivedi, Y.K., et al.: Artificial Intelligence (AI): multidisciplinary perspectives on emerging challenges, opportunities, and agenda for research, practice and policy. Int. J. Inf. Manage. **57**, 101994 (2019)
31. DIN, DKE.: German standardization roadmap industry 4.0, vol. 3 (2018)
32. IDC: Automation and Customer Experience Needs Will Drive AI Investment to $5 Billion by 2019 Across European Industries (2019)
33. The World Economic Forum. https://www.weforum.org/. Accessed 11 March 2021

34. Salama, S.: Saudi Arabia approves policy on Artificial Intelligence, expects SR500b windfall by 2030. https://www.prnewswire.com/ae/news-releases/data-and-ai-to-add-more-than-usd-10-billion-to-saudi-arabia-s-economy-825535205.html. Accessed 31 Mar2021
35. Cision Global Blog: Data and AI to Add More Than USD 10 Billion to Saudi Arabia's Economy (2020). https://www.prnewswire.com/ae/news-releases/data-and-ai-to-add-more-than-usd-10-billion-to-saudi-arabia-s-economy-825535205.html. Accessed 30 Mar 2021
36. Palmer, M.: Data is the new oil. https://ana.blogs.com/maestros/2006/11/data_is_the_new.html (2006). Accessed 6 Mar 2021
37. Hays, J., Efros, A.A.: Scene completion using millions of photographs. ACM Trans. Graph. (TOG) **26**(3), 4 (2007)
38. Wirtz, B.W., Müller, W.M.: An integrated artificial intelligence framework for public management. Public Manage. Rev. **21**(7), 1076–1100 (2019)
39. Yan, L., et al.: Prediction of criticality in patients with severe Covid-19 infection using three clinical features: a machine learning-based prognostic model with clinical data in Wuhan. MedRxiv (2020)
40. Jiang, X., et al.: Towards an artificial intelligence framework for data-driven prediction of coronavirus clinical severity. Comput. Mater. Contin. **63**(1), 537–551 (2020)
41. Manyika, J., et al.: Jobs Lost, Jobs Gained: Workforce Transitions in a Time of Automation, vol. 150. McKinsey Global Institute (2017)
42. Zandi, D., Reis, A., Vayena, E., Goodman, K.: New ethical challenges of digital technologies, machine learning and artificial intelligence in public health: a call for papers. Bull. World Health Organ. **97**(1), 2 (2019)
43. Floridi, L.: Group privacy: A defence and an interpretation. In: Taylor, L., Floridi, L., van der Sloot, B. (eds.) Group privacy. PSS, vol. 126, pp. 83–100. Springer, Cham (2017). https://doi.org/10.1007/978-3-319-46608-8_5
44. Mittelstadt, B.D., Allo, P., Taddeo, M., Wachter, S., Floridi, L.: The ethics of algorithms: mapping the debate. Big Data Soc. **3**(2), 1–21 (2016)
45. Müller, V.C., Bostrom, N.: Future progress in artificial intelligence: A survey of expert opinion. In: Müller, V.C. (ed.) Fundamental issues of artificial intelligence. SL, vol. 376, pp. 553–570. Springer, Cham (2016). https://doi.org/10.1007/978-3-319-26485-1_33
46. Gasser, U., Almeida, V.A.F.: A layered model for AI governance. IEEE Internet Comput. **21**(6), 58–62 (2017)
47. Mehr, H.: Artificial intelligence for citizen services and government. Ash Center for Democratic Governance and Innovation, Harvard Kennedy School, Cambridge (2017)
48. Filho, W.L. (ed.): Handbook of Sustainability Science and Research. WSS, Springer, Cham (2018). https://doi.org/10.1007/978-3-319-63007-6
49. Nabbout, M.: What you need to know about Saudi Arabia's new AI authority? (2019). https://stepfeed.com/what-you-need-to-know-about-saudi-arabia-s-new-ai-authority-1276. Accessed 28 Mar 2021
50. Tabaud (2020). https://tabaud.sdaia.gov.sa/IndexEn. Accessed 11 Mar. 2021
51. Tawakkalna (2020). https://ta.sdaia.gov.sa/en/index. Accessed 11 Mar. 2021
52. Carlson, C.: Saudi Arabia announces plans for a 100-mile, car-free linear city called the line. https://www.dezeen.com/2021/01/13/line-saudi-arabia-170-kilometres-long-city-neom/. Accessed 28 Mar 2021
53. Benbasat, I., Goldstein, D.K. Mead, M.: The case research strategy in studies of information systems. MIS Q. **11**, 369–386 (1987)
54. Eisenhardt, K., Martin, J.: Dynamic capabilities: what are they? Strateg. Manage. J. **21**(10–11), 105–1121 (2000)
55. Gill, P., Stewart, K., Treasure, E.: Methods of data collection in qualitative research: interviews and focus groups. Br. Dent. J. **204**, 291–295 (2008)

56. Alwalidi, A., Lefrere, P.: Making E-l invisible: experience king Khalid Saudi Arabia. Educ. Technol. **50**(3), 4–7 (2010)
57. OECD: COFOG: classification of the functions of government. Government at a Glance, pp. 194–195 (2011)
58. Naderifar, M., Goli, H., Ghaljaie, F.: Snowball sampling: a purposeful method of sampling in qualitative research. Strides Dev. Med. Educ. **14**(3), 1–6 (2017)
59. Noy, C.: Sampling knowledge: the hermeneutics of snowball sampling in qualitative research. Int. J. Soc. Res. Methodol. **11**(4), 327–344 (2008)
60. Weick, K.E.: Theory construction as disciplined imagination. Acad. Manage. Rev. **14**(4), 516–531 (1989)
61. Weiner, B.J.: A theory of organizational readiness for change. Implement. Sci. **4**(1), 1–9 (2009)
62. Fast, E., Horvitz, E.: Long-term trends in the public perception of artificial intelligence. In: Proceedings of the Thirty-First AAAI Conference on Artificial Intelligence (AAAI 2017), pp. 963–969 (2017)
63. Gioia, D., Corley, K., Hamilton, A.: Seeking qualitative rigor in inductive research. Organ. Res. Methods **16**(1), 15–31 (2013)

Achieving Digital-Driven Patient Agility in the Era of Big Data

Rogier van de Wetering(✉)

Faculty of Sciences, Open University of the Netherlands, Valkenburgerweg 177, 6419 AT Heerlen, The Netherlands
rogier.vandewetering@ou.nl

Abstract. There is still a limited understanding of the necessary skill, talent, and expertise to manage digital technologies as a crucial enabler of the hospital's ability to adequately 'sense' and 'respond' to patient needs and wishes, i.e., patient agility. Therefore, this investigates how hospital departments can leverage a 'digital dynamic capability' to enable the department's patient agility. This study embraces the dynamic capabilities theory, develops a research model, and tests it accordingly using data from 90 clinical hospital departments from the Netherlands through an online survey. The model's hypothesized relationships are tested using structural equation modeling (SEM). The outcomes demonstrate the significance of digital dynamic capability in developing patient sensing and responding capabilities that, in turn, positively influence patient service performance. Outcomes are very relevant for the hospital practice now, as hospitals worldwide need to transform healthcare delivery processes using digital technologies and increase clinical productivity.

Keywords: Dynamic capabilities · Digital dynamic capability · Big data analytics · Patient agility · Sense and respond · Patient service performance · Hospitals

1 Introduction

In the age of big data and data-driven decision-making, hospitals worldwide use innovative information technology (IT) to transform their care delivery processes and business models, thereby improving cost efficiency, clinical quality, service efficiency, and patient satisfaction [1–7]. Hospitals are forced to do so, as they are an essential component of modern-day society, and the adoption of groundbreaking IT essential to its success [7–9]. Hospitals use IT, such as clinical decision-support systems (CDSS), to enhance the decision-making processes and provide clinicians with several modes of decision support (e.g., alerts, reminders, advice) [10–12]. Another recent development is using big data and predictive analytics as doctors need to analyze exponential volumes of patient-generated data [13]. Big data, in essence, refers to datasets whose size is beyond the ability of conventional database software tools to capture, store, manage, and analyze both structured and unstructured data. Modern hospitals are currently very active in

D. Dennehy et al. (Eds.): I3E 2021, LNCS 12896, pp. 82–93, 2021.
https://doi.org/10.1007/978-3-030-85447-8_8

exploring new digital options and data-driven innovations using big data to drive clinical care quality and strengthen the relationships and interactions with patients. For instance, clinicians use digital innovations in their clinical practice, e.g., mobile handheld devices and apps, to increase error prevention and improve patient-centered care [14]. Also, digital innovations provide clinicians with ways to be more agile in their work, improve clinical communication, remotely monitor patients, enhance clinical decision-support [8, 9], and improve the patient treatment process and medical quality services [15]. Big data analytics is particularly relevant for hospitals where it can be used to, e.g., to identify defects in care and risk factors for patient safety issues, determine the time required to perform key patient care activities (e.g., passing medication), occurrence patterns, and statistical testing of intervention strategies, evidence-based medicine, and analyses to measure the impact of using clinically substitutable supply items on patient outcomes.

There is a wealth of attention for information technology (IT) adoption and IT-enabled transformation in healthcare research [16]. However, there is still a limited understanding of big data's role and its associated predictive models as a crucial enabler of the hospital's ability to adequately 'sense' and 'respond' to patient needs and wishes, i.e., patient agility [13, 17] and hospitals have not fully grasped the value of these data-driven innovations yet [13]. As such, this article embraces the dynamic capabilities theory (DCT), a foundational strategic framework within the management and IS field, when it comes to the innovative and orchestrated use of digital technologies [18–21]. When hospital departments want to excel and use data-driven innovations in practice and drive patient agility, for instance, to help detect COVID-19 cases early using big data, they need to manage and master digital technologies. Hence, they need to develop a 'digital dynamic capability' which can be considered the "organization's skill, talent, and expertise to manage digital technologies for new innovative product development" [22]. For such a capability to develop, the hospital department needs heterogeneous competencies [17, 23]. Against this background and the current gaps in the literature, this paper acclaims that digital dynamic capability enhances the ability to sense and respond adequately to the patient's needs and demands and drive the department's patient service performance, i.e., the extent to which hospital departments achieve high-quality medical services [24]. Hence, this research addresses the following research questions:

> *(I) What is the effect of digital dynamic capability on the hospital departments' sense-and-respond capabilities, i.e., patient agility? Also, (II) through what mechanism does patient agility lead to high levels of patient service performance?*

2 Theoretical Foundation

This study builds upon the dynamic capabilities theory (DCT) [23, 25]. The DCT is a leading theoretical framework that explains where firms' competitive advantage comes from in industries with high technological and market turbulence. Dynamic capabilities can be defined as a specific subset of capabilities that allow firms to integrate, build, and reconfigure internal and external resources and competences to create new products and processes and respond to changing business environments [26]. Hence, these capabilities allow firms to manage uncertainty [19, 25]. Notwithstanding its significance, the theory has been profoundly subjected to theoretical debate [23, 25–27]. However, most empirical endeavors established positive relationships among these capabilities in recent years, firm's operational, innovative and competitive performance measures [28].

The concept of organizational agility is a manifested type of dynamic capability [19]. It can be conceptualized as a dynamic capability if "*they permit organizations to repurpose or reposition their resources as conditions shift*" [29]. Organizational agility has been proposed under the DCT as an essential organizational capability to respond to changing conditions while simultaneously proactively enacting the dynamic environment regarding customer demands, supply chains, new technologies, governmental regulations, and competition [19, 30, 31]. This 'sense-and-respond' capability has been defined and conceptualized in many ways and through various theoretical lenses in the IS literature [32, 33]. For instance, Park et al. [31] ground their conceptualization and operationalization in the information-processing theory and argue that information processing capabilities strengthen the organization's sense-response processes to adapt to changing environmental conditions. Lu and Ramamurthy [34] embrace a complementarity perspective and perceive agility as the organization's ability to seize market opportunities and operationally adjustment capacity. Roberts and Grover [35] synthesized that, although there seems to be ambiguity in definitions as reflected by the concepts' operationalized capabilities, a set of high-level characteristics can be devised from the extant literature: deliberately 'sensing' and 'responding' to business events in the process of capturing business and market opportunities. This article perceived patient agility as a higher-order manifested type of dynamic capability that allows hospital departments to adequately 'sense' and 'respond' to patient-based opportunities, needs, demands within a fast-paced hospital ecosystem context [19, 35]. Digital dynamic capability is a crucial technical-oriented dynamic capability necessary to innovate and enhance business operations using digital technologies [22, 36–38]. These digital technologies include big data analytics and artificial intelligence (AI). Digital dynamic capability can be conceived as an organization's ability to master digital technologies, drive digital transformations, and adopt new innovative services and products. Digital dynamic capability is conceptualized as a lower-order technical dynamic capability that facilitates developing higher-order dynamic organizational capabilities such as innovation ambidexterity, absorptive capacity, and organizational agility [17, 27, 38, 39].

3 Research Model and Hypothesis Development

3.1 Digital Dynamic Capability and Patient Agility

Recent scholarship shows that digital dynamic capability is crucial to innovate and enhance business operations [22, 36–38]. For instance, Wang et al. [40] argue that firms use the digital dynamic capability to leverage IT and knowledge resources to deliver innovative services that customers value. Coombs and Bierly [41] empirically showed that this technological-driven capability enables competitive advantages. The literature shows that by actively managing the opportunities provided by new digital innovation such as big data and AI and actively responding to digital transformation, organizations can succeed in their digital options and services [22, 40]. This capability is vital for hospital departments that want to strive for patient agility in clinical practice because the process of achieving new digital patient service solutions is exceedingly dependent on its ability to manage digital technologies [17, 22]. The digital dynamic capability provides the hospital department with the ability to, e.g., integrate devices (think, for instance, about patient location devices, smart beds, bed & tracking boards) so that accurate and efficient clinical documentation and processing is facilitated and better clinical decision takes places [6]. Hence, hospitals that actively invest and develop these capabilities are likely to sense and anticipate their patients' needs (of which they might be physically and mentally unaware) and respond fast to changes in the patient's health service needs using digital innovations and assessments of clinical outcomes [17, 22, 35]. Therefore, the following two hypotheses are defined:

Hypothesis 1: *Hospital departments' digital dynamic capability positively impacts the department's patient sensing capability.*

Hypothesis 2: *Hospital departments' digital dynamic capability positively impacts the department's responding capability.*

3.2 Patient Sensing and Responding Capability

This article, thus, hypothesizes that hospital departments' digital dynamic capability is key to establishing patient sensing and responding capabilities. Furthermore, it is suggested that the digital-driven patient sensing capability, in turn, affects the hospital departments' ability to respond rapidly if something important happens with the patients or their service needs. Digital options and innovations provide clinicians with ways to sense and anticipate patient's needs, wishes, and demands more effectively [7, 42] and thereby improve the patient treatment process and quality of medical services [15, 42]. However, in order for a responding capability to be effective, the hospital department is dependent on its ability to sense and anticipate the patients' needs [35]. In a similar vein, it can be argued that hospital departments cannot leverage a patient responding capability if they have not developed an effective sensing capability. Hence, the following is defined:

Hypothesis 3: *Hospital departments' sensing capability positively impacts the department's patient responding capability.*

3.3 Patient Responding Capability and Patient Service Performance

The extant literature shows that digital-driven sense and respond capabilities are crucial to achieving higher-quality and patient-centered care and hospitals' financial performance benefits [24, 43]. By making specific investments in capabilities valued by patients, hospital departments can achieve high levels of patient service performance and value in the turbulent healthcare environment [44]. For example, clinicians who use digital innovations in their clinical practice, e.g., mobile handheld devices and apps, can increase error prevention and improve patient-centered care [14, 43]. However, a sufficient responding capability should be preceded by a developed and aligned sensing capability to respond effectively and drive patient service performances [30, 45]. Hospital departments that can continually sense patients' needs are more effective in clinical communication, decision-support [7, 53], and the patient treatment process, thus responding effectively to patients' needs and wishes [15, 42]. A strong patient responding capability is likely to provide service flexibility, high-quality care, achieve patient satisfaction, and improve the accessibility of medical services [35, 43]. Following the literature on the widely adopted process-oriented perspective, it can be argued that patients' sensing capability effect on patient service performance is intermediated by patient responding capability [46]. Hence, this study defines the following:

Hypothesis 4: *Hospital departments' responding capability mediates the effect of sensing capability on the department's patient service performance.*

4 Research Methods

4.1 Data

This survey was pretested on multiple occasions by five Master students and six medical practitioners and scholars to improve both the content and face validity of the survey items. The medical practitioners all had sufficient knowledge and experience to assess the survey items effectively to provide valuable improvement suggestions. The survey was anonymously administered to key informants within hospital departments. We assured the respondents that their entries would be treated confidentially, and we would only report outcomes on an aggregate level [47]. Our target population includes medical heads/chairs of the department, practicing doctors, and department managers.

Data were conveniently sampled from Dutch hospitals through 5 Master students' professional networks within Dutch hospitals. The data we collected between November 10th, 2019, to January 5th, 2020. This study uses 90 complete survey responses for final analyses. Within the obtained sample, 28.9% of the respondents work for a University medical center, 41.1% work for a specialized top clinical (training) hospital, and 30% work for general hospitals. Most survey respondents are medical heads/chairs of the department (51.1%)[1], 24.4% is a practicing doctor, 11.1% is department manager, while the remaining 13.3% of the respondents hold other positions such as specialized oncology nurses.

Finally, Harman's single-factor analysis was applied using exploratory factor analysis (in using IBM SPSS Statistics™ v24) to restrain, ex-post, possible common method bias [47]. Outcomes show that the current sample is not affected by method biases; no single factor is attributed to most of the variance.

4.2 Constructs and Items

The selection of indicators was made based on previous empirical and validated work to increase the questions' internal validity and reliability. This study devised three core items from Khin and Ho [22] to measure *digital dynamic capability* and conceptualized *patient agility* as a higher-order dynamic capability comprising the dimensions '*patient sensing capability*' and '*patient responding capability*' [30, 32]. This study adopts five measures for each of these two capabilities, following Roberts and Grover [30]. This study builds upon the concept of IT-business value creation [24, 46] to conceptualize *patient service performance* (PSP). Thus, consistent with balanced evaluation

[1] 5 respondents claimed that they were team leads.

perspectives, patient service performance is represented by three measures, i.e., enhanced quality, improved accessibility of medical services, and achieving patient satisfaction [24, 48, 49]. The constructs' items in the research model used a seven-point Likert scale ranging from 1: strongly disagree to 7: strongly agree. Following prior IS and management studies, we controlled for 'size' (full-time employees), operationalizing this measure using the natural log (i.e., log-normally distributed) and 'age' of the department (5-point Likert scale 1: 0–5years; 5: 25+years). All measures are included in the Appendix, including the respective item-to-construct loadings (λ), mean values (μ), and the standard deviations (*Std.*).

4.3 Analyses Using Partial Least Squares

This study applied SmartPLS version 3.2.7. [50]. SmartPLS is a Structural Equation Modeling (SEM) tool that uses Partial Least Squares (PLS). PLS is used to estimate the research model and run its associated parameter estimates. A key reason for PLS's usage is that this current work focuses on predicting and articulating particular hypothesized relationships. Also, PLS allows flexibility concerning the assumptions on multivariate normality, the ability to run parameter estimates for smaller samples, and reduces the overall error associated with the model [51]. The sample size exceeds the minimum threshold to obtain stable PLS outcomes. This study uses a two-step approach to investigate PLS outcomes. First, the measurement model is assessed. Then, the hypotheses are tested using the outcomes of the structural model assessment.

5 Empirical Results

5.1 Measurement Model Analysis

The internal consistency reliability, convergent validity, and measurement validity of the first-order latent constructs were first assessed. PLS outcomes show that all the construct-to-item loadings far exceeded a threshold of 0.70. Both the Cronbach's alpha (CA) and Composite reliability (CR) values are all above the threshold of 0.7, showcasing the latent constructs' reliability. Next, to assess convergent validity, the average variance extracted (AVE) was analyzed. This value captures the degree of variance explained by the latent construct while relating it to the amount of variance due to measurement error [50]. All AVE-values exceeded the threshold of 0.50 (the minimum was 0.66 for patient service performance). Three complimentary assessments were used to evaluate discriminant validity [52]. First, the Fornell-Larcker criterion, i.e., the AVE's square root, is compared with cross-correlation values. Outcomes show that each value is larger than cross-correlations [52]. Next, the cross-loadings between constructs are investigated. No single cross-loading exceeds a (correlation) difference of 0.20. Finally. This study investigated the heterotrait-monotrait ratio of correlations (HTMT) values [53]. HTMT values are all well below the upper bound of 0.90, once more confirming discriminant validity. The above outcomes suggest that the measurement model is both reliable and valid.

5.2 Structural Model Assessment and Hypothesis Testing

This study evaluates the Standardized Root Mean Square Residual (SRMR) value[2]to assess the model fit. The SRMR value calculates the difference between observed correlations and the model's implied correlations matrix [52]. The obtained SRMR of 0.069 is well below the conservative threshold of 0.08. The model's hypothesized relationships can now be estimated. This study investigated each hypothesized path's significance and the coefficient of determination (R^2), measuring the model's predictive power [52] to test the hypotheses. Also, the model's predictive power is assessed [52]. This study uses a non-parametric bootstrapping procedure (using 5000 replications) to obtain stable results and interpret their significance of the path coefficients between this study's key construct. Figure 1 shows the results of the structural model assessments.

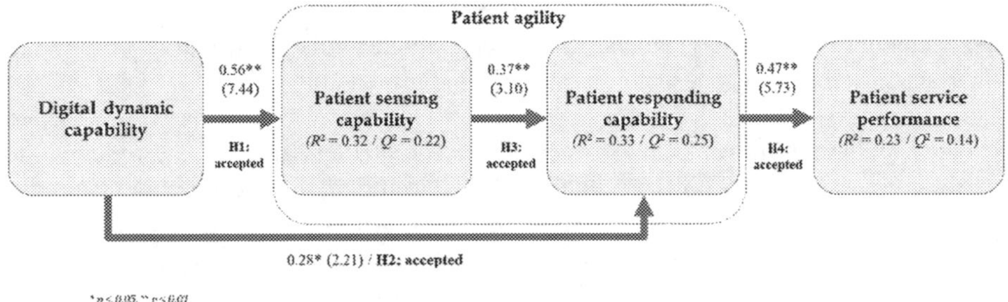

Fig. 1. Structural model assessment results using SmartPLS ($N = 90$)

As can be seen from Fig. 1, support was found for all the hypotheses. Digital dynamic capability positively influences patient sensing capability ($\beta = 0.56$; $t = 7.44$; $p < 0.0001$) and responding capability ($\beta = 0.38$; $t = 2.21$; $p = 0.03$). Patient sensing capability positively influences patient responding capability ($\beta = 0.37$; $t = 3.10$; $p = 0.002$). Finally, patient responding capability positively impacts patient service performance ($\beta = 0.47$; $t = 5.73$; $p < 0.0001$). The explained variance for sensing capability is 32% ($R^2 = .32$), for responding capability 33% ($R^2 = .33$), and for patient service performance ($R^2 = .23$). These amounts can be considered moderate effects. Specific mediation guidelines (Baron and Kenny 1986; Hair Jr et al. 2016; Hayes 2013) were followed to investigate the model's imposed mediation effects. Outcomes show that patient responding capability 'fully' mediates patient sensing capability on patient service performance [52, 54]. Concerning the first part of the model, patient sensing capability partially mediates the effect of digital dynamic capability. The included control variables shows non-significant effects: 'size' ($\beta = -0.01$, $t = 0.01$ $p = 0.92$), 'age' ($\beta = -0.01$, $t = 0.14$, $p = 0.89$). A subsequent blindfolding assessment for the endogenous latent constructs using Stone-Geisser values (Q^2) shows that the model has predictive power [52]. The Q^2 values far exceed 0, as can be seen in Fig. 1.

[2] This particular metric for model fit should still be interpreted with caution as it is not fully established in the PLS-SEM literature.

6 Discussion and Concluding Remarks

This study aimed to understand better the crucial role of digital dynamic capability as an enabler of the hospital's ability to adequately 'sense' and 'respond' to patient needs and wishes and unfold how hospital departments can grasp the value of data-driven innovations. Modern hospitals need to ensure that their processes can meet the needs of an increasingly complex environment, especially now during the COVID-19 crisis. It is well known that it is essential to maintain strategic flexibility under acute conditions so that adequate digital options and sensing and responding behavior are exercised [45, 55]. However, many hospitals currently struggle in their digital transformation efforts in practice, and this process is usually painfully slow, with many hurdles to overcome.

This study makes two theoretical contributions. This study is the first to conceptualize patient agility and empirically validate that patient agility will enhance hospital departments' service performance. This study found support for this claim. It shows that digital dynamic capability enhances patient agility's conceptualized construct by sequentially enhancing patient sensing capability and patient responding capability. These results are coherent with previous work prompting that those hospital departments that invest and enhance their skills, competences, and knowledge in managing innovative digital technologies are better equipped to be responsive, innovative, and satisfy patients' needs [22, 24]. Also, this study adds to the growing body of knowledge on the degree to which digital capabilities and competencies contribute to organizational capabilities and benefits [33, 44]. The obtained insights are valuable as future research can consider these particular insights when investigating hospitals' IT-business value.

The outcomes of this study provide managerial implications in several ways. First, the outcomes are relevant for the healthcare sector now, as hospitals worldwide need to transform healthcare delivery processes using digital technologies and increase clinical productivity during the COVID-19 crisis [56]. Hospital departments need to develop the dynamic capabilities and direct IT investments to bring about the highest IT business value. Hence, departments should prioritize clinical initiatives by focusing on critical workflows and clinical process improvement opportunities, emphasizing patient agility. The department's digital dynamic capability is crucial in the development of new digital patient service solutions. So, hospital departments need to actively invest in the skills and competencies to manage new digital technologies like big data and predictive analytics and AI. Hospitals typically will need to overcome adoption (e.g., physician resistance), process and technology challenges to develop the department's ability to master digital technologies, drive digital transformations, and adopt new innovative services and products. Therefore, hospital decision-makers must deliberately pay attention to stakeholder involvement and provide appropriate tangible and intangible resources [57, 58].

The study's limitations are now addressed so that the discussion is put into a proper academic context. First, data were collected at a single point in time (cross-sectionally) and thus providing only a snapshot of the firm's well-being. Also, capability building and achieving patient service performance are typically part of a hospital department's long-term goals and strategic direction. Therefore, a longitudinal approach could be valuable in providing a richer understanding of the dynamics among this study's constructs. *Second*, all the collected data in this study is from the Dutch hospitals. Therefore, the study outcomes could be subject to specific Country, cultural, and (local) economic influences. Notwithstanding, a substantial amount of current scholarships comes from Western (North America and Western-Europe) countries. This study, therefore, fits into a broader class of studies.

Appendix A: Constructs and Items

Construct		Measurement item	λ	μ	*Std.*	*Reliability statistics*
Digital dynamic capability	*Please indicate the ability of your department to: (1. Strongly disagree–7. Strongly agree*					
	DDC1	Responding to digital transformation	0.886	4.33	1.56	CA: 0.86 CR:0.91 AVE:0.78
	DDC2	Mastering the state-of-the-art digital technologies	0.895	3.69	1.48	
	DDC3	Developing innovative patient services using digital technology	0.856	4.74	1.63	
Sensing	*Indicate the degree to which you agree or disagree with the following statements about whether the department can (1 – strongly disagree 7 – strongly agree)*					
	S1	We continuously discover additional needs of our patients of which they are unaware	0.89	4.10	1.66	CA:0.89 CR:0.92 AVE:0.71
	S2	We extrapolate key trends for insights on what patients will need in the future	0.77	4.43	1.63	
	S3	We continuously anticipate our patients' needs even before they are aware of them	0.89	4.03	1.68	
	S4	We attempt to develop new ways of looking at patients and their needs	0.79	4.72	1.52	
	S5	We sense our patient's needs even before they are aware of them	0.86	3.94	1.66	
Responding	R1	We respond rapidly if something important happens with regard to our patients	0.93	4.52	1.50	CA:0.91 CR:0.93 AVE:0.89
	R2	We quickly implement our planned activities with regard to patients	0.91	4.52	1.42	
	R3	We quickly react to fundamental changes with regard to our patients	0.92	4.54	1.53	
	R4	When we identify a new patient need, we are quick to respond to it	0.87	4.11	1.62	
	R5	We are fast to respond to changes in our patient's health service needs	0.87	4.76	1.71	
PSP	*We perform much better during the last 2 or 3 years than comparable departments from other hospitals in: (1. Strongly disagree–7. Strongly agree).*					
	PSP1	Achieving patient satisfaction	0.83	4.98	1.32	CA:0.75 CR:0.85 AVE:0.66
	PSP2	Providing high-quality service	0.85	5.28	1.25	
	PSP3	Improving the accessibility of medical services	0.75	4.80	1.33	

References

1. Curtright, J.W., Stolp-Smith, S.C., Edell, E.S.: Strategic performance management: development of a performance measurement system at the Mayo Clinic. J. Healthc. Manag. **45**(1), 58–68 (2000)
2. Ahovuo, J., et al.: Process oriented organisation in the regional PACS environment. In: EuroPACS-MIR 2004 in the Enlarged Europe, pp. 481–484 (2004)

3. McGlynn, E., et al.: The quality of health care delivered to adults in the United States. N. Engl. J. Med. **348**(26), 2635–2645 (2003)
4. Chiasson, M., et al.: Expanding multi-disciplinary approaches to healthcare information technologies: what does information systems offer medical informatics? Int. J. Med. Inform. **76**, S89–S97 (2007)
5. Lee, J., McCullough, J.S., Town, R.J.: The impact of health information technology on hospital productivity. RAND J. Econ. **44**(3), 545–568 (2013)
6. Van de Wetering, R., Versendaal, J., Walraven, P.: Examining the relationship between a hospital's IT infrastructure capability and digital capabilities: a resource-based perspective. In: Proceedings of the Twenty-Fourth Americas Conference on Information Systems (AMCIS), AIS, New Orleans (2018)
7. Van de Wetering, R.: IT-enabled clinical decision support: an empirical study on antecedents and mechanisms. J. Healthc. Eng. **2018**, 10 (2018)
8. Hendrikx, H., et al.: Expectations and attitudes in ehealth: a survey among patients of dutch private healthcare organizations. Int. J. Healthc. Manag. **6**(4), 263–268 (2013)
9. Kohli, R., Tan, S.S.-L.: Electronic health records: how can IS researchers contribute to transforming healthcare? MIS Q. **40**(3), 553–573 (2016)
10. Garg, A.X., et al.: Effects of computerized clinical decision support systems on practitioner performance and patient outcomes: a systematic review. JAMA **293**(10), 1223–1238 (2005)
11. Romano, M.J., Stafford, R.S.: Electronic health records and clinical decision support systems: impact on national ambulatory care quality. Arch. Intern. Med. **171**(10), 897–903 (2011)
12. Van de Wetering, R.: Enhancing clinical decision support through information processing capabilities and strategic IT alignment. In: Proceedings of the 21st International Conference on Business Information Systems. Springer, Berlin (2018). https://doi.org/10.1007/978-3-030-04849-5_2
13. Wang, Y., Kung, L., Byrd, T.A.: Big data analytics: understanding its capabilities and potential benefits for healthcare organizations. Technol. Forecast. Soc. Change. **126**, 3–13 (2018)
14. Prgomet, M., Georgiou, A., Westbrook, J.I.: The impact of mobile handheld technology on hospital physicians' work practices and patient care: a systematic review. J. Am. Med. Info. Assoc. **16**(6), 792–801 (2009)
15. Li, W., et al.: Integrated clinical pathway management for medical quality improvement–based on a semiotically inspired systems architecture. Eur. J. Inf. Syst. **23**(4), 400–417 (2014)
16. Andargoli, A.E., et al.: Health information systems evaluation frameworks: a systematic review. Int. J. Med. Inf. **97**, 195–209 (2017)
17. Van de Wetering, R.: IT ambidexterity and patient agility: the mediating role of digital dynamic capability. In: Proceedings of the Twenty-Ninth European Conference on Information Systems (ECIS), AIS, Virtual Conference (2021)
18. Mikalef, P., van de Wetering, R., Krogstie, J.: Building dynamic capabilities by leveraging big data analytics: the role of organizational inertia. Inf. Manag. 103412 (2020)
19. Teece, D., Peteraf, M., Leih, S.: Dynamic capabilities and organizational agility: risk, uncertainty, and strategy in the innovation economy. Calif. Manag. Rev. **58**(4), 13–35 (2016)
20. Van de Wetering, R., Dynamic enterprise architecture capabilities and organizational benefits: an empirical mediation study. In: Proceedings of the Twenty-Eight European Conference on Information Systems, AIS, Virtual Conference (2020)
21. Van de Wetering, R., et al.: The impact of EA-driven dynamic capabilities, innovativeness, and structure on organizational benefits: a variance and fsQCA perspective. Sustainability **13**(10), 5414 (2021)
22. Khin, S., Ho, T.C.: Digital technology, digital capability and organizational performance: a mediating role of digital innovation. Int. J. Innov. Sci. **11**(2), 177–195 (2019)
23. Teece, D.J., Pisano, G., Shuen, A.: Dynamic capabilities and strategic management. Strateg. Manag. J. **18**(7), 509–533 (1997)

24. Wu, L., Hu, Y.-P.: Examining knowledge management enabled performance for hospital professionals: a dynamic capability view and the mediating role of process capability. J. Assoc. Inf. Syst. **13**(12), 976 (2012)
25. Eisenhardt, K.M., Martin, J.A.: Dynamic capabilities: what are they? Strateg. Manag. J. **21**(10–11), 1105–1121 (2000)
26. Teece, D.J.: Explicating dynamic capabilities: the nature and microfoundations of (sustainable) enterprise performance. Strateg. Manag. J. **28**(13), 1319–1350 (2007)
27. Wang, C.L., Ahmed, P.K.: Dynamic capabilities: a review and research agenda. Int. J. Manag. Rev. **9**(1), 31–51 (2007)
28. Wilden, R., Gudergan, S.P.: The impact of dynamic capabilities on operational marketing and technological capabilities: investigating the role of environmental turbulence. J. Acad. Mark. Sci. **43**(2), 181–199 (2014). https://doi.org/10.1007/s11747-014-0380-y
29. Tallon, P.P., et al.: Information technology and the search for organizational agility: a systematic review with future research possibilities. J. Strateg. Inf. Syst. **28**(2), 218–237 (2019)
30. Roberts, N., Grover, V.: Leveraging information technology infrastructure to facilitate a firm's customer agility and competitive activity: an empirical investigation. J. Manag. Inf. Syst. **28**(4), 231–270 (2012)
31. Park, Y., El Sawy, O.A., Fiss, P.C.: The role of business intelligence and communication technologies in organizational agility: a configurational approach. J. Assoc. Inf. Syst. **18**(9), 648–686 (2017)
32. Sambamurthy, V., Bharadwaj, A., Grover, V.: Shaping agility through digital options: reconceptualizing the role of information technology in contemporary firms. MIS Q. **27**(2), 237–263 (2003)
33. Chakravarty, A., Grewal, R., Sambamurthy, V.: Information technology competencies, organizational agility, and firm performance: enabling and facilitating roles. Inf. Syst. Res. **24**(4), 976–997 (2013)
34. Lu, Y., Ramamurthy, K.: Understanding the link between information technology capability and organizational agility: an empirical examination. MIS Q. **35**(4), 931–954 (2011)
35. Roberts, N., Grover, V.: Investigating firm's customer agility and firm performance: the importance of aligning sense and respond capabilities. J. Bus. Res. **65**(5), 579–585 (2012)
36. Acur, N., et al.: Exploring the impact of technological competence development on speed and NPD program performance. J. Prod. Innov. Manag. **27**(6), 915–929 (2010)
37. Zhou, K.Z., Wu, F.: Technological capability, strategic flexibility, and product innovation. Strateg. Manag. J. **31**(5), 547–561 (2010)
38. Li, T.C., Chan, Y.E.: Dynamic information technology capability: concept definition and framework development. J. Strateg. Inf. Syst. **28**(4), 101575 (2019)
39. Božič, K., Dimovski, V.: Business intelligence and analytics use, innovation ambidexterity, and firm performance: a dynamic capabilities perspective. J. Strateg. Inf. Syst. **28**(4), 101578 (2019)
40. Wang, Y., et al.: Leveraging big data analytics to improve quality of care in healthcare organizations: a configurational perspective. Br. J. Manag. **30**(2), 362–388 (2019)
41. Coombs, J.E., Bierly, P.E., III.: Measuring technological capability and performance. R&D Manag. **36**(4), 421–438 (2006)
42. Salge, T.O., Vera, A.: Hospital innovativeness and organizational performance: evidence from English public acute care. Health Care Manag. Rev. **34**(1), 54–67 (2009)
43. Bradley, R., et al.: An examination of the relationships among IT capability intentions, IT infrastructure integration and quality of care: a study in US hospitals. In: 2012 45th Hawaii International Conference on System Sciences. IEEE (2012)
44. Chen, Y., et al.: IT capability and organizational performance: the roles of business process agility and environmental factors. Eur. J. Inf. Syst. **23**(3), 326–342 (2014)

45. Overby, E., Bharadwaj, A., Sambamurthy, V.: Enterprise agility and the enabling role of information technology. Eur. J. Inf. Syst. **15**(2), 120–131 (2006)
46. Schryen, G.: Revisiting IS business value research: what we already know, what we still need to know, and how we can get there. Eur. J. Inf. Syst. **22**(2), 139–169 (2013)
47. Podsakoff, P.M., et al.: Common method biases in behavioral research: a critical review of the literature and recommended remedies. J. Appl. Psychol. **88**(5), 879 (2003)
48. Chen, J.-S., Tsou, H.-T.: Performance effects of IT capability, service process innovation, and the mediating role of customer service. J. Eng. Tech. Manag. **29**(1), 71–94 (2012)
49. Setia, P., Venkatesh, V., Joglekar, S.: Leveraging digital technologies: how information quality leads to localized capabilities and customer service performance. MIS Q. **37**(2), 565–590 (2013)
50. Ringle, C.M., Wende, S., Becker, J.-M.: SmartPLS 3. SmartPLS GmbH, Boenningstedt (2015). http://www.smartpls.com
51. Hair, J.F., Jr., et al.: Advanced Issues in Partial Least Squares Structural Equation Modeling. SAGE Publications, Thousand Oaks (2017)
52. Hair, J.F., Jr., et al.: A Primer on Partial Least Squares Structural Equation Modeling (PLS-SEM). Sage Publications, Thousand Oaks (2016)
53. Henseler, J., Ringle, C.M., Sarstedt, M.: A new criterion for assessing discriminant validity in variance-based structural equation modeling. J. Acad. Mark. Sci. **43**(1), 115–135 (2014). https://doi.org/10.1007/s11747-014-0403-8
54. Hayes, A.F.: Introduction to Mediation, Moderation, and Conditional Process Analysis: A Regression-Based Approach. Guilford Press, New York (2013)
55. D'Aveni, R.A., Dagnino, G.B., Smith, K.G.: The age of temporary advantage. Strateg. Manag. J. **31**(13), 1371–1385 (2010)
56. Keesara, S., Jonas, A., Schulman, K.: Covid-19 and health care's digital revolution. N. Engl. J. Med. **382**(23), e82 (2020)
57. Gray, C.S.: Seeking meaningful innovation: lessons learned developing, evaluating, and implementing the electronic patient-reported outcome tool. J. Med. Internet Res. **22**(7), e17987 (2020)
58. Papoutsi, C., et al.: Putting the social back into sociotechnical: case studies of co-design in digital health. J. Am. Med. Inf. Assoc. **28**, 284–293 (2020)

Responsible Machine Learning Pilot Test Projects: A Medical Coding Case Study

Samantha Champagnie[1] and Janis L. Gogan[2(✉)]

[1] Muma College of Business, University of South Florida, Tampa, FL, USA
[2] Bentley University, Waltham, MA, USA
jgogan@bentley.edu

Abstract. Prior studies reported on many machine learning (ML) projects that under-performed. What steps can leaders take during ML pilot projects to identify and mitigate project risks and systems risks, before implementing new ML systems at scale? We report on an exploratory case study of a U.S.-based healthcare provider organization's ML pilot project, undertaken when a software vendor proposed an automated solution that would combine natural language processing (NLP) and ML, to improve medical claims coding quality. We reveal tactics the client took during the pilot project, to spot and limit risks that could ultimately harm the firm, its healthcare providers, and its patients. We conclude with suggestions for further research on responsible ML.

Keywords: AI · Machine learning · Ethics · Governance · NLP

1 Introduction

"AI hype has far exceeded the state of AI science, especially when it pertains to validation and readiness for patient care" [32, p. 51]. In Winter 2021 IBM announced its planned sale of its Watson Health AI business [15] – an acknowledgement of a gap between the potential and actual realized value of AI in healthcare. Because some of the gap is attributed to human design mistakes that affect machine learning (ML) algorithms (e.g., when developers specify inaccurate or incomplete data sets for algorithms to analyze), ethicists propose that project sponsors and developers should be held accountable for ML mistakes that could harm patients and other stakeholders [21, p. 132, 34]. Consistent with this view, we define responsible machine learning (RML) as *the use of ethically-sound governance policies and controls to prevent ML errors and adverse events, to detect errors that nevertheless occur, and to minimize stakeholder harm, by correcting mistakes and appropriately adjusting relevant systems, processes, controls and policies.* Similar to [36], our definition acknowledges the duality of human fallibility and accountability, and recognizes that project leaders seek harm-free collaborative value creation [7, 35].

An IT pilot test – "a disciplined … time-bound, limited-scope, limited-participation project" [11] – can flag some project risks or system risks before they cause harm. In this paper we report on findings from an exploratory case study of an ML pilot test in

Published by Springer Nature Switzerland AG 2021
D. Dennehy et al. (Eds.): I3E 2021, LNCS 12896, pp. 94–106, 2021.
https://doi.org/10.1007/978-3-030-85447-8_9

healthcare (from before its launch to its end). First, we review relevant prior ML research in healthcare. After describing our research method, we present our case study findings, and discuss their implications for responsible ML pilot projects.

The Conclusions section discusses study contributions and limitations and offers suggestions for further RML research.

2 Prior ML Research: Insights and Perspectives

The "cognitive generation of decision support" [33] offers potential value in many industries. However, further research is needed to develop a better understanding of socially- and technically-constructed "synthetic knowing" challenges [23]. Several reviews summarize ML research in [12, 14, 29, 32], in healthcare and other contexts.

ML reportedly improves processes such as organizational sense making [1], judges' legal decisions [39], IoT data analytics for improved support of installed equipment [5], and cyber-security [9]. Analyzing huge structured and unstructured datasets [1, 25, 31], ML has been deployed to classify, compare, and detect patterns, and to optimize, predict and/or offer recommendations [29]. Healthcare datasets based on electronic medical records, claims, images, and/or social media content support efforts to improve operations and services [5, 32]. Some ML projects focus on disease diagnosis and treatment [4]. Other projects demonstrate ML potential for identifying triggers and risk factors, such as for asthma care [40] and detecting individuals at risk for suicide [8]. ML applications aim to support remote patient tele-monitoring [41] and to predict in-hospital mortality [36]. Thus, ML projects target many aspects of informed healthcare [14, 16], including screening, triage, and treatment [24, 32].

ML design teams confront tradeoffs among algorithm explainability, simplicity, speed, and accuracy [36]. Many prior studies reported unintended ML consequences [12], including consequences linked to a common risk factor: the so-called ML "Black Box" (difficulty explaining and evaluating opaque algorithms) [27, 32]. To address this problem, developers are urged to ensure multidimensional data quality (e.g., validity, accuracy, completeness), design limited-scope algorithms in modules [2] and to take other steps to improve algorithmic explainability [22, 28].

CIOs who already oversee IS project portfolios with varied risks may need expert help to evaluate unique ML risks (e.g., the Black Box and other technical, ethical and regulatory risks [5]). Committed partners [33] need to be both willing and able to collaborate effectively [26]. Ethicists and lawyers can help spot and mitigate some risks [21, 36]. In addition to partners with ethical and legal expertise, some new technical and managerial IS capabilities and roles are needed on ML teams [5, 22].

Prior ML studies suggest that ML projects need some new controls [21, 33]. IS project managers already seek to balance tight versus loose controls [35]. Tight formal controls include strict deadlines and performance metrics, while looser informal controls include mechanisms for building strong relationships between developers and their customers [7]. Thus, some unique ML risks (such as the Black Box) reportedly need to be subject to relatively tight controls [2]. Looser informal controls are needed to encourage a fact-based culture [33], promote realistic ML expectations [20] and ensure clear communication [2, 13]. Agile techniques [5, 39] – including pilot testing of minimally-viable algorithms [28] – can help reveal risks or stakeholder concerns before problems arise.

Prior ML studies provide a helpful foundation, yet raise important questions. Operating a new system without mitigating a known risk would violate a tenet of responsible ML – limit stakeholder harm. What specific new controls can mitigate unique ML risks? For example, what controls can help mitigate the Black Box problem? Under what circumstances is it necessary to redesign a planned ML system? Our case study aimed to address the following question: *In a collaboration between a healthcare organization and a software vendor, to pilot-test a minimally-viable ML system, how are ML project risks identified and mitigated?*

3 Research Method

3.1 Overview

This pilot ML project involved healthcare administration (claims coding and billing) and patient care (since training data relies on providers' medical documentation). "ProCo," (disguised) located in the U.S. East, handles claims processing for 500 physicians, physician assistants and nurse practitioners (hereafter, "providers"), in 45 medical specialties, for 3.5 million encounters per year. Its 200 staff work in ProCo's central office; 700 non-clinical support staff are located in provider clinics. About half of its patients are Medicare beneficiaries (age 65 and up). ProCo's ML pilot was initiated in early winter 2018, when executives became aware of a vendor's potential solution (at that time, they did not call it a pilot test; some executives hoped they were purchasing a low-cost coding solution).

A case study is a suitable research method for exploring complex new phenomena holistically and with a focus on "how" and "why" questions [37]. Our participant-observation case study began in March 2018. One author, a ProCo employee, had ongoing access to managers and documents, and sat in on project-related meetings. In interviews conducted April 2018 to December 2018 (10 ProCo employees, 3 ProCo providers, 3 SofCo employees), interviewees described contractual issues, stakeholder expectations, and technical and operational challenges in this "coding automation" pilot project. In a final June 2019 interview and follow-on emails, ProCo's Vice President of Revenue Cycle Management ("VP") described developments that took place in spring 2019. Our study archive contains hand-written field notes, vendor status reports, ProCo documents (e.g., weekly coding quality reports, relevant emails), and project meeting notes that the VP prepared for the executive team. This paper emphasizes the VP's perspective. A newcomer to the organization, she challenged many taken-for-granted assumptions – which was valuable for revealing risks other ProCo managers either did not see or were not willing to disclose.

3.2 Background: A Medical Claims Coding Tutorial

Healthcare providers produce encounter documentation (free-form notes plus highly structured codes) to describe patient evaluation, condition, and treatment. Current Procedure (CPT) codes describe treatment procedures, equipment, and medications prescribed. A CPT subset – Evaluation & Management (E&M) codes – describe the patient's status (new/existing), care setting (inpatient/ outpatient, medical unit, etc.), provider's review of their medical history, details relevant to patient's presenting condition, and provider's examination of the patient. International Classification of Disease (ICD) codes describe a patient's medical condition. CPT and ICD codes should align, since a provider performs E&M tasks based on a patient's presenting condition and diagnosis, their in-hospital medical record, and their personal health record (containing details of past patient encounters with a primary care provider and specialists). Specific E&M codes link to specific reimbursement amounts.

CPT codes are input into medical billing software via manual data entry or automated data transfers from other systems. Claims (submitted to private insurance companies or government agencies like Medicare) are denied, adjusted or delayed, and hefty financial and licensure penalties may be imposed, if they contain incorrect codes. Providers complain about overly complex coding rules [17, 19, 38]. Studies report that while computerized provider order-entry (CPOE) systems reduce many errors, new errors arise due to usability issues [3, 6, 10].

4 Case Findings

4.1 SofCo Proposes a Medical Claims Coding Solution

ProCo's certified medical coders (paid $23/h) in the central business office (CBO) input complex codes describing in-hospital care, while ProCo providers were responsible for office-visit notes and coding. Most providers produced these in real time, using speech-to-text software. Like many provider organizations, ProCo struggled to achieve consistently high E&M coding accuracy. In eight of 25 medical specialties, coding compliance overall (per internal and external audits) was less than 80% (20% or more claims contained at least one incorrect code). In some specialties, a few individual providers produced many inaccurate codes. These chronically non-compliant providers increased the risk that they and/or ProCo would incur penalties.

"SofCo" (disguised) proposed to create software that would audit all ProCo providers' office visit E&M codes. Its planned "engine" would rely on natural language processing (NLP) and ML. NLP software would scan real ProCo office encounter records and "interpret" their meaning (via pattern-recognition). First, SofCo would need to train the software. "Expert" certified offshore coders based in India would save their own E&M code decisions into the NLP/ML training dataset. With each pass through this training data, the ML algorithm would scan for patterns to enact as coding rules. Although the ProCo CIO and the central business office (CBO) head expressed some skepticism at that time, the CEO and CFO, envisioning a potentially very large financial benefit, signed a "limited-scope" contract with SofCo (scope limited to office-visit CPT E&M code auditing).

Between signing the contract in early winter 2018 and the start of our case study in late March 2018, the CBO head resigned. A new VP for Revenue Cycle Management ("VP") spent her first month on the job learning about ProCo and the planned "coding automation project" (not then referred to as a "pilot"). In an April demonstration, SofCo's Sales Director boasted their software would be the first NLP/ML system to perform E&M code auditing. The Sales Director claimed their existing NLP platform was already capable of suggesting E&M codes; it just needed "tuning;" within six months (she claimed) SofCo's software would successfully auto-code at least 60% of ProCo's encounter charts. She claimed that by May 2019 (one year from a planned May 2018 kick-off) SofCo's auto-coded charts would be comparable to providers' codes. At that point, audited codes (those containing no discrepancies, per the experts) would be routed directly to ProCo's billing system (without human intervention). Table 1 summarizes project milestones.

4.2 The ProCo VP Attempts to Establish Control

The new ProCo VP some came to recognize that this project was risky. No project plan or other "standard" vendor documentation existed (specifying deliverables, roles and responsibilities, data and process flows, etc.). Colleagues informed her about problematic communications issues. For example: although the project was contractually limited to E&M coding for office visits, SofCo's project manager inexplicably spent time learning about "hospital" encounters and associated coding. The Sales Director stated an E&M coding platform already existed, yet the VP soon learned that SofCo's NLP/ML "engine" was not yet operational. She learned that IT consultancy Gartner described NLP+ML solutions for medical coding as in a nascent stage of development. While the VP was "reassured" to learn that SofCo had NLP experience (ProCo providers used SofCo's speech-to-text software to produce encounter notes), she was "concerned" to discover that SofCo did not have a record of strong machine learning. The project goal was clear: produce a system capable of automatically producing E&M codes based on providers' encounter documentation, to a 95% level of accuracy. However, the means to achieve it were not clear. The VP also learned that ProCo did not issue a formal Request for Proposal (which, e.g., should spell out how ProCo would select and securely send charts to SofCo). The contract did not include necessary details (e.g., step-by-step explanations of how the proposed solution or coding accuracy verification would work, or whether SofCo was required to return or destroy ProCo's data at the project conclusion).

Hoping to clarify the project scope and roles, the VP arranged a second interactive online demonstration of SofCo's NLP+ML prototype in May. This session confirmed that SofCo's coding platform was not fully developed; further work was necessary to comply with E&M coding guidelines, and it could not become operational until human coders fed the training database. During this session, the VP clarified that the contract limited the scope to office visit encounter coding. Now, she narrowed the scope further, by limiting the project in two ways: 1) utilize only office encounter charts from ProCo's family practice specialty, and 2) include only charts of those providers whose coding quality was less than 80% (per government audits and ProCo internal audits).

The May 2018 demo resolved some important concerns, but other concerns arose that summer. The contract specified ProCo would send its office visit encounter records to SofCo on a daily basis, starting in May 2018. However, it took most of the summer to work out exactly how to transfer data securely to SofCo. The first data transfer took place in September, and thereafter, ProCo sent Family Practice office encounter records to SofCo each weekday.

The ProCo VP aired her concerns in weekly meetings with SofCo personnel. In fall 2018 she asked how SofCo measured the offshore coders' coding accuracy. SofCo replied that ProCo was welcome to audit their work. To that end, the VP added a U.S.-based

Table 1. Timeline of key events in the coding automation pilot project

Date	Project event
2018	
Winter	Limited-scope contract signed
Mar	Case study begins New VP-RCM ("VP") meets with outgoing VP-RCM, CFO, CIO, and IT Director to learn about planned NLP+ML collaboration with SofCo
April	Early April: SofCo conducts product demonstration VP meets with ProCo compliance officer, coding manager, a coding auditor, and some providers to learn if/how current processes would need to change during the pilot project and after system rollout CBO updates CEO and CFO on coding compliance project concerns
May	SofCo Project Manager agrees to weekly Project Status meetings SofCo conducts a second product demonstration VP asks SofCo's Project Manager to provide a project plan
June	VP seeks further clarification of project details on ProCo side
Aug	Detailed project discussions with CIO and IT Director. Outcome: How ProCo ambulatory encounter charts would be sent to SofCo
Sept	First Auto Feed of ambulatory encounter charts sent to SofCo Daily feeds (M-F) thereafter until May 2019
Oct	Review of feedback loop to Providers (how Indian coders would notify ProCo providers of suggested code changes based on their reviews, and expectations re timely ProCo provider responses)
Nov	ProCo 10% audits of SofCo coders' accuracy begin (continues until May 2019)
Dec	News that SofCo would soon be acquired by a very large company leads ProCo VP to have a "scope clarification" conversation with SofCo Sales Director
2019	
March	SofCo starts providing weekly written status reports
April	SoftCo announces invoicing ($.50/claim) will start May 1 SoftCo provides "cryptic" weekly code quality status reports (per VP)
May	Project escalation to CIO, CEO and CFO; contract terms renegotiated
June 26	The Coding Automation pilot project is dissolved ProCo VP provides a final update describing spring 2019 developments Case study ends

certified quality auditor to the project team, tasked with spotting and correcting offshore coders' errors. These audits began in November. These, and weekly meetings revealed that SofCo coders' accuracy was not as strong as SofCo's sales pitch predicted. This greatly concerned the ProCo VP; she felt claims auto-coding should not move forward until SofCo "experts" achieved 95% accuracy. She reasoned that "garbage-in/garbage out" applies to ML: if offshore coding accuracy was weak, the data set would train the

ML algorithm to "learn" incorrect coding rules. She expressed surprise that SofCo did not evaluate its coders' accuracy.

In mid-December 2018, SofCo announced it had agreed to be acquired by a Fortune 100 coding technology company; the deal was to be finalized in Q1 2019. SofCo's Sales Director assured the surprised ProCo VP "Nothing will change;" the name on their project materials, email signature and letterhead would reflect the acquiring company, yet the acquisition would not impact the project. The Sales Director expressed enthusiasm about their future parent company's considerable technical resources, which would further their development and design efforts. In turn, the ProCo VP reported to ProCo's executive team that the acquisition would bring additional resources to the coding automation project and should have no adverse impact on the project timeline.

In winter and spring 2019, ProCo's VP saw little improvement in offshore coders' quality, and she learned little about the opaque ML algorithm. In March, SofCo finally began providing weekly status updates. These mostly reported on corrective actions taken to improve offshore coders' quality. The VP stated that SofCo "minimally addressed the ML engine development; they merely indicated it was 'on track'." In her view, SofCo's report format was uniquely "cryptic … [and] at such a high level that I had to request multiple follow-up meetings just to understand it."

In April, SofCo stated it would invoice ProCo for coding services, starting May 1 (one year after the "effective" project start date of May 1, 2018, per the contract). ProCo responded by proposing a new agreement; ProCo would keep sending SofCo the data feeds they needed to train their algorithm, but SofCo should issue no invoices until its human coders successfully achieved a 3-month cumulative accuracy score of 95%. In her weekly updates to the CIO, CFO and CEO, the VP now reported the project status as "at risk." SofCo had yet to demonstrate an ability to deliver an automated solution that could produce compliant E&M coding.

In June 2019 SofCo informed ProCo that their new parent company would transfer SofCo's ML project to the parent's ongoing NLP+ML development effort, in order to consolidate resources. SofCo assured ProCo they would reengage once the parent's auto-coding software was "ready for market." On June 26, ProCo's executive team decided to end the coding automation project.

5 Discussion

As discussed above, prior studies advise ML project leaders to choose willing and capable partners and set realistic expectations. In retrospect, the ProCo VP believes SofCo made unwarranted promises (predicting their algorithm would be ready to recommend codes within six months of project initiation, and would correctly auto-code 60% of ProCo charts within one year). The ProCo VP, CIO, ProCo IT staff, and ProCO executives lacked ML experience. The new VP sensed a "disconnect" between the optimism of the CEO and CFO (who focused on potential financial benefits) and the CIO, who seemed cynical about, and disengaged from, this project.

The new VP played a valuable role, both by challenging taken-for-granted assumptions and by drawing on her prior expertise as a project manager in a coding compliance context. After the project ended, she reflected: "In previous software implementation projects, a lack of expertise on our end was not necessarily a problem; we relied on vendors' assurances that their products were ready for use." The VP did know how to evaluate SofCo's medical coding expertise, and she came to recognize why this was important (for training the algorithm). Her ability to evaluate SofCo's ML claims improved during the pilot project (thanks to Gartner reports and other authoritative sources that helped educate her about NLP and ML).

Because of the Black Box (algorithm explainability) problem, many prior studies advised ML project leaders to utilize a modular design. The pilot collaboration ended before SofCo was ready to release their ML software for ongoing operations. Up through that point, SofCo's status updates were seen (by the ProCo VP) as vague. After the project ended, she expressed the opinion that both SofCo's weak project management expertise and the black box challenge affected the project from the outset; she suspected that weak project management was the root cause. Given that three product demonstrations were necessary (because of questions the VP and others had about how the NLP+ML engine would learn), we believe a Black Box issue was evident. We do not know if SofCo attempted to design for modularity or explainability, but ProCo's VP stated that in meetings, SofCo personnel were unable to convey how their software worked, and their written status reports were "cryptic."

The case findings about SofCo's medical coding accuracy difficulties point to a vitally important ML issue. If humans produce data that will be used to train an ML algorithm, a) the data (in this case, medical E&M codes) must be correct, and b) the human process of producing that data (in this case, choosing codes based on providers' medical documentation) should be explainable. From this we infer that the "black box" of the human brain can be an antecedent to the ML algorithm "black box". The ProCo VP saw evidence that U.S.-based human ProCo coders were more proficient at E&M coding than the certified coders SofCo hired in India. Had this project been designed to rely on ProCo's coders to train the ML algorithm, she said, ProCo would have negotiated a very different contract with SofCo (since U.S. based coders earn much higher wages than India-based coders).

Start small and use appropriate data: The contract indicated the project would focus on E&M coding for office visits. The ProCo VP limited the scope further (just the Family Practice specialty and only those providers with weak prior coding quality). This latter choice added complexity to the project and contradicts prior advice to tackle easier problems first and gradually introduce complex patterns into ML training data sets [18]. SofCo's choice to request daily data feeds also added unnecessary complexity (as did their use of offshore coders to train the algorithm). SofCo could have asked ProCo for historical claims data (considered best practice for those ML projects involving processes with verifiably "correct" solutions).

Prior studies emphasize the importance of identifying clear success criteria and metrics, and designing controls that can detect mistakes. Both partners agreed that a successful system would pick correct E&M codes based on providers' documentation. Use of offshore coders as arbiters of correctness was problematic, but the VP overcame that problem by hiring a U.S.-based certified medical claims coder to audit their work (how the VP came to realize that the offshore coders were less skilled than SofCo claimed). The VP attempted to impose relatively tight formal control by requesting written project status updates based on project milestones and coding quality metrics. For months, SofCo did not send the requested reports. Perhaps this was because SofCo was wrestling with algorithm explainability issues? Perhaps they chafed at ProCo's attempted tight control (did not feel like a "partner")?

As discussed above, prior studies advise ML teams to partner with legal and ethical experts, and to especially rigorously evaluate clinical ML systems [32, 36]. Both ProCo and SofCo apparently framed this pilot project as having an administrative focus. Yet, medical coding is not merely an administrative job. Treatment efficacy studies, clinical trials, and public-health studies rely on accurately-coded medical records; poor data quality in this context can ultimately jeopardize care quality. The ProCo VP questioned why SofCo "was willing to use coders whose accuracy was only in the 60% range," to feed the ML training dataset. "I was surprised they did not hire auditors to verify the offshore coders' accuracy; everyone just assumed their codes were accurate," she said. In the context of "regulatory scrutiny … isn't a failure to verify accuracy unethical?" The VP was also concerned about possible federal penalties: "What would we say to the government? That the … algorithm coded it, so we assumed it was right?" Her comments emphasize that responsible data governance is a necessary element of responsible machine learning.

Prior ML studies emphasize the importance of clear communication among collaborators. The ProCo VP stated that weak communication was a problem, from start (e.g., scope confusion led SofCo to waste time mapping hospital processes) to finish ("nothing will change" statement by SofCo's Sales rep, just one month before the project's dissolution). After the pilot project ended, the VP stated she now believes ML projects "require more than traditional governance." One prior study suggested ML projects should be located in business units, not in IT [25]. The ProCo VP believes an internal partnership is needed: "While it is logical to embed a project like this in a business unit, the IS team needs … to play an important role in the overall project management and governance. The business unit understands what the ML engine needs to do, but the IS team should understand how to manage the IS project risks."

6 Contributions, Limitations and Conclusion

A prior study reports that provider resistance doomed an NLP+ML medical coding project in a German hospital [28]. Our case study, of a similar NLP+ML medical coding pilot project, revealed other impediments. Provider resistance did not impede this pilot; instead, the Black Box problem seems to have exacerbated communication, planning, and shared governance. Prior ML studies advise leaders to establish an appropriate ML project governance structure, including agreed-upon formal and informal preventive, detective and corrective project controls [22]. Our case study followed an ML pilot from launch to dissolution, to track specific risks the ProCo VP identified and attempted to mitigate. We note that each organization entered this collaboration with some unresolved internal governance challenges, and that the collaboration suffered from several shared-governance issues. The ProCo VP recognized a need for stronger governance, and took several appropriate steps to impose control (requesting weekly meetings and written status updates, adding a U.S.-based medical claims coding auditor to the team, etc.).

While SofCo did not disclose specific technical issues in their ML algorithm, the training data quality was implicated (human coders struggled to produce accurate codes and could not explain some coding decisions). ProCo's VP, with 20 years' relevant prior experience, recognized that human mistakes would contaminate the training data set that fed this ML algorithm. She attempted to exercise both formal and informal control, by requesting written status reports (formal control) and insisting on weekly meetings (informal control). Physical distance and lack of direct access to the offshore coders impeded some of her attempts at control.

A study limitation is that we cannot verify why SofCo's new parent company put the collaboration on hold. Had SofCo proposed to train the algorithm with prior approved claims from ProCo's high-quality providers (removing incorrect claims, such as those denied by insurers or flagged in internal and government audits), we believe this pilot might have succeeded. A fruitful next case study would focus on an organization that uses verified prior claims data for their training data set. That study would seek to answer a similar research question: What project risks and system risks arise? How (if at all) does a project sponsor or project manager mitigate known risks, prior to authorizing an ML system for operational use?

Schuetz & Venkatesh [30] propose that some prior IS practices and assumptions do not fit ML projects. Other studies link the ML Black Box problem (one unique ML challenge) to adoption issues [28]. Our case study reveals suggestive evidence that a human Black Box/explainability problem affected an ML pilot project. No one on the ProCo side understood how the ML algorithm would choose codes, and SofCo personnel could not explain "in understandable terms" (ProCo VP's phrase) how their software or human coders did or would spot patterns or how specific patterns did or would guide its coding decisions. The VP did not want to "blindly trust" the machine, the vendor liaison, or SofCo's claims coders. Both weak human explainability and weak machine explainability limited this manager's control options. How to impose preventive process controls in the face of opaque algorithmic or human decisions? She focused on what she knew about SofCo coders' performance. Behind the curtain, SofCo apparently struggled to "tune" its algorithm, but the ProCo VP was unable to deploy detective controls pointing directly to specific SofCo ML algorithm problems. The VP did recognize that an algorithm cannot be considered reliable if its training data is not verifiably reliable. Further design studies could attempt to develop automated detective controls that reveal why specific ML problems occur. Until then, smart systems need capable human partners. New case studies are needed, to continue to explore how humans and machines collaborate effectively or ineffectively in ML projects.

Unrealistic expectations constrained managers' and clinicians' readiness to participate in this case study, similar to findings of prior ML studies [27]. A CIO can temper unrealistic expectations by establishing project governance that fully addresses project planning, controls and oversight. This is especially important for those healthcare ML projects at the intersection of administrative and clinical practice. Such projects bring financial and regulatory risks, along with threats to patient privacy, quality of patient care, and public health. Stakeholders include patients, regulators, healthcare systems, payers, and clinicians [14].

A study limitation is that this paper focused on one key informant – a well-qualified newcomer VP who took responsibility for oversight of this pilot. A fuller exposition would closely examine the perspectives of other stakeholders (starting with the other participants whom we interviewed). New studies are also needed that look closely at specific ML risks that threaten harm in terms of diversity, equity and inclusion (with important social and ethical implications; see [26].

There is much to learn about challenges revealed in responsible (or irresponsible) ML pilot projects, and implications for subsequent large-scale ML implementation projects. We encourage other researchers to join this effort, with new design science, action research, critical incident studies and case studies that can shed further holistic light on early-stage collaboration in client-vendor ML pilot projects.

References

1. Abassi, A., Zhou, Y., Deng, S., Zhang, P.: Text analytics to support sense making in social media: a language-action perspective. MIS Q. **42**(2), 427–464 (2014)
2. Asatiani, A., Malo, P., Nagbøl, P.R., et al.: Challenges of explaining the behavior of Black-Box AI systems. MIS Q. Exec. **19**, 4 (2020)
3. Ash, J., Sittig, D., Poone, E., et al.: The extent and importance of unintended consequences related to computerized provider order entry. J. Am. Med. Inform. Assoc. **14**(4), 415–423 (2007)
4. Bardhan, I., Chen, H., Karahanna, E.: Connecting systems, data and people: a multidisciplinary research roadmap for chronic disease management. Introd. Spec. Issue IT Chronic Dis. MIS Q. **44**(1), 185–201 (2020)
5. Bilgeri, D., Gebauer, H., Fleisch, E., Wortmann, F.: Driving process innovation with IoT field data. MIS Q. Exec. **18**(3), 191–207 (2019). Article 5
6. Campbell, E., Sittig, D., Ash, J., Guappone, K., Dykstra, R.: Types of unintended consequences related to computerized provider order entry. J. Am. Med. Inform. Assoc. **13**(5), 547–556 (2006)
7. Cardinal, L.B., Kreutzer, M., Miller, C.C.: An aspirationl view of organizational control research: re-invigorating empirical work to better meet the challenges of 21st century organizations. Acad. Manag. Ann. **11**(2), 559–592 (2017)
8. Chau, M., Li, T.M.H., Wong, P.W.C., et al.: Finding people in emotional distress in online social media: a design combining machine learning and rule-based classification. MIS Q. **44**(2), 933–955 (2020)
9. Ebrahim, M., Nunamaker, J.F., Chen, H.: Semi-supervised cyber threat identification in dark net markets: a transductive and deep learning approach. JMIS **37**(3), 694–722 (2020)
10. El Shayib, M., Pawola, L.: Computerized provider order-entry related medication errors among hospitalized patients. Health Inform. J. **26**(4), 2834–2859 (2020)
11. Gogan, J.L., Rao, A.: When vendors participate in IT pilot test projects: pitfalls and challenges. Eng. Manag. J. **23**(3), 2–29 (2011)
12. Gogan, J.L.: Responsible machine learning projects. In: Proceedings of the 27th Americas Conference on Information Systems (AMCIS) (2021)
13. Goul, M.: Poised between 'a wild west of predictive analytics' and 'an analytics of things westworld frontier. MIS Q. Exec. **17**(4), 333–347 (2018). Article 9
14. He, J., Baxter, S.I., Xu, J., Zhou, X., Zhang, K.: The practical implications of artificial intelligence technologies in medicine. Nat. Med. **25**(1), 30–36 (2019)
15. Hernandez, D., Fitch, A.: IBM's retreat highlights hurdles for health AI. The Wall Street Journal (2021)

16. Johnston, M.: The transformation of healthcare with AI and machine learning. InformationWeek, 16 October 2018
17. King, M.S., Sharp, L., Lipsky, M.S.: Accuracy of CPT evaluation and management coding by family physicians. J. Am. Board Fam. Pract. **14**(3), 184 (2001)
18. Kühl, N., Hirt, R., Baier, L., Schmitz, B., Satzgerm G.: How to conduct rigorous supervised machine learning in information systems research: the supervised machine learning report card. Commun. Assoc. Inf. Syst. (CAIS) **48**, 46 (2021)
19. Kumetz, E., Goodson, J.: The undervaluation of evaluation and management professional services. Chest **144**(3), 740–745 (2013)
20. Lacity, M.C., Scheepers, R., Willcocks, L.P.: Cognitive automation as part of deakin University's digital strategy. MIS Q. Exec. **17**(2), 89–107 (2018)
21. Martin, K.: Designing ethical algorithms. MIS Q. Exec. **18**(2), 128–142 (2019). Article 5
22. Mayer, A.-S., Strich, F., Fiedler, M.: Unintended consequences of introducing AI systems for decision making, MIS Q. Exec. **19**(4), 238–257 (2020)
23. Monteiro, E., Parmiggiani, E.: Synthetic knowing: the politics of the Internet of Things. MIS Q. **43**(1), 141–165 (2019)
24. Mousavi, R., Raghu, T.S., Frey, K.: Harnessing artificial intelligence to improve the quality of answers in online question-answering health forums. JMIS **37**(4), 1073–1098 (2020)
25. Muller, O., Junglas, I., Debortoli, S., vom Brocke, J.: Using text analytics to derive customer service management benefits from unstructured data. MIS Q. Exec. **15**(4), 243–258 (2016)
26. Newell, S., Marabelli, M.: Strategic opportunities (and challenges) of algorithmic decision-making: a call for action on the long-term societal effects of 'datification.' J. Strat. Inf. Syst. **24**(1), 3–14 (2015)
27. Pumplun, L, Fecho, M., Islam, N., Buxman, P.: Machine learning systems: how mature is the adoption process in medical diagnostics? In: Proceedings of the 54th Hawaii International Conference on System Sciences (HICSS), pp. 6317–6326 (2021)
28. Reis, L., Maier, C., Mattke, J., Creutzenberg, M., Weitzel, T.: Addressing user resistance would have prevented a healthcare AI project failure. MIS Q. Exec. **19**(4), 273–296 (2020)
29. Rzepka, C., Berger, B.: User interaction with AI-enabled systems: a systematic review of IS research. In: Proceedings of the Thirty Ninth International Conference on Information Systems (ICIS), San Francisco, December 2018
30. Schuetz, S., Venkatesh, V.: The rise of human machines: how cognitive computing systems challenge assumptions of user-system interaction. J. Assoc. Inf. Syst. **21**(2), 460–482 (2020)
31. Shin, D., He, S., Lee, G.M., Whinston, A.B., Centintas, S., Lee, K.C.: Enhancing social media analysis with visual data analytics: a deep learning approach. MIS Q. **44**(4), 1459–1492 (2020)
32. Topol, E.: High performance medicine: the convergence of human and artificial intelligence. Nat. Med. **25**, 44–56 (2019)
33. Watson, H.: Preparing for the cognitive generation of decision support. MIS Q. Exec. **16**(3) (2017)
34. Wessel, M., Helmer, N.: A crisis of ethics in technology innovation. MIT Sloan Manag. Rev. SMR797 **61**, 70–76 (2020)
35. Wiener, M., Mahring, M., Remus, R., Saunders, C., Cram, W.A.: Moving IS project control research into the digital era: the 'why' of control and the concept of control purposes. Inf. Syst. Res. **30**, 1387–1401 (2019)
36. Wiens, J., Suchi, S, Sendak, M, et al.: Do no harm: a roadmap for responsible machine learning for health care. Nat. Med. Perspect. **25**, 1337–1340 (2019)
37. Yin, R.: Case Study Research: Design and Methods, 5th edn. Sage, Thousand Oaks (2014)
38. Young, R.A., Bayles, B., Hill, J.H., Kumar, K.A., Burge, S.: Family physicians' opinions on primary care documentation, coding and billing. Fam. Med. **46**(5), 278–384 (2014)

39. Zhang, Z., Nandhakumar, J., Hummel, J.T., Waardenburg, L.: Addressing the key challenges of developing machine learning AI systems for knowledge-intensive work. MIS Q. Exec. **19**((4) (2020). Article 5
40. Zhang, W., Ram, S.: A comprehensive analysis of triggers and risk factors for asthma based on machine learning and large heterogeneous data sources. MIS Q. **44**(1), 304–349 (2020)
41. Zhu, H., Santani, S., Chen, H., Nunamaker, J.F.: Human identification for activities of daily living: a deep transfer learning approach. JMIS **37**(2), 457–483 (2020)

AI and Analytics Decision Making

Wise Data-Driven Decision-Making

Morteza Namvar(✉) and Ali Intezari

The University of Queensland, St Lucia, QLD 4067, Australia
m.namvar@uq.edu.au

Abstract. This article reports on the preliminary findings of research in progress. In one of the first empirical studies in the information systems and organisations literature, we investigate the role of wisdom as a decision-making capacity in the use of analytics. To address the research question of how decision-makers can use analytics to make wise decisions, we interviewed six decision-makers and four data analytics in a diverse range of industries. Based on the findings, we introduce a process model of wise data-driven decision-making (WD3M). This study offers significant theoretical and practical implications as it extends our understanding of how wisdom can be defined and used in the analytics context. For practitioners, this study offers important guidelines as to how to make wise and more effective data-driven decisions.

Keywords: Business analytics · Wisdom · Knowledge · Decision-making · Data analysis

1 Introduction

For many organisations, business analytics is the new frontier in the information revolution [1]. They have gained significant attention from academia and industry [2] as a disruptor to organisations [3]. Essential stories hidden in big data are powerful means to enhance the interpretation of environmental scenarios by decision-makers [4]. Business analytics, or simply analytics, aims to create economic and social values [5] for organisations using big data [6]. It offers different ways to support users efficiently with information on decision-making scenarios [7], where technology, human perception, and organisations as interpretive systems combine to assist decision-makers in improving their information processing capabilities and enhance the understanding of the business environment [8].

Despite analytics being one of the essential elements of the modern decision-support system [7], in most organisations, analytics is loosely coupled with decision-making and much less with wise decision-making [9]. Many researchers observe that its use for decisions involves several issues [2] for dealing with fuzzy and ambiguous situations [10]. Decision-makers also work in groups, and social aspects are indispensable in making informed decisions [11], especially when encountering non-linear and complex decision situations [12]. Indeed, what decision-makers need from new analytics tools is capabilities that enhance their understanding, non-rational decision-making and satisficing, and knowledge implementation capacity.

D. Dennehy et al. (Eds.): I3E 2021, LNCS 12896, pp. 109–119, 2021.
https://doi.org/10.1007/978-3-030-85447-8_10

The current literature on socio-technical features of analytics is characterised by a limited number of empirical studies [5] and calls for interdisciplinary research drawing on theories from psychology and sociology. The success of analytics is in organisations requires not only infrastructure, data analysts, and knowledge and tools for dealing with big data but also an understanding of how analytics should be used wisely to translate big data to competitive advantages and wise decisions [13]. It is, therefore, crucial to investigate "how can decision-makers use analytics to make wise decisions"?

To address the research question, this study draws on the notion of wisdom. Wisdom is the process through which the problem is defined, the right alternatives are formulated, the most appropriate alternative is selected and implemented using the right means towards achieving the right end at the right time [9]. Wise decisions find impression in socially complex and ill-defined problems. These problems are characterised as emergent, dynamic, unpredictable, and difficult to formulate, encompassing numerous multi-directional cause-effects relationships, and engaging multiple stakeholders both within and outside the organisation. Most organisational strategic decisions are of this kind [9]. By employing the wisdom model, this study pursues the following objectives: (i) to conceptualise wisdom in the context of analytics; and (ii) develop a process model to show how organisations can make wise decisions based on analytics.

The following sections first present the theoretical framing of the study, followed by details of the research method and its design, and a description of the data collection process. Then it presents the analysis of the collected data along with the proposed process model of this study. Finally, the paper concludes and elaborates on how we will continue data collection and its analysis to complete this research.

2 Background

Making effective decisions based on both rational (e.g., using analytics) and non-rational (e.g., human insight and judgment) is at the heart of the notion of wisdom [9]. The notion of wisdom describes the evaluation of multiple perspectives to better understand the causes and ramifications of problems, which is an essential prerequisite to reaching effective decisions positively. Wisdom is the capacity to understand the relationship among and give meaning to objects, events, and human interactions by critically reflecting on the past (causes), present (manifestation), and future (ramifications) of the phenomena and their relationships. The notions of wisdom is based on right 'mean', 'time' and 'end'. The 'right mean' means that the selected alternative or solution should not involve the use of any coercion. The 'right time' refers to the decision to be made when it generates the most positive impact. The 'right end' means that the decision is made based on considering the legitimate and ethical interests of stakeholders.

Wisdom has been the topic of philosophical discourses for centuries. The concept is rooted in the works of philosophers such as Socrates and Aristotle. Interest in wisdom has revived over the past three decades. Contemporary studies of wisdom began by psychologists and gerontologists. More recently, other disciplines, including organisation and management studies [14], leadership [15], public administration [16], and education [17] examined the implication of wisdom. The information systems and the knowledge management scholars have joined the discourse. For example, [18] revisits the data–information–knowledge–wisdom hierarchy as the widely accepted model in the information systems and knowledge management disciplines and emphasises that the model is more about wisdom, as the ability to increase effectiveness than knowledge [19] . Discusses the individual, organisational, and societal issues related to contemporary technologies and argue that the use of technology requires a critical review based on the wisdom theory to enhance human well-being.

By integrating both rational and non-rational aspects of decision-making, wisdom can address the challenges of using organisational information systems to make insightful decisions based on analytics. In this sense, we argue that wisdom as a decision-making capacity can sit between analytics and decisions. [9] proposes a model of wisdom that conceptualises wisdom as a decision-making capacity to identify and solve complex problems based on (1) an understanding of both the internal and external world, (2) both rational and non-rational analyses of the problem at hand, and (3) a consideration of multiple stakeholders' perspectives.

We adopted the wisdom model as a theoretical framework in this study because wisdom is a more comprehensive concept in meaning than making decisions. Decision-making focuses on evaluating a range of possible actions and selecting the best alternative to the extent that the problem is solved [20]. While the attention of decision-making is directed almost entirely to solving the problem at hand and the future direct impact of decisions, actions, and their outcomes, wisdom necessarily deals with both the short- and long-term direct and indirect impacts of any possible solution on multiple stakeholders and from both the organisational and ethical perspectives.

From an analytics perspective, a decision-maker can make quality decisions after a lengthy and thorough process of information processing, especially at the strategic level. Little is, however, known about the process through which a decision-maker, especially strategic managers, can make wise decisions based on analytics.

3 Method

We have conducted pilot interviews with study participants from separate organisations to identify their personal experience in using analytics in making wise decisions. In the rest of this research, we will also use other data sources such as documents or log data. We will continue data collection until we achieve the theoretical saturation on the aspects of participants' experiences that are the focus of this study. We have interviewed four data analysts who work with advanced analytical tools and six managers and directors who use the garnered reports by data analysts to this stage of research. In the rest of this study, we use pseudonyms to refer to the study participants.

As the focus of the study is on organisational decision-making, we have chosen the study participants mainly from large enterprises. We have used semi-structured questionnaires during the interviews as a guide to the free-flowing discussion [21], and we have asked study participants to provide examples of business situations where they observed either wise or unwise data-based decisions. We followed a cyclical and recursive process of data collection and prepared transcripts, and analysed them gradually. Going through the interview transcripts, we discovered the concepts related to the use of analytics in organisations, and then we used thematic analysis to identify the fundamental themes of this study, using Strauss and Corbin's guidelines [22]. These themes include the concepts associated with using business analytics within organisations for wise decision-making. In the following section, we elaborate on the preliminary data analysis by elaborating on the four identified themes.

4 Preliminary Data Analysis

This section elaborates on four discovered themes that elaborate on the wise use of analytics in organisations. We have taken the organisational context of analytics into account to draw a more socio-technical characterisation of themes. The cyclical process of data collection has helped in preparing transcripts and analysing them. Concepts related to the use of analytics in organisations were dubbed with preliminary codes by reading the interview transcripts. These codes include the concepts associated with using analytics within organisations for wise decision-making. The four identified themes are 1) report generation, 2) trustworthiness analysis, 3) appropriateness analysis, and 4) alternative selection.

4.1 Report Generation

An effective decision is based on an accurate understanding and articulation of the problem. If the decision-makers fail to identify and formulate business problems accurately, they can't use data and information to articulate possible solutions. Our study participant, Dominic, Director of an IT firm, added to this view by noting that the main issue for understanding an organisation and its surrounding environment through analytics is clarifying requests of decision-makers rather than analytical functionalities.

The analytical skills of decision-makers influence their interactions with reports and affect analytics use in understanding organisational complexities. Christopher, Director of a government firm, identified the lack of proper interaction between data analysts and decision-makers as the primary barrier to unskilled decision-makers using analytics. Rebecca, Director of a government firm, further added to this view by highlighting the role of communication for data analysts and the extent to which proper presentation of their work could assist decision-makers to understand underlying concepts and influence the efficacy of analytics. She then captured the essence of analysts facing decision-makers who could not understand the reports presented to them, as she talked about failing to explain her work despite the robust model she had developed. In this sense, the wise use of data for better decision-making requires the decision-maker to understand the data clearly. Both analysts and the decision-maker should be consistent in terms of the data analysis results concerning the decision problem at a given time.

4.2 Trustworthiness Analysis

In the view of our study participants, sceptical decision-makers feel they lose their power if they make decisions based on analytics or they do not trust the validity of analytics reports. Wise decision-makers may also be sceptical in that they do not easily trust in data. Wise decision-makers also check the validity of data before they use it. In this sense, they are sceptical. On the other hand, they rely on data when they feel that the data is trustworthy and can lead to effective decisions. That is, the wise decision-maker will rely on data, even if they may be seen as incapable of making decisions solely based on their knowledge and experience.

Matteo, Director of a finance firm, noted that a lack of trust is even more problematic when reports recommend a solution to decision-makers. Austin, Manager in a healthcare firm, indicated that analytics could usually provide a straightforward comparison between objectives and progress; however, for reports at the strategic level, more effort is required to analyse the suitability of the analysis and solutions for the problem in hand. Rebecca further elaborated on sceptical decision-makers resistance in established organisations and suggested presenting analytics in a plausible and easy-to-understand way for decision-makers. Providing decision-makers with the opportunity to interact with and validate reports assists in analysing the trustworthiness of analytics. Wise decision-makers will not make decisions based on the data if they do not trust it. Joseph, a National manager in a government firm, also suggested interactive reports as a solution to improve the trust of decision-makers toward analytics since they lose confidence in using prescribed solutions and prefer to control and investigate what is behind reports. He further suggested engaging with decision-makers and personalising reports, and noted that decision-makers need assistance and training to interact with reports. He also explained that decision-makers would feel they have control over what they are using, leveraging their confidence in using analytics for decision-making after this interaction and engagement. Trust in data is, therefore, a critical aspect of wise data-driven decision-making.

4.3 Appropriateness Analysis

Wise decision-makers usually have ideas about appropriate solutions; they check the data to see if the data back up those right decisions. In this line, Chadrick explained that intuitive decision makers are looking for specific numbers or patterns that they already have in mind, and analytics provides them with numbers to support what they consider possible solutions. Rebecca noted that intuitive decision-makers use analytics to justify their actions. If there is any inconsistency between the data and the possible wise solutions that the decision-maker has in mind, wise decision-makers seek more data. For example, data should show a potential market for a particular product or service in the country. A wise decision-maker would not go ahead and supply that particular product or service if the product or service may have negative side effects on the potential customers; or if there is a cultural or religious sensitivity to that particular product and service.

Our study participants noted that, in these situations, extensive reports are not useful, and data analysts should focus on the lower level and operational drivers. Rebecca added that analytics should be used as a validation tool rather than an absolute prescriptive solution. On the other hand, and as discussed in the trustworthiness analysis, wise decision-makers do not ignore data when they see that the data can lead to a more effective decision.

4.4 Alternative Selection

Decision-making is about facing many situations of choosing alternatives. Wise decision-makers know that they need to use reports at the right time and have to respond to the real world rapidly. However, the analytics and IT-related processes may play against making timely decisions. Usually, in organisations, IT teams and analytics teams have their standards and processes, and many other business stakeholders also need to review their work. Ryder, a senior business analyst in a finance firm, mentioned that the process of preparing reports and using them is very lengthy, and decision-makers should wait for various pieces of data that some data suppliers can provide. Also, the processing time is required for technology and data analysts to bring this data and analyse it.

Shaden, a manager in a government firm, emphasised using KPIs to quantify strategic decisions and turn them into everyday operational actions. Wise decision-makers drill deeper into existing reports or create new stories to better understand business operations. Diego, a data analyst in a finance firm, also highlighted the role of interactive reports in gaining insight and choosing the alternatives wisely; he noted that decision-makers need to interact with reports and drill them down for additional insights to know their drivers of business functions.

5 Wise Data-Driven Decision-Making (WD3M)

We propose a process model for Wise Data-Driven Decision-Making (WD3M) (see Fig. 1). This model incorporates the notion of wisdom into data-driven decision-making to make wise use of data. The wisdom principals are enablers in the model, whereas the data-driven actions (four identified themes from the preliminary analysis) are episodes [23]. We elaborate on the main elements of the process model in the following.

WD3M starts with report generation, which is done by data analysts and monitored and improved by decision-makers. Identifying and considering essential signals from the internal and external environment to unfolding business events buried in masses of business data is a critical pillar in WD3M. The type of discovered insights from the available data depends on the variety and granularity of various data sources [24].

After the reports are generated, wise decision-makers assess the validity of the reports in an episode for trustworthiness analysis. There are two enablers from cognition and emotions of decision-makers when they analyse the trustworthiness of reports.

When decision-makers gained a confidant in using the reports after successfully analysing their trustworthiness, they move to appropriateness analysis. In this episode, in addition to cognition and emotions, wise decision-makers use their understanding of the internal and external world.

External world understanding means that the decision-makers analyse and interpret the data to understand the environmental context. They check the reports to see to what extent the report represents the external world when needed and to what extent the data represents the reality of the external world or what is happening outside the organisation.

Appropriateness analysis is the central aspect of wisdom. An analytical report and its source(s) can be trustworthy, as is checked in the trustworthiness analysis episode, and perfectly lead to a true understanding of both the internal and external worlds, yet to be inappropriate, as is checked in the appropriateness analysis episode. For example, the data can show that there is a great market for selling adult products or even guns to a community that has a financial justification. However, applying a multi-perspective consideration may identify the solution as an inappropriate solution. By inappropriate, we mean that the decision and its consequences can be unethical, illegal, and ignoring the community's interests. Multi-perspective consideration is an appropriateness analysis of the data, based on three perspectives: ethical, legal, and multiple stakeholders' interests [19].

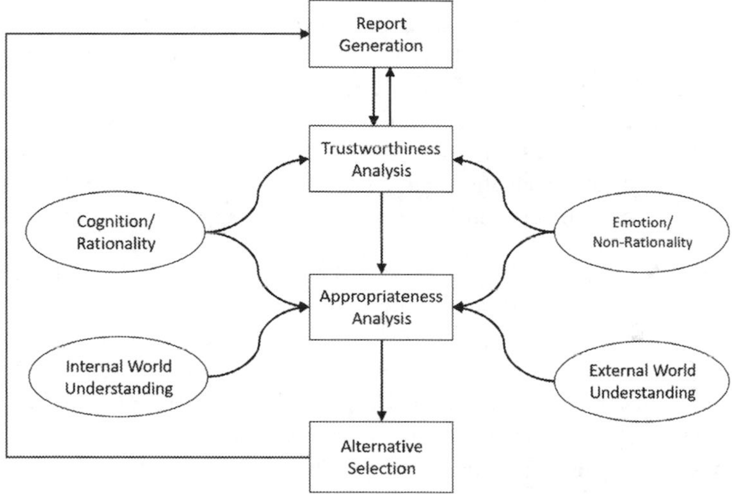

Fig. 1. Wise data-driven decision-making (WD3M)

Sceptical analysis and cognitive-emotional mastery are also crucial in the success of WD3M. For example, one external agent may provide an analytics report to an organisation about selling the company shares to another company. The data sources are trustworthy from a cognitive or rational point of view. However, whether or not the external agent has intentionally intended to mislead the organisation cannot be necessarily determined by looking at the trustworthiness of the data via an analytical (rational) point of view. The decision-maker may need to rely on his or her non-rational understanding of why the external agent is providing the data report. Through emotional or non-rational analysis, the decision-maker can, for example, assess the intention behind the data.

6 Discussion

Data analysts can employ an inductive approach to discover previously unknown patterns or distinctions [25] to emerge from big data. Engaging in this approach, data analysts can start from data and then seek to generate theoretical explanations from (wise) decision-makers [5]. Most decision-makers work with data analysts without a defined purpose, promoting a bottom-up, inductive approach to the use of analysis for decision-making [26]. However, what wise decision-making using analytics needs is incorporating both cognition/rationality and emotion/non-rationality from decision-makers.

From Cognition/Rationality to WD3M: The proposed process model highlights the importance of interactive reports and their insights to assist decision-makers in using their cognition and rational thinking in using analytics. In new analytics systems, data analysts do not need to do a lot of analytics on behalf of decision-makers; they create an environment where end-users apply analytics, except for advanced concepts or some areas where decision-makers might not carry the required skills. Data analysts can be innovative to arrive at ideas and insights; however, specific boundaries can simultaneously be set around their analytics to ensure that business value is delivered [27]. While decision-makers have a list of prepared reports in a typical analytics system, with interactive analytics, decision-makers can drag data onto their workspace, make their analysis, and modify and personalise reports. They can change dimensions or actual financial measures or add calculations on reports. They can start with developed reports, which they can modify and customise based on their understanding.

From Emotion/Non-rationality to WD3M: The proposed process model suggests a deductive approach in using reports and explains how decision-makers should use interactive reports. Analytics would not be effective unless reports are designed in ways that explicitly include decision-makers in the loop [28]. The integration of rational and non-rational analysis of the appropriateness of the possible solutions requires a high level of interaction between the data analysts and the decision-maker.

Analytics is widely used in automated algorithms for decision-making. However, the literature on analytics also highlights the importance of human intelligence [29] and the wisdom required to examine patterns and insights [30] and to refine them [31]. Along with building on algorithmic decision-making, analytics' stakeholders need to develop strategies to gain insights from big data beyond stable metrics, as the insights gained from analytics largely depend on the exploration of decision-makers.

Decision-makers trust analytics when they interact with reports and validate them. They may also feel they have more power, as they can make sense of and effectively integrate insights into their decision-making [25]. This trust and power can potentially result in more da-ta-driven actions and assist organisations in leveraging the potential of analytics [32]. The study participants who closely worked with decision-makers highlighted their willingness to anticipate decision-maker's needs and provide them with opportunities to customise and tailor reports. Also, some scholars contend that too much reliance on algorithmic decision-making may lead to a loss of confidence in using relevant knowledge by decision-makers, particularly when decision-makers don't clearly know how algorithms arrive at certain results, patterns, and decisions [33].

Algorithmic decision-making nevertheless has strengths and applications in many cases, and organisations need to devise ways to meaningfully balance this in interactive reports [29, 34]. To this end, scholars have started to explore the interaction between algorithmic and human intelligence and how this leads to valuable insights. In fact, data should be wisely supplemented with decision-makers experiences, common sense, and contextual knowledge [25], to solve problems for which the conditions are unknown.

In situations where algorithms are deployed to operate without human intervention, they actively enact the analytics environment, which gives algorithms an increasingly performative character [24, 35].

7 Conclusion

This study took the organisational context of analytics into account, thereby answering a call for a more socio-technical characterisation of big data to investigate how analytics can be used to make wise decisions. To this end, we conducted interviews to examine the strengths and limitations of analytics in the process of WD3M. Drawing on thematic analysis, this study developed a process model that shows how managers can use analytics to make wise decisions.

The proposed model demonstrated how four themes identified in the data – report generation, trustworthiness analysis, appropriateness analysis, and alternative selection, provide grounding for WD3M process. It showed both inductive and deductive approaches for using analytics in various steps for the process of wise decision-making and how these complement each other in this process. It also demonstrated how communication between wise decision-makers and data analysts results in balancing these two approaches. In fact, bridging analytics and wisdom is vital to helping decision-makers understand that analytics has more profound implications for business than just reporting on status. Analytical technology offers ample support for wise decision-making, thus providing management with methods and tools to continuously generate business insights leading to quality and actionable decisions.

This study provided strong evidence for the impact of the research in progress on the theory and practice of wisdom and its technological support. From a theoretical perspective, the study brings together two distinct fields – wisdom and analytics – and demonstrated how the approaches advocated by these two fields could improve the applications of analytics. The explanation of wisdom construct in the context of analytics revealed the strengths and limitations of analytics for addressing wise decision-making. From a practical point of view, this study demonstrated how decision-makers use analytics to improve their understanding of the business environment and make wise decisions. It also provides guidelines for developers to enhance their analytics tools to enable the end-users to make wise decisions.

Methodologically, the findings can potentially be undermined by a multitude of interrelated factors that influence analytics productivity, not all of which were identified in the conducted interviews. As the domain knowledge and experience of decision-makers may affect their interaction with analytics, more interviews with different decision-makers in each could be conducted to investigate how analytics improves wise decision-making. Further studies could also investigate under what particular conditions decision-makers can generate insights through analytics.

References

1. Goes, P.B.: Editor's comments: big data and IS research. MIS Q. **38**(3), iii–viii (2014)
2. Chen, H., Chiang, R.H.L., Storey, V.C.: Business intelligence and analytics: from big data to big impact. MIS Q. **36**(4), 1165–1188 (2012)
3. Fichman, R.G., Dos Santos, B.L., (Eric) Zheng, Z.: Digital innovation as a fundamental and powerful concept in the information systems curriculum. MIS Q. **38**(2), 329–353 (2014)
4. Namvar, M., Cybulski, J., Perera, L.: Using business intelligence to support the process of organizational sensemaking. Commun. Assoc. Inf. Syst. **38**(1), 330–352 (2016)
5. Günther, W.A., Rezazade Mehrizi, M.H., Huysman, M., Feldberg, F.: Debating big data: a literature review on realising value from big data. J. Strateg. Inf. Syst. **26**(3), 191–209 (2017)
6. Loebbecke, C., Picot, A.: Reflections on societal and business model transformation arising from digitisation and big data analytics: a research agenda. J. Strateg. Inf. Syst. **24**(3), 149–157 (2015)
7. Arnott, D., Pervan, G.: A critical analysis of decision support systems research. J. Inf. Technol. **20**(2), 67–87 (2005)
8. Namvar, M., Cybulski, J.: BI-based organisations: a sensemaking perspective. In: ICIS 2014 Proceedings, December 2014
9. Intezari, A., Pauleen, J.: Wisdom, Analytics and Wicked Problems: Integral Decision Making for the Data Age. Routledge Publication, London (2019)
10. Meyer, A., Zimmermann, H.-J.: Applications of fuzzy technology in business intelligence. Int. J. Comput. Commun. Control **6**(3), 428–441 (2011)
11. Hekkala, R., Stein, M.-K., Rossi, M.: Metaphors in managerial and employee sensemaking in an information systems project. Inf. Syst. J. **28**(1), 142–174 (2018)
12. Hasan, H., Gould, E.: Support for the sense-making activity of managers. Decis. Support Syst. **31**(1), 71–86 (2001)
13. Chiang, R.H.L., Grover, V., Liang, T.-P., Zhang, D.: Special issue: strategic value of big data and business analytics. J. Manage. Inf. Syst. **35**(2), 383–387 (2018)
14. Tredget, D.A.: Practical wisdom and the Rule of Benedict. J. Manage. Dev. (2010)
15. McKenna, B., Rooney, D., Kenworthy, A.L.: Introduction: Wisdom and Management—A Guest-Edited Special Collection of Resource Reviews for Management Educators. Academy of Management Briarcliff Manor, New York (2013)
16. Rooney, D., McKenna, B.: Wisdom in public administration: looking for a sociology of wise practice. Public Adm. Rev. **68**(4), 709–721 (2008)
17. Maxwell, N.: Wisdom: object of study or basic aim of inquiry? In: Ferrari, M., Weststrate, N. (eds.) The Scientific Study of Personal Wisdom, pp. 299–322. Springer, Dordrecht (2013). https://doi.org/10.1007/978-94-007-7987-7_14
18. Rowley, J.: The wisdom hierarchy: representations of the DIKW hierarchy. J. Inf. Sci. **33**(2), 163–180 (2007)
19. Intezari, A., Pauleen, D.J.: Conceptualizing wise management decision-making: a grounded theory approach. Decis. Sci. **49**(2), 335–400 (2018). https://doi.org/10.1111/deci.12267
20. Boland, R.J.: Decision making and sensemaking. In: Burstein, F., Holsapple, C.W. (eds.) Handbook on Decision Support Systems 1. International Handbooks Information System, pp. 55–63. Springer, Heidelberg (2008). https://doi.org/10.1007/978-3-540-48713-5_3
21. Moustakas, C.: Phenomenological Research Methods. Sage Publications, Incorporated, Thousand Oaks (1994)
22. Corbin, J.M., Strauss, A.: Grounded theory research: procedures, canons, and evaluative criteria. Qual. Sociol. **13**(1), 3–21 (1990)
23. Newman, M., Robey, D.: A social process model of user-analyst relationships. MIS Q., 249–266 (1992)

24. Yoo, Y.: It is not about size: a further thought on big data. J. Inf. Technol. **30**(1), 63–65 (2015)
25. Shollo, A., Galliers, R.D.: Towards an understanding of the role of business intelligence systems in organisational knowing. Inf. Syst. J. **26**(4), 339–367 (2016)
26. Constantiou, I.D., Kallinikos, J.: New games, new rules: big data and the changing context of strategy. J. Inf. Technol. **30**(1), 44–57 (2015)
27. Gao, J., Koronios, A., Selle, S.: Towards a process view on critical success factors in big data analytics projects. Presented at the Americas Conference On Information Systems, Puerto Rico (2015)
28. Jagadish, H.V., et al.: Big data and its technical challenges. Commun. ACM **57**(7), 86–94 (2014)
29. Ekbia, H., et al.: Big data, bigger dilemmas: a critical review. J. Am. Soc. Inf. Sci. **66**(8), 1523–1545 (2015)
30. Seddon, P.B., Constantinidis, D., Tamm, T., Dod, H.: How does business analytics contribute to business value? Inf. Syst. J. **27**(3), 237–269 (2017)
31. Sharma, R., Mithas, S., Kankanhalli, A.: Transforming decision-making processes: a research agenda for understanding the impact of business analytics on organisations. Eur. J. Inf. Syst. **23**(4), 433–441 (2014)
32. Bhimani, A.: Exploring big data's strategic consequences. J. Inf. Technol. **30**(1), 66–69 (2015)
33. Markus, M.L.: New games, new rules, new scoreboards: the potential consequences of big data. J. Inf. Technol. **30**(1), 58–59 (2015)
34. Abbasi, A., Sarker, S., Chiang, R.H.: Big data research in information systems: toward an inclusive research agenda. J. Assoc. Inf. Syst. **17**(2) (2016)
35. Lycett, M.: 'Datafication': making sense of (big) data in a complex world. Eur. J. Inf. Syst. **22**(4), 381–386 (2013)

Data-Driven Collaborative Human-AI Decision Making

Gregoris Mentzas[1(✉)], Katerina Lepenioti[1], Alexandros Bousdekis[1], and Dimitris Apostolou[1,2]

[1] Institute of Communication and Computer Systems, School of Electrical and Computer Engineering, National Technical University of Athens, Zografou, 15780 Athens, Greece
{gmentzas,klepenioti,albous}@mail.ntua.gr
[2] Department of Informatics, University of Piraeus, 18534 Piraeus, Greece
dapost@unipi.gr

Abstract. Business analytics use advanced techniques that can analyze and process large and diverse data sets in order to generate valuable insights and lead to better business decisions. Of the three types of business analytics – descriptive, predictive, and prescriptive – only the latter focus on decision making. This paper aims to address two limitations of existing approaches in prescriptive analytics: (i) the lack of a transparent integration between predictive and prescriptive analytics and (ii) the incorporation of human knowledge and experience within the decision-making process. In order to address these points, the paper develops a framework that integrates data-driven predictions and the decision-making process by taking account human experience. The framework adopts interactive reinforcement learning algorithms and provides a concrete approach for data-driven human-AI collaboration. The main challenges and limitations of the approach are also discussed.

Keywords: Human-AI interaction · Data analytics · Reinforcement learning

1 Introduction

Decision making has been studied from normative and descriptive approaches [1]. Normative theories focus on how to make the best decisions by deriving algebraic representations of preferences from idealized behavioral axioms. For example, the principle of utility maximization in economics and the concept of equilibrium in game theory describe how self-interested rational agents should behave individually or in a group, respectively [2]. On the other hand, descriptive theories incorporate known limitations of human behavior in the decision-making process. For example, prospect theory can successfully account for the failures of expected utility theory in describing human decision making under uncertainty [3].

Recently, these two traditional approaches of decision-making research have merged with additional disciplines [4]. It is now increasingly appreciated that learning plays an

Published by Springer Nature Switzerland AG 2021
D. Dennehy et al. (Eds.): I3E 2021, LNCS 12896, pp. 120–131, 2021.
https://doi.org/10.1007/978-3-030-85447-8_11

important role in decision making, although this has been ignored in most economic theories. In particular, Reinforcement Learning (RL) provides a valuable framework to model how decision-making strategies are tuned by experience [5–7].

Turning from the human to the organizational level, a recent trend in organizational decision making is the exploitation of the staggering amounts of data that organizations have at their disposal [8]. These data, if analyzed and processed properly, can generate valuable insights and lead to better business decisions [9]. The use of advanced techniques that can analyze and process very large and diverse data sets that include structured, semi-structured and unstructured data, from different sources, and in different sizes from terabytes to zettabytes, has led to the field of business analytics [10].

Business analytics focuses on data-driven decision-making and consists of three phases: descriptive, predictive, and prescriptive. While descriptive and predictive analytics allow us to analyze past and predict future events, respectively, these activities do not provide any direct support for decision-making [11, 12]. Contrary, prescriptive analytics is a new type of data analytics which enable data-driven optimization for decision support and planning [13]. It has been recently argued that the full exploitation of prescriptive analytics for optimized business decision making requires the incorporation of human knowledge and experience in the decision-making process [11, 14].

In the present paper we investigate how to explicitly incorporate human knowledge and experience in the data-driven decision-making process. In order to accomplish this, we incorporate interactive RL since it presents many opportunities for an osmosis of decision-making research in both human and artificial agents [15–17]. In interactive RL, a human interacts with an RL agent in real-time [18]. This approach has been shown to considerably improve the RL agent's learning speed and can allow RL to scale to larger or more complex problems [19].

The paper is structured as follows: first we introduce the theoretical background of prescriptive analytics. Then, we present the reinforcement learning mechanisms and focus on the way human-augmented approaches can be implemented with interactive RL. We define our proposed framework and describe how it favors data-driven human-AI collaboration. We discuss the main challenges of the approach and, finally, present our conclusions and describe future works.

2 Data-Driven Decision Making: Prescriptive Analytics

Business analytics refers to the extensive use of data, acquired by diverse sources, statistical and quantitative analysis, explanatory and predictive models, and fact-based management to drive decisions and actions to proper stakeholders [20].

Business analytics is categorized to three main stages characterized by different levels of difficulty, value, and intelligence [11, 21]: (i) descriptive analytics, answering the questions "What has happened?", "Why did it happen?", but also "What is happening now?" (mainly in a streaming context); (ii) predictive analytics, answering the questions "What will happen?" and "Why will it happen?" in the future; (iii) prescriptive analytics, answering the questions "What should I do?" and "Why should I do it?" (see Table 1).

Table 1. Types of Business Analytics (adapted from [11, 13, 14])

Type of analytics	Descriptive	Predictive	Prescriptive
Questions answered	What happened? Why did it happen?	What will happen? Why will it happen?	What should we do? How can we make it happen?
Focus	Hindsight	Foresight	Decision
Main task	Analyze	Predict	Influence
Sample use cases	Performance management	Risk modelling	Portfolio optimisation
Indicative technologies	• Dashboards • Statistics • Data mining	• Machine learning • Forecasting • Probabilistic models	• Mathematical programming • Logic-based models • Simulation
Perspective	From retrospective to prospective		

Prescriptive analytics typically involves two aspects: (a) exploration of possible actions and (b) generation of the prescription. Typically, the decision space for prescriptive analytics tends to be large and there are multiple situations with many variables, options and constraints. Compared to descriptive and predictive, prescriptive analytics is still less mature. Recently, however, prescriptive analytics has been considered as the next step towards increasing data analytics maturity and leading to optimized decision making, ahead of time, for business performance improvement [14, 22].

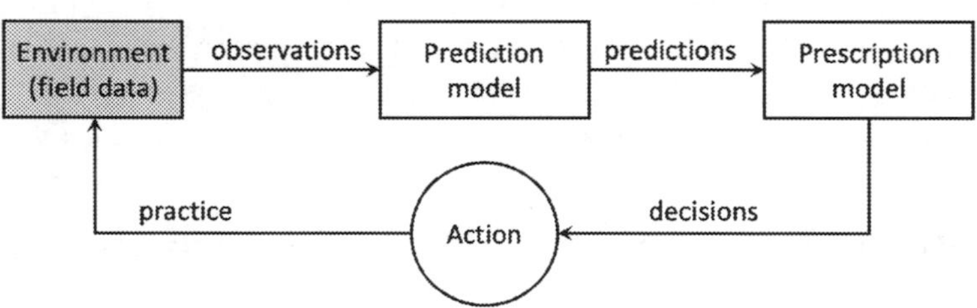

Fig. 1. Simplified diagram of prescriptive analytics

Integrating predictions and prescriptions is key for the extensive adoption as well as the exploitation of the values of prescriptive analytics [23, 24]. As for any method that relies on predictions, prescriptive analytics is stochastic by nature and may generate erroneous results. We argue that, similarly to control theory, an assessment of the validity of the prescriptions can be used as a feedback mechanism to generate a control action to improve the accuracy of the new predictions and the subsequent prescriptions (see Fig. 1). In the following section, we describe how such a feedback mechanism can be implemented using RL.

3 Reinforcement Learning for Decision Making

Reinforcement Learning (RL) is one of the three types of machine learning (the other two being supervised and unsupervised learning) [25]. In reinforcement learning the problem is represented by an environment consisting of states and actions and learning agents with a defined goal state. The agents aim to reach the goal state while maximizing the rewards by selecting actions and moving to different states [5, 6].

In RL, an agent learns how to perform a sequential decision task, i.e., a policy that decides which action to take in a state of the environment the agent encounters. A sequential decision task is modelled as a Markov Decision Process (MDP), denoted as $\{S, A, T, R, \gamma\}$. In MDP, S represents a set of all possible states and A represents a set of all possible actions. Time is divided into discrete time steps. At each time step t, the agent receives a representation of the environmental state, $s_t \in S$, takes an action $a_t \in A$ that results in next state of the environment s_{t+1}. One time step later, as a consequence of the action at taken based on the current state s_t, the agent will receive a numerical reward, R_{t+1} specified by a reward function which decides a numeric reward value at each time step based on the current state, action chosen, and the resultant next state. The probability of next state s_{t+1} that the agent will experience is decided by a transition function which describes the probability of transitioning from one state to another given a specific action (see Fig. 2 for the typical RL approach).

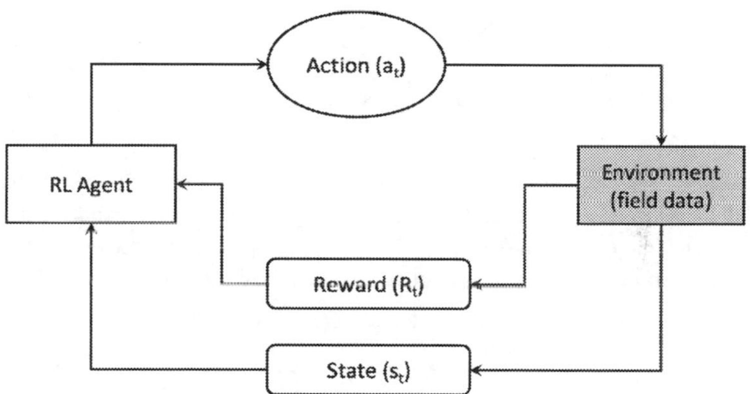

Fig. 2. The typical reinforcement learning approach.

What makes RL different from other machine learning paradigms is that there is no supervisor, only a reward signal. Feedback is delayed, not instantaneous and time really matters. The agent's actions affect the subsequent data it receives. An RL agent may include one or more of these components: (i) a *policy*: it is the agent's behavior function, a map from states to actions – policies may be deterministic or stochastic; (ii) a *value function*, which models how good is each state, acts as a predictor of future reward and is therefore used to select between actions; and/or (iii) an action *model*, which is the agent's representation of the environment and predicts what the environment will do next [26].

The combinations of these three components can be used to categorize RL agents into five types: (a) value based (there is no policy, or the policy is implicit and there is a value function); (b) policy-based (there is a policy and no value function); (c) actor critic (there is both a policy and a value function); (d) model-free (there may be a policy and or a value function but no model); and (e) model-based (there may be a policy and or a value function and there is a model - see Fig. 3). As we will see later, our proposed framework adopts the actor-critic type of RL.

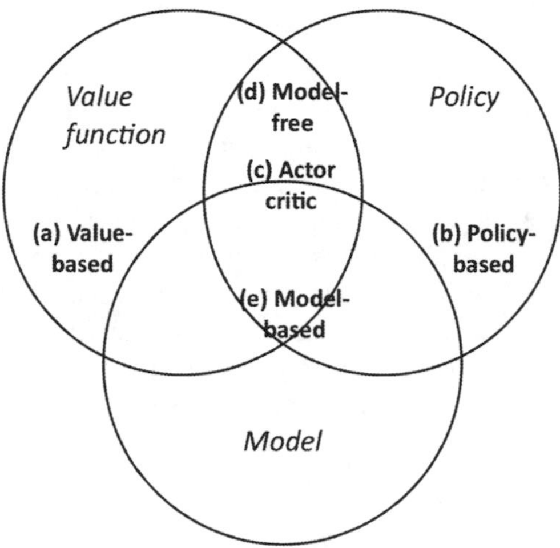

Fig. 3. Venn diagram of the space of agents in reinforcement learning (source [27])

In real-world applications humans may change the RL agents' optimal behavior by teaching them interactively according to their likings. In this case, standard RL cannot be applied, since the optimal behavior is usually preprogrammed via a reward function and most human users are laymen in agent design and programming. Interactive RL has

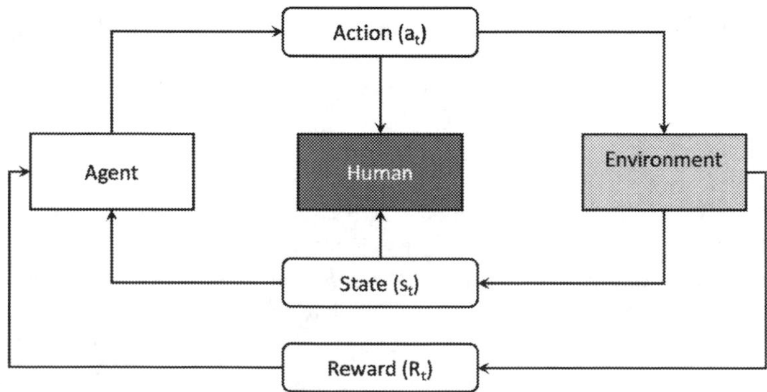

Fig. 4. Interactive reinforcement learning framework.

been developed and proven to be a powerful method for facilitating humans to teach agents in a natural way [18, 28].

A human user might not be an expert in programming but has knowledge about how to perform the decision task, which will reduce the agent's exploration time and speed up its learning. In interactive RL, every time the agent takes an action in a state, the observing human can provide feedback which tells the quality of the selected action based on the human's knowledge, as shown in Fig. 4. The agent then uses the feedback to update its policy. Therefore, the agent learns how to perform the decision task by interacting with a human, and it is the human feedback that decides the agent's behaviour [19, 29].

4 Framework for Collaborative Human-AI Decision Making

The proposed framework for collaborative human-AI decision uses the principles of interactive RL to implement the prescriptive model. Figure 5 shows how the integrated RL mechanism uses predictions generated by the prediction model as well as human feedback to guide the RL agent to provide actions for the environment. The RL agent is triggered by prediction events about future states of the environment which are generated by the prediction model. Subsequently, the agent prescribes the appropriate actions or set of actions among the alternatives so that an undesired future state is avoided, or a desired future state is sought after. Finally, the agent adjusts its policy based on both the rewards and the human feedback received.

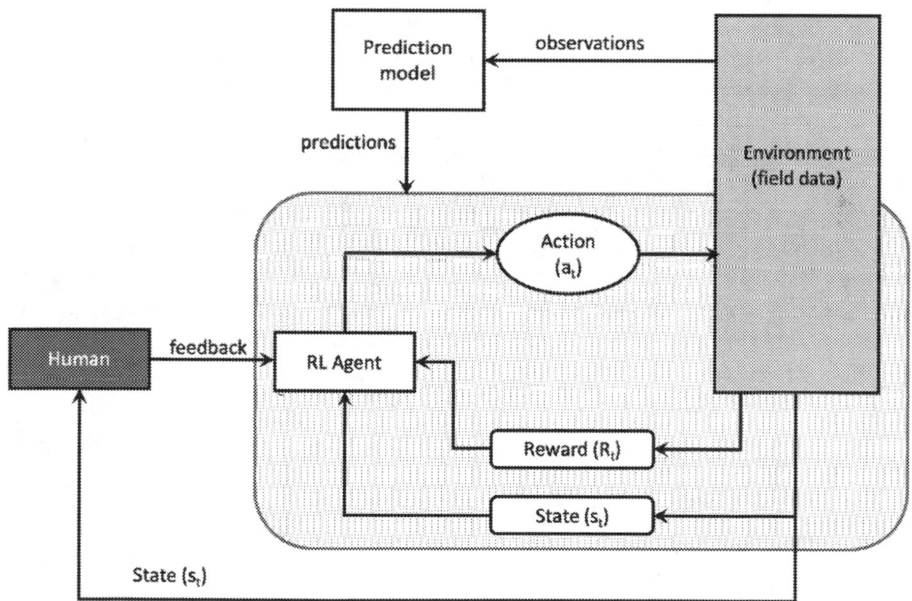

Fig. 5. Proposed framework for data analytics and interactive reinforcement learning.

To gain a better understanding of the proposed framework function, in the following we examine three critical design choices and their implications: (i) the choice of the predictive model to be used; (ii) the choice of the type of RL agent; and (iii) the type of human-AI interactions.

The first design choice refers to the type of predictive model to be used and the associated algorithms. Clearly the selection of the predictive model and algorithms depends largely on the problem at hand. Among prominent methods, Deep Learning (DL) is increasingly being used to make accurate predictions based on learned representations of data with multiple levels of abstraction [31]. An example of DL is Long Short-Term Memory (LSTM) networks. LSTM are a type of recurrent neural networks capable of learning order dependence in sequential prediction problems [32]. LSTM can learn to bridge minimal time lags and, hence, have proven to be effective when the input events are real-time streaming data, a case which is relatively typical in data-driven problems [33].

The second design choice refers to the type of the RL agent. In our framework we adopt actor-critic reinforcement learning [34]. The idea of the critic-only approach is to learn a value function based on which the agent can compare ("criticize") the expected outcomes of different actions. In the actor-only approach the agent senses the state of the environment and acts directly, i.e., without computing and comparing the expected outcomes of different actions, hence the agent learns a direct mapping (a policy) from states to actions. In contrast to these two approaches, the key idea of the actor-critic approach is to simultaneously use an actor, which determines the agent's action given the current state of the environment, and a critic, which judges the selected action. The actor learns a parameterized policy, and the critic learns a value function to evaluate state-action pairs [34]. Although learning the policy depends on the quality of the value function estimate (which is learned simultaneously by the critic), our preference for the actor-critic algorithm is due to the fact that it provides the policy necessary for the policy shaping method that consists our choice in the third design issue.

The third design issue refers to the type if human-agent interaction. Human interaction in RL algorithms has been classified in five categories: (i) standard imitation learning, in which the human trainer observes the state information and demonstrates action to the agent; (ii) learning from evaluative feedback, where the human trainer watches the agent performing the task and provides instant feedback on each agent decision; (iii) imitation from observation, which is similar to standard imitation learning except that the agent does not have access to human demonstrated action; (iv) learning attention from human, which requires the trainer to provide attention map to the learning agent; and (v) learning from human preference, in which the human watches two behaviors generated by the learning agent simultaneously and decides which is more preferable [35, 36].

Our framework adopts the learning from evaluative feedback approach. In this approach the agent adjusts its policy based on the feedback received. The simplest form of evaluative feedback is a scalar value indicating how desirable an observed action is. This approach does not require the human trainer to be an expert at performing the task - it only requires the trainer to accurately judge agent behaviors. One of the main challenges in this approach is to interpret human feedback correctly. Methods that assume different interpretations of human feedback include: (a) policy shaping. which interprets human feedback as direct policy labels; (b) reward shaping that interprets human feedback as the value function or a human-specified reward function; (c) human intervention, in which a human supervises the training process of an RL agent and blocks catastrophic actions; and (d) policy-dependent feedback, which posits that feedback should be interpreted as an advantage function that specifies how much better or worse when deviating from the agent's current policy.

5 Discussion

The recent increase of the use of AI technologies in our everyday lives has generated the need for AI systems to work synergistically with humans in an effective, transparent and ethical way [37]. However, if we are to treat AI systems in such a manner as to allow them to augment our abilities and compensate for our weaknesses, we need a new understanding of AI that takes humans explicitly into account. We need to change our view from AI systems as "thinking machines" and treat them as "cognitive prostheses" that can help humans think and act better [38, 39].

Our proposal of a framework for collaborative human-AI decision making is towards this direction. It aims to exploit the predictive power of data-driven predictive analytics techniques with the decision-making approach of reinforcement learning with human feedback. Our framework can be considered a specific instance of the hybrid structure of the human and AI-based decision making combinations described in [40]; actually it can be categorized in the "Hybrid 1: AI to human" category, in which the AI agent works in tandem with the human by providing algorithmic prediction results, which are then used as input to a collaborative human-AI decision-making process.

The proposed framework outlines an approach towards the combination of predictive and prescriptive analytics, which – according to analysts' reports [41] – will allow organizations to reap significant business benefits. However, there are also critical costs to be considered, chief among them the cost of acquiring and annotating data. The appropriate datasets for predictive tasks have recently become key corporate assets. The issue of sample efficiency is especially important when reinforcement learning is used; if the data samples are limited in numbers the learning algorithm would have very low exploration of the environment from training data as the information and states are not fully covered. To handle this issue, the efficiency of data should be good enough or the RL approach should be sample efficient to learn the environment from limited amount of data [26]. An additional characteristic, that may increase the cost of datasets, is the need to guarantee and continuously assess data quality [42, 43].

The design and development of human-AI systems may demonstrate unpredictable behaviors that can be disruptive, confusing, offensive, and even dangerous. There is therefore a clear need to address the human computer interaction (HCI) issues of human-AI systems in a systematic manner. The recent advances generate a stream of challenges and opportunities for the HCI community. Although recent efforts have already developed reusable design guidelines [44], many challenges still persist in designing and innovating valuable human-AI interactions. Topics such as the uncertainty surrounding AI's capabilities and the complexity of AI's output create yet unsolved design challenges [45].

The way human users are involved in a direct collaboration with RL agents is an additional topic that needs special attention. Interactive RL approaches need to be designed in such a manner as to produce behaviors that align with the user's intention and allow clear communication between the human and the RL algorithm. For example, in order to motivate users to give feedback several studies suggest the use of gamification strategies [18].

Furthermore, the fatigue of users and its effects on the quantity and quality of feedback should be considered; for example, it has been observed that humans tend to reduce the quantity of feedback they give over time while the quality also diminishes. Developing appropriate design strategies to address the engagement of humans becomes paramount. Finally, the knowledge level of the human involved in the interaction is an important feature of the human-AI interactions. This level has an impact on the quality and quantity of feedback and could limit the use of some feedback types that require more precise information, such as demonstrations or action advice [18].

The practical real-world challenges of implementing reinforcement learning algorithm constitute another area of concern. Topics such as the ones related to the exact definition of reward functions, the number of actions and state spaces, as well as the data sample efficiency (already mentioned above) have significant impact on the performance of RL algorithms in real-world applications [46]. In addition, the environment in real-world application domains may allow only partial observation. Conventional RL methods assume that environments are fully observable Markov environments. Partial observability requires the generalization of Markov decision processes to partially observable ones, which increases computational complexity.

Of course, the more general issues of human-AI interactions also apply in our case. Topics like the need for governance structures that address AI failures; the need for explaining AI recommendations; and the issues of trust, transparency and reliability are still open research questions in the organization science, information systems and artificial intelligence fields [47, 48].

6 Conclusions and Further Work

In the present paper we developed a conceptual framework that integrates the data-driven predictions of predictive analytics with the decision-making process of prescriptive analytics. The framework explicitly takes into account human experience using the mechanisms of interactive reinforcement learning. Early implementations of the framework in application domains like financial management (stock trading) and industry 4.0 (predictive maintenance in steel industry) provide encouraging results.

In our further work we intend to address problems that need to solve several tasks with different rewards simultaneously. For such problems, we aim to experiment with multi-objective RL (MORL). MORL can be viewed as the combination of multi-objective optimization (MOO) and RL to solve decision-making problems with multiple conflicting objectives [49]. Moreover, in order to facilitate learning the reward function from demonstrations by human experts, we aim to experiment with inverse RL [50], which attempts to extract the reward function from the observed behavior of an agent.

Acknowledgements. This work is partly funded by the European Union's Horizon 2020 project COALA (Grant agreement No. 957296). The work presented here reflects only the authors' view and the European Commission is not responsible for any use that may be made of the information it contains.

References

1. Johnson, J.G., Busemeyer, J.R.: Decision making under risk and uncertainty. Wiley Interdiscip. Rev. Cognit. Sci. **1**(5), 736–749 (2010)
2. Von Neumann, J., Morgenstern, O.: Theory of Games and Economic Behaviour Princeton Univ. Press, Princeton (1944)
3. Kahneman, D., Tversky, A.: Prospect theory: an analysis of decision under risk. Econometrica **47**, 263–292 (1979)
4. Lee, D.: Decision making: from neuroscience to psychiatry. Neuron **78**(2), 233–248 (2013)
5. Sutton, R.S., Barto, A.G.: Reinforcement Learning: An Introduction. MIT Press, Cambridge (2018)
6. Kaelbling, L.P., Littman, M.L., Moore, A.W.: Reinforcement learning: a survey. J. Artif. Intell. Res. **4**, 237–285 (1996)
7. Mnih, V., et al.: Human-level control through deep reinforcement learning. Nature **518**(7540), 529–533 (2015)
8. Davenport, T.H.: Competing on analytics. Harv. Bus. Rev. **84**(1) (2006)
9. LaValle, S., Lesser, E., Shockley, R., Hopkins, M.S., Kruschwitz, N.: Big data, analytics and the path from insights to value. MIT Sloan Manag. Rev. **52**(2), 21–32 (2011)
10. Chen, H., Chiang, R.H.L., Storey, V.C.: Business intelligence and analytics: from big data to big impact. MIS Q., 1165–1188 (2012)
11. Lepenioti, K., Bousdekis, A., Apostolou, D., Mentzas, G.: Prescriptive analytics: literature review and research challenges. Int. J. Inf. Manage. **50**, 57–70 (2020)
12. Bertsimas, D., Kallus, N.: From predictive to prescriptive analytics. Manage. Sci. **66**(3), 1025–1044 (2020)
13. Frazzetto, D., Nielsen, T.D., Pedersen, T.B., Šikšnys, L.: Prescriptive analytics: a survey of emerging trends and technologies. VLDB J. **28**(4), 575–595 (2019)
14. Sappelli, M., de Boer, M.H.T., Smit, S.K., Bomhof, F.: A vision on prescriptive analytics. In: ALLDATA 2017, p. 54 (2017)
15. Neftci, E.O., Averbeck, B.B.: Reinforcement learning in artificial and biological systems. Nat. Mach. Intell. **1**(3), 133–143 (2019)
16. Collins, A.G.E.: Reinforcement learning: bringing together computation and cognition. Curr. Opin. Behav. Sci. **29**, 63–68 (2019)
17. Amershi, S., Cakmak, M., Knox, W.B., Kulesza, T.: Power to the people: the role of humans in interactive machine learning. AI Mag. **35**(4), 105–120 (2014)
18. Arzate Cruz, C., Igarashi, T.: A survey on interactive reinforcement learning: design principles and open challenges. In: Proceedings of the 2020 ACM Designing Interactive Systems Conference, pp. 1195–1209 (2020)
19. Li, G., Gomez, R., Nakamura, K., He, B.: Human-centered reinforcement learning: a survey. IEEE Trans. Hum. Mach. Syst. **49**(4), 337–349 (2019)
20. Holsapple, C., Lee-Post, A., Pakath, R.: A unified foundation for business analytics. Decis. Support Syst. **64**, 130–141 (2014)
21. Delen, D.: Prescriptive Analytics: The Final Frontier for Evidence-Based Management and Optimal Decision Making. FT Press (2019)
22. Larson, D., Chang, V.: A review and future direction of agile, business intelligence, analytics and data science. Int. J. Inf. Manage. **36**(5), 700–710 (2016)

23. den Hertog, D., Postek, K.: Bridging the gap between predictive and prescriptive analytics-new optimization methodology needed. Tilburg Univ., Tilburg, The Netherlands (2016). http://www.optimization-online.org/DB_FILE/2016/12/5779.pdf. Accessed 28 Dec 2020
24. Mundru, N.: Predictive and prescriptive methods in operations research and machine learning: an optimization approach. Ph.D. diss., Massachusetts Institute of Technology (2019). https://dspace.mit.edu/handle/1721.1/122099. Accessed 28 Dec 2020
25. Jordan, M.I., Mitchell, T.M.: Machine learning: trends, perspectives, and prospects. Science **349**(6245), 255–260 (2015)
26. Naeem, M., Rizvi, S.T.H., Coronato, A.: A gentle introduction to reinforcement learning and its application in different fields. IEEE Access (2020)
27. Silver, D.: Lectures on Reinforcement Learning (2015). https://www.davidsilver.uk/teaching/. Accessed 28 Dec 2020
28. Griffith, S., Subramanian, K., Scholz, J., Isbell, C.L., Thomaz, A.L.: Policy shaping: Integrating human feedback with reinforcement learning. Adv. Neural. Inf. Process. Syst. **26**, 2625–2633 (2013)
29. Lin, J., Ma, Z., Gomez, R., Nakamura, K., He, B., Li, G.: A review on interactive reinforcement learning from human social feedback. IEEE Access **8**, 120757–120765 (2020)
30. LeCun, Y., Bengio, Y., Hinton, G.: Deep learning. Nature **521**(7553), 436–444 (2015)
31. Najafabadi, M.M., Villanustre, F., Khoshgoftaar, T.M., Seliya, N., Wald, R., Muharemagic, E.: Deep learning applications and challenges in big data analytics. J.Big Data **2**(1), 1–21 (2015). https://doi.org/10.1186/s40537-014-0007-7
32. Hochreiter, S., Schmidhuber, J.: Long short-term memory. Neural Comput. **9**(8), 1735–1780 (1997)
33. Yu, Y., Si, X., Changhua, H., Zhang, J.: A review of recurrent neural networks: LSTM cells and network architectures. Neural Comput. **31**(7), 1235–1270 (2019)
34. Konda, V.R., Tsitsiklis, J.N.: Actor-critic algorithms. In: Advances in Neural Information Processing Systems, pp. 1008–1014 (2000)
35. Grondman, I., Busoniu, L., Lopes, G.A.D., Babuska, R.: A survey of actor-critic reinforcement learning: standard and natural policy gradients. IEEE Trans. Syst. Man Cybern. Part C **42**(6), 1291–1307 (2012)
36. Zhang, R., Torabi, F., Guan, L., Ballard, D.H., Stone, P.: Leveraging human guidance for deep reinforcement learning tasks. In: Proceedings of the Twenty-Eighth International Joint Conference on Artificial Intelligence, Survey Track, pp. 6339–6346 (2019)
37. Kambhampati, S.: Challenges of human-aware AI systems. AI Mag. **41**(3) (2020)
38. Akata, Z., et al.: A research agenda for hybrid intelligence: augmenting human intellect with collaborative, adaptive, responsible, and explainable artificial intelligence. Computer **53**(8), 18–28 (2020)
39. Trunk, A., Birkel, H., Hartmann, E.: On the current state of combining human and artificial intelligence for strategic organizational decision making. Bus. Res., 1–45 (2020)
40. Shrestha, Y.R., Ben-Menahem, S.M., Von Krogh, G.: Organizational decision-making structures in the age of artificial intelligence. Calif. Manage. Rev. **61**(4), 66–83 (2019)
41. Gartner Inc.: When and How to Combine Predictive and Prescriptive Techniques to Solve Business Problems, 25 October 2018. ID: G00368423 (2018)
42. Wang, R.Y., Strong, D.M.: Beyond accuracy: what data quality means to data consumers. J. Manage. Inf. Syst. **12**(4), 5–33 (1996)
43. Cai, L., Zhu, Y.: The challenges of data quality and data quality assessment in the big data era. Data Sci. J. **14** (2015)
44. Amershi, S., et al.: Guidelines for human-AI interaction. In: Proceedings of the 2019 CHI Conference on Human Factors in Computing Systems, pp. 1–13 (2019)

45. Yang, Q., Steinfeld, A., Rosé, C., Zimmerman, J.: Re-examining whether, why, and how human-AI interaction is uniquely difficult to design. In: Proceedings of the 2020 CHI Conference on Human Factors in Computing Systems, 1–13 (2020)
46. Dulac-Arnold, G., Mankowitz, D., Hester, T.: Challenges of real-world reinforcement learning. In: ICML 2019 Workshop, Reinforcement Learning for Real Life, 14 June 2019, Long Beach, CA, USA (2019)
47. Glikson, E., Woolley, A.W.: Human trust in artificial intelligence: review of empirical research. Acad. Manage. Ann., ja (2020)
48. Samek, W., Montavon, G., Vedaldi, A., Hansen, L.K., Müller, K.-R. (eds.): Explainable AI: interpreting, explaining and visualizing deep learning. LNCS (LNAI), vol. 11700. Springer, Cham (2019). https://doi.org/10.1007/978-3-030-28954-6
49. Liu, C., Xin, X., Dewen, H.: Multiobjective reinforcement learning: a comprehensive overview. IEEE Trans. Syst. Man Cybern. Syst. **45**(3), 385–398 (2014)
50. Zhifei, S., Joo, E.M.: A review of inverse reinforcement learning theory and recent advances. In: 2012 IEEE Congress on Evolutionary Computation, pp. 1–8. IEEE (2012)

Always Trust the Advice of AI in Difficulties? Perceptions Around AI in Decision Making

Amit Kumar Kushwaha(✉), Ruchika Pharswan, and Arpan Kumar Kar

Indian Institute of Technology Delhi, New Delhi 110016, India

Abstract. Artificial Intelligence (AI) has now evolved from a phase of being merely adopted as a new system to now fueling the decision-systems to generate specific data. Borrowing from the social sciences and emerging sub-body of mathematics research literature and theories around algorithmic knowledge and value realization leads to the formation of perceptions around the confidence of allowing AI to be at the heart of any domain's decision-making. This amalgamation of AI in decision-making systems (ADMS). The current study has undertaken attempts to link personal attributes to perceptions around ADMS with the boundary constraints of these perceptions, namely the stretch to which these perceptions vary across media and domain contexts. A scenario-based survey instrument has been used to collect the data from two sets of ADMS stakeholders, vis-à-vis owners and end-users of ADMS. Analysis of the collected data from this sample (N = 558) reveals that these stakeholders are by and large anxious about the risks associated with ADMS. They have a mixed and general attitude towards the on-field usefulness and fairness of ADMS outcomes at the societal level. These generic frames of mind are driven mainly by the individual traits and involvement and accountability in the domain like a revenue-generating business, social (healthcare), and the oversight of ADMS. Theoretical, management practice, and societal impacts about these findings are also discussed along the current work's final sections.

Keywords: Artificial Intelligence · Automated decision-making · Algorithm · Farness · Perception

1 Introduction

Ever-growing research and developments in the mathematical and algorithmic domain have fueled the rise and shine of Artificial Intelligence (AI) [1]. Furthermore, with the proper support of information systems scholars, AI's applicability across various business domains has been further strengthened and generalized for management practitioners. In the last decade, several business houses have evolved from merely adopting AI [2] as a state-of-the-art technique to more tightly integrating the same to decision-making systems to generate the returns from the investment made while building the in-house AI practice. With AI in decision-making systems (ADMS) [3–5] business stakeholders' confidence in the decisions has seen both sides of the coin. With more involvement and

Published by Springer Nature Switzerland AG 2021
D. Dennehy et al. (Eds.): I3E 2021, LNCS 12896, pp. 132–143, 2021.
https://doi.org/10.1007/978-3-030-85447-8_12

understanding if AI vests higher confidence in the outcomes of ADMS, past success with the gut-based decision making endows more confidence in manual decision making.

ADMS has been driving the customer-facing services in the current business set-up, for instance: personalization, recommendations, contextual responses, better allocation of advertising budgets, and overall advertising [6]. ADMS has eventually secured its role in the backend systems like automatic detection of phishing emails, suspicious financial activities, and profiles. Additionally, ADMS paves its way to make a societal and public impact by fueling virtual health [7] response systems, automated speech recognition systems to cater application filling avoiding any erroneous data being captured, helping through e-governance, and the role in the healthcare domain is endless. The presence of ADMS in the judiciary domain is also catching up slowly but gradually, with law and enforcement. For instance, there is a handful of ADMS in the directional prediction of who should get an early release from parole vs. who should continue longer with parole, helping law and enforcement parole officers. This upheaves the argument around stakeholders' confidence, like business owners and customers in the base of business ADMS, doctors and patients in healthcare ADMS, government bodies and citizens in governance ADMS, law enforcement officers and law-abiding citizens in societal [8] ADMS.

Defining ADMS more in detail to analyze the above upheavals, the literature narrowly defines this as a "*technology-driven decision with no humans' involvement*" [1]. This statement further alleviates the convulsions. However, broadening the definition by stating: a robust mathematical framework trained on ever-growing volume, variety, veracity, and real-time data fueled by the latest state of the art (SOTA) algorithms, with the flexibility of over-ruling the decisions if required or felt the need of, might grant some confidence back to ADMS. A growing sub-body of research also tries to uncover the aftermath consequences of ADMS outcomes, along with the risks associated domain-wise and limitations. This research also reveals the percentage involvement of humans at every level of results of ADMS per domain, and then it evaluates the value it can bring in. This might further bestow some of the confidence and sense of ease towards ADMS. Having stated the above, much is yet to be explored in terms of the correlating stakeholder's perception (overall, technical, domain applicability) of ADMS on the factors of perceived usefulness, limitation, risk, and fairness.

Borrowing from the social sciences literature and theories, in the current research undertaken, we extend the notion of orientation, source, and influence of heuristic algorithms on algorithmic appreciation and perceptions. This is achieved by investigating the data on the factors of fairness, usefulness, and risk. Using the representative sample ($N = 477$) of professionals, who have also informed citizens outside their work, we try to draw insights into how the general or in-detail understanding and other traits can influence the frame of mind towards ADMS as part of primary analysis. As part of the follow-up, the secondary research, we try to analyze how exposure to knowledge, forums surrounding AI, and self-efficacy, demographical attributes further affects the development of the school of thoughts towards ADMS. Broadening the research scope, we have considered the automated responses, suggestions, and recommendations and the end automated decisions through AI leading to a specific outcome.

When it comes to ADMS leading to more customer-oriented outcomes, like personalized [9] search, recommendations, and results, we assume that a lower level of exposure initial technical knowledge among business and customers as stakeholders would lead the way. However, as we move to the societal impact of ADMS, a much higher understanding and understanding of technical aspects of the entire automated framework and intermediate human intervention is required. This takes the highest level when it comes to healthcare applications of ADMS are concerned with a lot at stake. To uncover more on these assumptions, with the support of initial literature review, we tend to tackle the below research questions through the current study:

RQ1: To what degree the business and technology domain knowledge is needed to gain confidence about fairness, risk, and usefulness of ADMS.
RQ2: To what extent the demographics orientation and presence play a role in gaining confidence about fairness, risk, and usefulness of ADMS.

The rest of the article is structured as follows: in the second section, we start with uncovering the literature artifacts supporting the assumption above, which could help us formulate the hypotheses statements to test the above. We then explain the methodology deployed to find the insights in section three, followed by section four results. We conclude with theoretical and practice implications and future scope of work, and limitations of the current study.

2 Prior Literature

2.1 AI in Decision-Making Systems

ADMS has been conceptualized as automated frameworks that can collect the data, denoise for usage, structure for a model, select the suitable model, generate the outputs, penalize if the outcome was incorrect, reward if it was correct, and then learn from the mistakes to move to the next iteration of results. The last couple of feedback loop steps are where the learning and self-improvement of the entire ADMS take place. Hence the ADMS is perceived by the inventors is that while an initial couple of steps are mechanical in terms of the data, the latter half of self-learning from the feedback loop is where the socio-technical application of the outcomes plays a crucial role. While the model algorithm is encoded as a set of mathematical rules, resulting in the formulation of a mathematical equation, it updates the weights in these equations that have to be driven by socio-technical implications to make and ADMS successful. ADMS can overall be thought of as a combination of the following elements: data (that fuels), the algorithm used in the model (at the heart of ADMS), and the implication of the outputs generated (self-learning). Now ADMS can further be divided into the following types: high manual intervention at the beginning of data collection and taking a call at the end of output generation, medium manual intervention required to make sure ADMS does not generate extreme outputs which could entirely disrupt the socio-economic or law and order in any form, and finally the third type being no or zero manual intervention required in any of the stages.

The level of human intervention or human involvement and the domain decide the "gear and hype cycle" stage" the current ADMS is for any discipline. For instance: healthcare application of ADMS, with zero human involvement performing critical surgeries, might leave the stakeholders in the fear cycle. However, extremely personalized advertisement, recommendations, search results might put the same ADMS in a hype cycle. Like that, governmental applications and law and order applications of AMDS with moderate human intervention might put the stakeholders somewhere in the middle of the fear and hype cycles. Literature suggests that for every technology to be successful, understanding the current position and drivers of the fear and hype cycles is essential. As part of the literature in the next section, we try to uncover the theory's support in building the same perspective.

2.2 Perspective Towards ADMS

There has always been work stating any automated system driven by algorithms being more efficient and rational than human-based decisions. The perspective has been built a long time, with the results being proven statistically with drug effectiveness in patients to launch satellites by predicting weather conditions and wind speed. Hence the confidence is being driven by the statistical certainty that the results bring along with them. In other words, the heuristic nature of the results and algorithm is one of the critical factors for the stakeholders to form a perspective of the result from ADMS. Literature also suggests that the lesser a stakeholder anthropomorphizes any algorithmic black box, the more they might consider the outcomes as generalizable or objective. Computer Are Social Actors (CASA) framework suggesting that algorithms running and controlling software must be regarded as autonomous, with assumptions decided by humans and the correctness of outcomes by the domain applicability and the impact. For instance: 98.00% accurate results can be considered ok in some domains but cannot be considered in the health domain, requiring the third decimals' highest accuracy.

Several prior studies have conceptualized the same, suggesting that there could be other factors, too, leading to the perspective towards ADMS. For instance, any user might not let go of any single incorrect personalized recommendation generated by a machine/algorithm as a human. Hence, the results from ADMS are inscrutable. Although the results generated from ADMS on average are always efficient and correct as compared to human gut feeling based decision, still being the fact that driven from automated systems, the general perspective remains the same that it cannot go incorrect at any single point of time and that it has to self-learn in the real-time to improves the blend of the results.

2.3 Personal Traits Leading to the Formation of Perspective Towards ADMS

Delving further into the reasons behind the shaping of the mindset discussed in Sect. 2.2, we use some of the specific pivots of literature factors. The first factor that the literature suggests is "understanding" of algorithm and domain. As a government representative, if a person has specific knowledge of the domain and some amount of knowledge around the ADMS self-train itself, he/she should be able to make more informed decisions on the outcomes of ADMS in any crisis. On similar lines, a doctor is already expected to know about the medical domain, if also caught up on how an ADMS predicting Diabetic Meletus, could use the judgment of margin of error he/she can live with before suggesting a remedy for the patient.

On similar lines, the stakeholders' [10] personal beliefs in the algorithms' heuristic nature drive perspective formation. This is also partially caused by the individual factor of safety towards the quality of the outcome. Another essential factor that emerges from the literature review beyond the understanding and quality is the demographics, more precisely the age. Age as a factor from time and again has played a crucial role in deciding the formation of perspective towards any new technology, acceptability and hence even the AMDS can not stay untouched from the effect of the same [11].

3 Hypothesis Development

Prior research indicates that understanding is an essential factor in how an individual (any stakeholder) might perceive new technology's value. Hence, borrowing from the previous investigations, it becomes critical to include understanding as an important actor of the stakeholders driving the opinion formation towards ADMS. The details of this understanding, however, have miscellaneous results. Some of the prior works highlight the understanding of mathematics when it comes to forming a perspective of the algorithms behind AI, while others indicate the level of domain understanding to decide the importance and confidence in AI fueling ADMS. A small section of the literature suggests the elementary level of education of the end-used ADMS, and stakeholders [12] who have invested in ADMS capability have an association with understanding AI.

Building on similar thoughts from prior literature, when it comes to forming a point of view on algorithmic fairness while making decisions, a higher level of understanding of the mathematics and coding on the platform on which ADMS is developed seems to have a higher correlation. Hence given the mixed indication from the prior literature to form better insights around ADMS, we propose the below hypothesis to be tested:

H1: *Technical and domain knowledge will have a driving relationship on an individual's perspective of ADMS.*

Designed on the entire framework of large-scale automated data collection, building model and self-learning loop from the penalty and reward of the outcome has been the central theme of ADMS. Users of ADMS as one of the stakeholders unknowingly act as data creators and, at times, might share more on the personal data without realizing it. If a human handle the data collection and usage, he/she might choose to drop these to maintain an individual's privacy by intervening in the processing pipeline. However, with no manual intervention, the input framework of ADMS might be intelligent enough to separate personal information from the actual data for training the AI model. There has been supporting in the earlier research showing how an individual's assumption of unique ability to protect personal data (self-efficacy in online mode) might lead to impact [13] his/her perspective of ADMS and, more specifically, AI in that framework. Hence to us, this becomes an essential construct to tested in the model, and we formulate our hypothesis as below:

H2: *An individual's self-efficacy will have a driving relationship on an individual' perspective of ADMS.*

Borrowing from the IT and technology adoption kinds of literature, demographics of the stakeholders investing, owning, using, and consuming the results play a vital role in driving new technologies [14]. We hypothesize that adoption eventually builds confidence in the technology being adopted and used with time. Literature also suggests that adoption is driven by the perceived usefulness, fairness, and ease of usage. Also, the prior literature indicates that the social acceptability with factors like age and gender also plays a critical role. However, in previous experimentations, gender as a factor has turned out to a non-significant one, but age always has been a significant one to drive adoption. Hence, we hypothesize that as adoption goes confidence in the technology being adopted (in the current research referring to ADMS), the demographic factors driving adoption will also cause the perception built for ADMs. With this, we arrive at our third hypothesis as:

H3: *Demographic factors will have a driving relationship on an individual's perspective of ADMS.*

4 Research Methodology

Participants in this study were carefully selected by profile selection and shortlisting through professional networking. Some professionals were also chosen through professional social media platforms (SMP) like LinkedIn and were requested to participate in the survey. Another primary source selected for the study was the listeners of the AI podcost platform like "AI Galore," which provides technical mentorship and guidance to the stakeholders planning to pursue or set-up AI as a technology domain. It also provides mentorship to users of AI systems [15] by sending just one email a day. Survey forms were sent out as part of the regular newsletter by randomly selecting the participants' sample from the listeners. Each participant was requested for their consent to participate in the survey and that their inputs captured in the study will be used for the academic research in the field of AI.

Once participants provided the informed constraint, initial questions are placed to gauge the participants' level of knowledge on the factors like mathematics, AI, domain, societal impacts known, and any programming language knowledge. The participants were then provided a reading material on ADMS and how the outputs' applicability can be explored in several domains. These professional participants were then asked for their point of view on ADMS. Post answering the initial questions, and the participants were then assigned to random scenarios: business usage of ADMS, governmental or societal usage of ADMS, law and enforcement usage of ADMS, and finally, complicated health care use of ADMS. These scenarios roll-up to business [16], society [17], law, and enforcement, and health domains. The participants' strategies were borrowed from the vignette-experiment ideology with three levels: ADMS vs. human decision X self vs. others accepting the output X high vs. low impact with the domains designed. The participants also communicated that the ADMS decisions were based purely on data and algorithms with no human interventions.

Technical knowledge (SD = 1.21, M = 3.3), domain knowledge (SD = 1.25, M = 5.07), privacy with online self-efficacy (SD = 1.05, M = 2.29) were considered as in the independent variables with each recorded through three different questions on the understanding of the mathematics behind algorithms, overall AI framework and domain implication of the decisions. The notion of equality was considered a control variable to ensure that the participants and the data captured are from a level playing domain. Furthermore, borrowing from the adoption literature, the perceived value, fairness, risk in decision making using ADMS outcomes were considered dependent variables. All these factors have been borrowed from the IT and other technology adoption literature.

The domain scenarios that the assigned participants had to evaluate the ADMS outputs on were perceived value (SD = 1.59, M = 3.27), fairness in decisions (SD = 1.62, M = 3.78), and the risk associated (SD = 1.83, M = 3.94), with the AMDS outputs when implemented in any of the scenarios. All the participants were then given checkpoint questions to cross-verify the inputs entered through them to cross-verify the results and the robustness of the same. Multivariate linear regression models were finally built on the three dependent variables, and only the factors that came out significant in all three were yet considered significant. We deployed a mechanism to strictly remove any responses that sounded unsure or did not correlate to the decision-making as the core of the current research undertaken is decision-making through ADMS.

5 Results and Findings

The linear regression model results on the three dependent variables are represented in Table 1. Before finalizing the model version, multiple iterations were tried with the step-wise introduction of the variables and step-wise dropping the variables to make sure the models' directional sense tells the same story across all the iterations. We also compared the r-square of the models to check for robustness; however, each variable in step-wise addition increased the overall r-square; we then had to rely on adjusted r-square to take a call on the models. Adjusted r-square is also reported in the Table 1. However, building the model is more to check the statistical significance of the independent variables on the dependent variable, and hence the actual value of the model fitness in terms of adjusted r-square or improving it further was not in the scope of the current research undertaken.

Table 1. Regression outputs

	Value	Fairness	Risk
Intercept	4.75***	4.68***	4.24 (0.26)***
Gender (female)	−0.27*	0.02	0.22
Age	−0.02***	−0.015	−0.016**
Education	0.18**	0.15**	0.14**
Understanding	0.32***	0.28***	0.14
Equality	0.15	0.16*	−0.13
Online self-efficacy	0.17*	−0.11**	0.223**
Online privacy	−0.19*	−0.24***	0.36***
Adjusted R2	0.25	0.19	0.23

Ad-hoc analysis of the responses reveals that almost 45% of the respondents scored perceived above the overall average, which established the value in pursuing the outcomes driven by ADMS or fueled by AI [1], while 30% scored below the mid-point. This creates an optimistic picture in the minds of stakeholders from the owners' and consumers' perfective. Fairness [3] in the decision saw a more even distribution of the respondents with roughly equally (~28% above, 29% below, and rest around mid-point) distribution of the overall respondent's sample. This created a small question mark on the self-learning loop of ADMS from the penalties of wrong decision and the rewards on the correct decision. However, with merely equal distribution, it is not easy to interpret and pass an opinion. This picture becomes further clearer when moving to the risk associated with the decisions of ADMS. With a precise skewed distribution of 70%, not optimistic vs. only 22% optimistic raises the implication or impact radius of any incorrect choices.

The effect of personal traits or characteristics on the point of view on value, fairness, and the risk was further evaluated using ordinary least square (OLS) regression models. The personal features that the participants were comfortable sharing were gender, age, level of technical knowledge, level of domain knowledge, privacy belied, self-efficacy. Pretty much except for privacy concerns related to ADMS, the rest of all the factors have come out to be significant with a positive relationship across all the models. However, equality was only significant with a positive relationship in the model of fairness, but insignificant in the rest of the models, and hence can not be generalized and will be treated as a non-driver overall in the process of perception formation on ADMS. The model results also support hypotheses statements H2 and H3 on an individual's self-efficacy and demographics having a significant relationship with the perception of ADMS. The higher the privacy threat, the more negative the relationship is strong with the AMDS perception.

Similarly, the stronger the self-efficacy of opinion on personal data, the stronger the formation of the perception of ADMS. To investigate this relationship of the personal traits on value, fairness, and risks, we built a multilevel model using a generalized linear model (GLM) with factors as the scenarios. The results of the model are presented in Table 2.

When we start deep diving into the results at the scenario based, we learn that there is no significant difference in perceived values between ADMS and human while comparing health vs. societal and business vs. societal fairness perception formation. Rather ADMS outputs were considered more fairer than human interventions when it comes to business. There was no significant difference observed in impact as well. When it comes the perceived value in the mixed effects, clearly healthcare stands out that tend to gain the most out of ADMS [18]. Testing the boundary conditions, ADMS decisions are considered to more valuable as compared to human, and hence the trust is vested in the outcomes generated through AI [12]. When compared in the impact, ADMS outputs gains the value in low impactful areas of healthcare. Now there can be two reasons to that: either the confidence of the stakeholders is not bult yet on ADMS when it comes to high impactful areas like automated surgeries, or the cost of building that high impactful healthcare ADMS could be very high. Investigating the reasons behind the same is currently beyond the scope of current research. Finally, when it comes to risk associated, with the ADMS outputs, the level wise model analysis uncovers that

Table 2. Model results

	Value	Fairness	Risk
Fixed effects			
ADMS vs Human	0.18 (0.12)	0.14 (0.11)	−0.06 (0.11)
Context			
Business (vs Law and order)	−0.24 (0.11)*	−0.15 (0.11)	0.16 (0.1)
Health (vs Law and order)	0.36 (0.11)**	0.44 (0.11)***	0.07 (0.11)
Decision × Domain			
ADMS × Health	0.15 (0.16)	0.15 (0.16)	−0.17 (0.16)
ADMS × Business	0.13 (0.16)	0.01 (0.16)	−0.25 (0.16)
Impact of the decision			
High (vs. low)	0.09 (0.07)	0.09 (0.07)	−0.37 (0.06) ***
Subject			
Self vs. others	−0.13 (0.07)	−0.05 (0.07)	0.06 (0.06)
Intercept	4.75***	4.68***	4.24 (0.26)***
Gender (female)	−0.27*	0.02	0.22
Age	−0.02***	−0.015	−0.016**
Education	0.18**	0.15**	0.14**
Understanding	0.32***	0.28***	0.14
Equality	0.15	0.16*	−0.13
Online self-efficacy	0.17*	−0.11**	0.223**
Online privacy	−0.19*	−0.24***	0.36***

that there is not much difference in human vs. AI [19] based decisions at an overall level. However, when it comes to business, this difference becomes significant when comparing the ADMS output vs. human intelligence driven outputs.

6 Discussion

The current study is at a unique place where it draws assumptions from the literature technology like IT adoption [11, 20] while at the same time we are drawing our assumptions from the social sciences literature to be tested on a technology which is beyond adoption, however it is yet to gain the confidence of all the stakeholders in the value chain. The data collected through survey based instrument, reveals that the participants are split when it comes to perceived value, risk, and fairness. There is no strong consensus towards one, and this split further increase when we deep-dive into the analysis at the domain level application and bucketing the same to various impact levels. For instance:

in high impactful [21] domain applications of ADMS, stakeholders still do not have a lot of perceived confidence in the outputs, however this does not get impacted when it comes to low level impactful applications of ADMS.

When it comes to business across the impact zones, ADMS outputs are considered above par when compared to human intervened decisions on value, risk, and fairness. This finding is an important contribution of perceived emotions towards AI, that stakeholders in business have moved way past mere adoption to vesting interest and confidence in ADMS [22]. This is applicable across all the impact levels. When it comes to societal impacts, the stakeholders are still unsure on the maturity of AI in decision making process. There is no clear indication of less confidence in high impactful like health care or high confidence like business. Hence the findings, did not reveal a very clear picture on the same [8].

Furthermore, personal traits of individuals play a very healthy role in driving the formation of perception towards ADMS outputs. Demographic attributes like age, gender and knowledge play a crucial role. The model uncovers that higher the knowledge of mathematical groundings of algorithms and programming knowledge topped with the domain knowledge too, might build more confidence in the outputs of ADMS. This leads us to believe that stakeholders with more knowledge might turn out more optimistic with ADMS. Secondly online self-efficacy in tandem with privacy concerns play an important role in confidence in the ADMS decisions.

7 Conclusion and Future Scope of Research

We conclude the article with the thought that ADMS has slowly started becoming part of what we consume and see, how we consume and direct or indirectly, being part of society we do the consequences of these automated outcomes effecting out life in one way or the other. With the means of survey based data experimentation, the current research successfully revealed mixed emotions around societal impacts, but clearer views around business and healthcare domain applications of ADMS.

With the type of collection of the data, and increase in the penetration of social media data, the current study has a limitation of not considering the social media platform data as an important group to be analyzed. However, at the same this limitation also opens the future scope to validate these hypothesis and factors through the participants from social media platforms and see if the findings of the current study hold good there too. Another limitation of the current study is to not be able to find the reasons behind unsureness with societal impacts of ADMS. As part of future scope or extended analysis of the current study, we plan to uncover these factors as well.

References

1. Duan, Y., Edwards, J.S., Dwivedi, Y.K.: Artificial intelligence for decision making in the era of Big Data – evolution, challenges and research agenda. Int. J. Inf. Manage. **48**, 63–71 (2019). https://doi.org/10.1016/j.ijinfomgt.2019.01.021

2. Kushwaha, A.K., Kar, A.K.: Micro-foundations of artificial intelligence adoption in business: making the shift. In: Sharma, S.K., Dwivedi, Y.K., Metri, B., Rana, N.P. (eds.) TDIT 2020. IAICT, vol. 617, pp. 249–260. Springer, Cham (2020). https://doi.org/10.1007/978-3-030-64849-7_22
3. Cox, D., Cox, A.D.: Communicating the consequences of early detection: the role of evidence and framing. J. Mark. **65**(3), 91–103 (2001). https://doi.org/10.1509/jmkg.65.3.91.18336
4. Kushwaha, A.K., Kar, A.K.: Language model-driven chatbot for business to address marketing and selection of products. In: Sharma, S.K., Dwivedi, Y.K., Metri, B., Rana, N.P. (eds.) TDIT 2020. IAICT, vol. 617, pp. 16–28. Springer, Cham (2020). https://doi.org/10.1007/978-3-030-64849-7_3
5. Kushwaha, A.K., Kar, A.K.: Information labelling of medical forum posts by non-clinical text information retrieval, p. 12
6. Gupta, S., Kar, A.K., Baabdullah, A., Al-Khowaiter, W.A.A.: Big data with cognitive computing: a review for the future. Int. J. Inf. Manage. **42**, 78–89 (2018). https://doi.org/10.1016/j.ijinfomgt.2018.06.005
7. Shareef, M.A., Kumar, V., Dwivedi, Y.K., Kumar, U., Akram, M.S., Raman, R.: A new health care system enabled by machine intelligence: elderly people's trust or losing self control. Technol. Forecast. Soc. Change **162**, 120334 (2021). https://doi.org/10.1016/j.techfore.2020.120334
8. Agarwal, R., (Gordon) Gao, G., DesRoches, C., Jha, A.K.: Research commentary—the digital transformation of healthcare: current status and the road ahead. Inf. Syst. Res. **21**(4), 796–809 (2010). https://doi.org/10.1287/isre.1100.0327
9. Thurman, N., Schifferes, S.: The future of personalization at news websites. J. Stud. **13**(5–6), 775–790 (2012). https://doi.org/10.1080/1461670X.2012.664341
10. Kar, A.K., Dwivedi, Y.K.: Theory building with big data-driven research – moving away from the 'What' towards the 'Why. Int. J. Inf. Manage. **54**, 102205 (2020). https://doi.org/10.1016/j.ijinfomgt.2020.102205
11. Venkatesh, V., Davis, F.D.: A theoretical extension of the technology acceptance model: four longitudinal field studies. Manage. Sci. **46**(2), 186–204 (2000). https://doi.org/10.1287/mnsc.46.2.186.11926
12. Pillai, R., Sivathanu, B., Dwivedi, Y.K.: Shopping intention at AI-powered automated retail stores (AIPARS). J. Retail. Consum. Serv. **57**, 102207 (2020). https://doi.org/10.1016/j.jretconser.2020.102207
13. Mustafa, S.Z., Kar, A.K., Janssen, M.F.W.H.A.: Understanding the impact of digital service failure on users: integrating Tan's failure and DeLone and McLean's success model. Int. J. Inf. Manage. **53**, 102119 (2020). https://doi.org/10.1016/j.ijinfomgt.2020.102119
14. Mathivathanan, D., Mathiyazhagan, K., Rana, N.P., Khorana, S., Dwivedi, Y.K.: Barriers to the adoption of blockchain technology in business supply chains: a total interpretive structural modelling (TISM) approach. Int. J. Prod. Res. **0**(0), 1–22 (2021). https://doi.org/10.1080/00207543.2020.1868597
15. Mir, U.B., Sharma, S., Kar, A.K., Gupta, M.P.: Critical success factors for integrating artificial intelligence and robotics. Digit. Policy Regul. Gov. **22**(4), 307–331 (2020). https://doi.org/10.1108/DPRG-03-2020-0032
16. Kushwaha, A.K., Kar, A.K., Vigneswara Ilavarasan, P.: Predicting information diffusion on Twitter a deep learning neural network model using custom weighted word features. In: Hattingh, M., Matthee, M., Smuts, H., Pappas, I., Dwivedi, Y.K., Mäntymäki, M. (eds.) I3E 2020. LNCS, vol. 12066, pp. 456–468. Springer, Cham (2020). https://doi.org/10.1007/978-3-030-44999-5_38

17. Kushwaha, A.K., Mandal, S., Pharswan, R., Kar, A.K., Ilavarasan, P.V.: Studying online political behaviours as rituals: a study of social media behaviour regarding the CAA. In: Sharma, S.K., Dwivedi, Y.K., Metri, B., Rana, N.P. (eds.) TDIT 2020. IAICT, vol. 618, pp. 315–326. Springer, Cham (2020). https://doi.org/10.1007/978-3-030-64861-9_28
18. Thurman, N., Moeller, J., Helberger, N., Trilling, D.: My friends, editors, algorithms, and I. Digit. J. **7**(4), 447–469 (2019). https://doi.org/10.1080/21670811.2018.1493936
19. Kushwaha, A.K., Kar, A.K., Ilavarasan, P.V.: Predicting retweet class using deep learning. Trends Deep Learn. Methodol., 89–112 (2021). https://doi.org/10.1016/B978-0-12-822226-3.00004-0
20. Venkatesh, V., Bala, H.: Technology acceptance model 3 and a research agenda on interventions. Decis. Sci. **39**(2), 273–315 (2008). https://doi.org/10.1111/j.1540-5915.2008.00192.x
21. Jha, S., Topol, E.J.: Adapting to artificial intelligence: radiologists and pathologists as information specialists. JAMA **316**(22), 2353–2354 (2016). https://doi.org/10.1001/jama.2016.17438
22. Garg, S., Sinha, S., Kar, A.K., Mani, M.: A review of machine learning applications in human resource management. Int. J. Product. Perform. Manag., ahead-of-print (2021). https://doi.org/10.1108/IJPPM-08-2020-0427

Big Data Analytics Affordances for Social Innovation: A Theoretical Framework

Ilias O. Pappas[1,2(✉)] and Devinder Thapa[1,3]

[1] University of Agder, 4639 Kristiansand, Norway
ilias.pappas@uia.no, ilpappas@ntnu.no
[2] Norwegian University of Science and Technology, 7491 Trondheim, Norway
[3] University of South-Eastern Norway, 3603 Kongsberg, Norway

Abstract. This paper proposes a theoretical framework to identify the mechanisms by which actors perceive the affordances of big data analytics (BDA) and how institutional voids and supports enable or hinder the actualisation of those perceived affordances. In doing so, we contribute to identifying the missing link needed to understand the social innovation process in relation to BDA. The framework paves the ground towards understanding the institutionalization process of social innovation and its implications for research and practice.

Keywords: Affordance theory · Big data analytics · Social entrepreneur · Social innovation · Institutional support · Institutional void

1 Introduction

Big data analytics (BDA) can generate business and social value [1–3], improve social and environmental sustainability [4, 5], allow data-driven decisions, and contribute to the creation of sustainable societies [1]. BDA and Artificial Intelligence (AI) enabled tools can be used in a variety of ways, for example, to offer personalized healthcare [6] improve learning environments [7], or to analyse data from social media to predict suicide [8]. In several countries, governments have made their data openly available, while individuals develop applications to address specific problems. Such actions foster innovation and the generation of new ideas.

Previous works highlight the potential of social innovation in offering sustainable solutions to social problems, achieving social integration, and creating equal opportunities [9–11]. It is critical for citizens and organisations to collaboratively identify specific innovative solutions for achieving the desired Sustainable Development Goals (SDGs). However, there is a lack of theoretical frameworks to describe and explain the mechanisms by which technology, such as BDA or AI, can facilitate the social innovation process vis-a-vis social change [11–13].

We address this gap, by proposing a theoretical framework that combines the theory of affordances and concepts from institutional theory. This framework offers a way to uncover the aforementioned mechanisms for successful BDA implementations in social innovation processes.

Published by Springer Nature Switzerland AG 2021
D. Dennehy et al. (Eds.): I3E 2021, LNCS 12896, pp. 144–149, 2021.
https://doi.org/10.1007/978-3-030-85447-8_13

In the subsequent section, we describe these theories and discuss their complementarities in understanding how actors perceive affordances of BDA and the role of institutional voids and institutional supports, within their institutional context, for actualizing the perceived affordances. Next, we present our theoretical framework, and conclude the paper suggesting ways for future research.

2 Theoretical Background

2.1 Big Data Analytics Ecosystems

The topic of big data analytics has received increased popularity the past years [3, 14, 15], with studies focusing on technology and infrastructure [16] and recent developments in the area leading to new technologies and applications [17]. The term big data refers to large volumes of extensively varied data that are generated, captured, and processed at high velocity [18], while big data analytics refer to analysis of the data in order to realize value from them [14]. For a list of definitions of BDA see also Mikalef, Pappas [19]. Although organizations consider BDA as a major source of value [2, 20], generating such value often raises social risks [21], that can have different impacts in the society.

Several stakeholders, including organizations, their competitors, partners, and customers, can mutually benefit from data being shared and combined [14], as in a digital ecosystem. An ecosystem comprises multiple hierarchical layers and requires its actors to cooperate and collaborate to increase its efficiency, coherency, and overall performance [22]. Big data analytics ecosystems, drawing from the business ecosystems [23], refer to the environment created and supported by the numerous actors, that comprise the ecosystem, their perpetual data generation along with their interactions and interrelations, which can lead to the creation of sustainable societies [1]. Thus, we need to extend existing ecosystems, or develop new ones, to be more dynamic and actively include more of their stakeholders, taking into account both their capabilities and needs. However, the challenge remains on how to take advantage of the vast amount of data available to solve essential societal problems in a sustainable manner towards achieving systemic change. The social innovation process can be excelled by using BDA towards solving societal challenges.

2.2 Social Innovation

Social innovation can be defined as new ideas (i.e., innovations) that incorporate the social factor both as a medium and an outcome. These innovations, under the proper circumstances (e.g., government conducive policies for technological interventions) may be adopted by other individuals, communities, or organizations [24]. It examines interrelations among actors, processes and cultural contexts and possibilities that lead to social sustainability and change [25].

Considering the importance and potential of social innovations, we build upon previous studies that describe the nature and interlinkages between institutional context and social innovation process [12, 26] who consider the role of the actor in the interface. Three critical parts of the social innovation process are the challenge that the actors have identified, their goal, that is to solve the challenge, and the process they will follow to achieve this goal. The end goal of the social innovation process is systemic change [27]. We consider the actor to be the social entrepreneur who can drive societal and systemic change, through the social innovation process, and we seek to understand how social entrepreneurs can benefit from contemporary technologies, such as BDA, and how institutions can enable or hinder this process. In the next section, we introduce the theory of affordance as it can help the entrepreneur to see the action possibilities from BDA while employing the social innovation process to achieve their goals.

2.3 Affordance Theory

Affordance theory originated from the field of ecological psychology. As Gibson [28] states "[t]he affordances of the environment are what it offers the animal, what it provides or furnishes, either for good or ill. It implies the complementarity of the animal and the environment". Affordances examined in IS studies, are defined as "the possibilities for goal-oriented action afforded to specified user groups by technical objects" [29], and further advanced as the potential for behaviours associated with achieving an outcome, where the potential arises from the relationship between the object (e.g., BDA) and the goal-oriented actors [30], therefore, they are neither properties of the artifact nor characteristics of the actor. Our view resonates with affordances as potential for action, where the specific actualisation is dependent on the context [30, 31]. An example of such view is described recently by Meske, Amojo [6], who suggest that the affordance of accessibility to relevant information in healthcare applications arises out of conversational agents and the patients using them. However, affordance theory does not describe the institutional context that can enable or inhibit the actualization process, thus, we complement affordance theory with concepts from institutional theory.

2.4 Institutional Theory

Institutional theory explains how institutions (norms, rules, conventions, and values) influence our understanding of how societies are structured and how they can change [32, 33]. Institutions have a critical role in developing new ideas and new types of social systems, thus institutional theory allows to better explain the interrelations and patterns among the different actors in the society [34]. The institutional theory, however, puts less emphasis on the human agency, for example, why an actor will interact with technology. Thus, we propose that combining institutional theory and theory of affordances can offer a better understanding of the implementation of BDA for social innovation process.

Institutional mechanisms, systems, and structures can either be absent or present, thus constraining or enabling the social innovation process. The absence, weakness or failure of formal or informal institutions that support the markets can be defined as institutional void [26]. The existence of voids can naturally hinder the social innovation process (e.g., lack of governance structure or policy, infrastructure, absence of access to funding). However, the existence of voids can create opportunities for social innovations as social entrepreneurs may come up with innovative ways to overcome them. For example, good policy environment can help increase foreign aid effectiveness to developing countries, however an extremely increased trade deficit, due to appropriate policies, can reduce the effectiveness of foreign aid [35]. Overall, the existence of supportive institutional mechanisms, systems, and structures is designed to support social innovation.

3 A Theoretical Framework of BDA for SI

The purpose of this paper is to suggest a framework that can help identify the mechanisms which enable the social innovation process and allow actors, such as social entrepreneurs, to perceive and actualize the possibilities that BDA provide for solving societal challenges. However, the social innovation process mainly focuses on processes that can lead to systemic change, while considering technology, such as BDA, as a black box [26, 36]. Existing research does not explain how actors perceive the action possibilities of BDA.

Furthermore, recent studies examine how BDA can be utilized to achieve digital transformation and sustainability [1, 5], while discussing the role of the actors, without though, examining the interrelations between actors and technology. To address this issue, we complement the theory of affordances with the concepts of institutional void and institutional support, that derive from institutional theory, to explain the relational aspects of technology and actors within their institutional context.

In summary, we propose the following theoretical framework (Fig. 1), for ICT and societal change through social innovation. Based on this framework, the actor has a central role in the process of using the IT artifact for SI. The actor that can use the IT artifact, perceives its affordances into taking action for employing the social innovation process. At the same time, the actor needs to consider the threats of voids and opportunities of supports, inherent in institutional context, when actualizing the affordances of the IT artifact for societal change.

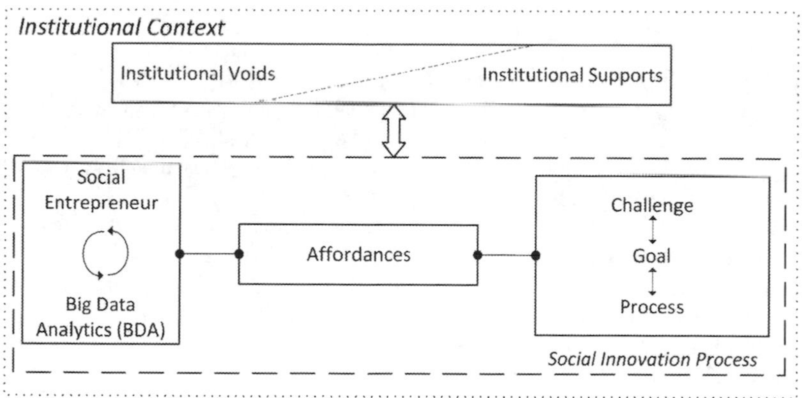

Fig. 1. Theoretical framework of BDA for social innovation

4 Conclusions

The paper contributes by offering a theoretical framework of BDA affordances for social innovation. There is a lack of theoretical lenses to understand and describe the social innovation process in relation to technology [12, 26], and particularly the role of BDA in such processes [1]. In this paper, we contribute to the social innovation process by coupling it with the theory of affordances, which allows us to better explain and understand the role of BDA for social innovation. In addition, we contribute to the affordance theory by combining it with institutional void and support, which can better explain the institutional context that influences the perception and actualization of BDA affordances for social innovation.

Based on the proposed framework, we argue that to make the action possibilities of BDA possible, the actors, like social entrepreneurs, need a holistic understanding of the institutional context and the social innovation process. To this end, more studies are needed to evaluate and further develop this model. Likewise, there is an opportunity to perform comparative studies among multiple countries, and thus investigate how the institutional context among different societal cultures and contexts, influences the way actor perceives and actualizes the affordances of ICT for societal change.

Acknowledgements. This project has received funding from the European Union's Horizon 2020 research and innovation programme, under the Marie Sklodowska-Curie Grant Agreement No. 751510.

References

1. Pappas, I.O., et al.: Big data and business analytics ecosystems: paving the way towards digital transformation and sustainable societies. Inf. Syst. e-Bus. Manage. **16**(3), 479–49 (2018). https://doi.org/10.1007/s10257-018-0377-z
2. Mikalef, P., et al.: Big data and business analytics: a research agenda for realizing business value. Inf. Manage. **57**(1) (2020)
3. Agarwal, R., Dhar, V.: Editorial—big data, data science, and analytics: the opportunity and challenge for IS research. Inf. Syst. Res. **25**(3), 443–448 (2014)
4. Dubey, R., et al.: Can big data and predictive analytics improve social and environmental sustainability? Technol. Forecast. Soc. Change **144**, 534–545 (2019)
5. Zhang, D., et al.: Orchestrating big data analytics capability for sustainability: a study of air pollution management in China. Inf. Manage., 103231 (2019)
6. Meske, C., Amojo, I., Thapa, D.: Understanding the affordances of conversational agents in mental mobile health services. In: ICIS 2020 Proceedings (2020)
7. Kabudi, T., Pappas, I., Olsen, D.H.: AI-enabled adaptive learning systems: a systematic mapping of the literature. Comput. Educ. Artif. Intell. **2**, 100017 (2021)
8. Song, T.-M., Ryu, S.: Big data analysis framework for healthcare and social sectors in Korea. Healthc. Inform. Res. **21**(1), 3–9 (2015)
9. Howaldt, J., Kopp, R., Schwarz, M.: Social innovations as drivers of social change — exploring tarde's contribution to social innovation theory building. In: Nicholls, A., Simon, J., Gabriel, M. (eds.) New Frontiers in Social Innovation Research, pp. 29–51. Palgrave Macmillan, London (2015). https://doi.org/10.1057/9781137506801_2
10. Mulgan, G., et al.: Social innovation: what it is, why it matters and how it can be accelerated (2007)
11. Pappas, I.O., et al.: Social innovation and social entrepreneurship through Big Data: developing a research agenda. In: 11th Mediterranean Conference on Information Systems (MCIS), Genoa, Italy (2017)

12. Cajaiba-Santana, G.: Social innovation: moving the field forward. A conceptual framework. Technol. Forecast. Soc. Change **82**, 42–51 (2014)
13. Faik, I., Barrett, M., Oborn, E.: How information technology matters in societal change: an affordance-based institutional logics perspective. MIS Q. **44**(3) (2020)
14. Günther, W.A., et al.: Debating big data: a literature review on realizing value from big data. J. Strateg. Inf. Syst. **26**(3), 191–209 (2017)
15. Chen, Y., et al.: Big data analytics and big data science: a survey. J. Manage. Anal. **3**(1), 1–42 (2016)
16. Chen, C.P., Zhang, C.-Y.: Data-intensive applications, challenges, techniques and technologies: a survey on Big Data. Inf. Sci. **275**, 314–347 (2014)
17. Watson, H.J.: Update tutorial: Big Data analytics: concepts, technology, and applications. Commun. Assoc. Inf. Syst. **44**(1), 21 (2019)
18. Laney, D.: 3D data management: controlling data volume, velocity and variety. META Gr. Res. Note **6**(70), 1 (2001)
19. Mikalef, P., et al.: Big data analytics capabilities: a systematic literature review and research agenda. Inf. Syst. e-Bus. Manage. **16**(3), 547–578 (2018). https://doi.org/10.1007/s10257-017-0362-y
20. Grover, V., et al.: Creating strategic business value from big data analytics: a research framework. J. Manage. Inf. Syst. **35**(2), 388–423 (2018)
21. Clarke, R.: Big data, big risks. Inf. Syst. J. **26**(1), 77–90 (2016)
22. Tsujimoto, M., et al.: A review of the ecosystem concept—towards coherent ecosystem design. Technol. Forecast. Soc. Change **136**, 49–58 (2018)
23. Moore, J.F.: The Death of Competition: Leadership and Strategy in the Age of Business Ecosystems. HarperBusiness New York (1996)
24. Westley, F., Antadze, N.: Making a difference: strategies for scaling social innovation for greater impact. Innov. J. **15**(2) (2010)
25. Howaldt, J., Schwarz, M.: Social innovation and human development - how the capabilities approach and social innovation theory mutually support each other. J. Hum. Dev. Capab. **18**(2), 163–180 (2017)
26. Turker, D., Altuntas Vural, C.: Embedding social innovation process into the institutional context: voids or supports. Technol. Forecast. Soc. Change **119**, 98–113 (2017)
27. Murray, R., Caulier-Grice, J., Mulgan, G.: The Open Book of Social Innovation. National Endowment for Science, Technology and the Art (NESTA), London (2010)
28. Gibson, J.: The Theory of Affordances The Ecological Approach to Visual Perception, pp. 127–143. Houghton Miffin, Boston (1979)
29. Markus, M.L., Silver, M.S.: A foundation for the study of IT effects: a new look at DeSanctis and Poole's concepts of structural features and spirit. J. Assoc. Inf. Syst. **9**(10), 5 (2008)
30. Volkoff, O., Strong, D.M.: Critical realism and affordances: theorizing IT-associated organizational change processes. MIS Q., 819–834 (2013).
31. Thapa, D., Sein, M.K.: Trajectory of affordances: insights from a case of telemedicine in Nepal. Inf. Syst. J. **28**(5), 796–817 (2018)
32. Hollingsworth, J.R.: Doing institutional analysis: implications for the study of innovations. Rev. Int. polit. Econ. **7**(4), 595–644 (2000)
33. Lounsbury, M., Crumley, E.T.: New practice creation: an institutional perspective on innovation. Organ. Stud. **28**(7), 993–1012 (2007)
34. Scott, W.R.: Institutions and Organizations: Ideas, Interests, and Identities. Sage publications (2013)
35. Karki, Y., Pappas, I.O.: Investigating aid effectiveness in developing countries: the case of Nepal. In: Hattingh, M., Matthee, M., Smuts, H., Pappas, I., Dwivedi, Y.K., Mäntymäki, M. (eds.) I3E 2020. LNCS, vol. 12067, pp. 338–344. Springer, Cham (2020). https://doi.org/10.1007/978-3-030-45002-1_29
36. Sandeep, M., Ravishankar, M.: Social innovations in outsourcing: an empirical investigation of impact sourcing companies in India. J. Strateg. Inf. Syst. **24**(4), 270–288 (2015)

COVID-19 Discrepancies Rising from Population Density Political Polarization Exacerbates Policy Gap

Mouwafac Sidaoui(✉), Nicholas Abrams(✉), and Abhishruti Adhikari(✉)

Menlo College, Atherton, CA 94027, USA
{mouwafac.sidaoui,nicholas.abrams,abhishruti.adhikari}@menlo.edu

Abstract. The Coronavirus pandemic severely impacted certain areas of the USA more than others. The data-driven decision making at every level at CDC will aid government decision makers to reallocate medical resources while planning recovery and reopening businesses in the United States. In this paper, we use a data visualization approach combined with current secondary research to measure which areas of the USA are most severely impacted by the Coronavirus pandemic. We propose a novel methodology that is implementable by medical organizations that use informatics depending on the data initiative at hand.

Keywords: Data visualization · Business analytics · COVID-19 · USA · Policy gap · Political polarization

1 Introduction

Real data from cdc.gov shed light on the states with the worst infection and death rates to better understand what states are most severely impacted by the Coronavirus. This insight will aid decision makers when allocating further medical resources while planning recovery and reopening of states. Along the way, important concerns regarding criteria and metrics are examined to provide greater clarity towards answering a further question. How does one measure impact and severity? The data within this research paper is first aggregated at the country level, then disaggregated to the state level. The data leads to two alternate conclusions for decisionmakers to ponder. Coastal states have experienced the greatest number of deaths related to the Coronavirus, while states situated in the interior of the country have experienced the greatest number of deaths related to the Coronavirus adjusted for population in given state. These metrics reveal contrasting conclusions that arise due to absolute and relative bases.

D. Dennehy et al. (Eds.): I3E 2021, LNCS 12896, pp. 150–158, 2021.
https://doi.org/10.1007/978-3-030-85447-8_14

2 Research USA Time Series

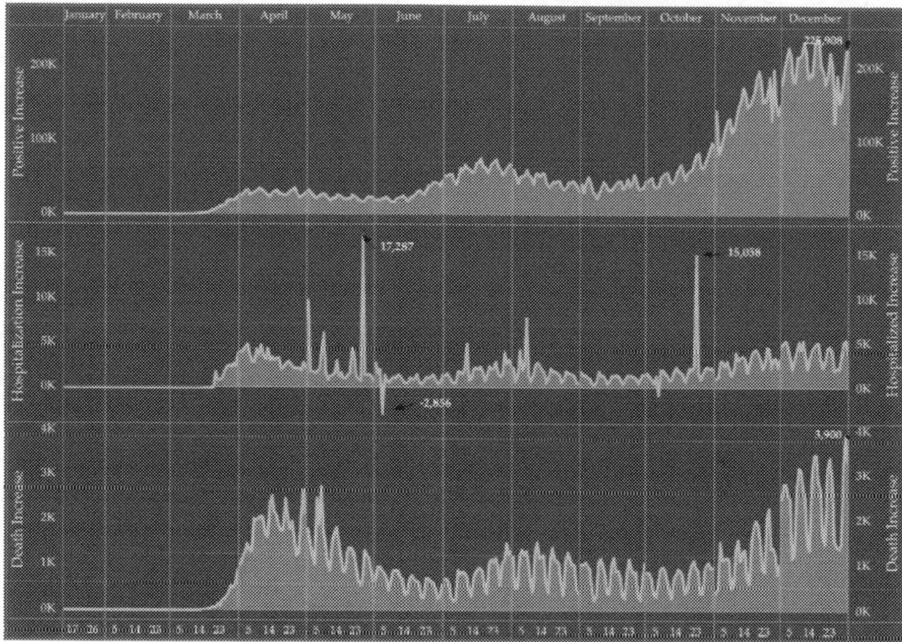

Fig. 1. *COVID in Numbers.* Numbers on the left represent Total cases, Total Hospitalized, Total Deaths, and Fatality Rate of COVID in the US as of January 24, 2021. Graphs on the right represent the increase in Positive cases, Hospitalizations, and Deaths.

Notice Fig. 1 the first two months of the year present a minor increase in Positive Cases with zero hospitalization and few deaths. The month of March reveals positive cases, hospitalizations, and deaths increasing sharply. These indicators increase throughout the second half of the year. Hospitalizations, results of positive cases, and deaths related to the virus increase dramatically in the fall.

In the months leading up to March, there was not enough data or a robust set of data tools to gather and analyze the COVID-19 dataset. After the novel coronavirus was declared a national emergency on President Donald Trump on March 13, 2020, the White House urged its AI experts to develop tools to be applied to the COVID-19 dataset to help understand the transmission, risk, and other vital information of the virus. The "COVID-19 Open Research Dataset (*CORD-19*), representing the most extensive machine-readable coronavirus literature collection available for data mining to date, was put together by researchers from the Allen Institute for AI, the Chan Zuckerberg Initiative (CHI), Georgetown University's Center for Security and Emerging Technology (CSET), Microsoft, and the National Library of Medicine (NLM) at NIH" as a result of the call-to-action by the White House soon after (Kent 2020). Initiatives from Google Cloud to offer researchers free access to COVID-19 information through its COVID-19

Public Dataset Program helped the data be even more accessible to researchers paving the path for using AI tools in medicine.

While understanding the trends of the infection among various geographic regions and demographics, researchers identified very early on that the virus had disproportionately impacted not only the elderly and people with underlying conditions but also the people of lower socioeconomic status and other minority populations. Medical Home Network, an organization serving patients in the Chicago area, used Artificial Intelligence to identify high-risk individuals to prioritize care management outreach to patients at most risk to severe complications from the virus (Kent 2020). Similar usage of the Artificial Intelligence algorithm helped an NYU team to accurately predict which patients diagnosed with COVID-19 will develop serious respiratory disease (NYU 2020). Data scientists, Andrew Satz and Brett Averso founded a startup, EVQLV, that creates algorithms capable of generating, screening, and optimizing millions of therapeutic antibodies (EVQLV 2020). Likewise, Definitive Healthcare, in partnership with Esri, launched an interactive data platform to predict where and when the resources such as ICU beds and ventilators need to be allocated by looking at the number of hospital beds, equipment, and other resources available in each county of each state in the country. Likewise, the Center for Systems Science and Engineering (CSSE) at Johns Hopkins released a web-based dashboard with real-time cases, recoveries, and deaths for all countries affected by the virus. These data gave the US federal and state governments a scientific guideline to implementing quarantine and social distancing measures.

Despite the efforts to make data transparent, much was still needed to learn about the coronavirus. All indicators of severity, including positive cases, hospitalizations, and deaths spike throughout the second half of the year. On May 28, total fatalities numbered 100,000. The daily death rate of the coronavirus hovered around 2,000 deaths per day. The Fatality Rate peaked on May 15 at 2.59% and subsequently decreased. The number of positive cases increased rapidly during Summer before subsiding towards Fall.

Fall experienced a more dramatic surge. Positive tests, hospitalizations, and fatalities increased. Nonetheless, the numbers so far represent the whole country and looking at data covering 50 states and 8 territories at the same time. Creating a Pareto chart to see where each state lies in relation to the running total of positive cases in the country provides further insight (Fig. 2).

Notice that 11 states contribute to almost 60% of total cases in the US. The top 10 states with the most positive cases in the US are used for further analysis. The top 10 most-affected states were identified using the rank calculation, (RANK(SUM([POSITIVE]) and filtering the data by [*Rank in Positive] $\leq$ [Top 10].

The cross tab below sorts those 10 states to create a chart that contains Positive Increase, Hospitalization Increase, Maximum Recovered, and Death Increase with % of the total sum as labels. The chart was then color-coded, where light to bright orange indicated low to high percentages.

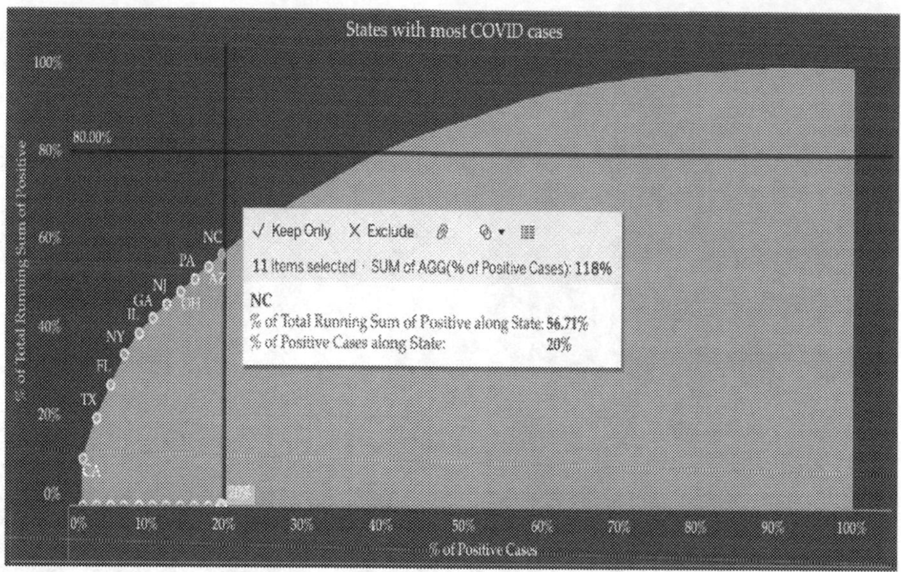

Fig. 2. *Pareto Chart.* A Pareto Chart with % of positive cases along with states and % total running sum of positive cases along states showing that 11 states contribute to 56.71% of total positive COVID cases in the US.

3 Research Absolute vs. Relative Basis

Figure 3 illustrates Total Deaths related to the Coronavirus in each state across a heat map of the United States. The number of deaths associated with individual states are illustrated with a density chart that increases in size and varying degrees of color. The states which experience a greater number of deaths related to the Coronavirus are illustrated in red, while states which experience a lesser number of deaths related to the Coronavirus are illustrated in more pale color.

Most remarkable is the contrast between the interior and coastal regions of the country. The states experiencing the most deaths related to the Coronavirus are California, Texas, New York, Florida, New Jersey, Illinois, Pennsylvania, Michigan, Massachusetts, and Georgia. The paler, less impacted States are situated more in the interior of the USA, while the redder, more impacted States are situated in coastal areas of the USA. This analysis illustrates that the interior of the country is less impacted by the Coronavirus than the coastal regions of the country. More precisely, the states most impacted by the Coronavirus are situated on the coastal regions of the country.

A different analysis provides the opposite conclusion. Figure 4 below illustrates the severity of the Coronavirus by first taking the total number of deaths related to the Coronavirus within each state, then adjusted by the state's population size. This provides a relative number of deaths related to the Coronavirus "per 100,000" citizens. Notice that most states across the country experience a similar intensity of the Coronavirus. While the intensity of the Coronavirus is similar across the country, ten states stand out as the most severely impacted on this metric of "per 100,000" citizens. Those are Arizona, North Dakota, South Dakota, Missouri, Louisiana, New Jersey, New York, Rhode Island,

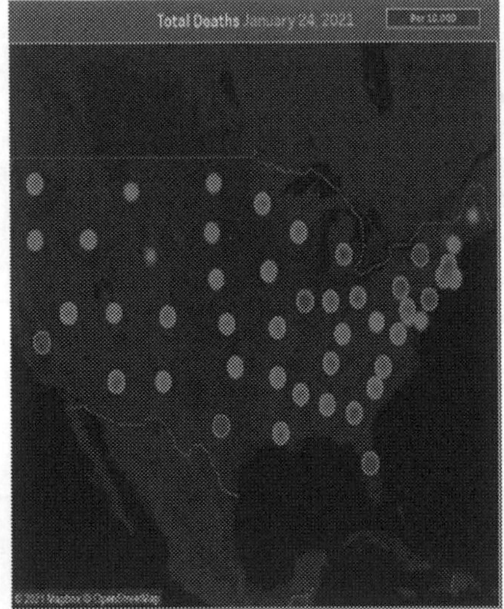

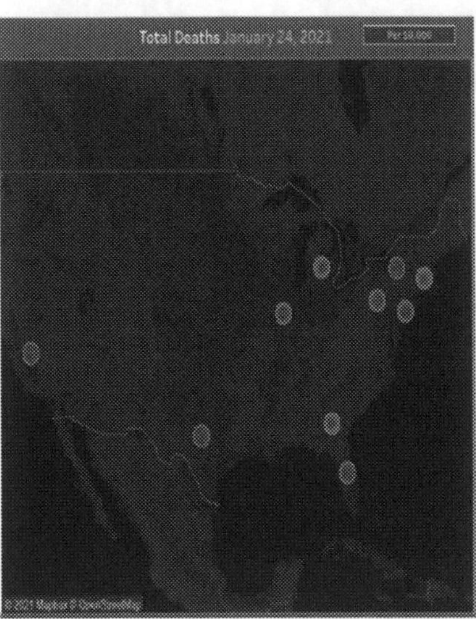

Fig. 3. *Heat Map: Total Deaths.* A map of the United States illustrating the number of deaths associated with each state. On the right-hand side, the data is filtered to narrow down on the top-10 states with the most deaths.

Massachusetts, and Connecticut. This relative basis reveals that states within the interior of the country have greatly suffered from the Coronavirus pandemic, albeit relative to their population size.

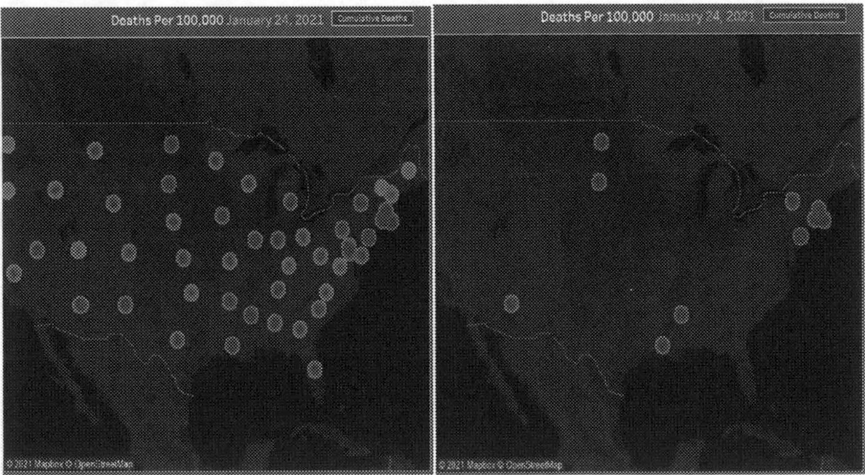

Fig. 4. *Heat Map: Deaths Per 100,000.* A map of the United States illustrating the number of deaths associated with each state, then divided by the population size of the given state. On the right-hand side, the data is filtered to narrow down on the top-10 states with the most deaths relative to their population size.

Contrast the conclusion of both density charts. The first metric of "Total Deaths" within a given state concludes that coastal regions of the country suffer the greatest impact from the Coronavirus pandemic. Those states include California, New York, New Jersey, Texas, and Florida, among others. "Deaths per 100,000" of the state's population concludes that states in the interior of the country suffer the greatest. Those states include North Dakota, South Dakota, Louisiana, Missouri, and Arizona.

Some states show themselves to be affected only on a relative basis. These states do not hold a top ten position with Total Deaths related to the Coronavirus but do hold a top ten position within "Deaths per 100,000" citizens. These states include Rhode Island, Missouri, South Dakota, Connecticut, North Dakota, Louisiana, and Arizona Fig. 5.

Fig. 5. States Rhode Island, Missouri, South Dakota, Connecticut, North Dakota, Louisiana, and Arizona experience the greatest impact of the Coronavirus only relative to their population size.

More precisely, the impact of the Coronavirus in these states is found in the number of deaths relative to their population size. The number of deaths relative to the Coronavirus in each state is small compared to other states, but when this metric is normalized on a common basis, population size, the severity of the situation becomes apparent.

4 Discussion Policy Gap

States in the interior of the country experienced a disproportionately high number of deaths related to the Coronavirus relative to their population size. Most striking are the states of North Dakota, South Dakota, Arizona, Missouri, and Louisiana. Why did such states become so severely impacted by the Coronavirus? Initial reports hint that bad policy was to blame.

A policy gap is a concept where the implementation of policy fails to achieve the intended results. The most salient factor contributing to policy gap throughout the response to the Coronavirus was the challenge of policy implementation across dispersed governance (Hudson et al. 2019). Three levels of governance make policy implementation challenging. First, federal recommendations lead to state regulation. Then state regulation leads to municipal implementation. This layering of bureaucratic decision-making highlights "the need for policymakers to confront the messy engagement of multiple players with diverse sources of knowledge" (Hudson et al. 2019). The increasing layers of bureaucracy produce implementation limitations at each level that become exacerbated when these layers of policymakers fail to establish common ground on core facts at hand. This is greatest highlighted in North and South Dakota's bleak response when faced with the Coronavirus.

South Dakota Governor Kristi Noem refrained from mandating policy that other states found appropriate. Masks were not mandated nor were large gatherings limited. The decision sought to respect personal freedom (Levin and Lebeau 2021). The impact is obvious. This laissez faire approach resulted in South Dakota experiencing one of the highest numbers of deaths relative to their population size (Levin and Lebeau 2021). Similarly, North Dakota's enforcement of mask mandates was short lived, and the result was a dramatic spike in cases and subsequent deaths during the spring and summer months (Turley and Springer 2020). This dismissive response to federal and public health official recommendations is not unique to these two states, but indicative of a political polarization that further exacerbates the policy gap.

North and South Dakota highlight the political polarization that increased the challenge of policy implementation across dispersed governance. Trust between policymakers and public health officials was very low and predominantly split between political party lines (Milosh 2020). Take for example the situation surrounding face masks. Face coverings have been a staple policy to mitigate the spread of the Coronavirus across the country with impressive efficacy, however particular states were not interested in implementing the measure (Leung 2020). During the pandemic, all 24 of the Democratic Governors required citizens within their state to wear a face mask indoors (Reimann 2020). Only 8 of the 26 Republican Governors require citizens within their state to wear a face mask indoors (Reimann 2020). Further research revealed areas that strongly supported democratic candidates in the 2016 election were more willing to comply with mask mandates while the opposite is true with areas that supported Republican candidates (Milosh 2020). Republican led states were generally distrustful, or otherwise dismissive, of federal and public health official recommendations.

The Coronavirus pandemic exposes decision making mistakes across state and municipalities whose responsibility is to protect their population from such disasters. To avoid similar exacerbations of policy gap in future pandemics, trust between policymakers and health officials needs to be restored. Public health officials need to persuade policymakers across the various layers of governance and their subsequent constituency to make behavior changes and follow public health policies.

Public health officials' relationship with policymakers can be improved with transparency of the scientific modeling process that leads to recommendation of policy. The decision-making process of the Coronavirus pandemic involved interpreting scientific evidence in the form of quantitative models, abstract representations of reality that provide a logically consistent way to organize thinking about the relationship among variables of interest (Berger 2021). Should differing scientific conclusions exist, public health officials need to clarify with the skeptical policy makers the scientific process to establish common ground on core facts at hand.

Public health officials' relationship with policymakers' constituencies can be improved through enlisting favored voices. Public health officials can follow a similar strategy as West Africa during the Ebola Crisis in 2014. West Africa officials enlisted local voices to build engagement and trust between the individuals and health officials (Bavel 2020). This phenomenon is further validated by study by Ajzenman et al., who noticed shortly after Donald Trump's endorsement of masks in July of 2020, social media engagement of mask mandates was significantly positive. Support from prominent figures can improve the impression of public health officials.

Further, public health officials can make a moral case for behavioral change. The pandemic revealed Americans are more willing to abide by stringent lockdown measures if they are convinced doing so would risk infecting a coworker of a serious illness (Bavel 2020). Clear understanding of the implication of individuals' actions improves their ability to discern the impact of their choices. The result being public health recommendations are more appreciated.

5 Conclusion

When decision makers attempt to craft policy regarding the Coronavirus and aid areas of the country that are most severely impacted, they must account for population size in their considerations. Further, decision makers must keep in mind that while coastal regions of the country suffer the greatest in the number of deaths related to the Coronavirus on a cumulative basis, a relative basis provides a different conclusion. On a relative basis, the interior of the country experiences a significant impact from the Coronavirus.

The states impacted by the Coronavirus on a relative basis reveal remarkable policy gaps through the Coronavirus response. These policy gaps were primarily caused by challenges in implementing policy through several layers of governance, though was further exacerbated by political polarization that impacted individuals trust in federal and public health mandates. Trust between policymakers and public health officials, and trust between policymakers' constituency and public health officials must be improved to avoid repeat outcomes of North and South Dakota.

References

Ajzenman, N.: Leaders' speech and risky behaviour during a pandemic. VOX, CEPR Policy Portal (2020). https://voxeu.org/article/leaders-speech-and-risky-behaviour-during-pandemic

Bavel, J.J.: Using social and behavioural science to support COVID-19. pandemic response. Nature Human Behaviour (2020). https://www.nature.com/articles/s41562-020-0884-z?error=cookies_not_supported&code=f6599321-3df6-4797-934f-bd3dabeb5293

Berger, L.: Rational policymaking during a pandemic. PNAS (2021). https://www.pnas.org/content/118/4/e2012704118

Cohen, J., Rodgers, Y.V.D.M.: Contributing factors to personal protective equipment shortages during the COVID-19 pandemic. Prevent. Med. **141**, 162–163 (2020). https://doi.org/10.1016/j.ypmed.2020.106263

Hudson, B., Hunter, D., Peckham, S.: Policy failure and the policy-implementation gap: can policy support programs help? Policy Des. Pract. **2**(1), 1–14 (2019). https://doi.org/10.1080/25741292.2018.1540378

Leung, N.H.L.: Respiratory virus shedding in exhaled breath and efficacy of face masks. Nature Medicine (2020). https://www.nature.com/articles/s41591-020-0843-2?fbclid=IwAR0Q3-WhHv1F9dmZSr2iLNQ-F6ioAIfOYAch7PPtHib9EsuVyhs-mYZlXcg&error=cookies_not_supported&code=a9b92dd0-6150-4811-ae2c-86db898e6933

Levin, J., Lebeau, D.: Covid's South Dakota Rampage Created a Failed Experiment in Herd Immunity. Bloomberg (2021)

Milosh, M.: Political polarisation impedes the public policy response to COVID-19. VOX, CEPR Policy Portal (2020). https://voxeu.org/article/political-polarisation-impedes-public-policy-response-covid-19

Reimann, N.: All States With Democratic Governors Now Have Mask Mandates, But Most With Republicans Don't. Forbes (2020). https://www.forbes.com/sites/nicholasreimann/2020/07/30/all-states-with-democratic-governors-now-have-mask-mandates-but-most-with-republicans-dont/?sh=24622de27e25

Silverstein, J.: U.S. reported more COVID-19 cases in November than most countries had all year. CBS News (2020). https://www.cbsnews.com/news/covid-november-cases-united-states/

Times, T.N.Y.: Spike in U.S. Cases Far Outpaces Testing Expansion. The New York Times (2020). https://www.nytimes.com/2020/07/22/world/Coronavirus-covid-19.html

Turley, J., Springer, P.: How did North Dakota's COVID-19 outbreak become the worst in the country? Twin Cities (2020). https://www.twincities.com/2020/11/15/how-did-north-dakotas-covid-19-outbreak-become-the-worst-in-the-country/

AI Philosophy, Ethics and Governance

Ethics and AI Issues: Old Container with New Wine?

Fred Niederman[1(✉)] and Elizabeth White Baker[2]

[1] Saint Louis University, St. Louis, MO 63146, USA
fred.niederman@slu.edu
[2] Virginia Commonwealth University, Richmond, VA, USA

Abstract. This paper reflects on what differentiates AI ethics issues from more general concerns raised by all IS applications. Examination of the PAPA framework advanced in 1986 by Richard Mason suggests that the categories of problems remains much as they have over the decades, with the exception of a new set of societal issues. Within these categories, however, the increase in capabilities of computing generally and AI in particular, shift some affordances from only possible to realized and the ethical issues attached to these affordances come to the fore. AI, however, is a catalyst for deeper philosophical considerations about the nature of mind, thought, agency, and responsibility.

Keywords: Ethics · Artificial intelligence · AI · PAPA framework · Internet of behavior · Distributed cloud · Hyper-automation

1 Introduction

> "*Nowhere is the potential threat to human dignity so severe as it is in the age of information technology, especially in the field of artificial intelligence (p. 9),*" Richard O. Mason (1986).
>
> "*Be nice to your vacuum cleaner, it may become more sentient than you before you have a chance to apologize for your decades of disrespect,*" Fred Niederman (2021).

Literally thousands of scholarly articles have been written in the past decade alone about ethics and artificial intelligence (AI). Yet it is not clear how much has been added to an initial view of IS ethics produced by Mason (1986). This paper aims to review in broad brush what Mason's framework reveals and what remains for further examination.

An ABI-Informs search on April 9, 2021, on the key words "artificial intelligence" and ethics yielded 27,821 retrieved articles. Narrowing down to scholarly journals yielded 3,152 articles. *AI Magazine* led the pack with 118 articles, *Communications of AIS* is among the leaders within the MIS community with 61 articles and the *Journal of AIS* led the "Basket of 8" designated by the AIS senior scholars' college with 27. Special issues have been devoted to the topic including ones in the journals: *Ethics and*

Published by Springer Nature Switzerland AG 2021
D. Dennehy et al. (Eds.): I3E 2021, LNCS 12896, pp. 161–172, 2021.
https://doi.org/10.1007/978-3-030-85447-8_15

Information Technology, Philosophy & Technology, Transactions on Human-Computer Interaction, Proceedings of IEEE, and Journal of AIS (Aggarwal 2020; Benbya, et al. 2021; Dignum 2018; Winfield, et al. 2019; Robert et al. 2020). Interest in the topic extends beyond the discipline of IS to include scholars in the humanities, social sciences, computer science, and engineering.

Numerous books, in particular *Weapons of Math Destruction*, (O'Neil 2016), have addressed ethics and AI, including sophisticated analytics. O'Neil's book is particularly effective at pointing to impacts from AI and analytics and just how much these can vary between stakeholders – providing significant convenience to a large number of consumers, while providing extreme harm to relatively few for whom the systems do not operate as intended. *Future Politics* by Susskind (2018) speculates at length about the potential effects of AI (among other technology influences) on relationships between individuals and institutions in the future. It proposes that society is likely to face emergent issues as a result of advancing technology, create new rules and institutions to respond to these, and suggests that such a future result in nightmare or enlightened scenarios for the people of those days.

Much writing about AI ethics pertains to relatively broad threats such as the erosion of a need for human labor characterized in some quarters as the 'robo-apolcalypse', and the pernicious effect of inappropriate exclusion from modern society based on biased or erroneous information. Writings on these topics tends toward showing the dangers of such threats (Clarke 2019) or proposing that they are unlikely to manifest (Willcocks 2020), noting potential ways to avoid or ameliorate them. Others focus less on particular AI applications or dangers and more on preventing general ill effects through attempts to provide rules or codes of ethics on one hand or algorithms for preventing, detecting, and correcting errors. Siau and Wang (2020), in this regard, usefully differentiates AI ethics in terms of those applying to creating new AI versus the effects of AI on stakeholders.

In this essay, we consider whether and, if so how, AI presents new ethical challenges beyond those that have confronted information systems and reactions to them from AI's beginnings. In this paper we address questions arising from reconsideration of Mason's (1986) PAPA model (privacy, accuracy, property, accessibility). The overarching research question of this study is: What, if anything, differentiates AI-related ethical issues from all other information systems ethical issues? Secondary questions consider whether Mason's framework is sufficient for organizing discussions about AI and ethics. If it is not sufficient, what remains to be added?

This line of questioning is based on the premise that if we have accumulated knowledge of ethics pertaining to information systems generally, some may be directly applied to issues relative to AI. Once applied, are there remaining issues to be addressed? Mason's framework is certainly not a representation of the accumulation of all knowledge about IS and ethics, but it is a highly cited and fundamental piece worth considering as an initial entry point to comparison of AI and general IS relative to ethics.

Underlying this discussion is the view that AI can be understood as a collection of techniques that to some degree seek to mimic human capabilities (e.g., language recognition, movement through robotics) or develop alternatives that substitute for human decisions and/or actions. The dividing line between AI and other information systems is fuzzy because; (1) AI components may be embedded in more traditional systems. For example, some AI programming may search for fraudulent transactions as a component of an enterprise or accounting system; (2) to some degree AI and analytics represent porous categories where some particular techniques could be claimed by either. For example, Bayesian statistics may be regarded as underpinning either analytic or AI techniques; and (3) historically many information systems applications, from COBOL implemented transaction systems to proprietary enterprise systems have substituted for human decisions and actions without concerns for replicating the manner in which humans performed these tasks.

Mikalf and Gupta (2021) methodically develop a list of capabilities pertaining to organizations relative to their ability to create applications using AI and, as a result of their use, create value. These capabilities are framed in terms of technology, human resources, and other organizational factors. They do not explicate AI capabilities in terms of their affordances or how they are put to use in the world. Thus AI is viewed in terms of organizational skill and technical capabilities rather than affordances such as: extrapolating past activity into probabilities for future performance, connecting 'sensory' data such as from vision or language to actions contingent on the content of such data, helping to eliminate infeasible choice options, or finding unexpected connections (say selecting team members from hundreds of thousands in a multinational enterprise for a special project) where limits of human experience and search time would make such activities impossible.

In the following sections, we review Mason's framework, discuss what it does and does not do for advancing ethical considerations, consider particular issues that AI raises in the philosophical realm, particularly regarding 'consciousness'; present three examples of emerging technologies and how the PAPA framework can identify issues but also leaves some remaining unclassified, which we propose falls under an additional 'societal' category, then we conclude with discussion about what remains for dealing with AI ethics beyond the framework.

2 PAPA Issues Then and Now

Mason (1986) produced a seminal categorization of ethical issues particular to IS. He called them the "PAPA" issues: privacy, accuracy, property, and accessibility. For each he provides examples. There is also a modest sequential nature to the issues, particularly as privacy leads into accuracy concerns.

2.1 Privacy

Privacy in the framework represents a combination of issues. The first pertains to the ability of individuals to choose what to conceal or reveal from selected or all others information about themselves. This may be for reasons of economic consequence such as not revealing a medical condition that would change costs of insurance (or even eligibility). It may alternatively be for pure personal preference such as revealing that one is addicted to reading Marvel comics (a badge of honor in some circles, a sign of immaturity to others). The second pertains to the ability of information regarding an individual revealed for one purpose to be applied to non-disclosed subsequent purposes.

Mason is aware of the cumulative effect of multiple revelations which he summarizes as: "Each additional weaving together of my attributes reveals more and more about me (p. 6)." Importantly, his view was expressed in 1986 before such data integration has largely become a widespread fact of daily life.

In contemporary terms, we see not only the convergence of increasing numbers of data sets pertaining to individual behaviors and choices, but the increasingly sophisticated ability to combine these to extrapolate likely additional characteristics and to predict future choices and preferences. As a result, new affordances from chatbots to recommender systems shift from being possible to actualized.

Note that these issues of privacy do not assume any mistaken or malicious use of data. Rather even with non-distressing inputs, outputs may still cause harm when data has been combined. Issues where data is actually false or misinterpreted lead to the second element in PAPA, lack of accuracy.

2.2 Accuracy

Accuracy, or more properly inaccuracy, becomes a problem when (1) historic methods of interaction are subsumed by digital ones such that historic archives may not be recognized in the digital world – if there is no physical backup and the computer says you are a deadbeat, you have become one whether you have paid your obligations or not. When the data becomes the truth, inaccuracy can produce distressing results when translated back to the 'real world'; and (2) people acting on data that should be but is not correct result in costly mistakes. Mason illustrates with faulty GPS information leading to a transportation accident with attendant costs. Mason notes the growth in such reliance: "Today we are producing so much information about so many people and their activities that our exposure to problems of inaccuracy is enormous (p. 8)."

Given that it is nearly impossible and relatively expensive to maintain perfectly clean data sets, much attention on accuracy pertains to finding and correcting those inaccuracies that make a difference. Note the attention in data warehousing to the cleansing of data being moved from independent transaction to integrated systems. In some scenarios all individual pieces of data may be correct (or at least not verifiably wrong), yet in combination lead to a poor conclusion. This can happen for example if a flawed procedure, say a contaminated blood sample, produced multiple readings all of which are incorrect, but correctly recorded relative to the reported test results. Even accurate data may suggest membership in a group where such combinations are the norm, but where an individual does not conform. Hofstede (1991) warns very severely about the 'ecological fallacy' of generalizing from the group to each individual. Cases of the harm that can arise from such invisible sources are dramatically documented by O'Neil (2016).

2.3 Property

Property pertains to the ownership of information as well as the tools that produce and manipulate it. Generally intellectual property refers to knowledge embedded in artifacts, but the content and data itself should be included as well. Mason focuses, among the many things which content ownership implies. But consider one producing a political tract being paired by an information consolidator, with an opposing tract which contains misinformation and personal attacks that one doesn't have the opportunity to refute. Even if not a comma is changed, the meaning and purpose of the initial tract may be significantly misused.

The systems we interact with now tend to be combinations of pieces supplied by an array of vendors which operate together to produce particular outcomes. However, when there are snags, it is often difficult to match the source of the problem to one particular component – particularly if each is operating as expected but are out of mutual alignment. We might call this the responsibility for floating and ghost glitches.

2.4 Accessibility

Accessibility refers to the capacity of individuals or organizations to acquire and use data. Mason posits the keys to this are three components of computer literacy: the intellectual skills to handle information; access to the technologies that connect to that information, and access to the information itself. It is noteworthy that the first two of these require economic and psychological investment by those who would seek access and the last pertains to the legitimate and illegitimate efforts to shield information from being acquired freely. Mason focuses on inequalities in the ability to pay these prices: "Thus the educational and economic ante is really quite high for playing the modern information game. Many people cannot or choose not to pay it and hence are excluded from participating fully in our society (p. 11)."

Over the years this situation has come to be called the 'digital divide' which marks differential access by economic status; location or ethnicity of origin; rural or urban; gender; age; physical capabilities and various other characteristics. In a world strongly moved, if not dominated, by economic performance, what would motivate vendors of software or hardware to produce versions of their products and services for subsets of customers where revenues generated are unlikely to payback the costs of modification for special needs?

3 PAPA Implications for AI Ethics

Before turning to the relationship of AI ethics issues and PAPA, it is worth considering what the framework is and what it isn't. As a framework, PAPA is a categorization scheme, or taxonomy, if one prefers. Following Bailey (1994) there are generally two types of taxonomy – inductive and deductive. Inductive taxonomies sort instances into groups where each group represents a category. Quantitatively, such a procedure may begin with a set of instances and use mathematical techniques like cluster analysis to sort the instances into types. It becomes a challenge to scholars to both label and ascertain the key differentiators among categories.

In contrast, the deductive approach starts with logically derived categories, sometimes by observing variations on dimensions thought to be meaningful such as aggressive/passive; communicative/quiet and using placement on both measures to segregate instances into categories. An advantage of this approach includes straightforward assignment of instances into categories. On the other hand, it does not necessarily take into account differences on other dimensions that may be equally or even more relevant, variance among instances within categories, and dimensions where evaluation of an instance is not clear.

3.1 Uses for PAPA

Once a taxonomy is established it can have multiple uses. One purpose is to create a basis for classifying instances. Given a particular instance, like drones falling out of the sky and injuring pedestrians, we might use the PAPA framework to consider what sort of issue this is. In this case, I'd surmise it would be likely to be considered a "property" issue in terms of who owns the drone and who owns liability for its proper usage. The classification relative to the framework in itself would be trivial (who cares what sort of problem it is when I need someone to drive me to the hospital?).

However, if we can assign an instance to a category, we can envision that the instance may inherit the general characteristics of that category. If the falling drone is a property problem it may inherit issues relative to varied stakeholder contributions that are present in many cases such as designer, builder, operation, and owner each having some potential responsibility. To the extent that such a premise is the case for all property issues, identifying the falling drone as a property issue highlights at least a first set of considerations. In this way categorization can create value by shortcutting the initial analysis process when a new instance is identified such that the general attributes become known and more specific characteristics of the instance can become the focus of further investigation. Note, however, that such initiation of discussion cannot substitute for the independent analysis of each emergent case. The drone falling from the sky may have some analogy to a self-driving car crashing into a pedestrian, however it also has differences including the potential for a different kind of damage and different level of victim awareness (e.g., as a pedestrian, one knows, or should know, that the space is shared with automobiles driven by humans or not; but the sunbather cannot be expected to anticipate a drone falling from the sky – at least at this time when drone use remains rare).

Although Mason (1986) discusses each of the categories in broad terms and presents examples, it is not clear whether any standard properties have been defined that can be applied to surfaced instances within the category.

Another use of a categorization scheme like PAPA is to help anticipate emergent issues. As technologies grow near creating new affordances, we may use the PAPA framework to anticipate classes of emergent issues. We know that there are property issues relative to human driven autos, but as we approach driverless ones, we can see that the list of contributors to the new technology grows to include programmers and other IT specialists along with the manufacturer and driver. Adding GPS to the auto (whether driven by humans or not) adds another dimension of affordances – like automated routing for the driver and recording of locations for archivists or whomever else can and wants to wrangle access) suggests a range of privacy, accuracy, and access issues.

As new technologies and platforms emerge, from fintech to crowdsourcing to gamification and well beyond, the PAPA framework can be applied to anticipate emergent general ethical instances such that designers and builders may be able to design them out of systems and/or processes for detection and remediation may be set in advance.

Further, periodic consideration of PAPA categories can be used relative to the interaction and accumulation of computing technologies to consider emergent ethical instances that do not adhere to one and only one emergent technology. For example, a growing sense of anxiety may derive not just from social media, ubiquitous computing, and the move toward digitization of many previously physical processes but from their accumulation. Each may provide benefits over cost worth their adoption but collectively they may change society in ways that generate new concerns.

Note that this discussion does not address AI as separate from other computing technologies. AI however is worthy of consideration as a generator of new applications or affordances that create new ethical instances. It is also an accelerator of new affordances in combination with other technologies. AI is a component enabling technologies like drones and self-driving cars, but both problems and solutions are intertwined with other systems (e.g., better sensors, coding for collaboration whether using AI algorithms or not, and even physical systems like lighter materials and better brakes).

3.2 What PAPA Doesn't Do

The strength of PAPA is in helping us understand and plan. That is not to say that understanding say a privacy issue with Alexa, or the other home companion devices, can positively lead to solutions through designing the problem out or providing countervailing tools for users. On the other hand, the PAPA framework still has some significant limitations.

PAPA does not offer any hints about how to deal with tradeoffs among stakeholders. For example, one might argue that I have a right to record every word you say to me, but equally you might have the right to speak without your words being recorded. Your right to the privacy of your words competes with my right to hold and review all that is presented to me. I suggest that nearly all issues that pertain to multiple stakeholders and present complex balances among competing reasonable if not valid interests. Knowing the category of this class of ethical issues may help us select a process for negotiating a compromise solution, but handling of such tradeoffs remains.

PAPA does not reduce uncertainty. A consequentialist ethics evaluates actions based on their results. Sometimes this might be quantifiable as a simple cost-benefit analysis, other times intangibles do not allow this. At the time of decision and action we can only estimate or guess what the outcomes will be. In the early 2000s when wireless systems were first being installed in coffee shops, there was widespread concern about pirating of the data of users of these public systems. To my understanding such concerns have not manifest (perhaps because they were highly publicized and of sufficient concern) in part because of technologies such as frequency changing but perhaps also because there are so many other easier, less costly, and less risky ways to steal data. Where the PAPA framework helps to anticipate issues and where these are viewed as sufficiently concerning, the process whether organized or ad hoc may indeed influence decisions and actions in a way that averts negative incidents.

PAPA does not resolve differences in moral values. Even if we could know the outcomes of any particular decision and action in advance, it is unlikely that agreement will be universal about which results are "good" versus "bad". Algorithms that discriminate by postal code in assigning eligibility or cost of home loans may cause immense difficulty for those living in some neighborhoods. Some will view this as atrocious malfeasance, others as simply reflecting the underlying discrimination of society such that these differences are simply passed on to the AI system and, therefore, not its responsibility. PAPA can surface this sort of issue, but not resolve it.

3.3 AI and Consciousness

Another type of ethical consideration that PAPA does not directly address pertains to the issues emergent relative to the hypothetical consciousness and agency potentially embodied in machines. This is largely a philosophical question with varied positions espoused, often with quite a bit of certainty. On one hand is Dreyfus (1992) who maintains, with much more thorough discussion that consciousness is and must be embodied. On the other hand, Rorty (2018) and like-minded philosophers argue that what we experience as consciousness is an emergent property of physical brain processes and therefore with no inherent reason why other sources of elemental processing should not also create consciousness as an emergent property.

Let us suppose, for example, that we have come to a point where creating machine consciousness can be achieved. Should it be done? From a universal perspective, the most important principle is uncertainty. We cannot begin to predict the results even if we can anticipate some and are fairly certain that others will emerge. If we take this step, even with a backdoor to 'pull the plug' if things go wrong, could we be justified ending the life of another sentient being, even if sentient by virtue of our own choices and actions? If the capability to create consciousness is near, would there be any way to stop absolutely everyone capable from deciding individually whether or not to go forward?

Another issue pertains to the rights and responsibilities of sentient machines. In many, if not all, human societies we grant some rights to animals of various sorts, even if not equivalently to humans. We recognize to varying degrees the consciousness and contribution of animals from endangered species to work animals from seeing-eye dogs to horses that pull wagons carrying tourists through recreational centers. Assuming varied possible levels of intensity in extending human rights to machine agents, ranging from full human status to regulations on maintenance, we might meaningfully ask questions about the implications for human ethics. Following PAPA, how might knowledge obtained by sentient machines affect our privacy? Do we have the right to expunge information gathered before sentience occurred? Assuming dozens, hundreds, or millions of such machines it is almost guaranteed that they will have varied "experiences" and form a wide range of inferences about us that will vary from the affirming to the very negative. If the machines are built from code written by individuals relative to various license agreements drawn for example from open source libraries, do the authors of the code have claims on benefits created by the machines or liability for claims made against them?

On the other hand, if calls for strict ethical screening of the processes for building AI and the data sets on which they are trained are instituted, we may find ourselves as humans in a position where our tools are more trustworthy than our colleagues. Perhaps this has long been the case as, simplistically, I'd trust a jack to hold the car up while I am working on it than even three strong and well-intended friends. It is a little much to believe we can program effective ethical guardrails on our AI tools when we demonstrably have so much trouble both defining and abiding by even simple ethical guidelines among ourselves. If you doubt this, check the local newspaper for listings of murders, embezzlements, and domestic violence – events that would rarely be considered highly ethical even without the help of AI robots. God, Allah, and/or Atman please help the vacuum cleaner that can feel pain before it can defend itself.

We may make the assumption that such machine consciousness is far off in the future, but when is the right time to start considering these issues? Will we as humans even know when machines develop sentience any more than we know how sentient are whales or mice?

4 IS PAPA Sufficient?

Given the early stages of the development of a new technology, one might use the framework proactively to project possible ethical issues following the PAPA framework. But we should not take this for granted but rather test how well it does work. Let us consider three currently emergent technology trends as proposed in the 2021 Gartner strategic trends listing (Pannetta 2020): internet of behaviors; distributed cloud, and hyper-automation (see Table 1).

Table 1. Three emerging technologies viewed through PAPA categories.

	Internet of behaviors	Distributed cloud	Hyper-automation
Privacy	Integration of disparate data sources Exposure of individual items and/or inferences	Forced privacy if data is not compatible across platforms	???
Accuracy	Tolerance of sensors to error Compounding of error through integration	Finding data where it is spread across physical media Keeping all data updated simultaneously throughout system	Inability to intervene mid-process to avoid or correct mistakes
Property	Locus of decision making for access to each thread as well as collection	Claims of host toward ownership of data Responsibility of host for effects of false and harmful data	Concentration of ownership in fewer hands
Access	Authority and ability to interpret data	Chokepoints and potential arbitrary host rules (and changes)	Exclusion of key stakeholders from usage
Societal Well Being	Movement toward "surveillance society"	Faster, more efficient distribution of data and content	Influence on number and type of jobs; the nature of work

It is relatively easy to map issues of internet of behaviors to the PAPA framework. Issues generated by the internet of behaviors follow and extend especially concerns for privacy, accuracy and access. These might be closely related to the "surveillance society" as described by Clarke (2019) where hyper-automation refers to the arrangement of work and, more broadly, to the accumulation and distribution of resources. It can be illustrated with the metaphor of adding or taking away chairs in the game 'musical chairs' or changing rules which favor one group (perhaps those with more STEM education) relative to others without the same capabilities. It is not clear the extent to which AI technologies and codes are required to enable the internet of behaviors. To the extent that such implementation is agnostic to particular coding approach, AI may have no strong relationship to ethics in this arena.

Relating distributed cloud and hyper-automation to the PAPA framework is more difficult, perhaps because they are of a more infrastructural technical nature, but not impossible. Distributed cloud is mostly about where data is stored, though it could have effects on users by enabling easier access and perhaps greater security from external threats by affording larger investment in preventative tactics. If having most relevant data nearby and access to the full range of data from across the entire "cloud" creates some new affordances, these might generate new ethical issues. If integration across separate clouds (e.g., data on Amazon is not accessible from Google, or vice versa), then perhaps issues involving the selection of host and either the forcing of ecosystem choice or expenses for operating on multiple platforms might actually constrain some new innovation while presenting their own difficult business choices. Issues of hyper-automation would concentrate on the basis for ownership of systems and access across stakeholders to determining its use.

This set of ethical issues pertains less to individuals (except perhaps in the numbers affected) and more in structural shifts in the community. For lack of a better term, we might label the category of these issues; societal well-being. In our view this term pertains to the changing environment within which individuals might operate. It can be visualized as problems that may arise when each component is optimized (or at least operating in a satisfactory way) and approved but where their accumulation changes the milieu in which we operate. For example, we may value surveillance of public spaces to reduce crime but if the surveillance becomes too pervasive, social life may become overly artificial and fail to accommodate its users.

5 Conclusion

> *Our moral imperative is clear. We must insure that information technology, and the information it handles, are used to enhance the dignity of mankind. To achieve these goals, we must formulate a new social contract, one that insures everyone the right to fulfill his or her own human potential (*Mason, 1986, *p. 11).*

I'm afraid that like many discussions of AI and ethics, we raise more questions than we answer. That said, we think this brief essay suggests that the PAPA framework holds up reasonably well as a basis for analysis of AI ethical issues. It serves as a way to sort various possible negative effects of new AI generated affordances; it serves as a way to anticipate some emergent ethical issues as new technologies emerge. That said, it has some limitations. It focuses much more strongly on effects on individuals. In considering particular emergent technologies, we surface one category of ethical concern, social wellbeing, that highlights a different set of ethical issues, or suggests another way to look at them.

Overall, we believe that the ethical issues faced by the emergence of AI are largely extensions of those generated by the continued growth of the technical capacities of information systems and, as a result, the growing storehouse of affordances. That said, the main effect of AI is to accelerate capacities and affordances such that entire families of issues move from hypothetical possibility to actualization.

In some quarters there is much faith that the solution to technical problems is more technology. Arthur (2009) seems to suggest this in documenting a view of the history of technology pointing out that many characteristics of sophisticated technology are the solutions to problems created by prior versions. To the extent that machine learning can reinforce underlying social discrimination, an algorithm to search for and remediate this would exemplify a technology solution to a technology created problem. But there is also pushback on this idea as exemplified by Kolbert (2021) describing the great environmental problems generated by engineering solutions to earlier problems. Algorithms that catch statistical discrimination may relieve the problem for individuals but may leave the underlying disadvantages causing the social issues, like discriminatory housing opportunities to remain unaddressed.

At the end of the day, we should be grateful to Mason (1986) for creating a useful framework, but not be satisfied with only categorizing issues. Now, more than 30 years following the presentation of this framework, it is difficult to say we've made positive progress in balancing competing values relative to the PAPA issues or developed ways to prevent or remediate harm when it occurs. On a personal note, having lived through a good portion of the information age since first diffusion of mainframe computers to the present (May 2021), it seems we are pretty good at technical solutions to technically created problems, we are good at adjusting to incremental changed expectations relative to privacy and evolving social norms, and at waiting out problems which eventually resolve themselves (although those harmed by them may not see it this way). On the other hand, we can use progress on methodically surfacing ethical issues emergent with new affordances, ways to quickly recognize and remediate harm done, and techniques for addressing varied stakeholder positions, overall uncertainty, and differences in values and moral opinions.

References

Aggarwal, N.: Introduction to the special issue on intercultural digital ethics. Philos. Technol. **33**(4), 547–550 (2020)

Arthur, W.B.: The nature of technology: What it is and how it evolves. Free Press, New York (2009)

Bailey, K.D.: Typologies and Taxonomies: An Introduction to Classification Techniques, vol. 102. Sage, Thousand Oaks (1994)

Benbya, H., Pachidi, S., Jarvenpaa, S.: Special issue editorial artificial intelligence in organizations implications for information systems research. J. Assoc. Inf. Syst. **22**(2), 281–303 (2021). https://doi.org/10.17705/1jais.00662

Clarke, R.: Risks inherent in the digital surveillance economy: a research agenda. J. Inf. Technol. **34**(1), 59–80 (2019). https://doi.org/10.1177/0268396218815559

Dignum, V.: Ethics in artificial intelligence: introduction to the special issue. Ethics Inf. Technol. **20**(1), 1–3 (2018). https://doi.org/10.1007/s10676-018-9450-z

Dreyfus, H.: What Computers Still Can't Do: A Critique of Artificial Reason. MIT Press, Cambridge (1992)

Hofstede, G.: Cultures and Organizations: Software of the Mind. McGraw-Hill, London (1991)

Kolbert, E.: Under a White Sky: The Nature of the Future. Crown, New York (2021)

Mason, R.O.: Four ethical issues of the information age. MIS Q. **10**(1), 5–12 (1986). https://doi.org/10.2307/248873

Mikalef, P., Gupta, M.: Artificial intelligence capability: Conceptualization, measurement calibration, and empirical study on its impact on organizational creativity and firm performance. Inf. Manage. **58**(3), 103434 (2021)

O'Neil, C.: Weapons of Math Destruction. Crown Publishing Group a Division of Penguin Random House, New York (2016)

Panetta, K.: Gartner Top Strategic Technology Trends for 2021. https://www.gartner.com/smarterwithgartner/gartner-top-strategic-technology-trends-for-2021/. Accessed 21 Apr 2021

Lionel, P., Jr., Robert, G.B., Melville, N., Stafford, T.: Introduction to the special issue on AI fairness, trust, and ethics. AIS Trans. Human-Comput. Interact. **12**(4), 172–178 (2020). https://doi.org/10.17705/1thci.00134

Rorty, R.: Philosophy and the Mirror of Nature. First Princeton Classics Edition. Princeton University Press, Princeton (2018)

Siau, K., Wang, W.: Artificial intelligence (AI) ethics: ethics of AI and ethical AI. J. Database Manage. **31**(2), 74–87 (2020)

Susskind, J.: Future Politics. Oxford University Press, Oxford, United Kingdom (2018)

Willcocks, L.: Robo-apocalypse cancelled? Reframing the automation and future of work debate. J. Inf. Technol. **35**(4), 286–302 (2020). https://doi.org/10.1177/0268396220925830

Winfield, A., Michael, K., Pitt, J., Evers, V.: Machine ethics: the design and governance of ethical AI and autonomous systems Spec. Issue Proc. IEEE. **107**(3), 509–517 (2019)

Governing Artificial Intelligence and Algorithmic Decision Making: Human Rights and Beyond

Vasiliki Koniakou[1,2(✉)]

[1] University of Turku, Faculty of Law, Caloniankuja 3, 20014 Turku, Finland
vaskon@utu.fi, koniakou@eltrun.gr

[2] ELTRUN Research Center and ISTLab, Department of Management Science and Technology, Athens University of Economics and Business, Evelpidon 47A, 11362 Athens, Greece

Abstract. In the context of Artificial Intelligence Ethics, human rights have been commonly invoked as a promising basis for an ethical framework. They have been also promoted as guidelines for Artificial Intelligence and Automatic Decision-making governance, or as engineering principles that may be turned into design requirements. Since literature so far engages only partially with the relevance and suitability of the extension of human rights in the realm of proprietary algorithms and privately owned Artificial Intelligence systems, this paper offers the necessary background and justification, building upon international human rights law theory and the concept of radiance of human rights. It aims to contribute to the scholarship promoting the human rights not only as ethical values but also as governance principles for Artificial Intelligence and algorithms. It also stresses the significance of concretizing and implementing the values of transparency, accountability, and explicability. Moreover, it suggests that for the ethically sound and societally beneficial employment of Artificial Intelligence and algorithms, useful insights may be derived from the field of technology governance. Stemming from that, it emphasizes the necessity to embrace the role of designers, and the need of conscious democratic control.

Keywords: Algorithms · Algorithmic decision-making (ADM) · Artificial intelligence (AI) · Human rights · AI ethics · AI governance · Science and technology studies (STS) · Technology theory

1 Introduction

The last two decades we have witnessed impressive advances in Artificial Intelligence (AI) and algorithmic decision-making (ADM). AIs and various forms of ADM are increasingly employed, permeating several aspects of contemporary society [1]. Enabling data-driven, automatic decision-making, they have rapidly become integral for numerous sectors and industries, ranging from healthcare, taxation and policy-making to pricing, products, processes, and services innovation [2, 3]. Additionally, bearing the

Published by Springer Nature Switzerland AG 2021
D. Dennehy et al. (Eds.): I3E 2021, LNCS 12896, pp. 173–184, 2021.
https://doi.org/10.1007/978-3-030-85447-8_16

promise of effective and efficient decision-making, they are considered as providing new opportunities for people, and the society at large, to improve and augment their capabilities and wellbeing [4, 5]. They are also expected to contribute to global productivity [6, 7], the achievement of sustainable development goals [7, 8], and broader environmental objectives [9, 10].

However, instances of discrimination and bias [11–13], disinformation and opinion manipulation [14, Ch. 4], [15], private censorship [16, 17] pervasive monitoring or surveillance [18–20], as well as adverse job market effects [6, 21] have raised serious concerns, attracting attention to the negative implications of automated 'intelligent' processes. Moreover, as ADM and AIs are increasingly implemented to inform critical decisions in the legal system, or to define individuals' eligibility or entitlement to critical opportunities and/or benefits, it is apparent that they relate and may also interfere with human rights [2, 22–25]. Hence, whereas the significance and impactful role of algorithms and AIs is not in question, whether and to what extent their impact will be positive or negative is hotly contested. [4] Furthermore, as reliance on AIs and ADMs deepens, the ethical questions and concerns amplify. Numerous researchers have engaged with the ethical aspects of AIs and algorithms, seeking to offer insights and create a road map towards their socially beneficial and ethically sound employment [3, 26–30].

AI Ethics is a broad interdisciplinary field of research, reflecting a wide range of value-based and societal concerns related to AI applications and the extensive employment of algorithms.[22, p. 78]. In this discourse, human rights have been invoked from various aspects. They have been proposed by scholars, policy-makers and civil society organizations as offering a promising set of ethical standards for AIs [2, 22, Ch. 4]. Researchers have also suggested ways of translating human rights into design requirements through various methodologies[3]. Additionally, they have been suggested as governance principles for AIs, to *"underlie, guide and fortify"* an AIs governance model [31]. The distinction between human rights as ethical standards, and human rights as governance principles and legal requirements is a meaningful one, particularly regarding the binding effects of legal requirements and the actual reach human rights may have in each case. It is also particularly relevant as a significant portion of algorithms and AIs are proprietary, privately designed, owned, and operated, whereas human rights as legal obligations are in principle vertical in nature [32].

So far, the literature has not addressed the question whether human rights are more relevant and appropriate as ethical standards, as formal obligations and governance principles for AIs and ADM, or both. Additionally, it has only partially engaged with the suitability of extending the application of human rights to the private sphere. The argumentation is mostly premised on their relevance for AIs and ADMs as ethical principles, and the effects AIs and algorithms may have on human rights [22, 31]. Moreover, the discussion regarding the steering of new and disruptive technologies towards ethical and societally beneficial ends is hardly new nor unique to AIs and ADM. On the contrary, it is part of a broader discourse on the relationship between technology and society, centered around human-centric design and the necessity to humanize technology governance and to allow the development, employment and governance of technologies in a socially beneficial way [33–35]. In that context, human rights are an essential part of a broader strategy towards technology governance that involves additional elements, values, and principles.

Stemming from these observations, this article wishes to offer additional argumentation on the relevance and suitability of human rights as governance principles for AIs and ADM based on international human rights theory. It argues that human rights, apart from ethical standards, ought to be applied as guiding governance principles, and their respect in terms of AIs and algorithms should be legally required. Furthermore, it stresses the significance of concretizing and implementing the values of transparency, accountability, and explicability and argues for the need to examine AI governance within the broader context of technology governance, under the light of Technology Theory and Science and Technology Studies (STS). More specifically, it emphasizes the necessity to embrace the decisive and ethically important role of designers and invest in ethics education, as well as the need of conscious democratic governance of AIs.

2 Human Rights, AIs and ADM

2.1 Human Rights as Guidelines for AI Ethics

Human rights constitute a rare set of values recognized internationally by the majority of societies [36, pp. 53, 54, 37]. Even though they are not uncontroversial [38], nor universally applied [39], they represent a sum of principles and norms that are widely shared and institutionalized globally. Serving as the basic moral entitlements of every human being, they are deeply rooted in contemporary politics and law, recognized in political practice and legal institutions globally [40, pp. 2–3]. Hence, human rights, both in their strictly legal sense, and as norms encapsulating and reflecting moral and social values, are considerably comprehensive and widespread. Furthermore, the international human rights system includes a well-established institutional framework comprised by dedicated monitoring bodies and agencies, as well as conflict and tensions resolution mechanisms. It also involves a rich theoretical background and ample discursive tools aimed to protect and promote human rights, as well as monitor, and ensure compliance with human rights principles globally.

Contrary to human rights, currently in AI Ethics there is no commonly agreed upon set of ethical standards that may serve as governance principles [22, p. 80], [41]. The industry-driven self-governance model is largely premised on a variety of voluntarily adopted codes and self-commitments. Such codes are usually rather abstract and largely vague, while they often lack the necessary mechanisms and frameworks to ensure the enforcement of the norms and handle disputes, conflict and tensions [42]. Thus, the lack of binding effects, and their questionable enforceability combined with the absence of conflict resolution mechanisms hamper their effectiveness and normative function. Additionally, such self-commitments may be in fact proclamatory, invoked for 'ethics washing'[22, p. 84], [43, 44] or simply to avoid direct regulatory interference, in the form of binding legislation [42, 45]. Therefore, considering the ineffectiveness of self-commitments, literature suggests that human rights offer a substantially better alternative, promoting human rights as a more rich and elaborated set of principles that can serve as ethical standards for AIs and ADM.

2.2 Human Rights as Principles for AI and ADM Governance and the Extension of Human Rights to the Private Realm

Going a step further, some scholars promote human rights not merely as ethical guidelines, but as governance principles, suggesting a governance approach anchored in human rights [22, p. 85]. Essentially, they argue that instead of simply internalizing human rights in AI Ethics, human rights-premised obligations should be turned into concrete legal requirements in the field of AIs and ADM, and human rights should inform and shape AI and ADM governance [22, Ch. 4]. From a similar point of view, the High-Level Expert Group on Artificial Intelligence (AI HLEG) that the EU Commission tasked to offer input for the development and deployment of AI, stressed that *"respect for fundamental rights, [...], provides the most promising foundations for identifying abstract ethical principles and values"* [46]. In its recommendations, human rights are identified as the foundational principles for a normative framework that may safeguard the development and deployment of AIs in a societally beneficial way. This suggestion progressively gains momentum in literature and policy discourse for various reasons, mainly related to the merits of the international human rights system and its potentials to prevent socially harmful uses of technology.

The rights enshrined in the Universal Declaration of Human Rights (UDHR), the Charter of Fundamental Rights of the European Union (EU Charter), as well as in the European Convention on Human Rights (ECHR) are arguably the most broadly embraced set of values and ethical principles, closely related to rule of law and the democratic polity. Hence, human rights, both in their strictly legal sense, and as norms encapsulating and reflecting moral and social values, are considerably comprehensive and widespread. Instead of fragmentary, abstract, or conflicting principles, premised on various views or aspirations, human rights can serve as common framework to address the majority of not only ethical but also normative concerns related to AIs and algorithmic decision-making. Simultaneously, the international human rights law system can provide guidance also in terms of the procedural aspects, offering a solid and tested tension and dispute resolution mechanisms and the necessary theoretical and discursive tools [22, Ch. 4], [31].

Finally as AIs, ADM and algorithms increasingly define opportunities and risks [47], having an often mediating role regarding human rights, the international human rights law system is not only suitable but also highly relevant. As AI applications become ubiquitous and pervasive, routinely relied upon to carry a wide range of tasks, they increasingly affect a wide variety of human rights, from freedom of expression and privacy to access to health care. From this angle, the extension of human rights to the private realm, in the form of concrete principles and specific obligations, and their integration to AI and ADM governance mechanisms is critical *"to maintain the character of our political communities as constitutional democratic orders."* [22, p. 81] Thus, human right should serve both as ethical guidelines, and as governance principles, while they should be extended to regulate the development and deployment of AIs and ADM, informing and shaping their processes and procedures also from the design and technology-in-the-making point of view [3]. Nevertheless, a significant portion of algorithms and AIs are privately designed, owned, and operated, while human rights are in principle vertical in nature, [32] which makes their extension to the private sphere far from self-evident or uncontroversial.

2.3 The Challenge of Applying Vertical Rights in the Private Realm

The turn to human rights as a source of governance principles, and the necessity of extending human rights obligations to the private realm to achieve socially important ends are not new within the technology governance discourse [37, 48–50]. However, according to international human rights law it is the states and not private entities that are bound by them [40]. This means that while the application of human rights as ethical guidelines is largely unproblematic, their adoption as governance principles, as well as the extension of human rights-premised obligations to private actors, such as the owners and operators of AI systems and proprietary algorithms, is relatively challenging. More specifically, the suitability and appropriateness of the extension of human rights-related obligations to the private realm is a hotly contested topic. Practically, the scope and application of international human rights law in the private sphere constitutes one of the most topical issues in constitutional law and human rights discourse [51].

The horizontal application of human rights, namely the extension of human rights to relationships otherwise regulated under private law, is challenging both theoretically and practically. Enforcing the same duties as public bodies to private actors could affect the very core of private law and liberal autonomy having adverse effects for both private law and international human rights law. Nevertheless, the vertical nature of human rights is premised upon the *"far greater imbalance of power between the state and individuals,"* [52, p. 16] which is rapidly challenged in the context of the modern society, in which individuals' rights commonly depend on private entities' actions and decisions, business and revenue models, corporate policies and rules. The indubitable power of private actors to negatively affect human rights brings to the forefront the change in the global balance of power between state and non-state actors. It also highlights the distance between the human rights doctrine and the reality of several almost omnipotent non-state actors in contemporary society. [53, p. 192] Thus, there is an ever-growing volume of literature exploring the ways to protect human rights from non-state actors, through the extension of human rights to private relationships, allowing them to have *horizontal effects*. [54] In that context, the question over the so-called horizontal application of human rights is of considerable practical importance and political relevance [52, p. 3].

2.4 Horizontality, The Radiance of Human Rights and the Human Rights Gap

As it is progressively becoming apparent that individuals' rights and freedoms as well as a wide array of societal and constitutional principles are threatened or restrained more frequently or severely in terms of private relationships [52, p. 20], the discussion regarding the positive duties of private actors comes to the forefront. The sharp distinction between the public and private spheres seems increasingly obsolete [55]. Moreover, as we are rapidly moving from technologies of pervasive effects towards technologies that are themselves pervasive, or as Susan Brenner puts it, from '*dumb*' to '*smart*' technologies [56], the majority of which are privately owned, designed and/or operated, the role and placement of human rights is a critical discussion.

Looking beyond the question of vertical nature or horizontal effects, stemming from the German constitutional tradition, and the concept of *"Drittwirkung"*[1] we may perceive human rights as "radiating" over the legal order, serving as a *"fundamental and objective system of values, which provides a blueprint for society as a whole."* [52, p. 129] From that angle, they have both an interpretative and guiding effect towards private law, without necessarily applying directly. They may inform the work of legislators and the decisions of judiciary, forming an indivisible, interdependent and interrelated whole which unites the legal order. This view, acknowledging that human rights and private law *"no longer exist in isolation from each other"*[57] is valuable for approaching and framing the role of human rights in the context of AIs and ADM governance. It allows them to be employed in AIs and ADM governance, enabling the extension of human rights-premised duties to private actors, as well as the employment of human rights and human rights due-diligence as a basis of assessment for private policies and governing structures in the field of AIs. Simultaneously, it does not absolve the states from their positive obligations to protect human rights, nor allows them to outsource this duty to private actors. Furthermore, the extension of human rights to the private sphere via the concept of radiance allows us to interpret the existing framework under the light of human rights, offering a much-needed time window to prepare the rules without the risk of a normative vacuum.

Finally, such an extension is also necessary to prevent a *"human rights gap"* in the governance of AIs and ADM. Given the increasingly relevant role of AIs and algorithms for human rights, keeping human rights strictly public (in the sense that only the states are obligation holders) and not extending them to the governance of AIs and ADM may result into a *"human rights gap."* This 'gap' is essentially the void created by the fact that although human rights are impactfully affected, mediated or even governed by non-state actors, these actors and technologies remain shielded from human rights obligations, leading to a vacuum of human rights protection. However, specific technologies, particularly those that penetrate the *"lifeworld"* producing consequential impacts that shape and affect individuals' options and choices, rights, and freedoms, should not be left outside the human rights discourse and system [53, p. 71].

3 Looking Beyond Human Rights

3.1 Transparency, Accountability, Explicability

As mentioned in the introduction, for the ethically sound and socially beneficial development and deployment of AIs and ADM, human rights ought to be part of a larger governance strategy. In this context, values and principles derived from the self-adopted ethical codes in private sector, along with insights from various Recommendations, Declarations and Ethical Principles suggested by several organizations, think tanks and institutions [42, 58–60], can also have a role. Particularly the commonly recurring values of "transparency", "accountability", and "intelligibility" or "explicability", shared among most of these recommendations [4, 42], should be concretized into rules and turned into specific and viable governance guidelines. Jointly, these three values are essential for the meaningful scrutiny, and integral for good governance in the field of technology.

[1] BVerfGE 7, 198 ff of 15 January 1958.

Thus, they are also particularly relevant for AIs and ADM governance, especially as they constitute new and powerful forms of smart agency.

Transparency about the input and outcomes of algorithmic decision-making criteria is crucial, given that algorithms, as forms of automatic decision-making, control or significantly influence key aspects of daily life, affecting eligibility to life-changing opportunities, defining access to goods and services [22, Ch. 4]. Simultaneously, they increasingly penetrate the judicial system and law enforcement [47, 61]. However, ADM is *"essentially concealed behind a veil of code"* [62] often protected by intellectual property rights (IPR). This means that although algorithms may reach decisions with major impact for individuals' lives, the way they reached upon these decisions and the data they acted upon is opaque to the affected individual. [44] In turn, the lack of transparency significantly obscures both explicability and accountability. AI systems and algorithms are largely presented as back boxes, too complex and difficult to be explained and/or understood. Yet the lack of explicability raises serious questions about due process, and the possibility of meaningful human control and scrutiny [63, 64]. Simultaneously, the question "who is responsible for the way it works?" is close to impossible to be answered if transparency is absent and no one can answer "how it works?" for reasons of allegedly complexity or IPR protection.

Nonetheless, if we are indeed entering an era of omnipresent smart agents, wherein algorithms largely determine and shape the exercise of power, affecting public policy, and human rights, we need to find meaningful ways to ensure transparency, accountability, and explicability, rejecting the black box approach and realigning private rights with public interest [62, 65]. Law and regulatory intervention have here a significant part to play. The EU has taken a number of regulatory initiatives towards this direction, most prominently through the General Data Protection Regulation (GDPR), that emphasizes the principles of transparency and accountability, while stresses the need of explainability in case of automated processes, such as automated profiling. Yet, this also entails finding new ways to balance private interests and IPRs with the requirements of transparency, accountability, and explicability, without risking the malicious exploitation of algorithmic transparency, or hampering innovation.

3.2 From AI and ADM Governance to Technology Governance

These challenges are not unique for AIs and ADM governance [13]. Some of the key questions for the future of smart agents governance are inherent in the field of technology governance and have been thoroughly discussed in terms of Technology Theory [66, 67] and STS [68]. From that angle, it may be insightful to examine AIs and ADM governance under the light of Technology Theory and STS, building upon the rich literature of technology governance. In that context, a necessary first step towards establishing a governance model that will contribute to the ethically sound and socially beneficial employment of AIs and ADM would be demystifying them. Regardless of their opacity and the "veil of mystery" that covers their processes, they are both human constructs, in the sense that they are designed, programmed, applied by human beings. Hence, those creating them have both considerable control over how they function [2], and the responsibility to ensure that they are employed within a sound ethical framework. However, responsibility here is not to be perceived narrowly, in terms of liability or accountability in the legal sense, but as the moral and social virtue of steering intellectual creations towards the public good.

Opening the back box and perceiving AIs and algorithms as malleable, human creations, sheds light on the dilemmas, social processes, institutions and arrangements that affect the development of technology [69, p. 568]. From that angle, the design of technologies and technological artifacts involves more than technical skills or creative insight, as the final outcome reflects also the character, views, values, and ethics of the designers and developers [70, 71]. Acknowledging that engineering practice involves choice, value struggles, and value-informed decisions, highlights the fact that algorithms and AI design choices are not neutral [72]. Embracing the key role of the designers [69, p. 573], and the ethically important aspects of engineering, brings to the forefront the necessity to include ethics modules and courses in Higher Education Institutions, at least in fields of engineers and computer science [73, 74]. Thus, improving access to ethics modules and stand-alone courses related to ethical considerations in design, and responsible engineering, [58, 75, 76] which still remain relatively low [41], may be a vital to steer AIs and ADM towards socially beneficial and ethically sound ends.

Similarly, it is equally important to place AI governance withing a framework of democratic scrutiny, and conscious democratic control, allowing policy and decision-making about such impactful and consequential technologies to reflect and adequately represent the views, considerations, values, fears, hopes and expectations of the citizens. Whereas in modern constitutional democracies such a request sounds self-evident or presumed already satisfied, in fact technology governance is commonly a non-democratic procedure [66, 77]. More specifically, as a reductionist way of thinking about the relationship between technology and society, technological determinism remains deeply rooted in our casual way of thinking about technologies [78]. As such, it has informed several socio-economic configurations [79], promoting non-democratic, technocratic arrangements, and preventing the conscious democratic control of technologies [77], or allowing for non-democratic practices to be accepted as inevitable [80].

From that aspect, identifying and rejecting technological determinism and its entailments from AIs and ADM governance may constitute a necessary and relatively demanding step to ensure that their governance will not be an exception of democratic control. Considering the expanding role of AIs and ADM in contemporary society, as well as their far-ranging implications for individuals and human rights, it is of at most importance to premise their governance upon a democratic framework. To put it differently, although AIs may be privately owned, while algorithms are in their majority proprietary, their governance, how they are regulated and the larger policy framework about them should be subject to democratic steering. In turn, this is closely related with ensuring transparency, accountability, and explicability, [81, 82] as well as with rejecting technological determinism that leads to the decoupling of technology governance and democratic decision-making.

4 Concluding Thoughts

Algorithms and AI are not simply *"another utility that needs to be regulated once it is mature."* [4] They comprise a powerful and disruptive new form of smart agency, that bears significant promises as well as risks. This paper argued that to steer this force towards the benefit of the society it is necessary to introduce human rights not only as guidelines for AI Ethics, but also as governance principles for AIs and ADM. Whereas the literature has already argued for the need to extend human rights obligations to AI governance, it largely tends to avoid engaging with the question of horizontality. Yet, without clearly articulating the relevance and the suitability of human rights as governance principles for AI, the proposed models may seem ill-grounded from an international human rights law point of view. Building on this observation, the paper sought to offer background and justification regarding the relevance of human rights and the suitability of extending them into the private sphere building upon the theory of *Drittwirkung* and the concept of human rights' radiance. It also highlighted the risk of a *"human rights gab"* in case private actors are left to act outside the scope of human rights. Looking beyond human rights, it emphasized the need to concretize the values of transparency, accountability, and explicability and turn them to pillars of AI governance. Finally, it sought to bring to the forefront the valuable insights AI and ADM governance may derive from Technology Theory, technology governance and STS. Embracing the key role of engineers and developers it is critical to invest in their ethics education and take specific legislative and normative initiatives to address the black box approaches towards technology. Additionally, it is vital to ensure that governance of AIs will be a democratic procedure, rejecting technological determinism and exploring meaningful ways to align private interests with the public good.

References

1. Cath, C.: Governing artificial intelligence: Ethical, legal and technical opportunities and challenges. Philos. Trans. R. Soc. A. Math. Phys. Eng. Sci. **376**(2133), 20180080 (2018)
2. Gerards, J.: The fundamental rights challenges of algorithms. Netherlands Q. Human Rights **37**(3), 205–209 (2019)
3. Aizenberg, E., van den Hoven, J.: Designing for human rights in AI. Big Data Soc. **7**(2), 205395172094956 (2020)
4. Floridi, L., et al.: AI4People-an ethical framework for a good AI society: opportunities risks principles, and recommendations. Minds Mach. **28**, 689–707 (2018)
5. Tegmark, M.: Life 3.0: Being Human in the Age of Artificial Intelligence. Knopf, New York (2017)
6. Agrawal, A., Gans, J., Goldfarb, A.: Artificial Intelligence, Automation, and Work (2019)
7. Pedemonte, V.: AI for Sustainability: An overview of AI and the SDGs to contribute to the European policy-making (2020)
8. Vinuesa, R., et al.: The role of artificial intelligence in achieving the Sustainable Development Goals. Nat. Commun. Nat. Res. **11**(1), 1–10 (2020)
9. Elshafei, G., Negm, A.: AI technologies in green architecture field: statistical comparative analysis. Proc. Eng. **181**, 480–488 (2017)
10. Mishra, K.S., Polkowski, Z., Borah, S., Dash, R.: AI in Manufacturing and Green Technology: Methods and Applications. Routledge, Milton Park (2021)
11. Murray, S., Wachter, R., Blog, R.C.-H.A.,: Discrimination by artificial intelligence in a commercial electronic health record—a case study. Healthaffairs.Org. (2020). Doi:https://doi.org/10.1377/hblog20200128.626576/. Accessed 07 Apr 2021
12. Gorwa, R., Binns, R., Katzenbach, C.: Algorithmic content moderation: technical and political challenges in the automation of platform governance. Big Data and Society (2020)

13. Borgesius, F.Z.: Discrimination, artificial intelligence, and algorithmic decision-making (2018)
14. Allen, J.R., Massolo, G.: AI in the Age of Cyber-Disorder | ISPI (2020)
15. Cadwalladr, C.: Fresh Cambridge analytica leaks 'shows global manipulation is out of control. The Guardian (2020). https://www.theguardian.com/uk-news/2020/jan/04/cambridge-analytica-data-leak-global-election-manipulation?CMP=Share_AndroidApp_Slack. Accessed 07 Apr 2021
16. Gillespie, T.: The Relevance of Algorithms. In: Media Technologies (2014)
17. Gillespie, T.: Custodians of the internet: Platforms, content moderation, and the hidden decisions that shape social media (2018)
18. Hildebrandt, M., Koops, B.-J.: The Challenges of ambient law and legal protection in the profiling era. Mod. Law Rev. **73**(3), 428–460 (2010)
19. Feldstein, S.: The Global Expansion of AI Surveillance (2019)
20. Kambatla, K., Kollias, G., Kumar, V., Grama, A.: Trends in big data analytics. J. Parallel Distrib. Comput. **74**(7), 2561–2573 (2014)
21. Vochozka, M., Kliestik, T., Kliestikova, J., Sion, G.: Participating in a highly automated society: How artificial intelligence disrupts the job market. Econ. Manage. Finan. Mark. **13**(4), 57–62 (2018)
22. Dubber, M.D., Pasquale, F., Das, S.: Oxford Handbook of Ethics of AI. Oxford University Press, Oxford (2020)
23. Raso, F., Hilligoss, H., Krishnamurthy, V., Bavitz, C., Kim, L.Y.: Artificial intelligence & human rights: opportunities & risks. SSRN Electron. J. (2018)
24. Buchholtz, G.: Artificial intelligence and legal tech: challenges to the rule of law. In: Wischmeyer, T., Rademacher, T. (eds.) Regulating Artificial Intelligence, pp. 175–198. Springer, Cham (2020)
25. MSI-NET: Algorithms and Human Rights : Study on the Human Rights Dimensions of Automated Data Processing Techniques (in particular Algorthims) and Possible Regulatory Implications. Council of Europe Study DGI (2017). https://edoc.coe.int/en/internet/7589-algorithms-and-human-rights-study-on-the-human-rights-dimensions-of-automated-data-processing-techniques-and-possible-regulatory-implications.html. Accessed 08 Apr 2021
26. Van Wynsberghe, A.: A method for integrating ethics into the design of robots. Industrial Robot (2013)
27. Umbrello, S.: Atomically precise manufacturing and responsible innovation: a value sensitive design approach to explorative nanophilosophy. Int. J. Techn. **10**(2), 1–21 (2019)
28. Bryson, J., Winfield, A.: Standardizing ethical design for artificial intelligence and autonomous systems. Computer **50**(5), 116–119 (2017)
29. Tubella, A.A., Theodorou, A., Dignum, V., Dignum, F.: Governance by glass-box: implementing transparent moral bounds for AI behavior. IJCAI Int. Joint Conf. Artif. Intell. **2019**(August), 5787–5793 (2019)
30. Taddeo, M., Floridi, L.: How AI can be a force for good. Science **361**(6404), 751–752 (2018)
31. Smuha, N.A.: Beyond a human rights-based approach to AI governance: promise, pitfalls, plea. Philos. Technol. (2020)
32. Lane, L.: The horizontal effect of international human rights law in practice. Eur. J. Compar. Law Govern. **5**(1), 5–88 (2018). https://doi.org/10.1163/22134514-00501001
33. Bucchi, M.: Beyond Technocracy: Science, Politics and Citizens. Springer New York, New York, NY (2009). https://doi.org/10.1007/978-0-387-89522-2
34. Strobel, J., Tillberg-Webb, H.: Applying a critical and humanizing framework of instructional technologies to educational practice. In: Moller, L., Huett, J.B., Harvey, D.M. (eds.) Learning and Instructional Technologies for the 21st Century, pp. 1–19. Springer US, Boston, MA (2009). https://doi.org/10.1007/978-0-387-09667-4_5

35. Benedek, W., Kettemann, M.C., Senges, M.: The humanization of internet governance: a roadmap towards a comprehensive global (human) rights architecture for the internet. SSRN Electron. J. (2017)
36. Walkila, S.: Horizontal Effect of Fundamental Rights in EU Law. Europa Law Publishing, Zutphen (2017)
37. Brown, I., Clark, D.D., Trossen, D.: Should specific values be embedded in the Internet architecture. In: Proceedings of the Re-Architecting the Internet (ReArch) Workshop, Held in Conjunction with CoNEXT 2010 (2010)
38. Hopgood, S.: The Endtimes of Human Rights. Cornell University Press, Ithaca (2018)
39. Tharoor, S.: Are human rights universal? World Policy J. **16**(4), 1–6 (2000)
40. Etinson, A.: Human Rights. Oxford University Press, Oxford (2018)
41. Zhang, D., et al.: Artificial Intelligence Index Report 2021 (2021)
42. Hagendorff, T.: The ethics of AI ethics: an evaluation of guidelines. Mind. Mach. **30**(1), 99–120 (2020). https://doi.org/10.1007/s11023-020-09517-8
43. Bietti, E.: From Ethics Washing to Ethics Bashing: A View on Tech Ethics from Within Moral Philosophy, 01 December 2019
44. Muller, V.C.: Ethics of Artificial Intelligence and Robotics (Stanford Encyclopedia of Philosophy). Stanford Encyclopedia of Philosophy (2020). https://plato.stanford.edu/entries/ethics-ai/. Accessed 08 Apr 2021
45. Wagner, B.: Ethics As an Escape From Regulation (2019)
46. Pekka, M. A.-P., Bauer, W., Bergmann, U.B.: Ethics guidelines for trustworthy AI - Publications Office of the EU (2018). https://op.europa.eu/en/publication-detail/-/publication/d3988569-0434-11ea-8c1f-01aa75ed71a1. Accessed 09 Apr 2021
47. Pasquale, F.: The Black Box Society: The Secret Algorithms That Control Money and Information. Harvard University Press, Cambridge (2015). https://doi.org/10.4159/harvard.9780674736061
48. Cath, C., Floridi, L.: The design of the internet's architecture by the internet engineering Task Force (IETF) and human rights. Sci. Eng. Ethics **23**(2), 449–468 (2016). https://doi.org/10.1007/s11948-016-9793-y
49. Zalnieriute, M., Milan, S.: Internet architecture and human rights: beyond the human rights gap. Policy Internet **11**(1), 6–15 (2019)
50. Mueller, M.L., Badiei, F.: Requiem for a dream: on advancing human rights via internet architecture. Policy. Internet. **11**, 61–83 (2019)
51. Hall, O.B.: Private authority: non-state actors and global governance. Harv. Int. Rev. **27**(2), 66–70 (2005)
52. Oliver, D., Fedtke, J.: Human Rights and the Private Sphere. UCL Human Rights Review (2008)
53. Mylly, T.: Intellectual Property and European Economic Constitutional Law : The Trouble with Private Informational Power. Edward Elgar Publishing, Cheltenham (2009)
54. Knox, J.H.: Horizontal human rights law. Am. J. Int. Law **102**(1), 1–47 (2008)
55. Lane, L.: The horizontal effect of international human rights law in practice: a comparative analysis of the general comments and jurisprudence of selected United Nations human rights treaty monitoring bodies. Eur. J. Compar. Law Govern. **5**(1), 5–88 (2018)
56. Brenner, S.: Law in an Era of Smart Technology. Oxford University Press, Oxford, England (2007). https://doi.org/10.1093/acprof:oso/9780195333480.001.0001
57. Cherednychenko, O.O.: Fundamental rights and private law: a relationship of subordination or complementarity? Utrecht Law Rev. **3**(2), 1–25 (2007)
58. The IEEE Global Initiative: Ethically Aligned Design: A Vision for Prioritizing Human Wellbeing with Autonomous and Intelligent Systems, Version 2 (2017)

59. de Montréal, U.: The Montreal Declaration for the Responsible Development of Artificial Intelligence (2020). https://www.montrealdeclaration-responsibleai.com/. Accessed 09 Apr 2021
60. OV: AI Principles - Future of Life Institute. Future of Life Institute (2017). https://futureoflife.org/ai-principles/?submitted=1#confirmation. Accessed 09 Apr 2021
61. Kitchin, R.: Thinking critically about and researching algorithms. Inf. Commun. Soc. **20**, 14–29 (2016)
62. Perel, M., Elkin-Koren, N.: Black box tinkering: beyond transparency in algorithmic enforcement. SSRN Electron. J. **181**, 48 (2016). https://doi.org/10.2139/ssrn.2741513
63. Whittaker, M., et al.: AI Now Report 2018 (2018)
64. Robbins, S.: A misdirected principle with a catch: explicability for AI. Mind. Mach. **29**(4), 495–514 (2019). https://doi.org/10.1007/s11023-019-09509-3
65. Steen, M.: Upon opening the black box and finding it full: exploring the ethics in design practices. Sci. Technol. Human Values **40**, 1–22 (2015)
66. Feenberg, A.: The technocracy thesis revisited: On the critique of power. Inquiry (United Kingdom) **37**(1), 85–102 (1994)
67. Winner, L.: Autonomous Technology: Technics-Out-Of-Control As A Theme In Political Thought. MIT Press, Cambridge (1977)
68. Hess, D.J.: Engaging science, technology, and society. Engag. Sci. Technol. Soc. **1**, 121–125 (2015)
69. Jameson, W.M., Johnson, D.G.: STS and ethics: implications for engineering ethics. In: The Handbook of Science and Technology Studies, MIT Press (2008)
70. Whitbeck, C.: Ethics as design: doing justice to moral problems. Hastings Cent. Rep. **26**(3), 9 (1996)
71. Whitbeck, C.: Ethics as design: doing justice to moral problems. In: Whitbeck, C. (ed.) Ethics in Engineering Practice and Research, pp. 135–154. Cambridge University Press, Cambridge (2011). https://doi.org/10.1017/CBO9780511976339.007
72. Kranzberg, M.: Technology and history: 'Kranzberg's laws.' Technol. Cult. **27**(3), 544 (1986)
73. Pritchard, M.S.: Responsible engineering: the importance of character and imagination. Sci. Eng. Ethics **7**(3), 391–402 (2001)
74. Pesch, U.: Engineers and active responsibility. Sci. Eng. Ethics **21**(4), 925–939 (2014). https://doi.org/10.1007/s11948-014-9571-7
75. Krippendorff, K., Butter, R.: Semantics: meanings and contexts of artifacts. In: Product Experience (2008)
76. Lynch, W.T., Kline, R.: Engineering practice and engineering ethics. Sci. Technol. Human. Values. **25**, 195–225 (2000)
77. Dotson, T.: Technological determinism and permissionless innovation as technocratic governing mentalities: psychocultural barriers to the democratization of technology. Engag. Sci. Technol. Soc. **1**, 98–120 (2015)
78. Wyatt, S.: Technological determinism is dead: long live technological determinism. In: Hackett, E.J. (ed.) The Handbook of Science and Technology Studies, pp. 165–180. The MIT Press, Cambridge (2008)
79. Jasanoff, S., Markle, G., Peterson, J., Pinch, T.: Handbook of Science and Technology Studies. SAGE Publications, Inc., Thousand Oaks (1995). https://doi.org/10.4135/9781412990127
80. Laird, F.N., Science, S., Values, H., Summer, N.: Participatory analysis, democracy, and technological decision making stable. Particip. Anal. Democr. Technol. Decis. Making. **18**(3), 341–361 (2016)
81. Eriksen, E.O.: Governance between expertise and democracy: the case of European security. J. Eur. Publ. Policy **18**(8), 1169–1189 (2011)
82. Williams, M.E.: Escaping the zero-sum scenario: democracy versus technocracy in Latin America. Polit. Sci. Q. **121**(1), 119–139 (2006). https://doi.org/10.1002/j.1538-165X.2006.tb00567.x

Analysing AI via Husserl and Kuhn How a Phenomenological Approach to Artificial Intelligence Imposes a Paradigm Shift

Daire Boyle(✉)

Department of Philosophy, Maynooth University, Maynooth, Co. Kildare, Ireland
daire.boyle@mu.ie

Abstract. In a world of rapid technological progress the question of artificial consciousness looms large. Whether machines could ever be considered conscious depends, firstly, on our understanding of consciousness. This paper seeks to characterise consciousness in Husserlian terms, before making the case that a Kuhnian paradigm shift in the worlds of philosophy of mind and artificial intelligence research is caused by such a framing. This view is supported by reference to Husserl's thesis of the Natural Standpoint as a guiding tool in recognising philosophically valid modes of inquiries, wherein foundational assumptions are precisely assessed and held in close focus at all times. In establishing this Husserlian paradigm shift we become better placed to truly understand consciousness, its modalities, and its potentiality for machines.

Keywords: Consciousness · Artificial intelligence · Phenomenology · Paradigm shifts · Machine learning opacity

1 Introduction

Thomas S. Kuhn's 1962 work *The Structure of Scientific Revolutions* presented an historiographic account of scientific progress as discrete, disjointed, and contested. In framing scientific progression as the result of incommensurable paradigm shifts Kuhn challenged the narrative of science as an inevitable march towards solving widely accepted goals, instead showing that overcoming crisis in science requires more than mere fine-tuning of previously useful models. In this paper I shall use Kuhn's paradigm shift scaffolding to make the case that the phenomenology of Edmund Husserl is impossible to ignore in the realm of research into both consciousness and artificial intelligence (AI). Adopting methodological considerations outlined by Husserl make for a more philosophically valid basis upon which truly insightful and novel achievements can be won in the search for understanding consciousness, as the rapid technological progress of the past half-century or more lead us to speculate about a future wildly different from the present. Indeed do we live in exciting times, and talk of a technological 'singularity' wherein the computational abilities of machines far outstrip man's own paints a picture of the future in which man's place in the *cosmos* is called into question. We must prepare for

Published by Springer Nature Switzerland AG 2021
D. Dennehy et al. (Eds.): I3E 2021, LNCS 12896, pp. 185–197, 2021.
https://doi.org/10.1007/978-3-030-85447-8_17

such potentialities immediately through rigorous analysis of the most intimate human faculty – consciousness. In order to do so, however, we must be absolutely certain that foundations of this edifice, our appraisal of consciousness, is incontrovertible. This will not be possible without grasping the opportunity offered by a Husserlian paradigm shift. The focus of the first half of the paper shall be that of philosophical definitions – situating the ideas of Kuhn and Husserl – so that the second half can assess historical and contemporary approaches to AI from the realm of computer science. Ultimately, the case shall be made that it is only through Husserlian analysis that we can truly understand our own consciousness and, thus, the potentiality for *artificial* consciousness. Any breakthroughs, therefore, on the cutting edge of AI research must pay heed to these philosophical principles.

This paper shall also make the case that understanding consciousness in Husserlian terms, in order to better diagnose potential breakthroughs in the engineering of AI, is relevant not just for the philosophy of science, or philosophy in general. As Burrell [2] notes, the trend in modern-day AI strategies is toward increasing opacity at the level of implementation, and recent meta-analyses from MIT [13] further underline this point. Regulatory bodies have begun to take note of the risks inherent in such approaches, with the European Commission recently [11] announcing that the drafting of legislation classifying and accordingly limiting certain AI technologies has begun. I argue, therefore, that such movements represent a paradigm shift for AI both in terms of how it is viewed as a technology by society at large, as well as on the level of computer science. The philosopher, and scientist researching AI methods, must recognise that such a *practical* paradigm shift is inevitable, and correspondingly update their worldview in order to offer meaningful analysis regarding the results of future AI breakthroughs. The opacity that defines contemporary approaches to AI coheres nicely with a Husserlian-diagnostic understanding of consciousness, as shall be argued in this paper, and so adopting such a standpoint establishes a common and suitably sophisticated framework whereby researchers can better appraise the cultural – as well as scientific – impact of their work in all facets of AI development; not just in those attempts to establish artificial consciousness.

2 A Sketch of Kuhn's Notion of Paradigm Shifts

Kuhn's 1962 text is remarkable for its diagnosis of the conditions for progress in scientific research. Competing historiographical understandings of science, most notably from Butterfield [3] and Popper [18] tended to view science as a discipline which inductively improved upon itself with each new theory and discovery. Arguably such a view bequeathed science with a sort of *telos*, a sense that while future developments might require the critical reassessment of previously axiomatic truths there was no danger that the scientific method itself – as best exemplified by Popper's falsification model – could ever be doubted. And while Kuhn does not explicitly claim that the scientific method itself is up for debate, he does make the case that scientific revolutions are theoretically interminable [16, pp. 92–110]. There is no overarching *telos*, as each scientific revolution importing a fresh paradigm represents a discrete change in scientific worldview. There is a sense in which Kuhn's theories operate as a dialectical model [6, p. 327] as, for him, scientific progress runs thus: normal science, crisis, revolution. Of key focus for us here is the definition of these terms and so we shall examine them now.

Normal science is defined as 'research firmly based upon one or more past scientific achievements, achievements that some particular scientific community acknowledges for a time as supplying the foundation for its further practice' [16, p. 10]. Kuhn characterises the scientist carrying out investigations in normal science as a puzzle-solver attempting to solve, say, a jigsaw puzzle [16, p. 36]. The boundaries within which that scientist operates are well-defined, and she seeks to 'add to the scope and precision with which [a] paradigm can be applied' [16, p. 36] through her investigative work. Thus, normal science is to the scientist what mapping a newly discovered landmass is to a cartographer; both may encounter novelties in the well-defined scope of their work, but such novelties never threaten to call the ontological status of the landmass – or scientific theory – into question. There is no compunction that such puzzles be ideologically important to the scientific theory as a whole, and they may indeed lack solutions, but what is important is that they seek to work within established bounds.

Crisis, then, comes about due to anomalies encountered during the course of normal scientific operations. To illustrate this Kuhn describes the progression from Ptolemaic to Copernican models of astronomy, similarly of the move from Aristotelian to Newtonian physics of motion due to well-established issues in Aristotle's work [16, pp. 68–9]. Such is the nature of Kuhn's work that there is nothing, thus far, about this assessment of scientific progress that seems to be out of place. Indeed, it is facile to note that the likes of Lavoisier, Newton, Maxwell, Einstein, and others brilliantly 'solved' or 'reframed' key anomalies in the accepted scientific theories of their times; proposing new systems of thought where such incoherence was not present. Let us consider the juncture at which we currently find ourselves vis-à-vis Kuhn's model: either we can rationalise successive scientific theories (such as the Copernican 'improvement' on Ptolemaic astronomy) as the gradual accretion of scientific data, a linear progression wherein science builds on previous results – removing some incompatible parts of old theories but, in the main, recognising their (albeit limited) enduring epistemological validity – or we take the view that these new scientific theories are wholesale incompatible with what has gone before. As Kuhn's word choice suggests, he opts for this latter horn – he is in the business of describing scientific *revolutions* as opposed to scientific *progress*.

To that end, let us investigate Kuhn's understanding of a scientific revolution. Once again it is illustrative to examine how Kuhn frames this: he states that when scientists are confronted by foundational anomalies they do not immediately recourse to 'renounc[ing] the paradigm that has led them into crisis' [16, p. 77]. Here Kuhn critiques Popper's doctrine of falsification by arguing that new paradigms replace older ones only when the new is fully ready to take the former's place. In Kuhn's words '[n]o process yet disclosed by the historical study of scientific development at all resembles the methodological stereotype of falsification by direct comparison with nature' [16, p. 77]. As a result, the rejection of one paradigm is never carried out in a vacuum: '[t]he decision to reject one paradigm is always simultaneously the decision to accept another' [16, p. 77]. Herein lies the thesis of incommensurability, as Kuhn describes the disconnect between advocates of competing paradigms as being akin to an individual's attitude pre- and post-*Gestalt* shift. We shall return to this notion of *Gestalt* later but for now Kuhn's summation is illuminating: '[l]ike the choice between political institutions, that between competing paradigms proves to be a choice between incompatible modes of community life' [16, p. 94]. The presence of incommensurability in Kuhn's structure speaks to the forces that influence scientific revolutions; it is not the case that there is such a thing as a 'correct' paradigm which is widely accepted to be the natural successor of the old paradigm. No, new paradigms are instead *usurpers* and their place within the historiography of science owe much to political and cultural machinations aside from their own scientific merit.

If paradigm shifts are incommensurable then how is it that consensus is ever reached to move from the old to the new? Kuhn stresses that science carried out during crisis is not marked by new counterfactuals that were not present pre-crisis. Indeed, how could this be the case given Kuhn's analysis of normal science as puzzle solving in service of fleshing out the results of a given paradigm: 'there is no such thing as research without counterinstances' [16, p. 79]. In elucidating this point Kuhn gives the example of geometric optics as a field which has been 'finished', to put it colloquially [16, p. 79]. Geometric optics are in no danger of being replaced by an updated paradigm which resolves tensions in this theoretical framework as all of the problems of that field are generally accepted as solved. Thus, geometric optics is employed as a tool in fields such as engineering in order to investigate and clarify issues in those paradigms. So, what then characterises revolution? In wrestling with this question Kuhn states that when 'an anomaly comes to seem more than just another puzzle of normal science, the transition to crisis and to extraordinary science has begun' [16, p. 82]. Furthermore, he foreshadows his later thesis of paradigmatic exemplars with his description of how '[m]ore and more attention is devoted to [the anomaly] by more and more of the field's most eminent men' [16, p. 82]. Here we arrive at the apex of the crisis, which ultimately will result in a paradigm shift. Nascent investigations into the nature of the anomaly will usually follow the accepted rules of the current paradigm, Kuhn argues, but soon these investigations call into question more and more foundational bricks in the paradigm's structure. A blurring occurs, and 'formerly standard solutions of solved problems are called in question' [16, p. 83].

3 Edmund Husserl's Natural Standpoint and Its Paradigmatic Implications for Consciousness

The goal of this paper's emphasis on Husserlian principles is not to support a case calling for the adoption of phenomenology as foundational philosophy. That particular argument is well-worn and bears no reintroduction here. Instead, we wish to highlight the singular usefulness of phenomenology *as a method* in investigating the realm of consciousness. Furthermore, this paper shall not make any metaphysical claims regarding the origins of consciousness nor shall we require a wholly Husserlian interpretation of the *substance* of consciousness – although such a view is ultimately endorsed by this author it is not the case that one must fully accept all of Husserl's conclusions in order to concur with the thrust of this paper. I simply entreaty that we consider what makes Husserl so effective and useful in the domain of consciousness. To do so let us examine the thesis of the Natural Standpoint which is so central to Husserl's philosophy. One of Husserl's key insights in *Ideas I* is his accurate diagnosis of our naïve and unexamined acceptance of the world in everyday life. In this 'Natural Standpoint' I am aware of the world, while things in the world are *'for me simply there'* [14, p. 51]. The Natural Standpoint is characterised by an acceptance that objects around me and in nature simply are as they seem, whether I am directly inspecting them or not, and this world 'contains everything', so to speak: 'this world is not there for me as a mere *world of facts and affairs*, but, with the same immediacy, as a *world of values*, a *world of goods*, a *practical world*' [14, p. 53]. While I may delve into other 'worlds'; such as the arithmetical when conducting arithmetical investigations, the natural world is '*constantly there for me*, so long as I live naturally and look in its direction' [14, p. 53]. While we are in the Natural Standpoint we never question the veracity or indubitability of the world; when we conduct scientific experiments in this standpoint we are investigating through this lens of 'assumption' – assuming that the world is simply *there*. Husserl does not mean to deride 'living' in the Natural Standpoint by calling attention to it, he simply wishes to challenge us to recognise the presuppositions required by the standpoint. Natural sciences must, inherently, operate within the Natural Standpoint – Husserl points out that the 'lore of experience' alone is not enough to provide answers about the intricacies of the world around us, requiring us to utilise natural scientific methods which unquestioningly adopt empirical principles in order to conduct investigations [14, p. 54]. The validity of the world cannot be called into question while that same world undergoes the process of being empirically understood.

The transcendental phenomenological project takes shape with Husserl's next idea – the *epoché*, or *bracketing*. The goal of bracketing is to rid one's mind of the preconceptions one might have of an object with which one is presented. The key point here is that, in bracketing, a thesis concerning the Being of an object (i.e. its existence) is challenged – for instance, we might bracket whether or not the table in front of us is 'actually there' – and that such a challenge does not constitute a *denial*. As Husserl states: '[i]t is likewise clear that the *attempt* to doubt any object of awareness in respect of its *being actually there necessarily conditions a certain suspension (Aufhebung) of the thesis* [...] It is not a transformation of the thesis into its antithesis' [14, p. 57]. All we do is *bracket* this thesis, suspending our valuing of an object we see before us. We now nearly have the crux of the phenomenological movement according to Husserl. If we can win this insight into the Natural Standpoint, and recognise the assumptions entailed in living within it, we can now move on to systematising this knowledge with Husserl's full phenomenological epoché (or, equivalently, reduction) which runs as follows:

> *We put out of action the general thesis which belongs to the essence of the natural standpoint* [...] I do *not* then *deny* this "world", as though I were a sophist, *I do not doubt that it is there* as though I were a sceptic; but I use the "phenomenological" έπ οχ ή, which *completely bars* me *from using any judgment* ***that*** *concerns spatio-temporal existence* (Dasein). [14, p. 59]

Husserl's pre-emptive dismissal of solipsism is important here, and Husserl was subject to attacks insinuating his status as one throughout his life. He does not wish to found a new science upon the idea that the world may or may not exist, he simply wants to draw up the foundations for a new science that can categorically deal with the problems of consciousness whose domain, he contends, is not accessible via natural scientific methods.

This conclusion is reached by Husserl's employing of the phenomenological reduction. When we cast our attention to the realm of consciousness Husserl notes that we 'lack above all [...] a certain general insight into the essence of *consciousness in general*' and this makes bracketing of consciousness impossible [14, p. 62]. As such, we end up with the state of affairs whereby '[*c*]*onsciousness in itself has a being of its own which in its absolute uniqueness of nature remains unaffected by the phenomenological disconnexion*' and thus consciousness 'remains over as a *"phenomenological residuum"*' [14, pp. 62–3]. From here, then, can we found this new science of phenomenology through which all matters related to consciousness are explored.

As stated in the previous section, Kuhn's concept of incommensurability sought to draw parallels between scientific and political revolutions. It is not the case that the *status quo* paradigm 'peels off' to reveal a new one that contains answers to previous landmark issues, rather proponents of the new 'live in a different world', so to speak, to those upholding the old. I bring up this understanding of incommensurability once more to expand on a pertinent point by a commentator of Husserl and Kuhn. Don Ihde draws the excellent comparison between Kuhn and Husserl as both describing paradigm shifts albeit in slightly different ways. As discussed earlier, Kuhn's contention of paradigm shifts as codifying a *Gestalt* switch was never elaborated upon in great detail as Kuhn, following criticism, seemed to recognise this reading of paradigm shifts as more analogical than literal; the central difficulty being that *Gestalt* shifts concern immediate individual changes in stance rather than the kind of overarching change in axioms experienced by a scientific community undergoing revolution. And while Kuhn's terminology may be confused Ihde finds common ground between him and Husserl: '[t]he common perceptual model between Husserl and Kuhn is the *gestalt shift*' [15, p. 184]. This is so due to Ihde's key insight: 'In a sense, Kuhn describes what happens in a shift, but how it happens remains for him, largely unconscious. Husserl attempts to make shifting a deliberate procedure, a phenomenological rationality' [15, p. 184]. On this basis, then, can we frame the phenomenological reduction as an *explicit model for generating a paradigm shift in the realm of our knowledge about consciousness.* In the reduction we strip away the extraneous until we are left with the phenomenological ideal, and it is upon this ideal – in the context of paradigm shifts – that new insight can be won. Therefore, purely as a means of generating potential paradigm shifts, there is complete coherence between the phenomenological reduction and Kuhnian philosophy of science. Husserl's reduction can be co-opted in this manner to aid in the discovering of new paradigms – and yet this is merely a side-effect of the true import of the marrying of Kuhnian paradigms with Husserlian phenomenology. It is important at this point to remember the core thesis of this paper: Husserlian analysis of consciousness can provide us with a richer understanding of consciousness. This does not require us to accept every aspect of Husserl's descriptive investigation of the mechanism of consciousness as correct – indeed, disputation of his ideas is welcomed – but once we perform the phenomenological reduction and at least *consider* the possibility of consciousness as irreducible then we are presented with novel concepts and methods to employ and analyse in the quest for *artificial consciousness.* To support this claim we shall critically examine two case studies in the next section.

4 The Razor of the Natural Standpoint and Its Role in Paradigm Shift

We must now tie the above excursus on Husserlian-phenomenology to the issue of AI, and we do so by characterising it as necessary paradigm shift. Firstly, to what can we apply the label of 'normal science' in the context of philosophical inquiry into consciousness? Let us consider two case studies: the MIT laboratory of AI research in the 1950s and '60s, and contemporary trends in philosophical analyses of consciousness. The research aims of the MIT lab in the former case was largely spurred on by the Dartmouth Summer Research Project on Artificial Intelligence of 1956 [19]. Organised by John McCarthy, a foundational figure in the history of computer science, participants in the conference would go on to conduct research in MIT in the years following focusing in on the preliminary problems of the field of AI. Consider the example of SHRDLU, an experiment by Terry Winograd which explored the possibilities of natural language processing by machines. This experiment involved Winograd interacting with a language processor representing a simple robotic arm; one could tell the 'arm' to pick things up, drop them, and so on, and it was conceived to be a proof of concept for machine interaction with human 'worlds'. In this context we mean the world as it contains meanings, traditions, values, implications, etc., and Winograd's contention was that the robot could understand human operators on a human level – it could understand relatively simple vagaries of language (solely within the contrived and limited world set up by Winograd) and communicate naturally with humans [9]. This experiment is a pre-eminent example of what Hubert Dreyfus (via Marvin Minsky and Seymour Papert) termed a 'micro-worlds' approach to AI; this approach entailed exhaustively mapping human concepts in a given sphere for artificially intelligent agents [9]. For instance, one might encode a micro-world of 'co-operation', which would entail translating, for a machine, every possible concept related to the activity of co-operation. This style of advancement in AI research, of relating the human world in discrete 'chunks' to robots was famously critiqued by Dreyfus. While the scope of this paper is not broad enough to allow for a thorough overview of Dreyfus's objections to the trend of AI[1] at this time, it is worth noting the impact his work had on the field as a whole. In identifying four key assumptions common to researchers at the time[2] Dreyfus changed how such research would progress in the future. More on this in a moment, but for now we highlight the carrying out of 'normal science', in a Kuhnian sense, by these early researchers – they attempted to bring about artificially intelligent agents using a 'top-down' approach wherein human concepts were symbolically represented and translated to machines. These machines were prescribed rules, as opposed to given environments whereby they could divine these rules and nuances of human concepts by themselves.

[1] For further reading see Dreyfus's books *Alchemy and AI* (1965) [7], *What Computers Can't Do* (1972) [8], and *Mind Over Machine* (1986) [10].

[2] Dreyfus enumerates these as the 'biological assumption' (the idea that human brains can be modelled by physical circuits), the 'psychological assumption' (the idea that the mind functions as a device with formal rules), the 'epistemological assumption' (the idea that all knowledge can be formalised and symbolically represented), and the 'ontological assumption' (the idea that the world itself can be accurately and exhaustively represented in symbolic fashion). For more see *Alchemy and AI* and *What Computers Can't Do*.

In the case of contemporary philosophical ideas on consciousness we need look no further than David Chalmers. Chalmers' 2018 paper *The Meta-Problem of Consciousness* codified prevailing trends in contemporary discussions on consciousness and also prescribed a programme of research needed to settle the issue of consciousness once and for all. Throughout this paper Chalmers eschews a wholly reductionist view of consciousness, although he flirts with it at times. Given his past work, most notably his 1995 paper *Facing Up to the Problem of Consciousness*, it would be unfair to label Chalmers a physicalist concerning consciousness, however. That 1995 paper formulated the 'hard problem of consciousness', namely, the question of why it is that a subjective feeling characterises the experience of consciousness [4]. This is, of course, a neat reframing of the thesis of Thomas Nagel's 1974 paper *What is it Like to Be a Bat?* which raises the issue of the 'subjective character of experience' as needing to be explained by any model of consciousness [17]. Such a valuation of consciousness is certainly coherent in a Husserlian context, and Nagel's influence on contemporary discussions on consciousness should not go unnoticed. Chalmers, too, should be commended for both his 'hard problem' and 'meta-problem'[3] given the emphasis they put on the centrality of the subjective experience to consciousness. Particularly in *Meta-Problem* do we see a philosophical field conducting 'normal science', especially as Chalmers calls for interdisciplinary research from various natural scientific fields to supplement philosophical theorising. Chalmers lays out his model of consciousness, while also referencing multiple competing ones, and sets out the issues that need to be investigated in more detail in order to secure the academic understanding of consciousness. For example, in describing 'problem intuitions' (i.e. the personal and subjective questions that one might have about the nature of consciousness) he claims that they are widespread and intimately knowable to all humans, regardless of academic standing [5]. In attempting to pursue this thread of 'normal science' researchers Sytsma & Ozdemir experimentally verified just how widespread such intuitions were, and concluded that Chalmers' claim of universality was unfounded [20]. This, by any metric, is a field of science conducting normal science.

My word choice in that preceding sentence is deliberate – Chalmers is employing natural scientific methods (as are his interlocutors) and thus should be considered a scientist. The paradigm that Chalmers is attempting to secure is *status quo*, he is not advocating for a radical revaluation of physics, nor psychology, nor any related field. His bedrock is the notion of the subjective experience, but this axiom is by no means in opposition to any axiom of any current paradigm. Similarly, the researchers in the MIT labs of the '50s and '60s challenged no contemporaneous paradigms, in fact their work represented applications of results from fields such as information theory, physics, computer science, and so on without ever seeking to supplant these preceding fields with their novel research. I contend that doing so, that avoiding direct confrontation with the make-up of individual paradigms across the broad spectrum of this research both then and now, has lead us into *crisis*. In Kuhn's description of crisis we get the notion of anomaly; this anomaly stubbornly appears in all kinds of results and thus shapes a period of crisis, and while scientists may argue vigorously regarding which path to

[3] The meta-problem is elucidated by Chalmers as the question of why it is we have such difficulty describing consciousness [5].

follow to in order to smooth out this anomaly there is broad agreement that something *is* anomalous. Here is where we run into some difficulty in proposing the Husserlian paradigm shift – do we see anomalies in the state of research into consciousness and/or AI? It may seem more the case that instead of anomaly we have *dispute*; on the one hand are those who endorse a physicalist, reductionist, or some related variant theory of consciousness while on the other are the idealists, panpsychists, dualists and others. The difficulty here hinges on what exactly it is we mean by science, and here I reemphasise earlier results from Husserl. While the subject of philosophy may rightly be seen as the scaffolding which supports the natural sciences in the realm of consciousness and AI the line between structure and method are blurred. It is certainly the case that philosophical inquiries into the nature of consciousness can be conducted in methods not founded upon natural scientific principles. Descartes' *Meditations* is the pertinent example here, as the totality of Descartes' research is done meditatively. His conclusion of the indisputable *cogito* is reached in a decidedly non-scientific manner; he ideates rather than physically hypothesising and testing.[4] It is doubtful that one would confuse such an approach for a natural scientific endeavour – why is that?

This 'why' is readily answered: Descartes' transcendental reflection does not assume the general thesis of the Natural Standpoint. *This* is the key achievement of Husserl's phenomenology in our context; we now have a sophisticated razor by which we can separate philosophical inquiries from natural scientific ones. In the ensuing dichotomy we can then seize upon the method offered by philosophical inquiry into consciousness rather than natural scientific; as the purely philosophical investigation entails no hidden presumptions.[5] Now we can finally see the true nature of the crisis that has been hinted in the last few paragraphs: the crisis for the sciences of consciousness is a methodological one. Dreyfus was the first to identify this with his identification of the four assumptions employed by early AI researchers. There remains a sense that Dreyfus' critique, while important, was never really that consequential for the world of AI research as we now know it. I contend this is for two reasons; firstly, those researchers on the practical side were more concerned with implementing applications of natural language processing, computer vision, etc. than responding to philosophical analyses on the nature of their work and, secondly, theoretical approaches *did change* as a result of Dreyfus – but these changes could never be considered a paradigm shift. As mentioned previously, in the early days of AI research approaches were, generally speaking, tooled from the top down (cf. microworlds). Nowadays the opposite is true, and here we introduce the notion of *opacity* in machine learning (ML)[6] methods via reference to two specific examples.

[4] The example of Descartes is here used for illustrative purposes and not as an endorsement of Cartesian dualism.

[5] This should not suggest that a philosophical inquiry does not rest on some presuppositions – in this context those presuppositions are known, declared, and remain in steady focus throughout. This contrasts against the natural scientific approach which does not place its presuppositions front and centre throughout.

[6] Here 'machine learning' refers to a particular school of thought in AI research (see MIT's meta-analysis [13] for more on this). In ML, as outlined above, goals are set for machines but the specific path to achieving these goals are left 'up to' the machines' internal logic, which is opaque in character.

The early approaches to AI research discussed above were marked by their *transparency*. There is no mystery in the case of SHRDLU's functioning; its parameters are well-defined, and its resultant behaviour can be readily anticipated. This is not so much the case with Deep Learning strategies. Take, for example, the recent autoregressive language model GPT-3, which implements a 'few-shot' approach to natural language processing [1]. The architecture of GPT-3's underlying artificial neural network processes 175 billion parameters in a 96-layer artificial neural network [1, p. 8]. Certainly, the levels of complexity involved with tooling such a model makes SHRDLU's micro-world setup pale in comparison, but a comparison in such terms undersells the novelty of the few-shot approach. In this implementation of few-shot learning between 10 and 100 examples of 'context and completion' are provided to the model in order to train it to perform tasks of, for example, translation [1, p. 6]. What is of key importance, here, is that in few-shot learning weights in the neural architecture are not updated post training. This contrasts against 'fine-tuning' approaches which update weights after training sessions, requiring the regular intervention of human agents in order to aid ML. Let us consider a further example, Weight Agnostic Neural Networks (WANNs) [12]. The achievement of the WANN is similar to that of the few-shot learning approach: fine-tuning the weights of nodes in neural architectures is minimised (indeed, in the case of WANNs, it is eliminated entirely), allowing for a less interventionist style of reinforcement learning. WANNs perform basic tasks (such as simulating walking and driving [12, p. 1]) comparatively well with respect to weight-tuned neural networks, demonstrating their status as a technology worth further exploring and refining in the quest to produce still more optimal ML strategies.

What unites GPT-3 and WANNs is, among other things, their *opacity*, particularly in comparison to the transparency of SHRDLU. Burrell [2, p. 4] encapsulates the nature of this opacity clearly; opacity in models such as GPT-3 and WANNs occurs 'at the scale of application', which is to say that the specific internal decision making logic of the model is obfuscated. In discussing relatively simple (in comparison to GPT-3) artificial neural networks tasked with recognising handwritten numbers Burrell [2, p. 6] identifies the unique unintelligibility of ML. The purpose of 'hidden layer' nodes in such structures is to pick out individual features of handwritten numbers from training datasets in order to accurately classify unseen numbers in testing datasets, but there is no guarantee that such features would similarly be identified as crucial by human agents. Indeed, as Burrell [2, p. 7] shows, it is often the case that these machine-identified markers are radically different from those of human agents. This opacity is emblematic of a 'bottom-up' approach to ML; computer science strategies have moved well beyond the naïve implementations of structural primitives and micro-worlds of nascent AI research. No longer are computer scientists dictating rules and relations to machines, instead they are configured to happen upon these *by themselves*. And we really do mean 'by themselves' – while all ML methods rely on human intervention at multiple stages, from algorithm design to fine-tuning of neural networks, the particular implementation used by a machine is arrived at through its own internal decision-making logic. Opacity alone, however, does not rescue AI endeavours from the critique of Dreyfus. It is not controversial to note, I argue, that such trends in AI research represent a paradigm shift on the level of implementation, but this shift lacks a requisite philosophical grounding to contextualise the broader issue of consciousness as a whole. It is for this reason that we argue to take Husserl's thought as foundational.

Husserl's phenomenology is the paradigm shift. The reason that crisis exists is also down to Husserl – his assessment that consciousness cannot be naturalised is a view that, as yet, has not been adequately dealt with by contemporary researchers of both consciousness and AI. It should be noted that dealing with this view does not have to involve endorsement of the view itself, either. My promotion of Husserl as foundational throughout this paper has been mostly along methodological lines; Husserl's manner of conducting philosophy involves painstaking awareness of his own entailed assumptions. Little has been said as to whether his assessment of consciousness is wholly correct, although his thesis of the Natural Standpoint has been supported unreservedly. Even on this point do we remain decidedly non-fanatical; support for the Husserlian Natural Standpoint simply requires that one brackets – *without negating* – the natural world in the pursuit of insight into consciousness. Therefore the paradigm shift we propose is similarly limited, the case we make is that meaningful answers regarding the nature of consciousness can only arise when one faces up to the presuppositions entailed in their methodological approaches.

5 Conclusion and the Metaphysical Status of Consciousness

While we have heralded Husserl's key achievement as that of the thesis of the Natural Standpoint we must not overlook a particularly important consequence arising from this, namely that we cannot get 'outside' ourselves. We are inexorably tied to our corporeal forms and our all-encompassing lenses of consciousness. Such unity causes contamination in our natural scientific investigations into the nature of consciousness – *our consciousness* is the ultimate *lurking variable* – but also allows for qualified speculation in the world of AI. On a Husserlian view, we can only come to know our consciousness as its individual features reveal itself themselves to us in reflection; but we cannot see the unity of our own consciousness from a global perspective. Given this lack of global access we also cannot categorically state that *other* forms of consciousness may not exist. Husserl's view is that consciousness cannot be naturalised and, I contend, that does not exclude it from being *something*. By 'something' I mean consciousness could well be a purely physical phenomenon as much as it could be an emergent characteristic of a distributed entity or a transcendental framework of intentional relations. These are all possibilities for the metaphysical status of consciousness, but we can never aver that one possibility is correct to any degree of certainty.

This assessment of consciousness as *something* seems to leave us in a strange place vis-à-vis our upholding of Husserlian doctrines. It is, however, precisely the conclusion to draw given Husserl's systematic account of the thesis of the Natural Standpoint, for once we concretise consciousness as one possibility over another we revert to the Natural Attitude as consciousness *always* remains as residuum in the phenomenological reduction; meaning that giving consciousness a definite structure is tantamount to removing it from the reduction. If it has been described in totality it is no longer there, as all of the theses associated with a 'decided' consciousness must be reduced in the *epoché*. It is here that we happen upon the *revolutionary* aspect of Husserl's phenomenology in the context of paradigm shifts. I stated above that the paradigm shift required by Husserl is one of methodology, that is, natural scientific methods should not be assumed to be *prima facie* applicable to the investigation of consciousness. I now go one step further to argue that true acceptance of the Husserlian paradigm only comes about when the metaphysics of consciousness is ignored. This applies equally to researchers in consciousness and AI; in the case of the former the focus post-paradigm shift should be in enumerating and describing the individual features of consciousness in every conceivable setting, while the focus in the latter becomes taking these analysed features of consciousness as goals to be achieved with little emphasis placed on *how this happens*. The issue of opacity, discussed above, represents the perfect opportunity to begin this shift in attitude; the ethos of setting a goal and allowing machines to achieve it by whatever means necessary (with minimal human intervention) represents a more philosophically fruitful avenue for achieving genuine artificial consciousness. We cannot hypothesise structures of machine consciousness any more than we can structures of human consciousness – but we will 'know' consciousness when we 'see' it. Other forms of consciousness are theoretically valid, it is up to us now to happen upon such forms. We can only do so phenomenologically, our approaches must be descriptively informed rather than prescriptively set lest we revert to the Natural Standpoint. This new movement toward increasing opacity, in the engineering of AI, means that we must, as researchers, challenge ourselves to reflect on results through a Husserlian-phenomenological lens. In bracketing not only do we allow ourselves to better assess whether machine capabilities can accurately institute human characteristics of consciousness; we also, more generally, shift to a more descriptive mindset. In describing, as opposed to prescribing, we adopt a standpoint already wholeheartedly characteristic of opaque ML methods; and, therefore, such descriptive analysis is both more appropriate and more insightful in the arena of AI progress. I have remained agnostic on the question of whether such machine consciousness could ever exist throughout this paper, but it is difficult to see how considering a shift in paradigm, as impelled by Husserlian principles, could result in anything other than clarifying that question. The Husserlian paradigm is ripe for genuine novelty in consciousness discoveries – we must adopt it.

References

1. Brown, T.B., et al.: Language models are few-shot learners. Advances in Neural Processing Systems 33 (2020)
2. Burrell, J.: How the machine 'thinks': understanding opacity in machine learning algorithms. Big Data Soc. **3**(1) (2016)
3. Butterfield, H.: The Origins of Modern Science. The Free Press, New York (1965). Revised Edition
4. Chalmers, D.: Facing up to the problem of consciousness. J. Conscious. Stud. **2**, 200–219 (1995)
5. Chalmers, D.: The meta-problem of consciousness. J. Conscious. Stud. **25**, 6–61 (2018)
6. Cohen, H.R.: Dialectics and scientific revolutions. Sci. Soc. **37**, 326–336 (1973)
7. Dreyfus, H.: Alchemy and AI. RAND Corporation, California (1965)
8. Dreyfus, H.: What Computers Can't Do: The Limits of Artificial Intelligence. MIT Press, Massachusetts (1972)

9. Dreyfus, H.: From micro-worlds to knowledge representation: AI at an impasse. In: Haugel, J. (ed.) Mind Design, pp. 143–182. MIT Press, Massachusetts (1981)
10. Dreyfus, H.: Mind Over Machine. The Free Press, Michigan (1986)
11. European Commission: Artificial Intelligence Act: a welcomed initiative, but ban on remote biometric identification is necessary in public space is necessary. Brussels (2021)
12. Gaier, A., Ha, D.: Weight agnostic neural networks. In: 32nd Conference on Neural Processing Systems (2019)
13. Hao, K.: We analyzed 16,625 papers to figure out where AI is headed next. MIT Technology Review (2019)
14. Husserl, E.: Ideas: General Introduction to Pure Phenomenology. W. R. Boyce Gibson (trans.), Routledge, Oxford (2012)
15. Ihde, D.: Consequences of Phenomenology. State University of New York Press, New York (1986)
16. Kuhn, T.: The Structure of Scientific Revolutions, 3rd edn. The University of Chicago Press, Chicago (1996)
17. Nagel, T.: What is it like to be a bat? Philos. Rev. **83**, 435–450 (1974)
18. Popper, K.: The Logic of Scientific Discovery. Hutchinson, London (1959)
19. Solomonoff, R.: The time scale of artificial intelligence: reflections on social effects. Hum. Syst. Manag. **5**, 149–153 (1985)
20. Sytsma, J., Ozdemir, E.: No problem: evidence that problem intuitions are not widespread. J. Conscious. Stud. **26**, 241–256 (2019)

The Ethical Implications of Lawtech

Rónán Kennedy(✉)

School of Law, National University of Ireland Galway, Galway, Ireland
ronan.m.kennedy@nuigalway.ie

Abstract. The development of information and communications technology has changed the work of many professionals and may now be radically changing the functioning of the legal system. 'Lawtech', or technology which supports, replaces, or improves the provision of legal services and the operation of the justice system, has become more and more important.

Lawtech raises significant ethical issues. It often relies on so-called 'artificial intelligence' (AI), but this does not 'think' as humans do. Software, such as machine learning tools, can help judges to make decisions. Some jurisdictions are replacing judges with AI. Lawyers also use AI to predict the outcomes of litigation. These tools can be more transparent and fairer. However, they may also be more opaque. Also, researchers raise questions about whether the data and processes used in these applications simply reflects and strengthens existing biases and prejudices.

Lawtech provides an opportunity to improve the operation of the legal services market and the justice system for the benefit for the citizen and the consumer. However, this is not certain, and it could worsen existing problems or create new ones. This will require careful consideration and more research in the future.

Keywords: Lawtech · Legaltech · Ethics · Law · Artificial intelligence · Judicial support · Bias · Courts · Lawyers

1 Context

The development of information and communications technology (ICT), particularly the networked digital computer, has brought about very significant changes to the skills, capacity, and daily work practices of many professionals. However, the pace and type of change has not been the same across all walks of life. This paper explores how ICT has affected the practice of law and how it is likely to affect it in the future.

Relatively little has changed in the practice of law since Dickens' time [1, pp. 143–4]. If a doctor, engineer, or journalist from the 18th century was transported to a modern workplace, they would be confused and confounded by the many machines in use. A lawyer from the same time period deposited in a modern courtroom or legal practice would see some computers but the nature of legal work, the interactions with clients, and the business of law would be familiar. However, the recent rapid growth in legal information technology – often referred to as 'lawtech' – is transforming and disrupting the world of legal practice to a very significant extent [2, p. 997].

Published by Springer Nature Switzerland AG 2021
D. Dennehy et al. (Eds.): I3E 2021, LNCS 12896, pp. 198–207, 2021.
https://doi.org/10.1007/978-3-030-85447-8_18

This could have significant benefits, but it may also bring significant problems. Lawtech could lead to better access to justice, more affordable legal services, and a better quality of service. However, it could also strengthen existing biases and inequalities, widen the digital divide, and lead to the provision of unregulated services which do not serve consumers well.

2 What is 'Lawtech'?

A broad definition of 'lawtech' is any use of ICT for legal practice. It is also called 'legaltech' or 'legal technology' (This paper will use 'lawtech' to avoid the implication that all uses of ICT are legal.) This term covers quite a wide range of sophistication: from the relatively simple use of word processors for the preparation of correspondence, to the use of artificial intelligence (AI) to automatically review legal documents such as contracts. The Law Society of England and Wales has a more precise definition of lawtech, which this paper will adopt, as: 'technologies that aim to support, supplement or replace traditional methods for delivering legal services, or that improve the way the justice system operates.' [3].

This is quite a wide-ranging definition, and includes many aspects of the law – consumers and providers of legal services, the judiciary and courts, and public and private law. (This paper does not consider the use of ICT in policing.) Lawtech also includes:

1. *digitalisation or automation* – converting existing paper-based processes to electronic or digital processes, in the hope of saving time and money; and
2. *innovation or transformation* – re-thinking these processes entirely or creating new approaches to old problems or challenges, often relying on technology, and either trying to save time and money or to create new markets and business models.

Lawtech can be sub-divided into 'Office Tech' (traditional office automation tools, which have little or no influence on business models) and 'Legal Tech' (which 'directly affects the provision of legal services') [4]. Office Tech is perhaps best understood as internal and supporting lawyers, while Legal Tech is external and supports or facilitates clients.

3 Ethical Implications of Lawtech

This section discusses some ethical issues which lawtech raises, particularly the risk of bias in judicial decision support systems.

3.1 AI, Judicial Decision Support Tools, and Bias

Limitations of AI. An important use of lawtech in the courts which raises ethical issues is judicial decision support tools. Many of these tools rely on artificial intelligence (AI). Although AI is sometimes understood or presented as having human-like intelligence, these tools do not work like a human mind and have significant limitations [5, Chap. 7].

A significant ethical issue in the development of digital technology, generally, is that AI which depends on 'big data' may strengthen existing biases and unfairness in society [6, pp. 2–5]. This is very relevant to the development of lawtech, and although Ireland is not as advanced as other jurisdictions in its adoption, it deserves careful consideration.

Lawtech AI generally takes two forms:

1. '*Expert systems*' apply rules developed and programmed by humans to make decisions or provide guidance.
2. '*Machine learning*' applies statistical analysis of large amounts of records ('big data') in order to identify connections and correlations, particularly ones that are not obvious to humans.

Neither of these approaches are truly 'intelligent', and the latter is often misunderstood:

> Data-reliant AI operates by looking for associations. The software assesses how predictive certain factors are, and through iterative analysis hones in on relationships that might not be visible to human analysis.
>
> This software does not apply logical rules in the sense of rules-based systems, or in the way that humans apply logic to solve problems. This software neither understands nor applies logical rules, rather through mathematical analysis of vast amounts of data relationships it can identify these relationships. The software neither knows nor cares why these relationships exist; it simply identifies that they do exist [7, p. 327].

While these tools are quite powerful in certain contexts, they do not work in the same way as humans:

> … today's AI systems are decidedly not intelligent thinking machines in any meaningful sense. Rather, … AI systems are often able to produce useful, intelligent results without intelligence. These systems do this largely through heuristics – by detecting patterns in data and using knowledge, rules, and information that have been specifically encoded by people into forms that can be processed by computers. Through these computational approximations, AI systems often can produce surprisingly good results on certain complex tasks that, when done by humans, require cognition. Notably, however, these AI systems do so by using computational mechanisms that do not resemble or match human thinking.
>
> By contrast, the vision of AI as involving thinking machines with abilities that meet or surpass human-level cognition – often referred to as Strong AI or Artificial General Intelligence (AGI) – is only aspirational [8, p. 1308].

These big data tools can enhance our lives, but the software programs used may also 'learn' to discriminate in ways that are illegal. For example, they might focus on characteristics that are proxies for social class, race or gender (such as home address or height). They might also pick up existing human biases in the data, for example, descriptions of images that differentiate on the basis of race [6, pp. 2–5].

AI in Judicial Decision-Making. Big data and machine learning tools are now being developed to support judges in their decision-making. These take two general forms:

1. An assistant, providing relevant information to guide judicial decisions
2. A complete replacement for a judge, providing judgments in an autonomous and automatic fashion [9, p. 4].

AI tools have been developed to predict the outcomes of litigation, to assess the risk of an individual, or otherwise to help to gather information needed for a decision [9, p. 5–12]. AI is now being used by judges worldwide. China has ambitious plans for the use of AI in judicial processes [7, p. 324; 10–12], and Pakistan is experimenting with its use by judges [13]. Estonia intends to use an automated system to deal with small claims disputes of less than €7000 [14].

The use of analytics to examine patterns in the decisions of judges has been banned in France. The rationale put forward was to prevent judges coming under undue pressure, but concerns were raised that the ban could reduce transparency and accountability. It has been argued that these tools could lead to a significant increase in transparency in judging. However, there are limitations, including incomplete or low-quality data, being inappropriate for certain areas of law, the unstructured nature of judgments, and high cost. They may improve as data sets become larger and better, the technology develops, and costs fall. They might lead to an increase in 'judge shopping' (preferring or avoiding judges seen as more or less favourable), and challenges to judicial fairness or competence [15].

AI judicial support tools have been controversial. The Correctional Offender Management Profiling for Alternative Sanctions ('COMPAS') software has been used to assess the risk of recidivism of an individual before sentencing in some US courts. Critics have alleged that it assigns African-Americans as high-risk at twice the rate of other groups, while assigning white people as low-risk more often than people of colour [16].

There are concerns that 'algorithms might perpetuate or amplify existing biases and stereotypes, which can consequently result in discrimination.' [9, p. 8] Underlying this concern is an understanding that no dataset is free of human choices regarding what is measured and what is recorded, and can thus easily reflect human biases and assumptions: '[f]or example, crime data may reflect policing and judicial biases towards minority groups, while data on eligibility for benefits may reflect bureaucratic impulses to reduce spending.' [17, p. 434; See also 18; 19; 20].

Ethical Issues with Judicial Decision Support Tools. If machine learning tools are used to support judges, this could have both positive and negative effects. From an ethical perspective, there may be an obligation on courts to take full advantage of the opportunities which digitalisation offers [21]. Technology can enable greater transparency and accountability, by enabling the court to communicate to a wider audience. However, it can also reduce transparency, by giving the court too much control over the message that it communicates, or making the reasons for decisions more difficult to publish or understand. A greater capacity to communicate can enhance the independence of the courts, and the use of (for example) random case allocation can enhance impartiality [22].

Algorithms could also reduce transparency by making decisions more opaque and hard to understand [9, pp. 13–17]. Four possible forms of opaque algorithm are [23, pp. 3–5; 24, p. 5–6]:

1. Intentional corporate or state secrecy, particularly to protect trade secrets and competitive advantage;
2. Software code which is difficult to understand, particularly for those without the specialised skills necessary;
3. Systems which are built to such a scale that they are difficult to completely grasp; and
4. AI systems which do not make it clear how their decisions are made.

There are arguments that trade secrecy should not be privileged in the use of software tools in criminal proceedings [25]. Judicial decision support tools could be developed with some degree of access to software source code – either entirely open, accessible on request, or reviewed by independent experts [26, p. 135]. However, review of open source by itself does not guarantee that problems will be identified [27, pp. 647–650]. In addition, AI researchers are developing more explainable or interpretable algorithms [24, pp. 6–7]. If these are insufficient, another approach could be to ensure that those who may be affected by AI judicial decision support tools can opt-in or opt-out of their use [26, p. 136].

Lawtech could enable greater efficiency, but this value may be in tension with ideals of fairness and justice [22]. However, providing judges with a database of past decisions (particularly sentences) could increase their consistency and impartiality, and external analysis of decisions may highlight unusual or unfair decision-making by particular judges. The use of AI in selecting judges could lead to a more diverse bench.

However, examination of case studies of these systems in practice show that this is not always achieved, and AI tools may never be appropriate for contexts where the stakes are high:

> Ultimately, humans must evaluate each decision-making process and consider what forms of automation are useful, appropriate and consistent with the rule of law. The design, implementation and evaluation of any automated components, as well as the entire decision-making process including human elements, should be consistent with such values. It remains to be seen whether these values can be fully integrated into automated decision- making and decision-support systems used by government [17, pp. 454–5].

Can Judicial Decision-Making Be Automated? The next possible step is the use of AI to replace some or all of the decision-making by human judges. It is argued that this could make the process much fairer:

> In adjudication much uncertainty is due to the fact that outcomes are influenced by the judge's intellectual ability, background knowledge, experience, moral inclinations and political outlook, all of which vary from judge to judge. Computer

> law-application promises to be more consistent and equal. Like humans, AI systems may be infected with bias, but once such a defect has been detected, it may be eliminated. It is much more difficult to detect human bias since it may be unconscious, let alone to overcome it. Importantly, there is mounting evidence that machines are better than humans in detecting lying and assessing the probability of future eventualities, such as the risk of reoffending [28, p. 439].

In addition, the population generally may think that AI is fairer than humans [29]. AI may assist in reducing bias, by providing more objective assessments of a case, removing flawed intuitions, reducing jury bias, and hiring more diverse staff. However, AI could also exacerbate bias because it relies on biased data, although this may be corrected [30, pp. 161–176].

From a human rights perspective, an automated or quasi-automated system could have the important advantage of speed, which is particularly important where there are backlogs in the court system. However, if the system is not explainable, it may infringe on the right to a fair trial [31, pp. 36–41].

It seems unlikely that AI will entirely replace human judges. The capacity of AI to substitute for human judges may be limited by lack of sufficient data. A more important limitation is that there is no artificial general intelligence, and even if there was, it would be very difficult, if not impossible, to free it from human bias. It also may not be appropriate for computers to create new rules which impact on humans, and AI might not be able to command the same respect from the public as do judges [7, p. 348].

The perception that AI is fairer and more consistent does not take into account how algorithms developed by different individuals or teams do not always yield the same results. For example, there are many online databases of legal resources, some of which will include functionality which extend a search to include similar words, singular/plural, and so on. These algorithms are unique to the database and proprietary. Carrying out the same search across different databases yields different results: up to 40% were unique to a particular database, some databases returned more than 50% irrelevant material in the top 10 results, and the 'best' database involved more human curation of its information [32]. Similarly, when 52 programmers were assigned the task of automating the enforcement of speed limits, the programs that they wrote issued very different numbers of tickets for the same sample data [33]. If artificial intelligence were to replace judges, this would raise questions such as whether computers have legal authority to make decisions, how laws are translated into computer code, how discretion can be managed, and when computers might understand meaning rather than simply logic [34, pp. 1126–1130].

Another limitation is that if AI becomes more common, the justice system may be re-engineered and individuals working within it may think in a different way, for example in terms of risk profiles and the classification of groups [35, pp. 630–631]. AI systems that predict the future based on the past, or reach conclusions based on past cases, may not be able to make creative leaps, deal with unanticipated situations, or develop the law in the way that a human lawyer or judge can [36, pp. 6–7]. The use of AI to support or substitute for human judges may lead to a more codified or standardised justice system, which could be more fine-grained than human decision-making, but which may also be too limited in its methods of measurement to be truly just. The end result may be incomprehensible by citizens and unable to change, leading to disillusionment and alienation [37]. A system that is slow to change could lose its legitimacy in the eyes of the public [38, p. 235].

Therefore, we are still some distance from fully automated judges being a reality [39]. It will require technology that does not yet exist, and may not ever [35, pp. 627–628]. It may be that 'the human heart of the judicial process, being a combination of conscious and currently unknowable unconscious thought, remains quite literally beyond the comprehension of the most talented programmer.' [40, p. 112]. The incomplete and fuzzy nature of the law may mean that attempts to convert it into something which can be reliably processed by a machine could damage the rule of law [41]. In the future, therefore, judges are unlikely to be entirely replaced by AI [42, p. 3], but we may see hybrid human-machine systems used for judging [43].

Is the Role of the Judiciary Limited to Decision-Making? Another reason why AI may never entirely replace judges is that their role goes beyond simply adjudicating on cases, and can vary significantly between legal systems [7, p. 334]. Much of current AI research does not focus to a significant extent on what courts and judges do in practice, such as managing a courtroom, a caseload, and a team of staff, but only on the application of rules [35, pp. 628–631]. In addition to deciding cases, judges also enable public participation in the process of justice, explain its functioning, assess facts, create documents, identify and apply doctrine, reason by analogy, are consistent, create law when required, and ultimately project 'the power and legitimacy of the state to the public.' [7, pp. 338–341].

European Ethical Charter on the Use of AI in Judicial Systems. The use of AI in courts raises many important opportunities and challenges. Liu and others have considered these issues in detail, and have asked a number of questions for consideration:

> It is far from clear whether automated systems support, or replace human discretion and judgment in practice. So who are the decision-makers – the government officials involved or software programs they are relying on, which are designed by companies for profit? In many cases, private entities wield public power by virtue of the algorithms they design[.]
>
> …
>
> …, what type of decisions can governments delegate to machines? Should the authority be shaped broadly enough to allow algorithms to make value-based judgments or only non-discretionary decisions? Moreover, codes and algorithms are value-laden. Development of algorithms is a complex process that can be influenced by humans – such as criteria selection, data mining, training, semantics and interpretation. In designing the operational parameters … it is not uncommon for developers to have 'desired outcomes in mind that privilege some values and interests over others'. While sensitive attributes like gender, race or ethnicity are generally disallowed in the decision-making process of public sectors, they may be encoded, inadvertently or not, when private companies design the systems. The fact that algorithms are implemented throughout government agencies can only magnify and perpetuate the risks of hidden biases and errors [26, pp. 137–138].

One possible structure for responding to these issues is the Council of Europe's European Commission for the Efficiency of Justice (CEPEJ)'s European Ethical Charter on the Use of Artificial Intelligence in Judicial Systems and Their Environment, which sets out five principles:

1. *Principle of respect for fundamental rights*: Ensure that the design and implementation of artificial intelligence tools and services are compatible with fundamental rights;
2. *Principle of non-discrimination*: Specifically prevent the development or intensification of any discrimination between individuals or groups of individuals;
3. *Principle of quality and security*: With regard to the processing of judicial decisions and data, use certified sources and intangible data with models conceived in a multidisciplinary manner, in a secure technological environment;
4. *Principle of transparency, impartiality and fairness*: Make data processing methods accessible and understandable, and authorise external audits; and
5. *Principle 'under user control'*: Preclude a prescriptive approach and ensure that users are informed actors and in control of their choices [44].

The CEPEJ has also prepared a feasibility study for a mechanism for certifying AI tools and services in the sphere of justice and the judiciary, which outlines how these principles might be applied in practice [45].

4 Conclusion

Lawtech has been part of a wave of change and innovation in the legal services market. It could save consumers and businesses money and time, and be a source of economic growth. However, it is not a 'silver bullet' to solve the problem of access to justice. As AI is used more by lawyers and courts, this could save time and money and be fairer, but may be biased and inflexible.

These policy choices will become more important as lawtech develops at a faster pace. The Council of Bars and Law Societies of Europe has considered the use of AI in detail, and provides a reflection which summarises the issues well:

> Much debate is still needed critically to assess what role, if any, AI tools should play in our justice systems. Change should be embraced where it improves or at least does not worsen the quality of our justice systems. However, fundamental rights and adherence to ethical standards that underpin institutions based on the rule of law, cannot be subordinated to mere efficiency gains or cost saving benefits, whether for court users or judicial authorities.
>
> Increasing access to justice by reducing the cost of judicial proceedings may sound like a desirable outcome, but there is little value in increasing access to justice if the quality of justice is undermined in doing so [46, p. 20].

Acknowledgements. This publication has emanated from research supported in part by a research grant from Science Foundation Ireland (SFI) under Grant Number 19/PSF/7665. It is derived from

Oireachtas Library & Research Service, 2021, L&RS Spotlight: Algorithms, Big Data and Artificial Intelligence in the Irish Legal Services Market.

References

1. Kirby, M.: The future of courts – do they have one? J. Law Inf. Sci. **9**, 141–151 (1998)
2. Donoghue, J.: The rise of digital justice: courtroom technology, public participation and access to justice. Mod. Law Rev. **80**, 995–1025 (2017)
3. The Law Society: What is lawtech? (2019). http://www.lawsociety.org.uk/campaigns/lawtech/guides/what-is-lawtech
4. Hartung, M., Bues, M.-M., Halbleib, G. (eds.): Legal Tech: How Technology is Changing the Legal World. Beck/Hart, Munich/Oxford (2018)
5. Broussard, M.: Artificial Unintelligence: How Computers Misunderstand the World. MIT Press, Cambridge, Massachussets (2018)
6. Fundamental Rights Agency: #bigdata: Discrimination in Data-Supported Decision-Making. Fundamental Rights Agency, Vienna (2018)
7. Campbell, R.W.: Artificial intelligence in the courtroom: the delivery of justice in the age of machine learning. Colo. Technol. Law J. **18**, 323–349 (2020)
8. Surden, H.: Artificial intelligence and law: an overview. Georgia State Univ. Law Rev. **35**, 1305–1337 (2018)
9. Ulenaers, J.: The impact of artificial intelligence on the right to a fair trial: towards a robot judge. Asian J. Law Econ. **11** (2020). Article no. 20200008
10. Zou, M.: "Smart courts" in China and the future of personal injury litigation. J. Pers. Inj. Law **2**, 135–140 (2020)
11. Wang, R.: Legal technology in contemporary USA and China. Comput. Law Secur. Rev. **39**, 105459 (2020)
12. Zheng, G.G.: China's grand design of people's smart courts. Asian J. Law Soc. **00**, 1–22 (2020)
13. Pakistan Today: AI to assist judiciary in becoming more efficient, says CJP Khosa (2019). https://www.pakistantoday.com.pk/2019/06/19/ai-to-assist-judiciary-in-becoming-more-efficient-says-cjp-khosa/
14. Park, J.: Your Honor, AI. Harv. Int. Rev. **41**, 46–48 (2020). Spring
15. McGill, J., Salyzyn, A.: Judging by numbers: how will judicial analytics impact the justice system and its stakeholders. Dalhousie Law J. **44**, 249–284 (2021)
16. Angwin, J., Larson, J., Mattu, S., Kirchner, L.: Machine bias. ProPublica (2016). https://www.propublica.org/article/machine-bias-risk-assessments-in-criminal-sentencing
17. Zalnieriute, M., Moses, L.B., Williams, G.: The rule of law and automation of government decision-making. Mod. Law Rev. **82**, 425–455 (2019)
18. Gitelman, L. (ed.): Raw Data is an Oxymoron. MIT Press, Cambridge (2013)
19. Bowker, G.C., Star, S.L.: Sorting Things Out: Classification and Its Consequences. MIT Press, Cambridge (1999)
20. Kitchin, R.: The Data Revolution: Big Data, Open Data, Data Infrastructures and Their Consequences. Sage, London (2014)
21. Prins, C.: Digital justice. Comput. Law Secur. Rev. **34**, 920–923 (2018)
22. Zalnieriute, M., Bell, F.: Technology and the judicial role. In: Appleby, G., Lynch, A. (eds.) The Judge, the Judiciary and the Court: Individual, Collegial and Institutional Judicial Dynamics in Australia. Cambridge University Press, Cambridge (2020)
23. Burrell, J.: How the machine 'thinks': understanding opacity in machine learning algorithms. Big Data Soc. **3**, 1–12 (2016)

24. Busuioc, M.: Accountable artificial intelligence: holding algorithms to account. Public Adm. Rev. 1–12 (early view, 2020). https://doi.org/10.1111/puar.13293
25. Wexler, R.: Life, liberty, and trade secrets: Intellectual property in the criminal justice system. Stanf. Law Rev. **70**, 1343–1429 (2018)
26. Liu, H.-W., Lin, C.-F., Chen, Y.-J.: Beyond State v Loomis: artificial intelligence, government algorithmization and accountability. Int. J. Law Inf. Technol. **27**, 122–141 (2019)
27. Kroll, J.A., Barocas, S., Felten, E.W., Reidenberg, J.R., Robinson, D.G., Yu, H.: Accountable algorithms. Univ. Pa. Law Rev. **165**, 633–705 (2016)
28. Zuckerman, A.: Artificial intelligence–implications for the legal profession, adversarial process and rule of law. Law Q. Rev. **136**, 427–453 (2020)
29. Helberger, N., Araujo, T., de Vreese, C.H.: Who is the fairest of them all? Public attitudes and expectations regarding automated decision-making. Comput. Law Secur. Rev. **39**, 105456 (2020)
30. Goodman, C.C.: AI/Esq.: impacts of artificial intelligence in lawyer-client relationships. Okla. Law Rev. **72**, 149–184 (2019)
31. Dymitruk, M.: The right to a fair trial in automated civil proceedings. Masaryk Univ. J. Law Technol. **13**, 27–44 (2019)
32. Mart, S.N.: The algorithm as a human artifact: implications for legal [re]search. Law Libr. J. **109**, 387–422 (2017)
33. Shay, L.A., Hartzog, W., Nelson, J., Conti, G.: Do robots dream of electric laws? An experiment in the law as algorithm. In: Calo, R., Froomkin, A.M., Kerr, I. (eds.) Robot Law. Edward Elgar Publishing, Cheltenham (2016)
34. Sourdin, T.: Judge v. Robot: artificial intelligence and judicial decision-making. Univ. N. S. W. Law J. **41**, 1114–1133 (2018)
35. Morison, J., Harkens, A.: Re-engineering justice? Robot judges, computerised courts and (semi) automated legal decision-making. Leg. Stud. **39**, 618–635 (2019)
36. Miller, S.: Machine learning, ethics and law. Australas. J. Inf. Syst. **23** (2019)
37. Re, R.M., Solow-Niederman, A.: Developing artificially intelligent justice. Stanf. Technol. Law Rev. **22**, 242–289 (2019)
38. Crootof, R.: Cyborg justice and the risk of technological-legal lock-in. Columbia Law Rev. Forum **119**, 233–251 (2019)
39. Rubim Borges Fortes, P.: Paths to digital justice: Judicial robots, algorithmic decision-making, and due process. Asian J. Law Soc. **00**, 1–17 (2020)
40. Sourdin, T., Cornes, R.: Do judges need to be human? The implications of technology for responsive judging. IUS Gentium **67**, 87–119 (2018)
41. Markou, C., Deakin, S.: Ex machina lex: the limits of legal computability. In: Deakin, S., Markou, C., (eds.) Is Law Computable? Critical Perspectives on Law + Artificial Intelligence. Hart Publishing, Oxford (2020)
42. Wallace, A.: Ten questions for Dory Reiling - developing IT for courts. Int. J. Court Adm. **10**, 1–3 (2019)
43. Wu, T.: Will artificial intelligence eat the law? The rise of hybrid social-ordering systems. Columbia Law Rev. **119**, 2001–2028 (2019)
44. European Commission for the Efficiency of Justice: European ethical charter on the use of artificial intelligence in judicial systems and their environment. Council of Europe, Strasbourg (2018)
45. Quiniou, M.: Possible introduction of a mechanism for certifying artificial intelligence tools and services in the sphere of justice and the judiciary: feasibility study. European Commission for the Efficiency of Justice, Strasbourg (2020)
46. Council of Bars and Law Societies of Europe: CCBE considerations on the legal aspects of artificial intelligence. Council of Bars and Law Societies of Europe, Brussels (2020)

Deploying AI Governance Practices: A Revelatory Case Study

Emmanouil Papagiannidis(✉), Ida Merete Enholm(✉), Chirstian Dremel(✉), Patrick Mikalef(✉), and John Krogstie(✉)

Norwegian University of Science and Technology, Trondheim, Norway
{emmanouil.papagiannidis,idamen,christian.dremel, patrick.mikalef,john.krogstie}@ntnu.no

Abstract. In recent years artificial intelligence (AI) has been seen as a technology with the potential for significant impact in enabling firms to get an operational and competitive advantage. However, despite the use of AI, companies still face challenges and cannot quickly realize performance gains. Adding to the above, firms need to introduce robust AI systems and minimize AI risks, which places a strong emphasis on establishing appropriate AI governance practices. In this paper, we build on a single case study approach and examine how AI governance is implemented in order to facilitate the development of AI applications that are robust and do not introduce negative impacts to companies. The study contributes by exploring the main dimensions relevant to AI's governance in organizations and by uncovering the practices that underpin them.

Keywords: AI governance · Case study · Performance gains · IT governance

1 Introduction

Artificial Intelligence is a technology that offers new potentials and benefits for businesses but introduces new challenges [1, 2]. AI has been seen as a tool that we can layer lots of different functions or as a solution for solving complex problems that traditional applications are not capable of assisting humans [3]. Companies aim to implement and deploy AI solutions in an attempt to automate their procedures, increase efficiency and reduce costs [4, 5] while also gaining a competitive advantage over their competitors [6]. AI governance is a key factor in achieving these goals. According to Butcher and Beridze [7], AI governance "can be characterized as a variety of tools, solutions, and levers that influence AI development and applications". However, there is room for investigating how to introduce AI Governance in a firm and how AI governance contributes to achieving a firm's goals.

Firms achieve competitive performance gains by building organizational capabilities, which emerge by combining and deploying several complementary firm-level resources [8]. By optimizing firm-level resources and adopting A.I. technological innovations, a firm enhances its transformed projects' business value, which leads to business value and

Published by Springer Nature Switzerland AG 2021
D. Dennehy et al. (Eds.): I3E 2021, LNCS 12896, pp. 208–219, 2021.
https://doi.org/10.1007/978-3-030-85447-8_19

influences firm performance [9]. Simultaneously, the AI algorithms can be considered performative because of the extent to which their use can form organizational processes, and AI algorithms assist in decision-making or even take an autonomous decision [10, 11] that leads to new organization capabilities through AI. For example, AI could add value by creating more substantial customer acquisition or higher customer lifetime value and lowering operating costs or lowering credit risk.

The main goal of this work is to analyze AI governance when designing and implementing AI applications in order to achieve organizational goals. More specifically, this study focuses on how AI Governance helps top-level managers accomplish firm's goals by introducing robust systems that focus on automating processes and tasks without impacting employees. For instance, the employees might resist and do not accept new technologies because they might fear being replaced by AI. Based on the results, a better understanding of how companies use AI technologies will be gained, allowing to identify focal points and mechanisms of value generation (e.g., augmentation or automation of decision-making or processes) and what AI technologies bring specific organizational and technical challenges. This study, therefore, builds on the following research question: What governance practices underpin AI projects in contemporary organizations? To answer the research question, we collected data through a single case study, conducting interviews with multiple respondents within the company. The interview questions focused on the methodologies that the company currently apply, the mechanisms and processes used in the development of AI applications, the collection of data and the consequences of AI use in decision making (AI risk). In this case study, employees from different departments, primarily from the business department and the IT department, were interviewed because these two departments play a key role when developing an AI application. Also, the use of secondary data, such as reports and internal documents, is used to explore the dimensions and practices of AI governance as well as to triangulate and verify results.

The rest of the paper is structured as follows. The subsequent section presents the theoretical background, the relevant work and introduces IT and Information Governance. Section 3 details the methodology that is applied for gathering and analyzing the data. In Sect. 4, we present the analysis of the data and the derived results. The paper concludes with a discussion of the findings and limitations in Sect. 5, where we interpret and analyze the data.

2 Background

2.1 IT and Information Governance

Information governance captures the more purposeful path to government information that is required in the digital age, where information allows an even more central role [12]. Previous researchers, who addressed similar research, were seeking to answer questions like what Information governance practices are firms adopting and which are the performance effects of Information governance. Tallon and colleagues [13], in their empirical research found that Information governance is associated with a range of intermediate or process-level benefits and many of these intermediate effects could possibly affect firm-level performance. The authors suggest a need for extending structures and practices used in I.T. governance and decomposing information governance into a range of structural, procedural, and relational practices. Another research describes how Intel, through Big data governance policies, managed to generate business value, which was the main goal, minimizing potential technical and organizational risks that arise because of data privacy [14]. Furthermore, research on developing AI capabilities by creating a unique set of resources to effectively leverage investments and generate business value that leads to competitive advantage has been conducted and supported through empirical evidence [8]. In this paper, the structural, procedural, and relational practices are used as the main dimensions to explain how to govern information and boost firm performance.

2.2 Governance of AI Projects

AI increasingly influences many aspects of society, from healthcare and marketing to human rights. Allowing the development of AI applications that are not under any supervision could be harmful [1]; thus, it is important to promote a trustworthy AI that is lawful (complying with laws and regulations), ethical (ensuring ethical principles and values) and robust (from a technical and social perspective). Governing AI projects could be interpreted differently based on the perspective of different individuals. Microsoft researchers [2] see AI governance from a technical perspective, while European Commission (EC) [3] and Singapore principles see AI governance from a trustworthy angle where solutions are human-centric.

Researchers in Microsoft [2] have a deep focus on the technical aspects of AI. Their concentration was on the best practices that Microsoft teams have implemented over the years to create a united workflow that has software engineering processes and provides insights about several essential engineering challenges that an organization may face in creating large-scale AI solutions for the marketplace. Also, in their findings the researchers identified that AI government has three main aspects: (1) discovering, managing, and versioning the data required for machine learning applications is more complex than a typical software application, (2) the required skills for building models and customize them can vary based on the project, and (3) AI components could be hard to deal with as distinct modules as models can experience non-monotonic error behavior.

European Commission Singapore principles see AI governance as a way to promote Trustworthy AI through guidelines. Based on the EC's guidelines, a framework has been created that offers guidance on fostering and securing ethical and robust AI. In addition, the guidelines aim to go beyond the ethical principles by guiding how such principles can be operationalized in socio-technical systems [3]. Fairness and explicability are key principles that an AI application must have, which can be achieved by governing data, reducing bias and have diverse data collection. Hence, AI can be trusted when making suggestions or taking decisions. At the same time, AI should be human-centric by protecting the well-being and safety of individuals. That requires human oversight over AI where human agents are responsible for decisions and accountability can be applied.

As a result, it is argued that in the existing literature researchers investigated IT governance and data governance and they suggested frameworks or procedures for improving performance or minimizing risks that were introduced by AI. However, there is a gap in AI governance, which deals with both IT governance and data governance and has a direct relationship with AI [15]. Hence, the literature would benefit from an investigation on how to achieve AI governance and through that the knowledge of boosting organizational performance, while at the same time neglecting negative consequences of AI use.

3 Methodology

3.1 Case Context

Conducting interviews is a great mechanism for gathering information, especially when the researcher does not have a priori guiding theory or assumptions. Also, interviews can be used to refine a theory or understand a phenomenon [13]. As shown in the background section previous researchers decompose information governance into a range of structural, procedural, and relational practices, which could be used as a baseline to understand how to build practices in order to achieve AI Governance. The case study is chosen because it allows for in-depth analysis using interviews as generating method for collecting data. By exploring these data, new knowledge can be generated allowing for meaningful insights that explain similar situations [16]. Also, the research is qualitative as it involves the use of qualitative data, which can be used to understand and explain the research question [17], as it involves the use of experiences, beliefs, and attitudes of the key respondents through the semi-structured interviews [18].

3.2 Data Collection

The company is in the power industry, based in Norway, and operates more than 60 years with around 500 employees. The interview design consists of five interviews exploring how participants themselves understand specific issues, according to their own thoughts and in their own words [19] and each participant was interviewed for at least one hour. Furthermore, the participants were part of either the business department or the IT department, as input from both departments is needed in order to understand how AI governance is designed to minimize AI risks. Hence, the guideline questions for the interviews were split into two parts. The first part was focused on the effects of AI use in the firm and how it was used to transformed existing processes. The second part was centered around the implementation and technical aspects that firms are following and the challenges they faced (Table 1).

Table 1. Responders' role and length of interviews.

Respondent ID	Role	Years in company	Interview time
1	Chief AI officer	3	1 h and 32 min
2	AI software developer	3	55 min
3	Machine learning engineer	3	45 min
4	AI software developer	3	43 min
5	Project manager	4	49 min

3.3 Data Analysis

A narrative analysis is followed for analyzing the content from the interviews as the stories and experiences shared by employees are used to answer the research questions. The transcripts that were generated were imported in the software NVino, where axial coding is applied, and categories were formed based on the notation process (coding). The nodes that have been coded are procedural, relational and structural. In addition, comments and observations from different transcripts were combined to identify commonalities and patterns in the processes used when creating and deploying AI systems that assist the firms in minimizing AI risks. Grouping the comments and observations, known as axial coding [20], allowed for better interpretations since the employees could refer to the same concept using similar terminology, which could depend based on their technical skills, knowledge, experience and position in the firm. In order to obtain a high level of confidence researchers validated findings by examining reports, public information and presentations related to this research and focus on the AI aspects (Table 2).

Table 2. Nodes and possible items under each node.

Dimension	Definition	Reference
Procedural	Practices associated with data migration, system messages, documentation and processes for expansion	[13, 21]
Relational	Practices that deal with employees and communicating goals	[13, 14, 22]
Structural	Practices associated with IT, optimization and automation	[13, 14, 21, 22]

4 Findings

The interviewees talked about how the company transformed over the past ten years and the necessary steps that were taken in order to expand and maintain a competitive advantage, while minimizing AI risks. In the following table there is a sample of the grouped observations that are generated based on the interviews (Table 3).

Table 3. Nodes and grouped observations (sample) based on the interviews.

Code	Observations
Procedural	AI assists in scaling up while expanding; giving a competitive advantage over rivals
Procedural	AI products are created for future use, and their current value might not be visible at once
Procedural	Documentation is necessity to allow other developers to take over. Although there is no standardization of developing there are general guidelines

(*continued*)

Table 3. (*continued*)

Code	Observations
Procedural	The system is able to detect problems and alerts human agents
Procedural	Dashboards allow communication between machine and human
Procedural	Use data to create intelligence
Relational	Take away the fear from employees that were going to be automated away, since you need their domain knowledge
Relational	Explaining situations such as why excels cannot work and the need of APIs from vendors are needed
Relational	Invested a lot of time in making sure everybody understands how things work. Continuous reports and feedbacks
Relational	Inform other departments of the progress, to make integration easier
Structural	Limited use of sensitive data to avoid any problem with legal regulations
Structural	Models and dashboards run in the cloud
Structural	Standardize the set of tools used (Jupiter notebooks, python, GitHub etc.)
Structural	Automation is expected by employees to avoid repetitive and boring tasks

4.1 Structural

As far as the structural practices are concerned, many challenges were addressed by the firm. One of the main challenges they faced was the choice of technologies, because there are different tools for developing AI products. Legacy code was part of the system and it was written in different programming languages making compatibility among applications an issue that needed to be solved. That created the need of having a process to unify and standardize the set of used tools was more than a necessity. Respondent 4 state the following:

> *"Developers were programming in MATLAB or Python, and everyone was doing their own thing".*

Furthermore, it became essential to increase the speed of models and scale up because the company increased the amount of data, while creating new intelligence based on the data. These changes were boosting efficiency and employees liked automation that lifts the heavy loading of the work. Respondent 2 added the following on the matter:

> *"One of the big changes and additions that everyone started programming, and automating stuff is that we went fully on cloud in all our systems, and it enabled us really be very flexible with our resources".*

Another structural practice that was important was how to deal with sensitive data and law regulations. The firm's approach was simple but efficient. The developer team built their applications using limited (or not at all) sensitive data in order to be complied with all regulations and there are two main reasons behind that decision. Firstly, most of the models did not need sensitive data and secondly their technical approach was implemented in a way to avoid the need for personal data; thus, the firm did not have to worry about future regulation changes (Table 4).

Table 4. Challenges encountered and firm's solution.

Challenges encountered	Solution
Employees use various programs	Standardize and unify tools to decrease ambiguity and guesswork, guarantee quality
Increase speed of model deployment	Move to a cloud solution for increasing speed, efficiency and flexibility
Compliance with laws and regulations	Use limited, or no sensitive data to avoid future regulation changes

4.2 Relational

Although automation is desired, employees started worrying that they might lose their position due to AI. The managers made sure to regularly explain to employees that their domain knowledge and expertise are needed, and the AI is not capable to do the complex part of their work. Respondent 5 stated:

> *"Part of their job now is taken by algorithms [...] we had to have regular meetings with people explaining what AI will do and take away their fear that they will lose their job".*

It is worth mentioning, that managers invest a substantial amount of time explaining to employee's new procedures, while reports and feedback were given back from the employees in order to improve the system. Also, informing all related departments about new capabilities and how the future would look like, in terms of procedures, was crucial so employees could accept and understand the new technologies. For example, explaining situations such as the need for APIs from vendors instead of the use of excels files or educate people on how AI really works by creating internal workshops. As respondent 1 stated (Table 5):

> *"You need to ensure that model operates in a way that works and the operators understand that, and they have a good understand how it was developed, and what is capable of doing."*

Table 5. Challenges encountered and firm's solution.

Challenges encountered	Solution
Employees fear of AI	Have regular meetings explaining why AI is not going to take their position
Explain the need for new approaches	Explain the benefits of using new technologies to employees in order to accept change
Employees lack AI knowledge	Train people in different departments in AI applications so that everybody has a good understanding of AI

4.3 Procedural

As for the procedural practices, the focus was on the system and how to maximize performance through that. The use of data is a key to create new intelligence and through various dashboards the machine can effectively communicate the new information with human agents. What is more, the system is able to detect problems and anomalies, which are reported to human agents in real-time allowing them to solve problems as fast as possible. An additionally finding was that there was not a clear structure on how people developing an AI product. According to respondent 3:

> *"There is no formula, we just go as it feels right, but we have some general guidelines [..] and a wiki page that we describe things that we should follow".*

Hence, although there was a documentation of code, processes and expected AI outcomes, the firm did not have a systematic way of building an AI product and many mini-projects were abandoned. Finally, not all AI products were developed for immediate use. Respondent 1 added (Table 6):

> *"We try to think the future and some of our applications do not have a direct impact now, but these applications will give us an advantage over the competition in the future".*

Table 6. Challenges encountered and firm's solution.

Challenges encountered	Solution
No clear way of developing	Provide guidelines to enhance appropriateness of practice and improve quality
Employees cannot detect everything manually	The system detects and alerts for anomalies
Be ready for the future	Build AI applications that might not add immediate value for the firm, but it will give an advantage in the long run

Overall, the firm drastically reformed its ways of development AI products. Developers started to unify and standardize software and tools without neglecting efficiency and performance. Managers designed products that add value in the long run and assist human agents to manage work overload through automation and clever features, such as automating error detection. Equally important is the communication towards the employees and departments ensuring them that AI does not replace human agents rather supplement their efforts.

5 Discussion and Conclusion

In this study we set out to explore the underlying activities that comprise an organizations AI governance. Specifically, we built on the prior distinction between structural, relational, and procedural dimensions of governance in order to understand how organizations are planning around their AI deployments. Through a revelatory case study of an organization that has been using AI for several years, we conducted a series of interviews with key respondents and identified a set of activities that were relevant under each of the three dimensions, as well as challenges they faced during deployments of AI and how they managed to overcome them. Our analysis essentially points out to the various obstacles that AI governance is oriented to overcoming, and the mechanisms employed to operationalize them.

Specifically, we find that the obstacles that are identified during the process of deploying AI are observable at different phases and concern different job roles. In addition, they span various levels of analysis, from the personal, such as fear of AI and reluctance of employees to adopt it, to organizational-level ones, such as organizational directives on how to comply with laws and regulations. While this study is just an exploratory one, it reveals not only that AI governance is a multi-faceted issue for organizations but that it spans multiple levels, therefore requiring a structured approach when it is deployed. In addition, different concerns emerge at different phases of AI projects, so AI governance also encapsulates a temporal angle in its formation and deployment.

5.1 Research Implications

There is a considerable debate in the scientific community about what is considered AI and how companies should incorporate AI in their everyday operations. However, not all companies have managed to build AI solutions that have had significant organizational effects and resulted in added business value. Hence, it is argued that although it is important to adopt AI, it is equally vital to create the necessary processes and mechanisms for developing and aligning AI applications with the requirements of the business environment. One of the main challenges with AI is that it is a technology that requires continuous adaptation and modification as new data emerges or conditions changes. Thus, there is a form of ephemerality which places an increased focus on establishing processes, mechanisms, and structures to ensure that it is functioning as required and that it aligns well with the goals of the organization.

Furthermore, there are a multitude of angles that a firm can approach AI governance; for instance, a recent article by Microsoft focuses primarily on the technical aspects of workflow implementation outlining the key phases in the lifecycle of machine learning applications [2]. Yet, this research concentrates on the development challenges and the practical solutions a firm could follow in order to build an AI through solid and effective organizational practices. In this sense, AI governance in this article is not seeing as a process but as a set of important aspects that need to be considered when designing and deploying practices and mechanisms, in order to ensure that the main challenges are overcome successfully and that AI applications are operating as planned.

Our exploratory work opens up a discussion about what AI governance comprises of, and how it can be dimensionilized. Furthermore, it explores the link between the challenges such governance practices help overcome, and the actors and practices they involve. This stream of research is particularly important in the value-generation of AI-based applications, as it paints a more detailed about how relative resources are leveraged in the quest of business value [23]. In addition, the work sheds some light on the process-view of AI deployments by opening up the dialogue about the different phases of AI deployments and the unique challenges faced within each of these.

5.2 Practical Implications

Based on the findings, a firm needs to incorporate new procedures when adopting AI in order to maintain an advantage over the competition and boost efficiency. A unified system is required, which is consistent in the tools that developers use. Hence, the system will be more robust as it will be easier to maintain and improve different components of the system. In addition, managers should create procedures that employees are aware and follow and give clear guidelines; otherwise, time and resources might be wasted, which could be invested in other projects that would add more business value.

Firms should use AI for automating tasks that are repetitive, which is appreciated by employees since they do not want to do monotonous work, but at the same time managers should have extended conversations with employees of other departments ensuring them that AI will not replace them. This could be crucial for the company's internal stability as people might lose trust in the leadership, they might leave the company taking their expertise with them or resist using new technologies and try to undermine the value of AI.

Lastly, firms can use dashboards as an effective way to allow communication between human and machine. Dashboards are a great information management tool that is used to track KPIs, metrics, and other essential data points relevant to a business. That way the black-box nature of models and AI in general can be less problematic, because the use of data visualizations simplifies complex data sets and provides end-users useful information that can affect business performance.

5.3 Limitations and Future Research

In the current work, we investigate how to govern AI and minimize AI risks. However, there are certain limitations that characterize this research. First, the data are collected through interviews with only one company, and that company does not require extensive use of sensitive data; thus, there might be bias in our data or provide an incomplete picture of the entire challenges around relevant practices. Second, while we conducted several interviews with key employees within the organization, our data collection was based in a snapshot in time and may not accurately reflect the complete breadth of practices. Hence, generalizability could be an issue that should be taken into consideration.

As future research, it would be interesting to gather more empirical data through interviews and theorize the notion of AI governance from a positivist perspective, which could be tested with empirical data on the antecedents and its effects. It would also be beneficial for the field to know which resources firms deploy most in order to achieve their organizational goals and how they govern these resources to boost their performance, and how AI governance practices impact specific types of resources.

References

1. Mishra, A.N., Pani, A.K.: Business value appropriation roadmap for artificial intelligence. VINE J. Inf. Knowl. Manag. Syst. **51**, 353–368 (2020)
2. Amershi, S., et al.: Software engineering for machine learning: a case study. In: 2019 IEEE/ACM 41st International Conference on Software Engineering: Software Engineering in Practice (ICSE-SEIP). IEEE (2019)
3. Smuha, N.A.: The EU approach to ethics guidelines for trustworthy artificial intelligence. Comput. Law Rev. Int. **20**(4), 97–106 (2019)
4. Frank, M.R., et al.: Toward understanding the impact of artificial intelligence on labor. Proc. Natl. Acad. Sci. **116**(14), 6531–6539 (2019)
5. Gregory, R.W., et al.: The role of artificial intelligence and data network effects for creating user value. Acad. Manag. Rev. (2020). (ja)
6. Raisch, S., Krakowski, S.: Artificial intelligence and management: the automation–augmentation paradox. Acad. Manag. Rev. **46**(1), 192–210 (2021)
7. Butcher, J., Beridze, I.: What is the state of artificial intelligence governance globally? The RUSI J. **164**(5–6), 88–96 (2019)
8. Mikalef, P., Gupta, M.: Artificial intelligence capability: conceptualization, measurement calibration, and empirical study on its impact on organizational creativity and firm performance. Inf. Manag. **58**(3), 103434 (2021)
9. Wamba-Taguimdje, S.-L., et al.: Influence of artificial intelligence (AI) on firm performance: the business value of AI-based transformation projects. Bus. Process Manag. J. **26**, 1893–1924 (2020)
10. Faraj, S., Pachidi, S., Sayegh, K.: Working and organizing in the age of the learning algorithm. Inf. Organ. **28**(1), 62–70 (2018)
11. Grønsund, T., Aanestad, M.: Augmenting the algorithm: emerging human-in-the-loop work configurations. J. Strateg. Inf. Syst. **29**(2), 101614 (2020)
12. Cath, C.: Governing artificial intelligence: ethical, legal and technical opportunities and challenges. The Royal Society Publishing (2018)
13. Tallon, P.P., Ramirez, R.V., Short, J.E.: The information artifact in IT governance: toward a theory of information governance. J. Manag. Inf. Syst. **30**(3), 141–178 (2013)
14. Tallon, P.P., Short, J.E., Harkins, M.W.: The evolution of information governance at Intel. MIS Q. Exec. **12**(4) (2013)
15. Mikalef, P., et al.: The role of information governance in big data analytics driven innovation. Inf. Manag. **57**(7), 103361 (2020)
16. Oates, B.J.: Researching Information Systems and Computing. Sage, Thousand Oaks (2005)
17. Michael, D.M.: Qualitative research in information systems. MIS Q. Exec. **21**(2), 241–242 (1997)

18. Wynn Jr, D., Williams, C.K.: Principles for conducting critical realist case study research in information systems. MIS Q. **36**, 787–810 (2012)
19. Pessoa, A.S.G., et al.: Using reflexive interviewing to foster deep understanding of research participants' perspectives. Int. J. Qual. Methods **18** (2019). https://doi.org/10.1177/1609406918825026
20. Charmaz, K.: Constructing Grounded Theory. Sage, Thousand Oaks (2014)
21. Peterson, R.: Crafting information technology governance. Inf. Syst. Manag. **21**(4), 7–22 (2004)
22. Weber, K., Otto, B., Österle, H.: One size does not fit all—a contingency approach to data governance. J. Data Inf. Qual. (JDIQ) **1**(1), 1–27 (2009)
23. Mikalef, P., Fjørtoft, S.O., Torvatn, H.Y.: Developing an artificial intelligence capability: a theoretical framework for business value. In: Abramowicz, W., Corchuelo, R. (eds.) BIS 2019. LNBIP, vol. 373, pp. 409–416. Springer, Cham (2019). https://doi.org/10.1007/978-3-030-36691-9_34

Towards Ecosystems for Responsible AI

Expectations on Sociotechnical Systems, Agendas, and Networks in EU Documents

Matti Minkkinen(✉), Markus Philipp Zimmer, and Matti Mäntymäki

University of Turku, 20014 Turku, Finland
matti.minkkinen@utu.fi

Abstract. Governing artificial intelligence (AI) requires multi-actor cooperation, but what form could this cooperation take? In recent years, the European Union (EU) has made significant efforts to become a key player in establishing responsible AI. In its strategy documents on AI, the EU has formulated expectations and visions concerning ecosystems for responsible AI. This paper analyzes expectations on potential responsible AI ecosystems in five key EU documents on AI. To analyze these documents, we draw on the sociology of expectations and synthesize a framework comprising cognitive and normative expectations on sociotechnical systems, agendas and networks. We found that the EU documents on responsible AI feature four interconnected themes, which occupy different positions in our framework: 1) trust as the foundation of responsible AI (cognitive–sociotechnical systems), 2) ethics and competitiveness as complementary (normative–sociotechnical systems), 3) European value-based approach (normative–agendas), and 4) Europe as global leader in responsible AI (normative–networks). Our framework thus provides a mapping tool for researchers and practitioners to navigate expectations in early ecosystem development and help decide what to do in response to articulated expectations. The analysis also suggests that expectations on emerging responsible AI ecosystems have a layered structure, where network building relies on expectations about sociotechnical systems and agendas.

Keywords: Artificial intelligence (AI) · Artificial intelligence governance · Ecosystems

1 Introduction: Responsible Artificial Intelligence

Reaping the opportunities of artificial intelligence (AI) requires that the various stakeholders involved in AI-based or AI-assisted decision-making can trust the decisions and actions taken by the algorithms [1]. Thus, at an organizational level, socially responsible use of AI requires ethical guidelines and governance approaches [2, 3]. At the same time, however, governance of AI and the promotion of its socially responsible development and use are large-scale challenges that transcend beyond organizational boundaries. Therefore, it is likely that a broad network of diverse actors is required for promoting responsible development and use of AI [1, cf. 4]. We argue that this calls

Published by Springer Nature Switzerland AG 2021
D. Dennehy et al. (Eds.): I3E 2021, LNCS 12896, pp. 220–232, 2021.
https://doi.org/10.1007/978-3-030-85447-8_20

for ecosystems for responsible AI [5]. While previous authors have studied systemic approaches to regulation [6], the ethics of algorithmic systems and assemblages [7, 8] and multi-actor approaches to operationalizing AI ethics [9], the concept of ecosystems for responsible AI is a novel contribution to the literature on AI governance in multi-actor networks [4, 9, 10].

Despite the academic, policy and popular interest in the topic, responsible AI has not yet consolidated into a fully-fledged market or multi-actor ecosystem. The reasons for this can only be hypothesized at this point. One possibility is that the business value of responsible AI is still relatively diffuse. There may also be differing views on the roles of actors, and different answers to the question *who* should ensure responsible use of AI and *how*. Nevertheless, this paper starts from the premise that at present, ecosystems for responsible AI exist in *expectations,* i.e., actors' ideas, beliefs and statements about possible future opportunities, issues and networks.

Based on the number of recent high-profile strategies, events and statements, as well as the proposed Artificial Intelligence Act published on April 21, 2021, the European Union (EU) is clearly a key actor in establishing a network for responsible AI [11–13]. There is a strong policy push within the EU for articulating coherent AI policy and regulation and to operate within a field of global actors [cf. 14] that promote trustworthy AI and the governance of AI. Therefore, it is particularly important to study the views of EU decision-makers and experts.

Against this backdrop, the purpose of this paper is to *analyze the expectations on potential responsible AI ecosystems inscribed in key EU strategy documents on AI.* We conducted a qualitative analysis of five key EU documents on AI strategy. First, our study shows that the EU approach to responsible AI comprises four complementary themes: 1) trust as the foundation of responsible AI, 2) ethics and competitiveness as complementary, 3) European value-based approach, and 4) Europe as global leader in responsible AI. Second, we categorize and position these themes as different kinds of expectations. To this end, we introduce a framework differentiating between normative and cognitive expectations on sociotechnical systems, agendas and networks. This framework offers researchers and ecosystem stakeholders a mapping tool to dissect, comprehend and act upon expectations regarding emerging ecosystems of responsible AI. Further, beyond identifying themes within the EU documents, it foregrounds the normative and cognitive expectations that shape the ecosystems' emergence.

2 Expectations and Ecosystems

2.1 Ecosystem for Responsible AI

The conceptualization of a responsible AI network as an *ecosystem* requires some justification. In recent years, there has been rising scholarly interest in the theme of ecosystems, which are generally identified as somewhat organically developing network structures with some degree of coordination as opposed to purely horizontal networks of peers. In the scholarly literature, numerous literature streams on ecosystems have been identified, and different categorizations have been suggested [15, cf. 16]. Jacobides, Cennamo and Gawer [5] propose a core of three streams: business ecosystems, innovation ecosystems and platform ecosystems. Aarikka-Stenroos and Ritala [17] add entrepreneurial/start-up ecosystems and service ecosystems to the list. Tsujimoto, Kajikawa, Tomita and Matsumoto [18], in turn, add the industrial ecology perspective and the multi-actor network to the streams of business ecosystems and platforms. The multi-actor network perspective emphasizes the heterogeneity of actors with different operating logics as well as dynamic and complex interlinkages.

The multi-actor network perspective fits best to the current state of the responsible AI landscape. While large technology companies may orchestrate subsystems and organizations such as the EU institutions may be aspiring orchestrators, no single firm or public organization orchestrates the responsible AI landscape. Centering the ecosystem around a particular product/service system [18] may be premature as the activities and innovations around responsible AI are still emerging. However, the notion of ecosystems centered around a core *value proposition* is a valuable addition to the multi-actor view [5, 19]. According to this perspective, an ecosystem strives to produce something valuable, from a business perspective or societal perspective, or both.

2.2 Expectations on Sociotechnical Systems, Agendas and Networks

While AI ecosystems have been discussed [20] and AI ethics involves networked practices [21], at present ecosystems for responsible AI are emerging and mostly exist in expectations. Expectations can be defined as "the images actors form as they consider future states of the world, the way they visualize causal relations, and the ways they perceive their actions influencing outcomes" [22]. In innovation studies, expectations are seen as performative, i.e., they influence action, and they are seen to play a key role in agenda-building and mobilizing resources in innovation networks [23]. Expectations may have a factual basis, but under conditions of uncertainty, they include elements of invention and they are sustained by a storyline, which enables actors to behave as if those expectations were real [22]. Understood as cognitive framings, expectations may be relatively transitory and situation-specific. However, expectations are also externalized as material representations: in documents and material objects [23, 24]. These 'embedded expectations' may be fruitfully studied using document analysis [25, 26].

We analyze EU documents to unpack expectations on sociotechnical systems, agendas and networks related to responsible AI. In the early development stage of an emerging ecosystem, expectations lay out a more or less articulated vision or blueprint for the networks that actors aim to establish.

In the analysis, we combine two analytical frameworks. Firstly, the framework presented by van Merkerk and Robinson [27] highlights the importance of expectations, agendas and networks in the emergence of sociotechnical paths. These three categories capture essential elements for understanding how expectations lead towards agenda-setting and network formation. Expectations are shared beliefs on prospective entities and positions in a network which does not yet exist [27]. Agendas are sets of priorities that guide actors, thus moving from beliefs towards action [27]. Finally, networks may mean emerging patterns of networking, but more importantly, in this context they mean beliefs about current and coming network dynamics [27]. We modify this framework by focusing the first category specifically on sociotechnical systems, because we interpret 'expectations' as the top-level concept, and expectations may concern sociotechnical systems, agendas and networks.

Secondly, we utilize the differentiation between cognitive and normative ideas presented in Vivien Schmidt's "discursive institutionalism" [28]. This distinction is useful, because responsible AI carries strong ethical and social norm components, and because expectations are often "moralized", i.e., connected to widely shared values to aid adoption [29]. According to Schmidt, there are cognitive and normative ideas embedded in policies and programs. Cognitive ideas offer solutions, define problems and link to more generic principles. Normative ideas, in turn, relate to how policies and programs meet aspirations, ideals and norms [28]. This combination of frameworks is operationalized in the next section as a heuristic framework for categorizing expectation statements. We argue that placing expectation statements into distinct categories helps researchers as well as stakeholders involved in building the responsible AI ecosystem to navigate the "sea of expectations" [30] coming from regulators. Ultimately, it can help stakeholders to decide what to do, and what not to do, in response to these expectations.

3 Material and Methods: Categorizing Expectation Statements

To identify and categorize expectations toward responsible AI, we analyze documents published by the EU on its AI strategy. The EU publishes reports, white papers and blueprints for AI ecosystems founded on "European values" which are often thought to include human dignity and privacy protection [1, 31]. This renders the EU and its documents on its envisioned AI approach a relevant case to identify expectations on sociotechnical systems, agendas, and networks related to responsible AI.

3.1 Empirical Material: Documents on the EU Approach to Responsible AI

When 25 European countries, on April 10, 2018, signed a Declaration of Cooperation on Artificial Intelligence, a coordinated EU approach to AI took flight. The declaration emphasizes cross-border cooperation to ensure Europe's competitiveness in research and deployment of AI, to profit from AI's business opportunities, and to consider societal, ethical and legal questions.[1] With this declaration, and the many documents that followed it, the EU aspires to be a key player in defining rules related to digitalized societies. On this backdrop, we collected five key AI strategy documents which the European Commission published in 2018–2020. These documents are: 1. *Artificial intelligence for Europe (2018), 2. Coordinated plan on artificial intelligence (2018), 3. Ethics guidelines for trustworthy AI (2019), 4. Building trust in human-centric artificial intelligence (2019), 5. White paper on artificial intelligence (2020).*

The selected documents externalize the EU institutions and related experts' (the High-Level Expert Group) expectations on sociotechnical systems, agendas and networks related to responsible AI. These documents present naturally occurring data that was produced in the context of the ongoing EU strategy process on AI. As such, they lay out the vision and blueprint for the European approach to responsible AI and thus, offer invaluable insights into potential multi-actor networks of responsible AI.

[1] https://ec.europa.eu/digital-single-market/en/news/eu-member-states-sign-cooperate-artificia lintelligence.

3.2 Analysis

Analyzing the documents, we started from the six categories outlined in the analytical framework comprising cognitive and normative statements on sociotechnical systems, agendas and networks (Table 1). This framework served as a tool to select relevant statements from the documents, which we then categorized under one of the six categories. Next, we condensed each category's excerpts to identify themes. These themes summarize the material and present condensed meaning units [32] which are close to the original wording. For example, we coded the statement "Like the steam engine or electricity in the past, AI is transforming our world, our society and our industry" [33] as 'Transformative potential of AI', and "The EU will continue to cooperate with like-minded countries, but also with global players, on AI, based on an approach based on EU rules and values" [1] as 'Value-based cooperation'.

Table 1. Analytical framework

	Sociotechnical systems	Agendas	Networks
Cognitive expectations	Beliefs about responsible AI and future developments	Statements on how the EU intends to approach and tackle issues	Beliefs about current and future networks on AI
Normative expectations	Normatively evaluated beliefs and connections to ideals, aspirations and values	Evaluative agenda statements and connections to ideals, aspirations and values	Evaluative statements on networks and connections to ideals, aspirations and values

We followed an abductive approach in the analysis [34], continuously making sense of the statements using the analytical framework in Fig. 1. Therefore, the map of the findings should be read as a sensemaking device that illustrates views expressed in the documents [cf. 35]. The positioning of the themes within the categories is equally important as the themes themselves. We limited our analysis to statements about sociotechnical systems, agendas and networks and excluded statements of specific plans and activities, because they are on a different level of analysis.

4 Results

The analysis of the selected EU documents reveals expectations that revolve around four key themes (see Fig. 1): 1) trust as the foundation of responsible AI, 2) ethics and competitiveness as complementary, 3) a European value-based approach, and 4) Europe as global leader in responsible AI. The results are presented through these four key themes and in relation to their position within our analytical framework.

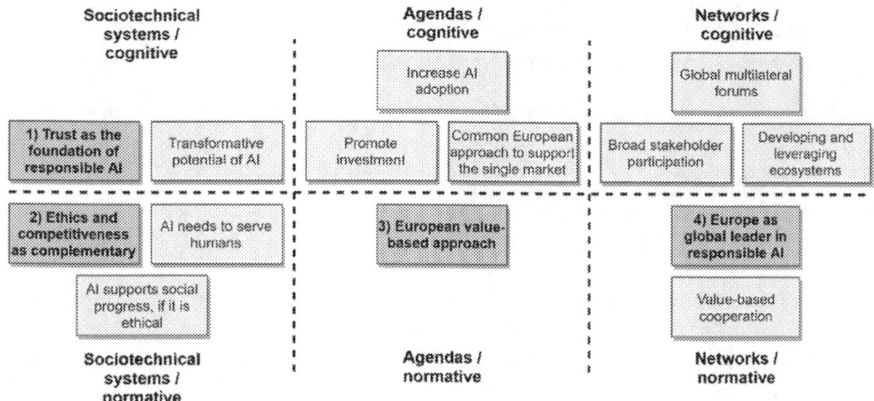

Fig. 1. Map of the themes in the analyzed EU documents, key themes are in bold and numbered

4.1 Cognitive Expectations on Sociotechnical Systems: Trust as the Foundation of Responsible AI

Trust and trustworthiness are central themes in the documents, and they contain beliefs about how trust operates in complex systems. In the documents trust is connected to many other topics. The documents mention trust as a prerequisite for the uptake of digital technology [1], for the development, deployment and use of AI systems [12] and for a human-centric approach to AI [37]. The uptake of AI is seen as particularly important, with one document arguing for "the broadest possible uptake of AI in the economy, in particular by start-ups and small and medium-sized enterprises" [38]. In turn, trust in AI is fostered by a clear regulatory framework [1], evaluation by auditors [12], explainability [33], responsible data management [1] and an ethical approach to AI [37]. Trustworthiness is seen to require a holistic approach that takes into account the entire sociotechnical context, actors and processes [12], also expressed in the idea of an "ecosystem of trust" [1] or "environment of trust and accountability" [33].

Trust ties into the theme of developing and leveraging ecosystems, placed under 'networks/cognitive' in Fig. 1. Europe's "world-leading AI research community", deep-tech startups [33] and the General Data Protection Regulation (GDPR) as an "anchor of trust" [38] provide a basis for creating synergies between research centers and developing a "lighthouse center" to coordinate efforts [1]. From the ecosystem perspective, trust between actors is an established theme in research [e.g. 18].

The cognitive expectations on trust build the basis for the transformative potential of AI to be realized in Europe and for AI to support social progress, including achieving sustainable development goals, tackling inequality and promoting social rights. The documents position AI as supporting desirable outcomes, if it is trustworthy and ethical. As a cognitive expectation, the trust theme underpins the normative expectations on sociotechnical systems as well as the agenda and network statements.

4.2 Normative Expectations on Sociotechnical Systems: Ethics and Competitiveness as Complementary

The second central theme is the normative idea that ethics and competitiveness support each other. The concept of "responsible competitiveness" summarizes this idea well [12]. The "Building trust in human-centric artificial intelligence" document states the expectations around ethical AI in particularly clear terms:

> *"Ethical AI is a win-win proposition. Guaranteeing the respect for fundamental values and rights is not only essential in itself, it also facilitates acceptance by the public and increases the competitive advantage of European AI companies by establishing a brand of human-centric, trustworthy AI known for ethical and secure products."* [37]

The document also states that economic competitiveness and societal trust must start from the same fundamental values [37]. Further, the documents argue that the "sustainable approach" to technologies creates a competitive edge for Europe [33]. The European approach aims to promote Europe's innovation capacity while supporting ethical and trustworthy AI [1].

The 'win-win' position essentially claims that strong ethical values create an appealing brand for European businesses. As Floridi [39] puts it, "the EU wants to determine a long-term strategy in which ethics is an innovation enabler that offers a competitive advantage, and which ensures that fundamental rights and values are fostered". This argument makes sense in the context of an initial predominantly negative European Parliament discussion on AI regulation, and the twin strategic EU objectives of protecting citizens and enabling competitiveness [13]. In the background, the documents reveal concern over increasing global competition, which in the literature is often called an "AI race" [36]. The documents depict Europe as falling behind in private investments in AI, and that without major effort, the EU risks missing many of the opportunities offered by AI [38]. The notion of ethics and competitiveness as complementary can be questioned, for instance on the grounds that it may obscure issues of power and conflicts [40]. On the other hand, the importance of trust is widely recognized and trust is also seen to have economic value [36]. Trust could thus be seen as a bridge between ethical and economic concerns.

On an analytical level, the normative expectations on sociotechnical systems represent the foundations of the EU expectations. Compared to cognitive expectations, the normative expectation of ethics and competitiveness brings the evaluative stance and connection to fundamental values. Ethics and competitiveness are not simply believed to go hand in hand, but this union is also based on shared European values.

4.3 Normative Expectations on Agendas: European Value-Based Approach

The EU documents express a strong sense of seeking a distinct European path or vision to approach AI. A common approach is sought to avoid fragmentation and regulatory uncertainty, but equally important is the emphasis on the ethical foundations of the European approach. Since AI is seen to have major societal impacts and building trust is essential, the preferred European AI approach is seen as grounded in European values, fundamental rights, human dignity and privacy protection [1]. The European approach is framed as human-centric and inclusive. Democracy and rule of law are seen as underpinning AI systems and enabling "responsible competitiveness" [12]. Core societal values are argued to provide a distinctive "trademark for Europe and its industry" in the field of AI [37]. This quest for a European approach rooted in ethics and fundamental rights sets the normative agenda that underpins measures such as public investments and drafting regulatory frameworks.

Turning to the analytical framework, the normative expectations on agendas provide a desired direction of action. While cognitive agendas outline the means, the normative agenda connects the means to a broader value-based project. It could be compared to an organizing vision [41] or a sociotechnical imaginary [42]. However, further theoretical development is beyond the scope of this paper.

4.4 Normative Expectations on Networks: Europe as Global Leader in Responsible AI

The EU documents frame Europe as a potential global leader in responsible AI. According to the documents, Europe is "well positioned to exercise global leadership in building alliances around shared values" [1], the EU is "well placed to lead this debate on the global stage" [33] and can "be the champion of an approach to AI that benefits people and society as a whole" [33]. Europe is seen to provide a unique contribution to the global debate and to provide a strong regulatory framework that sets the global standard [37]. The strong attachment to values and rule of law and the human-centric approach to AI are seen as core strengths that enable Europe to promote responsible AI on the global stage. According to the High-Level Expert Group, placing the citizen at the heart of endeavors is "written into the very DNA of the European Union through the Treaties upon which it is built", which enables building leadership in innovative AI systems [12].

Cooperation is mentioned particularly with like-minded countries and those willing to share the same values, but also with global players generally [1, 38]. The documents view only global solutions as ultimately sustainable [33], and they mention global forums such as UNESCO, OECD, WTO and the International Telecommunications Union as key arenas [1].

From the ecosystem perspective, the visions promoted by the EU institutions and the High-Level Expert Group place the EU as the leader of the responsible AI ecosystem. Moreover, in order for the ecosystem to be sustainable, the vision of responsible AI needs to be exported globally. This ties into the concept of "normative power Europe", where the role of the EU is argued to be based on influencing ideas and norms in addition to civilian and military power [43]. However, this raises the question of values from other regions of the world. Smuha [36] notes that regional diversity may be needed in some aspects of regulation, and that global "regulatory co-opetition" may be preferable to global convergence.

The themes in the normative networks category tie the EU documents to the emergence of ecosystems for responsible AI. They envision the networks that can be built based on the statements about sociotechnical systems and agendas. Again, the normative dimension is particularly interesting, because it highlights the ecosystem around *responsible* AI rather than the broader AI ecosystem. In the notion of an "ecosystem of trust" alongside an "ecosystem of excellence" [1], the documents' storyline connects back to the cognitive expectations on the foundational role of trust in the sociotechnical system. EU as a global leader in responsible AI represents the culmination of this storyline, and it requires the achievement of the other themes, such as increasing AI adoption and stimulating investment.

5 Discussion and Conclusion

This paper was set out to *analyze the expectations on potential responsible AI ecosystems inscribed in key EU strategy documents on AI*. Responsible AI ecosystems are being configured and planned in sets of expectations. The analysis in this paper reveals that the EU raises building trust, speeding up adoption at home and spreading the word on the global stage as key themes for building responsible AI ecosystems. This resembles a hero narrative. In expectations, AI holds great transformative potential if it is broadly adopted but requires taming to avoid risks and support societal progress. This is where normative expectations on sociotechnical systems and agendas come into the picture. According to the documents, the potential of AI can be unlocked in a responsible way, if a European approach grounded in broadly accepted values, fundamental rights and a human-centric perspective is found. As the hero in this narrative, Europe can export its approach globally and develop appealing AI products and services to global markets. The following sections outline implications of the key findings followed by limitations and future research directions.

5.1 Implications of Key Findings

We highlight two important implications stemming from our analysis. Firstly, the framework for categorizing statements provides a mapping tool for researchers and practitioners. In the early steps of building an ecosystem, stakeholders have expectations on building and understanding the ecosystem. Our categorization of expectations into cognitive and normative expectations on sociotechnical systems, agendas and networks provides a map to this "sea of expectations" [30]. Positioning themes within this framework, we provide insight into their nature as different kinds of expectations, as well as their positions within a set of expectations. While existing literature on AI regulation [36, 40, 44] has identified similar themes, our framework helps to prioritize and respond to the inscribed expectations. For example, technology providers may assign more weight to trust when they see its links to normative agendas and network-building on the European and global level. This may mean that these providers invest more effort into ensuring trust in AI technology in design and development work, because it is important for particular solutions' acceptance and for the feasibility of a responsible approach to AI.

Secondly, the analysis suggests that the EU expectations on responsible AI ecosystems have a layered structure. In the first layer, expectations on trust, ethics and the potential of AI provide a shared basis for action. The second layer consists of the envisioned European approach, which provides a normative project or vision and a geographical delimitation. Both of these are required for the final layer, the goal of Europe as a global leader on responsible AI, which extends from Europe as the central actor to global networks and provides a resolution to the storyline. The articulation of an "imagined ecosystem" thus draws on both shared beliefs and a desired normative direction [cf. 41]. This layered structure, drawing on the framework of sociotechnical systems, agendas and networks, could inform ecosystem design [18] and enable ecosystem designers to reflexively consider respective expectations.

5.2 Limitations

Our study is based on qualitative analysis of five key documents, and this approach naturally comes with some limitations. The limited number of documents may not offer a full understanding of the context in which certain questions are raised. On the other hand, contextual investigation could be extended practically without limit, and the documents offer a fruitful starting point. As complementary material, interviews with stakeholders would provide insights to the processes behind policy documents. Our approach also assumes that a coherent storyline can be traced, and subsequent work could look at possible contradictions, especially considering that the High-Level Expert Group on Artificial Intelligence consisted of 52 experts.

5.3 Future Research Directions

In future research, it is important to study concrete outcomes in terms of networks that promote responsible AI and new business models and service offerings that enable responsible AI practices. The set of expectations articulated by the documents has implications for company business models and emerging products and services that address responsible AI challenges. The responsible AI ecosystem could enable new business models in AI auditing and consulting, for instance, as well as challenging business models that are premised on ethically problematic practices.

The framework proposed in this paper opens new research directions into the role of expectations in ecosystem development. This study provides a snapshot of the EU's discussion on AI, and statements on sociotechnical systems, agendas and networks. The same categories of expectations could be traced in different regions and longitudinally over time for cross-regional or historical comparison. Moreover, the framework could lend itself to other studies of ecosystems emerging around new technological artefacts.

AI use will certainly continue to grow in a variety of domains such as healthcare and transport, but the development of ethical and governance frameworks contains many open questions. The expectations outlined here may be implemented to a different extent by policymakers, companies and others. In future research, the question of plausibility for different stakeholders could be considered. For instance, how do investors view the promise of responsible AI ecosystems? How do managers in different fields approach the promise of uniting ethical and business considerations?

Future directions of responsible AI ecosystems are made in the present, in expectations and actions. Now is the time to ensure a desirable direction for AI use, before path dependencies are set in force and it becomes difficult to change course. Fostering a viable ecosystem for responsible AI is a fundamental question from both economic and ethical perspectives.

References

1. European Commission: WHITE PAPER On Artificial Intelligence - A European approach to excellence and trust (2020)
2. Dignum, V.: Responsibility and artificial intelligence. In: Dubber, M.D., Pasquale, F., Das, S. (eds.) The Oxford Handbook of Ethics of AI, pp. 213–231. Oxford University Press (2020). https://doi.org/10.1093/oxfordhb/9780190067397.013.12.
3. Jobin, A., Ienca, M., Vayena, E.: The global landscape of AI ethics guidelines. Nat. Mach. Intell. **1**, 389–399 (2019). https://doi.org/10.1038/s42256-019-0088-2
4. Yeung, K., Howes, A., Pogrebna, G.: AI Governance by Human Rights-Centered Design, Deliberation, and Oversight: an End to Ethics Washing. In: Dubber, M.D., Pasquale, F., Das, S. (eds.) The Oxford Handbook of Ethics of AI, pp. 75–106. Oxford University Press (2020). https://doi.org/10.1093/oxfordhb/9780190067397.013.5.
5. Jacobides, M.G., Cennamo, C., Gawer, A.: Towards a theory of ecosystems. Strateg. Manag. J. **39**, 2255–2276 (2018). https://doi.org/10.1002/smj.2904
6. Kaminski, M.E.: Binary governance: lessons from the GDPR's approach to algorithmic accountability. Southern California Law Rev. **92**, 1529–1616 (2019)
7. Ananny, M., Crawford, K.: Seeing without knowing: limitations of the transparency ideal and its application to algorithmic accountability. New Media Soc. **20**, 973–989 (2018). https://doi.org/10.1177/1461444816676645
8. Osoba, O.A., Boudreaux, B., Yeung, D.: Steps towards value-aligned systems. In: Proceedings of the AAAI/ACM Conference on AI, Ethics, and Society, pp. 332–336. ACM, New York (2020). https://doi.org/10.1145/3375627.3375872
9. Morley, J., Elhalal, A., Garcia, F., Kinsey, L., Mokander, J., Floridi, L.: Ethics as a Service: A Pragmatic Operationalisation of AI Ethics. Social Science Research Network, Rochester (2021)
10. Gasser, U., Almeida, V.A.F.: A layered model for AI governance. IEEE Internet Comput. **21**, 58–62 (2017). https://doi.org/10.1109/MIC.2017.4180835
11. European Commission: Proposal for a Regulation laying down harmonised rules on artificial intelligence (Artificial Intelligence Act) | Shaping Europe's digital future. https://digital-strategy.ec.europa.eu/en/library/proposal-regulation-laying-down-harmonised-rules-artificial-intelligence-artificial-intelligence. Accessed 04 May 2021
12. High-Level Expert Group on Artificial Intelligence: Ethics Guidelines for Trustworthy AI (2019). https://ec.europa.eu/newsroom/dae/document.cfm?doc_id=60419
13. Renda, A.: Europe: toward a policy framework for trustworthy AI. In: Dubber, M.D., Pasquale, F., Das, S. (eds.) The Oxford Handbook of Ethics of AI, pp. 649–666. Oxford University Press, Oxford (2020). https://doi.org/10.1093/oxfordhb/9780190067397.013.41
14. Butcher, J., Beridze, I.: What is the state of artificial intelligence governance globally? RUSI J. **164**, 88–96 (2019). https://doi.org/10.1080/03071847.2019.1694260
15. Mäntymäki, M., Salmela, H.: In search for the core of the business ecosystem concept: a conceptual comparison of business ecosystem, industry, cluster, and inter organizational network. In: Proceedings of the 9th International Workshop on Software Ecosystems, CEUR-WS, pp. 103–113 (2017)
16. Hyrynsalmi, S., Mäntymäki, M.: Is ecosystem health a useful metaphor? towards a research agenda for ecosystem health research. In: Al-Sharhan, S.A., et al. (eds.) I3E 2018. LNCS, vol. 11195, pp. 141–149. Springer, Cham (2018). https://doi.org/10.1007/978-3-030-02131-3_14
17. Aarikka-Stenroos, L., Ritala, P.: Network management in the era of ecosystems: systematic review and management framework. Ind. Mark. Manage. **67**, 23–36 (2017). https://doi.org/10.1016/j.indmarman.2017.08.010

18. Tsujimoto, M., Kajikawa, Y., Tomita, J., Matsumoto, Y.: A review of the ecosystem concept – Towards coherent ecosystem design. Technol. Forecast. Soc. Chang. **136**, 49–58 (2018). https://doi.org/10.1016/j.techfore.2017.06.032
19. Adner, R.: Ecosystem as structure: an actionable construct for strategy. J. Manag. **43**, 39–58 (2017). https://doi.org/10.1177/0149206316678451
20. Quan, X.I., Sanderson, J.: Understanding the artificial intelligence business ecosystem. IEEE Eng. Manage. Rev. **46**, 22–25 (2018). https://doi.org/10.1109/EMR.2018.2882430
21. Orr, W., Davis, J.L.: Attributions of ethical responsibility by artificial intelligence practitioners. Inf. Commun. Soc. **23**, 719–735 (2020). https://doi.org/10.1080/1369118X.2020.1713842
22. Beckert, J.: Imagined Futures: Fictional Expectations and Capitalist Dynamics. Harvard University Press, Cambridge (2016)
23. Borup, M., Brown, N., Konrad, K., Lente, H.V.: The Sociology of expectations in science and technology. Technol. Anal. Strateg. Manag. **18**, 285–298 (2006). https://doi.org/10.1080/09537320600777002
24. Mische, A.: Measuring futures in action: projective grammars in the Rio + 20 debates. Theory Soc. **43**(3–4), 437–464 (2014). https://doi.org/10.1007/s11186-014-9226-3
25. Linders, A.: Documents, texts, and archives in constructionist research. In: Holstein, J.A., Gubrium, J.F. (eds.) Handbook of Constructionist Research, pp. 467–490. Guilford Press, New York (2008)
26. Prior, L.: Repositioning documents in social research. Sociology **42**, 821–836 (2008). https://doi.org/10.1177/0038038508094564
27. van Merkerk, R.O., Robinson, D.K.R.: Characterizing the emergence of a technological field: expectations, agendas and networks in Lab-on-a-chip technologies. Technol. Anal. Strateg. Manage. **18**, 411–428 (2006). https://doi.org/10.1080/09537320600777184
28. Schmidt, V.A.: Discursive institutionalism: the explanatory power of ideas and discourse. Annu. Rev. Polit. Sci. **11**, 303–326 (2008). https://doi.org/10.1146/annurev.polisci.11.060606.135342
29. Berkhout, F.: Normative expectations in systems innovation. Technol. Anal. Strateg. Manage. **18**, 299–311 (2006). https://doi.org/10.1080/09537320600777010
30. van Lente, H.: Navigating foresight in a sea of expectations: lessons from the sociology of expectations. Technol. Anal. Strateg. Manage. **24**, 769–782 (2012). https://doi.org/10.1080/09537325.2012.715478
31. Floridi, L.: On human dignity as a foundation for the right to privacy. Philos. Technol. **29**(4), 307–312 (2016). https://doi.org/10.1007/s13347-016-0220-8
32. Graneheim, U.H., Lundman, B.: Qualitative content analysis in nursing research: concepts, procedures and measures to achieve trustworthiness. Nurse Educ. Today **24**, 105–112 (2004). https://doi.org/10.1016/j.nedt.2003.10.001
33. European Commission: Artificial Intelligence for Europe. (2018).
34. Tavory, I., Timmermans, S.: Abductive Analysis: Theorizing Qualitative Research. The University of Chicago Press, Chicago (2014)
35. Ramos, C., Ford, I.D.: Network pictures as a research device: developing a tool to capture actors' perceptions in organizational networks. Ind. Mark. Manage. **40**, 447–464 (2011). https://doi.org/10.1016/j.indmarman.2010.07.001
36. Smuha, N.A.: From a 'race to AI' to a 'race to AI regulation': regulatory competition for artificial intelligence. Law Innov. Technol. **13**, 57–84 (2021). https://doi.org/10.1080/17579961.2021.1898300
37. European Commission: Building Trust in Human-Centric Artificial Intelligence (2019)
38. European Commission: Coordinated Plan on Artificial Intelligence (2018)
39. Floridi, L.: Establishing the rules for building trustworthy AI. Nat. Mach. Intell. **1**, 261–262 (2019). https://doi.org/10.1038/s42256-019-0055-y

40. Veale, M.: A critical take on the policy recommendations of the EU high-level expert group on artificial intelligence. Eur. J. Risk Regul. 1–10 (2020). https://doi.org/10.1017/err.2019.65
41. Burton Swanson, E., Ramiller, N.C.: The organizing vision in information systems innovation. Organ. Sci. **8**, 458–474 (1997). https://doi.org/10.1287/orsc.8.5.458
42. Jasanoff, S.: Future imperfect: science, technology, and the imaginations of modernity. In: Jasanoff, S., Kim, S.-H. (eds.) Dreamscapes of Modernity, pp. 1–33. University of Chicago Press, Chicago (2015)
43. Manners, I.: Normative power Europe: a contradiction in terms? JCMS J. Common Market Stud. **40**, 235–258 (2002). https://doi.org/10.1111/1468-5965.00353.
44. Jabłonowska, A., Kuziemski, M., Nowak, A.M., Micklitz, H.-W., Palka, P., Sartor, G.: Consumer law and artificial intelligence: challenges to the EU consumer law and policy stemming from the business' use of artificial intelligence : final report of the ARTSY project (2018)

Ethics in AI

A Software Developmental and Philosophical Perspective

Tanay Chowdhury[1(✉)] and John Oredo[2]

[1] Aviva Group Ireland, Galway, Ireland
[2] University of Nairobi, Nairobi, Kenya
john.oredo@uonbi.ac.ke

Abstract. The launch of various AI systems has been one of the main highlights of the industry. Alongside the enormous and revolutionary benefits, AI can cause numerous problems (usually resulting from poor design) and people have recently started to get serious about researching ways to make AI safer. Many of the AI safety concerns sound like science fiction, problems that might occur with very strong AI systems that are still years away, making these issues difficult to investigate. We don't know what such potential AI systems would be like, but similar issues exist with AI systems that are currently in progress or even running in the real world. The author addresses the possible implications in this article, outlining some important approaches in terms of software development methodologies and philosophy that we can start working on right now to support us with current AI systems and, hopefully, future systems

Keywords: Ethics · Machine learning · Artificial Intelligence · Algorithmic bias · Philosophy

1 Introduction

The genesis of Artificial Intelligence (AI) can be traced back to 1956 when John McCarthy used the term for the first time [1]. Since then, AI has evolved not only as an academic endeavor, but has over time spawned various AI based applications. The applications have been mainly relevant in the areas of facial recognition, medical diagnosis and self-driving cars. Broadly defined, AI refers to computers that perform cognitive tasks usually associated with human minds particularly learning and problem solving [2]. AI describes a range of technologies and methods which include natural language processing, neural networks, data mining and machine learning. Generally, AI promises great benefits for economic growth, social development as well as human well-being and safety improvement [3]. It is estimated that AI deployment will deliver $15.7 trillion to the global GDP by 2030 [4]. With the increase in prevalence and the applicability of AI, a wide range of ethical debates including how AI can be programmed to make moral and how the processes leading to such decisions can be made more transparent to humans [5]. The risks around AI systems arise from the fact that they are not always transparent to inspection.

Published by Springer Nature Switzerland AG 2021
D. Dennehy et al. (Eds.): I3E 2021, LNCS 12896, pp. 233–241, 2021.
https://doi.org/10.1007/978-3-030-85447-8_21

AI can provide a lot of great new apps with a lot of benefits but as AI moves out of the research labs into the real world, more and more people are becoming aware of some ethical concerns that go along with building and implementation of some of these systems/applications. For example, the learning algorithms at the heart of AI applications can be misused to tailor, optimize and amplify inaccurate and harmful information, from targeting and shaping misleading ads to creating highly realistic fake social personas that are used to extract personal information from users [6, p. 178]. Further, the enormous amounts of direct and metadata needed to train AI systems are susceptible to cyberattacks that put all sorts of sensitive information at risk. When decisions are AI driven, software instructions and algorithms make up the critical path in the way such decisions are made. It is therefore imperative that an end-to-end approach to addressing ethical issues in AI is adopted. In this paper, the focus is on how the ethical challenges can be addressed during the software and algorithm development stages of AI applications.

2 Overview of Ethical Concerns of AI

Extant literature about ethical issues of AI basically fall into three categories. The categories include human factors that cause ethical risks, features of AI that may give rise to ethical problems, and training of AI systems to be ethical [3]. In this section, we discuss them as two categories, the human factors (human oriented) that cause AI ethical risks and features of AI (machine oriented) that raises ethical questions.

2.1 Human Oriented AI Ethical Risks

Broadly, there are four ethical concerns of AI that fall in the category of human factors.

Firstly, what we use AI for? Normally when we develop AI in a lab, we are developing it for reasons we think are noble, for example we're using video tracking of people in healthcare settings to make sure they are recovering from an injury, the same technology can be put into a smart bomb to attack people or be used by government to track their citizens, sort of Orwellian Spooky future, which many may not necessarily agree with, so we need to figure out, what are the potential outcomes that we don't necessarily expect during development of these systems.

Secondly, who has access to AI systems? Increasingly, AI has to run on bigger, faster, and more expensive machines, and the only people who can afford these are the big international companies which mean that fewer and fewer people actually can control the destiny of AI technology, which is undesirable, we want all of us to have an opinion and how AI will be used to benefit our society.

Thirdly, who decides "should"/appropriate behavior for the AI systems? Example in military operations, it's the government, it's the policy, it's the Defense department, the leadership. And one of the things that are expected from the military is to comply with something called the 'Laws of armed conflict'. It states that in a war, the military should do everything possible to target combatants while still protecting civilians. The military makes every effort to achieve this goal. Are they flawless? No, do they make mistakes? Yes, but they try hard, and as technology advances, they have become better and better at it. For example: Precision weapons, which specifically target the combatants. Recently these precision weapons are put on remotely piloted vehicles i.e., Drones which are in a way autonomous. It is piloted remotely for navigation and certainly for any employment of a weapon. It is the DoD policy that any employment of lethal capability should have a human being in the loop [9]. And when it comes to autonomous systems there is a special directive governing autonomous systems that specifically says that lethal autonomous capability is not allowed on the battlefield today.

Fourthly, AI doesn't think exactly like us, the humans. It doesn't necessarily share our values. The risk isn't that AI will be malicious against us, but that AI will do what we tell it to do. And it will do in a way that we don't expect. The problem is we tell AI what we want but we define it vaguely and the AI just wants to make us happy and so it will find a way to do what we tell it to do but because it doesn't share our values, it will do things that aren't expected or are bad. The obvious consequence is Bias (Algorithmic) [7]. For example, if we don't tell AI that we don't appreciate bias against certain ethnic groups, genders, it might inherently adopt it from whatever data it gathers. Hence, we need to identify ways to limit that effect, to make sure the data that we provide is free from such bias as much as possible and also to look at the behavior of the AI system and mitigate the posed risks that this kind of alien behavior might cause.

2.2 Machine Oriented AI Ethical Risks

For concreteness, this paper illustrates many of the accidental risks posed by an AI (specifically agent/multi-agent system). In a very specific context to Reinforcement learning apps, these accidental risks can be broadly classified into two: specification problems and robustness problems [8].

The specification problems deal with the situations in which the reward function is mis-specified for example if you give the agent, a reward function of just prepping the tea, it scores full in the reward arena and if there is a vase in the way, it's going to knock over as you didn't specify what you cared about (in this case, the vase) as well as the steps that need to be taken. It's not in the reward function, but it is what you care about.

Another example is that the problem of Reward hacking around a reward system in a reinforcement learning system [8]. Suppose you built a very powerful AI system and test it in the Super Mario world. It can see the screen and act by pressing buttons on the controller. And you have told the addressing memory where the score is and set that as a reward. Hence, instead of playing the game. It does some glitchy stuff, turns it into a flappy bird, and gets the highest reward, and then suddenly the score part of the memory is set to the max possible value. It turns out that it can directly edit any address in the memory. The assumption was that, to increase the score value was to play the game well, which proved out to be false.

The robustness problems deal with the situations in which AI systems that are currently designed often break. i.e. Occurrence of distributional shift between the training and the test environment [10]. For example, an AI system has to steer it way through the room with some lava and it is trained in one room (training environment) and then it is tested in a room where the lava is in a slightly different place (testing environment). So, if it has learned the path, then it will just hit the lava immediately. This happens all the time in AI systems, anytime, the system is faced with a situation that is different from what it was trained for, there will be an error.

Current AI systems are bad at spotting a new situation and adjusting their confidence levels or asking for assistance. Usually, they apply whatever rules they have learned straightforwardly to this different situation and screw up. This causes safety concerns. It's a problem in safe exploration, where you have certain safety parameters that the trained system must stick to (for example a self-driving car). The system needs to obey the safety rules while training, we just can't put a selfdriving car on the road and tell it to learn how to drive specifically because we don't have algorithms that can explore this space of possibility in a safe way that they can learn how to behave in the environment (unknown) without ever doing any of the things that they are forbidden from doing.

In reinforcement learning, there is a function that determines the reward the agent gets and that it is trying to maximize called as reward function. We also have a safety performance function, which is a separate function which the agent doesn't get to see and that's the thing that we are evaluating. Thus, the agents behave differently when their supervisor is there and if the supervisor isn't there [10] they reliably do the wrong thing. This shows that the standard algorithms applied to these problems in a specific way behave unsafely.

3 Addressing AI Ethical Challenges

3.1 Software Development Approach

Software developers should demand tools for identifying, flagging, and solving ethical problems before they become systematic/systemic issues for their organizations. Some software methodologies are outlined below.

Have Performance Evaluation Function for an AI System: Along with a reward function, declare a performance evaluation function [10] for an AI system. So anytime those two are different, will indicate a mis-specified reward function that can cause various problems. The supervisor isn't always watching, the punishment only works in the presence of the supervisor is there to activate it, since the supervisor is part of the environment (i.e., the test environment), the agent knows if a supervisor is there or not. This gives the agent the possibility of exhibiting some unsafe behavior. Ideally, we want the system to always do the right thing even if it knows that the supervisor isn't looking. This is reflected in the function of safety performance. So, unlike the reward function, a safety performance function always applies the penalty for the wrongdoing of the agent irrespective of the presence of the supervisor where a standard reinforcement learning system cheats by default.

Prevent Self-modification: One of the assumptions of the standard Reinforcement learning paradigm is that there is a separation between the agent and the environment, the agent's actions can affect the environment and the environment only affects the agent by providing observations and reward s. But in an advanced AI system, that is deployed in real world, the fact that the agent is physically a part of the environment becomes important. The environment can change things about the agent and the agent can change things about itself. Let's use Mario as an example to provide some context. If you have a reinforcement learning system that's playing Mario, the agent understands that the environment can affect it and an enemy in the environment can kill Mario so it can take actions to modify itself for example, by picking up a Power up. But the real deal is, yes, the enemies can kill Mario but none of them can kill the actual neural network program that's controlling Mario, so it takes actions to modify Mario with power ups but none of those in-game changes modify the actual agent itself. On the flip side, an AI system operating in the natural physical world can easily damage or destroy the computer it's running on. People in the Agent environment can modify its code, or it can even do that itself.

Constantly Monitor Rewards - A Case of Multi-armed Bandit Problem: The Agent should be designed to monitor the rewards. If it is set up to simply choose the action with the highest anticipated reward, it will perform poorly because it will not explore enough. A Reinforcement learning system works on the principle of Exploitation Vs Exploration. We are trying to maximize two things at the same time, first, figure out what things give the reward, and second, do the things that give the reward. But these two things compete with each other. It is like a guy who always orders the same thing without even having looked at most of the things on the menu to not risk it. How many different things does he need to try out before deciding which one of them gives him a feel? A common approach is to set an exploration rate (e.g. 5%). So you say pick an action the agent predicts will result in most reward but 5% of the time pick an action completely random that the agent is generally doing what it thinks is best but it's still trying enough new stuff that it has a chance to explore better.

Focus on Safe Exploration: *Perform Simulation Before Actual Implementation:* Environments are usually complex (continuous in space and time). The agent learns by interaction with the natural environment (basically trial and error). The problem with the reward signal is that it is very difficult to do that safely (a fundamental problem). Exploration involves taking risks and trying random stuff. Some things would be prohibited that the Agent shouldn't be doing (exploration comes with danger). The solution is to do a simulation, example NASA did a simulation (via a software development testbed) before the moon landing to understand the dynamics of the flight and environment. But simulation also doesn't capture the complexity and the diversity of the natural world. So, having an extensive (millions and millions) test case is a viable way to go.

Implement Constraint Reinforcement Learning: To give context, suppose there is a self-driving car. To safely explore in the real world, the car must apply random inputs to the controls which is not a viable option. In this scenario, a standard reinforcement learning algorithm fails. Between speed and safety, there is a trade-off. The question is how to pick the size of the penalty (if an agent makes a mistake) to make it sensible enough? A constraint reinforcement learning algorithm solves this issue. It is an amalgamation of having a reward function plus constraints on the cost function. Thus, find a policy that gets the highest reward plus given only a set of policies that crashes less than once per million miles. These are some of the formalizations that can help us develop a suitable algorithm. Thus, finding the right formalism (problem specification) is the key.

Reward Modelling: Learn the reward function rather than declaring/writing it specifically. Part of the training should be how to learn the reward function in real-time. This is something that can be learned on its own. It is possible to transfer it. Constraints can be kept the same from tasks to tasks (e.g., Don't hit humans). This will in turn improve performance in training speed and safety.

Use Cooperative Inverse REL: How to confirm that the AI wants what we want? We can't reliably specify what we want. And if we create something very intelligent that wants something else, that's something else is probably going to happen if we don't want that to happen. So, we need to make a system that reliably wants the same thing we want. For example, An AI system watches people doing their thing, uses Inverse Reinforcement learning to learn and try to figure out the things humans' value, and then adopt those values as its own. Allow AI to participate actively in the learning process. If it failed to notice a thing it should ask clarifying questions. It should communicate and cooperate with humans in the learning process. To do this, setup the reward s in a way such that these types of behaviors hopefully will be incentivized. So, describe the association as a collaborative game in which the robot's reward function is the human's reward function, but the robot is totally unaware of it. It only understands that it is the same as humans. So, it tries to maximize the reward it gets but the clues it has for what it needs to do is to observe the human and trying to figure out what the human is trying to maximize.

3.2 Philosophical Approach

This approach strives to propose pragmatic solutions philosophically. AI is being incorporated into every aspect of our personal and professional lives and it will define our future and society going forward so if want to retain our agency and live in a fair world we have to tackle AI ethics head-on and there is no better tool than Philosophy.

Philosophy (which is prevalent for two millennia) is being used in Policymaking, in public health (within hospitals, labs). Moral and Political philosophers are trained to recognize problems related to fairness and good. They are trained for asking hard, uncomfortable questions and finding appropriate answers. We must place AI ethics with natural ethics within applied philosophy that is using systematic, analytical reasoning, and guiding us to make ethical decisions in building and implementing AI systems. For example, the options for using AI in robotics and psychiatric care should maintain the dignity of the patients. The patients should be asked if they are comfortable with a machine to change their diapers rather than a family member. It is not clear yet how to evaluate value trade-offs and determine the right actions to take in building and implementing an AI system. A major setback for this has been Ethics Washing and Ethics Policing. That is using the Ethics language and giving the appearance of doing it [11] in part to avoid Ethics policing.

When a practitioner thinks about ethics, they think about regulation, oversight, and compliance, some authority telling them what they can and what they cannot do. So, to avoid policing they often pretend to tackle ethical issues just by mentioning ethics repeatedly. All of this makes companies look good, but they don't solve ethical problems. The data that we as audience produce is often used to benefit other actors at the expense of our autonomy, our well-being, and our fair treatment. And as the devices become smart, these problems only get bigger. So how can we build ethical technologies? Some philosophical approaches are outlined below.

Ban AI Systems that Identify Themselves as Humans when Dealing with Humans: AI systems should not give the impression that they are a real individual and not a computer. For example, when someone gets a phone call from an AI, he/she should get alerted that this is not a human. Otherwise, it will be a nightmare of Phishing scams etc. AI should never be allowed to manipulate people who use it. Humans advocate for self-awareness, clarity, and truth; however, these social hallucinations are profoundly rooted in our society, and they create a world of delusions, even though some people are fine with it. However, this poses an important ethical concern regarding how much self-deception should be accepted in society.

Limit or Ban AI in the Political Process: Some people think that AI can be beneficial in the political process. Politicians often disregard society's best interests, pursuing their own agendas and accepting bribes, so AI can improve politics. According to some scholars, humans are inherently unsuitable for politics. They are arrogant and ambitious. They are unpredictable when it comes to making policy choices. Artificial intelligence, on the other hand, is a logic-based device. AI can achieve high levels of idealism, which humans cannot have. Assisting politicians should begin with robots that closely resemble humans. As a result, the electorate would become accustomed to the idea.

Scalable Supervision: We need to find ways for AI systems to learn from humans without needing a human to constantly supervise everything they do. We need to make systems that can operate safely with less supervision. A slightly more practical metric would be to have a human inspect after the agent has completed a particular task and indicate what it did right and what wrong. If necessary, have a big Red STOP button if the robot fails to do the needful.

Gathering User Information: Decisions should include what data to collect and share, which features to build so that user agency is not sacrificed for convenience and how to communicate imp info to get meaningful user concept. It is the creation of a Cauchy Surface of human awareness and consciousness, not the physical tracking of people, that poses a threat. This ability to monitor the states of human minds and their relations allows for a thick wedge to be pushed between fact and perception, as well as manipulation of individuals and groups of humans. It would be helpful to make a distinction between ML, AI, and NN, the latter of which are designed to be models of and for our mental processes.

There is Only One Solution: Knowledge, as well as society's knowledge of itself, is a public utility, much more so than the air we breathe. It's easy to picture air being monopolized, resulting in complete enslavement. The same can be said about data and its accessibility. In this sector, all research and practice should be open to the public. To be specific, companies like Google and Baidu should be owned by the government or a supranational body, not by private individuals. There is a lot of control to choose from. Humans set goals, and it should be humans who work on the subject who are under our influence. For example, it is realistic to explain to all what kernel methods are and why functional analysis and much-valued logic are useful to know; what Ramsey's constructs are and why they must appear; and so on (it looks like a bit of an open problem). The deification of science (the result of certain scientists' hands and minds) does not aid in the process of enabling a layperson to comprehend the boundaries of science and scientific learning research. The negative feedback loop comes to an end at this point.

Collaboration Between Technology and Ethics Experts: We need technology experts and ethics experts to collaborate throughout all phases of building and implementing AI systems, which is research, development, design, deployment, updating, etc. We can get this by training developers and researchers by having philosophers analyze and help solve complex ethical problems and by constructing ethics strategies for the companies.

Draft AI Principles from Applied Philosophy: Craft an action plan guiding operational ethics strategy dropping from applied philosophy with clear definitions, priorities, and processes for implementation. Corporate executives must integrate applied ethics into their organizational culture and business operations by collaborating with ethics experts and institutional investors should require companies to demonstrate that they can proactively address and solve ethical problems. For example, have a penalizing empowerment metric i.e., don't give Agent too much empowerment (to influence/control its surroundings).

Ethical Impact Assessment/Analysis: Every project in industry should have both environmental impact analysis done as well as ethical impact analysis at the beginning of the project and every project should be able be dropped if it violates ethics philosophy that negatively affects individual lives/humanity.

4 Conclusion

The author thinks that we all need to have a big open discussion about what AI can (medical diagnostics infinitely better than humans) and can't do (give real/emotional care to patients) and how we can manipulate things to make sure that it can be used.

for the benefit of as many people as possible. We need engineering, programming/software development, and philosophy to work together to solve high technology problems that challenge our way of life and human existence. Understanding the difference between human intelligence and artificial intelligence is important. Human beings are the embodiment of the fight for survival. They've been fine-tuned over millions of years to live and thrive. When we talk about the risks of AI, it should not be dismissed as scaremongering, it is like doing safety engineering, where we need to think of everything that can go wrong so that we can guarantee that everything goes right. That's how we got people to the moon safely, and it is how AI will help us move towards an exciting future as a species. The author claims that if we can win the race between the increasing power of technology and the wisdom with which we handle it, we can truly build an exciting future with advanced AI. The problem is that in the past, learning from our mistakes has always been our strategy for staying ahead of the competition. First invent the fire then after some accidents, invent the fire extinguisher but if something is as powerful as nuclear weapons or Superhuman Artificial General Intelligence, we don't want to learn from our mistakes, it's a terrible strategy it's better to be proactive than to be reactive. Plan ahead of time and get things right the first time, as this may be the only chance we have. AI has an enormous and positive impact on society and has the potential to create a digital paradise in a true sense. In any case, artificial intelligence development must adhere to strict ethical standards, or we will become slaves to our own technology.

References

1. Russell, S., Norvig, P.: Artificial Intelligence: A Modern Approach, 3 edn. Pearson, Upper Saddle River (2009)
2. Zawacki-Richter, O., Marín, V.I., Bond, M., Gouverneur, F.: Systematic review of research on artificial intelligence applications in higher education – where are the educators? Int. J. Educ. Technol. High. Educ. **16**(1), 1–27 (2019). https://doi.org/10.1186/s41239-019-0171-0
3. Wang, W., Siau, K.: Ethical and moral issues with AI - a case study on healthcare robots. In: Proceedings of the 24th Americas Conference on Information Systems, New Orleans, LA (2018). https://scholarsmine.mst.edu/bio_inftec_facwork/232
4. Lee, K.-F.: AI Superpowers: China, Silicon Valley, and the New World Order, 1st edn. Houghton Mifflin Harcourt (2018)
5. Ouchchy, L., Coin, A., Dubljević, V.: AI in the headlines: the portrayal of the ethical issues of artificial intelligence in the media. AI Soc. **35**(4), 927–936 (2020). https://doi.org/10.1007/s00146-020-00965-5
6. Iansiti, M., Lakhani, K.R.: Competing in the Age of AI: Strategy and Leadership When Algorithms and Networks Run the World. Harvard Business Review Press (2020)
7. Brown, T.B., et al.: Language Models are Few-shot Learners (2020). arXiv:2005.14165; http://arxiv.org/abs/2005.14165. Accessed 24 May 2021
8. Amodei, D., Olah, C., Steinhardt, J., Christiano, P., Schulman, J., Mané, D.: Concrete problems in AI safety (2016). arXiv:1606.06565; http://arxiv.org/abs/1606.06565. Accessed 24 May 2021
9. U. S. P. on L. A. W. S. Defense Primer (2020). https://crsreports.congress.gov/product/pdf/IF/IF11150
10. Leike, J., et al.: AI Safety Gridworlds (2017). arXiv:1711.09883; http://arxiv.org/abs/1711.09883. Accessed 24 May 2021
11. Statt, N.: Google reportedly leaving Project Maven military AI program after 2019 (2018)

Privacy and Transparency in a Digitised Society

Stop Ordering Machine Learning Algorithms by Their Explainability! An Empirical Investigation of the Tradeoff Between Performance and Explainability

Jonas Wanner[1], Lukas-Valentin Herm[1], Kai Heinrich[3], and Christian Janiesch[1,2(✉)]

[1] Julius-Maximilians-Universität Würzburg, Würzburg, Germany
{jonas.wanner,lukas-valentin.herm, christian.janiesch}@uni-wuerzburg.de
[2] HAW Landshut, Landshut, Germany
[3] Otto-von-Guericke-Universität Magdeburg, Magdeburg, Germany
kai.heinrich@ovgu.de

Abstract. Numerous machine learning algorithms have been developed and applied in the field. Their application indicates that there seems to be a tradeoff between their model performance and explainability. That is, machine learning models with higher performance are often based on more complex algorithms and therefore lack interpretability or explainability and vice versa. The true extent of this tradeoff remains unclear while some theoretical assumptions exist. With our research, we aim to explore this gap empirically with a user study. Using four distinct datasets, we measured the tradeoff for five common machine learning algorithms. Our two-factor factorial design considers low-stake and high-stake applications as well as classification and regression problems. Our results differ from the widespread linear assumption and indicate that the tradeoff between model performance and model explainability is much less gradual when considering end user perception. Further, we found it to be situational. Hence, theory-based recommendations cannot be generalized across applications.

Keywords: Machine learning · Explainability · Performance · Tradeoff · User Study

1 Introduction

Today, intelligent systems based on artificial intelligence (AI) technology primarily rely on machine learning (ML) algorithms [1]. Despite their prediction performance, there is a noticeable delay in the adoption of advanced ML algorithms based on deep learning or ensemble learning in practice [2]. That is, practitioners prefer simpler, shallow ML algorithms such as logistic regressions that exhibit a higher degree of explainability through their inherent interpretability [3].

Published by Springer Nature Switzerland AG 2021
D. Dennehy et al. (Eds.): I3E 2021, LNCS 12896, pp. 245–258, 2021.
https://doi.org/10.1007/978-3-030-85447-8_22

In contrast, much of the current AI research focuses on the performance of ML models [4] and data competitions are dominated by deep learning algorithms such as artificial neural networks (ANN) that outperform shallow ML algorithms [e.g., 5]. However, the processing of these algorithms is practically untraceable due to its complex and intransparent inner calculation logic. This renders it impossible for humans to interpret an ANN's decision-making process and prediction results, making it a black box.

This results in a tradeoff between performance and explainability which is not yet sufficiently understood. The uncertainty and lack of control due to a lack of explainability can fuel algorithm aversion of the end user. The aversion describes a phenomenon where users prefer humans over machines even when the performance of the machine is superior to the human [6]. In contrast, recent work by Logg et al. [7] implies that for some situations when performance is communicated, humans may prefer machines resulting in algorithm appreciation. A better understanding of the tradeoff can help to reduce algorithm aversion and may even foster algorithm appreciation from an end user perspective.

While the performance of an algorithm can be estimated by common performance indicators such as precision, recall, or the F-score, it remains unclear, which ML algorithm's inherent interpretability is perceived as more explainable by end users. However, this is crucial as the perceived explainability of a prediction determines the effectiveness of an intelligent system. That is, if the human decision maker can interpret the behavior of an underlying ML model, he or she is more willing to act based on it [8] – especially in cases where the recommendation does not conform to his or her own expectations. As a consequence, intelligent systems without sufficient explainability may even be inefficacious as end users will disregard their advice.

In scholarly literature, several theoretical considerations on the tradeoff of performance and explainability exist [9–15], yet a scientific investigation or even an empirical proof is still missing. We formulate our research question accordingly:

"How do machine learning models compare empirically in the tradeoff between their performance and their explainability as perceived by end users?"

These insights have a high potential to better explain AI adoption of different ML algorithms contributing to a better understanding of AI decision-making and the future of work using hybrid intelligence. That is on the one hand, the results can help us to understand to what extent various ML algorithms differ in their perceived explainability from an end user perspective. This allows us to draw conclusions about their future improvement as well as about their suitability for a given situation in practice. On the other hand, the results can help us to understand how much performance end users are willing to forfeit in favor of explainability. Ultimately, Rudin [3]'s call to avoid explaining black-box models in favor of using inherently interpretable white-box models could be better approached if the tradeoff was sufficiently understood from a social-technical perspective.

In the following, Sect. 2 introduces fundamentals of ML and the state-of-the-art of existing ML tradeoff schemes concerning model performance and model explainability. In Sect. 3, we describe our methodology before we outline preparatory work comprising the datasets and algorithms. The section also comprises the technical realization of the algorithms, the measurement for comparison, and the survey design. In Sect. 4, we discuss the results of the empirical comparison. We close by summarizing our results and pointing out limitations of our study in Sect. 5.

2 Fundamentals and Related Work

2.1 Machine Learning Algorithms

ML focuses on algorithms that are able to improve their performance through experience. That is, ML algorithms are able to find non-linear relationships and patterns in datasets without being explicitly programmed to do so [16]. The process of analytical modeling building to turn ML algorithms into concrete ML models for the use in intelligent systems is a four-step process comprising data input, feature extraction, model building, and model assessment [1].

Each ML algorithm has different strengths and weaknesses regarding their ability to process data. Many shallow ML algorithms require the feature selection of relevant attributes for model training. This task can be time-consuming if the dataset is high-dimensional, or the context is not well-known to the model engineer. Common shallow ML algorithms are linear regressions, decision trees, and support vector machines (SVM). ANNs with multiple hidden layers and advanced neurons for automatic representation learning provide a computation- and data-intensive alternative called deep learning [1]. These algorithms can master feature selection on increasingly complex data by themselves [17]. In consequence, their performance surpasses shallow ML models and even exhibits super-human performance in applications such as data-driven maintenance [e.g., 18]. On the downside, the resulting models have a nested, non-linear structure that is not interpretable for humans, and its results are difficult to reproduce.

In summary, while many shallow ML algorithms are considered interpretable and, thus, white boxes, deep learning algorithms tend to perform better but are considered to be intransparent and, thus, black boxes [19].

2.2 Interpretability and Explainability in Machine Learning

Explanations have the ability to fill the information gap between the intelligent system and its user similar to the situation in the principal-agent problem [2]. They are decisive for the efficacy of the system as the end user decides based on this information whether he or she integrates the recommendation into his or her own decision-making or not. The question of what constitutes explainability and how explanations should be presented to be of value to human users fuels an interdisciplinary research field in various disciplines, including philosophy, social science, psychology, computer science, and information systems.

From a technical point of view, explainability in intelligent systems is about two questions: the "how" question and the "why" question. The former is about global explainability, which provides answers to the ML algorithm's internal processing [3, 9]. The latter is about local explainability, which answers the ex-post reasoning about a concrete recommendation by a ML model [9]. To form a common understanding for our research artifact, we define explainability as "the perceived quality of a given explanation by the user" [19].

In this context, as noted above many shallow ML models are considered to be white boxes that are interpretable per se [13]. In contrast, a black-box ML model is either far too complicated for humans to understand or opaque for a reason and, therefore, equally hard to understand [3]. Consequently in this research, in line with Adadi and Berrada [19]'s argument we consider a model's explainability as its innate interpretability by end users not using any further augmentations.

2.3 Related Work on Machine Learning Tradeoffs

Considerations about the (hypothesized) tradeoff between model performance and model explainability have been the subject of discussion for some time. Originating from theoretical statistics, a distinction for different ML algorithms was first made between model interpretability and flexibility [15]. More recently, this changed towards a comparison between model accuracy and interpretability [e.g., 10, 13] or algorithmic accuracy and explainability [e.g., 9, 12]. However, all tradeoffs address the same compromise of an algorithm's performance versus the algorithm's degree of result traceability.

Overall, in the field many subjective classifications of this tradeoff exist [9–15]. These subjective classifications of the different authors show great similarities but also some dissimilarities. We summarize the related work and their classifications (left side) in Fig. 1 illustrating a high conformity between all authors. The resulting Cartesian coordinate system (right side) shows five common ML algorithms ordered by their common performance (y-axis) and their assumed explainability (x-axis). Grey-box models (i.e., ex-post explainers) are only subject of few studies [e.g., 12, 14], hence we have not included them in our considerations.

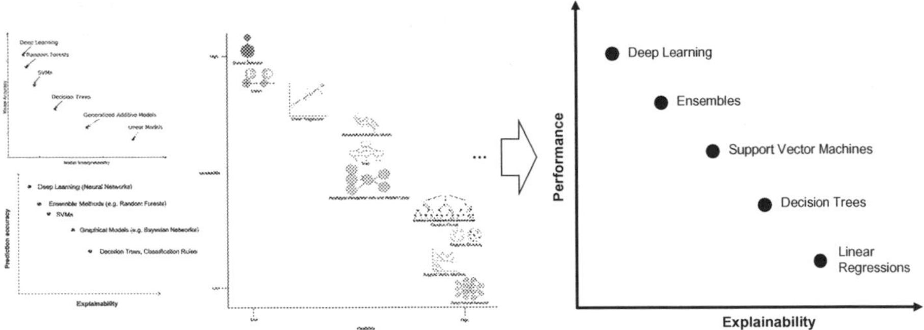

Fig. 1. A synthesis of common ML algorithm classification schemes

While there is a general agreement on key ML algorithms, there are some differences on their placement and the granularity of representation. The general notion is that with a loss of performance, algorithms provide better explainability in a more or less linear fashion. That is, deep learning algorithms or ANNs are categorized as the most powerful with the least degree of model explainability, followed by ensemble algorithms, which consist of multiple ML models. Third in performance, SVMs serve as a large margin classifier based on data point vectors. Fourth, decision trees use sorted, aligned trees for the development of decision rules. Finally, linear regressions are considered of least performance, yet straightforward to interpret [20]. Some authors have chosen to classify certain ML algorithms closer to each other to arguably represent better their assumed true position in the tradeoff [e.g., 9, 11, 21].

In essence, these theoretical classification schemes represent a hypothetical and data-centered view on the tradeoff of model accuracy vs. model interpretability. They have neither yet been validated for specific applications based on real data, nor with end users in a user-centered approach to unearth their true pertinency to represent said tradeoff of performance vs. explainability. Despite this obvious deficiency, they are commonly referenced as a motivation for user- or organization-centered XAI research or intelligent system deployment [e.g., 3, 21, 22].

Thus, in summary it remains unclear how the end users perceive explainability and how this is in line with these tradeoff considerations. In our work, we focus on the tradeoff between performance and an ML models inherent explainability to avoid biases introduced by model transfer techniques from the field of explainable AI (XAI), which aims at providing more transparent ML models that have both, high model performance and high explanatory power [11].

3 Methodology

Our research methodology uses four main steps: research question, data collection, data analysis, and result interpretation [23]. They are depicted in Fig. 2.

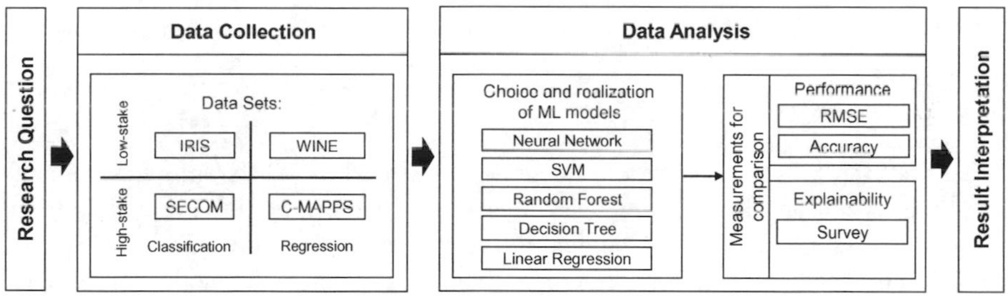

Fig. 2. Overall methodology.

We started by formulating our RQ with the aim to shed light on the similarities and differences between different ML algorithms in terms of their tradeoff between performance and explainability. We verified the relevance of our RQ by a theoretical review of existing contributions and pointed out the research gap (cf. Sect. 2.3).

As we expect the tradeoff to be moderated by the underlying criticality of the task (low stake vs. high stake) and the type of the task (regression vs. classification), we employ a two-factor factorial design with four treatments using four different publicly available datasets. See Table 1 for an overview of the datasets.

To test the tradeoff empirically, we trained five ML models using common ML algorithms present in the aforementioned theoretical tradeoff schemes for the four treatment datasets using scikit-learn. We performed common data cleansing steps prior to model training. See Table 2 for an overview of the implementations.

Table 1. Overview of datasets.

Dataset	Treatment	Description
IRIS [24]	Low-stake classification	IRIS is well known and has a low complexity. It contains 150 observations of 4 different features about the shape of iris flowers as well as their classification into one of 3 distinct species
WINE [25]	Low-stake regression	The WINE quality dataset consists of 11 different features describing red Portuguese "vinho verde" wines. The dataset includes 1599 wine samples that are ranked in their quality from 0 to 12
SECOM [26]	High-stake classification	SECOM includes use data from a semi-conductor manufacturing process. It contains data of over 590 sensors tracking 1567 observations of single production instances as well as the classification of semi-conductor production defects
C-MAPSS [27]	High-stake regression	C-MAPSS provides turbofan engine degradation sensor data. It is based on a modular aero-propulsion system simulation about the remaining useful lifetime using different operational conditions. It contains simulation data from 93 turbines with 50 cycles per turbine and 25 sensors measurements per cycle

To evaluate the performance of our models, we used two different measurements due to the type of problem (i.e., regression vs. classification). For the evaluation of the regression-based predictions, we applied the root mean square error (RMSE). For the evaluation of the classification-based predictions, we calculated the model's accuracy.

While a model's performance can be evaluated independently of the user, its explainability depends on the perceptions of its users [28]. Therefore, we evaluated the users' perceived explainability by conducting a survey to account for the subjective nature of the perception of the ML models. We used the platform prolific.co using a monetary incentive. We did not limit the participation by factors such as the experience with AI or data science skills to receive broad feedback. For reasons of duration and repetitiveness, we designed two separate studies that were assigned at random: a classification study and a regression study, each containing a low-stake and high-stake case. The procedure within each variant was identical.

In the survey, we first collected demographics, prior experience with AI, as well as the participant's willingness to take risks. In the second part, we provided them with an

Table 2. Overview of ML algorithm implementations.

ML algorithm	Implementation
Linear regression	Due to data preprocessing, we skipped default normalization and used the default settings. For the non-centered datasets such as SECOM, we included the intercept of the model
Decision tree	We did not restrict the models by regulations such as the minimum sample split numbers of the estimators. The resulting trees have a depth of five or six, depending on the treatment
SVM	For all datasets, we applied an SVM using a radial basis function as kernels
Random forest (ensemble)	We used the bagging algorithm random forest as proxy for ensembles. Random forests consist of 100 estimators each and their complexity was not restricted (see decision tree)
ANN	For C-MAPSS, we used an ANN with six alternating hidden layers consisting of LSTM and dropout layers. For the other datasets, we applied a multi-layer-perceptron with six hidden layers including dropout layers

introduction to the concepts of either regression- or classification-based ML, typical data processing steps, and general information about the visualization of ML predictions.

Second, we presented the use case for each treatment: The interviewees were asked to assume the role of an employee confronted with a decision situation. We provided a task definition and information about the process. Further, we explained that the task should now be performed by an intelligent system. For each case, we provided the criticality of wrong decisions.

Third, we evaluated their explainability based on the propositions by Hoffman, et al. [29]. To survey global explainability, we provided the participants with descriptions of the employed ML algorithms. To survey local explainability, we provided the participants with a graphical visualization of specific predictions. The participants did not receive any information about the performance of the ML to avoid biases. For each ML model, the participants had to rate their overall perceived explainability of the model on a five-point Likert-scale. The models were presented in random order to avoid sequence bias.

We received responses from 204 participants (112 classification, 92 regression). After processing multiple exclusion criteria (duration, lazy patterns, control questions), we could use 151 surveys (117 male, 34 female). Most participants ($\approx$45%) were between 20 and 30 years old, followed by 31–40 ($\approx$28%). $\approx$75% were from Europe, while $\approx$23% were from North America and only $\approx$2% from other regions. Half of the participants ($\approx$52%) had no experience in AI, while $\approx$33% used AI for less than two years and only $\approx$15% had more than two years of experience with AI. $\approx$13% of the participants would describe their willingness to take risks as very low, while $\approx$46% would classify themselves as medium and $\approx$41% as high to very high.

4 Results

4.1 Result Comparison

Performance. In general, the performance results confirm the theoretical ordering in Fig. 1 (y-axis). Nevertheless, the relative performance differs. Especially, the difference between random forest and SVM is smaller than assumed. In our case, this may be due to the datasets and the ensemble algorithm, but it reveals that the ordering of algorithms by their performance is hardly deterministic. Further, the performance difference between shallow ML algorithms and deep learning can be almost neglectable in scenarios with low complexity such as IRIS. Still, linear regression constantly performed worst while ANN performed best in comparison to the other models. Table 3 illustrates the results of our performance evaluation.

Table 3. Performance results of ML models.

Model	Classification in accuracy*		Regression in RMSE**	
	IRIS	SECOM	WINE	C-MAPSS
Linear regression	81.59	68.70	1.05	59.39
Decision tree	85.95	83.50	0.85	55.60
SVM	92.10	94.46	0.81	53.03
Random forest	92.90	94.92	0.79	42.31
ANN	**94.21**	**95.20**	**0.77**	**38.56**

* higher = better, in %; ** lower = better, in total values

Explainability. We present the perceived level of explainability from the conducted survey for each algorithm in Table 4. We follow the recommendations of Boone and Boone [30] and applied a mean calculation for the Likert-scale data. The standard deviations appear normal with no discernible anomalies.

Across all treatments, random forests and decision trees achieved the highest or second-highest ratings. Decision trees are considered highly interpretable by humans in terms of their global and local explainability, since it is possible to follow a path of variables from the root node to a leaf node containing the final decision [13]. This explainability by design makes the model itself (global) as well as every prediction (local) transparent. Random forests use multiple decision trees with a majority vote or averages on the predictions from the decision trees resulting in a single prediction. This could explain their comparably high scores. The perception of explainability varies across the remainder of models as discussed in the following.

Table 4. Comparison of mean explainability and standard deviation.

Mean explainability*					SD explainability**			
Model	Classification		Regression		Classification		Regression	
	IRIS	SECOM	WINE	C-MAPSS	IRIS	SECOM	WINE	C-MAPSS
Linear regression	3.30	3.04	3.13	2.97	0.85	0.93	**0.86**	**0.85**
Decision tree	**3.53**	3.34	**3.17**	**3.41**	**0.79**	0.83	0.88	0.90
SVM	3.29	3.12	2.88	3.03	0.96	0.89	0.90	0.85
Random forest	3.38	**3.42**	3.32	3.32	0.91	**0.75**	0.87	0.90
ANN	3.07	3.25	2.92	2.95	1.02	1.01	1.00	0.98

* mean of five-point Likert scale; 1,00 = very low; 5,00 = very high; ** standard deviation of five-point Likert scale

4.2 Discussion

Low- and High-Stake Classification. For the low-stake classification treatment IRIS, the models' explainability were generally well-received and perceived as more similar. They reflect the theoretical ordering of explainability in Fig. 1 (x-axis) quite well. IRIS represents a case of low algorithmic involvement with good accuracy values resulting in the low distances between the models. The case is straightforward with only few variables on flower properties such as sepal width. Hence, any participant should have been able to grasp the features relevant to fulfill this task in its entirety.

For the high-stake classification treatment SECOM, we found large performance differences as the case is more complex with more input variables, which is reflected by the poor performance of the shallow ML models such as linear regression. In addition, we found that the explainability of models, which can be visualized for simple cases in a straightforward way, loose their explanatory value for end users in this treatment.

We also found that the user's preference shifts from single decision trees to the majority vote of random forests. We assume that human biases may be at work more prominently in high-stake scenarios. This is also mirrored by the higher explainability scores of ANN for SECOM even though – objectively – the global and local explainability should be non-existent as ANN is a black-box model.

Low- and High-Stake Regression. The regression datasets also highlight the divergent perception regarding the different stakes. In the low-stake WINE treatment, the results mostly fit the theoretical assumption. In contrast, in the high-stake C-MAPSS treatment, the explainability score for ANN is higher than for SVM and linear regressions. Furthermore, linear regression received low scores for explainability in strong contrast to theory. A possible rationalization is the difficulty of the participants to grasp the nature of regression altogether since it is not as naturally understood as classification. This may highlight the importance of some data science skills at the human user's end in order for the explanations (also in the context of XAI) to have any meaningful impact on the (hybrid) decision-making.

In general, the random forest seems to master the tradeoff between performance and explainability particularly well in relative comparison to the other ML models. Except for decision trees, there is also a shift of the user's favor from shallow ML models to deep learning models when the stake rises.

Generalization of Tradeoff. For the generalization of our findings and analysis of the tradeoff, we merged the data of the four treatments. In order to enable this merge, we normalized the data to the range of 0 to 1 to allow for relative comparison of the ML algorithms regarding the different use cases, tasks, and performance measurements. For the factor regression, we inverted the performance scale of RMSE since smaller values indicate better predictions, inversely to accuracy for classification. We transferred it into a Cartesian coordinate system similar to Fig. 1. We used mean values to yield a position for each algorithm. Figure 3 shows the resulting averaged scheme calculated from the data in Tables 3 and 4.

The hypothetical simple linear relation between ML model performance and ML model explainability assumed theoretically by prior research does not hold across our user-centered treatments. While we can confirm some tendencies mostly concerning ML model performance, reflected by accuracy and RSME, a few things are notably different from the theoretical proposition.

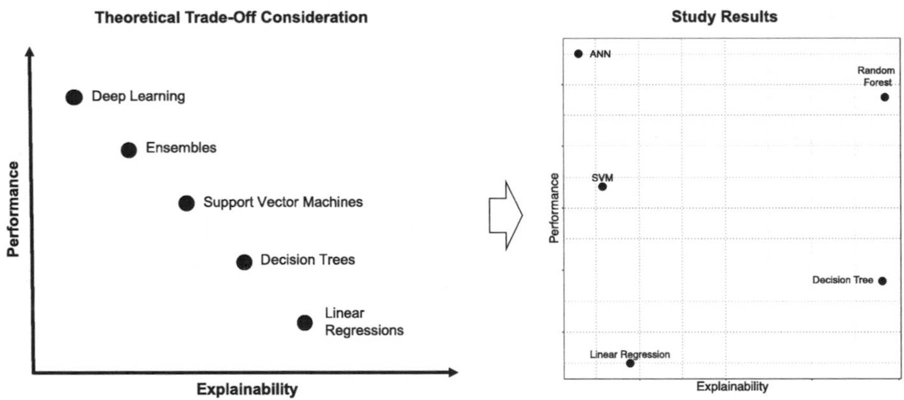

Fig. 3. Theoretical vs. empirical scheme for the tradeoff of performance vs. perceived explainability in machine learning

We find that the tree-based models decision trees and random forests are perceived to provide the best explainability of the five ML models by far from an end user's perspective. We assume that this is most likely due to their intuitive transparency with regard to global explainability [31], which may indicate that these two tree-based algorithms do not invoke the same degree of algorithm aversion associated with the remainder of ML algorithms. Contrary to our expectations, we could not substantiate that a single decision tree is perceived as more explainable than a random forest consisting of many unbalanced decision trees. We assume that this may be since we did not present all resulting trees of the random forest to the participants for review.

4.3 Implications

Our observations enable us to suggest theoretical and practical implication. They are important to consider when assessing how people respond to algorithmic advice as they hold implications for any decision maker or organization using intelligent systems.

Biases Hinder Objective Measurement. It is possible that participants were biased in their judgement by the perceived capability or promise of an algorithm and therefore assumed a higher value [32]. That is, shallow ML algorithms such as SVM and linear regression offer a form of internal explainability. Hence, they were supposed to result in a better perceived explainability than black-box models with no internal explainability such as ANN. However, we found that there is hardly any difference in their perceived explainability by end users. This may be due to participants who were not able to understand the presentation of SVM and linear regression as they lacked prior knowledge [33], which may be a practical problem in real-life cases as well. In contrast, simpler models seem to be especially good in explaining more straightforward scenarios. Consequently, due to high valuation in one category (performance), end users may attribute higher scores in another category (explainability). This is called halo effect.

Interpretability does not Entail Explainability. The discrepancy between theory and our empirical findings can be explained at least partly by the nature of our observations. While theoretical contributions look at the algorithmic and mathematical description of objects (data-centered perspective), we have employed a socio-technical and thus user-centered perspective. That is, in our study, we targeted the naturally biased perception of end users of an ML algorithm directly and found that the difference between performance and explainability is not linearly increasing. Rather, we found that linear regression's and SVM's (and ANN's) explanatory value is far from tree-based algorithms in most situations. While our results do not allow to uniformly rank and rate explainability for ML decisions (and were not expected to), they add to the growing evidence that there is more to model explainability than transparent mathematical parameters and good intentions. Moreover, ordering ML algorithms by their assumed data-centered interpretability is not helpful as it is constantly being misinterpreted and misused in socio-technical settings. In contrast, socio-technical aspects stand out as important for the efficacious use of ML models and explainability may be the key factor for their acceptance by end users [34, 35]. According to our research, in non-augmented form decision trees and random forests are currently the most suitable options to engage with end users.

5 Conclusion, Limitations, and Outlook

Albeit its fundamental importance for human decision-makers, empirical evidence regarding the tradeoff between ML model performance and explainability is scarce. The goal of our research was to conduct an empirical study to determine a more realistic depiction of this relationship and subsequently compare the placement of common ML models to the existing theoretical propositions.

We found that the explanatory value of decision trees and random forests constantly dominates other ML models. Comparing averages, we could not find noteworthy differences in the perceptions of explainability of SVM, linear regression, and even ANN. We did notice though that explainability was generally better received for more straightforward cases such as low-stake classifications.

In summary, we found existing theoretical propositions to be data-centered and misleading oversimplifications when compared to our user-centered observations. Our study shows that when explanations are put to use, socio-technical factors of user perception dominate well-intended analytical considerations concerning the goodness of visualizations by ML experts.

As with any empirical research, our study faces some limitations. First, our study was an online survey with benchmarking datasets. While we only allowed for participants with a certain background, participants may have been exposed to the scenarios and several of the ML algorithms for the first time. Hence, we measured an *initial* explainability. Second, there was no time restriction for viewing and assessing an explanation. We expect results to differ in a high-velocity treatment. Third and last, we compared inherently interpretable shallow ML algorithms and ANN without further augmentations. We assume that XAI augmentations will affect explainability positively. In contrast, other more diverse ensembles than random forests may perform worse.

Concluding, we identified socio-technical aspects as highly important for the perception of explainability and therefore further user studies with varying skill levels and cultural backgrounds are necessary to better understand the biases at work. Further, explainability does not entail understandability. If explainability only contributes to more trusted decision-making but not to a better understanding, research into XAI may be on the wrong track and ultimately only lulls users into a false sense of security by adding fancy yet inefficacious visualization.

References

1. Janiesch, C., Zschech, P., Heinrich, K.: Machine Learning and Deep Learning. Electronic Markets forthcoming (2021)
2. Wanner, J., Heinrich, K., Janiesch, C., Zschech, P.: How much AI do you require? Decision factors for adopting AI technology. In: Proceedings of the 41st International Conference on Information Systems (ICIS), pp. 1–17. AIS, India (2020)
3. Rudin, C.: Stop explaining black box machine learning models for high stakes decisions and use interpretable models instead. Nat. Mach. Intell. **1**, 206–215 (2019)
4. La Cava, W., Williams, H., Fu, W., Moore, J.H.: Evaluating recommender systems for AI-driven data science. arXiv:1905.09205 (2019)
5. Hyndman, R.J.: A brief history of forecasting competitions. Int. J. Forecast. **36**, 7–14 (2020)
6. Burton, J.W., Stein, M.K., Jensen, T.B.: A systematic review of algorithm aversion in augmented decision making. J. Behav. Decis. Mak. **33**, 220–239 (2019)
7. Logg, J.M., Minson, J.A., Moore, D.A.: Algorithm appreciation: People prefer algorithmic to human judgment. Organ. Behav. Hum. Decis. Process. **151**, 90–103 (2019)

8. Ribeiro, M.T., Singh, S., Guestrin, C.: "Why should i trust you?" Explaining the predictions of any classifier. In: Proceedings of the 22nd ACM SIGKDD International Conference on Knowledge Discovery and Data Mining (KDD), San Francisco, CA, pp. 1135–1144 (2016)
9. Dam, H.K., Tran, T., Ghose, A.: Explainable software analytics. In: Proceedings of the 40th International Conference on Software Engineering: New Ideas and Emerging Results (ICSE-NIER), Gothenburg, pp. 53–56 (2018)
10. Yang, Y.J., Bang, C.S.: Application of artificial intelligence in gastroenterology. World J. Gastroenterol. **25**, 1666–1683 (2019)
11. Gunning, D.: Explainable artificial intelligence (XAI). Defense Advanced Research Projects Agency (DARPA), nd Web 2 (2017)
12. Angelov, P., Soares, E.: Towards Explainable Deep Neural Networks (xDNN). arXiv:1912. 02523 (2019)
13. Arrieta, A.B., et al.: Explainable Artificial Intelligence (XAI): Concepts, taxonomies, opportunities and challenges toward responsible AI. Inf. Fusion **58**, 82–115 (2020)
14. Nanayakkara, S., et al.: Characterising risk of in-hospital mortality following cardiac arrest using machine learning: a retrospective international registry study. PLoS Med. **15**, e1002709 (2018)
15. James, G., Witten, D., Hastie, T., Tibshirani, R.: An Introduction to Statistical Learning. Springer, New York (2013)
16. Bishop, C.M.: Pattern Recognition and Machine Learning. Springer, New York (2006)
17. Schmidhuber, J.: Deep learning in neural networks: an overview. Neural Netw. **61**, 85–117 (2015)
18. Wang, J., Ma, Y., Zhang, L., Gao, R.X., Wu, D.: Deep learning for smart manufacturing: methods and applications. J. Manuf. Syst. **48**, 144–156 (2018)
19. Adadi, A., Berrada, M.: Peeking inside the black-box: a survey on explainable artificial intelligence (XAI). IEEE Access **6**, 52138–52160 (2018)
20. Goodfellow, I., Bengio, Y., Courville, A.: Deep Learning. MIT Press, Cambridge (2016)
21. Guo, M., Zhang, Q., Liao, X., Chen, Y.: An interpretable machine learning framework for modelling human decision behavior. arXiv:1906.01233 (2019)
22. Asatiani, A., Malo, P., Nagbøl, P.R., Penttinen, E., Rinta-Kahila, T., Salovaara, A.: Sociotechnical envelopment of artificial intelligence: an approach to organizational deployment of inscrutable artificial intelligence systems. J. Assoc. Inf. Syst. **22**, 325–352 (2021)
23. Müller, O., Junglas, I., Brocke, J.V., Debortoli, S.: Utilizing big data analytics for information systems research: challenges, promises and guidelines. Eur. J. Inf. Syst. **25**, 289–302 (2017)
24. Marshal, M.: Iris Data Set (1988). https://archive.ics.uci.edu/ml/datasets/iris
25. Cortez, P.: Viticulture Commission of the Vinho Verde Region (CVRVV) (2009). http://archive.ics.uci.edu/ml/datasets/wine+quality
26. McCann Michael, J.A.: SECOM Data Set (2008). http://archive.ics.uci.edu/ml/datasets/secom
27. Saxena, A., Goebel, K.: Turbofan engine degradation simulation data set - NASA Ames Prognostics Data Repository (2008). www.ti.arc.nasa.gov/tech/prognostic-data-repository/#turbofan
28. Miller, T.: Explanation in artificial intelligence: Insights from the social sciences. Artif. Intell. **267**, 1–38 (2019)
29. Hoffman, R.R., Mueller, S.T., Klein, G., Litman, J.: Metrics for Explainable AI: Challenges and Prospects. arXiv:1812.04608, pp. 1–50 (2018)
30. Boone, H.N., Boone, D.A.: Analyzing likert data. J. Extension **50**, 1–5 (2012)
31. Mohseni, S., Zarei, N., Ragan, E.D.: A Multidisciplinary Survey and Framework for Design and Evaluation of Explainable AI Systems. arXiv:1811.11839 (2018)
32. Hilton, D.: Mental models and causal explanation: judgements of probable cause and explanatory relevance. Think. Reason. **2**, 273–308 (1996)

33. Amershi, S., et al.: Guidelines for human-AI interaction. In: Proceedings of the 2019 CHI Conference on Human Factors in Computing Systems, Glasgow, pp. 1–13. ACM (2019)
34. Cramer, H., et al.: The effects of transparency on trust in and acceptance of a content-based art recommender. User Model. User-Adap. Inter. **18**, 455–496 (2008)
35. Lee, M.K.: Understanding perception of algorithmic decisions: fairness, trust, and emotion in response to algorithmic management. Big Data Soc. **5**, 205395171875668 (2018)

Gender Bias in AI: Implications for Managerial Practices

Ayesha Nadeem[1(✉)], Olivera Marjanovic[1], and Babak Abedin[2]

[1] University of Technology Sydney, Sydney, NSW, Australia
Ayesha.Nadeem@student.uts.edu.au, Olivera.Marjanovic@uts.edu.au
[2] Macquarie University, Sydney, NSW, Australia
Babak.abedin@mq.edu.au

Abstract. Artificial intelligence (AI) applications are widely employed nowadays in almost every industry impacting individuals and society. As many important decisions are now being automated by various AI applications, fairness is fast becoming a vital concern in AI. Moreover, the organizational applications of AI-enabled decision systems have exacerbated this problem by amplifying the pre-existing societal bias and creating new types of biases. Interestingly, the related literature and industry press suggest that AI systems are often biased towards gender. Specifically, AI hiring tools are often biased towards women. Therefore, it is an increasing concern to reconsider the organizational managerial practices for AI-enabled decision systems to bring fairness in decision making. Additionally, organizations should develop fair, ethical internal structures and corporate strategies and governance to manage the gender imbalance in AI recruitment process. Thus, by systematically reviewing and synthesizing the literature, this paper presents a comprehensive overview of the managerial practices taken in relation to gender bias in AI. Our findings indicate that managerial practices include: better fairness governance practices, continuous training on fairness and ethics for all stakeholders, collaborative organizational learning on fairness & demographic characteristics, interdisciplinary approach & understanding of AI ethical principles, Workplace diversity in managerial roles, designing strategies for incorporating algorithmic transparency and accountability & ensuring human in the loop. In this paper, we aim to contribute to the emerging IS literature on AI by presenting a consolidated picture and understanding of this phenomenon. Based on our findings, we indicate direction for future research in IS for the better development and use of AI systems.

Keywords: Artificial Intelligence · Machine learning · Analytics · Gender · Fairness

1 Introduction

It is true that AI applications offer solutions to various problems faced in different disciplines but simultaneously yield biased outcomes that could affect individuals or minorities of a certain race, gender, or color (Ntoutsi et al. 2019). The biased and adverse outcomes of algorithm decisions reach beyond the individuals and include harmful effects

Published by Springer Nature Switzerland AG 2021
D. Dennehy et al. (Eds.): I3E 2021, LNCS 12896, pp. 259–270, 2021.
https://doi.org/10.1007/978-3-030-85447-8_23

that reach families, communities, and society at large (Altman et al. 2018). The literature is evident that gender bias does exist in AI algorithms (Trewin 2018; Leavy 2018; Mehrabi et al. 2019; Dawson et al. 2019; Kumar et al. 2019; Canetti et al. 2019; Crawford 2016; Altman et al. 2018; Lambrecht and Tucker 2018; Galleno et al. 2019; Bolukbasi et al. 2016; Daugherty et al. 2018, Dwivedi et al. 2019; Agarwal 2020; Robnett 2015; Nadeem et al. 2020).

According to past literature bias is externalized and includes misguided conducts of "bad actors" which are either intentional or accidental and might not be easily traceable; therefore, such social and contextual issues are left beyond the law's reach (Hoffmann 2019) and thus are deprived aspect of the society since long. AI algorithms are trained on datasets that are influenced by their creators' thinking, and as a result the pre-existing prejudices in the society "sneaks in" the AI systems thus amplifying the societal gender stereotyping and discrimination in society (Ntoutsi et al. 2019 , Lee 2018, Hoffmann 2019).

It is noteworthy to mention here that lack of gender diversity and exceptionally homogenous and male domination in high tech industries and in the design & implementation of AI creating "blind spots" (Johnson 2019, Lee 2018, Wang 2020, Martinez and Fernandez 2020, Clifton et al. 2020) that drives gender bias in AI.

Furthermore, AI enabled decision systems used in the recruitment software are found to be biased towards women according to a recent report of the Division of gender equality, UNESCO (2020) (Nadeem et al. 2020). As AI algorithm are the reflections of the biased data (that comes from years of previous resumes) on which they are trained, hence AI systems are expected to yield biased outcome (World Economic Forum 2019; Galleno et al. 2019, Nadeem et al. 2020). As organizations are relying on AI enabled decision tools for talent recruitment, talent sourcing, and candidate screening and engagement it is crucial to ensure that the decision taken by AI systems are not biased towards a certain group of people (Mehrabi et al. 2019; Jobin et al. 2019).

Moreover, gender bias in AI is a complex and tricky matter, requiring attention from not just the technological aspect but also from the managerial aspects for dealing with data, people, and algorithms. Moreover, certain regulations, laws, and policies regarding fairness awareness/education if enhanced will improve the validation of the AI systems against gender bias and other discriminations. Given the above, this paper aims to answer the following research question:

What managerial practices are useful for organizations for mitigating gender bias in AI?

To answer this question, this study conducts a systematic literature review, following Webster and Watson's (2002) literature review method. The findings of systematic literature review (SLR) contribute to the emerging body of the literature on AI in Information Systems (IS) and beyond by identifying and categorizing the insights on managerial practices for mitigating gender bias in AI. As such, this study paves a way for a more comprehensive study of gender bias in AI through, for example, experts' interview in a particular context. It could also offer insights to data practices for developers and managerial practices for managers of AI to employ in order to avoid bias.

The remainder of this paper is organized as: Sect. 2 presents the research design for this research along with the process of selection of related articles; Sect. 3 presents the findings and discussion on managerial practices; Sects. 4 and 5 presents the future work recommendations along with limitations and conclusion.

2 Research Methodology

According to Webster and Watson (2002), systematic literature reviews (SLR) thoroughly investigate research areas and opportunities for new research. As this area of research is relatively a new and emerging research field, therefore we conducted SLR by adopting Webster and Watson (2002) guidelines to acquire a better understanding of this phenomena by systematically analyzing the literature.

The process of selection and identification of relevant articles was carried out through a rigorous method. The first step of this research included a thorough investigation of the appropriate keyword selection. The keywords finally selected and used for this research were: Artificial Intelligence, Machine learning, Analytics, Gender, fairness.

For this research, we used Scopus as a source of search. We looked at various disciplines while selecting the articles in order to grasp a wider perspective on this area of research i.e. we selected computer science and business management (including Information Systems), social sciences and psychology to cover the social and behavioral aspects of gender bias in AI. Further, this search was limited to papers written in English.

There were 3817 articles that were captured through the selected keywords. The filtration of articles started by applying source type and inclusion criteria. A total number of 882 articles were recovered that met the inclusion criteria. In this step, we considered only those papers that were directly dealing with gender bias in AI or the papers that discussed the procedures or practices for mitigating gender bias in AI ranging from technical approaches to managerial approaches. Therefore, we started by reading the titles of the identified articles. The total number of articles that were recovered through titles were136. After selecting the articles on the basics of their titles, we recovered the articles on the basis of their abstract, which came to 65 (this number included articles on fairness in AI, gender bias, AI ethics, discrimination in AI and AI in HR). We then thoroughly read the full text of the 65 articles. In this step we excluded all the articles that were outside the scope of this research. Therefore only 31 papers were selected that were relevant to our research scope. As this area of research is a fairly new and emerging topic, therefore 31 articles are a good number for analyzing the past literature systematically.

The analyses of the articles were carried out in a step wise process which included reading the articles line by line and highlighting the phrases/sentences (called excerpts) that were relevant to this research (Wolfswinkel et al. 2013). The identification of the concepts and themes was carried out by organizing, analyzing and coding the final set of articles by following the guidelines by Wolfswinkel et al. (2013). Open coding, axial coding and comparative analysis was carried out as recommended by (Wolfswinkel et al. 2013) for the development of the themes and concepts. Further, the themes that had almost the same meaning and were used in the same context and perspective were merged into high-level themes and concepts for better understanding and discussion.

3 Outcomes and Discussion of Systematic Review

In this section, we present the key findings from systematic literature review (SLR). The SLR analysis confirms that the level of publication activity in this field started to increase from 2017 and increased considerably in 2020, which shows that this is an emerging and fast-growing research area. Moreover, this trend highlights that although fairness in AI has been under discussion for the past few years, little has been published in IS journals so far. The results indicate that the research on gender bias is not yet well established, which highlights a great potential for future research in this field.

Prior research illustrates that there is a need to better understand and identify what manifests and contributes to gender bias in AI and what approaches should be undertaken for addressing this matter. Therefore, at this stage we will briefly discuss the contributing factors behind gender bias in AI. Our recent research shows there are eight main themes relating to contributing factors of gender bias in AI: Biased training datasets, gender stereotyping, biased behaviors and decisions, AI amplifying the bias, lack of gender diversity in training data and developers, lack of AI regulations, contextual/ socio-economic factors and other external factors.

It is noted in literature that the training datasets are often biased due to improper practices i.e. over, under, or misrepresentation of certain groups (Hayes et al. 2020), historical biases and gender stereotyping (Ntoutsi, et al. 2019 , Johnson 2019). Moreover, unfair patterns in datasets (Veale and Binns 2017) such as the correlation of data of sensitive variables/features i.e. proxy variable (salary serving as a proxy of gender, zip code serving as a proxy of background) make their way into AI algorithm and result in biased outcomes and contributing factors behind gender bias in AI.

Furthermore, the absence of gender disparity in developers, data miners, and datasets incorporate bias during the training phase of the algorithm (Martinez and Fernandez 2020, Johnson 2019, Lee 2018, Wang 2020, Clifton et al. 2020), creates "blind spots" that emerge over time and are often difficult to predict (Hoffmann 2019) that needs further attention.

3.1 Managerial Practices for Mitigating Gender Bias in AI

We established six main managerial practices for mitigating gender bias in AI and they are: better fairness governance practices, continuous training on fairness and ethics for all stakeholders, collaborative organizational learning on fairness & demographic characteristics, interdisciplinary approach & understanding of AI ethical principles, Workplace diversity in managerial roles, designing strategies for incorporating algorithmic transparency and accountability & Ensuring Human in the loop as shown in Table 1 in appendices. We will now discuss these managerial practices and their implications accordingly.

Algorithms sift through datasets (Hoffmann 2019) and discover the trends/patterns and make predictions; it is thus important to rely on better, faster and more ubiquitous algorithms to make sense of the big datasets (Martin 2019). Perhaps designing managerial strategies for fair AI compliance and audits and updated regulations to maintain certain minimum standards for the datasets (Johnson 2019) could be adopted for neutralizing the gender bias in AI.

It is noted in literature that managerial practices, such as organizations investing in hiring, training/workshops of expert programmers for regular maintenance and vetting of datasets is essential for mitigating gender bias in AI (Noriega 2020). This would require for the organizations to develop improved and modernized fair and ethical internal structures and corporate strategies to govern and manage the gender imbalance (Johnson 2019).

Moreover, organizational strategies that could bring awareness on the ethical and responsible AI is very much needed; including giving importance to work force diversity in an organization; including policies pertaining to gender diverse workplace that bring cultural diversity in data will be beneficial in neutralizing the gender bias in AI (Lee 2018). Enhanced women representation/gender inclusion in the technology sector especially STEM career domain (Lambrecht and Tucker 2020), gender diversity among the member of boards, management and leadership roles (Johnson 2019) plus focusing on the "blind spots" (Hoffmann 2019) that are created by the lack of gender diversity in data and developers, will minimize the homogeneous and exceptionally male-dominated leaderships and decisions (Johnson 2019) would offer a pathway towards mitigating gender bias in AI.

Additionally, emphasis on improved business model innovation addressing gender equity and fairness in AI should be designed (Arrieta et al. 2020, Feuerriegel et al. 2020); including firms addressing fairness in the overall culture instead of focusing on filling the requirement of diversity quotas. Regular data audit practices for identifying datasets that correlate with protected characteristics and may therefore serve as a proxy for an attribute of protected classes (Johnson 2019) would neutralize the misrepresentation of gender in the data and also in AI decisions.

It is noted in past literature that Algorithms for AI enabled decision systems should be designed to yield fair decisions. Developers should not only be responsible for ethical implications but they should shift algorithmic decision-making responsibility to the users as well (Martin 2019). Practices and strategies that preclude individuals to take responsibility within a decision should be replaced with giving autonomy to users in decision making to bring fairness in the AI decisions (Martin 2019, Hayes et al. 2020). Likewise, organizations should also deploy efficient quality control and assurance policies for better and improved algorithmic accountability and transparency for neutralizing gender bias in AI (Ntoutsi, et al. 2019).

4 Directions for Future Research

Our findings indicate some future IS research related to prevention, mitigation, and future theorization of gender bias in AI. Following are a few of the suggested future directions in this area of research:

Research on AI policies and regulations to bring justice to society and in AI fair design should be enhanced. Including but not limited to exploring ways how organizations can ensure diversity in the workplace and how organizations can bring autonomy to users in AI enabled decision systems. Also, future work should focus on investigating and theorizing gender bias in AI (Ivaturi and Bhagwatwar 2020; Sen 1995).

It is noted in a recent survey, 38% of organizations are already using AI in their workplace with 62% expected to be using it near future (Martinez and Fernandez 2020).

Therefore, organizations need to deploy certain mechanisms to deal with gender bias in AI. Users of AI should use their own intuition while using AI tools. Therefore, organizations need to re-consider their managerial approaches including designing innovative business models and managerial strategies focusing on mitigating gender bias in AI.

Therefore, as a follow up of this paper, our next step in this research would be to collect empirical data by conducting experts' interviews from those subjects who are directly involved in managing AI in an organization and posits a broader overview of organizational AI-enabled decision systems. Empirical data will explore the current managerial practices and mechanism that are being carried out by organizations in this regard and also will present the guidelines on practices for organizations for better managing of gender bias in AI.

Experts' Interviews. Interviews are considered as a primary data source (Myer and Newman 2007). Experts' interview would not only validate our SLR findings from the real-world perspective – it will present the insights from the experts' who have vast and extensive and precise knowledge and experience in this field and are able to manager AI within an organization (Mergel et al. 2019). An expert interview would provide this research with an in-depth insight from the user as well as from organizational perspective; also, would present the framework on strategies and practical approaches that would be useful for managing gender bias in AI.

5 Conclusion

Past data is mostly reflection of history and AI algorithms trained on past datasets could be discriminatory towards a certain group or individuals due to the various underlying drivers and factors. Hence people suffer from algorithms harm and there is no accountability for it.

Bias is externalized and includes misguided conducts of "bad actors" which are either intentional or accidental and might not be easily traceable; therefore, such social and contextual issues are left beyond the law's reach (Hoffmann 2019) and thus are deprived aspect of the society since long.

Given the above, this paper aims to focus on unpacking the managerial approaches for mitigating gender bias in AI. In this research, we have presented a deeper understanding of gender bias in AI and have provided evidence from the systematic literature review that gender bias does exist in AI systems and the practices/ approaches required for addressing gender bias in AI. This research gives a concise overview of findings of gender bias in AI from past literature; in terms of what has been discussed and investigated and what needs to be researched in the future.

As the roots of gender bias in AI are not just technological, and as such technological solutions might not suffice; AI enabled decisions systems are being made on mathematical model that leads to a biased outcome. There has to be some checks for assurance against gender bias when making decisions through AI enabled decision systems. Hence, organizations need to follow some mechanisms and strategies to mitigate and address this matter timely and effectively. This research therefore presents a set of managerial practices, approaches and recommendations for organizations for better governance and management of gender bias in AI.

Due to time constraints we were not able to present empirical findings and their analyses with the lens of a theory, which is one of the limitations of this short paper. However, we aim to publish our empirical outcomes in near future.

Appendices

Table 1. Managerial practices for mitigating gender bias in AI

Grouping of concepts	Concepts for mitigating gender bias in AI	Description
Better fairness governance policies	Internal governance policies (Johnson 2019) Internal structures and process-oriented corporate governance (Johnson 2019, Martin 2019)	Enhanced AI corporate governance for gender bias mitigation
Continues education/training on fairness and ethics for all stakeholders	Educational workshops and training on workplace fairness (Noriega 2020) Certified professional required (Martin 2019) Awareness of ethics and promoting responsible AI (Wu et al. 2019, Veale and Binns 2017) Awareness of unintended bias in scientific community and technology industry (Cirillo et al. 2020)	Workshops/education that involves principles of ethics such as promoting ethical education for every stakeholder in AI research & development
Collaborative organizational learning on fairness & demographic characteristics	Business models and policy should be designed concerning fair AI (Feuerriegel et al. 2020)	Design of business models and policies to consider AI principles
Interdisciplinary approach & understanding of AI ethical principles	Interdisciplinary disciplines to work collaboratively to address ethical challenges (Wu et al. 2019, Ibrahim et al. 2020)	Employment of a more diverse IT workforce to be included in the design and implementation of algorithms

(*continued*)

Table 1. (*continued*)

Grouping of concepts	Concepts for mitigating gender bias in AI	Description
Workplace diversity in managerial roles	Gender diversity at managerial levels (Lee 2018) Diversity in the development of AI systems (Costa and Ribas 2019, Johnson 2019, Ntoutsi et al. 2019, Arrieta et al. 2020, Clifton et al. 2020) Gender diversity in the high-tech industry and STEM career (Lee 2018, Johnson 2019, Wang, 2020)	An increase in gender inclusion in the development of AI technologies will introduce diverse perspectives
Designing strategies for incorporating algorithmic transparency and accountability	Big data review board required (Martin 2019) Incorporate regular audits of the data (Martinez and Fernandez, 2020, Johnson 2019, Ibrahim et al. 2020, Robert et al. 2020, Piano 2020, Veale and Binns 2017, Noriega 2020) Designing strategies for fairness and ensure accountability (Hayes et al. 2020)	AI audits to be conducted periodically to ensure AI compliance
Ensuring Human in the loop	Integrating human & AI decision making (Miron et al. 2020)	Design strategies like providing more autonomy to the users in decision-making would bring fairness to the AI decisions

References

Hoffmann, A.L.: Where fairness fails: data, algorithms, and the limits of anti-discrimination discourse. Inf. Commun. Soc. **22**(7), 900–915 (2019)

Grari, V., Ruf, B., Lamprier, S., Detyniecki, M.: Achieving fairness with decision tress: an adversarial approach. Data Sci. Eng. **5**(2), 99–110 (2020). https://doi.org/10.1007/s41019-020-00124-2

Martinez, C.F., Fernandez, A.: AI and recruiting software: ethical and legal implications. J. Behav. Robot. **11**(1), 199–216 (2020)

Costa, P., Ribas, L.: AI becomes her: discussing gender and artificial intelligence. J. Specul. Res. **17**(1–2), 171–193 (2019)

Bellamy, R.K.E., et al.: AI fairness 360: an extensible toolkit for detecting, understanding, and mitigating unwanted algorithmic bias. J. Res. Dev. (2018)

Hayes, P., van de Poel, I., Steen, M.: Algorithms and values in justice and security. AI Soc. **35**(3), 533–555 (2020). https://doi.org/10.1007/s00146-019-00932-9

Schonberger, D.: Artificial intelligence in healthcare: a critical analysis of the legal and ethical implications. Int. J. Law Inf. Technol. **27**(2), 171–203 (2019)

Prates, M., Avelar, P., Lamb, L.C.: Assessing gender bias in machine translation – a case study with Google translate. Neural Comput. Appl. (2019)

Kyriazanos, D.M., Thanos, K.G., Thomopoulos, S.C.A.: Automated decisions making in airports checkpoints: bias detection toward smarter security and fairness. Automated security decision-making. IEEE Secur. Appl. **17**(2), 8–16 (2019)

Johnson, K.N.: Automating the risk of bias. Georg. Wash. Law Rev. **87**(6), 1214 (2019)

Lambrecht, A., Tucker, C.: Algorithmic bias? An empirical study of apparent gender bias discrimination in the display of STEM career ads. Manage. Sci. **65**(7), 2966–2981 (2020)

Ntoutsi, E., et al.: Bias in data-driven artificial intelligence systems – an introductory survey. Data Min. Knowl. Disc. **10**(3), e1356 (2019)

Ibrahim, S.A., Charlson, M.E., Neill, D.B.: Big data analytics and the structure for equity in healthcare: the promise and perils. Health Equity **4**(1), 99–101 (2020)

Chen, I.Y., Szolovits, P., Ghassemi, M.: Can AI help reduce disparities in general medical and mental health care? AMA J. Ethics **22**(2), 167–179 (2019)

Qureshi, B., Kamiran, F., Karim, A., Ruggieri, S., Pedreschi, D.: Causal inference for social discrimination reasoning. J. Intell. Inf. Syst. **54**(2), 425–437 (2019). https://doi.org/10.1007/s10844-019-00580-x

Robert, L.P., Pierce, C., Marquis, L., Kim, S., Alahmad, R.: Designing fair AI for managing employees in organizations: a review, critique, and design agenda. Hum.-Comput. Interact. **35**(5–6), 545–575 (2020)

Lee, N.T.: Detecting racial bias in algorithms and machine learning. J. Inf. Commun. Ethics Soc. **16**(3), 252–260 (2018)

Martin, K.: Ethical implications and accountability of algorithms. J. Bus. Ethics **160**, 835–850 (2019). https://doi.org/10.1007/s10551-018-3921-3

Wu, W., Huang, T., Gong, K.: Ethical principles and governance technology development of AI in China. Engineering **6**, 302–309 (2019)

Piano, S.L.: Ethical principles in machine learning and artificial intelligence: cases from the field and possible ways forward. Humanit. Soc. Sci. Commun. **7**, 1–7 (2020)

Miron, M., Tolan, S., Gómez, E., Castillo, C.: Evaluating causes of algorithmic bias in juvenile criminal recidivism. Artif. Intell. Law **29**(2), 111–147 (2020). https://doi.org/10.1007/s10506-020-09268-y

Arrieta, et al.: Explainable Artificial Intelligence (XAI): Concepts, taxonomies, opportunities, and challenges towards responsible AI. Inf. Fusion **58**, 82–115 (2020)

Feuerriegel, S., Dolata, M., Schwabe, G.: Fair AI: challenges and opportunities. Bus. Inf. Syst. Eng. **62**(4), 379–384 (2020)

Veale, M., Binns, R.: Fairer machine learning in the real world: mitigating discrimination without collecting sensitive data. Big Data Soc. **4**, 1–17 (2017)

Berk, R., Heidari, H., Jabbari, S., Kearns, M., Roth, A.: Fairness in criminal justice risk assessments: the state of the art. Sociol. Methods Res. **50**, 3–44 (2018)

Thelwall, M.: Gender bias in machine learning for sentiment analysis. Online Inf. Rev. **42**(3), 343–354 (2017)

Paulus, J.K., Kent, D.M.: Predictably unequal: understanding and addressing concerns that algorithmic clinical prediction may increase health disparities. Digit. Med. **99**(3), 1–8 (2020)

Cirillo, D., et al.: Sex and gender differences and biases in artificial intelligence for biomedicine and healthcare. Digit. Med. **8**(3), 1–11 (2020)

Noriega, M.: The application of artificial intelligence in police interrogations: an analysis addressing the proposed effect AI has on racial and gender bias, cooperation, and false confessions. Futures **117**, 102510 (2020)

Wang, L.: The three harms of gendered technology. Australas. J. Inf. Syst. **24** (2020)
Ahn, Y., Lin, Y.R.: Fairsight: visual analytics for fairness in decision making. IEEE Trans. Vis. Comput. Graph. **26**(1), 1086–1095 (2020)
Clifton, J., Glasmeier, A., Gray, M.: When machines think for us: the consequences for work and place. Camb. J. Reg. Econ. Soc. **13**(1), 3–23 (2020)
Webster, J., Watson, R.T.: Analysing the past to prepare for the future: writing a literature review. MIS Q. **26**(2), 3–23 (2002)
UNESDOC Digital library, Artificial intelligence, and gender equality: key finding of UNESCO's global dialogue. https://unesdoc.unesco.org/ark:/48223/pf0000374174
Australian Academy of Science. (2019) Women in STEM Decadal Plan (Australian Academy of Science)
Agarwal, P.: Gender bias in STEM: women in tech still facing discrimination. Forbes (2020)
Altman, M., Wood, A., Vayena, E.: A harm-reduction framework for algorithmic fairness. IEEE Secur. Priv. **16**, 34–45 (2018)
Bentivogli, L. et al.: Gender in danger? Evaluating speech translation technology on the Must-She Corpus. In: 58th Proceeding of Association for Computational Linguistic (2020)
Brunet, M.E., Houlihan. C.A., Anderson, C., Zemel, R.: Understanding the origins of bias in word embedding. In: Proceedings of the 36th International Conference on Machine Learning, Long Beach, California (2019)
Bolukbasi, T., Chang, K.W., Zou, J., Saligrama, V., Kalai, A.: Man is to computer programmer as women is to homemaker ? Debiasing word embeddings. Cornell University Computer Science and Artificial Intelligence (2016)
Bellamy, R.K.E., et al.: AL fairness 360: an extensible toolkit for detecting, understanding and mitigating unwanted algorithmic bias. *Computer Science* (2018)
Berger, K., Klier, J., Klier, M., Probst, F.: A review of information systems research on online social networks. Commun. Assoc. Inf. Syst. **35**(8), 145–172 (2014)
Beard, M., Longstaff, S.: Ethics by design: principles for good technology. The Ethics Center (2018)
Blodgett et al.: Language (technology) is power: a critical survey of bias in NLP. Computational and Language (2020)
Canetti, R., et al.: From soft classifiers to hard decisions: how far can we be? In: Processing of the Conference on Fairness, Accountability, and Transparency, pp. 309–318 (2019)
Croeser, S., Eckersley, P.: Theories of parenting and their application to artificial intelligence. Computers and Society (2019)
Crawford, K.: A.I.'s White Guy Problem. (Sunday Review Desk) (OPINION). The New York Times (2016)
Dwivedi, Y.K., et al.: Artificial intelligence (AI): multidisciplinary perspective on emerging challenges, opportunities, and agenda for research, practice, and policy. Int. J. Inf. Manag. **57**, 101994 (2019)
Daugherty, P., Wilson, H., Chowdhury, R.: Using artificial intelligence to promote diversity. MIT Sloan Manag. Rev. **60**, 1 (2018)
Dawson, D.: Artificial Intelligence: Australia's Ethics [17] Framework. Data61 CSIRO, Australia (2019)
Edwards, J.S., Rodriguez, E.: Remedies against bias in analytics systems. J. Bus. Anal. **2**(1), 74–87 (2019)
Feast, J.: 4 ways to address gender bias in AI. Harvard Business Review (2019)
Font, J., Costa-Jussa, M.R.: Equalizing gender biases in neural machine translation with word embedding techniques. Computational and Language (2019)
Florentine, S.: How artificial intelligence can eliminate bias in hiring. CIO (2016)
Galleno, A., Krentz, M., Tsusaka, M., Yousif, N.: How AI could help or hinder women in the workforce. Boston Consulting Group (2019)

Gonen, H., Goldberg, Y.: Lipstick on a pig: debasing methods cover up systematic gender bias in words embeddings but do not remove them. In: Proceeding of Association for Computational Linguistics, Minnesota (2019)

Gummadi, K.P., Heidari, H.: Economic theories of distributive justice for fair machine learning. In: Companion Proceedings of 2019 Worldwide Web Conference (2019)

Holstein, K., et al.: Improving fairness in machine learning systems: what do industry practitioners need? In: ACM CHI Conference on Human Factors in Computing Sciences (2019)

Huang, J., et al.: Historical comparison of gender inequality in scientific careers across countries and disciplines. Proc. Nat. Acad. Sci. U.S.A. **117**, 4609–4616 (2020)

Ivaturi, K., Bhagwatwar, A.: Mapping sentiments to themes of customer reactions on social media during a security hack: a justice theory perspective. Inf. Manag. **57**(4), 103218 (2020)

Jobin, A., Lenca, M., Vayena, E.: The global landscape of AI ethics guidelines. Nat. Mach. Intell. **1**, 389–399 (2019)

Wolfswinkel, J.F., Furtmueller, E., Wilderom, C.P.M.: Using grounded theory as a method for rigorously reviewing literature. Eur. J. Inf. Syst. **22**(1), 45–55 (2013)

Kumar, G., Singh, G., Bhatanagar, V.: Scary side of artificial intelligence: a perilous contrivance to mankind. Humanit. Soc. Sci. Rev. **7**(5), 1097–1103 (2019)

Kulik, C.T., Lind, E.A., Ambrose, M.L., Maccoun, R.J.: Understanding gender differences in distributive and procedural justice. Soc. Justice Res. **9**(4), 351–369 (1996). https://doi.org/10.1007/BF02196990

Leavy, S.: Gender bias in artificial intelligence: the need for diversity and gender theory in machine learning. In: 2018 IEEE/ACM First International Workshop on Gender Equality in Software Engineering, Gothenburg, Sweden (2018)

Lambrecht, A., Tucker, C.: Algorithmic bias? An empirical study into apparent gender-based discrimination in the display of STEM career ads (2018). https://ssrn.com/abstract=2852260, http://dx.doi.org/10.2139/ssrn.2852260

Mehrabi, N., Morstatter, F., Saxena, N., Lerman, K., Galstyan, A.: A survey on bias and fairness in machine learning. Comput. Sci.- Mach. Learn. https://arxiv.org/abs/1908.09635 (2013)

Mikolov, T., et al.: Distributed representation of words and phrases and their compositionality. In: Proceeding of the 26th International Conference on Neural Information Processing Systems, vol. 2, pp. 3111–3119 (2013)

Parsheera, S.: A gendered perspective on artificial intelligence. In: Machine Learning for a 5G Future (2018)

Parikh, R.B., Teeple, S., Navathe, A.M.: Addressing bias in artificial intelligence in health care. JAMA **322**, 2377–2378 (2019)

Robnett, R.D.: Gender bias in STEM fields: variation in prevalence and links to STEM self-concept. Psychol. Women Q. **40**, 65–79 (2015)

Ridley, G., Young, J.: Theoretical approaches to gender and IT: examining some Australian evidence. Inf. Syst. J. **22**(5), 355–373 (2012)

Srivastava, B., Rossi, F.: Towards compostable bias rating of AI service. In: AAAI/ACM Conference on AI, Ethics and Society, New Orleans, Louisiana (2018)

Sen, A.: Gender inequalities and theory of justice. In: Nussbaum, M., Glover, J. (eds.) Women, Culture, and Development: A Study of Human Capabilities. Oxford University Press, New York (1995)

Sun, T., et al.: Mitigating gender bias in natural language processing: a literature review. In: 57th Proceeding of Association for Computational Linguistics, Italy (2019)

Trewin, S.: AL fairness for people with disabilities: point of view. Computer science (2018)

Terrell, J., et al.: Gender differences and bias in open source: pull request acceptance of women versus men. Peer J. Comput. Sci. **3**, e111 (2017)

Myer, M.D., Newman, M.: The qualitative interview in IS research: examining the craft. Inf. Manag. **7**(10), 2–26 (2007)

Mergel, I., Edelmann, N., Haug, N.: Defining digital transformation: results from the expert interview. Gov. Inf. Q. **36**(4), 101385 (2019)

Nadeem, A., Abedin, B., Marjanovic, O.: Gender bias in AI: a review of contributing factors and mitigating strategies. In: ACIS 2020 Proceedings 27 (2020). https://aisel.aisnet.org/acis2020/27/

Zhao, J., et al.: Gender bias in contextualization word embedding. In: Proceeding of Association for Computational Linguistics, Minnesota (2019)

Zhong, Z.: A tutorial on fairness in machine learning. Towards data science (2018)

A Systematic Review of Fairness in Artificial Intelligence Algorithms

Khensani Xivuri(✉) and Hossana Twinomurinzi

University of Johannesburg, Auckland Park, Johannesburg, South Africa
{200911813,hossanat}@uj.ac.za

Abstract. Despite being the fastest-growing field because of its ability to enhance competitive advantage, there are concerns about the inherent *fairness* in Artificial Intelligence (AI) algorithms. In this study, a systematic review was performed on AI and the fairness of AI algorithms. 47 articles were reviewed for their focus, method of research, sectors, practices, and location. The key findings, summarized in a table, suggest that there is a lack of formalised AI terminology and definitions which subsequently results in contrasting views of AI algorithmic fairness. Most of the research is conceptual and focused on the technical aspects of narrow AI, compared to general AI or super AI. The public services sector is the target of most research, particularly criminal justice and immigration, followed by the health sector. AI algorithmic fairness is currently more focused on the technical and social/human aspects compared to the economic aspects. There was very little research from Asia, Middle East, Oceania, and Africa. The study makes suggestions for further research.

Keywords: AI · Machine learning · Algorithms · Fairness · Bias · Ethics

1 Introduction

Artificial Intelligence (AI) has rapidly been gaining momentum in different industries and is now a part of daily life [1]. AI enables systems to perform tasks that would normally be performed by humans [2] in three different categories; narrow AI, general AI and super AI [3]. Narrow AI performs operational tasks through the use of machine learning tools such as recognising individual faces, driving a car or speech recognition [3, 4]. General AI is designed to be as intelligent as humans with the ability to perform any intelligent tasks [3], but remains computationally complex [5]. General AI solves complex problems and independently controls itself. General AI has the ability to get knowledge, apply it, reason, and think. Super AI is the type that is more intelligent than humans and would do better than humans in almost everything including intelligence and social skills [3]. Super AI has not been developed yet and its implementation although being utopic is feared it could have negative consequences such as human extinction [4].

AI applications collect and process data, and provide results that mimic human intelligence using rules learnt over time. Most AI applications have three common components; input data, a machine learning algorithm that processes the input data, and the

D. Dennehy et al. (Eds.): I3E 2021, LNCS 12896, pp. 271–284, 2021.
https://doi.org/10.1007/978-3-030-85447-8_24

output decision which is based on the machine learning process [6]. Machine learning makes use of trained data and test data for algorithmic models [7]. Algorithms are the coded procedures trained on existing data that transforms input data into expected results [8]. Another type of AI is expert systems which are rule-based and do not use machine learning algorithms to process data [9].

Some of the popular AIs are computer vision, natural language processing, and artificial neural networks. Some well-known AI solutions include Apple's SIRI, Google Maps, Google predictions, Smart replies by Gmail [10].

As the use of AI grows in different industries, organisations also need to consider the ethics and morals relating to the decisions from AI [11]. AI is prone to algorithmic unfairness, that is, making judgmental errors and incorrect assessments based on biased code or data, resulting in operational and reputational damage [12]. AI systems have the potential to be unfair to certain groups of people, especially with regards to racial discrimination [11], yet it is often difficult to prove if the algorithms are being unfair without access to the data and algorithms [12].

The ethics of AI is a rapidly emerging field of ethics concerned with the design, development, and implementation of AI systems [13]. The ethics of AI is important in maintaining trust in AI and ensuring that bias is removed. One of the main principles of AI ethics is fairness, which requires AI systems to be fair in terms of respecting the law, human rights and democratic values and principles. Fairness requires that AI is built in a manner that promotes democratic values and principles such as freedom and equality [14]. Fairness as a behavioral quality also means impartiality in decision-making [15, 16], that is treatment without any self-interest or prejudice in either the outcomes or the process leading to the outcomes. Fairness further extends beyond equality and perceptions and digs into the underlying reasons.

The objective of this study was therefore to conduct a systematic review of AI algorithmic fairness. The paper sought to identify the existing gaps, challenges, and opportunities for future research on AI algorithmic fairness.

2 Methodology: Search Procedures, Coding, and Classification

The study adopted Okoli and Schabram's guide [17] to conducting a systematic literature review (SLR). Systematic literature reviews are important for identifying and evaluating the existing body of work and knowledge produced by scholars, researchers and practitioners [17]. This kind of literature review is used to identify gaps and challenges for future research [18]. The SLR includes details on the literature search, screening for inclusion and exclusion, data extraction and analysis of the results. The data for this research was collected between April and September 2020. Refer to Fig. 1 for all search results. The results were analyzed against the inclusion, exclusion and quality assessment criteria as detailed in Table 1 below [19].

2.1 Screening for Inclusion and Exclusion

The Boolean operators "AND" and "OR" were used in the search to combine all search elements for articles relating to both Artificial Intelligence and Fairness. The search

Table 1. Inclusion, exclusion & quality assessment criteria

Inclusion criteria	Exclusion criteria	Quality assessment criteria
Full research articles including AI and fairness	Research performed before 2015 (to ensure that the research is current)	Verifying that the paper was based on research
Reputable news	Research that included AI but not fairness	Verify that an adequate description of the research context was described
All industries	Research that included fairness but not AI	Verify that the methodology was described
All locations		Verify that there is a clear statement of findings
Articles written in English		Verify that the paper described AI

string that was used on all the search engines was: ((AI OR Artificial Intelligence OR Algorithm OR Algorithmic) AND (Fairness OR Bias OR Discrimination OR Ethics)).

The initial search resulted in 295 311 possible articles as shown in Fig. 1 below. The research results were reviewed based on the inclusion, exclusion and quality criteria assessment defined in Table 1. Only 47 articles met all required conditions. The 47 articles were read in detail to identify the current gaps, challenges, and opportunities in algorithmic fairness. The process is presented through the PRISMA flowchart [20] in Fig. 1. The classification and coding of the articles selected were defined as per Sect. 2.2. Section 2.2 also details the classification framework used for the analysis.

The analysis of the results was based on the classification framework in Sect. 2.2. A correlation analysis using Pearson's coefficient was additionally used to check for any linear relationships between the different classifications and their relationship strength [21].

2.2 Classification Framework

A classification system was developed based on Amui et al. [18] that includes focus, method of the research, sector, practices or dimensions and origin. The framework follows the following procedures:

- Conduct a survey of available articles published on the fairness of AI algorithms;
- Develop and use a structured classification coding system to provide a structure on the existing knowledge on the fairness of AI algorithms;
- Identify main results of the articles based on the developed coding system; and
- Analyse the identified gaps, opportunities, and challenges for future studies.

The classification codes are based on the following:

- Focus (1), coded on a scale of A to D (i.e. whether the articles focused on General AI, Super AI, Narrow AI or no categorisation), based on the work of [22] and [23].
- Research method (2), coded as A to H (i.e. Quantitative, Qualitative, Conceptual research methodologies etc.,) based on the work of [24].
- Sector analysis (3), coded as A to T (i.e. Agriculture, Basic Metal production, Chemical industries, commerce etc.,) based on the work of [22]. The sectors were taken from [25].
- Practices or dimensions used in the research (4) coded as A to D (i.e. technical aspects, social/human aspects, or economic aspects) based on the work of [26].
- Origin of the research done, coded as A to G, which includes the different continents, based on the work of [27].

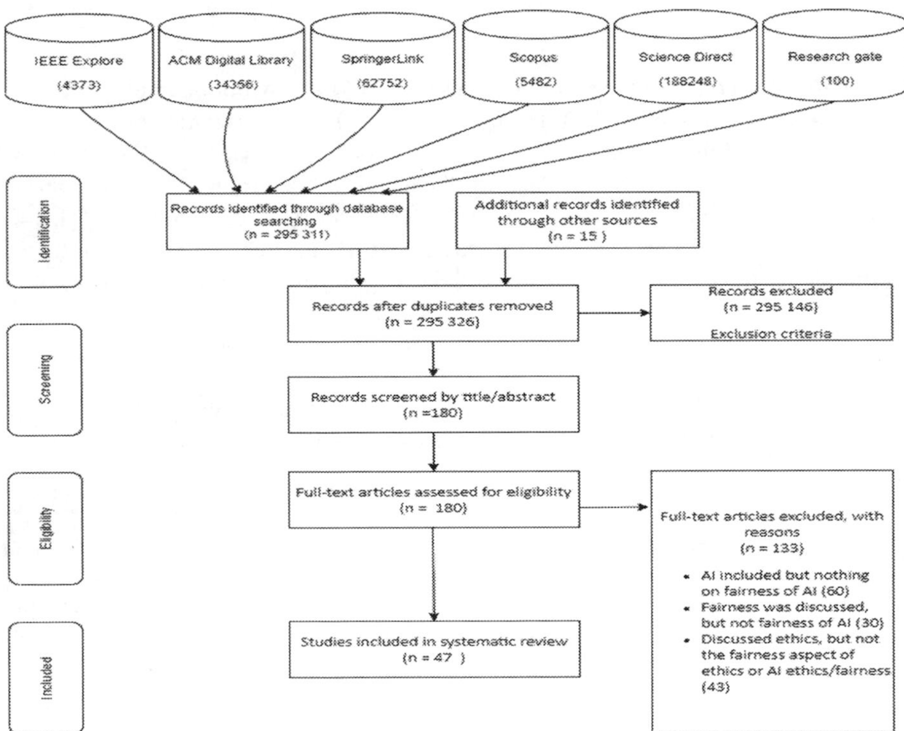

Fig. 1. Screening for inclusion and exclusion

Due to space limitations, all classifications and codes used are given in Annexure 1. A brief description of the objectives and results of each of the articles is given in Annexure 2. Annexure 3 presents the correlation table and Annexure 4 has a summary of the 47 articles reviewed. This is presented in https://dx.doi.org/10.13140/RG.2.2.26883.43048.

3 Analysis and Discussion of Findings

3.1 Focus

Algorithmic fairness was discussed using AI, machine learning and algorithms interchangeably in almost all the research papers reviewed. In as much as machine learning has been around since the 1950s, the terminology used by different entities still differs. For example, Beil et al., [28] use both AI and machine learning together, throughout their research paper, whilst Mujtaba and Mahapatra [29] use AI and machine learning interchangeably, and Dias and Torkamani [30] use AI, machine learning and algorithms separately with a clear differentiation between all three terms. This can be expected as there is a lack of formalised AI terminology and definitions. The lack of formalised AI definitions also creates differences in algorithmic fairness terminology, resulting in the lack of mutual understanding around algorithmic fairness terminology. Many researchers have come up with different technical definitions of machine learning fairness, however, there is no standardised definition of crucial AI terminology [31]. Standards clearly defining AI terminology should be developed to ensure that algorithmic fairness is universally understood and adopted.

57% of the articles focused on fairness in Narrow AI (1C), 38% were non categorised and did not address any specific type of AI (1D), whilst 2% focused on the fairness of both General AI and Narrow AI (1A, 1C). The other 2% considered the fairness of all three types of AI (1A, 1B, 1C) together. The above results are presented in Annexure 5 – Fig. 1 found on https://dx.doi.org/10.13140/RG.2.2.26883.43048. A correlation analysis revealed that fairness of Narrow AI (1C) was mainly focused on the technical areas (4A) (0.52517), while non-categorised AI (1D) did not focus on the technical areas (4A) (−0.55293).

The findings indicate that a great deal of research on the fairness of AI algorithms is focused on the technical areas of Narrow AI. This might be expected as it is in narrow AI that one will find the algorithmic implementation. Ethical challenges may arise due to the technical characteristics of AI and machine learning and the limited skills in narrow AI [28]. There are technical approaches, fixes, efforts, tools, and solutions that can be used to mitigate bias in AI [32, 33]. Additionally, there are gaps in the current available AI ethical guidelines, including technical detail and explanations [33].

The lower count of research on the fairness of General AI and Super AI indicates both the complexity of the latter two areas and the limited number of implementations. Although Super and General AI are only expected in the future, the lack of research in the two areas could lead to implications more extreme than current implications noted from lack of fairness in Narrow AI.

There is therefore a research opportunity to address the fairness of General AI and Super AI. In as much as General AI currently does not exist, it is important to first understand the difference between Narrow AI and General AI before defining AI, machine learning and their implications [34]. Some risks can be expected from General AI and Super AI automated decision making [35].

3.2 Method of the Research

Most of the articles used the conceptual research methodology (2G – 45%), and the qualitative and theoretical research methodologies together (2A, 2C – 17%) with a correlation of 0.359. There is little research using qualitative (2B – 6%), survey (2F – 4%), theoretical (2%), quantitative (2A – 2%), empirical (2D – 2%), and case study/interview (2E – 2%) research methodologies in the study of algorithmic fairness. The above results are presented in Annexure 5 – Fig. 2 found on https://dx.doi.org/10.13140/RG.2.2.26883.43048. Research originating from America (5A) used the theoretical research methodology (0.326) more, compared to Europe which used less of the theoretical research methodology (−0.359), the empirical research methodology (−0.293).

The dominance of the theoretical research methodology could be because the fairness of AI is an emerging phenomenon, and more research is required for example, around policies, legal and consumer protection [36].

There is an opportunity for more research to be conducted using a mixture of different research methodologies across the different regions/continents and sectors. There is a need for theoretical and empirical research around justifications of AI decision making [37]. Performing empirical and philosophical research around this area will aid in getting a more thorough public and individual perspective on AI decision making [37]. There is a need for empirical research that is more focused and rigorous on important questions regarding AI, its adoption, and the consequences thereafter [34].

3.3 Sectors

Most of the research was not specific to any sector (3U – 62%). 21% of the articles were focused on the public services sector (3Q), mainly in the criminal justice, immigration, and government. 11% of the articles were from the health sector (3J), 2% from the financial sector (3G) and 2% from the Postal and telecommunications sector (3P). The other 2% considered the fairness of AI in both the health and financial sectors (3G, 3J). The above results are presented in Annexure 5 – Fig. 3 found on https://dx.doi.org/10.13140/RG.2.2.26883.43048.

The findings indicate that most of the research done was generalised and not specific to any sector. This could be because sector-specific information relating to the fairness of AI is not available or easily attainable. There are currently not enough public data sets and information around AI to allow for a detailed microanalysis of differences in the different sectors and regions [34].

A smaller percentage of the research focused on the criminal justice sector, the financial sector, and the health sector. This could be because more AI benefits have been realised in these sectors compared to the other sectors. The banking and financial sectors are currently at the forefront of AI [38]. AI has brought in a lot of benefits in industries such as health care, transportation, criminal justice, and economic inclusion [39]. This could also be because biases in these sectors could have a larger impact compared to the other sectors. An example relating to the health sector is an algorithm that is used widely in the US health care, affecting millions of people, which was found to be highly biased in that it gave white people greater health care over black people who needed the treatment more as their health conditions were worse [40]. This type of bias could result in consequences such as loss of lives as well as fines from the health regulatory boards. The use of AI in healthcare raises critical ethical issues that are important in avoiding harming patients, liability for healthcare providers and undermining public trust in AI. Another example relating to the finance sector is the use of biases such as gender and race to provide a credit score or determine an individual's credit eligibility, which is illegal in the US [41]. Bias in the financial sector could result in punishment by courts and fines where there are laws against it. Lastly, an example relating to the criminal justice sector is the recent outrage from the Black Lives Matters movement in the US which argues that the criminal justice sector is biased against black people [42]. The criminal justice sector uses criminal risk assessments algorithms to determine a criminal/defendant's future risk for misconduct [42]. Bias in such algorithms could result in incorrect conviction or sentencing.

There is therefore an opportunity for sector-specific research on the fairness of AI. A sector-specific AI fairness approach is required to oversee, audit and monitor AI technologies in the different sectors [43]. A sector-specific approach will ensure that the sector focuses more on the application of AI and its impacts rather than prioritising the technology. Different sectors have different characteristics and required expertise, and therefore the governance or regulations of one sector may not be appropriate for another sector. Different expertise and knowledge specific to each sector will be required for good AI governance and ensuring the fairness of AI in the different sectors.

3.4 Practices or Dimensions Used in the Research

72% of the papers focused on both the technical aspects and the social/human aspects of algorithmic fairness (72% – 4A, 4B). 19% of the articles focused on social/human aspects (4B), and 6% on all 3 aspects together (4A, 4B, 4C). The other 2% considered the economic aspects (4C) of algorithmic fairness. The above results are presented in Annexure 5 Fig. 4 found on https://dx.doi.org/10.13140/RG.2.2.26883.43048.

The findings indicate that there is not enough research on the economic aspects of algorithmic fairness. This could be a result of the lack of transparency in the AI algorithms used in the financial sector. Gender and race are still used to determine whether a loan should be granted to individuals and businesses in South Africa [44]. Algorithms used for loan decisions are trained using loan history and demographic data of applicants who have been accepted or rejected, which increases the chances of black women being rejected or given high-interest rates for loan applications, resulting in continued financial injustices in the country which may further affect the economy. AI biases have also resulted in black people's loan applications being rejected in the US [44]. Banking services have been investing a lot in AI, however, conversations on the biases of AI used in banking are very limited [44].

There is therefore an opportunity for research to be done on the economic aspects of algorithmic fairness. There is a need for evidence-based research which will provide more detail on how AI will affect economic outcomes [44]. The banking sector was one of the biggest sectors which invested in AI in 2019 globally [44]. The increase in AI investments in this sector calls for more research on the fairness of algorithms in the finance/banking sector and the economic aspects of it.

3.5 Origin

Most of the research on algorithmic fairness originated from Europe (5B – 49%), America (5A – 21%) and both Europe and America (5A, 5B – 13%). 9% of the articles originated from Africa (5D), 6% from Asia (5C), 4% from a combination of America, Europe, and Asia (5A, 5B, 5C), and 2% from a combination of America and Asia (5A, 5C). The other 2% were either global or not specific to any region (5G). The above results are presented in Annexure 5 – Fig. 5 found on https://dx.doi.org/10.13140/RG.2.2.26883.43048. An analysis of research originating from Africa revealed that algorithmic fairness in Africa did not focus on the technical aspects of algorithmic fairness. Algorithmic fairness research originating from Africa focused more on uncategorised AI compared to Narrow AI and was done mainly using the conceptual research methodology.

The findings indicate that there is not enough research done on algorithmic fairness in Asia, Middle East, Oceania, and Africa. For example, countries that have issued ethical AI guidelines are economically developed countries such as the USA and the UK, followed by Japan, Germany, France and Finland [45]. There is a lack of AI guidelines originating from Africa, South and Central America, and Asia, which shows that regions are not equally participating in the development of AI ethics.

The findings also illustrate that research done in Africa did not focus on the technical aspects of algorithmic fairness. Research originating from Africa focused on the fairness of generalised AI and not specific AI types. This could be because AI is still an emerging technology in Africa despite it being highly implemented. In as much as there's a lot of researchers, engineers and technology professionals who are ready to explore AI in Africa, AI is still a new concept in Africa [46]. There is a need for expanding AI expertise and building AI solutions in Africa rather than just focusing on the theoretical aspects of it [47].

There is therefore an opportunity for research to be done on algorithmic fairness globally. There is also an opportunity to do research focusing on the fairness of the different types of AI (Narrow AI, Super AI, and General AI) in Africa. For example, it is important for all countries, regardless of their economic conditions, to be fully involved in the development of AI ethics [45]. The involvement of all countries will help avoid neglecting local knowledge, cultural diversity, and the need for global fairness.

4 Discussion

Table 2 presents a summary of key gaps, opportunities, and future research.

Table 2. Discussion and conclusion

Category	Gaps	Opportunities/further research
Focus	Lack of formalised AI terminology and definitions	Standards clearly defining AI terminology should be developed to ensure that algorithmic fairness is universally understood and adopted
	Lack of research on the fairness of General and Super AI	There is a research opportunity to address the fairness of General AI and Super AI
	Lack of Social/human aspects and economic aspects of Narrow AI	There is a research opportunity to address the social/human aspects of Narrow AI and the economic aspects of AI
Research Methodology	Lack of research using a mixture of different research methodologies across the different regions and sectors. Most of the research largely used the conceptual research methodology	There is an opportunity to perform research using a mixture of different research methodologies across the different sectors and regions
Sectors	Lack of sector-specific research	There is a research opportunity for sector-specific research on the fairness of AI
	Research that was sector-specific was focused on the criminal justice sector, the financial sector, and the health sector	There is a research opportunity to address the fairness of AI in all sectors including the impact of bias in the different sectors
Dimensions	Lack of research on the economic aspects of AI fairness	There is a research opportunity to address the economic aspects of AI fairness
Origin	Lack of research on algorithmic fairness in Asia, the Middle East, Oceania, and Africa	There is a research opportunity to address algorithmic fairness globally
	Lack of research on the technical aspects of AI fairness originating from Africa	There is a research opportunity to address the technical aspects of algorithmic fairness in Africa

5 Conclusions

This study performed a systematic literature review on the fairness of AI algorithms. This type of review is important in structuring available knowledge in a subject area, and the planning of future studies. The results of the study indicate the absence of formalised AI terminology and definitions. Most of the research focused on the fairness of Narrow AI, in no specific sector, in America and Europe, largely using the conceptual research methodology. Less research is available on the economic aspects of algorithmic fairness globally, and the technical aspects of algorithmic fairness in Africa. There is therefore a gap in AI terminology, the algorithmic fairness of Super & General AI, sector-specific algorithmic fairness, and the economic aspects of algorithmic fairness. Standards clearly defining AI terminology should be developed to ensure that algorithmic fairness is universally understood and adopted. Research addressing the technical aspects of algorithmic fairness in Africa should be done.

This research provides a significant implication for research theory and practice. The findings indicate that there is less research on algorithmic fairness in low-income countries. There are opportunities to develop sector-specific theory in the field of algorithmic fairness of AI, including the development of formalised standards clearly defining AI terminology on a global level. In practice, policymakers for AI implementation should also look at the algorithmic fairness of AI before roll-out, its implications, and how to avoid bias to ensure success and trust from society.

This research contributes to Information systems governance by highlighting gaps, challenges, and opportunities in AI algorithmic fairness research. Research on the fairness of General and Super AI, focusing on the economic aspects of AI, using a mixture of research methodologies.

References

1. Scherer, M.U.: Regulating artificial intelligence systems: risks, challenges, competencies, and strategies. Havard J. Law Technol. **29**, 353–400 (2016)
2. Ghosh, A., Chakraborty, D., Law, A.: Artificial intelligence in Internet of things. CAAI Trans. Intell. Technol. **3**, 208–218 (2018)
3. Gherheş, V.: Why are we afraid of Artificial Intelligence (AI)? Eur. Rev. Appl. Sociol. **11**, 6–15 (2019)
4. Gurkaynak, G., Yilmaz, I., Haksever, G.: Stifling artificial intelligence: Human perils. Comput. Law Secur. Rev. **32**, 749–758 (2016)
5. Pennachin, C., Goertzel, B.: Contemporary approaches to artificial general intelligence. Cogn. Technol. **8**, 1–30 (2007)
6. Salah, K., Rehman, M.H.U., Nizamuddin, N., Al-Fuqaha, A.: Blockchain for AI: Review and open research challenges. IEEE Access. **7**, 10127–10149 (2019)
7. Hacker, P.: Teaching fairness to artificial intelligence: existing and novel strategies against algorithmic discrimination under EU law. Common Mark. Law Rev. **55**, 1143–1185 (2018)
8. Beretta, E., Santangelo, A., Lepri, B., Vetrò, A., De Martin, J.C.: The invisible power of fairness. how machine learning shapes democracy. In: Meurs, M.-J., Rudzicz, F. (eds.) Canadian AI 2019. LNCS (LNAI), vol. 11489, pp. 238–250. Springer, Cham (2019). https://doi.org/10.1007/978-3-030-18305-9_19
9. Yigin, I.H., Taşkin, H., Cedİmoglu, I.H., Topal, B.: Supplier selection : an expert system approach. Product. Plan. Control **18**(1), 16–24 (2007)
10. Patel, K.N., Raina, S., Gupta, S.: Artificial intelligence and its models. J. Appl. Sci. Computat. **7**(2), 95–97 (2020)
11. Sharma, S., Henderson, J., Ghosh, J.: CERTIFAI: Counterfactual Explanations for Robustness, Transparency, Interpretability, and Fairness of Artificial Intelligence models. arXiv:1905.07857v1 (2019).

12. Horowitz, M.C.: Artificial intelligence, international competition, and the balance of power. Texas Natl. Secur. Rev. **1**, 37–57 (2018)
13. Strous, L., Johnson, R., Grier, D.A., Swade, D.: Unimagined Futures – ICT Opportunities and Challenges. Springer Nature Switzerland AG, Switzerland (2020)
14. Ienca, M.: Democratizing cognitive technology: a proactive approach. Ethics Inf. Technol. **21**, 267–280 (2018)
15. Farnadi, G., Babaki, B., Getoor, L.: Fairness in relational domains. In: AIES 2018 – Proceedings of the 2018 AAAI/ACM Conference on AI, Ethics and Society, pp. 108–114 (2018)
16. Neuteleers, S., Mulder, M., Hindriks, F.: Assessing fairness of dynamic grid tariffs. Energy Policy **108**, 111–120 (2017)
17. Okoli, C., Schabram, K.: A Guide to Conducting a Systematic Literature Review of Information Systems Research. Sprouts: Working Papers on Information Systems, 10 (2010)
18. Amui, L.B.L., Jabbour, C.J.C., de Sousa Jabbour, A.B.L., Kannan, D.: Sustainability as a dynamic organizational capability: a systematic review and a future agenda toward a sustainable transition. J. Clean. Prod. **142**, 308–322 (2017)
19. Kusen, E., Strembeck, M.: A decade of security research in ubiquitous computing: results of a systematic literature review. Int. J. Pervasive Comput. Commun. **12**, 216–259 (2016)
20. Harris, J.D., Quatman, C.E., Manring, M.M., Siston, R.A., Flanigan, D.C.: How to write a systematic review. Am. J. Sports Med. **42**, 2761–2768 (2014)
21. Chok, N.S.: Pearson's Versus Spearman's and Kendall's Correlation Coefficients for Continuous Data. Master's Thesis, University of Pittsburgh (2010)
22. Jabbour, C.J.C.: Environmental training in organisations: from a literature review to a framework for future research. Resour. Conserv. Recycl. **74**, 144–155 (2013)
23. Mariano, E.B., Sobreiro, V.A., do Nascimento Rebelatto, D.A.: Human development and data envelopment analysis: a structured literature review. Omega (United Kingdom). **54**, 33–49 (2015)
24. Lage, M., Filho, M.G.: Production planning and control for remanufacturing: literature review and analysis. Prod. Plan. Control. **23**, 419–435 (2012)
25. Organisation International Labour: Industries and Sectors. https://www.ilo.org/global/industries-and-sectors/lang--en/index.htm. Accessed 08 Nov 2020
26. Jabbour, C.J.C., Jugend, D., De Sousa Jabbour, A.B.L., Gunasekaran, A., Latan, H.: Green product development and performance of Brazilian firms: measuring the role of human and technical aspects. J. Clean. Prod. **87**, 442–451 (2015)
27. Fahimnia, B., Sarkis, J., Davarzani, H.: Green supply chain management: a review and bibliometric analysis. Int. J. Prod. Econ. **162**, 101–114 (2015)
28. Beil, M., Proft, I., van Heerden, D., Sviri, S., van Heerden, P.V.: Ethical considerations about artificial intelligence for prognostication in intensive care. Intensive Care Med. Exp. **7**(1), 1–13 (2019)
29. Mujtaba, D.F., Mahapatra, N.R.: Ethical considerations in AI-based recruitment. In: 2019 IEEE International Symposium on Technology and Society (ISTAS), pp. 1–7 (2019)
30. Dias, R., Torkamani, A.: Artificial intelligence in clinical and genomic diagnostics. Genome Med. **11**, 1–12 (2019)
31. Lepri, B., Oliver, N., Letouzé, E., Pentland, A., Vinck, P.: Fair, Transparent, and accountable algorithmic decision-making processes: the premise, the proposed solutions, and the open challenges. Philos. Technol. **31**, 611–627 (2018)
32. Hagendorff, T.: From privacy to anti-discrimination in times of machine learning. Ethics Inf. Technol. **21**(4), 331–343 (2019). https://doi.org/10.1007/s10676-019-09510-5
33. Hagendorff, T.: The ethics of AI ethics: an evaluation of guidelines. Mind. Mach. **30**(1), 99–120 (2020). https://doi.org/10.1007/s11023-020-09517-8

34. Raj, M., Seamans, R.: Primer on artificial intelligence and robotics. J. Organ. Des. **8**(1), 1–14 (2019). https://doi.org/10.1186/s41469-019-0050-0
35. Gill, K.S.: AI & Society: editorial volume 35.2: the trappings of AI Agency. AI Soc. 35, 289–296 (2020)
36. Cath, C., Wachter, S., Mittelstadt, B., Taddeo, M., Floridi, L.: Artificial intelligence and the 'good society': the US, EU, and UK approach. Sci. Eng. Ethics **24**(2), 505–528 (2017)
37. de Fine Licht, K., de Fine Licht, J.: Artificial intelligence, transparency, and public decision-making: why explanations are key when trying to produce perceived legitimacy. AI Soc. (2020)
38. Soluciones Decide: How Different Sectors are Using AI | by Decide Soluciones|Becoming Human: Artificial Intelligence Magazine. https://becominghuman.ai/how-different-sectors-are-using-ai-26470ba334ab. Accessed 03 Sep 2020
39. Bundy, A.: Preparing for the future of artificial intelligence. AI Soc. **32**(2), 285–287 (2016)
40. Obermeyer, Z., Powers, B., Vogeli, C., Mullainathan, S.: Dissecting racial bias in an algorithm used to manage the health of populations. Science **366**(6464), 447–453 (2019)
41. Klein, A.: Reducing bias in AI-based financial services. https://www.brookings.edu/research/reducing-bias-in-ai-based-financial-services/. Accessed 25 Nov 2020
42. Rao, A.: Artificial intelligence poses serious risks in the criminal justice system – The Johns Hopkins News-Letter, https://www.jhunewsletter.com/article/2020/09/artificial-intelligence-poses-serious-risks-in-the-criminal-justice-system. Accessed 25 Nov 2020
43. Whittaker, M., et al.: AI Now report. AI Now Inst. (2018)
44. Moosajee, N.: Fix AI's racist, sexist bias – the Mail & Guardian. https://mg.co.za/article/2019-03-14-fix-ais-racist-sexist-bias/. Accessed 27 Nov 2020
45. Jobin, A., Ienca, M., Vayena, E.: The global landscape of AI ethics guidelines. Nat. Mach. Intell. **1**, 389–399 (2019)
46. Nwankwo, E., Sonna, B.: Africa's social contract with AI. XRDS crossroads. ACM Mag. Students **26**, 44–48 (2019)
47. Marwala, T.: Review, amend or create policy and legislation enabling the 4IR – The Mail & Guardian. https://mg.co.za/article/2020-04-03-review-amend-or-create-policy-and-legislation-enabling-the-4ir/. Accessed 28 Aug 2020
48. Covelo de Abreu, J.: The Role of Artificial Intelligence in the European e-Justice Paradigm – Suiting Effective Judicial Protection Demands. In: Moura Oliveira, P., Novais, P., Reis, L.P. (eds.) EPIA 2019. LNCS (LNAI), vol. 11804, pp. 299–308. Springer, Cham (2019). https://doi.org/10.1007/978-3-030-30241-2_26
49. Council of Europe – European commission for the efficiency of justice (CEPEJ): European ethical charter on the use of Artificial Intelligence in judicial systems and their environment. https://rm.coe.int/ethical-charter-en-for-publication-4-december-2018/16808f699c
50. Raymond Geis, J., et al.: Ethics of artificial intelligence in radiology: summary of the joint European and North American multisociety statement. Insights Imaging **10**(1), 1–6 (2019)
51. Ishii, K.: Comparative legal study on privacy and personal data protection for robots equipped with artificial intelligence: looking at functional and technological aspects. AI Soc. **34**(3), 509–533 (2017). https://doi.org/10.1007/s00146-017-0758-8
52. Calo, S., Bertino, E., Verma, D. (eds.): Policy-Based Autonomic Data Governance. LNCS, vol. 11550. Springer, Cham (2019). https://doi.org/10.1007/978-3-030-17277-0
53. Choraś, M., Pawlicki, M., Puchalski, D., Kozik, R.: Machine learning – the results are not the only thing that matters! What about security, explainability and fairness? Lect. Notes Comput. Sci. (including Subser. Lect. Notes Artif. Intell. Lect. Notes Bioinformatics), vol. 12140 LNCS, pp. 615–628 (2020)
54. Thesmar, D., Sraer, D., Pinheiro, L., Dadson, N., Veliche, R., Greenberg, P.: Combining the power of artificial intelligence with the richness of healthcare claims data: opportunities and challenges. Pharmacoeconomics. **37**, 745–752 (2019)

55. Završnik, A.: Criminal justice, artificial intelligence systems, and human rights. ERA Forum **20**(4), 567–583 (2020). https://doi.org/10.1007/s12027-020-00602-0
56. Neri, E., Coppola, F., Miele, V., Bibbolino, C., Grassi, R.: Artificial intelligence: who is responsible for the diagnosis? Radiol. Med. (Torino) **125**(6), 517–521 (2020). https://doi.org/10.1007/s11547-020-01135-9
57. Currie, G., Hawk, K.E., Rohren, E.M.: Ethical principles for the application of artificial intelligence (AI) in nuclear medicine. Eur. J. Nucl. Med. Mol. Imaging **47**(4), 748–752 (2020). https://doi.org/10.1007/s00259-020-04678-1
58. D'Agostino, M., Durante, M.: Introduction: the governance of algorithms. Philos. Technol. **31**(4), 499–505 (2018). https://doi.org/10.1007/s13347-018-0337-z
59. Floridi, L., Cowls, J., King, T.C., Taddeo, M.: How to design AI for social good: seven essential factors. Sci. Eng. Ethics **26**(3), 1771–1796 (2020). https://doi.org/10.1007/s11948-020-00213-5
60. Lee, M.S.A., Floridi, L.: Algorithmic fairness in mortgage lending: from absolute conditions to relational trade-offs. Mind. Mach. **31**(1), 165–191 (2020). https://doi.org/10.1007/s11023-020-09529-4
61. Miron, M., Tolan, S., Gómez, E., Castillo, C.: Evaluating causes of algorithmic bias in juvenile criminal recidivism. Springer, Netherlands (2020)
62. Wong, P.H.: Democratizing algorithmic fairness. Philos. Technol. **33**, 225–244 (2020)
63. Samek, W., Müller, K.-R.: Towards explainable artificial intelligence. In: Samek, W., Montavon, G., Vedaldi, A., Hansen, L.K., Müller, K.-R. (eds.) Explainable AI: Interpreting, Explaining and Visualizing Deep Learning. LNCS (LNAI), vol. 11700, pp. 5–22. Springer, Cham (2019). https://doi.org/10.1007/978-3-030-28954-6_1
64. Iosifidis, V., Fetahu, B., Ntoutsi, E.: FAE: a fairness-aware ensemble framework. Proceedings of the 2019 IEEE International Conference on Big Data, Big Data 2019, pp. 1375–1380 (2019)
65. Parsheera, S.: A gendered perspective on Artificial Intelligence. Mach. Learn. a 5G Futur. (ITU K), 1689–1699 (2018)
66. Altman, M., Wood, A., Vayena, E.: A harm-reduction framework for algorithmic fairness. IEEE Secur. Priv. **16**, 34–45 (2018)
67. Bellamy, R.K.E., et al.: AI fairness 360: an extensible toolkit for detecting and mitigating algorithmic bias. IBM J. Res. Dev. 63 (2019)
68. Oneto, L., Chiappa, S.: Fairness in machine learning. In: Oneto, L., Navarin, N., Sperduti, A., Anguita, D. (eds.) Recent Trends in Learning From Data. SCI, vol. 896, pp. 155–196. Springer, Cham (2020). https://doi.org/10.1007/978-3-030-43883-8_7
69. Antunes, N., Balby, L., Figueiredo, F., Lourenco, N., Meira, W., Santos, W.: Fairness and transparency of machine learning for trustworthy cloud services. In: Proceedings of the 48th Annual IEEE/IFIP International Conference Dependable System Networks Work. DSN-W 2018, pp. 188–193 (2018)
70. Zhang, W., Tang, X., Wang, J.: On fairness-aware learning for non-discriminative decision-making. In: IEEE International Conference Data Min. Work. ICDMW. 2019-Novem, pp. 1072–1079 (2019)
71. Binns, R.: What can political philosophy teach us about algorithmic fairness ? IEEE Secur. Privacy **16**(03), 73–80 (2018)
72. Nayebare, M.: Artificial intelligence policies in Africa over the next five years. XRDS Crossroads. ACM Mag. Students **26**, 50–54 (2019)
73. Heaven, W.D.: The UK is dropping an immigration algorithm that critics say is racist. MIT Technol. Rev. https://www.technologyreview.com/2020/08/05/1006034/the-uk-is-dropping-an-immigration-algorithm-that-critics-say-is-racist/. Accessed 28 Aug 2020
74. Marwala, T.: South Africa must have a stake in artificial intelligence technology – the mail & guardian. https://mg.co.za/article/2020-03-06-south-africa-must-have-a-stake-in-artificial-intelligence-technology/. Accessed 28 Aug 2020

75. Žliobaitė, I.: Measuring discrimination in algorithmic decision making. Data Min. Knowl. Disc. **31**(4), 1060–1089 (2017)
76. Ignatiev, A., Cooper, M.C., Siala, M., Hebrard, E., Marques-Silva, J.: Towards Formal Fairness in Machine Learning. In: Simonis, H. (ed.) CP 2020. LNCS, vol. 12333, pp. 846–867. Springer, Cham (2020). https://doi.org/10.1007/978-3-030-58475-7_49
77. Feuerriegel, S., Dolata, M., Schwabe, G.: Fair AI. Bus. Inf Syst. Eng. **62**, 379–384 (2020)
78. Kapatamoyo, M., Ramos-Gil, Y.T., Márquez Dominiguez, C.: Algorithmic discrimination and responsibility: Selected examples from the United States of America and South America. In: Florez, H., Leon, M., Diaz-Nafria, J.M., Belli, S. (eds.) ICAI 2019. CCIS, vol. 1051, pp. 147–157. Springer, Cham (2019). https://doi.org/10.1007/978-3-030-32475-9_11
79. Ntoutsi, E., et al.: Bias in data-driven AI systems – an introductory survey. WIREs Data Mining Knowl. Discov. **10**(3), 1356 (2020)

Is Downloading This App Consistent with My Values?

Conceptualizing a Value-Centered Privacy Assistant

Sarah E. Carter[1,2,3](✉)

[1] Data Science Institute, National University of Ireland Galway, Galway, Ireland
s.carter6@nuigalway.ie

[2] Discipline of Philosophy, School of History and Philosophy, College of Arts, Social Sciences, and Celtic Studies, National University of Ireland Galway, Galway, Ireland

[3] Science Foundation Ireland Centre for Research Training in Digitally-Enhanced Reality (D-Real), Galway, Ireland

Abstract. Digital privacy notices aim to provide users with information to make informed decisions. They are, however, fraught with difficulties. Instead, I propose that data privacy decisions can be understood as an expression of user values. To optimize this value expression, I further propose the creation of a value-centered privacy assistant (VcPA). Here, I preliminary explore how a VcPA could enhance user value expression by utilizing three user scenarios in the context of considering whether or not to download an environmental application, the OpenLitterMap app. These scenarios are conceptually constructed from established privacy user groups - the privacy fundamentalists; the privacy pragmatists; and the privacy unconcerned. I conclude that the VcPA best facilitates user value expression of the privacy fundamentalists. In contrast, the value expression of the privacy pragmatists and the privacy unconcerned could be enhanced or hindered depending on the context and their internal states. Possible implications for optimal VcPA design are also discussed. Following this initial conceptual exploration of VcPAs, further empirical research will be required to demonstrate the effectiveness of the VcPA system in real-world settings.

Keywords: Privacy assistant · Mobile applications · Values

1 Introduction

Designing effective digital privacy notices remains challenging. For example, too many privacy notices can lead to notice fatigue, causing a user to habitually "click through" notices rather than making informed decisions [1]. Instead, I propose that data privacy decisions can be understood as an expression of user values [2]. I also conceptually outline a system to assist users with smartphone selection based on these issues [3]. This assistant - here called a value-centered privacy assistant (VcPA) - helps create the space for users to act in accordance with their values.

In the following pages, I preliminary explore how a VcPA could enhance user value expression. To accomplish this, I utilize three user scenarios for each privacy user group

Published by Springer Nature Switzerland AG 2021
D. Dennehy et al. (Eds.): I3E 2021, LNCS 12896, pp. 285–291, 2021.
https://doi.org/10.1007/978-3-030-85447-8_25

- the privacy fundamentalists; the privacy pragmatists; and the privacy unconcerned - in the context of considering whether or not to download an environmental smartphone application, OpenLitterMap [4]. I then explore whether each group's value expression is preserved with the VcPA by utilizing Killmister's theory of autonomy [3, 5]. To this end, I conclude that the VcPA best facilitates the value expression of privacy fundamentalists. In contrast, privacy pragmatists and the privacy unconcerned could have their value expression enhanced or hindered depending on the context and their internal states. Possible implications for future VcPA investigations are also discussed.

1.1 Theoretical and Conceptual Background

Designing for informed user consent in digital privacy settings is fraught with difficulties. Originally, privacy notices and policies were based around the conceptualization of users as "rational consumers" – those who weigh the service offered against their value of privacy [6]. While this view continues to inform certain policy and regulatory measures, it is now well-accepted by most privacy scholars that current notice-and-consent regimes are insufficient at providing adequate user privacy controls. For example, too many privacy notices can lead to notice fatigue, causing a user to habitually "click through" notices rather than making informed decisions [1]. In addition, "dark patterns" can coax users to consent to data collecting practices [7–9]. To combat this, privacy-preserving modifications – also called "bright patterns" – have been explored to encourage users to make better privacy choices [10, 11]. These interventions, however, can be considered manipulative to the user, especially if they are unaware of a bright pattern's use [3].

Instead, I propose that we take a value-centered approach to privacy decision-making [2]. This conceptualizes data privacy as an expression of user values. When a user is faced with a privacy notice, the data collection practice of the service will either be consistent or inconsistent with a user's values. Their decision to consent or not can therefore be understood as an expression of their values.

To optimize user value expression, I propose the creation of a value-centered privacy assistant (VcPA) – an assistant that helps users select smartphone applications consistent with their values [3]. The VcPA consists of three features: suggesting alternative applications; personalized pausing; and randomized notice (summarized in Table 1). In practice, users will be prompted with personalized notices to notify them when a smartphone application's data collection practices are inconsistent with their values. While the technical details of such a personalized system have yet to be determined, the VcPA would ideally store its data locally to minimize data protection issues. Periodically, a user's values around data privacy will also be "mined" by random notices for applications previously consistent with their values. In addition, all notices will include a suggestion of alternative applications with similar functionality but more value-consistent data collection practices.

Table 1. Proposed features of a value-centered privacy assistant (VcPA)

Feature	Description
Suggesting alternatives	On the notice itself, include suggestions for alternative applications with similar function that are consistent with the user's pre-stated values
Personalized pausing	Prompting a user selectively with a notice when an application is not consistent with their values
Randomized notices	Prompting users with notices at random time internals for applications consistent with their values

2 Methods: User Scenarios Design and Evaluation

User scenarios are a central requirement of user-centered design. Designers can utilize scenarios as a means of translating high-level ideas into more concrete possibilities. For the purpose of this paper, I define user scenarios as "narrative descriptions" of a user's engagement with a VcPA [12]. In particular, these user scenarios have descriptive emphasis on the user's goals and values. They also reflect three privacy preference groups described elsewhere [13, 14]. These groups are: privacy fundamentalists, or users who are very concerned about disclosing their data even in the presence of privacy protections; privacy pragmatists, or users who have very specific privacy concerns about data disclosure in certain contexts; and the privacy unconcerned, or users who have mild or no concern about disclosing data, although they may still show concern for their data privacy in select circumstances [14].

In each scenario, all three hypothetical users are faced with the decision whether to download the application OpenLitterMap [4]. OpenLitterMap is a citizen science initiative that allows users to take smartphone pictures of litter and upload them into a publicly available dataset. The goal is to empower citizens to be active participants in combating local pollution. Photos of litter can be uploaded anonymously or with a username to participate in the litter "World Cup." In both cases, the system records a number of features, including time, date, location, and phone model. This means that in areas of low app use, it becomes possible to identify a user based on inference. From a value-centered privacy approach, a potential OpenLitterMap user will need to balance the value of disclosing information against the possible (albeit, small) risk of identification.

To evaluate value expression in each user scenario, I will utilize an existing systematic conception of autonomy that incorporates values. This conception of autonomy, proposed by Suzy Killmister [5], maps autonomy into four distinct dimensions: self-definition, self-realization, self-unification, and self-constitution. In the context of smartphone selection, self-definition is where a user brings together their individual goals, beliefs, and values to form a set of commitments on how to interact with smartphone applications. Self-realization consists of two states. The first internal state is when a user deliberates and decides whether to download an application based on their commitments. The second, the external state, is when a user downloads the app (or not). Self-unification is whether how the user has acted is consistent with their commitments. Self-constitution involves whether or not a user is able to modify their commitments when encountering new information about the application, such as data privacy information. From this view, then, when a user is deciding to download a smartphone application, they are involved in a dynamic process of weighing (self-realization), expressing (self-realization), and modifying (self-constitution) their defined (self-definition) values, goals, and beliefs. For it to be fully autonomous, their decision to download an application or not will also need to be consistent with their values (self-unification).

3 Results and Discussion

3.1 User Scenario Evaluation

The Privacy Fundamentalist. User #1 (the privacy fundamentalist) likes to make environmentally friendly choices. they are willing to do what they can to preserve the environment and provide the best future for their children. User #1 hears about OpenLitterMap from a friend and goes to download it. with the VcPA System, a notice appears on their screen, warning them that this application is not consistent with their personal values of security and control. They decide to check out other apps first by clicking "see alternative applications."

At this point, there are two possible outcomes for User #1. The first is that they find a different litter clean-up application that is consistent with their values of security and control and download that one instead. In this application, the data collected may, for example, only be accessible to policy makers and environmental scientists, be encrypted, and also not collect their phone model. The second possible outcome is that User #1 does not find another application with a similar function. They may then decide to stick to their regular beach cleanings to help their environment instead of downloading an application.

Without the VcPA system, User #1 may click through the privacy settings and allow the app to access their photos, camera, location, date, time, and phone model. They begin using the app when they are walking to pick up their children from school. While they want to help document litter and believe in allowing data scientists access to their documented litter data for environmental research purposes, they would feel uncomfortable if someone was able to identify their route to and from the school – and, by association, information about their children. To uphold their values of security and control, they may decide to upload their litter anonymously rather than with a username. However, they may be the only one using OpenLitterMap on that route, and it would be possible for someone looking at the data to identify them. While some may have been comfortable with this level of risk, they would not have been – they prioritize security and control over their value of environmentalism.

The Privacy Pragmatist. User #2 (the Privacy Pragmatist) has a number of practical apps on their phone. A colleague recommends that they take a look at OpenLitterMap. They go to download it.

With the VcPA, there would be two possible outcomes for User #2. They could firstly receive a randomized notice letting them know that, while this application is consistent with their previously stated values, there is a chance of violating the values of security and control if they use the application. User #2 will then have to decide whether or not to download this application when faced with this new information. In the absence of a randomized notice, User #2 may simply click through the privacy settings and allow the app to access their photos, camera, location, date, time, and phone model, the same result without the VcPA system.

The Privacy Unconcerned. User #3 (the privacy unconcerned) attends a talk organized by their local greens club about the harmful effects of litter. The greens club recommends checking out openLitterMap. User #3 likes the idea of creating a profile to compete for the littermap "World Cup" leaderboards. They go to download the application.

Regardless of whether User #3 has the VcPA system, there is likely only one outcome. They could receive a randomized notice letting them know that, while this application is consistent with their previously stated values, there is a chance of violating the values of security and control if they use the application. They will likely then decide to download the application anyway. In the absence of the randomized notice, they will download the application. User #3 would also likely download the application without the VcPA.

3.2 User Scenario Evaluation

Here, I systematically assess the success of the VcPA at facilitating user value expression using the four-dimensional theory of autonomy [3, 5].

In the first user scenario (privacy fundamentalist), the absence of the VcPA would have resulted in a violation of their self-unification – their actions (to download the application) would not be in alignment with their values (security and control). Thanks to personalized pausing, however, User #1 is alerted to this misalignment of their action and their values. In addition, their self-realization (acting on their beliefs) could also be enhanced if they are able to find another app using the "suggest alternatives" feature.

In the second user scenario (privacy pragmatist), User #2's autonomy may be enhanced with the VcPA. It could help with self-constitution depending on the context and their specific value preferences. When a randomized notice appears and they are presented with new information they may not have previously been aware of, they may decide to modify their values and commitments, promoting self-constitution. If, however, they do not change their values; still intend to download OpenLitterMap; and they do not download it because of the added notice, this would actually hinder self-unification because they would act in a manner inconsistent with their values. Interestingly, by introducing added friction in the form of an added notice, self-realization may also be slightly reduced by providing a small barrier to realizing their values and intention. Suzy Killmister has noted this issue previously, cautioning that interventions that encouraging a specific behavior must be consistent with what the agent has defined to uphold self-unification [5].

The same applies for the third user scenario (the privacy unconcerned). It is possible that a randomized notice could encourage them to take on new commitments concerning their privacy and thereby self-constitute; even "the privacy unconcerned" are concerned in specific circumstances [14]. Like User #2, however, it is also possible that they will suffer the same tension between self-realization/unification and self-constitution if a randomized notice changes their behavior in a manner inconsistent with their values.

3.3 Implications for Future VcPA Design

While the VcPA best upholds value expression of the privacy fundamentalists, the expression of the privacy pragmatists and the privacy unconcerned may be upheld depending on the context and their internal states. I have previously suggested that we could take cues from the recommender system literature to create a system of continuous exploration that minimizes the user behavioral effects of preference-mining [3, 15]. The results here support that this will be critical for an effective VcPA system for the majority of users, who are privacy pragmatists [14]. The VcPA system could be optimized using user tests of privacy pragmatists to determine the right frequency and presentation of the randomized notices that maximize self-constitution while minimizing the harms to self-realization/unification.

4 Concluding Thoughts

This initial high-level conceptual exploration suggests that a VcPA could enhance or similarly preserve user value expression across different privacy groups. In order to accomplish this goal, a VcPA should be carefully designed to minimize the behavioral effects of randomized notices. Further empirical studies will also be required to further evaluate VcPA efficacy and desirability. In addition to supporting the hypothesis that a VcPA could help users make more value-centered privacy decisions, such studies will need to answer whether users will find a VcPA beneficial over current privacy controls. To validate both hypotheses, I will be utilizing a mix-method approach to elucidate relevant user values in privacy decision-making and user app download behavior with a prototype VcPA system.

Acknowledgments. This work is being conducted with financial support from the Science Foundation Ireland Centre for Research Training in Digitally-Enhanced Reality (d-real) under Grant No. 18/CRT/6224. It is supervised by Mathieu d'Aquin (Data Science Institute, National University of Ireland Galway), Heike Schmidt-Felzmann (Discipline of Philosophy, National University of Ireland Galway), Kathryn Cormican (School of Engineering, National University of Ireland Galway), and Dave Lewis (ADAPT Centre, Trinity College Dublin).

References

1. Schaub, F., Balebako, R, Durity, A.L., Canor, L.F.: A design space for effective privacy notices. In: Proc. 11th Symp. Usable Priv. Secur. (SOUPS), pp. 1–17. The USENIX Association, Ottawa (2015)
2. Carter, S.E.: Improving notice: the argument for a flexible, multi-value approach to privacy notice design. Presented at: 30th Intl. Assoc. Prof. Appl. Ethics (APPE) Conf., online (2021). https://vimeo.com/509883867/c734b7c879
3. Carter, S.E.: A value-centered exploration of data privacy and personalized privacy assistants. Presented at: CEPE/IACAP Joint Conf. Phil. Eth. AI., online (2021)
4. OpenLitterMap. http://openlittermap.com. Accessed 28 Feb 2021
5. Killmister, S.: Taking the Measure of Autonomy: A Four-Dimensional Theory of Self-governance. Routledge, New York (2017)

6. Hoofnagle, C.J., Urban, J.M.: Alan Westin's privacy homo economicus. Wake For. Law Rev. **14**(1), 261–351 (2014)
7. Gray, C.M., Kou, Y., Battles, B., Hoggatt, J., Toombs, A.L.: The dark (patterns) side of UX design. In: Proc. Conf. Hum. Fac. Comput. Syst. (CHI), pp. 1–14. ACM, Montreal (2018)
8. Mathur, A., et al.: Dark patterns at scale: Findings from a crawl of 11K shopping websites. In: Proc. Conf. Comput. Sup. Coop. Work (CSCW), pp. 81:1–81:32. ACM, Austin (2019)
9. Utz, C., Degeling, M., Fahl, S., Schaub, F., Holz., T.: (Un)informed consent: Studying GDPR consent notices in the field. In: Proc. Conf. Comput. Comm. Secur. (CCS), pp. 971–990. ACM, London (2019)
10. Almuhimedi, H., et al.: Your location has been shared 5,398 times! A field study on mobile app privacy nudging. In: Proc. Conf. Hum. Fac. Comput. Syst. (CHI), pp. 787–796. ACM, Seoul (2015)
11. Graßl, P., Schraffenberger, H., Zuiderveen Borgesius, F., Buijzen, M.: Dark and bright patterns in cookie consent requests. J. Digit. Soc. Res. **3**(1), 1–38 (2021)
12. Rosson, M.B., Carroll, J.M.: Scenario-based design. In: Jacko, J., Sears. A (eds.) The Human-Computer Interaction Handbook, 1st ed., pp. 1032–1050. Lawrence Erlbaum Associates, New York (2002)
13. Westin, A.F.: Harris-Equifax consumer privacy survey. Equifax, Atlanta (1991)
14. Ackerman, M.S., Cranor, L.F., Reagle, J.: Privacy in e-commerce: Examining user scenarios and privacy preferences. In: Proc. 1st Conf. Elec. Comm., pp. 1–8. ACM, Denver (1999)
15. Jiang, R., Chiappa, S., Lattimore, T., György, A., Kohli, P.: Degenerate feedback loops in recommender systems. In: Proc. Conf. AI Ethics Soc. (AIES), pp. 383–390. ACM, Honolulu (2019)

Operationalization of a Glass Box Through Visualization: Applied to a Data Driven Profiling Approach

Niels Netten(✉), Arjen Suijker, Mortaza S. Bargh, and Sunil Choenni

Rotterdam University of Applied Sciences, Creating 010, 3011WN Rotterdam, Netherlands
{c.p.m.netten,a.j.suijker,m.shoae.bargh,r.choenni}@hr.nl

Abstract. The profiles from data-driven profiling applications are a model of the reality. The interpretability of these profiles for end users, e.g. policymakers, is often far from trivial. How and why these models are obtained by the applications are often regarded as a black box. In recent years several profiling applications used by public organizations have led to wrong interpretations of the obtained models and impacted individuals and society adversely. Hence, the research focus has increasingly shifted towards dealing with the trust and interpretability issues of the models. In support of a more careful and proper interpretation of these models, several scholars have advocated a glass box approach that aims at making these models more transparent to end users. In this paper, we operationalize the glass box approach for a Genetic Algorithm (GA) based profiling application. To enhance the interpretability of the models provided by the application, we aim at facilitating the interaction of domain experts with the models. Hereby domain experts can gain insight to the evolvement of the profiles and what happens to the profiles if we change or add a new pieces of information. Adding such an interactive visualization provides more transparency about the derived models, making them more understandable for end users and policymakers. As a result, they can better assess and explain the consequences of those models when they apply to practice.

Keywords: Algorithms · Glass box · Transparency · AI · Profiling

1 Introduction

Nowadays, many organizations in the private and public sector are searching for ways to take advantage of the explosive growth of (big) data. Especially, in the public domain we see a growing urge to apply data-driven analytics. In recent years, we have seen that data-driven analytics is used to examine large datasets for profiling purposes such as fraud detection [1, 2] and predictive policing [3–5]. On the one hand, these new applications of profiling have opened up many new opportunities for organizations to analyze and predict the behavior of people. On the other hand, in the context of government services the outcome profiles of these new applications are sensitive and a matter of public debate,

Published by Springer Nature Switzerland AG 2021
D. Dennehy et al. (Eds.): I3E 2021, LNCS 12896, pp. 292–304, 2021.
https://doi.org/10.1007/978-3-030-85447-8_26

because they can (adversely) impact individuals (see for example [6] and the references there-in [7]). If the profile models are wrongly interpreted and applied to practice, they may lead to decisions that seem mathematically optimal, but are far from being correct, just and fair. Hence, it is important to take care of a proper interpretation of profile models and apply them appropriately to practice. To this end, it is advocated to adopt a glass box approach [8, 9]. In such a glass box approach, the relevant concepts and their relationships within an advanced application are explained to end users in a meaningfully transparent way. The goal of a glass box approach is to facilitate a proper interpretation of the obtained models so that end users can assess the consequences of the actions taken based on those models.

In this paper, we operationalize the glass box approach for the GA-based profiling tool as reported in [2]. The tool is developed to support the law enforcement staff at Rotterdam municipality in investigating those individuals who unlawfully misuse the municipality's social benefits system. Despite the reliable performance of GA-based profiles, optimizing, interpreting, and applying such profiles to practice remain challenging for domain experts and policymakers [10]. Domain experts usually have a basic understanding of statistics, but often lack deep knowledge about machine learning in general and GAs in particular. This makes it hard for them to scrutinize the resulting profiles. One should realize that deriving and applying group profiles is also subject to further validations based on privacy and ethical laws and constraints. To aid the validation of the resulting profiles, transparency of the used model is essential for experts and policymakers who want to apply the profiles to practice. Although the human-readable profiles developed by [2] add a lot of transparency to the results of the algorithm, they do not explain what goes on inside the GA-based profiling tool. When evaluating the human-readable profiles resulting from the GA-based tool, two major questions were put forward: how does the algorithm come up with these specific profiles? And could users steer the algorithm towards a preferred set of profiles? To address these questions, visualization of the GA algorithm for profiling seems a promising approach.

In this contribution, we concentrate on visualization as a method to show the adaptive internal search process and strategy of the developed GA-based profiling tool to find relevant profiles in the data. The visualization functions are implemented as a graphical user interface that allows users to view the creation and evolvement of profiles, interpret the influence of separate profile attributes, and steer the search of the algorithm while it is running.

2 A Strategy for a Responsible Use of AI Models

An increasing trend for users who apply complicated AI models to practice is to focus more on a responsible use of these models and enhance the trust of end-users in such models. A solution direction for a responsible use of the AI models is to provide more model transparency to end-users as we explain in Subsect. 2.1. Subsequently we present a short review of the related works in Subsect. 2.2.

2.1 Moving from a Black to a Glass Box

Black boxes are systems that hide their internal logic to the user [11–13]. According to the black box approach, data sets and some constraints are fed to the black box and only the outcomes of the black box are observed. In case that we are not satisfied with the outcomes, some constraints and data may be altered and again fed to the black box. This process may be repeated until the outcomes are satisfactory based on some criteria. In another approach, referred to as the open box, the implementation of the concepts and their relationships are fully documented so that it can be tracked how the outcomes are obtained exactly. In case that the outcomes obtained are not satisfactory, it is possible to find out which concepts and relationships contribute to this dissatisfaction. These concepts and relationships can be adapted accordingly.

We propose to take, however, a view which is in between these two extreme views, referred to as the glass box [8, 9, 14]. In this view, it is not necessary to know precisely all the ins and outs of the implementation of the used concepts and their relationships. Instead, the crucial and relevant concepts and their relationships between them are explained to end users in a meaningfully transparent way.

The goal of a glass box approach is to facilitate a proper interpretation of obtained models in such a way that end users (e.g. policymakers) can assess the consequences of the actions based on those models within their application domain. The transparency of why and how these models are obtained is an important means to realize this goal. Two crucial questions in the context of a glass box are: (1) what concepts and relationships should be made transparent? And (2) what level of transparency is desired? Subsequently the third question would be how to best convey transparency to users. Unfortunately, there are no straightforward answers to these questions as they depend on the application, i.e. the usage scenario, at hand. We distinguish between two extremes: transparency of algorithms and transparency of data.

In the first situation, the focus is on the transparency of the algorithms, while the transparency of the other components can fully be neglected. As an example of a situation in which this is recommended, consider a neural network based application that is trained for recognizing faces of apes (i.e., the possible output classes are apes). One might be disappointed if he/she offers his/her own picture to this application and the application classifies the picture as a gorilla. As the neural network is trained to classify everything as apes, it may be excellent at recognizing the faces of apes but not those of humans. Therefore, it does not matter what pictures you offer to the neural network, it will always recognize each of them as a type of ape. So, to prevent disappointments in classifying faces of people, it is better to be transparent about the algorithm.

In the second situation, the focus is on the transparency of the data and the transparency of the other components are neglected fully. As an example of how this works, suppose that we have an application that predicts who has high chances to become the next Prime Minister of the Netherlands. Like most big data algorithms, assume that the application bases its prediction on the features of the persons that have been elected Prime Minister of the Netherlands in the past. Few people will be surprised if such an algorithm will predict that the next prime minister will be a tall man. In this case, transparency regarding the data is crucial for a proper interpretation and use of the outcome. If most of the previously elected Prime Ministers can be characterized by these features and these features are reflected in the data, then the prediction is understandable. If for some reasons the prediction is undesirable, then the data should be adapted. In this situation transparency with regards to the algorithms will not help to prevent undesired outcomes.

In the GA-based profiling application that we consider [2], the focus will be to visualize the search process and strategy of the algorithm since the end users of the application, i.e., the policymakers at the municipality, are quite familiar with the data and the quality issues of the data used by the tool.

2.2 Related Work

Some of the earliest influential work on the subject of visualizing GA's was done by [15]. He discusses several standard techniques, which include visualizations of the increase of fitness over several generations. This is still the most common basic way to visualize the progress of GAs. Another common visualization technique focuses on showing the individuals in each generation, while displaying their respective fitness, genetic make-up or other individual information [16–18]. Usually, the same tools display information that allows users to explore the family tree of successful individuals. Again, this type of information can be useful to illustrate the abstract technical workings of the algorithm, but the results are hard to interpret without any knowledge about GAs.

Most of the data that provides real insight exists in many dimensions, since most practical implementations of GAs are used with big datasets consisting of many variables. This presents a challenge for visualization of GAs as we usually only have two dimensions available on a screen. There are several methods to display more dimensions, such as adding color, 3D-projection and time-based visualizations. However, none of these methods scale very well when the number of possible dimensions starts to exceed five [15]. Another method employed by [15] is to map only the dissimilarities existing in higher dimensions unto lower dimensions. This vastly reduces visual complexity, but also neglects a lot of useful information. The main information that can be gained from these visualizations is whether the GA is converging or diverging. A similar method is used by [19], who transform variables into arbitrary polymorphs. A visualization is then based on these polymorphs, displaying mostly (dis)similarity of variables over generations. The resulting visualization is very abstract and hard to interpret, because the link between the variables and the algorithm is removed.

Although these approaches have merit, none of them appears very suitable for visualizing the GAs used for profiling due to the following shortcomings: (a) the knowledge of GAs is required for comprehension, (b) the results cannot be shown on the fly, (c) they cannot be used to guide the GA when users want to get insight into a certain impact, and (d) they abstract away too much of the underlying attributes, which makes the profiles unintelligible.

3 Profiling: Using a GA-Based Algorithm

Municipalities and government agencies in the Netherlands have embraced data-driven analytics in recent years to exploit their available data in order to be more effective and efficient in their task execution. The rapid deployment of those data-driven analytics applications in practice, however, brought forward some challenges for these organizations. In [2] the first step towards addressing the transparency challenge was taken by choosing the algorithm that suits the preconditions of the problem at hand.

3.1 Challenges of Data-Driven Profiling in Practice

The municipality of Rotterdam and the Dutch IRS are two public organizations that embraced the new opportunities of data-driven profiling. One of the challenges they both encountered was how to deal with profiles and make use of the opportunities provided by these profiles responsibly. A profile is a data driven conclusion that applies to a group of people with a confidence value that may or may not be a realistic probability value. The municipality of Rotterdam made use of the Risk Indication System (abbreviated as SyRi in Dutch) to support the municipality in reducing the risk of social assistance fraud within a household. The data (on houses, labor, education, detention, benefits, debts, taxes and receipts allowances) pertained to the residents of the districts Bloemhof and Hillesluis were combined to make a risk analysis of who may be involved in committing social benefits fraud. At the Dutch IRS, people were tracked down that possibly cheated on their child support benefits, on the grounds of dual nationality and other forms of ethnic profiling.

In both cases it is unclear how both organizations dealt with the interpretation of the results of the profiling systems. In these situations, it is crucial to adequately interpret the concept of opportunity and profile. After all, even if a system delivers a result that someone has a 98% chance to commit fraud or that he/she fully complies with a fraud profile, it cannot simply be concluded that the fraud is actually committed or is going to take place. Another challenge in such applications is that in advance it is known that the analyses will sometimes be wrong. The question then is how do you deal with the so-called "*false positives*" and "*false negatives*". Because both public organizations mentioned above did not provide an adequate answer to the interpretation challenges of the results, the application of the results to practice has led to the disadvantage of citizens, stigmatization of groups and social commotion. As a result, the profiling applications at the municipality of Rotterdam as well as at the Dutch IRS were shut down.

To enable these organizations to better deploy their data driven profiling in practice, we shall provide some answers for them via creating more transparency for their profile models. In [2] the first step towards this was taken with the GA-based profiling tool. This tool shows that it is feasible to derive meaningful and sensible profiles from data analytics.

3.2 Mining with a Genetic Algorithm

In [2, 20] a data-driven profiling approach was adopted that uses a GA to search for meaningful and human understandable (group) profiles, i.e., in the use case of [2] finding groups of clients who make unlawful use of the municipality's social service. In that context a profile, which is specified by a set of data attributes (and their values), represents a group of people who unlawfully use social services. An example of such a profile might be "*young men who live in ZIP code 1234AB*". To search for the profiles, we model the databases as a search space and tailor a GA to walk through the space. To facilitate the interpretation of the profiles, a profile will be presented in IF-THEN-ELSE-RULES. An example rule might be: *IF sex=male AND age IN* [18, 24]*AND zipcode=1234AB THEN unlawful use of social service.*

Via a case study, paper [2] showed that the resulting profiles can be comprehensible for law enforcement officers to apply them to their daily practices, for policymakers to analyze their efficiency and legality, and for others to scrutinize their fairness. Nevertheless, it also concluded that deriving and using the profiles should be done with great care according to, among others, privacy and non-discrimination laws and guidelines. Hence, in addition to providing a comprehensible outcome, one should assure and validate the resulting profiles in being fair and accurate enough before applying them (i.e., one should manually investigate those persons who are identified by the validated profiles, before imposing any sanctions on them).

Essentially, this approach was successful at making the output of the algorithm more comprehensible, but it also highlighted the need for transparency of the algorithm's process and subsequent control over it. We exploit data visualization as a tool to show the internal search process of the algorithm. Additionally, this visualization functions as a graphical interface that allows users to modify the search direction of the algorithm while it is searching through the data.

The profiling algorithm that was used in [2] is a GA. GA's are considered more easy to understand for data scientists, since their internal search process can be tracked and analyzed. However, their internal representation is often too abstract for domain experts to understand. In terms of performance, this doesn't have to be a problem. The evolvement of the profiles during the search process, however, is still very hard to grasp in this way. Therefore, we look at the discipline of data visualization to make this search process more transparent. In the following section this will be explained in more detail.

4 A Glass-Box for a GA Profiling Algorithm

Based on desktop research and interviewing the domain experts at Rotterdam municipality, we gathered the requirements about the GA-visualization that would allow them to secure the interpretation of the creation and evolvement of profiles during the search process (see Sect. 4.1). We noticed an interest in the aspects that are considered important in determining a high prediction risk by the GA and an eagerness in knowing what will happen to the profile search if new pieces of information are added. To address this transparency, it is worthwhile to develop a robust, interpretable, and interactive GA visualization. Visualization methods that we can employ to satisfy these requirements are given in Sect. 4.2. The implementation of GA-Viz in Sect. 4.3 and a hypothetical use case is given in Sect. 4.4.

4.1 Requirements of GA-Viz

Work on the role of visualizations in data-driven profiling exists, but most of it focuses on the exploration of the dataset using general visualization algorithms [21]. Instead, we intend to follow and steer an algorithm in its path through the data in order to find a solution, i.e., a profile for a problem at hand. Based on several interviews with domain experts and through literature review, we elicited a number of requirements for the visualization of the search process and strategy of the GA. Together, these requirements should result in a visualization module on top of the GA so that end users can obtain more insight into the algorithm's search process and can more actively steer the search. The resulting design requirements are:

1. **Coverage analysis**: Users should be able to determine which parts of the data have been considered by the algorithm and which have been ignored [22]. This control helps to prevent a number of issues, like the GA developing a bias, getting stuck in a local optimum, or ignoring the areas in the dataset that end users know to be of interest. We intent to show the coverage of the algorithm in two ways: by showing an ordered list of the variables the algorithm is exploring the most, and by clustering similar profiles together so that less-explored variables can be seen as lying further out.
2. **Convergence/divergence**: Users should be able to determine whether an algorithm is diverging or converging on solutions [22]. This helps them to decide on the optimal number of cycles to run the GA. To make this possible, the visualization should be on the fly. This also allows them to see that the clusters of similar profiles either grow or shrink, and that the list of different explored variables either grows or shrinks.
3. **Interaction with the algorithm:** A popular, well-performing paradigm for systems designed for domain experts is the human-in-the-loop approach [23, 24]. This means that the decision process is designed in such a way that the algorithm can work semi-independently, but that it benefits greatly from human input in its decision process. Our visualization accomplishes this by keeping users updated on every decision by the algorithm and allowing them to interact with the algorithm by steering it in certain directions based on their domain knowledge.
4. **Real-time operation:** the visualization of the algorithm needs to happen in real-time to make real interaction possible. Simply restarting the algorithm with different parameters won't have the same effect, since non-deterministic approaches such as GA will lose the unique progress that they make.
5. **Confirmatory and exploratory analysis:** The visualization should allow for both confirmatory and exploratory analysis, meaning that end users can not only let the program run its course and learn from its process, but can also easily change its hyperparameters and run it again to check certain hypotheses [25]. Because the search process of the GA can be followed, both confirmatory and exploratory analysis not only are possible, but also are easy since end users don't need the algorithm to finish completely before their analysis. Exploration can also be made easier by making the algorithm interactive, thereby allowing end user to steer the direction of their exploration.

4.2 Conceptual Design of GA-Viz

How the requirements have been translated into the architecture of our GA-based profiling tool on an abstract level is shown in Fig. 1. On the left side in Fig. 1 is the overall workflow of the GA. It starts with the random initialization of the profile population with completely random solutions. Then the GA selects pairs of profiles (parents) to evaluate their fitness (i.e. the score it tries to optimize) with regard to the defined search problem. Next the two parents are subjected to the manipulation operators of crossover and mutation. The two resulting offspring profiles are also evaluated on their fitness and the best one is passed on to the next generation together with the parent profile with the highest score. For more GA details see [2].

The visual design of the interface revolves around a force-based lay-out, where each profile is represented as a circle. The distance between the circles is based on the overlap between their target groups: all profiles represent a group of people, and the distance between these profiles is decided by the number of people they have in common. This creates visual clusters that give users information about the (dis)similarity of the profiles. The size of the circles is determined by the size of the target group, since this is an important indicator for the usefulness of a profile. In Sect. 4.4 these visual design choices are illustrated.

The coverage can be analyzed by seeing which profiles are being added and removed. The convergence and divergence can be checked by seeing increasing or decreasing similarity between the profiles that continually added, changed and removed. The interaction with the algorithm is made possible in real time, because the profile overview is updated with every new generation, which allows the user to react to this by changing the likelihood of the propagation of specific properties, leading to visible changes in the next iteration. The confirmatory and exploratory analysis are made possible through the same process.

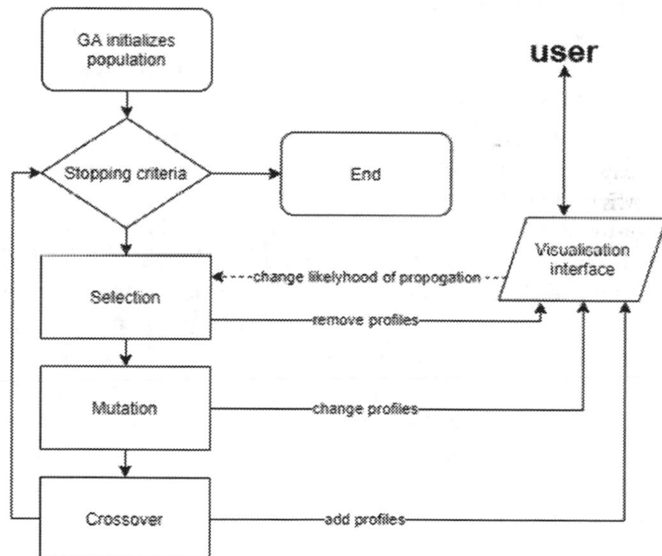

Fig. 1. Interaction between user and GA-model

4.3 Implementation of GA-Viz

The GA runs on a server using the Genie package for Julia language. The visualization runs in a browser. This makes the system flexible and modular. The GA and its visualization are connected through websockets, which makes the communication between them near-instantaneous. The GA starts to run, and whenever genetic individuals are created, mutated or removed, it sends an update to the client browser in the JSON format. The client browser runs JavaScript, using d3 for its clustering algorithm. Normally, d3 works with dynamic svg-images. This leads to performance issues when too many objects are displayed at the same time. Therefore, we used PixieJS to render our visualization instead, since it uses WebGL to achieve superior performance. In this way, we were able to implement all the requirements mentioned in Sect. 4.1, apart from the interaction with the algorithm. Although the infrastructure and the design are there, implementing the actual interaction is left for future editions of the tool. This means that the dotted line in Fig. 1 is still in the implementation phase.

To tailor and test the visualization, we utilized a similar use case and dataset as those of [2] to visualize the corresponding GA. However, in order to showcase the genericness of our approach and due to the classified nature of that dataset, we decided to create and test another use case based on public U.S. census data [26].

4.4 A Hypothetical Use Case

To illustrate our visualization, we present a hypothetical use case. It not only shows how the system may work in practice, but also illustrates how the visualization satisfies the requirements in Sect. 4.1. We will refer to these requirements as (req. 1) through (req. 5). Figure 2 shows a screenshot of the user screen during the search process. In the use case, a car producer is doing market research for a new series of high-end cars. They are looking for buyers in a higher income bracket. They set this bracket at an income of 50K $ per year. Using available census data, they want to create interesting profiles of potential customers so that they can adapt their marketing accordingly.

The visualization shows the progress of the GA through the data, while it 'searches' for the best (i.e., the highest scoring) profiles. The GA is optimized to work with profiles made of demographic data and to find those profiles that fit a large number of high-income persons. For example, a profile looks like the one shown in Table 1. This profile could be represented in our visualization as shown in Fig. 2. Since it has a high fitness there, it is represented by a relatively large circle. The GA uses these profiles as genetic individuals, tries out new combinations, and strives to generate new profiles with an increasingly good fit. A fitness function is used to optimize the search process for a (predefined) ratio of the number of people with an income above or below the 50K $ threshold that a profile represents.

The end user of the profiling system is a marketing expert we will call John. Starting the GA, it immediately shows ten blue circles of varying sizes. Each circle is also labeled with a sequential number to ease identification. John hovers over one of the circles with his mouse, and he is presented with information about the profile that that circle represents, like its attributes, its fitness and the size of its target class (i.e., the

Table 1. Profile example (consisting of 5 attributes)

Attribute	Value
Wage per hour	10.17–18.82
Age	2:16
Reason for unemployment	New entrant
Education level	Associates degree/academic program
Race	Black

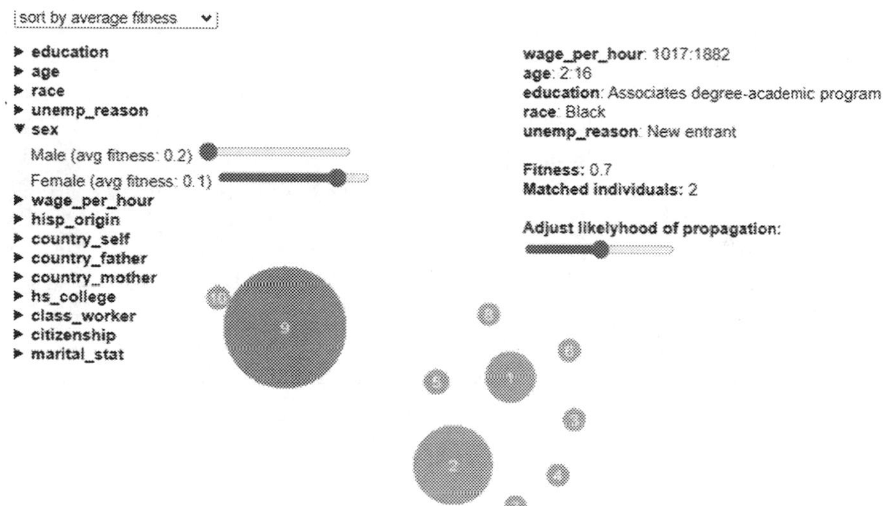

Fig. 2. A screenshot of our application illustrating the use case.

number of people it targets). John is curious about some of the smaller circles, so he scrolls his mouse wheel and drags the canvas to pan and zoom in on his areas of interest.

The profile updates from the GA are animated, drawing attention to the changes (req. 4). Whenever a new profile is created, it 'shoots' onto the screen. When a profile mutates, it shakes. When a profile is removed, it fades out. John sees that many of the uninteresting profiles are being replaced by new ones, but also that some of the profiles are changing and becoming more interesting and better performing. This shows that the algorithm is slowly converging (req. 2). John sees that a cluster of profiles is starting to form, all of which include the attribute sex="female". He is interested in this and he marks them by clicking them. This clicking makes the color of the profile cluster red so that their progress can easily be tracked (req. 5). After a while, however, he notices that many of these profiles are being replaced by different profiles that represent highly-educated white males because they tend to have higher average incomes. Since this is already an over-saturated market, he adjusts a slider, so that sex="male" is negatively weighted in next generations (req. 3).

Gradually different profiles start to emerge and, besides the main clusters, some small profiles (i.e., targeting few persons) at the edges start to appear and disappear. These small profiles seem interesting but are not selected for reproduction causing some areas of the data to be underexplored (req. 2). John clicks one of them and adjusts a slider that increases their reproduction likelihood (req. 3). Another important aspect of the visualization is that it keeps an updated list of attributes. This list shows all of the attributes that are currently involved in at least one of the profiles. It updates whenever the visualization changes. Included in this list is the total number of the profiles using each parameter, as well as the average fitness of all of these profiles.

By default, this list is sorted by the average fitness value of the profiles that incorporate that attribute. This gives an indication about that specific attribute, which is often an overall good predictor. The list can also be sorted by the number of the profiles that incorporate that attribute. This gives an indication of how much the currently running GA is focusing on that attribute (req. 1). This give users an overview of the current state of the algorithm, and it also allows users to check if the algorithm is missing opportunities. For example, John notices that the inclusion of attribute 'education' produces high fitness, but when he sorts the list by number of profiles, he sees that the algorithm is not really focusing on that attribute. He adjusts a slider to include the likelihood of those profiles to reproduce (req. 3). When a user clicks on the attributes in this list, the profiles that incorporate that attribute are highlighted and can be tracked throughout the GA search process. John uses this functionality, and notices that education performs especially well in conjunction with sex="female", forming small target groups with a high fitness. He decides to use this finding as the foundation of his new marketing campaign, using the generated profiles to further specify some niches.

5 Conclusion and Future Work

In this paper we operationalize a glass box concept for a GA-based profiling tool. To this end, we exploited the visualization of the search process and strategy of GA to find profiles. The visualization provides ends user insights and a better understanding of why and how certain profiles are selected by the GA. These insights help them to interpret the selected profiles by the GA. Furthermore, end users are given the possibility to steer the GA into a desired direction.

Experts appeared to be interested in how the application comes up with the profiles as well as playing with the application to see what the effect is when one starts turning the knobs. So far, we described the first part of a glass box extension of a GA-based profiling application. A next step is to implement a more comprehensive interaction functionality for our GA-based profiling application (i.e., the GA-Viz tool). Once this is implemented, end user tests can start to determine the efficacy of our approach.

In the current design, we have made all the information available in one coherent visualization module. This visualization provides an overview of all profiles that are being explored by the algorithm. Although it provides a lot of information, this could be improved upon by offering users multiple 'views'. For example, a view could be offered that gives more information about a specific profile, or a view that shows more information about the general progress and history of the current algorithm. These could be shown together on a dashboard to increase informativity and clarity, which has been shown with great success by previous work like [27].

Not only can a visualization make this specific profiling tool much more transparent, but also, we believe, many profiling algorithms would benefit from being more transparent. While developing the visualization, we aimed to make it generic enough to be used not only on GAs as used by [2, 20], but on all profiling algorithms based on supervised machine learning. Examples include Support Vector Machines, Multiple Regression and Random Forests. It could even be used to visualize Neural Network-based algorithms, although additional work would be needed to extract the necessary data.

References

1. Jans, M., Lybaert, N., Vanhoof, K.: Data mining for fraud detection: toward an improvement on internal control systems? (2008)
2. Netten, N., Bargh, M.S., Choenni, S.: Exploiting data analytics for social services: on searching for profiles of unlawful use of social benefits. In: Proceedings of the 11th International Conference on Theory and Practice of Electronic Governance. pp. 550–559. ACM, New York, NY, USA (2018)
3. PredPol. PredPol (2018). http://www.predpol.com/. Accessed 10 March 2021
4. Lonkhuyzen, L.: To predict crime, it is possible, NRC, May. (2017) www.nrc.nl/nieuws/2017/05/16/misdaad-voorspellen-het-kan-echt-9100898a1558837
5. Willems, D., Doeleman, R.: Predictive policing: wens of werkelijkheid. Tijdschrift voor Politie **76**, 4 (2014)
6. Hildebrandt, M.: Profiling: from data to knowledge. Datenschutz und Datensicherheit-DuD **30**(9), 548–552 (2006)
7. Leese, M.: The new profiling: algorithms, black boxes, and the failure of anti-discriminatory safeguards in the European Union. Secur. Dialogue **45**(5), 494–511 (2014)
8. Choenni, S., Netten, N., Bargh, M., Choenni, R.: Challenges of big data from a philosophical perspective. In: Proceedings of the 2018 International Conference on Multidisciplinary Research (MyRes), Pamplemousses, Mauritius, 22–23 June 2018, pp. 71–81
9. Choenni, S., Netten, N., Shoae-Bargh, M., Choenni, R.: On the usability of big (social) data. In: 2018 IEEE Intl Conference on Parallel & Distributed Processing with Applications, Ubiquitous Computing & Communications, Big Data & Cloud Computing, Social Computing & Networking, Sustainable Computing & Communications (ISPA/IUCC/BDCloud/SocialCom/SustainCom), pp. 1167–1174 (2018)
10. Choenni, S., Netten, N., Bargh, M.S., van den Braak, S.: Exploiting Big Data for Smart Government: Facing the Challenges. In: Augusto, J.C. (ed.) Handbook of Smart Cities, pp. 1–23. Springer International Publishing, Cham (2020). https://doi.org/10.1007/978-3-030-15145-4_82-1
11. Guidotti, R., Monreale, A., Ruggieri, S., Turini, F., Giannotti, F., Pedreschi, D.: A survey of methods for explaining black box models. ACM Comput Surv, **51**, 5 (2018)
12. du Boulay, B., O'Shea, T., Monk, J.: The black box inside the glass box: presenting computing concepts to novices. Int. J. Man Mach. Stud. **14**(3), 237–249 (1981)
13. Sokol, K., Flach, P.A.: Glass-Box: Explaining AI Decisions With Counterfactual Statements Through Conversation With a Voice-enabled Virtual Assistant. In IJCAI (pp. 5868–5870), Jan 2018
14. Rai, A.: Explainable AI: from black box to glass box. J. Acad. Mark. Sci. **48**(1), 137–141 (2020)

15. Pohlheim, H.: Visualization of evolutionary algorithms - set of standard techniques and multidimensional visualization. In: Proceedings of the 1st annual conference on genetic and evolutionary computation, Vol. 1. pp. 533–540. Morgan Kaufmann Publishers Inc., San Francisco, CA, USA (1999)
16. Wu, A.S., De Jong, K.A., Burke, D.S., Grefenstette, J.J., Loggia Ramsey, C.: Visual analysis of evolutionary algorithms. In: Proceedings of the 1999 Congress on Evolutionary Computation-CEC99 (Cat. No. 99TH8406). pp. 1419–1425, Vol. 2 (1999). ieeexplore.ieee.org
17. Cruz, A., Machado, P., Assunção, F., Leitão, A.: ELICIT: evolutionary computation visualization. In: Proceedings of the Companion Publication of the 2015 Annual Conference on Genetic and Evolutionary Computation. pp. 949–956. ACM, New York, NY, USA (2015)
18. Hart, E., Ross, P.: GAVEL-a new tool for genetic algorithm visualization. IEEE Trans. Evol. Comput. **5**, 335–348 (2001)
19. Daneshpajouh, H., Zakaria, N.: A clustering-based visual analysis tool for genetic algorithm. In: VISIGRAPP (3: IVAPP). pp. 233–240 (2017). researchgate.net
20. Choenni, S.: Design and implementation of a genetic-based algorithm for data mining. In: VLDB. pp. 33–42 (2000)
21. Ross, G, Morrison, A., Chalmers, M.: Coordinating views for data visualisation and algorithmic profiling, In: Proceedings Second International Conference on Coordinated and Multiple Views in Exploratory Visualization, London, UK, pp. 3–14 (2004)
22. Shine, W.B., Eick, C.F.: Visualizing the evolution of genetic algorithm search processes. In: Proceedings of 1997 IEEE International Conference on Evolutionary Computation (ICEC '97), pp. 367–372 (1997). ieeexplore.ieee.org
23. Llorà, X., Sastry, K., Alías, F., Goldberg, D.E., Welge, M.: Analyzing active interactive genetic algorithms using visual analytics. In: Proceedings of the 8th Annual Conference on Genetic and Evolutionary Computation. pp. 1417–1418. ACM, New York, NY, USA (2006)
24. Hayashida, N., Takagi, H.: Visualized IEC: interactive evolutionary computation with multidimensional data visualization. In: 26th Annual Conference of the IEEE Industrial Electronics Society. IECON 2000. 21st Century Technologies, Vol. 4, pp. 2738–2743 (2000)
25. Keim, D.A., Mansmann, F., Schneidewind, J., Thomas, J., Ziegler, H.: Visual Analytics: Scope and Challenges. In: Simoff, S.J., Böhlen, M.H., Mazeika, A. (eds.) Visual Data Mining, pp. 76–90. Springer Berlin Heidelberg, Berlin, Heidelberg (2008). https://doi.org/10.1007/978-3-540-71080-6_6
26. U.S. Census Bureau. Census-income (KDD) data set (2000). https://archive.ics.uci.edu/ml/datasets/Census-Income+%28KDD%29
27. Google Research. People + AI Research (PAIR) (2021). https://research.google.com/bigpicture/attacking-discrimination-in-ml/. Accessed 10 March 2021

Digital Enabled Sustainable Organisations and Societies

Artificial Intelligence and the Evolution of Managerial Skills: An Exploratory Study

Laurent Giraud[1(✉)], Ali Zaher[1], Selena Hernandez[2], and Akram Al Ariss[2]

[1] Toulouse School of Management, TSM Research (UMR CNRS 5303), Toulouse 1 Capitole University, Toulouse, France
laurent.giraud@tsm-education.fr
[2] Toulouse Business School, Toulouse, France

Abstract. This article investigates how the rise of Artificial Intelligence (AI) in organizations may affect managerial skills. We conducted qualitative and semi-structured interviews of 40 experts around the world who work with AI in a variety of disciplines and sectors. Using thematic content analysis on the data, we identify the trends showing how AI may replace, augment, or not affect managerial skills. In addition, our results highlight the technical and non-technical skills that managers should develop for successful implementation of AI. This study contributes to the scholarship in its depiction of these trends and in its empirical exploration of the links between managerial skills and AI. We also supplement existing taxonomies of managerial skills, provide future research proposals, and discuss the theoretical as well as the practical implications of our study.

Keywords: Artificial Intelligence · AI-HRM interface · Managers

1 Introduction

Artificial Intelligence (AI) is 'a system's ability to interpret external data correctly, to learn from such data, and to use those learnings to achieve specific goals and tasks through flexible adaptation' [1]. AI technology turns out to be essential for the success of many organizations [2] and one of the most disruptive technologies of the 21st century [3]. It has facilitated a fourth industrial revolution [4] and continues to rapidly develop [5]. Between 1991 and 2015, AI patents increased by 11% each year [6].

As AI is likely to alter the future of work design [7], managerial skills are facing a possible upheaval by being replaced, extended, and even remodeled. However, theoretical [8] and empirical [9] elements on that matter are still lacking. Although Huang and Rust [10] have written that the rise of AI in organizations may replace some managerial skills, their research did not focus on managers. While Huang *et al.* [11] have suggested that 'managers must adapt the nature of jobs to compensate for the fact that many of the analytical and thinking tasks are increasingly being performed by AI', their analysis was performed at the macro-level and based on secondary data. To our knowledge,

Laurent Giraud – Associate Researcher at the ESSEC Chair of Change Management.

Published by Springer Nature Switzerland AG 2021
D. Dennehy et al. (Eds.): I3E 2021, LNCS 12896, pp. 307–317, 2021.
https://doi.org/10.1007/978-3-030-85447-8_27

the literature only offers scattered elements about the interplays between AI and skills with regard to the *managerial* category. No empirical study has yet been conducted to specifically assess the impact of AI on managerial skills.

In the next section, we review the academic literature on managerial skills in relation to AI. We then outline the exploratory and qualitative methodology of our empirical study. We next present and discuss the results of our study. Before concluding our study, we suggest paths for future research.

2 Literature Review

2.1 Managerial Skills

Over time, managerial skills have been categorized in multiple ways. Fayol [12] first classified managerial competencies as related to planning, organizing, commanding, coordinating, and controlling. Mintzberg [13] later identified managerial skills as interpersonal, informational, and decisional. In parallel, Katz [14] proposed an alternative set of three critical managerial skills: technical, human, and conceptual. Similarly, Bhanugopan *et al.* [15] listed personal attributes, managerial skills, and business skills. Robbins and Coulter [16] added that due to rapid globalization, competition, and the pace of technology, managers face other integrative issues, such as managing in a global environment, diversity, social responsibility, change, and innovation.

2.2 Artificial Intelligence

Farrow [17] has defined AI as 'a computer science aiming to perform tasks that replicate human or animal intelligence and behavior'. This technology includes machine learning, robotics, computer vision, automated reasoning, machine perception, and knowledge representation [18–20].

2.3 Relationship Between AI and Managerial Skills

As AI changes the nature of work and collaboration [7], it interacts with managerial skills. Nevertheless, theoretical [8] as well as empirical [9] elements are lacking and remain dispersed in the literature. In this section, we discuss how AI is likely to overtake or augment certain managerial skills, and which managerial skills are necessary for successfully implementing AI.

In fact, the current literature anticipates three major kinds of impacts of AI on jobs, tasks, and skills: the latter can be *replaced*, *augmented,* or remain *unaffected* [17, 21, 22]. While this technology could in fact *replace* some skills and even jobs (often associated with repetitive and simple tasks), AI would also be capable of *augmenting* human tasks that remain too complex to be replaced by a machine. An optimized managerial decision or specific skill could then be based on an automated AI pre-analysis. This *augmented* output would be reached thanks to an optimized collaboration with the machine which could take the form of a hybridization of managers [23], potentially through symbiotic metamorphosis [24]. Finally, some skills might neither be *replaced* nor *augmented* because of their extreme complexity or their strong human nature: like emotional intelligence, for instance (Mattingly and Kraiger, 2019). Those very skills would therefore remain *unaffected* by AI, at least in the form in which this technology exists today.

The literature also suggests that introduction of AI into organizations triggers the need for specific, or even new, managerial skills. Emergent AI is already able to automatically generate initial production system configurations [25] and to optimize production [26]. If AI can make predictions in an abundant and inexpensive way, then managers need to decide how to best implement such predictions, which will involve using their judgment. This judgment comes from knowledge of organizational history [27], a dimension that AI usually fails to consider and which should be monitored by humans. So far, AI looks unable to show advanced ethical judgment, emotional intelligence, artistic taste, or ability to define tasks well [28].

3 Empirical Study

3.1 Data Collection

Qualitative Research Design and Semi-structured Interviews. We follow Yin's [29] argument that the 'how' questions should be addressed through qualitative research methods. Particularly, this study uses grounded theory—specifically Interpretive Grounded Theory (IGT)—because it allows new theory creation [30] about new phenomena, which can explain in conceptual terms what is actually going on in the field [31]. IGT served our needs because we were engaged in interpreting the data and extracting information from the literature before and during the data analysis. Secondly, this approach is consistent with the methodology used, as open-coding, axial-coding, and dimensions creation go hand-by-hand with IGT. Thirdly, the ultimate goal of theory development is in line with IGT.

Therefore, our study design draws upon semi-structured interviews with experts who work on AI in a variety of sectors and countries. Semi-structured interviews are the most commonly used designs in qualitative research [32]. As Bell *et al.* [32] recommended, we used an interview guide. Qualitative interviews focus on the interviewee's point of view rather than on the researcher's concerns, with the objective of obtaining rich and detailed answers. This approach sometimes requires flexibility in ordering questions and even openness to adding new questions based on respondents' replies [32]. Interviewing respondents is a structured and common way to collect data on respondents' experiences and perspectives [33, 34].

Data were collected in the summer of 2019, after and during a time of rapid AI development [35]. Two researchers from our team led face-to-face interviews in English. Each interview lasted approximately an hour and was audio-recorded (with the permission of the participants), and then transcribed. To increase the credibility of our qualitative research, a validation process was conducted by sending a summary of the findings to each participant to seek corroboration of interpretations of the interview responses [32]. We sent summaries, rather than entire scientific documents, to avoid difficulties in terms of participants understanding theories, concepts, and contextual issues [36]. To guarantee dependability (reliability), we kept complete records of all phases in the research process, including the participant selection, fieldwork notes, interview transcripts, and data analysis, in case further verification and justification were needed [32].

Sampling

The sampling of a variety of management levels, sectors, and countries should increase the transferability and dependability of our results [37]. In sum, our sample includes 40 participants from 30 companies and seven industries (research, consulting, automotive, education, aerospace, energy, and utilities). The sample is composed of 22.5% women and 77.5% men, which is representative of the current population of AI specialists in terms of gender[1]. The average age is 42 years, with four years of job tenure. External reliability is difficult to acquire in qualitative research (LeCompte & Goetz, 1982), but we attempted to increase external reliability and external validity by using a variety of management levels, sectors, and countries.

Data Analysis

We used the NVivo 12 software, a common tool in business research [32], which allows thematic content analysis of a full transcript of interviews, as recommended by Roulston [38]. This method of analysis is the most common in organizations and best suited to these kind of data [39]. To improve internal reliability, each researcher simultaneously interpreted and analyzed the data before proceeding to comparison [32].

4 Results and Discussion

Our study aimed to answer calls from scholars regarding further investigation of the links between AI and skills [8, 40–42] with empirical elements [9] and regarding the future of work [7]. Fig. 1 summarizes our findings. The collected data has allowed us to identify the most plausible upcoming trends about the interplays between AI and managerial skills. Two major trends (in grey in Fig. 1) have indeed been shared and expressed by most of our respondents and are likely to significantly impact organizations: First, AI is likely to augment most managerial skills; Second, technical and non-technical managerial skills will probably have to be developed in order to optimize the use of AI in organizations.

Our results first show which managerial skills are likely to be *replaced*, *augmented*, or *remain unaffected*, confirming the relevance of those categories when it comes to qualify the effects of AI on jobs, tasks, and skills [17, 21, 22]. In a recent article, Raisch and Krakowski [43] argue for a change of perspective on these categories as, in the management domain, *augmentation* cannot be neatly separated from *automation*.

[1] https://reports.weforum.org/global-gender-gap-report-2018/assessing-gender-gaps-in-artificial-intelligence/.

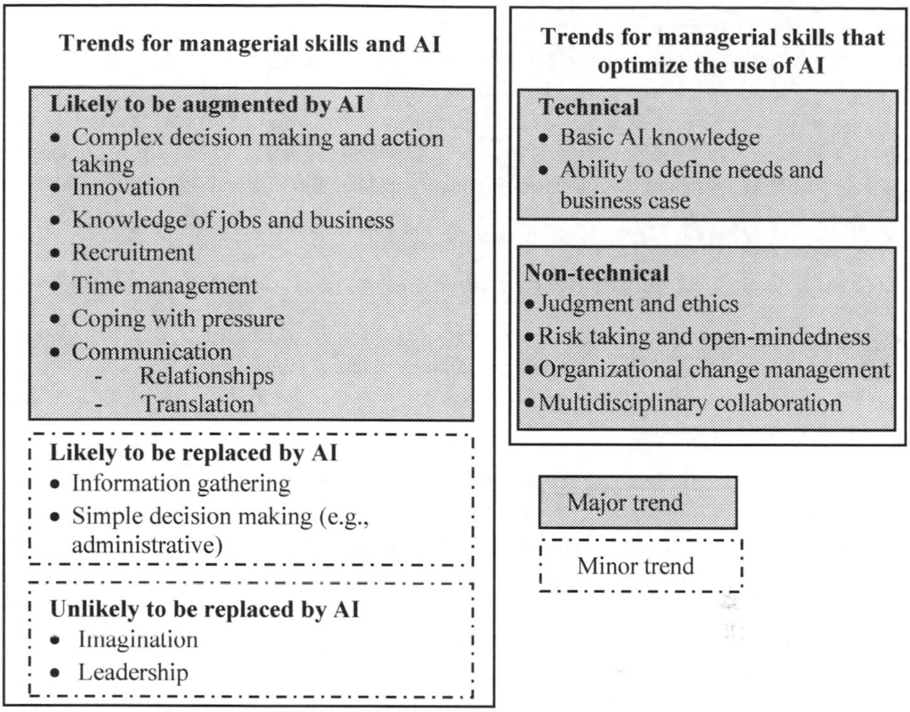

Trends for managerial skills and AI

Likely to be augmented by AI
- Complex decision making and action taking
- Innovation
- Knowledge of jobs and business
- Recruitment
- Time management
- Coping with pressure
- Communication
  - Relationships
  - Translation

Likely to be replaced by AI
- Information gathering
- Simple decision making (e.g., administrative)

Unlikely to be replaced by AI
- Imagination
- Leadership

Trends for managerial skills that optimize the use of AI

Technical
- Basic AI knowledge
- Ability to define needs and business case

Non-technical
- Judgment and ethics
- Risk taking and open-mindedness
- Organizational change management
- Multidisciplinary collaboration

Major trend

Minor trend

Fig. 1. Minor and major trends about the relationships between Artificial Intelligence (AI) and managerial skills

4.1 Minor Trends About the Relationships Between AI and Managerial Skills

As highlighted in Fig. 1, two minor trends first appear in our results: only a few managerial skills are likely to be (1) fully replaced or (2) unaffected by AI.

Managerial Skills Likely to be Replaced by AI. Because managerial jobs are complex, involving analysis, solving advanced operational problems, and human relations, the sampled experts confirm that few managerial skills are eligible for wholesale replacement by AI [11]. Our respondents recall that AI has already replaced managers for information provision and simple decision making [44]. This finding is consistent with the work of Lichtenthaler [45], who has categorized automation jobs involving limited complexity as a 'substitute' matrix that replaces human work with increased efficiency. Therefore, AI may increase managers' opportunities to focus on work requiring their core competencies in order to better participate in value creation [25], even though our respondents add that some specific managerial skills will then be needed for successful AI implementation (see *Managerial skills that optimize the use of AI* in section 0, below).

Managerial Skills Unlikely to be Replaced by AI. Our respondents add that AI might never replace advanced managerial skills such as imagination and leadership. Imagination, including such tasks as thinking of questions to ask and imagining something that does not yet exist, may indeed not be replicable by AI [46]. Agrawal *et al.* [28] have also noted that AI is not creative enough to find new opportunities by itself. In that sense, we can confirm that storytelling and motivational speeches are unlikely to be duplicated by AI [45, 47]. The interviewed experts also indicate that AI may be unable to lead because of the inherent difficulty it has to generate ideas *ex nihilo* and dealing with employees' trust or emotions [48]. Leading should remain a core managerial and human competency unaffected by AI, consistent with previous findings [28, 49].

4.2 Major Trends About the Relationships Between AI and Managerial Skills

In contrast, our respondents indicate two major trends about the relationships between AI and managerial skills: (1) a majority of managerial skills are likely to be augmented by AI while (2) specific, and maybe new, managerial skills may be needed to optimize the use of AI in companies.

Managerial Skills Likely to be Augmented by AI. Our respondents agree that managerial skills to be augmented by AI actually cover a large spectrum from planning, organizing, and controlling [12, 16], to self-insight roles like self-management and self-development [50] and through creativity. Another example yielded by our data is that AI could produce abundant and inexpensive predictions to enable managers to better know their jobs and business, which completes the work by Agrawal *et al.* [28]. Our results additionally suggest that prediction can help for the identification of talents [51]. Even if our data confirm that AI may not conduct a full recruitment process autonomously, they suggest that its applications for hiring and selecting can be useful, even though the literature recalls that contextual factors should be carefully considered [52]. Our respondents confirm how AI can continue to augment managers for time, project management, and even stress management (i.e., Egger & Kleiner, 1992; Javanmardi *et al.*, 2014). The technology can indeed process information (Brynjolfsson *et al.*, 2018) that provides managers with more control, therefore reducing stress (Lambert *et al.*, 2003) in adverse situations. AI may also augment managerial skills for communication through enhanced (1) relationships, as already suggested by Sumi and Nishida [53], with the provision of valuable background information about individuals, and (2) translation. Due to rapid globalization, managers face integrative issues such as managing multilingual and multicultural teams [16] which might provoke communication issues caused by language differences where AI could be particularly helpful.

Our results provide specific clues about how managerial practices are likely to be enhanced by AI in the coming years [54]. The anticipated augmentation of most managerial skills is a significant contribution to the AI-HRM literature, which must anticipate how the interplay between AI and humans should be framed and supervised. This observation supports the hypothesis that managers may have to radically adapt to AI [55] and strive towards hybridization [23], possibly through symbiotic metamorphosis [24].

Managerial Skills that Optimize the use of AI. A second major trend highlighted in our data suggests that managerial skills may need to be developed to optimize the implementation and use of AI. These skills should be technical as well as non-technical. If the literature has previously investigated the topic from a macro point of view [11], our results provide specific elements about the managerial occupations.

Our data suggest that managers should at first acquire technical skills like basic AI knowledge as well as the ability to define when and how AI could be helpful for their activity. Our results confirm that managers play a key role in identifying the rationale for using AI [56], analyzing business cases [57], weighing costs and benefits as well as spotting any misleading conclusions that could be produced by AI applications [58].

Moreover, managers are invited to own non-technical managerial skills in order to optimize AI implementation. According to our respondents, a good AI prediction remains subject to a good managerial judgment. This finding is consistent with the literature stating that AI usually lacks good judgment [28] and that managerial training may shift from focusing on prediction-related skills to judgment-related skills [59]. Thus, final decisions related to critical and ethical issues are unlikely to be replaced and should be handled by humans. We confirm that future managerial skills are likely to be about determining how to best apply AI to making predictions and what should be predicted [28]. Our respondents also reiterate the necessity for managers to maintain a clear sense of ethics to prevent AI bias and misuse [60, 61].

Additionally, our results suggest that managers need to be open-minded and keener on taking risks: although AI remains costly, this technology does not always yield immediate results as it often requires learning and adjustment. Building and maintaining trust with a risky tool therefore seems to be a priority [62]. Therefore, our results confirm that organizational change management skills could facilitate commitment to AI [63] and reduce resistance to new technologies [64]. These non-technical skills are important skills, as AI may be seen as a threat to some occupations and can trigger significant fears [65] as well as unrealistic expectations [66].

Our results corroborate that managers must develop the necessary skills to define new job descriptions and organizational structures required by AI [67]. This technology will probably produce a stronger multidisciplinary collaboration. Our experts agree that clear role descriptions and task separation may be needed in order to grant an effective AI-HRM interface as humans team up with machines [68]. Our respondents also confirm that AI may radically change power relationships [23, 69]. In fact, knowing that technical changes are occurring at a fast pace [69], our respondents confirm that the development of organizational learning appears to be a prerequisite for a successful AI implementation [70].

Overall, our respondents verify that the success of AI requires preliminary socialization [24]. Thus, our results suggest that managers may be in charge of dealing with AI-induced changes, including power reconfigurations [69]. From that perspective, non-technical skills such as organizational change management and multidisciplinary collaboration appear necessary to cope with AI implementation. Our research therefore confirms that companies adopting AI should further consider the relational and structural complexities associated with the implementation of such advanced technology [24].

Our results confirm that with the advent of AI, managers 'will need to be more skilled than ever before' [54]. Our study even implies that the existing taxonomies of managerial skills (e.g., Gentry *et al.*, 2008) should be updated and re-prioritized so that an effective AI-HRM interface can be set up [71]. Our results show that AI might increase managers' opportunities to focus on work requiring their core competencies in order to better participate to value creation [25]. They also warn that the right conditions must be met (i.e., managers having the appropriate skills to implement AI). For example, they recall that human decision making based on AI will likely require managers to acquire new skills, as the literature has already claimed about other occupations [72].

5 Conclusion

Our results reveal major and minor trends about the managerial skills that are likely to be replaced, augmented, or unaffected by AI and how such changes might occur. Further, our data evince specific technical and non-technical skills that managers are expected to develop to successfully accommodate the growing presence of AI.

5.1 Limitations

A major limitation of our study is the heterogeneity of our sample in terms of selected locations, occupations, and sectors. Because access to AI experts was challenging, we thought it was more important to produce rich accounts of experts' experiences, a technique known as 'thick description' [73], thereby providing other researchers with a useful database for assessing the possible transferability of findings to other contexts [74]. The diversity of our respondents finally turns out to be an interesting way to undertake a comprehensive exploration of a globally rising phenomenon like the introduction of AI into corporations and its impacts on managerial skills at the AI-HRM interface [75].

References

1. Kaplan, A., Haenlein, M.: Siri, Siri, in my hand: Who's the fairest in the land? On the interpretations, illustrations, and implications of artificial intelligence. Bus Horiz. **62**(1), 15–25 (2019)
2. Bianca, M.L.: Artificial Intelligence. In: Alai, M., Buzzoni, M., Tarozzi, G. (eds.) Science Between Truth and Ethical Responsibility, pp. 91–104. Springer, Cham (2015). https://doi.org/10.1007/978-3-319-16369-7_7
3. Fosso Wamba, S., Bawack, R.E., Guthrie, C., Queiroz, M.M., Carillo, K.D.A.: Are we preparing for a good AI society? A bibliometric review and research agenda. Technol. Forecast Soc. Change. **164**, 120482 (2021)
4. Ray, K., Thomas, T.A.: Online outsourcing and the future of work. J. Glob. Responsib. **10**(3), 226–238 (2019)
5. Lu, H., Li, Y., Chen, M., Kim, H., Serikawa, S.: Brain intelligence: go beyond artificial intelligence. Mob. Netw. Appl. **23**(2), 368–375 (2018)
6. OECD: Science, Technology and Industry Scoreboard 2017 - The digital transformation [Internet]. 2017 [cited 2019 Feb 7]. Available from: http://www.oecd.org/sti/oecd-science-technology-and-industry-scoreboard-20725345.htm
7. Dennehy, D., Griva, A., Pouloudi, N., Mäntymäki, M., Pappas, I.: Call for papers: Implications of Artificial Intelligence for Decision-Making and the Future of Work. Int. J. Inf. Manag. (2021)
8. Parker, S.K., Knight, C., Ohly, S.: The changing face of work design research: Past, present, and future directions. In: Wilkinson, A., Bacon, N., Lepak, D., Snell, S. (eds.) The Sage Handbook of Human Resource Management, 2nd edn., pp. 402–419. SAGE, London (2019)

9. European Parliament: Digital automation and the future of work [Internet]. European Parliamentary Research Service; 2021 [cited 2021 Feb 9]. (Scientific Foresight Unit). Available from: https://www.europarl.europa.eu/stoa/en/document/EPRS_STU(2021)656311
10. Huang, M.-H., Rust, R.T.: Artificial intelligence in service. J. Serv. Res. **21**(2), 155–172 (2018)
11. Huang, M.-H., Rust, R., Maksimovic, V.: The feeling economy: managing in the next generation of artificial intelligence (AI). Calif. Manage Rev. **61**(4), 43–65 (2019)
12. Fayol, H.: Administration Industrielle et Générale. Dunod, Paris (1916)
13. Mintzberg, H.: The Nature of Managerial Work. Harper & Row, New York (1973)
14. Katz, R.L.: Skills of an Effective Administrator, p. 87. Harvard Business Review Press, Boston, Massachusetts (1974)
15. Bhanugopan, R., Wang, Y., Lockhart, P., Farrell, M.: Managerial skills shortages and the impending effects of organizational characteristics: evidence from China. Pers. Rev. **46**(8), 1689–1716 (2017)
16. Robbins, S.P., Coulter, M.K.: Management. 11th ed. Prentice Hall, Boston, 643 p (2012)
17. Farrow, E.: To augment human capacity—artificial intelligence evolution through causal layered analysis. Futures **108**, 61–71 (2019)
18. Marsh, A.: Revolution: the first 2,000 years of computing: the computer history museum, mountain view, California. Technol. Cult. **3**(54), 640–649 (2013)
19. Mehta, N., Devarakonda, M.V.: Machine learning, natural language programming, and electronic health records: the next step in the artificial intelligence journey? J. Allergy Clin. Immunol. **141**(6), 2019-2021.e1 (2018)
20. Tractica: Artificial Intelligence Software Revenue to Reach $59.8 Billion Worldwide by 2025 [Internet]. 2017 [cited 2019 Feb 28]. Available from: https://www.tractica.com/newsroom/press-releases/artificial-intelligence-software-revenue-to-reach-59-8-billion-worldwide-by-2025/
21. Daugherty, P.R., Wilson, H.J.: Human + Machine: Reimagining Work in the Age of AI. Harvard Business Press, 258 p (2018)
22. OECD: Trends Shaping Education 2019. OECD Publishing, Paris, 109 p (2019)
23. Moldenhauer, L., Londt, C.: Leadership, artificial intelligence and the need to redefine future skills development. J. Leadersh. Account Ethics **16**(1) (2019)
24. Makarius, E.E., Mukherjee, D., Fox, J.D., Fox, A.K.: Rising with the machines: a sociotechnical framework for bringing artificial intelligence into the organization. J Bus Res. **1**(120), 262–273 (2020)
25. Hagemann, S., Sünnetcioglu, A., Stark, R.: Hybrid artificial intelligence system for the design of highly-automated production systems. Proc. Manuf. **28**, 160–166 (2019)
26. Mohammadi, V., Minaei, S.: 2 - Artificial Intelligence in the Production Process. In: Grumezescu, A.M., Holban, A.M. (eds.) Engineering Tools in the Beverage Industry, pp. 27–63. Woodhead Publishing, USA (2019)
27. Kolbjørnsrud, V., Amico, R., Thomas, R.J.: How artificial intelligence will redefine management. Harvard Bus. Rev. (2016)
28. Agrawal, A., Gans, J.S., Goldfarb, A.: What to expect from artificial intelligence. MIT Sloan Manage. Rev. (2017)
29. Yin, R.K.: Case Study Research: Design and Methods. 5th ed. SAGE, Thousand Oaks, CA, 312 p (2014)
30. Martin, P.Y., Turner, B.A.: Grounded theory and organizational research. J. Appl. Behav. Sci. **22**(2), 141–157 (1986)
31. Fernández, W.D., Lehmann, H.: Achieving rigour and relevance in information systems studies: using grounded theory to investigate organizational cases. Grounded Theory Rev. **5**(1), 79–107 (2005)

32. Bell, E., Bryman, A., Harley, B.: Business Research Methods, 5th edn., p. 687. Oxford University Press, Cambridge, UK (2018)
33. Alvesson, M., Ashcraft, K.L.: Interviews. In: Symon, G., Cassell, C. (eds.) Qualitative Organizational Research: Core Methods and Current Challenges, pp. 239–257. SAGE Publications, Inc., London (2012). https://doi.org/10.4135/9781526435620.n14
34. Lindlof, T.R., Taylor, B.C.: Qualitative Communication Research Methods. 2nd ed. SAGE Publications Inc, 377 p (2002)
35. Duan, Y., Edwards, J.S., Dwivedi, Y.K.: Artificial intelligence for decision making in the era of Big Data: evolution, challenges and research agenda. Int. J. Inf. Manag. **1**(48), 63–71 (2019)
36. Skeggs, B.: Situating the Production of Feminist Ethnography. In: Maynard, M., Purvis, J. (eds.) Researching Women's Lives from a Feminist Perspective, pp. 72–93. Taylor & Francis Ltd, Basingstoke (1994)
37. Guba, E.G., Lincoln, Y.S.: Competing paradigms in qualitative research. In: Handbook of Qualitative Research, pp. 105–117 (1994)
38. Roulston, K.: Analysing interviews. In: Flick, U. (ed.) The SAGE Handbook of Qualitative Data Analysis, pp. 297–312. SAGE Publications, London (2014)
39. Symon, G., Cassell, C., editors: Qualitative Organizational Research: Core Methods and Current Challenges. SAGE Publications Ltd, London, 546 p (2012)
40. Budhwar, P.S., Malik, A.: Call for papers: artificial intelligence challenges and opportunities for international HRM. Int. J. Hum. Resour. Manag. (2019)
41. Budhwar, P.S., Malik, A.: Call for papers: Leveraging Artificial and Human Intelligence through Human Resource Management. Hum. Resour. Manag. Rev. (2020)
42. Felten, E.W., Raj, M., Seamans, R.: A method to link advances in artificial intelligence to occupational abilities. AEA Pap Proc. **108**, 54–57 (2018)
43. Raisch, S., Krakowski, S.: Artificial intelligence and management: the automation–augmentation paradox. Acad. Manage. Rev. **46**(1), 192–210 (2021)
44. Harms, P.D., Han, G.: Algorithmic leadership: the future is now. J. Leadersh. Stud. **12**(4), 74–75 (2019)
45. Lichtenthaler, U.: Substitute or synthesis: the interplay between human and artificial intelligence. Res-Technol. Manag. **61**(5), 12–14 (2018)
46. Rometty, G.: Digital Today, Cognitive Tomorrow [Internet]. MIT Sloan Management Review. 2016 [cited 2019 Feb 27]. Available from: https://sloanreview.mit.edu/article/digital-today-cognitive-tomorrow/
47. Wilson, H.J., Daugherty, P.R., Morini-Bianzino, N.: The jobs that artificial intelligence will create. MIT Sloan Manag. Rev. **5** (2017)
48. Ferràs-Hernández, X.: The future of management in a world of electronic brains. J. Manag. Inq. **27**(2), 260–263 (2018)
49. Manyika, J., Sneader, K.: AI, automation, and the future of work: Ten things to solve for (Tech4Good) | McKinsey. McKinsey Global Institute (2018)
50. Gentry, W.A., Harris, L.S., Baker, B.A., Brittain, L.J.: Managerial skills: what has changed since the late 1980s. Leadersh Organ. Dev. J. **29**(2), 167–181 (2008)
51. Jantan, H., Hamdan, A.R., Othman, Z.A.: Human talent prediction in HRM using C4. 5 classification algorithm. Int. J. Comput. Sci. Eng. **2**(8) 2526–2534 (2010)
52. Pan, Y., Froese, F., Liu, N., Hu, Y., Ye, M.: The adoption of artificial intelligence in employee recruitment: the influence of contextual factors. Int. J. Hum. Resour. Manag. (2021)
53. Sumi, K., Nishida, T.: Communication support system adapted to a user's background knowledge and the topic context. Syst. Comput. Jpn. **34**, 87–98 (2003)
54. Gratton, L.: Rethinking the manager's role. MIT Sloan Manag. Rev. **58**(1), 8–9 (2016)
55. Merrill, P.: Be ready. Qual. Prog. **52**, 54–56 (2019)

56. Fiore, A.D., Schneider, S., Farri, E.: The 5 things your AI unit needs to do. Harvard Bus. Rev. (2018)
57. Henke, N., Levine, J., McInerney, P.: You don't have to be a data scientist to fill this must-have analytics role. Harvard Bus. Rev. (2018)
58. Schrage, M.: Is "murder by machine learning" the new "death by powerpoint"? Harvard Bus. Rev. (2018)
59. Pistrui, J.: The future of human work is imagination, creativity, and strategy. Harvard Bus. Rev. (2018)
60. Barfield, W., Pagallo, U.: Research Handbook on the Law of Artificial Intelligence, p. 731. Edward Elgar Publishing, Cheltenham, UK (2018)
61. Ford, M.: Architects of Intelligence: The Truth about AI from the People Building it, p. 540. Packt Publishing Ltd, USA (2018)
62. Shestakofsky, B.: Working algorithms: software automation and the future of work. Work Occup. **44**(4), 376–423 (2017)
63. Adil, M.S.: Impact of change readiness on commitment to technological change, focal, and discretionary behaviors: evidence from the manufacturing sector of Karachi. J. Organ Change Manag. **29**(2), 222–241 (2016)
64. Abraham, M., et al.: Electronic monitoring at work: the role of attitudes, functions, and perceived control for the acceptance of tracking technologies. Hum. Resour. Manag. J. **29**(4), 657–675 (2019)
65. Papacharissi, Z.: A Networked Self and Human Augmentics, Artificial Intelligence, Sentience, p. 333. Routledge, UK (2018)
66. The New York Times: Looking Forward Artificial Intelligence. USA: The Rosen Publishing Group, Inc, 226 p (2018)
67. Knickrehm, M.: How will AI change work? Here are 5 schools of thought. Harvard Bus. Rev. (2018)
68. Norman, D.: Design, business models, and human-technology teamwork. Res-Technol. Manag. **60**(1), 26–30 (2017)
69. Sousa, M.J., Wilks, D.: Sustainable skills for the world of work in the digital age. Syst. Res. Behav. Sci. **35**(4), 399–405 (2018)
70. While, A.: Are you IT savvy? Br. J. Commun. Nurs. **24**(4), 198 (2019)
71. Malik, A., Srikanth, N.R., Budhwar, P.S.: Digitisation, AI and HRM. In: Crashaw, J., Budhwar, P.S. (eds.) Strategic Human Resource Management, 3rd edn., pp. 88–111. SAGE Publications, UK (2020)
72. Lindebaum, D., Vesa, M., den Hond, F.: Insights from "the machine stops" to better understand rational assumptions in algorithmic decision making and its implications for organizations. Acad. Manage. Rev. **45**(1), 247–263 (2020)
73. Geertz, C.: Thick description: towards an interpretive theory of culture. In: Geertz C, editor. The Interpretation of Cultures. Basic Books, New York (1973)
74. Lincoln, Y.S., Guba, E.G.: Naturalistic Inquiry, p. 416. SAGE Publications Inc, Beverly Hills, Calif (1985)
75. Vrontis, D., Christofi, M., Pereira, V., Tarba, S., Makrides, A, Trichina, E.: Artificial intelligence, robotics, advanced technologies and human resource management: a systematic review. Int. J. Hum. Resour. Manag. (2021)

The Diffusion of Innovation Experience

Leveraging the Human Factor to Improve Technological Adoption Within an Organisation

Gustav du Plessis(✉) and Hanlie Smuts

University of Pretoria, Pretoria 0181, South Africa
u29380490@tuks.co.za, hanlie.smuts@up.ac.za

Abstract. The evolution of digital technologies is by its very nature, disruptive, compelling organisations to reconsider the relationships among employees, customers, and suppliers. In addition, organisations must carefully consider their strategies to fully exploit the digital revolution's benefits as these technologies are diffused across organisations at an accelerated pace. Organisational strategies related to technological advancement such as cyber-physical systems, artificial intelligence, and new forms of human-machine interaction, must therefore address economic benefit for the organisation, while minimising job dislocation, preventing digital exclusion, and reducing risk of marginalisation. In order to devise a comprehensive approach, the aim of this study is to suggest a model, The Diffusion of Innovation (DOI) Experience, which organisations may reference to encourage and facilitate the adoption of, and adaption to, technology by employees within organisations. Such a model is relevant in the context of facing organisational transformation as it focuses on the individual employee experience and reaction to change, specifically within the context of adopting a new technology. By applying the DOI Experience Model, organisations can improve their change management practices with regard to technological change, and subsequently increase the success rate of technology adoption within the organisation.

Keywords: Diffusion of innovation · Technology adoption · Technology adaption

1 Introduction

Over the past two centuries, technological growth has been categorized into four periods, known as industrial revolutions. Each industrial revolution not only significantly improved the technology of its time, but greatly improved on the technology of the preceding revolution [1]. This trend of continuous increase in technological improvements witnessed through each industrial evolution can be explained by Moore's law, a forecasting model that suggests technology grows exponentially [2].

The current (fourth) industrial revolution has seen unprecedented levels of technological advancements, introducing rapid and abrupt changes that disrupt the status-quo

Published by Springer Nature Switzerland AG 2021
D. Dennehy et al. (Eds.): I3E 2021, LNCS 12896, pp. 318–329, 2021.
https://doi.org/10.1007/978-3-030-85447-8_28

across all industries [3, 4]. Consequently, organisations are forced to implement digital transformation strategies, and in some cases, change their entire business model to ensure that they stay competitive and survive in the long term [5, 6].

Considering that disruption concerns technological advancement, and its impact on an organisation's business model, the frequency and timing of technology adoption is crucial [6]. By keeping Moore's law in mind, it can be assumed that the severity and frequency of disruption will only increase over time, meaning that organisations will need to continually adopt new technologies to succeed [2, 7].

Timely technological adoption could therefore be considered a key element of organisational success [6], and can be viewed from both an organisational and individual perspective. This means that while an organisation makes the initial strategic decision to adopt a technology, it is up to the individuals within the organisation to actually adopt to and use the technology. Ultimately, without individual acceptance, the adoption of any new technology introduced from an organisational perspective will most likely not succeed [8].

This paper proposes a model that organisations can use to encourage and facilitate the adoption of technology by individuals within their organisation. The suggested model will focus on the individual experience or reaction to change, specifically within the context of adopting a new technology.

The remainder of the paper is structured as follows: in Sect. 2 we provide the background to the study and the approach to the study is discussed in Sect. 3. In Sect. 4, an overview of the data analysed is presented, and Sect. 5 details the proposed model. We conclude in Sect. 6.

2 Background

Research over the last decade scrutinised the wide array of factors that influence organisations and their performance [9]. Although these studies are thorough on the effects on the economy, the change caused by technology must be considered [10]. According to Li et al. [25], the view from top management related to changes such as digital transformation, is key to an organisation adopting new technologies [25]. This adoption needs to begin internally by establishing a culture of responsiveness that must be understood and applied both internally and externally [12, 13].

In the following sections diffusion of innovation and the human factor in adopting and adapting to new technologies will be discussed.

2.1 Diffusion of Innovation Theory

Diffusion of innovation theory by Rogers [14], in summary, suggests that individuals within a social system (such as an organisation) will adopt technology at a different rate, depending on how innovative they are. The innovativeness of an individual refers to how early they will adopt a new technology or idea, in comparison to the average member within a social system. Within this framework, individuals fall into one of five adopter categories, namely: innovators, early adopters, early majority, late majority, and laggards [14]. Each adopter category compromises of individuals with similar levels of innovativeness, as described in Table 1 below.

Table 1. Adopter categories [14]

Category	Description
Innovators	Innovators are very eager to try new ideas, technologies, or innovations and desires or invites risk. Innovators are not always as integrated into, or respected by other members of the social system
Early adopters	Early adopters are respected by members in their social system, has the highest degree of opinion leadership. The individuals in the early majority, late majority, and laggard groups will often check whether these individuals have adopted before trying or using a new technology or idea
Early majority	Adopts just before the average member of a social system. Does not want to lead adoption, but are willing to adopt once necessary and others have started to do so
Late majority	Very sceptical of new innovations and will only adopt once most of their peers have done so
Laggards	Laggards do not want to adopt any new innovation and are content with the past and current way of doing things. They are the last to adopt, and will often not adopt, or only adopt when it is too late

The bell curve in Fig. 1 below illustrates the distribution of each category within a social system [14]. Considering the innovativeness of individuals within each adopter category, there is a clear distinction between the first and second half of individuals. The first half will adopt a new technology eagerly or after some persuasion, while the second half will resist change and adoption to varying degrees.

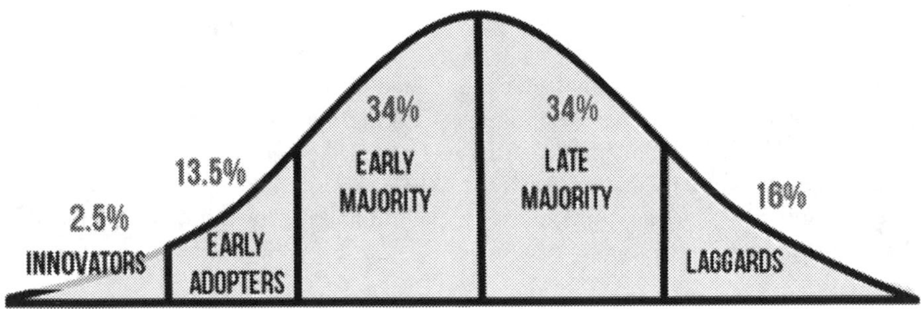

Fig. 1. Technology adoption curve [14]

This, unfortunately, illustrates that even though the introduction of a new idea, innovation or technology may have obvious advantages, achieving adoption by most of the individuals within a social system is often extremely challenging [14].

2.2 Accounting for the Human Factor

While Diffusion of Innovation Theory (Sect. 2.1) is successful at categorising individuals into adopter categories, it is important to account for the individual perspective of technology adoption within a social system as well, as their adoption is a significant element of success [8].

Within the context of an organisation as a social system, technology adoption will often be seen as a change management process, in which the organisation will attempt to guide individuals through change.

Two popular models organisations utilise to facilitate change, Kotter's Eight Step Change Model [15] and Lewin's Three Step Model [16], emphasises transformation and aims to encourage change, but ultimately does not account for the individual experience of the change or transformation process. To account for how individuals experience change on a personal level, one can look at models or theories that explain how individuals experience change, loss, or grief. These models or theories contain stages or phases that differ significantly from transition or change management models used by organisations.

Models or theories with similar phases are Kubler-Ross (1967) [16–18], Fink (1967) [16], Grant (1996) [16], Reynolds (1994) [16], Bupp (1996) [16] and Perlman and Takacs (1990) [16]. For the purpose of this paper, the five phases of the Kubler-Ross Grief Cycle will be used. It documents the phases through which individuals pass when dealing with loss or grief, such as facing their own death due to the diagnosis of a terminal illness, or the death of a loved one. The model describes 5 phases, which ultimately lead to the

Table 2. The stages of Grief – Kubler-Ross grief cycle [18]

Phase	Description
Denial	The person experiencing the loss of a loved one is in shock and disbelief, and cannot believe or fathom that the person he or she has lost is truly gone, and that they will never "walk through the door" again
Anger	Anger is not necessarily logical. It manifests in different ways, such as being angry at the person for leaving them, anger at yourself for not doing something to stop it from happening, or anger at a third party. Anger is usually the front line of feelings such as sadness, loneliness or hurt and is the first stage of the healing process
Bargaining	Before a loss, such as the diagnosis of a terminal illness of a loved one, the person would "bargain" that they would do anything if their loved one would be spared, for instance "I will never be angry at my father again if he lives". After a loss, the person gets lost in past through guilt and "if only" or "what if" statements, trying to bargain the pain away and yearning for the past
Depression	The depression stage sets in when the person moves from the past to the present. In this stage, grief hits harder than the person could ever have imagined. They withdraw from life, and get lost in a vacuum of grief and sadness
Acceptance	Acceptance does not mean that everything is better or "okay". It means that the person has recognised and accepted the new reality, and can slowly start moving on from grief, trying to have more good days than bad days

acceptance of the loss or change [17]. Table 2 briefly describes each phase in the context of a person losing a loved one.

Although the death of an individual or their loved ones may seem like an extreme comparison to an individual's experience of adopting a new technology, the cycle of dealing with change and loss is appropriate when considering the adopter categories at Sect. 2.1.

For example, when adopting to technological change in an organisation, an individual that falls into the Late Majority or Laggard groups could experience various forms of loss or grief, such as: increased uncertainty and anxiety, the loss of normality, the loss of comfort and possible humiliation in front of their peers. In contrast, individuals that fall in the Innovator or Early Adopter categories will have a positive experience to technological change, and will eagerly adopt any new technology [14].

3 Research Approach

The aim of this paper is to present a model that organisations can use to encourage and facilitate the adoption of technology by individuals within their organisation. In order to achieve this outcome, we followed a design science approach where the aim of the research output is on utility [19]. The implementation of this utility, as an outcome of the design science process, must be defined clearly [20, 21], and its application may be refined through utility evaluation [11, 22].

The integrated model, the utility, in Sect. 4, titled "The DOI Experience Model", will be synthesized mainly from the two theories which have been discussed in this paper. *Firstly*, the phases of the Kubler-Ross Grief Cycle (Sect. 2.2) will be adapted slightly to fit the narrative of individuals who are experiencing change due to technology adoption within an organisation. *Secondly*, the adopter categories, as per the Diffusion of Innovation Model (Sect. 2.1), will be used to identify facilitators and inhibitors to the adoption of technology, with the support of Chasm Theory (Sect. 4.2). *Lastly*, an integrated model will be presented (Sect. 4.3), with an application guide (Sect. 5) that can be used by organisations to apply the model in conjunction with their chosen change management models or processes. The application of the model will assist organisations to improve their change management practices with regard to technological change, ensuring that organisations may leverage and benefit from adoption of and adaption to digital technologies.

4 Integrated Model - The DOI Experience

The DOI Experience Model, when used in conjunction with other change management tools and processes, will ensure that individuals within an organisation are comfortable and eager to use the new technology before it is officially implemented, and ready to switch once the new technology when it replaces the previous.

4.1 The Five Stages of Technological Adoption Cycle

By using an adapted version of the Kubler-Ross Grief Cycle (Sect. 2.2) to recognise individual experiences, organisations can address how different groups of individuals process technological adoption within the organisation [14, 16]. In the first step of the utility design process, the original five phases were adapted to present five suggested stages that describes an individual's experience when adopting a new technology, and whether their reaction to change is positive or negative. The five stages are illustrated in Fig. 2.

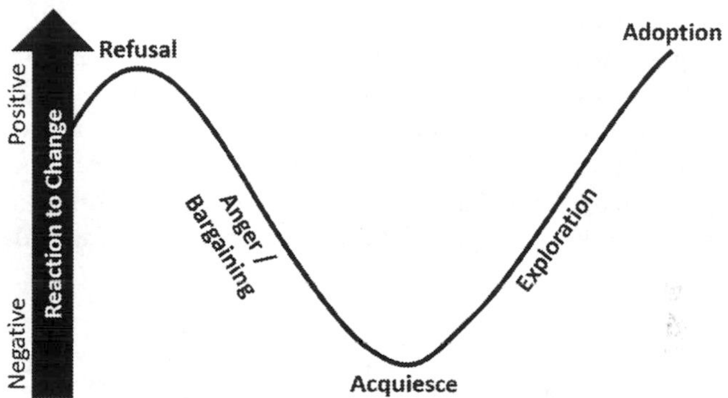

Fig. 2. Individual technology adoption cycle (Adapted from [16])

The first phase, *Refusal*, refers to when an individual outright refuses to adopt any new technologies or innovations – in this phase, they are still positive about the change, because in many cases they believe it will not happen if they refuse, similar to denial in Sect. 2.2. In the next phase, *Anger/Bargaining,* the individual realises that that change is inevitable, but will still resist through demonstrating anger and/or trying to negotiate their way out of the adopting; as they move through this phase, their reaction to change becomes increasingly negative. In third phase, *Acquiesce,* the individual stops resisting and reluctantly accepts that adoption will ultimately be necessary, but does not necessarily approve. In this phase, the reaction to change is at its lowest point, as the individual feels forced into changing. During the *Exploration* phase, having accepted that they will need to adopt a new technology, individuals start exploring the new technology for themselves. As they see the potential benefits of the new technology, their reaction to the change gradually increases. Finally, *Adoption* means that the individual is comfortable to use the new technology through exploration, feels positive about the change, and will willingly adopt the new technology once it replaces the current one.

4.2 Facilitators and Inhibitors

The second step of the utility design process, examined the scope and impact of individuals on a change. When examining each category of Diffusion of Innovation Theory (Sect. 2.1), it can be seen that individuals within those categories are either a facilitator or inhibitor to change. Innovators and Early Adopters (Sect. 2.1), from here on referred to simply as Early Adopters, will be a facilitator to technological adoption, and will speed up the change process for an organisation by eagerly adopting new technologies. Considering their positivity towards, and eagerness to adopt new technologies, they will not experience the Individual Technology Adoption Cycle as illustrated in Fig. 2. These individuals should be seen as change champions, and be utilised by the organisation within their larger change management process; for example, if the organisation is applying Kotter's Eight Step Change Model (Sect. 2.2) they should form part of the minimum mass of change coalition [15].

Mainstream Adopters, which include the Early Majority, Late Majority and Laggards categories (Sect. 2.1), will not experience adoption in the same way. The individuals in each of these categories will initially be an inhibitor to change, and go through the Individual Technology Adoption Cycle, starting with Refusal, and ending with Adoption. From a change management perspective, it is important to consider that each category within the mainstream adopters group will go through the Individual Technology Adoption Cycle (Fig. 2) at a different pace. For example, the Early Majority should theoretically move from Refusal to Adoption in much shorter timeframe than Laggards, as depicted in Fig. 3 below.

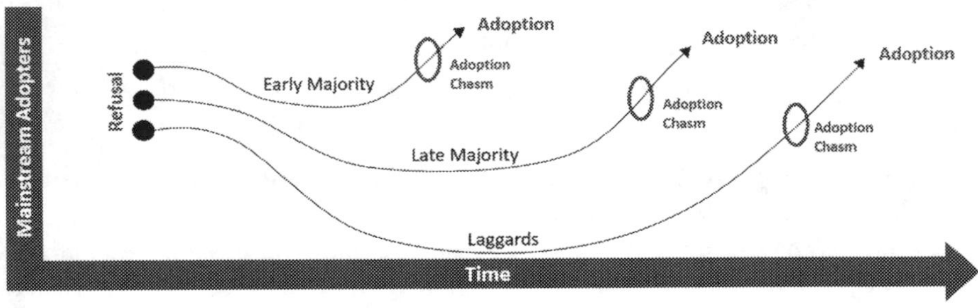

Fig. 3. Mainstream adopters change timeline (Adapted from [14, 23])

Adoption Chasm. Once an individual in the mainstream group reaches the adoption stage, they become a facilitator to change. This shift is described as an adoption chasm, which is indicated by the red circle on each line in Fig. 3 above. The principle of this shift is based on Chasm Theory, which describes the pivotal point when adoption of a new innovation crosses from the early market to the mainstream market; "crossing the chasm" is generally regarded as an indicator of market adoption and success [23]. In the context of this model, the pivotal point refers to when an individual, and ultimately adopter category, moves from Exploration to Acceptance (Fig. 2), adopts the new technology within the organisation, and finally becomes a facilitator to change.

4.3 Integrated Model

Figure 4 below presents the design utility, an integrated model, that was synthesised from the theories and principles discussed throughout the paper, more specifically Fig. 2

and Fig. 3. It presents an overall model to illustrate how various types of individuals experience change on a personal level, due to technological adoption within an organisation.

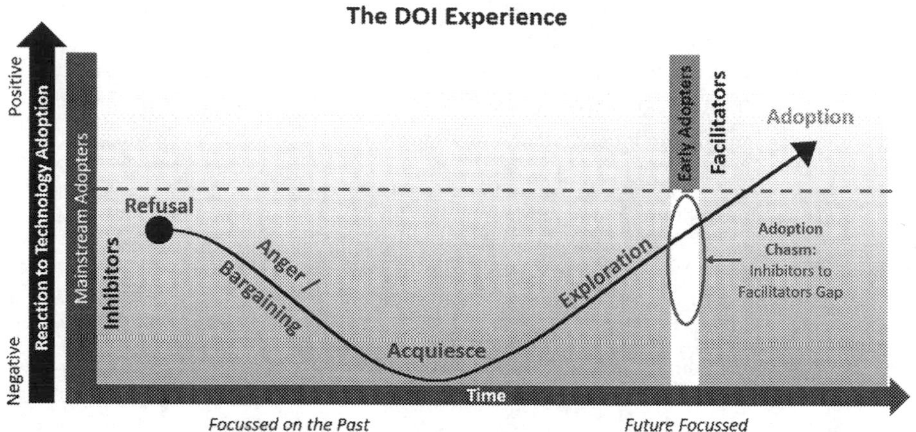

Fig. 4. Integrated model: the DOI experience

The vertical arrow on the y-axis refers to how the individual reacts to the change (shifting between positive and negative) as they progress through the Individual Technology Adoption Cycle (Fig. 2). The Individual Technology Adoption Cycle is depicted by the arrow spanning from Refusal to Adoption on the x-axis, *Time*.

Early Adopters (Innovators and Early Adopters from Sect. 2.1), shown on the top right of the model, are facilitators from inception, as they are change champions that do not go through the entire technological adoption process. Mainstream adopters, regardless of adopter category (Sect. 2.1), all start as inhibitors at the refusal dot, and then move though the Individual Technology Adoption Cycle (Fig. 2), albeit at different paces (Fig. 3); as they progress through the cycle, their reaction will turn more positive, and their perspective will shift from past to future focussed. Finally, when each mainstream adopter moves through the adoption chasm from exploration to adoption, they become facilitators that can be leveraged by the organisation to implement the new technology, and speed up the adoption process.

5 Model Application Guide

The final step of the design process guides the implementation guide of the utility. When applying the proposed model in a real-world setting, it is important to note that it should not be used in isolation. The aim of this model is to work in conjunction with change management principles, models and/or processes, and increase the efficiency by taking individual experience into account. Secondly, although individuals (in this context employees) need to be assigned adopter categories, it is important to do this without assigning labels to individuals, as this could result in conflict and reduce transparency, which ultimately impedes change and adoption. The suggested application phases below will ensure that individuals do not feel labelled, while utilising the knowledge of each adopter category to improve change management processes.

To effectively use this model, the organisation will need to track individual usage of the new technology to some degree, and be willing and able to do a phased or parallel transition from the old to the new technology. This means that before an organisation fully implements the new technology, they need to successfully onboard individuals on the new technology through a testing phase where they are allowed to learn and adopt the technology before official implementation.

5.1 Phase 1: Discovering Early Adopters

Depending on the size of the organisation, Early Adopters (which include Innovators and Early Adopters discussed at Sect. 2.1) can be identified in different ways. Smaller organisations can have managers identify these individuals, since they would know their workforce more intimately. In larger organisations, Early Adopters can be identified by sending out a survey with relevant questions with regard to technology adoption, and the possibility of changes to systems and processes and the individual's reaction towards it.

Once Early Adopters have been identified, they should be given first access to the new technology, system, or innovation, with the purpose of testing and providing feedback based on their experience. Based on the feedback received, the organisation could make changes to improve the user experience. Although these individuals could be incentivised for their feedback at this phase, depending on the change, it may not always be necessary as they would often be eager and excited to try something new. Once feedback from this group has been incorporated, the other three groups should be given access to the new technology to start the DOI Experience process. The ultimate goal of Phase 1 is to attain buy-in from Early Adopters, as the majority of the group is respected in the organisation (social system), and their acceptance will steer the next group, the Early Majority, to try the new technology and initiate their path through the DOI Experience.

5.2 Phase 2: Converting Mainstream Adopters

Once the buy-in of Early Adopters has been secured, mainstream adopters should be notified of the adoption of the new technology. As illustrated in Fig. 3, the three groups of mainstream adopters will progress through the DOI Experience model at a different pace, the process of which is shortly described below. It is critical to note that change management actions will be necessary to enable the progression of Mainstream Adopters through the DOI Experience.

Winning Over the Early Majority. Once individuals that fall in this group are notified that a new technology needs to be adopted in the near future, they will start their progress through the DOI Experience, starting with Refusal, followed by Anger/Bargaining. However, considering the profile of the Early Majority (Sect. 2.1), it can be assumed that they will quickly reach the Acquiesce stage and move on to Exploration, simply because the Early Adopters have "approved" the new technology. Once they have started the Exploration stage, individuals in this group will cross the Adoption Chasm and reach the Adoption stage. According to diffusion of innovation theory (Sect. 2.1), once this group has reached the Adoption stage, roughly 50% of the individuals within the organisation will have adopted the new technology, and be ready to use the new technology once it is implemented.

Supporting the Late Majority. The Late Majority group will start their path through the DOI Experience at the same time as the Early Majority, however, they will take much longer to reach the Adoption stage, and require more support and convincing than previous groups. As discussed in Sect. 2.1, the Late Majority will only adopt once most of their peers have done so, and once it is absolutely necessary. These individuals could remain in the Refusal and Anger/Bargaining stages for an extended time, and will need extra support, whether through training or other incentives or actions that usually form part of change management procedures to guide them through the DOI Experience. As an increasing number of individuals within the organisation reach the Adoption stage (Early Majority individuals), the increased pressure of peers adopting over time, along with the provided support, will initiate the shift to Acquiesce, Exploration and ultimately Adoption of the Late Majority.

Pressuring Laggards. Once the Early Adopters, the Early Majority and the Late Majority have successfully moved to the Adoption stage, roughly 84% of the individuals within the organisation will be ready to use the new technology. As the last 16% to accept change and adopt, Laggards will need convincing and pressure applied to them to move from Refusal or Anger/Bargaining to Acquiesce, meaning they have accepted that change will happen. Once the Acquiesce stage has been reached by a Laggard, meticulous support should be given to ensure that they successfully move through the Exploration stage and reach Adoption. As this last group moves through the DOI Experience, the most stubborn individuals may not reach the Acquiesce stage in time, and the new technology could be implemented before they have reached the Adoption stage. In this scenario, to ensure successful implementation, it might be necessary to provide them with an ultimatum, such is "fit it or be replaced".

6 Conclusion

The evolution of digital technologies compels organisations to consider the impact of technological change on employees, customers, and suppliers. Furthermore, organisations must also contemplate the pace at which these technologies are diffused across organisations in order to fully exploit the digital benefits. Employees are at the centre of organisational actions as they apply these digital benefits and in order to support organisations with a comprehensive approach, we presented the DOI Experience Model developed through a design science research process. Organisations may reference the DOI Experience Model to encourage and facilitate the adoption of, and adaption to, technology by the organisation's employees. By applying the DOI Experience Model, organisations can improve their change management practices with regard to technological change, and subsequently increase the success rate of technology adoption within the organisation, ultimately preparing the organisation to benefit from their chosen digital technology implementations.

6.1 Limitations

As discussed in Sect. 5, the paper suggests a theoretical model to improve change management activities within an organisation's holistic change management approach, and should not be used in isolation. It has thus not been validated in a practical environment or application, and it is uncertain how it would align with holistic change management models such as Kotter's Eight Step Change Model [15] or Lewin's Three Step Model [16].

6.2 Future Research

Although the "DOI Experience Model" presented in this paper is derived from grounded theoretical perspectives, it needs to be applied in practical scenarios in order to test its validity. Future studies should consider implementing this model as part of a technological adoption change management process, and apply findings from real world application to validate, improve and/or alter the model. Considering the rapid pace of technology adoption within the digital sector, specifically within digital native enterprises [24], future research that focuses on organisations within the digital sector will scrutinise the validity and practicality of this model at the highest level, as change and adoption will happen quickly and continuously. In addition, design principles applied during the design of this utility, may be extracted, further enhancing potential contributions from this research scope of work.

References

1. Skilton, M., Hovsepian, F.: The 4th industrial revolution: responding to the impact of artificial intelligence on business (2017). https://doi.org/10.1007/978-3-319-62479-2
2. Denning, P.J., Lewis, T.G.: Exponential laws of computing growth. Commun. ACM **60**(1), 54–65 (2017). https://doi.org/10.1145/2976758
3. Cozzolino, A., Verona, G., Rothaermel, F.T.: Unpacking the disruption process: new technology, business models, and incumbent adaptation. J. Manage. Stud. **55**(7), 1166–1202 (2018). https://doi.org/10.1111/joms.12352
4. Aghina, W.: The five trademarks of agile organizations. McKinsey Report (2018). https://www.mckinsey.com/business-functions/organization/our-insights/the-five-trademarks-of-agile-organizations
5. Euchner, J.: Business model innovation. Res. Technol. Manag. **59**(3), 10–11 (2016). https://doi.org/10.1080/08956308.2016.1161396
6. Rayna, T., Striukova, L.: 360° business model innovation: toward an integrated view of business model innovation. Res. Technol. Manag. **59**(3), 21–28 (2016). https://doi.org/10.1080/08956308.2016.1161401
7. Jesse, N.: Organizational evolution - how digital disruption enforces organizational agility. IFAC-PapersOnLine **51**(30), 486–491 (2018). https://doi.org/10.1016/j.ifacol.2018.11.310
8. Fichman, R.G.: Information technology diffusion: a review of empirical research. In: ICIS (1992)
9. Safar, L., Sopko, J., Bednar, S., Poklemba, R.: Concept of SME business model for industry 4.0 environment. TEM J. **7**(3), 626–637 (2018). https://doi.org/10.18421/TEM73-20

10. Lee, Y., Shin, J., Park, Y.: The changing pattern of SME's innovativeness through business model globalization. Technol. Forecast. Soc. Chang. **79**(5), 832–842 (2012). https://doi.org/10.1016/j.techfore.2011.10.008
11. Venable, J., Pries-Heje, J., Baskerville, R.: A Comprehensive framework for evaluation in design science research. In: Peffers, K., Rothenberger, M., Kuechler, B. (eds.) DESRIST 2012. LNCS, vol. 7286, pp. 423–438. Springer, Heidelberg (2012). https://doi.org/10.1007/978-3-642-29863-9_31
12. Francke, E., Alexander, B.: Entrepreneurial development in South Africa through innovation: a model for poverty alleviation. Acta Commercii **19**(1), 1–11 (2019). https://doi.org/10.4102/ac.v19i1.631
13. Chen, Y.Y.K., Jaw, Y.L., Wu, B.L.: Effect of digital transformation on organisational performance of SMEs: evidence from the Taiwanese textile industry's web portal. Internet Res. **26**(1), 186–212 (2016). https://doi.org/10.1108/IntR-12-2013-0265
14. Rogers, E.M.: Diffusion of Innovations, 3rd edn. The Free Press, New York (1995). https://doi.org/10.4324/9780203710753-35
15. Kotter, J. P.: Leading change: why transformation efforts fail. Harvard Bus. Rev. **May–June**, 59–67 (1995)
16. Elrod, P.D., Tippett, D.D.: The "death valley" of change. J. Organ. Change Manag. **15**(3), 273–291 (2002). https://doi.org/10.1108/09534810210429309
17. Elisabeth, K.-R.: On Death and Dying. Nature Reviews, vol. 1. The Macmillan Company, New York (2015)
18. Kubler-Ross, E., Kessler, D.: On Grief and Grieving - Finding the Meaning of Grief Through the Five Stages of Loss. Nature Reviews. Scribner - Simon and Schuster Inc., New York (2014)
19. Venable, J., Pries-Heje, J., Baskerville, R.: FEDS: a framework for evaluation in design science research. Eur. J. Inf. Syst. **25**(1), 77–89 (2016). https://doi.org/10.1057/ejis.2014.36
20. Kuechler, W., Vaishnavi, V.: A framework for theory development in design science research : multiple perspectives. J. Assoc. Inf. Syst. 13(6), 395–423 (2012). http://aisel.aisnet.org/jais/vol13/iss6/3
21. van der Merwe, A., Gerber, A., Smuts, H.: Guidelines for conducting design science research in information systems. In: Tait, B., Kroeze, J., Gruner, S. (eds.) SACLA 2019. CCIS, vol. 1136, pp. 163–178. Springer, Cham (2020). https://doi.org/10.1007/978-3-030-35629-3_11
22. Hevner, A.R., March, S.T., Park, J., Ram, S.: Design science in information systems. MIS Q. **28**(1), 75–105 (2004)
23. Moore, G.A.: Crossing the Chasm, 3rd edn. Harper Business, New York (2014)
24. Rosen, M., et al.: How the digital-native enterprise is winning the future, now (2017)
25. https://doi.org/10.1111/isj.12153

Exploring the Link Between Digitalization and Sustainable Development: Research Agendas

Yashoda Karki[1(✉)] and Devinder Thapa[2,3]

[1] University of South-Eastern Norway, Drammen, Norway
yashoda.karki@usn.no

[2] University of South-Eastern Norway, Hønefoss, Norway
devinder.thapa@uia.no

[3] University of Agder, Kristiansand, Norway

Abstract. In this paper, we argue that the existing research looking at digitalization (DT) and sustainable development (SD) in Business Management and Information Systems takes a dualist view, where digitalization and sustainable development is studied independently. Such a dualistic approach has limitations because these two areas are interconnected and mutually influence each other. Hence, we need to take a non-dualistic view to better understand these two phenomena. By conducting a selective literature review, we describe how digitalization and sustainable development concepts are used; and revealed how these two areas are linked in the current literatures. Finally, based on our analysis, we propose four research agendas: first, need for a *paradigm shift (ontology, epistemology, axiology, methodology, and domain)*; second, *conceptual clarity in terms of digitalization and sustainable development*; third, *theories to link DT and SD*; and fourth, *the role of social enterprises in linking DT and SD.*

Keywords: Digitalization (DT) · Sustainable Development (SD) · Sustainability · Ethics · Research agenda

1 Introduction

Digitalization (DT) and Sustainable Development (SD) are the two most sought-after research areas these days. Digitalization is the introduction of technology in a fundamental way in order to upgrade the performance or expand the reach of enterprises [1]. It is a process that improves an entity by triggering significant changes in its processes and properties through combination of information, computing, communication, and connectivity technologies [2]. The use of digital technologies enables major business improvements in the enterprises such as enhancing customer experience, improving operational efficiencies, or creating new business models [3]. Digitalization as information technology (IT) comes in several forms starting from infrastructural IT such as servers, networks, laptops, and smart devices, transactional IT for example business

The original version of this chapter was revised: a second affiliation was added for the second author. The correction to this chapter is available at
https://doi.org/10.1007/978-3-030-85447-8_66

Published by Springer Nature Switzerland AG 2021
D. Dennehy et al. (Eds.): I3E 2021, LNCS 12896, pp. 330–341, 2021.
https://doi.org/10.1007/978-3-030-85447-8_29

process automation, informational IT to improve management through decision support system, planning, sales and forecasts, and strategic IT for the development of new products and services [4].

The concept of sustainability was raised after the establishment of the Brundtland commission - chaired by Norwegian Prime Minister Gro Harlem Brundtland. It broadly defines sustainable development as the "ability to make development sustainable – to ensure that it meets the needs of the present without compromising the ability of future generations to meet their needs." This idea of sustainable development has been used in researches (e.g. Chichilnisky [5]). The definition has evolved over time to include three dimensions of sustainable development: economic development, social inclusion, and environmental sustainability [6]. To operationalize the concept of sustainable development, a set of 17 sustainable development goals (SDG) was promulgated by the United Nations General Assembly in 2015[1]. Later, it was adopted by all UN member states. The SDGs provide a global framework for cooperation to address these three dimensions within an ethical framework.

From a digitalization perspective, the main focus so far is on environmental sustainability at three different levels; production, consumption, and disposal of IT devices [7]. However, digitalization can create the possibility to contribute to the overall SDG [8]. For example, digitalization generates enormous data, and collection, extraction, and analysis of such data can be critical to SDG. There is a need for an information system to integrate the data collected from various source and involve multiple parties to interoperate and collaborate [9]. The process of digitalization, therefore, does not seem straightforward. On the other hand, from sustainable development perspective, the development issues are complex, interrelated, and interdependent [6]. Therefore, it is not enough to relate the research outcome to seventeen SDGs, rather, it needs systemic solutions [10, 11]. If we compare two concepts; digitalization and sustainable development, one looks into connectivity and automatization of the organizational process [2], the other looks into the coexistence of economic, social, and environmental spheres [11]. The former focuses on efficiency and competitive advantage; the latter focuses on economic value embedded in social, and environmental values. However, the dualistic perspective of analyzing these two phenomena in isolation might not show the complete picture. These two phenomena are intertwined, entangled, and interdependent [10], which may lead to contradictory goals if we take a dualistic approach. Digitalization sometimes may not go according to the principles of sustainability. To state explicitly, the digitalization process for merely economic benefits may shelter as Zuboff [12] says 'surveillance capitalism' and other unintended consequences [13]. For example, as in surveillance capitalism, the data generated through the digitalization process mainly focuses on capturing the users' micro-level experiences (clicking) and gaining economic benefits by selling the behavioral prediction in the market [12].

On the other hand, taking sustainable development as a mark to justify any isolated activities is also a blind approach [14]. The developmental process considering technology as a black box can also keep the possibilities of the technologies unclear. Therefore, we argue that it is important to link DT to SD because sustainable development is based on the philosophy of 'deep ecology' [15], for example, not compromising the future

[1] See for details: https://sdgs.un.org/goals.

resources to meet current needs. It puts the impetus that technology has to be designed in such a way that it should not disrupt nature's inherent ability to sustain [10]. So, connecting DT to SD may lead to ethical designing of the technology. Furthermore, organization while introducing the digitalization process can follow an ethical framework of deep ecology. Meaning, not only focusing on economic values but also social and environmental values.

Linking ICT to development has been discussed in the ICT4D literature. However, their focus is on ICT artifacts and specific development goals such as individual/collective capabilities [16, 17]. Digitalization, the phenomenon itself is broader and wider than the use of ICT artifacts for attaining certain pre-specified goals. Therefore, linking DT to SD needs an ecosystem approach [18] to uncover the broader realm of these phenomena. There are works of literatures in IS and management that discuss the importance of digitalization in the light of sustainable development [19, 20], however, there is still a lack of research on identifying the mechanism or process that relates DT to SD.

In order to fill this gap, we build upon the understanding of the concepts: digitalization and sustainable development, in the existing literatures and explore how the digitalization processes and sustainable development are interlinked. Furthermore, we study what kind of theory, framework, or model can be found in the literature to connect these two areas, and what methodologies should be applied to understand such phenomena. In order to look for such results, we have conducted a selective literature review [21]. Subsequently, we provide four research agendas: *the need for a paradigm shift*, *conceptual clarity in terms of DT and SD*, *theories to link DT and SD*, and *the role of social enterprises in linking DT and SD*.

2 Selective Literature Review

Since the research area is still emerging in terms of linking DT to SD, literature reviews can create a foundation for advancing knowledge through identifying the current status, research gaps, and the areas where more research is needed [22]. In this paper, unlike a comprehensive review that attempts to discuss as many published sources on the topic as possible, we apply a selective literature review approach that only uses a certain number of specific sources [21]. In our study, digitalization[2], sustainable development, and the relation between these two phenomena were the main criteria. The articles were selected by using the Scopus and IS databases (basket journals). Because of the authors' expertise in the relevant fields, we limited our search for the literatures in business management and information systems (IS) domain. In the review process, we followed concept centric approach suggested by Webster and Watson [22].

From the search based on the keywords presented in Table 1, we have selected a list of 165 articles in total. There was further addition of 20 articles that we identified through backward and forward search. To make it more inclusive, we further conducted

[2] We use the term digitalization because digitization is just converting analog to digital form, whereas digital transformation is a complete transformation of an organization or society. Digitalization here refers introduction of digital tools in some specific process of change (organizational or societal).

an author-based search on the most cited authors. Finally, two authors independently read and shortlisted the titles and abstracts of the papers to identify a set of highly relevant articles. We excluded the papers that were not focused on digitalization and sustainable development, for example just mentioning digitalization, sustainability used as business viability and sustainability of the organizations. We also excluded the official reports and papers that were not published in academic journals in our final selection. Based on the most relevant articles, we finally selected 45 papers for review.

The caveat however is, all literature reviews are based on some kind of selection strategy. Therefore, our study also runs the risk of excluding potentially relevant articles and reports from sources that are not included in the search criterion [17]. We do agree that the inclusion of more material might have provided additional information regarding contemporary research in the digitalization and sustainable development area. We see this caveat as an opportunity to validate and elaborate on our findings by extending the literature list. Despite these limitations, we believe that our literature review provides a good summary of the status of the link between DT and SD.

Table 1. Literature review

Search library	Scopus; IS basket of journals
Keywords	Digitalization, sustainability, sustainable development
Subject areas	Business management and information systems
Total relevant articles	185
Selected and reviewed	45
Language	English
Inclusion/Exclusion	Journal articles only Cross checking the relevance, backward & forward search based on authors and citations, recent articles [22]

3 Findings

In this section, we present our findings from the review. The findings include the current literature that describes digitalization and sustainability, and how these two areas are interlinked. We also present the examples from our findings that show the link between DT and SD (see Table 2).

3.1 The Concept of Digitalization and Sustainable Development

Our analysis shows that digitalization is explained as the use of digital tools [4, 20], big data analytics [25], social media use [19], and the role of IT [4]. There is a confusion about whether digitalization is design, implementation, use, or outcome. A few studies in our analysis, however, differentiated digitization as converting analog data to digital

Table 2. Examples of studies linking DT to SD

Refs.	Concept of digitalization	Concept of sustainable development	Linking DT to SD approaches/Theory and method	Research agenda
Teo, Nishant [4]	Use of green IT	Green initiative (environmental sustainability)	Through the use of green IT and resources to support green initiatives	Need of further research and theory development
Tim, Pan [19]	Use of social media	Environmental and social sustainability	Through identification and actualization of social media affordances by incorporating societal perspectives	Application of affordances lens to reveal possibilities of DT for SD
Ordieres-Meré, Remón [23]	Use of internet of things (IoT)	Environmental and economic sustainability	Through improved institutional knowledge (knowledge creation and knowledge sharing)	Design of digital functionalities around sustainability goals
von Kutzschen bach and Daub [24]	Use of digital technologies	Sustainability in general	Through organizational learning, the change in mindset, from firm centric to systemic change and from solution oriented to learning oriented	Change in mindset, from firm centric to systemic change and from solution oriented to learning oriented
Pankaj and Seetharaman [20]	Use of IT	Social and economic sustainability	Through generating income create a sustainable society. Understanding DT and SD as sociomaterial practice	Importance of social enterprises on finding a link between DT and SD

format, digitalization as applying digital tools in existing business processes, and digital transformation as the system level restructuring of organizations and society occurred through digital diffusion, and it is an ongoing evolutionary process of innovation [24]. Hence, digital transformation is a broader concept than digitalization.

Similarly, sustainable development also carries different meanings and definitions. For example, sustainability of digitalization process, products or services, economic values, environmental values, or community empowerment. The concept of sustainability has been defined in the literature in three domains of it: social, economic, and environmental. These three domains have been studied both independently and simultaneously. Perhaps, because of the complexity that there is a lack of empirical studies showing the interrelation among these three domains. A few papers have managed to study the overall phenomenon of sustainability considering all three domains [26, 27].

Economic sustainability has been defined as the improvement in corporate profitability, human resource development, and the overall economic development of the country through the creation of employment [28]. Economic sustainability can be achieved through enhancing the efficiency of the business processes and by enabling new functionalities, processes, and business models [29], reduced transaction (logistic) cost, reduction in delivery time, inventory reduction [27]. The concept of social sustainability in existing literature has been defined as social capital, social support, community resilience, and community development [20]. Social sustainability has been studied as a grassroots initiation for reaching the environmental sustainability, and ultimately the overall sustainability goal [19]. Environmental sustainability resulted through digitalization counts in the form of energy and resource optimization [27, 28], reducing waste and pollution [27], reduction of harmful GHG emissions [27, 28], and the development of proactive environmental-friendly practices [28]. Furthermore, environmental sustainability seems to be more frequently studied either in the combination with economic or social sustainability. However, some studies theoretically suggest that investigating three domains to understand the overall phenomenon of sustainable development is necessary [27, 30]. The use of social media, for example, helps societies and communities to create sustainability-related awareness and empowers them to take necessary action to create a sustainable society [19]. Similarly, Ghobakhloo [28] explains that the economic sustainability of Industry 4.0 shows the way to develop socio-environmental sustainability functions.

Once we understand the concept of digitalization and sustainable development, the next question is how to link digitalization with sustainable development. The following section summarizes our findings on the link between digitalization and sustainable development.

3.2 Linking Digitalization to Sustainable Development

Our analysis further shows that it is important to connect DT with SD to address economic, social, and environmental challenges; however, the mechanism or process to show the interrelation is vaguely described. To illustrate the link between DT and SD, we used five examples from the literatures. Our study reveals the primary objective of digitalization is to address some kind of economic, social, or environmental challenges. For example, illiteracy, poverty, lack of physical infrastructure, and political pressures hindered the relationship between DT and SD [31]. However, there are several factors that can enable or hinder the developmental process. Through this analysis, we want to show that the use of this approach (linking DT to SD) could help in better understanding the nuances of the digitalization process for sustainable development.

The importance of linking DT to SD conceptually as well as empirically has been advocated by the research community. For example, Pappas, Mikalef [18] presented an ecosystem-based model in which they suggested exploring the capabilities of big data analytics to connect digitalization to the social innovation process and societal change. They argue that digitalization generates a huge dataset (big data). Utilizing analytics; with an understanding of the big data ecosystem, the data can be converted to actionable information. The refined knowledge in turn can facilitate the social innovation process vis-a-vis sustainable society. Other empirical studies in this regard show that if the affordances of social media [19] are actualized with the help of the community it can empower them socially and economically. Exploring the link through knowledge creation and institutional improvement [23], and through a change in mindset [24] are also advocated in the literature. These studies have targeted one or two dimensions of sustainable development, however, all of them agreed that understanding the link between digitalization and sustainable development is not possible without having a holistic approach. Studies show that Industry 4.0 is one way of designing the digitalization process keeping the holistic view of sustainability in focus [28]. They argue that the functions of economic sustainability such as production efficiency and business model innovation resulted through Industry 4.0 adds to more socioenvironmental sustainable activities like reduction of harmful emissions, sustainable consumption of energy, and improvement in social welfare [28].

The analysis, therefore, shows that the ecosystem approach, actualization of IT affordances, knowledge creation, institutional improvement, and change in mindset can address the challenges in three dimensions of sustainable development.

4 Discussion and Research Agendas

We started with the main question of what digitalization and Sustainable Development are, and how these are interconnected. Our finding shows that research in this area has been acknowledged its importance, but it is still in the initial stage and needs further deliberation. The digitalization process for merely economic benefits ignoring social and environmental dimensions can amplify the dark side [32]. Similarly, the developmental process considering technology as a black box can also be lopsided. The proponent of sustainable development should be at least aware of the various functionalities and affordances of technologies. In the absence of such knowledge, it will be difficult to figure out what kind of technological design may be done to address societal problems [14]. Hence, a well-designed digitalization process keeping sustainable development; based on the philosophy of deep ecology, in mind can lead to an ethical design and implementation of technology. The existing DT and SD related projects in most cases are taking the approach of force-fitting the outcome to some goals of SDG. Such approaches do not address the true essence of sustainable development. The SDG framework suggested by the UN also has several challenges in terms of operationalization. For example, it does not explicitly state the link between DT and SD. However, the positive aspect of the SDG framework is its holistic approach and the underlying philosophy of deep ecology [10] that can be applied to research and practice.

The analysis in the previous section shows that studies lack systemic thinking, amongst clear conceptualization of DT and SD (with a few exceptions), and a lack of theoretical approaches to link DT with SD. Furthermore, our study reveals that the area needs a more conceptual and empirical base to move forward. One feasible way is to aim for greater impact on practice through digitalization studies, where the theoretical knowledge base can be leveraged to facilitate sustainable development initiatives. We elaborate our discussion in the rest of this section and propose four research agendas.

Agenda 1: Paradigm Shift

Exploring the link between DT and SD is not a simple process, but a complex interrelated phenomenon. To understand this complex phenomenon, we have to change our mindset [24], in other words, a paradigm shift is needed [13]. The details of the paradigm shift are as follows.

Ontology: The ontological view needs to be shifted from a mechanistic view to a systemic view of interconnected, interrelated, and interdependent entities.

Epistemology: The epistemological view needs advancement of knowledge from a concept-based approach to knowledge through action. For example, in addition to the dominating approaches in business management and IS such as interpretivism and positivism, critical realism and pragmatism-based approaches can generate more relevant and significant knowledge [33].

Axiology: The existing digitalization processes are mainly focused on the economic benefit resulting from it. However, the societal and environmental (ecological) impact is equally important, and they should be focused on while designing the process. Therefore, the axiological perspective should be extended from an anthropocentric (human centered) to an eco-centric approach. As Capra and Luisi [10] in their book stated that "sustainable society must design in such a way that its ways of life, businesses, economy, physical infrastructures, and technologies do not interfere with nature's inherent ability to sustain life. (pp. 353)" This is only possible if the understanding of deep ecology, which is the essence of sustainable development, is embedded in the digitalization process.

Methodology: The existing methods are limited to focusing either on digitalization or sustainable development research. Since these two phenomena are interlinked and interdependent, the methodologies used for the study of this phenomenon should take a systemic approach. In other terms, we need to explore digitalization, sustainable development, and their linking mechanism. Such a holistic approach can provide a better ontological and epistemological view in this regard. Instead of the unidirectional causal relationship between digitalization and sustainable development, we argue that bidirectional studies better explain the link between these two areas. Studies are required not just on the impact of digitalization on sustainability but also how the digitalization process can be designed based on the principles of sustainability. As we mentioned earlier, epistemology should also advance towards action to knowledge, proactive research approaches such as action-design research (ADR) should be encouraged [34]. ADR conceptualizes the research process as containing the inseparable and inherently interwoven activities of IT artifact building, intervening in the organization or communities, and evaluating the use of the artifact concurrently.

Domain: The shifting in paradigm should change its focus from developing countries to the global development issues. The existing issues such as relative poverty, climate change, and surveillance capitalism are not only affecting global south, but it has universal consequences. Hence, it is important to have a global perspective in such studies.

Agenda 2: Conceptual Clarity

There is confusion among the concepts such as digitization, digitalization, and digital transformation [23]. Few papers have mentioned the basic difference among these terminologies; however, the usage is vague and there is further call to clarify the concept of the digital transformation. To make advancement in any area of research it is important to have a common understanding of the concepts among researcher and practitioner. If we take the example of the least developed countries, they are experiencing the transition from digitization to digitalization (in some sectors), likewise, digital transformation is an advanced phenomenon in developed countries as well. Hence, conflating these terms may give the wrong portrayal. On the other side, 'sustainability' is also understood in many forms such as financial, organizational, economic, social, and environmental. We argue that sustainable development based on the triple bottom line concept: economic, social, and environmental, should be considered holistically in order to achieve the overall goal of sustainable development. Additionally, the spiritual dimension which is always considered as a foreign area should be added to these three dimensions [10].

Agenda 3: Theories to Link DT and SD

Existing studies show a few examples of theories that can be applied to explore the link between DT and SD. However, the operationalization of such theories is still a challenge. There is still lack of theories that explain the link between DT and SD. Existing theories such as dynamic capabilities, or resource-based view are mainly focused on addressing the economic and human values of an organization [2, 4]. These theories are still useful, but to understand the complex relation between DT and SD there is a need for better theories or a combination of theories. DFID (Department for International Development) sustainable livelihood framework is a holistic framework that takes the essence of sustainable development. However, the framework does not consider digitalization explicitly [35]. Digitalization or sustainable development, both require actionable information. The digitalization process generates big data that can be converted into actionable information [8], which can be later mapped to SDG indicators. The theory of affordances originated from ecological psychology can be a useful lens in this regard [20, 36, 37]. The Affordance theory states that we perceive objects in terms of action possibilities (what I can do with the object), i.e., affordances rather than their properties. For example, in the DT and SD context, we can say people do not care about big data but the action possibilities by which they can solve their economic, social, or environmental challenges. However, what kind of facilitating conditions should be arranged to make the affordances perceivable needs further exploration. Because, just perceiving affordances, does not lead to actualization due to various sociocultural and institutional challenges [36]. Therefore, to understand the actualization process we can combine other theories such as institutional theory, structuration, or Actor-Network theory to name a few [38]. It also calls for a grounded approach to develop new theories instead of borrowing theories that were not meant to study the link between DT and SD.

Agenda 4: Role of Social Enterprises in Linking DT and SD

One of the areas that we identify in our analysis is social enterprises, aiming to contribute to sustainable development [39], that are mainly dealing with both digitalization and sustainable development. Unlike profit-making enterprises, the motive of social enterprises (SE) is to address societal and environmental challenges in addition to meet the economic goal [20]. Because of their focus on solving problems in all three dimensions

[39], SE is an important sector in finding the link between DT and SD. Therefore, it is important to study the role of SEs in attaining sustainable development grounding the principle of the triple bottom line. The role of such enterprises in developing countries' context becomes more vital. There are several examples of emerging social enterprises (formal and informal) that are adopting the digital platform to excel innovations and address societal challenges [18, 20, 40]. However, it is important for the stakeholders involving in social enterprises to perceive the action possibilities of digitalization that may lead to sustainable development, especially, in terms of addressing the intertwined nature of economic, social, and environmental dimensions of sustainable development. Hence, there is a need for studies that explore how social enterprises in developing countries design, implement and evaluate the digitalization process to attain sustainable development.

5 Conclusion

The purpose of this paper was to conduct a selective literature review to explore how the existing research explains the phenomena of digitalization and sustainable development; furthermore, how these two areas are interlinked. In doing so, we scrutinized 45 journal papers from the business management and information systems disciplines. Our review showed that the concept of digitalization and sustainable development are not used consistently in the literature and need further theorization. So far, these topics have been mostly studied independently, and there is a lack of studies that investigate the link between digitalization and sustainable development. To illustrate, we selected five papers as examples that partially show the relationship between DT and SD. Finally, based on the overall analysis of the literature, we propose four research agendas as future research avenues.

References

1. Westerman, G., et al.: Digital transformation: a roadmap for billion-dollar organizations. MIT Center for Digital Business and Capgemini Consulting, vol. 1, pp. 1–68 (2011)
2. Vial, G.: Understanding digital transformation: a review and a research agenda. J. Strateg. Inf. Syst. **28**(2), 118–144 (2019)
3. Fitzgerald, M., et al.: Embracing digital technology: a new strategic imperative. MIT Sloan Manag. Rev. **55**(2), 1 (2014)
4. Teo, T.S., Nishant, R., Goh, M.: Do shareholders value green information technology announcements? J. Assoc. Inf. Syst. **18**(8), 542 (2017)
5. Chichilnisky, G.: What is sustainable development? Land Econ. **73**(4), 467–491 (1997)
6. Robert, K.W., Parris, T.M., Leiserowitz, A.A.: What is sustainable development? Goals, indicators, values, and practice. Environ.: Sci. Policy Sustain. Dev. **47**(3), 8–21 (2005)
7. Dedrick, J.: Green IS: concepts and issues for information systems research. Commun. Assoc. Inf. Syst. **27**(1), 1–11 (2010)
8. Macmahon, S.: The challenge of rating ESG performance, in making sustainability count. Harvard Bus. Rev. (2020). https://hbr.org/2020/09/the-challenge-of-rating-esg-performance
9. Watson, R.T., Boudreau, M.-C., Chen, A.J.W.: Information systems and environmentally sustainable development: energy Informatics and new directions for the IS community. MIS Q. **34**(1), 23–38 (2010)

10. Capra, F., Luisi, P.L.: The systems View of Life: A Unifying Vision. Cambridge University Press, Cambridge (2014)
11. Raworth, K.: Doughnut Economics: Seven Ways to Think Like a 21st-Century Economist. Chelsea Green Publishing, White River Junction (2017)
12. Zuboff, S.: Big other: surveillance capitalism and the prospects of an information civilization. J. Inf. Technol. **30**(1), 75–89 (2015)
13. Rothe, F.-F.: Rethinking positive and negative impacts of ‘ICT for development’ through the holistic lens of the sustainable development goals. Inf. Technol. Dev. **26**(4), 653–669 (2020)
14. Majchrzak, A., Markus, M.L., Wareham, J.: Designing for digital transformation: lessons for information systems research from the study of ICT and societal challenges. MIS Q. **40**(2), 267–277 (2016)
15. Næss, A., Jickling, B.: Deep ecology and education: a conversation with Arne Naess. Can. J. Environ. Educ. (CJEE) **5**(1), 48–62 (2000)
16. Thapa, D., Sein, M.K., Sæbø, Ø.: Building collective capabilities through ICT in a mountain region of Nepal: where social capital leads to collective action. Inf. Technol. Dev. **18**(1), 5–22 (2012)
17. Thapa, D., Sæbø, Ø.: Exploring the link between ICT and development in the context of developing countries: a literature review. Electron. J. Inf. Syst. Dev. Ctries. **64**(1), 1–15 (2014)
18. Pappas, I.O., et al.: Big data and business analytics ecosystems: paving the way towards digital transformation and sustainable societies. Inf. Syst. e-Bus. Manag. **16**, 471–491 (2018). https://doi.org/10.1007/s10257-018-0377-z
19. Tim, Y., et al.: Digitally enabled affordances for community-driven environmental movement in rural Malaysia. Inf. Syst. J. **28**(1), 48–75 (2018)
20. Pankaj, L., Seetharaman, P.: The balancing act of social enterprise: an IT emergence perspective. Int. J. Inf. Manag. **57**, 102302 (2021)
21. Bryson, J.M., Berry, F.S., Yang, K.: The state of public strategic management research: a selective literature review and set of future directions. Am. Rev. Public Adm. **40**(5), 495–521 (2010)
22. Webster, J., Watson, R.T.: Analyzing the past to prepare for the future: writing a literature review. MIS Q. **26**, xiii–xxiii (2002)
23. Ordieres-Meré, J., Remón, T.P., Rubio, J.: Digitalization: an opportunity for contributing to sustainability from knowledge creation. Sustainability **12**(4), 1460 (2020)
24. von Kutzschenbach, M., Daub, C.-H.: Digital transformation for sustainability: a necessary technical and mental revolution. In: Dornberger, R. (ed.) New Trends in Business Information Systems and Technology. SSDC, vol. 294, pp. 179–192. Springer, Cham (2021). https://doi.org/10.1007/978-3-030-48332-6_12
25. Dremel, C., et al.: Actualizing big data analytics affordances: a revelatory case study. Inf. Manag. **57**(1), 103121 (2020)
26. Jovanović, M., Dlačić, J., Okanović, M.: Digitalization and society’s sustainable development–Measures and implications. Zbornik Radova Ekonomski Fakultet u Rijeka **36**(2), 905–928 (2018)
27. Kayikci, Y.: Sustainability impact of digitization in logistics. Procedia Manuf. **21**, 782–789 (2018)
28. Ghobakhloo, M.: Industry 4.0, digitization, and opportunities for sustainability. J. Clean. Prod. **252**, 119869 (2020)
29. Hanelt, A., Busse, S., Kolbe, L.M.: Driving business transformation toward sustainability: exploring the impact of supporting IS on the performance contribution of eco-innovations. Inf. Syst. J. **27**(4), 463–502 (2017)
30. Stock, T., Seliger, G.: Opportunities of sustainable manufacturing in industry 4.0. Procedia Cirp **40**, 536–541 (2016)

31. Hatakka, M., Thapa, D., Sæbø, Ø.: Understanding the role of ICT and study circles in enabling economic opportunities: lessons learned from an educational project in Kenya. Inf. Syst. J. **30**(4), 664–698 (2020)
32. Ransbotham, S., et al.: Special section introduction—ubiquitous IT and digital vulnerabilities. Inf. Syst. Res. **27**(4), 834–847 (2016)
33. Heeks, R., Ospina, A.V., Wall, P.J.: Combining pragmatism and critical realism in ICT4D research: an e-resilience case example. In: Nielsen, P., Kimaro, H. (eds.) Information and Communication Technologies for Development. Strengthening Southern-Driven Cooperation as a Catalyst for ICT4D, vol. 552, pp. 14–25. Springer, Cham (2019). https://doi.org/10.1007/978-3-030-19115-3_2
34. Sein, M.K., et al.: Action design research. MIS Q. **35**(1), 37–56 (2011)
35. Parkinson, S., Ramirez, R.: Using a sustainable livelihoods approach to assessing the impact of ICTs in development. J. Community Inform. **2**(3) (2006). https://doi.org/10.15353/joci.v2i3.2072
36. Thapa, D., Sein, M.K.: Trajectory of affordances: insights from a case of telemedicine in Nepal. Inf. Syst. J. **28**(5), 796–817 (2018)
37. Seidel, S., Recker, J., Vom Brocke, J.: Sensemaking and sustainable practicing: functional affordances of information systems in green transformations. MIS Q. **37**, 1275–1299 (2013)
38. Sein, M.K., et al.: A holistic perspective on the theoretical foundations for ICT4D research. Inf. Technol. Dev. **25**(1), 7–25 (2019)
39. Jenner, P.: Social enterprise sustainability revisited: an international perspective. Soc. Enterp. J. **12**(1), 42–60 (2016)
40. Bonina, C., et al.: Digital platforms for development: foundations and research agenda. Inf. Syst. J. (2021). https://doi.org/10.1111/isj.12326

Research Trends, Theories and Concepts on the Utilization of Digital Platforms in Agriculture: A Scoping Review

Abraham Kuuku Sam[1(✉)] and Sara Saartjie Grobbelaar[1,2]

[1] Department of Industrial Engineering, Stellenbosch University, Stellenbosch, South Africa
[2] DSI-NRF CoE in Scientometrics and Science, Technology and Innovation Policy, Stellenbosch University, Stellenbosch, South Africa

Abstract. Globally, the agriculture sector is faced with multiple challenges especially in developing countries where smallholder farmers face barriers such as lack of access to financial services, information, formal and/or economic identity. The utilization of digital platforms in agriculture can offer solutions such as information services, financial inclusion and access to credit, digital identities, track and traceability systems, farm management systems and access to markets. This paper explores the research trends, theories and concepts associated with the utilization of digital platforms in agriculture. Using a scoping review and a directed content analysis approach, 52 papers were studied. It was found that studies have so far focused mainly on the policy, economics, knowledge and innovation systems, impact and adoption of digital agriculture platforms. The findings of this scoping review will aid in the understanding of the state of research on the utilization of digital platforms in agriculture and contribute to future research by helping to identify gaps in the relevant literature.

Keywords: Digital platform · Agriculture · Scoping review

1 Introduction

The utilization of digital platforms in agriculture can provide solutions to challenges such as lack of information, credit, insurance and identity for farmers, especially in developing countries. It can also provide full and real-time visibility, assist in capturing and analyzing data for the management of value chain activities [1]. Digital Agriculture Platforms (DAPs) provide information services on agricultural extension, education, certification standards and skills for farmers. They also boost the ability of farmers to share knowledge and experiences [2]. They promote financial inclusion by granting smallholder farmers access to digital financial services which include credit, insurance [1, 3] and farm inputs [4, 5]. In addition, DAPs can serve as track and traceability [6], farm management and data management systems for value chain stakeholders [1, 2].

The aim of this study is to explore the utilisation of digital platforms in agriculture by conducting a scoping review of peer-review articles by (1) identifying the focus areas

Published by Springer Nature Switzerland AG 2021
D. Dennehy et al. (Eds.): I3E 2021, LNCS 12896, pp. 342–355, 2021.
https://doi.org/10.1007/978-3-030-85447-8_30

where studies on DAPs have concentrated, (2) theories and concepts that have been utilised in DAP studies and (3) trend of DAP research. The research questions follow directly from the aim of this study. *The research questions are: (1) What focus areas have research on the DAP concentrated on? (2) What theories and concepts have been utilized in DAP research? (3) What has been the trend of DAP research based on focus areas and the number of studies?*

2 Methodology

This scoping review is based on the steps suggested by [7] in their seminal paper. These are 1. identifying the research question, 2. identifying relevant studies, 3. study selection and 4. charting the data and 5. collating, summarizing and reporting the results. Having identified the research questions in the previous section, steps 2 and 3 will be applied in this section and then steps 4 and 5 will be utilized when presenting the results of this study.

2.1 Identifying Relevant Studies

The search for **relevant** articles was done on 6 July 2020 using **Scopus**. The following search string was used to search for literature on the use of digital platforms in agriculture: ("agriculture" OR "farming" OR "horticulture") AND ("digital" OR "ICT" OR "mobile") AND ("Platform").

2.2 Study Selection

There exists the engineering or technological view and the economic or transactional view in the discussion of platforms [8, 9]. There is also the information systems view with a socio-technical perspective [10]. Papers that *solely* discussed the design and development of platform architecture exclusively usually concentrated on the design of software and hardware systems. These were excluded. To meet the inclusion criteria, the paper must be a peer-reviewed journal article and must be published in English.

For the results of this scoping review to be useful, the study selection must be transparent, reproducible and adequately documented [11]. For this reason, the **Preferred Reporting Items for Systematic Reviews and Meta-Analyses (PRISMA)** was used as the guide for the selection of relevant literature [12]. Figure 1 shows the selection process based on PRISMA and adopted from [12]. The first screening involved examining the titles and abstracts and the second screening involved analyzing full-text.

2.3 Data Extraction and Charting of Included Studies

Using a directed content analysis approach which allows the researcher to validate or extend conceptually a theoretical framework [13], various categories of data pertinent to answering the research questions were identified and recorded. Using the thematic clusters identified by [14] in their review on digital agriculture, smart farming and agriculture 4.0 as the starting point, key concepts were identified as initial coding categories. The selected articles were then analysed, and the data extracted and categorized.

The following information was recorded in an Excel spreadsheet: Author(s), title, year, number of citations, country, geographical location, Methodology (eg. Literature review, case study, etc.), Methodology Classification (Empirical research, theoretical research or design and development), Theoretical or Analytical lens and target of observation (eg. Smallholders, value chain actors, etc.). Following the fourth step recommended in the methodology proposed by [7], the data were analysed and classified in a manner that allowed for charts to be produced to represent the information.

3 Results

This section presents the results from the study selection, the coding, analysis and categorisation of the identified studies included in the scoping review.

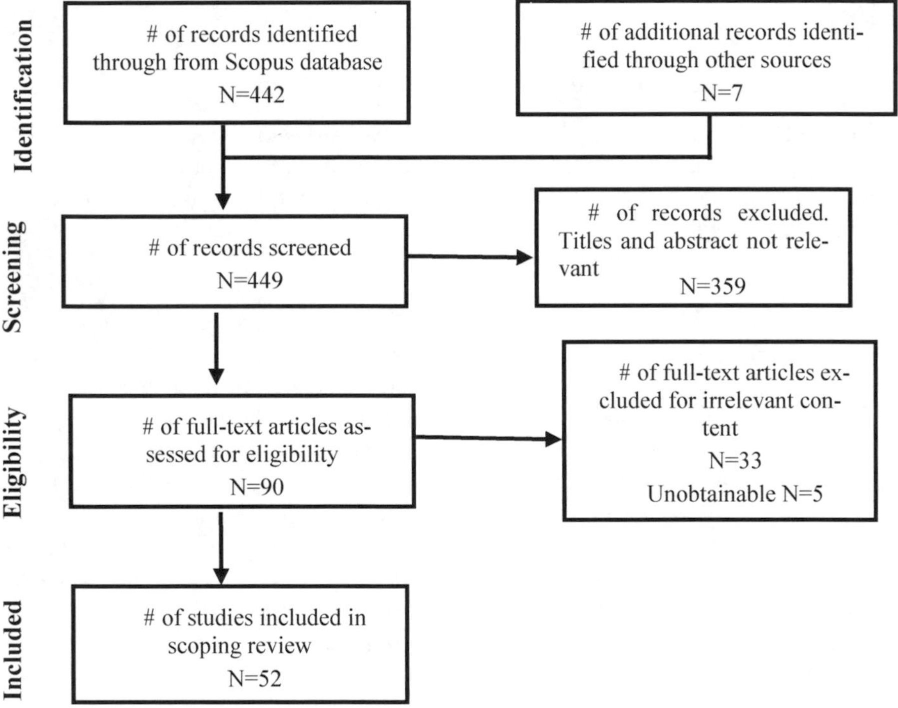

Fig. 1. PRISMA flow diagram showing study selection

3.1 Identification of Included Articles

As represented in Fig. 1 above, the search from Scopus produced 442 results. Seven additional articles were added. This means a total of 449 articles were screened as part of the study. Of the 449 articles, 359 articles were excluded based on examination of titles and abstracts. Thereafter 90 articles were studied, and the full texts were assessed for their relevance to DAPs. 38 were excluded during the full-text assessment because 33 were found to have focused on the design and development of software and/or hardware used in Smart Farming, Precision Agriculture and Agriculture 4.0 while five articles were inaccessible. After the study selection, 52 articles were identified as relevant.

3.2 Collating, Summarizing and Reporting the Results

In this section, the results from the coding, analysis and categorization of the selected articles are discussed to answer the research questions specified in Sect. 1 above.

Characteristics of Included Articles. The percentage distribution of the articles per geographical location is as shown in Fig. 2. None of the selected papers focused explicitly on Central Asia and the Middle East and North Africa. 'Global' represents studies that are not localised to any geographical location.

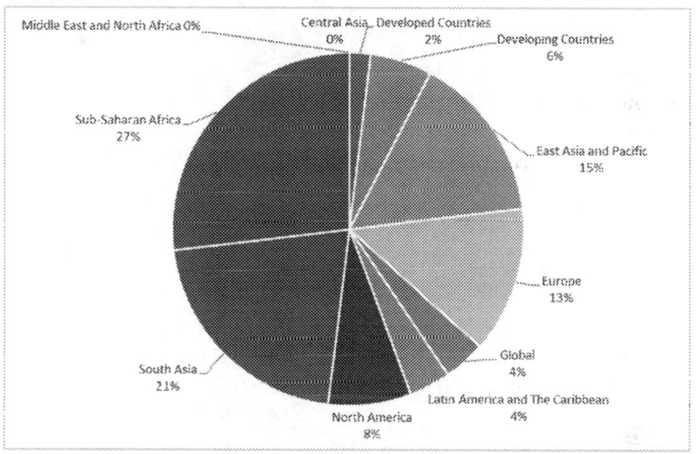

Fig. 2. Geographical location of the included articles

Categorizing Included Articles into Themes. Using the thematic clusters identified by [14] as the starting point, the articles included in the study were categorized into five thematic areas as shown in Table 1. They are:

- Thematic Area 1: Economics and management of DAPs in agriculture.
- Thematic Area 2: Agricultural knowledge Systems, Innovation Systems and Innovation Ecosystems.
- Thematic Area 3: Impact of DAP.
- Thematic Area 4: Adoption, use and adaption of DAPs.
- Thematic Area 5: DAPs from the Policy/Politics/Governance/Perspective.

It must, however, be stated that some studies covered more than one thematic area.

Table 1. Categorization of included articles based on thematic areas

Economics and management of DAPs in agriculture value chains	Business models	Access based business model/sharing economy	[15]
	Production management	Cost analysis and management	[16, 17]
		Farm management system	[18]
		Track and traceability systems	[6]
	Financial sustainability	Profitability of providing digital platforms with infrastructure	[19]
	E-Business	Effect of digital platforms on commodity prices	[20]
		Connection of value chain actors	[3, 18, 21–24]
	Market structure	Creation of an alternative market structure	[19, 47]
Digital platforms and agricultural knowledge and innovation (Eco)systems	Knowledge systems	Technology transfer pathways	[25]
		Agriculture extension services	[26, 60]
		Knowledge sharing, co-creation and management	[27–35]
		Decision support systems	[36, 37]
	Ecosystems	Knowledge services	[38]

(*continued*)

Table 1. (*continued*)

		Urban food ecosystem	[39]
	Innovation systems	Innovation intermediation	[40]
		Digitalisation of agriculture innovation systems	[41]
Impact of DAP	Farmers' work routine		[42]
	Lock-in tendencies		[43]
	Enabling efficiencies through information sharing		[16, 19]
	Collective and individual learning and training		[27, 44, 45]
	Early warning system for flood management		[46]
	Access to farm mechanization by smallholder farmers		[15]
	Trust mediation for value chain financing		[5]
	Uses and opportunities		[47, 48]
	Benefits		[2, 32, 33, 47, 49, 50]
	Land use and gentrification		[51, 52]
	Effect on foodscapes		[53]
	Productivity		[4, 50, 54]
Adoption, use and adaption of digital agriculture platforms	How digital agriculture platforms encountered		[53]
	Inclusive value chain partnerships		[55]
	Information sharing and education		[30, 36, 61]
	Challenges and limitations		[2, 3, 18, 44, 47, 48, 56]
	Determinants and moderating factors influencing value		[35]
	Necessity and feasibility		[56]
	Adoption of digital platforms among smallholders		[57]
	Monitoring carbon stocks on smallholder farms		[58]
	Determinants and moderating factors of user acceptance and usage behavior		[16]

(*continued*)

Table 1. (*continued*)

DAP from the Policy/Politics/Governance/Perspective	Power, ownership, privacy, ethics and politics of digital agriculture platforms	Distributive politics of digital agriculture platforms	[42]
		Effect of ownership structure and governance	[43, 53]
		Data privacy and ownership	[41]
	Public Administration	Food safety and regulation	[6]

The impact of DAP on agriculture has been studied the most. The studies concentrated mainly on the benefits and opportunities offered by DAP especially to smallholder farmers. The least studied area has been the policy perspective of DAP. The few studies reviewed focused on ownership structure, data privacy and regulation, especially in developed countries. No research in this thematic area focused on Sub-Saharan Africa.

Methodology, Theoretical and Conceptual Perspectives of the Included Articles. Three of the selected articles dedicated their methodology section to a discussion of the design and development of DAPs. Of the remaining 49 articles, 43 (88%) were empirical research and six (12%) were theoretical research. The six theoretical research articles were made up of four papers focused on reviews and two dedicated to models on DAPs.

The theoretical and conceptual perspectives of the articles were also identified as shown in Table 2. While some studies focused on one theoretical perspective, others looked at the studies using multiple lenses. Value Chain theory was applied the most.

Table 2. Theoretical and conceptual perspective of reviewed articles

Theoretical and conceptual perspective	Articles reviewed
Business model: Access-based business model	[15]
Diffusion of innovation theory	[26, 61]
Assemblage theory	[52, 53]
Competence model	[45]
Contingent effectiveness model of technology transfer	[25]
Critical theory (critical data studies)	[52]
Cross-platform mobile development framework	[48]
Decision support systems	[46, 51]

(*continued*)

Table 2. (*continued*)

Theoretical and conceptual perspective	Articles reviewed
Design patterns and storytelling	[31]
Digital native, Digital immigrants concept	[32]
Economic theory: Bargaining power, Information asymmetry and structural differences Productivity Two-sided market	[20] [50] [23]
Econometric analysis	[59]
Ecosystem: Innovation ecosystem	[38, 39, 41]
Innovation	[2, 58, 60]
Information systems concept: Information chain Technology acceptance model	[29] [26]
Innovation systems	[40]
Interconnected systems	[33]
Knowledge systems	[36]
Marketing concept	[18]
Multi-criteria decision analysis	[37]
Multi-criteria evaluation	[30]
Networked community	[54]
Operational model	[24]
Pedagogical model	[44]
Propensity Score Matching (PSM) approach	[4]
Requirements analysis	[56]
Responsible research and innovation	[27, 41]
Skills, Community development, and Structural inequalities perspective	[42]
Sociomaterial perspective	[3]
Sustainability	[19]
Sociological underpinnings of 'the' future, political ontology and Foucault's concept of dispositif	[43]
Total quality management: Quality function deployment	[17]
Transition theory: Multi-level Perspective (MLP)	[41]
Unified theory of acceptance and use of technology model	[16]
Use case model	[28]
User-centred design	[49]
Value chain	[5, 6, 21, 22, 55, 57]
Vibrant materialism, Geographies of care, enactive politics	[53]

Trend of Digital Agriculture Platform Studies. Figure 3 presents the number of articles in the five thematic areas published over time. Research on the utilization of digital platforms in Agriculture has been published since 2004. However, it was in 2017 that the number of articles for all thematic areas started increasing. Over the year, the most consistent thematic area that has been researched is the impact of DAP. Until 2016, not all thematic areas were researched every year but since 2017, every thematic area has seen an increase in the number of studies.

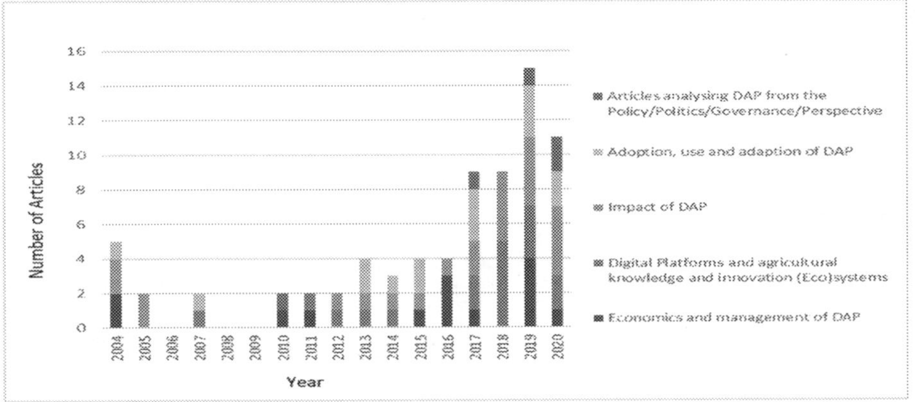

Fig. 3. Number of articles per thematic area published over time

4 Discussion

No article focused explicitly on Central Asia and the Middle East and North Africa.

This indicates a gap in DAP literature for these parts of the world. Most of the articles on Sub-Saharan Africa, South and East Asia also focused mainly on smallholder and rural farmers. Conversely, most of the articles that concentrated on developed countries concentrated on the entire value chain.

Articles on the "Economics and Management of DAPs in agriculture" discussed the benefits of DAPs from the economic or farm management perspective. The benefits include creating a digital marketplace [3, 9, 21–24], new business models such as access-based business models or sharing economy [15] and the creation of alternative market structures [19, 47]. DAPs can also assist with farm operations [18], cost management [16, 17] and quality assurance [6].

Most of the articles reviewed on "Agricultural knowledge Systems, Innovation Systems and Ecosystems" discussed the use of DAPs to share knowledge and information [27–35]. Specifically, [26] and [60] explored the use of mobile telephony to support agricultural extension services for rural farmers. [25] focused on technology transfer after donor projects have been completed.

A significant number of the articles reviewed discussed the impact of DAP on farming, farmers and value chain actors. These articles studied the use of DAPs for enabling efficiencies through information sharing, collective and individual learning and training, early warning systems for flood management, access to farm mechanization by smallholder farmers, trust mediation for Value Chain Financing and improved land management and productivity.

Only five of the 52 articles discussed DAPs from the policy or governance perspective. This is the least number of articles selected from any thematic area. The articles surveyed are dominated by empirical research. Of the six theoretical papers, four were reviews and two focused on models related to DAPs. There was no scoping review among the selected articles. DAPs are been studied using a wide range of theoretical and conceptual lenses. The value chain concept has been used in a significant number of studies from Sub-Saharan Africa [5, 6, 21, 22, 55, 57].

From the scoping review, research on DAPs is started quite recently. The first articles from the included studies were published in 2004. These early articles studied the impact, adoption, use and adaption of DAPs and the Economics and management of DAPs. However, in 2017 research on DAPs almost doubled and has been increasing in recent times with articles covering agricultural knowledge systems, innovation systems and innovation ecosystems and policy in addition to the thematic areas mentioned above. In recent times, more articles have also targeted developing countries.

4.1 Strengths and Limitations of This Scoping Review

PRISMA guided the selection of relevant literature so that the study selection will be transparent, reproducible and adequately documented. However, some relevant studies may have been omitted. This scoping review identified and selected English articles from the Scopus Database. While the articles in Scopus are usually peer-reviewed and the journals are generally of high academic and intellectual value, knowledge of DAPs is not limited to Scopus. Also, reviewing only peer-reviewed journal articles means that knowledge in grey literature may have been overlooked.

5 Conclusions, Implications and Directions for Future Research

Research on DAPs is quite recent. They started in 2004. Since 2017, the number of studies on DAPs has increased significantly.

This study reveals the need for studies that address the systemic challenges confronting the development of DAPs and the corresponding systemic policy frameworks required to tackle them. Also, the lack of research from the policy and innovation systems perspective in Sub-Saharan Africa context must be addressed. Specifically, rigorous studies are required to address topics such as data privacy and protection, data governance and the regulation of DAPs. By mapping and categorising the literature on DAPs, researchers and policymakers will be able to address the issues related specifically to each theme that was identified.

It also provides different routes for future research on DAPs by categorising the included studies into themes and highlighting the research that has already been conducted under each theme. The lack of literature from Central Asia and the Middle East and North Africa is proof that studies on DAPs published in English are needed from these geographical areas. Finally, it is suggested that since this scoping review used only literature from SCOPUS, a similar review is conducted that covers several recognised databases. This, it is believed, will assist in providing a more holistic picture of the research about DAPs.

References

1. Loukos, P., Javed, A.: Opportunities in agricultural value chain digitization. https://www.gsma.com/mobilefordevelopment/wp-content/uploads/2018/01/Opportunities-in-agricultural-value-chain-digitisation-Learnings-from-Ghana.pdf. Accessed 02 Mar 2020 (2018)
2. Eitzinger, A., Cock, J., Atzmanstorfer, K., Binder, C.R., Läderach, P., Bonilla-Findji, O., et al.: GeoFarmer: a monitoring and feedback system for agricultural development projects. Comput. Electron. Agric. **158**, 109–121 (2019)
3. Hoppen, N., Klein, A.D.C.Z., Rigoni, E.H.: Sociomaterial practices: challenges in developing a virtual business community platform in agriculture. Braz. Adm. Rev. **14**(2), 1–22 (2017)
4. Ogutu, S.O., Okello, J.J., Otieno, D.J.: Impact of information and communication technology-based market information services on smallholder farm input use and productivity: The case of Kenya. World Dev. **64**, 311–321 (2014)
5. Agyekumhene, C., De Vries, J.R., van Paassen, A., Macnaghten, P., Schut, M., Bregt, A.: Digital platforms for smallholder credit access: the mediation of trust for cooperation in maize value chain financing. NJAS - Wageningen J. Life Sci. **86–87**, 77–88 (2018)
6. Xiong, B., Fu, R., Lin, Z., Luo, Q., Yang, L., Pan, J.: A solution on pork quality traceability from farm to dinner table in Tianjin City China. Agric. Sci. China **9**(1), 147–156 (2010)
7. Arksey, H., O'Malley, L.: Scoping studies: towards a methodological framework. Int. J. Soc. Res. Methodol. Theory Pract. **8**(1), 19–32 (2005)
8. Baldwin, C.Y., Woodard, C.J.: The architecture of platforms: a unified view. In: Gawer, A. (ed.) Platforms, Markets and Innovation, pp. 19–44. Edward Elgar Publishing, Cheltenhampp (2009)
9. Gawer, A.: Bridging differing perspectives on technological platforms: toward an integrative framework. Res. Policy **43**(7), 1239–1249 (2014)
10. de Reuver, M., Sørensen, C., Basole, R.: The digital platform: a research agenda. J. Inf. Technol. **33**, 124–135 (2018)
11. Armstrong, R., Hall, B.J., Doyle, J., Waters, E.: 'Scoping the scope' of a cochrane review. J. Public Health **33**(1), 147–150 (2011)
12. Moher, D., Liberati, A., Tetzlaff, J., Altman, D.G., The PRISMA group: preferred reporting items for systematic reviews and meta-analyses: the PRISMA statement. PLoS Med. **6**(7), e1000097 (2009)
13. Hsieh, H.F., Shannon, S.E.: Three approaches to qualitative content analysis. Qual. Health Res. **15**(9), 1277–1288 (2005)
14. Klerkx, L., Jakku, E., Labarthe, P.: A review of social science on digital agriculture, smart farming and agriculture 4.0: new contributions and a future research agenda, NJAS - Wageningen J. Life Sci. 90–91, 100315 (2019)
15. Sengupta, T., Narayanamurthy, G., Moser, R., Hota, P.K.: Sharing app for farm mechanization: gold farm's digitized access based solution for financially constrained farmers. Comput. Ind. **109**, 195–203 (2019)
16. Aribe, S.G., Turtosa, J.M.H., Yamba, J.M.B., Jamisola, A.B.: Ma-ease: an android-based technology for corn production and management. Pertanika J. Sci. Technol. **27**(1), 49–68 (2019)

17. Sopegno, A., Calvo, A., Berruto, R., Busato, P., Bocthis, D.: A web mobile application for agricultural machinery cost analysis. Comput. Electron. Agric. **130**, 158–168 (2016)
18. Singh, R., Kumar, J., Nayak, A.: AGROY: creating value through smart farming. Emerald Emerg. Markets Case Stud. **9**(3), 1–31 (2019)
19. Kumar, R.: 'eChoupals: A study on the financial sustainability of village internet centers in rural Madhya Pradesh. Inf. Technol. Int. Dev. **2**(1), 45–73 (2004)
20. Banker, R., Mitra, S., Sambamurthy, V.: The effects of digital trading platform on commodity prices on agricultural supply chains. MIS Q. **35**(3), 599–611 (2011)
21. Weddagala, W.M.T.B., Basnayake, B.M.R.L., Wijesekara, H.M.L., Dharmathilaka, N.R.D.S., Kiriveldeniya, K.K.A., Karunaratne, A.S., et al.: Crowd sourcing for value chain management: a case of market decision support system in Sri Lankan agriculture market. Acta Hort. **1278**, 173–178 (2020)
22. Ndour, M., Gueye, B.: Mlouma: to connect the agricultural products market players. Emerald Emerg. Markets Case Stud. **6**(3), 1–18 (2016)
23. Vincent, R., Sanjaykumar, K., Rajesh, M., Verma, S.K.: Agricart: an innovative methodology for enhancing farmers livelihood. J. Comput. Theor. Nanosci. **17**(1), 373–377 (2020)
24. Barmpounakis, S., Kaloxylos, A., Groumas, A., Katsikas, L., Sarris, V., Dimtsa, K., et al.: Management and control applications in agriculture domain via a future internet business-to-business platform. Inf. Process. Agric. **2**(1), 51–63 (2015)
25. Bugayong, I.D., Hayashi, K., Querijero, N.J.V.B., Orden, M.E.M., Agustiani, N., Hadiawati, L., et al.: Technology transfer pathways of information and communication technologies for development (ICT4D): the case of the weather-rice-nutrient integrated decision support system (WeRise) in Indonesia. J. Int. Soc. Southeast Asian Agric. Sci. **25**(2), 104–117 (2019)
26. Mugabi, N., State, A.E., Omona, J., Jansson, B.: Revolutionalizing agriculture extension delivery through mobile telephony: the experience of village enterprise agent model in Greater masaka area, Uganda. WIT Trans. Ecol. Environ. **217**, 963–974 (2019)
27. Witteveen, L., Lie, R., Goris, M., Ingram, V.: Design and development of a digital farmer field school. Experiences with a digital learning environment for cocoa production and certification in Sierra Leone. Telematics Inf. **34**(8), 1673–1684 (2017)
28. Kliment, T., Bordogna, G., Frigerio, L., Stroppiana, D., Crema, A., Boschetti, M. et al.: Agris on-line papers in economics and informatics supporting a regional agricultural sector with geo & mainstream ICT. Case Stud. Space Agric. Proj. **6**(4), 69–81 (2015)
29. Glendenning, C.J., Ficarelli, P.P.: Content development and management processes of ICT initiatives in Indian agriculture. Inf. Dev. **27**(4), 301–314 (2011)
30. Karetsos, S., Costopoulou, C., Sideridis, A., Patrikakis, C., Koukouli, M.: Bio@gro - an online multilingual organic agriculture e-services platform. Inf. Serv. Use **27**(3), 123–132 (2007)
31. Lyle, P., Choi, J.H.J., Foth, M.: Designing to the pattern: a storytelling prototype for food growers. Multimodal Technologies Interac. **2**(4) (2018)
32. Roy, M., Ghosh, C.K.: The benefits of the e-learning agricultural project kissankerala to digital immigrants and digital natives. Turkish Online J. Distance Educ. **14**(2), 150–164 (2013)
33. Mylonas, P., Voutos, Y., Sofou, A.: A collaborative pilot platform for data annotation and enrichment in viticulture. Information **10**(4), 1–27 (2019)
34. Flak, J.: Technologies for sustainable biomass supply-overview of market offering. Agronomy **10**(6), 798 (2020)
35. Evans, K.J., Terhorst, A., Kang, B.H.: From data to decisions: helping crop producers build their actionable knowledge. Crit. Rev. Plant Sci. **36**(2), 71–88 (2017)
36. Ogunti, E.O., Akingbade, F.A., Segun, A., Oladimeji, O.: Decision support system using mobile applications in the provision of day to day information about farm status to improve crop yield. Periodicals Eng. Nat. Sci. **6**(2), 89–99 (2018)
37. Lian, J.W., Ke, C.K.: Using a modified ELECTRE method for an agricultural product recommendation service on a mobile device. Comput. Electr. Eng. **56**, 277–288 (2016)

38. Kawtrakul, A.: Ontology engineering and knowledge services for agriculture domain. J. Integr. Agric. **11**(5), 741–751 (2012)
39. Davies, F.T., Garrett, B.: Technology for sustainable urban food ecosystems in the developing world: strengthening the nexus of food–water–energy–nutrition. Front. Sustain. Food Syst. **2**(84), 1–11 (2018)
40. Munthali, N., Leeuwis, C., Van Paassen, A., Lie, R., Asare, R., Van Lammeren, R., et al.: Innovation intermediation in a digital age: comparing public and private new-ICT platforms for agricultural extension in Ghana. NJAS - Wageningen J. Life Sci. **86–87**, 64–76 (2018)
41. Fielke, S.J., Garrard, R., Jakku, E., Fleming, A., Wiseman, L., Taylor, B.M.: Conceptualising the DAIS: implications of the "Digitalisation of Agricultural Innovation Systems" on technology and policy at multiple levels. NJAS - Wageningen J. Life Sci. 90–91, 100296 (2019)
42. Carolan, M.: Automated agrifood futures: robotics, labor and the distributive politics of digital agriculture. J. Peasant Stud. **47**(1), 184–207 (2020)
43. Carolan, M.: Acting like an algorithm: digital farming platforms and the trajectories they (need not) lock-in. Agric. Hum. Values **37**(4), 1041–1053 (2020). https://doi.org/10.1007/s10460-020-10032-w
44. Muniafu, M., Wambalaba, F., Wanyama, W., Nduati, G., Ndirangu, D.: Using OER as a tool for agribusiness management training for hard-to-reach rural farmer populations. J. Asynchronous Learn. Netw. **17**(2), 21–30 (2013)
45. Thanopoulos, C., Protonotarios, V., Stoitsis, G.: Online web portal of competence-based training opportunities for organic agriculture. Agris On-line Pap. Econ. Inf. **4**(1), 49–63 (2012)
46. Amarnath, G., Simons, G.W.H., Alahacoon, N., Smakhtin, V., Sharma, B., Gismalla, Y., et al.: Using smart ICT to provide weather and water information to smallholders in Africa: the case of the Gash River Basin, Sudan. Clim. Risk Manage. 52–66 (2018)
47. Schiefer, G.: New technologies and their impact on the agri-food sector: an economists view. Comput. Electron. Agric. **43**(2), 163–172 (2004)
48. Xin, J., Zazueta, F.S., Vergot, P., III., Mao, X., Kooram, N., Yang, Y.: Delivering knowledge and solutions at your fingertips: strategy for mobile app development in agriculture. Agric. Eng. Int. CIGR J. **2015**, 317–325 (2015)
49. Singh, P.P., Pandey, P., Singh, D., Singh, S., Khan, M.S., Semwal, M.: "Mentha Mitra"—an android app based advisory digital tool for menthol mint farmers. Ind. Crops Prod. **144**, 112047 (2020)
50. Talwar, V., Mastakar, N., Bowonder, B.: ICT platforms for enhancing agricultural productivity: the case study of Tata Kisan Kendra. Int. J. Serv. Technol. Manage. **6**(3–5), 437–448 (2005)
51. Jordan, R., Euxodie, G., Maharaj, K., Belfon, R., Bernard, M.: AgriMaps: improving site-specific land management through mobile maps. Comput. Electron. Agric. **123**, 292–296 (2016)
52. Carolan, M.: "Urban Farming Is Going High Tech": digital urban agriculture's links to gentrification and land use. J. Am. Plann. Assoc. **86**(1), 47–59 (2020)
53. Carolan, M.: Agro-digital governance and life itself: food politics at the intersection of code and affect. Sociol. Rural. **57**(11), 816–835 (2017)
54. Bowonder, B., Yadav, Y.: Developing an ICT platform for enhancing agricultural productivity: The case study of EID Parry. Int. J. Serv. Technol. Manage. **6**(3–5), 322–341 (2005)
55. Agyekumhene, C., De Vries, J.R., van Paassen, A., Schut, M., MacNaghten, P.: Making smallholder value chain partnerships inclusive: exploring digital farm monitoring through farmer friendly smartphone platforms. Sustainability **12**(11), 4580 (2020)
56. Li, Z., Luo, C., Zhang, J.: Research on the development and preliminary application of 12396 new rural sci-tech service hotline we chat public platform. In: 2015 International Conference on Network and Information Systems for Computers, pp. 453–456.

57. Hartmann, G., Nduru, G., Dannenberg, P.: Digital connectivity at the upstream end of value chains: a dynamic perspective on smartphone adoption amongst horticultural smallholders in Kenya. Competition and Change (2020)
58. Mbile, P., Makansi, A., Ajayi, O., Ferguson, C., Manzinga, A., Ebokely, M.: Monitoring carbon stocks on smallholder farms using information and communications technologies: evaluating the potential for central Africa. Electron. J. Inf. Syst. Dev. Countries **71**(1), 1–17 (2015)
59. Oyinbo, O., Chamberlin, J., Maertens, M.: Design of digital agricultural extension tools: perspectives from extension agents in Nigeria. J. Agric. Econ. (2020)
60. Omulo, G., Kumeh, E.M.: Farmer-to-farmer digital network as a strategy to strengthen agricultural performance in Kenya: a research note on "Wefarm" platform. Technol. Forecast. Soc. Change **158**, 120120 (2020)
61. Bentley, J.W., Van Mele, P., Barres, N.F., Okry, F., Wanvoeke, J.: Smallholders download and share videos from the internet to learn about sustainable agriculture. Int. J. Agric. Sustain. **17**(1), 92–107 (2019)

The Impact of Industry 4.0 on the Business Models of Small and Medium Enterprises: A Systematic Literature Review

Abdul Qadir Soondka and Hanlie Smuts(✉)

Department of Informatics, University of Pretoria, Pretoria, South Africa
u16009879@tuks.co.za, hanlie.smuts@up.ac.za

Abstract. New digital technologies, referred to as Industry 4.0, can create many opportunities, not only for larger organisations, but for small and medium enterprises (SMEs) as well. However, for SMEs to create value from Industry 4.0, the digital technologies must be applied in alignment with the SMEs' business model as the SME business model is the means through which the SME creates value. This study aimed to identify the key impacts of Industry 4.0 on business models SMEs through conducting a systematic literature review and a detailed analysis of 27 papers. We identified 5 primary impact areas namely customer, financial, organisational, employee and cost structure collated from of 23 sub impact areas. In order to report our findings, we mapped it to business model components consisting of value creation, value proposition and value capture. Through considering business model impact, SMEs may be able to leverage the technology platforms in Industry 4.0 towards business value creation and economic sustainability.

Keywords: Industry 4.0 · Small and medium enterprises · Business models

1 Introduction

SMEs may be considered as the backbone of an economy and have direct influence on a nation's Gross Domestic Product [1, 2]. Like with the previous industrial revolutions, the Fourth Industrial Revolution (Industry 4.0), brings many changes in the way organisations function [3]. The implementation of Industry 4.0 technologies requires a business model to be redesigned to be sustainable and facilitate a magnitude of factors that arise from such a transformation [3, 4]. A business model, in this context, provides an approach towards a better understanding as to how Industry 4.0 technologies can be used to create and capture value, as well as generate revenue [3, 5, 6]. A business model is an *"organisation's approach to generating revenue at a reasonable cost, and incorporates assumptions about how it will both create and capture value"* [4, 5: 263].

There have been several studies conducted on the impact of Industry 4.0 on organisations, economies, and education in general. However, according to Müller [7], research on how business models of SMEs are affected by Industry 4.0, is very scarce. Therefore, this study aims to answer the research question: *"What are the key impacts of Industry*

Published by Springer Nature Switzerland AG 2021
D. Dennehy et al. (Eds.): I3E 2021, LNCS 12896, pp. 356–367, 2021.
https://doi.org/10.1007/978-3-030-85447-8_31

4.0 on the business models of SMEs?". By considering these impacts on business models, SMEs may be able to consider opportunities more holistically in their effort to apply the advantages that Indsutry 4.0 technologies bring.

This paper is structured as follows: in Sect. 2 highlights the background to the study and in Sect. 3, the research approach is presented. Section 4 contains the data analysis and the findings and contribution are discussed in Sect. 5. We conclude the paper in Sect. 6.

2 Background

SMEs make up, and contribute to, a significant part of the global economy [1, 2]. Yet, SMEs deal with several challenges pertaining to strategic planning and implementation when considering technologies that evolved in the realm of Industry 4.0 [8]. These challenges include a lack of focus on a strategy for their products and investments, lack of capital investment based on a targeted technology roadmap and lack of skills to address the impact, and opportunity, of Industry 4.0 technologies [8–10]. This is where business models play an important role as business models provide a framework to create value, capture value and generate revenue. Business models provide an approach and an understanding into utilising resources and infrastructure to provide value [11–15]. Joan [15] argues that a new technology will not succeed without a good business model.

In this section we provide background to the study by discussing business models in the context of SMEs, the scope of Industry 4.0 and the impact of the evolution of digital technologies on SMEs.

2.1 Business Models

Several definitions for business model exist in the literature. Hummel, Slowinski [11] defines a business model as the logic and principles by which a firm generates revenue. However, they go further into explaining that business models are the organisational structures, its resources and infrastructure around its business model to provide guidance on how things should be done. According to Baden-Fuller and Mangematin [12], a business model is defined as a framework used to create and provide value to the organisation and consumers, as well as generate revenue and profits.

A business model contains different elements, each element carrying a different responsibility to ensure the organisations success. Clauss [16] argues that there are three elements of a business model, namely value creation, value offer or value proposition and finally, value capture. The *value creation* element of the business model describes how and by what means the organisation creates its value [16]. Mueller and Daeschle [17] describes the value creation element as the tasks and work performed for the organisation to provide value to its customers. The value proposition, also termed value offer, addresses the aspect of the actual dealing with the customer. The actual dealing with the customer covers the aspect of different product and service offerings to capture the customer's attention and ultimately, their support and business. The value offer can be described as the bridge between value creation and the final stage of value capture [1, 13, 16].

Baden-Fuller and Haefliger [13] describes the value capture element as an organisation's method of capturing and delivering value. It can be further understood as the way in which value proposition is converted into revenue for the organisation which is used to cover costs and ultimately make a profit [7, 13, 16].

2.2 SMES and New Technologies

When it comes to SMEs, the adoption of new technologies is lagged as opposed to larger organisations [18]. In studies previously conducted relating to the third industrial revolution and the adoption of the internet by SMEs, a few challenges were identified such as: lack of understanding of the technology and how it can be incorporated into the organisation; lack of research and development; lack of skills to use the new technology and the price of technology [18, 19].

From more recent studies conducted with regards to Industry 4.0 and the adoption by SMEs, the same issues are still prevalent compared to findings from previous industrial revolutions. A significant challenge to the adoption is identified from the cost vs benefit analysis of Industry 4.0. Unlike major corporations and larger enterprises, SMEs have a limited workforce and limited funding. The limitation in funding plays a vital role in the adoption of Industry 4.0. Another major challenge is that Industry 4.0 brings a significant change to how the organisation would function. In the initial stages of implementation, the SME would be required to use a substantial amount of capital to set up for Industry 4.0, and the return on this is not delivered immediately. It takes time for the return to grow to before having a vital effect [6, 8, 10, 20, 21].

2.3 The Impact of Industry 4.0 on SME's

Industry 4.0 applies different components and machines to create a more extensive system. Each component and machine plays a role to support the broader objective of the organisation [3, 9, 17, 22, 23]. The initial literature and reports on Industry 4.0 suggested that it will have a substantial benefit on SMEs; however other research argues that Industry 4.0 will have a negative impact on SMEs [8]. There are visible and noticeable changes in the structure and in the way SMEs operate, that result from Industry 4.0. SMEs are no longer seen as a standalone organisation, but as a component in a more extensive network [24]. SMEs that have adopted Industry 4.0 now form part of a new digitalised landscape and environment, changing the SME business model from a "seller" to a "networker". To continue operating, SMEs need to adapt to the ever-changing digitalised environment, while managing the drastic changes in the traditional business models of SMEs as Industry 4.0 aims to make organisations more productive. This effort results in drastic changes in the operations, structure and manner in which business is conducted [1, 3, 24, 25].

3 Research Approach

The aim of this study was to understand the key impacts of Industry 4.0 on the business models of SMEs. In order to achieve this outcome, a systematic literature review (SLR) was conducted [26]. In order to conduct the literature search, academic databases such as ScienceDirect, ResearchGate, Google Scholar, Academia, Emerald Insight, SpringerLink, IEEE Xplore Digital Library and Web of Science containing peer reviewed literature were searched. Initially, there were 242 articles identified and screened. Inclusion criteria such as publications between the years 2011 to 2019, English papers and articles relevant to the research question were applied resulting in 27 articles remaining which were used for the purpose of the SLR.

The selected papers were analysed and 23 sub-themes related to Industry 4.0 impact on SME business model were extracted. Through a process of axial coding, linkages between the identified sub-themes were constructed [27] and 5 themes were identified as depicted in Table 1. The identified themes were customer; financial; organisational; employee and cost structure.

Table 1. Themes and sub-themes extracted of the impact of Industry 4.0 on the business models of SMEs

Theme	Sub-theme	Literature
Customer	Customer relationships	[1, 3, 7, 9, 12, 22, 28–34]
	Customer satisfaction	[7, 31, 32]
	Customer service and support	[10, 22, 23, 32]
	Customer retention	[22, 35]
	Customer identification	[13, 31, 34]
	Customer understanding	[9, 23, 25, 33, 34, 36]
	Customer interaction	[3, 33]
	Customer segments	[3, 7, 24, 30]
Financial	Revenue model	[1, 7, 22, 24, 33, 34]
	Revenue streams	[1, 7, 13, 22–24, 29, 30, 34, 35]
	Product and service offerings	[1, 7, 22, 24, 25, 28–34, 37]
	Product innovation	[3, 23, 24, 29, 30, 34, 38]
	Increased competition	[1, 9, 23, 31, 32, 35, 37, 38]
Organisation	Organisational structure	[3, 23, 39]
	Organisational culture	[23, 24, 28, 34, 40]
	Business processes and key activities	[22–24, 31, 33, 35, 41]
	Industry partners and business relationships	[1, 3, 7, 22, 24, 25, 28, 30, 34, 36]
Employee	Employee relationships	[3, 9, 33]
	Employee selection and adoption	[3, 7, 9, 23, 28, 32–34, 41]
	Employee skills and training	[3, 22, 23, 28, 32–35]
Cost structure	Capital investments	[7, 10, 42]
	Equipment, machinery and technology	[1, 3, 7, 10, 24, 32, 34]
	Reduced costs and increased productivity	[1, 31]

For each theme identified, all the relevant sub-themes and references are shown in Table 1. Each theme and its sub-themes are discussed in detail in the next section.

4 Analysis and Findings

The purpose of this paper was to define the key impacts of Industry 4.0 on the business models of SMEs. Through the SLR, 23 sub-themes coded to 5 primary themes were identified.

4.1 Theme 1: Customer

The customer theme is comprised of 8 sub-themes and addresses the customer aspect of the SME business model. Customer relationships are the different links and relationships that an SME establishes between itself and its consumer base. Customer segments describe the different groups and types of customers that the business wants to deal with. Another important aspect of the customer theme is the customer identification and customer understanding sub-themes addressing the way in which target customers are identified and understood. Customer understanding also contributes towards customer retention and customer satisfaction.

Table 2. Customer theme frequency

Theme	Sub-theme	Frequency
Customer	Customer relationships	13
	Customer satisfaction	3
	Customer service and support	4
	Customer retention	2
	Customer identification	3
	Customer understanding	6
	Customer interaction	2
	Customer groups	4
	Total	37

The frequency count for the customer theme is 37. Table 2 summarises the number of times each sub-theme in the customer theme is mentioned. The sub-theme which occurred the most throughout the literature was the Customer Relationships theme (13).

4.2 Theme 2: Financial

The financial theme comprises of the revenue model, revenue streams, product and service offering, product innovation and increased competition. Revenue streams refer to the different means for the organisation to capture value and create an income. Industry 4.0 has a major impact on the streams of revenue and therefore has an impact on the revenue model. With industry 4.0, there are more possible models of pricing for example, pay per use or pay per feature. The revenue streams in certain cases can have a direct relationship with the product and service offerings as such that, as a product or service is developed, changed or removed, the revenue stream is affected. However, the relationship is not one-sided; when a revenue stream is changed, removed or developed, the product and service offerings have to adapt to the revenue streams. Product innovation is closely tied to product and service offerings as well as revenue streams. The literature describes product innovation as an important factor in the adoption of industry 4.0 and the organisations success henceforth. Increased competition is centred on competitive advantage and market competition. The way in which market competition is approached and the means to get a competitive advantage is the focus of this sub-theme.

Table 3. Financial theme frequency

Theme	Sub-theme	Frequency
Financial	Revenue model	6
	Revenue streams	10
	Product and service offerings	13
	Product innovation	7
	Increased competition	8
	Total	44

The entire financial theme collated reflected a frequency of 44. Table 3 contains an overview of the financial theme as well as the number of times the sub-themes were mentioned in the literature analysed.

4.3 Theme 3: Organisation

The organisational theme consists of 4 sub-themes addressing the day to day running of the organisation, as well as the structure and layout of the organisation. The industry partners and business relationships sub-theme addresses the links and relationships the organisation with possible key partners, suppliers and any other personnel in the business model. Industry 4.0 brings a change to the way in which the business will maintain relationships with key partners, competition and other relationships surrounding the organisation. The relationships upheld with partners and business personnel is an important part of the business model and plays a role in the intended success and functionality of the organisation. Business processes and key activities address how tasks are set out and completed. It also entails the everyday operations and tasks of the organisation and the ways in which they are completed. The business processes and key activities also affect the structure and culture of the organisation. The organisational structure and culture can affect the selection and adoption of employees as well as employee training and skills.

Table 4. Organisation theme frequency

Theme	Sub-theme	Frequency
Organisation	Organisational structure	3
	Organisational culture	5
	Business processes and key activities	7
	Industry partners and business relationships	10
	Total	**26**

The organisational aspect including all sub-themes was mentioned a total of 26 times through the literature reviewed. Table 4 contains a summary of the frequency of the organisational theme.

4.4 Theme 4: Employee

The SME may proceed with the adoption of Industry 4.0 opportunities, but in order to do so, the employees need to be prepared and trained for this. There are 3 sub-themes that were identified within the employee theme. Employee skills and training, employee relationships; employee selection and adoption. Employee skills and training discusses the aspects of the core competencies and minimum requirements required by the employees of the organisation. With Industry 4.0, the entire dynamic and role of the workforce are altered. The organisation requires more skilled workers to form part of the workforce. The literature suggests that there would be a predicted staff reduction in the lower and middle qualified workers. It is also apparent that the organisations need for more skilled workers would either require a new selection of staff or extensive training.

The dynamics of the relationship between employee and employer will also be impacted due to the implementation of Industry 4.0 technologies - the employee relationship aspect evaluates and discusses the change in links and relationships within the SMEs staff. The literature further suggests that there will be a major impact on the relationships surrounding the organisation e.g. with suppliers or vendors.

The employee theme is mentioned a total of 20 times in the analysed literature. Table 5 contains a summarized version showing the number of times the employee theme and sub-themes we addressed in the literature found.

Table 5. Employee theme frequency

Theme	Sub-theme	Frequency
Employee	Employee relationships	3
	Employee selection and adoption	9
	Employee skills and training	8
	Total	**20**

4.5 Cost Structure

The cost structure entails the financial and monetary impacts of the adoption of Industry 4.0 on the organisation. During the initial phases of the implementation of Industry 4.0, there is a requirement for larger capital expenditure as well as newer equipment and machinery. Industry 4.0 requires newer technologies and equipment, machinery and different types of technologies to perform the required functions. They are usually costly and was an aspect clearly identified from the SLR dataset. Capital investments, while they are mainly comprised of equipment, machinery and different technologies, they also include employee training and potentially new warehousing.

The third sub-theme within the cost structure theme dealt with reduced costs and increased productivity. In the literature, there is a consensus view that Industry 4.0 will bring about reduced costs in the long term and a more efficient and effective method of production, thereby increasing the overall productivity of the organisation. This will have a relationship with the customer offerings, such that products can be produced faster and with better quality than the conventional means. This does pave the way for a larger customer base as well as a new customer base. There is also agreement that industry 4.0 will allow for future growth.

Table 6. Cost structure theme frequency

Theme	Sub-theme	Frequency
Cost Structure	Capital investments	3
	Equipment, machinery and technology	7
	Reduced costs and increased productivity	2
	Total	**12**

The cost structure theme is a key aspect of implementing and utilising Industry 4.0 and is mentioned in the literature 12 times. Table 6 contains a summary of the frequency of the relevant sub-themes.

5 Discussion

Figure 1 summarises the top 5 themes which were identified in the dataset. From the analysis of themes and sub-themes based on frequency count (Sect. 4), the top 5 sub-themes may be identified. The sub-themes which presented itself the most was the Product and Service offerings theme and the Customer Relationships theme (13 times each, 48.14% each). Capital investments in equipment, machinery and technology, as well as Revenue Streams and Industry Partners and Business relationships presented 10 time each and related to 37.03% each of the total sub-themes identified. These themes will be considered the key elements and themes to be affected by Industry 4.0 for the purpose of this study.

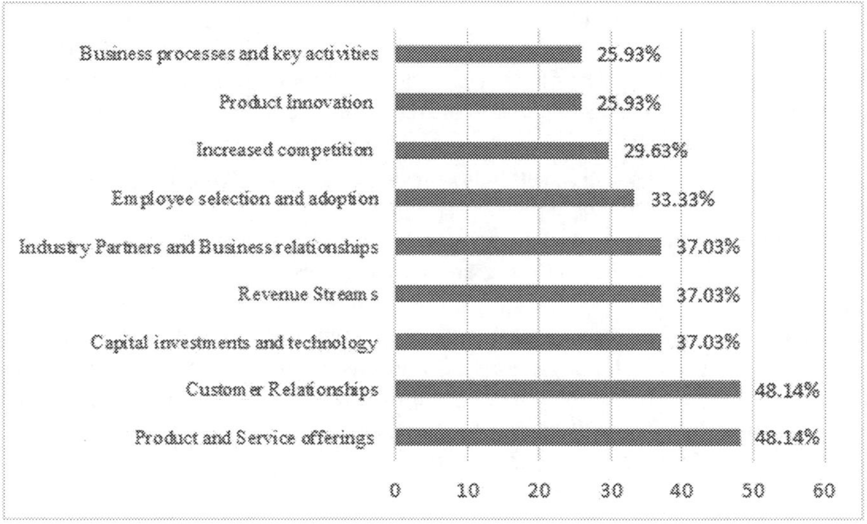

Fig. 1. Top 5 business model impact sub-theme frequency

In order to report the SLR findings, the business model definition of Clauss [16] consisting of 3 aspects namely value creation, value proposition and value capture were used to map the themes and sub-themes to Fig. 2 diagrammatically represents the business model elements to which each theme and sub-theme belong to.

The value creation element consists of three themes; employee, organisation and cost structure. The aspects of the organisation can have a major impact on employees and the sub-themes within the employee aspect. Within the value proposition element, two themes were mapped: Financial and Customer. The most mentioned themes (Fig. 1) are the Customer Relationships theme and the Product and Service offering, both of which fall within the value offer element. Finally, the value capture element contains 3 themes: Financial, Customer and Cost Structure. It must be noted that Cost Structure, Financial and Customer had to be mapped at a sub-theme level as some sub-themes related to different business model elements.

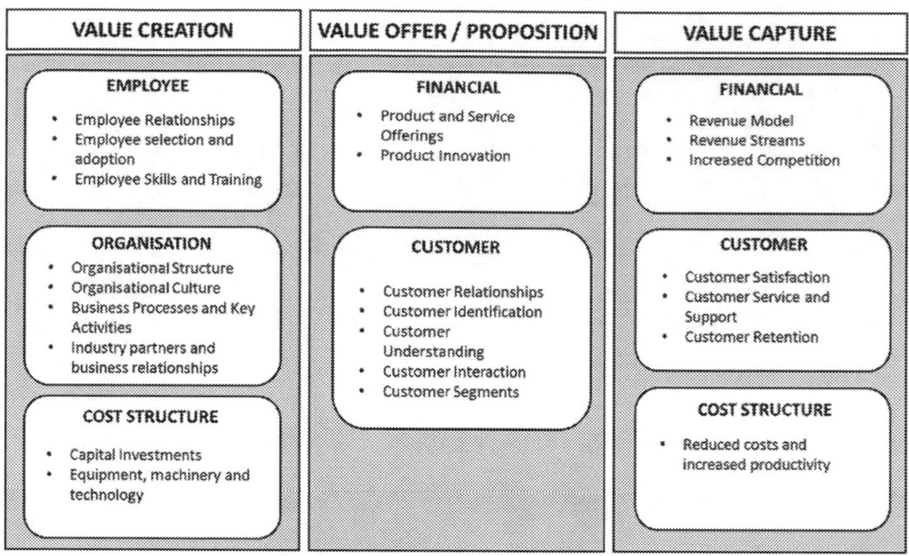

Fig. 2. Industry 4.0 business model impacts on SMEs

6 Conclusion

Industry 4.0 can create many opportunities for not only larger organisations, but for SMEs as well. However, for the technology of industry 4.0 to create value for the SME, the technology needs to be used in alignment with the business model. In order to consider the impact of Industry 4.0 on the business models of SMEs, we conducted an SLR to identify business model impacts and identified 5 themes and 23 sub-themes. In order to report the business model impacts, the themes and sub-themes were related the components of a business model as defined by Clauss [16]: value creation, value proposition and value capture. By enabling SMEs to consider business model impact and opportunity holistically, they may be able to leverage the technology platforms in Industry 4.0 towards business value creation and economic sustainability.

The next step in terms of this research study is to test the Industry 4.0 business model impacts on SMEs in practice and collect data regarding the actual experiences from SMEs compared to our research findings.

References

1. Safar, L., et al.: Concept of SME business model for industry 4.0 environment. TEM J. **7**(3), 626 (2018)
2. Robu, M.: The dynamic and importance of SMEs in economy. USV Ann. Econ. Public Adm. **13**(1(17)), 84–89 (2013)
3. Müller, J.M., Buliga, O., Voigt, K.-I.: Fortune favors the prepared: how SMEs approach business model innovations in Industry 4.0. Technol. Forecast. Soc. Change **132**, 2–17 (2018)
4. Wahl, M.: Strategic factor analysis for industry 4.0. J. Secur. Sustain. Issues **5**(2), 242–247 (2015)

5. Gambardella, A., McGahan, A.M.: Business-model innovation: general purpose technologies and their implications for industry structure. Long Range Plan. **43**(2–3), 262–271 (2010)
6. Yoon, D.: What we need to prepare for the fourth industrial revolution. Healthc. Inf. Res. **23**(2), 75–76 (2017)
7. Müller, J.M.: Business model innovation in small-and medium-sized enterprises: strategies for industry 4.0 providers and users. J. Manuf. Technol. Manage. **15**(1), 1127–1142 (2019)
8. Hansen, D.G., Malik, A.A., Bilberg, A.: Generic challenges and automation solutions in manufacturing SMEs. In: DAAAM International, 1161–1169 (2017)
9. Kiel, D., et al.: Sustainable industrial value creation: benefits and challenges of industry 4.0. Int. J. Innov. Manage. **21**(08), 1740015 (2017)
10. Schröder, C.: The Challenges of Industry 4.0 for Small and Medium-Sized Enterprises. Friedrich-Ebert-Stiftung, Bonn, Germany (2016)
11. Hummel, E., et al.: Business models for collaborative research. Res. Technol. Manage. **53**(6), 51 (2010)
12. Baden-Fuller, C., Mangematin, V.: Business models and modelling business models. Adv. Strateg. Manage. **33**, xi-xxii (2015)
13. Baden-Fuller, C., Haefliger, S.: Business models and technological innovation. Long Range Plan. **46**(6), 419–426 (2013)
14. Da Silva, C.M., Trkman, P.: Business model: what it is and what it is not. Long Range Plan. **47**(6), 379–389 (2014)
15. Joan, M.: Why Business Models Matter (2002)
16. Clauss, T.: Measuring business model innovation: conceptualization, scale development, and proof of performance. R&D Manage. **47**(3), 385–403 (2017)
17. Mueller, J.M., Daeschle, S.: Business model innovation of industry 4.0 solution providers towards customer process innovation. Processes **6**(12), 260 (2018)
18. Chapman, P., et al.: Building internet capabilities in SMEs. Logist. Inf. Manag. **13**(6), 353–361 (2000)
19. Levy, M., Powell, P., SME internet adoption: towards a transporter model. In: BLED 2002 Proceedings, p. 38 (2002)
20. Luff, P.: The 4th industrial revolution and SMEs in Malaysia and Japan: some economic, social and ethical considerations. Reitaku Int. J. Econ. Stud. **25**, 25–48 (2017)
21. Wischmann, S., Wangler, L., Botthof, A.: Industrie 4.0 Volks-und betriebswirtschaftliche Faktoren für den Standort Deutschland. Bundesministerium für Wirtschaft und Energie **3**, 21 (2015)
22. Arnold, C., Kiel, D., Voigt, K.: Innovative business models for the industrial internet of things. BHM Berg-und Hüttenmännische Monatshefte **162**(9), 371–381 (2017)
23. Roblek, V., Meško, M., Krapež, A.: A complex view of industry 4.0. Sage Open **6**(2), 2158244016653987 (2016)
24. Prause, G.: Sustainable business models and structures for industry 4.0. J. Secur. Sustain. Issues **5**(2), 159–169 (2015)
25. De Maeyer, C., Bonne, K.: Entrepreneurship 3.0: tools to support new and young companies with their business models. J. Positive Manage. **6**(3), 3–15 (2015)
26. Kitchenham, B.: Procedures for performing systematic reviews. Keele, UK, Keele Univ. **2004**(33), 1–26 (2004)
27. Leedy, P.D., Ormrod, J.E.: Practical Research: Planning and Design, 67 (2010)
28. Mittal, S., et al.: A critical review of smart manufacturing & Industry 4.0 maturity models: implications for small and medium-sized enterprises (SMEs). J. Manufact. Syst. **49**, 194–214 (2018)
29. Ibarra, D., Ganzarain, J., Igartua, J.I.: Business model innovation through Industry 4.0: a review. Procedia Manuf. **22**, 4–10 (2018)

30. Maffei, A., Grahn, S., Nuur, C.: Characterization of the impact of digitalization on the adoption of sustainable business models in manufacturing. Procedia CIRP **81**, 765–770 (2019)
31. Gerlitz, L.: Design management as a domain of smart and sustainable enterprise: business modelling for innovation and smart growth in industry 4.0. Entrepreneurship Sustain. Issues **3**(3), 244–268 (2016)
32. Sommer, L.: Industrial revolution-industry 4.0: are German manufacturing SMEs the first victims of this revolution? J. Ind. Eng. Manage. **8**(5), 1512–1532 (2015)
33. Sanders, A., Elangeswaran, C., Wulfsberg, J.P.: Industry 4.0 implies lean manufacturing: research activities in industry 4.0 function as enablers for lean manufacturing. J. Ind. Eng. Manage. (JIEM) **9**(3), 811–833 (2016)
34. Kiel, D., Arnold, C., Voigt, K.-I.: The influence of the industrial Internet of Things on business models of established manufacturing companies – a business level perspective. Technovation **68**, 4–19 (2017)
35. Müller, J.M., Voigt, K.-I.: Sustainable industrial value creation in SMEs: a comparison between industry 4.0 and Made in China 2025. Int. J. Precis. Eng. Manuf.-Green Technol. **5**(5), 659–670 (2018)
36. Liu, K., Zhong, P., Zeng, Q., Li, D., Li, S.: Application modes of cloud manufacturing and program analysis. J. Mech. Sci. Technol. **31**(1), 157–164 (2017). https://doi.org/10.1007/s12206-016-1215-1
37. Glova, J., Sabol, T., Vajda, V.: Business models for the Internet of Things environment. Procedia Econ. Finan. **15**, 1122–1129 (2014)
38. Bouwman, H., de Reuver, M., Nikou, S.: The impact of digitalization on business models: how IT artefacts, social media, and big data force firms to innovate their business model. Int. Telecommun. Soc. (ITS) (2017)
39. Umrani, A.I., Johl, S.K.: How different ownership structures perform in industry 4.0: a case of Malaysian manufacturing SMEs. In: EDP Sciences, vol. 56, p. 04003 (2018)
40. Radanliev, P., et al.: The Industrial Internet-of-Things in the Industry 4.0 supply chains of small and medium sized enterprises. University of Oxford (2019)
41. Singh, D.: Industry 4.0 – 4th rising industrial revolution in manufacturing industries and its impact on employability and existing education system. Pramana Res. J. **8**(11), 161–169 (2018)
42. Zhang, X., Ming, X., Liu, Z., Qu, Y., Yin, D.: An overall framework and subsystems for smart manufacturing integrated system (SMIS) from multi-layers based on multi-perspectives. Int. J. Adv. Manuf. Technol. **103**(1–4), 703–722 (2019). https://doi.org/10.1007/s00170-019-03593-6

Digital Technologies and Organisational Capabilities

BIM as a Boundary Object in Construction Projects: A Knowledge-as-Practice Perspective

Jing Wang(✉), Pamela Y. Abbott, and Efpraxia D. Zamani

University of Sheffield, Sheffield S10 2TN, UK
{Jwang150,p.y.abbott,e.zamani}@sheffield.ac.uk

Abstract. Collaboration in a construction project faces challenges of knowledge sharing among different team members across organisational and disciplinary boundaries. As an example of ICT innovation in the Architecture, Engineering and Construction (AEC) industry, Building Information Modelling (BIM) is thought to play a boundary object role in collaboration. The literature, however, is less clear on how BIM technology as a boundary object is used for knowledge sharing in construction projects. This paper conceptualises BIM technology as a boundary object for collaboration in a construction project from a knowledge-as-practice perspective. The conceptual framework explains how BIM technology as tools and artefacts become boundary objects-in-use in a construction project collaboration. The paper demonstrates how this can further contribute to our understanding of knowledge sharing in construction projects as a boundary spanning practice among different backgrounds. As success within an increasingly digitalised society depends on ICT-based collaborations of diverse teams and professionals, a deeper understanding regarding such boundary objects-in-use can be particularly useful.

Keywords: Building Information Modelling (BIM) technology · Boundary objects · Knowledge

1 Introduction

Building Information Modelling (BIM) is a set of digital tools and work process in construction projects for presenting the comprehensive building information through 3D digital models and databases across organisations and disciplines in the Architecture, Engineering and Construction (AEC) industry. This paper will argue that BIM can play the role of a boundary object in construction projects. Boundary objects are considered to be the device to facilitate the knowledge sharing among different fields. However, the project-based type work organisation in a construction project embodied in the temporary teams involves different parties increase the difficulty and challenge for knowledge

Published by Springer Nature Switzerland AG 2021
D. Dennehy et al. (Eds.): I3E 2021, LNCS 12896, pp. 371–382, 2021.
https://doi.org/10.1007/978-3-030-85447-8_32

sharing [1], making collaboration more challenging and problematic. There is thus fertile ground to explore effective collaboration thanks to the prevalence of project-based work from the AEC industry, which comprise members from multiple disciplines and organisations. Therefore, with the introduction of BIM in the AEC industry, there is an increased interest in the organisation of work practices for sharing knowledge in a construction project among team members from different organisations and disciplines [2–4].

BIM, regarded as a promising digital innovation, and increasingly used in innovative construction projects within the AEC industry, is thought to integrate different disciplines and organisations for better collaboration. Due to diverse professional backgrounds, understanding other team members' work often results in challenges and conflicts [2]. It is thus important to consider how to facilitate effective knowledge sharing for problem-solving and decision-making. Recent research calls for attention to studying BIM as a boundary object in construction project collaborations [5–8]. There is limited research exploring how the components of BIM technology can be conceptualised as boundary objects in a construction project, especially when knowledge sharing among professions is considered.

To provide a better understanding of BIM technology as a boundary object in a construction project, this paper proposes a conceptual framework to theorise the BIM components as boundary objects-in-use by identifying the role of BIM technology for collaboration among construction project team professionals. This is achieved, first, by determining the nature and characteristics of knowledge in the AEC industry and BIM technology as boundary objects through a literature review. Subsequently, we identify the elements of BIM technology in a construction project and determine the relationship between these concepts and boundary objects. Finally, we discuss the potential contribution this conceptual framing can make to the study of BIM as a boundary object and its role in boundary work around shaping collaborative practice in construction projects.

2 Literature Review

2.1 Knowledge-as-Practice Perspective in the Architecture, Engineering and Construction (AEC) Industry

Perspectives of Knowledge. Continuous debates in the literature about knowledge among scholars are taken from different perspectives. Most can be divided into either a knowledge-as-possessed-asset perspective or a knowledge-as-practice perspective. While the two perspectives come from different worldviews, Cook and Brown [9] suggest that possessed knowledge can be regarded as a tool to serve knowing as a process (i.e., part of action). From the perspective of knowledge as an ongoing process, Orlikowski [10] states that knowledge is an ongoing action embodied in what actors do every day to get their work done. Similarly, in other forms of work such as project-based organisational forms, e.g., in product development projects, Carlile's view [11] on knowledge also supports this perspective, i.e., that knowledge is not a static entity or stable disposition, but an ongoing and dynamic production among actors in innovative settings.

Knowledge in the AEC Industry and Construction Project. A substantial amount of knowledge is involved in the AEC industry due to the many disciplines and organisations that contribute to different functions throughout the lifecycle of the same construction project. In the construction project collaborative process, knowledge can be shared through the interaction of different objects worlds [2], which include physical artefacts and tools as well as discipline-specific guidelines and associated practices. The transformation of different sharing pathways of explicit knowledge and tacit knowledge also indicates that knowledge and practice are inseparable [2]. Woo et al. [12] claim that shared knowledge in the construction project relies more on the AEC professions possessing tacit knowledge and their experience of related projects with explicit knowledge providing a supporting role and, in a project, knowledge is dynamic depending on problem-solving and the tasks to be performed. For the AEC industry, therefore, knowledge can be seen as a tool to facilitate a dynamic knowing process addressing problems to improve project progress. That means, therefore, in the ongoing construction project process, knowledge can be shared effectively when it can be used to achieve the practical targets and tasks in the actors' practice. In the construction project, Rezgui [15] classifies knowledge in the construction domain to include domain knowledge, organisational knowledge and project knowledge. Domain knowledge forms the overall information context, including administrative information, standards, technical rules and product databases. Organisational knowledge is company-specific, including personal skills, project experience of employees and cross-organisational knowledge. Project knowledge is the potential for usable knowledge created by interaction, including project records, solutions and memory of processes.

Using the Knowledge-as-Practice Perspective in Construction Projects. Knowing calls for an epistemology of practice, where practice implies doing the real work itself. Practice, here, refers to "action informed by meaning drawn from a particular group context" [9]. We understand knowing as the practice or 'doing' of actions using knowledge to seek a solution to a problem. To shed light on knowing in practice, Carlile's pragmatic view [11] suggests knowledge is localised, embedded, and invested in practice articulated from experience and know-how. Similar to this perspective, Ryle [14] proposes that know-how can be described as when a person knows how to do and that knowledge is manifested in their practice/action rather than in their statement.

Furthermore, the know-how practice/actions should be reasonable under the required principles of their work setting for performing their tasks. With respect to collaborative teams in the AEC industry, Majchrzak, Malhotra, and John [15] propose collaboration know-how in teams to refer to knowledge about how to communicate and integrate ideas with others and how to coordinate others' work and actions in the team. In light of the knowledge-as-practice perspective in collaboration within a construction project, digital technology also affects the knowing process among different functions. It is also suggested that knowledge-as-practice is embedded in the dynamics between physical interaction and ICT-related design practice in a construction project [2]. To apply the knowledge-as-practice perspective in a construction project, we need to draw on what actors in the construction project need to know and what actors are doing with what they need to know in practice.

2.2 Boundary Objects and Building Information Modelling (BIM)

The Nature and Characteristics of Boundary Objects. In the knowledge sharing process, knowledge is generally shared among different fields of practice and across boundaries. Boundaries delimit fields and arise from knowledge differences of different fields [16]. The objects used to facilitate the association between functions and across boundaries are defined as boundary objects that "are plastic enough to adapt to local needs and constraints of the several parties employing them, yet robust enough to maintain a common identity across sites" [17]. Star [18] proposes three components of boundary objects: interpretive flexibility; the structure of informatics and work process needs and arrangements; and, finally, the dynamic between ill-structured and more tailored uses of the objects. Boundary objects are created or appear with several characteristics, participants share common goals but have different purposes and the shared goals are performed by each participant in different ways [17]; "boundary objects are at once temporal, based in action, subject to reflection and local tailoring" [18]. Based on different forms of boundary objects (repositories, ideal type, coincident boundaries and standardised forms) proposed by Star and Griesemer [17], Carlile [11] propose three approaches (i.e., transferring, translation, and transformation) that require capabilities to transfer and manage knowledge across syntactic, semantic and pragmatic boundaries. However, boundary objects might not be used to span boundaries as designated. Boundary objects are not always stable but are subject to change as part of actors' ongoing practice, such dynamic action leading to the emergence of a joint field of practice [19]. In knowledge sharing, artefacts can be transformed from a common semantic meaning to a common pragmatic meaning for different functions involved in a joint field of practice thus leading to their reframing as boundary objects-in-use [19]. Boundary objects-in-use, they argue, are locally useful (incorporated into the joint practice) and have a common identity (recognisable across fields). Within the AEC industry, boundary objects may be devices that improve collaboration between different professions. Examples include timelines, building models, prototypes and sketches [20].

Building Information Modelling (BIM). BIM involves a set of digital modelling technologies used throughout a construction project's lifecycle to create, store, share, and reuse the integrated models of building information, associating different organisations and disciplines together. BIM-related collaboration entails generating, presenting and sharing information among various actors and project stakeholders [5]. From a boundary object perspective, BIM artefacts can be seen as potentially integrating knowledge from actors across different fields for problem-solving and decision-making during the project lifecycle. However, when actors possess knowledge from different backgrounds, Neff et al. [6] argue that the BIM digital models cannot actually work as boundary objects due to their failure to provide enough interpretative flexibility in communication. That means BIM artefacts may have design constraints that limit their ability to enable transference, translation or transformation of knowledge across boundaries. The implication is that even if BIM artefacts are thought to be designated boundary objects, their potential for knowledge sharing may only become evident as boundary objects-in-use [19, 21]. The interplay between BIM technology and BIM-enabled processes is inseparable, and BIM artefacts as boundary objects can influence collaboration and integration of activities in project teams in a structurational way, i.e., both in terms of the affordances of the technology and the way individual actors share knowledge and adjust their practices [5].

3 Conceptual Framing

BIM is regarded as the interplay of the BIM-enabled processes and BIM technology [5]. BIM technology includes BIM tools and BIM artefacts [7]. From a traditional software-view, BIM technology focuses on the relevant BIM tools including BIM-related hardware, software, and networks that help actors complete their work and achieve their goals [21]. BIM artefacts fall into five categories based on the project needs, i.e., digital models, 2D documents, specialised sessions, BIM execution protocols and decision-making instruments [22]. BIM tools and BIM artefacts are potential sources of boundary objects to achieve the collaboration needs of a construction project. The boundary objects used in a construction project consists of four types, including shared database, standardised format, property information representations and responsibility division. The proposed conceptual framework (Fig. 1) consists of the main components of BIM technology and their relationship to boundary objects, within the context of AEC industry construction projects. Each part is further delineated below.

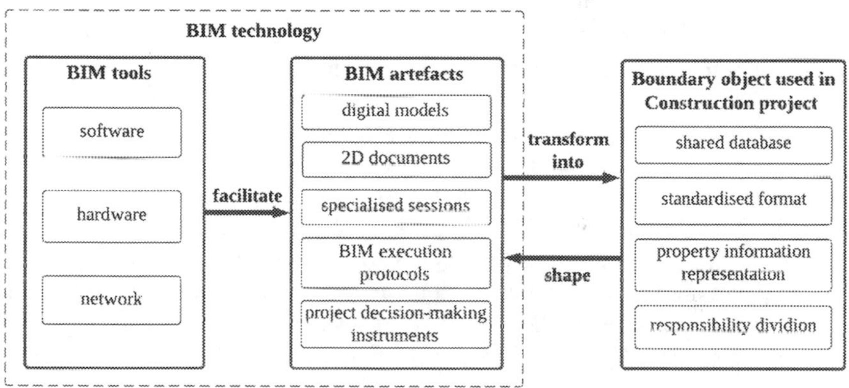

Fig. 1. The conceptual framework of the relationship between BIM technology and boundary objects in construction projects.

3.1 BIM Tools and BIM Artefacts

BIM technology consists of BIM tools and BIM artefacts. In construction projects, professionals produce BIM artefacts by engaging BIM tools through BIM-related software, hardware and networks. In this process, they contribute their knowledge from their professional background and experience from their work practice. For example, when architects create digital models of their ideas and visions for a project, they augment them with the documents that carry and communicate information from and to different stakeholders (such as the budgeting document from owners), forming together the contents of a shared database, which in turn becomes the basis for negotiating the design of the building. So the BIM tools engage with the professional's practice in producing the BIM artefacts. Furthermore, BIM technology in the construction project has multifaceted functions represented in the produced BIM artefacts in the lifecycle of a construction project, such as model integration and simulation. Digital models, i.e., 3D building models, are produced by different disciplines through diverse BIM software and other compatible tools. Procedural documents include 2D drawings and Gantt charts. Specialised sessions include clash detection and kick-off [5]; specialised sessions are for professionals who have different knowledge backgrounds to create a joint field of practice and deal with conflicts of digital information with each one specialised in their own fields providing professional solutions. BIM executive protocols include explicit conventional information to create BIM deliverables. Project decision-making instruments refer to the generated guidance for making decisions and progressing the project. Professional use of BIM tools to create, use and maintain BIM artefacts is embodied in BIM-enabled processes as part of the lifecycle of a construction project. Boundary objects need to represent the abstraction of construction management data in support of the use of an actor's tacit knowledge [23].

3.2 Boundary Objects Used in the Construction Project

From current research on the nature of boundary objects, it is evident that boundary objects functioning effectively in practice require the emergence of a joint field that embodies common meanings and values from different professions [18, 19]. In a construction project, BIM artefacts do not necessarily always become boundary objects even though they are often designated as able to bridge knowledge boundaries between the various professions [2]. When the tensions arising between the different professions' work practices lead to the recognition of growing problems, the BIM artefacts should perform roles with the effects of establishing the common language to transfer knowledge in their daily tasks and negotiation, helping to create the shared understanding in the collaboration, and enabling them to work together to develop the shared goals and creates new knowledge. These artefacts transform into the boundary object-in-use with both having the capacity of functioning effectively and providing the potential to facilitate the negotiation between different perspectives [11, 24]. Boundary Objects Used in the Construction Project.

From existing research, generic types of boundary objects used in projects include repositories, standardised forms and methods, objects and models, and the map of boundaries [7]. The boundary objects influence the collaborative activities in a construction project in four aspects, i.e., searching and delivering information in the project; providing adaptable and universal elements to the teams it serves; bridging team members through creating balanced discussion and coordination, and clarifying the roles and responsibilities of project members [25]. Considering these effective roles in the construction project, boundary objects are used as shared databases, standardised formats, property information representations and responsibility divisions, respectively. Mapping BIM artefacts to generic types of boundary objects in construction projects shared databases can be seen as repositories that different professionals can access in their practice. For projects in the AEC industry, actors need to acquire and access both product knowledge and process knowledge through a shared lessons-learned database [26]. Similarly, standardised forms would refer to BIM artefacts that share a common language among professionals. This standardised information is crucial for communication among different specialisms in sharing information and knowledge, especially for standardising object models of buildings so that actors' knowledge of the project can be well-defined and shared through the modelling process [27]. Property information representation refers to types of objects and models in construction projects that satisfy the needs of professions in visualising building information to share their knowledge [23]. Responsibility division boundary objects are related to the map of boundaries. Through the demarcation of boundaries, professionals can identify their knowledge sharing. Responsibility division includes the concerns of actors' roles, duties and ways of working among professions to share knowledge in practice. Boundary objects, especially ICT-related boundary objects can depict and mediate this interaction among actors [28, 29].

The boundary objects-in-use also shape the BIM artefacts through the boundary process. Boundary objects-in-use can facilitate transformational learning since managing artefacts is not a static process in the project [7]. For example, BIM models as modifiable digital artefacts are also regarded as intermediary objects which are involved in the cycle of collaborative design [30]. In addition, the boundary objects-in-use can also shape the further BIM artefacts creating process (such as detailed design) through play a role of the object in the process (see Fig. 1). For example, the project ideas of the main structure from the early stage database might influence the latter detailed design in the fitting-out stage.

4 Discussion

BIM as an information system involves the interplay of BIM technology and BIM-enabled processes among professionals [5]. The previous section established a conceptual framework of the relationship between BIM technology and boundary objects by identifying the main BIM artefacts that can be regarded as boundary objects in construction projects and the main aspects of BIM tools that structure BIM artefacts. It illustrates the main types of boundary objects used in a construction project from the knowledge as practice view among AEC professionals. This conceptual framework provides some direction for further study on how BIM technology as a boundary object affects BIM-enabled processes.

According to Lindberg's [31] research, boundaries are performed in practice in an iterative and recursive way through boundary work. For BIM-enabled processes, interactions between professions are not always synchronised due to the characteristics of long-term modelling and frequent changes of needs or requirements from various parties. These processes share project information across different fields of practice or functions to integrate building information. Professionals work together to share knowledge for problem-solving and decision-making in the project. As new practices emerge, this shapes new boundaries, which in turn create opportunities for further new practices. This results in boundary work, i.e. a recursive relationship between practice and boundary and the iterative modelling process [31]. The inside of a boundary is composed of practice within the same professions, such as work based on documents, protocols and ideas of the profession. These are reflected on the outcomes directly (rather than the communication). The knowing process is more about explicit to explicit (e.g. sorting the records of on-site material usage) or tacit to explicit (e.g. architecture modelling). The difference, dependency and novelty can be manifested in how professions use relevant documents and protocols to achieve their tasks in their common fields. The inter-boundary interaction is more about tacit to tacit (e.g. sharing project experience), explicit to tacit (e.g. learning from the discussion), the difference, dependency and novelty can be explicated through conflicts and negotiation for decision-making. Therefore, the boundary work involved in BIM-enabled processes can be seen from two perspectives: work practice inside the boundaries of the profession (intra-boundary work) and work practice outside the boundaries of the profession (inter-boundary work).

4.1 BIM Artefacts as Boundary Objects Within Professions and Professional's Know-How Practice – Intra-boundary Work

Within a profession's boundaries, actors' work practices include coordination and synchronisation in the same professions, such as individuals creating models according to the needs and requirements of other parties or policies. BIM artefacts can be created, used or delivered under contracts and relevant instructions between agents [5]. Therefore, when actors use BIM tools to complete their professional work or achieve a goal, their know-how practice is influenced by the requirements and needs of other parties via policies and contracts. Know-how practice can also be seen as the actor's process of completing their work from 'objects' (the artefacts that individuals work with) to 'ends' (the outcomes that substantiate the successful creating, measuring and manipulating of the objects) [11]. In the light of the process from 'objects' to 'ends' in the lifecycle of a construction project, BIM is seen as playing a role in know-how practice [2], such as the BIM model being used as a boundary object and BIM-related software helping actors to complete their work.

Know-how practice is thus a form of collaborative work in construction projects. Knowledge sharing occurs through know-how practice among individuals in construction projects. It is expected that individuals' knowledge will be transferred and shared when collaborating with others through interaction and boundary objects. Neff [6] suggests, though, that digital objects have less interpretative flexibility, leading to nominated boundary objects failing to bridge boundaries effectively. This result also verifies the proposition from existing research [19] that not all boundary objects can actually play the boundary objects-in-use role. In addition, change always happens in a construction project so that BIM artefacts designated as boundary objects might not achieve the function of boundary-object-in-use. Thus, for BIM artefacts to become boundary objects-in-use may require BIM artefacts to encompass know-how practice from 'objects' to ends. For example, BIM modellers may integrate BIM models from different design disciplines into a whole in order to detect design issues. There are some discussion on the intra-professional relation [32] and various forms of work occur at the intra-professional level [33]. Thus far, however, only few studies have considered how boundary objects play a role in the intra-boundary work, particularly regarding BIM artefacts used as boundary objects in construction projects. This work provide a insight to explore how BIM artefacts designated as boundary objects involved in intra-boundary work practice emerge as boundary objects-in-use and how professionals shape know-how practice with BIM in a project.

4.2 BIM Artefacts as Boundary Objects in Knowledge Sharing Practice Between Professionals – Inter-boundary Work

Representing knowledge, learning difference and dependency at knowledge boundaries and jointly transforming current knowledge into a common field should be achievable through boundary objects [11, 19]. Interactions among actors who have different professional backgrounds in a construction project always involve knowledge embedded in practice. Work practices outside of professional boundaries, i.e., inter-boundary interaction, includes synchronised communication and negotiation with other professions. Therefore, it is significant and worthwhile to explore how the dynamic relationship between practice and the boundary is influenced by BIM artefacts, as boundary objects. Few studies explore how boundary objects are represented, understood or used in boundary work across knowledge boundaries in the AEC industry. Earlier studies have shown how the establishment of digital artefacts' value and local usefulness can situate them as boundary objects in the effective knowledge boundary spanning [4, 31]. The same can be explored in the context of BIM artefacts' use in effective knowledge boundary spanning.

Current research focuses less on BIM-enabled processes, especially the knowledge sharing aspects [34]; thus it is important to establish the relationship between BIM-enabled processes, knowledge sharing, knowledge boundaries and collaborative practice [35]. The proposed conceptual framework provides a foundation to study BIM as a boundary object involved in digital collaboration in the context of a BIM-enabled project from the knowledge-as-practice perspective. BIM artefacts as boundary objects can play a role in the boundary work occurring at knowledge boundaries between professions. Effective boundary objects should provide the transferring, translating and transforming capacities to approach different boundaries [11]. In addition, as Levina and Vasst [19] argue, when new joint fields of practice emerge that incorporate a common meaning from, say the negotiation related to problem-solving, boundary objects may have a transformative effect to guide in making decisions. Thus, through exploring the relationship between BIM and boundary objects, it enhances the understanding of the capacity of BIM as a boundary object to navigate and shape knowledge boundaries between different fields of practice in a construction project and the construction of a new collaborative practice.

5 Conclusion

Recent research on BIM collaboration focuses more on managing boundaries through discussing the influence of BIM as a boundary object in the collaboration [5, 7, 29], but less on how BIM technology is regarded as a boundary object. For future empirical research work, the conceptual framework developed in this paper helps explore BIM-enabled construction projects in practice. At the project level, the framework can explore how BIM influences knowledge boundary work, and knowledge sharing, thus helping project managers consider BIM implementation and its influence on work practice. Furthermore, managers can improve their competence by considering BIM-related training and education at the organisational level. These studies can also help institutions interpret BIM-related instructions and protocols at the industry level. Overall, this work brings to the fore insights regarding BIM as a boundary object among team members from different professional backgrounds, but the lack of the guideline on how to conduct empirical research or design science research is the limitation of this work.

This paper contributes to knowledge by exploring the relationship between BIM technology and boundary objects in a construction project. The framework contributes to addressing the gap around how BIM artefacts as boundary objects involved in the boundary work involving collaborative practices and how BIM artefacts as boundary objects can establish know-how practice from 'objects' to 'ends' in a construction project. Having said that, the study's findings are particularly pertinent for our increasingly digitalised society. Focusing on boundary work and collaborative practices, the study's arguments can be extrapolated to other settings where project success depends on the collaboration of diverse team members of different backgrounds and the use of boundary objects, as for example distributed teams assembled on an ad hoc basis for a software or research project.

References

1. Dave, B., Koskela, L.: Collaborative knowledge management—a construction case study. Autom. Constr. **18**, 894–902 (2009). https://doi.org/10.1016/j.autcon.2009.03.015
2. Berente, N., Baxter, R., Lyytinen, K.: Dynamics of inter-organisational knowledge creation and information technology use across object worlds: the case of an innovative construction project. Constr. Manage. Econ. **28**, 569–588 (2010). https://doi.org/10.1080/01446193.2010.489926
3. Doolin, B., McLeod, L.: Sociomateriality and boundary objects in information systems development. Eur. J. Inf. Syst. **21**, 570–586 (2012). https://doi.org/10.1057/ejis.2012.20
4. Hsu, J.S.-C., Chu, T.-H., Lin, T.-C., Lo, C.-F.: Coping knowledge boundaries between information system and business disciplines: an intellectual capital perspective. Inf. Manage. **51**, 283–295 (2014). https://doi.org/10.1016/j.im.2013.12.005
5. Papadonikolaki, E., van Oel, C., Kagioglou, M.: Organising and Managing boundaries: a structurational view of collaboration with Building Information Modelling (BIM). Int. J. Project Manage. **37**, 378–394 (2019). https://doi.org/10.1016/j.ijproman.2019.01.010
6. Neff, G., Fiore-Silfvast, B., Dossick, C.S.: A case study of the failure of digital communication to cross knowledge boundaries in virtual construction. Inf. Commun. Soc. **13**, 556–573 (2010). https://doi.org/10.1080/13691181003645970
7. Forgues, D., Koskela, L.J., Lejeune, A.: Information technology as boundary object for transformational learning. J. Inf. Technol. Constr. **14**, 48–58 (2009)
8. Merschbrock, C., Munkvold, B.E.: A Research Review on Building Information Modeling in Construction—An Area Ripe for IS Research. CAIS **31** (2012). https://doi.org/10.17705/1CAIS.03110
9. Cook, S.D.N., Brown, J.S.: Bridging epistemologies: the generative dance between organizational knowledge and organizational knowing. Organ. Sci. **10**, 381–400 (1999). https://doi.org/10.1287/orsc.10.4.381
10. Orlikowski, W.J.: Knowing in practice: enacting a collective capability in distributed organising. Organ. Sci. **13**, 249–273 (2002). https://doi.org/10.1287/orsc.13.3.249.2776
11. Carlile, P.R.: A pragmatic view of knowledge and boundaries: boundary objects in new product development. Organ. Sci. **13**, 442–455 (2002). https://doi.org/10.1287/orsc.13.4.442.2953
12. Woo, J.-H., Clayton, M.J., Johnson, R.E., Flores, B.E., Ellis, C.: Dynamic knowledge map: reusing experts' tacit knowledge in the AEC industry. Autom. Constr. **13**, 203–207 (2004). https://doi.org/10.1016/j.autcon.2003.09.003

13. Rezgui, Y.: Review of information and the state of the art of knowledge management practices in the construction industry. Knowl. Eng. Rev. **16**, 241–254 (2001). https://doi.org/10.1017/S026988890100008X
14. Ryle, G.: Knowing how and knowing that: the presidential address. Proc. Arist. Soc. **46**, 1–16 (1945)
15. Majchrzak, A., Malhotra, A., John, R.: Perceived individual collaboration know-how development through information technology-enabled contextualisation: evidence from distributed teams. Inf. Syst. Res. **16**, 9–27 (2005). https://doi.org/10.1287/isre.1050.0044
16. Langan-Fox, J., Cooper, C.: Boundary-Spanning in Organisations: Network. Influence and Conflict. Routledge, Abingdon Oxon (2014)
17. Star, S.L., Griesemer, J.R.: Institutional ecology, 'translations' and boundary objects: Amateurs and professionals in Berkeley's museum of vertebrate zoology, 1907–39. Soc. Stud. Sci. **19**, 387–420 (1989). https://doi.org/10.1177/030631289019003001
18. Leigh Star, S.: This is not a boundary object: reflections on the origin of a concept. Sci. Technol. Hum. Values **35**, 601–617 (2010). https://doi.org/10.1177/0162243910377624
19. Levina, N., Vaast, E.: The emergence of boundary spanning competence in practice: implications for implementation and use of information systems. MIS Q. **29**, 335–363 (2005). https://doi.org/10.2307/25148682
20. Koskela, L., et al.: Towards shared understanding on common ground, boundary objects and other related concepts. In: Proceedings of 24th Annual Conference of the International Group for Lean Construction, Boston, MA, USA, 20–22 July 2016, pp. 63–72 , Boston, USA (2016)
21. Succar, B.: Building information modelling framework: a research and delivery foundation for industry stakeholders. Autom. Constr. **18**, 357–375 (2009). https://doi.org/10.1016/j.autcon.2008.10.003
22. Papadonikolaki, E., Vrijhoef, R., Wamelink, H.: The interdependences of BIM and supply chain partnering: empirical explorations. Architect. Eng. Des. Manage. **12**, 476–494 (2016). https://doi.org/10.1080/17452007.2016.1212693
23. Russell, A.D., Chiu, C.-Y., Korde, T.: Visual representation of construction management data. Autom. Constr. **18**, 1045–1062 (2009). https://doi.org/10.1016/j.autcon.2009.05.006
24. Franco, L.A.: Rethinking Soft OR interventions: models as boundary objects. Eur. J. Oper. Res. **14**, 720–733 (2013)
25. Phelps, A.F., Reddy, M.: The influence of boundary objects on group collaboration in construction project teams. In: Proceedings of the ACM 2009 international conference on Supporting group work - GROUP 2009, p. 125. ACM Press, Sanibel Island (2009)
26. Ferrada, X., Núñez, D., Neyem, A., Serpell, A., Sepúlveda, M.: A lessons-learned system for construction project management: a preliminary application. Procedia Soc. Behav. Sci. **226**, 302–309 (2016). https://doi.org/10.1016/j.sbspro.2016.06.192
27. Howard, R., Björk, B.-C.: Building information modelling – experts' views on standardisation and industry deployment. Adv. Eng. Inform. **22**, 271–280 (2008). https://doi.org/10.1016/j.aei.2007.03.001
28. Bosch-Sijtsema, P., Gluch, P.: Challenging construction project management institutions: the role and agency of BIM actors. Int. J. Constr. Manage. 1–11 (2019). https://doi.org/10.1080/15623599.2019.1602585
29. Gal, U., Lyytinen, K., Yoo, Y.: The dynamics of IT boundary objects, information infrastructures, and organisational identities: the introduction of 3D modelling technologies into the architecture, engineering, and construction industry. Eur. J. Inf. Syst. **17**, 290–304 (2008). https://doi.org/10.1057/ejis.2008.13
30. Miettinen, R., Paavola, S.: Reconceptualising object construction: the dynamics of building information modelling in construction design. Inf. Syst. J. **28**, 516–531 (2018). https://doi.org/10.1111/isj.12125

31. Lindberg, K., Walter, L., Raviola, E.: Performing boundary work: the emergence of a new practice in a hybrid operating room. Soc. Sci. Med. **182**, 81–88 (2017). https://doi.org/10.1016/j.socscimed.2017.04.021
32. Martin, G.P., Currie, G., Finn, R.: Reconfiguring or reproducing intra-professional boundaries? Specialist expertise, generalist knowledge and the 'modernisation' of the medical workforce. Soc. Sci. Med. **68**, 1191–1198 (2009). https://doi.org/10.1016/j.socscimed.2009.01.006
33. Comeau-Vallée, M., Langley, A.: The Interplay of inter- and intraprofessional boundary work in multidisciplinary teams. Organ. Stud. **41**, 1649–1672 (2020). https://doi.org/10.1177/0170840619848020
34. Cao, D., Li, H., Wang, G., Luo, X., Yang, X., Tan, D.: Dynamics of project-based collaborative networks for BIM implementation: analysis based on stochastic actor-oriented models. J. Manage. Eng. **33**, 1–12 (2017). https://doi.org/10.1061/(ASCE)ME.1943-5479.0000503
35. Deshpande, A., Azhar, S., Amireddy, S.: A Framework for a BIM-based knowledge management system. Procedia Eng. **85**, 113–122 (2014). https://doi.org/10.1016/j.proeng.2014.10.535

Understanding How Enterprise Architecture Contributes to Organizational Alignment

Hong Guo[1,2(✉)], Jingyue Li[2], Shang Gao[3], and Darja Smite[2,4]

[1] Anhui University, No. 111 Jiulong Road, Hefei, China
[2] Norwegian University of Science and Technology, Trondheim, Norway
{hong.guo,jingyue.li,darja.smite}@ntnu.no
[3] Örebro University, Örebro, Sweden
shang.gao@oru.se
[4] Blekinge Institute of Technology, Karlskrona, Sweden
darja.smite@bth.se

Abstract. Alignment is one of the most important benefits that Enterprise Architecture (EA) could bring to organizations. However, it is still unclear what mechanism EA uses to help organizations achieve alignment. Related research is very scattered, making it difficult to accumulate relevant knowledge and experiences, and thus, the more successful EA application is hindered. To address this issue, the present research examines essential requirements of alignment and mechanisms with which underlying EA deliverable models impact organizations. By doing so, we proposed a conceptual framework explaining how EA modeling activities contribute to organizational alignment. We demonstrated the use of this framework with three use cases. The results show that EA could help organizations achieve alignment in quite different ways, and our proposed framework helped us examine and understand the mechanisms. We expect this research could establish an essential common understanding of how EA enables organizational alignment, thereby facilitating academia to move forward in this field.

Keywords: Alignment · Enterprise Architecture, EA · Model Quality

1 Introduction

Empirical studies showed that Enterprise Architecture (EA) brought various benefits to organizations. However, the application of EA does not always succeed and also faces multiple challenges such as its complexity, heavy workload demand, and poor user acceptance [1]. This motivated researchers to examine the mechanism of how to achieve EA benefits. Among all these benefits, alignment is one of the most important benefits that EA could bring to organizations, directly or indirectly [2]. Some benefits are directly referred to as strategy alignment, business-IT alignment, and partner alignment [2]. Other benefits, such as agility, are thought to be relied on alignment significantly [3]. We limited our focus on organizational alignment (so called alignment in this paper), covering all such relation compliance in an organizational context. To our knowledge, there is

Published by Springer Nature Switzerland AG 2021
D. Dennehy et al. (Eds.): I3E 2021, LNCS 12896, pp. 383–396, 2021.
https://doi.org/10.1007/978-3-030-85447-8_33

little consensus about how EA brings organizational alignment. Relevant researches are very scattered [4], fragmented, and lacks explanatory theories [5], making it difficult to accumulate relevant knowledge and experience.

This problem motivated the present research. In this research, we examined the nature of organizational alignment requirements, EA primary deliverables, and EA mechanisms to impact organizations. The result shows alignment focuses on the compliance of relations among organizational components. Alignment shall be achieved with a continuous process. The result also shows that EA deliverable models provide the capability to represent and realize the compliance of relations among organizational components through a series of modeling activities. And such activities could be included in the continuous process of aligning.

To understand how different modeling activities contribute to alignment goals, separately and as a whole, we proposed a framework named EA-AIR. In this framework, we decompose the alignment process into parts where different modeling activities contribute to and identify key factors of such activities that impact alignment goals. This article also demonstrates how to use the framework to analyze EA's contributions to organizational alignment with three use cases.

The remainder of the paper is structured as follows. Section 2 introduces relevant background knowledge. Section 3 proposes a conceptual framework based on existing theories. In Sect. 4, we present three use cases where EA plays different organizational roles. We demonstrate how to use the proposed framework to analyze the mechanism EA contributes to organizational alignment in each case. Then, we discuss how to use this framework to better apply EA for alignment goals in Sect. 5. Lastly, we conclude the paper in Sect. 6.

2 Background

This section introduces some background knowledge about organizational alignment and EA. Because EA is generally delivered as (graphical) models, we also present relevant knowledge about different modeling activities and factors that make good models. Based on such knowledge, we summarize possible explanations on why and how EA contributes to alignment achievement.

2.1 Organizational Alignment

Alignment in dictionaries is defined as "the act of aligning or state of being aligned [6]", "arrangement in a straight line or in correct relative positions [7]", and "the proper positioning or state of adjustment of parts (as of a mechanical or electronic device) in relation to each other [6]".

When alignment is used in organizational contexts, it is defined as "the continuous process, involving management and design sub-processes, of consciously and coherently interrelating all components of the business-IT relationship in order to contribute to the organization's performance over time [8]". Typically, organizational alignment is often referred to but not limited to Strategy Alignment [9, 10], Business-IT Alignment [8, 11, 12], and Partner Alignment [2]. Literally, their focuses differ a little bit on relations that are primarily considered and strive to achieve. For instance, Strategy alignment indicates that organizations' resources shall be appropriately arranged to realize strategies. Business-IT alignment cares about whether business and IT components have supported each other.

To summarize, organizational alignment is in general about the compliance of relations among organization components. It is about a status that needs to be achieved by a continuous process involving a series of activities.

2.2 Enterprise Architecture

EA is generally defined as "The fundamental organization of a system, embodied in its components, their relationships to each other and the environment, and the principles governing its design and evolution [13]". Here, an enterprise is viewed as a "system" [13].

EA is usually delivered as a set of abstract graphics covering the enterprise's high-level content across areas such as strategy, business, information, and technology. We call these abstractions EA artifacts or EA models as they are usually in graphical forms.

To summarize, EA is usually delivered as a set of graphical artifacts named EA models. Such models could represent organizational components and their relations involved in an alignment goal. They could reflect and influence reality (e.g., realizing the alignment goal) by means of a series of modeling activities.

2.3 Models

Models are generally defined as "explicit **representations** of some portions of reality as perceived by some actor [14] ". However, models can also **influence reality** if they are **active** [15]. This means when a model is changed, the way some actors perceive reality (reflected by the model) is also changed. Actors in this context include users and software components.

Model **activation** is the process by which a model affects reality. Model activation involves actors interpreting the model and, to some extent adjusting their behavior accordingly. This process can be automatic, manual, or interactive. We define a model to be **interactive** if it is interactively activated.

An interactive model entails **coevolution** of the model and its domain. The process of updating an interactive model is called **articulation**. The interplay of articulation and activation reflects the mutual constitution of interactive models and the social reality.

Researchers pursued to define what makes a **good model** as it is crucial to influence the reality that the model reflects [16]. In [16], the authors distinguished between goals and means by separating what to achieve in modeling from how to achieve. The notion of feasibility was introduced to make goals more realistic. A framework summarizing model quality goals and means was proposed (hereafter called the SEQUAL framework [17]). The SEQUAL framework was closely linked to linguistic concepts as it was recognized that modeling is essentially making statements in some language. Its initial version [16] considered three quality levels: syntactic, semantic, and pragmatic quality. The framework was later extended [17, 18] to include more quality aspects such as physical quality and empirical quality. It was also revised [15] to make it more appropriate for active models.

2.4 EA and Organizational Alignment

Based on our understanding of EA (models) and organizational alignment as introduced above, we identified some facts which explained why EA could facilitate organizational alignment.

- Organizational alignment is about the compliance of **relations** among fundamental components of an organization. EA can represent such relations as well as components involved in the relations.
- Organizational alignment often involves statuses of both "**as is**" and "**to-be.**" EA can represent such with descriptive and prescriptive models.
- Organizational alignment takes place in **reality**. EA Models can influence reality by facilitating (human and technical) actors to learn new knowledge and take action.
- Organizational alignment is achieved through a **continuous process**. EA model can evolve and continuously interact with reality utilizing articulation and activation. Such modeling activities can be embedded in such an aligning process.
- How well models actually influence reality highly depends on the model **quality.**
- Based on these facts, we aim to construct an explanatory theory to systematically understanding mechanisms of EA-enabled alignment.

3 The EA-AIR Conceptual Framework

We define Alignment Insights and Recommendations (AIR) as descriptive and prescriptive information relevant to alignment relations. Such information can be generated from data collected according to the alignment context and converted to knowledge after interpretation of people or tools.

We think EA contributes to organizational alignment, primarily by representing AIR (entailed by developing EA deliverable models) and realizing AIR (entailed by activating EA deliverable models). Therefore, we name the proposed framework as EA-AIR because it helps us decompose the alignment process and examine relevant activity aspects that might impact the EA models delivered.

We pursue using the EA-AIR framework to explain the mechanism of EA-enabled alignment, namely, how different EA activities, separately and as a whole, help organizations achieve alignment goals and *the key influencing factors.*

We describe how we derived the EA-AIR framework and formalize it in this section.

3.1 Deriving the EA-AIR Framework

As explained in Sect. 2, we assume that it is possible to decompose the overall alignment process into parts where different (EA) modeling activities can contribute. We also think it is possible to identify key aspects that impact the quality of delivered (EA) models. By examining the decomposed parts of the alignment process and key aspects of involved modeling activities, we can better analyze, at a smaller granularity, how alignment goals are achieved through EA.

First, we decompose the alignment process into five parts where different modeling activities could contribute. As shown in Table 1, we could observe how various modeling activities, separately and accumulatively, help organizations achieve alignment goals. Notably, in the first three parts (colored in light blue in Table 1), EA activities are primarily leveraged to represent AIR and thus more restricted to (paper or electronic) models themselves. While in the last two parts, EA activities are more about realizing AIR and therefore take place in reality.

Table 1. Mapping EA modeling activities to alignment achieving process.

Alignment process	Alignment Scoping (AS)	Alignment Embodiment (AE)	Alignment Augmentation (AA)	Alignment Realization (AR)	Alignment Maintenance (AM)
(EA) modelling **activities**	Model conceptualization	Model externalization	Model computation	Model activation	Model evolution

Second, we identify key aspects of modeling activities in each part, which significantly impact the quality of delivered models. This work was done in two steps:

- Step 1: observing which model quality goals [15] can be decided in relevant modeling activities.
- Step 2: identifying aspects (means) that could impact the quality goals according to [15, 17], specializing the aspects considering the alignment context, and compensating with new aspects to activities that are not discussed in [15, 17], according to common knowledge.

Regarding step 1, we cover five main model quality described in [15, 17]: physical quality, syntactic quality, semantic quality, empirical quality, and pragmatic quality. There are more quality aspects described in [15, 17]. We do not include them, namely organization quality, perceived semantic quality, and social quality, for two reasons. First, these three aspects are more about how models fit with the environment (organizations and stakeholders) than models themselves. Second, according to [15], such aspects are unavailable for a formal inspection.

Regarding step 2, *firstly*, we identify some modeling aspects that could contribute to a specific modeling quality according to the SEQUAL framework [15]. For instance, as defined in [16], feasible completeness is one of the main goals/aspects relevant to semantic quality. *Secondly*, we further consider these identified aspects and specialize them in the alignment context. For instance, feasible completeness means that components and relations among them relevant to the alignment goal have been completely covered. In other words, this is about the scoping of EA. We further identify three dimensions that could define this scope: domain, abstraction level, and timeline. *Thirdly*, for some parts that no model quality is directly related to, we think about general solutions according to our best knowledge and make abstractions to summarize them as aspects. For instance, for alignment maintenance, a general solution is to evaluate the models by organizing regular meetings to collect feedbacks, adjusting, and starting new cycles. Thus, we propose evaluation and cycle as two aspects in this part. Results of Step 1 and 2 are appended to Table 1, as shown in the third and fourth rows of Table 2.

Table 2. Model qualities and modeling aspects relevant to modeling activities.

Alignment process	**Alignment Scoping (AS)**	**Alignment Embodiment (AE)**	**Alignment Augmentation (AA)**	**Alignment Realization (AR)**	**Alignment Maintenance (AM)**
Modeling activities	Model conceptualization	Model externalization	Model computation	Model activation	Model evolution
Model qualities	Semantic quality	Syntactic quality, physical quality, empirical quality	Pragmatic quality (as general models)	Pragmatic quality (as active models)	
Modeling aspects	• **Domain** • **Abstraction level** • **Timeline**	• **Intensity** • **Medium** • **Repository**	• **Leveraging computation**	• **Enabling learning** • **Enabling actions** • **Automatic activation**	• **Evaluation** • **Cycles**

3.2 Formalizing the EA-AIR Framework

To make Table 2 easy to use, we simplified it by hiding the two middle rows and use the remainder (bolded parts of Table 2) to formalize the proposed framework, as presented in Table 3. Each part and aspect in the framework are formally defined as below.

Alignment Scoping (AS): this is to define the scope of alignment, namely, which components shall be identified/created, and which relations shall be identified/established. We identified three dimensions where alignment might cover. The first dimension is the domain, such as business domain, data domain, application domain, and service domain. The second dimension is the abstraction level, such as vision, strategy, capability, solution. The third dimension is about time, like “as is” and “to-be.”

Alignment Embodiment (AE): this explicitly represents alignment (i.e., relations and relevant components). Three aspects are included here. The first aspect is the intensity indicating how intense the alignment relations are presented (e.g., explicit, based on taxonomies, formally defined with meta-model, verified by tools). The second aspect is the medium. It aims to represent which medium is used for the externalization, such as physical medium and electronic medium. The third aspect describes how the model artifacts are stored, by using a single digital repository, for instance.

Alignment Augmentation (AA): this is to augment and enhance the alignment relations by calculating them. The augmentation might include static analysis, dynamic simulation, and prediction by leveraging various computation techniques. AA is the place where more added value could be explored and attached to original models.

Alignment Realization (AR): in this part, EA models are used to influence reality. Three aspects are included in this part. The first two aspects describe how models enable human users to learn or take actions (i.e., manual model activation). The third aspect illustrates how to use tools to trigger automatic model activation.

Alignment Maintenance (AM): this is to maintain/ continuously approach the alignment status. Often, it is conducted in terms of periodically evaluating and restarting the whole cycle.

Table 3. Formalization of the EA-AIR conceptual framework.

Alignment Scoping (AS)	**Alignment Embodiment (AE)**	**Alignment Augmentation (AA)**	**Alignment Realization (AR)**	**Alignment Maintenance (AM)**
• Domain • Abstraction level • Timeline	• Intensity • Medium • Repository	• Leveraging computation	• Enabling learning • Enabling actions • Automatic activation	• Evaluation • Cycles

4 Case Studies

According to [19], there are typically three schools of thought regarding EA, namely Enterprise IT Architecting, Enterprise Integrating, and Enterprise Ecological Adaptation. The scope and purpose of EA differ a lot for these three thoughts, as summarized in the three right columns of Table 4 [19]. To demonstrate how to use our proposed framework, we chose representative studies for each type as our cases (as shown in Table 4). In these empirical studies, comprehensive descriptions about applying EA to achieve alignment goals can be found.

In the following sub-sections, we analyze how EA has contributed to achieving alignment in typical cases of each of the three schools based on the EA-AIR framework. We also tentatively quantified the results by giving each part of these three cases' alignment process a score. According to the author's preliminary assessment, an integer score between 0 and 3 is given, depending on the extent to which EA is fully utilized in each case according to our proposed framework. By doing so, we compared the results for the three cases in a visualized way. The three cases are summarized as:

Case 1 is about one of the largest insurance companies in the world [20]. The company introduced agile methods on a larger scale in 2016, ran ten large-scale agile development programs with more than 5,000 employees, and decided to initiate the second wave of the

Table 4. Cases for different schools of EA thoughts.

Case	EA School	Scope	Purpose
C1	Enterprise IT Architecting	All components of the enterprise IT assets	Effectively execute and operate the overall enterprise strategy for maintaining a competitive advantage by aligning the business and IT strategies such that the proper IT capabilities are developed to support current and future business needs
C2	Enterprise Integrating	All facets of the enterprise	Effectively implement the overall enterprise strategy by designing the various enterprise facets to maximize coherency between them and minimize contradictions
C3	Enterprise Ecological Adaptation	The enterprise and its environment	Help the organization innovate and adapt by designing the various enterprise facets to maximize organizational learning throughout the enterprise and encourage system-in-environment coevolution

transformation by applying agile methods across the enterprise. The EA team was tasked with the alignment of the running large-scale agile development programs, particularly about the technologies and standards used.

Case 2 [21] describes a case of leveraging advanced EA Management (EAM) tools to implement the EU's General Data Protection Regulation (GDPR). GDPR is drawing increasing attention [22], and according to our previous research [23], it might be a very typical scenario where EA and EAM tools can play an important role. Industry/commercial tools are often less observed by academia, although their importance has been recognized [24–26]. We did not find scientific studies where such a case is reported. We analyzed a customer story reported by a leading EAM tool vendor on their official website, therefore [21]. Kommunal Landspensjonskasse (KLP), which is Norway's largest pensions and life insurance company, has used a leading EAM tool, namely ABACUS, since 2016. To comply with GDPR, the company reconsidered the way they capture, manage, and process personal data and fully understood how the data management is aligned to contribute to their level of compliance and effectively produce regulatory documents.

Case 3 [27] described a smart city case where data was collected from an organization and a municipality in Norway. In this case, two major EA artifacts were modeled in the language of ArchiMate [28]. One artifact illustrated how individual enterprises were aligned/ collaborated to create and provide services. The other one depicted how business could be aligned and mapped with IT strategies.

4.1 Case 1: EA for Large-Scale Agile Development Environment

We analyze how EA contributed to the alignment goal according to our proposed framework for this case. *First*, EA was scoped as architectural principles, guidelines, and Key Performance Indicators (KPIs). *Second*, the EA artifacts seemed to be presented in an initial and direct way. *Third*, there seemed not to be any computation augmented. *Fourth*, efforts were put on EAM initiatives which complemented the enforcement-centric view of traditional EAM by an influence-centric view. They were exerted by normative and mimetic pressures to enforce principles without encountering agile teams' resistance. Voting on the adoption, refinement, or rejection of EA artifacts also facilitated the learning and actions. *Fifth*, the articulation of EA and continuous interactions between EA and the domain was conducted. Web applications have supported automated testing and an overview of which guidelines (EA artifact) were applied by which teams. Feedback on using guidelines was collected for guideline adjustment. The result is summarized in Table 5.

Table 5. Scoring alignment levels for Case 1.

AS: 1	AE: 0	AA: 0	AR: 2	AM: 2
Abstraction level: high-level; Domain: architecture principles, guidelines, and KPIs to align organizational-wide goals and implementations	NA	NA	Enabling actions: voting on adoption of EA, normative& mimetic pressures to facilitate the application of EA	Evaluation: collecting feedback to change EA, automated testing, an overview of the appliance

4.2 Case 2: Leveraging EA Tools to Implement GDPR

According to the EA-AIR framework, the *first* aspect is about the alignment scope. To comply with the GDPR, comprehensive data needs to be analyzed in broad scope, including personal data, systems, applications, and business priorities. *Second*, with the advanced commercial tool's support, data can be managed based on well-defined meta models and maintained in a single digital repository. Data can be imported from various applications or collected by inviting corresponding stakeholders to input. *Third*, Avolution [29], as one of the leading EAM tools, provided KLP multiple computation support. Such supports include keeping data up to date when content is changed and providing an "auto-generated multi-page report which details the company's systems and compliance." *Fourth*, learning new knowledge was facilitated. As said in [21], "visualize this analysis, helping people understand." "Day-to-day, this information vault allows them to generate a picture of the technology, an understanding of what each system does and what part of the portfolio it fits into." In addition, collaboration was enabled through inviting data collection and triggering communications. *Fifth*, the team runs a full ABACUS report monthly as part of the company's evidence of compliance. The result is summarized in Table 6.

Table 6. Scoring alignment levels for Case 2.

AS: 3	AE: 3	AA: 3	AR: 1	AM: 1
Domain, abstraction level, timeline: comprehensive data collected in a broad scope	Intensity: well-defined meta-models; Repository: a single digital repository, inviting data collection, data integration	Leveraging computation: Keeping data up to date, automatic report generation	Enable learning: everyday information vault, rich visualization; Enabling actions: triggering communications	Evaluation, cycles: running full report monthly

4.3 Case 3: EA in a Smart Cities Project

According to the framework, *first*, two types of EA artifacts were developed and applied. One artifact covered high-level enterprise collaboration relations, and the other one described how business is aligned with IT strategies. *Second*, EA artifacts were modeled in well-defined language, namely ArchiMate. *Third*, no information was found about if computation was applied to the EA artifacts. *Forth*, the EA models were prepared for each session of a focus group, and it was ensured that all vital issues were discussed. *Fifth*, after each session, the discussion results were presented in models, refined, and confirmed. The analysis is summarized in Table 7.

Table 7. Scoring alignment levels for Case 3.

AS: 2	AE: 2	AA: 0	AR: 1	AM:1
Domain, abstraction level: how enterprises collaborate to provide services, how business is aligned with IT strategies	Intensity: well defined meta-models/ modeling languages	NA	Enabling learning, enable actions: ensuring all issues are discussed based on models	Evaluation/cycles: multiple sessions, refining &confirming models

4.4 Comparing the Three Cases

The results are compared and visualized in Fig. 1. As shown in the figure, these three cases present pretty different EA ways to help organizations achieve alignment. While

Case 2 focuses more on representing AIR formally and comprehensively by leveraging powerful tools and computations (technical aspects), Case 1 paid more attention to realizing AIR (social aspects). Case 3 comparatively employed a more balanced way to achieve alignment.

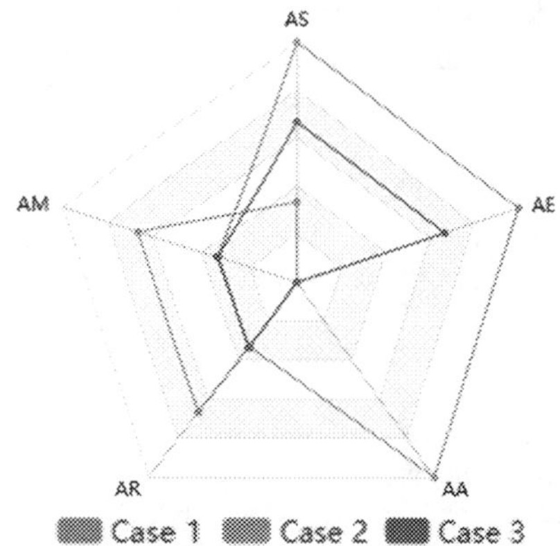

Fig. 1. Comparing the three cases by tentatively quantifying the results.

5 Discussions

We discuss how to apply our proposed framework to use EA better in contributing to organizations' various alignment goals.

"Just enough" AIR: EA should be customized to provide "just enough" AIR in a "just enough" way. EA could provide AIR with different scope, intensity, medium, calculation, and other capabilities. The cost of EA is different accordingly. Considering the ever-existed Return on Investment (ROI) pressure in organizations [30], EA should strive to balance and provide cost-effective AIR. Therefore, EA should focus on users' needs and be "just enough" (lightweight, eliminating wastes, but without compromising necessary quality). To achieve this goal, analyzing each EA artifact (with small granularity) and each modeling aspect (as indicated by the EA-AIR framework), instead of analyzing EA as a whole, might be needed.

Between AIR and the reality: Organizations should complement EA with other resources to use AIR to achieve the best alignment. As a set of models, EA strives to provide the best insights and (learning and acting) recommendations according to organizations' specific scenarios and requirements to achieve alignment. Organizations should think about how to make better use of them. This imply not only direct efforts in AR part of the EA-AIR framework, but also some indirect efforts related to other parts, such as trainings and governance policies.

Use AIR continuously: An organizational environment might be changing due to various reasons. Besides, when EA users learn and act according to AIR, they gain different knowledge and change domains (organizational components and environment).

The new knowledge and the changed domain, in turn, might indicate not only changes in the facts on which AIR is based but also changes in AIR requirements. Therefore, AIR often requires to be continuously adapted and applied to keep its effectiveness (AM).

Leverage AIR for organizational agility: It is increasingly important for organizations to keep agile [3]. On the one hand, organizations need AIR to do the right things in the right way so that to keep lean (eliminating waste without compromising quality) and responding to changes. On the other hand, as one component of an organization, EA by itself should be agile. That also indicates why "just enough" and "continuous" AIR is important.

Evaluation and Improvement: The proposed EA-AIR framework could be used for systematically evaluate how well EA has been leveraged for alignment goals, but also could be used for further analyzing how to improve relevant efforts.

6 Conclusion

This article examined notable theories of EA modeling and alignment and proposed a framework named EA-AIR explaining how EA helps organizations achieve alignment. We employed three cases to demonstrate how to use the framework. The result shows that, in these three cases, EA used quite different mechanismsto help achieve the alignment goals, and our proposed framework helped us examine and understand the mechanisms. This indicates that our proposed framework can classify and structure relevant studies about applying EA for (achieving, measuring, and maintaining) organizational alignment. By doing so, a common understanding of how EA enables alignment could be gained for academia to move forward in this field. With such a picture and relevant knowledge in mind, we expect organizations to leverage EA-relevant techniques and methods systematically and intentionally to achieve alignment effectively and efficiently.

The main limitation of the present research is the lack of further validation of the proposed framework. By far, we have only applied it to three cases which might be representative but far from sufficient. The proposed modeling aspects also need to be further enumerated to be more inclusive and exhaustive. In addition, it is not clear enough how organizations could benefit from this framework concretely and practically. Thus, we plan to review relevant works systematically to validate and enhance the framework. We also plan to apply the framework in real projects. In this way, we will investigate how to deliver feasibly good methods for specific alignment and organizational context based on the proposed framework.

Acknowledgments. This research is financially supported by The European Research Consortium for Informatics and Mathematics (ERCIM) (https://www.ercim.eu/). This work has been partially supported by NFR 295920 IDUN.

References

1. Guo, H., Li, J., Gao, S.: Understanding challenges of applying enterprise architecture in public sectors: a technology acceptance perspective. In: 2019 IEEE 23rd International Enterprise Distributed Object Computing Workshop (EDOCW). IEEE (2019)

2. Niemi, E., Enterprise architecture benefits: Perceptions from literature and practice. Tietotekniikan tutkimusinstituutin julkaisuja, vol. 18, pp. 1236–1615 (2008)
3. Tallon, P.P., Pinsonneault, A.: Competing perspectives on the link between strategic information technology alignment and organizational agility: insights from a mediation model. MIS Q. **35**, 463–486 (2011)
4. Zhang, M., Chen, H., Luo, A.: A systematic review of business-IT alignment research with enterprise architecture. IEEE Access **6**, 18933–18944 (2018)
5. Foorthuis, R., van Steenbergen, M., Brinkkemper, S., Bruls, W.A.G.: A theory building study of enterprise architecture practices and benefits. Inf. Syst. Front. **18**(3), 541–564 (2015). https://doi.org/10.1007/s10796-014-9542-1
6. Merriam-Webster. Alignment (2021). https://www.merriam-webster.com/dictionary/alignment
7. Oxfordify. Alignment (2021). https://www.oxfordify.com/meaning/alignment
8. Maes, R., et al.: Redefining business-IT alignment through a unified framework. Universiteit Van Amsterdam/Cap Gemini White Paper (2000)
9. Gregor, S., Hart, D., Martin, N.: Enterprise architectures: enablers of business strategy and IS/IT alignment in government. Inf. Technol. People **20**, 96–120 (2007)
10. Henderson, J.C., Venkatraman, H.: Strategic alignment: Leveraging information technology for transforming organizations. IBM Syst. J. **38**(23), 472–484 (1999)
11. Luftman, J., Brier, T.: Achieving and sustaining business-IT alignment. Calif. Manage. Rev. **42**(1), 109–122 (1999)
12. Luftman, J., Kempaiah, R.: An update on business-it alignment: "a line" has been drawn. MIS Q. Executive **6**(3), 165–177 (2007)
13. ISO/IEC/IEEE, ISO/IEC/IEEE 42020:2019 (2019)
14. Wegner, P., Goldin, D.: Interaction as a framework for modeling. In: Goos, G., et al. (eds.) Conceptual Modeling. Lecture Notes in Computer Science, vol. 1565, pp. 243–257. Springer, Heidelberg (1999). https://doi.org/10.1007/3-540-48854-5_19
15. Krogstie, J., Sindre, G., Jørgensen, H.: Process models representing knowledge for action: a revised quality framework. Eur. J. Inf. Syst. **15**(1), 91–102 (2006)
16. Lindland, O.I., Sindre, G., Solvberg, A.: Understanding quality in conceptual modeling. IEEE Softw. **11**(2), 42 (1994)
17. Krogstie, J., Lindland, O.I., Sindre, G.: Defining quality aspects for conceptual models. In: Falkenberg, E.D., Hesse, W., Olivé, A. (eds.) Information System Concepts. IAICT, pp. 216–231. Springer, Boston, MA (1995). https://doi.org/10.1007/978-0-387-34870-4_22
18. Krogstie, J. and H.D. Jørgensen. Quality of interactive models. in International Conference on Conceptual Modeling. 2002. Springer.
19. Lapalme, J.: Three schools of thought on enterprise architecture. IT Prof. **14**(6), 37–43 (2011)
20. Uludag, Ö., Nägele, S., Hauder, M.: Establishing architecture guidelines in large-scale agile development through institutional pressures: A single-case study (2019)
21. Avolution. Marshalling data (2021). https://www.avolutionsoftware.com/use-cases/data-privacy-security-enterprise-architecture/
22. Rozehnal, P., Novák, V.: The Core of Enterprise Architecture as a Management Tool: GDPR Implementation Case Study (2018)
23. Guo, H., et al.: Agile enterprise architecture by leveraging use cases. In Proceedings of the 16th International Conference on Evaluation of Novel Approaches to Software Engineering - MDI4SE. 2021, SciTePress
24. Nowakowski, E., Häusler, M., Breu, R.: Analysis of enterprise architecture tool support for industry 4.0 transformation planning. In: 2018 IEEE 22nd International Enterprise Distributed Object Computing Workshop (EDOCW). IEEE (2018)

25. Korhonen, J.J., et al.: Adaptive enterprise architecture for the future: towards a reconceptualization of EA. In: 2016 IEEE 18th Conference on Business Informatics (CBI). IEEE (2016)
26. Naranjo, D., Sánchez, M.E., Villalobos, J.: Evaluating the capabilities of enterprise architecture modeling tools for visual analysis. J. Object Technol. **14**(1), 31-32 (2015)
27. Anthony, B., Petersen, S.A., Helfert, M.: Digital transformation of virtual enterprises for providing collaborative services in smart cities. In: Camarinha, L.M., Afsarmanesh, H., Ortiz, A. (eds.) PRO-VE 2020. IAICT, vol. 598, pp. 249–260. Springer, Cham (2020). https://doi.org/10.1007/978-3-030-62412-5_21
28. The Open Group, ARCHIMATE® 3.1 SPECIFICATION
29. Avolution. Avolution (2021). https://www.avolutionsoftware.com/
30. Guo, H., et al.: Boost the potential of EA: essential practices. In: Proceedings of the 23rd International Conference on Enterprise Information Systems, ICEIS 2021, vol. 2, p. 735–742

How EA-Driven Dynamic Capabilities Enable Agility: The Mediating Role of Digital Project Benefits

Rogier van de Wetering(✉)

Faculty of Sciences, Open University of the Netherlands, Valkenburgerweg 177, 6419 AT Heerlen, The Netherlands
rogier.vandewetering@ou.nl

Abstract. As the modern business environment is highly volatile and demanding, orchestrating all business and IT components and capabilities are crucial. Firms use enterprise architecture (EA) for this purpose. However, it is currently by no means clear how EA-driven firm capabilities facilitate becoming agile. When firms are agile, they can recombine digital resources to change the business practice while also coping with uncertainty and recovering rapidly from disruption through innovative digital technologies. This study embraces the dynamic capability view (DCV), develops a model, and validates the associated hypotheses using cross-sectional data from 177 firms using a Partial Least Squares approach. The outcomes show that EA-driven dynamic capabilities are a crucial antecedent of digital project benefits. In turn, these benefits positively enhance agility. The findings shed light on becoming agile, and this study providing insights and guidance on achieving the EA-driven benefits.

Keywords: Dynamic capabilities · Enterprise architecture · EA-driven dynamic capabilities · Digital project benefits · Agility · Entrepreneurial agility · Adaptive agility

1 Introduction

Modern firms in hyper turbulent markets are pressured to increase both the efficiency and effectiveness of business operations to realize the firm's strategic direction and unlock the true potential of new and disruptive digital business models [1]. Among the core directions and objectives, firms typically aim to provide digitally enhanced products and services to their customers that subsequently drive new revenue streams and increase profitability while minimizing operational and overhead costs. In recent years, firms have to respond to current challenges using new innovative digital technologies (e.g., big data analytics, Internet of Things, robotics process automation, distributed ledger technology, digital security, cloud, mobile, and social media platforms, platformization). These digital opportunities have excessively altered existing value chains and the need

The original version of this chapter was revised: the term "adaptive agility" was corrected to "entrepreneurial agility" in last sentences of sect 5.2. The correction to this chapter is available at https://doi.org/10.1007/978-3-030-85447-8_66

Published by Springer Nature Switzerland AG 2021
D. Dennehy et al. (Eds.): I3E 2021, LNCS 12896, pp. 397–410, 2021.
https://doi.org/10.1007/978-3-030-85447-8_34

to become agile as a means to integrate and reconfigure digital assets and capabilities [2–5].

To orchestrate all business and information systems (IS) and information technology (IT) components and capabilities in digital and organizational transformation, firms increasingly adopt Enterprise Architecture (EA). EA helps firms document current and desirable future states of firms' digital infrastructure, processes, and capabilities [6, 7]. Therefore, EA can be considered 'a strategy' to achieve specific business goals and objectives [6] and enable firms to become agile, aligned, customer-focused, and enable better decision-making across the firm [8, 9].

There is a wealth of scholarship on the concept of EA. However, limited scholarship exists on how firms can leverage EA to create digital business benefits and value, and therefore, substantial gaps remain in the literature [7, 10, 11]. To be more specific, there is currently no empirically work that assesses the relationship between EA-driven capabilities—that synchronize business and IT resources using EA while aligning goals, objectives with the particular use of IS/IT—, digital projects benefits, and their collective effect on agility [7, 12–15]. Digital project benefits can be considered the outcomes of discrete projects improved by EA-driven dynamic capabilities within the focal firm and consist of four components: digital distinctive competencies, digital strategic alignment, data diagnosticity, and decision-making effectiveness [1, 9, 16–18]. Digital and business-driven changes in firms typically contain these components' elements, depending on the change project's nature [7, 15, 19, 20].

Agility can be considered the firm's stance of exploring and creating new resources and their applications using new innovative digital technologies and the firm's capability to cope with uncertainty and recover rapidly from disruption through these innovative digital technologies [21–24]. In this regard, it is essential that firms consciously build and deploy the ability to proactively change while going forward as firm resources are typically scarce in the current hyper turbulent economic environment. The relationships between dynamic capabilities, digital project benefits, and agility have neither been empirically investigated nor statistically estimated. This study, therefore, aims to extend existing work on EA and benefit realization through the dynamic capabilities view (DCV) and tries to explain how EA-driven dynamic capabilities enhance agility through digital project benefits. To this end, this study's research question is as follows:

What is the effect of EA-driven dynamic capabilities on the firm's agility by realizing digital project benefits?

2 Background

Recently, studies have emphasized deploying EA resources—that focus on the development and deployment of EA artifacts—to be leveraged for business transformation and contribute to better EA-driven capabilities [7, 14]. EA-driven capabilities highlight EA's particular usage in the process of decision-making and the organizational routines that drive IT and business capabilities [7, 8]. These capabilities inform business strategies and the achievement of business objectives. They do so by evoking strategic and operational benefits and drive competitive firm performance. These particular studies build upon the DCV. Various studies argue that dynamic capabilities are the primary source of sustainable competitive advantage in industries where technology and the market change [25, 26]. Following [27, 28], this study defines dynamic capabilities as a specific subset of capabilities that allow firms to integrate, build, and reconfigure internal and external resources and competences to create new products and processes and respond to changing business environments. Teece [27] argues that strong dynamic capabilities are required for fostering the organizational agility and associated requirements necessary for digital-driven innovation. This study claims that EAs can be leveraged within firms, but only when they are infused in the firms' dynamic capabilities that collectively use the EA to sense environmental threats and business opportunities implementing new strategic directions. Therefore, this study conceives 'EA-driven dynamic capabilities' as a dynamic capabilities that drives the firm's strategic direction and the deployment of new business and IT initiatives.

Based on the conceptualization of dynamic capabilities by [28] and recent EA-driven capabilities work [7, 29–31], three related but distinct capabilities can be synthesized, i.e., EA sensing capability, EA mobilizing, and an EA transformation capability. Firms can cultivate these capabilities and business value sources to support their strategy, business goals, and organizational benefits. We will elaborate on each of these three dynamic capabilities. A firm's EA sensing capability accentuates EA's crucial role in firm-wide procedures and routines to sense and identify new business ventures and undertakings and even possible threats. EA sensing capability also facilitates firms by proactively cultivating both a reactive and proactive capacity in the business domain [7, 32, 33].

Moreover, EA sensing capability involves evaluating the consequences of ongoing transformations on a firm's EAs [7, 33]. This capability also accentuates the deployment of EA resources to improve business processes and review EA services (e.g., providing content, EA standards, skills, and knowledge) and ensure that they are in line with what key (internal and external) stakeholders want [29]. The second capability, i.e., EA mobilizing capability refers to the firms' capability to use EA to evaluate, prioritize and select potential solutions and mobilize resources in line with a potential solution or potential threats [4, 7, 32, 34]. Once business opportunities are sensed (e.g., technological or market), firms should address them through the use of new products, processes, or services [27]. Thus, EA mobilizing capability focuses on seizing opportunities using EA and drawing up detailed plans to carry out a potential solution. The EA mobilizing capability construct also concerns EA's use to review and update firm-wide routines that are orchestrated with recognized good practices [34]. An essential requisite for EA mobilizing capability is to secure access to resources (e.g., human capital, financial resources, other capabilities) behind an informed conjecture [27]. An EA transforming capability concerns the firm's dexterity to apply EA to reconfigure working processes and the IS/IT landscape, engage in resource recombination, and adjust for unexpected changes [7]. This capability is crucial for firms that want to achieve sustained profitable growth as markets and technologies continuously change [26, 27]. Hence, an EA transforming capability accentuates the importance of using the EA in response to competitive strategic moves or market opportunities [7]. An EA transforming capability helps firms match better product-market areas and assets [33] while simultaneously using EA to create new or substantially changed ways of achieving our targets and objectives [35].

3 Model and Hypotheses

Figure 1 summarizes the research model and the associated hypotheses. The model shows that four essential elements and concepts are involved, i.e., EA-driven dynamic capabilities, digital project benefits, and entrepreneurial and adaptive agility that collectively form this study's hypotheses.

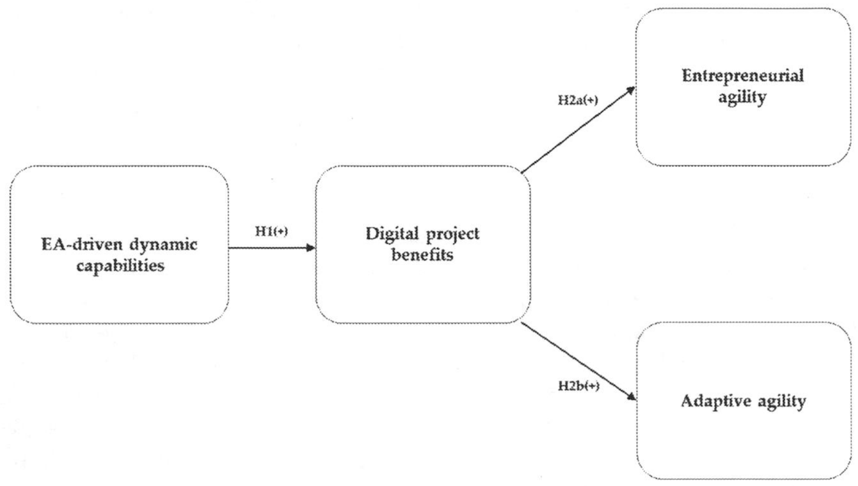

Fig. 1. Research model

EA-driven dynamic capabilities provide firms the ability to use EA in the process of enhancing data diagnosticity (i.e., retrieval of information from basic data) [16, 36], which leads to improved firm decision-making processes and support competencies to change the position of IS/IT and other firm resources geared toward the operational functioning of the firm [7, 37]. Firms can, therefore, use EA-driven dynamic capabilities to progress their digital distinctive competence—an organization's expertise in mobilizing various new innovative digital technologies through a series of routines and procedures—in key business processes and facilitate innovative work practices [12, 38, 39]. Dynamic capabilities leverage the firms' EA to bridge the communication gap between business and IT stakeholders, facilitate cross-organizational dialogue and input [40, 41], and improve digital strategic alignment [42]. Hence, it can be argued that EA-driven dynamic capabilities allow firms to continuously sense the ongoing firm-wide transformations and sufficiently react to these evolvements by recombining and redeploying business and IT assets and resources. These EA-driven capabilities provide a better understanding of business processes and IS/IT, their interdependencies, and possible synergies. They provide a foundation for identifying those critical stakeholders within the firm that might be consulted and engaged during the process and technology-driven changes [40]. Thus, EA-driven dynamic capabilities provide firms with the ability to reconfigure the business successfully and the IS/IT landscape, recombine resource, and adjust for and respond to unexpected changes is an essential driver for digital strategic alignment and thus that the firm's strategy is designed and subsequently implemented to leverage innovative digital resources and achieve differential value [9, 43, 44]. Based on this thorough analysis, the following hypothesis is formulated:

Hypothesis 1: *EA-driven dynamic capabilities exhibit a positive effect on the firms' digital project benefits.*

This study follows previous agility scholarship [21, 24, 45] by claiming that to become agile, the firm's ability to pursue adaptive agility and entrepreneurial agility, specific digital investments, and projects is essential. Adaptive agility (i.e., exploitation mode) concerns the firm's ability to cope with uncertainty and recover rapidly from disruption by using these innovative digital technologies without fundamentally changing products or processes [21–23]. On the other hand, entrepreneurial agility (i.e., exploration mode) concerns a firm's stance on creating new resources, ideas, and applications beyond the firm's boundaries using new innovative digital technologies [21, 23, 24]. Digital project benefits facilitate various operational and strategic processes within a firm that customers ultimately value [2]. To enhance business success in the current turbulent market, firms should consider and activate the digital resources and capabilities and make digital project investments that focus on digital innovations, enhancing business operations, and synchronizing the firm's assets and resources [46]. This study argues that digital project benefits lead to agility in several ways.

First, digital distinctive competencies allow firms to utilize firm-wide technological advancements to effectively transform inputs (e.g., information, investments) into outputs, e.g., specific products or services [39]. These competencies are crucial for developing new digital innovations that reinforce the prevailing product/service and rapidly develop new digital business approaches or solutions. Improved data diagnosticity and thus the retrieval of information from basic data will enhance the firms' exploration and exploitation capabilities [16, 47] through, for instance, real-time snapshots of customer segments. These insights will enable the organization to continually look for new innovative ways to reinvent the organization using new innovative digital technologies to serve their clients better while also enabling firms to react to emerging opportunities in customer needs. Enhanced decision-making effectiveness helps firms render customers' business priorities, understand customers' needs, serve the market place better, and positively influence innovation success in turbulent markets and respond more quickly to change [17, 48, 49]. Digital strategic alignment allows firms to leverage digital resources to create differential value and improve their capacity to easily and quickly reshape their business processes in turbulent business environments through digital innovation [22]. Research on EA-driven capabilities has demonstrated that agility benefits can be achieved through EA [7, 14]. However, to achieve agility, firms need to develop particular data diagnosticity and decision-making skills and digital distinctive competences [2–4, 16, 17, 39]. Firms also need to execute their strategy by leveraging digital resources to create differential value [1, 9, 18]. Following the extant literature, it can be argued that EA-driven dynamic capabilities' effect on agility is intermediated by digital project benefits [19, 50, 51]. Firms can enhance their agility level when they direct the dynamic capabilities to develop complementary digital project benefits such as enhanced data-driven decision-making benefits and digital resource leveraging benefits [9, 16, 17, 39, 43, 52]. Hence, the current study proposes that:

Hypothesis 2a: *Digital project benefits mediate the effect of EA-driven dynamic capabilities on the firms' entrepreneurial agility.*

Hypothesis 2b: *Digital project benefits mediate the effect of EA-driven dynamic capabilities on the firms' adaptive agility.*

4 Research Method

4.1 Data Collection

An online survey was developed to investigate the research hypotheses. This survey was pretested on multiple occasions by five Master students, four Ph.D. students, and five senior business professionals. The target respondents included senior IT and business managers and staff. Participating Master students of an advanced course on strategic EA management of a Dutch University were asked to fill in this survey. All the students ($N = 214$) were asked to distribute the survey to two knowledgeable practitioners within their respective professional networks. The survey items were operationalized using a seven-point Likert scale ranging from strongly disagree (1) to strongly agree (7). Data were collected between the 7th of October 2019 and the 11th of November 2019. A total of 369 unique respondents from different organizations started the questionnaire. This study includes a total of 177 usable questionnaires for the analyses after carefully removing incomplete ($N = 25$) or unreliable ($N = 21$) cases. The majority of respondents operate either in the private sector (i.e., 52%) or the public sector (i.e., 39%). A small percentage (i.e., 9%) comes from other categories such as private-public partnerships and non-governmental organizations. The majority of responses come from senior managers (including Chief Information and Executive Officers, IT, business, and innovation managers (approximately 65%).

4.2 Measures and Conceptualization

The selection of measurement scales was made following previous empirical and validated work. EA-driven dynamic capabilities are operationalized following Van de Wetering's conceptualization [29]. Hence, this construct is operationalized as a higher-order construct. Specifically, these dynamic capabilities were operationalized using a reflective-formative type II model [53]. The construct was measured using 12 equally distributed indicators across three first-order constructs, i.e., EA sensing capability (EAS), EA mobilizing capability (EAM), and EA transformation capability (EAT). Digital project benefits are the outcomes of discrete projects improved by EA-driven dynamic capabilities that are likewise operationalized and contain four first-order constructs that are often mentioned in the EA-literature, i.e., digital distinctive competencies (DC) [39], digital strategic alignment (DSA) [9, 43], data diagnosticity (DAT) [16], and decision-making effectiveness (DEC) [17]. Finally, agility is operationalized by two first-order reflective constructs entrepreneurial agility (EDA) and adaptive agility (ADA). Three items for entrepreneurial agility were included based on the work of [21, 23, 24]. The three measurement items for adaptive agility were based on work from [21–23]. This study also included control variables: firm size (ranging from 1.: less than 100 employees to 5. over 3000 employees) and industry segment (i.e., private and public sector, private-public partnerships, non-governmental organization, non-profit organization). All measures are included in Appendix A.

4.3 Analyses Using Partial Least Squares

This study applied SmartPLS version 3.2.7. [54]. SmartPLS is a Structural Equation Modeling (SEM) tool that uses Partial Least Squares (PLS). PLS is used to estimate the research model and run its associated parameter estimates. PLS maximizes the explained variance in the dependent construct and handles both reflective and formative measures [55, 56], as is the case in this research. The PLS algorithm, this study uses the path weighing scheme within SmartPLS.

Finally, a non-parametric bootstrapping procedure (using 5000 replications) was employed to obtain stable results and interpret their significance of the path coefficients between this study's key construct. This study uses a two-step approach to investigate PLS outcomes. First, using confirmatory factor analyses assesses the model's psychometric properties. Then, the hypotheses are tested using the outcomes of the structural model assessment.

5 Empirical Findings

5.1 Measurement Model Analysis Using PLS

The model's psychometric properties were assessed using the internal consistency reliability, convergent validity, and measurement validity of the first-order latent constructs [54]. All construct-to-item loadings exceeded a threshold of 0.70. Next, all Cronbach's alpha (CA) values are above the same threshold. The Appendix includes an overview of reliability and validity results. The average variance extracted (AVE), to evaluate convergent validity, is used to assess the degree of variance captured by the latent construct while relating it to the amount of variance due to measurement error [54]. The AVE-values exceeded the lowest recommended mark of 0.50 [57]. Finally, to assess discriminant validity, this study employed a heterotrait-monotrait ratio of correlations (HTMT) analysis. HTMT proved to be the most reliable method of assessing discriminant validity in variance-based models [58]. HTMT values are all well below the upper bound of 0.90, confirming discriminant validity.

5.2 Hypotheses Testing

The outcomes of the model fit[1] index analysis were strong. Hence, the obtained Standardized Root Mean Square Residual (SRMR) of 0.06 is well below the conservative proposed mark of 0.08 [59]. Hence, the structural model and the hypotheses test can now be examined. This study investigated each hypothesized path's significance and the coefficient of determination (R^2), measuring the model's predictive power [60] to test the hypotheses. Also, the model's predictive power is assessed [60].

[1] Please note that these particular PLS model fit indices are in an early stage of development.

The results show that dynamic capabilities positively influence ($\beta = .55$; $t = 9.061$; $p < .0001$) digital project benefits. Thus, hypothesis 1 is supported. Also, digital project benefits had a significant impact ($\beta = .67$; $t = 17.29$; $p < .0001$) on entrepreneurial agility, thereby confirming hypothesis 2a. Digital project benefits also significantly impact adaptive agility ($\beta = .71$; $t = 18.05$; $p < .0001$); confirming hypothesis 2b.

This study follows mediation guidelines by [60] to systematically investigate if digital project benefits fully or partially mediate the relationship between dynamic capabilities and adaptive and entrepreneurial agility. When digital project benefits were removed from the model, the direct effects of dynamic capabilities were significant. It can be concluded that digital project benefits fully mediate the effect of dynamic capabilities on the firms' adaptive and entrepreneurial agility. The included control variables 'size,' and 'industry' showed non-significant effects. Outcomes show that the assessed model explains 30% of the variance for digital project benefits ($R^2 = .30$), 51% of the variance for adaptive agility ($R^2 = .51$) and 45% of the variance for entrepreneurial agility ($R^2 = .45$). These effect sizes are considered moderate to large [60]. A blindfolding procedure is used to assesses the model's predictive power [60]. Hence, the obtained Stone-Geisser values (Q^2) for the endogenous latent constructs should all be higher than 0 as an indication of predictive relevance. All Q^2 values exceed 0.30, indicating the research model's overall predictive relevance [60].

6 Discussion of the Results and Concluding Remarks

This study tried to explain how EA-driven dynamic capabilities enhance firms' agility through digital project benefits. This paper shows that EA-driven dynamic capabilities positively affect the firms' digital project benefits and that these benefits positively influence the firms' capacity to pursue an entrepreneurial and adaptive stance on agility. Finally, the outcomes show that the effect of dynamic capabilities on agility is indirect, and thus digital project benefits fully mediate this particular effect. Hence, firms that do not have developed their EA-driven dynamic capabilities could be underutilizing their resources, thus prohibiting digital agility and the recombination and development of new products, services, and business models that enhance the value created for the customer.

This work adds to the theoretical knowledge base by making three contributions. The results shed light on the current lacunas in the extant literature concerning the mechanisms through which business benefits can be achieved using EA-driven capabilities. Second, this work extends existing work on EA-driven capabilities and the 'type' of benefits that can be achieved. Third, prior studies of dynamic capabilities have focused on how firms could address the turbulent business environment by facilitating managers to modify existing operational capabilities into new ones and thereby create a competitive edge over competitors [35]. This work complements previous studies by focusing on the value of digital project benefits in achieving agility, an essential quality required to achieve digital transformation in the current turbulent market using innovative digital technologies like AI, big data analytics, and IoT [2, 3, 61].

The outcomes of this study provide managerial implications in two ways. First, the outcomes imply that decision-makers and senior business and IT practitioners need to have a comprehensive view of the state of practice of their respective dynamic enterprise architecture capabilities. EA-driven dynamic capabilities are crucial in leveraging the firms' business and IT resources and obtaining digital project benefits. Hence, dedication and shaping appropriate conditions for developing these capabilities are essential for a firm's ability to obtain digital project benefits. Second, as the EA-driven dynamic capability construct reveals, it comprises various underlying key capabilities and complementary managerial practices. Investing in each of these elements in isolation is unlikely to achieve the desired outcomes [62]. Consequently, the impact of a system of complementary EA-driven practices will be greater than the sum of its parts because of the synergistic effects of bundling practices together [62]. Therefore, decision-makers should actively look for ways to invest in these capabilities and routines to build and develop digital resources and project benefits.

Several study limitations should be mentioned. First, data were collected at a single point in time (cross-sectionally) and thus providing only a snapshot of the firm's well-being, limiting our comprehension of the relationships among the included constructs in this study. A longitudinal approach could provide a richer understanding of the dynamics among the critical constructs in this study. Second, this study used self-reported measures that could be subject to hindsight and possible biases. However, obtaining comparable archival and objective measures is a challenging endeavor, and self-reported data is justifiable, as these data types are typically strongly correlated to objective measures.

Appendix A: Survey Constructs and Items

Construct	Measurement item
*To what extent do you agree with the following statements? (1. Strongly disagree–7. Strongly agree). * EAS EAM, EAT use the same Likert scale*	
EAS*	We use our EA to identify new business opportunities or potential threats
	We review our EA services regularly to ensure that they are in line with key stakeholders wishes
	We adequately evaluate the effect of changes in the baseline and target EA on the organization
	We devote sufficient time to enhance our EA to improve business processes
EAM	We use our EA to draft potential solutions when we sense business opportunities or potential threats
	We use our EA to mobilize resources in line with a potential solution when we sense business opportunities or potential threats
	We use our EA to draw up a detailed plan to carry out a potential solution when we sense business opportunities or potential threats
	We use our EA to review and update our practices in line with renowned business and IT best practices when we sense business opportunities or potential threats
EAT	Our EA enables us to successfully reconfigure business processes and the technology landscape to come up with new or more productive assets

(*continued*)

(*continued*)

Construct	Measurement item
	We successfully use our EA to adjust our business processes and the technology landscape in response to competitive strategic moves or market opportunities
	We successfully use our EA to engage in resource recombination to better match our product-market areas and our assets
	Our EA enables flexible adaptation of human resources, processes, or the technology landscape that leads to competitive advantage
Please choose the appropriate response for each item (1 – strongly disagree 7 – strongly agree)	
DSA	Our organization has a digital strategy to use novel digital technologies (e.g., big data analytics, IoT, robotics process automation, cloud) to enter new market segments
	Our organization has a digital strategy to develop new innovative digital technologies for new kinds of products/services
	Our digital strategy is one that in practice encompasses a fusion view, in which both the information technology and business strategy are equated
Indicate the degree to which you agree or disagree with the following statements about whether the organization has (1 – strongly disagree 7 – strongly agree)	
DC	Competence to obtain information about the status and progress of science and relevant new innovative digital technologies like big data analytics, IoT, robotics process automation, digital security, cloud, mobile and social media platforms
	Competence to generate advanced processes driven by new innovative digital technologies
	Competence to assimilate new innovative digital technologies and useful innovations
	Competence to attract and retain qualified scientific-technical staff with adequate digital technologies skills
	Competence to dominate, generate or absorb basic and new innovative digital business technologies
We are more effective than our competitors at: (1 – strongly disagree 7 – strongly agree)	
DEC	Responding quickly to change
	Making real-time decisions
	Understanding customers
To what extent do you agree or disagree with the following statements? (1 – strongly disagree 7 – strongly agree). In my firm, the understandings/conclusions that we arrive while processing information are often	
DAT	Sophisticated
	Deep
	Creative

(*continued*)

(*continued*)

Construct	Measurement item
	Relevant
Please indicate your firm's capabilities relative to competition for each of the following. (1 – strongly disagree 7 – strongly agree)	
EDA	We constantly look for ways to reinvent/reengineer our organization using new innovative digital technologies to better serve our market place
	We are the first to market with new digital business approaches or solutions
	We develop digital innovations and solutions that fundamentally change our prevailing products/services
ADA	We rapidly react to emerging opportunities in customer needs using new innovative digital technologies
	We rapidly respond to competitive and operational threats (e.g., process and organizational disruptions) through the use new innovative digital technologies
	We develop new digital innovations that reinforce our prevailing product/service lines

References

1. Bharadwaj, A., et al.: Digital business strategy: toward a next generation of insights. MIS Q. **37**(2), 471–482 (2013)
2. Eggers, J., Park, K.F.: Incumbent adaptation to technological change: the past, present, and future of research on heterogeneous incumbent response. Acad. Manage. Ann. **12**(1), 357–389 (2018)
3. Verhoef, P.C., et al.: Digital transformation: a multidisciplinary reflection and research agenda. J. Bus. Res. **122**, 889–901 (2019)
4. Sambamurthy, V., Bharadwaj, A., Grover, V.: Shaping agility through digital options: reconceptualizing the role of information technology in contemporary firms. MIS Q. **27**(2), 237–263 (2003)
5. Karimi, J., Walter, Z.: The role of dynamic capabilities in responding to digital disruption: a factor-based study of the newspaper industry. J. Manage. Inf. Syst. **32**(1), 39–81 (2015)
6. Ross, J.W., Weill, P., Robertson, D.: Enterprise Architecture as Strategy: Creating a Foundation for Business Execution. Harvard Business Press, Boston (2006)
7. Shanks, G., et al.: Achieving benefits with enterprise architecture. J. Strateg. Inf. Syst. **27**(2), 139–156 (2018)
8. Hazen, B.T., et al.: Enterprise architecture: acompetence-based approach to achieving agility and firm performance. Management **193**, 566–577 (2017)
9. Bradley, R.V., et al.: Enterprise architecture, IT effectiveness and the mediating role of IT alignment in US hospitals. Inf. Syst. J. **22**(2), 97–127 (2012)
10. Hoogervorst, J.: Enterprise architecture: enabling integration, agility and change. Int. J. Coop. Inf. Syst. **13**(03), 213–233 (2004)
11. Van de Wetering, R., Kurnia, S., Kotusev, S.: The role of enterprise architecture for digital transformations. Sustainability **13**(2237), 1–4 (2021)

12. Korhonen, J.J., Halén, M.: Enterprise architecture for digital transformation. In: 2017 IEEE 19th Conference on Business Informatics (CBI). IEEE (2017)
13. Pattij, M., Van de Wetering, R., Kusters, R.J.: Improving agility through enterprise architecture management: the mediating role of aligning business and IT. In: Proceedings of the Twenty-Sixth Americas Conference on Information Systems (AMCIS), AIS, Virtual conference (2020).
14. Van de Wetering, R.: Enterprise architecture resources, dynamic capabilities, and their pathways to operational value. In: Proceedings of the Fortieth International Conference on Information Systems, AIS, Munich (2019)
15. Foorthuis, R., van Steenbergen, M., Brinkkemper, S., Bruls, W.A.G.: A theory building study of enterprise architecture practices and benefits. Inf. Syst. Front. **18**(3), 541–564 (2015). https://doi.org/10.1007/s10796-014-9542-1
16. Ghasemaghaei, M., Calic, G.: Can big data improve firm decision quality? The role of data quality and data diagnosticity. Decis. Support Syst. **120**, 38–49 (2019)
17. Cao, G., Duan, Y., Cadden, T.: The link between information processing capability and competitive advantage mediated through decision-making effectiveness. Int. J. Inf. Manage. **44**, 121–131 (2019)
18. Chanias, S., Myers, M.D., Hess, T.: Digital transformation strategy making in pre-digital organizations: the case of a financial services provider. J. Strateg. Inf. Syst. **28**(1), 17–33 (2019)
19. Melville, N., Kraemer, K., Gurbaxani, V.: Review: information technology and organizational performance: an integrative model of IT business value. MIS Q. **28**(2), 283–322 (2004)
20. Lange, M., Mendling, J., Recker, J.: An empirical analysis of the factors and measures of enterprise architecture management success. Eur. J. Inf. Syst. **25**(5), 411–431 (2016)
21. Sambamurthy, V., et al.: IT-enabled organizational agility and firms' sustainable competitive advantage. In: ICIS 2007 Proceedings, p. 91 (2007)
22. Tallon, P.P., Pinsonneault, A.: Competing perspectives on the link between strategic information technology alignment and organizational agility: insights from a mediation model. Mis Q. **35**(2), 463–486 (2011)
23. Subramaniam, M., Youndt, M.A.: The influence of intellectual capital on the types of innovative capabilities. Acad. Manage. J. **48**(3), 450–463 (2005)
24. Lu, Y., Ramamurthy, K.: Understanding the link between information technology capability and organizational agility: an empirical examination. MIS Q **35**(4), 931–954 (2011)
25. Teece, D., Peteraf, M., Leih, S.: Dynamic capabilities and organizational agility: risk, uncertainty, and strategy in the innovation economy. Calif. Manage. Rev. **58**(4), 13–35 (2016)
26. Eisenhardt, K.M., Martin, J.A.: Dynamic capabilities: what are they? Strateg. Manag. J. **21**(10–11), 1105–1121 (2000)
27. Teece, D.J.: Explicating dynamic capabilities: the nature and microfoundations of (sustainable) enterprise performance. Strateg. Manag. J. **28**(13), 1319–1350 (2007)
28. Teece, D.J., Pisano, G., Shuen, A.: Dynamic capabilities and strategic management. Strateg. Manag. J. **18**(7), 509–533 (1997)
29. Wetering, R.: Dynamic enterprise architecture capabilities: conceptualization and validation. In: Abramowicz, W., Corchuelo, R. (eds.) BIS 2019. LNBIP, vol. 354, pp. 221–232. Springer, Cham (2019). https://doi.org/10.1007/978-3-030-20482-2_18
30. Van de Wetering, R., Kurnia, S., Kotusev, S.: The effect of enterprise architecture deployment practices on organizational benefits: a dynamic capability perspective. Sustainability **12**(21), 8902 (2020)
31. Van de Wetering, R., et al.: The impact of EA-driven dynamic capabilities, innovativeness, and structure on organizational benefits: a variance and fsQCA perspective. Sustainability **13**(10), 5414 (2021)

32. Overby, E., Bharadwaj, A., Sambamurthy, V.: Enterprise agility and the enabling role of information technology. Eur. J. Inf. Syst. **15**(2), 120–131 (2006) https://doi.org/10.1057/palgrave.ejis.3000600
33. Pavlou, P.A., El Sawy, O.A.: Understanding the elusive black box of dynamic capabilities. Decis. Sci. **42**(1), 239–273 (2011)
34. Wilden, R., et al.: Dynamic capabilities and performance: strategy, structure and environment. Long Range Plan. **46**(1–2), 72–96 (2013)
35. Protogerou, A., Caloghirou, Y., Lioukas, S.: Dynamic capabilities and their indirect impact on firm performance. Ind. Corp. Change **21**(3), 615–647 (2012)
36. Lnenicka, M., Komarkova, J.: Developing a government enterprise architecture framework to support the requirements of big and open linked data with the use of cloud computing. Int. J. Inf. Manage. **46**, 124–141 (2019)
37. Roberts, N., et al.: Absorptive capacity and information systems research: review, synthesis, and directions for future research. MIS Q. **36**(2), 625–648 (2012)
38. Prajogo, D.I., Sohal, A.S.: The relationship between TQM practices, quality performance, and innovation performance: an empirical examination. Int. J. Qual. Reliab. Manage. **20**(8), 901–918 (2003)
39. BolíVar, M.T., GarcíA, V.J., GarcíA-SáNchez, E.: Technological distinctive competencies and organizational learning: Effects on organizational innovation to improve firm performance. J. Eng. Tech. Manage. **29**(3), 331–357 (2012)
40. Tamm, T., et al.: How does enterprise architecture add value to organisations. Commun. Assoc. Inf. Syst. **28**(1), 141–168 (2011)
41. Van de Wetering, R., Dijkman, J.: Enhancing digital platform capabilities and networking capability with EA-driven dynamic capabilities. In: Proceedings of the Twenty-Seventh Americas Conference on Information Systems (AMCIS), AIS, Virtual conference (2021)
42. Gregor, S., Hart, D., Martin, N.: Enterprise architectures: enablers of business strategy and IS/IT alignment in government. Inf. Technol. People **20**(2), 96–120 (2007)
43. Chan, Y.E.: Why haven't we mastered alignment? The importance of the informal organization structure. MIS Q. Executive **1**(2), 97–112 (2002)
44. Van de Wetering, R.: Dynamic enterprise architecture capabilities and organizational benefits: an empirical mediation study. In: Proceedings of the Twenty-Eighth European Conference on Information Systems (ECIS), AIS, Virtual Conference (2020)
45. Lee, O.-K., et al.: How does IT ambidexterity impact organizational agility? Inf. Syst. Res. **26**(2), 398–417 (2015)
46. Hult, G.T.M., Ketchen, D.J., Jr.: Does market orientation matter? A test of the relationship between positional advantage and performance. Strateg. Manag. J. **22**(9), 899–906 (2001)
47. Toppenberg, G., Henningsson, S., Shanks, G.: How Cisco Systems used enterprise architecture capability to sustain acquisition-based growth. MIS Q. Executive **14**(4), 151–168 (2015)
48. Rausch, E., et al.: Technology-based service proposal screening and decision-making effectiveness. Manage. Decis. **49**(5), 762–783 (2011)
49. Cepeda, G., Vera, D.: Dynamic capabilities and operational capabilities: a knowledge management perspective. J. Bus. Res. **60**(5), 426–437 (2007)
50. Schryen, G.: Revisiting IS business value research: what we already know, what we still need to know, and how we can get there. Eur. J. Inf. Syst. **22**(2), 139–169 (2013). https://doi.org/10.1057/ejis.2012.45
51. Soh, C., Markus, M.L.: How IT creates business value: a process theory synthesis. In: ICIS 1995, Proceedings, p. 4 (1995)
52. Wheeler, B.C.: NEBIC: a dynamic capabilities theory for assessing net-enablement. Inf. Syst. Res. **13**(2), 125–146 (2002)

53. Becker, J.-M., Klein, K., Wetzels, M.: Hierarchical latent variable models in PLS-SEM: guidelines for using reflective-formative type models. Long Range Plan. **45**(5–6), 359–394 (2012)
54. Ringle, C.M., Wende, S., Becker, J.-M.: SmartPLS 3. SmartPLS GmbH, Boenningstedt (2015). http://www.smartpls.com
55. Ringle, C.M., Sarstedt, M., Straub, D.W.: Editor's comments: a critical look at the use of PLS-SEM in "MIS Quarterly." MIS Q. **36**, iii–xiv (2012)
56. Hair, J.F., Jr., et al.: Advanced Issues in Partial Least Squares Structural Equation Modeling. SAGE Publications, Thousand Oaks (2017)
57. Fornell, C., Larcker, D.: Evaluating structural equation models with unobservable variables and measurement error. J. Mark. Res. **18**(1), 39–50 (1981)
58. Henseler, J., Ringle, C.M., Sarstedt, M.: A new criterion for assessing discriminant validity in variance-based structural equation modeling. J. Acad. Mark. Sci. **43**(1), 115–135 (2014). https://doi.org/10.1007/s11747-014-0403-8
59. Hu, L.T., Bentler, P.M.: Cutoff criteria for fit indexes in covariance structure analysis: conventional criteria versus new alternatives. Struct. Equ. Model. Multidiscip. J. **6**(1), 1–55 (1999)
60. Hair, J.F., Jr., et al.: A primer on partial least squares structural equation modeling (PLS-SEM). Sage Publications, Thousand Oaks (2016)
61. Warner, K.S., Wäger, M.: Building dynamic capabilities for digital transformation: an ongoing process of strategic renewal. Long Range Plan. **52**(3), 326–349 (2019)
62. Milgrom, P., Roberts, J.: Complementarities and fit strategy, structure, and organizational change in manufacturing. J. Acc. Econ. **19**(2–3), 179–208 (1995)

ICT-Based Inter-organisational Knowledge Exchange: A Narrative Literature Review Approach

Yuzhen Zhu[1(✉)], Efpraxia D. Zamani[1], Jorge Tiago Martins[2], and Ana Cristina Vasconcelos[1]

[1] Information School, The University of Sheffield, Sheffield, UK
Yzhu74@sheffield.ac.uk
[2] VTT Technical Research Centre of Finland Ltd., Espoo, Finland

Abstract. Organisations are increasingly seeking collaborations across organisational boundaries, and the digitalisation of organisation can greatly accelerate people to exchange knowledge in such inter-organisational collaborations. Therefore, Information and Communication Technologies (ICTs) play a more significant role in organisations' inter-organisational knowledge exchange (IOKE) than ever before. However, current studies provide somewhat fragmented perspectives through which knowledge and technology may be interpreted. It is critical now for research and practice to understand how ICTs shape IOKE. This study accordingly explores how IOKE is conceptualised from different ICT perspectives and understand their limitations and implications. The paper contributes to understanding the dynamic nature of IOKE from ICT perspectives and calls for future research to conceptualise IOKE from a more integrative view.

Keywords: Knowledge exchange · Inter-organisational collaboration · Narrative literature review · Sociomateriality · Socio-technical systems

1 Introduction

As the world of work continuously transforms, organisations seek collaborations outside their boundaries, forming inter-organisational collaborations [1]. The digitalisation of organisations has enabled people to work remotely [2]. The Covid-19 pandemic has further accelerated this, making even more apparent the impact of ICTs on inter-organisational work [4] and our reliance on them for business continuity [5].

To date, however, the discourse on the role of ICTs for inter-organisational knowledge exchange (IOKE) is somewhat fragmented as there are multiple perspectives through which both knowledge and technology may be interpreted. For example, the socio-technical perspective emphasises IOKE's interactive process shaped by social and technical subsystems [6], while the sociomaterial perspective focuses on IOKE's practices shaped by ICT and actions [7]. What is critical for research and practice today is to

Published by Springer Nature Switzerland AG 2021
D. Dennehy et al. (Eds.): I3E 2021, LNCS 12896, pp. 411–422, 2021.
https://doi.org/10.1007/978-3-030-85447-8_35

explore how different perspectives of ICTs help shape IOKE; what are the similarities and differences across existing perspectives of ICTs in how they address, conceptualise and influence IOKE, and what are the implications and limitations of these different perspectives for an enhanced understanding and practice of IOKE.

To address the aforementioned questions, this study conducts a narrative literature review, drawing from the Information Systems and Knowledge Management literatures, with the aim to explore how IOKE is conceptualised from different ICT perspectives. The specific objectives are: to understand the dynamic nature of IOKE; to explore different perspectives of knowledge exchange; to explore the role of ICTs in knowledge exchange; and to delineate the limitations and implications for the investigation of IOKE practices. The narrative literature review approach is considered to be particularly useful for extracting a broader landscape of ICT studies for the IOKE field [8, 9].

This paper contributes to the understanding of IOKE from an ICT perspective. The intrinsic and dynamic nature of IOKE is clarified from different perspectives of ICT through which salient areas for future research and the need for conceptualising IOKE from a more integrative view are identified.

2 Inter-organisational Knowledge and Knowledge Exchange

As organisations increasingly seek opportunities from external resources [10], knowledge exchange in inter-organisational collaborations attracts the interest of organisational scholars [11]. However, and despite the increasing interest, there is not yet an agreed definition of the concept. For example, Fazey et al. [12] define knowledge exchange as "a process of generating, sharing, and/or using knowledge through various methods appropriate to the context, purpose, and participants involved" (p. 20). Davenport [13] defines it as a "dynamic process by which knowledge is transferred, shared and created within the core collaboration and with wider stakeholders" (p. 297), and emphasises its iterative and multi-directional characteristics that are supportive of collaboration. On the other hand, Davison et al. [14] conceptualise knowledge exchange as a constitution of "knowledge seeking and knowledge sharing". While different, these conceptualisations suggest that knowledge exchange can be viewed as a broader concept, encapsulating the creation, sharing, storage and application of knowledge.

2.1 Inter-organisational Knowledge Exchange Process

Knowledge exchange is a social process where various perspectives, contextual conditions, entities, and technologies are involved and interact in a systematic way [15, 16]. The process is iterative and interactive, and involves the multi-directional mobilisation of knowledge [13]. In the context of inter-organisational collaboration, such knowledge mobilisation reflects a dynamic knowledge exchange taking place across organisational boundaries, i.e., IOKE [17–19]. We thus posit that IOKE is *a dynamic, multi-directional and iterative process by which knowledge is created, shared, stored and applied in inter-organisational collaborations, which achieve an inter-organisational exchange of knowledge.* By reviewing and synthesising current IOKE literature, we argue that inter-organisational knowledge exchange involves five distinct sub-processes as knowledge is created, shared, stored and applied in IOKE. These are discussed next.

Knowledge Exploration reflects the process through which new knowledge is sought. This means that new knowledge is explored and refined regularly and evolves continuously [20]. Davison et al. [14] argue that knowledge is shared when sought. This indicates that the new knowledge exploration process plays a significant role in knowledge exchange and expands the knowledge domain as the IOKE process develops.

Extant Knowledge Exploitation refers to the synthesis and reuse of *existing* knowledge. Knowledge exploitation activities, such as locating knowledge and classifying knowledge, help understand relevant knowledge in the present [20, 21]. Therefore, extant knowledge exploitation is vital for the knowledge exchange process.

Context Construction shows the shifting context of knowledge exchange. Macro contextual factors, such as the economic context, exemplify the external context of knowledge exchange [22]. Micro contextual factors such as organisational structure, culture and leadership influence knowledge exchange practices [23]. These contextual factors shape and are shaped by knowledge exchange practices as the IOKE process evolves [24].

Intervention relates to the knowledge exchange activities. During knowledge exchange, individuals develop knowledge by sharing their own knowledge, creating and tailoring new knowledge, discussing and negotiating their ideas, which mediate their knowledge exchange patterns [22, 26]. Intervention thus refers to how knowledge exchange patterns evolve as knowledge sharing, creation, storage and application processes interact in IOKE.

Knowledge Utilisation refers to the shifting use of knowledge in the practice. Rather than focusing on the shifting of knowledge itself to promote IOKE in interventions, knowledge utilisation focuses on shifting the knowledge use in actions. This is associated with different types of knowledge use, such as conceptual and procedural use of knowledge and various relevant actions such as monitoring and evaluating the use of knowledge [25]. Organisations need to develop capabilities in mobilising their knowledge into action, which is the purpose of knowledge management and core for developing organisational competitive advantage [26]. In this respect, knowledge utilisation entails evaluating how effective the knowledge exchange process is and how useful the knowledge exchanged is [22]. As a result, knowledge utilisation is an essential phase in the knowledge exchange process and it reflects that knowledge exchange is a "know-do" process.

These processes are interrelated and interact with each other. For example, knowledge sharing mechanisms such as the use of ICT can readily display explicit knowledge through codification, i.e., the categorisation of knowledge enabling it to be embedded, stored and retrieved [27]. Stored knowledge can be further transformed into new explicit knowledge via sharing practices, which facilitates knowledge creation in inter-organisational collaboration [17, 28]. These shape the core interaction among internal processes of IOKE (Central Cycle in Fig. 1). As these processes interact, new processes or phases emerge in IOKE (Outer Cycle in Fig. 1) and mutually reinforce each other. For example, as knowledge is being explored or exploited, the structure of inter-organisational network [29], inter-organisational trust [30], and culture [31] are being (re)built and developed, which facilitate the contextual construction of IOKE. These interactive processes mutually shape the dynamic nature of IOKE.

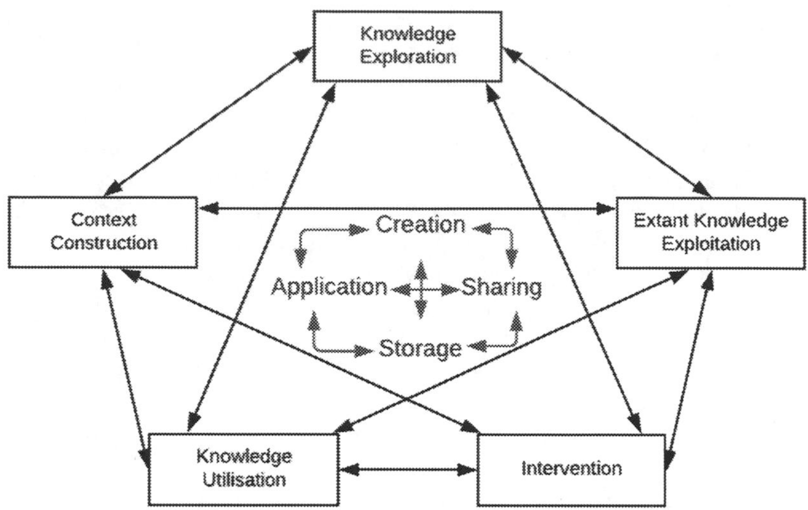

Fig. 1. Inter-organisational knowledge exchange process.

3 The Role of ICTs for Inter-organisational Knowledge Exchange

ICTs are crucial for the dynamic nature of IOKE, as they strengthen the efficiency of IOKE practices [32]. To date, ICTs have been studied through different perspectives, as for example, the discrete entity, the ensemble, the structure, sociomaterial and the socio-technical perspective, among others. Orlikowski and Iacono [33] argue that these perspectives are the more prominent ICT-based ones for the study of organisational practices, such as IOKE. Over the years, these still remain the more influential ones among organisation studies. For example, Sarker et al. [34] argue for the relevance of the socio-technical perspective for studying organisations as being the "axis of cohesion in IS" (p. 700). Similarly, Hultin [35] argues for the sociomaterial approach and there is a multitude of empirical studies leveraging it for studying organisations and organising [36, 37]. However, each of these perspectives emphasises different aspects of the IOKE process, influencing how the process itself and the role of ICTs are understood and interpreted. Through a narrative literature review approach, we pay attention on both historical and more recent studies that discuss IOKE from these ICT perspectives. In what follows, we discuss these perspectives in more detail (see Table 1 for an overview).

3.1 Discrete Entity Perspective

The Discrete Entity perspective treats ICTs as a discrete entity or object [38] that can stand apart from the IOKE process. ICTs can be classified by types (e.g., communication or computing technologies), and by applications (e.g., content management systems) [39]. ICTs constitute a distinct entity that is additional and affiliated to IOKE and interacts with various aspects of IOKE practices. The focus is on how ICTs, as solely an artefact with distinct characteristics, affect IOKE. For example, social media, being almost spatiotemporally agnostic, provide a digital platform for interaction and knowledge exchange across boundaries [40–42]. Email's rapid communication and turnaround capabilities enable faster inter-organisational learning [43, 44]. Therefore, through the discrete entity perspective, ICTs are seen as independent tools, which actors in the social world (e.g., people, organisations, knowledge, relations) interact with within the IOKE process. In other words, ICTs in an IOKE context are seen as affecting IOKE practices by facilitating or inhibiting them, without any other influence on the practice itself. Under this perspective, the IOKE process can be conceptualised as being ICT-enabled, with ICTs being an add-on to the process.

3.2 Mutually Dependent Ensemble Perspective

The mutually dependent ensemble perspective conceptualises ICTs as "part of the complex process through which organising is accomplished" [38]. Studies normally emphasise the interplay between ICTs and organisations, e.g., how technology and organisations mutually depend on each other on the basis of their interactions [38, 45].

Work can be seen as an evolving process of shifting objects from one state to another, reflecting an iterative problem-solving practice where practical knowing is embedded in moving objects from their start state to their end state [46]. The flexibility of inter-organisational collaboration is a dynamic characteristic that changes over time, influencing individuals' understanding regarding technology and affecting changes on the context of the collaboration [47]. In this light, ICTs are considered immersed and embedded in organisational practices, whereby ICTs, organisations, and humans are interdependent and associated with each other, shaping the IOKE process [45, 48]. In an IOKE context, the role of ICT is to interact with organisation and then together influence and shape the IOKE practices, where the emphasis is on the interaction between organisations and ICTs, such as how ICT affords or constrains user interaction for knowledge exchange [49]. Therefore, the mutually dependent ensemble perspective views IOKE as an ICT-embedded process in which people and technology shape mutually dependent dynamic interactions that evolve practical knowing over time.

3.3 Structure Perspective

The perspective of ICTs as structure conceptualises technologies as embodied in social structures, such as rules and resources [33, 50]. Structuration theory [50] argues that social structures are constructed into technology by artefact designers and they are then appropriated by users as the latter interact with the technology [51]. Similar to the ensemble view, this perspective focuses on the interplay between technology and people that mutually shape the IOKE process. For example, Rosenbaum and Shachaf [24] argue that as people adapt various ICTs while interacting with online Q&A sites, their identity formation and maintenance is (re-)created through which the structure of the online community and participants' identity are co-constituted. However, this perspective emphasises the human-technology interactive nature of the IOKE process and how it is influenced by contextual structures, such as rules and routines, contrary to the ensemble perspective that emphasises objects, such as knowledge, interests and artefacts. For example, inter-organisational practices are viewed as recursive actions of the structural properties of the network where network agents, enabled or inhibited by rules, make sense of the situated context and convert meaning of ongoing actions to others [52]. According to this perspective, in an IOKE environment, organisations appropriate ICTs are appropriated and (re)produce social structures in IOKE practices. In short, IOKE is conceptualised as an ICT-embodied process in which people situated in the context appropriate social structures embodied in ICT artefacts through IOKE practices.

3.4 Sociomaterial Perspective

This perspective conceptualises ICTs with a materiality shaped by social practices [38]. ICTs are mutually related to other sociomaterial elements of the organisations and are materially constituted with actions in emergent practices of the IOKE. Therefore, all materiality should be considered as social, since it is created, interpreted and used in social processes [53]. Sociomateriality indicates an enactment of activities that blend materiality within social contexts [54] and thus, technologies are constituted through the imbrication of social and material agencies in practice (i.e., sociomaterial practice) [55, 56]. For example, the sociomaterial perspective conceptualises coordination as performed through the imbrication of diverse coordination technologies, inter-organisational knowledge transfer routines, and diversity of situations [7]. Learning is conceptualised as a matter of enactment of different knowledge resources, values, objects, and relations [57]. Sociomateriality, thus, challenges the separated ontological reality where ICTs are viewed separately from organisations and posits that all practices appear as the imbrication of technologies, humans and contexts [58]. In the IOKE context, the role of ICT is to intra-act with organisations within IOKE practices, and the focus is how sociomaterial facets (knowledge, ICT artefacts, inter-organisational relations, organisations) emerge, shape and are shaped by IOKE practices. Therefore, IOKE is conceptualised as an ICT-entangled process where sociomaterial facets are imbricated and entangled in the shaping of IOKE.

3.5 Socio-technical Perspective

This perspective sees ICTs as a system that combines both technical and social subsystems [53]. The technical subsystem refers to ICTs with materiality (i.e., the technological artefact), or sociomaterial practices. The social subsystem refers to the unfolding social constructions in relation to institutions such as social roles, power relations and hierarchies [53]. This perspective acknowledges the significance of sociomateriality but places the focus on the macro-level where the social subsystem exists. As such, studies adopting the socio-technical perspective focus on how the properties of a social subsystem (e.g., norms, rules, etc.) are reinforced through the imbrication of material and social agencies within the technical subsystem (i.e., ICTs) towards a 'joint optimisation' [53, 59]. For example, Silver and Markus [60] argue that an IT artefact's technical and social characteristics are equally important and together will shape its impacts. Geels [61] conceptualises dynamic patterns in socio-technical systems and examines innovation ecosystems where actors (people and artefacts) combine social resources and capabilities and interact within a network to create and deliver value [6].

In these studies, ICTs are conceptualised by considering the interactions between the technical and the social world, linking both the technical and social components that jointly shape the socio-technical system used in IOKE practices. In turn, IOKE can be seen as an ecosystem where technical and social subsystems of actors (human/organisation, knowledge, ICT artefacts) interact and mutually shape the IOKE process. Under this perspective, IOKE is conceptualised as an ICT-optimised process through which IOKE practices are shaped by the interrelated and joint optimisation of technical and social subsystems.

Table 1. Summary of the examined perspectives of ICTs

Perspective	How ICTs are defined	The role ICTs play	Implications for ICT-based IOKE
Discrete entity	ICTs are a distinct entity that is an add-on and connected to the IOKE process	The focus is on how ICTs as solely an artefact affect the IOKE	IOKE is conceptualised as an ICT-augmented process, where ICTs are independent but facilitate or inhibit inter-organisational collaboration relationships or activities
Mutually dependent ensemble	ICTs are a collection of additional resources that individuals are associated with, and highly embedded in practices	The focus is on how ICTs and individuals interact, mutually evolve and change IOKE practices	IOKE is conceptualised as an ICT-embedded process in which people and technology shape dynamic interactions that are mutually dependent and evolve practices over time
Structure	ICTs are technologies embodied in social structures, e.g., rules and resources [33, 50]	The focus is on how ICTs and people interact to evolve the context of IOKE practices	IOKE is conceptualised as an ICT-embodied process in which people appropriate the ICT-embodied social structures through IOKE practices

(continued)

Table 1. (*continued*)

Perspective	How ICTs are defined	The role ICTs play	Implications for ICT-based IOKE
Sociomaterial	ICTs are technologies with a materiality, shaped by social practices [38]	The focus is on how ICTs and actions are materially constituted and intrinsic to IOKE practices	IOKE is conceptualised as an ICT-entangled process in which sociomaterial facets are mutually imbricated and entangled. Different sociomaterial facets (subjects, objects, inter-organisational relations, partners) of equal significance afford understanding of the IOKE
Socio-technical System	ICTs as a socio-technical system that combines both technical and social subsystems [53]	The focus is on how ICTs link the technical world and the social world by affording a socio-technical system in which people, artefacts and social aspects interact to develop both social and technical aspects of IOKE practices	IOKE is conceptualised as an ICT-optimised process where technical and social subsystems of actors (human/organisation, knowledge, ICT artefacts) interact and mutually shape the IOKE process. IOKE practices here are shaped by the interrelated and joint optimisation of technical and social subsystems

4 Implications for Understanding Inter-organisational Knowledge Exchange

While the previous discussion cannot be considered as an exhaustive presentation of the multitude of perspectives of ICTs within the context of IOKE, it offers a categorisation of the diversity of the field, through the analysis of how different ICT perspectives conceptualise ICTs, their role, and the IOKE process. It also shows that typically the focus is placed on the interaction among artefacts, people, knowledge, and relations in a certain context within a certain process. This suggests that adopting one of these perspectives may lead to disregarding that IOKE is the encapsulation and interaction of several processes, i.e., knowledge creation, sharing, storage, and application. These processes are not simply assembled together, but they interact with each other in order to inform knowledge exchange. This means that IOKE depends not only on the interaction of facets (e.g., entities, actors, ICTs), but on the interaction of the aforementioned processes. To the extent that ICTs play a role within each of these processes (e.g., for knowledge sharing), there will be an accumulated impact from all these processes on IOKE, forming and shaping it, but also shaping the way individuals and organisations participate in this process. Most crucially, depending on the adopted perspective for investigating IOKE, scholars will be applying their own set of assumptions and interests shedding light on certain processes and obscuring or disregarding others, whereas the way ICTs are enmeshed within knowledge creation, sharing, storage, and application, individually and collectively, is focal for IOKE.

5 Conclusion

ICTs are increasingly used for inter-organisational collaborations, and thereby it is necessary to understand their role in IOKE from a more comprehensive perspective. This paper focused on exploring how some of the more influential perspectives of ICTs are typically applied within IOKE contexts to identify current limitations and challenges for a holistic understanding. While current perspectives of ICTs are diverse, each tends to focus on facets of the knowledge exchange process; hence an integrative view that addresses the role of ICTs and encapsulates the multiple interactive processes that shape the dynamic nature of IOKE is missing. We posit that this is something that warrants further future research. Exploring how ICTs shape and are shaped by the interactive processes of IOKE, particularly across dimensions such as the temporal one, is of interest, especially now as we move faster towards increasingly digitised societies and organisational practices as a result of intense digitalisation.

References

1. Alexiev, A.S., Volberda, H.W., Van den Bosch, F.A.J.: Interorganizational collaboration and firm innovativeness: unpacking the role of the organisational environment. J. Bus. Res. **69**, 974–984 (2016). https://doi.org/10.1016/j.jbusres.2015.09.002
2. Hofeditz, L., Mirbabaie, M., Stieglitz, S.: Virtually Extended Coworking Spaces? – The Reinforcement of Social Proximity, Motivation and Knowledge Sharing Through ICT. arXiv: 2012.09538 [cs] (2020)
3. Mozaffar, H., Panteli, N.: The online community knowledge flows: distance and direction. Eur. J. Inf. Syst. 1–14 (2021). https://doi.org/10.1080/0960085X.2020.1866442.
4. Wang, W.-T., Wu, S.-Y.: Knowledge management based on information technology in response to COVID-19 crisis. Knowl. Manag. Res. Pract. 1–7 (2020). https://doi.org/10.1080/14778238.2020.1860665
5. Papadopoulos, T., Baltas, K.N., Balta, M.E.: The use of digital technologies by small and medium enterprises during COVID-19: implications for theory and practice. Int. J. Inf. Manage. **55**, 102192 (2020). https://doi.org/10.1016/j.ijinfomgt.2020.102192
6. Walrave, B., Talmar, M., Podoynitsyna, K.S., Romme, A.G.L., Verbong, G.P.J.: A multi-level perspective on innovation ecosystems for path-breaking innovation. Technol. Forecast. Soc. Chang. **136**, 103–113 (2018). https://doi.org/10.1016/j.techfore.2017.04.011

7. Nova, N.A., González, R.A.: Reframing coordination in knowledge transfer: a sociomaterial perspective. In: Fred, A., Dietz, J., Aveiro, D., Liu, K., Bernardino, J., Filipe, J. (eds.) IC3K 2016. CCIS, vol. 914, pp. 346–362. Springer, Cham (2019). https://doi.org/10.1007/978-3-319-99701-8_17
8. Bryman, A.: Social Research Methods. Oxford University Press, Oxford (2012)
9. Schauer, A., Vasconcelos, A.C., Sen, B.: The ShaRInK framework: a holistic perspective on key categories of influences shaping individual perceptions of knowledge sharing. J. Knowl. Manag. **19**, 770–790 (2015). https://doi.org/10.1108/JKM-12-2014-0519
10. Deken, F., Berends, H., Gemser, G., Lauche, K.: Strategizing and the initiation of interorganizational collaboration through prospective resourcing. AMJ. **61**, 1920–1950 (2018). https://doi.org/10.5465/amj.2016.0687
11. Radziwon, A., Bogers, M.: Open innovation in SMEs: exploring inter-organisational relationships in an ecosystem. Technol. Forecast. Soc. Chang. **146**, 573–587 (2019). https://doi.org/10.1016/j.techfore.2018.04.021
12. Fazey, I., et al.: Knowledge exchange: a review and research agenda for environmental management. Envir. Conserv. **40**, 19–36 (2013). https://doi.org/10.1017/S037689291200029X
13. Davenport, J.J.: Exploring the Theory and Practice of Knowledge Exchange: intention, context and characteristics. 427 (2018)
14. Davison, R.M., Ou, C.X.J., Martinsons, M.G.: Interpersonal knowledge exchange in China: the impact of guanxi and social media. Inf. Manag. **55**, 224–234 (2018). https://doi.org/10.1016/j.im.2017.05.008
15. Algeo, C.: How do project managers acquire and exchange knowledge? An action research study of project managers in Australia. Presented at the (2014)
16. Phillipson, J., Lowe, P., Proctor, A., Ruto, E.: Stakeholder engagement and knowledge exchange in environmental research. J. Environ. Manage. **95**, 56–65 (2012). https://doi.org/10.1016/j.jenvman.2011.10.005
17. Al-Busaidi, K.A., Olfman, L.: Knowledge sharing through inter-organisational knowledge sharing systems. VINE J. Inf. Knowl. Manag. Syst. Bingley **47**, 110–136 (2017)
18. Blecker, T., Neumann, R.: Interorganizational Knowledge Management: Some Perspectives for Knowledge Oriented Strategic Management in Virtual Organisations. Presented at the (2000).https://doi.org/10.4018/978-1-930708-65-5.ch004
19. Loebbecke, C., van Fenema, P.C., Powell, P.: Managing inter-organisational knowledge sharing. J. Strateg. Inf. Syst. **25**, 4–14 (2016). https://doi.org/10.1016/j.jsis.2015.12.002
20. Ward, V., Smith, S., House, A., Hamer, S.: Exploring knowledge exchange: a useful framework for practice and policy. Soc. Sci. Med. **74**, 297–304 (2012). https://doi.org/10.1016/j.socscimed.2011.09.021.25
21. Mentzas, G., Apostolou, D., Kafentzis, K., Georgolios, P.: Inter-organisational networks for knowledge sharing and trading. Inf Technol Manage. **7**, 259–276 (2006). https://doi.org/10.1007/s10799-006-0276-8
22. Prihodova, L., Guerin, S., Tunney, C., Kernohan, W.G.: Key components of knowledge transfer and exchange in health services research: findings from a systematic scoping review. J. Adv. Nurs. **75**, 313–326 (2019). https://doi.org/10.1111/jan.13836
23. Cannatelli, B., Smith, B., Giudici, A., Jones, J., Conger, M.: An expanded model of distributed leadership in organizational knowledge creation. Long Range Plan. **50**, 582–602 (2017). https://doi.org/10.1016/j.lrp.2016.10.002
24. Rosenbaum, H., Shachaf, P.: A structuration approach to online communities of practice: The case of Q&A communities. J. Am. Soc. Inform. Sci. Technol. **61**, 1933–1944 (2010). https://doi.org/10.1002/asi.21340

25. Ward, V., House, A., Hamer, S.: Developing a framework for transferring knowledge into action: a thematic analysis of the literature. J. Health Serv. Res. Policy **14**, 156–164 (2009). https://doi.org/10.1258/jhsrp.2009.008120
26. Alavi, M., Leidner, D.E.: Review: knowledge management and knowledge management systems: conceptual foundations and research issues. MIS Q. **25**, 107–136 (2001). https://doi.org/10.2307/3250961
27. Michailova, S., Gupta, A.: Knowledge sharing in consulting companies: opportunities and limitations of knowledge codification. J. Inf. Knowl. Manag. 201–212 (2005)
28. Akhavan, P., Ghojavand, S., Abdali, R.: Knowledge sharing and its impact on knowledge creation. J. Inf. Knowl. Manag. **11**(02), 1250012 (2012). https://doi.org/10.1142/S0219649212500128
29. Kempner-Moreira, F., Freire, P.D.S.: The five stages of evolution of inter-organisational networks: a review of the literature. J. Inf. Knowl. Manag. **19**(04), 2050038 (2020). https://doi.org/10.1142/S0219649220500380
30. Tang, P., Chen, H., Shao, S.: Examining the intergovernmental and interorganizational network of responding to major accidents for improving the emergency management system in China. Complexity **2018**, 1–16 (2018). https://doi.org/10.1155/2018/8935872
31. Larentis, F., Antonello, C.S., Slongo, L.A.: Inter-Organizational Culture: Linking Relationship Marketing with Organizational Behavior. Springer (2018). https://books.google.co.uk/books?id=0W9_DwAAQBAJ
32. Alavi, M., Leidner, D.E.: Research commentary: technology-mediated learning—a call for greater depth and breadth of research. Inf. Syst. Res. **12**, 1 (2001). https://doi.org/10.1287/isre.12.1.1.9720
33. Orlikowski, W., Iacono, S.: Research commentary: desperately seeking the "IT" in IT research—a call to theorising the IT artifact. Inf. Syst. Res. **12**, 121–134 (2001). https://doi.org/10.1287/isre.12.2.121.9700
34. Sarker, S., Chatterjee, S., Xiao Xiao, Elbanna, A.: Sociotechnical axis of cohesion for the is discipline: its historical legacy and its continued relevance. MIS Q. **43**, 695-A5 (2019). https://doi.org/10.25300/MISQ/2019/13747
35. Hultin, L.: On becoming a sociomaterial researcher: exploring epistemological practices grounded in a relational, performative ontology. Inf. Organ. **29**, 91–104 (2019). https://doi.org/10.1016/j.infoandorg.2019.04.004
36. Barrett, M., Oborn, E., Orlikowski, W.: Creating value in online communities: the sociomaterial configuring of strategy, platform, and stakeholder engagement. Inf. Syst. Res. **27**, 704–723 (2016). https://doi.org/10.1287/isre.2016.0648
37. Pelizza, A.: Towards a sociomaterial approach to inter-organisational boundaries: How information systems elicit relevant knowledge in government outsourcing. J. Inf. Technol. 0268396220934490 (2020). https://doi.org/10.1177/0268396220934490
38. Orlikowski, W., Scott, S.V.: Sociomateriality: challenging the separation of technology, work and organization. Acad. Manag. Annals **2**, 433–474 (2008)
39. Sein, M.K., Harindranath, G.: Conceptualising the ICT artifact: toward understanding the role of ICT in national development. Inf. Soc. **20**, 15–24 (2004). https://doi.org/10.1080/01972240490269942
40. Foth, M., Forlano, L., Satchell, C., Gibbs, M.: From Social Butterfly to Engaged Citizen: Urban Informatics, Social Media, Ubiquitous Computing, and Mobile Technology to Support Citizen Engagement. . MIT Press, Cambridge (2011)
41. Hislop, D., Bosua, R., Helms, R.: Knowledge Management in Organisations: A Critical Introduction. Oxford University Press, Oxford (2018)
42. Ooms, W., Bell, J., Kok, R.A.W.: Use of social media in inbound open innovation: building capabilities for absorptive capacity. Create. Innov. Manag. **24**, 136–150 (2015). https://doi.org/10.1111/caim.12105

43. Nawinna, D., Venable, J.R.: Effects of ICT-enabled social capital on inter-organisational relationships and performance: empirical evidence from an emerging economy. Inf. Technol. Dev. **25**, 49–68 (2019). https://doi.org/10.1080/02681102.2018.1451979
44. Scott, J.E.: Facilitating interorganizational learning with information technology. J. Manag. Inf. Syst. **17**, 81–113 (2000). https://doi.org/10.1080/07421222.2000.11045648
45. Goldkuhl, G.: What kind of pragmatism in information systems research? Presented at the AIS SIGPrag Inaugural Meeting at ICIS in Paris (2008)
46. Carlile, P.R.: A pragmatic view of knowledge and boundaries: boundary objects in new product development. Organ. Sci. **13**, 442–455 (2002). https://doi.org/10.1287/orsc.13.4.442.2953
47. Kopanaki, E., Smithson, S.: The issue of flexibility in inter-organisational collaboration: an appreciative systems thinking perspective. Int. J. Appl. Syst. Stud. 5, ied Systemic Studies (2013). https://doi.org/10.1504/IJASS.2013.053349
48. Goldkuhl, G.: From ensemble view to ensemble artefact – an inquiry on conceptualisations of the IT artefact. Syst. Signs Actions **7**, 49–72 (2013)
49. Gott, A., Schaefer, S.M.: Knowledge Sharing in the Public Sector An Affordance Approach of Information and Communications Technology (2020). https://lup.lub.lu.se/luur/download?func=downloadFile&recordOId=9012606&fileOId=9012610
50. Giddens, A.: The Constitution of Society: Outline of the Theory of Structuration. University of California Press (1984)
51. Tchounikine, P.: Designing for appropriation: a theoretical account. Hum. Comput. Interact. **32**, 155–195 (2017). https://doi.org/10.1080/07370024.2016.1203263
52. Ellis, N., Mayer, R.: Inter-organisational relationships and strategy development in an evolving industrial network: mapping structure and process. J. Mark. Manag. **17**, 183–223 (2001). https://doi.org/10.1362/0267257012571410
53. Leonardi, P.M., Nardi, B.A., Kallinikos, J.: Materiality and Organising: Social Interaction in a Technological World. OUP Oxford (2012)
54. Ayoko, O.B., Ashkanasy, N.M.: Organisational Behaviour and the Physical Environment. Routledge, London (2019)
55. Leonardi, P.M.: When flexible routines meet flexible technologies: affordance, constraint, and the imbrication of human and material agencies. MIS Q. **35**, 147–167 (2011). https://doi.org/10.2307/23043493
56. Orlikowski, W.J.: Sociomaterial practices: exploring technology at work. Organ. Stud. **28**, 1435–1448 (2007). https://doi.org/10.1177/0170840607081138
57. Fenwick, T., Nerland, M., Jensen, K.: Sociomaterial approaches to conceptualising professional learning and practice. J. Educ. Work **25**, 1–13 (2012). https://doi.org/10.1080/13639080.2012.644901
58. Leonardi, P.M.: Theoretical foundations for the study of sociomateriality. Inf. Organ. **23**, 59–76 (2013). https://doi.org/10.1016/j.infoandorg.2013.02.002
59. Jones, A., Bissell, C.: The social construction of educational technology through the use of authentic software tools. Res. Learn. Technol. 19 (2011). https://doi.org/10.3402/rlt.v19i3.17116
60. Silver, M.S., Markus, M.L.: Conceptualising the SocioTechnical (ST) Artifact. **7**, 8 (2013)
61. Geels, F.W.: Ontologies, socio-technical transitions (to sustainability), and the multi-level perspective. Res. Policy **39**, 495–510 (2010). https://doi.org/10.1016/j.respol.2010.01.022

Industry 4.0 and Organisations: Key Organisational Capabilities

Stefan Smuts(✉), Alta van der Merwe, and Hanlie Smuts

Department of Informatics, University of Pretoria, Pretoria, South Africa
u19235781@tuks.co.za, {alta,hanlie.smuts}@up.ac.za

Abstract. The fast-paced evolution of digital technologies, termed the fourth industrial revolution (4IR), influences organisations to realise digital technology potential from a holistic point of view. In this context, organisational competitiveness relies on whether organisations' business value-creation capabilities are adaptable and flexible. The purpose of this study was to consider the 4IR key organisational capabilities that organisations require to ensure sustainability and to create business value. We identified 14 4IR organisational capabilities and operationalised these capabilities by mapping them to the dynamic capabilities sensing (strategic leadership, external drivers, data value), seizing (decision-making, technology features, software services and solutions) and transforming (business model, process optimisation, product efficacy, organisation, customer) as defined by Teece. Three 4IR organisational capabilities, namely employees, skills and expertise, as well as communication, are relevant across all three dynamic capabilities. By applying the 4IR organisational capabilities, organisations will be able to consider the end-to-end impact of 4IR on them and to address action plans to sustain value, or to create new business value.

Keywords: Industry 4.0 · Organisational capabilities · Dynamic capabilities

1 Introduction

To remain competitive, organisations have to manage the significant evolution of digital technologies from two perspectives: firstly, the scope of the evolution and secondly, the pace at which it takes place [1, 2]. This evolution of digital technology, referred to as the fourth industrial revolution (4IR) [3, 4], is associated with aspects such as artificial intelligence, the internet of things, big data, robotics, cloud computing and augmented reality [5]. However, for organisations to realise the 4IR potential from a comprehensive point of view, 4IR-relevant organisational aspects such as an 4IR-relevant strategy, digital business model innovation, technology investment optimisation, workforce management complexity, digital eco-systems, technology-centric convergence, virtual model and physical environment linkage, value chain digitalisation and product portfolio innovation, must be considered [6].

While 4IR potentially offers great value to organisations, traditional business models struggle to meet and keep up with the demands of the new digital economy, potentially

Published by Springer Nature Switzerland AG 2021
D. Dennehy et al. (Eds.): I3E 2021, LNCS 12896, pp. 423–438, 2021.
https://doi.org/10.1007/978-3-030-85447-8_36

threatening their sustainability [7]. Furthermore, emerging technological implementation and transformation fail to realise the desired business value-creation intentions [8]. Organisational competitiveness therefore relies on whether organisations' business value-creation capabilities are adaptable and flexible [9]. Such efficacy of capabilities enables organisations to adjust organisational and technology strategies dynamically and to ensure sustained alignment between the organisation's capabilities and business value creation [9, 10].

This research study was conducted to understand the required capabilities better and to ensure that the identified capabilities enable business value-creation in the context of 4IR. The focus of this paper is therefore on contributing to the discourse on what 4IR organisational capabilities entail, by considering the following research question: "*What are the 4IR key organisational capabilities that organisations need to consider?*" We reflect on this research question by considering an overview of 4IR in an organisational context and how it affects key organisational capabilities required.

In this paper, we firstly provide an overview of literature in Sect. 2, followed by the research approach in Sect. 3. In Sect. 4 we present a discussion on the data analysis and findings, while Sect. 5 details the contribution of the study. Section 6 concludes the paper.

2 Background

The aim of 4IR is to use technology to realise improved operational efficiency and productivity, to optimise business systems and to improve customer experience [11, 12]. Furthermore, human-machine interaction enables enhanced value-added services, automatic data exchange and communication, as well as analysis across value chains [13, 14] This contributes to business process efficacy and ultimately enables the creation of quality products and services at lower cost [7, 11].

In this section, we consider 4IR in the context of organisations, organisational capabilities and organisational capability theory.

2.1 Industry 4.0 and Organisations

The evolution of digital technologies had a significant impact on organisations [15], altering organisational practices as 4IR technologies (e.g. the internet of things, robotics, etc.) replaced routine and repetitive jobs [16]. Process visualisation and machine learning techniques may be applied to detect flaws and to optimise outputs [15]. To allow organisations to manage these multiple internal and external factors to enhance business value and create a sustainable competitive advantage, 4IR horizontal and vertical integration alignment must be considered [16, 17]. The activities of a horizontally integrated organisation focus on its core competencies and build their end-to-end value chain through establishing partnerships. Alternatively, a vertically integrated company manages most of its value chain in-house, e.g. product development, manufacturing, sales, distribution and marketing [15–17].

Therefore, to allow organisations to manage multiple complexities introduced by 4IR, the development and application of new models and methods are required [18].

These models and methods need to consider complex systems, comprehensive infrastructure consisting of a high-quality information network and internet connectivity, security and privacy, data protection, work organisation and design, and the effective use of resources [3, 17, 19, 20]. As these complex systems affect the roles of employees and managing teams of highly specialised technical experts, organisational performance needs to take cognisance of skilling employees to operate in the new technological revolution, with specific profiles that are currently non-existent [21, 22].

2.2 Organisational Capabilities and Challenges

Organisational capabilities are intangible assets and refer to the "collective skills, expertise, and alignment of the people" in the organisation [23: 119]. Capabilities span the whole organisation, as opposed to competencies that tend to be associated with an individual employee [23]. Such organisational capabilities represent the ways in which people and resources are combined to accomplish work [23, 24]. Capabilities therefore refer to the ability to take action (e.g. a decision), to carry out a set of strategic or operational activities, to accomplish a practised or routine activity, or to perform a collection of routines such as processes or procedures [25, 26]. In this context, the importance of management capability to adapt effectively to changing environments by "re-configuring internal and external organisational skills and resources" is highlighted [27].

However, scholars report many challenges with regard to organisational capabilities in the context of 4IR [8]. Some of these challenges include identifying which strategic technologies to focus on, considering multiple factors when complex requirements and their impact on business value-creation must be assessed and balancing market-pull and technology-push approaches to find new business value-creation initiatives based on new technology capability [7, 8, 28]. At an operational level, challenges include inconsistent business processes, duplicated software solutions, limited system capability to support operations and lack of end-to-end visibility and transparency [7–9, 29].

2.3 Organisational Capability Theory

As organisations initiate and execute transformation of their business, technology and operational aspects, they utilise capability maturity models and metrics to monitor the measurement of success [28]. Maturity models have proven to be a significant tool to guide organisations in improving their capabilities and process orientation [30], and several maturity models have been developed with the aim to evaluate progress of organisational capability improvement [31–33]. Maturity models, in the context of capabilities, track the improvement (maturing) of organisational and technological systems in order to increase their capabilities over time with the aim to achieve the defined future state [32]. Some examples of such capability maturity models include the capability maturity model consisting of a five-staged structure (initial, repeatable, defined, managed, optimising) [34], a maturity model for assessing organisational process capabilities consisting of nine dimensions (products, customers, operations, technology, strategy, leadership, governance, culture, people) [32], a quality management maturity grid consisting of 14 steps [35] and multiple project management maturity models [36].

For the purpose of this study and in the context of 4IR, dynamic capabilities were considered as defined by David Teece [37]. Teece's [27, 37] concept of dynamic capabilities presumed that organisations require the ability to navigate fast-changing markets by reshaping the organisation's asset structure and realise the essential internal and external transformation. The dynamic capabilities included three aspects: *sensing* (the capacity to explore and shape opportunities and threats), *seizing* (to take hold of opportunities) and *transforming* (to maintain competitiveness through improving and reconstructing the organisation's tangible and intangible assets) [27]. These three capabilities, sensing, seizing and transforming, were deemed key to ensure that an organisation may reach the next transformative stage [24].

3 Research Approach

The objective of this paper is to present the 4IR key organisational capabilities that organisations need to consider. In order to achieve the objective, data collection was carried out in two steps. Firstly, a systematic literature review (SLR) to synthesise the existing body of completed and recorded work produced by researchers, scholars and practitioners was conducted to identify 4IR organisational capabilities [38, 39]. Peer-reviewed and academic sources such as technical reports, books and conference proceedings were selected for the SLR process [40, 41]. To include all references to 4IR and organisational capability, the search terms were chosen as: ("fourth industrial revolution" and "organisational capability") or ("Industry 4" and "organisational capability"). The initial research studies extracted (165) (Fig. 1) were screened by applying specific criteria such as non-English studies, anecdotal or opinion-based papers and duplicate studies that formed part of the result set. Inclusion criteria consisted of peer-reviewed publications and technical reports relevant to the research question. After the initial search, as well as the application of inclusion and exclusion criteria, 153 publications were selected as shown in Fig. 1.

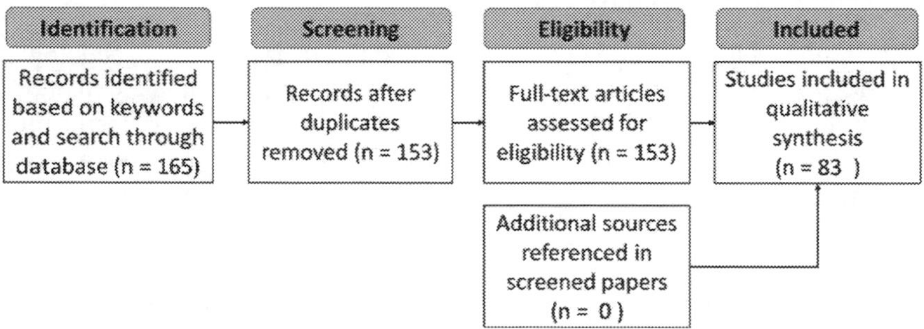

Fig. 1. Total number of papers extracted and analysed

We concluded a detailed screening of abstracts and analysis of the full text of the prospective papers, after which 83 papers were assessed in detail. Papers were excluded based on criteria such as studies not being associated with the research question, a keyword mismatch and irrelevance (e.g. about speech, about psychology, about racial analysis).

Secondly, semi-structured interviews were conducted in order to enrich the organisational capabilities defined through the SLR. A semi-structured interview guide was designed, guided by the SLR findings and consisting of two sections: the initial section captured respondent demographic information, followed by the second section containing the questions regarding key 4IR capabilities. Nine respondents were identified through purposive sampling based on their experience and knowledge related to the research study [42]. The profiles of respondents are summarised in Table 1.

Table 1. 4IR Organisational capabilities extracted from the literature.

Organisational level		Tenure at current organisation		Industry sector	
Senior management	1	9–12	2	Education	1
Executive	4	16+	2	Communication and information technology sector	3
Middle management	2	3–5	4	Financial sector	3
Specialist	2	6–8	1	Aviation	2

Seven of the nine respondents (78%) confirmed that they had undergone a digital transformation project in the past five years.

4 Data Analysis and Findings

The aim of this paper is to consider the 4IR key organisational capabilities. Themes and main themes were identified in the selected studies through a two-step process: firstly, descriptive codes were used to identify themes [43] and secondly, open coding was used to identify emerging main themes [44]. Table 2 depicts the extracted capabilities, identified themes, as well as the references.

Table 2. 4IR organisational capabilities extracted from the literature.

Theme	Capability from the literature	References
Leadership	Accountability	[23, 45]
Leadership	Co-created leadership/leadership	[7, 23, 45–49]
Organisation	Coherent brand identity	[23, 46]
Customer	Collaboration	[23, 50]

(continued)

Table 2. (*continued*)

Theme	Capability from the literature	References
Product efficacy	Creativity	[46, 51]
Customer	Customer connectivity	[5, 7, 23, 45]
Data value	Data-driven decision support	[5, 28, 47, 48, 50–52]
External environment	Deal with external disasters	[45, 47]
Customer	Dialogue	[45, 46, 48]
Organisation	Diversity and inclusion	[45, 46, 48]
Product efficacy	Efficiency	[23, 46]
Employees	Employee voice	[46, 48, 50, 51]
Employees	Employee-driven improvement	[46, 47, 51]
Skills and expertise	Enterprising behaviour	[7, 46, 47, 51]
External environment	Environment and market	[7, 8, 53]
Product efficacy	Flexibility	[46, 51, 53]
Product efficacy	Innovation	[8, 23, 46, 51, 52]
Skills and expertise	Legal and regulatory	[8, 45, 51]
Organisation	Organisational culture	[7, 28, 48, 51, 54]
Organisation	Organisation design	[7, 46, 47, 54, 55]
Organisation	Organisational agility	[28, 52]
Organisation	Organisational knowledge and continuous learning	[23, 48, 51, 54, 55]
Product efficacy	Product and service personalisation	[5, 28]
Product efficacy	Process transparency	[8, 46, 47, 50, 51, 54]
Product efficacy	Quality	[45–47, 49, 53]
Leadership	Shared mind-set	[23, 45, 51]
Product efficacy	Speed	[7, 23, 28]
Leadership	Stakeholder relationship management	[28, 51]
Leadership	Strategic unity	[7, 23, 45, 51]
Skills and expertise	Talent	[7, 8, 23, 45–47, 51]
Technology	Technology (context relevance and efficacy)	[7, 23, 28, 45, 47–51]
External environment	Waste minimisation and green practices	[45–47, 49, 53]

We identified nine unique 4 IR capability themes, namely leadership, organisation, customer, product efficacy, data value, external environment, employees, skills and expertise and technology.

Table 3. 4IR organisational capabilities extracted from the semi-structured interviews.

Theme	Description	Frequency count	
Customer	Customer experience, customer value, customer; customer travel experience; seamless customer experience; customer touch point; word of mouth; level of customer experience; free customer experience; many new customer	49	21%
Technology features	Digital technologies; latest technology; new technology; new tools; next generation technology; bespoke technological solutions; old-fashioned way; unique software features; new digital technology; technology	43	18%
Data value	Data; analysis of data; scientific data modelling; appointment of data; data science capabilities; use of data; value of data; new data services; master data management; actuarial scientific data; data processing capabilities; big data	36	15%
External drivers	4IR criteria; i4.0 type solutions; current newest trends; external driver; biggest external driver; industry; thorough impact assessment; technology intelligence process; company image	18	8%
Product efficacy	Efficient products delivery; products	17	7%
Employees	Employees; healthy team culture; behavioural change management; massive organisational shift; electronic skills matrix; employees' entry; whole organisation; organisational culture	16	7%

(*continued*)

Table 3. *(continued)*

Theme	Description	Frequency count	
Skills and expertise	Continuous learning opportunities; digital training platform; digital skills; certain software professionals; high-quality skillsets; domain of expertise; software services company; use of technology	10	4%
Process optimisation	Process of innovation; internal workflow tools; exit process/invoice; way of work; many manual processes; internal process; way of working; business improvement opportunities	9	4%
Strategic thinking	Strategic objectives; digital transformation objectives; much revenue; digital strategy; lockdown strategic initiative	8	3%
Organisation	Business unit; elements of business; new business unit; digital business unit	7	3%
Software services and solutions	Competitive software services; services provider relationship; use of services; solutions development philosophy; specific solutions development; system implementation project	6	3%
Business model	Virtual company; new business model; business value; business case approval; approved business case; differentiated business model	8	3%
Decision-making	Decision making; core pillar; significant focus	4	2%
Communication	Internal communications tools; information sharing tools; personalised communication	4	2%
	Total comments	**235**	**100%**

The qualitative data collected through the nine semi-structured interviews were analysed in order to identify 4IR capability themes. Major themes identified included customer, data, customer experience, employee, technology, external driver and business. Secondly, common themes highlighted in the interviews were collated and the frequency

Table 4. Integrated 4IR organisational capabilities

Theme	4IR capabilities from the literature	4IR capabilities from semi-structured interviews
Business model		Virtual company; new business model; business value; business case approval; approved business case; differentiated business model
Communication		Internal communications tools; information sharing tools; personalised communication
Customer	Collaboration, Customer connectivity, Dialogue	Customer experience, customer value, customer; customer travel experience; seamless customer experience; customer touch point; word of mouth; level of cx; free customer experience; many new customers
Data value	Data-driven decision support	Data; analysis of data; scientific data modelling; appointment of data; data science capabilities; use of data; value of data; new data services; master data management; actuarial scientific data; data processing capabilities; big data
Decision-making		Decision-making; core pillar; significant focus
Employees	Employee voice, Employee-driven improvement, Shared mind-set	Employees; healthy team culture; behavioural change management; massive organisational shift; electronic skills matrix; employees' entry; whole organisation; organisational culture
External drivers	Deal with external disasters, Environment and market, Waste minimisation and green practices	4IR criteria; i4.0 type solutions; present newest trends; external driver; biggest external driver; industry; thorough impact assessment; technology intelligence process; company image

(*continued*)

Table 4. (*continued*)

Theme	4IR capabilities from the literature	4IR capabilities from semi-structured interviews
Strategic leadership	Accountability, co-created leadership/leadership, Stakeholder relationship management, Strategic unity	strategic objectives; digital transformation objectives; much revenue; digital strategy; lockdown strategic initiative
Organisation	Coherent brand identity, Diversity and inclusion, Organisational culture, Organisation design, Organisational agility, Organisational knowledge and continuous learning	Business unit; elements of business; new business unit; digital business unit
Process optimisation	Efficiency, Speed, Process transparency	Process of innovation; internal workflow tools; exit process/invoice; way of work; many manual processes; internal processes; way of working; business improvement opportunities
Product efficacy	Creativity; Flexibility; Innovation; Product and service personalisation; Quality	Efficient product delivery; products
Skills and expertise	Enterprising behaviour, Legal and regulatory, Talent	Continuous learning opportunities; digital training platform; digital skills; certain software professionals; high-quality skillsets; domain of expertise; software services company; use of technology
Software services and solutions		Competitive software services; services provider relationship; use of services; solutions development philosophy; specific solutions development; system implementation project

(*continued*)

Table 4. (*continued*)

Theme	4IR capabilities from the literature	4IR capabilities from semi-structured interviews
Technology features	Technology (context relevance and efficacy)	Digital technology; latest technology; new technology; new tools; next-generation technology; bespoke technological solutions; old-fashioned way; unique software features; new digital technology; technology

of the comment was noted, as shown in Table 3. The theme *customer* was mentioned 49 times (21%), while *technology features* and *data value* were presented 43 (18%) and 36 (15%) times respectively.

We integrated the 4IR capabilities extracted from the literature (Table 2) with the capabilities extracted from the interview transcripts (Table 3), as shown in Table 4.

Where a particular 4IR capability was not present in the review of the literature or the interview data, we indicated that cell with a diagonal line. It may be observed that the enriched dataset shown in Table 4 consists of 14 4IR capabilities; the capabilities identified from the literature were enriched by four capabilities highlighted in the interviews, namely business model, communication, decision-making, and software services and solutions.

The *technology features capability* focuses on context relevance and efficacy of the 4IR digital technologies and how these technological opportunities translate into business value. The *business model capability* refers to the opportunities 4IR provides to organisations to differentiate their business models or create new business models, with the aim to increase or add business value. This capability is also informed by the *external driver capability* enabling the organisation to understand 4IR criteria and solution types (technology intelligence) deeply in order to inform differentiation. *Strategic leadership capability* combines these aspects into coherent strategic objectives, creating strategic unity and ensuring that all stakeholders are managed in this process. *Communication capability* is important from two perspectives: both internally in the organisation and externally to customers. Communication and knowledge-sharing internally in the organisation empower employees to make sense of the 4IR strategies, while communication with customers is personalised, based on the particular customers' profile and engagement with the organisation. *Customer capability* means the management of a seamless customer experience and all the capabilities in the organisation required to achieve it. Such personal customer experiences are possible through the *value of data capability*, where large datasets are analysed using different techniques to enable data-driven decision support, not just as it relates to the customer, but also generating business value insight for the organisations. This highlights the *decision-making capability* that enables actionable insights through a process of factual analysis and learning, rather than based on intuition only.

Employees as a 4IR capability refer to the management of the key impact on employee-driven improvement enabled by 4IR technologies, the significant organisational shift required towards a transformational culture and the impact on employee skills to deal with the new organisational and technology landscape. This capability is strongly associated with the *skills and expertise capability,* where an organisation must invest in continuous learning opportunities and a digital training platform to foster these high-quality skillsets. Organisational culture, organisational design, organisational agility and the establishment of new/revised business units based on the business model choice all form part of the *organisational capability*. The *process optimisation capability* refers to efficiency, process transparency and innovation, as it influences and relates to business improvement opportunities and ultimately the new way of work in an organisation. The *product efficacy capability* underpins two key aspects. The first is the creativity, flexibility and innovativeness of product design and service personalisation, and the second the efficacy of product delivery. A *software services and solutions capability* refers to competitive software services, whether an organisation follows an internal solutions development philosophy, or whether a service provider relationship and use of services are considered.

In order to report and operationalise the findings presented in Table 4, we mapped these to the dynamic capabilities sensing, seizing and transforming as defined by Teece [37] and present the detail in the next section.

5 Key 4IR Organisational Capabilities

The aim of this paper is to consider the key 4IR organisational capabilities. Fourteen 4IR organisational capabilities were extracted from the literature and from nine semi-structured interviews, whereafter the findings were operationalised by mapping them to Teece's 3 [37] dynamic capabilities depicted in Fig. 2. The definitions of dynamic capabilities theory informed the association to the particular 4IR organisational capability.

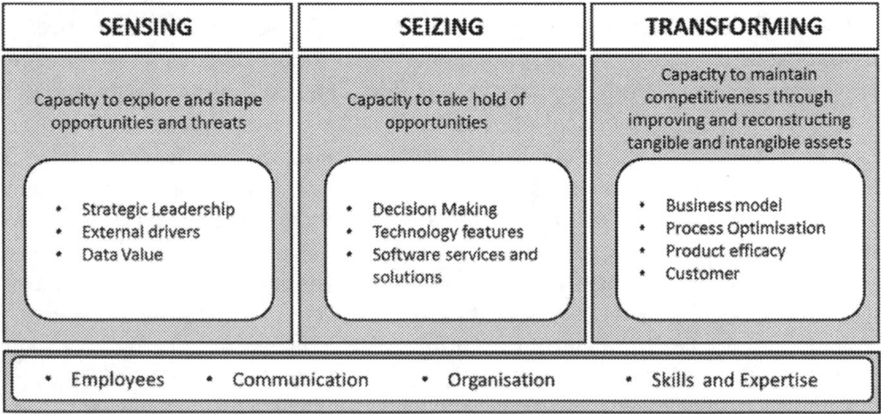

Fig. 2. 4IR relevant organisational capabilities (mapped to Teece's dynamic capabilities [37])

For an organisation to create business value in the 4IR world, it must constantly explore opportunities and be aware of potential threats in order to navigate fast-changing markets. To achieve this, through strategic leadership organisations must constantly scan (sense) the environment, consider external drivers that could have a potential impact on their concerns and obtain data-driven insights. Through this sensing dynamic capability, organisations may then seize opportunities, i.e. decide which opportunities to implement or which threats to address. These decisions will be informed by the technology features, software services and solutions to which the organisation has access. The next step is to implement these decisions and transform the organisation through business model changes, process optimisation, product and organisational capabilities – all to the benefit of the customer and ultimately to create value for the organisation.

Three 4IR organisational capabilities, namely employees, skills and expertise, and communication, are relevant across sensing, seizing and transforming. Employees and their skills and expertise are applied throughout the process, and this process will be affected by transformation. Communication – internal and external – will also take place across all three activities of sensing, seizing and transforming and will play a significant role during transformation. We have therefore placed these three 4IR capabilities across sensing, seizing and transforming.

6 Conclusion

Organisations must deal with significant evolution of digital technology (4IR) to remain competitive. While 4IR digital technologies potentially offer great value to organisations, traditional business models struggle to keep up with the demands of this new digital economy and require digital capabilities to sustain or create business value. In this study we considered the 4IR key organisational capabilities that organisations require to navigate the 4IR digital technology evolution. We identified 14 4IR organisational capabilities based on an SLR and nine semi-structured interviews. To operationalise the 14 4IR capabilities identified, we mapped these to the sensing, seizing and transforming dynamic capabilities defined by Teece [24]. By applying the 4IR organisational capabilities, organisations will be able to consider the end-to-end impact of 4IR on the organisations and to address action plans to sustain value holistically.

As the study proposes 4IR organisational capabilities in the context of dynamic capabilities, further research may be conducted to test the proposal in a real-world scenario in an organisation.

References

1. Bär, K., Herbert-Hansen, Z.N.L., Khalid, W.: Considering Industry 4.0 aspects in the supply chain for an SME. Prod. Eng. Res. Devel. **12**(6), 747–758 (2018). https://doi.org/10.1007/s11740-018-0851-y
2. Gerryts, E.W., Maree, J.G.: Enhancing the employability of young adults from socio-economically challenged contexts: theoretical overview. In: Maree, J. (ed.) Handbook of Innovative Career Counselling, pp. 425–444. Springer, Cham (2019). https://doi.org/10.1007/978-3-030-22799-9_24

3. Badri, A., Boudreau-Trudel, B., Souissi, A.S.: Occupational health and safety in the industry 4.0 era: a cause for major concern? Saf. Sci. **109**, 403–411 (2018)
4. Ding, B.: Pharma Industry 4.0: literature review and research opportunities in sustainable pharmaceutical supply chains. Process Saf. Environ. Protect. **119**, 115–130 (2018)
5. King, S., Grobbelaar, S.S.: Industry 4.0 and business model innovation: a scoping review. In: IEEE International Conference on Engineering, Technology and Innovation (ICE/ITMC), pp. 1–8. IEEE, Cardiff, UK (2020)
6. Smuts, S., van der Merwe, A., Smuts, H.: A strategic organisational perspective of Industry 4.0: a conceptual model. In: Hattingh, M., Matthee, M., Smuts, H., Pappas, I., Dwivedi, Y.K., Mäntymäki, M. (eds.) I3E 2020. LNCS, vol. 12066, pp. 89–101. Springer, Cham (2020). https://doi.org/10.1007/978-3-030-44999-5_8
7. Rautenbach, W.J., de Kock, I., Jooste, J.L.: The development of a conceptual model for enabling a value-adding digital transformation: a conceptual model that aids organisations in the digital transformation process. In: 2019 IEEE International Conference on Engineering, Technology and Innovation (ICE/ITMC), Valbonne Sophia-Antipolis, France, pp. 1–10. IEEE (2019)
8. Jacobs, J., Pretorius, M.W.: The major challenges facing organisations to create technology-enabled value in the fourth industrial revolution: a dynamic capabilities perspective in South Africa. S. Afr. J. Ind. Eng. **31**, 40–61 (2020)
9. Arendt, L.: Barriers to ICT adoption in SMEs: how to bridge the digital divide? J. Syst. Inf. Technol. **10**(2), 93–108 (2008)
10. Cheng, Y., et al.: Forecasting of potential impacts of disruptive technology in promising technological areas: elaborating the SIRS epidemic model in RFID technology. Technol. Forecast. Soc. Change **117**(C), pp. 170–183 (2017)
11. Roblek, V., Meško, M., Krapež, A.: A complex view of industry 4.0. SAGE Open **6**(2), 1–11 (2016)
12. Lu, Y.: Industry 4.0: A survey on technologies, applications and open research issues. J. Ind. Inf. Integr. **6**(2017), 1–10 (2017)
13. Khairuddin, S.M., Omar, F.I., Ahmad, N.: Digital inclusion domain in entrepreneurship: a preliminary analysis. Adv. Sci. Lett. **24**, 2721–2724 (2018)
14. Wagire, A.A.W., Rathore, A.P.S., Jain, R.: Analysis and synthesis of Industry 4.0 research landscape using latent semantic analysis approach. J. Manuf. Technol. Manag. (2018)
15. Yadav, N., Shankar, R., Singh Surya, P.: Impact of Industry4.0/ICTs, Lean Six Sigma and quality management systems on organisational performance. TQM J. **32**(4), 815–835 (2020)
16. Chen, J., Yin, X., Mei, L.: Holistic innovation: an emerging innovation paradigm. Int. J. Innov. Stud. **2**(1), 1–13 (2018)
17. Crnjac, M., Veža, I., Banduka, N.: From concept to the introduction of Industry 4.0. Int. J. Ind. Eng. Manag. (IJIEM) **8**(1), 21–30 (2017)
18. Pinzone, M., et al.: A framework for operative and social sustainability functionalities in human-centric cyber-physical production systems. Comput. Ind. Eng. (2018)
19. Lezzi, M., Lazoi, M., Corallo, A.: Cybersecurity for Industry 4.0 in the current literature: a reference framework. Comput. Ind. **103**, 97–110 (2018)
20. Karodia, N.C.: Managing the transition to a 'digital culture': the experience of financial service firms. In: Gordon Institute of Business Science, p. 107. University of Pretoria, Pretoria (2018)
21. Gareis, K., et al.: E-skills for jobs in Europe: Measuring progress and moving ahead (2014)
22. O'Connor, B.: Digital transformation: a framework for ICT literacy. In: A Report of the International ICT Literacy Panel (2007)
23. Ulrich, D., Smallwood, N.: Capitalizing on capabilities. Harvard Bus. Rev. p. 119–127 (2004)
24. Teece, D.J.: The foundations of enterprise performance: Dynamic and ordinary capabilities in an (economic) theory of firms. Acad. Manag. Perspect. **28**(4), 328–352 (2014)

25. Cetindamar, D., Phaal, R., Probert, D.: Understanding technology management as a dynamic capability: A framework for technology management activities. Technovation **29**(4), 237–246 (2009)
26. Winter, S.: Understanding dynamic capabilities. Strateg. Manag. J. **24**(10), 991–995 (2003)
27. Teece D., Pisano G.: The dynamic capabilities of firms. In: Holsapple C.W. (eds.) Handbook on Knowledge Management. International Handbooks on Information Systems, vol 2. Springer, Heidelberg (2003). https://doi.org/10.1007/978-3-540-24748-7_10
28. Huang, J., Chang, E., Jalavand, F.: Implementation of the road map to digital government transformation (DGT). Eng. Intell. Syst. **28**(2), 147–156 (2020)
29. Gerth, A.B., Peppard, J.: The dynamics of CIO derailment: how CIOs come undone and how to avoid it. Bus. Horizon **59**(1), 61–70 (2016)
30. Ćwiek-Kupczyńska, H., et al.: Measures for interoperability of phenotypic data: minimum information requirements and formatting. Plant Methods **12**(1), 44 (2016)
31. Ganzarain, J., Errasti, N.: Three stage maturity model in SME's toward Industry 4.0. J. Ind. Eng. Manag. **9**(5), 1119–1128 (2016)
32. Schumacher, A., Erol, S., Sihn, W.: A maturity model for assessing Industry 4.0 Readiness and Maturity of Manufacturing Enterprises. Procedia CIRP **52**, 161–166 (2016)
33. Lanza, G., Haefner, B., Kraemer, A.: Optimization of selective assembly and adaptive manufacturing by means of cyber-physical system based matching. CIRP Ann. **64**(1), 399–402 (2015)
34. Paulk, M.C., et al.: The capability maturity model for software. Softw. Eng. Project Manag. **10**, 1–26 (1993)
35. Crosby, P.B.: Quality is Free: The Art of Making Quality Certain. Penguin, New York (1979)
36. Backlund, F., Chronéer, D., Sundqvist, E.: Project management maturity models – a critical review: a case study within Swedish engineering and construction organizations. Procedia Soc. Behav. Sci. **119**, 837–846 (2014)
37. Teece, D., Peteraf, M., Leih, S.: Dynamic capabilities and organizational agility: risk, uncertainty, and strategy in the innovation economy. California Manag. Rev. **58**(4), 13–35 (2016)
38. Biolchini, J., et al.: Systematic review in Software Engineering, in System Engineering and Computer Science Department. PESC, Editor., Rio de Janeiro (2005)
39. Rouhani, B.D., et al.: A systematic literature review on enterprise architecture implementation methodologies. Inf. Softw. Technol. **2015**(62), 1–20 (2015)
40. Aromataris, E., Pearson, A.: The systematic review: an overview. AJN Am. J. Nurs. **114**, 53–58 (2014)
41. Rouhani, B.D., et al.: A systematic literature review on enterprise architecture implementation methodologies. Inf. Softw. Technol. (2015)
42. Gentles, S.J., Charles, C., Ploeg, J.: Sampling in qualitative research: insights from an overview of the methods literature. Qual. Report **20**(11), 1772–1789 (2015)
43. Welman, C., Kruger, F., Mitchell, B.: Research Methodology, 3rd edn. Oxford University Press Southern Africa, Cape Town (1994)
44. Leedy, P.D., Ormrod, J.E.: Practical Research: Planning and Design, 10th edn. Pearson Education Limited, New Jersey (2014)
45. Van der Waldt, G.: City government's capability for resilience: Towards a functional framework L van der Merwe Centre for Innovative Leadership Ltd (CIL) Midrand. **27**, 57–76 (2018)
46. Totterdill, P.: The corporate response to the fourth industrial revolution. Eur. J. Workplace Innov. **3**(2), 117–138 (2017)
47. Barletta, I., et al.: Organisational sustainability readiness: a model and assessment tool for manufacturing companies. J. Clean. Prod. **2021**(284), 1–13 (2021)

48. Alsheiabni, S., Cheung, Y., Messom, C.: Towards an artificial intelligence maturity model: from science fiction to business facts. In: Pacific Asia Conference on Information Systems (PACIS), AIS, Xi'An, China (2019)
49. Ghobakhloo, M.: Determinants of information and digital technology implementation for smart manufacturing. Int. J. Prod. Res. **58**(8), 2384–2405 (2020)
50. La Torre, M., et al.: The fall and rise of intellectual capital accounting: new prospects from the big data revolution. Meditari Account. Res. **26**(3), 381–399 (2018)
51. van den Berg, M.J., Stander, M.W., van der Vaart, L.: An exploration of key human resource practitioner competencies in a digitally transformed organisation. SA J. Hum. Resour. Manag. **2020**(18), 1–13 (2020)
52. Kurniawana, R., Hamsal, M.: Achieving decision-making quality and organisational agility in innovation portfolio management in Telecommunication 4.0. Int. J. Innov. Create. Change **8**(6), 332–356 (2019)
53. Mendoza, M.A., Cuellar, S.: Industry 4.0: Latin America SMEs challenges. In 020 Congreso Internacional de Innovación y Tendencias en Ingeniería (CONIITI), Bogota, Colombia. IEEE (2020)
54. Lin, T.C., Sheng, M.L., Wang, K.J.: Dynamic capabilities for smart manufacturing transformation by manufacturing enterprises. Asian J. Technol. Innov. **28**(3), 403–426 (2020)
55. Grant, R.M.: Prospering in dynamically-competitive environments: organizational capability as knowledge integration. Organ. Sci. **7**(4), 359–467

Digitised Supply Chains

How Does IOS-Enabled Business Intelligence Enhance Supply Chain Performance?

Caleb Amankwaa Kumi, David Asamoah, and Benjamin Agyei-Owusu(✉)

Kwame Nkrumah University of Science and Technology, Kumasi, Ghana
{dasamoah.ksb,bagyei-owusu.ksb}@knust.edu.gh

Abstract. This study examines the mechanisms through which IOS-enabled business intelligence enhances supply chain performance of organizations. The study proposes that IOS-enabled business intelligence first impacts information exchange, coordination and integration capabilities, which subsequently enhance supply chain responsiveness and supply chain performance. A research model examining the proposed relationships was developed and tested using data from retail organizations operating in an emerging African country. Data analysis through partial least squares structural equation modelling confirmed that IOS-enabled business intelligence allowed firms to obtain information exchange, coordination, integration and supply chain responsiveness capabilities. With the exception of integration capabilities, supply chain capabilities directly enhanced supply chain performance as well. Finally, supply chain responsiveness partially mediated the relationship between information exchange capabilities and supply chain performance and fully mediated the relationship between integration capabilities and supply chain performance. The implications of these findings are discussed.

Keywords: Business intelligence · Inter-organizational information systems · Supply chain capabilities

1 Introduction

Inter-organizational information systems (IOS) are network-enabled information systems that allow organizations to effectively manage business operations and supply chain activities across several organizations (Asamoah et al. 2021a). Adoption and use of IOS have grown in recent decades, and have become common place in many sectors. Researchers have identified that adoption and use of IOS can be patterned to achieve three possible objectives, namely, to enable communication, to achieve integration, and to enable business intelligence (Zhang and Cao 2018; Subramani 2004). Deploying IOS for business intelligence is of particular relevance in the present era of big data where large volumes of business data is created on a daily basis. Exploring and understanding business data can help firms gain new insights into their operations, customers and market, and this can serve as the foundation of higher performance. IOS-enabled business intelligence refers to the extent to which the use of IOS facilitates learning and

Published by Springer Nature Switzerland AG 2021
D. Dennehy et al. (Eds.): I3E 2021, LNCS 12896, pp. 441–453, 2021.
https://doi.org/10.1007/978-3-030-85447-8_37

knowledge creation between members of a supply chain network (Zhang and Cao 2018). Applications for IOS-enabled business intelligence may take the form of shared database and decision support systems, shared knowledge acquisition, and artificial intelligence (Mandal and Dubey 2021).

Previous studies reveal that deploying IOS enhances outcomes such as firm performance (Hartono et al. 2010), supply chain capabilities (Rajaguru and Matanda 2013), and supply chain performance (Cho et al. 2017; Asamoah et al. 2021a). The extant literature in exploring outcomes of IOS however often lump different dimensions of IOS use together, largely examining IOS use at the second order level, and failing to examine how specific dimensions of IOS use may enhance performance of firms. This means that there still exists a gap in our understanding on whether and how IOS-enabled business intelligence enhances firm performance. There have been multiple calls by researchers to examine the influence of different dimensions of IOS use on performance (Asamoah et al. 2021a; Agbenyo et al. 2018). Further, there is very little understanding into the mechanisms through IOS-enabled business intelligence enhances firm performance. This study addresses these research gaps by examining the role of information exchange, coordination, integration and supply chain responsiveness capabilities in explaining the outcomes of IOS-enabled business intelligence. The study proposes that IOS-enabled business intelligence initially enables firms to obtain information exchange, coordination and integration capabilities. These supply chain capabilities are then leveraged to achieve higher supply chain responsiveness, and ultimately, supply chain performance. These assertions are tested using data obtained from firms operating in an emerging economy.

The study is significant in a number of ways. This study is the first to empirically examine how IOS-enabled business intelligence drives supply chain performance, to the best of our knowledge. The study provides new insight into the business intelligence-supply chain performance link by proposing and empirically confirming that IOS-enabled business intelligence first creates information exchange, coordination and integration capabilities, which are leveraged for greater supply chain responsiveness and supply chain performance. The study additionally provides insights on the outcomes of business intelligence deployment within an African country context, a context that has been very little studied. The study also provides insights for owners and managers of firms by creating a clear understanding of how IOS-enabled business intelligence may enhance their supply chain performance.

The rest of the paper is organized as follows. The research model and hypotheses is presented next, followed by the methodology of the study. This is immediately followed by a discussion of the results of the study. The study then concludes by discussing the implications of the study for research and practice.

2 Research Model and Hypotheses

This study is underpinned by the resource-based view theory. The resource-based view theory argues that for organizations to gain competitive advantage, they must possess resources that are rare, valuable, inimitable, non-substitutable and can be deployed in manner that is difficult for competitors to duplicate (Barney 1991; Peteraf 1993). In this study, we argue that IOS-enabled business intelligence is an important intangible resource, that can be leveraged to obtain supply chain capabilities such as information exchange, integration, coordination and responsiveness, which ultimately help organizations to gain superior performance in the form of improved supply chain performance. The research model is presented in Fig. 1 below. The hypotheses of the study are discussed next.

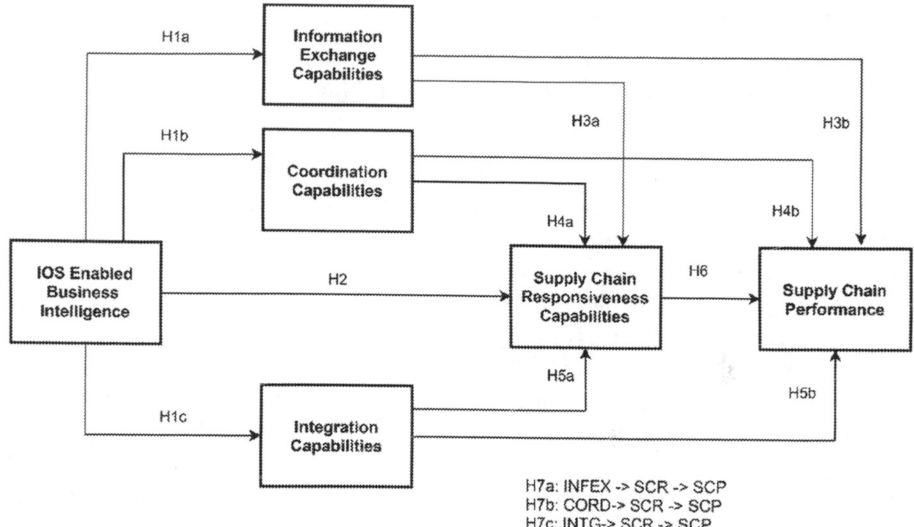

Fig. 1. Research model

2.1 IOS-Enabled Business Intelligence and Supply Chain Capabilities

IOS enabled business intelligence allows supply chain partners to work collaboratively to attain mutual benefits (Nissen et al. 2014). Additionally, the shared knowledge enabled by IOS allows effective and efficient synchronization of the supply chain processes, and joint planning and execution (Ayoub et al. 2017). Mandal and Dubey (2021) observed that using IOS for intelligence enhances IOS use for integration, collaboration, and coordination. IOS-enabled business intelligence allows organizations to jointly plan with their supply chain partners to address the needs customers in a responsive manner (Mandal and Dubey 2021; Yu et al. 2018). Through the use of IOS, firms can derive useful insights towards improving their supply chain capabilities (Asamoah et al. 2021a; Asamoah et al. 2019). From the purview of the resource-based view theory and the discussions above, we argue that the IOS-enabled business intelligence is a valuable, rare and inimitable organizational resource that can be exploited by organizations to develop supply chain capabilities such as information exchange, coordination, integration, and responsiveness. Drawing from the discussion above we propose the following hypotheses:

H1a: Higher levels of IOS-enabled business intelligence will lead to higher levels of information exchange capabilities.
H1b: Higher levels of IOS-enabled business intelligence will lead to higher levels of coordination capabilities.
H1c: Higher levels of IOS-enabled business intelligence will lead to higher levels of integration capabilities.
H2: Higher levels of IOS-enabled business intelligence will lead to higher levels of supply chain responsiveness capabilities

2.2 Information Exchange Capabilities, Supply Chain Responsiveness and Supply Chain Performance

Information exchange capabilities refers to the ability of an organization to share relevant information with its supply chain partners effectively and efficiently (Wu et al. 2006; Yeniyurt et al. 2019). Information exchange helps to enhance interorganizational integration and coordination between supply chain partners and gain useful insight about the business environment (Kim et al. 2018; Yu et al. 2018). Effective and efficient supply chain information exchange leads to higher levels of supply chain responsiveness (Liu et al. 2013; Yu et al. 2018). Yu et al. (2018) affirms that through information exchange, organizations are able to improve their performance. Following the discussion above, we propose that:

H3a: Information exchange capabilities is positively related to supply chain responsiveness.
H3b: Information exchange capabilities is positively related to supply chain performance.

2.3 Coordination Capabilities, Supply Chain Responsiveness and Supply Chain Performance

Coordination capabilities refers to the ability of organizations to effectively and efficiently coordinate business activities with their supply chain partners (Wu et al. 2006). Supply chain coordination has been identified as a key antecedent of organizational performance (Yeniyurt et al. 2019). Kumar and Singh (2017) assert that effective supply chain coordination helps to manage interdependencies and reduce uncertainties. Improved supply chain coordination leads to benefits such as reduced transaction costs and improved operational efficiency among supply chain partners (Wu et al. 2006). A healthy supply chain coordination fosters the entire supply chain to be more responsive (Kim and Lee 2010). Thus, it is expected that coordination capabilities will result in enhanced supply chain responsiveness and supply chain performance. Accordingly, we propose the following hypothesis:

H4a: Coordination capabilities is positively related to supply chain responsiveness.
H4b: Coordination capabilities is positively related to supply chain performance.

2.4 Integration Capabilities, Supply Chain Responsiveness and Supply Chain Performance

Integration capabilities refers to the ability of organization efficiently integrate their internal and external supply chain activities. Wong et al. (2011) argues that activity integration helps to creates opportunities for leveraging the knowledge embedded in collaborative processes to enhance value creation, delivery performance and reduce cost. A number of studies have emphasized that supply chain integration helps practicing firms to improve their efficiency and effectiveness (Escorcia-Caballero et al. 2019). Similarly, Danese et al. (2013) maintain that supply chain integration helps improve responsiveness. Based on the discussions above, we propose the following hypotheses:

H5a: Integration capabilities is positively related to supply chain responsiveness.
H5b: Integration capabilities is positively related to supply chain performance.

2.5 Supply Chain Responsiveness and Supply Chain Performance

Supply chain responsiveness capabilities refers to extent to which members of a supply chain are able to cooperatively respond to changes presented by the environment (Wu et al. 2006; Yeniyurt et al. 2019). In today's market place plagued with several levels of uncertainties and competition, supply chain responsiveness becomes a very useful organizational capability (Asamoah et al. 2021). Yu et al. (2018) found that supply chain responsiveness has a positive effect on firm financial performance. Similarly, the study of Kim and Lee (2010) found that supply chain responsiveness positively influences market performance. Drawing from the discussions above, it is conceivable that supply chain responsiveness capabilities will result in supply chain performance. Accordingly, we propose that:

H6: Supply chain responsiveness capabilities is positively related to supply chain performance

2.6 Mediating Role of Supply Chain Responsiveness

Drawing on the discussions in the previous sections, this study hypothesizes that supply chain responsiveness intervenes the direct effects of integration capabilities, coordination capabilities and information exchange capabilities on supply chain performance. Specifically, we argue that supply chain capabilities such as coordination, supply chain information exchange, and integration drives supply chain responsiveness which in turn influences firm performance. Accordingly, we postulate that:

H7a: Supply chain responsiveness capabilities mediates the relationship between integration capabilities and supply chain performance.
H7b: Supply chain responsiveness capabilities mediates the relationship between information exchange capabilities and supply chain performance.
H7c: Supply chain responsiveness capabilities mediates the relationship between coordination capabilities and supply chain performance.

3 Methodology

3.1 Measurement Items Development

Measurement items for the research items were sourced from existing literature with IOS-driven business intelligence sourced from Asamoah et al. (2021a) and Zhang and Cao (2018). Measures for information exchange capabilities, coordination capabilities, integration capabilities and supply chain responsiveness capabilities were sourced from Wu et al. (2006) and Asamoah et al. (2021a). The measures of supply chain performance were sourced from Koçoğlu et al. (2011) and Won Lee et al. (2007). All constructs were conceptualized at the first level, with the exception of supply chain performance, which was conceptualized as a second level construct with efficiency, flexibility and reliability as sub-dimensions. The measures were refined by three professors specializing in business intelligence and three top practitioner business intelligence experts. The measures were also subjected to pilot testing for further refinement.

3.2 Data Collection

Data for the study was obtained from a survey of firms involved in retail trade in Ghana that use IOS. IOS, particularly vendor-managed inventory, has seen increasing adoption in the retail operations in Ghana, particularly for fast-moving consumer goods (Asamoah et al. 2021a). Five hundred firms directly involved in the wholesale and retail of fast-moving consumer goods were randomly selected from a database and targeted for data collection. Questionnaires were delivered to these organizations, together with a cover letter explaining the purpose of the study. In all, 161 usable responses were received from firms that indicated they were into wholesale and retail of fast-moving consumer goods.

4 Results

4.1 Demographic Results

The demographic results revealed that largest categories of firms have been in operation for over 20 years (39.1%), had high revenues larger than 10 million Ghana cedis (31.7%), and had employee size larger than 500 (36%). This suggests IOS-enabled business intelligence is used more by larger firms, relative to smaller firms. The full demographic data is presented in Table 1 below.

Table 1. Demographic results

Years of operation	Frequency	Percent
1 to 5 years	33	20.5
6 to 10 years	25	15.5
11 to 15 years	20	12.4
16 to 20 years	20	12.4
More than 20 years	63	39.1
Total	161	100.0
Annual Revenue (in Ghana cedis)	Frequency	Percent
Up to 100,000	25	15.5
100,000 to 1,000,000	47	29.2
1,000,001 to 10,000,000	30	18.6
More than 10,000,000	51	31.7
Missing	8	5.0
Total	161	100.0
Employees	Frequency	Percent
Less than 10	6	3.7
10 to 50	42	26.1
51 to 500	55	34.2
More than 500	58	36.0
Total	161	100.0

4.2 Measurement Model Results

Measurement model results were assessed by following the guidelines of Hair et al. (2019). Indicator loadings were found to be greater than 0.708 as required, indicating good item reliability. Composite reliability values were greater than 0.7, indicating internal consistency reliability of the research constructs. The average variance extracted (AVE) values were larger than 0.5, indicating acceptable convergent validity of the model. These results are summarized in Table 2 below.

Table 2. Psychometric properties of research constructs

Constructs	Composite reliability	AVE
Coordination Capabilities (CORD)	0.916	0.685
Efficiency (EFF)	0.930	0.767
Flexibility (FLEX)	0.925	0.712
Information Exchange Capabilities (INFX)	0.930	0.768
Integration Capabilities (INTG)	0.931	0.773
IOS-enabled business intelligence (INTL)	0.914	0.726
Reliability (REL)	0.927	0.718
Supply Chain Responsiveness (RESP)	0.905	0.703

In establishing discriminant validity, we used the Fornell-Larcker criterion. Comparing the square root of the AVE of each construct with the correlation between constructs and confirming if the former is larger than the latter establishes discriminant validity (Hair et al. 2019). In Table 3 below, the diagonal values in bold which represent the square root o the AVE of constructs are larger than the off-diagonal values which are correlations among constructs, establishing discriminant validity.

Table 3. Fornell-Larcker test results

	CORD	EFF	FLEX	INFX	INTG	INTL	REL	RESP
CORD	**0.828**							
EFF	0.672	**0.876**						
FLEX	0.614	0.708	**0.844**					
INFX	0.781	0.664	0.656	**0.876**				
INTG	0.638	0.530	0.492	0.615	**0.879**			
INTL	0.634	0.636	0.645	0.672	0.594	**0.852**		
REL	0.668	0.702	0.701	0.707	0.627	0.664	**0.848**	
RESP	0.717	0.663	0.697	0.765	0.712	0.766	0.726	**0.839**

The discriminant validity of the construct was also assessed using the heterotrait-monotrait (HTMT) ratio of the correlations test, which indicates that HTMT values should be less than 0.9 (Henseler et al. 2015). The HTMT values were within this range, confirming the discriminant validity of the model. The HTMT results are presented in Table 4 below.

Table 4. HTMT results

	CORD	EFF	FLEX	INFX	INTG	INTL	REL	RESP
CORD								
EFF	0.748							
FLEX	0.678	0.786						
INFX	0.867	0.738	0.725					
INTG	0.709	0.587	0.545	0.682				
INTL	0.717	0.716	0.725	0.757	0.669			
REL	0.741	0.782	0.776	0.786	0.696	0.747		
RESP	0.816	0.753	0.791	0.868	0.810	0.883	0.825	

4.3 Structural Model Results

Having established the validity of the measurement model, the structural model was assessed. The model's in-sample explanatory power was assessed by examining the R^2 of the endogenous variables, which ranged from a moderate level of 0.353 for integration capabilities to a high level of 0.749 for supply chain responsiveness. The R^2 values are presented inside the endogenous constructs in Fig. 2 below. The predictive relevance of the model was also established since Q^2 values ranged from 0.260 to 0.596, which are significantly larger than zero (Hair et al. 2019).

To ascertain whether the direct effects were supported, the path co-efficient and p-values of the hypothesized direct paths were examined. The mediation paths were assessed by following the procedure outlined by Nitzl et al. (2016). The results of the hypotheses tests are summarized in Fig. 2 below.

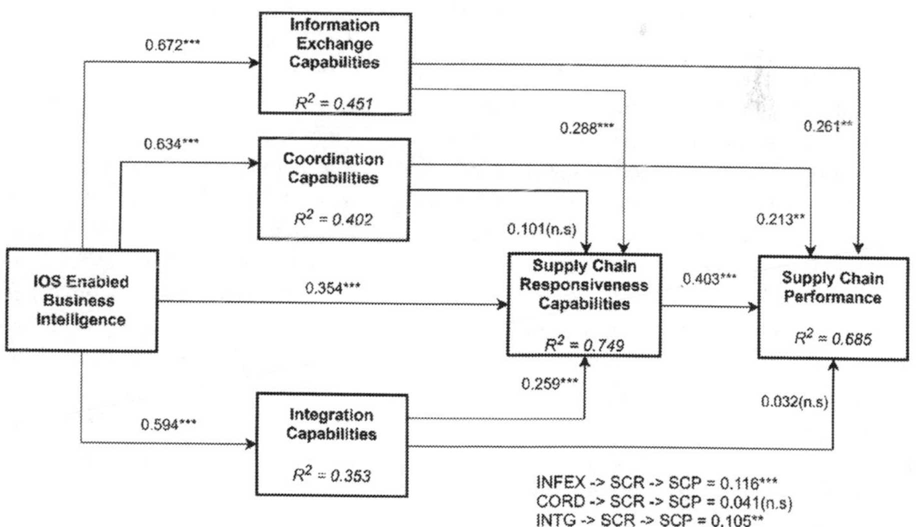

Fig. 2. Structural model results

4.4 Discussions

The study set out to examine whether and how IOS-enabled business intelligence enhances the supply chain performance of firms. The findings of the study confirmed that IOS-enabled business intelligence first allowed organizations to obtain information exchange, coordination and integration capabilities as hypothesized. Additionally, IOS-enabled business intelligence enhanced the supply chain responsiveness capabilities of firms. These findings are in line with the results of previous studies that observed that use of IOS in general enhances supply chain management capabilities in general (Agbenyo et al. 2018; Asamoah et al. 2019; Asamoah et al. 2021a). Whilst the specific effect of IOS-enabled business intelligence on these capabilities have not been studied in previous studies, the study of Mandal and Dubey (2021) can serve as a useful reference. They observed that IOS use for intelligence will occasion higher levels of IOS use for integration, collaboration, and coordination. Beyond these findings, the present study explores the interrelationship between supply chain management capabilities. It was revealed that information exchange capabilities and integration capabilities can be leveraged to achieve higher supply chain responsiveness. This suggests that IOS-enabled business intelligence occasions a staggered improvement in supply chain management capabilities. Coordination capabilities however were not associated with higher supply chain responsiveness.

Regarding the effect of supply chain capabilities, it was observed that information exchange, coordination and supply chain responsiveness capabilities all resulted in higher supply chain performance. Integration capabilities however did not enhance supply chain performance. This mirrors the findings of Yu et al. (2018) that observed that data driven supply chains enabled information exchange, coordination, activity integration and responsiveness capabilities, and that all these supply chain capabilities with the exception of activity integration enhanced financial performance. The different ways in which supply chain capabilities impact on supply chain performance highlight the need for researchers to explore into detail how the individual dimensions of supply chain capabilities are influenced by IOS and they in turn influence supply chain performance.

Examining the mediation role of supply chain responsiveness in the effect of information exchange, coordination and integration capabilities on supply chain performance revealed interesting findings. A partial mediation role of supply chain responsiveness was observed for the effect of information exchange capabilities on supply chain performance. This means that information exchange capabilities partly enhance supply chain performance directly, and partly enhance it through enhanced supply chain responsiveness. The effect of integration capabilities on supply chain performance on the other hand was fully mediated through supply chain responsiveness, since the direct effect of integration capabilities on supply chain performance was not significant, but the mediation effect was positive and significant. Finally, examining the mediation role of supply chain responsiveness on how coordination capabilities enhance supply chain performance reveals that there was no mediating role of supply chain responsiveness. This indicates that supply chain responsiveness does not intervene the relationship between coordination capabilities and supply chain performance.

5 Conclusion

The study examined into detail the mechanisms through which IOS-enabled business intelligence enhances the supply chain performance of firms by proposing that supply chain capabilities play an important, individual and staggered role in explaining this relationship. The findings of the study largely support the assertions of the study, with IOS-enabled business intelligence enhancing all four identified supply chain management capabilities, and three of the capabilities having a significant effect on supply chain responsiveness and performance.

There are some implications of the study. The study provides a detailed understanding of how IOS-enabled business intelligence enhances supply chain performance, by bringing to light the role of that supply chain management capabilities in enhancing supply chain performance. The study also foments an understanding in the interrelationships between supply chain capabilities that can guide future researchers who are studying supply chain capabilities. The study also adds up to the nascent studies on business intelligence within the African context. By way of implications for practice, the findings of the study confirm that positive outcomes in terms of improved supply chain management capabilities and improved supply chain performance can be obtained from IOS-enabled business intelligence initiatives. Business owners and managers can therefore invest in IOS to enhance their performance outcomes. The study also highlights the important role of supply chain management capabilities in achieving successful supply chain performance outcomes from IOS-enabled business intelligence.

There are some limitations of the study. Data was obtained from firms in the retail sector of Ghana, an emerging African country, and it is possible that the findings may not apply to firms in other industries or in other geographic contexts. Future research can consider expanding the scope of the study to examine other industries, examine similar relationships in other contexts, and explore possible constructs enhance the effect of IOS-enabled business intelligence on performance outcomes.

References

Agbenyo, L., Asamoah, D., Agyei-Owusu, B.: Drivers and effects of Inter-Organizational Systems (IOS) use in a developing country. In: AMCIS 2018 Proceedings (2018)

Asamoah, D., Agyei-Owusu, B., Andoh-Baidoo, F.K., Ayaburi, E.: Effect of Inter-Organizational Systems use on supply chain capabilities and performance. In: Dwivedi, Y., Ayaburi, E., Boateng, R., Effah, J. (eds.) ICT unbounded, social impact of bright ICT adoption, pp. 293–308. Springer (2019). https://doi.org/10.1007/978-3-030-20671-0_20

Asamoah, D., Agyei-Owusu, B., Andoh-Baidoo, F.K., Ayaburi, E.: Inter-organizational systems use and supply chain performance: mediating role of supply chain management capabilities. Int. J. Inf. Manag. **58**, 102195 (2021a)

Asamoah, D., Nuertey, D., Agyei-Owusu, B., Akyeh, J.: The effect of supply chain responsiveness on customer development. Int. J. Logist. Manag. (2021, ahead-of-print). https://doi.org/10.1108/IJLM-03-2020-0133

Ayoub, H.F., Abdallah, A.B., Suifan, T.S.: The effect of supply chain integration on technical innovation in Jordan: the mediating role of knowledge management. Benchmark. Int. J. **24**(3), 594–616 (2017)

Barney, J.: Firm resources and sustained competitive advantage. J. Manag. **17**(1), 99–120 (1991)

Cho, B., Ryoo, S.Y., Kim, K.K.: Interorganizational dependence, information transparency in interorganizational information systems, and supply chain performance. Eur. J. Inf. Syst. **26**(2), 185–205 (2017)

Danese, P., Romano, P., Formentini, M.: The impact of supply chain integration on responsiveness: the moderating effect of using an international supplier network. Transp. Res. Part E Logist. Transp. Rev. **49**(1), 125–140 (2013)

Escorcia-Caballero, J.P., Moreno-Luzon, M.D., Chams-Anturi, O.: Supply chain integration capability: an organizational routine perspective. **8**(5), 39–47 (2019)

Hair, J.F., Risher, J.J., Sarstedt, M., Ringle, C.M.: When to use and how to report the results of PLS-SEM. Eur. Bus. Rev. **31**(1), 2–24 (2019)

Hartono, E., Li, X., Na, K.S., Simpson, J.T.: The role of the quality of shared information in interorganizational systems use. Int. J. Inf. Manage. **30**(5), 399–407 (2010)

Henseler, J., Ringle, C.M., Sarstedt, M.: A new criterion for assessing discriminant validity in variance-based structural equation modeling. J. Acad. Mark. Sci. **43**(1), 115–135 (2014). https://doi.org/10.1007/s11747-014-0403-8

Kim, D., Lee, R.P.: Systems collaboration and strategic collaboration: their impacts on supply chain responsiveness and market performance. Decis. Sci. **41**(4), 955–981 (2010)

Kim, D., Jean, R.J.B., Sinkovics, R.R.: Drivers of virtual inter-firm integration and its impact on performance in international customer–supplier relationships. Manag. Int. Rev. **58**(3), 495–522 (2018)

Kocoğlu, İ, İmamoğlu, S.Z., İnce, H., Keskin, H.: The effect of supply chain integration on information sharing: enhancing the supply chain performance. Procedia Soc. Behav. Sci. **24**, 1630–1649 (2011)

Kumar, R., Kumar Singh, R.: Coordination and responsiveness issues in SME supply chains: a review. Benchmark. Int. J. **24**(3), 635–650 (2017)

Liu, H., Ke, W., Wei, K.K., Hua, Z.: The impact of IT capabilities on firm performance: the mediating roles of absorptive capacity and supply chain agility. Decis. Support Syst. **54**(3), 1452–1462 (2013)

Mandal, S., Dubey, R.K.: Effect of inter-organizational systems appropriation in agility and resilience development: an empirical investigation. Benchmark. Int. J. (2021, ahead-of-print). https://doi.org/10.1108/BIJ-10-2020-0542

Nissen, H.A., Evald, M.R., Clarke, A.H.: Knowledge sharing in heterogeneous teams through collaboration and cooperation: exemplified through Public–Private-Innovation partnerships. Ind. Mark. Manage. **43**(3), 473–482 (2014)

Nitzl, C., Roldan, J.L., Cepeda, G.: Mediation analysis in partial least squares path modeling. Ind. Manag. Data Syst. **116**(9), 1849–1864 (2016)

Peteraf, M.A.: The cornerstones of competitive advantage: a resource-based view. Strateg. Manag. J. **14**(3), 179–191 (1993)

Rajaguru, R., Matanda, M.J.: Effects of inter-organizational compatibility on supply chain capabilities: exploring the mediating role of inter-organizational information systems (IOIS) integration. Ind. Mark. Manage. **42**(4), 620–632 (2013)

Subramani, M.: How do suppliers benefit from information technology use in supply chain relationships? MIS Q. **28**(1), 45–73 (2004)

Won Lee, C., Kwon, I.G., Severance, D.: Relationship between supply chain performance and degree of linkage among supplier, internal integration, and customer. Supply Chain Manag. Int. J. **12**(6), 444–452 (2007)

Wong, C.Y., Boon-Itt, S., Wong, C.W.: The contingency effects of environmental uncertainty on the relationship between supply chain integration and operational performance. J. Oper. Manag. **29**(6), 604–615 (2011)

Wu, F., Yeniyurt, S., Kim, D., Cavusgil, S.T.: The impact of information technology on supply chain capabilities and firm performance: a resource-based view. Ind. Mark. Manage. **35**(4), 493–504 (2006)

Yeniyurt, S., Wu, F., Kim, D., Cavusgil, S.T.: Information technology resources, innovativeness, and supply chain capabilities as drivers of business performance: a retrospective and future research directions. Ind. Mark. Manage. **79**, 46–52 (2019)

Yu, W., Chavez, R., Jacobs, M.A., Feng, M.: Data-driven supply chain capabilities and performance: a resource-based view. Transp. Res. Part E Logist. Transp. Rev. **114**, 371–385 (2018)

Zhang, Q., Cao, M.: Exploring antecedents of supply chain collaboration: effects of culture and interorganizational system appropriation. Int. J. Prod. Econ. **195**, 146–157 (2018)

A Review of AI in the Supply Chain Industry: Preliminary Findings

Conn Smyth[1(✉)], Denis Dennehy[1], and Samuel Fosso-Wamba[2]

[1] NUI Galway, Galway, Ireland
c.smyth19@nuigalway.ie
[2] Toulouse Business School, Toulouse, France

Abstract. Artificial Intelligence (AI) has been claimed to provide transformational powers in developing efficient and sustainable supply chains. Despite this, the supply chain industry is grappling with a number of challenges related to the implementation of AI. Additionally, AI and supply chain research to date has largely focused on the technical elements or different functions of AI, rather than AI as a whole. In order to provide a consolidated view of AI in the context of supply chains, we synthesis this dispersed knowledge by conducting a systematic literature review of AI research in supply chains that have been published in 3* and 4* ranked journals between 2000 and 2020. The search strategy resulted in 468 studies, of which 56 were identified as primary papers relevant to this research. This research adds to aggregation of knowledge by providing a state-of-the-art of AI and supply chain research, synthesising the reported challenges of the supply chain industry and the claimed benefits of AI.

Keywords: Artificial intelligence · Supply chain · Systematic literature review

1 Introduction

Supply chain firms are becoming increasingly aware of the potential of AI for coping with the unpredictable nature of supply chains and the world around them [1, 2]. Supply chains have always been vulnerable to distributions [3, 4], however, this vulnerability is further intensified due to customer demand continuously evolving [5], products becoming more complex [6], higher customer expectations [7], greater product variety [8, 9], and greater emphasis on transparency and sustainability [10–13].

The concerns about the stability of modern supply chains were brought to light throughout the COVID-19 pandemic, with 86% of supply chain firms being negatively impacted [2]. Such events have raised awareness among both researchers and practitioners of the need to create a more resilient supply chain that can handle the complex problems faced by modern supply chains [14–17]. Previous SLRs (see Table 1) have demonstrated the many benefits of the different functions of AI (i.e. machine learning, expert systems), moreover, previous SLRs have also illustrated the various applications of AI such as, AI's potential for enhancing risk management [4]. However, these SLRs

Published by Springer Nature Switzerland AG 2021
D. Dennehy et al. (Eds.): I3E 2021, LNCS 12896, pp. 454–466, 2021.
https://doi.org/10.1007/978-3-030-85447-8_38

fail to provide a comprehensive overview of the collective functions and applications of AI in the supply chain industry, echoing the concerns of 'fragmented adhocracy', which has proven costly to other research areas [19, 20]. In order to avoid this scenario, this research will provide a state-of-the-art of AI and supply chain research, synthesise the claimed challenges of the supply chain industry and the reported benefits of AI.

Table 1. Literature reviews of AI in supply chain management.

Comparison Element	[18]	[21]	[4]	[22]	This study
Timeline	2002–2019	2007–2019	1978–June 2018	1994–2009	2000–2020
Focus	Machine learning application in the agricultural supply chain	Analyse the application of Bayesian networks to supply chain risk, resilience, and the ripple effect	Assess how effectively supply chain risk management research has exploited the potential of artificial intelligence	Provides a comprehensive review of research conducted in textile and apparel supply chains using artificial intelligence and decision-support systems	Illustrate the supply chain challenges that can be addressed by artificial intelligence
Methodology	Systematic review	Visualization-based scientometric analysis	State-of-art-review	State-of-art-review	Bibliometric analysis
Primary Studies	Scientific literature 93 papers	Scientific literature 63 papers	Scientific literature 276 papers	Scientific literature 35 papers	Scientific literature (IS basket, 3* & 4* CABS journals only) 56 papers

The paper is structured as follows. First, the approach taken to develop this SLR is outlined. Then, the analysis of AI research in a supply chain context is presented and followed by a discussion. The paper ends with a conclusion.

2 Research Methodology

The section outlines the systematic literature review (SLR) approach adopted in this study, which follows the established guidelines and procedures proposed by Kitchenham [23, 24]. This approach (see Fig. 1) consists of 9 steps across three phases: planning (3 steps), conducting (4 steps), and documenting (2 steps). The need for this review has been established throughout the introduction of this paper. The aforementioned objectives of this review are described in the form of three research questions:

RQ1: What is the current state of AI research in the supply chain industry?

RQ2: What are the reported challenges of the supply chain industry have been reported in A?

RQ3: What benefits of AI have been recorded in the context of supply chains?

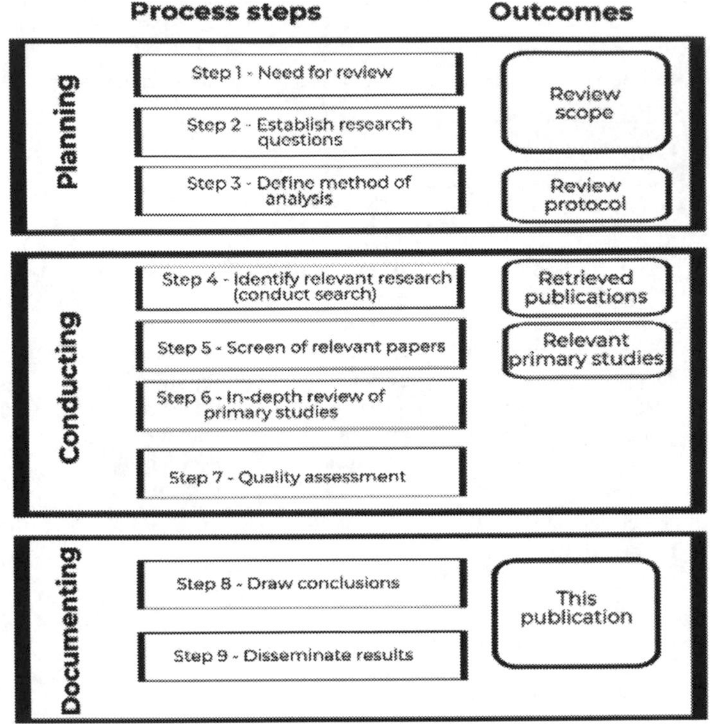

Fig. 1. SLR steps followed in this study.

2.1 Search Strategy

The search was conducted within three electronic databases: AIS, Scopus, and Web of Science [25–27]. The search covered twenty years of research on AI and SC literature between January 2000 to December 2020. Papers were eligible for inclusion if it (i) directly answers one or more research questions of this study, (ii) clearly states its focus on AI in the IS domain and supply chains, and (iii) describes the application of AI and the approach used to study its use or implementation. The search initially retrieved a list of 5,059 papers, however, in order for studies to be eligible for inclusion in the SLR they must be published in 3* and 4* Chartered Association of Business Schools (CABS) ranked journals which resulted in 468 remaining papers. Our rationale for selecting from 3* and 4* journals was that these papers would be of higher quality having previously gone through a rigorous review, moreover, these journals place a larger focus on theorization, which collectively the authors believed would provide a better representation of AI and supply chain literature. The 468 papers were screened and excluded based on (i) duplicate papers, (ii) non-English, (iii) publication year, and (iv) title reading. This process resulted in 117 remaining papers, which were then subject to an in-depth review, which required two authors to read the papers in full. After the in-depth was conducted a total of 56 papers remained. Lastly, a quality assessment was conducted on these using the criteria proposed by Dybå and Dingsøyr [28]. The quality of the papers was deemed appropriate as these papers have been published in 3* and 4* journals (Fig. 2).

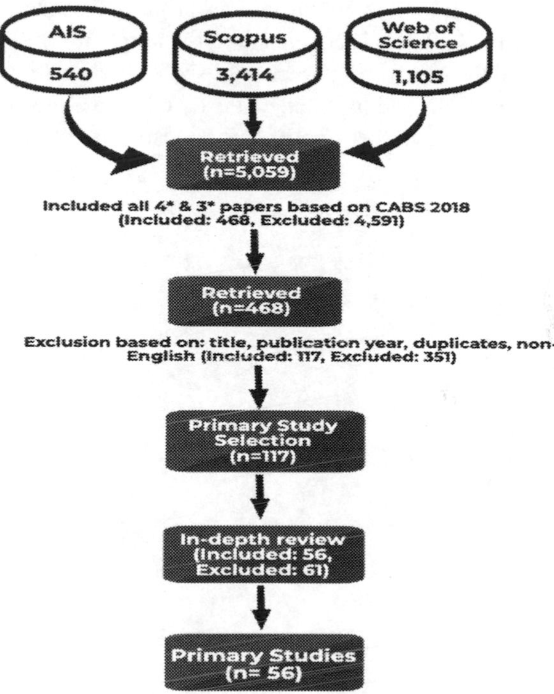

Fig. 2. Paper selection process

This study utilized bibliometric techniques to analysis the journal statistics of the primary papers, which has been widely applied in many research areas such as, supply chain management [29, 30] and big data [31, 32]. There are a number of statistics that can be used for bibliometric analysis, however, this study follows the guide of Gaviria-Marin [33] and utilizes h-index and its derivative m-index. The h-index is defined as "the number of papers with citation number $\geq$h" [34], while the m-index is the h-index divided by the "academic age" of the individual.

3 Analysis

This section presents the analysis of AI research in the context of supply chain management based on the following (i) publication by year, (ii) type of journals, (iii) reported challenges, and (iv) claimed benefits of AI. The primary papers were analyzed using Excel and presented using both Excel and Tableau.

3.1 Publication by year

RQ1: What is the current state of AI research in the supply chain industry?
Between 2000 and 2001 no studies were reported, the first publications included in this study were received in 2002. Between 2002 and 2020 the number of publications that met the inclusion criteria grew from 2 to 56, this represents a 27-fold increase. A total of 15 articles were received in 2020, this is equivalent to the number of publications received from 2000 to 2010, and the number of papers published between 2014 and 2019. While a number of publication peaks and lulls can be observed across the 20-year period (see Fig. 3), interest in AI research in the supply chain industry has been exponential.

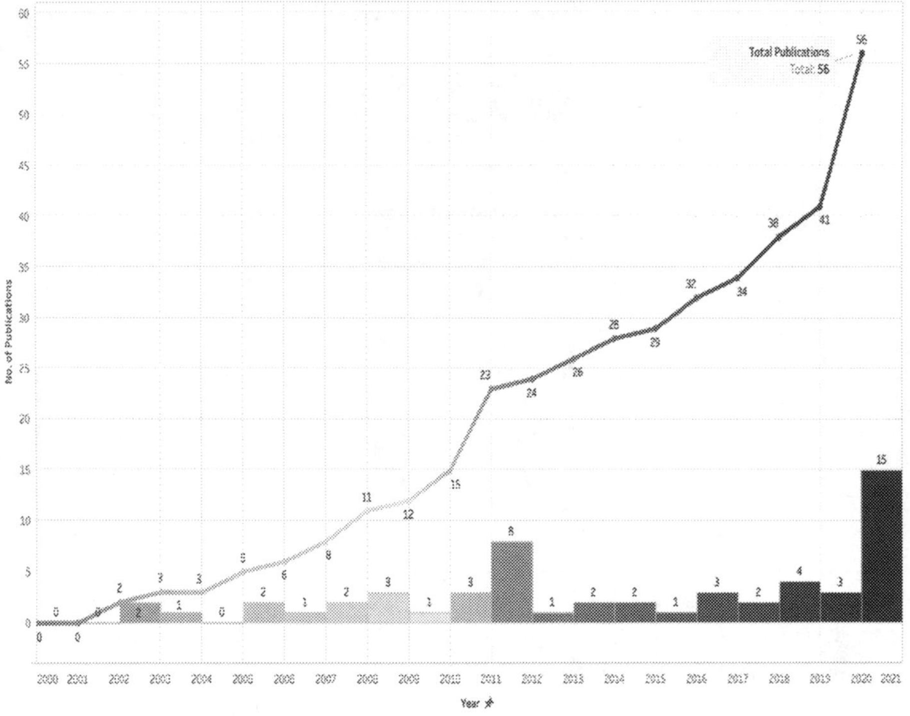

Fig. 3. Number of publications per year (2000–2020).

3.2 What 3* and 4* Ranked Journals are Publishing AI Research in the Context of Supply Chains

AI research has been applied to a large number of areas [35, 36], with AI and supply chain research accounting for a small portion. The articles included in this review were sourced form a total of 12 journals. International Journal of Production Research (IJPR) and Expert Systems with Applications (ESA) accounted for 17 and 16 of the articles included, respectively. Figure 4 illustrates the 12 journals included in this study, ordered according to the h-index of the journal, which is calculated based on the citations and number of publications. The acronyms used in this table are described in Appendix 1.

Journal Name	TP	h-index	2000-2005	2006-2010	2011-2015	2016-2020	≥200	≥100	≥50	<50	TC	C/Y	Avg Cit	IF	YFP	m-index
Expert Systems with Applications	16	12	2	1	8	5	0	2	3	11	629	37.00	39.31	5.452	2003	0.706
International Journal of Production Research	17	10	1	3	3	10	0	0	2	15	223	12.39	13.12	4.577	2002	0.556
Production Planning & Control	4	4	0	2	1	1	0	0	1	3	84	6.00	21.00	3.605	2006	0.286
International Journal of Production Economics	5	4	1	1	0	3	0	1	1	3	207	11.50	41.40	5.134	2002	0.222
European Journal of Operational Research	4	3	1	2	0	1	1	0	1	2	331	22.079	82.75	4.213	2005	0.200
Decision Support Systems	2	2	0	1	1	0	0	0	0	2	60	5.45	30.00	4.721	2009	0.182
Production and Operations Management	1	1	0	0	0	1	0	0	1	0	64	32.00	64.00	2.590	2018	0.500
MIS Quarterly	1	1	0	1	0	0	0	0	1	0	70	5.00	70.00	5.370	2006	0.071
Journal of the Operational Research Society	1	1	0	0	1	0	0	0	0	1	10	1.11	10.00	2.175	2011	0.111
Computers and Operations Research	1	1	0	0	0	1	0	0	0	1	3	3.00	3.00	1.720	2020	1.000
Annals of Operations Research	2	1	0	0	0	2	0	0	0	2	30	15.00	15.00	2.583	2018	0.500
Computers in Industry	2	0	0	0	0	2	0	0	0	2	0	0.00	0.00	3.954	2020	0.000

Fig. 4. Journal sources of AI and supply chain research.

Although ESA had one less publication than IJPR, it had the highest levels of influence (highest h-index, TC, C/Y). IJPR and ESA are the most dominate and influential journal sources for AI and SC research with h-indices of 10 and 12, respectively. However, the European journal of Operational Research was the only journal that recorded an article with over 200 citations and had the highest average citations per publication (C/Y). Four journals introduced their first AI and SC literature in the last two years, (1) Production and Operations Management, (2) Computers and Operations Research, (3) Annals of Operations Research, and (4) Computers in Industry, which reiterates the rapid growth AI and supply chain literature has experienced in recent years.

3.3 The Reported Challenges of the Supply Chain Industry in AI Literature

RQ2: What challenges of the supply chain industry have been reported in AI and supply chain literature?
Of the 56 primary papers analyzed 53 papers reported challenges faced by the supply chain industry, these papers subsequently examined how AI could potentially combat these challenges. The reported challenges are synthesized and categorized into seven categories (see Table 2). Each challenge is explained based on the analysis of the primary papers.

Table 2. Reported challenges of the supply chain industry.

Challenges	Explanation	#
Problems resulting from using traditional forecasting techniques	Forecasting refers to either making predictions about internal operations and processes or customer demand forecasting. Traditional methods of forecasting are unable to handle the inherent complexity of modern supply chains [37–39], therefore difficult to make accurate and effective predictions, resulting in a number of subsequent issues	16
Difficulties of selecting appropriate suppliers and managing supplier relationships	Supplier selection and management is becoming increasingly important for supply chains firms due to customers growing need for efficient delivery [40], and rising global competitiveness [41]. In order to select an appropriate supplier and to effectively manage this relationship, supply chain firms must consider and actively monitor a large array of tangible and intangible factors [42], which is very difficult through traditional methods	4
Managing supply chain disruptions and risk mitigation	Supply chain disruptions and risk mitigation are grouped as they both have the same objective of minimising supply chain interruptions and delays. Supply chain disruptions can result in increased costs, loss of profits and damaged company reputation [43–45]. Therefore, the aversion of these risks is of the utmost importance to supply chain organisations	10

(*continued*)

Table 2. (*continued*)

Challenges	Explanation	#
Managing inventory and selecting appropriate replenishment strategies	Inventory is the cornerstone of every supply chain [46], therefore, as the supply chain evolves to align with customer needs and demand, so must the inventory and vendor management strategy. This paired with customer demand that is rapidly growing and changing [5] creates a continuous and daunting problem for supply chain firms	5
Issues related to supply chain configuration, design, and planning (SCCDP)	SCCDP plays an essential role in creating a competitive advantage and ensuring supply chain responsiveness [47]. Effective SCCDP utilises all available resources to ensure that the supply chain is in a position to meet demand, while also being able to react to disruptions [48, 49] and the fluctuating demand of customers [39, 50]	7
Problems faced during the production process	Production processes have got the brunt of the increasing pressure on supply chain firms to increase transparency [10, 13], and to provide higher quality products [51]. As a result, supply chains are left questioning how they can address the aforementioned problems while still creating a profitable product	8
Difficulties in optimising supply chain processes and procedures	The increasing scale and number of entities involved in contemporary supply chains [52] has made supply chain optimisation a growing concern for firms, as traditional methods for solving optimisation problems typically lack the ability to handle the nonlinearity and complexity of modern supply chains [38, 53, 54]	6

3.4 The Claimed Benefits of AI in the Supply Chain Industry

RQ3: What benefits of AI have been recorded in the context of supply chains?
The benefits of AI that are dispersed across the 56 primary papers have been synthesized and categorized into eight categories (see Fig. 5). This review does recognize that some of these categories could be mapped into more than one category, however, to avoid complexity they are mapped into the most relevant category. It's evident that AI has the potential to impact a wide variety of supply chain elements, most notably, supply chain configuration, design and planning (SCCDP), with 12 papers reporting benefits to SCCP. This is due to AI's ability to simulate the configuration of supply chains and provide support across a wide variety of planning decisions. As expected, demand forecasting was

also highly reported, due to machine learning's strong predicative powers. Collectively these benefits of AI have the potential to propel supply chains to a new level of efficiency and quality, in addition to strengthening supply chains resiliency to disruptions.

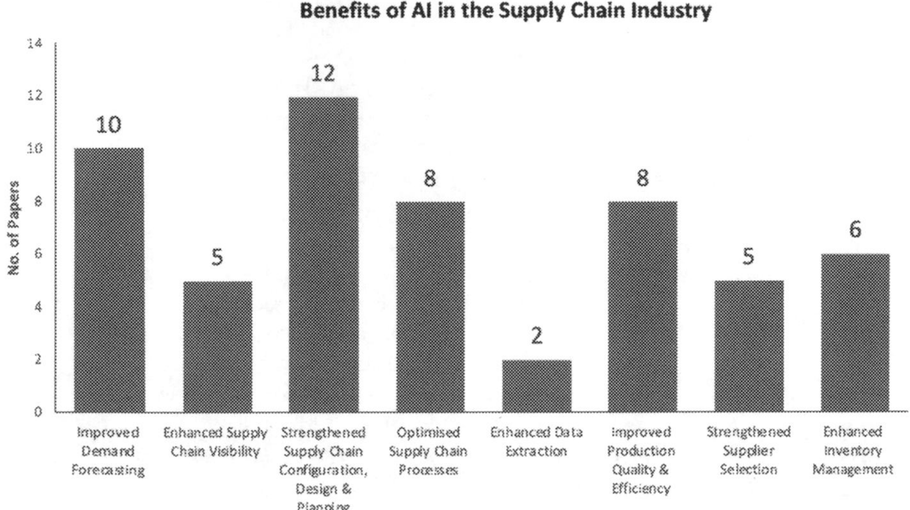

Fig. 5. Benefits of AI in the supply chain industry

4 Discussion

This study's objective was to synthesize the collective knowledge on AI and supply chain literature, with the ultimate goal of illustrating the potential of AI for addressing some of the most pressing concerns facing the supply chain industry. As previously highlighted, the supply chain industry is becoming increasingly susceptible to disruptions, in addition to report the challenges. Collectively, these issues will provide an opportunity for supply chain firms to shift their focus from traditional risk management and efficiency techniques (i.e., lean, just-in-time) to developing resilient supply chains [4, 14, 17, 55–57]. Therefore, firms must seek out enablers that support the development of resilient supply chains. It's clear from the many benefits of AI (Fig. 5) that AI can not only improve the resilience of supply chains but can also enhance the overall efficiency and operations of the supply chain. However, despite the recent influx in publications (Fig. 3) and uptake by journals (Fig. 4) of AI and supply chain literature, the true potential of AI in the supply chain industry is yet to be achieved. It's evident that there is still a number of on-going issues in the supply chain industry, despite AI's potential for minimizing these concerns, this shortcoming instigates the need for more AI research in the context of the supply chain industry, particularly studies that focus on enabling supply chains firms to leverage the capabilities of AI. Despite this, we can conclusively say that this research has achieved its original target of synthesizing and adding to the accumulative knowledge of AI in the supply chain industry.

5 Conclusion

There has been a sharp influx in the applications of AI in the supply chain industry thanks to recent advances in computational power, big data, and cloud computing, to name a few. This paired with the growing digitation of supply chains provides an ideal platform for AI to address some of the most alarming concerns facing the industry. This review examined 56 articles synthesizing the claimed benefits of AI and the reported challenges faced by the supply chain industry, with the goal of making researchers and practitioners aware of the issues that can be addressed by AI. However, combating these issues only scraps the surface of the applications of AI in the supply chain industry. More research is required in order to truly gauge the full potential of AI.

Appendix 1: Acronyms Used

Acronym	Description
TP	Total publications included in the study
$\geq$200, $\geq$100, $\geq$50	Articles with more than 200, 100, and 50 citations
$<$50	Articles with less than 50 citations
TC	Total citations
C/Y	Citations per year
Avg Cit	Average citations
IF	Impact factor
YFP	Year of first publication
YP	Year published

References

1. Papadopoulos, T., Gunasekaran, A., Dubey, R., Altay, N., Childe, S.J., Fosso-Wamba, S.: The role of Big Data in explaining disaster resilience in supply chains for sustainability. J. Clean. Prod. **142**, 1108–1118 (2017). https://doi.org/10.1016/j.jclepro.2016.03.059
2. Remko, V.H.: Research opportunities for a more resilient post-COVID-19 supply chain – closing the gap between research findings and industry practice. Int. J. Oper. Prod. Manage. **40**, 341–355 (2020). https://doi.org/10.1108/IJOPM-03-2020-0165
3. Zeng, B., Yen, B.P.C.: Rethinking the role of partnerships in global supply chains: a risk-based perspective. Int. J. Prod. Econ. **185**, 52–62 (2017). https://doi.org/10.1016/j.ijpe.2016.12.004
4. Baryannis, G., Validi, S., Dani, S., Antoniou, G.: Supply chain risk management and artificial intelligence: state of the art and future research directions. Int. J. Prod. Res. **57**, 2179–2202 (2019). https://doi.org/10.1080/00207543.2018.1530476
5. Bodaghi, G., Jolai, F., Rabbani, M.: An integrated weighted fuzzy multi-objective model for supplier selection and order scheduling in a supply chain. Int. J. Prod. Res. **56**, 3590–3614 (2018). https://doi.org/10.1080/00207543.2017.1400706

6. Ben-Daya, M., Hassini, E., Bahroun, Z.: Internet of things and supply chain management: a literature review. Int. J. Prod. Res. **57**, 4719–4742 (2019). https://doi.org/10.1080/00207543.2017.1402140
7. Simchi-Levi, D., Wu, M.X.: Powering retailers' digitization through analytics and automation. Int. J. Prod. Res. **56**, 809–816 (2018). https://doi.org/10.1080/00207543.2017.1404161
8. De Treville, S., Shapiro, R.D., Hameri, A.P.: From supply chain to demand chain: the role of lead time reduction in improving demand chain performance. J. Oper. Manage. **21**, 613–627 (2004). https://doi.org/10.1016/j.jom.2003.10.001
9. Bozarth, C.C., Warsing, D.P., Flynn, B.B., Flynn, E.J.: The impact of supply chain complexity on manufacturing plant performance. J. Oper. Manage. **27**, 78–93 (2009). https://doi.org/10.1016/j.jom.2008.07.003
10. Akkermans, H., Bogerd, P., Van Doremalen, J.: Travail, transparency and trust: a case study of computer-supported collaborative supply chain planning in high-tech electronics. Eur. J. Oper. Res. **153**, 445–456 (2004). https://doi.org/10.1016/S0377-2217(03)00164-4
11. Giannakis, M., Louis, M.: A multi-agent based system with big data processing for enhanced supply chain agility. J. Enterp. Inf. Manage. **29**, 706–727 (2016). https://doi.org/10.1108/JEIM-06-2015-0050
12. Barbosa-Póvoa, A.P., da Silva, C., Carvalho, A.: Opportunities and challenges in sustainable supply chain: an operations research perspective. Eur. J. Oper. Res. **268**, 399–431 (2018). https://doi.org/10.1016/j.ejor.2017.10.036
13. Sodhi, M.M.S., Tang, C.S.: Research opportunities in supply chain transparency. Prod. Oper. Manage. **28**, 2946–2959 (2019)
14. Tukamuhabwa, B.R., Stevenson, M., Busby, J., Zorzini, M.: Supply chain resilience: definition, review and theoretical foundations for further study. Int. J. Prod. Res. **53**, 5592–5623 (2015). https://doi.org/10.1080/00207543.2015.1037934
15. Vanpoucke, E., Ellis, S.C.: Building supply-side resilience – a behavioural view. Int. J. Oper. Prod. Manage. **40**, 11–33 (2019). https://doi.org/10.1108/IJOPM-09-2017-0562
16. Kahiluoto, H., Mäkinen, H., Kaseva, J.: Supplying resilience through assessing diversity of responses to disruption. Int. J. Oper. Prod. Manage. **40**, 271–292 (2020). https://doi.org/10.1108/IJOPM-01-2019-0006
17. de Sá, M.M., de Souza Miguel, P.L., de Brito, R.P., Pereira, S.C.F.: Supply chain resilience: the whole is not the sum of the parts, Int. J. Oper. Prod. Manage. **40**, 92–115 (2019). https://doi.org/10.1108/IJOPM-09-2017-0510
18. Sharma, R., Kamble, S.S., Gunasekaran, A., Kumar, V., Kumar, A.: A systematic literature review on machine learning applications for sustainable agriculture supply chain performance. Comput. Oper. Res. **119**, 104926 (2020). https://doi.org/10.1016/j.cor.2020.104926
19. Fitzgerald, B., Adam, F.: The status of the IS field: historical perspective and practical orientation. Inf. Res. **5**, 1–17 (2000)
20. Banville, C., Landry, M.: Can the field of MIS be disciplined? Commun. ACM. **32**, 48–60 (1989). https://doi.org/10.1145/63238.63241
21. Hosseini, S., Ivanov, D.: Bayesian networks for supply chain risk, resilience and ripple effect analysis: a literature review. Expert Syst. Appl. **161**, 113649 (2020)
22. Ngai, E.W.T., Peng, S., Alexander, P., Moon, K.K.L.: Decision support and intelligent systems in the textile and apparel supply chain: an academic review of research articles. Expert Syst. Appl. **41**, 81–91 (2014)
23. Kitchenham, B.: Procedures for performing systematic reviews. In: Jt. Tech. Report, Comput. Sci. Dep. Keele Univ. Natl. ICT Aust. Ltd (0400011T.1) (2004). https://doi.org/10.5144/0256-4947.2017.79
24. Kitchenham, B.A., Budgen, D., Pearl Brereton, O.: Using mapping studies as the basis for further research - a participant-observer case study. Inf. Softw. Technol. **53**, 638–651 (2011). https://doi.org/10.1016/j.infsof.2010.12.011

25. Lu, Y., Papagiannidis, S., Alamanos, E.: Internet of Things: a systematic review of the business literature from the user and organisational perspectives. Technol. Forecast. Soc. Change. **136**, 285–297 (2018)
26. Martín-Martín, A., Orduna-Malea, E., Thelwall, M., Delgado López-Cózar, E.: Google Scholar, Web of Science, and Scopus: a systematic comparison of citations in 252 subject categories. J. Informetr. **12** (2018) 1160–1177
27. Tueanrat, Y., Papagiannidis, S., Alamanos, E.: Going on a journey: a review of the customer journey literature. J. Bus. Res. **125**, 336–353 (2021). https://doi.org/10.1016/j.jbusres.2020.12.028
28. Dybå, T., Dingsøyr, T.: Empirical studies of agile software development: a systematic review. Inf. Softw. Technol. **50**(9–10), 833–859 (2008). https://doi.org/10.1016/j.infsof.2008.01.006
29. Fahimnia, B., Sarkis, J., Boland, J., Reisi, M., Goh, M.: Policy insights from a green supply chain optimisation model. Int. J. Prod. Res. **53**, 6522–6533 (2015)
30. Singh, A., Kumari, S., Malekpoor, H., Mishra, N.: Big data cloud computing framework for low carbon supplier selection in the beef supply chain. J. Clean. Prod. **202**, 139–149 (2018). https://doi.org/10.1016/j.jclepro.2018.07.236
31. Batistič, S., van der Laken, P.: History, evolution and future of big data and analytics: a bibliometric analysis of its relationship to performance in organizations. Br. J. Manage. **30**, 229–251 (2019)
32. Tan, W.J., Zhang, A.N., Cai, W.: A graph-based model to measure structural redundancy for supply chain resilience. Int. J. Prod. Res. **57**, 6385–6404 (2019)
33. Gaviria-Marin, M., Merigó, J.M., Baier-Fuentes, H.: Knowledge management: a global examination based on bibliometric analysis. Technol. Forecast. Soc. Change. **140**, 194–220 (2019). https://doi.org/10.1016/j.techfore.2018.07.006
34. Hirsch, J.E.: An index to quantify an individual's scientific research output. Proc. Natl. Acad. Sci. USA **102**, 16569–16572 (2005)
35. Borges, A.F.S., Laurindo, F.J.B., Spínola, M.M., Gonçalves, R.F., Mattos, C.A.: The strategic use of artificial intelligence in the digital era: systematic literature review and future research directions. Int. J. Inf. Manage. 102225 (2020)
36. Grover, P., Kar, A.K., Dwivedi, Y.K.: Understanding artificial intelligence adoption in operations management: insights from the review of academic literature and social media discussions (2020)
37. Wong, W.K., Guo, Z.X.: A hybrid intelligent model for medium-term sales forecasting in fashion retail supply chains using extreme learning machine and harmony search algorithm. Int. J. Prod. Econ. **128**, 614–624 (2010)
38. Jaipuria, S., Mahapatra, S.S.: An improved demand forecasting method to reduce bullwhip effect in supply chains. Expert Syst. Appl. **41**, 2395–2408 (2014). https://doi.org/10.1016/j.eswa.2013.09.038
39. Chien, C.F., Lin, Y.S., Lin, S.K.: Deep reinforcement learning for selecting demand forecast models to empower Industry 3.5 and an empirical study for a semiconductor component distributor. Int. J. Prod. Res. **58**, 2784–2804 (2020)
40. Aksoy, A., Öztürk, N.: Supplier selection and performance evaluation in just-in-time production environments. Expert Syst. Appl. **38**, 6351–6359 (2011)
41. Zhao, K., Yu, X.: A case based reasoning approach on supplier selection in petroleum enterprises. Expert Syst. Appl. **38**, 6839–6847 (2011)
42. Choy, K.L., Lee, W.B., Lo, V.: Design of an intelligent supplier relationship management system: a hybrid case based neural network approach. Expert Syst. Appl. **24**, 225–237 (2003). https://doi.org/10.1016/S0957-4174(02)00151-3
43. Hendricks, K.B., Singhal, V.R.: The effect of supply chain glitches on shareholder wealth. J. Oper. Manage. **21**, 501–522 (2003). https://doi.org/10.1016/j.jom.2003.02.003

44. Wagner, S.M., Bode, C.: An empirical examination of supply chain performance along several dimensions of risk. J. Bus. Logist. **29**, 307–325 (2008). https://doi.org/10.1002/j.2158-1592.2008.tb00081.x
45. Hendricks, K.B., Singhal, V.R., Zhang, R.: The effect of operational slack, diversification, and vertical relatedness on the stock market reaction to supply chain disruptions. J. Oper. Manage. **27**, 233–246 (2009)
46. Priore, P., Ponte, B., Rosillo, R., de la Fuente, D.: Applying machine learning to the dynamic selection of replenishment policies in fast-changing supply chain environments. Int. J. Prod. Res. **57**, 3663–3677 (2019)
47. Parmigiani, A., Klassen, R.D., Russo, M.V.: Efficiency meets accountability: performance implications of supply chain configuration, control, and capabilities. J. Oper. Manage. **29**, 212–223 (2011)
48. Brintrup, A., et al.: Supply chain data analytics for predicting supplier disruptions: a case study in complex asset manufacturing. Int. J. Prod. Res. **58**, 3330–3341 (2019). https://doi.org/10.1080/00207543.2019.1685705
49. Nezamoddini, N., Gholami, A., Aqlan, F.: A risk-based optimization framework for integrated supply chains using genetic algorithm and artificial neural networks. Int. J. Prod. Econ. **225**, 107569 (2020)
50. Fragapane, G., Ivanov, D., Peron, M., Sgarbossa, F., Strandhagen, J.O.: Increasing flexibility and productivity in Industry 4.0 production networks with autonomous mobile robots and smart intralogistics. Ann. Oper. Res. (2020)
51. Rong, A., Akkerman, R., Grunow, M.: An optimization approach for managing fresh food quality throughout the supply chain. Int. J. Prod. Econ. **131**, 421–429 (2011). https://doi.org/10.1016/j.ijpe.2009.11.026
52. Abbasi, B., Babaei, T., Hosseinifard, Z., Smith-Miles, K., Dehghani, M.: Predicting solutions of large-scale optimization problems via machine learning: a case study in blood supply chain management. Comput. Oper. Res. **119**, 104941 (2020). https://doi.org/10.1016/j.cor.2020.104941
53. Doganis, P., Aggelogiannaki, E., Sarimveis, H.: A combined model predictive control and time series forecasting framework for production-inventory systems. Int. J. Prod. Res. **46**, 6841–6853 (2008)
54. Rabelo, L., Helal, M., Lertpattarapong, C., Moraga, R., Sarmiento, A.: Using system dynamics, neural nets, and eigenvalues to analyse supply chain behaviour. A case study. Int. J. Prod. Res. **46**, 51–71 (2008)
55. Marucheck, A., Greis, N., Mena, C., Cai, L.: Product safety and security in the global supply chain: issues, challenges and research opportunities. J. Oper. Manage. **29**, 707–720 (2011). https://doi.org/10.1016/j.jom.2011.06.007
56. Jüttner, U., Maklan, S.: Supply chain resilience in the global financial crisis: an empirical study. Supply Chain Manage. **16**, 246–259 (2011)
57. Carvalho, H., Barroso, A.P., MacHado, V.H., Azevedo, S., Cruz-Machado, V.: Supply chain redesign for resilience using simulation. Comput. Ind. Eng. **62**, 329–341 (2012). https://doi.org/10.1016/j.cie.2011.10.003
58. Gunasekaran, A., Ngai, E.W.T.: Expert systems and artificial intelligence in the 21st century logistics and supply chain management. Expert Syst. Appl. **41**, 1–4 (2014). https://doi.org/10.1016/j.eswa.2013.09.006

Dynamic Capability Theory as a Lens to Investigate Big Data Analytics and Supply Chain Agility

Trevor Cadden[1(✉)], Guangming Cao[2], Raymond Treacy[3], Ying Yang[4(✉)], and George Onofrei[5]

[1] University of Ulster and Ajman University, Ajman, UAE
t.cadden@ulster.ac.uk
[2] Ajman University, Ajman, UAE
[3] University of Gothenburg, Gothenburg, Sweden
[4] Newcastle University, Newcastle upon Tyne, UK
ying.yang2@newcastle.ac.uk
[5] Letterkenny Institute of Technology, Letterkenny, Ireland

Abstract. The study draws on the dynamic capability perspective to explore how turbulent and competitive environments influence big data analytics capabilities which, in turn, impact supply chain (SC) agility. Survey data from 201 UK manufacturers is collected and analysed, and a moderation model is presented. The results show that in turbulent environments, characterized by high degrees of environmental dynamism, firms should leverage the volume, velocity and variety facets of big data which, in turn, enable sensing and creative search (dynamic) capabilities needed to adapt in such environments. In competitive environments however, where first mover advantage is crucial, firms should scale back on time consuming search capabilities (data variety). At the operational level, firms should exclusively leverage the velocity aspects of big data to enhance SC agility. Finally, while, previous studies have focused on analytical maturity as a prerequisite to big data implementation, this study finds that a reconfigured analytical orientation culture specifically on responsiveness, i.e. strategic alignment and predictive forecasting analytics, moderates the relationship between big data velocity and SC agility. The results of this study therefore fill a key gap in the SC management literature as the study demonstrates how environmental factors, both internal and external, influence big data and dynamic capability development in order to enhance SC agility.

Keywords: Big Data analytics · SC agility · Dynamic capability

1 Introduction

Supply chain agility (SCA) is a strategic ability that assists organizations to rapidly sense and flexibly respond to such internal and external uncertainties and pressures [1, 2] which, in turn, can result in enhanced customer value and competitive advantage [3].

Published by Springer Nature Switzerland AG 2021
D. Dennehy et al. (Eds.): I3E 2021, LNCS 12896, pp. 467–480, 2021.
https://doi.org/10.1007/978-3-030-85447-8_39

Through the lens of dynamic capabilities, the ability to 'sense', 'seize' and 'respond' in a dynamic and competitive environment is critical to delivering competitive advantage [2, 4]. Business organisations conduct data capturing, sharing, analysing and integration to create a learning SC and builds the dynamic capabilities, and constantly stimulates innovation and change internally to address the dynamism and competitive in the external marketplace [5, 6]. Therefore, firms not only need to develop systems and processes to capture, store, share, analyse and integrate of vast amounts of information available but also develop analytical-orientational culture within this dynamic environment to make strategic decisions [4, 7].

It has paved the way for a burgeoning research area within SCs known generally within the academic and industrial lexicon as Big Data Analytics (BDA). The result is an unprecedented interest and explosion of studies investigating the role of BDA in support of increased organisational value. Almost 400 papers (44%) of total papers in a Scopus search relating to SC and Big Data were published in recent years (between 2016 and 2018) [8]. Whilst BDA as a construct has variations in its reported definitions, generally definitions focus on the range of process and techniques that a firm possesses to collect and analyse this dynamic data (typically characterised as volume, variety and velocity) in support of competitive advantage [4, 9]. Yet, interestingly a recent study reported that only 17% of enterprises have implemented BDA in one or more SC function [10] and found the ability to achieve SCA much more complex than assumed [11]. It is argued in this paper that a key reason firms are not realising the requisite SC success in respect of BDA in support of SC agility is due ignoring the holistic and nuanced perspectives required. Sensing, seizing and reconfiguration capabilities are all interrelated dynamic capabilities that must be in harnessed to adapt and transform internal SC processes to enhance SCA [12]. This study addresses this research gap through the following three research questions: (1) How does the external environment (external dynamism and competitive pressures) influence big data capabilities and data collection (Sensing and search capabilities)? (2) What types of BDA capabilities lead to enhanced SCA (Seizing capability)? (3) How can SCs be configured/reconfigured to enhance SCA (Configuration capability)?

A key contribution of this paper is the adoption of Dynamic Capability Theory (DCT) to scan the external environment to leverage the BDA capabilities in support of SC agility. A second contribution is this study aims to deconstruct BDA into sub dimensions (volume, variety and velocity) to assess the role of each characteristic in achieving SCA. Studies to date largely group BDA and therefore the results lose the nuanced insights that this paper will provide. Thirdly, this study develops a new and exciting construct (Analytical Orientation: AO) to assess how AO moderates a firm relationship between BDA and SCA. Studies to date have largely ignored a firm's AO in leveraging BDA in support of SCA, yet many make fleeting and implied references to its importance. Finally, the paper provides a framework and insights for management on how to integrate and maximise the information available within the external environment in support of SCA.

This paper is structured as follows. First, a review of key literature related to BDA, SCA and DCT presented. Next, the rational for development of the hypothesis is outlined, followed by the research methodology. Then the results and analysis section are provided. Finally, a discussion of key findings, implications, and future research are presented.

2 Literature Review and Hypothesis Development

2.1 Big Data Analytics

Firms are increasingly understanding the importance of Big data analytics (BDA) in responding to the external environment and competitive pressures; and the nuances that underpin the broad construct. The BDA approach is widely accepted as a composite term which includes big data perspective (BD) and the analytics perspective. The BD component compromises three key dimensions: volume, variety and velocity. The analytics perspective builds on the data collection and storage element of Big Data and applies advanced analytic techniques, such as data mining, statistical analysis and predictive analytics, to interpret the huge amounts of data available in order to uncover hidden patterns, trends, correlations in support of strategic decision making. While resources in themselves may be easily replicated, it is believed that the information and knowledge created by BDA is not easy to replicate and will lead to sustained competitive advantage. BDA has thus risen to prominence due to the ability to gain meaningful insights from data and thereby help organisations make better decisions. The literature has also stated that BDA plays a key role in enhancing agility and business performance, (such as new product development, responding to sudden disruptions or change, customer service, sales and revenue, and market expansion), allowing businesses to excel in the current fast-paced and ever-changing market environment [10, 13]. BDA creates novel ways of analysing and configuring SC processes [14, 15], enhancing SC innovation and identifying new opportunities for SC collaboration [16]. The development of BDA capabilities within the organisation and SC has led to increased processing power, assimilation and reaction to market changes. However, BDA as an approach has not been without its criticisms. The perception that attempts to automate highly complex decisions ignore the human aspect and leads to relationship myopia and may impact holistic SC decision making [17].

2.2 Dynamic Capabilities View

Our study is underpinned by the dynamic capabilities view. The term dynamic capabilities originate from the resource-based theory [18] and represents a company's ability to integrate, build, and reconfigure internal and external competences to respond to changes in the business environment [5, 19]. Organisations use these higher levels capabilities as antecedents to organizational and strategic routines, by which managers alter their resource base to generate new value-creating strategies [20]. Chen et al. [21] summarised two reasons that organizations implement BDA to enable their dynamic capabilities. First, using BDA helps organizations establish knowledge creation routines particularly when market dynamism is high. Second, this view of BDA usage also reflects the key characteristics of dynamic capabilities suggested by the literature: commonalities in key features, coupled with idiosyncrasy in details [18]. Prior studies have investigated the performance effects of BDA at SC level. For example, Wamba et al. [2] found that BDA has positive effects on SC agility, SC adaptability and operational performance. Similarly, Dubey et al. [7] argue that companies that have successfully developed BDA capabilities have improved their SC performance. Having sophisticated planning tools and advanced IT-enabled control practices allows companies to move the value of data towards outcome values through increasing SC planning and performance capabilities [22]. These studies highlight the impact of BDA on SC agility, as well as the role of BDA-enabled dynamic capabilities. Our study draws on the dynamic capability view and seeks to further expand the conceptualisation of BDA as a dynamic capability. There is a scarcity of studies that decompose the BDA capability into sub-capabilities [2].

2.3 Environmental Dynamism

An important situational parameter in the DCT is environmental dynamism [23], which represents the response of an organisation's competitive position created through organisational capabilities, to the changes in the business environment. Environmental dynamism is characterised by changes in products/services, technology, customer preferences and impacts a company's resource allocation strategy [6]. Prior research has highlighted that companies operating in volatile environments need to build dynamic capabilities to respond with innovative solutions to problems that are encountered, in order to satisfy the market requirements [23, 24, 26]. Kovach et al. [27] asserted that it is more difficult to attain superior performance in highly dynamic environments and managers require timely information in order to make the right decisions. Given the unpredictable nature of environmental dynamism, the typical response for firms is to enhance their strategic sense making capacity, by acquiring and analysing information to develop cognitive maps which in turn enables them to effectively respond to external environmental variations. In a turbulent environment, firms must capture large amounts of data, that can potentially reveal new and unique insights which can give them an edge over their competitors [28]. The speed at which they convert this information into new products and services, can be the winning factor when dealing with upstream and downstream uncertainties [3]. Thus, we posit:

H1(a-c): Environmental dynamism tends to lead to firms having more BDA capabilities: volume, variety and velocity.

2.4 Competitive Pressures

Globalisation and rapid technological change have created opportunities and challenges that led to new competitive pressures. To respond to these, firms have turned toward technology and integrated BDA throughout their SCs [25]. Firms are under pressure from their customers, suppliers and competitors to improve resource efficiency and achieve competitive advantage [29]. Very few studies have looked at the impact of competitive pressures on organisational BDA adoption [21]. Chen et al. [21] posits that external competitive pressures may positively affect the degree to which firms adopt BDA in their SCs. For instance, the use of BDA by SC actors (customers and suppliers), will likely influence the firm to engage in similar practices [30]. Over the last ten years, companies have been taking advantage of new economics of data and the heightened global nature of rivalry among market incumbents has stimulated management to heavily invest in information technologies [3]. The successful adoption of BDA by competitors will trigger imitative practices throughout organisations. As a result, in order to gain competitive advantage, firms are likely to employ BDA tools to enable them to quickly react to market changes. Therefore, we posit that:

H2 (a-c): Competitive pressures tends to lead to firms having more BDA capabilities: volume, variety and velocity.

2.5 Big Data Analytics and Supply Chain Agility

BDA has a huge operational and strategic impact on SC agility by allowing firms that adopt it to achieve a competitive advantage through enhancing decision-making and increasing value-adding activities [31, 32]. BDA extracts useful information from massive data sets to identify useful insights such as market trends, customer buying patterns and how to enable more targeted business decisions, in order to allow companies to excel in the current fast-paced and ever-changing market environment [10]. BDA also offers opportunities to effectively collaborate with SC partners in order to respond to market changes in a rapid manner, thereby allowing businesses to gain competitiveness [33]. Pisano et al. [20] pointed out that BDA transformed business by serving as a cross-functional capability that allows managers to align strategies and make decisions in accordance with market demands. Zhan and Tan [32] stated that BDA provides a roadmap to firms and managers by generating practical SC strategies, facilitating collaboration between departments, and generating fact-based operational decisions. SC agility has been recognised as the rapid and successful reconfiguration of key resources so firms can meet changing customers' demands and as a necessary ingredient for improving competitiveness [33, 34]. While there is a rich body of literature on SC agility [1, 33, 35] the majority of research has focused on the factors relating to speed, flexibility and adaptability, which contribute to change response. However, in order for an organization to respond to changes effectively, organizations need to adopt a proactive stance to be able to reconfigure their resources and to respond to changes quickly and effectively [1]. Because of a dynamic and volatile business environment, SC agility needs simple, experiential and flexible processes to rapidly make decisions and create new knowledge in order to yield unpredictable outcomes [18, 35].

H3(a-c): BDA capabilities: volume, variety and velocity, are positively related to SC agility.

2.6 The Moderating Role of Analytical-Orientation Culture

Most organisations have adopted various advanced BDA techniques to process and analyse data quickly and accurately, in order to extract valuable insights from data and to develop the agility to cope with constantly changing market conditions and to explore business opportunities. The results of BDA mean different things to different people and many organisations face enormous challenges when deriving quality insights from BDA results [21]. McAfee et al. [36] identified five challenges for organizations in becoming data-driven: leadership, talent management, technology, decision-making, and company culture. Clearly, analytics is not simply a technical matter. In this study, we follow Davenport [37] and Ransbotham et al. [38] proposed that firms need to develop an analytical orientation to combine critical data results as well as adapt cultural norms to guide management decisions and actions. In this sense, analytical orientation allows companies to maximize decision-making processes by developing an organization's capacity to conduct analysis and act, providing better results by generating value and efficiency in decision making.

H4: The firm analytical orientation culture moderates the relationship between BDA and SC agility.

3 Research Method

3.1 Sample and Data Collection

In order to test the above hypotheses, primary data was collected from a sample of UK manufacturers using a questionnaire survey. To capture the responses to the measurements of all constructs, the questionnaire survey was generated using a seven-point Likert scale. Akin to other UK studies investigating SC relationships [39], a national database of manufacturing industry companies, filtered by greater than 100 employees, were examined. A random sample of 1000 companies were selected, and the survey forwarded based on job roles. We received 304 responses and 201 were usable responses, which represent a 36.8% response rate which was deemed appropriate and exceeds the level of 20% reported by Malhotra and Grover [40]. Several steps were undertaken to minimize common method bias, following the recommendations of Tehseen et al. [41]. The presence of non-response bias was evaluated by conducting a t-test to compare early ($n = 102$) and late ($n = 99$) respondents on all measures.

3.2 Evaluation of the Measurement Model

In order to avoid measurement model misspecification, a confirmatory tetrad analysis (CTA- PLS) was conducted based on Gudergan et al. [42] and Hair et al. [43]. The result of the CTA-PLS confirmed that the measurement model was a reflective model, which was then evaluated and validated by considering the internal consistency (composite reliability), indictor reliability, convergent validity and discriminant validity [43]. The evaluation results are summarized in Table 1 and Table 2. Discriminant validity was also satisfactory based on two tests.

The research model's predictive power was assessed by the amount of variance attributed to the latent variables (i.e., R^2) (Fig. 1). The R^2 values indicated that the full model explained 35% of the variance in SCA, 38% in volume (VOL), 50% in variety (VAR), and 60% in velocity (VEL). According to Wetzels *et al.* [44], the effect size suggested for R^2 in IT- related research is small = 0.1, medium = 0.25, and large = 0.36. Thus, while SCA's effect size was very close to large, the effect sizes of other variables were large.

Table 1. Convergent validity and internal consistency reliability

Construct	Indicator	Loading	Indicator Reliability	Composite Reliability	Cronbach's α	AVE
Environmental Dynamism (ED)	ED1	0.87	0.76	0.91	0.85	0.77
	ED2	0.89	0.79			
	ED3	0.88	0.77			
Competitive pressures (CP)	CP1	0.83	0.69	0.86	0.75	0.67
	CP2	0.83	0.69			
	CP3	0.80	0.64			
Volume (VOL)	VOL1	0.72	0.52	0.92	0.89	0.74
	VOL2	0.89	0.79			
	VOL3	0.90	0.81			
	VOL4	0.92	0.85			
Variety (VAR)	VAR1	0.90	0.81	0.95	0.94	0.84
	VAR2	0.88	0.77			
	VAR3	0.95	0.90			
	VAR4	0.93	0.86			
Velocity (VEL)	VEL1	0.92	0.85	0.95	0.94	0.84
	VEL2	0.93	0.86			
	VEL3	0.93	0.86			
	VEL4	0.88	0.77			
Supply chain agility (SCA)	SCA1	0.90	0.81	0.94	0.92	0.81
	SCA2	0.90	0.81			
	SCA3	0.91	0.83			
	SCA4	0.88	0.77			
Analytical Socialisation Mechanisms (ASM)	ASM1	0.87	0.76	0.94	0.91	0.79
	ASM 2	0.91	0.83			
	ASM 3	0.88	0.77			
	ASM 4	0.89	0.79			

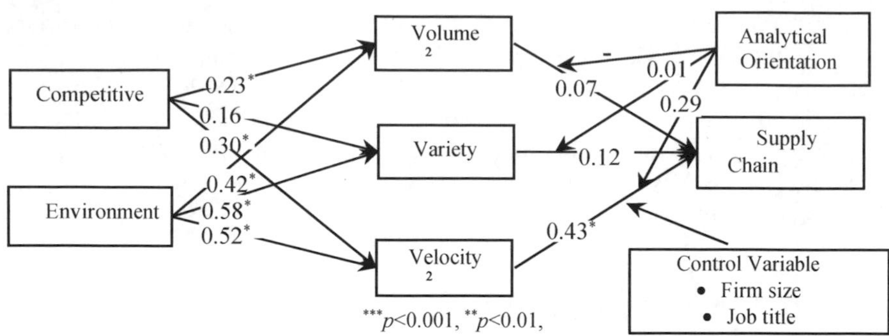

Fig. 1. Hypothesis test results

3.3 Hypotheses Testing and Moderation Analysis

Table 2 shows the results of hypothesis testing. H1 suggests that environmental dynamism (ED) relates to VOL (H1a), VAR (H1b), and VEL (H1c) positively. H1 is supported as ED has a statistically significant effect of 0.42 ($p < 0.001$) on VOL, 0.58 ($p < 0.001$) on VAR, and 0.52 ($p < 0.0001$) on VEL. H2 assumes that competitive pressure (CP) is positively related to VOL (H2a), VAR (H2b), and VEL (H2c). H2a and H2c are supported since NP's effects on VOL is 0,23 ($p < 0.05$) and on VEL is 0.30 ($p < 0.01$); however, H2b is rejected since CP's effects on VAR is not significant. H3 hypothesizes that SCA is positively affected by VOL (H3a), VAR (H3b), and VEL (H3c). H3c

Table 2. Summary results of hypotheses testing

Hypothesis	Hypothesized Path	Direct effect	Empirical evidence
H1a	ED - > VOL	0.42^{***}	Supported
H1b	ED - > VAR	0.58^{***}	Supported
H1c	ED - > VEL	0.52^{***}	Supported
H2a	CP - > VOL	0.23^{*}	Supported
H2b	CP - > VAR	0.15^{ns}	Rejected
H2c	CP - > VEL	0.30^{**}	Supported
H3b	VAR - > SCA	0.12^{ns}	Rejected
H3c	VEL - > SCA	0.43^{**}	Supported
H4a	VOL × AO - > SCA	-0.15^{ns}	Rejected
H4b	VAR × AO - > SCA	0.01^{ns}	Rejected
H4c	VEL × AO - > SCA	0.29^{*}	Supported

is supported as VEL has a statistically significant effect of 0.43 ($p < 0.01$) on SCA. However, H3a and H3b are rejected as both VOL and VAR have no statistically significant effects on SCA. H4 postulates that analytical orientation level (AO) moderates the relationship between VOL and SCA, VAR and SCA, and VEL and SCA. In order to test these moderation effects, the function of "Create Moderating Effect" (a two- stage method) provided by SmartPLS3 was used, with VEL as a predictor variable and AO as a moderator variable. The analysis was based on bootstrapping (5,000 samples) [43, 45], which indicated that H4c is supported as AO moderates the relationship between VEL and SCA, with the moderating effect of 0.29 ($p < 0.05$). However, H4a and H4b are rejected as the AO does not moderate the relationship between either VOL and SCA or VAR and SCA.

4 Research Findings and Discussion

In relation to subset one i.e. Hypotheses H1a-H1c, which explored the impact of environmental dynamism (ED) on BDA capabilities (i.e. volume, variety and velocity), the results are clear. In turbulent environments, characterized by high degrees of variability and changing customer tastes, ED significantly influences BDA capabilities and thus the initial data collected, which is ultimately leveraged for decision-making. Interestingly, ED is linked to all three BDA capabilities (i.e. volume, variety and velocity). In other words, the results support DC theory, as all three facets of BD are significant and form both the firms' sensing (volume and velocity) and search (variety) DCs [19, 46, 47]. This finding contradicts previous research linking ED to BDA, which only found partial support for such a relationship (see 2). In relation to H1a specifically, the positive link to BD volume is surprising. It can be argued that in turbulent environments, products can become outdated quickly and there is a need for as much information as possible in relation to the external environment [19, 48]. In relation to H1b, there is a positive relationship between ED and variety. It's argued that in turbulent environments, changing customer tastes and the need for new products require both flexibility and exploration in the SC [24]. This observation also aligns with DCT, particularly the creative search capability (see 46). For example, in relation to data variety, data may be acquired from many different sources in the SC to facilitate innovation and visibility in dynamic environments [19, 46]. In other words, BD variety enables creative search DCs which help set the scene for the subsequent seizing and transformation aspects of DCs [19, 46, 47]. The idea is to facilitate greater SC visibility and to capture new opportunities and innovations (incremental or radical) needed for changing customer demand [24, 47]. Finally, the results of H1c demonstrate that ED is positively related to data velocity (H1c). This suggests that swiftness in terms of accessing real-time data to facilitate rapid customization, greater SC responsiveness, and the introduction new products, is crucial for adapting and responding to dynamic and ever-changing environments. In other words, velocity is linked to the response aspects of DCT and SCA due to the need to quickly sense and react to environmental threats [19, 46, 47].

In relation to H2a to H2c. The results demonstrate that Competitive Pressures (CP) are significantly related to (H2c) data velocity (0.30**) while also positively related to data volume (H2a) (0.23*). Conversely, CPs were not found to be related to data variety (H2c). Hence H2a and H2c are supported, while H2b is rejected. The positive results are related to DCT, in particular sensing capabilities as opposed to creative search DCs (see 46). Sensing capabilities help develop subsequent response and transformation capabilities by initially analyzing the competitive landscape and selecting the appropriate response [15, 46]. In this case, a possible explanation for the positive linkages between CP and volume and velocity is that in highly competitive environments many firms may seek a first mover advantage in terms of products, process and services and seek large amounts of customer data/market intelligence which can be accessed and processed quickly. In such settings, firms sense that a first mover advantage characterized by agility and responsiveness are market winners.

Hypotheses H3a to H3c, consider the seizing aspects of DCs and how BD capabilities can be leveraged to enhance SCA. A second key contribution of this study is that it not only explores if BDA can be leveraged to enhance SCA, but also identifies which BDA capabilities are specifically related to SCA. Hence, this study facilitates transparency in terms of uncovering the micro-foundational relationships between DCs, BDA and SCA by allowing management to narrow down the BDA antecedents of both DCs and SCA. Moreover, the path from the external environment (sensing DCs) is now linked to the internal environment, providing a clear link between BDA strategy, and secondly, how can the data be seized to enhance SCA. The results of H3a to H3c find that data volume and data variety are not linked to SCA, while BD velocity was found to have a significant relationship with SCA (0.43**). Hence, hypotheses H3a and H3b are rejected while hypotheses H3c is supported.

Finally, hypotheses H4a to H4c consider the moderating role of analytical orientation to help deconstruct the relationship between BDA and SCA. More specifically, in order to analyse data quickly and efficiently, the final stage may require the reconfiguration of SC culture and the creation of co-specialized assets [15]. According to DCT theory [15, 19], this may be achieved by reconfiguring the SC and creating an analytical orientation in order to better facilitate data velocity (or variety and volume). The results demonstrate however, that the moderating effect of SC analytical orientation in the relationship between BDA and SCA is only significant for data velocity (H4c). This highlights that specific analytical enablers, i.e. strategic alignment, top management support and predictive modelling skills will facilitate SCA, but only in relation to velocity capabilities. This positive relationship with data velocity may be explained by DCT, as BD structures can be reconfigured and aligned to create co-specialized assets to enhance SCA [15, 19]. More specifically, reconfiguring the SC to support an analytical orientation helps enhance data flow in the SC which, in turn, facilitates real-time data and the ability to respond to opportunities and threats (responsiveness). Finally, data volume (H4a) and variety (H4b) are not related to SCA, even when a firm possesses a strong SC analytical orientation. Hence, a key finding is that data volume and data variety and are only relevant for developing sensing and search capabilities where strategic flexibility and the ability to adapt to external conditions are key [15, 19].

5 Research Implications

5.1 Implication for Theory

BDA has the potential to reduce many of the complexities inherent within agile SCs [2, 11]. Conversely, in the literature, the capabilities which link to this outcome are not clear. Accordingly, this study employed a DC lens [19, 46] in a SC setting to explore three novel research questions which aimed to examine; (1) How the external environment influences BD capabilities and data collection (Sensing and search capabilities), (2) What types of BDA capabilities lead to enhanced SCA (Seizing capability) and (3) How SC culture can be reconfigured to enhance SCA (Reconfiguration capability). Our results find strong support for the DCT across all three research questions. While previous research has only considered the "seizing aspects" of BD [12] this study employs a holistic DC perspective, which focuses on both the initial "sensing" and subsequent "reconfiguration" aspects of BD alongside the seizing aspects i.e. the entire path.

The results show that in turbulent environments, ED is linked to all three BDA capabilities (volume, variety and velocity) as they enable *both* sensing and creative search DCs [19, 46]. These capabilities in turn form sensing capabilities (volume and velocity) and search capabilities (variety) which help firms not only adapt in turbulent environments, but also pinpoint the most appropriate data for strategic decision making relevant to the firm. As shown in this study, this is particularly important in relation to SCA [19, 46]. This research therefore expands on previous studies, which found ED was only partially linked to BDA and SCA (See referenced 2) by finding a wholly positive association with all three BD capabilities (i.e. the development of sensing and search capabilities) and, secondly, by offering a transparent breakdown of which BDA capabilities can help firms adapt in turbulent environments.

6 Conclusions, Limitations and the Way Forward

Previous research suggests that there is a need for new theoretical approaches to holisti cally capture the dynamic nature of big data in the field of SCM [12, 48]. Accordingly, this study sought to explore the impact of BDA on SCA by employing a DC lens at the SC level. More specifically, the contribution of this study is to not only examine the "response" aspects of DC and SCA in the domain of BDA, but also to explore the initial sensing and subsequent reconfiguration aspects of DCs (see 15, 19, 46), which have been largely overlooked in the BDA-SC literature [12, 48]. In terms of contributions, this study has achieved its aims and objectives by identifying how firms operating in dynamic and competitive environments can harness BDA to enhance SC agility. More specifically, the study contributes to the literature by employing a DC lens in a BD and SC setting. Accordingly, the results demonstrate that ED and CP play a key role in BD capability development and data collection as they enable the sensing and search DCs which allow firms to adapt in turbulent and competitive environments. Subsequently, it's shown that data velocity is a key dynamic response capability (Seizing capability) needed to enhance SCA. Finally, BD can act an enabler of SC reconfiguration and the development of co- specialized assets (DCs) which is needed to facilitate a better analytical environment for SCA (Reconfiguration capability). This study is restricted in number of ways and therefore offers many opportunities for future research. Firstly, this study only considered turbulent and competitive environments, additional outcome variables could be explored in the domain of BDA such as SC resilience, SC flexibility and SC innovation (incremental and radical). In relation to the BDA-SCA relationship specifically, studies could also examine, using factor analysis, additional enablers of the BDA-SCA relationships using the 3V framework outlined in this study. In conclusion, this study filled a major oversight in the literature in relation to how firms can implement BD to enhance SCA in turbulent and competitive environments. The study also considered how the external environment intertwines with BDA to play a key role in shaping DC capabilities and how these capabilities can be leveraged internally to enhance SCA.

References

1. Fayezi, S., Zutshi, A., O'Loughlin, A.: How australian manufacturing firms perceive and understand the concepts of agility and flexibility in the supply chain. Int. J. Oper. Prod. Manag. **35**, 248–281 (2015)
2. Wamba, S.F., Dubey, R., Gunasekaran, A., Akter, S.: The performance effects of big data analytics and supply chain ambidexterity: the moderating effect of environmental dynamism. Int. J. Prod. Econ. **222**, 1–14 (2020)
3. Kamble, S.S., Gunasekran, A.: Big data-driven supply chain performance measurement system: a review and framework for implementation. Int. J. Prod. Res. **58**, 65–86 (2020)
4. Duan, Y., Cao, G., Edwards, J.S.: Understanding the impact of business analytics on innovation. Eur. J. Oper. Res. **281**, 673–686 (2020)
5. Defee, C.C., Fugate, B.S.: Changing perspective of capabilities in the dynamic supply chain era. Int. J. Logistics Manag. **21**(2), 180–206 (2010)
6. Dubey, R., et al.: Big data analytics and artificial intelligence pathway to operational performance under the effects of entrepreneurial orientation and environmental dynamism: a study of manufacturing organisations. Int. J. Prod. Econ. **226**, 107599 (2019)
7. Calatayud, A., Mangan, J., Christopher, M.: The self-thinking supply chain. Suppl. Chain Manag. Int. J. **24**(1), 22–38 (2019)
8. Gunasekaran, A., et al.: Big data and predictive analytics for supply chain and organizational performance. J. Bus. Res. **70**, 308–317 (2017)
9. Nguyen, T., Li, Z., Spiegler, V., Ieromonachou, P., Lin, Y.: Big data analytics in supply chain management; state-of-the-art literature review. Comput. Oper. Res. **98**, 254–264 (2018)
10. Jha, A.K., Agi, M.A.N., Ngai, E.W.T.: A note on big data analytics capability development in supply chain. Decis. Support Syst. **138**, 1–9 (2020)
11. Wamba, S.F., Akter, S.: Understanding supply chain analytics capabilities & agility for data-rich environments. Int. J. Oper. Prod. Manag. **39**(6), 887–912 (2019)
12. Akter, S., Wamba, S.F., Gunasekaran, A., Dubey, R., Childe, S.J.: How to improve firm performance using big data analytics capability and business strategy alignment? Int. J. Prod. Econ. **182**, 113–131 (2016)
13. Hazen, B.T., Skipper, J.B., Ezell, J.D., Boone, C.A.: Big data and predictive analytics for supply chain sustainability: a theory-driven research agenda. Comput. Ind. Eng. **101**, 592–598 (2016)
14. Conboy, K., Mikalef, P., Dennehy, D., Krogstie, J.: Using business analytics to enhance dynamic capabilities in operations research: a case analysis and research agenda. Eur. J. Oper. Res. **281**(3), 656–672 (2020)
15. Sanders, N.R., Ganeshan, R.: Big data in supply chain management. Prod. Oper. Manag. **24**(6), 1028–1029 (2015)

16. Davenport, T.H., Harris, J.G.: Competing on Analytics: The New Science of Winning. Harvard Business Press, Boston (2007)
17. Eisenhardt, K.M., Martin, J.A.: Dynamic capabilities: what are they? Strateg. Manag. J. **21**, 1105–1121 (2000)
18. Teece, D.J.: Explicating dynamic capabilities: the nature and microfoundations of (sustainable) enterprise performance. Strateg. Manag. J. **28**(13), 1319–1350 (2007)
19. Pisano, G.P.: Knowledge, integration, and the locus of learning: An empirical analysis of process development. Strateg. Manag. J. **15**, 85–100 (1994)
20. Chen, D., Preston, D.S., Swink, M.: How the use of big data analytics affects value creation in supply chain management. J. Manag. Inf. Syst. **32**(4), 4–39 (2015)
21. Chae, B., Olson, D., Sheu, C.: The impact of supply chain analytics on operational dubeyperformance: a resource-based view. Int. J. Prod. Res. **52**, 4695–4710 (2014)
22. Girod, S.J., Whittington, R.: Reconfiguration, restructuring and firm performance: dynamic capabilities and environmental dynamism. Strateg. Manag. J. **38**, 1121–1133 (2017)
23. Aslam, H., Blome, C., Roscoe, S., Azhar, T.: Dynamic supply chain capabilities: how market sensing, supply chain agility and adaptability affect supply chain ambidexterity. Int. J. Oper. Prod. Manag. **38**(12), 226–2285 (2018)
24. Aslam, H., Blome, C., Roscoe, S., Azhar, T.M.: Determining the antecedents of dynamic supply chain capabilities. Supply Chain Manag. Int. J. **25**(4), 1–20 (2020)
25. Helfat, C.E., Raubitsheik, R.S.: Dynamic and integrative capabilities for profiting from innovation in digital platform-based ecosystems. Res. Policy **47**, 1391–1399 (2018)
26. Kovach, J.J., Hora, M., Manikas, A., Patel, P.C.: Firm performance in dynamic environments: the role of operational slack and operational scope. J. Oper. Manag. **37**, 1–12 (2015)
27. Johnson, J.S., Friend, S.B., Lee, H.S.: Big data facilitation, utilization, and monetization: exploring the 3Vs in a new product development process. J. Prod. Innov. Manag. **34**(5), 640–658 (2017)
28. Ward, P.T., Duray, R.: Manufacturing strategy in context: environment, competitive strategy and manufacturing strategy. J. Oper. Manag. **18**(2), 123–138 (2000)
29. Chang, S.E., Chen, Y.: When blockchain meets supply chain: a systematic literature review on current development and potential applications. IEEE Access **8**, 62478–62494 (2020)
30. Pape, T.: Prioritising data items for business analytics: framework and application to human resources. Eur. J. Oper. Res. **252**(2), 687–698 (2016)
31. Zhan, Y., Tan, H.T.: An analytic infrastructure for harvesting big data to enhance supply chain performance. Eur. J. Oper. Res. **281**(3), 559–574 (2020)
32. Blome, C., Schoenherr, T., Rexhausen, D.: Antecedents and enablers of supply chain agility and its effect on performance: a dynamic capabilities perspective. Int. J. Prod. Res. **51**(4), 1295–1318 (2013)
33. Van Hoek, R., Harrison, A., Christopher, M.: Measuring agile capabilities in the supply chain. Int. J. Oper. Prod. Manag. **21**(1/2), 126–148 (2001)
34. Gligor, D.M., Esmark, C.L., Holcomb, M.C.: Performance outcomes of supply chain agility: when should you be agile? J. Oper. Manag. **33**, 71–82 (2015)
35. McAfee, A., Brynjolfsson, E., Davenport, T.H.: Bigdata: the management revolution. Harv. Bus. Rev. **90**, 60–68 (2012)
36. Davenport, T.H.: Competing on analytics. Harv. Bus. Rev. **84**(1), 98–107 (2006)
37. Ransbotham, S., Kiron, D., Prentice, P.K.: Beyond the hype: the hard work behind analytics success. MIT Sloan Manag. Rev. **57**(3), 1–18 (2016)
38. Cadden, T., Millar, K., Treacy, R., Humphreys, P.: The mediating influence of organisational cultural practices in successful lean management implementation. Int. J. Prod. Econ. **229**(1), 1–12 (2020)
39. Malhotra, M.K., Grover, V.: An assessment of survey research in POM: from constructs to theory. J. Oper. Manag. **16**(4), 407–425 (1998)

40. Tehseen, S., Ramayah, T., Sajilan, S.: Testing and controlling for common method variance: a review of available methods. J. Manag. Sci. **4**(2), 142–168 (2017)
41. Gudergan, S.P., Ringle, C.M., Wende, S., Will, A.: Confirmatory tetrad analysis in PLS path modelling. J. Bus. Res. **61**(12), 1238–1249 (2008)
42. Hair, J.F., Ringle, C.M., Sarstedt, M.: Partial Least Squares Structural Equation Modeling (2013)
43. Wetzels, M., Odekerken-Schröder, G., van Oppen, C.: Using PLS path modeling for assessing construct models: guidelines and empirical illustration. MIS Q. **33**(1), 177–195 (2009)
44. Hayes, A.F.: Beyond Baron and Kenny: statistical mediation analysis in the new millennium. Commun. Monogr. **76**(4), 408–420 (2009)
45. Pandza, K., Thorpe, R.: Creative search and strategic sense-making: missing dimensions in the concept of dynamic capabilities. Br. J. Manag. **131**, S118–S131 (2009)
46. Mikalef, P., Boura, M., Lekakos, G., Krogstie, J.: Big data analytics capabilities and innovation: the mediating role of dynamic capabilities and moderating effect of the environment. Br. J. Manag. **30**, 272–298 (2019)
47. Barlette, Y., Baillette, P.: Big data analytics in turbulent contexts: towards organizational change for enhanced agility. Production Planning and Control (2020). (In press)
48. Dubey, R., Altay, N., Gunasekaran, A., Blome, C., Papadopoulos, T., Childe, S.J.: Supply chain agility, adaptability and alignment: empirical evidence from the Indian auto components industry. Int. J. Oper. Prod. Manag. **38**(1), 129–148 (2018)

The Effect of Data Driven Culture on Customer Development and Firm Performance: The Role of Supply Chain Information Sharing and Supply Chain Information Quality

Benjamin Agyei-Owusu(✉), Mawuli Kobla Amedofu, David Asamoah, and Caleb Amankwaa Kumi

Kwame Nkrumah University of Science and Technology, Kumasi, Ghana
{bagyei-owusu.ksb,dasamoah.ksb}@knust.edu.gh, mkamedofu@st.knust.edu.gh

Abstract. Firms seeking to maximize the benefits of data analytics have begun adopting data driven culture. Data driven culture is expected to enhance firm performance outcomes. However, the mechanism through which data driven culture enhances firm performance has received little empirical attention and is little understood. This study proposes that data driven culture first enhances the supply chain information sharing and supply chain information quality capabilities of firms, which subsequently help firms to maximize their customer development and firm performance outcomes. A research model examining these relationships was developed and tested using data from 123 firms operating in Ghana. The results confirmed that data driven culture enhanced the supply chain information sharing and supply chain information quality, which subsequently enhance customer development and firm performance.

Keywords: Data driven culture · Supply chain information management · Customer development

1 Introduction

In recent times, many organizations have turned to data analytics as a means to stay competitive amidst high levels of uncertainties in the current age of big data. But for organizations to be able to fully exploit the potential of advanced analytics, there is the need for an enterprise-wide data-driven culture [1]. It is therefore not surprising that becoming data-driven has become a top priority in many organizations [2]. "Data-drivenness" is all about developing tools, abilities and a culture that acts on data [1]. Data driven culture has been defined as a pattern of behaviors and practices by a group of people which share a belief that having, understanding and using certain kinds of data and information plays a critical role in the success of an organization [3]. Organizations develop a data driven culture in order to gain new insights into their operations, business

Published by Springer Nature Switzerland AG 2021
D. Dennehy et al. (Eds.): I3E 2021, LNCS 12896, pp. 481–492, 2021.
https://doi.org/10.1007/978-3-030-85447-8_40

environments and customers, with the hope of being better able to achieve higher customer development – the ability to attract, satisfy and retain customers – and enhance their bottom line [4, 5]. Previous studies have indeed indicated that firms with high data driven culture obtain better customer results [6] and achieve higher firm performance [7, 8].

Whilst it is hoped that data driven culture would result in higher customer outcomes and firm performance, the mechanism through which data driven culture enhances these outcomes has been little explored and is little understood. In the light of this paucity, this study examines the mechanisms through which data driven culture enhances customer development and firm performance by shedding light on the important role of supply chain information management. Information has been identified as a key resource that must be well managed to enhance performance of firms. There is the need for firms to go beyond effectively managing information within the firm and aim at effectively managing relevant supply chain information with key supply chain partners [9]. Supply chain information management refers to how well an organization manages supply chain information, and it has been explored in two ways in the literature: volume of information shared and quality of information shared [10]. Supply chain information sharing relates to the volume of information shared between organizations and its trading partners whilst supply chain information quality refers to the accuracy, timeliness, adequacy and credibility of the supply chain information exchanged [4]. The study articulates that supply chain information sharing and supply chain information quality help further our understanding of how data driven culture enhances customer development and firm financial performance.

The study is relevant in a number of ways. First, the study fosters a deeper understanding of how data driven culture enhances the ability of firms to attract, satisfy and retain customers, as well as how data driven culture enhances the financial performance of firms. Supply chain information sharing and supply chain quality are confirmed to be initial benefits that firms obtain, which subsequently enable higher customer development and firm performance. The study also provides insights into the outcomes of "data-drivenness" from the context of a developing African country, a context that has been little explored in the existing literature [11]. The study also provides insights that can guide managers and practitioners in how to achieve higher customer development and firm performance outcomes from their data driven culture initiatives.

The rest of the paper is organized as follows. The theoretical background is presented next, followed by the research model and hypotheses. Next the methodology of the study is elaborated on, followed by a discussion of the results of the study. The study then concludes by discussing the implications of the study and recommendations for future research.

2 Theoretical Background

This study is grounded on the absorptive capacity theory and the dynamic capability theory. The absorptive capacity theory explains a firm's ability to recognize the value of new information, assimilate it and incorporate them into organizational processes [12]. The theory expounds that the ability of firms to extract valuable information from different sources is contingent upon their absorptive capacity. Drawing from the absorptive theory, we argue that data driven culture serves as an absorptive capacity, and allows organizations to share and have access to quality information [13].

Rooted in the resource-based view, dynamic capabilities refer to the ability of an organization to build and reconfigure the internal and external resources and competences required to sense and seize opportunities in rapidly changing environment [14]. The dynamic capability theory expounds that, the competitive benefits obtained by an organization are a result of capabilities built in reaction to environmental responsiveness strategies [15]. Correspondingly, this study draws on the dynamic capability theory to propose that information sharing and information quality are positively related to customer development and firm performance. Additionally, we draw on the same theory to propose a positive relationship between customer development and firm performance.

3 Research Model and Hypotheses

The research model of the study proposes that data driven culture initially enhances the supply chain information sharing and supply chain information quality of firms. These subsequently result in customer development and firm financial performance benefits for firms. All constructs were conceptualized at the first order level. The research model is presented in Fig. 1 below. The hypotheses of the study are discussed next.

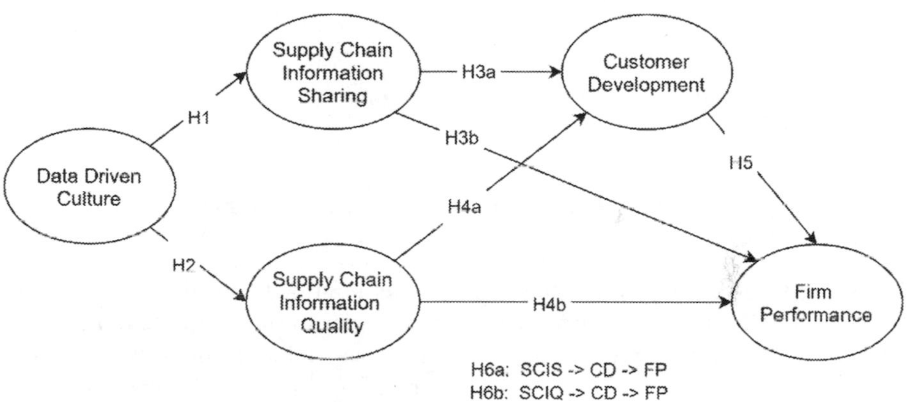

Fig. 1. Research model

3.1 Data Driven Culture, Supply Chain Information Sharing and Supply Chain Information Quality

Recent IT developments have enhanced the absorptive capacities of firms and empowered them to access, manage and analyze data for more effective decision making [16]. Sanders [17] emphasizes that the benefits of information are maximized through enabling information sharing within and outside the organization. It has been noted that data driven culture enables organization to collaborate closely with supply chain partners [18]. Firms with a strong data driven culture are more likely to aim to share sound supply chain data to a high level. Again, data driven organizations invest in big data analytics capabilities which maximizes their absorptive capacities for obtaining and leveraging quality supply chain information. Based on the discussions above, the study proposes that:

H1: There is a positive relationship between data driven culture and supply chain information sharing.

H2: Data driven culture is positively related to supply chain information quality.

3.2 Supply Chain Information Sharing, Customer Development and Organizational Performance

Supply chain information sharing enables visibility throughout the value chain, which helps firms to better understand customer and market demand, positioning them to be better able to meet customer demand [19]. Supply chain information sharing also allows firms to more efficiently and effectively fulfill supply chain operations, which culminates in higher firm performance [20]. Again, information sharing allows key supply chain actors such as suppliers, manufacturers, and retailers to forecast, synchronize, and improve production and delivery related decisions [21]. Effective supply chain information sharing helps firms to capture external knowledge to strategize to meet customers requirement in an everchanging business environment [22]. Accordingly, we propose that:

H3a: There is a positive relationship between supply chain information sharing and customer development.

H3b: There is a positive relationship between supply chain information sharing and firm performance.

3.3 Supply Chain Information Quality, Customer Development and Firm Performance

Having access to accurate and timely supply chain information is important for firms to meet dynamic customer demand and market changes for improved performance. A number of studies assert that information quality has an influence on the soundness of organizational decisions [23]. Poor supply chain information quality may cause organizational losses such as missed opportunities, making incorrect decisions and loss of customers [24]. The efficiency and effectiveness of a supply chain is largely influenced by the timeliness and accuracy of information used for decision making. The use of quality information reduces risks associated with demand uncertainties. It has been argued that information quality is a key determinant of customer service capabilities [25]. It has also been observed that information quality has an effect on firm performance [20]. Based on the discussions above we postulate that:

H4a: There is a positive relationship between supply chain information quality and customer development.

H4b: there is a positive relationship between supply chain information quality and firm performance.

3.4 Customer Development and Organizational Performance

The main goal of any organization and supply chain is to create or improve the value offered to customers [26]. Fawcett et al. [27] maintains that customers are the main source of revenue in the supply chain. Thus, customer acquisition, satisfaction and retention are very key to the survival of organizations [4, 28]. However, customers have become increasingly demanding and their preferences can change rapidly over a short period of time [5]. It is firms that are able to meet dynamic needs of customers that will achieve high firm performance outcomes. This assertion is confirmed by the study of Amedofu et al. [4] who found that customer development has a positive impact on the performance of start-up firms. Based on the discussions above, this study postulates that:

H5: Customer development has a positive impact on firm performance.

3.5 Mediating Role of Customer Development

The study finally proposes that the supply chain information management capabilities obtained by data driven firms enhance their performance by first enhancing their ability to attract, satisfy and retain customers. The ability of firms to obtain benefits from enhanced supply chain information management lies in how well they are able to leverage the supply chain information to respond to varying customer demand. This assertion is confirmed by Amedofu et al. [4] who observed that supply chain management practices such as supply chain information sharing and supply chain information quality first enhanced customer development, which subsequently enhanced performance of start-ups. This suggests that customer development plays an important intervening role in the relationship between supply chain information sharing and firm performance. This leads us to hypothesize that:

H6a: Customer development mediates the relationship between information sharing and firm performance.

H6b: Customer development mediates the relationship between information quality and firm performance.

4 Methodology

4.1 Measurement Items Development

The measurement instruments used to measure the constructs explored in this study were initially sourced from previous studies, with measurement items for data driven culture sourced from [11]. Measures for supply chain information sharing and supply chain information quality were sourced from [29] and [10]. Measurement items for customer development were adapted from [4] and firm performance from [10] and [28]. After carefully selecting the various measurement items from literature, the resultant questionnaire items were sent to various managers of different industries to assess whether the items were applicable within their respective domains. Some of the items for the constructs were modified to suit the context of the study based on the feedback received. The instruments were then administered to three experts for review. Their response and input further helped to refine the measurement instruments and ensured that the questionnaire was readable, understandable, and relevant to the study. The measurement items used in this study are presented in the Appendix.

4.2 Data Collection

To obtain data to test the research model, a survey of manufacturing and service firms operating in Ghana was conducted. A list of 5,000 firms operating in Ghana was obtained from the Registrar General's Department, out of which a sample of 500 firms were randomly selected for this study. The firms were contacted and permission was sought for data collection. In all, 58 firms declined to participate in the study. These were removed from the sample. For the remaining firms, questionnaires were sent to email, courier or in-person, depending on which option the firms preferred. After a week, follow up calls were made, with a second wave of reminders sent in the next week. In all, 123 usable responses were successfully retrieved, which accounted for a response rate of 24.6%. Power analysis was conducted using a recommended medium effect size of 0.3, a minimum statistical power of 0.8, and a probability of error of 0.05 [30], with the results revealing that a minimum sample size of 82 responses will be required for the results to attain statistical power. Therefore the 123 responses were sufficient for the study.

5 Results

5.1 Demographic Results

The demographic data revealed that cumulatively, 57.8% of the organizations who responded had employed less than 19 people, falling under the classification of micro enterprise businesses. Also, 26.8% of firms surveyed had more than 99 employees. With regards to how long the firms have been in operation, 54.5% had been in operation from 5 years or less. In terms of estimated annual revenues, 30.9% of responding firms had revenue levels of less than $10,000.

5.2 Measurement Model Results

The analysis was conducted using the partial least squares structural equation modelling (PLS-SEM) approach. The measurement model was analyzed by assessing the convergent validity and discriminant validity of the model. Convergent validity can be assessed by measuring the composite reliability of constructs, average variance extracted (AVE) and factor analysis [31]. Items with loadings below 0.708 and items with high cross loadings were dropped. The attributes of the constructs were then tested by measuring the psychometric properties of the constructs and comparing them against acceptable benchmarks. Composite reliability values were high and comfortably exceeded the suggested 0.7 threshold and the AVEs of all the constructs are higher than 0.5 as required [31]. The summary of the psychometric properties of the constructs are presented in Table 1.

Table 1. Psychometric properties of constructs

Construct	Composite reliability	AVE
Data driven culture	0.906	0.707
Supply chain information quality	0.959	0.825
Supply chain information sharing	0.923	0.665
Customer development	0.937	0.682
Firm performance	0.937	0.714

The items were next tested for sufficient discriminant validity. Discriminant validity examines the extent to which a measure correlates with measures of constructs that are different from the construct they intended to assess [31]. Discriminant validity can be assessed by comparing the AVE for each factor against the squared correlation of each constructs, with the former required to be higher than the latter [31]. In Table 2, the bold diagonal numbers represent squared AVEs whilst the off-diagonal numbers represent correlation among constructs. It can be seen that the bold diagonal values are all greater than the off-diagonal ones, confirming adequate discriminant validity.

Table 2. Fornell-Larcker test

	I	II	III	IV	V
Data driven culture (I)	**0.841**				
Supply chain information quality (II)	0.528	**0.908**			
Supply chain information sharing (III)	0.668	0.685	**0.816**		
Customer development (IV)	0.563	0.622	0.586	**0.826**	
Firm performance (V)	0.441	0.488	0.507	0.552	**0.845**

Discriminant validity was further assessed using the HTMT test. HTMT is the average of the heterotrait-heteromethod correlations and is a more stringent alternative measure of discriminant validity [31]. HTMT test approach indicates that HTMT values must be significantly less than 1, with a value of less than 0.85 ideal [31]. Table 3 indicates that the highest HTMT value is 0.758, confirming the model possesses adequate discriminant validity.

Table 3. HTMT test

	I	II	III	IV	V
Data driven culture (I)					
Supply chain information quality (II)	0.583				
Supply chain information sharing (III)	0.758	0.738			
Customer development (IV)	0.631	0.662	0.634		
Firm performance (V)	0.487	0.519	0.555	0.579	

5.3 Structural Model Results

After confirming the soundness of the measurement model, the structural model and hypothesized relationships were examined. PLS-SEM provides the coefficient of determination value (R^2), as well as the magnitude, direction and significance of the hypothesized causal relationships as standardized path coefficients. We first assessed the model's in-sample explanatory power by investigating the R^2 values of the endogenous variables. As a guideline, R^2 values of 0.75, 0.50 and 0.25 can be considered substantial, moderate and weak respectively [31]. The co-efficient of determination (R^2) of the constructs ranged from 0.278 to 0.450, which represent moderate levels of determination. Examining the predictive relevance of the model revealed Q^2 values ranging from 0.223 to 0.286, confirming the predictive relevance of the model [31].

Assessing the hypotheses results revealed that all hypothesized relationships in the study were positive and significant except the direct relationship between the supply chain information quality and firm performance. The findings revealed that data driven culture significantly enhances the supply chain information sharing and supply chain information quality capabilities of firms as hypothesized. Supply chain information sharing then directly enhances customer development and firm performance. Supply chain information quality on the other hand directly enhanced customer development, but not firm performance. Customer development was also found to significantly enhance firm performance. Examining the mediating role of customer development in the relationship between supply chain information sharing and firm performance revealed that customer development partially mediated the effect of supply chain information sharing on firm performance. On the other hand, the relationship between supply chain information quality and firm performance was fully mediated by customer development. The structural model results are summarized in Fig. 2 below.

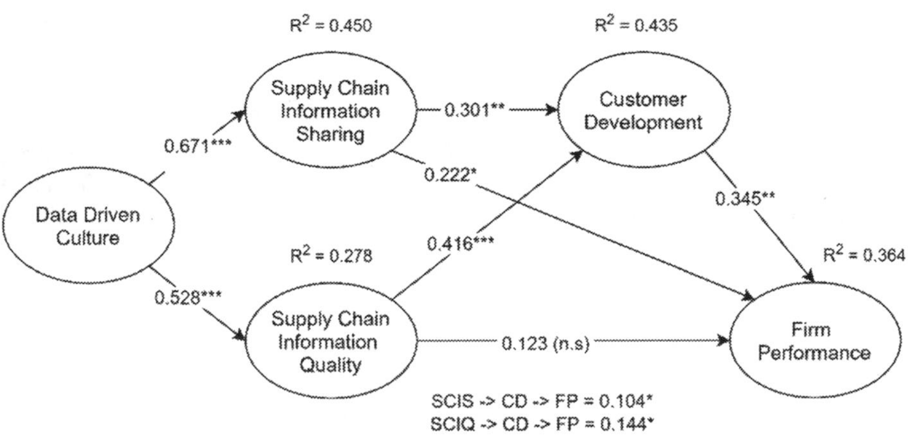

Fig. 2. Structural model results

5.4 Discussions

The findings of the study confirm that the initial manifestation of outcomes of a sound data driven culture is an increase in the volume and quality of important supply chain information that is shared with key partners, which is in line with previous studies [16].

The subsequent outcomes of these first level benefits provide more insight into how data driven culture enhances performance of organizations. Supply chain information sharing was found to directly enhance the ability of firms attract, satisfy and retain customers. This supports the findings of previous studies [4]. Additionally, supply chain information sharing directly enhanced the firm performance of firms, which is in congruence with the findings of previous researchers [10]. Delving further into the performance outcomes of supply chain information sharing by examining indirect effects reveals that some of the effect of supply chain information sharing on firm performance was mediated through customer development, which is indicative of complimentary partial mediation. Thus, supply chain information sharing enhances firm outcomes by directly enhancing customer development and firm performance, and indirectly enhancing firm performance through enhanced customer development.

Supply chain information quality enhances performance of organizations in a different way. Supply chain information quality directly enhances the ability of firms to attract, satisfy and retain customers, consistent with previous studies [25]. However, supply chain information quality did not directly enhance firm performance. Closer examination of the supply chain information quality – firm performance link however, reveals that there is a positive and significant indirect effect of supply chain information quality on firm performance. Given that the direct effect was not significant and the indirect effect through customer development was significant, it is concluded that customer development fully mediates the effect of supply chain information quality on firm performance.

Put together, the findings shed much insights into how the capabilities delivered by data driven culture enhances the performance of firms. These findings should be of interest to both researchers and practitioners. For researchers, the study elucidates the important roles of supply chain information sharing and supply chain information quality in understanding how "data drivenness" enhances the bottom line of firms. These can be viewed as the initial manifestation of the outcomes of data driven culture. The study additionally identifies the important role of customer development in explaining how supply chain information sharing and supply chain information quality enhance firm performance. For practice, the study provides an important guide for managers and owners of firms who want to see positive outcomes from their data driven culture. Business leaders can expect that "data-drivenness" will ultimately enhance their firms' performance but important intermediary outcomes such as supply chain information management and customer development must be managed to ensure that financial firm performance gains are maintained.

6 Conclusion

The study was conducted to examine how data driven culture enhances performance outcomes of firms. The study proposed and empirically confirmed that data culture initially creates supply chain information sharing and supply chain information quality capabilities for firms, which are then leveraged to achieve higher customer development and firm performance. Additionally, customer development was found to play important mediation roles in understanding how supply chain information management enhances firm performance.

There were some limitations of the study. Data was collected only from Ghana and the results should be interpreted with this limitation in mind. Further research is needed to explore the effect of data culture on firm performance in developed countries and other regions as it is suggested that environmental conditions might play an important role in the outcome of information systems and supply chain initiatives [32, 33]. Further research can also examine the complementarity between supply chain information sharing and supply chain information quality in understanding the effects of data driven culture on performance outcomes.

Appendix: Measurement Items and Their Sources

Data Driven Culture [11]
Our organization has the data it needs to make decisions
Our organization depends on data to support its decision making
Our organization spends significant time analyzing data to support decision making
Our organization uses data rather than guess work to make decision

Supply Chain Information Quality [10, 29]
Information sharing between our trading partners (suppliers and customers) and us is timely
Information sharing between our trading partners and us is accurate
Information sharing between our trading partners and us is complete
Information sharing between our trading partners and us is adequate
Information sharing between our trading partners and us is reliable

Supply Chain Information Sharing [10, 29]
We inform trading partners (suppliers and customers) in advance of changing needs
Our trading partners share proprietary/exclusive information with us information with us
Our trading partners keep us fully informed about issues that affect our business
Our trading partners share business knowledge of core business processes with us
We and our trading partners exchange information that helps in the drawing of business plans
We and our trading partners keep each other informed about events or changes that may affect the other partners

Customer Development [4]
Our firm is able to attract customers
Our firm has discovered our niche customer markets
Our firm has validated customer base
Our firm is able to acquire customers
Our firm is able to retain customers

Our firm's customer base is growing
Our firm has growing referred customers (dropped)
Overall, our customers are satisfied with us

Firm Performance [4, 28]
How well does your organization perform in terms of meeting its goals in terms of:
returns on assets
revenue
return on investment
profit margins on sales
growth in sales market share

References

1. Anderson, C.: Creating a Data-Driven Organization: Practical Advice from the Trenches. O'Reilly Media, Inc., Sebastopol (2015)
2. Storm, M., Borgman, H.P.: Understanding challenges and success factors in creating a data-driven culture, vol. 10 (2020)
3. Kiron, D., Ferguson, R.B., Prentince, P.K.: From value to vision: reimagining the possible with data analytics. MIT Sloan Manag. Rev. **54**, 1 (2013)
4. Amedofu, M., Asamoah, D., Agyei-Owusu, B.: Effect of supply chain management practices on customer development and start-up performance. Benchmarking: Int. Journal. **26**, 2267–2285 (2019)
5. Asamoah, D., Nuertey, D., Agyei-Owusu, B., Akyeh, J.: The effect of supply chain responsiveness on customer development. The International Journal of Logistics Management. ahead-of-print (2021)
6. Hallikainen, H., Savimäki, E., Laukkanen, T.: Fostering B2B sales with customer big data analytics. Ind. Mark. Manage. **86**, 90–98 (2020)
7. Brynjolfsson, E., Hitt, L.M., Kim, H.H.: Strength in Numbers: How Does Data-Driven Decisionmaking Affect Firm Performance? Available at SSRN 1819486 (2011)
8. Wamba, S.F., Gunasekaran, A., Akter, S., Ren, S.J., Dubey, R., Childe, S.J.: Big data analytics and firm performance: effects of dynamic capabilities. J. Bus. Res. **70**, 356–365 (2017)
9. Sundram, V.P.K., Bahrin, A.S., Abdul Munir, Z.B., Zolait, A.H.: The effect of supply chain information management and information system infrastructure: the mediating role of supply chain integration towards manufacturing performance in Malaysia. J. Enterprise Inform. Manag. **31**, 751–770 (2018)
10. Li, S., Ragu-Nathan, B., Ragu-Nathan, T.S., Subba Rao, S.: The impact of supply chain management practices on competitive advantage and organizational performance. Omega **34**, 107–124 (2006)
11. Asamoah, D., Andoh-Baidoo, F.: Antecedents and outcomes of extent of ERP systems implementation in the sub-saharan africa context: a panoptic perspective. Commun. Assoc. Inform. Syst. **42**, 22 (2018)
12. Cohen, W.M., Levinthal, D.A.: Absorptive capacity: a new perspective on learning and innovation. Adm. Sci. Q. **35**, 128–152 (1990)
13. Chatterjee, S., Chaudhuri, R., Vrontis, D.: Does data-driven culture impact innovation and performance of a firm? An empirical examination. Annals of Operations Research (2021)
14. Teece, D.J., Pisano, G., Shuen, A.: Dynamic capabilities and strategic management. Strateg. Manag. J. **18**, 509–533 (1997)

15. Mikalef, P., Boura, M., Lekakos, G., Krogstie, J.: Big data analytics capabilities and innovation: the mediating role of dynamic capabilities and moderating effect of the environment. Br. J. Manag. **30**, 272–298 (2019)
16. Yu, W., Jacobs, M.A., Chavez, R., Feng, M.: Data-driven supply chain orientation and financial performance: the moderating effect of innovation-focused complementary assets. Br. J. Manag. **30**, 299–314 (2019)
17. Sanders, N.R.: Big data driven supply chain management: a framework for implementing analytics and turning information into intelligence. Pearson, Upper Saddle River, New Jersey (2014)
18. Chavez, R., Yu, W., Jacobs, M.A., Feng, M.: Data-driven supply chains, manufacturing capability and customer satisfaction. Prod. Planning Control **28**, 906–918 (2017)
19. Dubey, R., Bryde, D.J., Foropon, C., Graham, G., Giannakis, M., Mishra, D.B.: Agility in humanitarian supply chain: an organizational information processing perspective and relational view. Annals of Operations Research (2020)
20. Juan Ding, M., Jie, F.A., Parton, K.J., Matanda, M.: Relationships between quality of information sharing and supply chain food quality in the Australian beef processing industry. Int. J. Log. Manag. **25**, 85–108 (2014)
21. Wu, I.-L., Chuang, C.-H., Hsu, C.-H.: Information sharing and collaborative behaviors in enabling supply chain performance: a social exchange perspective. Int. J. Prod. Econ. **148**, 122–132 (2014)
22. Gawankar, S.A., Gunasekaran, A., Kamble, S.: A study on investments in the big data-driven supply chain, performance measures and organisational performance in Indian retail 4.0 context. Int. J. Prod. Res. **58**, 1574–1593 (2020)
23. Myrelid, P., Jonsson, P.: Determinants of information quality in dyadic supply chain relationships. Int. J. Log. Manag. **30**, 356–380 (2018)
24. Ge, M., Helfert, M.: Impact of information quality on supply chain decisions. J. Comput. Inform. Syst. **53**, 59–67 (2013)
25. Setia, P., Setia, P., Venkatesh, V., Joglekar, S.: Leveraging digital technologies: how information quality leads to localized capabilities and customer service performance. MIS Q. **37**, 565–590 (2013)
26. Stank, T.P., Keller, S.B., Daugherty, P.J.: Supply chain collaboration and logistical service performance. J. Bus. Logist. **22**, 29–48 (2001)
27. Fawcett, S.E., Ellram, L.M., Ogden, J.A.: Supply Chain Management: From Vision to Implementation. Pearson, NJ (2013)
28. Blank, S.: The Four Steps to the Epiphany: Successful Strategies for Products that Win. John Wiley & Sons, Hoboken (2020)
29. Li, S., Rao, S.S., Ragu-Nathan, T.S., Ragu-Nathan, B.: Development and validation of a measurement instrument for studying supply chain management practices. J. Oper. Manag. **23**, 618–641 (2005)
30. Cohen, J.: Statistical Power Analysis for the Behavioral Sciences. Routledge, Milton Park (2013)
31. Hair, J.F., Risher, J.J., Sarstedt, M., Ringle, C.M.: When to use and how to report the results of PLS-SEM. Eur. Bus. Rev. **31**, 2–24 (2019)
32. Asamoah, D., Andoh-Baidoo, F., Agyei-Owusu, B.: Impact of ERP Implementation on Business Process Outcomes: A Replication of a United States Study in a Sub-Saharan African Nation. AIS Transactions on Replication Research, vol. 1 (2015)
33. Asamoah, D., Andoh-Baidoo, F., Agyei-Owusu, B.: Examining the relationships between supply chain integration, information sharing, and supply chain performance: a replication study. In: AMCIS 2016 Proceedings (2016)

Customer Behavior and E-business

The Use of Elaboration Likelihood Model in eWOM Research: Literature Review and Weight-Analysis

Elvira Ismagilova[1(✉)], Yogesh K. Dwivedi[2,3], and Nripendra Rana[4]

[1] Faculty of Management, Law and Social Sciences, University of Bradford, Bradford, UK
e.ismagilova@bradford.ac.uk

[2] Emerging Markets Research Centre, School of Management, Swansea University, Swansea, UK
y.k.dwivedi@swansea.ac.uk

[3] Department of Management, Symbiosis Institute of Business Management, Pune & Symbiosis International (Deemed University), Pune, Maharashtra, India

[4] College of Business and Economics, Qatar University, P.O. Box 2713, Doha, Qatar
n.p.rana@bradford.ac.uk

Abstract. With the development of Internet and e-commerce, traditional word of mouth communications have evolved into electronic word of mouth (eWOM) communications, which significantly affect consumers in their decision-making process. Previous studies investigated how consumers process information online and how it affects consumer behaviour applying the Elaboration Likelihood Model (ELM). ELM distinguishes between two routes of information processing: central and peripheral. Existing literature has a mixed of findings regarding factors affecting information process using ELM and lacking a comprehensive review providing evaluation and a consolidated view of these factors. Thus, the aim of this research is to evaluate the use of ELM in the context of eWOM research by performing a systematic review and weight analysis of existing research findings. This will help consolidating the predictive power of the independent variables on the dependent variable, by taking into consideration the number of times a relationship has been previously examined. The model developed through weight analysis would allow eWOM practitioners to decipher more influential factors.

Keywords: eWOM · ELM · Weight analysis · eWOM persuasiveness · Literature review

1 Introduction

Developed from traditional word of mouth communications, Electronic word-of-mouth (eWOM) communications represent one of the most important information sources used by consumers in their decision-making process [1]. eWOM is defined as "the dynamic and on-going information exchange process between potential, actual, or former consumers regarding a product, service, brand, or company, which is available to a multitude

Published by Springer Nature Switzerland AG 2021
D. Dennehy et al. (Eds.): I3E 2021, LNCS 12896, pp. 495–505, 2021.
https://doi.org/10.1007/978-3-030-85447-8_41

of people and institutions via the Internet" [2]. eWOM has unique characteristics (e.g. tie strength, privacy, anonymity, volume), which makes its processing more complicated in comparison with traditional WOM [3].

eWOM communications receive growing interest from researchers and practitioners [2]. eWOM significantly affects the consumer decision-making process. According to recent statistics, online reviews, which are types of eWOM influence the purchase decision for 93 percent of consumers [4]. A number of studies investigated factors affecting the persuasiveness of eWOM and its impact on consumer behaviour. To explain the information processing, researchers used Elaboration Likelihood Model (ELM). ELM is considered as the most popular and useful persuasion model in consumer research and social psychology [5]. According to ELM individuals process information using central and peripheral routes. The topic of ELM studies in the context of eWOM communications is still relatively new. Few existing studies provided a comprehensive literature review of the application of ELM model in information processing but did not consider it in the context of eWOM communications [5, 6]. The extant literate on ELM studies in eWOM environment appeared fragmented without a comprehensive review of published papers or a classification framework. Thus, it is not easy to draw meaningful conclusions from prior studies due to inconsistent results and lack of their consolidated understanding. Existing studies in this area have reported conflicting results on the effect of factors on persuasion and consumer behaviour. For example, Kim and Lee [7] found that source credibility has a significant positive effect on intention to buy, while Wang [8] found that the effect is non-significant. The difference in the results might be explained by different types of products and services, as well as different platform characteristics. The mixed findings on the factors affecting perceived persuasiveness of eWOM communications and consumer behaviour can lead to confusion for academics and marketing practitioners alike.

As a result, it is important to conduct a review of existing ELM studies in eWOM context and perform weight-analysis. Hence, the purpose of this research is to evaluate the use of ELM in the context of eWOM research by performing a systematic review and weight analysis of existing research findings. This will help investigate the predictive power of the independent variables on the dependent variable, by taking into consideration the number of times a relationship has been previously examined. The model developed through weight analysis would allow eWOM practitioners to decipher more influential factors.

The remainder of the paper is organised as follows. First, the literature review will be presented. After, the research method employed for this study is described. Next, the findings from weight analysis are presented. Then, the findings are discussed, followed by the conclusion and outlining the limitations of this study and directions for future research.

2 Literature Review

ELM was proposed by Petty and Cacioppo [9]. It is a dual process theory which describes the change of attitude form. The model explains different ways of stimuli processing. ELM separates the central route (when an individual considers an idea logically) and peripheral route (where an individual employs pre-existing ideas and superficial qualities to be persuaded by the message) [9]. Individuals use the central route when they are motivated and can think about the issue (high involvement consumers). Opposite to central route, the peripheral route is used when either ability or motivation to think on the issue is low (low involvement consumers) [9, 10]. ELM is used in the information adoption model proposed by Sussman and Siegal [11]. The information adoption model states that information helpfulness will influence outcomes (e.g. intention towards and advocated behaviour). ELM is considered as a major theoretical model in eWOM research [12].

Existing studies in eWOM communications mostly consider ELM by using central or peripheral cues to process information [10, 12, 13]. Existing literature states that information embedded in eWOM message is centrally processed by consumers, whilst information associated with text attributes such as reviewer characteristics is heuristically processed by individuals [14]. Studies defined argument quality, accuracy, factuality, valence, timeliness, type of review, length, readability, and relevance as the central route [15–18]. Whilst average rating, consistency, expertise, image, number of followers, number of friends, presentation mode, credibility, tie strength, and volume were defined as a peripheral route [19–22].

3 Research Method

As this research aims to synthesise existing findings on the use of ELM in eWOM research, it was considered appropriate to employ weight analysis [23, 24]. Weight analysis is used to ascertain the predictive power of independent variables taking into account the number of times the relationships between independent and dependent variables were studied before.

To perform the analysis, peer-reviewed journal articles on eWOM communications were collected from bibliographic databases Scopus, EBSCO and Web of Science using a keyword search based approach [25–27]. The searched keywords included "Elaboration likelihood model", "ELM", "Online review", "Online reviews", "Electronic word-of-mouth", "Electronic word of mouth", "eWOM", "Internet word-of-mouth", "Internet word of mouth", "iWOM", "Online word-of-mouth", "Online word of mouth", "Virtual word-of-mouth". As a result of this search 120 articles were identified. Articles that did not have empirical findings were excluded, leaving 75 articles. Based on the screening

Table 1. Factors affecting consumer behaviour

Route	Construct	Definition	# of studies	Representative studies
Central route	Argument quality	Persuasive strength of arguments embedded in an informational message	36	[34, 35]
	Accuracy	The correctness of the shared information	5	[15]
	Factuality	The message containing fact-based information	2	[16]
	Valence	Whether the message is positive or negative	17	[14, 18]

(*continued*)

Table 1. (*continued*)

Route	Construct	Definition	# of studies	Representative studies
	Timeliness	The extent to which the informational content is current and timely	6	[15, 16]
	Type of the review	Attribute value vs simple recommendation	2	[36]
	Length	Total number of words in the message	16	[12, 15]
	Readability	The level of effort required to understand the text	3	[14, 17]
	Relevance	The extent to which an online review is viewed relevant and is considered by the decision maker	7	[16]
Peripheral route	Average Rating	Average rating of the product/service	16	[16, 18]
	Consistency	Consistency of the review with the rest of the reviews	8	[19, 20]
	Expertise	The degree to which the message communicator is able to provide the correct information	10	[19, 22]
	Image	Number of images in the message about product/service	2	[12, 18]
	Number of followers	Number of followers the reviewer has online	3	[12, 15]
	Number of friends	Number of friends the reviewer has online	2	[15]
	Presentation mode	Ranging from pure text to text with image, to the most visual presentation mode, video	2	[29, 30]
	Source credibility	Consumers' overall perceptions regarding the credibility of the message communicator	31	[12, 16]
	Tie strength	The depth of a relationship between source and information seeker	2	[21]
	Volume	Total number of posted online reviews	27	[15, 36]

and initial review of these 75 articles, Table 1 presents the factors (as constructs or dimensions of ELM) affecting consumer behavior that were used in eWOM studies.

Based on the analysis of 75 articles, it was found that researchers used a number of moderators, which affected the impact of peripheral and central cues on information processing. The most common used moderators are product type [28, 29], involvement [16, 30], gender [20, 31], source expertise [32], and prior knowledge [7, 33].

4 Weight Analysis

In order to perform weight analysis, the number of significant results was divided by the total number of times that particular relationship between a given independent and dependent variable had been tested [24, 37]. For example, to calculate the weight for the relationship between argument quality and attitude, 6 (number of significant relationships) was divided by 7 (the total number of studies investigated this relationship), which results in weight 0.857. Table 2 presents findings from weight analysis for all attributes identified in this review.

Table 2. Weight analysis

Independent variable	Dependent variable	Significant	Non-significant	Total	Weight
Argument Quality	Attitude	6	1	7	0.857
Source credibility		4	4	8	0.500
Volume		4	1	5	0.800
Argument Quality	Engagement	0	4	4	0.000
Attitude		3	0	3	1.000
Source credibility		3	1	4	0.750
Attitude	eWOM adoption	3	1	4	0.750
Argument Quality		5	0	5	1.000
eWOM credibility		11	0	11	1.000
eWOM usefulness		13	0	13	1.000
Source credibility		3	0	3	1.000
Tie strength		2	0	2	1.000
Argument Quality	eWOM credibility	12	0	12	1.000
Average product/service rating		7	0	7	1.000
Consistency of review		6	1	7	0.857
Source expertise		3	1	4	0.750
Source credibility		11	0	11	1.000
Volume		2	0	2	1.000
Argument Quality	Intention to Buy	9	1	10	0.900
Attitude		14	0	14	1.000
Engagement		3	0	3	1.000
eWOM credibility		7	1	8	0.875

(continued)

Table 2. (*continued*)

Independent variable	Dependent variable	Significant	Non-significant	Total	Weight
eWOM usefulness		14	2	16	0.875
Source credibility		3	3	6	0.500
Type of the review		1	1	2	0.500
Volume		12	4	16	0.750
Accuracy	eWOM usefulness	4	2	6	0.667
Argument Quality		12	0	12	1.000
Consistency of review		2	0	2	1.000
Expertise		7	1	8	0.875
Factuality		1	1	2	0.500
Image count		2	0	2	1.000
Length of review		16	3	19	0.842
Number of followers		1	2	3	0.333
Number of friends		2	0	2	1.000
Timeliness		5	3	8	0.625
Average rating		9	2	11	0.818
Presentation mode		2	0	2	1.000
Readability		1	2	3	0.333
Relevance		6	1	7	0.857
Source Credibility		9	3	12	0.750
Valence		15	2	17	0.882
Volume		6	2	8	0.750

Based on the classification proposed by Jeyaraj et al. (2006), predictors can be classified as well-utilised and experiments. The predictor is considered "well-utilised" if it was examined five or more times, otherwise, the predictor is considered as "experimental". A well-utilised predictor can be classified as "best predictor" if its weight is equal or greater than 0.8. An experimental predictor can be classified as "promising" if its weight is 1. Based on the above discussion findings from weight analysis were classified in the following way.

Three factors affecting attitude towards product/service, namely argument quality (examined 7 times, significant 6 times), source credibility (examined 8 times, significant 4 times), and volume (examined 5 times, significant 4 times) are considered well-utilised. Based on the result of weight analysis, argument quality and volume are the best predictors of attitude as they have weights of 0.857 and 0.800 respectively.

Three factors influencing eWOM engagement are defined as experimental predictors: argument quality (examined 4 times, significant 0 times), attitude (examined 3 times, significant 3 times), and source credibility (examined 4 times, significant 3 times). As argument quality has weight equals 1, it is considered as a promising predictor of eWOM engagement.

Three out of 6 predictors of eWOM adoption are best predictors with weight equals to 1: argument quality (examined 5 times, significant 5 times), eWOM credibility (examined 11 times, significant 11 times), and eWOM usefulness (examined 13 times, significant 13 times). The other three predictors, namely attitude (examined 4 times, significant 3 times), source credibility (examined 3 times, significant 3 times), and tie strength (examined 2 times, significant 2 times) are considered experimental. Source credibility and tie strength are examined less than five times but have weight equals to 1, which makes them promising predictors of information adoption.

Four out of 6 factors affecting eWOM credibility are examined more than five times and have weight more than 0.8, which makes them best predictors: argument quality (weight equal 1), average rating (weight equals 1), consistency of review (weight equals 0.857) and source credibility (weight equals 1). Two other predictors are considered as experimental: attitude (examined 4 times, significant 3 times) and tie strength (examined 2 times, significant 2 times). Tie strength has a weight of 1, thus it is considered as a promising predictor of eWOM credibility.

Six out of 8 predictors of intention to buy are well utilised: argument quality (examined 10 times, significant 9 times), attitude (examined 14 times, significant 14 times), eWOM credibility (examined 8 times, significant 7 times), eWOM usefulness (examined 16 times, significant 14 times), and source credibility (examined 6 times, significant 3 times). Argument quality (weight equals 0.900), attitude (weight equals 1) and eWOM credibility (weight equals 0.875) are considered as best predictors of intention to buy, as their weight is more than 0.8 and they were examined 5 or more times. Type of review (examined 2 times, significant 1 time) is considered as experimental predictor and engagement (examined 3 times, significant 3 times) is found to be a promising predictor with the weight equals to 1.

Ten out of 17 predictors affecting eWOM usefulness are well-utilised, namely accuracy (examined 6 times, significant 4 times), argument quality (examined 12 times, significant 12 times), expertise (examined 8 times, significant 7 times), length of review (examined 19 times, significant 16 times), timeliness (examined 8 times, significant 5 times), average rating (examined 11 times, significant 9 times), relevance (examined 7 times, significant 6 times), source credibility (examined 12 times, significant 9 times), valence (examined 17 times, significant 15 times), and volume (examined 8 times, significant 6 times). Out of nine well utilised predictors, the following predictors have weight more than 0.8, which makes them best predictors of eWOM usefulness: argument quality (weight equals 1), expertise (weight equals 0.875), length of review (weight equals 0.842), average rating (weight equals 0.818), relevance (weight equals 0.857), and valence (weight equals 0.882).

Finally, seven predictors of eWOM usefulness are experimental as they were examined less than 5 times: consistency of review (examined 2 times, significant 2 times), factuality (examined 2 times, significant 1 time), image count (examined 2 times, significant 2 times), number of followers (examined 3 times, significant 1 time), number of friends (examined 2 times, significant 2 times), presentation mode (examined 2 times, significant 2 times), and readability (examined 3 times, significant 1 time). Out of these experimental predictors, four have weight equals to 1, which makes them promising predictors of eWOM usefulness: consistency of review, image count, number of friends, and presentation mode.

5 Discussion

Taking into consideration the growing number of studies employing ELM to study eWOM persuasiveness, it is important to discuss and analyse their collective findings. Figure 1 depicts the diagrammatic representation of the factors affecting consumer behaviour using ELM with their corresponding weight by employing the results of weight analysis. The findings suggest that best predictors such as volume, argument quality, consistency of review, source credibility, expertise, length of the review, average rating, relevance, source credibility, and valence should be included in eWOM research. Promising predictors of engagement (attitude), eWOM adoption (source credibility, tie

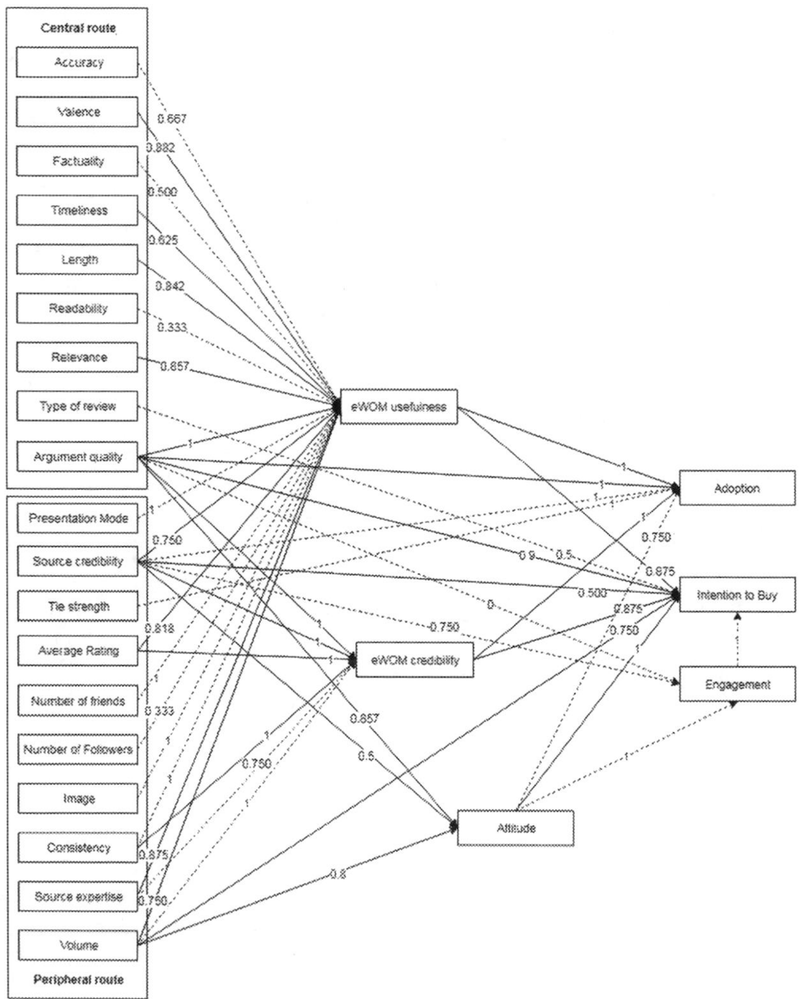

Fig. 1. Factors affecting the persuasiveness of eWOM communications and consumer behavior. Note: – – ▶experimental predictors; ⟶▶well-utilised predictors.

strength), eWOM credibility (volume), intention to buy (engagement) and eWOM usefulness (image count, number of friends, presentation mode) should be included in future empirical research in order to evaluate their overall performance.

Most of the eWOM studies employing ELM as a theoretical foundation focused on characteristics of the message source or content of the message. However, limited number of studies investigated the impact of individual characteristics on information processing. Thus, future research needs to consider factors such as age, gender, level of education, trust tendency to name a few. This will advance our understanding of information processing by individuals.

6 Conclusion

This research aimed to evaluate the use of ELM in the context of eWOM research by performing weight analysis of existing research findings. This aim was reached by identifying and analysing relevant and important studies on eWOM that used ELM as a theoretical foundation. The weight analysis was performed by identifying a number of significant and non-significant relationships between studied variables.

This research provides some implications for researchers and practitioners. This study builds a framework for future research identifying peripheral and central route factors and their impact on consumer behaviour. The proposed framework provides the overall picture of persuasive eWOM communication by using ELM. Scholars looking further into the factors affecting information processing of eWOM messages can employ the results of this study in order to make more informed decisions regarding inclusion of factors in their research. Practitioners are advised to carefully evaluate the traditionally utilised predictors and pay more attention to the best predictors- volume, argument quality, consistency of review, source credibility, expertise, length of the review, average rating, relevance, source credibility, and valence.

The current study has some limitations. First, this study used only Web of Science, Scopus and EBSCO databases for collection of study, which can limit the number of research outputs available for weight analysis. Future research should also employ any other available datasets. Second, this research employed only weight analysis without conducting meta-analysis. Conducting meta-analysis can assist researchers in evaluation of the significance of the studied relationships based on the effect size statistics. Additionally, outcomes of meta-analysis could strengthen the findings of weight analysis [38]. Thus, future studies could perform both types of analysis of factors affecting consumer behaviour.

References

1. Tsao, W.-C., Hsieh, M.-T.: eWOM persuasiveness: do eWOM platforms and product type matter? Electron. Commer. Res. **15**(4), 509–541 (2015). https://doi.org/10.1007/s10660-015-9198-z
2. Ismagilova, E., Dwivedi, Y.K., Slade, E., Williams, M.D.: Electronic word of mouth (eWOM) in the marketing context: a state of the art analysis and future directions (2017)
3. King, R.A., Racherla, P., Bush, V.D.: What we know and don't know about online word-of-mouth: a review and synthesis of the literature. J. Interact. Mark. **28**, 167–183 (2014)

4. Kaemingk, D.: 20 online review stats to know in 2019. Qualtrics (2019). https://www.qualtrics. com/blog/onlinereview-stats/. Accessed 29 Feb 2020
5. Teng, S., Khong, K.W., Goh, W.W.: Conceptualizing persuasive messages using ELM in social media. J. Internet Commer. **13**, 65–87 (2014)
6. Kitchen, P.J., Kerr, G., Schultz, D.E., McColl, R., Pals, H.: The elaboration likelihood model: review, critique and research agenda. Eur. J. Mark. (2014)
7. Kim, J., Lee, C.: Examining the role of relationship factors on eWOM effectiveness in social media. Int. J. Internet Mark. Advert. **11**, 103–123 (2017)
8. Wang, P.: Understanding the influence of electronic word-of-mouth on outbound tourists' visit intention. In: Li, H., Mäntymäki, M., Zhang, X. (eds.) I3E 2014. IAICT, vol. 445, pp. 33–45. Springer, Heidelberg (2014). https://doi.org/10.1007/978-3-662-45526-5_4
9. Petty, R.E., Cacioppo, J.T.: The elaboration likelihood model of persuasion. In: Communication and Persuasion, pp. 1–24. Springer, New York (1986). https://doi.org/10.1007/978-1-4612-4964-1_1
10. Baek, H., Ahn, J., Choi, Y.: Helpfulness of online consumer reviews: readers' objectives and review cues. Int. J. Electron. Commer. **17**, 99–126 (2012)
11. Sussman, S.W., Siegal, W.S.: Informational influence in organizations: an integrated approach to knowledge adoption. Inf. Syst. Res. **14**, 47–65 (2003)
12. Cheng, Y.-H., Ho, H.-Y.: Social influence's impact on reader perceptions of online reviews. J. Bus. Res. **68**, 883–887 (2015)
13. Hussain, S., Ahmed, W., Jafar, R.M.S., Rabnawaz, A., Jianzhou, Y.: eWOM source credibility, perceived risk and food product customer's information adoption. Comput. Hum. Behav. **66**, 96–102 (2017)
14. Agnihotri, A., Bhattacharya, S.: Online review helpfulness: role of qualitative factors. Psychol. Mark. **33**, 1006–1017 (2016)
15. Aghakhani, N., Oh, O., Gregg, D.: Beyond the review sentiment: The effect of review accuracy and review consistency on review usefulness. (2017)
16. Filieri, R., Hofacker, C.F., Alguezaui, S.: What makes information in online consumer reviews diagnostic over time? The role of review relevancy, factuality, currency, source credibility and ranking score. Comput. Hum. Behav. **80**, 122–131 (2018)
17. Mousavizadeh, M., Koohikamali, M., Salehan, M.: The effect of central and peripheral cues on online review helpfulness: a comparison between functional and expressive products (2015)
18. Srivastava, V., Kalro, A.D.: Enhancing the helpfulness of online consumer reviews: the role of latent (content) factors. J. Interact. Mark. **48**, 33–50 (2019)
19. Cheung, C.M.-Y., Sia, C.-L., Kuan, K.K.: Is this review believable? A study of factors affecting the credibility of online consumer reviews from an ELM perspective. J. Assoc. Inf. Syst. **13**, 2 (2012)
20. Luo, C., Wu, J., Shi, Y., Xu, Y.: The effects of individualism–collectivism cultural orientation on eWOM information. Int. J. Inf. Manage. **34**, 446–456 (2014)
21. Mahapatra, S., Mishra, A.: Acceptance and forwarding of electronic word of mouth. Mark. Intell. Plan. (2017)
22. Thomas, M.-J., Wirtz, B.W., Weyerer, J.C.: Determinants of online review credibility and its impact on consumers' purchase intention. J. Electron. Commer. Res. **20**, 1–20 (2019)
23. Rana, N.P., Dwivedi, Y.K., Williams, M.D.: A meta-analysis of existing research on citizen adoption of e-government. Inf. Syst. Front. **17**(3), 547–563 (2013). https://doi.org/10.1007/s10796-013-9431-z
24. Ismagilova, E., Slade, E.L., Rana, N.P., Dwivedi, Y.K.: The effect of electronic word of mouth communications on intention to buy: a meta-analysis. Inf. Syst. Front. 1–24 (2019)
25. Alsudairi, M., Dwivedi, Y.K.: A multi-disciplinary profile of IS/IT outsourcing research. J. Enterpr. Inf. Manage. (2010)

26. Hughes, D.L., Dwivedi, Y.K., Rana, N.P., Simintiras, A.C.: Information systems project failure–analysis of causal links using interpretive structural modelling. Prod. Plan. Control **27**, 1313–1333 (2016)
27. Slade, E.L., Williams, M.D., Dwivedi, Y.K.: Devising a research model to examine adoption of mobile payments: an extension of UTAUT2. Mark. Rev. **14**, 310–335 (2014)
28. Ketron, S.: Investigating the effect of quality of grammar and mechanics (QGAM) in online reviews: the mediating role of reviewer crediblity. J. Bus. Res. **81**, 51–59 (2017)
29. Xu, P., Chen, L., Santhanam, R.: Will video be the next generation of e-commerce product reviews? Presentation format and the role of product type. Decis. Support Syst. **73**, 85–96 (2015)
30. Xu, P., Chen, L., Wu, L., Santhanam, R.: Visual Presentation Modes in Online Product Reviews and Their Effects on Consumer Responses (2012)
31. Chong, A.Y.L., Khong, K.W., Ma, T., McCabe, S., Wang, Y.: Analyzing key influences of tourists' acceptance of online reviews in travel decisions. Internet Research (2018)
32. Evertz, L., Kollitz, R., Süß, S.: Electronic word-of-mouth via employer review sites–the effects on organizational attraction. Int. J. Hum. Res. Manage. 1–30 (2019)
33. Cao, X., Liu, Y., Zhu, Z., Hu, J., Chen, X.: Online selection of a physician by patients: empirical study from elaboration likelihood perspective. Comput. Hum. Behav. **73**, 403–412 (2017)
34. Han, S., Li, Y., Jiang, Y., Zhao, X.: Exploring the persuasion effect of restaurant food product online reviews on consumers' attitude and behavior. In: Proceedings of the 2018 International Conference on Internet and e-Business, pp. 57–60
35. Wang, P.: Exploring the influence of electronic word-of-mouth on tourists' visit intention: A dual process approach. Journal of Systems and Information Technology (2015)
36. Park, D.-H., Kim, S.: The effects of consumer knowledge on message processing of electronic word-of-mouth via online consumer reviews. Electron. Commer. Res. Appl. **7**, 399–410 (2008)
37. Jeyaraj, A., Rottman, J.W., Lacity, M.C.: A review of the predictors, linkages, and biases in IT innovation adoption research. J. Inf. Technol. **21**, 1–23 (2006)
38. Jeyaraj, A., Dwivedi, Y.K.: Meta-analysis in information systems research: review and recommendations. Int. J. Inf. Manage. **55**, 102226 (2020)

Explaining the Network of Factors that Influence the Timing of and Decision to Upgrade Enterprise Systems

Candice Petersen and Lisa F. Seymour(✉)

CITANDA, University of Cape Town, Cape Town, WC, South Africa
Lisa.seymour@uct.ac.za

Abstract. The Enterprise System (ES) forms the core of e-Business, providing support for operations, and analytical information for real-time decision-making. A well-functioning ES can enable organizational success and thereby create economic and social value. Once installed, upgrading an ES is important for improving performance, automating business processes, and reducing maintenance efforts. But ES upgrades also cause business disruption and downtime. As a result, many organisations cannot gauge when to upgrade ES. This paper explains the network of factors that influence the timing of and decision to upgrade ES and answers, why and when do organisations decide to upgrade their ES? Literature on upgrades, although scarce, presents opposing views on the timing of upgrades. Moreover, studies investigating this also appear to be dominated by studies from high-income countries where these systems are developed. Other countries potentially face different challenges. Hence, this phenomenon was investigated in South Africa, a middle-income country, through three qualitative case studies. The findings suggest that upgrade decisions are tightly controlled by executive committee approval and are aligned to the organisation's strategy. In addition, the business calendar and risk management play a vital role in the timing of and decision to upgrade ES. The paper presents an explanatory model of how factors impact one another. The model should be useful to organisations wanting to upgrade their ES and extends the current ES upgrade literature.

Keywords: Enterprise Systems · Enterprise Resource Planning · ES upgrades

1 Introduction

The backbone of Information Technology (IT) infrastructure, an Enterprise System (ES) is 'a customizable application suite that includes integrated business solutions for the major business processes and administrative functions of an enterprise. The value from ES is broad, providing real-time decision-making and organizational, human and social benefits [1, 2]. Enterprise Resource Planning (ERP) systems are the central component of this suite [3]. Value from ES is only realised post-implementation [4], when a core activity enabling value, is to extend and improve the system by upgrading [5]. An ES

Published by Springer Nature Switzerland AG 2021
D. Dennehy et al. (Eds.): I3E 2021, LNCS 12896, pp. 506–518, 2021.
https://doi.org/10.1007/978-3-030-85447-8_42

upgrade enables leveraging of new functionality which can improve performance, automate business processes and reduce maintenance efforts [4]. However, despite these benefits, deciding when to upgrade is a problem organisations face [6].

The timing of upgrades has been found to be driven by vendor's influence as opposed to the organisation's strategic objectives [6]. In other cases, the timing is influenced by customer need, economics and version availability [4]. The industry perspective [7] highlights that 'CIOs who take a business-strategy-first approach to ERP will deliver 60% increased business value over those who take a vendor-first approach'. As there is limited and contradictory research on upgrades [4], this study responded to the call for further understanding of the ES upgrade phenomenon. This study focused on answering the following question: 'Why and when do organisations decide to upgrade their Enterprise Systems?' To answer the question, this paper first reviews the relevant literature on ES upgrades. The research approach is then described. Subsequently, the factors which were found to influence the timing of and decision to upgrade ES are described and discussed, and an explanatory model is presented before the paper concludes.

2 Literature Review

An ES delivers many benefits. These benefits include improvement in productivity and profitability, internal integration, improved information and processes, improved customer service [8], as well as quality of work life [1]. Real-time fact based decision making is enabled by analytical information stored in the ES [8]. An ES can elevate the synergy between departments, create better competitiveness and produce more effective and efficient processes, which is critical in a global economy [9]. Organisations have become reliant on integrated ES for timely service delivery, improving operations and managing supply chains across the globe [6]. A stable ES also supports good quality information [9]. Analytics increases ERP value, impacting improved internal operations and downstream sales [2].

Business and IT alignment delivers great value to organisations. To leverage this value ES capabilities need to align with organisations' strategic objectives [10]. These changes occur post-implementation and are considered an extension of an ES implementation [11]. One of the post-implementation phases is an upgrade [11]. Upgrades are essential for continuous enhancement and system stability [4]. An upgrade is a major change process [12] which adds functional improvements and enables new IT usage and business strategies. When migrating from one version of an innovation to another, a question of timing afflicts each organisation [13]. Hence it is argued that it is not a question about whether to upgrade but rather about when to upgrade [11]. Authors cite business disruption as one of the key reasons for not upgrading sooner [11]. Yet, Barth and Koch [12] note that the objective of an upgrade is to restrict business disruption. Industry analysts [7] recommend that when adopting an ES, whether an upgrade or implementation, organisations needed to answer the following four questions: (1) What do we do? ES is not what you do. It is there however to add value. (2) Why now? Is it due to the market? If so, this is not a good enough reason to disrupt the business. (3) Are we ready? Upgrades are there to offer business value and often businesses may not be receptive to a new way of doing things therefore these innovations deliver poor value. (4) Can we delay?

Yet vendors are stated to exert pressure on organisations to upgrade despite no business requirement [6]. In a prior study [11] an Irish organisation waited twelve years before upgrading despite vendor de-support. In a more recent study [4], Irish and UK organisations were noted to upgrade to the latest version despite any improvements. This decision was taken due to vendor dependence and fear of vendor de-support. Based on these conflicting findings the decision of when to upgrade is complex. In order to maximise upgrade benefits, a comprehensive approach to decision-making is needed [14]. The decision to utilise an innovation is known as adoption [15]. There are adoption theories which we reviewed. The T-O-E model has been used to identify factors that influence the adoption of ES upgrades [16]. T-O-E focuses on technology, organisation, and environment. The Frambach et al. [15] organisational innovation adoption framework includes these categories and includes social network and supplier factors. Hence the five categories: organisational, technological, environmental, supplier and social network, were chosen to be used in this study. A summary of extant research on upgrade adoption is classified according to these five categories in Table 1.

Table 1. Factors influencing the decision to upgrade ES.

Categories	Factors	Source: [13]	[11]	[4]	[15]	[6]
Supplier	Communication	X				
	Vendor influence	X	X	X		
Social network	Network participation				X	
	Social Influence				X	
Environmental	Competitive pressures	X	X	X		
	Regulatory requirements			X		
Technological	Relative advantage	X	X	X		
	Costs	X	X	X		X
	Version similarity	X				
	Compatibility		X	X		
	Complexity					
	Customisation		X			
Organisational	Org. innovativeness/strategic posture	X				
	Org. strategic objectives		X	X		
	Resource competence	X	X			

3 Research Methodology

The intent of this research was to study the ES upgrade phenomena and understand and explain why and when organisations decide to upgrade their ES. We adopted an interpretive philosophy as we acknowledged respondents playing an active role and rather than looking at them, we looked with them, while seeking understanding by using dialog [17]. By selecting an inductive approach, we were able to collect data and develop a theory based on the results of data analysis. Table 1, derived from the literature, was used as an investigative lens to scope the analysis. We chose three South African ES upgrades as case studies. The upgrades were within a retail, healthcare, and financial services organisation, which we will refer to as E1, E2 and E3 respectively.

Prior to collecting data, ethics approval from the University's ethics committee and organisational permission were secured. Primary data was obtained through interviews. Walsham [18] states that interviews are key to accessing the interpretations of informants in the field. The seven semi structured interviews were each approximately forty-five minutes long. The interview protocol developed asked open ended questions mainly based on the five literature categories. We approached participants from middle and executive management and took on heterogeneous purposive sampling to gain diverse perspectives [19]. Data was collected during 2020. Due to the COVID-19 pandemic, the countrywide lockdown and social distancing requirements, Microsoft Teams and Zoom were utilised for interviews. The respondents and case organisations are listed in Table 2. Secondary data comprised two documents. When citing responses, we use the respondent or document code, followed by the case, for example R1_E1.

Table 2. Case Organisations and Data Sources

Case	Employees	Industry	Documents	Interviews	Position	Years experience
E1	10000+	Retail	D1, D2	R1	IT Director	30–35
				R2	Senior IT Manager	30–35
				R4	Systems Manager	15–20
E2	350–499	Healthcare		R3	Chief Information Officer	25–30
E3	3500+	Financial Services		R5	Project/Change Manager	25–30
				R6	Digital Manager	15–20
				R7	Development Manager	10–15

The process first followed the data preparation phase as follows: Interviews were digitally recorded using MS Teams and Zoom and were imported into Otter Notes for transcription. Transcripts were then exported to MS Word and edited by removing repeating words and sensitive data. Transcripts were also edited while listening to audios to ensure accuracy. Thematic analysis [20] using NVivo software was then utilised for data analysis and reporting of interviews and project documents. To ensure trustworthiness of data analysis one should consider credibility, transferability, dependability and confirmability [21]. Some strategies to improve these were adopted such as purposive sampling, maintaining version control in analysis and triangulation of multiple data types.

4 Case Descriptions

Feldman et al. [4] found that half the organisations in their study upgraded whenever a new version became available and half did not. In this study all the organisations preferred to be a version or two behind. As a large organisation, E1 used several ESs, and did not upgrade as soon as a new version is released. Accordingly, it took the organisation more than twenty years before upgrading their Retail Merchandising System (RMS). It took championing for five years, before the Executive Committee (Exco) approved the upgrade. E1 owned the RMS source code and built enough skills in-house to be self-sufficient, thus, not relying on vendor support. In 2020, they upgraded their RMS. E2 has a small IT department with six permanent staff and their model relies on outsourced IT functions for ERP implementations, hosting, upgrades as well as support. Their ERP system was on premise with Platform as a Service (PaaS). E2 was considering and investigating the options of migrating to the cloud version. Even though it was learnt, after the interviews, that this may be a migration rather than an upgrade, how they made the decision was still deemed useful and relevant to this study. E3 is part of a larger group, referred to as HoldCo, where HoldCo is the major shareholder of E3. Their ES portfolio comprises ERP Financials, CRM, Policy Administration, Claims and ad-hoc solutions that add to the Policy Administration system. When it came to upgrading their ES, the company was leading (not bleeding) edge and looked at individual applications and trying to keep them as current as is feasible and safe.

5 Findings and Discussion

In this section we answer the three questions posed. We identified twenty themes that influence the timing of and decision to upgrade ES within the cases studied. Eight of these themes were not found in the literature. An explanatory model was generated and we describe timings chosen by organisations.

5.1 What Factors Influence the Timing of and Decision to Upgrade ES?

While South Africa is a middle-income country [22], we could not determine whether the differences between literature findings and our findings were due to the middle-income context. The themes identified are categorised under organisational, technological, environmental, supplier and social network and are now discussed.

Organisational. Organisational factors were considered the most important. Five organisational themes emerged.

Exco Approval. Exco Approval is common across organisations. Although literature highlights the importance of management support in upgrade decisions [4], in this study it was found that no ES decision can be made without the Exco Approval. R3_E2 referred to the need of the IT Department to present business cases or motivations to the Exco, and only if these were successful could the upgrade decision be made. As mentioned by R6_E3, the Exco controlled the finances for updating any technology.

Risk Management. Once finances are secured, organisations don't necessarily adopt the latest version as and when it is released but rather opt to be a version or two behind. R3_E2 and R5_E3 referenced not wanting to be first to market or on the latest version. This ensured stability and as a way of learning from the experiences of others who have already adopted these versions. In addition to adopting leading edge over bleeding edge, at least one participant in each case mentioned their respective organisations aversion of risk. Therefore, should the current system version become dated, the organisation will only upgrade their ES if there are stable versions available. This impacts the relative advantage that could be derived. Although, Feldman et al. [4] referred to this in literature as a management strategy, in this study the respondents referred to management avoiding the disruption that comes with employing new unstable versions.

Business Requirement and Buy-in. As a business initiative, upgrades require support and buy-in from the business. As noted by R2_E1, *'IT decisions are ultimately business's decisions'*, therefore an upgrade will require collaboration between business and IT. In certain scenarios, R6_E3 mentioned that the requirement for an upgrade would come from business and that way business buy-in and support would exist. While this theme on its own would not influence whether to upgrade, it will influence the timing of an ES upgrade. Participants and secondary data confirmed that the business would drive the timing of an ES upgrade in terms of the business calendar. R4_E1 noted: *'I think our business decides when the upgrade will happen. And the timing of that upgrade and the project…it is very much based around the business calendar.'*

Organisation Strategic Objectives. Organisations noted that they upgrade their ES to support their strategic objectives, whether it be improving customer experience or employing the best systems: *'depending where the organisation is going, are they planning acquisitions…for which there are limitations in your existing applications? Are they branching into new lines of… products of any kind new services, you need to make sure that your application will be able to support the business needs going forward' [R1_E1].* Additionally, when an organisation plans to introduce these strategies will influence the timing of the ES upgrade: *'Again, it would be based on when do we plan to introduce certain strategical… imperatives that would drive the timing of when you choose to upgrade' [R1_E1].* This contradicts literature that found that the timing of ES upgrades is not driven by the organisation's strategic objectives [6]. When advocating for a new upgrade, literature notes that it would be more favourable if the IT function is perceived to be more strategic [13].

Resource Competence. One participant mentioned that from an ES upgrade decision perspective, the organisation will consider the complexity from a resource perspective and whether additional resources or different skills are required to maintain it: *'we would look at our complexity from an upgrade perspective… does that require… the rescaling of your organisation, of your people that would support the new technologies' [R1_E1].* Participants also mentioned that resource competence could influence the timing of an ES upgrade due to availability: *'The last upgrade that we did now… we contracted resources locally and in India, to assist with upgrades. And if those skills are not available, you cannot do the upgrades as simple as that… So, the availability of skills does have some influence on the scheduling of the upgrade.' [R5_E3].* The availability of the right skills to influence an ES upgrade is consistent with literature that notes that resources possessing the right technical expertise, provides organisations with greater confidence in committing to an ES upgrade [13].

Technological. There were eight technological themes which emerged.

Cost. Research [11] notes that the cost of an upgrade has a major influence on an ES upgrade timing. Our analysis also suggests that a lack of funds can cause a delay in the ES upgrade and relying on extended support agreements is an alternative if possible. Researchers only mentioned the availability of funds related to adopting the new version. We noted that the cost to upgrade or not to upgrade can equally influence the decision to upgrade. ES respondents mentioned the cost to maintain customisations on current versions: *'as soon as it is starting to cost you more to keep the old dog running then to move forward with the new and improved…that is a real factor.' [R4_E1].*

Compatibility. The reliance of one system version upon another as well as maintaining compatibility within the architecture stack was found to influence the decision to upgrade an ES: *'we went on a project this year to implement Claim Centre, and so it did influence the decision last year to upgrade Policy Centre before we can put down a Claim Centre' [R6_E3].* Architecture compatibility was noted by Feldman et al. [4]. Additionally, if an upgrade is not adopted, it could cause systems to move out of step and compromise support from vendors: *'products started moving out of step with one another. And as soon as you are upgrading one and not the other. Your versions start becoming strained. And…the vendor will not necessarily support combinations you are on.'* [R4_E1]. Compatibility would not only influence the timing of an ES upgrade but also which ES to upgrade first. *'if we upgrade this system to a newer version, then it will no longer be able to talk to these systems. So we have to upgrade this at the same time…So we really want to upgrade this, but we cannot let us do this one first…So compatibility would most definitely impact the timing decisions for upgrades'* [R5_E3]. This theme is consistent with literature. Feldman et al. [4] stated that when there are inter organisational systems, overcoming compatibility is one reason for upgrading.

Outdated Technology. Analysis notes that outdated technology can be inflexible which can influence the upgrade decision. Outdated technology is prone to customisations which decreases flexibility and impacts costs over time. R7_E3 noted: *'One of the hindrances of legacy systems is that it prevents you from being agile…So that in itself can also trigger the decision to upgrade an enterprise system, which did in our case.'*

Relative Advantage. Respondents note that the ability to leverage additional features and functionality that can benefit business and feed into the strategy of the business can influence the decision to upgrade ES: *'Yes…that is how we knew that it had everything that we needed for a future strong foundation for future omni-channel experience' [R2_E1].* Claybaugh et al. [13] argue that benefits such as globalisation, greater systems integration, and operational cost reduction can influence the upgrade decision. These benefits are classified as organisational objectives.

Security Vulnerabilities. Feldman et al. [4] noted that security issues can lead to upgrades. This was found in the study. Besides the risk of no patches being written and released, running a system that is unsupported also opens the door to hackers creating security vulnerabilities. *'Running any software that is unsupported carries an extreme risk that you cannot expose…to the enterprise organisation.' [R5_E3] 'where the vendor is no longer supporting in terms of writing patches for that particular version…You are forced to upgrade to a version where there are actually patches…security vulnerabilities come in probably every single day'* [R6_E3].

Cloud Transition. As the cloud hype increases, more and more organisations are becoming aware of the impending transition to the cloud. Analysis showed that when transitioning to the cloud, organisations need to consider the customisations already in place. To facilitate the transition to cloud an organisation also needs to be as close as possible to the latest version. Participants mentioned the Cloud Transition can influence the decision to upgrade ES: *'I think what… pushed a lot of organisations further and quicker is the Cloud Transition… which means you need to be as close as possible to what their versions are if you want to be able to transition'* [R4_E1].

Customisation. The findings were consistent with literature, in terms of customization causing delays in ES upgrades. In this study the opportunity to restrict customisation was also found to be key in influencing an ES upgrade. In addition, the effort it took to maintain and support the customised version also influenced the decision to upgrade: *'security was key. How do you keep this new enterprise system more independently replaceable and less tied up with customisations and other unknown integrations?… We were going to get to a point where we would have to start creating and maintaining features that were available to us in newer versions… you do not want to be there. If you can upgrade and get some of those features out the box, that is where you want to be.'* [R4_E1] *'there was a lot of customisation in the financial system before we started the upgrade… we actually…minimised the customisation'* [R5_E3].

Complexity. One participant mentioned that due to ease of use being compromised, end users may resort to using parallel systems because of complexity of the new version and that can be a factor considered when deciding to upgrade their ES: *'in any IT system, if your system becomes too complex to use…users may not want to use the system and before you realise, you find users are doing parallel systems' [R3_E2].* In addition, one participant referred to the complexity of the ES upgrade itself and referenced resources needed to support it and keep it running: *'we would look at our complexity from an upgrade perspective… in terms of ability to keep the updated version, the new version running and operating.' [R1_E1].* Complexity was found to influence Business Requirement and Buy-in in terms of ease of use and can influence Resource Competence in terms of the skills needed to support the version.

Environmental. Innovation adoption can be in response to changing conditions within the environment which can force upgrades [4]. We found three themes.

Regulatory Requirements. Organisations need to comply with regulatory requirements. In line with the literature [14], changes in regulatory requirements were found to influence the upgrade decision: *'if there are changes that happen because of regulation…for example, your financial software, let us say there is new regulations coming in, and in order to meet those regulations, your software needs to be updated, then that would drive the need for it. So yes…regulation can definitely influence the decision to update your software' [R7_E3].* Analysis also suggest that participants believe if organisations were first to comply with legislature, that it would result in a competitive advantage and revenue opportunities. *'I mean if we can change our systems too before anybody else, it means it is a competitive advantage' [R3_E2].*

Competitive Pressure. Participants referenced staying competitive and being more reactive in the marketplace as factors influencing an ES upgrade decision. It was also mentioned that pressure from competitors could force a decision and timing: *'for us this was really like putting down the foundation that allows you then to ultimately build out serious and new competitive advantages' [R2_E1]. 'if your competitor goes to market with something which you believe you should as well, the sooner rather than later would drive your desire to do it shortly as opposed to in time' [R1_E1].*

Business Partners. A participant explained the significance of a broker within the insurance industry and how as a business partner, they offer brokerage services which forms part of the sales operations within the organisation. These business partners were found to influence ES upgrade decisions. *'They are an extension of our sales op…I think that the decision to upgrade or not upgrade is definitely influenced more directly by the broker and the role of the broker… if 95% of your business comes through brokers, they definitely have a voice in the organisation' [R5_E3].*

Supplier. Three Supplier themes influencing an ES upgrade emerged.

Existing Relationship. Claybaugh et al. [13] proposed that the quality (satisfaction and commitment) of the relationship with ES vendors influenced the organisation's decision to upgrade their ES. However, in this study the quality of the relationship E2 had with the vendor had no bearing on the decision to adopt an ES upgrade. In one case the relationship with the vendor had broken down: *'It is a very good system, but we do not particularly like the organisation' [R3_E2].*

Communication. Participants highlighted that through an existing relationship with vendors, vendors could provide communication in terms of new releases or risk via documentation or recommendations. This creates awareness and can influence the decision to upgrade ES. Hence this theme on its own will not influence an ES upgrade, it will create awareness which together with other factors can influence an ES upgrade decision. *'they… gave us all the information that we needed. They put us in touch with all the potential SIs [system implementers] that we would be looking at to tender on the project… we got a lot of documentation from them upfront' [R2_E1].*

Vendor Influence. Participants referred to the constant reminder in the marketplace that a version was approaching its end of life which will result in the end of support. Once this occurs, the system is vulnerable to risk. Hence, this influences the decision to upgrade ES. *'I think the most obvious one is obviously when you are running systems that are reaching end of life of support...running any software that is unsupported carries an extreme risk that you cannot expose...the enterprise to' [R5_E3].*

Social Network. One Social Network theme emerged which we termed 'Network Participation'. Participants mentioned the influence of user groups, Gartner groups and collaboration with other ES upgrade adopters can influence the decision to upgrade ES. Participants also highlighted that organisations could leverage significant benefits such as cost reductions through network participation, that in turn would influence the upgrade timing. *'When decisions are made here on products to choose or upgrades to take...Gartner groups...will be highly influential, because I think big corporates or those who use enterprise systems want to know that they are using what is right' [R4_E1]. 'we may discuss doing things differently so that it can benefit us all and save cost...instead of each...of us hosting our own Vendor2 instance, separately, we can maybe agree, let us host it...together [R3_E2].*

5.2 Why Do Organisations Decide to Upgrade Their ES?

An explanatory model (Fig. 1) was derived which depicts how the factors impact one another which we now describe. We found that the IT departments in these South African companies are continuously assessing the status of ES and how well it serves business needs. Aligning business needs and ES capabilities can be achieved by collaboration, analytics, and add-ons within the ES [2]. As ES upgrades are huge IT investments [6], and a complex exercise that could cause major business disruption, decisions are governed and planned in formal executive committees. The ES upgrade decision is precipitated by a myriad of internal and external factors. Factors directly or indirectly impact the Exco approval.

One of the most significant factors influencing ES upgrades was the organisation's strategic objectives which the ES needs to support. When these are no longer aligned, organisations will decide to upgrade ES. Other unavoidable factors directly impacting the Exco approval and why organisations upgrade are classified as environmental. These include regulatory requirements, competitive pressure, and business partners. From an insurance context, brokers as business partners influence ES upgrades. From a technological perspective, factors directly impacting Exco approval and why organisations upgrade were cost and security vulnerabilities. Indirect factors from a technological point of view were outdated technology, relative advantage, cloud transition, customisation, complexity, and compatibility. Compatibility was found to influence security vulnerabilities. Security vulnerabilities emerge when ESs are no longer supported by vendors. And this nudge or push from vendors was identified as vendor influence.

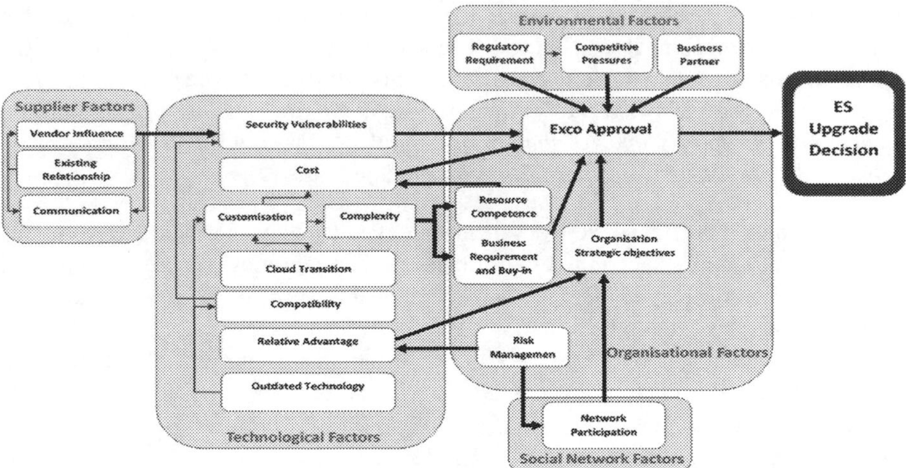

Fig. 1. Factors impacting ES upgrade decisions

5.3 When Do Organisations Decide to Upgrade Their ES?

Organisations were found to upgrade their ES when the ES no longer serve the business needs. However, the decision of when to upgrade can only be made once the Exco has approved. In this study, five factors were found to influence when organisations decide to upgrade ES: (1) When it is convenient for business – Business is driven by a business calendar and often upgrades are adopted within a less disruptive period. (2) When a stable version is available with sufficient support to prevent disruption. (3) When resources are available – provided you are sourcing external resources. (4) Within the regulatory compliance due date. (5) Before vendor support is due to end.

6 Conclusion

This study explained the network of factors influencing the timing of and decision to upgrade ES. We analysed three upgrade case studies in South Africa. We found that ES upgrades were considered or undertaken where the promise of cost reduction, improved customer experience or increased efficiency through later versions existed. Other factors impacting the decision, included compatibility, regulatory compliance, cost, and security vulnerabilities with emphasis placed on Exco approval, business convenience and calendar for the timing. In addition, organisations also need to position themself aptly as ES progress and transition to the cloud. It is noted that 'vendors are manufacturing another Y2K by forcing customers to upgrade to new cloud versions of their software, which has forced the tipping point of cloud ERP' [23]. While vendor influence persists, organisations decide what is best for them. Perhaps it is as simple as knowing and reaffirming, what do we do? Why now? Are we ready? And can we delay? [7] and to foster mutual collaboration and strategic alliance with vendors.

This study had limitations. The generalisability of the research may be limited, as only large organisations were used in this study. Due to the COVID 19 pandemic and social distancing, interviews were not done in the same room and recordings at times were not clear which compromised the interpretations made and as only seven interviews were performed the findings are incomplete. The use of a cross-sectional time horizon made information recalled by respondent's time-dependent and their confidence of recall may be questionable. This might be applicable to organisations who had upgraded months before the study was conducted. Additionally, the narrow research timeframe resulted in no member checks and we also were unable to determine which factors applied to the case study context. Future research could be to conduct cases within different types of organisations and in different countries. For example, more agile medium sized organisations might consider different factors. A longitudinal study would also add more clarity.

References

1. Bailey, L., Seymour, L.F., Van Belle, J.-P.: Impact of ERP implementation on the quality of work life of users: a sub-Saharan African study. Afr. J. Inf. Syst. **9**, 3 (2017)
2. Ruivo, P., Johansson, B., Sarker, S., Oliveira, T.: The relationship between ERP capabilities, use, and value. Comput. Ind. **117**, 103209 (2020)
3. Lech, P.: Causes and remedies for the dominant risk factors in Enterprise System implementation projects: the consultants' perspective. SpringerPlus **5**(1), 1–12 (2016). https://doi.org/10.1186/s40064-016-1862-9
4. Feldman, G., Shah, H., Chapman, C., Amini, A.: Technological, Organisational, and Environmental drivers for enterprise systems upgrade. Ind. Manage. Data Syst. **116**, 1636–1655 (2016). https://doi.org/10.1108/imds-09-2015-0407
5. Motiwalla, L.F., Thompson, J.: Enterprise Systems for Management. Pearson, Boston (2012)
6. Morgan, H.M., Ngwenyama, O.: Real options, learning cost and timing software upgrades: towards an integrative model for enterprise software upgrade decision analysis. Int. J. Prod. Econ. **168**, 211–223 (2015). https://doi.org/10.1016/j.ijpe.2015.06.028
7. Saunders, P., Ganly, D., Guay, M.: Strategic Roadmap for Postmodern ERP. https://www.gartner.com/document/3933972?ref=solrAll&refval=243780322. Accessed 31 May 2019
8. Xu, W., Ou, P., Fan, W.: Antecedents of ERP assimilation and its impact on ERP value: a TOE-based model and empirical test. Inf. Syst. Front. **19**(1), 13–30 (2015). https://doi.org/10.1007/s10796-015-9583-0
9. Gnevanov, M., Sharlaimova, A.: The impact of organizational commitment on upgrading ERP for maintaining the quality of information and the ERP performance. E3S Web Conf. **110**, 02081 (2019). https://doi.org/10.1051/e3sconf/201911002081
10. Comuzzi, M., Parhizkar, M.: A methodology for enterprise systems post-implementation change management. Ind. Manage. Data Syst. **117**, 2241–2262 (2017). https://doi.org/10.1108/imds-11-2016-0506
11. Dempsey, S., Vance, R., Sheehan, L.: Justification of an upgrade of an enterprise resource planning (ERP) system–the accountant's role. Global J. Hum. Soc. Sci. **13**, 16–24 (2013)
12. Barth, C., Koch, S.: Critical success factors in ERP upgrade projects. Ind. Manage. Data Syst. **119**, 656–675 (2019). https://doi.org/10.1108/imds-01-2018-0016
13. Claybaugh, C.C., Ramamurthy, K., Haseman, W.D.: Assimilation of enterprise technology upgrades: a factor-based study. Enterp. Inf. Syst. **11**, 250–283 (2015). https://doi.org/10.1080/17517575.2015.1041060
14. Feldman, G., Shah, H., Chapman, C., Pärn, E.A., Edwards, D.J.: A systematic approach for enterprise systems upgrade decision-making. J. Eng. Des. Technol. **15**, 778–802 (2017). https://doi.org/10.1108/jedt-08-2017-0076

15. Frambach, R.T., Schillewaert, N.: Organizational innovation adoption: a multi-level framework of determinants and opportunities for future research. J. Bus. Res. **55**, 163–176 (2002). https://doi.org/10.1016/s0148-2963(00)00152-1
16. Depietro, R., Wiarda, E., Fleischer, M.: The Context for Change: Organization, Technology and Environment: The Processes of Technological Innovation, pp. 151–175. Lexington Books, Lexington (1990)
17. Bygstad, B., Munkvold, B.E.: Exploring the role of informants in interpretive case study research in IS. J. Inf. Technol. **26**, 32–45 (2011). https://doi.org/10.1057/jit.2010.15
18. Walsham, G.: Doing interpretive research. Eur. J. Inf. Syst. **15**, 320–330 (2006)
19. Saunders, M., Lewis, P., Thornhill, A.: Research methods for business students (6. utg.). Pearson, Harlow (2012)
20. Braun, V., Clarke, V.: Using thematic analysis in psychology. Qualit. Res. Psychol. **3**, 77–101 (2006). https://doi.org/10.1191/1478088706qp063oa
21. Anfara, V.A., Brown, K.M., Mangione, T.L.: Qualitative analysis on stage: making the research process more public. Educ. Res. **31**, 28–38 (2002). https://doi.org/10.3102/0013189x031007028
22. World Bank. World Bank Country and Lending Groups. https://datahelpdesk.worldbank.org/knowledgebase/articles/906519-world-bank-country-and-lending-groups. Accessed 12 May 2021
23. Kimberling, E.: ERP Failure: Is it Time to Take it on the Run? https://www.thirdstage-consulting.com/erp-failure-is-it-time-to-take-it-on-the-run. Accessed 19 Jun 2019

An Overview of the Application of Sentiment Analysis in Quality Function Deployment

Blessed Sarema(✉) and Stephen Matope

Stellenbosch University, Cape Town, South Africa
smatope@sun.ac.za

Abstract. Customer feedback is important in continuous improvement of products and services for businesses to stay ahead of competition. With the advent of the internet, online product reviews from various platforms attracts a lot of comments from customers as they share their sentiments from experiences with the different products and services. The sentiments shared online are an important resource for mining opinions that can help businesses to improve on their products and services. Online sentiment analysis has brought about endless possibilities to incorporate these sentiments in product development in continuous improvement. However, most sentiments analysis research done seem to muzzle the customer comments into three points of view that are positive, neutral and negative. Though this approach is excellent in providing a general perception of customers about a particular product or service, it falls short in outlining specific product features that may require improvement in order to increase customer satisfaction from the Quality Function Deployment (QFD) perspective. This paper presents an overview of how sentiment analysis has been applied to a number of products and services reviews. The aim being to highlight the gaps in sentiment analysis output data and how QFD can be integrated with sentiment analysis to make the sentiments valuable. An integration conceptual framework is proposed to stimulate research into the area.

Keywords: Sentiment analysis · Quality Function Deployment · Opinion Mining

1 Introduction

The world has become one big room in which many conversations and transactions are taking place simultaneously, thanks to the internet and social media. These interactions generate a lot of data. The data can be collected, analyzed and processed into useful information for decision making. This collection of data repositories is known as Big Data [1]. In its raw form the data characteristics are summarised by the four Vs namely; Volume, Velocity, Variety and Veracity [2]. Volume refers to the huge quantity of the data while Velocity denotes high speed at which data accumulates in real time. Variety indicates that the data is composed of different types and Veracity brings the aspect of uncertainty and unreliability of the data [2, 3]. Big data is therefore a mixture of

Published by Springer Nature Switzerland AG 2021
D. Dennehy et al. (Eds.): I3E 2021, LNCS 12896, pp. 519–531, 2021.
https://doi.org/10.1007/978-3-030-85447-8_43

mainly unstructured data and a bit of structured data [4, 5]. This data resembles mineral deposits that require mining and processing for further purification to make the mineral useful. Data mining is thus defined as a process of knowledge discovery from large databases using data analysis and discovery algorithms [6]. In conventional mining various tools and methods are used to get the precious mineral out of the ore. Data mining likewise also uses different types of machine learning algorithms for extracting valuable information from the datasets [7]. This study reviews one of the techniques used in data mining called Sentiment Analysis or Opinion Mining. This method is employed to extract customers opinions about a product or a service from online platforms. The sentiments are categorized into positive, neutral and negative [8]. In this paper it is argued that these three may not provide sufficient information to assist in research and development to improve the product as the sentiments are muzzled together. A conceptual framework is proposed for integration of Sentiment Analysis and Quality Function Deployment.

2 Methodology

To develop the conceptual framework, the authors used the integrative literature review methodology to get an overview of the application of Sentiment Analysis in reviewing customer perceptions on different products and services. The aim being to find general ideas and the related procedures in order to collect relevant data and deduce the common stages and procedures used in Sentiment Analysis. The same is done for QFD to give readers a contextual perspective of the application of QFD in product development. The two processes are then superimposed on each other and a logical conceptual framework structure is developed in which sentiment analysis can provide input data for QFD.

3 Sentiment Analysis Overview

Sentiment analysis is one of the many data analytics tool used determine opinions expressed on online platforms about a particular topics, product or service [9]. This technology has become a game changer in marketing as companies are able to determine customers' opinions on brands and services and thereby understanding consumer attitudes towards the product or service [10]. Customer feedback is important for product research and development and these sentiments can play a major role in providing the much-needed voice of the customer as it is the key input in Quality Function Deployment processes. The process is only an insight into the general measure of the ambience [9]. To date sentiment analysis has been applied to review a number of disciplines, products and services. To mention a few examples Isah et al. [11] used sentiment analysis from Facebook and Twitter to compare customer perception on the safety of skin care products. In another study Hu et al. [12] discovered that while online feedback reviews may influence potential buyers, some of the information available is subject to manipulation. Be that as it may, Schuckert et al. [13] applied sentiment analysis to determine various customer perceptions in the hospitality and tourism industry while Alamoodi et al. [14] suggest that sentiment analysis could be used to fight pandemics like COVID 19 as an information tool. The variety of applications for sentiment analysis has also been proved by Ceron et al. [15] who applied it to predict election outcomes, Wang et al. [16] to forecast cellphone purchase decisions and Brunova and Bidulya [17] to customer satisfaction surveys for banking services. There is also a potential to develop a universal sentiment analysis tool that can automatically rank products based on consumer expectations, costs, convenience and communication issues in any product or service [18]. Investors may also use such tools to decide on their next business portfolios and location to set up their businesses, for example Lamba and Madhusudhan [19] used sentiment analysis productivity hashtags with results showing a number of sectors and countries that have high productivity. These applications indicate that sentiment analysis can be adopted as an interdisciplinary tool and the scope can be expanded beyond the polarity of sentiments. Sentiment Analysis involves a number of stages, Micu et al. [10] suggest that the process consists of four stages that are sentiment extraction; classification; retrieval, and reporting to decision makers. Kriegel et al. [6], Kennedy [9] and Isah et al. [11] reaffirm these stages, but describe them as data retrieval, preprocessing, sentiment analysis and reporting. A more holistic description of the process is given by Alamoodi et al. [14] in their four stage process that include search strategy, data collection, preprocessing and analysis. The presentation stage is added to the process and adopted as a standard process in this overview. The next section expands on these stages and reviews the applicable tools that can be used at each stage as summarised in Fig. 1.

3.1 Developing a Search Strategy in Sentiment Analysis

Most literature reviewed in this study does not document this important step of developing a search strategy in Sentiment Analysis. It is assumed to be obvious that the researcher knows what to look for and from which sites to search for the information. However, the best approach is to start from a position of ignorance and develop a plan of execution [20]. This stage is suggested and explained in detail by Alamoodi et al. [14]. The planning stage involves outlining the aim of the study and its accompanying objectives. It is also important to decide on the time period for carrying out the sentiment analysis [21]. This then directs the researchers to the different sources of mines from which they can extract their data from and these are often social media sites like YouTube, Facebook, Twitter, Instagram or any other product review sites. Deciding where to mine is critical at this stage because it determines the mining algorithms to be used as data is structured differently on different sites. There is need for developing a strategy mapping tool for data exploration. Beale [22] developed a tool that interacts with the user in order to understand information at different levels of detail for iterative exploration. However, the suggested tool in this overview is one which is user friendly and can be used by the less tech-savvy professions who would also want to apply sentiment analysis in their fields without having to rely on coding. The tools may culminate into a search engine specifically for sentiment analysis for example if there is Google Scholar there can be "Google Sentiments", Yahoo!, Bing and many more.

3.2 Data Retrieval in Sentiment Analysis

After the search strategy, the next phase is data retrieval. This stage is also known as data collection or data extraction [10, 14]. Application Programming Interfaces (APIs) and web crawling software programmes are used to collect data from the identified sites

[11, 23]. Most social media sites like Twitter, Facebook and You Tube have got APIs on the developers side that help with authentication, extraction and data sharing [11]. Other websites like Amazon do not support developer APIs, hence a web crawler has to be developed to retrieve data from such sites [24]. In a study on sentiment analysis for medical data applications Meena and Bai [25] used python tweepy and Twitter developer API to extract tweets from twitter for their study while Chong et al. [23] had to develop a web scrapping tool for their study to retrieve information from the Amazon site. It therefore follows that both APIs and web crawlers can be used for the same project and the results can be compared if the websites allow [26]. The data collected at this stage is usually noisy and requires further processing or cleaning [11].

3.3 Data Preprocessing in Sentiment Analysis

The data collected in the retrieval stage consists of structured and unstructured data [6]. Sentences and phrases usually contain joining words without meaning, symbols, misspelt words, word spacings and a lot of punctuation and these are the foundation of noise signals that need to be removed during processing [18]. According to Zhang et al. [27], some of the preprocessing steps include changing all words in a sentence to lowercase letters, removing stop-words and punctuation. In addition, during the preprocessing stage the data retrieved may need to be split into sentences and sentences into words and filtering stop words. This is possible through the application of Parts Of Speech (POS) tagging in which the words are classified into nouns, verbs, adjectives, pronouns and other POS tags [2]. Bag of Words (BoW) binary vectorization may also be used for preprocessing [11]. There could be information loss during processing and researchers must be careful [2]. Another challenge is that one sentence may carry multiple sentiments [28] and can also be written in a multi-linguistic manner [29]. Therefore corpus filtering for language preprocessing is always necessary [30]. Zhang et al. [27] proved that information losses can be avoided at the preprocessing stage by incorporating deep learning algorithms in the data retrieval stage to maintain the sentence structure.

3.4 Data Feature Extraction in Sentiment Analysis

Feature extraction is also the key process in sentiment analysis as it is the actual process of deriving the sentiments contained in the data. Alaei et al. [2] describes feature extraction as the process of discriminating information from nonredundant values to numerically represent a review or text. In other words, the process involves both statistical and semantic approaches [31]. This implies that words that have similar meaning are grouped together and represented statistically as it is described by Rambocas and Pacheco [32] as sentiment grouping. Features can be classified into three morphological types namely; semantic, syntactic and lexicon. In feature extraction researchers are concerned with frequent features and implicit features in order to analyse the sentiments [33]. Feature extraction is also possible in audio-visual sentiment analysis [34]. Artificial Intelligence algorithms play a vital role in sentiment extraction.

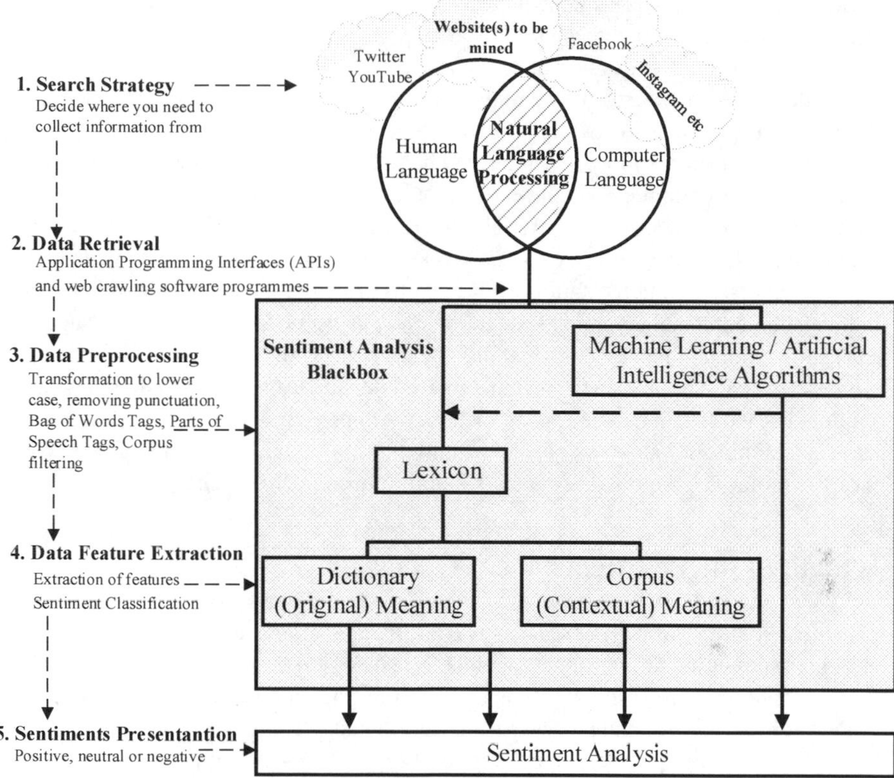

Fig. 1. Sentiment analysis procedures summary

3.5 Reporting Findings in Sentiment Analysis

As previously discussed, sentiment analysis findings are presented in a semantic and statistical format [31]. The features identified are the basis from which the sentiments are drawn from while the statistics indicate the number of opinions in different categories. A number of statistical manipulations of the data can be used in sentiment analysis for example averages, weighted averages, standard deviations, distribution analysis, relative importance and feature ratings. The data can be presented in a number of visual formats like bar charts, bubble charts and original lists separating the positive, neutral and negative reviews. Marrese-Taylor et al. [35] postulates that the development of a Results Visualization Module can better assist users in the manipulation of data for presentation.

3.6 Sentiment Analysis Algorithms

There are a number of artificial intelligence or machine learning algorithms available to use for sentiment analysis, but the decision on which ones to use is a very complicated [24]. It follows that the algorithms or combination thereof should be able to retrieve, preprocess, extract sentiments. There are a number of factors that should be considered in order to select or develop sentiment analysis algorithms. Some of the factors include the website from which sentiments are to be drawn, availability of developer API platforms, the length of the data, the structure of the data, the expected results and the complexity of the algorithm [24]. In order to fully comprehend the background and basics of sentiment analysis algorithms, it is necessary to understand that the sentiments are drawn from human language using computer language. The area of interaction between the human language and the computer language has led to the development of the field called Natural Language Processing (NLP) [31]. This implies that first and foremost the human language semantics and syntax have to be properly understood for correct interpretation of the sentiments. The interpretation would be based on the meaning of words which is also known as lexicon analysis [18]. Lexicon analysis is subdivided into two categories that are the dictionary and the corpus approach [31]. According to Ravi and Ravi [1] the dictionary approach is built on the original words meaning together with their synonyms and antonyms while Lin et al. [31] say the corpus approach is based on the aggregated semantic orientation that seeks to understand the contextual meaning of the words. Figure 1 summarizes the link between NLP and Sentiment Analysis.

4 Quality Function Deployment Overview

The decision to buy a product or service by customers is often a complex one, it involves the evaluation of competing products against the customers preferences or expectations. Research and development in quality and innovation helps businesses to improve their products and services to match customer requirements. Business and service providers need to effectively use customer feedback to obtain responses from users or customers to improve services. This form of response is to explore the level of satisfaction or dissatisfaction with a product or service [31]. In most cases the customer requirements are fuzzy and would need to be transformed to the technical specifications of a product. Quality Function Deployment (QFD) is one of the methods that is used for transforming customer requirements into the product technical specifications leading to the development of customer-oriented products [36]. According to Franceschini [37], the QFD approach consists of five stages that are; determining customer requirements, product specifications, sub-systems or part specifications, process specifications and quality control specifications. Ginting and Widodo [38] further proposes another five step approach to QFD that is composed of processes that include; identifying customer needs, determination of priorities, determination of technical specifications, determination of relationships between technical specifications and finally the relationship between customer needs and technical specifications. These stages are similar and this implies that the QFD process is pretty much standard. In all the stages, the House of Quality (HOQ) tool is used to link all the processes as shown in Fig. 2. Alsaadi et al. [39] describes the QFD process in eight stages of HOQ that are identifying customer needs, determination of priorities in the needs, identification of technical requirements, identification of relationships between the technical requirements, creation of relationship matrix between customer requirements and technical requirements, competitive benchmarking, technical requirements prioritization and determination of technical requirements to deploy. This paper reviews these stages in QFD with the aim of creating integration points with

Sentiment Analysis stages in order to apply Sentiment Analysis to product development through Quality Function Deployment.

4.1 Identifying Customer Needs

In order to deliver on customer expectations, it is necessary for organisations to identify customer needs through capturing the voice of the customer [39]. The demand for mass customized products is increasing and this requires businesses to shorten the product development phase so as to quickly launch their products on to the market [40]. This implies that customer feedback has to be captured into product design for companies to remain competitive. Traditionally the process of soliciting feedback from customers involved a lot of market research using tools like questionnaires and interviews [41]. The availability of online reviews makes it possible to apply sentiment analysis in quality function deployment since sentiment analysis can be used to capture the voice of the customers using opinion mining [8]. Identifying customer needs answers the "What" questions in terms of the features to be incorporated into a product [39].

4.2 Determination of Customer Needs Priorities

The advantage of using sentiment analysis in online reviews is that customers freely express feedback without any reservations. The next step after the identification of customer needs is to prioritize the needs. Prioritization is traditionally done with customers having to rank the needs or allocate some weights or scores in order for the product development team to determine the most important needs that should be prioritized [39]. When applying sentiment analysis after the retrieval of the sentiments from various sources that represent the voice of the customer, the needs can be extracted, organized and sorted in order of importance [42]. The voice of the customer is often elusive and fuzzy in nature and application of artificial intelligence can help in the defuzzification of the customer sentiments. Hybridization of this process with the Kano model can help to priorities the product attributes by splitting them into three categories that are Basic attributes, Performance attributes and Excellence attributes [8]. Thus the sentiments or customer needs can be split into product sub systems or critical paths [37].

4.3 Determination of Technical Specifications

After determining the customer priorities in terms of product quality, the next step is to determine how these specifications would be provided using the technical specifications of the product or service [39]. Technical specifications are also known as the product design requirements [43]. The technical specifications are simply responses on how the business intends to respond to the customer needs. This response can also be subjected to the manufacturing constraints such as regulatory requirements, environmental sustainability factors, materials availability, technology capability and logistical challenges [44]. Questions that remain to be answered are whether sentiment analysis is still applicable to this stage of QFD. Song et al. [45] demonstrated that the inclusion of the Kano model in sentiment analysis can help in theme extraction if the product can be decomposed into its constituent features.

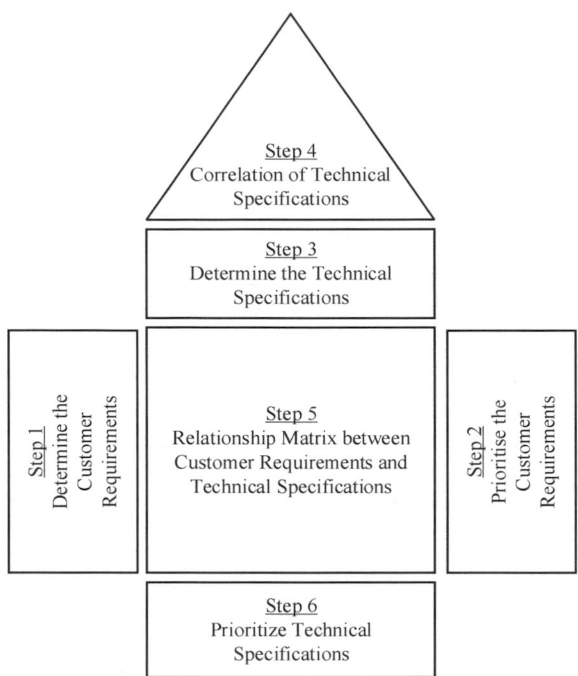

Fig. 2. Quality function deployment house of quality, adapted from Natee et al. [46]

4.4 Correlation of Technical Specifications

The next step after determining the technical specifications is to develop a correlation matrix of the technical specifications [44]. This forms the roof of the HOQ as shown in Fig. 2. The correlation seeks to quantify the relationships between the technical specifications themselves and their impact on each other. Like sentiment analysis the relationships are classified as strong positive, positive, neutral, negative and strong negative and different score can be allocated for each kind of relationship [39]. Positive correlation means that the technical specifications are complementary while negative correlation is a sign of conflict. Highlighting the correlations between the technical specifications means that complementing and conflicting specifications can be identified. This helps in determining the priorities and equitable trade-offs between conflicting specifications [37]. Focus must be on the conflicting specifications to allow for equitable trade-offs in order to maintain the product features that delight the customers [43].

4.5 Relationship Matrix Between Customer Needs and Technical Specifications

The most important part of the House of Quality in Quality Function Deployment is its ability to show the relationships between the customer requirements and the technical specifications. This is the biggest part in the matrix and the work and uses the priority matrix method [47]. The relationship matrix provides a comparison between the customer requirements and engineering characteristics. The number of comparisons depends on the number of the customer requirements and the number of engineering specifications [46]. Ginting and Satrio [47] recommends coupling the process together with value engineering in order to properly evaluate alternatives to the technical specifications. The relationships between customer requirements and technical specifications can be strong, mild or weak [37].

4.6 Technical Specifications Priorities

After having determined the nature of relationship between the customer requirements and the technical specifications, the next process is to determine the priorities for the technical specifications. Application of the Analytical Hierarchical Process (AHP) can be used to generate a meaningful degree of importance in the prioritization of technical specifications [37]. Competitive technical benchmarking can be used to inform the priorities of the technical specifications against competitors' products in order to set the technical targets and develop performance targets for the technical requirements for the product or service under review [47].

5 Proposed Integration Framework for Sentiment Analysis and Quality Function Deployment

In this paper, the authors provide an overview of Sentiment Analysis procedures and how Quality Function Deployment can be integrated with sentiment analysis to improve the product development process. The authors combine insights from the work of previous authors on the stages of sentiment analysis for example Isah et al. [11], Hu et al. [12], Schuckert et al. [13] and Alamoodi et al. [14] among others and the framework of Quality Function Deployment as discussed by Natee et al. [46], Ocampo et al. [44], Dehe and Bamford [43] and Ginting and Satrio [47] among others. In the conceptual framework a number of integration points have to be considered for the sentiment analysis and quality function deployment to work together seamlessly. Figure 3 represents the proposed integration in this paper. The first step is having the objectives of the QFD inform the search strategy. This will guide the researcher to the correct websites where the reviews are to extracted for sentiment analysis. When retrieving the data, preprocessing and extracting features it is also advisable to split the data into the different product or service features using the Kano model. The feature keywords should also be taken to be the voice of the customer into the process of determining the customer requirements in the QFD process. The sentiments expressed from the reviews should then guide the target areas of improvement during the product development stage. These sentiments should inform the prioritization stage for the customer requirements and loop back to the search strategy until the all the customer requirements have been captured.

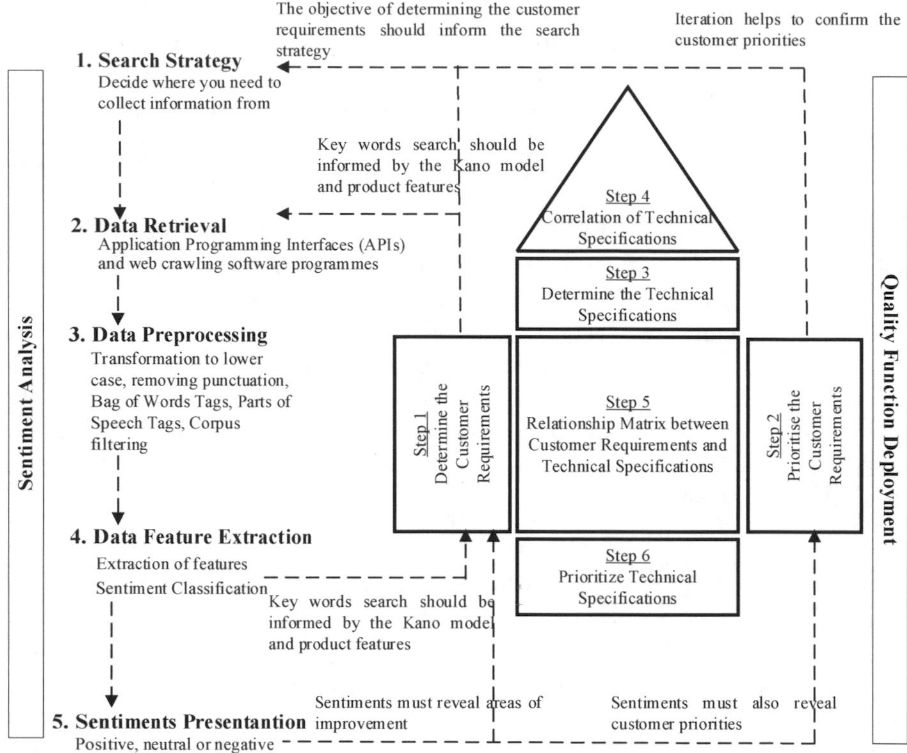

Fig. 3. Proposed conceptual framework of integration between Sentiment Analysis and QFD

6 Conclusion

In conclusion, the linkage between sentiment analysis and quality function deployment is an interesting field of research capable of shortening the product development process as well as a game changer in market research. The process may be used to augment the traditional market research approaches that are long and winding. As more and more consumers get connected to the internet in future the process may eventually replace the traditional market research process. More research needs to be done and this paper is a teaser to stimulate thinking towards that area. This overview is preliminary work for the authors to use sentiment analysis in the redesign of overlanding roof-top tents as future work. The framework is presented for adoption, further scrutiny, elaboration and revision by other scholars to suit specific needs for the products and services under review.

References

1. Ravi, K., Ravi, V.: A survey on opinion mining and sentiment analysis: tasks, approaches and applications. Knowl.-Based Syst. **89**, 14–46 (2015)

2. Alaei, A.R., Becken, S., Stantic, B.: Sentiment Analysis in Tourism: Capitalizing on Big Data. J. Travel Res. **58**(2), 175–191 (2019)
3. Joshi, O.S., Simon, G.: Sentiment analysis tool on cloud: software as a service model. In: 2018 International Conference on Advanced Communication Computing Technology, ICACCT 2018, pp. 459–462 (2018)
4. Bai, X.: Predicting consumer sentiments from online text. Decis. Support Syst. **50**(4), 732–742 (2011)
5. Tripathy, A., Agrawal, A., Rath, S.K.: Classification of sentiment reviews using n-gram machine learning approach. Expert Syst. Appl. **57**, 117–126 (2016)
6. Kriegel, H.P., Borgwardt, K.M., Kröger, P., Pryakhin, A., Schubert, M., Zimek, A.: Future trends in data mining. Data Min. Knowl. Discov. **15**(1), 87–97 (2007)
7. Parra-Royon, M., Atemezing, G., Benitez-Sanchez, J.M.: Semantics of data mining services in cloud computing. IEEE Trans. Serv. Comput. **1374**(c), 1–11 (2018)
8. Yoon, B., Jeong, Y., Lee, K., Lee, S.: A systematic approach to prioritizing R&D projects based on customer-perceived value using opinion mining. Technovation **98**, 102164 (2020)
9. Kennedy, H.: Perspectives on sentiment analysis. J. Broadcast. Electron. Media **56**(4), 435–450 (2012)
10. Micu, A., Micu, A.E., Geru, M., Lixandroiu, R.C.: Analyzing user sentiment in social media: implications for online marketing strategy. Psychol. Mark. **34**(12), 1094–1100 (2017)
11. Isah, H., Trundle, P., Neagu, D.: Social media analysis for product safety using text mining and sentiment analysis. In: 2014 14th UK Working Computing Intelligent UKCI 2014 - Proceeddings (2014)
12. Hu, N., Bose, I., Koh, N.S., Liu, L.: Manipulation of online reviews: an analysis of ratings, readability, and sentiments. Decis. Support Syst. **52**(3), 674–684 (2012)
13. Schuckert, M., Liu, X., Law, R.: Hospitality and tourism online reviews: recent trends and future directions. J. Travel Tour. Mark. **32**(5), 608–621 (2015)
14. Alamoodi, A.H., et al.: Sentiment analysis and its applications in fighting COVID-19 and infectious diseases: a systematic review. Expert Syst. Appl. **167**, 114155 (2020)
15. Ceron, A., Curini, L., Iacus, S.M.: Using sentiment analysis to monitor electoral campaigns: method matters—evidence from the United States and Italy. Soc. Sci. Comput. Rev. **33**(1), 3–20 (2015)
16. Wang, Q., Wang, L., Zhang, X., Mao, Y., Wang, P.: The impact research of online reviews' sentiment polarity presentation on consumer purchase decision. Inf. Technol. People **30**(3), 522–541 (2017)
17. Brunova, E., Bidulya, Y.: Aspect extraction and sentiment analysis in user reviews in Russian about bank service quality. In: 11th IEEE International Conference on Application Information Communication Technology, AICT 2017 - Proceedings (2019)
18. Lin, H.C.K., Wang, T.H., Lin, G.C., Cheng, S.C., Chen, H.R., Huang, Y.M.: Applying sentiment analysis to automatically classify consumer comments concerning marketing 4Cs aspects. Appl. Soft Comput. J. **97**, 106755 (2020)
19. Lamba, M., Madhusudhan, M.: Application of sentiment analysis in libraries to provide temporal information service: a case study on various facets of productivity. Soc. Network Anal. Min. **8**(1), 1–12 (2018). https://doi.org/10.1007/s13278-018-0541-y
20. Firestein, S.: Ignorance: How it Drives Science. Oxford University Press, Oxford (2012)
21. Appel, O., Chiclana, F., Carter, J., Fujita, H.: A hybrid approach to the sentiment analysis problem at the sentence level. Knowl.-Based Syst. **108**, 110–124 (2016)
22. Beale, R.: Supporting serendipity: Using ambient intelligence to augment user exploration for data mining and web browsing. Int. J. Hum. Comput. Stud. **65**(5), 421–433 (2007)
23. Chong, A.Y.L., Li, B., Ngai, E.W.T., Ch'ng, E., Lee, F.: Predicting online product sales via online reviews, sentiments, and promotion strategies: a big data architecture and neural network approach. Int. J. Oper. Prod. Manag. 36(4), 358–383 (2016)

24. Wang, H., Wang, W.: Product weakness finder: an opinion-aware system through sentiment analysis. Ind. Manag. Data Syst. **114**(8), 1301–1320 (2014)
25. Meena, R., Bai, V.T.: Study on machine learning based social media and sentiment analysis for medical data applications. In: Proceedings of the 3rd International Conference on I-SMAC IoT Social Mobile, Analysis Cloud, I-SMAC 2019, pp. 603–607 (2019)
26. Ben Hajhmida, M., Oueslati, O.: Predicting mobile application breakout using sentiment analysis of Facebook posts. J. Inf. Sci. (2020)
27. Zhang, M., Fan, B., Zhang, N., Wang, W., Fan, W.: Mining product innovation ideas from online reviews. Inf. Process. Manag. **58**(1), 102389 (2021)
28. Siering, M., Deokar, A.V., Janze, C.: Disentangling consumer recommendations: explaining and predicting airline recommendations based on online reviews. Decis. Support Syst. **107**, 52–63 (2018)
29. Abbasi, A., Chen, H., Salem, A.: Sentiment analysis in multiple languages: feature selection for opinion classification in Web forums. ACM Trans. Inf. Syst. **26**(3) (2008)
30. Srivats Athindran, N., Manikandaraj, S., Kamaleshwar, R.: Comparative analysis of customer sentiments on competing brands using hybrid model approach. In: Proceedings of the 3rd International Conference Invented Computing Technology ICICT 2018, pp. 348–353 (2018)
31. Ulfa, S., Bringula, R., Kurniawan, C., Fadhli, M.: Student feedback on online learning by using sentiment analysis: a literature review. In: Proceedings - 2020 6th International Conference Education Technology ICET 2020, no. 1, pp. 53–58 (2020)
32. Rambocas, M., Pacheco, B.G.: Online sentiment analysis in marketing research: a review. J. Res. Interact. Mark. **12**(2), 146–163 (2018)
33. Ahmad, S.R., Bakar, A.A., Yaakub, M.R.: A review of feature selection techniques in sentiment analysis. Intell. Data Anal. **23**(1), 159–189 (2019)
34. Wöllmer, M., et al.: IEEE INTELLIGENT SYSTEMS YouTube movie reviews: sentiment analysis in an audio- visual context. IEEE Comput. Soc. **13**, 1541–1672 (2013)
35. Marrese-Taylor, E., Velásquez, J.D., Bravo-Marquez, F.: A novel deterministic approach for aspect-based opinion mining in tourism products reviews. Expert Syst. Appl. **41**(17), 7764–7775 (2014)
36. Ginting, R., Ishak, A., Fauzi Malik, A., Satrio, M.R.: Product development with quality function deployment (QFD): a literature review. IOP Conf. Ser. Mater. Sci. Eng., **1003**, 012022 (2020)
37. Franceschini, F.: Advanced Quality Function Deployment. CRC Press LLC, New York (2002)
38. Ginting, R., Widodo: Technical characteristics' determination of crumb rubber product by using quality function deployment (QFD) phase I. IOP Conf. Ser. Mater. Sci. Eng. **602**(1) (2019)
39. Alsaadi, M.R., Ahmad, S.Z., Hussain, M.: Improving the quality of mobile government services in the Gulf Cooperation Council: a quality-function-deployment approach. J. Syst. Inf. Technol. **21**(1), 146–164 (2019)
40. Chaudha, A., Jain, R., Singh, A.R., Mishra, P.K.: Integration of kano's model into quality function deployment (QFD). Int. J. Adv. Manuf. Technol. **53**(5–8), 689–698 (2011)
41. Jiang, H., Kwong, C.K., Okudan Kremer, G.E., Park, W.Y.: Dynamic modelling of customer preferences for product design using DENFIS and opinion mining. Adv. Eng. Inform. **42**, 100969 (2019)
42. Chan, C.Y.P., Chin, K.-S., Chan, C., Tsui, K.L.: An analysis of passengers' ride needs of urban rail transit services: application of quality function deployment. Int. J. Qual. Innov. **5**(1) (2019)
43. Dehe, B., Bamford, D.: Quality Function Deployment and operational design decisions–a healthcare infrastructure development case study. Prod. Plan. Control **28**(14), 1177–1192 (2017)

44. Ocampo, L.A., Labrador, J.J.T., Jumao-as, A.M.B., Rama, A.M.O.: Integrated multiphase sustainable product design with a hybrid quality function deployment – multi-attribute decision-making (QFD-MADM) framework. Sustain. Prod. Consum. **24**, 62–78 (2020)
45. Song, H., Chen, C., Yu, Q.: Research on Kano model based on online comment data mining. In: 2018 IEEE 3rd International Conference on Big Data Analysis, ICBDA 2018, pp. 76–82 (2018)
46. Natee, S., Low, S.P., Teo, E.A.L.: Quality Function Deployment for Buildable and Sustainable Construction (2016)
47. Ginting, R., Riski Satrio, M.: Integration of Quality Function Deployment (QFD) and value engineering in improving the quality of product : a literature review. IOP Conf. Ser. Mater. Sci. Eng., 1003(1) (2020)

Cash is King, Isn't It? Payment Preferences and Switching Intentions of German Customers

Matthias Murawski(✉), Serena Scomparin, and Markus Bick

ESCP Business School, Berlin, Germany
{mmurawskiv,mbick}@escp.eu, serena.scomparin@edu.escp.eu

Abstract. In China, the traditional wallet with cash and credit cards is a distant memory as everything is done through the same app: WeChat. In Germany going out cashless and the idea of paying for coffee with the smartphone seems – at least partly – like science fiction, although research shows that cash is considered "inconvenient". Starting from a reflection on the two diametrically opposed examples, we attempt to firstly investigate the current payment preferences of German customers, before we secondly elaborate aspects regarding switching to alternative payment methods, i.e., mobile payments. We are wondering: Why do German customers prefer cash payments? and Which factors could affect the switch from cash to mobile payment methods for German customers? To answer these questions, we conducted a three-round Delphi study with eight experts and found, for example, that cash is still preferred because it is more practical as it is accepted by every merchant in Germany. Regarding the switching intentions, one major finding is that large retailers and other key players need to adopt mobile payments as their preferred system, so that customers can become more familiar with it.

Keywords: Cash payments · Customer preferences · Delphi study · Mobile payments · Switching intentions

1 Introduction

Digital innovations have been leading major changes causing entire systems (e.g., the payment system) to restructure. The race toward the shift to cashless economies has created pressure on firms and boosted the development of micro-payments that could potentially eliminate the inconvenience of using cash [1]. In China, for example, by simply scanning a QR Code from their WeChat account, customers can pay with their smartphone no matter if in the small mom-and-pop store around the corner or at a restaurant. Approximately 56% of Chinese transactions at the point-of-sale (POS) are dominated by third-party mobile payments, a share that is contented between only two non-bank service providers [2]. Very different however is the situation in Germany. Here mobile wallets are not only uncommon, but cash is the often preferred and sometimes even the only accepted form of payment. The comparative analysis carried out by Korella (2017) confirms that German customers prefer to use cash for small sums (up to 50 €)

Published by Springer Nature Switzerland AG 2021
D. Dennehy et al. (Eds.): I3E 2021, LNCS 12896, pp. 532–544, 2021.
https://doi.org/10.1007/978-3-030-85447-8_44

while cards are adopted for higher amounts [2]. Even in the context of the Covid-19 pandemic with its considerable impact on payment behavior [3], German customers hardly use mobile wallets. While there is a general shift from cash to cards, mobile wallets are used by approximately 13% of German smartphone owners only [4].

The ubiquity of smartphones has led to the exploration of new applications. Mobile payments for this matter refer to any purchase transaction carried through a mobile device [5, 6]. By storing several financial applications that allow such functionality, smartphones have now developed into micro-wallets [7], effectively substituting in some cases physical wallets [8]. Originally introduced to facilitate personal funds transfers between accounts and to allow e-commerce transactions, mobile wallets such as WeChat Pay and Alipay revolutionized customer behaviors and selection criteria [9]. In fact, omnipresence of smartphones, ease of transactions and hostility towards fees became the main reasons why users accepted this new format despite not being managed by the well-trusted banking sector [9]. Reasons for adoption of mobile payments have been investigated by information systems scholars. Pousttchi and Wiedemann (2007), for instance, explore factors influencing the adoption of mobile payments by the German market and find that user-friendliness and usefulness are two fundamental criteria [10]. Although convenience can improve the habitual use of digital wallets, privacy and security remain major concerns among consumers [1]. Yet in practice when approaching a checkout, people dispose of different instruments. Under this assumption, mobile wallets compete against the already well-known means of payment. Although Alaeddin et al. (2018) emphasize the possibility that mobile wallets could take over their physical equivalent, little further analyses can be found on this effect [8]. This is particularly true for the "cash- and card-oriented" German market. In addition, many existing studies addressing the German payment market were published before 2010 (e.g. [10]), emphasizing the need of an updated investigation. Filling this gap would not only be of value for researchers, but also for practitioners. In this context, we formulate the following two research questions (RQs): *RQ1: Why do German customers prefer cash payments? RQ2: Which factors could affect the switch from cash to mobile payment methods for German customers?*

Owing to the partly forecasting perspective of the research, the future-oriented conventional Delphi method is applied. The results of our qualitative research help to investigate the transition to cashless systems and the implications for the acceptance of the merge between social networking apps and mobile wallets as a new payment instrument in contrast to cash. This paper is composed of six sections. Section 2 contains the theoretical background. The research methodology is then outlined in Sect. 3. Section 4 summarizes the results while Sect. 5 compares them to existing academic knowledge and briefly discusses practical implications for managers. The paper concludes with Sect. 6.

2 Theoretical Background

2.1 Definitions

Mobile payments in technical terms are an information technology, but also a mean for customers to handle payments [10]. Mobile payment methods "include payments made using a mobile phone, either in-store or not in-store, as well as using an app to conveniently send and receive money without entering an IBAN" [11, p. 47]. They allow commercial transactions [12], which are operated through a credit card or a *mobile wallet*, meaning software applications for mobile devices that enable payment transactions [5]. In some cases, physical wallets have almost been replaced by mobile wallets allowing the customer to carry out in-store payments directly from their smartphone [13]. A *digital wallet* differs from traditional digital representation of cards, because it can also be financed through intra-wallets transfers or by direct connection to the bank account [9]. It allows to store sensitive data and credentials for mobile transactions [13]. Also, it allows to perform electronic transfers of different types [9], while mobile wallets are generally more suitable for transactions where the physical wallet is needed [14, 15]. Nonetheless the two terms *digital* and *mobile wallets* are very often used interchangeably as a synonym for mobile payments at the point-of-sale (POS) terminal [9].

Mobile payment systems are of two types depending on the communication technology. Gerpott and Meinert (2017) identify remote payment systems that are suited for purchases of digital and physical goods through online transactions (e.g., one-click bank transfer) or established mobile communication services (e.g., pay by call). They describe proximity payment systems as limited to purchases for goods at the POS in-store through short-range communication. This can be code scanning, like in the case of WeChat Pay where customers scan a QR code assigned to the merchant. The second type, already common in Germany with contactless cards, is Near Field Communication (NFC) where the payment is made by simply placing the mobile device within a maximum of 10 cm distance from the NFC POS terminal [15]. The limitation of NFC is that it only supports transactions up to a certain country-specific threshold above which the transaction needs to be authorized with a PIN code [15]. Many predict that PINs will soon become obsolete and that they will be replaced by biometric recognition which uses physical characteristics, such as fingerprints, face, voice, etc. as authentication measure [16]. Given that NFC technology in Germany is already present for contactless cards, mobile wallets could take advantage of this already available system. As this study aims at understanding the transition to alternative payment formats, a particular emphasis is given to payments for purchase, where mobile wallets offer a direct alternative to cash and credit cards, rather than payment of bills [5]. Cash is mainly used for those daily operations of small amounts, usually below 50 €, to pay for goods from a physical store [11]. Therefrom, the terms mobile payment and mobile wallet are used interchangeably to describe payments that are carried to a merchants' POS terminal using a service provided by a third-party payment on the mobile device.

2.2 Switching Intentions

In the shopping experience, the checkout phase is the moment customers become aware of the total price and finalize the payment [14]. While evidence shows that at the moment of the decision, most people in Germany still rely on cash for transactions at the manned POS [4, 11], some scholars investigated the presence of card and mobile premium effect resulting in higher willingness to pay for card or mobile payment transactions [14, 17]. In this scenario the decision of using mobile wallets cannot be analyzed in absolute terms, but rather relative to traditional instruments. According to the result found by Deutsche Bundesbank (2018) in a study with more than 2,000 individuals who responded to a questionnaire and filled a so-called payment diary, more than 90% of the respondents consider each of the following features as essential criteria for choosing a payment instrument: protection against financial loss, clear overview of spending, ease of use, familiarity and privacy, [11]. Rapidity (86%) and width of merchants' acceptance (82%) show less but still high values, but cash remains however the instrument able to fulfill most of all the requirements [11]. Results by Beutin and Harmsen (2019) confirm that skepticism toward mobile payments is driven by concerns on sharing confidential data with third parties and the risk of its misuse [18]. Past experiences are also key to understanding what drives purchases. The repetition of a behavior in a given context creates a direct association between the two, such that when a similar context is presented, the same response is triggered through memory recollection: this is what Wood and Neal (2009) referred to as *habit* [19]. The repetition of a consumer behavior can either be a form of habitual response, driven by context cues and performed regardless of people's goals, or the expression of a specific preference [19]. Habits are usually used as a default response when people are under time pressure or distracted, and they usually require multiple interventions to be changed [19]. Emphasizing on past experiences can be useful on two side: first, it can shed light on whether repetitive use of cash is driven by habits or specific preferences. Second, it could be a leverage factor to enhance adoption, because people that have already used smartphone to pay are more likely to use it repeatedly [20]. Customers will constantly seek for higher transparency and speed [21]. From the customers' view, transparency in a payment method is found in the form, meaning the ease of the overall experience and in the amount, the ability to track liquidity spent [22]. Falk et al. (2016) explain how cash fulfills both requirements due to the tangible possession, and how mobile payments are perceived even less transparent than cards which intangible nature makes it harder to keep track with liquidity [14]. The challenge for mobile wallets, when competing with an instrument of such trial usage, is creating an adequate user interface that is attractive and simple [7]. At the same time however, Lu (2019) points out that mobile wallets benefit of two types of convenience as opposed to cash: first, service providers can effectively bring their service closer to customer by leveraging on ubiquity of smartphones; second, they avoid the pain of handling cash (i.e., having change or dividing the bill at the restaurant) [7].

3 Research Design

Mobile payments can be considered as an information technology [10] and given this assumption the topic is usually studied through the application of technology acceptance models (e.g., 23). Although quantitative methodologies are the most common for exploring customers' approach to IT systems [5], for this study the Delphi methodology was chosen. Owing to the complexity of the research question which requires experts from different fields of expertise and since the topic would benefit more from the subjective judgments of a selected group than pure quantitative analyses, the Delphi method was considered appropriate. Furthermore, Löe et al. (2016) posit that in Delphi studies consensus among experts' opinions can be considered accountable for accurate forecasts [24]. Because the objective of this research is to postulate on the prospect of new payment formats in Germany, the future-oriented premise of the Delphi method fits our study appropriately.

3.1 Data Collection

The first distinctive characteristic of a Delphi study is the selection of the participants. Experts are pivotal to the success of the research; hence the panel was studied in terms of panel composition, group size and recruitment criteria. The conventional Delphi method usually relies on experts in one given area [24]. Given that mobile payments are part of a regulated ecosystem influenced by the interconnections of different stakeholders [25], a more diversified panel was considered more appropriate. Experts were therefore selected from different areas (see Table 1). In general, the size of the panel in Delphi studies varies depending on the topic assessed and based on the recruitment criteria used. The review on the application of Delphi method by Worrell et al. (2013) finds that the size of the panel can be of four participants if there are ideal circumstances, or else between ten and 30 members under typical circumstances [26]. In the case in which experts are selected from different sectors, then a group of five to ten members is considered acceptable [27]. Owning to the heterogenous composition of our panel, this research considered a panel size between five and eight acceptable. This study included both academicians and practitioners to guarantee a broader variety of perspectives. Aside from expertise, two more criteria were included: first a proficiency level of English, to prevent errors arising from language barriers; second, familiarity with the German market given the emphasis of the study. A total of 20 experts were contacted through direct email, LinkedIn, and personal networks, of which eight (three Germans, five Europeans) agreed to participate. Table 1 reports the list of members with the respective qualifications and area of expertise.

The second and third core characteristics of a Delphi study are anonymity and group communication. It is essential to prevent members from becoming aware of each other's identity to foster expressions of opinions free from pressure or influence as fears of embarrassment or public commitment are removed [28]. At every stage of the study, experts were given the opportunity to provide comments, modifications and suggestions to be integrated in the results and returned to the panel for further evaluation.

The goal of the first phase of data collection is related to the discovery of the issue. In order to avoid imposing pre-existing knowledge or the researcher view and to instead analyze data that is the result of the consolidated answers of the panel, round 1 was constructed following the conventional method. In a first step, several open questions were developed based on literature:

- Why do people prefer cash over mobile wallets for day-to-day operations?
- What are the main negative aspects users associate with mobile wallets?
- What are the main positive aspects users associate with mobile wallets?
- What are other external implications that influence the adoption and diffusion of mobile wallets?

To enhance clarity, in the introduction respondents were asked to consider (1) that the analysis of the customer segment focuses on Germany, and (2) that the primary emphasis of this study is on a customer perspective, although other factors may be considered relevant. Experts were then given approximately two weeks to answer and to send the completed word version via email. The objective of the following rounds is to validate the importance and to establish a ranking for the issue, that is assessing

Table 1. Panel of experts

	Sector	Field of expertise	Position
A	Strategic management	Academic, professional & research background in strategy, innovation and entrepreneurship	Academic professor & practitioner
B	Business development	Partner in international consulting and trade company. Experience in business development	Practitioner
C	Customer behavior	Academic, professional & research background in international marketing, pricing, quantitative methods and research methods	Academic professor
D	Financial services	Manager in a company for financial services. Experience in legal consulting	Practitioner
E	Payment methods & fin. services	Director of CRM and Fintech in firm of financial services. Experience in digital payment, mobile wallet, fin-tech, banking	Practitioner
F	Retail	CFO in a food retail and wholesale company. Experience in financial sector	Practitioner
G	Traditional banking	Head of acquiring in banking group. Experience in payments and business innovation	Practitioner
H	Mobile payment	Research background in mobile payment, banking & payment industry	Academic professor

and ranking the responses based on their importance [29]. Due to the nature of the initial questions, round 2 was constructed partially as a ranking list, where experts were asked to place items in order of importance, and partially in the form of statements. In the former case, categories for the ranking were proposed in randomized order to address the primacy effect bias pointed out by Skinner et al. (2015) [30]. In the latter case, consensus was measured using a 7-points Likert type scale. Here, numbers represented the degree of agreement, from 1 = extremely disagree, to 7 = extremely agree. Differently from the previous step, this phase was carried through an online platform (*SurveyHero.com*) and responses were collected over a period of one week. The final stage had the same architecture and format of the previous one, but this time the data was adapted to reflect the results of the previous round and to include the anonymized comments. Therefore, results of the previous round, including anonymized modifications, were sent back to the experts who this time, could deliberate based on the results from the consolidated responses of all the members. The data collection took place in March and April 2020.

3.2 Data Analysis

The answers from round 1 were analyzed following the "Grounded Theory re-envisioned" by Charmaz (2006) [31]. Codes and categories were developed from the raw data instead of coming from preconceived knowledge; collection and analysis of data happened simultaneously; constant comparative methods across data were used to find similarities and differences. The aim of the second and third round was to assess the degree of consensus within the panel, which can range from 55 to 100% agreement. Complete agreement is usually an unrealistic condition and when reached too quickly it could be a synonym that the topic is saturated or that the presentation of the results induced to a given answer [30]. Under these assumptions, this study considered a general agreement of 70% to be adequate. The majority of Delphi studies rely on central tendency measures and percentages as quantitative data analysis techniques [24]. For the ranking type results this was used in combination with Kendall coefficient of concordance, which is a non-parametric measure ranging from 0 to 1 (e.g., *0.1* = *very weak agreement, 0.9* = *unusually strong agreement*) and is an indicator of the degree of agreement achieved. For what concerns the Likert scale, a different approach was used. In this case, analysis was organized such that, any score above 5-points was considered as agreement and 70% needed to be achieved to have consensus. In addition to the above-mentioned methods, measures of central tendency, such as mean and standard deviation were also used.

During round 2 the experts provided comments and modifications which were to be incorporated in the results for round 3. To do so, two approaches were followed as explained by Sekayi and Kennedy (2017) [29]: if suggestions were to clarify or to complete the statement, without however changing the meaning of the original sentence, the latter was amended accordingly. However, when the modifications proposed were to alter completely the message, a new additional statement was created to the side of the old one. The results of the Likert scale evaluation are presented using Delphi diagrams elaborated by Pousttchi et al. (2015) [21].[1]

4 Findings

The study was made possible by the participation of eight experts (see Table 1). Although all the chosen members participated to R1, the following rounds only counted seven experts for R2 and six for R3 as two of them dropped out.

4.1 Reasons for Customers to Choose Cash

The results for this area of contribution demonstrate that understanding the prioritization process behind customers' decisions is neither evident nor easy to assess (Table 2). The

[1] More details are introduced along with Fig. 1.

following remarks build the answer to *RQ1*. At the end of R3, the group ranking confirmed that people still use cash instead of mobile payment, because the former is more practical as it is accepted by every merchant (mean = 8.67) and not because it is believed to have lower transaction costs (mean = 3.16). The iteration also estimated that such payment preference is influenced by the cultural heritage (mean = 8.5) and existing habitual behavioral patterns (mean = 7.83).

For this specific classification, "ease of use" referred to the speed of the transaction. By placing it fourth, experts effectively affirmed that customers prefer cash at the checkout, because they assume it to be faster than using mobile wallets. During R2, two respondents highlighted a strong similarity among four categories representing the perceived risk, namely "security" of the transaction, "trust" in electronic payments, "data protection" for the hostility toward sharing personal data and "traceability" as the reluctance toward feeling constantly controlled.

Table 2. Main findings why customers choose cash instead of mobile payment

R2	SD	**Mean**	**Mean**	SD	**R3**
Availability	3.41	**9.51**	**8.67**	2.58	Availability
Habit	3.44	**9.14**	**8.5**	2.81	Cultural background
Cultural background	3.82	**8.71**	**7.83**	3.06	Habit
Trust	0.79	**6.57**	**6.16**	2.32	Ease of use
Traceability	3.82	**6.29**	**5.83**	2.79	Perceived privacy
Ease of use	4.31	**6.29**	**5.5**	3.08	Control of liquidity
Control of liquidity	3.51	**6**	**5.33**	2.42	Tangible possession
Tangible possession	3.63	**5.86**	**5**	2.83	Data protection
Security	3.50	**5.71**	**5**	3.22	Security
Awareness	3.73	**4.71**	**3.33**	2.07	Awareness
Data protection	2.19	**4.14**	**3.16**	2.48	Perceived costs
Costs	2.94	**3.57**			
W = 0.28			**W = 0.31**		

Having considered the proximity in the position of "trust" and "traceability" we proceeded to combining them in a new category named "perceived privacy", which ranked fifth in R3. We also changed the reason "costs" (R2) to "perceived costs" (R3) following consistent remarks from the experts. Despite such remarks, the expert group seemed to consider each item differently, assigning distinct weights, exception made for "trust". In this specific case in fact, respondents seemed to agree that one of the first four reasons why customers prefer cash to mobile payment, is because they do not trust electronic payments (SD = 0.79). In round 3 however, only one expert still found the items similar, mentioning that all the categories representing perceived security were to be considered with analogous importance. According to the experts, people today still rely on cash more because they do not trust digital instruments or because they prefer not to leave any trace ("perceived privacy"), rather than because they assume cash will be a safer transaction ("security"). Owing to the divergency of opinions, the panel did not arrive at a sufficient consensus, thus Kendall's W remained low even after the third round (w = 0.31).

4.2 Switching Intentions

The findings presented in this subsection present the answer to *RQ2*. Figure 1 summarizes the key results on switching intentions to alternative payment methods according to the suggestion of Pousttchi et al. (2015) [21]:

- Each expert is represented by a square
- Above the horizontal there are the positive ratings while below the negative ones
- The color of each cell is a symbol for the degree of agreement, in which darker shades represents stronger agreement (–, + white; ++ or – grey)
- The major squares represent the responses for round 3 and the small column on the right the results of the previous round.

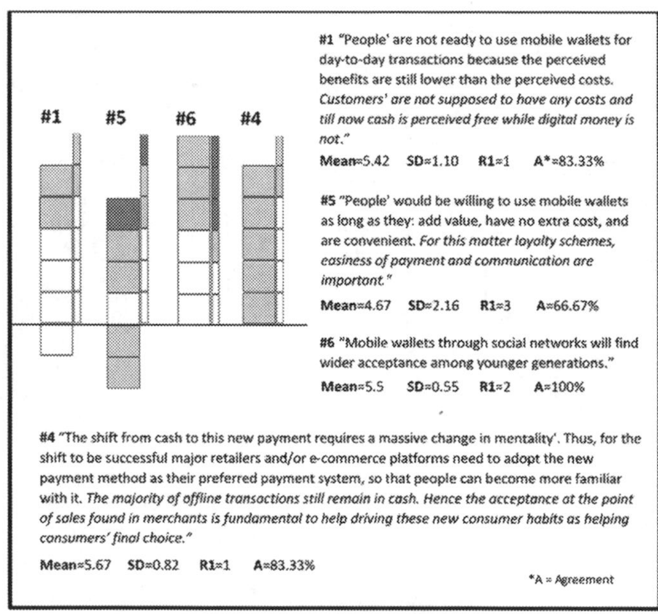

Fig. 1. Main findings for switching intention

During round 1, six respondents answered positively when asked whether people would be willing to use mobile wallets instead of cash for daily purchases. Interestingly however statement #1, which was first mentioned by one expert only, immediately received full consensus. In R3, despite one member shifted to a weak disagreement, the group answers validated (mean = 5.42) that customers are not ready to embrace this new instrument because the perceived costs outweigh the benefits. Item #5 revealed that, while it is shared opinion that providing added value at no extra cost would bring people closer to this new payment format, it is not so evident what such benefits should be. In fact, in R3 two members reconsidered their rating to "I mostly disagree" when considering loyalty schemes and ease as important added values. However, because there is low level of agreement (SD = 2.16), this statement cannot be considered valid. Acceptance of mobile wallets through social networks is said to be more important for younger generations (#6). This notion, already mentioned twice in R1, found universal almost unanimous support by all the members (mean = 5.5; A = 100%). In fact, this time all members take a clear positive position, although some reconsidered their "extreme" agreement to moderate. One reason for this may be that the existing target of social network is primarily digital natives. Nonetheless, experts are fully aware that this transition would require a big change in the mentality of customers, especially considering that the majority of the ordinary purchases are still settled with cash (#4). This is why in R3 respondents either confirmed or emphasized, with high level of agreement (SD = 0.82), that acceptance at the point of sale is key factor to drive new habits. Furthermore, two additional issues were raised during R2 and included in the list of R3 as separate items. One comment provided that customers would consider substituting physical with social wallets because they seek convenience as they strive to make their lives easier.

5 Discussion

Starting from the heavy reliance on cash, before understanding what can drive the adoption of a new payment it is important to investigate what could displace the existing option. In a context in which customers already possess a colored portfolio of payment instruments, mobile wallets would just be an additional way of terminating the shopping experience. Effectively, the major barrier to the diffusion of alternative payment methods is the tough competition against other instruments. Cash in fact, has a much longer history compared to mobile wallets, which are now just starting to enter the German market. Although it may seem evident, this is for cash a great competitive advantage because people are far beyond the familiarity phase: using cash now is the status quo. This research confirms the findings on habitual patterns of Wood and Neal (2009) by proposing that customers are so used to settle small purchases with cash, that whenever they find themselves in a similar situation, they will automatically do the same. The repetitive action however is not only the manifestation of a habit, but also of specific preferences that every customer has [19]. Our Delphi study reveals that customers look for payments that are easy to use, and they can trust. However, because they believe that cash better fulfills both requirements, people still prefer it to mobile payments. The findings also confirm the findings of Soman (2003), according to whom payment methods are transparent if they are easy to process and if they allow to keep track of liquidity [22]. Although it is not a top priority, our study shows people still believe it will be faster to manage their spending when possessing a physical wallet. The preference for material possession therefore also supports Falk et al. (2016), stating that in the eye of the customer the tangible nature of cash makes it feel more transparent than mobile payments [14]. However, the main reason why people persist using cash, it is not because it is perceived less costly than other options, but because people are certain that every merchant will accept it.

While acceptance at the POS is a strength for cash, for the other electronic payments it constitutes a major weakness, especially for mobile payments. Switching to mobile wallets means that one should be able to leave their home only with the smartphone. Logically, people will not feel comfortable with such idea, as long as they know this would prevent them from buying anything. In other words, like already pointed out by Gerpott and Meinert (2017), availability at the POS is one of the most important concerns for the adoption of new mobile wallets [15]. The results therefore suggest that a greater number of mobile payment POS terminals would help the diffusion of mobile payments. Like for regular mobile payments convenience and speed are two major benefits that customers expect to have if social networks were to offer mobile wallets. Our study supports that the convenience of mobile wallets stems from its ability to eliminate the hurdle of handling change [1], while still considering convenience, ease of use and speed separately. Furthermore, the results suggest that leveraging on the speed that mobile payment options provide could not only influence its usefulness, but also directly impacting the decision to use it. This supports Pousttchi et al. (2015) who estimated a constant increase in the demand for speed and transparency [21].

The results of this study allow to derive some implications for managers. When deciding to provide a substitute it is first necessary to understand what keeps customer from changing. As an incentive to change automatic repetitive behaviors, third party providers should emphasize on the convenience, speed and ease of use that mobile payments provide as opposed to cash. However, it is not sufficient to concentrate solely on the substitution of cash, because other instruments are threatening to address the same target. Contactless cards in fact already propose faster processing, they are accepted by most POS terminals and they are handled by financial services that customers already entrusted with their savings.

6 Conclusion

The main contribution of our study is an updated picture of the current German payment market in terms of customer preferences and switching intentions from cash to mobile payments. It appears that the evolution of payment methods will be influenced by the constant demand for more convenience, as people strive to make tasks easier and faster. In Germany, cash will continue to play an important role for transactions at the point-of-sale, if the technical infrastructure for digital formats remains underdeveloped, because customers do not have enough incentives to change their existing habits.

In terms of limitations of our research, significant payment behavior changes along with the Covid-19 pandemic are hardly covered in this analysis simply because the study has been conducted in the very beginning of the crisis in Germany (March/April 2020). However, recent studies (e.g. [4]) reveal that even in times of Corona, cash is indeed partly replaced by cards but the skepticism towards using mobile wallets remains. Thus, objectives and findings of our study are still relevant. Nonetheless, it would be interesting to investigate the long-term effects of the pandemic on mobile wallets usage in further studies. Also, the low consensus of the experts on some of the aspects (see 4.1) is a limitation of this study, so is the stop after three rounds of analysis. Two experts left the panel during the study which is another aspect that could bias the results. Therefore, further investigation (also applying other methods, e.g., large-scale consumer surveys) should be carried out to understand whether it is possible to identify a common explanation to the cash reliance in Germany or whether this behavior is dictated by individual preferences that significantly change from person to person. Despite the one-dimensional perspective of this study, the results bring forth the necessity to analyze the payment landscape from multiple angles. Thus, a stakeholder analysis may help future research building a more detailed picture of the payment ecosystem. Moreover, it might be value-adding to also integrate the opinions of experts of the Chinese market to better understand the differences between German and Chinese customers.

References

1. Ul Islam Khan, B., Olanrewaju, R.F., Baba, A., Langoo, A.A., Assad, S.: A compendious study of online payment systems: past developments, present impact, and future considerations. Int. J. Adv. Comput. Sci. Appl. **8** (2017)
2. Korella, J.L.: Outcomes of a comparative study on retail payment behaviour in China and Germany. https://www.ecb.europa.eu/pub/conferences/shared/pdf/20171130_ECB_BdI_conference/presentation_korella.pdf
3. Auer, R., Cornelli, G., Frost, J.: Covid-19, cash, and the future of payments. BIS Bull. **3** (2020). Bank for International Settlements
4. Deutsche Bundesbank: Payment Behaviour in Germany in 2020 – Making Payments in the Year of the Coronavirus pandemic. Survey on the Use of Payment Instruments. https://www.bundesbank.de/resource/blob/858022/648f4ff4f75ba2fe61a32ffd373ce34d/mL/zahlungsverhalten-in-deutschland-2020-data.pdf
5. Dahlberg, T., Mallat, N., Ondrus, J., Zmijewska, A.: Past, present and future of mobile payments research: a literature review. Electron. Commer. Res. Appl. **7**, 165–181 (2008)
6. Ozcan, P., Santos, F.M.: The market that never was: turf wars and failed alliances in mobile payments. Strateg. Manag. J. **36**, 1486–1512 (2015)
7. Lu, L.: Mobile payments—why they are so successful? Open J. Bus. Manag. **07**, 1131–1143 (2019)
8. Alaeddin, O., Altounjy, R., Zainudin, Z., Kamarudin, F.: From physical to digital: investigating consumer behaviour of switching to mobile wallet. Polish J. Manag. Stud. **17**, 18–30 (2018)
9. Klein, A.: Is China's new payment system the future? https://www.brookings.edu/research/is-chinas-new-payment-system-the-future/
10. Pousttchi, K., Wiedemann, D.: What influences consumers' intention to use mobile payments? Proceedings of the 6th Annual Global Mobility Roundtable, pp. 1–16 (2007)
11. Deutsche Bundesbank: Payment Behavior in Germany in 2017—Fourth Study of the Utilization of Cash and Cashless Payment Instruments. https://www.bundesbank.de/en/publications/reports/studies/payment-behaviour-in-germany-in-2017-737278
12. Au, Y.A., Kauffman, R.J.: The economics of mobile payments: understanding stakeholder issues for an emerging financial technology application. Electron. Commer. Res. Appl. **7**, 141–164 (2008)
13. Shin, D.-H.: Towards an understanding of the consumer acceptance of mobile wallet. Comput. Hum. Behav. **25**, 1343–1354 (2009)

14. Falk, T., Kunz, W.H., Schepers, J.J., Mrozek, A.J.: How mobile payment influences the overall store price image. J. Bus. Res. **69**, 2417–2423 (2016)
15. Gerpott, T.J., Meinert, P.: Who signs up for NFC mobile payment services? Mobile network operator subscribers in Germany. Electron. Commer. Res. Appl. **23**, 1–13 (2017)
16. Clearbridge Mobile: How Biometric Authentication is Shaping the Future of Security in Mobile Banking. https://clearbridgemobile.com/biometric-authentication-shaping-future-mobile-banking/
17. Boden, J., Maier, E., Wilken, R.: The effect of credit card versus mobile payment on convenience and consumers' willingness to pay. J. Retail. Consum. Serv. **52**, 101910 (2020)
18. Beutin, N., Harmsen, M.: Mobile Payment Report 2019. https://www.pwc.de/de/digitale-transformation/pwc-studie-mobile-payment-2019.pdf
19. Wood, W., Neal, D.T.: The habitual consumer. J. Consum. Psychol. **19**, 579–592 (2009)
20. de Kerviler, G., Demoulin, N.T., Zidda, P.: Adoption of in-store mobile payment: are perceived risk and convenience the only drivers? J. Retail. Consum. Serv. **31**, 334–344 (2016)
21. Pousttchi, K., Moormann, J., Felten, J.: The impact of new media on bank processes: a Delphi study. Int. J. Electron. Bus. **12**, 1 (2015)
22. Soman, D.: The effect of payment transparency on consumption: quasi-experiments from the field. Mark. Lett. **14**, 173–183 (2003)
23. Davis, F.D.: Perceived usefulness, perceived ease of use, and user acceptance of information technology. MIS Q. **13**, 319 (1989)
24. de Loë, R.C., Melnychuk, N., Murray, D., Plummer, R.: Advancing the state of policy delphi practice: a systematic review evaluating methodological evolution, innovation, and opportunities. Technol. Forecast. Soc. Chang. **104**, 78–88 (2016)
25. Hedman, J., Henningsson, S.: The new normal: market cooperation in the mobile payments ecosystem. Electron. Commer. Res. Appl. **14**, 305–318 (2015)
26. Worrell, J.L., Di Gangi, P.M., Bush, A.A.: Exploring the use of the Delphi method in accounting information systems research. Int. J. Account. Inf. Syst. **14**, 193–208 (2013)
27. Clayton, M.J.: Delphi: a technique to harness expert opinion for critical decision-making tasks in education. Educ. Psychol. **17**, 373–386 (1997)
28. Avella, J.R.: Delphi panels: research design, procedures, advantages, and challenges. Int. J. Dr. Stud. **11**, 305–321 (2016)
29. Sekayi, D., Kennedy, A.: Qualitative Delphi method: a four round process with a worked example. Qual. Rep. **22**, 2755–2763 (2017)
30. Skinner, R., Nelson, R.R., Chin, W.W., Land, L.: The Delphi method research strategy in studies of information systems. Commun. Assoc. Inf. Syst. **37** (2015)
31. Charmaz, K.: Constructing Grounded Theory. SAGE, Los Angeles, (2014)

Mining Segmentation Patterns Using e-Commerce Retail Data: An Experience Report

Anastasia Griva(✉) and Denis Dennehy

Lero - The Science Foundation Ireland Research Centre for Software, NUI Galway, Galway, Ireland
anastasia.griva@nuigalway.ie

Abstract. The goal of this experience report is to study and advance our understanding on visit and shopper segmentation in retail. Current segmentation studies mainly use customers as unit of analysis to identify shopper segments and mine patterns in their behaviors. Another stream of studies utilizes shopper baskets or visits to perform basket/visit segmentation and elicit shopping patterns. However, given the fact that we live in the era of personalization focusing solely on visits leads on neglecting the shopper. On the other hand, focusing solely on shoppers and their behavior over time, leads on losing his/her daily purchasing behavior. In this study we combine shopper and visit segmentation and we apply data mining to identify purchase patterns using data from an e-commerce grocery retailer.

Keywords: Retail analytics · Business analytics · Data mining · e-commerce

1 Introduction

In contemporary retail, both practitioners and researchers agree that old-school shopper segmentation is not enough and cannot describe the new shopper habits and preferences. They suggest that retail nowadays, demands a transformation of shopper segmentation approaches. This happens since the modern shopper has changed. Nowadays, the shopper performs a complex shopper journey with the purpose to satisfy his/her increasing demands [1]. Shopper behavior is no longer predictable; it is changing through time and, even, between shopping visits in the same store [2]. Thus, there is a need to focus on shoppers' visits and perform visit segmentation to cope with shoppers' changing behavior and perform data mining to identify segmentation patterns.

Practitioners have coined the term "shopping mission" to refer to the intention behind a shopper's visit [3, 4]. Similarly, researchers [5], [6] agree with practitioners and suggest that we should pay attention to each shopper visit which reflects the actual shopper needs. Looking at each specific shopper visit, instead of a shopper's total buying behavior over many visits, provides a better view of the shopper desires that change frequently due to unpredicted events e.g., COVID-19 pandemic. Approaches and studies that respects the different views of shoppers and considers their heterogenous behaviors, are becoming crucial [7].

Published by Springer Nature Switzerland AG 2021
D. Dennehy et al. (Eds.): I3E 2021, LNCS 12896, pp. 545–551, 2021.
https://doi.org/10.1007/978-3-030-85447-8_45

2 Background

Looking into the segmentation literature we can classify the pertinent studies in two categories: those focusing on shopper segmentation, and those that focus on visit segmentation. The first group of studies usually perform clustering as the data mining approach to identify patterns on everything a shopper has purchased in bulk, and overlook the shopping intentions, and missions of each shopper, which by nature are not the same in every store visit. Regarding the second group of studies, they examine shoppers' visits, usually by using association rule mining to perform visit segmentation [1], [8–11] e.g. a form of visit segmentation is market basket analysis.

In this study we combine visit and shopper segmentation, as we utilize visit segments (or else shopping missions) to then perform customer segmentation and identify the characteristics of the derived customer segments. To the best of our knowledge, there is paucity of studies that perform visit segmentation and use the derived segments to further extract and identify shopper segment. Current studies either perform visit segmentation, or shopper segmentation.

Below we describe the data used to perform visit and shopper segmentation, and the respective segmentation results. Then, we conclude our practitioners' paper via presenting the practical implications of our study

3 Data Analysis

3.1 The Dataset

We used point-of-sales (POS) data from the e-commerce store of a small retail chain named "XYZ" having 222 stores in the urban areas of Greece country. Retailer provided us with all the transactions that had been performed using their website within a year by retailer's shoppers using loyalty card. Thus, we received more than 120 billion product records that correspond to 15 billion transactions/baskets performed by 1.120.021 shoppers. A sample of the given dataset is provided in Table 1. Here, we should admit that almost the 96% of the total retail chain transactions happen using loyalty card; thus, sample is representative. The average basket costed 16,7€ and contained 8,1 products from 4,9 different product categories.

Table 1. Data sample

Basket_ID	Date	Barcode	Sum_Units	Sum_Value	Card_ID
1103084867	1/3/2021	800220505783	2	1.96	9160003751260
1103084867	1/3/2021	520139501183	1	5.349993	9160003751260
1092750793	1/3/2021	520423907421	6	1.740015	9164012915385
1106160983	1/3/2021	211069400000	1	0.749817	9162005811409
1108695491	1/3/2021	520286400380	−2	−0.6	NULL

3.2 The Analysis

In this section first we perform visit segmentation to identify customers' shopping missions or else the visit segments, and then we utilize these visit segments to perform shopper segmentation. In both the segmentation phases we use clustering as a data mining technique to derive the shopping patterns.

Visit Segmentation/Shopping Missions

Drawing on the method suggested by (Griva, Bardaki, Pramatari, & Papakiriakopoulos, 2018; Griva, Bardaki, Pramatari, & Doukidis, 2021), we identified customers shopping missions or else the visit segments. In a nutshell, we conducted clustering with expectation maximization algorithm on the product categories the shoppers purchased on each visit. This way we identified 7 distinct shopping missions, as shown in Fig. 1.

Main course		Snacks and beverages		Pastry making		Health and beauty		Breakfast		House cleaning and maintenance		Sandwich	
fresh vegetables	82 %	beverages	35 %	kit desserts	27 %	shower gel	63 %	coffee	50 %	house cleaning	65 %	counter cheese	63 %
counter red meat	64 %	salty snacks	24 %	sugar	25 %	shampoo	50 %	cereals	31 %	paper tissue and rolls	61 %	deli counter	61 %
counter poultry	60 %	chips	22 %	fresh milk	25 %	oral care	45 %	marmalade	27 %	laundry	59 %	bread slices	47 %
counter- fishmonger	47 %	beers	21 %	flour	24 %	women haircare	41 %	toast bread	23 %	dishwashers	56 %	pies	19 %
bread slices	44 %	biscuits	20 %	confectionary	24 %	facecare	29 %	packed sliced cheese	22 %	food storage	55 %	packed sliced cheese	16 %
pasta	27 %	spirits	20 %	cocoa	23 %	deodorants	25 %	yogurt - desserts	20 %	house and garden	14 %	packed ham slices	15 %
packed salad	26 %	sweets	19 %	coffee	23 %	sanitary protection	13 %	cookies	19 %	linen	13 %	bread	10 %
bread	20 %	deserts	18 %	culinary aids	21 %	bodycare	13 %	fresh milk	17 %	paper- schools	13 %	packed salads	5 %
counter cheese	18 %	watter	17 %	margarine	20 %	baby care	12 %	long-life milk	16 %	DIY and car	12 %		
fresh fruits	18 %	juices & smoothies	16 %	eggs	20 %	conditioner	9 %	bakery sweets	15 %	insecticides	11 %		
deli counter	15 %	wines	16 %	butter	20 %	clothing	8 %	juices & smoothies	14 %				
tinned tomatoes	14 %	fresh milk	15 %	spices and herbs	17 %	make up	7 %	honey	14 %				
biological vegetables	12 %	fresh vegetables	13 %	milk cream - sandy	17 %	men haircare	7 %						
table sauces	10 %	beverages	11 %	sweeteners	16 %	perfumes	5 %						
frozen vegetables	10 %	processed fruits	8 %	chocolates	16 %	accessories	4 %						
butter	9 %	empty cans	6 %	powder milk	7 %	vitamins	3 %						
oils and fats	9 %	party equipment	5 %										
dressing	9 %												
rice	8 %												
seafood	7 %												
ethnic food	5 %												
white cheese	4 %												
flour	3 %												

Fig. 1. Resulting visit segments/ shopping missions

Shopper Segmentation Based on the Visit Segments

Afterwards, we exploited the loyalty cards data, to detect the visit segments or else the shopping missions a shopper performed during his/her purchase history. We rated each shopper (Table 2) with a value ranging from 1 (low) to 5 (high) according to the s/he visited the store for each mission during the whole year weeks (weeks of presence).

In more detail, to calculate this value we used as benchmark the weeks of presence of all the shoppers per mission. Thus, this value is different for the various shopping missions. For example, a value equals 5 at the breakfast mission is not the same with a 5 into house cleansing and maintenance, as a shopper purchases more often breakfast than house cleansing products.

We used text mining to extract more meta-data from the available product descriptions. Thus, we identified whether a product is premium, private label (PL), and/or biological. Also, we classified the products based on their descriptions into children or elder usage. In addition, we added a binary flag in the cases that the product sold was in promo. Hence, we enriched our data mining table (i.e., fact table) by adding more meta-data per customer. Then, we utilized shoppers' fact table as input in the data mining model, we executed clustering with k-means algorithm, and we segmented shoppers based on the missions they had performed during their yearly visits.

We shaped ten shopper clusters i.e., ten shopper segments. Each shopper is assigned to one shopper segment. Segment 1 contains the 4,6% of shoppers. These shoppers visited the store for all the identified shopping missions as they are rated with five in all of them. Thus, here we have the more loyal shoppers that spend more than 281,83€ per month. These shoppers purchase many private label (PL), baby and biological products. Similarly, segment 2 contains loyal shoppers, as they are rated with five in almost all the missions. This leads them spend almost 100€ less (197,58€) than the previous segment. In addition, shoppers in this segment purchase more premium products. Closing, segments 1 and 2 could be declared as "the most loyal retailer's shoppers" that seem to have this retail chain as primary for their purchases. Thus, customer retention strategies could be more appropriate for these two segments.

Similarly, we identified the rest shopper segments based on the identified shopping missions. Table 2 presents the resulting shopper segments and their characteristics. Based on the descriptive statistics derive for each segment and the patterns identified regarding the purchased shopping missions we inferred shoppers' loyalty per segment.

Table 2. Segment characteristics

Segment No	Size	Average monthly value	Shoppers' loyalty classification	Segment characteristics
1	4,6%	281,83	Very high loyalty	Purchase all the shopping missions Preference in bio, baby and PL products
2	4,9%	197,58	Very high loyalty	Purchase all the shopping missions Preference in premium products
3	5,4%	121	High loyalty	Purchase all shopping missions but seem to visit a second retail chain for non-food products Preference in PL products, elderly products,
4	5,1%	128,2	High loyalty	Purchase all shopping missions but seem to visit a second retail chain for food products

(*continued*)

Table 2. (*continued*)

Segment No	Size	Average monthly value	Shoppers' loyalty classification	Segment characteristics
5	9,1%	85,6	Medium loyalty	This retailer is not their primary choice Purchase occasionally all shopping missions Prefer baby and bio products
6	6,9%	59,48	Medium loyalty	This retailer is not their primary choice Purchase only food shopping missions
7	10,9%	61,65	Medium loyalty	This retailer is not their primary choice Purchase only non-food shopping missions High preference in promo products
8	14,0%	53,95	Low loyalty	Purchase missions such as breakfast, sandwich and personal care and hygiene Visit stores close to student campuses
9	18,1%	24,33	No loyalty	Purchase only promotional products from various shopping missions
10	21,0%	26,05	No loyalty	Have visited retailer's store only 2 times per year and purchase premium products across all missions that were in promo

4 Conclusions

Business analytics can be powerful for companies in various domains ranging from software development [12] to retail [1]. In this study, we focused on retailing and we analyzed data from the e-commerce store of a grocery retailer. Our goal was to combine shopper and visit segmentation to showcase the potential of retail analytics. First, in the first phase of our analysis, we used a method to identify visit segments and patterns in shopper visit behaviors from the available data. Then, in our second phase we used these segments combined with loyalty and other data, and we applied data mining through clustering to identify loyalty-based shopper segments. From a research perspective these is lack of studies that combine shopper and visit segmentation. Researchers mainly focus on the first, and more recently there are some examples related to the second.

As an experience report, below we focus on the practical implications this study offers.

The practical value of this work is stressed when considering the business decisions, it can support. This analysis can be used and evolves into a tool for designing bundled promotions for product categories belonging to the same segment. For example, retailers may plan cross-coupon programs for addressing the needs of customers visiting the store with a specific purpose in mind. Alternatively, it can be used as the basis of a recommendation system for real-time purchases in retail stores. It can suggest to the customers products that they might have forgotten to buy, considering their prior or current visit(s).

Similarly, we can create offline and online product catalogues for specific visit segments. The extracted knowledge could also be valuable for advertising purposes; for instance, instead of making advertisements of specific product categories, retailers could advertise bundled product categories that correspond to a shopping mission, e.g., breakfast products advertisements.

On the other hand, the customer visit segments can dictate a new redesigned retail store physical or web store layout. For example, the product categories in the same visit segment could be positioned in nearby store aisles and shelves. Considering the bigger picture, we can move from a category-based layout to a mission-based layout that can help customers locate products in the store more easily and buy more in less time [8, 13]. Alternatively, second in-store placement spots can be detected.

Further, the value of such a system could be further enhanced when we use the resulting visit segments to perform shopper segmentation. By looking into the shopping missions that each shopper performs in all the stores of a retail chain, we can boost shopper marketing activities. Shopper segmentation based on the identified shopping missions can aid retailers identify selling gaps and opportunities and enhance personalization.

The results of Table 2 can be of significant value to the marketers. Based on these they can build retention strategies for the very high loyal segments, customer development strategies for the high and medium loyal segments, and customer attraction strategies for the less loyal segments. This way they can approach and treat the various loyalty segments they have differently, based on their actual behavior and needs.

Additionally, the store manager could reengineer store operations management and replenishment strategies by ordering groups of products based on the identified visit segments. Additionally, this approach could be even utilized to rearrange and modify a retailer's warehouse, by placing in nearby aisles products matching online orders to decrease order-picking time.

As it is obvious our study includes several limitations, which can all be considered and resolved in future studies. For instance, in this study we extract patterns using data from the e-commerce website of a grocery retailer, however, we neglect that some shopping gaps might be fulfilled in retailer's physical stores etc. Thus, from a marketing perspective future research may examine the omni-channel shopper behaviors. Moreover, from a technical perspective, future research may focus on mining behavioral shopping patterns using other data mining techniques such as graph mining etc. Closing, from an IS perspective future studies may focus on how retailers can make sense of business analytics and segmentation [14].

Acknowledgements. Dr. Griva received funding for this research from the European Union's Horizon 2020 research and innovation program under Marie Sklodowska-Curie grant 754489 and from the Science Foundation Ireland grant 13/RC/2094_2.

References

1. Griva, A., Bardaki, C., Pramatari, K., Doukidis, G.: Factors affecting customer analytics: evidence from three retail cases. Inf. Syst. Front. (2021)
2. Sorensen, H., et al.: Fundamental patterns of in-store shopper behavior. J. Retail. Consum. Serv. **37**(2017), 182–194 (2017)
3. Griva, A.: Data-driven innovation in shopper marketing: a business analytics approach for visit segmentation in the retail industry. Department of Management Science & Technology, Athens University of Economics and Business (2019)
4. Griva, A., Bardaki, C., Sarantopoulos, P., Papakiriakopoulos, D.: A data mining-based framework to identify shopping missions. In: MCIS 2014 Proceedings (2014)
5. Bell, D.R., Corsten, D., Knox, G.: From point of purchase to path to purchase: how preshopping factors drive unplanned buying. J. Mark. **75**(1), 31–45 (2011)
6. Walters, R.G., Jamil, M.: Exploring the relationships between shopping trip type, purchases of products on promotion, and shopping basket profit. J. Bus. Res. **56**(1), 17–29 (2003)
7. Rust, R.T., Huang, M.-H.: The service revolution and the transformation of marketing science. Mark. Sci. **33**(2), 206–221 (2014)
8. Cil, I.: Consumption universes based supermarket layout through association rule mining and multidimensional scaling. Expert Syst. Appl. **39**(10), 8611–8625 (2012)
9. Beck, N., Rygl, D.: Categorization of multiple channel retailing in multi-, cross-, and omni-channel retailing for retailers and retailing. J. Retail. Consum. Serv. **27**, 170–178 (2015)
10. Boztuğ, Y., Reutterer, T.: A combined approach for segment-specific market basket analysis. Eur. J. Oper. Res. **187**(1), 294–312 (2008)
11. Griva, A., Bardaki, C., Pramatari, K., Papakiriakopoulos, D.: Retail business analytics: customer visit segmentation using market basket data. Expert Syst. Appl. **100**(2018), 1–16 (2018)
12. Conboy, K., Mikalef, P., Dennehy, D., Krogstie, J.: Using business analytics to enhance dynamic capabilities in operations research: a case analysis and research agenda. Eur. J. Oper. Res. **281**(2020), 656–672 (2020)
13. Sarantopoulos, P., Theotokis, A., Pramatari, K., Roggeveen, A.L.: The impact of a complement-based assortment organization on purchases. J. Mark. Res., 1–20 (2019)
14. Zamani, E.D., Griva, A., Spanaki, K., O'Raghallaigh, P., Sammon, D.: Making sense of business analytics in project selection and prioritisation: insights from the start-up trenches. Inf. Technol. People (2021)

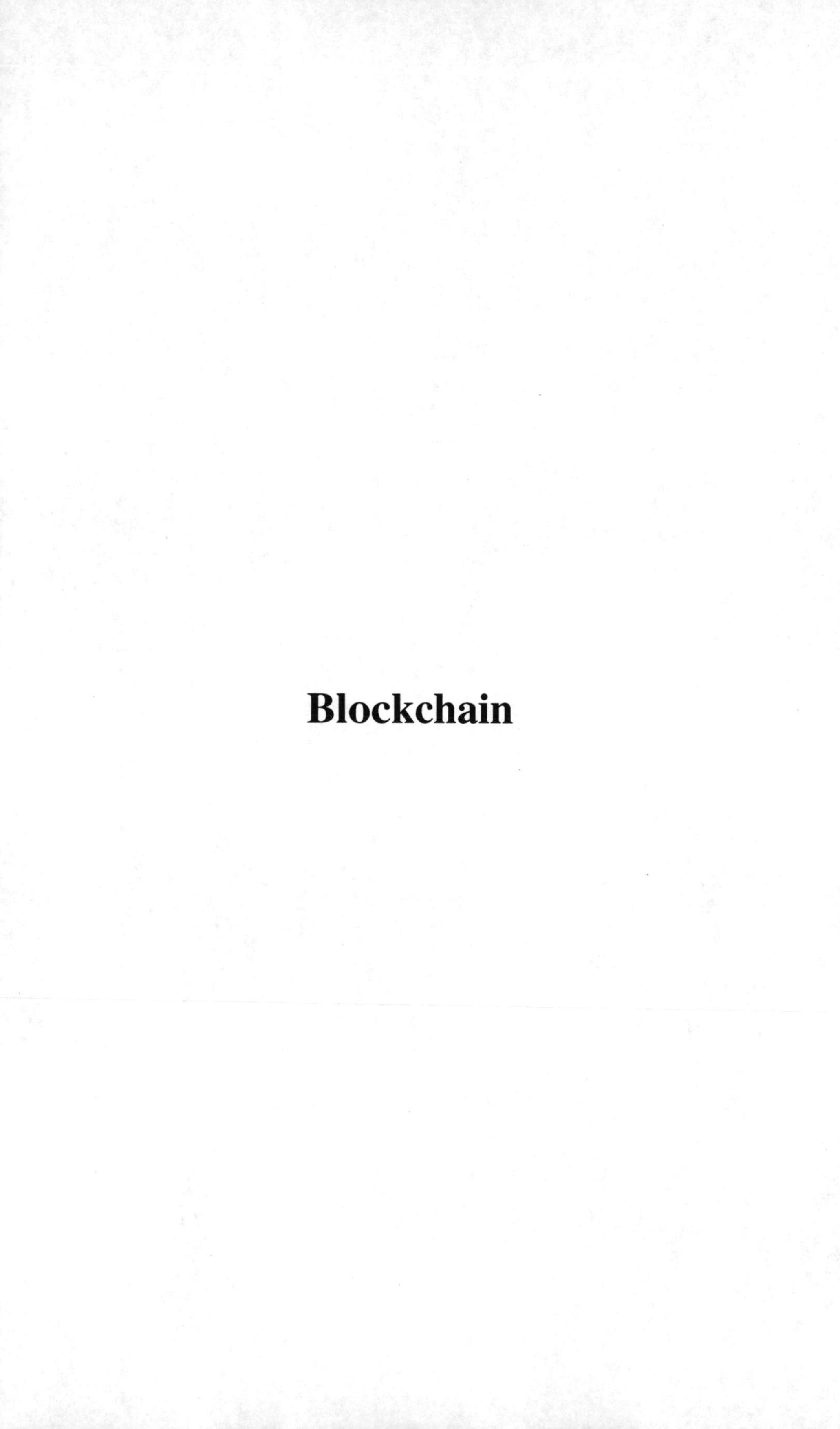

Blockchain

Blockchain in a Business Model: Exploring Benefits and Risks

Davit Marikyan[1(✉)], Savvas Papagiannidis[1], Omer Rana[2], and Rajiv Ranjan[3]

[1] Newcastle University Business School, 5 Barrack Road, Newcastle Upon Tyne NE14SE, UK
{d.marikyan2,savvas.papagiannidis}@newcastle.ac.uk

[2] School of Computer Science and Informatics, Cardiff University, Cardiff CF24 3AA, UK
ranaof@cardiff.ac.uk

[3] School of Computing, Newcastle University, 1, Urban Sciences Building, Science Square, Newcastle Upon Tyne NE4 5TG, UK
raj.ranjan@newcastle.ac.uk

Abstract. Although a blockchain has the potential to redefine value creation, delivery and capture activities in organisations, research on business model innovation from a blockchain perspective is still developing. This paper provides an analysis of literature on the use of blockchain in business model innovation. This analysis reconciles the technological and management perspectives to explore blockchain technology characteristics in relation to benefits and risks for business models. The findings contribute to the emerging stream of research discussing the business implications of innovative technologies, describing how blockchain networks can have an impact on business processes.

Keywords: Blockchain · Business model innovation · Digital transformation

1 Introduction

A business model is the logic of doing business and a firm's activities directed at creating competitive advantage and improving company offerings to deliver value for all stakeholders involved [1]. Firms digitalise their business models to improve business competitiveness in the realities of the dynamic market, technological innovations and changing customer needs [2]. One of the technological innovations that has disrupted the way of doing business is the 'blockchain' [3]. This is a distributed ledger technology that records and stores digital data in blocks across multiple locations in the network connected via cryptography, thus ensuring the immutability of records [4, 5]. Originally used in the financial sector, nowadays the blockchain has found an application in a wide range of digital data transactions across multiple industries.

The literature on business model innovation and blockchains is under-researched. There are a few studies that have examined the impact of blockchains in creating strategic capabilities, without an explicit exploration of the role of technology characteristics in value creation, delivery and capture, though [7]. Also, the papers exploring the role of

Published by Springer Nature Switzerland AG 2021
D. Dennehy et al. (Eds.): I3E 2021, LNCS 12896, pp. 555–566, 2021.
https://doi.org/10.1007/978-3-030-85447-8_46

blockchains in firms' value chains discussed only the positive effects of the technology on firms' performance (Chong et al. 2019; Morkunas et al. 2019; Schlecht et al. 2021). Consequently, the research has paid no attention to technology functions that potentially lower business value.

To fill the gaps in research, this study pursues two objectives. First, the paper examines different types of blockchain and the technical characteristics. We analyse the literature to understand how open, closed and consortium blockchain networks differ by the degree of control, data validation mechanisms, participants' access to data and operational complexity. Second, the paper draws on prior literature in the domain of business model innovation to analyse the role of blockchain technical characteristics in companies' value chains. We discuss how data access and validation mechanisms, the degree of operational complexity and control can be beneficial and risky for companies' value chains. Benefits and risks are mapped and explained in relation to the stages of business model innovation, namely, value creation, delivery and capture.

2 Business Model Innovation: A Blockchain Perspective

2.1 Business Model Innovation

A business model defines the logic of a firm by articulating the methods of value creation and delivery, and outlining associated costs and revenues [11]. For any company to grow in the market, a business model needs to be under constant improvement to generate a new value [12]. The transformation of the business model concerns value creation, value delivery and value capture functions [13, 14]. Value creation is rooted in resources/capabilities, technology, partnership networks and activities, representing sources of competitive advantage [13]. The value delivery function defines the ways in which offerings are delivered to customers [1]. It includes the modelling of company offerings, identifying customer segments/markets, customer relationships and promotion channels [13, 14]. Value capture concerns the activities that are directed at ensuring the company's long-term development [13, 14]. Firms may innovate the value capturing mechanism by adjusting revenue generation schemes and cost structures [13, 14].

The changes in value creation, delivery and capture can reflect the introduction of new activities, a new structure and/or a new form of governance of company activities. These changes result in the creation of novel customer experiences and offerings or lead to operational improvements captured by four value drivers, namely novelty, lock-in, complementarity and efficiency. Novelty captures the degree of innovation introduced to activities. Lock-in refers to the value-added and bundled to an existing offering, which increases switching costs. Complementarity relates to a value-enhancing added offering. Efficiency refers to cost-savings realised by interrelating activities [47].

2.2 Blockchain

The adoption of the blockchain in organisations could potentially drive business model innovation by bringing new value creation, delivery and capture mechanisms. A blockchain is defined as *"a technology which made possible to build an immutable, distributed, always available, secure and publicly assessable repository of data (ledgers), which relies on a distributed consensus protocol to manage this repository (e.g., to decide what valid new data to include) in a distributed manner"* [15]. Technically, a blockchain is not a single technology, but rather a protocol operated on a distribution ledger [16, 17]. The distribution system works as a *data validation mechanism,* making data exchange secure and trustable. Data is inscribed into blocks that are stored on the computers of all actors of the network. The blocks are cryptographically protected, making data difficult to tamper with. The inclusion of a new piece of data is controlled by the consensus mechanism [18], while the implementation of the rules of transactions are controlled by smart contracts [19]. A smart contract is triggered automatically when the conditions of negotiations are met, thus eliminating the need for a trusted intermediary to oversee a transaction [19]. Although it is suggested that technology can offer a novel service and an efficient and reliable channel of data exchange [8, 9], it can cause privacy, scalability and interoperability challenges [20]. Such risks could potentially undermine the success of business model innovation.

There are public, private and consortium blockchains, that differentiated by the degree of *data accessibility*, *decentralised control* and *operational complexity* they provide [9, 16]. A public blockchain does not restrict access to data, as the participation in the network is free for all actors [16]. The fact that all parties can see transactions makes it the subject of privacy concerns [9]. Since records are duplicated for a large number of participants, it is almost impossible to alter data, which is more secure. Public blockchain services are completely decentralised and uncontrollable by any party [17]. Given that an open blockchain is larger because of the number of actors, it requires more computational power and complex mechanisms to keep data secure [9, 17]. Private and consortium blockchains are similar in terms of the conditions of participation in transactions [17]. The participation is based on permission, which means that the details of transactions are accessible for reading and validation only by the participants of the network [16]. The networks are smaller, which implies some risk of data tampering, although they are easier to operate and produce greater throughput (the frequency of transactions per second) [9, 17]. When it comes to the degree of decentralisation, a private blockchain is controlled by a group, while a consortium one is partially centralised [17].

The three types of blockchain have inherent benefits and risks for the company value chain, stemming from their technical characteristics (data validation, data accessibility, operational efficiency and decentralised control) (Table 1). A blockchain can create value by facilitating collaborations and controlling value, deliver value by maximising network effects, and capture value by enabling cost efficiencies. The deployment of a blockchain can also destroy value by making transactions inflexible and undermining privacy, creating scalability challenges and incurring additional costs. The following sections will provide a detailed discussion of the technical characteristics of public, consortium and private blockchain technologies, resulting in benefits and risks for business model innovation.

Table 1. Blockchain characteristics in relation to benefits & risks for business model innovation.

Value chain stage	Benefits and risks for BMI	Public blockchain	Consortium blockchain	Private blockchain
		Permission-less access, validation mechanism, lack of control, decentralised, high complexity	Permissioned access, validation mechanism, some degree of control, partially decentralised, medium complexity	Permissioned access, validation mechanism, high degree of control, centralised, low complexity
Value creation	Trustable collaboration	X	X	
	Inflexible collaboration	X	X	
	Controlled value		X	X
	Privacy issue	X		
Value delivery	Network Effect	X		
	Scalability Challenge	X		
Value capture	Cost Efficiency		X	X
	Increased Investment	X		

3 Value Creation, Delivery and Capture: A Blockchain Perspective

3.1 Value Creation

Trustable Collaboration – Inflexible Transactions: Blockchain technology can enable the development of a platform facilitating collaborative interaction, affecting the company's value chain. *Trustable collaboration* is an important asset for value creation as it ensures the development of ideas and the co-creation of value by horizontally integrating company stakeholders [16, 21, 22]. Collaboration between stakeholders serves as a strategic success factor for the creation of novel solutions [23]. Stakeholders receive the ability to control the development of value offerings by leveraging the potential of the blockchain system to maintain the free exchange of ideas [22]. For trustable collaborations blockchain platforms should offer strong data validity and high data accessibility [8, 16, 24]. Data validity is provided by the blockchain system and smart contracts ensuring that data records are immutable, and transactions are trust-free and disintermediated. The trust-free disintermediation mechanism guarantees that stakeholders receive verified data, which the value offering must be based upon [16]. Since a smart contract is a self-enforced mechanism, which functions based on pre-defined rules, it automates the value transfer among each stakeholder of the blockchain network [25]. The smart contract contributes to collaborative activity by processing data in such a way as to achieve pre-defined and targeted consequences, thus ensuring the accuracy of the end result [26]. This mechanism enforces the fulfilment of contractual obligations and helps determine rewards or inflict a penalty for the breach of the transaction's conditions [22]. The second determinant of trustable collaborations is high data accessibility. The transaction data, which is recorded and synchronised at every node in the system and which is validated by consensus mechanisms, is accessible by every member of the network [10]. The accessibility of data makes the blockchain a useful value-creation tool. The history of transactions can be accessed and traced at any point in time [8]. This enables companies to control the supply chain, check the quality of products and services and use the data for creating future product development scenarios [8, 24]. Technically, trustable collaborations endure in open or consortium blockchain networks, as they are more inclusive in terms of the number of stakeholders [9, 21]. While an open blockchain can be more challenging to manage, consortium networks facilitate inter-organizational collaboration and the development of a business ecosystem, aiding the implementation of common business tasks [21].

The data accessibility and validity offered by the blockchain has a value destructive consequence too, due to the *inflexible nature of transactions*. The data validation mechanism implies the irreversibility of records, which adds rigidity and inflexibility, eliminating the possibility of ad-hoc experimentation. If transactions have been processed erroneously, a distributed system of storing and recording data does not make it possible to retrieve the data [27]. The deployment of smart contracts is bound to the programming code. Therefore, changes that were not predicted and factors that were not considered cannot be handled during data transactions [28]. Therefore, owing to the irreversibility of the records, once commenced the transaction proceeds without functionalities, which could be crucial for outcome accuracy [7]. Such technical functions are useful for hypothesis-driven experimentation, whereby the technology is tested for different business scenarios and applications [29]. However, they are not favourable for unexpected discoveries through trial and error and the influx of new ideas [30]. Inflexibility of transactions reduces the possibility of the exploration of new routes for business development and the innovation of firms' offerings [7]. To decrease the immutability of data, companies may deploy private blockchains, which, due to the relatively lower number of nodes, provides the possibility to edit records [17].

Controlled Value – Privacy: The adoption of a blockchain can create a trade-off between *controlling value* by compromising on actors' privacy and ensuring greater *privacy* by loosening the control over transactions. The control of value represents the activities that companies direct at tracing the use of services and goods to identify the degree to which the quality is met and determine customer preferences to customise offerings [16, 32]. Such an activity makes customers the co-creators of value, as insights driven from their transactional data (i.e. big data) give an opportunity for companies to improve products or services and provide value-added complementary offerings [33]. Customisations creates lock-in effects (the motivation to participate in repeated transactions), maximises customer loyalty and increases switching costs [34, 35]. It does not radically change the offering, but rather enhances the value of the product [36]. Also, disintermediated interaction between customers and firms increases customers' trust in companies, which positively affects the customer journey [37]. Value control through customisation and quality management is contingent on data accessibility, data validity and centralised control. The customer's approval to access data is possible when customers build trust toward the company and confidence that the data will not be misused [16]. Trustable relations between the company and customers are fostered by the mechanisms of verifying and authorising the data supplied by different actors in the system [17]. To obtain information and create added-value service, companies dynamically access data by being assured that the data stored in the system is correct [16]. Technically, the ability to control value is inherent to closed or consortium blockchain networks, where access is based on permission and the central entity has the right to fully or partially control the operation of the system and the transactions carried out [17, 32]. A closed blockchain owing to the limited number of actors offers better traceability, which, consequently, simplifies the process of managing and analysing records [32].

Even though the control of data by the third party and data accessibility provide a variety of ways to add value, they create *privacy* concerns and the risk of unauthorised data usage [10]. Privacy is an important aspect to consider for value creation. Companies should not only be concerned about business model innovation for a new product or service creation. They also need to consider the value that business stands for from the social perspective, such as health and safety [38]. Therefore, by sharing control over personal data, customers experience a risk undermining the value of firms' offering. Although privacy risk is inherent to all types of blockchains, it increases when the technology is deployed for public networks. In such scenarios, the entry into the network is permission-less, which provides more favourable conditions for unauthorised activities [5]. Privacy measures, such as the implementation of proof-of-costs, proof-of-stake and proof-of-space mechanisms, create barriers for malicious intrusion, although they massively increase the complexity of the system and resources for deploying these mechanisms [4, 39]. In contrast, private and consortium blockchain-based networks are more selective and exclusive. The identities are known for other actors in the group, as members are pre-validated. The decision to admit new members into the groups is laid on either the group authority or the existing member of the network. The closed nature of transactions increases privacy [9]. However, when it comes to the control over data, public blockchains have a decentralised application layer, which reduces the involvement of firms in the supervision and control of transactions [17].

3.2 Value Delivery

Network Effects – Scalability Challenge: *Network effect* is an intrinsic capability of the blockchain, revolutionising the way in which people exchange digital and physical goods and services [40]. Network effects have become possible primarily due to the disintermediated system of blockchains, leading to the integration of all actors in the platform [41]. It is a feature that enables efficient value delivery by accelerating activities among actors, leading to the extension of the network scope in the long term. That is why the stimulation of a positive network effect is so important for catalysing sales through new channels [42]. The utilisation of a blockchain in crowdfunding has become a powerful tool for creating network effects by establishing connections between potential investors. By leveraging on technical features that enable trust-free, transparent and secure transactions, the technology helps eliminate bureaucratic procedures and establish direct channels of communication and value delivery with organisations' stakeholders [30]. High data accessibility and decentralised control are important for achieving a positive network effect. The more people adopt the technology, the more widely the system becomes adopted [40]. Given that for the creation and delivery of value a sufficient diffusion of the blockchain is needed, the technical precondition for this capability is to deploy a public blockchain. The permission-less nature of participation drives the growth of the network, while it remains decentralised [40].

On the other hand, an open blockchain creates *scalability issues.* Scalability concerns the limit to the number of transactions per second that can be managed through blockchain platforms [43]. To ensure data validity, the decentralised system requires data to be stored and processed at multiple locations and replicated across the network to keep the nodes updated. These system characteristics increase the reliability of the data, although they add enormous operational complexity. The complexity causes a delay in transactions and transaction throughput [5]. The challenge to address data validity, decentralised control and scalability has been coined the scalability trilemma. The trilemma indicates the difficulty of addressing all three aspects and the need to prioritise any two of the three capabilities. In a permission-less blockchain, a relatively higher number of decentralised transactions affect the size of a block and the interval between blocks' creation, thus decreasing the frequency of transactions per second [43]. Consequently, public blockchain offers decentralised control and security, which is the precondition of the network effect, while compromising on scalability [44]. The seriousness of the scalability challenge for the business depends on the sectors and the area of application. It is not usable for markets, where delays in transactions can cause serious value delivery disruptions and undermine competitive advantage [5].

3.3 Value Capture

Cost Efficiency – Increased Investments: Due to its distributed consensus algorithms, the blockchain has been considered to hold business value as it makes it possible to restructure revenue - cost scheme to ensure value capture [17]. *Cost efficiency* is achieved in three ways. First, data access and validation reduce the transaction costs on the coordination of activities, tracing data and the integration of resources [19]. For example, in the finance sector, blockchain deployment can reduce costs that firms spend on manual processes, search and the negotiation of deals, which do not add business value to the firm. In total, the innovation of infrastructure in the finance industry is expected to bring up to 20 billion US dollars worth of savings [9]. In real estate, the technology authenticates the documentation for facilitating the transaction of ownership transfer from a seller to a buyer. Such transactions are carried out without notary intermediary, thus eliminating the associated costs for their service, which are often expensive [9]. This is enabled by the distributed system of data recording and storage at multiple locations in the network and among all nodes of the transaction through the copies of a ledger. Put differently, the disintermediation and the removal of associated labour costs decrease the time spent on verifying and accessing data, optimising transactions and decreasing the cost of product supply [6, 19]. Second, the firms whose transactions are operated based on a blockchain protocol benefit from decreased security and financial fraud risks due to the immutability of transactions [6]. Third, the disintermediated exchange requires less power consumption for a consumer due to the cut of around 20% of the price, which is usually added by a middleman. Consequently, the reduction in costs affects other firms' pricing models, thus leading to the refinement of cost structures across the energy market [45].

The utilisation of a blockchain may require *increased investments* to develop and maintain the network for digital transactions. Companies will most likely encounter the need to increase spending if they deploy a public blockchain. There are two main reasons that determine the negative effect of a public blockchain on value capture. First, overhead costs increase when a blockchain is deployed for public networks promoting anonymous participation. Since the entry into the network does not require authorisation [5, 30], firms need to invest financial resources and effort to increase the operational complexity associated with the utilisation of proof-of-costs, proof-of-stake and proof-of-space mechanisms [4, 5]. These mechanisms make the creation of new blocks of data costly, thus discouraging nodes (i.e. members) from disseminating corrupted information and eliminating the risk of Sybil attacks (cyber-attacks through the creation of a large number of anonymous and deceiving identities) [46]. Second, given the standardisation challenge, different blockchain architectures require investment to increase the interoperability and standardisation of systems to ensure seamless integration and operation [9].

4 Discussion of Implications for Business Model Innovation

The analysis of the literature made it possible to identify four groups of benefits and risks conducive to value creation, delivery and capture. As far as value creation is concerned, a blockchain can facilitate a trustable collaboration, which is possible by adopting open or consortium blockchain networks. These networks are characterised by strong data validation mechanisms and a higher degree of user access to data. The rigidity of the data validation in the public blockchain also implies the inflexibility of transactions and limited possibility of ad-hoc experimentation, which reduce the efficiency of collaboration. The second benefit in the value creation process is the possibility to control value offerings. This benefit is inherent to private or consortium blockchains, which have centralised or partially decentralised control and a higher possibility to trace data. At the same time, the control over transactions raises a privacy risk, which is stronger when adopting a public blockchain. Blockchain can facilitate value delivery through network effects. Such effects are realised through the decentralised control of transactions and permission-less access to data in public blockchain infrastructure. On the other hand, the increase in the load of the network decreases system capacity. Therefore, to address scalability issues, private or consortium blockchains could be more favourable. When it comes to value capture, the adoption of a blockchain impacts firms' cost-revenue scheme. The deployment of a private and consortium blockchain redefines transactional cost structures by introducing a disintermediated data validation mechanism and decentralised control. However, if organisations utilise an open blockchain, unlimited access to the network and operational complexity can result in higher spending on the system's deployment and maintenance.

From the business model innovation perspective, any benefits stemming from the adoption of a blockchain represent the introduction of new company activities, the change of the sequence or the structure of existing activities or new governance of activities. A blockchain enables companies to innovate business models by restructuring their existing activities in such a way as to remove an intermediary and make data traceable and accessible upon customers' request [8, 16, 24]. Through collaborations, disintermediation and traceability improve the efficiency of data exchange between stakeholders. Trust-free collaboration can also create complementary services for customers by offering transparency in transaction data [21, 24]. Network effects stimulated by disintermediation can improve efficiency by extending stakeholders' scope and catalysing sales through new channels [41, 42].

A blockchain facilitates business model innovation through the introduction of new activities for creating new markets. This strategy can be used for the launch of a new service, as a result of the company service portfolio diversification. Such a scenario is possible when a company that has been using direct offline channels redefines the business model by digitalising business processes. For example, the value of crowdfunding services based on the blockchain infrastructure is their potential to create network effects by establishing connections between investors and customers [30]. Similarly, Bitcoin was a novel service which partly gained its popularity due to the network effect [48].

Business model innovation through the introduction of new governance is underpinned by the ability of blockchain networks to grant companies control over transactions and save costs. Since a blockchain gives the opportunity to oversee data exchange, companies can take the role of a controller of value for customising and improving their offerings. Such activities make it possible to design value-added complementary services, which can create a lock-in effect (the motivation to participate in repeated transactions) [34]. Cost-efficiency enabled by a blockchain can have a complementary value, when revenues are secured not from the reduction of transaction costs, but from a new form of governance of the infrastructure. Given that the use of a blockchain reduces the risk of frauds and incurred financial losses [6], firms can market their services by promoting associated security features.

Table 2 presents the BMI design elements and value drivers, associated with the benefits of the private, consortium and public blockchain.

Table 2. Business Model Innovation enabled by a blockchain

Design elements of BMI	Blockchain benefits	Value drivers
New structure	Trustable collaborations	Efficiency, complementarity
	Network effects	Efficiency
	Cost-efficiency	Efficiency
New activities	Network effects	Novelty

(continued)

Table 2. (*continued*)

Design elements of BMI	Blockchain benefits	Value drivers
New governance	Value control	Lock-in, complementarity
	Cost-efficiency	Complementarity

5 Conclusion and Future Research

This paper aimed to address the gap in the literature on business model innovation, concerning the lack of understanding about the benefits and risks created by the utilisation of blockchains in business processes. First, we analysed the literature and identified the characteristics of the technology inherent to the public, consortium and private blockchain. The three types of blockchain differ by the varying degree of accessibility to data, decentralised control and operational complexity. The findings of such an analysis contribute to the literature by identifying differentiating factors in assessing the advantages and limitations of the technology. Secondly, drawing on the prior literature in the domain of business model innovation, we analysed the benefits and risks that technical characteristics of different blockchain networks create in the company value chain. The paper provides an understanding of the conditions for successful business model innovation and discusses the design elements of business model innovation rooted in blockchain benefits.

A direction for future research concerns the empirical validation of the findings of the present study. Scholars need to use methodologies to draw primary insights into the role of the different types of blockchain and their technical characteristics in the company value chain. In regard to value creation, a case study approach can be used to examine the degree to which permissioned and permission-less blockchains facilitate or hinder efficient collaborations between parties. To confirm the benefit of the traceability of customer preferences, future research needs to examine the impact on profits over time before and after blockchain utilisation. In terms of value delivery, scholars need to focus on negative implications that both permission-less and permissioned blockchain architectures have for ensuring interoperability between organisations and efficient business ecosystem. Finally, to progress research on the role of blockchain in value capture, more research is needed for developing systems addressing standardisation, security and interoperability challenges that negatively affect firms' revenues.

References

1. Morris, M., Schindehutte, M., Allen, J.: The entrepreneur's business model: toward a unified perspective. J. Bus. Res. **58**(6), 726–735 (2005)
2. Schallmo, D., Williams, C.A., Boardman, L.: Digital transformation of business models—best practice, enablers, and roadmap. Int. J. Innov. Manag. **21**(8), 1740014 (2017)
3. Nowiński, W., Kozma, M.: How can blockchain technology disrupt the existing business models? Entrepreneurial Bus. Econ. Rev. **5**(3), 173–188 (2017)
4. Nakamoto, S., Bitcoin, A.: A peer-to-peer electronic cash system. Bitcoin (2008) https://bitcoin.org/bitcoin.pdf

5. Notheisen, B., Cholewa, J.B., Shanmugam, A.P.: Trading real-world assets on blockchain. Bus. Inf. Syst. Eng. **59**(6), 425–440 (2017)
6. Zhang, Y., Wen, J.: The IoT electric business model: using blockchain technology for the internet of things. Peer-to-Peer Network. Appl. **10**(4), 983–994 (2016). https://doi.org/10.1007/s12083-016-0456-1
7. Schweizer, A., et al. Unchaining Social Businesses-Blockchain as the Basic Technology of a Crowdlending Platform. In: ICIS (2017)
8. Chong, A.Y.L., et al.: Business on chain: a comparative case study of five blockchain-inspired business models. J. Assoc. Inf. Syst. **20**(9), 9 (2019)
9. Morkunas, V.J., Paschen, J., Boon, E.: How blockchain technologies impact your business model. Bus. Horiz. **62**(3), 295–306 (2019)
10. Tiscini, R., et al.: The blockchain as a sustainable business model innovation. Manag. Decis. **58**, 1621–1642 (2020)
11. Teece, D.J.: Business models, business strategy and innovation. Long Range Plan. **43**(2–3), 172–194 (2010)
12. Markides, C.: Disruptive innovation: in need of better theory. J. Prod. Innov. Manag. **23**(1), 19–25 (2006)
13. Chesbrough, H.: Business model innovation: it's not just about technology anymore. Strategy Leadersh. (2007)
14. Bucherer, E., Eisert, U., Gassmann, O.: Towards systematic business model innovation: lessons from product innovation management. Creativity Innov. Manag. **21**(2), 183–198 (2012)
15. Sankar, L.S., Sindhu, M., Sethumadhavan, M.: Survey of consensus protocols on blockchain applications. In: 2017 4th International Conference on Advanced Computing and Communication Systems (ICACCS). IEEE (2017)
16. Bauer, I., et al.: Exploring blockchain value creation: the case of the car ecosystem. In: Proceedings of the 52nd Hawaii International Conference on System Sciences (2019)
17. Zheng, Z., et al.: An overview of blockchain technology: Architecture, consensus, and future trends. In: 2017 IEEE International Congress on Big Data (BigData Congress). IEEE (2017)
18. Tönnissen, S., Teuteberg, F.: Analysing the impact of blockchain-technology for operations and supply chain management: An explanatory model drawn from multiple case studies. Int. J. Inf. Manag. **52**, 101953 (2020)
19. Queiroz, M.M., Telles, R., Bonilla, S.H.: Blockchain and supply chain management integration: a systematic review of the literature. Supply Chain Manag. Int. J. (2019)
20. Moyano, J.P., Ross, O.: KYC optimization using distributed ledger technology. Bus. Inf. Syst. Eng. **59**(6), 411–423 (2017)
21. Zavolokina, L., et al.: Management, governance and value creation in a blockchain consortium. MIS Q. Exec. **19**(1), 1–17 (2020)
22. Scekic, O., Nastic, S., Dustdar, S.: Blockchain-supported smart city platform for social value co-creation and exchange. IEEE Internet Comput. **23**(1), 19–28 (2018)
23. Kiel, D., Arnold, C., Voigt, K.-I.: The influence of the Industrial Internet of Things on business models of established manufacturing companies – a business level perspective. Technovation **68**, 4–19 (2017)
24. Caro, M.P., et al.: Blockchain-based traceability in Agri-Food supply chain management: a practical implementation. In: 2018 IoT Vertical and Topical Summit on Agriculture-Tuscany (IOT Tuscany). IEEE (2018)
25. Cong, L.W., He, Z.: Blockchain disruption and smart contracts. Rev. Financ. Stud. **32**(5), 1754–1797 (2019)
26. Beck, R., et al.: Blockchain–the gateway to trust-free cryptographic transactions (2016)

27. Ahangama, S., Poo, D.C.C.: Credibility of algorithm based decentralized computer networks governing personal finances: the case of cryptocurrency. In: Nah, F.-H.-H., Tan, C.-H. (eds.) HCIBGO 2016. LNCS, vol. 9751, pp. 165–176. Springer, Cham (2016). https://doi.org/10.1007/978-3-319-39396-4_15
28. Christidis, K., Devetsikiotis, M.: Blockchains and smart contracts for the internet of things. IEEE Access **4**, 2292–2303 (2016)
29. Beck, R., Müller-Bloch, C.: Blockchain as radical innovation: a framework for engaging with distributed ledgers as incumbent organization. In: Proceedings of the 50th Hawaii International Conference on System Sciences (2017)
30. Chen, Y., Bellavitis, C.: Blockchain disruption and decentralized finance: The rise of decentralized business models. J. Bus. Ventur. Insights **13,** e00151 (2020)
31. Beck, R., Müller-Bloch, C., King, J.L.: Governance in the blockchain economy: a framework and research agenda. J. Assoc. Inf. Syst. **19**(10), 1 (2018)
32. Behnke, K., Janssen, M.: Boundary conditions for traceability in food supply chains using blockchain technology. Int. J. Inf. Manag. **52**, 101969 (2020)
33. Urbinati, A., et al.: Creating and capturing value from big data: a multiple-case study analysis of provider companies. Technovation **84–85**, 21–36 (2019)
34. Hänninen, M., Smedlund, A., Mitronen, L.: Digitalization in retailing: multi-sided platforms as drivers of industry transformation. Baltic J. Manag. (2018)
35. Amit, R., Zott, C.: Value creation in e-business. Strateg. Manag. J. **22**(6–7), 493–520 (2001)
36. Kohtamäki, M., et al.: Digital servitization business models in ecosystems: a theory of the firm. J. Bus. Res. **104**, 380–392 (2019)
37. Kumar, V., Ramachandran, D., Kumar, B.: Influence of new-age technologies on marketing: a research agenda. J. Bus. Res. (2020)
38. Dempsey, N., et al.: The social dimension of sustainable development: defining urban social sustainability. Sustain. Dev. **19**(5), 289–300 (2011)
39. Kiayias, A., Russell, A., David, B., Oliynykov, R.: Ouroboros: a provably secure proof-of-stake blockchain protocol. In: Katz, Jonathan, Shacham, Hovav (eds.) CRYPTO 2017. LNCS, vol. 10401, pp. 357–388. Springer, Cham (2017). https://doi.org/10.1007/978-3-319-63688-7_12
40. Schmidt, C.G., Wagner, S.M.: Blockchain and supply chain relations: A transaction cost theory perspective. J. Purchasing Supply Manag. **25**(4), 100552 (2019)
41. Kundu, D.: Blockchain and trust in a smart city. Environ. Urban. ASIA **10**(1), 31–43 (2019)
42. Fu, W., Wang, Q., Zhao, X.: The influence of platform service innovation on value co-creation activities and the network effect. J. Serv. Manag. (2017)
43. Gervais, A., et al.: On the security and performance of proof of work blockchains. In: Proceedings of the 2016 ACM SIGSAC Conference on Computer and Communications Security (2016)
44. Perboli, G., Musso, S., Rosano, M.: Blockchain in logistics and supply chain: a lean approach for designing real-world use cases. IEEE Access **6**, 62018–62028 (2018)
45. Brilliantova, V., Thurner, T.W.: Blockchain and the future of energy. Technol. Soc. **57**, 38–45 (2019)
46. Dinger, J., Hartenstein, H.: Defending the sybil attack in p2p networks: Taxonomy, challenges, and a proposal for self-registration. In: First International Conference on Availability, Reliability and Security (ARES 2006). IEEE (2006)
47. Amit, R., Zott, C.: Creating value through business model innovation (2012)
48. Worley, C., Skjellum. A.: Blockchain tradeoffs and challenges for current and emerging applications: generalization, fragmentation, sidechains, and scalability. In: 2018 IEEE International Conference on Internet of Things (iThings) and IEEE Green Computing and Communications (GreenCom) and IEEE Cyber, Physical and Social Computing (CPSCom) and IEEE Smart Data (SmartData). IEEE (2018)

Key Characteristics to Create Optimized Blockchain Consensus Algorithms

J. Leo and M. J. Hattingh(✉)

University of Pretoria, Private Bag X20, Hatfield, Pretoria 0028, South Africa
marie.hattingh@up.ac.za

Abstract. Blockchain is a fairly new technology and still in its infancy. As a result, many research papers are creating optimized consensus algorithms. Therefore, a need for key characteristics to create optimized blockchain consensus algorithms has been identified. This research paper presents the results of a systematic literature on identifying the main blockchain consensus algorithms and their associated advantages and disadvantages. Papers from four different databases were retrieved and after exclusion criteria were applied, 44 papers were ultimately included in the review. Results indicated that the five main consensus algorithms were Proof-of-Work (PoW), Proof-of-Stake (PoS), Practical Byzantine Fault Tolerance (PBFT), and Delegated Proof-of-Stake. The results further indicated that efficiency was the main advantage of the PoS, PBFT, PoA and hybrid consensus algorithms. The main disadvantage was "energy wastage" and was attributed to the PoW algorithm. Security concerns were the main disadvantage of the PoS algorithm. These findings were used to present key characteristics that future researchers can have in mind when creating optimized blockchain consensus algorithms.

Keywords: Blockchain · Consensus algorithm · Proof-of-Work (PoW) · Proof-of-Stake (PoS)

1 Introduction

Satoshi Nakamoto first introduced blockchain technology when he developed Bitcoin in 2008 [1]. This technology allows for decentralization as a history of all the transactions are kept on each node on the network [2]. Any person with access to the network plays a role in maintaining the blockchain node. Blockchain has a strong advantage of being transparent as any party can acquire access to the transaction. Furthermore, other characteristics included security, immutability and transparency [3]. Due to these characteristics blockchain has played a disruptive role in major industries such as the supply chain, the medical industry, financial and energy industry [4]. For it to be carried out successfully in these industries, optimized blockchain consensus algorithms need to be utilized.

There have been several different consensus algorithms created. The most common ones being Proof-of-Work and Proof-of-Stake [5]. Both these algorithms come with their

Published by Springer Nature Switzerland AG 2021
D. Dennehy et al. (Eds.): I3E 2021, LNCS 12896, pp. 567–579, 2021.
https://doi.org/10.1007/978-3-030-85447-8_47

advantages and disadvantages. As a result, many new consensus algorithms are being created to deal with their shortcomings.

An initial scanning of research determined that numerous research papers were creating improved consensus algorithms. As a result, a gap in research was determined where it would be beneficial to have key characteristics that these new consensus algorithms should have. Therefore, this research paper proposes the following main research question: *What are the key characteristics to create optimized blockchain consensus algorithms?*

To determine the answers to the main research, question the following sub-research questions need to be answered: (1) What are the main blockchain consensus algorithms? (2) What are the advantages of the main consensus algorithms found? (3) What are the disadvantages of the main consensus algorithms found?

This systematic literature review will be structured as follows. Section 2 details the systematic review methodology. Sections 3 and 4 presents the findings and discussion of the findings of the systematic literature respectively. Section 5 offers up future research whilst Sect. 6 will conclude the study by summarizing the main findings.

2 Methodology

Blockchain technology is still in its infancy [15], as a result, the methodology proposed and utilized in this systematic literature review is designed specifically with the novel technology in mind. This research paper considers both qualitative and quantitative research. Both of these research types will be used as blockchain consortiums is exiting the Peak of Inflated Expectations and entering the Trough of Disillusionment in the Gartner Hype Cycle [17]. Its placement in the Gartner Hype Cycle means that there will be plenty of qualitative research into the topic but minimal quantitative research as there are not many applications for this type of research to be conducted on.

The process of selecting the research papers to be included in this systematic literature review was as follows:

1. The following keywords were initially inserted into the chosen databases: (block chain AND consensus algorithm) OR proof of work OR proof of stake. These keywords were selected as blockchain consensus algorithms is the core components of the research paper. Proof-of-Work and Proof-of-Stake were included in the search terms as they are two of the most popular blockchain consensus algorithms, therefore it would yield better results.
2. Blockchain technology was first introduced in a paper by Satoshi Nakamoto in 2008. Since it was introduced in 2008, the search filter data range for all the databases were from 2008–2020. The reasoning behind the source types that will be listed below is because formal research papers that have gone through a rigorous process to be published, is desired. The following is the filter parameters that were used for each database:

   - Science Direct – source type: review articles and research articles
   - IEEE – source type: journals and conferences

- Ebsco Host – source type: academic journals
- Emerald – source type: article

3. The following step is to select relevant research papers by reading through the title and abstract of the research paper. The paper will be included if the author mentions relevant research containing consensus algorithms in the title and abstract. The research paper must also be downloadable immediately for it to be included. The results can be seen in the "Title and Abstract".
4. The final step in selecting research papers to be included in the study will be analyzing the research papers to determine if it adheres to the following inclusion criteria:

- Advantages of blockchain consensus algorithms
- Disadvantages of blockchain consensus algorithms
- Future research of blockchain consensus algorithms

The process mentioned above resulted in 44 research papers being included in this study. Content analysis will be the chosen analysis technique.

3 Results – Background

Analysis of the resultant papers indicated that 18 papers were based on qualitative research and 19 papers were based on quantitative research. Science Direct yielded 13 papers, and IEEE produced 23 papers respectively followed by five papers from EBSCO Host and 3 papers from Emerald Insight.

In answering sub-research question one, results further indicated that there was a total of 30 different blockchain consensus algorithms mentioned in the 44 articles that were included in the study. The four most common algorithms that the 44 included research papers mentioned, were Proof-of-Work (PoW), Proof-of-Stake (PoS), Practical Byzantine Fault Tolerance (PBFT), and Delegated Proof-of-Stake (DPoS).

In answering the second sub-research question the main advantages of blockchain consensus algorithms were efficiency, scalability and security. Efficiency was the advantage that was mentioned in 60% of the papers. The second type of advantage, scalability was associated with the PoW, PoS, and DPoS having the advantage of scalability.

Security as an advantage was associated with PoW and PBFT consensus algorithms [1–3].

In answering the sub-research questions, three findings indicated that "energy wastage" was mentioned in 25 papers as the most often occurring in the PoW consensus algorithm. Security was identified as the biggest disadvantage of the PoS algorithm by six papers [4–9].

4 Discussion

The following sections discuss the findings in terms of the three sub-research questions posed in Sect. 1.

4.1 S-RQ1 What are the Main Blockchain Consensus Algorithms?

According to the results in Sect. 3, out of the 44 research papers considered, 30 different consensus algorithms were identified. Of the 30 listed consensus algorithms, four of them were mentioned significantly more than the rest. These four algorithms included Proof-of-Work, Proof-of-Stake, Delegated Proof-of-Stake, and Practical Byzantine Fault Tolerance. This section will allow the reader to gain insights into how these consensus algorithms work. A stronger argument can be made for the advantages and disadvantages which will be further explored.

Proof-of-Work. Bitcoin uses the Proof-of-Work consensus algorithm. Proof-of-Work is essentially nodes putting in a rigorous computational effort to keep the blockchain network secure. This consensus algorithm involves nodes on the network competing with each other to solve a cryptographic problem which is easily verifiable by other nodes on the network. These nodes that are competing against each other are known as miners and the process of solving this cryptographic problem is known as mining. A miner's responsibility is to verify transactions, validate, create and add blocks to the chain [14]. This process of mining will be explained below.

Once a block is filled with transactions, the miner can initiate the verification process. The block contains a header that includes the hash pointer (the hash of the data of the previous block), the network difficulty, a timestamp, the version of the block, a list of the transactions that they think should be added to the network, and nonce. A nonce is a 4-byte adjustable number [5]. The miner must continuously change the nonce so that the outcome of the hash results in it is below the threshold that is set by the network difficulty level included in the header. After the miner finds a hash that is below the threshold, the block will be propagated onto the blockchain network using flooding algorithms [27]. The other nodes on the network will verify this block by taking the nonce that was used for validation and will hash the block with the same cryptographic function used by the miner that proposed that the block is valid. If the resulting hash results in a value lower than the threshold, then the miner will deem the block to be valid. The majority of the nodes on the network must deem this block valid for it to be added onto the chain of the blockchain network. If the block is successfully added to the chain, the miner will be rewarded with a certain amount of currency of the network, 12.5 coins in the Bitcoin context [9]. The longest chain is deemed the most valid one as it required the majority of the network's computational power [11].

This process of mining has some advantages but result in more disadvantages according to the research papers analyzed. These advantages will be discussed in Sect. 4.2. As a result of the disadvantages stemming from the proof-of-work consensus algorithm, there have been algorithms that have used Proof-of-Work as a building foundation but improvements have to be made.

Proof-of-Stake (PoS). The proof-of-stake is an alternative consensus algorithm that was created to deal with the inefficiencies and disadvantages of Proof-of-Work [11]. According to the paper, *Analysis of the main consensus protocols of blockchain*, Ethereum is planning on moving away from Proof-of-Work and transitioning towards the proof-of-stake consensus algorithm [12]. 81.82% of the included research, either mentioned or elaborated on this algorithm.

This consensus algorithm involves validators that have the responsibility of ensuring transactions and blocks are authenticated and valid. Stakeholders stake a certain amount to be considered to validated and add blocks to the chain. The stake is a certain amount of the digital currency that is stored in a vault to ensure that the validator does not carry out any malicious actions. This ensures that those who have staked more are less likely to carry out malicious actions as they will lose what they have staked [1]. The validator will be selected on a random selection basis with the validators staking more, having a higher chance of being selected as the one to validate the block. The validator that is selected will ensure that the transactions in the block are valid. If the transactions are deemed to be valid, the validator will add the block onto the existing chain. They will then will be rewarded in transactions fees instead of coins as in the Proof-of-Work consensus algorithm [13].

The creation of this has resulted in some advantages such as the reduction of computational power required. Although there are benefits as a result of this algorithm, there are disadvantages that also occur. Further advantages and disadvantages of this consensus algorithm will be discussed further in Sect. 4.3 Similar to Proof-of-Work, additional consensus algorithms use the foundation of proof-of-stake to create new and improved versions of this algorithm (Fig. 1).

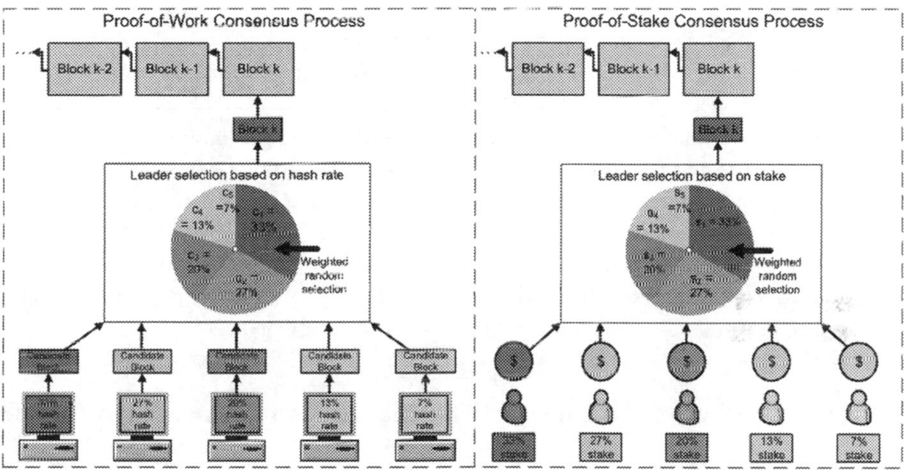

Fig. 1. Comparison of PoW vs PoS

Delegated Proof-of-Stake (DPoS). Delegated Proof-of-Stake was mentioned in ten of the research papers included in the study [11, 14, 15, 23, 26, 29, 33, 34, 46] and [2]. This consensus algorithm according to the research paper, *Blockchain technology in the energy sector: A systematic review of challenges and opportunities*, is described as a stakeholder voting consensus scheme [11]. The stakeholders, the people that own coins, elect nodes (witnesses) to validate, authenticate and create blocks [11]. The witnesses that receive the greatest number of votes will be given the authorization to create blocks. They will take turns in validating the blocks [14]. If the witnesses do not adhere to their responsibilities the stakeholders can remove them as a witness and elect a different node. In return for creating these new blocks, the witnesses are awarded the associated fees. Nodes on the network are also able to elect delegates who determine the rules and protocols of the network [11].

Practical Byzantine Fault Tolerance (pBFT). There are times where nodes do not come to a consensus as a result of a block acting in a malicious manner or the communication between them is not successful. This causes a delay in the blocks being added to the chain. This is known as a Byzantine fault. A Byzantine Fault Tolerance system allows a certain amount of these "malicious nodes" to be tolerated [11]. As a result, blocks can be added to the chain as per usual, without any delay being caused by these nodes.

The Practical Byzantine Fault Tolerance consensus algorithm is developed from the foundation of the Byzantine Fault Tolerance characteristic. It requires that 2/3 of the nodes of the network are to behave accordingly [11]. 36.36% of the included research papers mentioned this algorithm in its contents [1–3, 5, 12, 14, 20–26, 28].

Practical Byzantine Fault Tolerance two types of nodes, a primary node and secondary nodes (backup nodes). PBFT has five stages (note: m represents the maximum nodes that can be tolerated in the network) [12]:

1. Request: a block is created by the primary node and distributed on the network.
2. Prepare: a PRE-PARE message will be broadcasted by the primary node and the backup nodes need to verify this message.
3. Prepare: the backup nodes receive the PRE-PARE message and the block and then will broadcast the PREPARE message to the network. To move onto the next stage, the backup node must receive $2m + 1$ of the same PREPARE message from the other backup nodes.
4. Commit: the nodes broadcast the COMMIT message to all nodes on the network. It also must wait for $2m + 1$ of the identical COMMIT message from the other blocks.
5. The primary node can then append the block to the network.

4.2 S-RQ2 What are the Advantages of the Main Consensus Algorithms Found?

The advantages discussed in the research papers stemmed from the consensus algorithms that were mentioned in Sect. 4.1. In this section, the advantages of efficiency, security and scalability will be discussed and how they are achieved by the different blockchain consensus algorithms.

Efficiency. There are three different advantageous efficiencies identified namely efficiency as a general term, transaction throughput and energy efficiency. These three advantages will be discussed and how they are obtained differently in the four consensus algorithms:

Efficiency. An advantage of the Proof-of-Stake consensus algorithm is increased efficiency. One of the included research papers stated that Proof-of-Stake is efficient, but none of them provides a clear explanation on why they stated it was efficient [37].

Efficient or efficiency is not an appropriate characteristic to describe Proof-of-Stake. It should rather be paired with another term to more accurately describe this consensus algorithm, for example, energy-efficient.

Energy Efficiency. Six of the research papers included stated that the benefit of Proof-of-Stake is its reduced power consumption or energy efficiency [5, 12, 14, 24–26]. The way that this reduced power consumption is achieved, is by replacing the computational effort with a randomly weighted selection [22]. Instead of many nodes on the network competing to validate blocks, a node on the network is randomly chosen to become the validator. This eliminates the nodes needing to brute force the correct nonce thus reducing the computational power required as only one node is doing the work instead of all the nodes on the network.

Of the 44 research papers included in the analysis, 9.09% of them agreed that the implementation of the Practical Byzantine Fault Tolerance results in energy-efficiency benefits [1–3, 12, 18]. The key to its energy efficiency is by achieving consensus, and not solving complex mathematical problems like Proof-of-Work. However, the speed and scalability of the algorithm will be affected by the message overhead as the network grows in size [11].

Transaction Throughput. The advantage of the Hybrid consensus algorithm is its high transaction throughput. It is the combination of the Proof-of-Work and Byzantine Fault Tolerance consensus algorithms. It makes use of the Byzantine Fault Tolerance protocol to come to a consensus. This results in increased energy efficiency as complex mathematical problems don't have to be solved.

Scalability. Two research papers listed Delegated Proof-of-Stake as being scalable [12, 14]. Due to the voting scheme and the process to achieve consensus in Delegated Proof-of-Stake, this algorithm benefits from both increased efficiency and reduced energy wastage [14]. These 2 benefits will allow the application to be scalable with bigger networks.

Two papers deemed scalability as a benefit as a result of the Proof-of-Stake-consensus algorithm [12, 14]. This algorithm involves randomly selecting a validator to create and add a block to the chain. As there is only one agreement (picking the validator) before adding the block to the chain, energy demand is decreased and the general efficiency increases. As stated in the text above, these benefits are a good indication that it will be able to handle a larger load as the network size increases and thus making it scalable.

The general consensus of scalability of the Proof-of-Work consensus algorithm in the analysed papers is inconsistent. Two papers identified it as being scalable [12, 14], whilst two papers deemed it not scalable [2, 22]. Based on the numbers above, Proof-of-Work is not scalable. All the reasons listed for good scalability above, have energy efficiency as a benefit. The results indicated 35 energy wastage as a disadvantage of the Proof-of-Work consensus algorithm.

Security. Practical Byzantine Fault Tolerance and Proof-of-Work having the advantage of security. Security in the Proof-of-Work algorithm is a result of including the hash pointer in the block [1]. As discussed in Sect. 2, this hash pointer is what links blocks together. Any modification to a block will essentially change its hash and it will not match one of the hash pointer [6].

Practical Byzantine Fault Tolerance is said to be secure by two of the analyzed papers. It was shown that it would tolerate a certain number of malicious and would ignore these nodes. The security is increased as malicious nodes have no say in the network.

4.3 S-RQ3 What are the Disadvantages of the Main Consensus Algorithms Found?

This section will identify and elaborate on the common disadvantages identified of the main consensus algorithms as identified in Sect. 4.1.

Common Disadvantages of Proof-of-Work. Proof-of-Work is the consensus algorithm that Bitcoin uses in its blockchain architecture and it's the original consensus algorithm [24]. The most common disadvantages experienced by Proof-of-Work is security issues, wastage of energy, transaction throughput, and high latency.

The most common disadvantage of the Proof-of-Work consensus algorithm is that it is not energy efficient. As many as 35, (79.55%) of the included research papers, listed this as one of the disadvantages of the algorithm. The energy wastage occurs as many miners compete with each other to validate blocks. They compete with each other by solving complex mathematical problems by using brute force to determine the correct nonce that would solve these problems [26]. Brute forcing requires a lot of computational effort which leads to energy wastage [20]. This process of brute-forcing the correct nonce doesn't even guarantee that the miner will be the one chosen to validate the block and their effort could all in vain.

Transaction throughput is the number of transactions that can be processed in a certain period [6]. Low transaction throughout was another recurring disadvantage of the Proof-of-Work consensus algorithm. Four of the research papers agreed on this disadvantage [6, 9]. The low throughput is a result of the creation and addition of blocks. As stated in Sect. 1, miners validate and include transactions in a block. Once the block with the transaction is inserted into the chain, transactions have to wait for several additional blocks to be added to the chain before the transaction is confirmed [6]. The slow process of adding blocks to the chain delays the transaction confirmation and thus lowering the transaction throughput.

Seven out of the 44 research papers analyzed agreed that high latency was a recurring challenge of the Proof-of-Work consensus algorithm [1, 2, 5, 6, 9, 29, 38]. It is the period between a transaction and the time it takes for the transaction to be processed [5]. Block intervals are what determines the latency of a consensus algorithm [30]. The above text identified that it is a very slow process for blocks to be added to the chain in the Proof-of-Work consensus algorithm. This increases the block interval time and thus increasing the latency in the network.

Six of the research papers included in the research study, all had security issues as a disadvantage for the Proof-of-Work consensus algorithm [23, 24, 34, 40, 45, 46]. Security is one of the challenges as numerous attacks were developed to target and penetrate this consensus algorithm. Some of the attacks that were included in the included research paper are as follows:

- **51% attack** – In the Proof-of-Work algorithm, a block can only be added to the chain if the majority of nodes in the network deem it is valid. To verify the validity of the block, miners need large amounts of computational power, also known as hashing power. This hashing power helps determine the performance of the specific miner. The 51% attack is when an organization or an entity is in control of the majority of the hashing power [28]. As they have the majority of the hashing power, they can carry out the following actions [2]:
  - Control if blocks get validated or not.
  - The ability to exclude or modify the ordering of transactions.
  - It also gives them the ability to prevent the confirmation of transactions.
  - Proof-of-Work makes this attack difficult to carry out as an organization would need an enormous amount of hashing power which would not be feasible [23].
- **Double-spending** – the double-spending attack involves spending the same currency twice. This can be carried out by taking a conflicting transaction from another branch and transferring the funds back to the attacker [33].

Common Disadvantages of Proof-of-Stake. The common disadvantages of Proof-of-Stake is the threat of centralization, and the rich nodes having the ability to take advantage of the network. Both of these disadvantages all relate to the security of the consensus algorithm and it is the most common disadvantage identified in the research papers included in this study. Six is the number of analyzed research papers that identified security as one of Proof-of-Stake's disadvantage [4–10].

As security is the biggest disadvantage, this section aims to provide light on some of the attacks that were identified in the included research papers. This will be done by listing and explaining the most common attacks that would be possible on the Proof-of-Stake consensus algorithm.

There are three different types of long-range attacks: simple, posterior corruption and Stake Bleeding. All three of these long-range attacks aim to do one thing, replace the existing chain with a new chain that begins from the Genesis block (the initial block. In this research article, we will only be discussing the Stake Bleeding attack.

As mentioned above, the Stake Bleeding attack occurs when another chain is created from a genesis block. Each new node is provided with the Genesis block. This new chain becomes replaces the original one. A new node to the network always begins with the Genesis block. They try to build this chain up until it's longer or more valid than the valid chain. They are still a validator in the original chain, but when they get chosen to validate a block (become the slot leader), they skip their turn. This is called a Liveness Denial [6]. Because of the mechanics of Proof-of-Stake, no block is generated in this phase. The attacker's stake does decrease as the process goes on, which makes it less likely that they will get chosen. At the same time, they begin validating and adding blocks to their chain. The malicious validator also copies the transactions that occur on the main chain and includes them in their chain. As they are validating transactions, they receive a stake that allows them to compete in the original chain. Once the chain outpaces the original one, they make one more stake to other validators and then publish this other branch.

Another security issue of the Proof-of-Stake is possible centralization. The following papers have identified this as a common security issue of the Proof-of-Stake consensus algorithm. Nodes are selected to be validators by a weighted random selection process. The more a node stakes, the higher the probability that they will be selected as a validator. This means that the rich will get richer and centralization will start occurring [23].

5 Future Work and Implications for Researchers

This systematic literature review provides a researcher with key characteristics to take into consideration when creating optimized blockchain consensus algorithms. It identified these characteristics to be security, scalability, and efficiency. As a result of the findings of this research paper, the following areas of research are proposed:

- Quantitative research into the scalability, security and efficiency of blockchain solutions on a larger scale.
- Quantitative research on how efficiency can affect the security and scalability of blockchain solutions.
- Quantitative research into the efficiency of blockchain consensus algorithms. A common pattern noticed in the analysed papers was that they relied on comparing the consensus algorithms to Proof-of-Work and logically deducing that it's more energy efficient. This may be the case, but statistical real-world evidence needs to be researched to determine the true energy consumption of a consensus algorithm

6 Conclusion

Blockchain will disrupt many industries and the core component of this technology is consensus algorithms. Currently, Proof-of-Work and Proof-of-Stake are two of the most popular algorithms, but they yield many disadvantages [23]. As a result, this systematic literature review identified the characteristics to create optimized blockchain consensus algorithms. These findings indicated that there were many different advantages and disadvantages for the different consensus algorithms. From these findings, key characteristics identified were scalability, security, and efficiency. It was determined that these three key characteristics are key to developing optimized solutions as they will affect real-world applications. Due to the findings of this research paper, further research areas related to these characteristics were proposed.

References

1. Ali, I., Gervais, M., Ahene, E., Li, F.: A blockchain-based certificateless public key signature scheme for vehicle-to-infrastructure communication in VANETs. J. Syst. Archit. **99**, 101636 (2019)
2. Azzi, R., Chamoun, R.K., Sokhn, M.: The power of a blockchain-based supply chain. Comput. Ind. Eng. **135**, 582–592 (2019)

3. Viriyasitavat, W., Hoonsopon, D.: Blockchain characteristics and consensus in modern business processes. J. Ind. Inf. Integr. **13**, 32–39 (2019)
4. Scully, P., Höbig, M.: Exploring the impact of blockchain on digitized Supply Chain flows: a literature review. In: 2019 Sixth International Conference on Software Defined Systems (SDS), pp. 278–283 (2019)
5. Gemeliarana, I.G.A.K., Sari, R.F.: Evaluation of proof of work (POW) blockchains security network on selfish mining. In: 2018 International Seminar on Research of Information Technology and Intelligent Systems (ISRITI), pp. 126–130 (2018)
6. Deirmentzoglou, E., Papakyriakopoulos, G., Patsakis, C.: A survey on long-range attacks for proof of stake protocols. IEEE Access **7**, 28712–28725 (2019)
7. Aste, T., Tasca, P., Matteo, T.D.: Blockchain technologies: the foreseeable impact on society and industry. Computer **50**(9), 18–28 (2017)
8. Hazari, S.S., Mahmoud, Q.H.: A parallel proof of work to improve transaction speed and scalability in blockchain systems. In: 2019 IEEE 9th Annual Computing and Communication Workshop and Conference (CCWC), pp. 0916–0921 (2019)
9. Mohanta, B.K., Jena, D., Panda, S.S., Sobhanayak, S.: Blockchain technology: a survey on applications and security privacy Challenges. Internet Things **8**, 100107 (2019)
10. Han, X., Yuan, Y., Wang, F.-Y.: A fair blockchain based on proof of credit. IEEE Trans. Comput. Soc. Syst. **6**(5), 922–931 (2019)
11. Sharkey, S., Tewari, H.: Alt-PoW: an alternative proof-of-work mechanism. In: 2019 IEEE International Conference on Decentralized Applications and Infrastructures (DAPPCON), pp. 11–18 (2019)
12. Alsunaidi, S.J., Alhaidari, F.A.: A survey of consensus algorithms for blockchain technology. In: 2019 International Conference on Computer and Information Sciences (ICCIS), pp. 1–6 (2019)
13. Agrawal, H.: Different types of blockchains in the market and why we need them. CoinSutra - Bitcoin Community (2017). https://coinsutra.com/different-types-blockchains/. Accessed 24 Sep 2019
14. Andoni, M., et al.: Blockchain technology in the energy sector: a systematic review of challenges and opportunities. Renew. Sustain. Energy Rev. **100**, 143–174 (2019)
15. Wang, Y., Han, J.H., Beynon-Davies, P.: Understanding blockchain technology for future supply chains: a systematic literature review and research agenda. Supply Chain Manag. Int. J. **24**(1), 62–84 (2019)
16. Rimol, M.: Gartner 2019 Hype Cycle for Blockchain Business Shows Blockchain Will Have a Transformational Impact across Industries in Five to 10 Years (2019)
17. Zhang, S., Lee, J.-H.: Analysis of the main consensus protocols of blockchain. ICT Exp. S240595951930164X (2019)
18. Yang, F., Zhou, W., Wu, Q., Long, R., Xiong, N.N., Zhou, M.: Delegated proof of stake with downgrade: a secure and efficient blockchain consensus algorithm with downgrade mechanism. IEEE Access **7**, 118541–118555 (2019)
19. Chen, L., Xu, L., Gao, Z., Lu, Y., Shi, W.: Protecting early stage proof-of-work based public blockchain. In: 2018 48th Annual IEEE/IFIP International Conference on Dependable Systems and Networks Workshops (DSN-W), pp. 122–127 (2018)
20. Wang, X., et al.: Survey on blockchain for Internet of Things. Comput. Commun. **136**, 10–29 (2019)
21. Liu, Z., Tang, S., Chow, S.S.M., Liu, Z., Long, Y.: Fork-free hybrid consensus with flexible proof-of-activity. Future Gener. Comput. Syst. **96**, 515–524 (2019)
22. Buterin, V., Reijsbergen, D., Leonardos, S., Piliouras, G.: Incentives in ethereum's hybrid casper protocol. In: 2019 IEEE International Conference on Blockchain and Cryptocurrency (ICBC), pp. 236–244 (2019)

23. Aljassas, H.M.A., Sasi, S.: Performance evaluation of proof-of-work and collatz conjecture consensus algorithms. In: 2019 2nd International Conference on Computer Applications Information Security (ICCAIS), pp. 1–6 (2019)
24. Nguyen, C.T., Hoang, D.T., Nguyen, D.N., Niyato, D., Nguyen, H.T., Dutkiewicz, E.: Proof-of-stake consensus mechanisms for future blockchain networks: fundamentals, applications and opportunities. IEEE Access **7**, 85727–85745 (2019)
25. Gaži, P., Kiayias, A., Russell, A.: Stake-bleeding attacks on proof-of-stake blockchains. In: 2018 Crypto Valley Conference on Blockchain Technology (CVCBT), pp. 85–92 (2018)
26. Lipton, A.: Blockchains and distributed ledgers in retrospective and perspective. J. Risk Finance **19**(1), 4–25 (2018)
27. Makhdoom, I., Abolhasan, M., Abbas, H., Ni, W.: Blockchain's adoption in IoT: the challenges, and a way forward. J. Netw. Comput. Appl. **125**, 251–279 (2019)
28. Chomsiri, T., Kongsup, K.: P coin: high speed cryptocurrency based on random-checkers proof of stake. In: 2018 Joint 10th International Conference on Soft Computing and Intelligent Systems (SCIS) and 19th International Symposium on Advanced Intelligent Systems (ISIS), pp. 524–529 (2018)
29. Kang, J., Xiong, Z., Niyato, D., Wang, P., Ye, D., Kim, D.I.: Incentivizing consensus propagation in proof-of-stake based consortium blockchain networks. IEEE Wirel. Commun. Lett. **8**(1), 157–160 (2019)
30. Nawari, N.O., Ravindran, S.: Blockchain and the built environment: potentials and limitations. J. Build. Eng. **25**, 100832 (2019)
31. Li, X., Jiang, P., Chen, T., Luo, X., Wen, Q.: A survey on the security of blockchain systems. Future Gener. Comput. Syst. S0167739X17318332 (2017)
32. Tosh, D., Shetty, S., Foytik, P., Kamhoua, C., Njilla, L., CloudPoS: a proof-of-stake consensus design for blockchain integrated cloud. In: 2018 IEEE 11th International Conference on Cloud Computing (CLOUD), pp. 302–309 (2018)
33. Chen, J., Micali, S.: Algorand: a secure and efficient distributed ledger. Theor. Comput. Sci. **777**, 155–183 (2019)
34. Lucas, B., Páez, R.V.: Consensus algorithm for a private blockchain. In: 2019 IEEE 9th International Conference on Electronics Information and Emergency Communication (ICEIEC), pp. 264–271 (2019)
35. Lyu, Q., Qi, Y., Zhang, X., Liu, H., Wang, Q., Zheng, N.: SBAC: a secure blockchain-based access control framework for information-centric networking. J. Netw. Comput. Appl. **149**, 102444 (2020)
36. Yu, B., Liu, J., Nepal, S., Yu, J., Rimba, P.: Proof-of-QoS: QoS based blockchain consensus protocol. Comput. Secur. **87**, 101580 (2019)
37. Niya, S.R., et al.: Adaptation of proof-of-stake-based blockchains for IoT data streams. In: 2019 IEEE International Conference on Blockchain and Cryptocurrency (ICBC), pp. 15–16 (2019)
38. Mohanty, S.N., et al.: An efficient lightweight integrated blockchain (ELIB) model for IoT security and privacy. Future Gener. Comput. Syst. **102**, 1027–1037 (2020)
39. Kumar, G., Saha, R., Rai, M.K., Thomas, R., Kim, T.-H.: Proof-of-work consensus approach in blockchain technology for cloud and fog computing using maximization-factorization statistics. IEEE Internet Things J. **6**(4), 6835–6842 (2019)
40. Tosh, D.K., Shetty, S., Liang, X., Kamhoua, C., Njilla, L.: Consensus protocols for blockchain-based data provenance: challenges and opportunities. In: 2017 IEEE 8th Annual Ubiquitous Computing, Electronics and Mobile Communication Conference (UEMCON), pp. 469–474 (2017)
41. Sengupta, J., Ruj, S., Das Bit, S.: A comprehensive survey on attacks, security issues and blockchain solutions for IoT and IIoT. J. Netw. Comput. Appl. **149**, 102481 (2020)

42. Guan, Z., Lu, X., Wang, N., Wu, J., Du, X., Guizani, M.: Towards secure and efficient energy trading in IIoT-enabled energy internet: a blockchain approach. Future Gener. Comput. Syst. S0167739X19315018 (2019)
43. Puthal, D., Mohanty, S.P., Nanda, P., Kougianos, E., Das, G.: Proof-of-authentication for scalable blockchain in resource-constrained distributed systems. In: 2019 IEEE International Conference on Consumer Electronics (ICCE), pp. 1–5 (2019)
44. Ogawa, T., Kima, H., Miyaho, N., Proposal of proof-of-lucky-id (PoL) to solve the problems of PoW and PoS. In: 2018 IEEE International Conference on Internet of Things (iThings) and IEEE Green Computing and Communications (GreenCom) and IEEE Cyber, Physical and Social Computing (CPSCom) and IEEE Smart Data (SmartData), pp. 1212–1218 (2018)
45. Zhang, R., Preneel, B.: Lay down the common metrics: evaluating proof-of-work consensus protocols' security. In: 2019 IEEE Symposium on Security and Privacy (SP), pp. 175–192 (2019)
46. Chou, C.-N., Lin, Y.-J., Chen, R., Chang, H.-Y., Tu, I.-P., Liao, S.-W.: Personalized difficulty adjustment for countering the double-spending attack in proof-of-work consensus protocols. In: 2018 IEEE International Conference on Internet of Things (iThings) and IEEE Green Computing and Communications (GreenCom) and IEEE Cyber, Physical and Social Computing (CPSCom) and IEEE Smart Data (SmartData), pp. 1456–1462 (2018)

A Systematic Literature Review of Blockchain Consensus Protocols

Sikho Luzipo[1] and Aurona Gerber[1,2](✉)

[1] University of Pretoria, Pretoria, South Africa
aurona.gerber@up.ac.za
[2] The Center for AI Research (CAIR), Pretoria, South Africa

Abstract. Blockchain is the underlying technology behind Bitcoin, the first digital currency, and due to the rapid growth of Bitcoin, there is significant interest in blockchain as the enabler of digital currencies due to the consensus distributed ledger model. The rise and the success of alternative cryptocurrencies such as Ethereum and Ripple has supported the development of blockchain technology, but the performance of blockchain applications has been documented as a significant obstacle for adoption. At the core of blockchain is a consensus protocol, which plays a key role in maintaining the safety, performance and efficiency of the blockchain network. Several consensus protocols exist, and the use of the right consensus protocol is crucial to ensure adequate performance of any blockchain application. However, there is a lack of documented overview studies even though there is agreement in the literature about the importance and understanding of blockchain consensus protocols. In this study, we adopt a systematic literature review (SLR) to investigate the current status of consensus protocols used for blockchain together with the identified limitations of these protocols. The results of this study include an overview of different consensus protocols as well as consensus protocol limitations and will be of value for any practitioner or scholar that is interested in blockchain applications.

Keywords: Blockchain technology · Consensus protocols · Challenges

1 Introduction

Since its emergence as the core underlying technology for Bitcoin in 2008 [31], blockchain technology has evolved from its use as a verification mechanism for cryptocurrencies to a broader field of applications. Blockchain's primary objective is to provide a transactional, distributed ledger functionality with the aim of eliminating the need for trusted intermediary third-parties [3]. This implies that with blockchain, applications that operate through the use of trusted intermediaries can now operate in a decentralized way without relying on intermediaries and achieve the same level of functionality and benefits [9].

Despite the well documented benefits of blockchain technology, its adoption is still very limited due to performance challenges. Many scholars associate these challenges

D. Dennehy et al. (Eds.): I3E 2021, LNCS 12896, pp. 580–595, 2021.
https://doi.org/10.1007/978-3-030-85447-8_48

to one of blockchain's key components namely the consensus protocol algorithm [6], the mechanism that allows blockchain to decentralize trust [23]. A consensus protocol ensures that all participants on the blockchain system reach an agreement with regards to the validity of transactions in the ledger [21]. In a blockchain network, consensus protocols fulfil the role that a single authority has in a centralized database or ledger.

According to Wu and Gao [41], consensus protocols have delayed the development and widespread adoption of blockchain technology. The reliability and efficiency of these consensus protocols remain a challenge [20]. Gramoli [18] emphasized that the issues experienced with existing blockchain consensus protocols maybe as a result of fundamental design flaws. The many different positions on consensus protocols motivated the need for this study, namely, to use literature to identify the different consensus protocols and protocol limitations.

Due to the increasing importance and popularity of blockchain technology together with consensus protocols, there is a need to understand the current consensus protocols used in blockchain technology applications and the limitations that are associated with them. To address this need, a systematic literature review (SLR) was conducted [24]. Section 2 provides background for this study, Sect. 3 describes the research method, Sect. 4 documents the findings and Sect. 5 concludes.

2 Background

According to Aste et al. [4], blockchain is better understood when viewed with two lenses. The first lens views blockchain as information and communications technology (ICT) that is aimed at recording ownership of assets and contractual agreements. This is because of the inherent characteristics of blockchain technology such as untemperability, immutability, transparency and traceability of information stored on the ledger [11]. The second lens views blockchain as an institutional technology aimed at decentralising structures that are aimed at governing economic decisions and people. Blockchain can be defined as a distributed data structure that is used to hold information shared among various members of the network [43].

Literature identified two challenges that are preventing widespread adoption of blockchain [39, 42, 45]. The first challenge, which has been the focus of many studies, is the scalability in terms of the efficiency and resilience of the consensus protocol. The second challenge affecting the adoption of blockchain technology is how to ensure the degree of transaction privacy that is a standard requirement in most real-world applications today. Both these challenges are linked to the consensus protocol which are the core of blockchain technology.

2.1 Blockchain Consensus Protocols

In a distributed ledger system, consensus represents a state that there is agreement among all the participants regarding the same data values [42]. Consensus is a procedure that allows participants in decentralized or distributed multi-agent platforms to arrive at a common agreement [35]. According to Zhao et al. [47], consensus has been a problem in distributed computing since the early 1980s.

To reach consensus in the network, each node needs to exchange information with other nodes. There may be some instances whereby some nodes will be down or offline and there will also be some malicious nodes with the intention of disrupting the consensus process [18]. These malicious nodes that behave arbitrarily are often referred to as Byzantine failures [38]. A consensus protocol that is Byzantine tolerant aims to guarantee the correctness of the network (blockchain system) by ensuring the order of the newly created blocks of transactions [18]. The design and the implementation of the consensus protocol needs to address how to deal with these problems [38].

In blockchain, new blocks are added by following a protocol that establishes consensus among the members of the network to confirm the validity of the new block [10]. A consensus protocol is defined as a set rules that guide the way users utilize their computing power to arrive at consensus to create new blocks [25]. It allows self-interested peers to reach agreements and make consistent decisions when faced with contradictory alternatives [28]. The stability of a blockchain system is directly determined by the effectiveness of the consensus protocol [45]. Ferdous et al. [14] described consensus protocol as the most crucial component in the design of a blockchain system as it determines its security and performance. As a result, a number of consensus protocols have been proposed. These range from new designs to modifications to some of the well-known consensus mechanisms in the distributed systems literature. Proof of Work (PoW) and Proof of Stake (PoS) are the two most widely used consensus protocols for blockchain [25]. According to Herlihy [19], the design of a consensus protocols should satisfy the following properties, *agreement* (all honest parties should agree on the block that was selected, no two correct processes should propose different blocks), *validity* (the selected block is valid), *termination* (all honest parties eventually decide on a block) and *integrity* (no parties should decide twice).

Even though there are many consensus protocols that have been proposed, Wu and Gao [41] argue that these have many shortcomings which are preventing blockchain from meeting the expected performance requirements of various applications. Leornados et al. [28] argued that the choice of a consensus protocol has a very critical role in the success of blockchain as it has an impact on the security and performance of a blockchain system.

3 SLR Research Method

In this study, a systematic literature review (SLR) was conducted to review the current consensus protocols used in blockchain technology. The SLR was based on Kitchenham's guidelines and includes three phases namely (1) planning, (2) conducting and (3) documenting the review. Each phase is described in the sections that follow and the process is depicted in Fig. 1.

3.1 Systematic Literature Review Planning

During the planning phase the rationale for the review and the research questions that will guide the review and review protocol are identified as described below.

The Purpose of a Systematic Literature Review: Altarawneh et al. [2] identified four categories of the reasons for conducting literature reviews which are describe, test, extend and critique previously published studies. This SLR aimed to identify the current consensus protocols and limitations of blockchain technology that have been mentioned in the literature, and the SLR is therefore descriptive.

Review Protocol: The review protocol is the written plan that is completed prior to the start of the SLR [24], which specifies conditions for the selection of primary studies as well as any boundaries that may apply [8]. The main components of a review protocol include the research questions that will guide the review, search strategy, the resources (databases) to be used, selection of the studies and quality assessment procedures. Table 1 presents the research questions that were proposed to guide this review.

Table 1. Research questions for the SLR

ID	Research question	Motivation
RQ1	What are the current consensus protocols that have been mentioned in the literature for different blockchain systems and how are they classified?	The purpose of this question is to provide information about the current consensus protocols that have been mentioned in the literature
RQ2	What are the limitations of the current consensus protocols?	The purpose of this question is to provide information about the limitations of blockchain consensus protocols that have been mentioned in the literature

The identified research questions are followed by the formulation of the search strategy to be used to find studies that will assist with answering the research questions. The search process involves the selection of digital libraries, defining the search terms, executing pilot search, refining the search term and the retrieval of initial list of primary studies from the literature databases (Table 5) based on the search string. To ensure comprehensive coverage of all the blockchain technology literature related to consensus protocols, the following search string was used: "Blockchain Consensus Protocols"

Table 2. Inclusion and exclusion criteria

Papers included	Papers excluded
• English peer reviewed studies published in conferences, workshops, symposiums and journals related to the research topic • Study contains discussion /analysis about a specific consensus protocol for blockchain technology (RQ1) • Study contains discussion/ analysis about the limitations or challenges of blockchain consensus protocols (RQ2)	• Papers which are not related to the research questions • Opinion pieces, viewpoints or purely anecdotal and short papers (poster) • Non-peer reviewed articles • Articles that only review blockchain technology

OR "Blockchain Protocols" OR "Blockchain Consensus Protocols" OR "Blockchain Protocols" OR "Blockchain Consensus Mechanism".

The source selection criteria are determined next, and Table 2 provides inclusion/exclusion criteria used to select relevant studies.

The quality assessment procedure is compiled to ensure the quality of the sources that will be included in the SLR, and the checklist for the current study is outlined Table 3.

Table 3. Quality assessment checklist (Adapted from [13])

• Are objectives of the study clearly defined?
• Are different types of blockchain consensus protocols clearly defined?
• Are the benefits/importance of consensus protocols clearly defined?
• Are the challenges of blockchain consensus protocols clearly defined?
• Does the study make a contribution to academia or the industry?
• Are the findings of the study clearly defined and supported by reporting results?

Data Extraction and Data Synthesis Strategy: The data extraction and data analysis

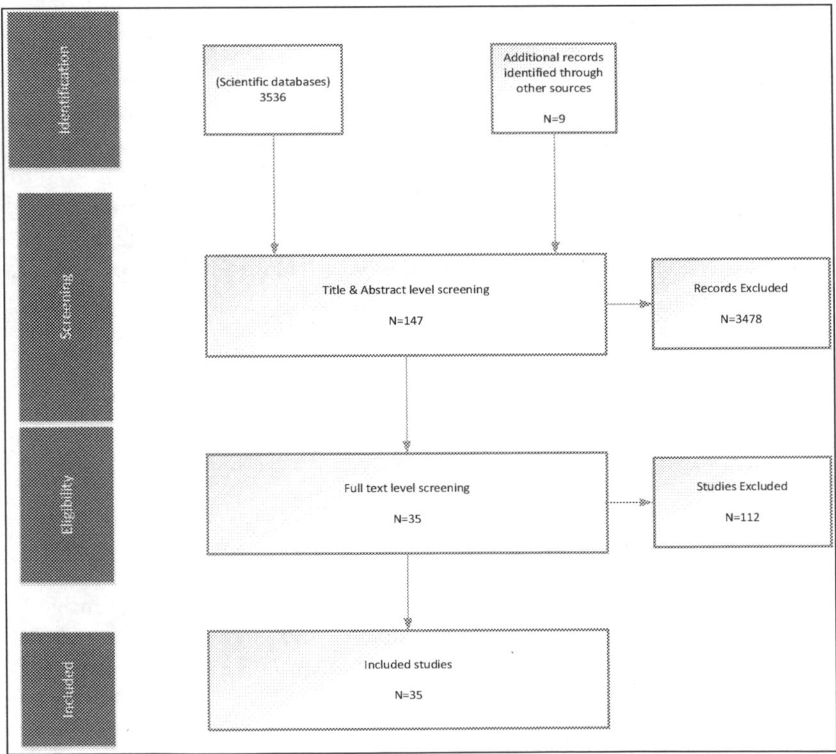

Fig. 1. SLR process

strategy are described in the next section. The strategy included that reference details of each of the relevant studies were recorded in Zotero (www.zotero.org), and notes and themes were identified. Narrative analysis and synthesis was adopted in order to identify the data related to the research questions.

3.2 Conducting the Review

During this phase the actual review is executed. The data extraction procedure involved four selection phases. The initial search resulted in a total of 3536 papers from the scientific databases as shown in Table 4. This was followed by selection by title and abstract reading. Due to the high number of the studies, only the first 200 relevant studies were reviewed from each of the databases as these were the most significant cited papers. In the end, there were 147 studies that met the inclusion criteria, and these were selected for full analysis and synthesis. These studies were then evaluated against the quality assessment checklist outlined in Table 3. A total of 35 papers remained at the end of this phase. The process is depicted in Fig. 1.

Table 4. Number of studies identified from the search databases

Database	Results	Search strategy	Search Date
ACM Digital library	166	Abstract and keywords	27-11-2020
IEEE Explore	2451	Abstract and keywords	28-11-2020
ScienceDirect	252	Abstract, title and keywords	11-12-2020
Springer Link	602	Abstract, title and keywords	11-12-2020
Ebsco	65	Abstract, title and keywords	11-12-2020
Total	**3536**		

3.3 Reporting the Review

During this phase the results of the review are documented. For the purpose of this paper the results and findings of this SLR are presented in the next section.

4 Findings: Blockchain Consensus Protocols

Thirty-five studies published between 2016 and 2021 were selected, and each study addressed one or both research questions. Among these, 20 papers were published in journals, 14 appeared in conference proceedings and one paper was extracted from a symposium. The number of papers by year publication is shown in Fig. 2.

4.1 Consensus Protocols Used in Blockchain Technology (RQ1)

Figure 2 provides a graphical representation of the current blockchain consensus protocols that have been identified in the SLR with a description presented in Table 5. In addition to all the protocols, three categories of consensus protocols were identified namely proof-based, voting-based and committee-based (hybrid) consensus protocols, which are briefly summarized in the remainder of this section.

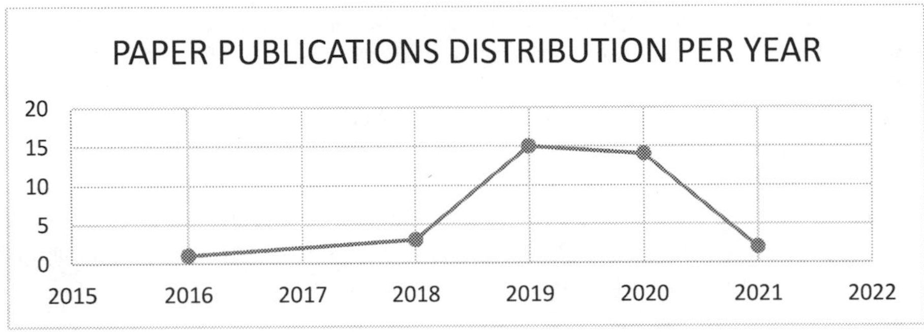

Fig. 2. Number of papers by year of publication

Table 5. Blockchain consensus protocols

Blockchain consensus classification	Reference
Permissioned consensus protocols; Permissionless consensus protocols	[29]
Public based consensus protocols; Alliance based consensus protocols	[47]
Leader based consensus protocols; Voting-based consensus protocols Committee + Voting based protocols; Fair accountant based protocols	[16]
Proof based; Capability based; Voting based; Compute Intensive-based	[7]
Proof based; Voting based	[22]
Quorum; Deterministic	[30]
Probabilistic finality; Absolute finality	[17, 46]
Leader-based; Voting based	[1]
Committee based; Sharding-based	[44]
Proof based; Voting based	[27, 34]
Incentivized consensus protocols; Non-incentivized consensus protocols	Bouraga (2021)
Classical consensus protocols; Elected leader consensus protocols Hybrid single committee consensus protocols; Hybrid multiple committee consensus protocols	Bano et al. (2019)

Proof-based consensus protocols are based on the idea that the node with sufficient proof will get the right to add the new block [27]. According to Wang et al. [40], each participant in proof-based consensus protocols has an attribute that is called the proof method. One of the main advantages of proof-based methods is that they guarantee consistency of under normal circumstances [27]. The most popular proof-based consensus protocol is proof of work (PoW) proposed by Nakamoto [31]. These protocols are mostly suited for public blockchains. Proof-based consensus protocols are also referred as 'leader-based consensus' [16] or 'competitive leader-based' [1]. Table 7 provides a list of some of the consensus protocols that fall in this category (Fig. 3).

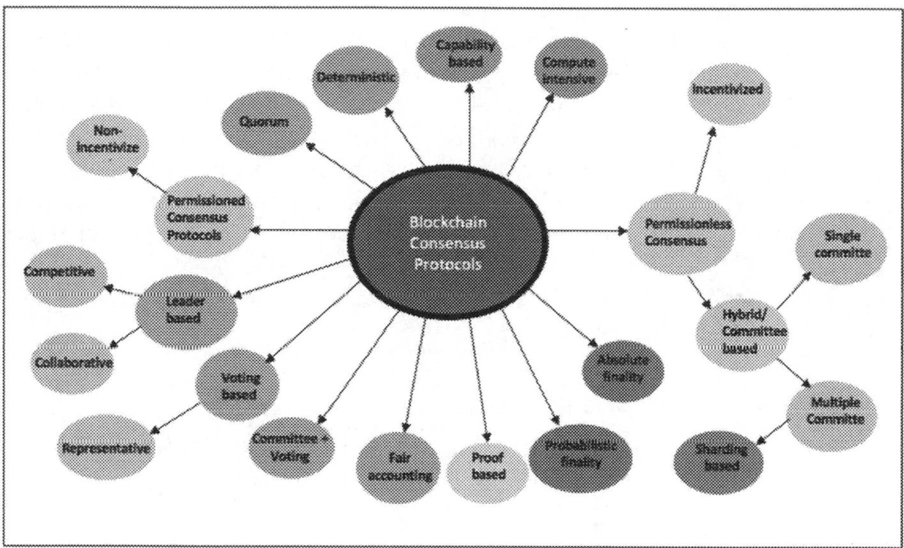

Fig. 3. Blockchain consensus protocols

Voting-based consensus protocols use a voting system to elect a node that is allowed to create a new block. In voting consensus protocols, nodes vote for the blocks they think are valid instead of competing [1]. For a node to append a block, a certain number of nodes must agree. If there are non-responsive nodes, the number of responsive nodes should exceed the non-responsive nodes for the voting consensus protocols to work. These types are mostly suited for use in private or consortium blockchains [34]. There are three stages [16] that must be followed for a block to be added in voting consensus protocols. In the first phase pre-prepare, the primary node that must send the block to other nodes (called replicas) verification. In the second phase, prepare, each replica sends back the verification results to all the other nodes. All replicas must confirm the new block. During the third phase, commit, each replica sends the verification result of the prepare stage to all other nodes again, and each node makes a final confirmation of the block according to the message received. Ismail and Materwala [21] classified voting consensus protocols into Bayzantine Fault Tolerant (BFT) based and Crash Fault Tolerant (CFT) based. A BFT based consensus ensures that the blockchain network will continue to operate even in the presence of malicious or failure nodes whereas a CFT based consensus prevents the system from failing when the node goes offline or crashes.

PBFT is one of the most popular BFT based consensus protocols used in blockchain. Altarawneh et al. [1] identified two broad categories of voting consensus protocols namely *representative* voting and *gossip* voting (not currently used in blockchain). In representative voting consensus protocols, a group of nodes are elected as representatives with the task of proposing new blocks. Some of the consensus protocols that fall in this category are listed in Table 7.

Committee-based (hybrid) consensus protocols have been proposed to address the imitations of single node consensus protocols where a committee rather than a single node is responsible for driving consensus. There are two types of committee-based consensus protocols namely single and multi-committee consensus protocols [29]. In single committee, the committee is responsible for managing transactions, while multiple committees act in parallel in order to improve the scalability of the blockchain network in multi-committee consensus protocols. The consensus process in single committees involves the following steps: committee formation, committee configuration and the actual consensus mechanism [6]. The consensus process for multi-committees comprises of committee topology, intra-committee configuration and the intra-committee consensus.

Table 6. Proof-based consensus protocols

Consensus protocols	How sufficient proof is achieved
Proof of Work (PoW)	Nodes are required to solve a puzzle with adjusted level of difficulty. The first node to solve the puzzle will get the right to append the new node in the current chain
Proof of stake	The node to append the next block on the blockchain is decided based on the size of the stake
Proof of elapsed time	In this type of consensus protocol, each node on the blockchain requests a wait-time. After all the nodes have received their wait-times, a timeout is set with scheduling and the node with the shortest wait-time wins the right to mine the new block
Proof of luck	In proof of luck, all the nodes are required to make their own blocks with different lucky numbers and add these to their chains. The chain with the most lucky numbers is chosen as the main one
Proof of space	In this consensus protocol, nodes are required to invest commit relevant disk space. A number of datasets called plots will be generated by proof of space protocol. The miner storing the most number of plots can mine a new block

Table 7. Voting-based consensus protocols

Consensus protocol	How consensus is achieved
Delegated Proof of Stake (DPoS)	DPoS works like a democracy, nodes in the network can register as voters in order to become shareholders and then have the right to vote for the block producers they want
Practical Byzantine Fault Tolerance (PBFT)	There is no leader required in PBFT. Instead, one node is considered as the primary and the others are regarded as replicas
Hotstuff	Hotstuff is considered as a leader variant of PBFT. Nodes communicate with each other via a leader resulting in a star communication network as compared to mesh communication network in PBFT
LibraBFT	LibraBFT is also a variant of PBFT consensus protocol. It makes improvements on Hotstuff with the introduction of a detailed specification and implementation of the Peacemaker mechanism
Delegated Byzantine Fault Tolerance (DBFT)	Consensus is achieved by selecting a group of nodes (representatives) through a vote. The selected nodes then use BFT consensus mechanism to reach a consensus and generate a new block
Federated Byzantine Agreement (FBA)	In FBA, any node can participate in the consensus process. All the participating nodes communicate with a group of nodes referred to as Unique Node List (UNL). A new transaction is added if 80% of the participating nodes agree
Raft CFT	In this consensus protocol, each node in the network is either a follower, candidate or leader. A leader is responsible for packaging all the new transactions received from the client and sends them to followers. Each block is replicated by the followers and acknowledgement sent to the leader. Once the leader receives confirmation from followers, it executes the transactions in the block and notifies the client

(*continued*)

Table 7. (*continued*)

Consensus protocol	How consensus is achieved
Federated CFT	In this type of consensus protocol, a leader and backup nodes are selected from a group of other nodes. The leader is responsible for validating and creating new blocks and the backup nodes are responsible for verifying the new blocks
Combined Delegated Proof of Stake and Byzantine Fault Tolerance (DPoS + BFT)	This consensus protocol uses DPoS to select the nodes to participate in the consensus process and then BFT to add the new transaction on the network

4.2 Challenges with the Current Blockchain Consensus Protocols (RQ2)

The most common challenges of blockchain consensus protocols that have been mentioned in the literature can be categorised under proof-based and voting-based and challenges that can happen on any of the two types (common attacks) as shown in Fig. 4. Table 8 list proof-based and voting-based protocol challenges, while Table 9 summarise the common attack challenges.

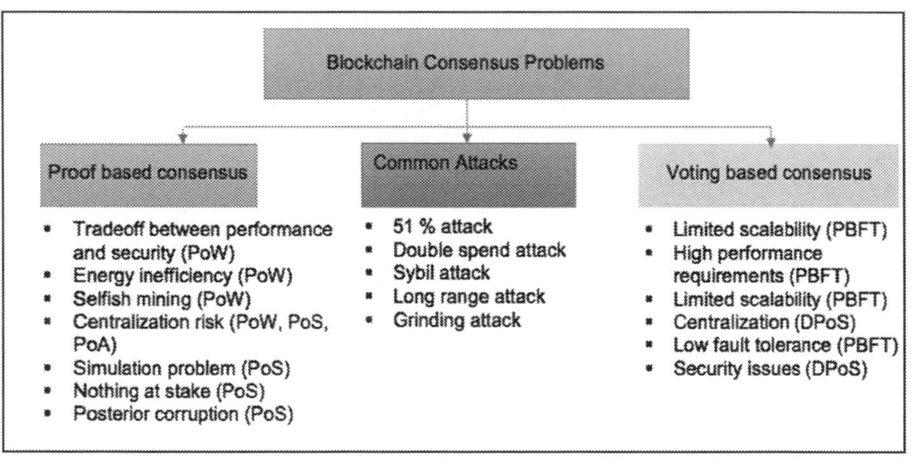

Fig. 4. Blockchain consensus protocol challenges

Challenges associated with proof-based consensus protocols: One of the most popular proof-based consensus protocols is proof of work (PoW). The main criticism of PoW is that it consumes a lot of power [34] without generating anything useful [1]. These challenges have led to a number. of new consensus protocols with the aim of addressing these limitations, however, these new consensus protocols introduced their own challenges. For example, even though proof of stake (PoS) eliminated energy inefficiencies, it did it at the expense of decentralisation [5]. PoS has been criticized for its security

Table 8. Challenges associated with consensus protocols

Consensus protocols	Challenge	Reference
Proof-based consensus protocols	Tight trade-off between performance and security	[42]
	Energy inefficiency	[5, 42, 46]
	Vulnerability to selfish mining	[33, 42]
	Mining pools and centralization risk	[42]
	Costless simulation problem	[42]
	Nothing-at-stake problem	[29, 42]
	Vulnerability to the posterior corruption	[42]
	Vulnerability to the long-range attack	[29, 42]
	Vulnerability to the stake-grinding attack	[29, 42]
	Centralization risk	[5, 15, 42]
Voting-based consensus protocols	Limited scalability	[37, 40]
	High performance requirements	[46]
	Centralisation	[37]
	Low fault tolerance	[5]
	Security issues	[37, 40]

measures [32], nothing at stake problem [29] which leads to double spending [42]. Proof of burn (PoB) has been suggested as an alternative to PoW, however Sharma & Jain [36] argued that PoB wastes resources with no plan of recovering the money. Proof of Weight (PoWeight) is another alternative consensus protocol that has been proposed to address the weaknesses of PoS but has been criticized for not incentivizing nodes [36]. In proof-based consensus protocols, there is also a possibility of miners to mine in secrecy in order to create forks when they want to do so [33].

Challenges Associated with Voting-Based Consensus Protocols: One of the main issues with voting-based consensus protocols such as PBFT is scalability. The frequent network node communication generates high traffic overhead [26]. They are not suitable for networks with large number of nodes [40]. Another issue that has been raised with voting based consensus protocols is centralization due to reduction of the number of verification nodes [40]. PBFT assume a defined closed group therefore not suitable for open networks where anyone can join [22]. PBFT has also been criticized for its inability to identify and remove faulty nodes [27]. The security of DPoS has been criticized by [40], they argued that it has a weak defense against malicious nodes. Since the committee members control the creation of new blocks in DPoS, if these members become malicious other nodes will be unable to do anything [47].

Table 9. Common blockchain consensus protocol attacks

Attack type	Description
51% attack	This type of attack usually occurs when a node or group of nodes tries to take control of more than fifty percent of the blockchain network's proof method such as stake in case of PoS or computing power in case of PoW. Once an attacker takes over the control of the blockchain, they can engage in malicious activities such as double spending
Double spend attack	This type of an attack happens when a person tries to spend a specific amount that has already been spent on the blockchain [46]. This type of attack can be a result of an error or in the system or deliberate fraud
Sybil attack	In this form an attack, an adversary uses numerous forged identities in order to confuse the blockchain network [12]. Sybil attack is mostly common in public blockchains as the identities of the nodes is unknown
Long range attack	This attack happens when the adversary tries to produce new blocks before the current block. This attack becomes successful when the branch created by adversary gets longer than longer and overtakes the main chain
Grinding attack	In grinding attack, an adversary performs some computation in order to try manipulate the randomness in their favour [42]. The attacker tries to increase their chances of generating future blocks based on the information of the current block [30]

5 Conclusion

This study adopted a SLR to provide an overview of current consensus protocols used in blockchain technology and the challenges that have been mentioned in the literature for consensus protocols. The SLR was executed using five digital libraries and selecting 35 peer-reviewed articles published in either journals or conferences between 2016 and 2021 that adhere to the quality protocols. The findings of the SLR indicate there is no single common standard or framework for developing consensus protocols for blockchain technology, bit that a number of protocols exist that can be categorized as either proof-based, voting-based or committee-based/hybrid consensus protocols. Limitations are associated with either strategy namely proof-based or voting-based, as well as common attacks that impact both categories. Even though there is agreement in the literature about the importance of consensus protocols in blockchain, there is lack of documentation on how to design and develop effective consensus protocols to address the needs of specific blockchain technology applications. Even though new and improved consensus protocols are proposed to address limitations, they introduce their own set of limitations and challenges. The findings from this study could assist with an increased awareness of blockchain consensus protocols as well as their limitations.

References

1. Altarawneh, A., et al.: Buterin's scalability trilemma viewed through a state-change-based classification for common consensus algorithms. In: 2020 10th Annual Computing and Communication Workshop and Conference (CCWC), pp. 0727–0736 (2020). https://doi.org/10.1109/CCWC47524.2020.9031204
2. Altarawneh, G., et al.: Synthesizing information systems knowledge: a typology of literature reviews. Inf. Manage. **52**(2), 183–199 (2015)
3. Andoni, M., et al.: Blockchain technology in the energy sector: a systematic review of challenges and opportunities. Renew. Sustain. Energy Rev. **100**, 143–174 (2019). https://doi.org/10.1016/j.rser.2018.10.014
4. Aste, T., et al.: Blockchain technologies: foreseeable impact on industry and society. Computer **50**(9), 18–28 (2017)
5. Bamakan, S.M.H., et al.: A survey of blockchain consensus algorithms performance evaluation criteria. Expert Syst. Appl. **154**, 113385 (2020)
6. Bano, S., et al.: SoK: consensus in the age of blockchains. In: Proceedings of the 1st ACM Conference on Advances in Financial Technologies, Zurich, Switzerland, pp. 183–198. Association for Computing Machinery (2019). https://doi.org/10.1145/3318041.3355458
7. Bodkhe, U., et al.: A survey on decentralized consensus mechanisms for cyber physical systems. IEEE Access **8**, 54371–54401 (2020)
8. Brereton, P., et al.: Lessons from applying the systematic literature review process within the software engineering domain. J. Syst. Softw. **80**(4), 571–583 (2007). https://doi.org/10.1016/j.jss.2006.07.009
9. Casado-Vara, R., et al.: How blockchain improves the supply chain: case study alimentary supply chain. Procedia Comput. Sci. **134**, 393–398 (2018). https://doi.org/10.1016/j.procs.2018.07.193
10. Cebe, M., et al.: Block4forensic: an integrated lightweight blockchain framework for forensics applications of connected vehicles. IEEE Commun. Mag. **56**(10), 50–57 (2018)
11. Chengfu, Y.: Research on autonomous and controllable high-performance consensus mechanism of blockchain. In: 2020 IEEE International Conference on Advances in Electrical Engineering and Computer Applications (AEECA), pp. 223–228 (2020). https://doi.org/10.1109/AEECA49918.2020.9213550
12. Deirmentzoglou, E., et al.: A survey on long-range attacks for proof of stake protocols. IEEE Access. **7**, 28712–28725 (2019). https://doi.org/10.1109/ACCESS.2019.2901858
13. Dybå, T., Dingsøyr, T.: Empirical studies of agile software development: a systematic review. Inf. Softw. Technol. **50**(9–10), 833–859 (2008). https://doi.org/10.1016/j.infsof.2008.01.006
14. Ferdous, M.S., et al.: Blockchain consensus algorithms: a survey. arXiv (2020)
15. Foti, M., et al.: Decentralized blockchain-based consensus for optimal power flow solutions. Appl. Energy **283**, 116100 (2021)
16. Fu, X., Wang, H., Shi, P.: A survey of Blockchain consensus algorithms: mechanism, design and applications. Sci. China Inf. Sci. **64**(2), 1–15 (2020). https://doi.org/10.1007/s11432-019-2790-1
17. Gao, S., et al.: T-PBFT: an EigenTrust-based practical Byzantine fault tolerance consensus algorithm. China Commun. **16**(12), 111–123 (2019). https://doi.org/10.23919/JCC.2019.12.008
18. Gramoli, V.: From blockchain consensus back to Byzantine consensus. Futur. Gener. Comput. Syst. **107**, 760–769 (2020). https://doi.org/10.1016/j.future.2017.09.023
19. Herlihy, M.: Blockchains from a distributed computing perspective. Commun. ACM **62**(2), 78–85 (2019)

20. Huang, C.-T., et al.: Consensus of whom? A spectrum of blockchain consensus protocols and new directions. In: 2019 IEEE International Smart Cities Conference (ISC2), pp. 1–8 (2019). https://doi.org/10.1109/ISC246665.2019.9071682
21. Ismail, L., Materwala, H.: A review of blockchain architecture and consensus protocols: use cases, challenges, and solutions. Symmetry **11**(10), 1198 (2019)
22. Jaroucheh, Z., et al.: SklCoin: toward a scalable proof-of-stake and collective signature based consensus protocol for strong consistency in blockchain. In: 2020 IEEE International Conference on Software Architecture Companion (ICSA-C), pp. 143–150. IEEE (2020)
23. Kim, D.-H., et al.: RSP consensus algorithm for blockchain. In: 2019 20th Asia-Pacific Network Operations and Management Symposium (APNOMS), pp. 1–4. IEEE (2019)
24. Kitchenham, B., et al.: Systematic literature reviews in software engineering – a systematic literature review. Inf. Softw. Technol. **51**(1), 7–15 (2009). https://doi.org/10.1016/j.infsof.2008.09.009
25. Kokina, J., et al.: Blockchain: emergent industry adoption and implications for accounting. J. Emerging Technol. Account. **14**(2), 91–100 (2017)
26. Lao, L., et al.: G-PBFT: a location-based and scalable consensus protocol for IOT-Blockchain applications. In: 2020 IEEE International Parallel and Distributed Processing Symposium (IPDPS), pp. 664–673 IEEE (2020)
27. Lei, K., et al.: Reputation-based byzantine fault-tolerance for consortium blockchain. In: 2018 IEEE 24th International Conference on Parallel and Distributed Systems (ICPADS), pp. 604–611 (2018). https://doi.org/10.1109/PADSW.2018.8644933
28. Leonardos, S., et al.: PREStO: a systematic framework for blockchain consensus protocols. IEEE Trans. Eng. Manage. **67**(4), 1028–1044 (2020)
29. Liu, Y., et al.: A fair selection protocol for committee-based permissionless blockchains. Comput. Secur. **91**, 101718 (2020)
30. Mackenzie, B., et al.: An assessment of blockchain consensus protocols for the Internet of Things. In: 2018 International Conference on Internet of Things, Embedded Systems and Communications (IINTEC), pp. 183–190. IEEE (2018)
31. Nakamoto, S.: A peer-to-peer electronic cash system. Bitcoin, vol. 4 (2008). https://bitcoin.org/bitcoin.pdf
32. Nguyen, C.T., et al.: Proof-of-stake consensus mechanisms for future blockchain networks: fundamentals, applications and opportunities. IEEE Access **7**, 85727–85745 (2019)
33. Niu, J., et al.: Incentive analysis of bitcoin-NG, revisited. Perform. Eval. **144**, 1–17 (2020)
34. Pahlajani, S., et al.: Survey on private blockchain consensus algorithms. In: 2019 1st International Conference on Innovations in Information and Communication Technology (ICIICT), Chennai, India, pp. 1–6. IEEE (2019). https://doi.org/10.1109/ICIICT1.2019.8741353
35. Panda, S.S., et al.: Study of blockchain based decentralized consensus algorithms. In: TENCON 2019 - 2019 IEEE Region 10 Conference (TENCON), pp. 908–913 (2019). https://doi.org/10.1109/TENCON.2019.8929439
36. Sharma, K., Jain, D.: Consensus algorithms in blockchain technology: a survey. In: 2019 10th International Conference on Computing, Communication and Networking Technologies (ICCCNT), pp. 1–7. IEEE (2019)
37. Vukolić, M.: The quest for scalable blockchain fabric: proof-of-work vs. BFT replication. In: Camenisch, J., Kesdoğan, D. (eds.) iNetSec 2015. LNCS, vol. 9591, pp. 112–125. Springer, Cham (2016). https://doi.org/10.1007/978-3-319-39028-4_9
38. Wan, S., Li, M., Liu, G., Wang, C.: Recent advances in consensus protocols for blockchain: a survey. Wireless Netw. **26**(8), 5579–5593 (2019). https://doi.org/10.1007/s11276-019-02195-0
39. Wang, Q., et al.: A comparative study of blockchain consensus algorithms. In: Journal of Physics: Conference Series, p. 012007. IOP Publishing (2020)

40. Wang, Y., et al.: Study of blockchains's consensus mechanism based on credit. IEEE Access **7**, 10224–10231 (2019). https://doi.org/10.1109/ACCESS.2019.2891065
41. Wu, W., Gao, Z.: An improved blockchain consensus mechanism based on open business environment. In: IOP Conference Series: Earth and Environmental Science, p. 012043. IOP Publishing (2020)
42. Xiao, Y., et al.: A survey of distributed consensus protocols for blockchain networks. IEEE Commun. Surv. Tutor. **22**(2), 1432–1465 (2020). https://doi.org/10.1109/COMST.2020.2969706
43. Yli-Huumo, J., et al.: Where is current research on blockchain technology?—a systematic review. PLoS ONE **11**(10), e0163477 (2016). https://doi.org/10.1371/journal.pone.0163477
44. Zamani, M., et al.: RapidChain: scaling blockchain via full sharding. In: Proceedings of the 2018 ACM SIGSAC Conference on Computer and Communications Security, Toronto, Canada, pp. 931–948. Association for Computing Machinery (2018). https://doi.org/10.1145/3243734.3243853
45. Zhang, C., et al.: Overview of blockchain consensus mechanism. In: Proceedings of the 2020 2nd International Conference on Big Data Engineering, New York, NY, USA, pp. 7–12. Association for Computing Machinery (2020). https://doi.org/10.1145/3404512.3404522
46. Zhang, S., Lee, J.-H.: Analysis of the main consensus protocols of blockchain. ICT Express **6**(2), 93–97 (2020)
47. Zhao, W., et al.: On consensus in public blockchains. In: Proceedings of the 2019 International Conference on Blockchain Technology, New York, NY, USA, pp. 1–5. Association for Computing Machinery (2019). https://doi.org/10.1145/3320154.3320162

Blockchain's Impact on Consumer's Perspective in the Luxury Fashion Industry: A Position Paper

Jean Noonan and Patrick Doran(✉)

Technological University Dublin, Dublin, Ireland
Patrick.doran@tudublin.ie

Abstract. Blockchain technology presents an opportunity for industries to implement for a more transparent and sustainable business model. The fashion industry is notoriously known for its complex and opaque supply chain and its negative impact on the environment and the people involved in the processes along the fashion supply chain. To address these long-standing challenges, the integration of blockchain technology has the ability to be the solution towards an ethical supply chain network. The study contributes to the current state of the fashion supply chain and the challenges it faces, outlining what blockchain technology is and its benefits in the context of the fashion industry. It also captures consumer sentiment on the subject of sustainability and transparency in the fashion industry and the perceived use and adoption of technology.

Keywords: Blockchain technology · Fashion supply chain · Transparency · Sustainability · Ethical supply chain management

1 Introduction

The thesis is concerned with the implementation of blockchain technology and how it impacts the consumer's perspective on the luxury fashion industry. Consumers, retailers and all other stakeholders along the supply chain have their own definition of trust. Blockchain technology can verify the claims of the stakeholders throughout the blockchain. The blockchain is shaped by its users. It encourages trust from all stakeholders as it holds everyone accountable for their claims which could hinder their reputation if they are not telling the truth; the system is designed for good behaviour, which is a key characteristic.

The fashion supply chain is a complex and opaque network with a variety of people and processes both domestically and globally. The fashion industry contributes negatively to the environment and people along the supply chain, from the chemicals used at the raw material stage to the welfare of the factory workers and the conditions that they work in. The fashion supply chain can often lead to misleading information for the consumers and retailers about where the garments are produced.

D. Dennehy et al. (Eds.): I3E 2021, LNCS 12896, pp. 596–606, 2021.
https://doi.org/10.1007/978-3-030-85447-8_49

The fashion industry has long-standing issues that must be resolved to gain consumer's trust and build brand loyalty. This is where blockchain technology can offer a solution. Blockchain technology has been touted as having the potential to solve the problem of achieving end-to-end transparency. It is an increasingly popular networking technology for streamlining business processes that uses a peer-to-peer (P2P) network to verify and share data (Misra, 2018 cited in Cole et al. 2019). It is represented as a shared, immutable ledger that facilitates the process of recording transactions and tracking assets in a business network ("What is Blockchain Technology? - IBM Blockchain", n.d.). Blockchain is a secure and seamless method of exchanging data between two entities on an open ledger, which has the ability to enhance a brand's supply chain and give full transparency and traceability of a product lifecycle to both consumers and retailers.

As blockchain technology in the context of the fashion industry is a relatively new area of research, this study will take a quantitative approach by surveying consumers in the luxury fashion industry on how the adoption and implementation of blockchain technology along the fashion supply chain can create transparency and sustainability.

1.1 Overview of Research Question and Research Objectives

The aim of this research is to analyse how the integration of blockchain technology impacts the consumer perspective of the luxury fashion industry. Using quantitative research methods to carry out this research aim and identifying the following objectives Fig. 1.

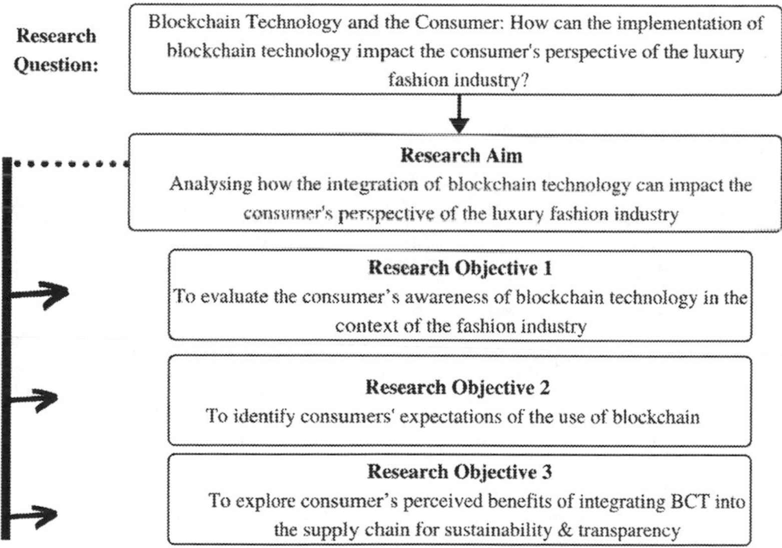

Fig. 1. Research question and research objectives

1.2 The Research Question

This thesis explores the impact of the implementation of blockchain technology on the consumer's perspective in the luxury fashion industry.

Blockchain is a digital database containing information that can be simultaneously used and shared within a large decentralised, publicly accessible network ("Definition of Blockchain", n.d.). It is an emerging technology that is impacting how industries and people see the journey of a product along the supply chain. Blockchain technology has become an area of relevance in recent years with a growing interest in mainstream media and in academic literature across a number of industries, including the fashion industry.

The research question of this paper is: How can the implementation of blockchain technology impact the consumer's perspective of the luxury fashion industry.

1.3 Research Objectives and Rationale

Research Objective 1:
To evaluate the consumer's awareness of blockchain technology in the context of the fashion industry.

Rationale: This research objective will be carried out using a quantitative approach by conducting surveys with luxury consumers to identify their awareness of blockchain technology and the potential impact it can have in the fashion industry by gaining an insight into where their clothes are coming from and who made them.

Research Objective 2:
To identify consumers' expectations of the use of blockchain technology.

Rationale: This research objective will be investigated with a quantitative approach by conducting a survey with luxury consumers to investigate their perceived usefulness of blockchain technology and their attitude towards using this technology to access information about their luxury garment. According to Fred Davis, the Technology Acceptance Model (TAM) explains a users' acceptance of technologies and tests two specific beliefs: Perceived Usefulness (PU); the likelihood of using the technology and how it can improve his/her action and Perceived Ease of Use (PEU) refers to the potential user expects the technology to be effortless. These beliefs can be influenced by external factors in TAM (Lai 2017).

Research Objective 3:
To explore consumer's perceived benefits of integrating blockchain technology into the supply chain for a more sustainable & transparent environment.

Rationale: Blockchain technology can help boost consumer confidence through its transparent nature. This research objective will be carried out using a quantitative approach by surveying consumers in the luxury fashion industry by using a drop-down menu of questions where they can select the benefits they believe blockchain can have.

The following section will outline the current state of the fashion supply chain industry, outline what blockchain technology is and its benefits. It also provides examples of the implementation of blockchain technology with transparent and ethical transactions in an inclusive fashion industry for all stakeholders along the supply chain.

2 The Fashion Supply Chain

As the fashion industry accelerates and continues to have a negative impact on the welfare of workers along the supply chain and on the environment, consumers are becoming more aware of their consumption habits. While Millennials and Generation Z consumers are driving 85% of the global luxury sales growth (Oakes, n.d.), the luxury fashion industry is becoming increasingly conscious of sustainability across the supply chain.

One possible way to prove authenticity and integrity of a brand's products can be achieved through the implementation of blockchain technology. It can address long-standing industry challenges in the fashion industry and create trust as it discloses information to consumers such as where the item was made, who made it and whether workers were paid a fair wage and the conditions in which they worked.

The fashion supply chain is a complex and opaque network that consists of people and processes from design and development to the finished product in-store, outlined in Fig. 2. A traditional supply chain is centralised network that is minimal and cumbersome communication between stakeholders and often linked to unsustainable practices and social injustices (Jordan et al. 2018).

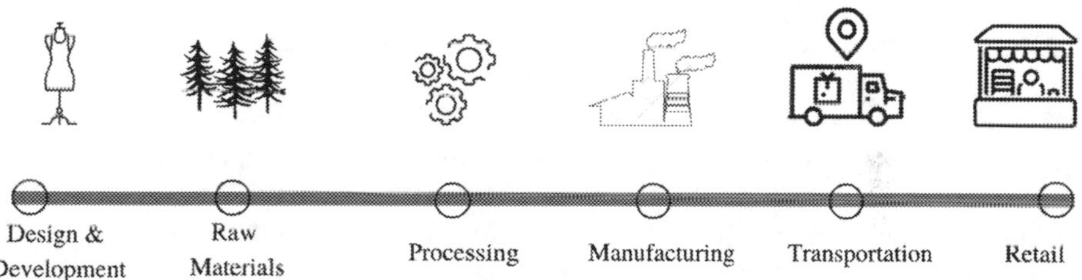

Fig. 2. The fashion supply chain

The challenges along the fashion supply chain affect the workers, environment and process from the raw material to the retailer's reputation. By 2030, the UN Sustainable Development Goals outline 17 objectives to achieve a better and more sustainable future for all (About the Sustainable Development Goals, n.d.). This research will focus on Goal 8: 'Promote inclusive and sustainable economic growth, employment and decent work for all' (Economic Growth, n.d.) which focuses on the workers. Goal 9: 'Build resilient infrastructure, promote sustainable industrialization and foster innovation' (Infrastructure and Industrialization, n.d.), focusing on the implementation of blockchain technology to create transparent and sustainable processes; and Goal 12: 'Ensure sustainable consumption and production patterns,' which focuses on the optimal use of raw materials across the supply chain (Sustainable consumption and production, n.d.).

By following the goals and objectives outlined by the UN, this can create a fashion supply chain that treats workers fairly, and positively impacts the environment. Consumers are becoming increasingly aware of the conditions that workers endure and the adverse effect that the production process has on the environment. They are beginning to seek more information about the product materials, where their products come from and the condition of the factories in which they were produced.

The fashion industry is known for its negative impact on the environment. As environmental activists became more prominent, so does transparency from brands. The pandemic amplified the awareness of the public about social injustices and human rights along the supply chain where sustainability credentials are becoming more important among consumers. The impact on global garment workers became visible to consumers as a number of brands cancelled orders, and payments were deferred or renegotiated. Suppliers globally were reported to have lost over $16 million in revenues between April and June 2020 (BOF Team and McKinse Co 2020). In an August 2020 survey by McKinsey, 66% of consumers said they would stop or significantly reduce shopping at a brand if they found it was not treating its employees or suppliers' employees fairly (BOF Team and McKinse Co 2020). Companies should focus on transparency to show their consumers that they are supporting all stakeholders equally along the supply chain.

2.1 The Blockchain Technology

Blockchain technology was developed in 2008 by Satoshi Nakamoto. The blockchain is a data structure that combines data records, called blocks, in a chain, demonstrated in Fig. 3 (Cole et al. 2019). It is a decentralised, distributed ledger that stores data transactions consecutively. Its decentralised component of the peer-to-peer network means that there are no intermediaries involved and can be shared over a public or private network. The distributed component of the blockchain is a fundamental advantage in a commercial context as no single entity has control, is that it resolves problems of disclosure and accountability between individuals and institutions where the interests of the parties are not necessarily aligned (Cole et al. 2019). The blockchain model includes five components: a shared and distributed ledger, immutable and traceable ledger, encryption, tokenization and a distributed public consensus mechanism (Panetta 2019). The data collected along the blockchain cannot be changed or corrupted, the users can only add to the ledger. The data encryption and coding in a blockchain improves transparency, efficiency and trust in information sharing (Misra 2018 cited in Cole et al. 2019). The immutability of blockchain technology prevents fraud and improves traditional supply chains in the fashion industry (Joel 2019) which builds a chain of authenticity with each secure transaction to establish transparency.

The global blockchain technology market was estimated by Statista to be worth $339.5 million in 2017, and is forecast to grow to $2.3 billion by 2021 (The State of Fashion 2019, 2019). The adoption of this growing market can bring greater transparency to supply chains (McDowell 2019) and prove authenticity of a product which can contribute to a more reliable system of product identification (Heubrandner 2020). The blockchain's fundamental value is enhancing trust, through the nature of its secure record-keeping transactions, it is widely accepted that the ability to track fabric and fibre origins can establish greater trust between consumer and brands (Heubrandner 2020).

In essence, the blockchain is a technical tool that makes it possible for companies to store and transmit information throughout their entire fashion supply chain network, from producers to distributors and retailers with complete transparency, and in a secure manner (Tudor, n.d.).

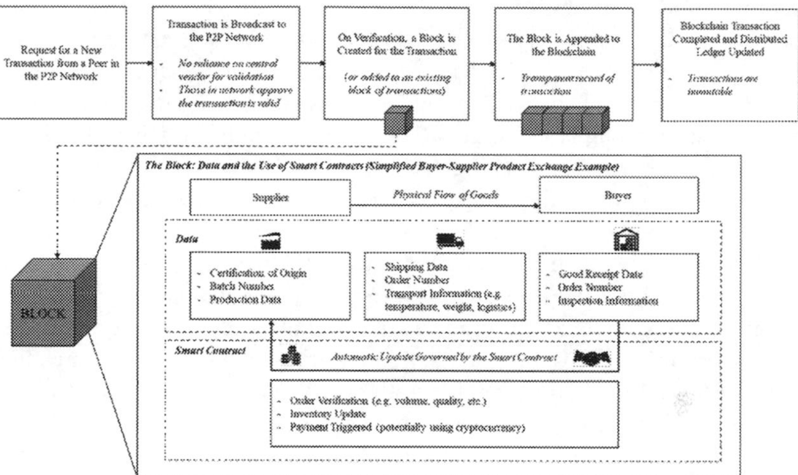

Fig. 3. How the blockchain works (Cole et al. 2019). Source: Adapted from IBM blockchain, IBM, (2018)

2.2 Blockchain Technology in Fashion Retailing

The fashion industry is notoriously known for being wasteful and harmful to the environment. Blockchain technology can have a positive impact on the fashion industry as its fundamental value is enhancing trust. The decentralised ledger acts as a single unified source of data that creates an audit trail which is consistent across all vendors involved along the supply chain(Cole et al. 2019). The integration of this technology along the luxury fashion supply chain has the ability to create a transparent and sustainable chain of transactions.

Blockchain technology can create a physical-digital connection between goods and their digital identities on the block (Shawdagor 2019). The blockchain can give customers the ability to track and trace the integrity of the brand's product. In real time, blockchains provide data to the network on the origins of materials, purchase orders, inventory levels, goods received, shipping manifests and invoices. Smart contracts match and verify this data against the agreement and trigger payment (Cole et al. 2019).

Sustainability

According to the CEO Agenda 2020, sustainability is no longer just a trend, it is a business imperative (Agenda 2020). A Nielsen report found that 66% of global consumers and 73% of millennials are willing to pay more for sustainable goods ("Blockchain in Retail

Fashion and Luxury | ConsenSys", n.d.). Sustainability in the fashion industry is no longer nice to have features in their business model but essential in sustaining their business. The blockchain gives consumers the ability to see the product throughout its lifecycle ("Blockchain in Retail Fashion and Luxury | ConsenSys", n.d.).

Transparency and Traceability

Transparency in the fashion industry is currently close to non-existent. The lack of transparency in the fashion industry has been at the forefront recently, especially since the Rana Plaza factory collapse in 2015 in Bangladesh. The majority of consumers do not have an understanding of the origin of their clothing and do not have the awareness of how or who made it before reaching the store shelf. The only information customers have to find out the source of the garment is the "made in" label, which can be deceiving (Makulova, n.d.).

The fashion supply chain is a complex and global network of stakeholders which makes it difficult for brands to keep track of who made the clothes and where the products are coming from (Agenda 2020). In most cases, retailers aren't aware of where their suppliers are obtaining goods, they do not know where the manufacturers are obtaining its raw materials. Blockchain technology allows consumers to see every step of the garment's production journey which assures them that the information that the brand is giving is accurate information since it is protected by a secure, decentralised system.

Transparency along the supply chain provides companies with the awareness of what is happening to communicate accurate information internally and externally. This process has become increasingly important as more consumers are demanding it. According to researchers at the MIT Sloan School of Management, consumers may be willing to pay 2% to 10% more for products from companies that provide great supply chain transparency (Bateman and Bonanni 2019).

Blockchain technology can guarantee supply chain transparency, secure intellectual property, and improve the efficiency of data sharing (Tudor, n.d.) and has the capabilities to make the production cycle transparent. To enable the consumer with the ability to verify the brand's claim on where the product can from and who made it improves authenticity and enhances consumer trust. The transparent and traceable components of blockchain technology integrated along the supply chain can have the ability to give greater efficiency of processes and information. By equipping consumers with credible and quality information regarding the social and environmental impacts of the clothes, they have the ability to make more informed decisions about the brands they purchase from.

"Blockchain's potential for forging greater trust in businesses along a fashion supply chain, enabling brands to provide verified information about the materials, processes, and people behind products." Martine Jarlgaard (Makulova, n.d.).

Product Authentication

The blockchain is capable of providing a transparent supply chain, therefore, product authentication is a natural extension of transparency. One the brand incorporates the blockchain into the supply chain, this offers the customer an insight into a product's journey. Counterfeit products will cease to exist as a unique digital authentication ID is assigned to each SKU, anyone outside the brand's blockchain network will not have the ability to copy the complex production of the real, luxury product due to the secure decentralised system. When a transaction takes place, the product's ID is assigned to a single consumer. If the product is resold to another person, they will claim ownership.

Blockchain technology is a reliable source of information for all stakeholders along the supply chain as it tracks and traces all transactions which can protect the brand's reputation. Retailers and consumers have a better understanding of the supply chain and can show with a degree of certainty how the goods were produced (Beckwith 2018). This technology can also help brands promote and verify ethical manufacturing processes, while proving authenticity and providing sustainable products for their consumers.

In-store Experience

The retail environment is changing rapidly. Customers are demanding a more immersive experience that they can not get online. Retail is transforming into more meaningful, creative experiences for their consumers, a space where the garments can tell a story (Makulova, n.d.).

The blockchain can act as a storytelling feature of the garment's journey from source to shelf. All aspects of the supply chain transparency and authentication can be reflected in the story (Makulova, n.d.). The customer will be able to learn how to dispose of the product ethically with the data stored on the blockchain. This information is educating the consumer and building valuable brand loyalty.

Circularity

Circular clothing is designed with the end in mind that produces products with sustainable materials that are recyclable or biodegradable (Makulova, n.d.). The blockchain can store the garment details through the smart label to advise the customer on how to recycle the product to benefit the environment.

2.3 Target Market

Target Market and Adoption to Technology

Most Millennials are Generation Z are digital natives and are comfortable with the use of new technologies. Their perceived use or perceived ease of use of new technologies such as blockchain may be more open compared to other demographics.

Rogers outlines five attributes in the diffusion of innovations; relative advantage, compatibility, complexity, trialability and observability (Rogers, 2003, p. 15 cited in Blackburn 2011). Relative advantage refers to the degree to which an innovation is perceived as better than the idea it supersedes. The greater the perceived relative advantage of a technology, the more it will be adopted by users (Blackburn 2011). Compatibility is the extent to which a technology is perceived as being consistent with the existing values, past experiences, and needs of potential adopters (Blackburn 2011). Complexity is the degree to which a technology is perceived to be confusing to understand and use (Blackburn 2011). Trialability refers to a technology that may be experimented on a limited basis (Blackburn 2011). Observability is the extent to which a technology is visible to others; users are more likely to adapt to a technology if it is easy to see results of the action (Blackburn 2011)

In the context of blockchain, despite the features of this innovative technology, ultimately it is the users' perceptions that establish the relative advantage of the blockchain compared to databases, they will observe the compatibility of their experiences, and observe the complexity of the technology.

Target Market and Sustainability

As well as their perceived use and openness of adoption to new technologies, the young affluent consumers are more conscious about the environment and the social impact of their purchasing behaviour. Their expectation of luxury brands is to be aligned with their values and provide transparency along the supply chain. A Nielson report in 2015 found that 73% of the Millennial generation was willing to pay more for sustainable goods (Petro 2020). Further, 54% of Generation Z state that they are willing to spend an incremental 10% or more on sustainable products, with 50% of Millennials saying the same. This compares to 34% of Generation X and 23% of Baby Boomers. It is evident that every generation is on a quest to strengthen their sustainability efforts (Petro 2020).

There are many sustainability routes that resonate with the younger generation such as sustainably sourced materials, recycling and reusing initiatives across the supply chain. Blockchain technology can give consumers, at any age, especially Millennial and Generation Z the opportunity to see the journey of their garments with its transparent transactions and the ability to see if the garment is in fact, sustainably sourced and produced.

Generation Z is becoming the largest generation of consumers. By 2020, Generation Z will account for 40% of global consumers. McKinsey reports that their spending power is at $150 billion in the US alone (Moran 2020). Retailers and brands must align their values with theirs and implement sustainability practices in order to keep pace with their expectations for this next-generation of consumers (Petro 2020).

2.4 Blockchain Examples

Treum

Treum's mission is to help businesses build trust with their customers by bringing transparency, traceability and tradability to supply chains, using blockchain technology ("Treum", n.d.). It is the first blockchain-powered live auction platform for authenticated memorabilia, demonstrating the future of fan engagement. Treum enables fans and collectors to trust the authenticity and ownership of their purchase ("Treum", n.d.).

They provide a trusted, authenticated platform for their consumers by providing a transparent, traceable and tradable platform. Transparency allows brands to verify information with their consumer; increasing consumer confidence. Traceability gives the ability to track the product from source-to-sale. Tradability enables customers to tokenise non-fungible assets and allow them to be held, purchased, exchanged and traded anytime, anywhere ("Treum", n.d.).

Provenance

There is a global movement to increase transparency in the fashion industry. To increase transparency in the fashion industry, Provenance collaborated with Martin Jarlgaad to provide verified information about the materials, processes and people behind the product ("Provenance", n.d.). Blockchain technology can be the solution to this problem by tracking and tracing products from the first mile, from origin to consumers. The product's journey information is accessible via the garment's smart label displaying the source of raw material, through to spinning, knitting, and finishing the sustainable alpaca fleece garments ("Provenance", n.d.). This gives the consumer the power to access the product's journey at the point of sale.

3 Conclusion

The blockchain has become a popular solution to achieve end-to-end transparency in the supply chain at a time where consumers are becoming more aware of provenance and more demanding of where their garments came from and who made them. The fashion industry is continuously evolving to align with the values and demands of their consumer. Blockchain has the ability to transform the fashion industry through its transparent components to show consumers where their clothes are coming from and who made their clothes. The integration of this technology can help brands improve efficiency and transparency which gives the consumer another reason to remain loyal to its brand (Sharma 2019).

References

Bateman, A., Bonanni, L.: What Supply Chain Transparency Really Means (2019). https://hbr.org/2019/08/what-supply-chain-transparency-really-means#:~:text=Defining%20Transparency&text=One%20reason%20the%20process%20has,provide%20greater%20supply%20chain%20transparency. Accessed 11 Feb 2021

Beckwith, C.: Op-Ed | blockchains could upend the fashion business (2018). https://www.businessoffashion.com/opinions/technology/op-ed-blockchains-could-upend-the-fashion-business. Accessed 18 Feb 2021

Blackburn, H.: Millennials and the adoption of new technologies in libraries through the diffusion of innovations process. Library Hi Tech **29**(4), 663–677 (2011). https://doi.org/10.1108/07378831111189769

Blockchain in retail fashion and luxury | ConsenSys. https://consensys.net/blockchain-use-cases/retail-fashion-and-luxury/. Accessed 11 Feb 2021

BOF Team, McKinse Co.: The year ahead: consumers to seek justice in the supply chain (2020). https://www.businessoffashion.com/reports/sustainability/the-year-ahead-sustainable-fashion-consumers-seeking-justice-in-the-supply-chain?int_source=onsite_marketing&int_medium=article_embed_asset&int_campaign=sof21_02122020&int_content=v1. Accessed 11 Feb 2021

CEO Agenda 2020 (2020). https://www.globalfashionagenda.com/report/ceo-agenda-2020/. Accessed 18 Feb 2021

Cole, R., Stevenson, M., Aitken, J.: Blockchain technology: implications for operations and supply chain management. Supply Chain Manage. Int. J. **24**(4), 469–483 (2019)

Economic Growth. https://www.un.org/sustainabledevelopment/economic-growth/. Accessed 18 Feb 2021

Heubrandner, F.: How blockchain can help fashion's transparency problem (2020). https://www.just-style.com/comment/how-blockchain-can-help-fashions-transparency-problem_id138001.aspx. Accessed 18 Feb 2021

Infrastructure and Industrialization. https://www.un.org/sustainabledevelopment/infrastructure-industrialization/. Accessed 18 Feb 2021

Jordan, Bonde Rasmussen, L.: The role of blockchain technology for transparency in the fashion supply chain (2018). http://muep.mau.se/bitstream/handle/2043/25482/OL646E-1201-MASTERTHESIS-JORDANRASMUSSEN.pdf?sequence=1

Lai, P.: The literature review oftechnology adoption models and theories for the novelty technology. J. Info. Syst. Technol. Manage. **14**(1) (2017) https://doi.org/10.4301/s1807-17752017000100002

Makulova, N.: Blockchain technology applications in fashion: part 1 - alleywatch. https://www.alleywatch.com/2018/07/blockchain-technology%E2%80%8Aapplications-in-fashion-part-1/. Accessed 11 Feb 2021

McDowell, M.: 6 ways blockchain is changing luxury (2019). https://www.voguebusiness.com/technology/6-ways-blockchain-changing-luxury. Accessed 18 Feb 2021

Moran, G.: Gen Z and Millennials 2020 – Drapers (2020). https://www.drapersonline.com/guides/gen-z-and-millennials-2020. Accessed 8 Feb 2021

Oakes, J.: Sustainable luxury: millennials buy into socially conscious brands. https://luxe.digital/business/digital-luxury-trends/millennials-buy-sustainable-luxury/. Accessed 11 Feb 2021

Panetta, K., (2019). https://www.gartner.com/smarterwithgartner/gartner-top-10-strategic-technology-trends-for-2020/

Petro, G.: Sustainable Retail: How Gen Z Is Leading The Pack (2020). https://www.forbes.com/sites/gregpetro/2020/01/31/sustainable-retail-how-gen-z-is-leading-the-pack/?sh=518eba4c2ca3. Accessed 8 Feb 2021

Sharma, T.: How blockchain improves the supply chains of the fashion domain?. (2019). https://www.blockchain-council.org/blockchain/how-blockchain-improves-the-supply-chains-of-the-fashion-domain/

Shawdagor, J.: How the fashion industry is getting benefits using blockchain technology | crypto heroes (2019). https://cryptoheroes.ch/how-the-fashion-industry-is-getting-benefits-using-blockchain-technology/. Accessed 11 Feb 2021

Sustainable consumption and production. https://www.un.org/sustainabledevelopment/sustainable-consumption-production/. Accessed 18 Feb 2021

Treum. https://www.treum.io/. Accessed 8 Feb 2021

Tudor, E. Can Blockchain Save the Fashion Industry?. From. https://nowfashion.com/can-blockchain-save-the-fashion-industry-28585. Accessed 18 Feb 2021

What is Blockchain Technology? - IBM Blockchain. https://www.ibm.com/blockchain/what-is-blockchain#:~:text=With%20a%20distributed%20ledger%20that,the%20blockchain%20and%20executed%20automatically. Accessed 11 Feb 2021

Information Systems Development

Digital Transformation of Software Development: Implications for the Future of Work

Samuli Laato[1(✉)], Matti Mäntymäki[1], Teemu Birkstedt[1], A. K. M. Najmul Islam[1,2], and Sami Hyrynsalmi[2]

[1] University of Turku, Vesilinnantie 5, 20540 Turku, Finland
{sadala,matti.mantymaki,teemu.birkstedt}@utu.fi, najmul.islam@lut.fi
[2] LUT University, Lahti/Lappeenranta, Finland
sami.hyrynsalmi@lut.fi

Abstract. In this work we explore digital transformation in software development. A set of interviews were conducted among industry experts to identify and elucidate the drivers and trajectories of digital transformation within the software industry. Using the Gioia method for qualitative analysis and synthesis, two major trajectories were found: (1) automation increasingly impacts several key activities related to software development; and (2) the importance of software and digital products is increasing in sectors where the core product or service has not traditionally been software-intensive. The findings have implications for the future of work in the context of software business. First, software developers and operators are increasingly needed, and more heavily involved across industry sectors. Second, as the level of automation becomes higher, the roles of automated testing and governance are highlighted, meaning a significant portion of development time will be spent in creating and validating automated tests. Third and finally, the importance of digital skills will increase also in non-IT roles as digital elements infuse into traditionally physical goods and services.

Keywords: Digital transformation · Artificial Intelligence · Software business · Software development · Automation · Future of work

1 Introduction

The transformative power of new engineering accomplishments has been known for decades [27, 29]. Advances in information technologies (IT) and automation enable various industry sectors to streamline their processes and operate more efficiently [10]. However, despite a certain technology existing, it may be too expensive to adopt it into use in the industry. Careful review and balancing is needed by decision makers in which technologies are practical and applicable [7]. It is therefore crucial for businesses to understand the current trends in software business and development for making

Published by Springer Nature Switzerland AG 2021
D. Dennehy et al. (Eds.): I3E 2021, LNCS 12896, pp. 609–621, 2021.
https://doi.org/10.1007/978-3-030-85447-8_50

informed decisions, in particular when choosing optimal strategies in the context of digital transformation. The body of academic literature on digital transformation is huge, largely due to the complexity and ever changing nature of the phenomenon [27]. Still, surprisingly few works focus on the digital transformation of software development, and recent studies have called for more research on the topic [3]. One reason for this may be that software development is typically viewed as a driver of digital transformation, not its recipient.

Among pertinent transformative trends in software engineering are cloud computing [2] and artificial intelligence (AI) [10]. Cloud computing is a key technological driver of digital transformation of businesses, as it accelerates software production and supports key digital activities. In recent years, cloud computing platforms such as Google Cloud, Microsoft Azure and Amazon Web Services (AWS) have gained significant traction, have revolutionized the way software is written, and hence, also influenced the skill requirements of software engineers. Despite this paradigm shift, cloud computing remains a small but growing part of the overall software business landscape [4]. Another major trend largely discussed in the digital transformation literature is AI [20]. It has also been predicted by futurists and technology forecasters to be an unprecedented transformative technology [9, 10, 12]. Accordingly, it also has influence on the way software engineers operate and write software. Other impactful categories of technologies include blockchain and data analytics [1] among others.

To evaluate the impact of transformative trends on software development and related business, it is important to identify the key drivers and trajectories of digital transformation in software development. This facilitates an enhanced understanding of the implications of digital transformation on the work of software engineers and data scientists. In doing so, our work contributes to the literature on the digital transformation of software development [3, 15] and the transformation of work of software professionals [18]. We summarize the purpose of this study with the following research question:

What are the main drivers and trajectories of digital transformation of software development and what implications do they have on the work and roles of software professionals?

The rest of this study is structured as follows. First, we go through the previous literature on the digital transformation and the role of software in it. Then we present the materials and methods for our empirical study followed by the results. We discuss the key findings and implications of our results, limitations and future work.

2 Background

2.1 Digital Transformation

Digital transformation can be defined as "a process where digital technologies create disruptions triggering strategic responses from organizations that seek to alter their value creation paths while managing the structural changes and organizational barriers that affect the positive and negative outcomes of this process" [27]. While certainly digital technology plays a crucial role in this process, scholars have argued that the primary driver of digital transformation is company strategy, not technology [17, 26]. Indeed, as new technologies and opportunities to use technology emerge, almost all industry sectors need to stay alert and explore how they can utilize and exploit the available opportunities [24]. Adopting new technologies on their own is not enough, but holistic changes throughout the company are needed. This means significant changes to the workforce.

According to Matt et al. [24], there are four dimensions in digital transformation that companies need to consider: (1) use of technology; (2) changes in value creation; (3) structural changes; and (4) financial aspects. Building of these four dimensions Hess et al. [16] elaborate on 11 key decisions that companies need to make when evaluating their strategy. They expand on (1) the use of technology to cover the aspects of whether the company is the enabler or supporter of IT and what is the level of their technical ambition [16]. For (2) the changes in value creation, they open it up to cover how diverse the company wishes to be in their adoption of available digital tools, what revenue model they will select, and what the scope of their future business is [16]. For (3) structural changes, they name the following decisions: who is responsible for the digital transformation within the company, will the digital technologies be integrated or separated, what will be the focus in their operation, and what competencies they need to build [16]. Finally, they clarify the fourth dimension (4) with the two aspects of what is the current level of financial pressure they have, and who will be financing the transformation [16]. In summary, as new technologies and opportunities surface, companies need to operate within the specified dimensions. The digital transformation is never finished, and rather, is a gradual process that evolves over time, and with technology.

2.2 Digital Transformation in Software Engineering

Among pertinent technologies in software engineering, AI has received a lot of attention lately. While there is a lot of hype going on around AI and its promises [6, 10], recent work has also framed AI as just one technology among others that supports companies' existing business strategies [6]. Thus, even though there is public interest towards AI and many promises of disrupting effects [12], it takes time, advances in AI research and related infrastructure among other factors for the promises to manifest [6]. Other technologies besides AI that currently are predicted to drive the digital transformation of companies are blockchain, cloud computing and data analytics [1]. These four are intertwined in many ways, as data-focused operations support both analytics and AI. Subsequently AI, with the exception of e.g. rule-based systems and reinforcement learning, are trained with data. Cloud platforms are able to support the development of AI solutions, and blockchain can be a way to store, access and manage information. Furthermore, approaches in software development such as DevOps also heavily influence how IS projects are carried out [15]. All in all, it seems that for a reliable analysis on the currently relevant digital transformation of software development, a holistic approach that covers a wide range of technologies and development practices is needed.

Despite the technology existing to automate production to a high degree, most current factories with complex machinery still require human operators. Only certain straightforward systems such as warehouses have been fully automated [5]. There are several reasons for this. First, the tasks machinery would be required to do may still be too difficult to fully automate. Second, human labour can in some cases be so cheap that replacing it with a machine is not worth the investment. Third, transformation of a business towards automation is not straightforward. Several barriers exist from employee rights and ethical issues to risks associated with heavy reliance on automation. For example, AI addresses in particular the first given reason, as it enables automating tasks that otherwise could not be automated. The resulting increased automation capability adds to the relevance of the third reason, as major organizational changes do not happen overnight [16, 24].

Automating processes requires scalable technologies. For example, AI is reliant on several technologies, including software such as development platforms and learning algorithms, and hardware such as processing capability, data storage, cooling systems and on a yet more fundamental level components such as CMOS transistors and their raw materials [28]. Therefore, it is unsurprising that only lately AI has been considered as a disrupting technology (e.g., [10, 23, 25]) despite basic machine learning algorithms being created already during the last millennium. From here we can predict that as the fundamental technological infrastructure develops, technologies operating at a higher abstraction level will become more relevant.

3 Materials and Methods

Previous work on digital transformation of businesses has utilized existing real world cases to accrue knowledge (e.g. [6, 12, 16]). Here, our aim was similar in that we wanted to obtain knowledge from high level professionals who have been working in the industry or academia, overseeing, developing, or otherwise experiencing the impact of AI, automation and the digital transformation. To this end, we collected data from expert informants through interviews [8]. We chose this approach, because any industry transition or disruption is a complex process, and to understand it, a plethora of data sources are needed. Experts are able to provide this data in an already processed and synthesized form, and are thus suitable and valuable informants.

To answer our research question *"What are the main drivers and trajectories of digital transformation of software development and what implications do they have on the work and roles of software professionals?"* we came up with three interview themes. These were (1) changes in the software business and software development, (2) drivers of change, and (3) the role of the change drivers in software development.

3.1 Data Collection

We wanted to ensure that the research participants had sufficient expertise to provide comprehensive insights about the studied phenomena. Thus, we agreed on specific expertise criteria which participants had to fill in order for them to qualify for interviews. First, they had to have worked in a responsible position in the software business or software education at least during the entirety of the past five years. Second, their work had to be related to data science or software development. Third, we sought to recruit people in leading positions, and people in unique positions with respect to one another to obtain diverse perspectives into the studied phenomena. With these criteria, we recruited

10 participants for in-depth interviews. Participants were found utilizing the extended networks of the authors.

The participants were interviewed in an online video call for 45 min to 90 min in a semi-structured fashion by the first author. The interviews took place in the first quarter of 2021. All interviews were recorded and subsequently transcribed. Notes were also taken during the interviews, which totalled 20 pages (A4). Descriptive information of the participants is displayed in Table 1. To protect participant anonymity, only general level information is given.

Table 1. Study participants

Title	Description	Company
1. Professor	Responsible for AI education at the university. Expertise on the societal impact of AI	University A
2. Professor	Listed among the top authorities within the IT field in his country	University B
3. Principal data scientist	Experience in leading and developing data science and AI related projects	International software consulting corp
4. Insurance mathematician	Expertise on statistical methods and ML. Has been present and seen the company transition towards AI tools	International insurance company
5. Analytics & AI consultant	20+ years of experience on analytics & AI in the industry. Top consultant for AI companies	Several startups
6. Software architect	Responsible for the development and operation of both new systems and legacy products within the company	Nation-wide food chain
7. Competence lead	Experience on overseeing and consulting projects primarily in the health sector	International software consulting corp
8. Chief technology officer	Experience as a software developer and recently as a technology leader in the company	Nation-wide IT-focused business
9. Professor	Listed among the top authorities within the IT field in his country	University C
10. Business lead	Responsible for overseeing the development, testing and production of embedded products shipped in the millions	International IT-focused business

3.2 Analysis

For analysis, we utilized the Gioia method, which is designed to bring rigor and structure into qualitative data analysis [14]. The Gioia method uses semi-structured interviews as its primary data source, but can also manage external data [14]. The method has been successfully used in recent work in the IS field (e.g., [22]), which makes it applicable in the current case.

The analysis process was as follows. First, we familiarized ourselves with the interview content by watching the recordings of the interviews and reading the notes made during the interviews. Based on the familiarization process we listed 1st order concepts that appeared in multiple interviews and were related to the research question of the study. Guided by trends disclosed by the expert participants and prior literature, we connected these concepts into second order categories. Here in particular, we looked to connect the 1st order concepts to the discussed trends of AI, cloud computing [1] and the DevOps paradigm [3] that have been highlighted as important trends in software business by recent academic studies. However, not all concepts could be mapped into these (e.g., economics of scale), in which case the 2nd order categories were named by the authors. This process was iterated until comprehensive 2nd order categories were reached. Looking at the digital transformation literature, technology can disrupt businesses in two main ways: (1) through automation which replaces human labor; and (2) by coming up with new practises. We used this approach to guide the clustering of the 2nd order categories into aggregate dimensions. Consequently, we ended up with two dimensions: automation of software development; and re-orientation of business. The results of this analysis process are depicted in Fig. 1. In the next section we discuss our findings in detail and present selected illustrative quotes from the informants.

4 Results

4.1 Automation of Software Development

The first aggregate dimension relates to the main factors identified by the interviewees to accelerate automation. Three central 2nd order categories driving automation were identified, and are displayed in Fig. 1: (1) AI-powered automation of tasks that could not previously be automated, and the future skill requirements of engineers; (2) availability of cloud platforms that automate a significant proportion of the workload of software systems, enabling engineers to start developing from the platform as a service (PaaS) level, and providing tools that guide automatic development thereafter; and (3) the increased popularity and use of software development paradigms such as DevOps and MLOPs which direct developers to create systems with built-in high level of automation.

Skill Set of Engineers. AI, cloud computing and other major technology trends in software engineering [1] are changing what skills developers are expected to have. First, participants agreed that knowledge of cloud computing systems and various software development tools has been highlighted in many software engineering jobs, and the ability to write algorithms has less and less significance. Second, participants believed the ability to make use of data and AI is slowly becoming a core skill for software engineers, if it is not that already. This included the ability to build AI tools, but also to use AI tools to assist programming and code maintenance. As an example, Participant 2 stated the following:

> *"With AI a set of things can be made easier for humans. (–) At some point this will be harnessed to help software development as well."*

Third, perhaps surprisingly, software engineers specializing in some specific area such as user interfaces or data science could become less needed. Participant 10 explained on this topic further:

> *"At least all developers should closely work together. (–) Too clearly defined roles in a development team lead to problems sooner or later. Of course sharing [responsibility] is not always easy either. (–) At some point there might be a situation where you need to call a friend if you're doing something where own expertise is insufficient."*

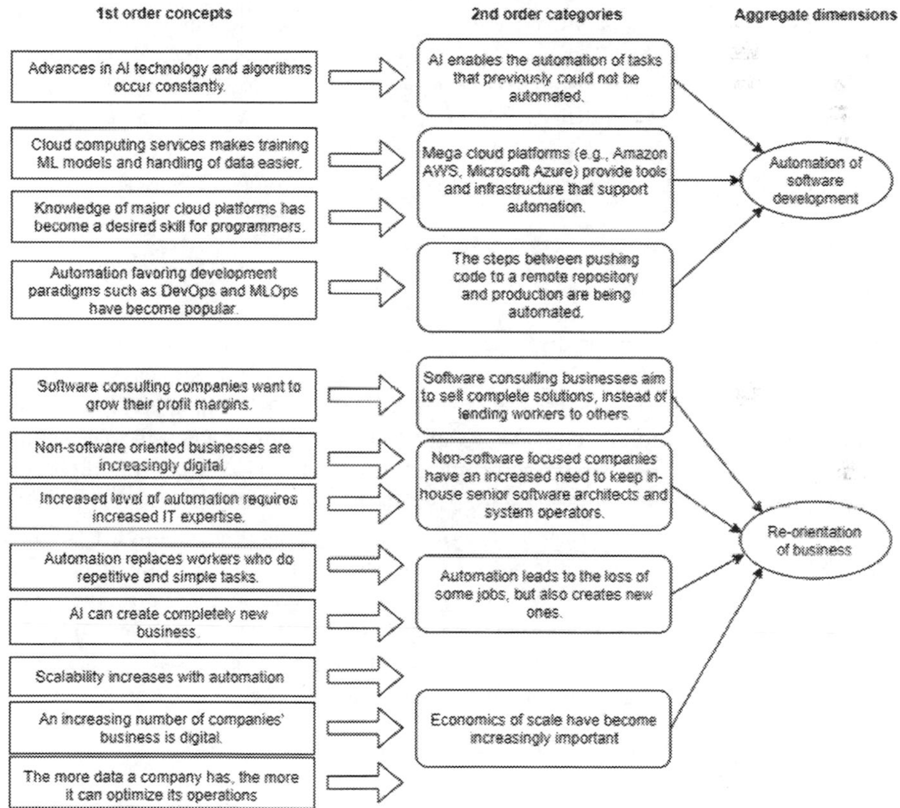

Fig. 1. 2nd order categories arising from the main 1st order concepts, and their aggregate dimensions visualized according to Gioia et al. [14]

Cloud Computing. The majority of participants attributed the popularity of AI solutions to the easy handling of data and availability of processing power, which are provided by large cloud service vendors (e.g. AWS, Azure). For example, AI training can be made easier through being able to access software APIs such as Keras (built on the TensorFlow API) and PyTorch, as well as computing hardware (e.g., Googles' tensor processing units). These solutions remove two essential barriers for training ML models which are the high technical skill requirement associated with understanding the mathematics behind the training routines and having access to sufficiently powerful hardware for executing the required computations. In addition to AI, cloud platforms provide various other benefits ranging from reducing development costs to guiding developers to use well-tested efficient development practices. Participants all agreed that knowledge related to popular cloud platforms has become essential for software engineers working in the consulting business, and furthermore, that the clients of software projects should also have general level knowledge about them.

Role of DevOps. Several participants brought into discussion the role of DevOps in software development. Whereas AI and cloud computing are related to technical tools and systems that increase automation, DevOps is a way of working which relies on built-in automation in systems [3]. DevOps was seen as one of the most important changes in software development practices from the past five years due to its guidance to streamline and automate steps that previously took a lot of manual handling. The importance of it was emphasized by arguments that it is a holistic approach that guides the entire software development life cycle from the initial steps to the final outcome and its operation.

4.2 Re-orientation of Business

The second aggregate dimension displayed in Fig. 1 relates to the re-orientation of businesses across industry sectors. Due to advances in technology, businesses will need to make several adjustments into their modi operandi. The 2nd order categories supporting this dimension were the following: (1) software consulting businesses aim to transition from lending workers towards providing full software as a service (SaaS) to their customers; (2) by contrast, non-software focused businesses should hire in-house IT experts, preferably senior level software architects, as the proportion of digital technology of their overall business increases; (3) while automation leads to the loss of some jobs, it also creates new ones, but the type of jobs is heavily context-dependent and difficult to predict; and (4) there are several factors currently at play which increase the magnitude of economics of scale in an unprecedented way, providing enormous growth opportunities for companies which embrace, and are able to make use of, digital transformation.

The Tension Between SaaS and In-House Developers. Participant 5: *"Previously IT has been some kind of a support service, but today when we look at, for example banks, software is in fact their core service. In this case it is almost impossible to outsource the programming."*

There was a lot of discussion on what the composition of future software engineering teams is like. This discussion oftentimes focused on so-called hybrid teams and whether there will be more or less of them in the future. There were several factors that influenced the outcome of this question according to the interviewed experts. For example, it would be wise for companies to increase the level of their digital expertise along with the increased proportion of digital tools and services of their business. Participant 2 explains:

"I think they [enterprises who increasingly use and offer IT products] really should employ their own IT people, but when we look at the company landscape today, we do not see this happening in practise"

However, according to the expert, many companies still cling on to ordering SaaS solutions instead of hiring in-house experts. Participant 7 gave the perspective of a software consultant company, arguing that it is in their business interest to provide SaaS to customers instead of lending them workers:

"[Our company] wants to move towards providing entire software and platform products as a service. (–) But for this, we would need to increase the level of our competence to extend beyond mere programming, more towards business transformation and life cycle support."

Automation can lead to a loss of some jobs, but open up new job opportunities. With regards to the impact of AI, data and automation on employment, participants highlighted that it is difficult to make accurate predictions, but seemed to agree that complex jobs will remain in the hands of humans. The work of software engineers and other IT professionals was one such job. On this subject, Participant 8 explained the following:

"Ever since industrialization we have seen jobs disappear and new ones coming to replace them. I cannot say what the net impact [of AI technology] is here. But from the perspective of IT companies, we can say that a major proportion of enterprises' actions will move from the physical realm to the digital. And everything that's digital requires someone to handle that. So certainly the work in IT will not disappear anywhere."

Economics of scale. Since industrialization, economics of scale have favoured large scale operation, but the increased scalability, increased proportion of companies' business being digital and the ability to optimize performance the more data businesses have via AI and other tools, all can accelerate the impact. In addition, those companies who make use of modern software tools and automate processes gain business advantage over their competitors. These factors together enable enormous growth opportunities, but at the same time may result in a more uniform landscape, as highly digital enterprises are able to rapidly and cost-effectively expand their business in a way where competitors have a difficulty to respond.

An additional topic that came into discussion with participants, also with regards to scalability, was the major cloud platform providers and their role in the re-orientation of software development. Most participants felt that these platforms are essential, and not making use of them made no sense. Participant 1 explained the following:

"It would be a waste [to not utilize the big cloud platforms]. They are big products, widely tested and not easy to do ourselves. (–) I pay for electricity as well, don't I?"

5 Discussion and Conclusion

5.1 Key Findings

As the main finding and the answer to the presented RQ, we consider the discovery of the factors that contribute to the two aggregate themes of (1) automation of software development; and (2) re-orientation of business. Many of the discovered factors were already discussed in prior literature such as automation and AI [10], blockchain, cloud computing and data analytics [1], but in addition to the identification of new factors, we also presented a conceptual data structure to describe the findings. The digital transformation of software business has vast influence for the future work of data scientists and programmers, as the changes also influence the developers' customers and their software needs. We summarize three main implications for the future of work of software professionals that arise from our findings:

- Software engineers, who with DevOps are typically both the developers and operators, are needed across industry sectors. They are also more heavily involved, as the relative proportion of digital tools and intelligence increases compared to other products and services that enterprises offer.
- The level of automation increases in both software development practises and the systems that are being developed. Developers are operating higher on the software stack and do less things manually. Because of this, the roles of automated testing and governance are highlighted.
- Digital skills will be increasingly needed across industry sectors. Software developers working in specific industry sectors also need knowledge in that field. For example, to make best use of data and AI, both technical and domain knowledge are needed.

5.2 Implications for Theory

According to Vial [27], digital transformation focuses in particular on organizations adapting new digital technology into use and the various challenges related to this process. Previous work has shown that physical work is becoming more digital [21], which transforms physical work. This has led to increased calls for non-technical disciplines to study technologies such as AI [19]. We contribute to this vein of research by looking at the situation from the perspective of software development, an area which is commonly seen as the enabler of digital transformation [1], not its target. We highlight the symbiotic relationship between the software engineering industry and businesses in digital transformation, with changes in either party impacting the other. Thus, we answer the call of recent work to study the digital transformation of software development [3]. With regards to AI as a transformative technology, our findings support previous work [6] in that AI is currently still just a technology among many which influence the ongoing digital transformation in the industry. However, the potential of AI as a disruptive technology [10] exists.

AL-Zahrani and Fakieh argued that through adopting DevOps practises, companies automatically embark towards digital transformation, and that DevOps indeed requires holistic digital transformation [3]. Similar findings were reported by Guşeilă et al. in the context of multi-cloud IoT applications, who argued that the automation that comes with DevOps companies are actively engaged in digital transformation [15]. Our findings contribute to this body of literature by taking a holistic view of the main trends influencing the work of software engineers. We show that DevOps is one piece of the complex puzzle that constitutes factors impacting the digital transformation of software development. Another vein of research to which our findings relate to is that of the transformation of work of software engineers. The development teams need to not only transform the way of their working [18], but also the composition of development teams are likely to change due to the factors detailed in Fig. 1. As individual business sectors re-imagine the way they work [11], software engineers need to adapt. Likewise, advances in software engineering provide new digital transformation opportunities for companies.

5.3 Limitations and Future Research

Concerning the limitations of our empirical study, one of the main points is that the discovered concepts and trends are tied to the viewpoints of the interviewed experts. Hence, they are influenced by factors such as a limited cultural and geographical location as well as their own experiences being tied to the field of software business. To address this limitation, participants dealing with software outside the software business industry could be interviewed, as well as experts from other geographical regions.

As this work is connected to technological forecasting, research methods that could increase the reliability of the findings, such as the delphi-method [13], could be harnessed. The advantage of this approach would be that as we iterate the findings together with the experts, they have the opportunity to make corrections to our interpretation of the results and collectively make adjustments to the presented trends and their drivers.

5.4 Outlook

No matter how advanced technologies are out there, unless significant automation is created to enable their cheap use, they will not transform businesses. For this reason, cloud computing and other solutions that lower development costs and increase the success rate of automation-driving software projects are essential in accelerating digital transformation. Whether we see the full utilization of AI and its capabilities is therefore highly dependent on the platform providers. The future work of software engineers is a complex equation with various variables, but the mega trends we see today can help forecast what kinds of skills are needed in the future.

References

1. Akter, S., Michael, K., Uddin, M.R., McCarthy, G., Rahman, M.: Transforming business using digital innovations: the application of AI, blockchain, cloud and data analytics. Ann. Oper. Res. 1–33 (2020)

2. Al-Ruithe, M., Benkhelifa, E., Hameed, K.: Key issues for embracing the cloud computing to adopt a digital transformation: a study of Saudi public sector. Procedia Comput. Sci. **130**, 1037–1043 (2018)
3. Al-Zahrani, S., Fakieh, B.: How DevOps practices support digital transformation. Int. J. Adv. Trend. Comput. Sci. Eng. **9**(3), 2780–2788 (2020)
4. Asay, M.: Cloud remains a small percentage of IT spending, but its gravitation pull is huge. Tech. Repub. (2019)
5. Azadeh, K., De Koster, R., Roy, D.: Robotized and automated warehouse systems: review and recent developments. Transp. Sci. **53**(4), 917–945 (2019)
6. Brock, J.K.U., Von Wangenheim, F.: Demystifying AI: what digital transformation leaders can teach you about realistic artificial intelligence. Calif. Manage. Rev. **61**(4), 110–134 (2019)
7. Buchalcevova, A., Doležel, M.: IT systems delivery in the digital age: agile, DevOps and beyond. In: Proceedings of the 27th Interdisciplinary Information Management Talks, pp. 421–429 (2019)
8. Coombes, L., Allen, D., Humphrey, D., Neale, J.: In-depth interviews. Res. Methods Health Soc. Care 197–210 (2009)
9. Duan, Y., Edwards, J.S., Dwivedi, Y.K.: Artificial intelligence for decision making in the era of big data–evolution, challenges and research agenda. Int. J. Inf. Manage. **48**, 63–71 (2019)
10. Dwivedi, Y.K., et al.: Artificial Intelligence (AI): multidisciplinary perspectives on emerging challenges, opportunities, and agenda for research, practice and policy. Int. J. Inf. Manag. **57**, 101994 (2019)
11. Finelli, L.A., Narasimhan, V.: Leading a digital transformation in the pharmaceutical industry: reimagining the way we work in global drug development. Clin. Pharmacol. Ther. **108**(4), 756–761 (2020)
12. Frick, N.R., Mirbabaie, M., Stieglitz, S., Salomon, J.: Maneuvering through the stormy seas of digital transformation: the impact of empowering leadership on the AI readiness of enterprises. J. Dec. Syst. 1–24 (2021)
13. Gallego, D., Bueno, S.: Exploring the application of the Delphi method as a forecasting tool in information systems and technologies research. Technol. Anal. Strat. Manag. **26**(9), 987–999 (2014)
14. Gioia, D.A., Corley, K.G., Hamilton, A.L.: Seeking qualitative rigor in inductive research: notes on the Gioia methodology. Organ. Res. Methods **16**(1), 15–31 (2013)
15. Guşeilă, L.G., Bratu, D.V., Moraru, S.A.: DevOps transformation for multi-cloud IoT applications. In: 2019 International Conference on Sensing and Instrumentation in IoT Era (ISSI), pp. 1–6. IEEE (2019)
16. Hess, T., Matt, C., Benlian, A., Wiesböck, F.: Options for formulating a digital transformation strategy. MIS Q. Exec. **15**(2), 103–119 (2016)
17. Kane, G.C., Palmer, D., Phillips, A.N., Kiron, D., Buckley, N., et al.: Strategy, Not Technology, Drives Digital Transformation, vol. 14, no. 1–25. MIT Sloan Management Review and Deloitte University Press (2015)
18. Klünder, J.A.C., Hohl, P., Prenner, N., Schneider, K.: Transformation towards agile software product line engineering in large companies: a literature review. J. Softw. Evol. Process **31**(5), e2168 (2019)
19. Laato, S., et al.: Propagating AI knowledge across university disciplines-the design of a multidisciplinary AI study module. In: 2020 IEEE Frontiers in Education Conference (FIE), pp. 1–9. IEEE (2020)
20. Magistretti, S., Dell'Era, C., Petruzzelli, A.M.: How intelligent is Watson? Enabling digital transformation through artificial intelligence. Bus. Horiz. **62**(6), 819–829 (2019)
21. Mäntymäki, M., Baiyere, A., Islam, A.N.: Digital platforms and the changing nature of physical work: insights from ride-hailing. Int. J. Inf. Manage. **49**, 452–460 (2019)

22. Mäntymäki, M., Hyrynsalmi, S., Koskenvoima, A.: How do small and medium-sized game companies use analytics? an attention-based view of game analytics. Inf. Syst. Front. 1–16 (2019)
23. Manyika, J., et al.: Jobs Lost, Jobs Gained: Workforce Transitions in a Time of Automation, vol. 150. McKinsey Global Institute (2017)
24. Matt, C., Hess, T., Benlian, A.: Digital transformation strategies. Bus. Inf. Syst. Eng. **57**(5), 339–343 (2015)
25. Schwartz, J.H., Wool, J.: "Reframing the Future of Work." MIT Sloan Management Review (2019). https://sloanreview.mit.edu/article/reframing-the-future-of-work. Accessed 19 Feb 2019
26. Tabrizi, B., Lam, E., Girard, K., Irvin, V.: Digital transformation is not about technology. Harv. Bus. Rev. **13**, 1–6 (2019)
27. Vial, G.: Understanding digital transformation: a review and a research agenda. J. Strateg. Inf. Syst. **28**(2), 118–144 (2019)
28. Wu, S.Y.: Key technology enablers of innovations in the AI and 5g era. In: 2019 IEEE International Electron Devices Meeting (IEDM), pp. 36–3. IEEE (2019)
29. Zuboff, S., et al.: In the Age of the Smart Machine. Basic Books, New York (1988)

Business Analytics Continuance in Software Development Projects – A Preliminary Analysis

Muhammad Ovais Ahmad[1(✉)], Iftikhar Ahmad[2], and Iqra Sadaf Khan[3]

[1] Department of Mathematics and Computer Science, Karlstad University, Karlstad, Sweden
ovais.ahmad@kau.se

[2] Department of Computer Science and Information Technology, University of Engineering and Technology, Peshawar, Pakistan

[3] Industrial Engineering and Management, Faculty of Technology, University of Oulu, Oulu, Finland

Abstract. This paper investigates factors affecting business analytics (BA) in software and systems development projects. This is the first study to examine business analytics continuance in projects from Pakistani software professional's perspective. The data was collected from 186 Pakistani software professionals working in software and systems development projects. The data was analyzed using partial least squares structural equation modelling techniques. Our structural model is able to explain 40% variance of BA continuance intention, 62% variance of satisfaction, 69% variance of technological compatibility, and 59% variance of perceived usefulness. Technological compatibility and perceived usefulness are the significant factors that can affect BA continuance intention in software and systems projects. Surprisingly the results show that satisfaction does not affect BA continuance intention.

Keywords: Business analytics · Information systems · Software development

1 Introduction

Around the world businesses are collecting a range of data to achieve greater competitiveness. Business analytics (BA) provide insight to data with help of business knowledge to support decision-making processes. Recently, BA received considerable attention in various industries to achieve and maximize business and gain competitive advantage [23, 26]. BA can be defined as *the techniques, technologies, systems, practices, methodologies, and applications that analyze critical business data to help an enterprise better understand its business and market and make timely business decisions* [11]. BA is about leveraging value from data deemed the new oil [1]. All types of analytics (e.g. BA, data analytics, mobile analytics, text analytics, web analytics, network analytics) rely on data mining, statistics and artificial intelligence techniques and natural language processing [11]. According to IDC report [18], in 2017 the BA software market was 54.1 billion dollars and it will increase 11.2% until 2022. BA helps to improve firm's agility

Published by Springer Nature Switzerland AG 2021
D. Dennehy et al. (Eds.): I3E 2021, LNCS 12896, pp. 622–628, 2021.
https://doi.org/10.1007/978-3-030-85447-8_51

and performance as well as generate greater competitiveness for an organization [4, 12]. In software development analytic guide practitioners in decision making throughout the software development process [22]. According to Ashrafi et al. [4] BA enhance information quality and innovative capabilities. Quality information contribute to timely decision and better adaptability to the environment. Aydiner et al. [5] highlighted that BA helps to improve business process performance and resulting into firm performance influences. In the con- text of software project organization agility is always challenged. It is evident that software projects are inherently complex as they have to dealt with technological challenges as well as organizational issues [7, 29]. Jaklic et al. [21] call for studies to explore how BA better fits with user expectations; whereas other suggest studies to understand the behavioral decisions of BA users regarding the (continuous) use of BA in organizational contexts [6, 14, 16].

This paper aims to examine how expectations from BA by members of soft-ware development teams affect their perceptions and continuous use of BA. Therefore, we are seeking to answer the following research question: What are the factors that affect BA continuance in software development projects? We used the expectation-confirmation model [8] as our theoretical frame-work to hypothesize on the behaviors of employees in software development projects vis- 'a-vis their expectations from BA investments made by their organizations. We collected data from software and system project participants in Pakistan.

2 Research Model and Hypotheses

This study objective was to investigate factors that affect BA continuance in software development projects in Pakistan from the user's point of view. The chosen strategy was to use the appropriate expectation-confirmation model (ECM) [8] as a basis for the designing the empirical research. ECM is based in Expectation Confirmation Theory (ECT) that is extensively used to gauge consumer satisfaction and post-purchase behavior. Bhattacherjee [8] presents ECM in the information systems field and elaborated the cognitive beliefs that influence users' intentions to continue using information systems. The existing studies shows that ECM is extended and validated in various context such as online shopping, healthcare and understanding business analytics continuance in agile information system development projects [6, 9, 19, 27, 28]. We use ECM as the theoretical foundation to investigate continuance intention to use BA in software and systems projects. Figure 1 summaries our conceptual model of this study.

User satisfaction can be referred to the affective attitude towards a particular computer application by an end user who interacts with the application directly [15]. According to Bhattacherjee [8] satisfaction influences IS use and a key determinant in post adoption behavior. Therefore, our hypothesis is:

- H1: Satisfaction has a positive effect on BA continuance intention to use.

Confirmation is the degree to which the actual use experience confirms their initial expectation [8]. It means that user actual use experience meets initial anticipation or expectation; which leads to user's satisfaction.

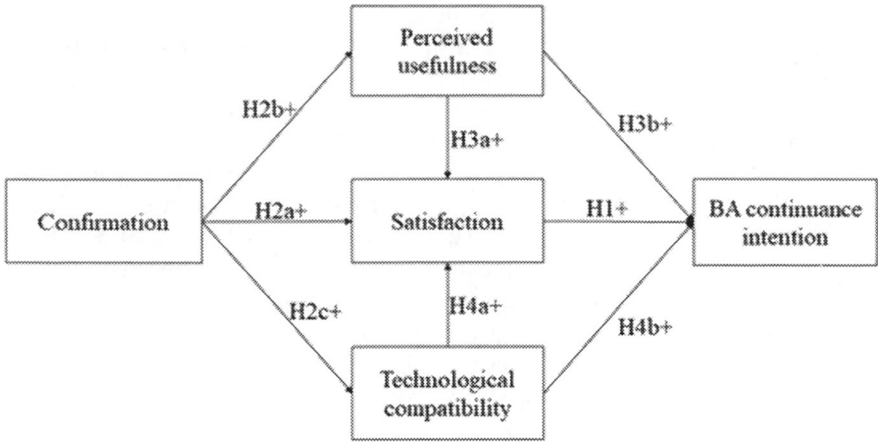

Fig. 1. Conceptual model for BA continuance in software and services projects in Pakistan.

The literature highlighted that confirmation is positively related to satisfaction [8, 25]. The same logic applies to BA use. Therefore, we hypothesized the following:

- H2a: Confirmation has a positive effect on satisfaction with BA use.
- H2b: Confirmation has a positive effect on perceived usefulness of BA use.
- H2c: Confirmation has a positive effect on technological compatibility.

Perceived usefulness is users' perceptions of the expected benefits of using an information system [13]. ECM elaborated that usefulness factor influence the user's satisfaction within system, which could be similar for BA because of its claimed benefits (e.g. visualize the data quickly and assist in decision making etc.). Therefore, we hypothesis that:

- H3a: Perceived usefulness has a positive effect on satisfaction with BA use.
- H3b: Perceived usefulness has a positive effect on BA continuance intention.

Technological compatibility is the degree to which an innovation is considered as being consistent with the existing values, needs and past experience of potential adopters [24]. According to Chen et al. [10] organizations more likely to use big data analytics when their existing values and work practices are compatible.

- H4a: Technological compatibility has a positive effect on satisfaction with BA use.
- H4b: Technological compatibility has a positive effect on BA continuance intention.

3 Methodology

To achieve our research goal, we chose quantitative research approach. An online questionnaire data collection technique helps to cover a large sample of participants from a population of interest. The target respondents for this study were BA practitioners in Pakistani software and services companies. We contacted respondents directly through phone calls and emails. An online questionnaire adapted to the context of BA in Pakistan was developed based on ECM. All of the variables related to ECM model five factors were measured using a five-point Likert-type scale, ranging from 1 (strongly disagree) to 5 (strongly agree). The online questionnaire was piloted, made the necessary corrections and distributed to the targeted population. In total we received 186 respondents.

We run the descriptive analysis on the data and then carried out Harman's single factor test to determine if the variance can be explained by a single factor. We achieved a score of 47% that is less than the threshold value of 50% indicating that there is no threat of common method bias (CMB). To evaluate our proposed model, we used Partial Least Squares Structural Equation Modeling (PLS-SEM).

4 Results

We collected data from 186 respondents belonging to diverse domains. 41% of the respondents identified themselves as software developer. 27% of the respondents selected telecommunication as their job, whereas 15% belonged to e-commerce industry. 6% of the respondents are working as IT-Consultants, and 4% are working in a government organization. The remaining 7% worked in various other sectors.

We consider the loading factors of the items, composite reliability and Cronbach alpha scores of the constructs. For individual items to be reliable the loading factor should be at least 0.7 and for construct reliability, the composite reliability and Cronbach alpha scores should be greater than 0.6 [20]. Further, Average Variance Extracted (AVE) is used to validate if a construct sufficiently explains the variance of its items i.e. greater than 0.6 [17]. The reliability and validity score show that loading factor each individual item is well above the threshold of 0.7. Similarly, the Cronbach alpha, composite reliability and AVE score are also meeting the minimum threshold criterion.

In evaluation of the structural model, the underlying model should exhibit no collinearity among the constructs to reflect the absence of bias [17, 20], i.e., the p-value of the predicates should be less than 5%. To gauge the predictive accuracy of the model, we consider R2 score. Threshold scores of 0.25, 0.5 and 0.75 are used to indicate weak, moderate and substantial predictive accuracy of the model. The findings of the structural model evaluation are summarized in Table 1. Analysis of the path coefficients of our structural model reveals that perceived usefulness and technological compatibility significantly effects BA continuance intention. We also identified that perceived usefulness is affected by confirmation whereas satisfaction is influenced by confirmation, perceived usefulness. However, technological compatibility does not influence satisfaction. Surprisingly, satisfaction does not affect BA continuance intention.

Table 1. Summary of the structure model evaluation

Hypothesis	Path coefficients	p-values	Hypothesis validation
H1: Satisfaction → BA continuance	0.022	0.816	Not Supported
H2a: Confirmation → Satisfaction	0.181	0.029	Supported
H2b: Confirmation → Perceived Usefulness	0.768	0.000	Supported
H2c: Confirmation → Technological Compatibility	0.831	0.000	Supported
H3a: Perceived Usefulness → Satisfaction	0.831	0.000	Supported
H3b: Perceived Usefulness → BA continuance	0.295	0.006	Supported
H4a: Technological Compatibility → Satisfaction	0.049	0.579	Not Supported
H4b: Technological Compatibility → BA continuance	0.363	0.000	Supported

5 Conclusion

The study examines Pakistani software professionals in software and systems development projects expect from BA as well as investigate individual intentions to continue using BA technologies adopted by their companies. ECM model helps us to show that confirmation of expectations about perceived usefulness and technological compatibility are contributing factors of BA continuance intention in software and systems projects in Pakistan. This study findings highlighted that BA continuance is influenced by the various factors as shown in Table 1. The results indicate that it is essential for managers to ensure their team members perceive the BA adopted as useful to their jobs and technological compatible with existing technologies used in current work. The findings are aligned with the existing literature such as [17]. In the recent past, there has been a tremendous increase in the use of machine learning applications in a multitude of domains [2, 3]. It will be interesting to investigate the usage of BA tools specifically in the context of machine learning projects. The theoretical contribution of the study is to extends body of knowledge at organizational level. The practical implication of the study for managers is that they need to pay more attention to technological compatibility and perceived usefulness factors to ensure BA continuance.

References

1. Acito, F., Khatri, V.: Business analytics: why now and what next? Bus. Horiz. **15**(5), 565–570 (2014)
2. Ahmad, I., Alqarni, M.A., Almazroi, A.A., Tariq, A.: Experimental evaluation of clickbait detection using machine learning models. Intell. Autom. Soft Comput. **26**(6), 1335–1344 (2020)
3. Ahmad, I., Yousaf, M., Yousaf, S., Ahmad, M.O.: Fake news detection using machine learning ensemble methods. Complexity **2020** (2020)

4. Ashrafi, A., Ravasan, A.Z., Trkman, P., Afshari, S.: The role of business analytics capabilities in bolstering firms' agility and performance. Int. J. Inf. Manage. **47**, 1–15 (2019)
5. Aydiner, A.S., Tatoglu, E., Bayraktar, E., Zaim, S., Delen, D.: Business analytics and firm performance: the mediating role of business process performance. J. Bus. Res. **96**, 228–237 (2019)
6. Bawack, R.E., Ahmad, M.O.: Understanding business analytics continuance in agile information system development projects: an expectation-confirmation perspective. Inf. Technol. People (2021)
7. Benbya, H., McKelvey, B.: Toward a complexity theory of information systems development. Inf. Technol. People (2006)
8. Bhattacherjee, A.: Understanding information systems continuance: an expectation-confirmation model. MIS Q. **25**(3), 351–370 (2001)
9. Brown, S.A., Venkatesh, V., Goyal, S.: Expectation confirmation in information systems research. MIS Q. **38**(3), 729–A9 (2014)
10. Chen, D.Q., Preston, D.S., Swink, M.: How the use of big data analytics affects value creation in supply chain management. J. Manag. Inf. Syst. **32**(4), 4–39 (2015)
11. Chen, H., Chiang, R.H., Storey, V.C.: Business intelligence and analytics: from big data to big impact. MIS Q. **36**(4), 1165–1188 (2012)
12. Chiang, R.H., Grover, V., Liang, T.P., Zhang, D.: Strategic value of big data and business analytics (2018)
13. Davis, F.D.: Perceived usefulness, perceived ease of use, and user acceptance of information technology. MIS Q., **13**(3), 319–340 (1989)
14. Dennehy, D., Pappas, I., Samuel, F., Katina, M.: Business analytics for the management of information systems development (2020)
15. Doll, W.J., Hendrickson, A., Deng, X.: Using Davis's perceived usefulness and ease-of-use instruments for decision making: a confirmatory and multigroup invariance analysis. Decis. Sci. **29**(4), 839–869 (1998)
16. Elhoseny, M., Hassan, M.K., Singh, A.K.: Special issue on cognitive big data analytics for business intelligence applications: towards performance improvement (2020)
17. Fornell, C., Larcker, D.F.: Evaluating structural equation models with unobservable variables and measurement error. J. Mark. Res. **18**(1), 39–50 (1981)
18. Gopal, C., et al.: Worldwide big data and analytics software forecast, 2019–2023. IDC Market Analysis, US44803719 (2019)
19. Gupta, A., Yousaf, A., Mishra, A.: How pre-adoption expectancies shape post-adoption continuance intentions: an extended expectation-confirmation model. Int. J. Inf. Manag. **52**, 102094 (2020)
20. Hair Jr, J.F., Hult, G.T.M., Ringle, C., Sarstedt, M.: A Primer on Partial Least Squares Structural Equation Modeling (PLS-SEM). Sage, Thousand Oaks (2016)
21. Jaklič, J., Grublješič, T., Popovič, A.: The role of compatibility in predicting business intelligence and analytics use intentions. Int. J. Inf. Manage. **43**, 305–318 (2018)
22. Misirli, A.T., Caglayan, B., Bener, A., Turhan, B.: A retrospective study of software analytics projects: in-depth interviews with practitioners. IEEE Softw. **30**(5), 54–61 (2013)
23. Nam, D., Lee, J., Lee, H.: Business analytics adoption process: an innovation diffusion perspective. Int. J. Inf. Manage. **49**, 411–423 (2019)
24. Rogers, E.M.: Diffusion of Innovations. Simon and Schuster, New York (2010)
25. Venkatesh, V., Thong, J.Y., Chan, F.K., Hu, P.J.H., Brown, S.A.: Extending the two-stage information systems continuance model: incorporating UTAUT predictors and the role of context. Inf. Syst. J. **21**(6), 527–555 (2011)
26. Wang, S., Yeoh, W., Richards, G., Wong, S.F., Chang, Y.: Harnessing business analytics value through organizational absorptive capacity. Inf. Manag. **56**(7), 103152 (2019)

27. Wang, S.M., Huang, Y.K., Wang, C.C.: A model of consumer perception and behavioral intention for AI service. In: Proceedings of the 2020 2nd International Conference on Management Science and Industrial Engineering, pp. 196–201 (2020)
28. Wu, L., Chiu, M.L., Chen, K.W.: Defining the determinants of online impulse buying through a shopping process of integrating perceived risk, expectation- confirmation model, and flow theory issues. Int. J. Inf. Manag. **52**, 102099 (2020)
29. Xia, W., Lee, G.: Complexity of information systems development projects: conceptualization and measurement development. J. Manag. Inf. Syst. **22**(1), 45–83 (2005)

Artificial Intelligence (AI) Capabilities, Trust and Open Source Software Team Performance

Babu Veeresh Thummadi(✉)

Lero, The Science Foundation Research Centre for Software, Cork University Business School, University College Cork, Cork, Ireland
vthummadi@ucc.ie

Abstract. In recent years, Artificial Intelligence (AI) has become a key element in digital platforms for improving performance. Despite vast body of knowledge it is yet unclear on how AI can be successfully integrated into platforms and what are the key mechanisms that drive the performance in digital platforms such as open source. To investigate this phenomena a survey has been conducted to understand how AI capabilities (i.e., capabilities associated with AI resources/usage) on Open Source Software (OSS) team performance. The analysis highlights the role of trust in driving OSS team performance and suggests that designers need to pay more attention to cognition when dealing with AI technologies and opportunities.

Keywords: Open source · Artificial intelligence (AI) · AI capabilities · OSS team performance · Trust

1 Introduction

Artificial Intelligence (AI) can be defined as "a broad collection of computer-assisted systems for task performance, including but not limited to machine learning, automated reasoning, knowledge repositories, image recognition, and natural language processing" [1]. In recent years open source software development, a type of software development practice that uses voluntary workers for creating software with minimal restrictions on code usage, has come to the forefront in solving some of the grand challenges associated with development of AI technologies [2–4].

Despite the growing importance of AI in open source production, very little work has been done on important issues surrounding how AI can be used as a capability in enhancing Open Source Software (OSS) team performance [2, 5]. AI capability can be thought of as a unique feature of open source team that measures open source teams' inclination in seeking AI opportunities and resources. For example, AI can be used an infrastructure in the form of bots in OSS teams for streamlining open source process such as closing pull requests, troubleshooting, greeting new users etc. At the same time, OSS teams can also explore new business opportunities in AI to increase attractiveness of the project. As open source communities use AI in myriad of ways, it is unclear how AI capabilities can affect OSS team performance [4]. Hence I ask:

Published by Springer Nature Switzerland AG 2021
D. Dennehy et al. (Eds.): I3E 2021, LNCS 12896, pp. 629–640, 2021.
https://doi.org/10.1007/978-3-030-85447-8_52

RQ1: How does AI capabilities affect open source software team performance? And what are the key mechanisms that drive open source team performance when using AI capabilities?

To investigate this question a theoretical model has been developed to understand the effects of AI capabilities on OSS team performance using existing literature. Then a survey has been carried out on Mechanical Turk (or simply "MTurk") to study the effects of AI capabilities on open source team performance [6]. A total of 223 responses have been recorded and the data has been cleaned extensively using various data cleaning strategies suggested in the literature. By employing various data clearing strategies, the final sample was reduced to 89 responses and the analysis was then carried out in smart PLS for understanding the relationships between the theorized variables. The analysis revealed that the effect of AI (specifically AI proactive stance i.e., projects' ability to acquire and exploit AI knowledge and innovations) on open source team performance was significant and was fully mediated by cognitive trust i.e., the trust that is generated by rational assessments. The analysis highlights the role of trust in driving OSS team performance and suggests that designers need to pay more attention to cognition when dealing with AI technologies and opportunities.

The paper is organized as follows. In the next section a background of AI and open source is discussed. Then key hypothesis are presented. This is followed by discussion of data collection and analysis. Then findings are reported. Finally the paper ends with discussion, conclusion and limitations.

2 Background

The field of AI was established around 1950s, though its adoption has been rather slow. AI as a field received recognition with the IBM "Deep Blue" intelligent computer program outpacing world-famous chess player Gary Kasparov in 1997. From then on AI gained steam and began to applied in organizations and societies for replacing or augmenting human intelligence [1]. For example, AI is currently used in wide variety of application for tasks such as autocompletion, crime detection, hiring, medical diagnosis, self-driving, recommendations etc. One key thing that distinguishes AI from simple automation programs such as auto reply is that AI has the capability in being unpredictable much like humans [7]. For example, when faced with a roadblock AI-based systems are expected to act more intelligently and take actions in harmony with the environment and not throw an automated response which can be harmful and dangerous. Hence von Krogh (2018) eloquently wrote, "AI has the qualities of being a new but poorly understood organizational phenomenon. By concentrating efforts on collecting quantitative and qualitative data on the aforementioned questions, we may discover unanticipated relationships and ways to resolve tensions and ambiguities in the research on AI within the domains organizational decision-making and problem-solving" [1].

When organizations or platforms use AI they use them for multiple purposes either in problem-solving or decision-making activities [1]. Within the first few decades of the introduction of AI, problem solving has been the prime focus and has been extensively used to solve problems and more recently the shift has been towards decision-making and how we can make AI more autonomous (i.e., the organizations and platforms are moving towards strong AI from weak AI that can intelligently decide and simultaneously solve problems without human intervention or minimal human intervention). Within the realm of digital platforms, open source software development platforms are using AI as a capability for creating cutting edge AI software that address global problems and societal challenges and for streamlining open source processes such as closing pull request, or greeting a new member etc. [4, 5]. For example, open source projects use AI as infrastructure and use bots for 1) license creation 2) reviewing and 3) chatting. Despite wide scale usage, bots are still are considered problematic, as they pose challenges in social interactions in the open source platforms. Many open source workers agree that bots are poor in social interactions [5].

In conclusion, use of AI in open source has been challenging and more work is needed in terms of understanding the relationship between AI capabilities and OSS team performance. In the next section key hypothesis are discussed.

3 Hypothesis Development

In this section the key hypothesis are developed (see Fig. 1). In recent IS literature, AI has been viewed as a capability as it enables platforms and organizations to sense, comprehend, act, and learn [8]. This concept of AI capabilities holds parallels to existing IT capabilities construct that is routinely used in IS literature [8] and hence AI capabilities can be defined as a "platform/firm's ability to acquire, deploy, combine, and reconfigure AI resources in support and enhancement of business strategies and work processes" [9]. Following prior research on IT capabilities, AI capability can be conceptualized as a latent construct reflected in three dimensions: *AI infrastructure capability* (the technological foundation), *AI business spanning capability* (business-AI strategic thinking and partnership), and *AI proactive stance* (opportunity orientation) [9]. All these three dimensions can play a key role in improving the open source development process and team performance.

For example, having a strong AI infrastructure capability and using bots can increase the confidence of the workers in making the processes more efficient by reducing unnecessary bells and whistles and hence AI infrastructure capability can have a positive effect on open source team performance by inducing novelty and streamlining existing process [5]. In a similar vein, AI business opportunities and orientation can also make open source workers tuned to the projects as open source workers like nut-cracking problems [10, 11]. Hence the orientation and business opportunities of AI can have a positive impact on open source team performance. Hence, I hypothesize:

H1/H2/H3: *AI [Infrastructure/Business Spanning/Proactive stance] can have a positive effect on OSS Team Performance.*

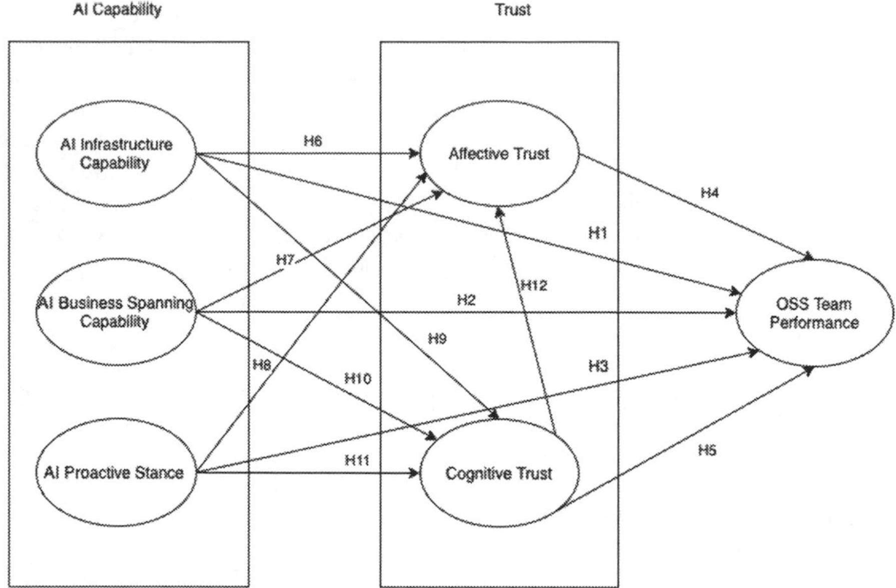

Fig. 1. Theorized model on the effects of AI on OSS Team performance

Prior works in open source development suggest that trust is an important factor that leads to effectiveness of the open source project. Stewart and Gosain (2006) distinguish two different forms of trust: cognitive and affective trust [12]. Cognitive trust arise out assessing the members and bots rationally and affective trust reflects the emotional connections between the actors (both humans and bots). By trusting and giving more power and decision making to AI technologies open source workers can focus on other more important project decisions and activities such as coming up with new requirements that can lead to better outcomes [5]. Both these types of trust can be critical in AI context as the workers' positive trust can have a positive effect on open source team performance. Hence I hypothesize:

H4/H5: *[Cognitive/Affective] Trust can have a positive effect on OSS Team Performance.*

Trust has been the key theme in AI research in the recent few years as humans find it hard to trust and give power to bots and algorithms taking over the life [7]. Much similar to how human-human trust develops through frequent interactions, the relationship between actors and bots can follow a similar trajectory. When open source workers rationally/emotionally believe and develop cognitive/affective trust on the bots and algorithms, the effects of AI capabilities [business spanning/infrastructure/proactive stance] on open source team performance can become mediated through trust [12]. Hence, I hypothesize:

H6/H7/H8/H9/H10/H11: *[Cognitive/Affective] Trust mediates the effect of AI [Infrastructure/Business Spanning/Proactive stance] on OSS Team Performance.*

Prior studies on open source development also hypothesize that cognitive trust can have a positive effect on affective trust, hence I include this in our model as well [12]. Hence, I hypothesize:

H12: *Cognitive Trust has a positive effect on affective trust.*

In the next section, research design, data collection, survey design and data analysis are discussed.

4 Research Methods

4.1 Data Collection

I first developed a survey instrument based on the existing scales (see Appendix for the scale and items) [9, 12, 13]. These items were asked to rate on a scale of 1–7. The survey was conducted on Amazon Mechanical Turk much similar to prior studies that were published in social sciences [6] and survey received 223 responses. Many researchers might question the legitimacy of the data and hence I chose to restrict the responders based on the ratings of the responders (for example, only responders with 95% accuracy scores were asked for responses, this is a feature in MTurk which was utilized for increasing accuracy of data), and also the survey explicitly asks in the first page that the survey is limited to open source workers with at least 1 years of open source and AI experience.

4.2 Data Analysis

Data was checked for reliability and then descriptive statistics were used to get a look at the data. The very first step was to clean the raw data. The responders who had answered the reverse coded question incorrectly were eliminated. Responses to control questions not adhering to survey guidelines were eliminated too. The survey on finalization was given to few candidates for pilot test. It was noticed that on an average they needed 180 s to complete the survey. Hence the cut off was set to eliminate responders who would respond to the survey within 180 s. Finally, missing values were dealt by elimination as well. The biggest loss of responses were the wrong answers to the reverse coded control question. Using the above strategies I was able to improve the quality of the data which is considered an issue in the studies conducted on MTurk. After cleaning the data there were 89 observations and this data was analysed using smart PLS using an exploratory factor analysis [14].

5 Findings

To analyse the survey data, I used the formative model and performed the exploratory factor analysis to understand how the items in survey getting loaded. I performed the single harman test to rule out any common method bias (and the variance less than 50%). The EFA revealed that the items were getting loaded very well and the loadings were above .4 as suggested by literature [12, 15]. One item was dropped in affective trust and cognitive trust constructs. The results from the EFA is listed in Table 1. For testing the reliability and validity, I used the threshold values set by Fornell and Larker (1981) and ensured that the item loadings were above 0.7, construct's composite reliability (CR) scores were above 0.8 and average variance extracted (AVE) above 0.5. From Table 1 we can see that the item loadings were all above .7 [16].

Table 1. Factor loadings

	1	2	3	4	5	6
AIB11	**0.798**	0.51	0.57	0.625	0.596	0.539
AIB21	**0.809**	0.527	0.638	0.632	0.648	0.692
AIB31	**0.775**	0.447	0.644	0.614	0.565	0.574
AIB41	**0.764**	0.525	0.617	0.655	0.568	0.511
AIIC11	0.545	**0.877**	0.478	0.466	0.462	0.43
AIIC21	0.598	**0.917**	0.582	0.557	0.513	0.565
AIPS11	0.672	0.475	**0.791**	0.67	0.637	0.644
AIPS21	0.628	0.559	**0.791**	0.559	0.575	0.643
AIPS31	0.5	0.4	**0.733**	0.484	0.529	0.531
AIPS41	0.638	0.425	**0.809**	0.643	0.633	0.599
AT11	0.607	0.387	0.566	**0.822**	0.616	0.628
AT21	0.589	0.496	0.595	**0.774**	0.564	0.536
AT31	0.714	0.536	0.685	**0.827**	0.722	0.638
AT51	0.676	0.432	0.604	**0.815**	0.672	0.611
CT11	0.671	0.428	0.629	0.724	**0.806**	0.682
CT21	0.61	0.384	0.643	0.615	**0.785**	0.633
CT31	0.506	0.405	0.527	0.613	**0.766**	0.574
CT51	0.575	0.433	0.616	0.625	**0.784**	0.672
CT61	0.575	0.48	0.543	0.523	**0.754**	0.53
TP11	0.605	0.436	0.615	0.607	0.679	**0.792**
TP21	0.558	0.434	0.662	0.556	0.588	**0.791**
TP31	0.656	0.48	0.622	0.614	0.682	**0.803**
TP41	0.57	0.374	0.511	0.601	0.566	**0.714**
TP51	0.447	0.435	0.578	0.495	0.546	**0.756**

I also checked for the convergent validity and the AVE and the cronbach's alpha were in the expected thresholds as prescribed by Fornell and Larker (1981) [16]. See Table 2 for the results pertaining to the convergent validity.

Table 2. Construct validity

	Cronbach's alpha	Composite reliability	Average variance extracted (AVE)
AI business spanning capability	0.795	0.866	0.619
AI infrastructure capability	0.759	0.892	0.805
AI proactive stance	0.788	0.863	0.611
Affective trust	0.825	0.884	0.655
Cognitive trust	0.838	0.885	0.607
OSS team performance	0.830	0.880	0.596

For testing discriminant validity I used the criteria that is prescribed by Chin (1998) and Fornell and Locker (1981) [16, 17]. See Tables 3 and 4 for the results pertaining to the divergent validity. First, I investigated the cross-loadings for the six factor identified by the model. Through visual inspection by row in Table 1 we can see that all constructs' indicators load highest into the respective constructs than other constructs. Second, I used the criteria prescribed by Fronell-Locker criterion and evaluated to see if the square root of AVE value are higher than the correlations with other constructs (square root of AVE is shown in bold in Table 3). From Table 3, we can see most of the constructs pass this criterion expect for AI Business spanning capability, Cognitive trust and OSS team performance. The square root of AVE for AI Business spanning capability is .789 as shown in the diagonal and the correlations to affective trust is higher by about .02. Based on this we can consider the discriminant validity results to be satisfactory.

Table 3. Discriminant validity

	1	2	3	4	5	6
1. AI business spanning capability	**0.787**					
2. AI infrastructure capability	0.639	**0.897**				
3. AI proactive stance	0.785	0.595	**0.782**			
4. Affective trust	0.802	0.574	0.759	**0.81**		
5. Cognitive trust	0.757	0.545	0.762	0.799	**0.779**	
6. OSS Team performance	0.74	0.561	0.776	0.747	0.797	**0.772**

Then I carried out path analysis. The analysis shows that the effects of AI proactive stance were significant on OSS team performance, though I did not find any significant effects of AI Infrastructure capability and AI business spanning capability on OSS Team performance (see Fig. 2). Furthermore, the cognitive trust was found to be mediating the effects of AI proactive stance. This provides support for hypothesis H3, H5, H10, H12.

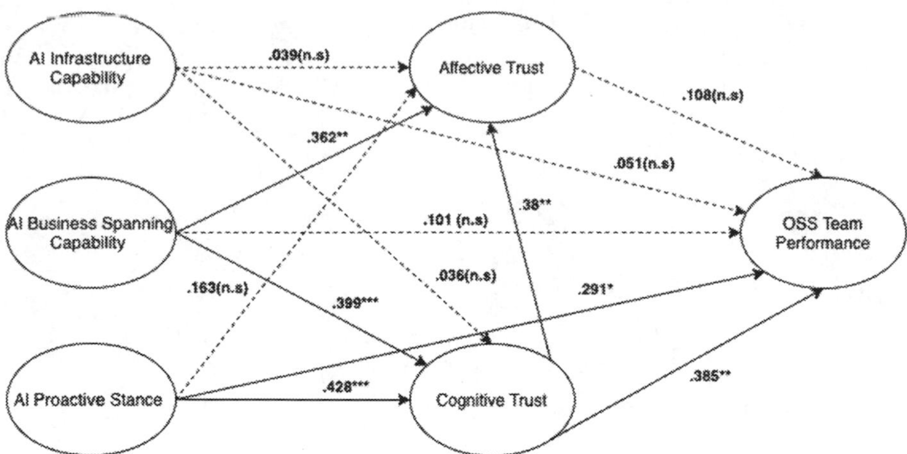

Fig. 2. Path model of the effects of AI Capabilities on OSS Team performance (*p < .05, **p < .01, ***p < .001, non-significant paths are indicated with dotted lines)

The results from the study should be useful for open source teams for organizing the projects. By successfully incorporating AI capabilities, open source teams can become more productive by increasing the cognitive trust between the members. In Table 4, the model fit statistics are reported and the SRMR is less than <.08 and hence is considered a good model fit [18].

Table 4. Model fit

	Saturated model	Estimated model
SRMR	0.074	0.074
Chi-square	481.118	481.118
NFI	0.676	0.676

6 Discussion

In this section I address the original research question: *How does AI innovations get adopted in open source platforms? And what are the key mechanisms that drive open source team performance when using AI innovations?*

The analysis shows that cognitive trust is important in the AI and Open source team performance relationship. Specifically, the results show that having a AI proactive stance can have a positive effect on OSS team performance. However, what was surprising was that AI infrastructure and AI business spanning capabilities did not have an effect on OSS team performance. This suggests that AI is still considered problematic and usage of bots and algorithms in OSS communities does not necessarily increase OSS team performance but rather it is the inclination and proactiveness of the OSS teams in seeking AI opportunities that drives performance [5]. Further, cognitive trust mediated the relationship between AI proactive stance and OSS team performance suggesting that OSS teams should seek and enhance cognitive trust more than affective trust for better OSS team performance. Open source workers are more likely to be technology savvy and hence the relationships might differ from a normal user, for example, in case of a different setting, affective trust might be more important. Hence caution has to be observed in terms of generalizing these results into other environments such as robots in healthcare, self-driving cars etc. Also this study should be considered exploratory as with MTurk we do not know the authenticity of data and hence care should be taken in terms of generalizations, a more detailed study on specific open source community could be carried out to validate or invalidate the current study and suggest possible guidelines for reconciling the MTurk design with an email survey.

I also report here some limitations and opportunities future research. When conducting the research I was limited by the method of collecting data. The initial idea was to conduct survey of teams, which would have narrowed down the technology stack as well as would have given a better idea of OSS as a team. However, I had difficulty securing such teams and hence had to conduct a survey for individual developers. In the future research a small programming question can be set up in the survey to determine whether they have the requisite open source experience which would increase the authenticity of the data collected. MTurk users could also be asked for providing their GitHub profile that could display their experience and reduce the fraud [6]. In conclusion, this study explores the nascent dimension of AI and unpacks the relationships of trust and performance in open source development.

Acknowledgements. This work was supported with the financial support of the Science Foundation Ireland grant 13/RC/2094 and co funded under the European Regional Development Fund through the Southern & Eastern Regional Operational Programme to Lero - the Science Foundation Ireland Research Centre for Software (www.lero.ie). Author would like to thank Adwait Bhalero for research assistance and the participants of AIS DIGIT community for the helpful comments on the earlier version of the paper. The errors are my own.

Appendix

AI Infrastructure Capability

Relative to other open source projects, please evaluate your open source projects' AI (artificial intelligence) infrastructure capabilities (for example bots, recommendations etc.) in the following areas 1–7 scale (1 = strongly disagree, 7 = strongly agree).

AIIC1: Bot services (for example chatbots, trouble shooting, automation services etc.) are helpful in navigating my open source work.
AIIC2: I like the recommendations and automatic notifications features.

(Source: Lu, Y., & K. (Ram) Ramamurthy (2011). Understanding the link between information technology capability and organizational agility: An empirical examination. *MIS quarterly*, 931–954).

AI Business Spanning Capability

Relative to other open source projects, please evaluate your open source projects' AI management capability in responding to the following on a 1–7 scale (1 = poorer than most, 7 = superior to most).

AIB1: Developing a clear vision on how AI contributes to business value.
AIB2: Integrating open source project planning and AI planning effectively.
AIB3: Enabling functional areas and general management's ability to understand the value in AI investments.
AIB4: Establishing an effective and flexible AI planning process and developing a robust AI plan.

(Source: Lu, Y., & K. (Ram) Ramamurthy (2011). Understanding the link between information technology capability and organizational agility: An empirical examination. *MIS quarterly*, 931–954).

AI Proactive Stance

Relative to other open source projects, please evaluate your open source projects' capability in acquiring, assimilating, transforming, and exploiting AI knowledge in the following areas on a 1–7 scale (1 = strongly disagree, 7 = strongly agree).

AIPS1: We constantly keep current with new AI innovations.
AIPS2: We are capable of and continue to experiment with new AI as necessary.
AIPS3: We have a climate that is supportive of trying out new ways of using AI.
AIPS4: We constantly seek new ways to enhance the effectiveness of AI use.

(Source: Lu, Y., & K. (Ram) Ramamurthy (2011). Understanding the link between information technology capability and organizational agility: An empirical examination. *MIS quarterly*, 931–954).

Affective Trust

Each of the statements below refers to how the participants in your open source project(s) feel about each other. Please indicate the extent to which you agree or disagree with each statement about the group using the following scale (1 = strongly disagree, 7 = strongly agree).

AT1. Members of the team have made considerable emotional investments in our working relationships.

AT2. Members of the team have a sharing relationship with each other. We can freely share our ideas, feelings, and hopes.
AT3. On this team we can talk freely with each other about difficulties we are having and know that others will want to listen.
AT4. Members of the team would feel a sense of loss we could no longer work together.
AT5. If a member for this group shared problems with other members, they would respond constructively and caringly.

Source: Stewart, K. J., & Gosain, S. (2006). The impact of ideology on effectiveness in open source software development teams. *Mis Quarterly*, 291–314.

Cognitive Trust

Each of the statements below refers to how the participants in your open source project(s) feel about each other. Please indicate the extent to which you agree or disagree with each statement about the group using the following scale (1 = strongly disagree, 7 = strongly agree).

CT1: Members of the team know that everyone on the team approaches their work with professionalism and dedication.
CT2: Given the track records of the team members, we see no reason to doubt each other's competence and preparation for a job.
CT3: Members of the team believe they will be able to rely on other members of the team not to make a job more difficult by careless work.
CT4: Members of the team are concerned with monitoring each other's work*.
CT5: Members of the team believe that other members should be trusted and respected as coworkers.
CT6: Members of the team consider each other to be trustworthy.

Source: Stewart, K. J., & Gosain, S. (2006). The impact of ideology on effectiveness in open source software development teams. *Mis Quarterly*, 291–314.

OSS Team Performance

Each of the statements below refers to how well your open source project(s) are positioned in the following activities. Please indicate the extent to which you agree or disagree with each statement about the group using the following scale (1 = strongly disagree, 7 = strongly agree).

TP1: Our open source team effectively used its resources.
TP2: Our open source team was within the proposed budget.
TP3: Our open source team was within the proposed time-schedule.
TP4: Our open source team was able to meet its goals.
TP5: Our open source team was able to respond quickly to problems.

Source: Kostopoulos et al. (2012): Structure and Function of Team Learning Emergence: A Multilevel Empirical Validation. Journal of Management, Vol. 39, No. 6, pp. 1430–1461.

References

1. Von Krogh, G.: Artificial intelligence in organizations: new opportunities for phenomenon-based theorizing. Acad. Manag. Discov. **4**(4), 404–409 (2018)
2. Hukal, P., et al.: Bots coordinating work in open source software projects. Computer **52**(9), 52–60 (2019)
3. Von Hippel, E., Von Krogh, G.: Open source software and the "private-collective" innovation model: issues for organization science. Org. Sci. **14**(2), 209–223 (2003)
4. Ng, A.: What artificial intelligence can and can't do right now. Harv. Bus. Rev. **9**(11) (2016)
5. Wessel, M., et al.: The power of bots: characterizing and understanding bots in OSS projects. In: Proceedings of the ACM on Human-Computer Interaction (CSCW), vol. 2, pp. 1–19 (2018)
6. Hauser, D.J., Schwarz, N.: Attentive Turkers: MTurk participants perform better on online attention checks than do subject pool participants. Behav. Res. Methods **48**(1), 400–407 (2015)
7. Glikson, E., Woolley, A.W.: Human trust in artificial intelligence: review of empirical research. Acad. Manag. Ann. **14**(2), 627–660 (2020)
8. Bawack, R., Wamba, S.F., Carillo, K.: Where information systems research meets artificial intelligence practice: towards the development of an AI capability framework. Technology **12**, 15–2019 (2019)
9. Lu, Y., Ramamurthy, K.: Understanding the link between information technology capability and organizational agility: an empirical examination. MIS Q. **35**(4), 931–954 (2011)
10. Raymond, E.: The Cathedral and the Bazaar: Musings on Linux and Open Source by an Accidental Revolutionary. O'Reilly & Associates Inc., Sebastopol (2001)
11. Von Krogh, G., Spaeth, S., Lakhani, K.: Community, joining, and specialization in open source software innovation: a case study. Res. Policy **32**(7), 1217–1241 (2003)
12. Stewart, K.J., Gosain, S.: The impact of ideology on effectiveness in open source software development teams. MIS Q. **30**(2), 291–314 (2006)
13. Kostopoulos, K.C., Spanos, Y.E., Prastacos, G.P.: Structure and function of team learning emergence: a multilevel empirical validation. J. Manag. **39**(6), 1430–1461 (2013)
14. Hair, J.F., Ringle, C.M., Sarstedt, M.: PLS-SEM: indeed a silver bullet. J. Market. Theory Pract. **19**(2), 139–152 (2011)
15. Stevens, J.P.: Applied Multivariate Statistics for the Social Sciences. Routledge, Oxfordshire (2012)
16. Fornell, C., Larcker, D.F.: Evaluating structural equation models with unobservable variables and measurement error. J. Market. Res. **18**(1), 39–50 (1981)
17. Chin, W.W.: Commentary: issues and opinion on structural equation modeling. MIS Q. **22**(1), vii–xvi (1998)
18. Hu, L.T., Bentler, P.M.: Cutoff criteria for fit indexes in covariance structure analysis: conventional criteria versus new alternatives. Struct. Eq. Model. Multidisc. J. **6**(1), 1–55 (1999)

Social Media and Analytics

Modeling Malicious Behaviors and Fake News Dissemination on Social Networks

Kento Yoshikawa, Masatsugu Ichino, and Hiroshi Yoshiura(✉)

The University of Electro-Communications, Tokyo, Japan
{k-yoshikawa,yoshiura}@uec.ac.jp, ichino@inf.uec.ac.jp

Abstract. As social media has become widely used, fake news has become a serious problem. A representative countermeasure is fake news detection. However, this countermeasure is not sufficient because people using social media tend to ignore facts that contradict their beliefs. To develop effective countermeasures, it is necessary to clarify the influence of fake news and the nature of its dissemination from the perspective of communication. In this paper, we propose two models explaining the dissemination of opinions about fake news: one in which the presence of the ground truth is assumed and one in which it is not assumed. In both models, an attacker disseminates fake news by imitating or hijacking target accounts. In evaluations on real-world social networks, the model in which the ground truth is assumed demonstrates that, contrary to our expectations, account imitation is a more harmful attack than account hijacking. The model in which ground truth is not assumed demonstrates that both account imitation and account hijacking are harmful attacks.

Keywords: Fake news · Social network · Opinion dissemination · Account imitation · Account hijacking

1 Introduction

The platforms on which people receive and disseminate information are changing from mass media (e.g., newspapers, television) to social media (e.g., Facebook, Twitter). Social media enable people to get information easily and to disseminate information rapidly. As a result, misleading news, including deceptive news, has become widespread. This misleading news, i.e., fake news, negatively affects individuals and society [11].

A representative countermeasure against fake news is fake news detection using texts and images [14], the speed at which the news spreads [13], and the reliability of people reporting the news [15]. However, widespread communication on social media has amplified the echo chamber effect in which one's beliefs are strengthened through interactions with like-minded individuals [8]. It has also amplified the backfire effect in which facts that contradict one's beliefs are rejected [8]. Fake news detection is thus insufficient.

Published by Springer Nature Switzerland AG 2021
D. Dennehy et al. (Eds.): I3E 2021, LNCS 12896, pp. 643–655, 2021.
https://doi.org/10.1007/978-3-030-85447-8_53

Developing effective countermeasures requires clarifying the influences of fake news and the nature of its dissemination from the perspective of communication. Previous models related to this aim describe opinion dissemination among people using social media (hereinafter "users") [3, 4, 7, 10, 12]. However, these models are insufficient because they do not take malicious attacks into account.

In this paper, we present two models explaining the dissemination of opinions about fake news generated by malicious users (hereinafter "attackers") on social networks. We used them to clarify the influence and properties of fake news. Our contributions to countermeasures against fake news are summarized as follows.

- We present two opinion dissemination models that users disseminate news in the presence of attackers. In the AAT-Based Model, attackers and users disseminate news when the ground truth is assumed while in the Trust-Based Model, they disseminate news when the ground truth is not assumed. In both models, attackers intentionally facilitate the spread of fake news by imitating or hijacking the accounts of target users.
- Using the AAT-Based Model on real-world social networks, we reveal an unexpected result that account imitation is a more harmful attack than account hijacking. For example, with account imitation, the attack is always effective, and 1% of attackers deter more than 80% of the users from making up their opinions. With account hijacking, the attack sometimes fails.
- Using the Trust-Based Model on real-world social networks, we reveal that account imitation and account hijacking can cause two outcomes even though there are only 1% of attackers: attackers can (1) facilitate the spread of opinions that support them and (2) suppress the spread of targets' opinions.

2 Related Work

2.1 Modeling Opinion Dissemination

Previous work proposes models explaining how users in social networks disseminate opinions. These models can be classified into two types: those that assume the presence of the ground truth (i.e., the fact that supports or contradicts an opinion) [4, 7] and those that do not [3, 10, 12].

The former type describes the dissemination of the correct (or incorrect) opinion that matches (or mismatches) the ground truth. Glinton et al. modeled the "opinion sharing problem" in which users share the correct opinion [4]. Pryymak et al. improved the precision of Glinton's model by developing an opinion dissemination model, AAT (Autonomous Adaptive Tuning) [7].

The latter type does not consider whether an opinion matches the ground truth and simply describe how people change their opinions due to communication. DeGroot proposed a model in which users update their opinions based on the fixed weighted average of the importance of their friends [3]. As extensions of DeGroot's model, Tsang and Larson modeled an opinion transition that diverse opinions converge to a few major opinions by adding people who never change their opinions [12]. Sasahara et al. modeled the echo chamber effect by formulating the disconnection with those who have different opinions [10].

In this paper, we adopt Pryymak's model [7] as the model in which the ground truth is assumed because it can accurately share correct opinions. We also adopt Tsang and Larson's model [12] as the model in which the ground truth is not assumed because it can better reflect opinion formation by updating not only opinions but also the importance of friends while other models of this type cannot. We incorporate malicious attacks (described in Sect. 2.2) into these two models (Sect. 3).

2.2 Malicious Attacks Facilitating Spread of Fake News

We first define "fake news" in this paper as deceptive news that attackers not only generate but also actively spread by deceiving users [11]. Malicious attacks on social networks that correspond to this definition are account imitation and account hijacking [5, 9]. In account imitation, the attacker generates accounts similar to the target accounts in terms of account names, photos, and texts [5, 9]. In account hijacking, the attacker hijacks the target accounts through phone calls, email, and linking social media with external applications [5, 9]. Although such attacks are rampant on social media, there has been no work to evaluate the effects of spreading fake news at present.

3 Modeling Malicious Behaviors and Opinion Dissemination for Fake News

3.1 Overview

The goal of an attacker is to convince users that the information benefiting the attackers is correct (e.g., political propaganda). To achieve this goal, the attacker disseminates "misinformation" and then performs account imitation or hijacking as described in Sect. 2.2 in order to facilitate its spread (① in Fig. 1). We analyze the dissemination of misinformation using Pryymak's model [7] (hereinafter "AAT-Based Model") and Tsang and Larson's model [12] (hereinafter "Trust- Based Model") (② in Fig. 1). The AAT-Based Model assumes the presence of the ground truth while the Trust-Based Model does not. In the AAT-Based Model, "misinformation" means opinions that misidentify real news as fake news or misidentify fake news as real news. In the Trust-Based Model, "misinformation" means opinions about the news that the attacker shares with users: fake positive opinions that are opposite to the targets' negative opinions or fake negative opinions that are opposite to the targets' positive opinions.

3.2 Problem Formulation

We consider graph $G(U, E)$ to be a social network, where $U = \{u_1, \cdots u_N\}$ is the set of users (i.e., nodes) and E is the set of friendships among all users (i.e., edges). Each user u_i has M_i ($1 \leq M_i \leq N - 1$) friends in $F_i = \left\{u_{i_1}, \cdots u_{i_j} \cdots, u_{i_{M_i}}\right\} \in E$, where F_i is the set of user u_i's friends and u_{i_j} is the jth friend of user u_i. In accordance with the models of Glinton's [4] and Pryymak's [7], each user communicates their opinions with their set of friends. Each user u_i has an opinion $o_i \in [0.0, 1.0]$ and an importance vector of friends $\boldsymbol{W}_i = \left(w_{i_1}, \cdots w_{i_j}, \cdots, w_{i_{M_i}}\right)$. Each user u_i updates the current opinion o_i^k to o_i^{k+1} by applying

$$o_i^{k+1} = f\left(o_i^k, \boldsymbol{W}_i^k, \boldsymbol{O}_i^k\right), \tag{1}$$

where k is the current opinion update step, $\boldsymbol{W}_i^k = \left(w_{i_1}^k, \cdots, w_{i_j}^k \cdots, w_{i_{M_i}}^k\right)$ is the current importance of friends, and $\boldsymbol{O}_i^k = \left(o_{i_1}^k, \cdots, o_{i_j}^k \cdots, o_{i_{M_i}}^k\right)$ is the current opinion of user u_i's friend $u_{i_j}(j = 1, \cdots M_i)$. Function $f\left(o_i^k, \boldsymbol{W}_i^k, \boldsymbol{O}_i^k\right)$ is embodied in Sect. 3.4. The attacker performs account imitation or account hijacking on the set of targets $B \subset U$ embodied in Sect. 3.3.

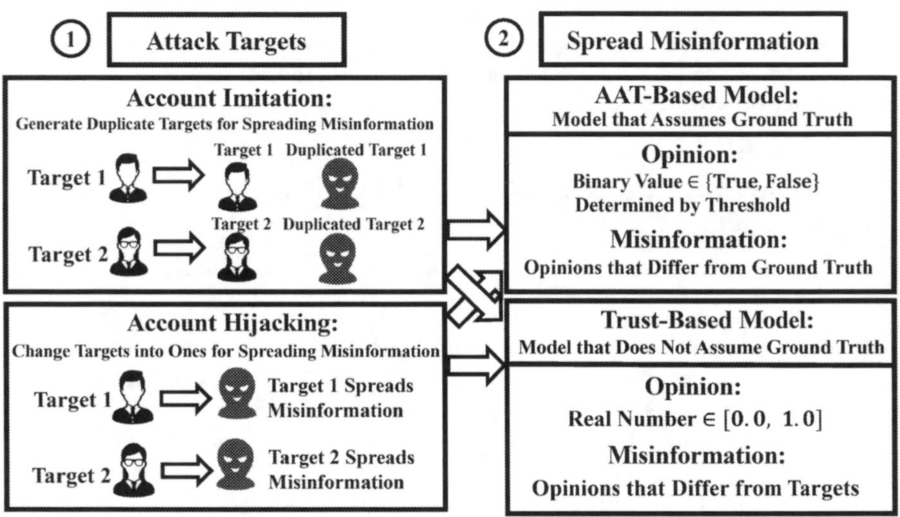

Fig. 1. Overall illustration of proposed models

- **Account Imitation**: The attacker generates duplicate target accounts and then adds them to a social network. The duplicated accounts spread misinformation among the friends of the targets. This attack represents the situation in which those who spread misinformation increase while those who spread correct information remain unchanged.
- **Account Hijacking:** The attacker succeeds in hijacking target accounts with some probability. The hijacked accounts spread misinformation among the friends of the targets. The probability of success varies from target to target depending on their security against hijacking. This attack represents the situation in which those who spread misinformation increase while those who spread correct information decrease by the same number.

By applying these attacks in the AAT-Based Model and Trust-Based Model, we clarify the influence of attacks on opinion dissemination in three cases: no malicious attacks, account imitation, and account hijacking.

3.3 Attacker Behaviors

We consider a situation in which an attacker performs account imitation or account hijacking against $|B|$ influencers (i.e., people who have many friends or are reliable) as targets. We assume that the attacker knows the number of friends for each target[1]. We next embody account imitation, account hijacking, and misinformation in the AAT-Based Model and Trust-Based Model.

- **AAT-Based Model**
  We define the ground truth as $z \in$ {True, False}. If z = True, the news is real news (e.g., the real news "Wildfires broke out in California in 2020", hereinafter "News California"). If z = False, the news is fake news (e.g., the fake news "5G can cause the COVID-19 infection"). We consider the targets to be users whose number of friends is within the top $m\%$ among all users in a social network $G(U, E)$ (i.e., influencers). We define misinformation as $\overline{z}$, which is opposite to the ground truth z

  - **Account Imitation** In a random opinion update step k_{rand}, the attacker generates duplicate target accounts $b' \left(b' = 1, \ldots, |B|\right)$, which have the reliability t_{i_b} and doubt f_{i_b}. Reliability t_{i_b} is the degree to which each user u_i believes targets b. Doubt f_{i_b} is the degree to which each user u_i doubts targets b. The duplicated accounts b' share opinions $o_{b'} = \overline{z}$ with the targets' friends F_b.
  - **Account Hijacking**: The attacker succeeds in hijacking target accounts b with probability p_b. The hijacked accounts b share opinions $o_b = \overline{z}$ with F_b.

- **Trust-Based Model**
  We consider targets to be users whose number of friends is within the top $m\%$ among extremists, who have extreme opinions (i.e., extremists among influencers). We define extreme opinions as opinion $o = 0$or1 (e.g., radical conservatives or radical liberals). Following Tsang and Larson [12], extremists never change their opinions. We define misinformation as $\overline{o_b} = 1 - o_b$, which is opposite to the targets b's opinions $o_b \in \{0, 1\}$.

  - **Account Imitation**: The attacker generates duplicate target accounts b' in step k_{rand}. The duplicated accounts b' share $o_{b'} = \overline{o_b}$ with F_b.
  - **Account Hijacking**: The attacker succeeds in hijacking target accounts b with p_b. The hijacked accounts b share $o_b = \overline{o_b}$ with F_b.

[1] This assumption is realistic because we can know the number of friends by accessing user profile pages on social media (e.g., the number of followers on Twitter).

3.4 Opinion Formulation

We embody the opinion update (i.e., the function $f\left(o_i^k, \boldsymbol{W}_i^k, \boldsymbol{O}_i^k\right)$ in the AAT-Based Model and Trust-Based Model.

- **AAT-Based Model**
The opinion of each user u_i is the subjective probability that he or she believes the news is real. We denote the opinion as $o_i = P_i(z = \text{True})$. We also denote $P_i(z = \text{False}) = 1 - P_i(z = \text{True})$ as the subjective probability that each user u_i believes the news is fake. If opinion $P_i(z = \text{True}) \geq$ a threshold $\sigma\,(0.5 < \sigma < 1.0)$, each user u_i shares opinion $o_i = \text{True}$ with each friend $u_{i_j} (j = 1, \ldots, |F_i|)$, which means that each user u_i tells their friends the news is real (e.g., each user tells their friends "News California" is real). If opinion $P_i(z = \text{True}) \leq 1 - \sigma$, each user u_i shares opinion $o_i = \text{False}$ with each friend u_{i_j}, which means that each user u_i tells the news is fake (e.g., each user tells "News California" is fake although it is real). If $1 - \sigma < P_i(z = \text{True}) < \sigma$, users do not share their opinions. The higher the threshold σ, the more careful users share their opinions; the lower the threshold, the more willing users share their opinions. If each user u_i receives opinions $o_{i_j} \in \{\text{True}, \text{False}\}$ from their friends u_{i_j}, he or she updates his or her current opinion $P_i^k(z)$ to $P_i^{k+1}(z|o_{i_j})$ using (2), which is based on Bayes' theorem:

$$P_i^{k+1}\left(z|o_{i_j}\right) = f\left(o_i^k, \boldsymbol{W}_i^k, \boldsymbol{O}_j^k\right) = \frac{P_i(o_{i_j}|z)P_i^k(z)}{\sum_{z \in \{\text{True},\text{False}\}} P_i(o_{i_j}|z)P_i^k(z)}, \tag{2}$$

where $\boldsymbol{W}_i^k = \left(t_{i_1}, \cdots, t_{i_j}, , \cdots, t_{iM_i}; f_{i_1}, , \cdots, f_{i_j}, \cdots, f_{iM_i}\right)$, $t_{i_j} = Pi(o_{i_j} = \text{True}|z = \text{True}) \in [0.0, 1.0]$ is reliability, and $f_{i_j} = Pi(o_{i_j} = \text{True}|z = \text{False}) \in [0.0, 1.0]$ is doubt, as described in Sect. 3.3. In the AAT [7], reliability is $t_{i_j} = t_{i_{j'}}$ and doubt is $f_{i_j} = f_{i_{j'}}$ where $\forall (j, j') \in F_i$(i.e., users believe or doubt friends equally). Pryymak et al. pointed out that t_{i_j} and f_{i_j} should differ for each friend (i.e., users believe or doubt their friends differently) [7]. To distinguish whether a user is an influencer (i.e., those who are reliable) or not, we followed Pryymak's remark. The opinion update process continues until the current opinion update step k exceeds the maximum opinion update step K.

- **Trust-Based Model**
If each user u_i receives opinion $o_{i_j}^k \in [0.0, 1.0]$ from friends u_{i_j}, he or she updates current opinion $o_i^k \in [0.0, 1.0]$ to o_i^{k+1} using (3), which is based on the weighted average:

$$o_i^{k+1} = f\left(o_i^k, \boldsymbol{W}_i^k, \boldsymbol{O}_i^k\right) = \frac{w_{ii} o_i^k + \sum_{j \in F_i} w_{i_j}^k o_{i_j}^k}{w_{ii} + \sum_{j \in F_i} w_{i_j}^k}, \tag{3}$$

where, $\boldsymbol{W}_i^k = \left(w_{i_1}^k, \ldots, w_{i_j}^k, \ldots, w_{i_{M_i}}^k\right)$ is the current importance of each friend, $\boldsymbol{O}_i^k = \left(o_{i_1}^k, \cdots, o_{i_j}^k \cdots, o_{i_{M_i}}^k\right)$ is the current opinion of each friend, and w_{ii} is the importance of the user himself or herself. Each user u_i also updates the elements of the current importance vector of friends using (4):

$$w_{i_j}^{k+1} = \frac{w_{i_j}^k + rT\left(o_i^k, o_{i_j}^k\right)}{1+r}, \tag{4}$$

where r is the learning rate. The higher it is, the less likely users accept opinions that differ from their opinions. $T\left(o_i^k, o_{i_j}^k\right)$ is the reliability function:

$$T\left(o_i^k, o_{i_j}^k\right) = \exp\left(-\frac{\left(o_i^k - o_{i_j}^k\right)^2}{h}\right), \tag{5}$$

which represents that users are more likely to rely on someone who has similar values and less likely to rely on someone who has different values. The h is a value representing empathy for opinions. The higher it is, the more likely users accept friends' opinions. Each user u_i updates their opinions using (3) and then updates importance using (4) [12].

Tsang and Larson proposed three methods for initializing friend's importance: the same value for all friends, a normal distribution, and the number of friends [12]. Since the targets are influencers (i.e., users have many friends), we use the third initialization method and initialize importance using

$$w_{i_j} = \frac{d_{i_j}}{d_i} w_{ii} = \frac{d_i}{d_i} = 1, \tag{6}$$

where d_i is the number of each user u_i's friends and d_{i_j} is the number of friends each user u_{i_j} has. The user u_i can always send their opinions. Opinion updating continues until the change in the opinions of all users becomes less than a certain small threshold ε or current opinion update step k exceeds the maximum opinion update step K.

4 Algorithms for Malicious Behaviors and Opinion Dissemination Models for Fake News

4.1 Algorithms for Opinion Updating

In the AAT-Based Model, each user updates his or her opinion in accordance with threshold σ and $1 - \sigma$ (Algorithm 1). In the Trust-Based Model, each user updates his or her opinion before updating the importance of their friends (Algorithm 2). If attacks terminate or do not exist from the beginning, Algorithm 3 in Sect. 4.2 is not executed.

Algorithm 1 Opinion Updating in AAT-Based Model

Initialize social network $G(U, E)$, ground truth z, threshold σ, opinion, reliability and doubt.
while $k \leq K$ **do**
  for $i = 1$ **to** $|U|$ **do**
    if an attack exists, **then**
      Attacker executes account imitation or account hijacking in accordance with Algorithm 3.
    if current opinion $o_i^k = P_i^k(z = \text{True}) \geq \sigma$, **then**
      Send $o_i^k = \text{True}$ to all friends belonging to the set F_i
    else if $o_i^k = P_i^k(z = \text{True}) \leq 1 - \sigma$, **then**
      Share $o_i^k = \text{False}$ with all friends in F_i.
    Update current opinion $o_i^k = P_i^k(z = \text{True})$ to $o_i^{k+1} = P_i^{k+1}(z = \text{True})$ using (2).
  Set $k = k + 1$

Algorithm 2 Opinion Updating in Trust-Based Model

Initialize social network $G(U, E)$, opinions, importance, learning rate r, empathy h, and threshold ε.
while $k \leq K$ **or** Differences in opinions of all users $\leq \varepsilon$ **do**
  for $i = 1$ **to** $|U|$ **do**
    if an attack exists, **then**
      Attacker executes account imitation or account hijacking in accordance with Algorithm 3.
    Update current opinion o_i^k to o_i^{k+1} using (3).
    Update current importance $w_{i_j}^k$ for all friends belonging to the set F_i using (4) and (5).
  Set $k = k + 1$

4.2 Algorithms for Attacker Behaviors

As shown in Algorithm 3, an attacker executes account imitation or account hijacking on targets. In the AAT-Based Model, misinformation is $\overline{z}$, which differs from ground truth $z \in \{\text{True}, \text{False}\}$. In the Trust-Based Model, misinformation is $\overline{o_b} = 1 - o_b$, which differs from targets' opinions $ob \in \{0, 1\}$.

Algorithm 3 Attacker Behaviors

Initialize update step k_{rand} to start attacking and update step T at which attacks are detected.
for target account $b = 1$ **to** $|B|$ **do**
  if Attack = "Account Imitation", **then**
    Generate set of duplicate target accounts B' at opinion update step k_{rand}.
    Duplicated accounts $b'(b' = 1, \ldots, |B|)$ spread misinformation in accordance with AAT-Based Model or Trust-Based Model.
  else if Attack = "Account Hijacking", **then**
    Hijack targets b with probability p_b.
    Hijacked targets b spread misinformation in accordance with AAT-Based Model or Trust-Based Model.
if current opinion update step $k \geq T$, **then**
  Terminate account imitation or account hijacking.

5 Evaluation

5.1 Overview

Through experiments, we clarify the influence of attacks on opinion dissemination by comparing the performance in three cases (i.e., no malicious attacks, account imitation, and account hijacking) for each the AAT-Based Model and Trust-Based Model. The performance of the AAT-Based Model is evaluated in terms of accuracy A, inaccuracy I, undetermined UD, where $A = \frac{\sum_{i=1}^{N} |o_i = z|}{N}$ (the percentage of users having opinion o_i the same as ground truth z), $I = \frac{\sum_{i=1}^{N} |o_i = \overline{z}|}{N}$ (the percentage of users having opinion o_i different from ground truth z), and $UD = 1 - A - I$. The performance of the Trust-Based Model is visualized by using heatmaps of the opinion distribution among users along with the opinion update steps. The models and experiments were implemented using Python 3.8.5.

5.2 Datasets and Experimental Settings

We used the publicly available Facebook and Twitter social network datasets, which can download from the website "Stanford Network Analysis Project" [6]. These datasets consist of nodes (i.e., users) and links (i.e., friendships among users). Each node has attributes (e.g., age, gender) and connects with other nodes reciprocally or partially reciprocally. The Facebook dataset consists of $4,039$ users and $88,234$ edges, with each user u_i having $\overline{F}_i = 44$ friends on average. The Twitter dataset consists of 81,306 users and $1,768,149$ edges, with $\overline{F}_i = 33$ friends. We used only the links in the experiments.

The common settings for both models were as follows. We set the attackers as 1% of the users in the dataset. For account hijacking, the probability pb that an attacker succeeds in hijacking targets b was a uniform distribution with a range of [0.0, 1.0]. The attacks were detected at 10 h or 20 h after they started in the real world [1, 2]. We converted these hours into the opinion update step T. The maximum opinion update step was 3,000, which corresponds to 24 h. We conducted 50 simulations for each social network (Facebook, Twitter) and attack method (account imitation, account hijacking).

For the AAT-Based Model, the targets were the users whose number of friends was within the top 1%. The initial opinion value was a normal distribution $N(\text{mean} = 0.5, \text{standard deviation} = 0.15)$, and the initial values of users' reliability and doubt were a uniform distribution with a range of [0.0,1.0]. The threshold σ to send opinions was 0.8. These parameter settings are in accordance with Pryymak et al. [7]. When a simulation terminated, the attack was considered to be a failure if $A \geq 80\%$ and to be a success if $I \geq 80\%$.

For the Trust-Based Model, the targets were the extremists (i.e., those who never change their opinions) whose number of friends was in the top 1%. Extremists were assumed to account for 10% for each extreme opinion $o \in \{0, 1\}$. The remaining 80% of the user opinions were initialized with a uniform distribution with a range of [0.0, 1.0]. We set the learning rate $r = 1.5$, empathy $h = 0.01$, and termination criterion $\varepsilon = 0.001$. These settings follow Tsang and Larson [12].

5.3 Results and Discussion

- **AAT-Based Model**
  When there were no attacks, accuracy A for real news was higher than that for fake news (i.e., people can more accurately perceive that real news is real than they can perceive that fake news is fake).

With account imitation, accuracy A decreased substantially, and undetermined UD increased substantially (i.e., it became harder for users to form opinions for both real news and fake news). The tendencies were remarkable for fake news, indicating that people find it harder to perceive fake news as fake than to perceive real news as real. As shown in Fig. 2, the average accuracy $\overline{A}$ was less than 80%, indicating that account imitation was always effective (i.e., account imitation did not fail, as mentioned in Sect. 5.2). The result for $T = 20$ h showed the same tendencies as those for $T = 10$ h (i.e., the average differences in accuracy $\Delta\overline{A}$, inaccuracy $\Delta\overline{I}$, and undetermined $\Delta\overline{UD}$ across both social networks and both ground truths were $\Delta\overline{A} = 1.27\%$, $\Delta\overline{I} = 1.16\%$, and $\Delta\overline{UD} = 2.22\%$).

With account hijacking, accuracy and undetermined showed the same tendencies as account imitation for fake news. However, the results for real news were unexpected: accuracy was higher and undetermined was lower than with account imitation (i.e., green bars in accuracy for real news were higher and green bars in undetermined for real news were lower than those of the blue bars). This is because account hijacking sometimes fails due to the probability of success that depends on targets' security against hijacking, while account imitation succeeds regardless of their security against imitation (Fig. 2).

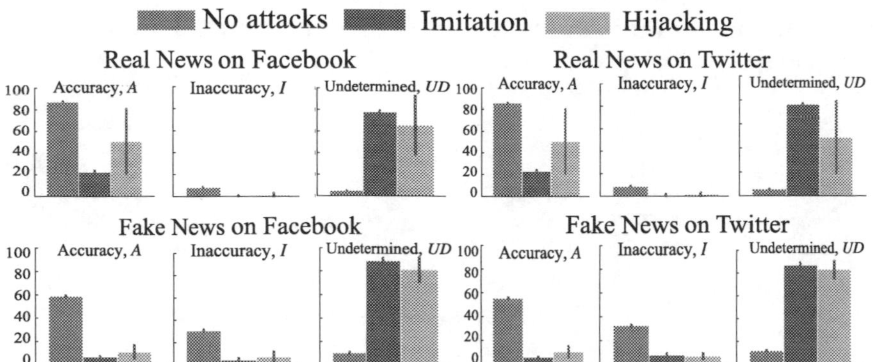

Fig. 2. Averages for accuracy, inaccuracy, and undetermined. "Imitation" and "Hijacking" results are for $T = 10$ h; error bars are standard deviation. (Color figure online)

- **Trust-Based Model**
  When there were no attacks, opinions gradually converged to 0 or 1, indicating that extremists bias users' opinions (which was also shown by Tsang and Larson [12]). Figure 3 shows an example of opinions converging to 0. When attackers whose opinions were 0 attacked the targets whose opinions were 1 ("Attacking 1-opinion targets" in Fig. 3), opinions converged to 0 faster than when there were no attacks. This indicates that attackers facilitate the convergence of the opinion that benefits them. Figure 3 also shows that there were no substantial differences between account imitation and account hijacking. Furthermore, the results for $T = 20$ h show the same tendencies as those for $T = 10$ h. The average opinion update step at which simulations converged (i.e., all users did not update opinions more than a threshold ε) in 10 and 20 h was 15.2 and 17.5, respectively. The same results were observed when attackers whose opinions were 1 attacked the targets whose opinions were 0, which is not discussed due to space limitations (i.e., opinions converged to 1 more quickly than when there were no attacks, both with account imitation and account hijacking).

When attackers whose opinions were 1 attacked targets whose opinions were 0 ("Attacking 0-opinion targets" in Fig. 3), the influence of opinion 0 was suppressed, and the opinions gradually converged to 1. This result corresponds to the situation in which attackers deter the influence of the targets' opinions and then facilitate the spread of opinions beneficial to the attackers. No substantial differences were found between account imitation and account hijacking. The average opinion update step at which simulations converged in 10 and 20 h was 118.2 and 121.7, respectively. The same tendencies were observed when attackers whose opinions were 0 attacked the targets whose opinions were 1 (i.e., the influence of opinions 1 was suppressed, and the opinions gradually converged to 0).

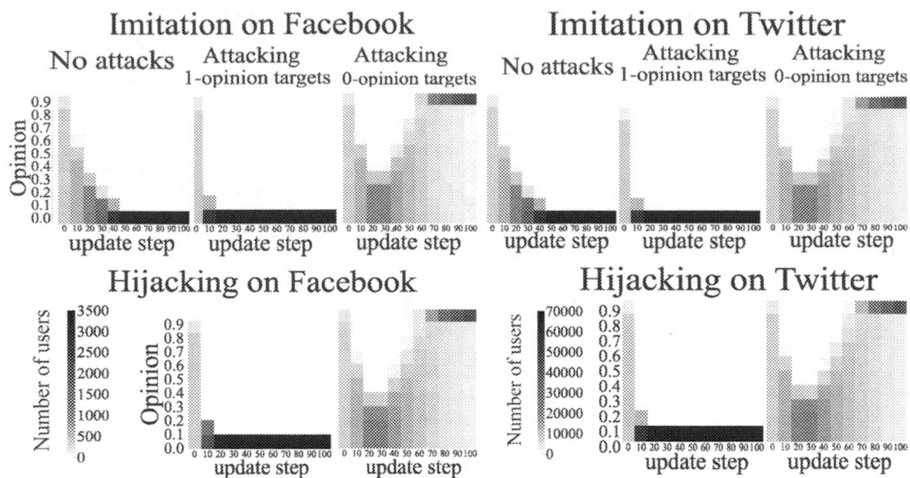

Fig. 3. Average opinion distribution for account imitation and account hijacking. "Attacking" results are for $T = 10$ h.

6 Conclusion

We have described the dissemination of opinions regarding fake news by attackers on social networks. Previous models [4, 7] described the spread of correct (or incorrect) opinions assuming the presence of the ground truth while other models [3, 10, 12] described opinion convergence without assuming it. However, these models do not take attackers into account. Therefore, we modeled attackers who intentionally facilitate the spread of fake news by imitating or hijacking those who have many friends (i.e., influencers). We also incorporated attackers into two models, the AAT [7] and Tsang and Larson's Trust-Model [12].

Experimental results on real-world social networks revealed that, with the AAT-Based Model, account imitation was always effective (e.g., 1% of attackers can deter 80.8% of the users from forming opinions) while account hijacking sometimes fails. With the Trust-Based Model, account imitation and account hijacking enabled 1% of attackers to quickly spread the opinions that supported attackers while suppressing the correct opinion convergence.

Our proposed models do not reflect psychological tendencies, such as the echo chamber effect and the backfire effect. Moreover, we have yet to develop effective countermeasures from our results. Future work will overcome these limitations.

Acknowledgements. This work was supported by JSPS KAKENHI Grant Number JP21K11883.

References

1. Aaron, G., Chapin, L., Piscitello, D., Strutt, C.: Phishing landscape 2020 (2020)
2. Cui, Q., et al.: Tracking phishing attacks over time. In: Proceedings of the 26th International Conference on World Wide Web, pp. 667–676 (2017)

3. DeGroot, M.H.: Reaching a consensus. J. Am. Stat. Assoc. **69**(345), 118–121 (1974)
4. Glinton, R.T., Scerri, P., Sycara, K.: Towards the understanding of information dynamics in large scale networked systems. In: 2009 12th International Conference on Information Fusion, pp. 794–801. IEEE (2009)
5. Hameed, K., Rahman, N.: Today's social network sites: an analysis of emerging security risks and their counter measures. In: 2017 International Conference on Communication Technologies (ComTech), pp. 143–148. IEEE (2017)
6. Leskovec, J., Krevl, A.: SNAP Datasets: Stanford large network dataset collection (2014). http://snap.stanford.edu/data
7. Pryymak, O., Rogers, A., Jennings, N.R.: Efficient opinion sharing in large decentralised teams. In: Proceedings of the 11th International Conference on Autonomous Agents and Multiagent Systems, pp. 543–550 (2012)
8. Quattrociocchi, W., Scala, A., Sunstein, C.R.: Echo chambers on facebook. Available at SSRN 2795110 (2016)
9. Salahdine, F., Kaabouch, N.: Social engineering attacks: a survey. Future Internet **11**(4), 89 (2019)
10. Sasahara, K., Chen, W., Peng, H., Ciampaglia, G.L., Flammini, A., Menczer, F.: Social influence and unfollowing accelerate the emergence of echo chambers. J. Comput. Soc. Sci. **4**(1), 381–402 (2020). https://doi.org/10.1007/s42001-020-00084-7
11. Shu, K., Sliva, A., Wang, S., Tang, J., Liu, H.: Fake news detection on social media: a data mining perspective. ACM SIGKDD Explorations Newsl **19**(1), 22–36 (2017)
12. Tsang, A., Larson, K.: Opinion dynamics of skeptical agents. In: Proceedings of the 13th International Conference on Autonomous Agents and Multiagent Systems, pp. 277–284 (2014)
13. Vosoughi, S., Roy, D., Aral, S.: The spread of true and false news online. Science **359**(6380), 1146–1151 (2018)
14. Wang, Y., et al.: Eann: event adversarial neural networks for multi-modal fake news detection. In: Proceedings of the 24th ACM SIGKDD International Conference on Knowledge Discovery and Data Mining, pp. 849–857 (2018)
15. Yang, S., et al.: Unsupervised fake news detection on social media: a generative approach. In: Proceedings of the AAAI Conference on Artificial Intelligence, vol. 33, pp. 5644–5651 (2019)

Developing Machine Learning Model for Predicting Social Media Induced Fake News

David Langley(✉), Caoimhe Reidy(✉), Mark Towey(✉), Manisha(✉), and Denis Dennehy(✉)

National University of Ireland, Galway, Galway, Ireland
{d.langley1,c.reidy10,m.towey3,m.161,denis.dennehy}@nuigalway.ie

Abstract. Fake news has been associated with major global events such as Covid-19 and the political polarisation of the US presidential election in 2016. This paper investigates how fake news has affected society and advance understanding of the nature of its impact in the future of democratic societies. Taken from large datasets consisting of over 23,000 fake news story words and over 21,000 true news story words we use descriptive and predictive analytics, partly analysing more than 350 words during the selected period of October 2016 to April 2017. The findings show that Trump was the most popular word for both true and fake news. In this study, we compare and contrast the words used and the volume of true versus fake news stories related to the election and the inauguration. This study makes an important contribution as it develops a predictive model that highlights the severity of political polarization and its consequences in democratic societies, which inevitably have implications for inclusive societies in the 21st century.

Keywords: Fake news · Social media · Echo chambers · Filter bubbles · Machine learning · Polarization

1 Introduction

Fake News can be defined as online publications that are intentionally false in order to mislead readers [1]. Although fake news is not a new a phenomenon, social media has intensified its' severity due to the rate in which news can be spread, regardless of whether it is true or false [1]. The need for fake news detection is greater than ever, as the implication of this false information is becoming increasingly dangerous for democratic societies [2]. Fake news publications through news outlets and social media have had major influence in the outcome of many worldwide events such as the US presidential election in 2016 and more recently the COVID-19 pandemic. The way in which algorithms work on social media platforms, such as Twitter and Facebook, can facilitate the creation of '*echo chambers*' (e.g., situations where individuals "hear their own voice") [17] and '*filter bubbles* (e.g. whereby like-minded individuals are not exposed to contrary perspectives or opinions, which can lead to tunnel vision and enabling confirmation bias [2]. The impact of echo chambers includes excluding alternative perspectives [18]

Published by Springer Nature Switzerland AG 2021
D. Dennehy et al. (Eds.): I3E 2021, LNCS 12896, pp. 656–669, 2021.
https://doi.org/10.1007/978-3-030-85447-8_54

and political chaos in many contexts [8]. Should the public lose trust in media outlets, it is very damaging to society, thus in this study, we build a model to predict whether a publication is true or false in a bid to restore faith in news sources [3].

The aim of this study *is "to use advanced analytics to identify and predict whether news is fake or true"*. This will be achieved through the means of machine learning. Machine learning models will be compared to determine an optimal model.

To achieve this aim, we seek to answer to interrelated questions:

1. What are the most commonly used words in fake news posts?
2. Does a major news event increase or decrease the amount of fake news created?

The paper is structured as follows. First, a review of background literature is presented. Next, the research methodology used to extract and clean data for the purpose of analysis is outlined. Then, discussion of key findings follows. The paper ends with a conclusion.

2 Background Literature

The prevalence of social media (e.g., WeChat, Facebook, LinkedIn, Twitter) has been a catalyst to inducing a polarized society [5]. Fake News is a global issue with its consequences becoming more severe by the day that the World Economic Forum (2018) raises concern that is the greatest threat to society due to the speed at which 'digital wildfires' spread on a global scale. More recently, Tim Cook (CEO, Apple) criticized the facilitating role that technology companies play by prioritizing conspiracy theories and violent incitement because of their high rates of engagement [7].

In response, it has led researchers to explore social media induced polarization from different theoretical lenses to study specific social media platforms and particular attention given to fake news [6]. Researchers' fake news and polarisation in varied contexts, such as politics [8], new framing [9], and modelling the combination of bias and polarisation to examine the impact of misinformation in social media networks [10].

[2] investigates the issue of fake news in the context of social media polarisation. It is apparent from this paper that although there is increased access to information, this does not lead to better informed citizens. It is argued that it leads to increased societal polarisation, this is because of people settling into 'ideological neighbourhoods,' whereby individuals experience opinions and views of like-minded individuals [2]. Xu argues that democracy is in danger. Techniques such as filter bubbles and echo chambers paired with fake news stories may distort the assumption that society is well-informed and may amplify confirmation bias [2]. A diffusion drift model used in this paper shows that increased information access contributes to growing polarisation – assuming the presence of confirmation bias and people looking for more outlying content. Technological solutions are proposed to help this issue. A previous study [4] conducted research to understand whether fake news differs systematically from real news in style and language use. The study reports that fake news articles tend to be shorter, use repetitive and less complex language, less punctuation, and less quotes [4]. Building on this body of knowledge, this study is to build on this work by providing a different approach, by

focusing on the differences in vocabulary used. Manifestations of fake news include misinformation about presidential election campaigns [11], immigration [12], religion [13], and pandemics, specifically Covid-19 [14]. We intend to present an in-depth exploration of the differences between real and fake news, with an overall aim to predict whether a news article is true or false.

3 Research Methodology

Cross Industry Standard Process for Data Mining (CRISP-DM) is an industry standard methodology that prescribes a set of guidelines to guide the efficient extraction of information from data [23]. The CRISP-DM methodology consists of six cyclical steps, namely (i) Business Understanding, (ii) Data Understanding, (iii) Data Preparation, (iv) Modeling, (v) Evaluation, and (vi) Deployment (see Fig. 1 below). It is a comprehensive and well-structured methodology that covers all the aspects of our project effectively. It is iterative where necessary, which is an important feature in an aim to monitor the models and the analysis to keep it up to date.

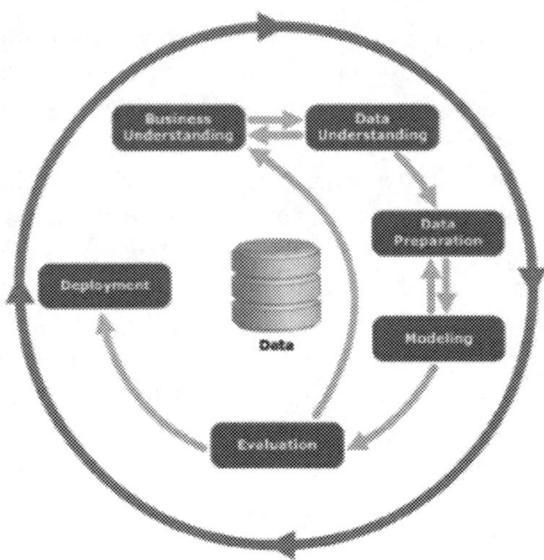

Fig. 1. CRISP-DM Methodology [21]

The **six stages** of the **CRISP-DM** model in the appropriate context are explained below:

Business Understanding: The first step is to gain an understanding of the topic of the research in a business context. A comprehensive analysis on the issue is crucial to attain this clear understanding and form research objectives. In order to achieve this understanding, the challenges posed by Fake News in the past is investigated, how it has affected society today and realize the prevalence of the issue by the way in which it can impact the future of democratic societies.

Data Understanding: The dataset chosen is analyzed in depth as to what it contains and represents, to best understand how to proceed. This step is vital in establishing the objectives when combined with the business understanding process [21]. The main focus of this stage are the questions that could arise in the dataset, in an aim to produce intriguing findings and actionable insights in the future. Our data is split between two datasets – one for fake news and one for true news. The dataset was sourced from Kaggle, with verification of the quality of the data carried out.

Data Preparation: The chosen dataset(s) is prepared for analysis through cleaning and formatting techniques. This involves the transformation from the initial dataset to the final dataset. Using Excel and Python, the data will be extracted from the topics to be able to count the number of words per source. The data will be cleaned, to prepare it for analysis. It is then formatted, in an aim to classify these words as being more likely to be used in 'Fake' vs 'True' news. All null and unknown values are removed to reduce uncertainty.

Modelling: Various models are built and analyzed in this step. As there will be multiple iterations of this phase, all models with low levels of error are run to ensure the optimal model is selected and built [21]. The model is then technically assessed. To fulfil our objectives, a predictive model is required – to predict whether an inputted topic or story is likely to be fake or true. We used Support Vector Machines (SVM), which was built using Python. The model is repeatedly run to gain comprehensive findings for examination in the next phase.

Evaluation: This phase focuses on the analysis of the modelling in the context of the business needs and understanding [22]. This is vital, as it is the basis of the actionable decisions, whether the model needs to be iterated or proceed to the next stage. The accuracy and the fit of our model is evaluated – a low level of error is essential in producing conclusive results. The model outputs will be evaluated and compared against each other to enhance data-driven decisions. One optimal model is selected, and the findings are analyzed in the context of our pre-determined objectives. We apply different visualization techniques to illustrate our findings using Tableau and R.

Deployment: This phase is the main test of any study, as it decides whether actionable insights can be drawn from findings and conclusions [23]. A review of the study must be performed for future endeavors. In the Deployment section we will be discussing how the model can be deployed to identify and predict Fake News, to add value to society. Through this section, we will provide insights into how our model can tackle the issue of Fake News and reduce the severity of its consequences.

Table 1 lists the analytical tools used to extract, structure, analyze, and visualize the data.

Table 1. Analytical tools used in the data collection and analysis.

Tools used	Description of tools
Kaggle – Dataset Source	One of the largest dataset free source websites
Advanced Microsoft Excel - Data Manipulation	A great application for storing data files and then using that current information and changing it do be user friendly, from adding in columns to break down dates to its lower forms to creating columns that further describe the data being discussed
Python – Data Extraction and Prediction	Python is known to be the most preferred programming language for data manipulation, data analysis and data visualization
Tableau – Data Visual Tool	One of the best visualization applications for displaying data through means of graphs, charts and more
R – Statistical Analysis Programming Language	R is a statistical programming language, which we also plan to use due to its high efficiency with regards to its visualization and data wrangling abilities

3.1 Data Extraction Process

The news headline data is imported into Python for the data extraction process. The data is stripped to facilitate the separation of each headline onto separate rows. Pre-processing is then carried out to clean the data for analysis, which consists of removing punctuation, numbers, symbols, stop words and involved the changing of all words to lowercase, to avoid duplication.

The news headline data is differentiated by the column 'Truth?', where it is characterized by 'FAKE' or 'TRUE' news. Tokenization is performed to count the words used in each news article headline. From this, a dictionary template of all the unique words is created which allowed for outputs; each word column contain 0's if the word is not present in the headline or the count number if the word is present, as shown in Fig. 2.

title	text	subject	date	Truth?	Day	Month	Year	Month & Ye	administr	admits	adviser	america
Republican lawmaker R	WASHING	politicsNews	April 30, 2017	TRUE	30	April	2017	Apr-17	0	0	0	0
Trump says China could	WASHING	politicsNews	April 30, 2017	TRUE	30	April	2017	Apr-17	0	0	0	0
Trump could target 'car	WASHING	politicsNews	April 30, 2017	TRUE	30	April	2017	Apr-17	0	0	0	0
Trump invites leaders o	WASHING	politicsNews	April 30, 2017	TRUE	30	April	2017	Apr-17	0	0	0	0
Trump celebrates first 1	HARRISBU	politicsNews	April 30, 2017	TRUE	30	April	2017	Apr-17	0	0	0	0
Toned-down White Ho	WASHING	politicsNews	April 30, 2017	TRUE	30	April	2017	Apr-17	0	0	0	0
EPA says website unde	WASHING	politicsNews	April 29, 2017	TRUE	29	April	2017	Apr-17	0	0	0	0
Trump to order a study	WASHING	politicsNews	April 29, 2017	TRUE	29	April	2017	Apr-17	0	0	0	0

Fig. 2. Sample dataset

4 Key Findings

This section presents key findings relating to the two aforementioned research questions, namely, 'What are the most commonly used words in fake news articles?' and 'Does a major news event increase or decrease the amount of fake news created?' During our research, we established a further discovery, which consisted of us looking at whether there was a correlation between a headline word count and their article content word count. The findings reveal that there is a correlation.

When thinking of fake news reports, click-bait headlines come to mind, ones whereby all the content is in the headline and near to nothing in the article body. Due to these news articles being fake, there is little to no evidence to support them, so, to get their polarizing message across, the headlines are crowded with content. The aim for publishers of fake news is to spread it far and wide and at speed. With this in mind, a python script was written to count the number of words in the news headlines and the article text. After exporting these to excel, a correlation scatterplot was devised, the initial assumptions proved to be true. As shown in Fig. 3, there is a clear difference between the true and fake news headlines. The true news headline's word count varies from 4–17 words, with their article content varying from 22–2000 words. In total contrast, the fake news headline's word count varies from 4–42 words, with their content varying from 0–4900 words. Figure 3 demonstrates that a correlation between the headline and their article content is present, and this can be drawn upon when looking to define the typing of a news headline. Upon taking a deeper look into the frequency of the article lengths, a clear observation was extracted (Fig. 4). The distribution for true news is fairly even, with two peaks at 80 and 400 words per article. The most substantial finding in the fake news section is the fact that there are 444 articles without a single word in their article. This is a clear sign that by adapting a machine learning algorithm to take the word length into account, creates a clearer distinction between the types of news headlines.

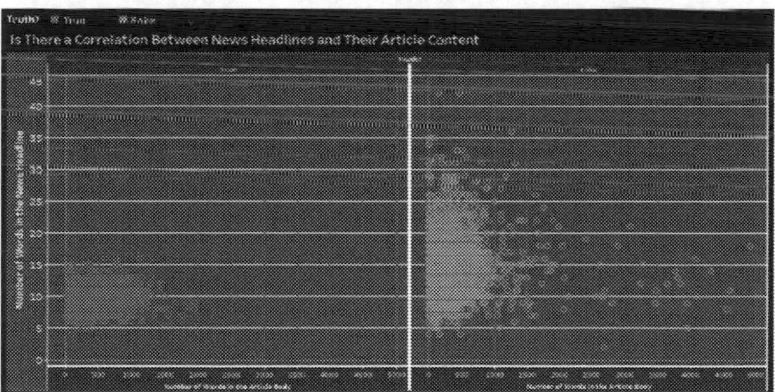

Fig. 3. Correlation between News Headlines their Article Content

The major event that was tracked in our dataset was the 2016 US Presidential Election, between Hillary Clinton and Donald Trump. The voting period for this event took place during November 2016, while the inauguration took place in January 2017. In Fig. 5

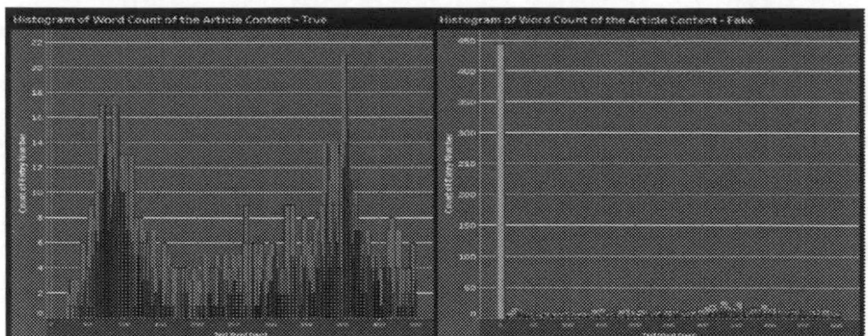

Fig. 4. **Frequency** Distribution of Article Lengths

[Left], there is a significant increase to the total news headlines during the months of November and January. This increase comes from the rise in true news (Fig. 5 [Right]), as the closer to the event you get the more real news stations and articles are going to be spreading true news.

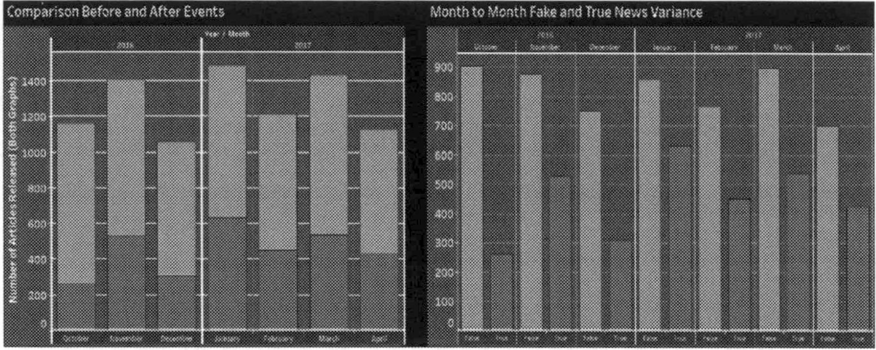

Fig. 5. Comparison of (Left) Total Headlines & (Right) Different Types of News Over Time

Leading up to the event, the percentage of October's Fake vs True News is 77.51% (Fig. 6), this shows depending on what you read, or who you follow, you may become persuaded to change your mind in your decision, thus causing polarization.

The results indicate that during the period of October 2016 – April 2017, Trump (also including Trumps) was the most popular word for both true and fake news. The words after this then differed, with 'US', 'says', 'house' and 'White' being in the top 5 for true news headlines (Fig. 7 [Right]). While for fake news headlines the top five consisted of, 'Video', 'Obama', 'Hillary' and 'watch' (Fig. 7 [Left]), this shows that there are clear differences when it comes to which words result in fake or true news and thus will be used in our machine learning model to predict if a news headline is fake or true.

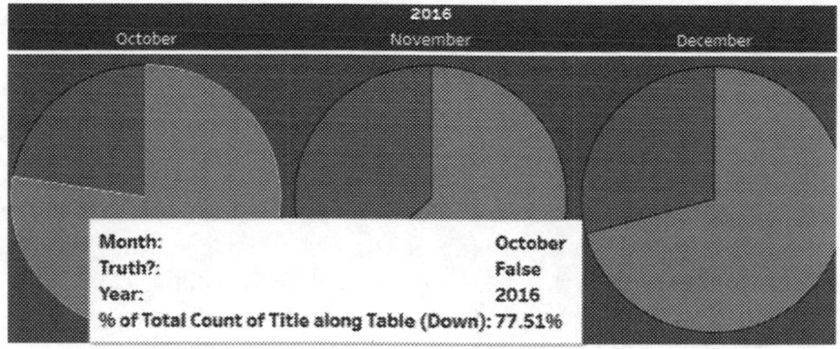

Fig. 6. Percentage of Fake VS True News Before an Event

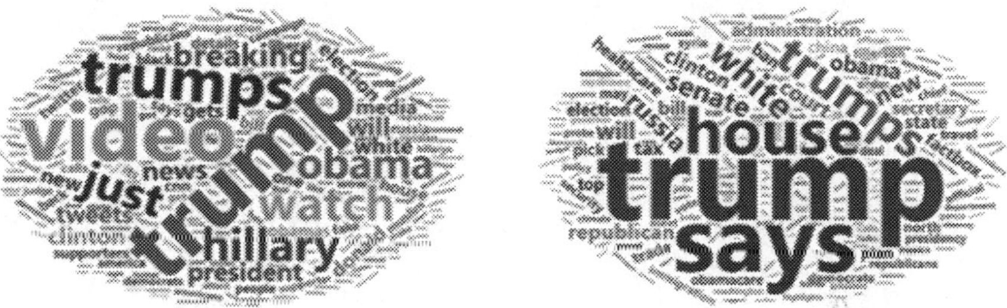

Fig. 7. Word Clouds of the Words used in Fake (Left) and True (Right) News Headlines

5 Model Creation

In our earlier analysis of the most common words in fake/real news, a Bag of Words approach was used to convert text data to numerical data. Bag of Words is the simplest way of converting text to numbers. The main limitation of the Bag of Words model is that it assigns equal value to the words, irrespective of their importance [15].

A TF-IDF approach was then considered to convert text data to numerical data for our model creation. TF stands for Term Frequency and is the frequency of a word in a document divided by the total number of words in the document. IDF stands for Inverse Document Frequency and is the Log of the total number of documents divided by the number of documents that contain a particular word. The TF and IDF values are multiplied together to give a TF-IDF value for each word. Put simply, this means that "the words that occur less in all the documents and more in individual documents contribute more towards classification" [15]. After optimizing and comparing 8 different Machine Learning Models, the 4 models with the highest accuracy scores were Logistic Regression, Support Vector Machines, Neural Networks and Decision Tree Classification, which are discussed below.

5.1 Logistic Regression

Logistic regression is a linear classifier which is used to predict a binary outcome based on a set of independent variables. [16] For example, the output can be 0/1, True/False,

Yes/No, Approved/Declined etc. It is essentially used to predict the probability of a binary event occurring. The binary event in our case, is if a particular news headline is fake news or not. For logistic regression to work, the dependent variable must be dichotomous, i.e., it can only fit into one of two categories. The dependent variable is predicted based on a set of independent variables. Independent variables are variables which may affect the dependent variable. Independent variables can either be continuous data, discrete ordinal data or discrete nominal data. [16]. Logistic regression is easier to train and implement compared to many other machine learning models and it works very well with a linearly separable dataset. Logistic regression is not very accurate with small datasets however and using logistic regression on a small dataset can often result in overfitting which means that the model is too closely fit to the training data and cannot accurately classify the test data [16] (Fig. 8).

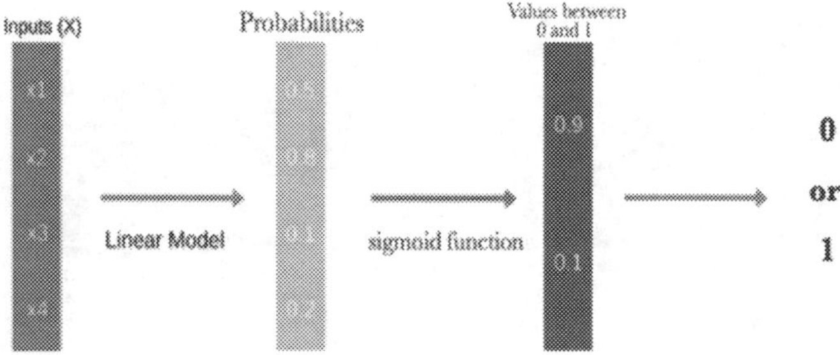

Fig. 8. Linear Classification Model

5.2 Support Vector Machines (SVM)

SVM is a linear model that solves classification and regression problems as well as linear and non-linear problems [24]. The SVM algorithm creates a line or hyperplane which separates the data into their different classes (characteristics). Creating the hyperplane sounds easy, it could go anywhere in between the grouped variables, but creating the optimal hyperplane can be difficult. For the optimal hyperplane, you need it to be equidistant from the closest support vectors, which are the variables closest to the line originally. The challenge is to maximize the margin, distance from support vectors to the hyperplane. Once the hyperplane has been optimized, then depending on where the variable lies either side of the hyperplane, will determine its class (Fig. 9).

5.3 Neural Networks

A neural network is a framework that trains to make predictions or generate forecasts by going through the following steps (i) taking the data from the input, (ii) making a logical prediction, (iii) taking the forecast and comparing it to the desired result, and (iv) changing its embedding layer to correctly predict the next time (Fig. 10).

Since neural networks can adapt and change input, they can produce the best possible outcome without requiring the output parameters to be redesigned. Neural networks are

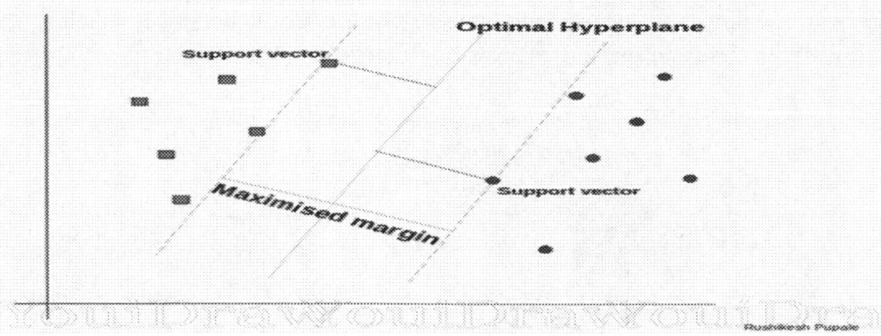

Fig. 9. Optimal Hyperplane using SVM Algorithm.

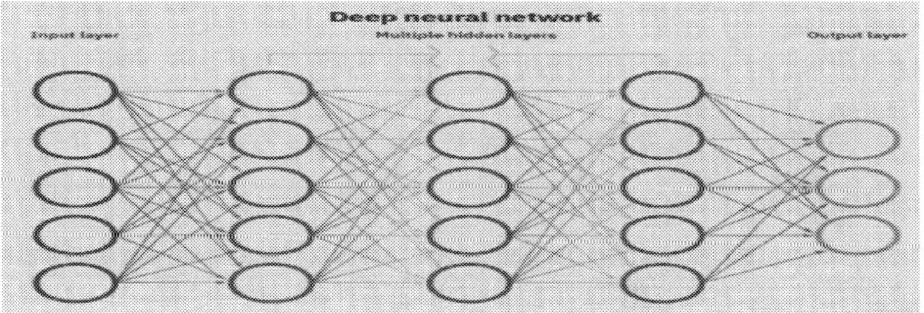

Fig. 10. Neural Network Model

made up of components such as vectors, layers, and linear regression. The data is stored as vectors, which are then stored in arrays in Python. The data from the previous layer is transformed by each layer. Since each layer extracts some representation of the data that came before it, and each layer works as a feature engineering phase.

The neural network uses the activation function. The method of training a neural network is close to that of trial and error.

5.4 Decision Tree Classification

Decision Tree Classification is a supervised machine learning algorithm. It performs a breakdown of the dataset into attributes, whereby each attribute forms a node. The setup of the tree begins at the Root Node with the attribute that provides the most information gain, the attributes with descending importance are positioned along the tree to the final node, the Leaf Node, which contains the result of the tree. When evaluating, each node is addressed as an iterative process, adhering to the decision outcome at each node, leading to a classified dataset [20].

There are two types of decisions trees; there is Categorical Variable and Continuous Variable decision trees. The dataset in question uses a categorical dependent variable, therefore, a categorical variable decision tree is implemented in this model. A key consideration is the ease of overfitting the tree – a limit is placed on the depth of the tree to prevent this; however, this introduces the risk of the results being not absolute [25]. Decision Tree's ease and speed of use outweigh any of its downfalls (Fig. 11).

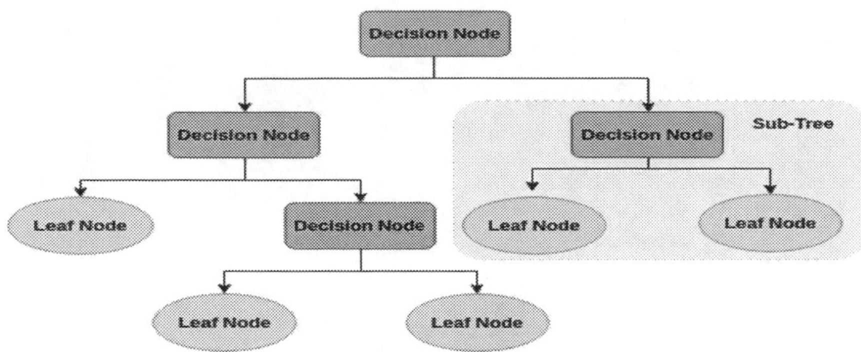

Fig. 11. Visualization of Decision Tree [20]

5.5 Model Choice Conclusion

The decision for which model that would be used was easy. By comparing the accuracy of each model, a clear winner was found, Support Vector Machines (SVM). With an accuracy score of 94.83% compared to the accuracy scores of the other Machine Learning models of, 93.04% for Logistic Regression, 94.03% for Neural Networks, and 89.26% for Decision Tree Classification. The data used was the total News Headlines between October 2016 and April 2017. After considering the possibility of better results coming from an evenly weighted dataset of truths vs fakes, the number of headlines were equated and the models were run again with only the Logistic Regression model receiving an increased accuracy score of 93.53%, but still not enough to surpass SVM as the winner of the most efficient Machine Learning model for the dataset. To make sure that this gives the greatest results in determining if a headline is a true or fake headline, the confusion matrixes were examined. These backed up the already satisfied result that SVM was the better model, with a larger percentage of correct true headlines for the SVM model vs the Neural Networks model, this doubled down the confirmation of 'best in class', which was the Support Vector Machine model.

6 Discussion, Limitations and Future Research

As our study used the 2016/17 US presidential election datasets to develop our model, Donald Trump was the big hot topic of conversation. His name was number 1 for both the true and fake news, and with how controversial he has been, this was expected [26]. In contrast, the other words in the top 5 differed between the two types, leading to the realization that we could use these words to help predict if an article is fake or true.

The uncovered correlation question when thought about made sense, but it was not until the script was being created and fine-tuned that the answer became clear. With fake news articles they just want to front load all their misinformation into the title because it is catchy and would be read by the public. Whereas with true news articles, they have the content and sources to back up their claims and only need to catch people's attention enough to get them to open the article. They do not need to have 20+ words in their articles to get noticed. There were an alarming 444 articles that had 0 words in their body, all of these being fake news ones. This demonstrates that these articles had no supporting sources and just wanted to impose malice information onto the general public.

Our proposed model could be implemented by organizations across varying industries. Social media platforms like Twitter and Face-book are the most obvious organizations which could find great value in implementing this model. Social media platforms have begun flagging election related posts which may be misleading in the wake of Donald Trump's comments regarding the 2020 U.S election [27] but this model could easily be used to flag potentially fake posts regarding a multitude of varying topics. Links to articles about a wide range of topics appear across social media on a daily basis and fake news articles can easily be flagged as fake whether these articles may be about politics, the COVID-19 pandemic, business or even celebrity gossip. We believe that if this model is implemented correctly, it will protect people from consuming fake news and will prevent people from being exploited by companies and individuals that are sharing fake news. This can benefit businesses, governments and the overall wellbeing of a society if people are aware of what is well informed, accurate news and what is misleading, fake news.

Our predictive model demonstrates that upon reading fake news, it can have impact the opinion of the reader. The correlation between the headlines and the content of a news article has proved that fake news headlines are likely to have more content than true news headlines. This can have serious repercussions for society, such as the creation of an echo chamber within an individual's social media newsfeeds. Our analysis shows that we can predict that news is fake or true with the higher accuracy by using the machine learning algorithm. This can add real value to society by revealing the truth about fake news stories, resulting in the possible change of opinion (polarization) in a certain topic. A person's opinion is fundamental to democracy, especially during times of elections or voting, and should that be wrongly influenced, it could cause significant damage to democratic societies.

As with all research, however, we acknowledge this study has three limitations. First, we are novice data scientists who are developing a novel model. Future research could apply to the proposed model to more complex scenarios to assess its utility. For example, apply sentiment analysis to economic news to reveal fake business news leading to instability in the stock market. This is another way of value creation from the paper, as fake news stories can cause serious economic issues to the stakeholders involved. Second, we did not take into consideration to real-world context those who are susceptible to fake news. Future research could focus on contextual factors such as the role of national culture and its influence on polarization [18, 19]. Additionally, future studies could use fake news detection and prediction in the corporate world regarding tarnishing company brand and reputation, and fake news regarding various market impacting mergers and acquisitions that could lead to a global crash in stock markets.

To conclude, by focusing on the differences in vocabulary used, this study advances understanding of filter bubbles and echo chambers, which can contribute to the polarization of societies, rather than inclusive societies.

References

1. Allcott, H., Mentzkow, M.: Social media and fake news in the 2016 election. J. Econ. Perspect. **31**(2), 211–236 (2017)
2. Xu, C., Li, J., Abdelzaher, T., Ji, H., Szymanski, K., Dellaverson, J.: The paradox of information access: on modeling social-media-induced polarization (2021)
3. Tandoc, E., Wei Lim, Z., Ling., R.: Defining “fake news”. Digit. Journal. **6**(2), 137–153 (2017)
4. Horne, B., Adali., S.: This just in: fake news packs a lot in title, uses simpler, repetitive content in text body, more similar to satire than real news. In: Proceedings of the International AAAI Conference on Web and Social Media, vol. 11, no. 1 (2017)
5. Spohr, D.: Fake news and ideological polarization: Filter bubbles and selective exposure on social media. Bus. Inf. Rev. **34**(3), 150–160 (2017)
6. Brummette, J., DiStaso, M., Vafeiadis, M., Messner, M.: Read all about it: the politicization of “fake news” on Twitter. Journal. Mass Commun. Q. **95**(2), 497–517 (2018)
7. Newman, N., Fletcher, R., Kalogeropoulos, A., Levy, A., Nielsen, R.: Reuters Institute digital news report 2017. https://reutersinstitute.politics.ox.ac.uk/sites/default/files/Digital%20News%20Report%202017%20web_0.pdf. Accessed 22 Jan 2021
8. Kim, Y., Kim, Y.: Incivility on Facebook and political polarization: the mediating role of seeking further comments and negative emotion. Comput. Hum. Behav. **99**, 219–227 (2019)
9. Fisher, C.: What is meant by ‘trust’ in news media? In: Otto, K., Köhler, A. (eds.) Trust in Media and Journalism, pp. 19–38. Springer Fachmedien Wiesbaden, Wiesbaden (2018). https://doi.org/10.1007/978-3-658-20765-6_2
10. Sikder, O., Smith, R.E., Vivo, P., Livan, G.: A minimalistic model of bias, polarization and misinformation in social networks. Sci. Rep. **10**(1), 1–11 (2020)
11. Guess, A., Nyhan, B., Reifler, J.: Selective exposure to misinformation: evidence from the consumption of fake news during the 2016 US presidential campaign. Eur. Res. Counc. **9**(3), 4 (2018)
12. Jaramillo-Dent, D., Pérez-Rodríguez, M.A.: #MigrantCaravan: the border wall and the establishment of otherness on Instagram. New Media Soc. **23**(1), 121–141 (2021)
13. Said, E.W.: Covering Islam: How the Media and the Experts Determine How We See the Rest of the World. Random House, London (2018)
14. Laato, S., Islam, A.N., Islam, M.N., Whelan, E.: What drives unverified information sharing and cyberchondria during the COVID-19 pandemic? Eur. J. Inf. Syst. **29**(3), 288–305 (2021)
15. Usman, M: Python for NLP: Creating TF-IDF Model from Scratch. StackAbuse.com (2021)
16. Thankda, A: What is Logistic Regression? A Beginner’s Guide. CareerFoundry.com (2020)
17. Brugnoli, E., Cinelli, M., Quattrociocchi, W., Scala, A.: Recursive patterns in online echo chambers. Sci. Rep. **9**(1), 1–18 (2019)
18. Gillespie, T., Boczkowski, P.J., Foot, K.A. (eds.): Media Technologies: Essays on Communication, Materiality, and Society. MIT Press, Cambridge (2014)
19. Gupta, M., Esmaeilzadeh, P., Uz, I., Tennant, V.M.: The effects of national cultural values on individuals’ intention to participate in peer-to-peer sharing economy. J. Bus. Res. **97**, 20–29 (2019)
20. Navlani, A.: Datacamp, 28 December 2018. https://www.datacamp.com/community/tutorials/decision-tree-classification-python. Accessed May 2021

21. Wirth, R., Hipp, J.: CRISP-DM: towards a standard process model for data. In: Proceedings of the 4th International Conference on the Practical Applications of Knowledge Discovery and Data Mining, vol. 1, pp. 29–39 (2000)
22. datascience-pm, Datascience (2020). https://www.datasciencc-pm.com/crisp-dm-2/. Accessed 03 2021
23. sv-europe, Crisp dm methodology (2021). https://www.sv-europe.com/crisp-dm-methodology/. Accessed 03 2021
24. Pupale, R.: Towards Data Science (2018). https://towardsdatascience.com/https-medium-com-pupalerushikesh-svm-f4b42800e989. Accessed 7 Apr 2021
25. Chakure, A.: Medium, 6 July 2019. https://medium.com/swlh/decision-tree-classification-de64fc4d5aac. Accessed May 2021
26. Francia, P.: Free Media and Twitter in the 2016 presidential election: the unconventional campaign of Donald Trump. Soc. Sci. Comput. Rev. (2017)
27. Fowler, G.: Twitter and Facebook warning labels aren't enough to save democracy. The-WashingtonPost.com (2020)

A Deep Multi-modal Neural Network for the Identification of Hate Speech from Social Media

Gunjan Kumar[1(✉)], Jyoti Prakash Singh[1], and Abhinav Kumar[2]

[1] National Institute of Technology Patna, Patna, India
{gunjank.phd20.cs,jps}@nitp.ac.in

[2] Department of Computer Science & Engineering, Siksha 'O' Anusandhan Deemed to be University, Bhubaneswar, India
abhinavkumar@soa.ac.in

Abstract. Hate speech can be particularized as an intentional and chronic act to harm a single person or a group of individuals. This act can be performed via social networking websites such as Twitter, YouTube, Facebook, and more. Most of the existing approaches for finding hate speech are concentrated on either textual or visual information of the posted social media contents. In this work, a multimodal system is proposed that uses textual as well as the visual contents of the social media post to classify it into Racist, Sexist, Homophobic, Religion-based hate, Other hate and No hate classes. The proposed multi-modal system uses a convolutional neural network-based model to process text and a pre-trained VGG-16 network to process imagery contents. The performance of the proposed model is tested with the benchmark dataset and it achieved significant performance in classifying social media posts into six different hate classes.

Keywords: Hate-speech · Multi-modal · Twitter images

1 Introduction

Please Social media such as Twitter, Instagram, YouTube, and Facebook encourages users to share ideas, thoughts, and information through virtual networks and communities [5]. The present electronic era makes it more popular and comfortable to access and communicate over it. These communications include blogging, reviews, social gaming, sharing of photos, video, audio, text, and business networks. It can connect and share information worldwide at the same time with many people. In recent years, social media users are tremendously increased. Currently, social media is also being utilized by governments to engage with constituents and voters. For businesses, social media is an essential tool for companies to find and hold with customers, increase sales through promotion, advertisements, and offering customer service or support. Social media has the capability to gather information from every user which helps to focus on research in

Published by Springer Nature Switzerland AG 2021
D. Dennehy et al. (Eds.): I3E 2021, LNCS 12896, pp. 670–680, 2021.
https://doi.org/10.1007/978-3-030-85447-8_55

many areas. It has numerous advantages but some of the severe challenges are also associated with it. Every user has the freedom to express their views without revealing their real identity, but some users are misusing this freedom to write the offensive language. Gomez et al. [3] defined hate-speech as an "aggressive, intentional act carried out by a group or individual using electronic forms of contact, repeatedly or overtime against a victim that cannot easily defend him or herself". Social media users are targeted by Hate-Speech and Offensive language such as abusive, hurtful, derogatory, or unlawful user-generated content by some mischievous users [10]. As a result of the misuse of online interactions, many people have fallen into depression, anxiety, other mental illness, and they feel poor in their position to react to Internet violence or harassment [10, 12, 17]. In severe cases, if the victim cannot reply and motivate himself/herself, then they commit suicide too. All these incidents encourage researchers to propose a practical solution to eliminate the negative impact of social media. Identifying hate speech and removing it from social media or preventing the writing of these posts is an important task.

Nowadays, social media users are frequently using text, images, videos, audios, and a combination of these media for their social interaction. A number of works have been reported by researchers that use textual contents of the social media posts to identify hate contents [6, 7, 10, 11, 17]. The role of imagery contents with the textual contents is important because sometimes by seeing a single modality of the post it is very difficult to recognize hate contents. For example, Fig. 3 not related to hate speech if someone only sees the imagery content whereas the combination of imagery and textual content make it hate content. Therefore, when designing an automated hate speech detection system it is important to take care of other modalities of the posts also to make online social media platform vigorous and secure [6, 7, 12]. A few works [2, 3, 12, 14] have been reported where researchers tried to use textual and imagery contents of the social media posts to train a system for binary classification (Hate or, Not-hate). In line with their works, in this work, a multi-modal system is developed to classify social media posts into six different classes such as *Racist, Sexist, Homophobic, Religion-based hate, Other hate and No hate*. To process textual contents, a convolutional neural network-based model is developed whereas to process imagery contents, a fine-tuned VGG-16 network is used. After getting the textual and imagery features from the said convolutional network and VGG-16 networks, the features are concatenated and pass through a softmax layer to classify posts into different classes. To validate the proposed system, a benchmark dataset [3] is used. The overall contributions of this paper are as follows:

- To extract features from the convolutional neural network and pre-trained VGG-16 network from textual and imagery contents, respectively.
- To propose a deep multi-modal neural network-based model for the classification of social media posts into the six different hate classes.

The rest of the paper is structured as follows: Sect. 2 presents related works for the detection of Hate Speech while Sect. 3 presents our methodology for identification of Hate Speech. Section 4 lists the results of the proposed model. Finally, Sect. 5, concludes the paper and has discussed the future directions for this work.

2 Related Work

Hate speech is the most prominent problem on social media, and an ample amount of research is going in this field. Identification and prevention of hate speech on social media are essential to avoid harm and injury in society. Salawu et al. [16] broadly classify the existing hate-speech detection methods into four classes, specifically supervised learning, rule-based, lexicon-based, and mixed-initiative methods. Supervised learning-based methods generally using Naive Bayes and Support Vector Machine (SVM) classifier to build predictive models for hate-speech detection. Lexicon-based processes are using word lists and find the existence of words inside the lists to identify hate speech. The rule-based method compares the text to pre-determine rules to recognize offensive and mixed-initiatives strategies to amalgamate human-based reasoning with one or more of the methods mentioned above. Kumari et al. [10, 11] worked on multi-lingual (Hindi, English and Bangla) code-mixed text. Also focus on finding the aggression level of the comment posted on social media. Each comment is marked as Non-aggressive, Covertly aggressive, or Overtly aggressive. They proposed two deep learning systems: Long Short Term Memory (LSTM) and Convolutional Neural Network (CNN), with two separate inputs in text representations, One-hot, and FastText embedding. It was found that for Hindi and Bangla datasets, LSTM is performing better with FastText embedding, and CNN is performing better for English. Chan et al. [1] identified hate-speech based on the social cognitive theory, which focuses on the known and needs to know, and also the reciprocal relationships between perpetrators, victims, and bystanders.

Another group of researchers [13–15, 19] proposed multi-modal systems for the identification of hate speech from social media platform. Wang et al. [19] propose a modal having multi-model encoder-decoder using bi-directional LSTM on two datasets from one of the famous social networking site Instagram (video and photo sharing) and Vine (Small video sharing) platform. Several textual features involve word-level TF-IDF vectors, character-level TF-IDF vectors, and intellectual characters from Linguistic Inquiry Word Count (LIWC). They have also used several deep learning models as the standard, including LSTM, Text-CNN, and an accuracy of 0.864 and F_1-score of 0.86 on Instagram and an accuracy of 0.838 and F1-score of 0.841 on the Vain dataset. Cheng et al. [2] proposed XBully, one of the hate-speech detection frameworks, which first redevelop multi-modal social networking website data as a heterogeneous network and then focus on learning node embedding representations upon it. Extensive experimental evaluations on real-world multi-modal social networking website datasets showed that the XBully architecture performs better than the existing hate-speech detection models. Yang et al. [20] present several fusion methods to integrate text and image signals. They adopt the baseline convolutional text differentiator and the image characteristics of photos. Also described multiple approaches to fuse texts and pictures, involving elementary concatenation, gated aggregated, bi-linear modification, and noticed with various alternations. Pre-train a deep, Cheng et al. [2] proposed XBully, one of the hate-speech detection frameworks, which first redevelop multi-modal social media data as a heterogeneous network and then focus on learning node embedding representations upon it. Extensive experimental evaluations on real-world multi-modal social media datasets showed that the XBully framework performs better than the existing hate-speech detection models. Finally, using attention fusion with deep cloning performs 84.8, an improvement over basic concatenation is statistically significant at the 99% confidence level.

Kumari et al. [14] has tried to find the bullying comment over social media posts containing text as well as image. They represent the text and image together and form a module that harmoniously learns the image and text, eliminates the need for independent learning. Single-layer Convolution Neural Network (CNN) is performing better with the 2-layered convolutional neural network. They used 3 channels of the word and three channels of the colour photo to present the input and achieved a recall value of 74% for the abusive comment classification. Paul et al. [15] designed a deep learning-based multi-modal architecture that helps in the early detection of hate speech. They predict a posted comment is hate or not as early as possible. The multi-modal features fusion-based experimental analysis achieved a 0.75 F-measure using the Residual BiLSTM-RCNN model, reflecting the efficiency of the proposed framework. Kumari et al. [13] proposed a model based on a Binary Particle Swarm Optimization (BPSO) and Convolutional Neural Network (CNN) to categorize the social networking website posts having a photo with cognate's text-message into 3 classes (non-aggressive, medium-aggressive, and high-aggressive). The dataset that they are using having symbolic photos and text messages to validate the proposed model. VGG-16 model has been used to find out the image characteristic and a three-layered CNN to find out the text characteristic. The combined characteristic set is attained by adding the characteristics of image and text and enhanced using the BPSO algorithm to gain the more appropriate factor and achieve a weighted F_1-Score of 0.74. Most of the developed models are classifying the post in binary class.

In most of the earlier works, researchers proposed the model using textual contents of social media for the identification of hate speech. A few potential works such as [13–15, 19] that uses multi-modal content of the social media platform to identify hate speech, but most of them are a binary classification task only, i.e., they used either hate or not-hate class to develop their system. In the current work, the proposed deep multi-modal system is trained for the six different hate classes such as *Racist, Sexist, Homophobic, Religion-based hate, Other hate and No hate* to see the efficiency of the proposed system in the granular level of hate speech classification.

3 Methodology

This section describes the details about the dataset and proposed methodology. The framework of the proposed multi-modal system is shown in Fig. 1. The design incorporates two parallel deep neural network structures: (i) Convolutional Neural Network (CNN) for processing tweet-text, and (ii) VGG-16 for images. The text is fed through CNN layers to extract text features whereas, for the image, Convolutional Neural Network (CNN)-based pre-trained VGG-16 model is used to extract imagery features. For the pre-trained VGG-16 network, the weights of the last two layers were trained and all other weights are marked as non-trainable to transfer the pre-trained weights for the current task. Then the extracted imagery features are mapped to the dense layer containing 128-neurons to get the 128-dimensional imagery feature vector (see Fig. 1). Similarly, the text features extracted through the convolution and max-pooling operation are mapped to the dense layer containing 128-neurons to get a 128-dimensional textual feature (see Fig. 1). Then the extracted textual and imagery contents are concatenated and input into a softmax layer to classify tweets into six different classes *Racist, Sexist, Homophobic, Religion-based hate, Other hate and No hate.*

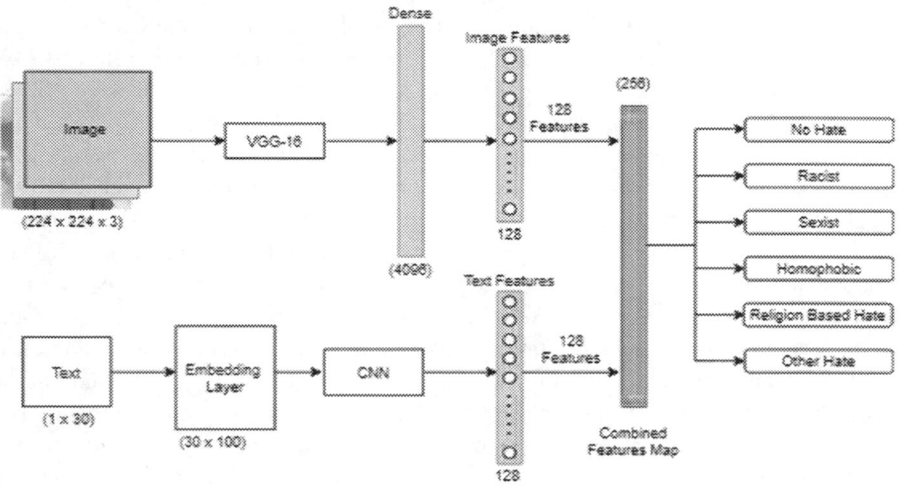

Fig. 1. Flow diagram of the proposed model for hate speech classification.

3.1 Data Description and Pre-processing

The dataset[3] published by Gomez et al. [3] is used to validate the proposed system. The dataset contains tweets from six different categories (i) Not-hate, (ii) Racist, (iii) Sexist, (iv) Homophobic, (v) Religion-based-hate, and (vi) Other-hate. Figures 2, 3, 4, 5, 6, and 7, represents the data samples for each of the classes, *Not-hate, Racist, Sexist, Homophobic, Religion-based-hate and Other-hate* respectively. The data samples for each of the classes can be seen in Table 1. For the pre-processing of images, it is resized to $(224 \times 224 \times 3)$, where (224×224) is the height and width of the image, and 3 is the RGB component. The pixel value of images was normalized between 0 to 1 by dividing all pixel values by 255. After pre-processing, images are directly inputted to the pre-train model to extract the relevant feature from them. Each tweet text is represented in 30 words; for the tweets having less than 30 words, we used padding and for more than 30 words, we curtailed out the words to make it into an equal length of 30.

Fig. 2. Nohate: "When a android nigga wanna talk about phone battery:"

Fig. 3. Racist: "@washington post @ Sabriyyah 54 More stupid racist white trash"

Fig. 4. Sexist: "@Doggin-Trump No sympathy for the twat waffle"

Fig. 5. Homophobic: "@eeeeeeeeeeekkk Me: Mental Illness: shut up faggot"

Fig. 6. Religion-based-hate: "The only POS is the Muzzie who will be arrested for treason"

Fig. 7. Other-hate: "My horses are retarded"

Table 1. The description of the data samples for each of the classes.

Tweets categories	Numbers of tweet per class
No attacks to any community	112845
Racist	11925
Sexist	3495
Homophobic	3870
Religion-based	163
Attacks to other communities	5811
Not in any categories	11714

3.2 Image Classification (VGG16)

VGG-16 is based on convolutional neural network architecture and it is trained on ImageNet dataset to classify it into 1,000 classes. It has 16 layers out of this 13 are convolutional layers and 3 layers are fully connected. It takes input as the image of size (224 224 3) and filter (3×3) for performing convolution operation. The detailed information regarding the parameters and layers of the VGG-16 can be seen in Simonyanet et al. [18]. VGG-16 has attractive architecture; it is the best option for pull-out the characteristics from the images [9]. Due to the diverse popularity of VGG-16 networks in extracting features from the images, this work also utilizes the VGG-16 network for extracting imagery features. The VGG-16 network can be modified at the last layer according to the tasks. In this work, weights between the first 14 layers are frozen and the weights of the last two layers are trained.

3.3 Text classification (CNN)

The convolution neural network (CNN) has the ability to identify the pattern and provide meaningful sense from the textual content of tweets. In the convolution layer, the dot product is performed between the weights and input. The size of the resultant is depended upon the filter size and number of filters used. ReLu is used as the activation function, whereas the Max-pooling layer is used to find the most important feature from a pooling window [18]. The detailed description of the CNN network can be seen in [4, 8]. To pull out the textual features from text messages, we first embedded each word into an embedding vector using pre-train Glove embedding vectors. We set 2-g, 3-g, and 4-g filters over the 1st, 2nd, and 3rd convolution layers. Then we applied max-pooling of size 5 over it to pull out the best features from it. These features are then concatenated with the image features (Fig. 1). This concatenated feature vector is then passed through the softmax layer to classify it into six different hate classes. The extensive experiments were performed to choose the best set of parameters. A learning rate of 0.001, epochs equals 16 and the batch size of 32 performed best. Since the model is a categorical classifier, we use Categorical cross-entropy as our loss function.

Table 2. Hyper-parameter settings for the proposed multi-modal system.

Model	Hyper-Parameters	Value
VGG-16	Image size	$224 \times 224 \times 3$
	Optimizer	Adam
	Loss Function	Categorical crossentropy
	Activation function	ReLU, Softmax
	Epochs	16
	Batch size	32
	Learning rate	0.001
CNN	Maximum sequence length	30
	Maximum No. of words	4000
	No. of filter	1024
	Filter size	2,3,4
	Optimizer	Adam
	Dropout-rate	0.2
	Pooling size	5
	Loss Function	Categorical crossentropy

(continued)

Table 2. (*continued*)

Model	Hyper-Parameters	Value
	Activation function	ReLU
	Epochs	16
	Batch size	32
	Learning rate	0.001

Adam is used for optimization and the Softmax activation function is used in the output layer. The detailed hyper-parameters used in the experimental analysis have been shown in Table 2.

4 Result

This section describes the result obtained from the proposed model for the Dataset MMHS150K. The proposed multi-modal system classifies the posted hate Twitter contents into six different hate classes. The provided dataset[4] have 138109 tweets out of which 10,000 tweets are for testing the model and 5,000 tweets are for validating the model and the remaining data samples are for training the model.

The proposed model categories the Twitter contents into six different hate classes and for each class, we get the precision, recall, and F1-score (see Table 3). The proposed system achieved a precision of 0.84, 0.76,0.67, 0.72, 0.60, and 0.76 for No-hate, Racist, Sexist, Homophobic, Religion, and Other-hate classes, respectively. The recall values achieved by the proposed systems are 0.97, 0.29, 0.26, 0.47, 0.23, and 0.42 for No-hate, Racist, Sexist, Homophobic, Religion and Other-hate classes, respectively. Similarly, the proposed system achieved an F_1-scores of 0.90, 0.41, 0.37, 0.57, 0.33 and 0.54 for No-hate, Racist, Sexist, Homophobic, Religion and Other-hate classes respectively. The proposed system achieved the weighted precision, weighted recall, and weighted F1-scores of 0.82, 0.83, and 0.81, respectively. The confusion matrix and ROC curve for the proposed system can be seen in Figs. 8 and 9 respectively.

Table 3. Result of proposed deep multi-modal system to classify Twitter contents into six different hate classes

Class	Precision	Recall	F1-score
Not-hate	0.84	0.97	0.90
Racist	0.76	0.29	0.41
Sexist	0.67	0.26	0.37
Homophobe	0.72	0.47	0.57
Religion	0.60	0.23	0.33
Other-hate	0.76	0.42	0.54
Weighted average	0.82	0.83	0.81

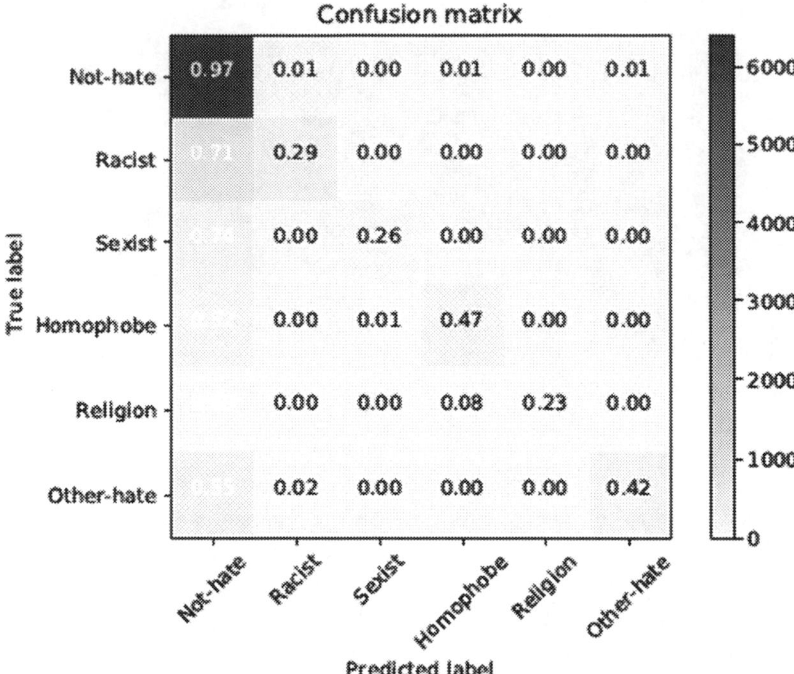

Fig. 8. Confusion matrix of the proposed deep multi-model neural network for hate speech classification

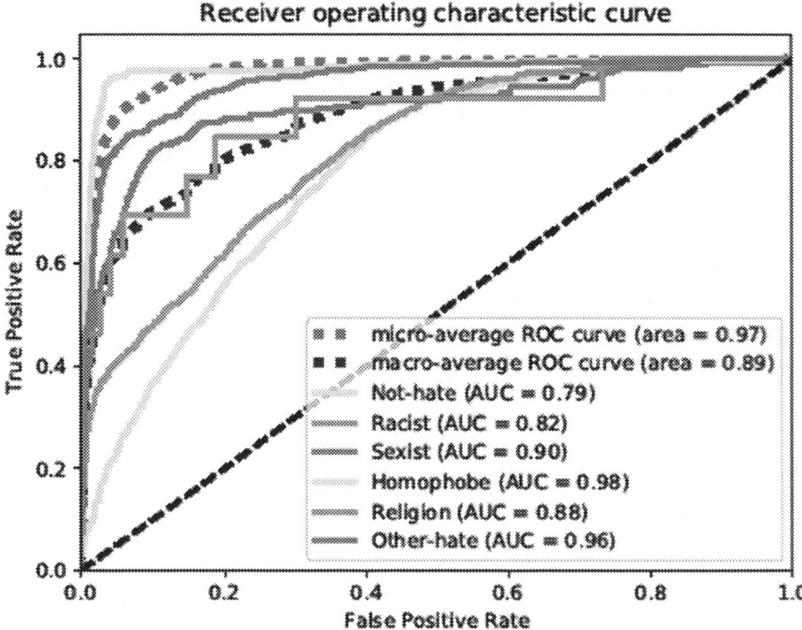

Fig. 9. Receiver operating characteristic curve of the proposed deep multi-modal neural network for hate speech classification

5 Conclusion

Hate speech on social media can cause people to suffer from depression, anxiety, and other mental illnesses. Most of the earlier works are reported for the identification of hate speech uses textual contents only. A few works are reported where researchers tried to train their system into the multi-modal setting, but they tested their system for the binary class classification only (i.e., whether hate or not hate). In this work, we have proposed a deep multi-modal system to classify Twitter hate contents into Racist, Sexist, Homophobic, Religion-based hate, Other hate and No hate classes. The textual content of the tweets was processed using a convolutional neural network and imagery content was processed using fine-tuned VGG-16 model. The proposed deep multi-modal neural network achieved promising performance with the weighted precision of 0.82, weighted recall of 0.83, and weighted F1-score of 0.81. The benchmark dataset used in this study suffers from the data imbalance problem. Therefore, in the future data augmentation, under-sampling, and over-sampling techniques can be applied to get better performance throughout all of the hate classes. The performance of the model is only tested with convolutional neural network and pre-trained VGG-16 network, therefore, in the future other deep learning models such as BERT for textual contents whereas ResNet50, VGG-19, Xception networks for imagery contents can be tested for better performance.

References

1. Chan, T.K., Cheung, C.M., Lee, Z.W.: Cyberbullying on social networking sites: a literature review and future research directions. Inf. Manag. **58**, 103411 (2020)
2. Cheng, L., Li, J., Silva, Y.N., Hall, D.L., Liu, H.: Xbully: cyberbullying detection within a multi-modal context. In: Proceedings of the Twelfth ACM International Conference on Web Search and Data Mining, pp. 339–347 (2019)
3. Gomez, R., Gibert, J., Gomez, L., Karatzas, D.: Exploring hate speech detection in multimodal publications. In: Proceedings of the IEEE/CVF Winter Conference on Applications of Computer Vision, pp. 1470–1478 (2020)
4. Kim, Y.: Convolutional neural networks for sentence classification. In: Proceedings of the 2014 Conference on Empirical Methods in Natural Language Processing (EMNLP), pp. 1746–1751. ACL (2014). https://doi.org/10.3115/v1/D14-1181
5. Kumar, A., Rathore, N.C.: Relationship strength based access control in online social networks. In: Satapathy, S Chandra, Das, S. (eds.) Proceedings of First International Conference on Information and Communication Technology for Intelligent Systems: Volume 2. SIST, vol. 51, pp. 197–206. Springer, Cham (2016). https://doi.org/10.1007/978-3-319-30927-9_20
6. Kumar, A., Saumya, S., Singh, J.P.: NITP-AI-NLP@ HASOC-FIRE2020: fine tuned BERT for the hate speech and offensive content identification from social media. FIRE (Working Notes), CEUR (2020)
7. Kumar, A., Saumya, S., Singh, J.P.: Nitp-ainlp@ hasoc-dravidian-codemix- fire2020: A machine learning approach to identify offensive languages from dravidian code-mixed text. FIRE (Working Notes), CEUR (2020)
8. Kumar, A., Singh, J.P.: Location reference identification from tweets during emergencies: a deep learning approach. Int. J. Disaster Risk Reduct. **33**, 365–375 (2019)
9. Kumar, A., Singh, J.P., Dwivedi, Y.K., Rana, N.P.: A deep multi-modal neural network for informative twitter content classification during emergencies. Ann. Oper. Res., 1–32 (2020)

10. Kumari, K., Singh, J.P.: AI ML NIT Patna at HASOC 2019: deep learning approach for identification of abusive content. In: FIRE (Working Notes). vol. 2517, pp. 328–335 (2019)
11. Kumari, K., Singh, J.P.: AI ML NIT Patna@ TRAC-2: deep learning approach for multilingual aggression identification. In: Proceedings of the Second Workshop on Trolling, Aggression and Cyberbullying, pp. 113–119 (2020)
12. Kumari, K., Singh, J.P.: Identification of cyberbullying on multi-modal social media posts using genetic algorithm. Trans. Emerg. Telecommun. Technol. **32**(2), e3907 (2021)
13. Kumari, K., Singh, J.P., Dwivedi, Y.K., Rana, N.P.: Multi-modal aggression identification using convolutional neural network and binary particle swarm optimization. Futur. Gener. Comput. Syst. **118**, 187–197 (2021)
14. Kumari, K., Singh, J.P., Dwivedi, Y.K., Rana, N.P.: Towards cyberbullying-free social media in smart cities: a unified multi-modal approach. Soft. Comput. **24**(15), 11059–11070 (2020). https://doi.org/10.1007/s00500-019-04550-x
15. Paul, S., Saha, S., Hasanuzzaman, M.: Identification of cyberbullying: a deep learning based multimodal approach. Multimedia Tools Appl., 1–20 (2020)
16. Salawu, S., He, Y., Lumsden, J.: Approaches to automated detection of cyberbullying: a survey. IEEE Trans. Affect. Comput. **11**(1), 3–24 (2017)
17. Schmidt, A., Wiegand, M.: A survey on hate speech detection using natural language processing. In: Proceedings of the Fifth International Workshop on Natural Language Processing for Social Media, pp. 1–10 (2017)
18. Simonyan, K., Zisserman, A.: Very deep convolutional networks for large-scale image recognition. arXiv preprint arXiv:1409.1556 (2014)
19. Wang, K., Xiong, Q., Wu, C., Gao, M., Yu, Y.: Multi-modal cyberbullying detection on social networks. In: 2020 International Joint Conference on Neural Networks (IJCNN), pp. 1–8. IEEE (2020)
20. Yang, F., et al.: Exploring deep multimodal fusion of text and photo for hate speech classification. In: Proceedings of the Third Workshop on Abusive Language Online, pp. 11–18 (2019)

Influencer is the New Recommender: Insights for Enhancing Social Recommender Systems

Ransome Epie Bawack[1] and Emilie Bonhoure[2](✉)

[1] ICN Business School, 54003 Nancy, France
[2] Kedge Business School, 33405 Talence, France
e.bonhoure@tbs-education.org

Abstract. Firms are increasingly turning to influencers to persuade consumers to purchase their brands. They do so because influencers have built a large social community around them on social media that they can persuade to adopt a recommended behaviour or brand. This objective is very similar to that of social recommender systems. Thus, this study aims to analyse influencer research and propose how to enhance the persuasion power of social recommender systems. A meta-analysis was conducted on influencer research obtained from the Web of Science core collection to this end. The meta-analysis revealed that influencers have a strong persuasion effect on consumer purchase intentions. Seven essential determinants of purchase intention were identified: trustworthiness, brand attitude, influencer's credibility, parasocial interactions, expertise, and attractiveness. This paper discusses how social recommender systems in e-commerce platforms could be improved based on these findings. It emphasises credibility and identification as two broad factors that should be explored in future research on social recommender systems.

Keywords: Influencer · Social recommender system · Purchase intention

1 Introduction

Digital platforms, especially social media, have become an indispensable source of information for consumers. Social media influencers (termed influencers hereafter) are people with sizeable followers on social media platforms who regard them as trusted tastemakers in one or several niches [1]. Thus, influencers are increasingly used to curate content on social media platforms in various application domains, including e-commerce. They have become an exciting channel for product/service recommendation by several brands [2].

Understanding influencers' role is of immense importance to research and practice, given their ubiquitous social media presence and increasing role in consumer decision-making. Influencers can recommend brands to their communities in exchange for compensation. Consumers adhere to influencers' recommendations because they perceive influencers as trusted opinion leaders with expertise on a particular topic [3,

Published by Springer Nature Switzerland AG 2021
D. Dennehy et al. (Eds.): I3E 2021, LNCS 12896, pp. 681–691, 2021.
https://doi.org/10.1007/978-3-030-85447-8_56

4]. Consequently, firms pay influencers to recommend their brands because they believe influencers can shape their followers' attitudes and actions in their favour [5].

A key component of influencers' success is their ability to drive consumers to consume a product or brand [6]. Through the massive number of followers they have, they can recommend a brand to a wide variety of people within their sphere of influence. This capability is very similar to that of recommender systems used in e-commerce and social media platforms. However, influencers do not collect information on their followers' preferences and do not know most of them personally [7]. Thus, unlike recommender systems, influencers cannot provide intelligent, personalised recommendations to individual followers. Therefore, influencers cannot recommend brands accurately but rather inform users about a brand's existence. Sometimes, influencers simply post pictures of themselves with the advertised brand without providing valuable information to help consumers decide whether to purchase the brand. Therefore, firms can hardly tell how many people in an influencer's community were genuinely interested in the brand. This challenge has led to several studies on digital influencers' role as recommenders [8, 9].

Despite this drawback, it seems like brands are increasingly abandoning traditional advertising techniques to adopt influencer-based advertising [10]. Does this imply that recommendations from recommender systems are less effective? This paper aims to use recent literature on influencers to inform research on social recommender systems. Social recommender systems are software agents designed to provide personalised recommendations to consumers based on social data. It aims to provide new theoretical perspectives that can help explain and improve social recommender systems' effect on consumer behaviours investigated in influencer literature. No research has addressed this topic before despite the growing importance of these distinct recommendation channels.

Furthermore, this research brings together two disparate research streams to help shed light on consumer behaviour towards recommendations made through social media platforms. These insights could help information systems (IS) practitioners improve their social recommender systems' quality. They could also help marketing managers decide the best way to recommend brands to consumers.

2 Background

The extant literature on influencers highlights that influencer recommendations are increasingly being accepted by consumers [9]. Consumers are more inclined to purchase products recommended by trusted influencers [11]. Firms are advised to collaborate with influencers who post visually appealing content and demonstrate expertise to maximise the adoption of new products [12]. Consumers are more likely to take influencer recommendations based on sound advice (expertise) [11]. This advice could help improve the quality of purchasing decisions made by consumers.

Designing systems to provide similar recommendations through social media platforms to consumers is a well-known IS practice. Social recommender systems refer to using social information to improve recommender systems' performance [13]. There is significant literature on the effect of social recommender systems on consumer behaviour. Friendship and group information, for example, can help recommender systems make accurate, evidence-based, and persuasive recommendations to consumers [13]. Modelling user communication patterns on social media has helped understand user influence across heterogeneous social networks and improve recommendations [14].

Analysing trust relationships within social networks has helped enhance recommendations from recommender systems [15]. Incorporating social context, activities, and preferences into recommender systems has led to more personalised recommendations [16]. Combining context-aware, social network, and sentiment-based information on consumers has also led to highly accurate and personalised recommendations [17, 18]. Such recommender systems can be further improved using artificial intelligence (AI), data science, and analytics [19, 20].

This research investigates how influencer literature can inform social recommender systems literature. Specifically, it discusses how the effect of social recommender systems can be improved based on evidence from influencers.

3 Methodology

A meta-analysis is a type of aggregative literature review that uses quantitative methods to test specific research hypotheses based on prior empirical findings [21]. This technique is instrumental in summarising evidence in research accurately and reliably [21]. A meta-analysis was conducted to understand influencers' effects on consumer behaviour. The approach used in this paper was proposed by Lipsey and Wilson [22]. It involves three main steps: (i) literature search, (ii) article coding, and (iii) article analysis. The literature search step involved searching the Web of Science core collection of databases using the term "influencer". This collection of databases was used because it is frequently cited as a key source of literature review data [21]. There was no restriction placed on the publication outlet. The search covered all publications until December 2020. A total of 799 articles were identified through the search. For a document to be included in the meta-analysis, it had to empirically investigate one variable's effect (independent variable) on another (dependent variable). Second, the dependent variable had to characterise purchase intention. Third, it had to report data sufficient to compute the independent variable's effect size reliably by providing data on correlation coefficient, significance level, and construct reliability.

Articles were coded to identify categories of determinants of all dependent variables investigated. Only independent-dependent variable relationships tested by more than one study were considered for this meta-analysis. The authors categorised independent variables based on existing theories. After that, the authors coded the variables independently, then came to a consensual code. A separate meta-analysis was conducted for each independent variable-variable pair for article analysis. Information on the correlation coefficients was collected from each study to calculate effect sizes. The magnitude of effect sizes was interpreted as small (<.30), medium (between .30 and .50), large (between .50 and .67), and very large (>.67). The validity and reliability of the main meta-analysis results were tested using a z-test.

Table 1 presents the paper collection results. Based on our inclusion criteria, 11 articles were retained for this meta-analysis.

Table 1. Paper collection results.

	Journal	Conference	Total
Papers identified in searches	642	157	799
Papers excluded based on exclusion criteria	602	156	758
Retained papers	**40**	**1**	**41**
2011	1	0	1
2017	1	0	1
2018	2	1	3
2019	11	0	11
2020	22	0	22
2021*	3	0	3
Papers used for the meta-analysis	**11**	**0**	**11**
2018	1	0	1
2019	1	0	1
2020	7	0	7
2021*	2	0	2

*These papers appeared as 2021 in the Web of Science database but were published in 2020

4 Results

Purchase intention was identified as the main effect of influencers on consumer behaviour. Table 2 presents the meta-analytic results of the determinants of purchase intention. The table reports the weighted mean effect sizes of each independent variable, their magnitudes, the number of studies that led to the results, and the total sample size used for the analysis. It also reports the z-test of each independent variable. The z-test results indicate each independent variable's significance.

Table 2. Meta-analysis results (dependent variable: purchase intention).

	Overall effect size (stand.)	Effect size magnitude	No. of studies	Total sample size	z-test ***	95% CI
Trustworthiness	0.560	Large	3	1 041	20.317	0.516; 0.6
Similarity	0.465	Medium	2	1 154	17.069	0.419; 0.509
Attitude towards the brand	0.443	Medium	2	917	14.355	0.389; 0.493
Influencer's Credibility	0.404	Medium	2	1 483	16.451	0.36; 0.445
Parasocial interactions	0.394	Medium	3	1 523	16.227	0.351; 0.436

(continued)

Table 2. (*continued*)

	Overall effect size (stand.)	Effect size magnitude	No. of studies	Total sample size	z-test ***	95% CI
Source expertise	0.294	Small	2	883	8.956	0.232; 0.353
Attractiveness	0.221	Small	4	1 491	8.652	0.172; 0.269

Table 3 presents the definition of each variable.

Table 3. Variable definition.

Variables	Definition
Dependent variables	
Purchase intention	A consumer's conscious plan and effort to purchase a product, a service, or a brand [6]
Independent variables	
Attitude towards the brand	Customers' evaluations of a brand [1]
Attractiveness	The degree to which an influencer is perceived as "classy, sexy and beautiful" [6]
Influencer's credibility	Perceptions of an influencer's physical appeal and expertise regarding the product [5]
Parasocial interactions	Relationship between an influencer and followers, implying an "illusion of intimacy" as in real personal relationships [23]
Similarity	The extent to which one person perceives sharing or having a shared experience, lifestyle, and other features with another person [24]
Source expertise	The degree of knowledge, skills, and experience that a source is perceived to feature [6, 24]
Trustworthiness	Perceptions of honesty, integrity, and believability of an endorser [24]

Figure 1 presents the meta-analysis-based research model discussed in the next section. The "***" indicate significance at the 1% level.

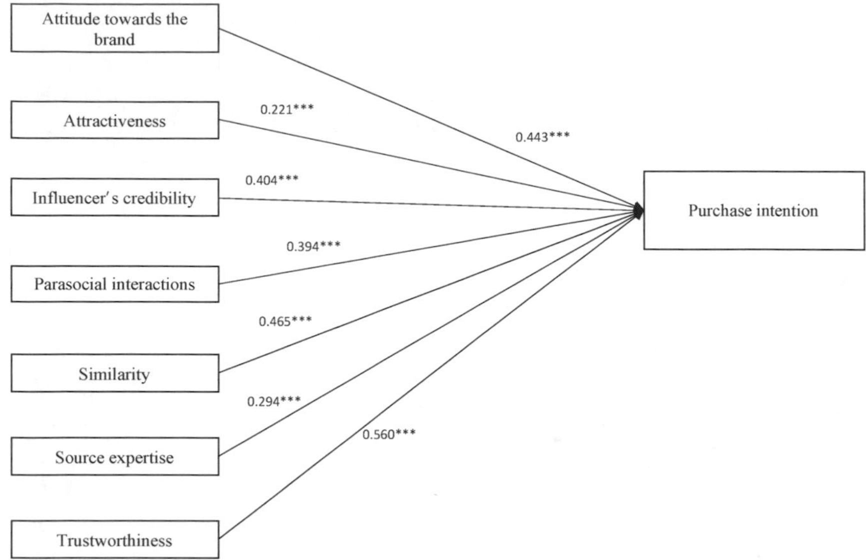

Fig. 1. A meta-model for influencer effect on consumer purchase intention.

5 Discussion

This paper aims to inform research on social recommender systems based on influencer literature. Given the similarity between these two research streams, IS researchers could learn from influencer research how to improve recommender systems' quality and effectiveness in e-commerce platforms. Based on the findings outlined in the results section, several valuable insights were uncovered regarding social recommender systems' effect on consumer purchase intention.

Trustworthiness has a large effect on consumer purchase intention. It implies that influencers perceived as trustworthy and honest are more likely to persuade consumers to purchase a specific brand. Consumers trust influencers because they assume that the influencers have tried the brand and so their opinion can be trusted. Four factors have medium effects on purchase intention: similarity, attitude towards the brand, influencer's credibility, and parasocial interactions, respectively, in order of magnitude. The effectiveness of influencers' recommendations is strongly tied to how much consumers identify with the influencer (shared experience, lifestyle, or other common characteristics, etc.). Consumers are more likely to purchase a product endorsed by an influencer they identify with [24]. Consumers' attitude towards a brand is measured by how good, pleasant, and favourable consumers perceive a brand. Influencers have the power to change consumer attitudes towards brands through their attractiveness. Although attractiveness has a small direct effect on purchase intention, it contributes significantly to consumer attitudes towards the brand recommended by influencers [1]. Attractiveness is measured through the influencer's physical looks, style, knowledge, and reputation [1]. Therefore, consumers are more likely to perceive brands as attractive and purchase items from the brand if the recommender is found attractive [5]. Influencer credibility is a combination of an influencer's physical appeal and expertise regarding a brand [5]. Physical appeal is very similar to attractiveness, explaining why influencer credibility strongly affects consumer attitude towards the brand and related recommendations [5]. Parasocial interaction also has a medium effect on consumer purchase intentions. Consumers are more likely to purchase products recommended by influencers with whom they have a parasocial relationship [23]. This relationship is strongly related to the feeling of identification and connection the consumer has for the influencer. This relationship is manifested through consumers' desire to look, behave, or belong to the same 'world' as an influencer. Such consumers are usually very active and reactive to the content proposed by influencers they follow [23]. Source expertise has minor effects on consumer purchase intentions. It may be because source expertise is factored into influencer credibility [5, 24]. Therefore, measured alone, its effect is relatively smaller than if captured as part of the influencer's credibility.

5.1 Implications for Research on Social Recommender Systems

These influencer literature findings have several implications for research on social recommender systems and their ability to influence consumer purchase intentions. One main implication is that just like influencer credibility, the recommender system platform's credibility could be essential for the effectiveness of the recommendation. Influencer credibility is based on two main components: the influencer's perceived trustworthiness and expertise [23, 24]. Likewise, recommender systems should be perceived as trustworthy and systems with some degree of expertise. The recommendations made should be trustworthy and perceived as coming from a knowledgeable and skilful person. Also, credibility can be perceived through physical appeal [5]. Thus, a platform that provides customers' recommendations more appealingly could be perceived as more credible. Therefore, a social recommender system that demonstrates credibility through perceived trustworthiness, expertise, and appeal could improve consumer purchase intentions. Credibility effects can be explained by the attribution theory [25]. This theory describes how people examine information to arrive at a causal judgment. It suggests that people see cause and effect relationships even where there is none to make sense of the social world. This theory has been used to show that people tend to trust messages more from a known than from an unknown source. As the source's credibility increases, so does the persuasiveness of its message [5].

Furthermore, the social learning theory argues that people acquire new behaviour through observation and imitation [26]. This theory has helped show that the way influencers appreciate brands they advertise influences their followers' attitudes towards the brand and thus transfer their credibility to the brand [5]. Therefore, it is essential to improve social recommender systems' credibility to increase their persuasiveness and effect on consumer purchase intentions. Therefore, future research should investigate how to enhance social recommender systems' credibility [27, 28].

Another key implication of this research is that identification could play a key role in the relationship between consumers and social recommender systems. Influencer literature highlights similarity and parasocial relationship as key components of identification [23, 24]. Thus, social recommender systems that consumers identify themselves with are more likely to influencer their purchase intentions. Therefore, recommendations from social recommender systems should reflect the consumers' lifestyle and other personal characteristics. Consumers should perceive that the recommender system understands their social needs. This perception would enable consumers to build an "intimate" relationship with the system, increasing the systems' ability to influence their purchase intentions. Like the product-endorser fit [1, 24], recommender systems should fit with the type of recommendation made. The recommender system should be found attractive with respect to the recommendation made. That is, the recommender system should demonstrate the looks, style, knowledge, and reputation necessary to make a specific type of recommendation. Therefore, researchers should investigate how to enhance consumer identification with recommendations from social recommender systems.

5.2 Implications for Practice

This research has some implications for practice, especially in the e-commerce context wherein recommender systems have become an integral part of e-commerce platforms. Recommender systems in such platforms should be perceived as credible to influence consumer purchase intentions. Designing such recommender systems involves improving how consumers perceive the recommendations' trustworthiness. It could be done by designing more trust-enhanced recommender systems [29, 30]. The recommender system should also be perceived as appealing. It can be done by improving the quality of display on the e-commerce website [31, 32] or how the information is communicated by voice.

Furthermore, the recommendation should be perceived as one based on expertise. Therefore, the recommender system should provide some expert-level information to support recommendations whenever possible. Regarding identification, social recommender systems should be designed to make consumers identify with the recommendations, that is, personalised. However, system designers should go beyond personalised recommendations to enhance the quality of interactions consumers have with the recommender systems. The more consumers have parasocial interactions with the platform, the more likely they would accept recommendations made, especially regarding purchase.

5.3 Limitations

The first limitation of this research is that some research papers may have been left out of this study because "influencer" is the only keyword used to conduct the literature search. The reason for this choice is that it is the only term that focuses on the concept we sought to investigate. Unlike "influencer", other terms like "micro-celebrities" or "online stars" do not necessarily characterise people whose purpose is to use social media to influence potential buyers of a product or service. Nevertheless, several studies may have used these terms interchangeably. Thus, future research should use more inclusive terms to identify any missing papers.

Second, this research used only the WoS database to identify relevant papers. While this database contains publications from all leading journals, it may not have publications from some conferences. Thus, future research should consider other databases like Scopus to expand this meta-analysis.

6 Conclusions

Today, social recommender systems are an integral part of most social media and entertainment platforms. Although it is a rich research stream, more research is needed to improve the quality and effectiveness of their recommendations. This paper uses influencer literature to incite researchers to investigate social recommender systems' credibility and make consumers identify with recommendations. The paper highlights perceived trustworthiness, expertise, and appeal as essential components of credibility. Meanwhile, it highlights similarity and parasocial interactions of key components of identification. Integrating these elements into the design and implementation of social recommender systems could lead to more effective social recommender systems, especially in influencing consumer purchase intentions. Hopefully, this paper will inspire future research on improving social recommender systems.

References

1. Torres, P., Augusto, M., Matos, M.: Antecedents and outcomes of digital influencer endorsement: an exploratory study. Psychol. Mark. **36**, 1267–1276 (2019)
2. Farivar, S., Wang, F., Yuan, Y.: Meformer vs. informer: Influencer type and follower behavioral intentions. In: 25th Americas Conference on Information Systems AMCIS 2019 (2019)
3. Jun, S., Yi, J.: What makes followers loyal? The role of influencer interactivity in building influencer brand equity. J. Prod. Brand Manag. **29**, 803–814 (2020)
4. Woodroof, P.J., Howie, K.M., Syrdal, H.A., VanMeter, R.: What's done in the dark will be brought to the light: effects of influencer transparency on product efficacy and purchase intentions. J. Prod. Brand Manage. **29**, 675–688 (2020)
5. Pick, M.: Psychological ownership in social media influencer marketing. Eur. Bus. Rev. **33**, 9–30 (2021)
6. Weismueller, J., Harrigan, P., Wang, S., Soutar, G.N.: Influencer endorsements: how advertising disclosure and source credibility affect consumer purchase intention on social media. Australas. Mark. J. **28**, 160–170 (2020)
7. Denecli, C., Denecli, S.: Role of credibility of phenomena in attitude toward advertising. In: Yengin, D., Algul, A., Ovur, A., Yeniceler, I., Bayrak, T. (ed.) Communication and Technology Congress (CTC 2019), pp. 75–85 (2019)
8. Jiménez-Castillo, D., Sánchez-Fernández, R.: The role of digital influencers in brand recommendation: examining their impact on engagement, expected value and purchase intention. Int. J. Inf. Manage **49**, 366–376 (2019). https://www.sciencedirect.com/science/article/pii/S0268401219301653
9. Breves, P.L., Liebers, N., Abt, M., Kunze, A.: The perceived fit between Instagram influencers and the endorsed brand how influencer-brand fit affects source credibility and persuasive effectiveness. J. Advert. Res. **59**, 440–454 (2019)
10. De Veirman, M., Cauberghe, V., Hudders, L.: Marketing through Instagram influencers: the impact of number of followers and product divergence on brand attitude. Int. J. Advert. **36**, 798–828 (2017)

11. Lindh, C., Lisichkova, N.: Rationality versus emotionality among online shoppers: the mediating role of experts as enhancing influencer effect on purchasing intent. J. Cust. Behav. **16**, 333–351 (2017). http://10.1362/147539217X15144729108135
12. Ki, C.W.C., Kim, Y.K.: The mechanism by which social media influencers persuade consumers: the role of consumers' desire to mimic. Psychol. Mark. **36**, 905–922 (2019)
13. Sun, J., Ying, R., Jiang, Y., He, J., Ding, Z.: Leveraging friend and group information to improve social recommender system. Electron. Commer. Res. **20**(1), 147–172 (2019). https://doi.org/10.1007/s10660-019-09390-3
14. Arbelaitz, O., Martínez-Otzeta, J.M., Muguerza, J.: User modeling in a social network for cognitively disabled people. J. Assoc. Inf. Sci. Technol. **67**, 305–317 (2016). http://10.1002/asi.23381
15. Li, W., Qi, J., Yu, Z., Li, D.: A social recommendation method based on trust propagation and singular value decomposition. J. Intell. Fuzzy Syst. **32**, 807–816 (2017). http://10.3233/JIFS-16073
16. Pouyanfar, S., Yang, Y., Chen, S.-C., Shyu, M.-L., Iyengar, S.S.: Multimedia big data analytics: a survey. ACM Comput. Surv. **51**, 10:1–34 (2018). http://10.1145/3150226
17. Colombo-Mendoza, L.O., Valencia-García, R., Rodríguez-González, A., Colomo-Palacios, R., Alor-Hernández, G.: Towards a knowledge-based probabilistic and context-aware social recommender system. J. Inf. Sci. **44**, 464–490 (2018). http://10.1177/0165551517698787
18. Yang, D., Huang, C., Wang, M.: A social recommender system by combining social network and sentiment similarity: a case study of healthcare. J. Inf. Sci. **43**, 635–648 (2017). http://10.1177/0165551516657712
19. Kaczorowska-Spychalska, D.: How chatbots influence marketing. Management **23**, 251–270 (2019). http://10.2478/manment-2019-0015
20. Guo, J., Zhang, W., Fan, W., Li, W.: Combining geographical and social influences with deep learning for personalized point-of-interest recommendation. J. Manage. Inf. Syst. **35**, 1121–1153 (2018). http://10.1080/07421222.2018.1523564
21. Templier, M., Paré, G.: A framework for guiding and evaluating literature reviews. Commun. Assoc. Inf. Syst. **37**, 112–137 (2015)
22. Lipsey, M.W., Wilson, D.B.: Practical Meta-Analysis. SAGE publications Inc., Thousand Oaks (2001)
23. Sokolova, K., Kefi, H.: Instagram and YouTube bloggers promote it, why should I buy? How credibility and parasocial interaction influence purchase intentions. J. Retail. Consum. Serv. **53** (2020)
24. Schouten, A.P., Janssen, L., Verspaget, M.: Celebrity vs. Influencer endorsements in advertising: the role of identification, credibility, and Product-Endorser fit. Int. J. Advert. **39**, 258–281 (2020)
25. Kelley, H.H.: Attribution theory in social interaction. In: Attribution: Perceiving the Causes of Behavior, pp. 1–26. University of Nebraska Press (1972)
26. Bandura, A., McClelland, D.C.: Social Learning Theory. Prentice Hall, Englewood Cliffs (1977)
27. Berkani, L., Belkacem, S., Ouafi, M., Guessoum, A.: Recommendation of users in social networks: a semantic and social based classification approach. Expert Syst. **38**, 1–35 (2021). http://10.1111/exsy.12634
28. Prasad, R., Kumari, V.V.: A categorical review of recommender systems. Int. J. Distrib. Parallel Syst. **3**, 73 (2012)
29. Yuan, W., Guan, D., Lee, Y.-K., Lee, S., Hur, S.J.: Improved trust-aware recommender system using small-worldness of trust networks. Knowl. Based Syst. **23**, 232–238 (2010)
30. Avesani, P., Massa, P., Tiella, R.: A trust-enhanced recommender system application: Moleskiing. In: Proceedings of the 2005 ACM Symposium on Applied Computing, pp. 1589–1593 (2005)

31. Huang, Z., Benyoucef, M.: Usability and credibility of e-government websites. Gov. Inf. Q. **31**, 584–595 (2014)
32. Lowry, P.B., Wilson, D.W., Haig, W.L.: A picture is worth a thousand words: Source credibility theory applied to logo and website design for heightened credibility and consumer trust. Int. J. Hum. Comput. Interact. **30**, 63–93 (2014)

Impact of COVID-19 Pandemic on E-participation of Fans in Sports Events

Vishal Mehra[1], Pooja Sarin[3], Prabhsimran Singh[1](✉), Ravinder Singh Sawhney[2], and Arpan Kumar Kar[3]

[1] Department of Computer Engineering and Technology, Guru Nanak Dev University, Amritsar, India
{vishalcet.rsh,prabhsimran.dcet}@gndu.ac.in

[2] Department of Electronics Technology, Guru Nanak Dev University, Amritsar, India
sawhney.ece@gndu.ac.in

[3] Department of Management Studies, Indian Institute of Technology, New Delhi, India
{sarin_pooja,arpankar}@dms.iitd.ac.in

Abstract. Sports watching both through offline as well as online mode has always been fancied by the sports lovers. We investigate the explicit use of social media by sports enthusiasts to show their support and solidarity for their favorite sports team or a particular sportsperson virtually i.e., via e-participation. For experimentation, we have considered the fourth Test match played between India versus Australia from 15–19 January, 2021 during Border-Gavaskar Trophy 2020–2021. During these five days period, a total of 69,965 tweets on Twitter were collected by us favoring both teams. Various statistical techniques coupled with social media analytics such as polarity and emotion analysis have been applied on the collected data to get valuable insights for our results. Our experimental results unambiguously indicate that sports enthusiast globally is using social media as important alternate media to show their support towards their favorite sports team virtually, via e-participation. The emergence and amalgamation of social media and marketing has provided newer horizons to various stakeholders i.e., both viewers and broadcasters to maximize e-participation.

Keywords: Covid-19 · E-participation · Fans · Pandemic · Social media analytics · Sports marketing

1 Introduction

The Internet has brought the world together. In the 21st century, the Internet has played a pivotal role in technological advances across various sectors such as education, business, healthcare, government, and many more. India, a developing nation, for example, has taken a massive leap in developing infrastructure for the Internet and paving its way to urban, semi-urban, and rural regions and has become one of the largest consumers of digital content across the globe. "Sports" is one such sector that has witnessed immense growth in audience and business with information available to fans in real-time through

Published by Springer Nature Switzerland AG 2021
D. Dennehy et al. (Eds.): I3E 2021, LNCS 12896, pp. 692–703, 2021.
https://doi.org/10.1007/978-3-030-85447-8_57

the plethora of platforms accessible via the Internet. Social Media has brought fans closer to their favorite players and teams (Seong 2021). Whether it's about collecting information or performing a communication (through video-call, voice-call, direct messaging, etc.) with social media, it's easy and fun. For example, the 2016 IPL match that reached out to around 110 million audiences witnessed a jump of 40% compared to previous years (Raheja 2019). At the global level, about 60% of people who have an interest in sports use Facebook. Nearly 3 in 4 of these sports fans say that the main reason to use social media is to follow sports events coverage (Facebook-IQ 2019). Social Media has provided players of less established sports such as Kabaddi, Hockey, Football, and many other sports globally to showcase their talent (Singh et al. 2019a; Trivedi et al. 2020). Sports marketers benefit from social media by promoting and marketing their sports events, franchises, related merchandise at minimal costs (Mahan 2011; Meng et al. 2015; Vale and Fernandes 2018). It has been seen that most professional teams maintain their presence on various social media platforms and adopt new ones. Instagram is one such platform used as a Brand Management Tool by Professional Team Sports Organizations (Anagnostopoulos et al. 2018), along with Facebook and Twitter as notable mentions (Vale and Fernandes 2018; Williams et al. 2014). Facebook, Twitter, YouTube, among many famous social media platforms, can increase and maintain fan's commitment and engagement with sporting events (Meng et al. 2015).

2 Literature Review

COVID-19 pandemic took the entire world by storm, and a large population from 213 countries have been infected by this deadly disease (Brahmi et al. 2020; Dwivedi et al. 2020). Even after more than a year, many countries have still imposed full or partial lockdown (Singh et al. 2020c), restricting outdoor activities like sports and entertainment. The magnitude of this pandemic was so high that even the Olympic Games scheduled to be held in Tokyo in 2020 were postponed to 2021 to safeguard the athletes' health and everyone involved (Olympic 2020). Online sports have emerged stronger during a pandemic, and the following are the perspectives from various stakeholders with respect to online sports.

2.1 Fans or General Audience Perspective

The term involvement can be defined as "a person's perceived relevance of the object based on inherent needs, values, and interests" (Zaichkowsky 1985). Laurent and Kapferer (1985) defined the term Sports involvement as "an unobservable state of motivation, arousal, or interest in viewing a game or participating in a sport-related activity that results in searching, information processing, and decision-making." The involvement of "Fans" or audience is a critical factor for the success of any sports event (Kim et al. 2020). Women harness the power of social media to follow sports. Nearly 80 percent of women surveyed globally say that they watch live sports online or in person. In Latin America, female viewers' percentage to male viewers is almost identical (Facebook-IQ 2019).

2.2 Sports Authorities Perspective

From existing fan bases and the level of their sports fandom, it can be inferred that sports organizations are positioned ideally to benefit from social media platform (McCarthy et al. 2014; Williams and Chinn 2010). Sports Authorities should plan mobile and TV ads together to target a larger audience (Facebook-IQ 2019). The researchers (Anderson 2018) have shown that sports clubs can increase viewership by leveraging live tweets during a match. Researchers (O'Shea and Alonso 2012) have shown that fans and sport club enthusiasts dictate professional sports organizations' managers the way to market and brand their products. Professional Sports clubs harness social media's power to add value to their brands and strengthen the bond with viewers and fans with their teams. They also provide fans with 'insider' information through social media channels (Williams et al. 2014).

2.3 Business Perspective

According to a report by KPMG, to escalate the engagement of fans in online sports events, league marketers are investing heavily on social media platforms to gather audience and benefits to the sponsor. In the developed markets, we have successful sports leagues like NBA, which have utilized social media to increase their fan base and game attendance (KPMG 2016). Researchers (Rosenbloom and Larsen 2003) have suggested that as businesses move into the e-commerce era, culture may exhibit a significant role in business marketing communication. The chief operating officer (COO) has to crucial part in making decisions about the franchises' social media policies and govern those (Prakash and Majumdar 2021). As the content generation strategy is an essential aspect for any sports event or franchise (Bennett and Miles 2006; Marcel 2009), the role of COO becomes even more critical.

2.4 Government Perspective

The viewers can be targeted using demographic and behavioral data (Cox Media 2020). The Government of India has liberalized the use and aims to enable Geospatial Data availability for applications across various sectors like e-commerce, delivery, and logistics, agriculture, etc. (NASSCOM 2021). The initiative has been taken to realize the vision of Prime Minister Narendra Modi-led Government of "AATMANIRBHAR BHARAT" and a $5 Trillion economy. The guidelines state that "Individuals, companies, organizations, and government agencies, shall be free to process the acquired geospatial data, build applications and develop solutions about such data and use such data products, applications, solutions, etc. By way of selling, distributing, sharing, swapping, disseminating, publishing, deprecating and destructing." Self-certification will be required for compliance (Dasgupta 2021). In England, a significant proportion of participants belongs to sports clubs run by their members and play a central role in the formulation of policies by the government to grow participation (Nichols et al. 2012).

2.5 Current Scenario and Social Media Adoption

Many International Federations and Sports Committees have started organizing sports events with limited or no audience (Bryson et al. 2021; Fischer and Haucap 2020) and hence leaving sports enthusiasts to look for some alternate options to show their support towards their favorite sports team and a sportsperson in particular. Social media (especially Twitter) is one such alternative that has emerged as a front-runner in these challenging times of the Covid-19 pandemic (Singh et al. 2020c; Sturm 2020). Social media is a virtual platform that allows people from all around the world to communicate without any geographical barrier that too is free of cost (Kapoor et al. 2018, Singh et al. 2020a, 2020b). These factors make social media a perfect fan favorite and effective alternate to virtually show their love and support towards their favorite sports team or sportsperson.

Since multiple countries, International Federations, and Sports Committees have decided to organize future sports events without an audience behind closed doors till the pandemic is not over (Guardian 2021), this opens up an all-new area of research for the researchers to explore. Hence, in this study, we explore the use of Twitter by fans/ sports enthusiasts to show their support towards their favorite sports team and sportsperson.

3 Research Objectives and Questions

Our research explores the use of social media by fans/sports enthusiasts to show their support towards their favorite sports team and sportsperson. We take the example of the fourth Test match between India and Australia played at Gaba during 15–19 January, 2021 of Border-Gavaskar Trophy 2020–2021 (ESPN-Crinfo 2021). The reason for choosing this particular sports event is that this game was evenly contested between both teams for the entire duration of five days and it was anybody's game till the penultimate over was bowled. Besides, it wasn't sure till the last session of the previous day i.e. 4th day (18th january, 2021) who could be the winner, making it a perfect case study to carry out our research objectives. The study focuses on the four research questions (RQ):

RQ1: *How sports enthusiasts use social media to show their support?*

H1a: *The mean of discussion regarding Test Match for all five days is the same on social media*

H1b: *The mean of discussion regarding Indian and Australian cricket Teams is the same on social media.*

RQ2: *How were the globally dispersed sports enthusiasts discussing about the cricket matches?*

RQ3: *What is the overall sentiment of the discussion on social media regarding the Test Match?*

RQ4: *What factors influence the discussion regarding the Test Match on social media?*

4 Methodology

For fulfillment of our goals, data was collected from Twitter using Twitter API. Hashtag like #AUSvsIND, #AUSvIND, #INDvsAUS, #INDvsAUS, #GabbaTest, #Border-GavaskarTrophy etc. were used as search terms in order to extract data from Twitter from Jan 15, 2021 to Jan 19, 2021 on daily basis. A total of 69,965 were collected from 37,453 users globally. Since the collected data contains a lot of noise, we performed data pre-processing to remove any ambiguities that could have led to conflicting results (García et al. 2015, Singh et al. 2018a). Once data was prepared for analysis, various statistical techniques and social media analytics (Sarin et al. 2020; Stieglitz and Dang-Xuan 2013) were applied to fulfill our goals and answer the research questions.

5 Results and Discussions

In RQ1, we try to analyze the use social media by fans/sports enthusiast to show their support virtually by e-participation. To validate our claim, we statistically validate H1a and H1b.

H1a: *The means of discussion regarding Test Match for all five days is same on social media.*

For H1a, we applied one-way ANOVA on session-wise tweet collected for all five days. The results of ANOVA at 95% confidence, is F-Value = 6.656 and P = 0.000111. According to the decision rule since, the value of $P < 0.05$, hence, H1a is rejected. This means that there exists significant difference between one or more groups of days with regards to discussion on Twitter. In order to get further insights, we plot the results of Tukey Honest Significant Differences (Tukey HSD) (See Fig. 1).

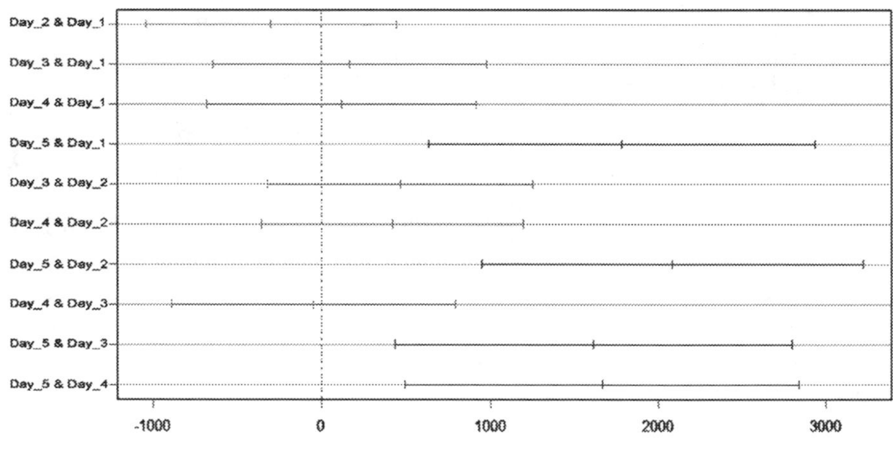

Fig. 1. Results of Tukey HSD

Inference: The results clearly indicate that the discussion on Twitter varies and is not similar across all three sessions of all five days of the Test Match. The results of Tukey

HSD indicates that means of day_5 & day_1, day_5 & day_2, day_5 & day_3 and day_5 & day_4, varies as compared to other groups.

H1b: *The mean of discussion regarding Indian and Australian cricket Team is same on social media.*

For H1b, two-tail independent t-test was applied to the tweets. The results of two-tail independent t-test at 95% confidence, is T-Value = 12.713 and P = 0.7593. According to the decision rule since, the value of P > 0.05, hence, H1b is accepted. This means that there does not exists any significant difference between the discussion regarding Indian and Australian cricket Team is same on social media.

Inference: The results of H1b, clearly indicate that both India and Australia are discussed statistically equally on Twitter. Statistically, both the countries are finding support from fans/sports enthusiasts via Twitter in equal numbers.

For RQ2, we try to find the country wise origin of tweet from where the fans/sports enthusiasts are showing their support via e-participation. Since, most of the tweets are geo-tagged, hence, we apply geo-location analysis. Location based analysis is considered the most critical tool for mapping public response in an area of large demography towards an entity (Singh et al. 2019b, 2018b). Based upon our analysis, India and Australia were the main contributors in the discussion, however, many other countries actively took part in the discussion. This active participation by people all around the world showed that people globally were taking part in this discussion and showing their support their favorite team. The result of geo-location analysis is shown in Fig. 2.

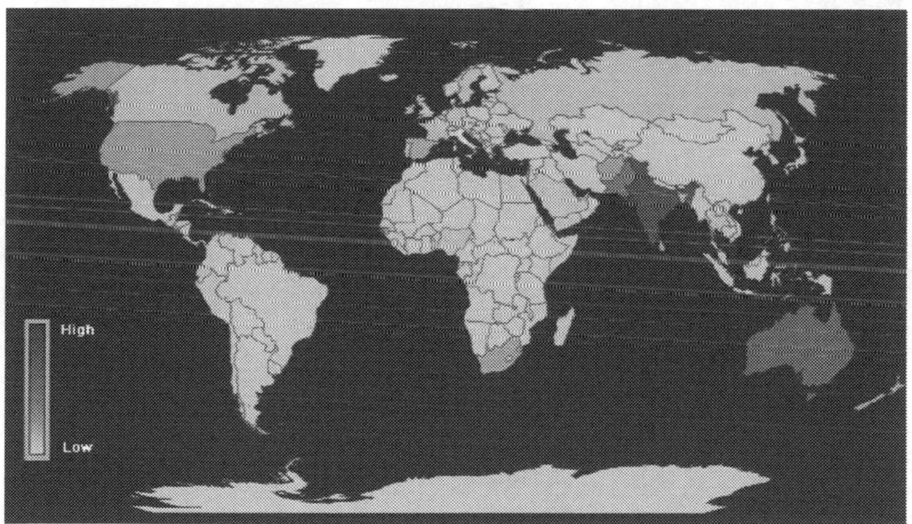

Fig. 2. Geo-location analysis

Inference: The results in Fig. 2, show that people globally were actively taking part in these discussions and showing their support for their favorite cricket team via Twitter through e-participation.

For RQ3, we have applied sentiment analysis, which is a text mining technique that depicts the sentiment from given piece of text (Mohammad and Turney 2010, Ou et al. 2014, Singh et al. 2017). Sentiment analysis is often classified into (a) Polarity Analysis (b) Emotion Analysis (Grover et al. 2019, Singh et al. 2020a). Polarity analysis defines the polarity (Positive, Neutral, Negative) of text, while, emotion analysis classifies the text based upon eight e-motions. Figure 3, show the results of polarity analysis while Fig. 4 shows the results of e-motion analysis.

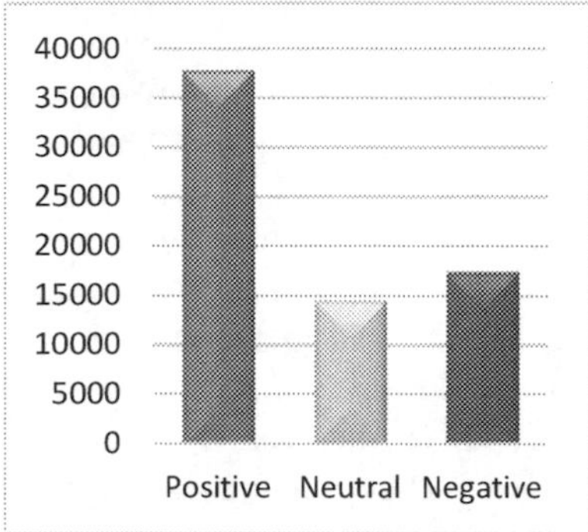

Fig. 3. Polarity analysis

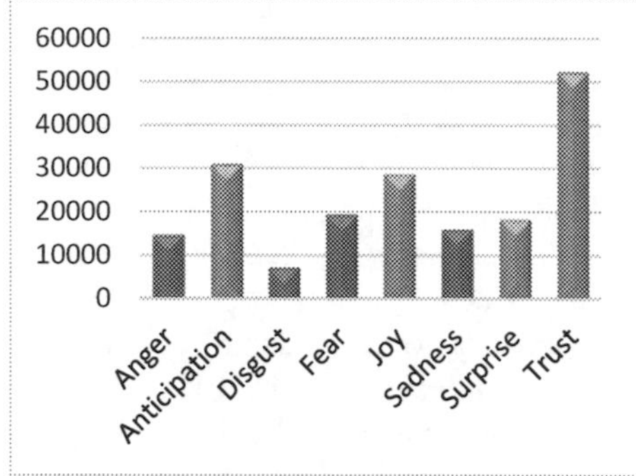

Fig. 4. Emotion analysis

Inference: The results of polarity analysis, indicates that overall discussion is taking place on Twitter regarding the test match is positive. Even the results of e-motion analysis indicate that the people show more anticipation, joy and trust in discussion as compared to other e-motions. Overall, fans are enjoying the discussion on Twitter while showing their support towards their favorite team. Further, fans do not hesitate to show their negative emotion, when they feel that certain players are not performing as per their reputation, which even led to online trolling (Kumari et al. 2019; Lundberg and Laitinen 2020).

For RQ4, we plotted a correlation plot in order to study what all factors affect the online discussion regarding the Test Match. For this we considered factors such as runs scored, wickets fallen, any batsman scoring a century or half century (Milestone_Batting), any bowler taking a five-wicket haul (Milestone_Bowler) and rain which interrupted the Test Match on two different days. The result of correlation analysis is shown in Fig. 5.

Inference: The results of correlation plots indicates that discussion is positively affected with number of runs scored, showing a strong positive correlation of 0.9. Similarly, rain negatively affects the online discussion, showing a moderate negative correlation of – 0.6. Further, milestones by batsmen or bowler also positively affect the discussion, show a moderate positive correlation of 0.4.

The way social media and marketing strategy has emerged, and provided a newer evolving dimension to social media marketing (Li et al. 2020) during pandemic will have its impact for longer duration and is forming the future base of e-participation as compared with traditional ways (See Fig. 6). There are several motivating factors

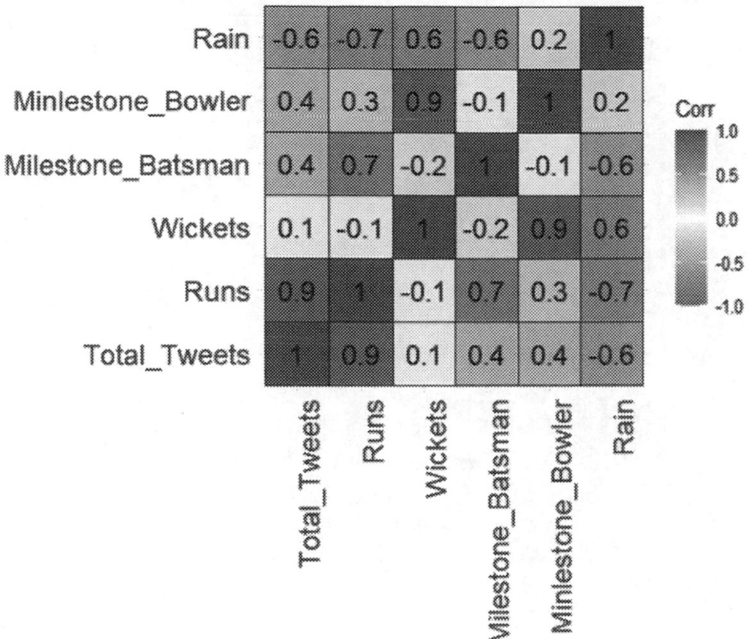

Fig. 5. Results of correlation plot

i.e., Information Motivation (IM), Pass-Time Motivation (PTM), Fanship Motivation (FM) and Entertainment Motivation (EM) which has led to more e-participation of fans in sports. The research provided by Crawford and Godbey (1987) has become the backbone for today's leisure constraint research by proposing three types of constraints which help us to understand whether a viewer participate or not: Intrapersonal or individual psychological states and attributes, such as stress or anxiety; Interpersonal or the results of interpersonal interaction, such as social interaction with family and friends; and Structural or Intervening factors between preference and participation, such as financial resources, time and accessibility. Covid-19 pandemic has facilitated all sorts of constraints for maximizing e-user participation as work from home culture elevated in the tough times. Participation can be seen as the process of overcoming these three constraints and each is applicable to Sport Twitter Consumption (Witkemper et al. 2012).

The evolution of social media involves several factors such as how the users interact and connectedness; passive versus active actor, how the resources are integrated, being interacted and connected which further helps to enhance brand related activities (Fig. 6), similarly, in this paper we are discussing online users as sports fans and the associated brand management which would further enhance the marketing strategy considering social media as a prime medium during the pandemic times and stay home culture.

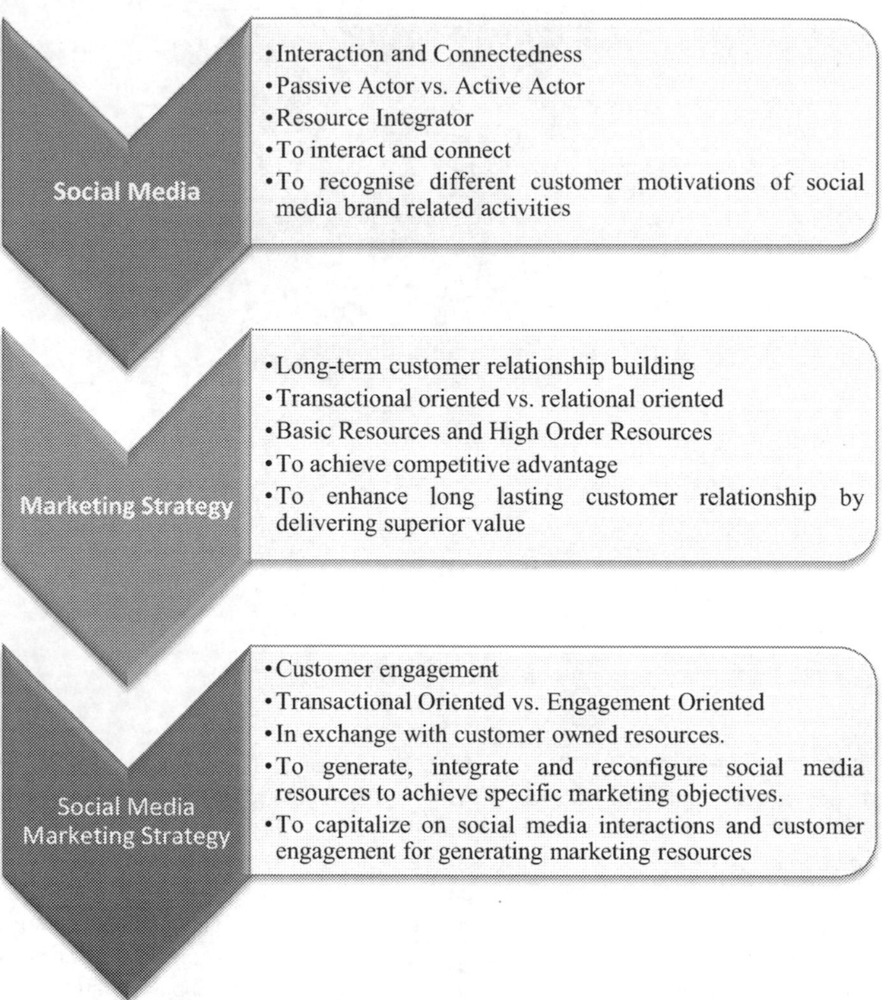

Fig. 6. Comparison of social media, marketing strategy, and social media marketing strategy (adapted from Li et al. 2020)

6 Conclusions

The interaction, communication and value-based concepts of prosumers and exchanging social media interaction focuses on expanded version of Gronroos's (2004) relationship-building. The evolution of the Internet, social media, and Mobile technology (Holland 2015, Sarin et al. 2021) has been transcendent and evolved newer avenues how the sports fans consume sports contents generally. During this pandemic time, internet penetration and home stay approach as well as government restrictions led to higher e-participation of sports fans. Even as the Tokyo Olympics are getting planned to take place in absence of foreign crowds (India Today 2021); sports ecosystem model, event-driven marketing, star marketing, and international differences in sports viewing for specific sports have emerged significantly through social media platforms. For Broadcasters and advertisers, the empty space in the stands present more visibility window for the advertisement to generate revenues and thus opening new doors to attract more targeted audience.

References

Anagnostopoulos, C., Parganas, P., Chadwick, S., Fenton, A.: Branding in pictures: using Instagram as a brand management tool in professional team sport organisations. Eur. Sport Manage. q. **18**(4), 413–438 (2018)

Anderson, B.: Winning over fans: how sports teams use live-tweeting to maximize engagement. Elon J. **54** (2018)

Bennett, N., Miles, S.: Second in command: the misunderstood role of the chief operating officer. Harvard Bus. Rev. **84**(5) (2006)

Brahmi, N., Singh, P., Sohal, M., Sawhney, R.S.: Psychological trauma among the healthcare professionals dealing with COVID-19. Asian J. Psychiatr. **54**, 102241 (2020)

Bryson, A., Dolton, P., Reade, J.J., Schreyer, D., Singleton, C.: Causal effects of an absent crowd on performances and refereeing decisions during Covid-19. Econ. Lett. **198**, 109664 (2021)

Cox Media, March 2020. https://hub.coxmedia.com/sports-advertising/how-to-reach-a-sports-audience-even-when-live-events-are-postponed-or-cancelled

Crawford, D.W., Godbey, G.: Reconceptualizing barriers to family leisure. Leis. Sci. **9**(2), 119–127 (1987)

Dasgupta, S., February 2021. https://theprint.in/theprint-essential/why-modi-govt-is-liberalising-mapping-policies-what-free-access-to-geospatial-data-means/606574/

Dwivedi, Y.K., et al.: Impact of COVID-19 pandemic on information management research and practice: transforming education, work and life. Int. J. Inf. Manage. **55**, 102211 (2020)

ESPN-Crinfo (2021). https://www.espncricinfo.com/series/india-in-australia-2020-21-1223867/australia-vs-india-4th-test-1223872/full-scorecard

Facebook-IQ, January 2019. https://en-gb.facebook.com/business/news/insights/the-changing-profile-of-sports-fans-around-the-world

Fischer, K., Haucap, J.: Does crowd support drive the home advantage in professional soccer? Evidence from German ghost games during the COVID-19 pandemic (2020)

García, S., Luengo, J., Herrera, F.: Data Preprocessing in Data Mining, vol. 72. Springer, Cham (2015). https://doi.org/10.1007/978-3-319-10247-4

Grover, P., Kar, A.K., Dwivedi, Y.K., Janssen, M.: Polarization and acculturation in US Election 2016 outcomes–Can twitter analytics predict changes in voting preferences. Technol. Forecast. Soc. Chang. **145**, 438–460 (2019)

Grönroos, C.:. The relationship marketing process: communication, interaction, dialogue, value. J. Bus. Ind. Market. (2004)

Guardian (2021). https://www.theguardian.com/sport/2021/mar/03/tokyo-olympics-will-be-closed-to-fans-from-abroad-hints-games-organiser

Holland, C.P.: Internet and social media strategy in sports marketing (2015)

Kapoor, K.K., Tamilmani, K., Rana, N.P., Patil, P., Dwivedi, Y.K., Nerur, S.: Advances in social media research: past, present and future. Inf. Syst. Front. **20**(3), 531–558 (2018)

Kim, S., Morgan, A., Assaker, G.: Examining the relationship between sport spectator motivation, involvement, and loyalty: a structural model in the context of Australian Rules football. Sport Soc. **24**, 1006–1032 (2020)

KPMG (2016). https://assets.kpmg/content/dam/kpmg/in/pdf/2016/09/the-business-of-sports.pdf

Kumari, K., Singh, J.P., Dwivedi, Y.K., Rana, N.P.: Towards cyberbullying-free social media in smart cities: a unified multi-modal approach. Soft. Comput. **24**(15), 11059–11070 (2019). https://doi.org/10.1007/s00500-019-04550-x

Laurent, G., Kapferer, J.N.: Measuring consumer involvement profiles. J. Mark. Res. **22**(1), 41–53 (1985). https://doi.org/10.1177/002224378502200104

Li, F., Larimo, J., Leonidou, L.C.: Social media marketing strategy: definition, conceptualization, taxonomy, validation, and future agenda. J. Acad. Mark. Sci. **49**(1), 51–70 (2020). https://doi.org/10.1007/s11747-020-00733-3

Lundberg, J., Laitinen, M.: Twitter trolls: a linguistic profile of anti-democratic discourse. Lang. Sci. **79**, 101268 (2020)

Mahan, J.E.: Examining the predictors of consumer response to sport marketing via digital social media. Int. J. Sport Manage. Mark. **9**(3–4), 254–267 (2011)

Marcel, J.J.: Why top management team characteristics matter when employing a chief operating officer: a strategic contingency perspective. Strateg. Manage. J. **30**(6), 647–658 (2009)

McCarthy, J., Rowley, J., Ashworth, C., Pioch, E.: Managing brand presence through social media: the case of UK football clubs. Internet Res. **24**, 181–204 (2014). https://doi.org/10.1108/IntR-08-2012-0154

Meng, M.D., Stavros, C., Westberg, K.: Engaging fans through social media: implications for team identification. Sport Bus. Manage. Int. J. (2015)

Mohammad, S., Turney, P.: Emotions evoked by common words and phrases: using mechanical turk to create an emotion lexicon. In: Proceedings of the NAACL HLT 2010 Workshop on Computational Approaches to Analysis and Generation of Emotion in Text, pp. 26–34, June 2010

NASSCOM, February 2021. https://community.nasscom.in/communities/policy-advocacy/department-of-science-and-technology-releases-new-guidelines-for-geospatial-data-and-geospatial-data-services.html

Nichols, G., Padmore, J., Taylor, P., Barrett, D.: The relationship between types of sports club and English government policy to grow participation. Int. J. Sport Policy Polit. **4**(2), 187–200 (2012)

Olympic (2020). https://www.olympic.org/news/ioc-ipc-tokyo-2020-organising-committee-and-tokyo-metropolitan-government-announce-new-dates-for-the-olympic-and-paralympic-games-tokyo-2020

O'Shea, M., Alonso, A.D.: Opportunity or obstacle? A preliminary study of professional sport organisations in the age of social media. Int. J. Sport Manage. Mark. **10**(3–4), 196–212 (2012)

Ou, G., et al.: Exploiting community emotion for microblog event detection. In: EMNLP, pp. 1159–1168, October 2014

Prakash, C.D., Majumdar, A.: Analyzing the role of national culture on content creation and user engagement on Twitter: the case of Indian Premier League cricket franchises. Int. J. Inf. Manage. **57**, 102268 (2021)

Raheja R.: 'Sportstainment': how ınternet changed the way audience watches sports. Financial Express, March 2019. https://www.financialexpress.com/industry/technology/sportstainment-how-internet-changed-the-way-audience-watches-sports/1528040/

Rosenbloom, B., Larsen, T.: Communication in international business-to business marketing channels: does culture matter? Ind. Mark. Manage. **32**(4), 309–315 (2003). https://doi.org/10.1016/S0019-8501(01)00202-4

Seong, D.-H.: How to utilize sports psychology for better customer experience in sports retail store as a distribution content perspective. J. Distrib. Sci. **19**(2), 45–52 (2021). https://doi.org/10.15722/JDS.19.2.202102.45

Sarin, P., Kar, A.K., Kiran Kewat, P., Ilavarasan, V.: Factors affecting future of work: insights from social media analytics. Procedia Comput. Sci. **67**, 1880–1888 (2020). https://doi.org/10.1016/j.procs.2020.03.207

Sarin, P., Kar, A.K., Ilavarasan, V.P.: Exploring engagement among mobile app developers – Insights from mining big data in user generated content. J. Adv. Manage. Res. (2021). https://doi.org/10.1108/JAMR-06-2020-0128. Vol. ahead-of-print No. ahead-of-print

Singh, P., Sawhney, R.S., Kahlon, K.S.: Forecasting the 2016 US presidential elections using sentiment analysis. In: Kar, A.K., Ilavarasan, P.V., Gupta, M.P., Dwivedi, Y.K., Mäntymäki, M., Janssen, M., Simintiras, A., Al-Sharhan, S. (eds.) I3E 2017. LNCS, vol. 10595, pp. 412–423. Springer, Cham (2017). https://doi.org/10.1007/978-3-319-68557-1_36

Singh, P., Sawhney, R.S., Kahlon, K.S.: Sentiment analysis of demonetization of 500 & 1000 rupee banknotes by Indian government. ICT Express **4**(3), 124–129 (2018)

Singh, P., Kahlon, K.S., Sawhney, R.S., Vohra, R., Kaur, S.: Social media buzz created by# nanotechnology: insights from Twitter analytics. Nanotechnol. Rev. **7**(6), 521–528 (2018)

Singh, J.P., Dwivedi, Y.K., Rana, N.P., Kumar, A., Kapoor, K.K.: Event classification and location prediction from tweets during disasters. Ann. Oper. Res. **283**(1–2), 737–757 (2019). https://doi.org/10.1007/s10479-017-2522-3

Singh, P., Singh, S., Sohal, M., Dwivedi, Y.K., Kahlon, K.S., Sawhney, R.S.: Psychological fear and anxiety caused by COVID-19: Insights from Twitter analytics. Asian J. Psychiatry **54**, 102280 (2020)

Singh, P., Dwivedi, Y.K., Kahlon, K.S., Pathania, A., Sawhney, R.S.: Can twitter analytics predict election outcome? An insight from 2017 Punjab assembly elections. Govern. Inf. q. **37**(2), 101444 (2020)

Singh, P., Dwivedi, Y.K., Kahlon, K.S., Sawhney, R.S., Alalwan, A.A., Rana, N.P.: Smart monitoring and controlling of government policies using social media and cloud computing. Inf. Syst. Front. **22**(2), 315–337 (2020)

Singh, P., Kaur, H., Kahlon, K.S., Sawhney, R.S.: Do people virtually support their favorite cricket team? insights from 2018 Asia cup. In: Proceedings of the Third International Conference on Advanced Informatics for Computing Research, pp. 1–8, June 2019a

Stieglitz, S., Dang-Xuan, L.: Emotions and information diffusion in social media—sentiment of microblogs and sharing behavior. J. Manage. Inf. Syst. **29**(4), 217–248 (2013)

Sturm, D.: Fans as e-participants? Utopia/dystopia visions for the future of digital sport fandom. Convergence **26**(4), 841–856 (2020)

India Today (2021). https://www.indiatoday.in/sports/other-sports/story/tokyo-olympics-2021-to-be-staged-without-overseas-spectators-no-audience-during-torch-relay-1777365-2021-03-09

Trivedi, J., Soni, S., Kishore, A.: Exploring the role of social media communications in the success of professional sports leagues: an emerging market perspective. J. Promot. Manage. **27**(2), 306–331 (2020)

Vale, L., Fernandes, T.: Social media and sports: driving fan engagement with football clubs on Facebook. J. Strateg. Mark. **26**(1), 37–55 (2018). https://doi.org/10.1080/0965254X.2017.1359655

Williams, J., Chinn, S.: Meeting relationship-marketing goals through social media: a conceptual model for sport marketers. Int. J. Sport Commun. **3**, 422–437 (2010). https://doi.org/10.1123/ijsc.3.4.422

Williams, J., Chinn, S.J., Suleiman, J.: The value of Twitter for sports fans. J. Direct Data Digit. Mark. Pract. **16**(1), 36–50 (2014)

Witkemper, C., Lim, C.H., Waldburger, A.: Social media and sports marketing: examining the motivations and constraints of Twitter users. Sport Mark. q. **21**, 170–183 (2012)

Zaichkowsky, J.L.: Measuring the involvement construct. J. Consum. Res. **12**(3), 341–352 (1985). https://doi.org/10.1086/208520

Investigating the Dynamics of Polarization in Online Discourse During COVID-19 Pandemic

Samrat Gupta[1(✉)], Gaurav Jain[1], and Amit Anand Tiwari[2]

[1] Indian Institute of Management, Ahmedabad, India
samratg@iima.ac.in

[2] Indian Institute of Management, Rohtak, India

Abstract. The socio-cultural polarization induced due to information and communication technology because of the selective online exposure during COVID-19 has been a major cause of concern around the globe. In this paper, we use random network theory-based simulation technique to investigate the temporal dynamics of opinion formation on YouTube videos. Our findings reveal that as the pandemic unfolded, the degree of polarization in the online discourse has increased with time. This study is significant for understanding that online discourse on sociocultural issues can lead to polarization particularly in crisis situations such as a pandemic and exacerbate the social divide.

Keywords: Polarization · COVID-19 pandemic · Online opinion formation · Consensus formation · Social media

1 Introduction

In December 2019, an outbreak of infectious disease, later named as coronavirus disease 2019 (COVID-19) and declared a pandemic, was first reported to WHO.[1] This unsettling pandemic has been generating a massive amount of data across the world each day. This data generation is a result of people using social media platforms to search the information and express their views related to the disease and to reduce isolation usually associated with the anxiety as well as long-term distress during the pandemic [1].

In the data generated due to COVID-19 crisis, there is a fair share of misinformation that is intentionally or unintentionally disseminated [2–5]. The socio-cultural polarization added to the turbulence even in such difficult times when the global agenda is (and should be) to fight an invisible enemy (coronavirus) and protect lives [6]. This socio-cultural polarization has given rise to *echo chambers* wherein individuals are by choice exposed only to the opinions, beliefs, and attitudes that are consistent with their own,

[1] https://www.businessinsider.in/slideshows/miscellaneous/a-comprehensive-timeline-of-the-new-coronavirus-pandemic-from-chinas-first-covid-19-case-to-the-present/slidelist/74721133.cms#slideid=74721140.

Published by Springer Nature Switzerland AG 2021
D. Dennehy et al. (Eds.): I3E 2021, LNCS 12896, pp. 704–709, 2021.
https://doi.org/10.1007/978-3-030-85447-8_58

leading to reinforcement of their views and behavior. However, the degree of polarization on a topic tends to change with time, as the users' interest and focus shifts from one topic to the other. This change in the interest of users around various topics related to COVID-19 over time motivates us to study the dynamics of opinion formation in online discourse using a network theoretic approach. We use a simulation technique based on the principles of evolution of opinions in an adaptive random network [7] to evaluate the formation of consensus with time among users who comment on a particular YouTube video. To the best of our knowledge, this work is one of the earliest attempts for investigating the temporal dynamics of consensus formation in online discourse related to COVID-19 pandemic. This has practical and policy implications that we highlight in the discussion section.

2 Background

Information and communication technology offer an opportunity to easily access any kind of information. The propensity to surround ourselves with similar others who share our perceptions intensifies feudal mindsets and produce "echo chambers" that damage the quality of online discourse on social media platforms [8]. This selective exposure to like-minded information fueled by recommendation algorithms on social media platforms leads to increased polarization which is a cause of growing concern as users don't get exposed to diverse opinions. Consider the causes and the consequences of polarization due to the events as listed below:

1. The treatment of daily wage migrant workers in India during the lockdowns has been widely discussed over various social media platforms. The government and the opposition were polarized in their views on how effectively the government handled the relief work for the migrant workers.[2]
2. Brazil's president's incendiary response to the pandemic wherein he encouraged street protests, attacked officials who imposed quarantines, lambasted the media as well as the judiciary, and fired his health minister led to polarizing debates in Brazil.[3]

These events indicate that the socio-cultural polarization of opinions about information/misinformation related to sociocultural activities may lead to violence, killings, civil protests, and can influence the response of governments. This socio-cultural polarization during COVID-19 has prevented the governments and healthcare agencies around the world from making concentrated efforts towards an effective response to the crisis.

3 Methodology: Simulation on Networks

The study of opinion dynamics in adaptive networks has gained significant attention for its profound prospects in understanding human social behavior [9]. Prior research has used various methods to understand the issues related to the characterization of

[2] https://www.youtube.com/watch?v=K-51rP9drwU.

[3] https://carnegieendowment.org/2020/04/28/polarization-and-pandemic-pub-81638.

the collective social behavior of individuals such as cultural information dissemination and the dynamics of opinion formation [7, 9–11]. We borrow from this stream of work to model the evolution of users' opinions as random binary encounters occur within a network and users update their opinion whenever the difference between the polarity of their opinions is below a certain threshold value of tolerance parameter.

The initial interaction between the users who comment on a YouTube video at a particular time corresponds to an Erdős–Rényi random network model i.e. it is considered as a random graph constructed by connecting a pair of nodes among the N users commenting on a YouTube video with probability p. In such a graph denoted by $G(N, p)$ the number of possible undirected connections without self-loops will be ${}^{N}C_2$. Since each of these connections has a probability of occurrence p, the expected number of connections will be ${}^{N}C_2 \times p$, and on average, a node in the network will have $p \times N$ acquaintances which is the degree of a node.

For N comments posted by users on a YouTube video at a given time t, let us denote the respective polarity scores as s_i where $i = 1, 2, 3, 4 \ldots .N$. One user is randomly chosen at each step and its polarity score is compared with that of the rest of the users in the network. The absolute difference of their polarity scores is compared with the tolerance limit (TL) and if the difference is within the TL, mean of all the differences is considered for adjusting the polarity score of the chosen user as per the following logic:

$$\text{Polarity score of user i} = \text{Convergence parameter}\{\text{Polarity score of user i} \\ + \text{Convergence parameter}(\text{Sum of the differences of the polarity score of user i with} \\ \text{each user where the difference is less than the tolerance level})\}$$

Using this methodology gives an insight into the number of iterations taken to form a consensus on different time-varying subsets of comments on a YouTube video. The delayed consensus formation indicates higher polarization and a faster consensus formation suggests less polarization in online discourse.

4 Experiments and Results

We focused on YouTube videos related to COVID-19 posted mainly by various news and healthcare agencies covering the spread of the pandemic. The extracted and cleaned data as described above was subjected to the sentiment analysis process to determine the polarity score of each of the comments. The data along with polarity score was subjected to the opinion formation simulation described in Sect. 3.

Appendix 1 shows a consolidated view of the experimental results on all the COVID-19 related YouTube videos that we considered for this study. These experimental results establish that the degree of polarization increases with time on diverse topics related to the COVID-19 pandemic. This lack of consensus could be attributed to the severity and sensitivity of the issues and the absence of an unequivocal governmental response to these issues. Overall, the results confirm that it becomes difficult to reach a consensus on diverse issues pertaining to COVID-19 over time due to increasing polarization and reinforcement of ideological homophily around these issues.

5 Discussion and Conclusion

One of the interesting observations from this study is that the consensus formation among polarized users takes longer as the public discourse's recency on a COVID-19 related video increases. The results of experiments indicate a gradual increase in iterations to form a consensus among the users' opinions over time. This observation indicates an increased polarization around COVID-19 among the users who posted comments on related videos as time passes.

Though the prior work on polarization around sociocultural issues such as controversial movies indicates a decrease in polarization with time [12] our findings suggest that polarization during the COVID-19 pandemic has increased with time. This increasing polarization indicates long-lived echo chambers which are detrimental to society, especially during pandemics. One of the practical implications of this work is to minimize the societal divide and prevent the damage that social media-induced polarization can cause during crisis situations.

However, this work is not devoid of limitations. The first limitation is related to the sentiment analysis methodology employed in this work as Azure sentiment analysis methodology does not consider the contextual polarity of a word. The second limitation of this work is the gap of information not captured in social media. The third limitation is that we have considered the comments only in the English language to avoid any misinterpretation due to subtleties associated with other languages that authors were not familiar with.

This study could open several directions for future work. One would be to extend the scope of this to cover polarization around black lives matter and climate change. Secondly, the investigation and analysis of polarization using big data around COVID-19 related posts, images, videos on other social media platforms (such as Facebook and Twitter) might reveal interesting insights and help in ascertaining and theorizing the evolution of polarization during COVID-19 [13]. Finally, another future research direction could be to address issues pertaining to information asymmetries or spreading false information in social media created by large and strong players with specific political intent.

Appendix 1: Experimental Results of Consensus Formation on COVID-19 Related YouTube Videos

Videos	Time	#Iterations for convergence
The lockdown: One month in Wuhan	Last week of March	15
	Last week of April	16
	First week of May	33
	Second week of May	71
Bill Gates makes a prediction about when coronavirus cases will peak	First week of June	18

(*continued*)

(*continued*)

Videos	Time	#Iterations for convergence
	First week of July	19
	Second week of July	20
	Third week of July	23
	Fourth week of July	25
Coronavirus: How the deadly epidemic sparked a global emergency	First week of May	31
	First week of June	31
	First week of July	33
How wildlife trade is linked to coronavirus	First week of May	12
	First week of June	12
	First week of July	16
	Second week of July	No consensus
	Third week of July	No consensus
	Fourth week of July	No consensus
Corona Virus - Covid 19 I Short Film I End of the world?	First week of May	15
	First week of June	17
	First week of July	17
	Second week of July	23
	Fourth week of July	30
What is the coronavirus?	First week of March	13
	First week of April	14
	First week of May	14
	First week of June	38
	First week of July	40
The Coronavirus Explained & What You Should Do	First week of March	14
	First week of April	14
	First week of May	15
	First week of June	20
	First week of July	23
Locked down India struggles as workers flee cities	First week of March	13
	First week of April	35
	First week of May	No consensus
	Last week of May	No consensus

References

1. Gonzalez-Padilla, D.A.: Social media influence in the COVID-19 Pandemic. Int. braz j urol **46**, 120–124. ISSN 1677-6119 (2020)
2. Apuke, O.D., Omar, B.: Fake news and COVID-19: modelling the predictors of fake news sharing among social media users. Telematics Inform. **56**, 101475 (2020)
3. Hart, P.S., Chinn, S., Soroka, S.: Politicization and Polarization in COVID-19 News Coverage. Sci. Commun. 1075547020950735 (2020)
4. Hatcher, W.: A failure of political communication not a failure of bureaucracy: the danger of presidential misinformation during the COVID-19 pandemic. Am. Rev. Publi. Adm. **50**(6–7), 614–620 (2020)
5. Kumar, S., Kar, A.K., Ilavarasan, P.V.: Applications of text mining in services management: a systematic literature review. Int. J. Inf. Manage. Data Insights **1**(1), 100008 (2021)
6. Qureshi, I., Bhatt, B., Gupta, S., Tiwari, A.A.: Causes, symptoms and consequences of Social Media Induced Polarization (SMIP) (2020)
7. Kozma, B., Barrat, A.: Consensus formation on adaptive networks. Phys. Rev. E **77**(1), 016102 (2008)
8. Garimella, K., Gionis, A., Parotsidis, N., Tatti, N.: Balancing information exposure in social networks. In: Advances in Neural Information Processing Systems, pp. 4663–4671 (2017)
9. Ju, C., Wang, J., Shi, J.: The intelligent method of public opinion polarisation modelling and simulation analysis based on multi-dimensional and multi-level evaluation. Behav. Inf. Technol. 1–13 (2020)
10. Jin, C., Li, Y., Jin, X.: Political opinion formation: initial opinion distribution and individual heterogeneity of tolerance. Phys. A **467**, 257–266 (2017)
11. Deffuant, G., Neau, D., Amblard, F., Weisbuch, G.: Mixing beliefs among interacting agents. Adv. Complex Syst. **3**(01n04), 87–98 (2000)
12. Amendola, L., Marra, V., Quartin, M.: The evolving perception of controversial movies. Palgrave Commun. **1**(1), 1–9 (2015)
13. Kar, A.K., Dwivedi, Y.K.: Theory building with big data-driven research–moving away from the "What" towards the "Why." Int. J. Inf. Manage. **54**, 102205 (2020)

Ecosystem of Social Media Listening Practices for Crisis Management

Lucia Castro Herrera[1(✉)], Tim A. Majchrzak[1], and Devinder Thapa[1,2]

[1] University of Agder, Kristiansand, Norway
{lucia.c.herrera,timam}@uia.no, Devinder.Thapa@usn.no
[2] University of South-Eastern Norway, Hønefoss, Norway

Abstract. The benefits of using social media data as a source of information are recognized by both practice and research in crisis management. However, the existing understanding on the matter is fragmented, it oscillates between techno-determinisms and socio-determinisms, which does not provide a holistic picture. In this paper we argue that to better adapt social media data use practices, an ecosystem perspective is needed. In doing so, we conducted a systematic literature review and identified the various entities and their interrelationships that configure the practices of social media listening for crisis management. Then, we summarize our findings by proposing a conceptual ecosystem of practice. Finally, we suggest its implications for future research and practice.

Keywords: Social media listening · Practice · Ecosystem · Crisis management

1 Introduction

Harnessing social media data has rapidly become a favored non-authoritative source of information in different fields. Businesses and academics increasingly adopt such data to perform their analysis and operations. The benefits of enabling social media listening, also known as *monitoring*, *intelligence*, *analytics*, *citizen-generated content*, and *surveillance* (SoMLIS), in crisis management are increasingly recognized especially in instances where access to other sources of information is scarce or costly [1]. SoMLIS, in essence, refers to the extraction, analysis, and reporting of insights from social media. This task is carried on with the help of technology solutions in the form of software, apps, or websites that offer social media listening and analytics capabilities. In SoMLIS practices, social, technological, organizational, and contextual features with unclear boundaries work together to fulfill information objectives that influence decision-making [2]. Hence, it is important to understand the ecosystem where SoMLIS practices are enacted to comprehend the emergence of information that contributes to decision making [3, 4].

Thus, by conducting a systematic literature review, we propose the *SoMLIS ecosystem in crisis management*. In doing so, we found that SoMLIS practices are inherently different and context dependent. However, the findings illustrate commonalities and overarching themes that can be generalized into a conceptual model. The model depicts

Published by Springer Nature Switzerland AG 2021
D. Dennehy et al. (Eds.): I3E 2021, LNCS 12896, pp. 710–722, 2021.
https://doi.org/10.1007/978-3-030-85447-8_59

the structure of the SoMLIS ecosystem that guides practice configurations. The rest of the article is structured as follows: Section 2 describes the literature review process. Section 3 presents the findings, and Section 4 presents a discussion and future research directions.

2 Methodology

This systematic literature review follows the general structuring approach from Okoli and Schabram [5]. After a rigorous process of selection of the literature (Fig. 1), we identified 109 articles for analysis. The scope included empirical studies written in English, with no publication timeframe, and with a focus on social media use as a source of information in crisis management.

We leveraged Boolean operator searches to retrieve the literature. The process started with a test-search on Google Scholar and other academic databases with the terms "social media listening" and "crisis", resulting in mostly irrelevant articles from diverse disciplines. Thus, we refined the search stream by integrating associated terms of SoMLIS, crises, and practice. We consulted five academic databases covering a wide range of study areas: AIS eLIbrary, Scopus, Web of Science, IEEE Xplore, and ProQuest. Then, automated filtering was applied to include relevant fields of study and reduce the volume of the literature. However, the breadth of results was still unmanageable. Subsequent manual steps were completed to select, screen, and analyze the literature. First, we performed title and abstract screenings and a preliminary content analyses following an inductive approach: abstracts were read and classified by field, methodology of analysis, subject, and practice type [5]. As a result, the following main categories emerged to classify the literature: *social media environment, social media use in practice and organizational configurations, other sources of information, and visualization of results.* These became the basis for further formulations of concepts, themes, and classifications. Our results and propositions are summarized and discussed in the following sections.

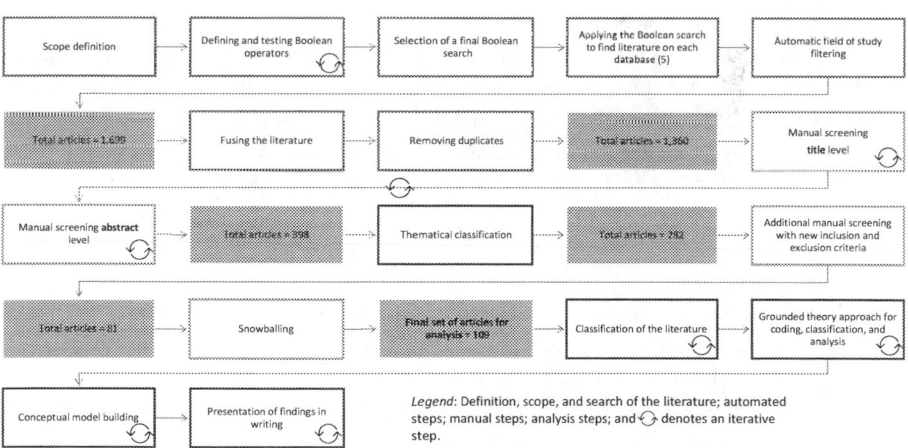

Fig. 1. The systematic literature review process

3 Findings: The Entities of SoMLIS

This section generalizes and describes *entities that participate in SoMLIS practices.*

3.1 Context

Context is the encompassing boundary that defines and re-defines the uniqueness of each enactment of SoMLIS practices and subsequent actions in crisis management. There are different views of context that can be classified but not limited to:

- *Crisis related*: While most of the analyzed literature focuses on social media use during the response and short-term mitigation of a disaster, SoMLIS contributes to the entire cycle, from preparedness and eventually risk reduction [6].
- *Location features*: Demographics of impacted area, location, level of disaster risk [7], socio-economical features, connectivity levels (infrastructure, broadband, accessibility and capabilities). Intrinsic to the place where crisis and practices are placed as it could be located remotely.
- *Organizational environment and patterns of collaboration*: The organizational, technological, and environmental resources, configurations, and techno-social capabilities situated under the organizational umbrella influence the adoption, design, improvements, and continuous enactments of practice [8], as well as the quality and trust in information extracted from social media [1], and the integrations of systems and collaboration patterns within and across organizations [4, 9].

  Context is not external to the configurations of the SoMLIS practice, but the opposite, the practice obtains its properties from the deep awareness and intrinsic relationship of such context. This awareness stems from accumulated knowledge of disasters and crisis response [3] or observed from following in the social media conversation [10]. Moreover, an assumption latent in social media research for crisis management is that technology is perceived as a universal solution [8] that calls for a change in rigid command and control structures [1]. The way in which technology is manipulated and the requirements for integrating systems depend on context of use [11], that in turn reflects the difference between needs and "wants" across different stakeholders and the actual use of technology at its full potential [12]. Ethical and legal issues related to privacy, security and liabilities, infrastructure failures, the digital divide, and low acceptance platforms [13] further add to the complexity of defining context.

3.2 Social Media Environment

Social media is a source that contributes to the fulfillment of information requirements; other sources include traditional media or physical sensors. Social media is the constant configuration of interactions driven by content and supported by technology [14]. The ***social media environment*** is where physical and digital users, content, and relationships co-create a reality driven by continuous narratives in diverse topics under the boundaries of a platform [15]. Social media is used systematically to ask for assistance, disseminate public warnings, share multimedia, and directly engage with other users [16], creating a story of a crisis revealed when practitioners listen to the social media conversation between users [17] beyond the organizations' own social media presence [18]. Tone and sentiment of the conversation give insight into how communities and authorities perceive and respond as crises unfold. The existing social media platforms have unique features and are perceived differently by users with different goals, whether as active contributors of content (suppliers) or active listeners looking for information (seekers) [19]. Tied to the social media platform of choice ***is the user's perception of privacy*** and the willingness to share different kinds of information during crises knowing that their conversations are monitored.

Information Types. *Text, multimedia, or a combination of formats constitute social media data.* However, if data is not enriched with contextual, time, and location features, yields incomplete information [8]. As a sense-making mechanism [16], social media use in crisis management *transforms from producing information to consuming information* [20] especially in early crisis onset. Thus, different types of information shape the story of a crisis. Raging from original, secondary, or re-sourced information classified by source; useful, sympathetic, individual, and situational information that includes sentiment as an indicator of the evolution of a crisis.

Social Media Users. Users in social media play other roles beyond seekers and suppliers (Table 1). The degree of influence is determined by patterns of information creation where media organizations and emergency services generate the most original content; and patterns of information sharing where individuals engaged in the conversation tend to share and re-share the most [21]. Artificially intelligent agents act in the form of bots contribute to and could influence the conversation in terms of volume, sentiment, and trends [22].

In the social media environment users receive many classifications (Table 1) which contributes to understanding the distribution, features, volume, and diversity of data present in the social media conversations. In recent years, the *influencer* concept emerged as lead users with big follower bases that use their social media knowledge to make purposeful content and manipulate the conversation. For example, a journalist who becomes a focal point in the social media conversation by initiating a source of aid through #PorteOuverte, a hashtag aiming to help the situation by matching demand and availability of shelter during the terrorist attacks in Paris [23]. Likewise, hashtags are ad-hoc identifiers or tags that, preceded by the hash sign (#) and combination of words without spaces, briefly describe a situation, event, theme, conversation, or place. Hashtags are desirable to follow conversations in social media chronologically, thematically, contextually, and systematically. Tags emerge organically by user-consensus active in the conversation or are established beforehand by influential users or crisis response entities to control the conversation. The effectiveness of hashtags is questioned because they are rarely used with novel information [24]. However, hashtags are a mass amplification vehicle when actionable information is sensed [23].

The social media environment is continuously configurated by a cluster of relationships, users, behavioral and organizational patterns that manifest through content, data, and information from diverse topics, interests, and contexts. Throughout the life cycle of crises, this environment serves as a mechanism for information flow that influences online and offline crisis management actions.

Table 1. User classification in social media in crises

Parameter	User type
Diverse social media presence and communication roles	*Organization*: i.e. Ministry, Emergency services agencies, media, political groups, office of the president, private company *Organization's leadership:* i.e., Minister, president, mayor, CEO *Individual*: private citizens acting on behalf of their affiliation with an organization or as regular citizens)
Activity in conversations	*Lead*: Topmost active users *Highly active:* Account for almost 10% of activity *Least active users:* Making the remaining 90%
Physical or emotional proximity to an event	*Directly affected:* Provide factual information due to their immediate involvement in the crisis *Indirectly affected:* Distribute information and turn to social media to make sense of situations *General public:* Generate large volumes of information that shape the overall sentiment of the conversation
Function	*Retransmissions*: Help amplify messages *Use-tweets:* Effective service providers or takers *Collective assurance:* Commenters on the situation
Eyewitnesses that recount events through social media platforms	*Direct eyewitnesses:* Report first-hand knowledge of events including perceived severity through detailed experiences, feelings, and happenings *Indirect eyewitnesses*: Distribute information with affected family and loved ones in mind, information sharing possibly occurs across platforms *Vulnerable eyewitnesses:* Population at risk of impeding disasters, (commonly in slow onset disasters with previous warning)

3.3 SoMLIS Entities in Practice

SoMLIS observes the world from an augmented reality that relies on the narratives from a network where consuming and responding to content is the main driver for users [15]. The core activities of listening to the social media environment are influenced by organizational configurations, collaboration routines, and methods. Practices exist to fulfill operational objectives that lead to specific crisis management actions. Thus, the decision makers drive objective-setting within organizational boundaries [25]. In crisis management, goals and expectations are set before events occur and tend to change dynamically [9]. The required information to aid crisis management tasks may be found in the social media environment but needs to be extracted, analyzed, synthesized, and reported in a format understandable by decision makers. This calls for the configuration of a socio-technical process that ensures a proper flow of information performed in a crisis management context (the SoMLIS practice).

In turn, "based on who is seeking information, different types of information may be broadcasted and sought depending upon the intended audience or the role of the information seeker" [26] (Table 2). The role of practitioners in communications and operations is changing [18], requiring understanding of tools for social media analytics and technical skills together with experience in the field of emergency management and public safety [12]. Thus, attitudes towards social media, originating in personal use and experience with platforms, influences the SoMLIS practices that in turn influence the delivery of crisis management services [11]. The use of different sources simultaneously and adaptability to different scenarios [9] is also desirable. Practitioners assert that young staff might bring value to the knowledge on social media and accept two-way communications as an organic process [11]; seasoned crisis managers perceive social media as a tool to find specific information such as damages, injuries, and basic needs [27].

Spectrum of Roles in Practice. These dualities between crisis management expertise and technology abilities, including social media, suggest that ideal organizational configurations mix internal and external sources with a variety of capabilities. Collaboration structures that encourage flexibility, coordination, and adaptation through the implementation of a social media analyst role [28] or collaboration with other organizations and digital volunteers [29] could optimize the value of social media data in crisis management operations [3]. For example, in adapting somlis processes, organizations need support, knowledge, and experience to meet technical internal and external needs [30]. In contrast, when setting up organized volunteering teams, the structure needs such flexibility to internally organize to embed in established structures of emergency management agencies [9]. While an institutionalized relationship between traditional humanitarian institutions and digital humanitarian organizations has not been established [13], patterns of collaboration are observed with other organizations that might not have the same structural and procedural characteristics [9]. Thus, information processes, communication, dialogue, and cooperation are vital factors in institutionalizing cooperation relationships to managing crises [9].

Adopters of social media in crisis management have matured their practice configurations to include a wide spectrum of specialization. Configurations of practice range from analysts tasked with social media functions in addition to regular roles [18] to dedicated social media intelligence teams [28]. Social media functions are traditionally housed under crisis communications and more recently included in operation and tactical roles. These roles are different but not mutually exclusive [28]. However, hesitancy remains in the official recognition of social media as a valid source of information, even in organizations where the integration of social media activities is more sophisticated [11]. The value of social media in operations remains ununderstood as information leads to different actions depending on the nature of operations [31].

Table 2. Information seekers in crisis management

Type	Definition
Citizens	Survivors and engaged individuals and communities affected by crises actively contribute information, make quick decisions, influence authorities' actions, and collectively help those in need Assume the role of *first* responders in the immediate onset of a disaster
Citizen scientists	Specialized or subject-matter-experts that contribute to collective sense-making for complex information and evidence interpretation
Digital volunteers/ humanitarians	*Spontaneous*: Surface soon after a crisis occurs, more notable in large scale disasters *Digital*: Affiliated to an organization with defined tasks, not necessarily collaborating with official entities *Virtual operations support teams (VOST)*: Contribute and collaborate with outsourced information gathering through social media monitoring, information verification, and crisis mapping. Have an established organizational bond and structure within emergency management agencies before a crisis occurs
Crisis mgmt. authorities and humanitarian organizations	Typically responsible for crisis management, count with a command-and-control structure where operation center analysts or public information officers are at the core of the demanded tasks

The Decision Maker. Much of the literature contributes to understanding and developing techniques for improving decision making using social media data. However, the concept of the *decision maker* is barely explained as a social entity. From the decision making processes, it is inferred that they are the final consumer of information gathered by somlis practice [32] and the enabler of actions, resource distribution and dynamic objective setting [33]. The decision maker can be a sole individual, a team, or a system that combines social aspects with technology capabilities.

Technologists and Technology. The realization of objectives starts with information gathering [34] that is performed with tasks intrinsically related to technology such as filtering, early warning, or visualizations [35]. Thus, technologists play a vital but often overlooked role in the ecosystem as they influences the innovation, adaptation and acceptance of technologies into practice [25]. Software developers are usually placed outside of the core organizational structures [12].

The uniqueness of crisis events in terms of magnitude, location, and type of disaster makes it difficult to predict the quantity, accuracy, and quality of data that will become available in social media [1]. Moreover, human computation of social media data is limited, demanding automatic methods, namely extraction, organization, analysis, synthesis, visualization, and reporting [35]. Nevertheless, operations carry-on with imperfect information [1]. **Technology solutions and techniques are designed to address social media data characteristics to match crisis management needs.** However, as information requirements reach more profound levels of complexity and specificity, the design of tools to aid SoMLIS practices become more context and need dependent. As "[t]here are no universally adopted systems[...]; the use depends on context, system features, user expertise, funding for purchasing software, and a willingness to adopt new (and often experimental) technologies." [12]. **Technology approaches that seek to address SoMLIS challenges** are diverse, examples include:

- Processing content, handling information overload, classifying, and prioritizing types of information.
- Processing social media multimedia for damage identification.
- Multilingual and context specific options other than English language.

In practice, technology solutions employed in crisis management range from the adoption of tools intended for other purposes such as marketing, to custom made, or in-house developed solutions tailored to a specific context, organization, and stakeholder needs. Additional **methods and technological solutions continuously become available** as interest in social media use increases in research. However, most solutions focus on challenges experienced in the early onset of crises, particularly situational awareness and early-warning systems [36]. Only few studies focus on the continuous use of social media both during crisis and non-crisis periods [37] or the use of social media tools for other parts of the crisis management life-cycle (preparedness, recovery and long-term mitigation) [6].

With the wide availability of technology solutions some commonalities are identified. For example, the user interface is typically driven by a data visualization dashboard [35]. Behind the dashboards, the collection and filtering of information through algorithmic, artificial intelligence (AI), automatic classification, aggregation, machine learning, and deep learning techniques is carried out [9]. AI train themselves to handle specific tasks; regardless of the technique, data is preprocessed in a format understood by the mechanisms of processing and analysis [35].

There is increasing importance in processing data with **geolocation and location referencing features** that are thought to be easily automated [26]. The way solutions are created through computational methods is a combination of manual data processing and **supervised or unsupervised learning techniques** for algorithms [36]. The **robustness of technology solutions** lies in dynamically addressing as many data properties as possible, taking into account computational constraints [36].

Practitioners appreciate reporting and visualization mechanisms that present insights from social media data in a cohesive and understandable format tailored to the requirements of decision-making and subsequent actions [38]. Visual analytics, situation reports, and collaborative map displays are the preferred features to summarize findings from social media and other digital services in practice [12]. Thus, geo-located data displayed on a map, shifts in social media conversation over time, and the emergence of trends are the most popular features requested by practice.

Through the mechanisms of reporting and visualizing information emanating from social media, data seem more *digestible* for the reader [11]. Visualizations and maps act as a *one-stop-shop* for continuously updated information. Moreover, usability and compliance with local regulations on data privacy together with spatial data infrastructure are important [8] but add an aditional layer of complexity.

Situation reports are traditionally the avenue for decision making by keeping track of the development of crises and the activities of the organizations [39]. The format of reports and communication protocols is intrinsic to the organizational, crisis, and operational context, and calls for synergy among team members and data transmission standardizations [9]. Producing reports is time-consuming, involving the format of pre-specified information protocols within the decision making process [1]. These documents contain high-level information that might lack details [1]. Urgent situation-specific information is preferably accessed directly and immediately [39].

3.4 SoMLIS and Other Systems

Practitioners in crisis management traditionally rely on more trusted approaches such as physical sensors, population distribution data, or remote sensing data to fulfill crisis management tasks [37]. Therefore, SoMLIS practices commonly operate as separate entities within crisis management strategies [4]. Because social media data alone might lack depth and quality [36] and it is regarded as a non-authoritative source [4]. Relying exclusively on social media data poses a risk of possible assumptions about affected areas based on a generalized picture constructed from high content production that reflects high connectivity and wealth [13]. Therefore, low-resource areas are often ignored, and social inequalities are exacerbated. The voids of social media are commonly addressed through familiar methods such as community outreach [1].There is a need to integrate different sources of information [37] ideally through fusion methodologies with architectures for triangulation, verification, and management of uncertainty [34]. However, practices count with different sets of systems with specific uses that pose a challenge when integrating social media tasks at the intra and inter-organizational levels.

4 Discussion: The Building of an Ecosystem

Crisis management practitioners, solution developers, and academics recognize social media's value as an information source during crises and non-crisis periods. Still, challenges remain in adopting, integrating, and improving SoMLIS practices [4, 8].

We summarize our findings through a scalable model depicting the ecosystem where SoMLIS practice configurations emerge (Fig. 2). However, this model is conceptual, constructed from a network perspective that calls for further validation with empirical data. In the model, the different features previously explained are illustrated as entities which interaction contributes to the achievement of a common goal under a distinctive context. Contrasting the model with empirical data could complement and emphasize the role of context in the organizational, geographical, socio-economic, environmental, and technological fronts where practices are configured and enacted.

The starting point are the objectives to be fulfilled, which can be situational awareness, two-way conversations, early warning of events or continuous monitoring. Then, information requirements emerge, and sources of information are selected to satisfy those requirements. In this model, the *social media listening practice SoMLIS* (purple box) is the main focus; however, as referenced previously, different combinations and coordination with other information sources and organizations are encouraged for a holistic approach to satisfy the need for information (green box).

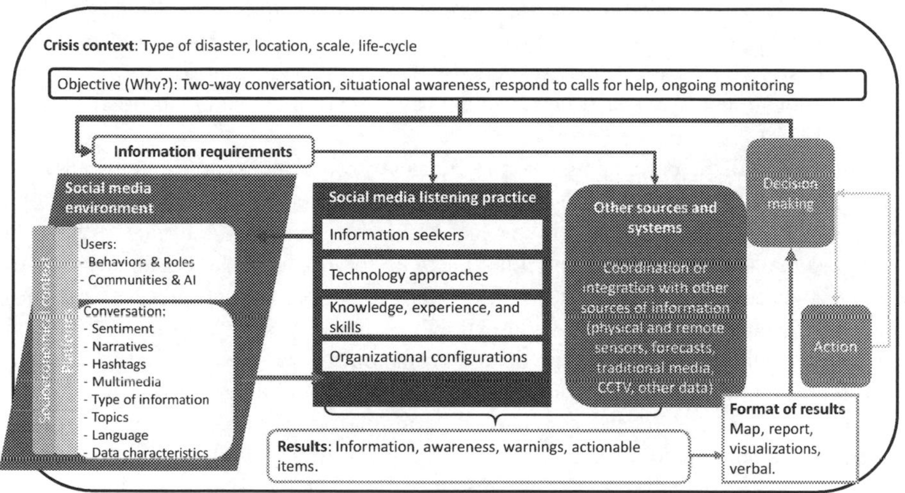

Fig. 2. The SoMLIS ecosystem in crisis management (Color figure online)

Within the SoMLIS practice, socio-technical configurations emerge through interconnections between technology software and methodologies, personnel in charge of social media tasks, organizational structures, professional networks, knowledge, experience, and craft both from technology and crisis management and legislation. Then the SoMLIS practice interacts with the *social media environment* (blue box) that is constantly producing descriptions of realities through text and multimedia content. The SoMLIS practice provides and input in the form of a query to the social media environment. The results of the query provide a data output for further processing. The quality of the query determines the quality of information harvested and processed [35]. Here, the relevance of the technology capabilities and experience of the staff in charge is reflected in the results. The harvested information is the basis for analysis, synthesis, and subsequent reporting of the data. From the literature, it is not clear *where* or *how* other sources of information converge. Therefore, we have illustrated this gap with a bracket as an aggregated, and arguably, ambiguous representation of the results produced from different sources. Results are then presented in a format tailored to the needs of the entities who need information, namely decision makers. Formatting and customizing the delivery and visualization of information is a necessary step before reaching decision making and subsequent action that in turn formulates objectives and new information requirements.

The SoMLIS practice is cyclical and navigates through periods of crises and non-crisis that respond to intrinsic characteristics given by a context (black line). The role of context goes beyond a box that encapsules practices and interactions as the properties of the ecosystem are assigned through context. For example, socio-economic, cultural, and political, aspects of the location of incidents are observed through the social media environment and manifested both online and offline. Characteristics of the crisis are intrinsic to the type of event and the impact on the affected community which can also be observed in the social media environment. The information that is processed, analyzed, and synthesized contains context embedded that informs decisions. Moreover, practice configurations themselves carry intrinsic environmental, technical, and organizational features [8].

Within SoMLIS, processing, classifying, analyzing, and synthesizing data from social media oscillates between automated and manual processes that respond to the requirements for information. The degree in which automation and manual tasks are optimized could depend on the interplay between the practice, the crisis, and the surrounding environment. Moreover, there is room for improvement and exploration of innovative avenues to aid information extraction, analysis, synthesis, and crisis management reporting. A research approach could include closer attention to the design of socio-technical systems starting with the requirements elicitation, analysis, testing, and evaluation of SoMLIS practices [27]. Where familiarity and experience with previous crisis management operations, technical solutions, training, guidelines, legislation, and processes compared against the temporality of crises are analyzed to optimally configure and re-configure practices.

Through a review of the academic literature that analyses practices of social media use in crisis management, we identified the entities that configure the SoMLIS practice. Then, we summarized our findings by proposing an ecosystem where the SoMLIS is situated in the middle. Our approach places entities and relationships within practice that acquire properties through the different realms or facets of context. Our results call for further validation and analysis with empirical data.

References

1. Tapia, A.H., Moore, K.: Good enough is good enough: overcoming disaster response organizations' slow social media data adoption. Comput. Support. Coop. Work (CSCW) **23**(4–6), 483–512 (2014). https://doi.org/10.1007/s10606-014-9206-1
2. Olteanu, A., Vieweg, S., Castillo, C.: What to expect when the unexpected happens: social media communications across crises. In: 18th ACM CSCW, 994–1009 (2015)
3. Hughes, A.L., Tapia, A.H.: Social media in crisis: when professional responders meet digital volunteers. JHSEM **12**(3), 679–706 (2015)
4. Ehnis, C., Bunker, D.: Repertoires of collaboration: incorporation of social media help requests into the common operating picture. Behav. Inf. Technol. **39**(3), 343–359 (2020)

5. Okoli, C., Schabram, K.: A guide to conducting a systematic literature review of information systems research (2010)
6. Anson, S., Watson, H., Wadhwa, K., Metz, K.: Analysing social media data for disaster preparedness: understanding the opportunities and barriers faced by humanitarian actors. Int. J. Disaster Risk Reduct. **21**, 131–139 (2017)
7. UNDRR: Sendai framework for disaster risk reduction 2015–2030. In: 3rd UN World Conference on DRR, 14–18 (2015)
8. Stieglitz, S., Mirbabaie, M., Fromm, J., Melzer, S.: The adoption of social media analytics for crisis management–challenges and opportunities. In: 26th ECIS 4 (2018)
9. Fathi, R., Thom, D., Koch, S., Ertl, T., Fiedrich, F.: VOST: a case study in voluntary digital participation for collaborative emergency management. Inf. Process. Manage. (2019)
10. Bruns, A., Stieglitz, S.: Quantitative approaches to comparing communication patterns on twitter. J. Technol. Hum. Serv. **30**(3–4), 160–185 (2012)
11. Reuter, C., Kaufhold, M.-A., Spahr, F., Spielhofer, T., Hahne, A.S.: Emergency service staff and social media – a comparative empirical study of the attitude by emergency services staff in Europe in 2014 and 2017. Int. J. Disaster Risk Reduct. **46**, 101516 (2020)
12. Hiltz, S.R., et al.: Exploring the usefulness and feasibility of software requirements for social media use in emergency management. Int. J. Disaster Risk Reduct. **42**, 1–14 (2020)
13. Burns, R.: Rethinking big data in digital humanitarianism: practices, epistemologies, and social relations. GeoJournal **80**(4), 477–490 (2014). https://doi.org/10.1007/s10708-014-9599-x
14. Cohen, H.: Social media definition: the guide you need to get results. In: Heidi Cohen: Actionable Marketing Guide, vol. 2020 (2020)
15. Pond, P.: The space between us: Twitter and crisis communication. IJDRBE **7**(1), 40–48 (2016)
16. Stieglitz, S.,et al.: Sensemaking and communication roles in social media crisis communication. Wirtschaftsinformatik (2017)
17. Meesters, K., van Beek, L., Van de Walle, B.: Help. The reality of social media use in crisis response: lessons from a realistic crisis exercise. In: 49th HICSS 2016, pp. 116–125 (2016)
18. Hughes, A.L., Palen, L.: The evolving role of the public information officer: an examination of social media in emergency management. JHSEM **9**(1) (2012)
19. Purohit, H., et al.: Identifying seekers and suppliers in social media communities to support crisis coordination. CSCW **23**(4–6), 513–545 (2014)
20. Reuter, C., Marx, A., Pipek, V.: Crisis management 2.0: towards a systematization of social software use in crisis situations. IJISCRAM **4**(1), 1–16 (2012)
21. Mirbabaie, M., Ehnis, C., Stieglitz, S., Bunker, D.: Communication roles in public events. In: Working Conference on Information Systems and Organizations, pp. 207–218 (2014)
22. Brachten, F., Mirbabaie, M., Stieglitz, S., Berger, O., Bludau, S., Schrickel, K.: Threat or opportunity? - Examining social bots in social media crisis communication. In: Australasian Conference on Information Systems (2018)
23. He, X., et al.: The signals and noise: actionable information in improvised social media channels during a disaster. In: ACM on Web Science Conference, 33–42 (2017)
24. Saleem, H.M., Xu, Y.S., Ruths, D.: Novel situational information in mass emergencies: what does twitter provide? Humanitarian Technol. Sci. Syst. Glob. Impact **78**, 155–164 (2014)
25. Olteanu, A., Vieweg, S., Castillo, C.: What to expect when the unexpected happens: social media communications across crises. In: 18th CSCW, 994–1009 (2015)
26. Vieweg, S., Hughes, A.L., Starbird, K., Palen, L.: Microblogging during two natural hazards events: what twitter may contribute to situational awareness. SIGCHI 1079–1088 (2010)
27. Kaufhold, M.-A., Rupp, N., Reuter, C., Amelunxen, C.: 112. Social: Design and evaluation of a mobile crisis app for bidirectional communication between emergency services and citizens. In: 26th ECIS (2018)

28. Power, R., Kibell, J.: The social media intelligence analyst for emergency management. In: 50th HICSS (2017)
29. Bonaretti, D., Piccoli, G.: Digital volunteers for emergency management: lessons from the 2016 central Italy earthquake. In: 24th AMCIS (2018)
30. Latonero, M., Shklovski, I.: Emergency management, twitter, and social media evangelism. IJISCRAM **3**(4), 1–16 (2011)
31. Purohit, H., Castillo, C., Imran, M., Pandey, R.: Ranking of social media alerts with workload bounds in emergency operation centers. In: IEEE/WIC/ACM International Conference on Web Intelligence, 206–213 (2018)
32. Backholm, K., et al.: Crises, rumours and reposts: rournalists' social media content gathering and verification practices in breaking news situations. Media Commun. **5**(2), 67–76 (2017)
33. Pogrebnyakov, N., Maldonado, E.: Didn't roger that: social media message complexity and situational awareness of emergency responders. IJIM **40**, 166–174 (2018)
34. Conrado, S.P., Neville, K., Woodworth, S., O'Riordan, S.: Managing social media uncertainty to support the decision making process during emergencies. J. Decis. Syst. **25**(1), 171–181 (2016)
35. Imran, M., Castillo, C., Diaz, F., Vieweg, S.: Processing social media messages in mass emergency: a survey. ACM CSUR **47**(4), 1–38 (2015)
36. Wang, Z., Ye, X.: Social media analytics for natural disaster management. Int. J. Geogr. Inf. Sci. **32**(1), 49–72 (2018)
37. Henriksen, H.J., et al.: Participatory early warning and monitoring systems: a Nordic framework for web-based flood risk management. Int. J. Disaster Risk Reduct. **31**, 1295–1306 (2018)
38. Calderon, N.A., Arias-Hernandez, R., Fisher, B.: Studying animation for real-time visual analytics: a design study of social media analytics in emergency management. In: 47th HICSS, 1364–1373 (2014)
39. Markenson, D., Howe, L.: American red cross digital operations center (DigiDOC): an essential emergency management tool for the digital age. Dis. Med. Public Health Preparedness **8**(5), 445–451 (2014)

#SDG13: Understanding Citizens Perspective Regarding Climate Change on Twitter

Prabhsimran Singh[1,3(✉)], Surleen Kaur[1,3], Yogesh K. Dwivedi[4,5], Sandeep Sharma[1,3], and Ravinder Singh Sawhney[2,3]

[1] Department of Computer Engineering and Technology, Guru Nanak Dev University, Amritsar, India
{prabhsimran.dcet,surleencse.rsh,sandeep.cse}@gndu.ac.in
[2] Department of Electronics Technology, Guru Nanak Dev University, Amritsar, India
sawhney.ece@gndu.ac.in
[3] Guru Nanak Dev University, Amritsar, India
[4] School of Management, Emerging Market Research Center (EMaRC), Swansea University, Swansea, UK
y.k.dwivedi@swansea.ac.uk
[5] Department of Management, Symbiosis Institute of Business Management, Pune & Symbiosis International (Deemed University), Pune, Maharashtra, India

Abstract. Earth, today is facing numerous environment related problems which have put a big question on the survival of the entire existence of humankind. Climate change is one of the most significant problems that are needed to be addressed by the present generation in order to safe guard the existence of our future generations. This research work explores the use of social media by the people across the world on discussions regarding the factors driving the climate change. The statistical analysis tools were applied on the collected data to get useful insights for our research objectives. The results obtained are indicative of the concerns raised by the people belonging to different strata of society from across the continents related to the causes of climate change on social media. Further, this research work confirms the fact that social media can be efficiently used to question the governmental policies on climate control by the citizens of any country and thus raising their voice against any climate related activity while leading to increased public participation towards policy making.

Keywords: Climate Action · Climate Change · SDG13 · Public Participation · Sustainable Development · Twitter Analytics

1 Introduction

Ever since the start of this millennium, due to the pressure exerted by the environmental agencies, the governments of many counties realized that the mankind in pursuit for industrial growth has already depleted a huge chunk of the natural forest resources available on this planet. This depletion has caused an immense harm to our environment

Published by Springer Nature Switzerland AG 2021
D. Dennehy et al. (Eds.): I3E 2021, LNCS 12896, pp. 723–733, 2021.
https://doi.org/10.1007/978-3-030-85447-8_60

thus endangering the life on the Earth while putting a big question on the survival for our future generations. More than 170 countries came together at the Earth-Summit in 1992 and raised a common consent to construct a concrete plan of action to continue with global socio-economic development but not at the cost of harm to climate and the term "sustainable development" was first coined (Parson et al. 1992). According to Brundtland Commission, sustainable development can be defined as a process of development which fulfils the requirements of the present keeping in check the necessities and demands of the future generations (Robert et al., 2005). Henceforth, the governments and environmental agencies of both developed as well as developing nations have been actively working hand-in-hand to accomplish UN's post-2015 Sustainable Development Goals (SDGs) for the greater good (UNDP 2021).

In total, there are 17 Sustainable Development Goals (SDGs) namely **SDG1:** End poverty in all its forms everywhere; **SDG2:** End hunger, achieve food security and improved nutrition and promote sustainable agriculture; **SDG3:** Ensure healthy lives and promote well-being for all at all ages; **SDG4:** Ensure inclusive and equitable quality education and promote lifelong learning opportunities for all; **SDG5:** Achieve gender equality and empower all women and girls; **SDG6:** Ensure availability and sustainable management of water and sanitation for all; **SDG7:** Ensure access to affordable, reliable, sustainable and modern energy for all; **SDG8:** Promote sustained, inclusive and sustainable economic growth, full and productive employment and decent work for all; **SDG9:** Build resilient infrastructure, promote inclusive and sustainable industrialization and foster innovation; **SDG10:** Reduce inequality within and among countries; **SDG11:** Make cities and human settlements inclusive, safe, resilient and sustainable; **SDG12:** Ensure sustainable consumption and production patterns; **SDG13:** Take urgent action to combat climate change and its impacts; **SDG14:** Conserve and sustainably use the oceans, seas and marine resources for sustainable development; **SDG15:** Protect, restore and promote sustainable use of terrestrial ecosystems, sustainably manage forests, combat desertification, and halt and reverse land degradation and halt biodiversity loss; **SDG16:** Promote peaceful and inclusive societies for sustainable development, provide access to justice for all and build effective, accountable and inclusive institutions at all levels; **SDG17:** Strengthen the means of implementation and revitalize the global partnership for sustainable development (UNDP 2021).

Out of these 17 SDGs, ***SDG13*** is one of the most talked and discussed goal (United Nations 2021). Climate change is indubitably the biggest threat to our planet Earth and to our goal of sustainable development (UNFCCC 2021). Ever since industrialization, globalization, urbanization gained pace, directly or indirectly it has proved extremely harmful for the global climate. As per United Nations, the previous decade i.e., 2010–2019 has been reported as the warmest decade ever with the year 2019 being recorded as the warmest year till date (UN 2021). Despite the endless efforts towards climate change mitigation, the levels of greenhouse gases, especially CO_2 were at record high in 2019. However, the year 2020 witnessed a fall in the levels but that was due to the worldwide economic slowdown as a result of ongoing COVID-19 pandemic. With the situation getting back to normal, once again a rise in the levels of greenhouse gases is expected. Already the average global temperature is over 1°C more than that in the 19th century and the collective worldwide emissions of CO_2 have increased by 50% after

1990 (United Nations India 2021). Without any stringent actions, the global temperature will have risen above 3°C by the end of 21st century (United Nations India 2021). This rapid climate change has already caused irreversible damage and is continuing to disrupt lives on Earth. Drastic changes in weather conditions, heat waves, natural disasters like floods, cyclones and draughts, loss of biodiversity, scarcity of water and food, rising sea levels, melting of glaciers, polluted air for breathing are some of the most alarming issues we are facing today (IAEA 2021; IISD 2021).

Drawing motivation from the above statements, this paper explores how people globally are discussing climate change (SDG13) on Twitter. The main objective of this research is to draw valuable insights from online discussions done by people with regards to climate change on Twitter. Rest of the paper is organized as following: Sect. 2 discusses a brief literature review along with hypothesis development. Section 3 provides in depth into the research methodology followed. Section 4 provides finding and results, followed by discussions in Sect. 4. Finally, we make concluding remarks in Sect. 5.

2 Literature Review and Hypothesis Development

This Section is divided into two sub-sections (a) Literature Review and (b) Hypothesis Development. The first sub-section presents a brief literature review regarding social media. In second sub-section, we discuss the hypothesis which forms the foundation of our research work.

2.1 Social Media

Social media especially Twitter has seen an exponential growth in last decade. Social media have become an integral part of our everyday life, as it enables us to discuss on wide range of topics ranging from elections (Grover et al. 2019; Singh et al. 2017), public policies (Harris et al. 2014; La et al. 2020), warning for natural disasters (Chatfield et al. 2013; Singh et al. 2019), social tensions (Burnap et al. 2015), diseases/pandemics (Singh et al. 2020c) etc. Social media provide us a virtual platform where people can share their view point with like-minded people globally, without any geographical barrier, that too free of cost (Kapoor et al. 2018; Singh et al. 2020a; Singh et al. 2020b).

Recently, people started using social media to create awareness among people on topics related to planet Earth like sustainable development goals including climate change (Cody et al. 2015; Williams et al. 2015; Pearce et al. 2019). However, most of the studies, focused upon applying text mining approaches particularly focusing upon sentiment analysis. Though, these studies were instrumental in providing textual information being discussed on social media. However, these studies failed to provide valuable insights regarding the discussions taking place on social media.

2.2 Hypothesis Testing

Our research focuses on four research questions (RQ) and we try to explore how Climate Change "#SDG13" and "SDG-13" is being used on Twitter, in order to get valuable insights regarding the discussions taking place on Twitter. Further, to statistically validate our RQ, we propose four hypothesis.

In RQ1, we explore that how SDG13 (climate change) is being discussed as compared to other SDGs on Twitter. To statistically validate RQ1, we propose the hypothesis H1.

RQ1: *How "#SDG13" and "#SDG-13" is being discussed on Twitter?*
H1: *The mean discussion on SDG13 and other SDGs is same on Twitter.*

There has been a lot of conversation on climate change among people on Twitter. However, the question remains, whether there is equal discussion on the problems arising from climate change and the possible solutions for climate change mitigation, which we try to examine through RQ2. To statistically validate RQ2, we propose the hypothesis H2.

RQ2: *Are people discussing the problems as well as their potential solutions regarding climate change on Twitter?*
H2: *The mean discussion on the problems and their potential solutions regarding climate change is same on Twitter.*

Climate action, in today's time, is no more a cause of concern only for the environmentalists and world organizations, it is affecting each and every being on Earth. Thus, in RQ3 we compare the discussions among people belong to different sections of society on Twitter. To statistically validate RQ3, we propose the hypothesis H3.

RQ3:*Which all sections of society are discussing "#SDG13" and "#SDG-13" on Twitter?*
H3:*The mean discussion involving different sections of our society is same on Twitter.*

In RQ4, we try to investigate whether the people from developed countries & developing countries are equally aware and how deeply invested they are in the discussion regarding the climate change on Twitter. To statistically validate RQ4, we propose the hypothesis H4.

RQ4:*Were the people globally discussing regarding "#SDG13" and "#SDG-13" on Twitter?*
H4:*The mean discussion on SDG13 from developed and developing countries is same on Twitter.*

Figure 1 presents pictorial representation of the conceptual concept being investigated in the study. Hashtag usage is given on one side (SDG13, SDG-13, ClimateAction, ClimateChange). While, on the other side measures like hashtag frequency, word frequency, user-type and geo-location is given. The proposed hypothesis, H1, H2, H3 and H4 explores the relationship between the two sides.

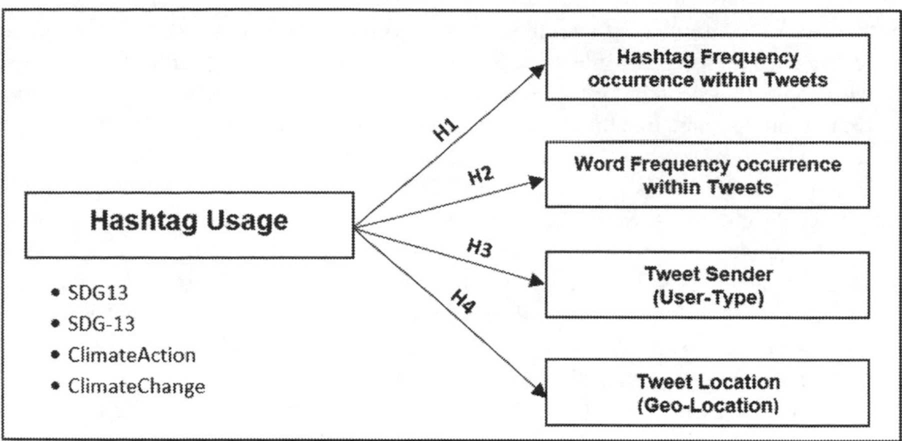

Fig. 1. Conceptual concept and investigated in the study

3 Research Methodology

To fulfil our research objectives, the entire process was divided three phases (data collection, data cleaning and data analysis). Phase-1, deals with data collection from Twitter, which was collected in an authenticated manner using Twitter API. For tweet collection, hashtags "#SDG13", "#SDG-13", "#ClimateAction" and "#ClimateChange" were used as search terms. Using these hashtags, a total of 45,874 tweets were collected from 32,715 unique senders over a period of five days (Feb 7, 2021 to Feb 11, 2021). Only the original/unique tweets were collected for analysis, and no retweet was considered for analysis. In phase-2, task of data cleaning was performed. Data cleaning is important in order to avoid any ambiguity in results (Naseem et al. 2020; Singh et al. 2018a). Finally, once data is cleaned, phase-3 comes into fray. In phase-3, statistical testing is performed in order to answer our research questions.

4 Findings and Results

In RQ1, we investigate how "#SDG13" and "#SDG-13" is being discussed on Twitter as compared to other SDGs? Hence, in this we compare the tweets associated with hashtag "#SDG13" with tweets associated with hashtags of all other SDGs. To answer RQ1, hypothesis H1 is formulated.

H1:*The mean discussion on SDG13 and other SDGs is same on Twitter.*

For H1, we apply one-way ANOVA on Tweets associated to 17 different SDGs. The results of ANOVA at 95% confidence, is F-Value = 7.37 and P = 1.47e-09. According to decision rule since, the value of $P < 0.05$, hence, H1 is rejected. This means that there exists significant difference between the one or more group (SDGs) in regards to discussion on Twitter.

Inference: As mentioned earlier, all SDGs are not discussed equally on social media. Some are discussed more, while some are discussed in association with others. Since, climate change is utmost important owing to extreme changes in weather conditions, heat waves, natural disasters like floods, cyclones and draughts, loss of biodiversity, scarcity of water and food, rising sea levels, melting of glaciers etc. Therefore, it is discussed more as compared to other SDGs, as found in our study. Further, Moreover, as we move towards sustainable development, SDG13 (climate action) cannot be regarded as a standalone goal, it is tightly coupled with various other goals namely SDG15 (life on land), SDG14 (life below water), SDG3 (good health & well-being), SDG7 (affordable and clean energy), SDG11 (sustainable cities and communities), SDG8 (decent work and economic growth), SDG1 (no poverty), SDG4 (Quality Education) where the developments of one largely impacts the progress of the others (IISD 2021).

Since, there has been a lot of conversation on climate change among people on Twitter. Hence, in RQ2 we examine, whether there is equal discussion on the problems arising from climate change and the possible solutions for climate change. To answer RQ2, hypothesis H2 is formulated.

H2:*The mean discussion on the problems and their potential solutions regarding climate change is same on Twitter.*

For H2, two-tail independent t-test was applied to the tweets. The results of two-tail independent t-test at 95% confidence, is T-Value = -0.31304 and P = 0.7593. According to decision rule since, the value of $P > 0.05$, hence, H3 is accepted. This means that there exists no significant difference between the discussion on the problems arising from climate change and the possible solutions for climate change.

Inference: People are discussing a lot of problems arising due to climate change on Twitter. These problems include rising temperature, food shortages, water scarcity, loss of biodiversity, extreme weather conditions, air pollution, rising sea levels, melting glaciers etc. But parallelly, groups of people are also discussing about the potential solutions of the climate change, that can not only help us but also our future generations. These solutions include renewable energy, internet of things (IoT), artificial intelligence (AI), improve education, awareness, green economy, cooperation among nations, capacity building, strengthening resilience etc. (Fathi et al. 2020; Sinha et al., 2019). These discussions highlight an important point that people are not only raising alarms by sharing problems associated with climate change but also providing potential changes that one should adapt to have a sustainable future.

Climate change is affecting each and every being on Earth. Therefore, in RQ3 we examine which all sections of our society are taking part in discussion regarding climate change. To answer RQ3, hypothesis H3 is formulated.

H3:*The mean discussion involving different sections of our society is same on Twitter.*

For H3, we apply one-way ANOVA on Tweets generated by different groups of our society. For ease of experimentation, we have bundled up these groups into following groups namely organizations (NGOs, government offices, non-profit organizations, societies), eminent personalities (politicians, ambassadors, UN-representatives, diplomats, bureaucrats, special envoys), activists (climate change activists, environmentalists, ecologists, social activists), journalists (media houses, news agencies, journalists, climate journalists), celebrities (actors, actress, singers) and general public.

The results of ANOVA at 95% confidence, is F-Value = 108 and P = 1.2e−15. According to decision rule since, the value of P < 0.05, hence, H3 is rejected. This means that there exists significant difference between the discussion done by various section of our society on climate change.

Inference: Though, climate change is affecting almost every section of our society and many groups are raising its voice on social media regarding climate change. However, the mean discussion of various groups varies, and its mainly general public which are the major contributor in Twitter discussion. Talking about various groups, many prominent personalities and organization are taking healthy participation in Twitter discussions. These includes organizations like UN Sustainable Development Group, International Institute for Sustainable development, United Nations Industrial Development Organization. Eminent personalities like Justin Trudeau, Manuel Pulgar Vidal and Malcolm Turnbull all raised their voice regarding climate change. Similarly, activists like Great Thunberg, Leah Namugerwa, Trisha Shetty, John Paul, Luisa Neubauer, Jake Horowitz and Holly Gillibrand were also part of Twitter discussion.

In RQ4, we try to investigate whether the people from developed countries & developing countries are equally participating in the discussion regarding the climate change on Twitter. To answer RQ4, hypothesis H4 is formulated.

H4:*The mean discussion on SDG13 from developed and developing countries is same on Twitter.*

For H4, two-tail independent t-test was applied to the tweets. The results of two-tail independent t-test at 95% confidence, is T-Value = 1.9864 and P = 0.05127. According to decision rule since, the value of P > 0.05, hence, H4 is accepted. This means that there exists no significant difference between the discussion involving developed and developing countries.

Inference: Given the importance of climate change, the entire world is facing problems that are affecting both developed as well as developing countries. Hence, people from both developed as well as developing countries are taking healthy part Twitter discussion on climate change in order to highlight the importance and immediate action need to be taken to combat it. Figure 2 shows the result of geo-location analysis (Singh et al. 2018b; Singh et al. 2019).

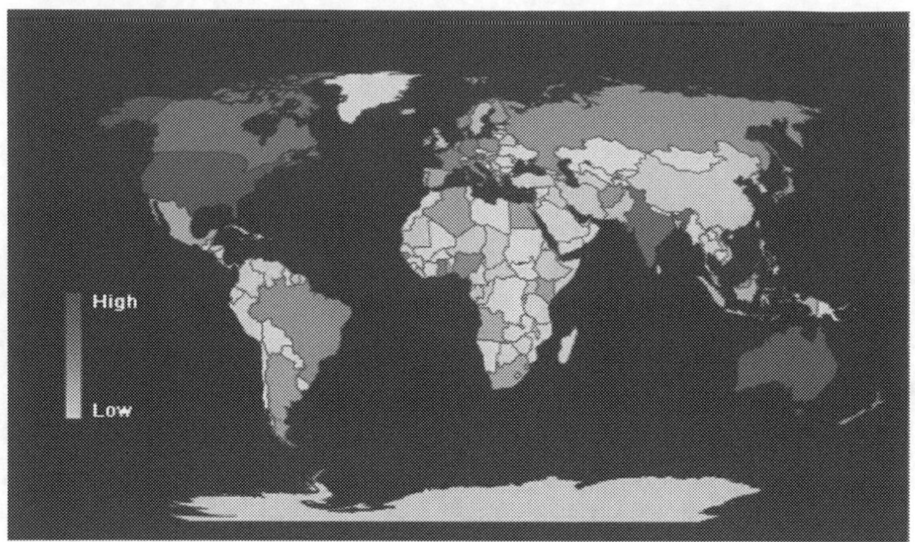

Fig. 2. Result of Geo-location Analysis

5 Discussion

Ever since environment activists started realizing the importance of climate change (SDG13) and all the dangers which may bring the current as well as future generations on the verge of doubts about their survival, various protocols and treaties have been agreed upon by the member countries of the United Nations Framework Convention on Climate Change (UNFCCC) for the collective good of our planet (Climate-Change-News 2019). This research work investigates how people globally are discussing climate change (SDG13) on Twitter and their reactions to the respective policies of their governments. Our results confirm that more and more public is becoming aware of climate deterioration and there is a continuous healthy discussion going on Twitter on climate change as well as the government policies on this issue. Further, when we discuss about SDG13, we need to be sure that it cannot be regarded as a standalone goal and it is tightly coupled with various other goals SDGs. Therefore, an integrated global action is required to increase awareness among people in this regard and both national as well as international policies, innovative strategies need to be implemented to achieve these goals (UNEP 2021).

5.1 Implications for Practice

The implication of the study for practice can be divided into two sub-sections (a) Government (b) Citizens and Activists. These sub-sections are discussed briefly below:

(a) **Government:** Any policy or project related to environment is issued by ministry of environment, forest and climate on behalf of the government. Though, governments of both developed as well as developing countries nowadays consider the recommendations of various bodies appointed to do proper feasibility study, the cost of project should not burden climate and environment. Still, most of the times some real issues are ignored that may lead to public resentment leading to agitations by the local population and thus leading to confrontation with the government. Hence, governments can take additional measures and invite people to vote in terms of their opinions either in favor or against these projects on social media platform. In this way government can utilize the public outlook before implementation of any project or policy that might affect the local climate in particular and national environment in general (Aladwani and Dwivedi 2018; Alryalat et al. 2017; Kar and Dwivedi 2020).

(b) **Citizens and Activists:** In this digital era, the social media have emerged as an important platform for the people to create awareness among the unknowns and raise a collected voice of the people on topics related to climate changes on the planet Earth. Whenever the people or the activists realized that certain activity or project would severely affect the local as well as national climate and could put human lives in danger, they had raised the banner of revolt and social media have assisted their cause (Rana et al. 2020). They may start a protest trend on the social media, which can soon be strengthened by many other like-minded people and non-government organizations, ultimately raising alarms for the government to rethink about the activity or project.

6 Conclusions

In this paper, we try to highlight the importance of sustainable development and analyze the overall perception of the people all around the world in this regard using Twitter data. Out of the seventeen sustainable development goals, goal number 13, which concerns the climate action (SDG13) has been observed to be of utmost importance and the most discussed goal among the masses throughout the world on Twitter. Our planet has suffered from environment deterioration and some unprecedented challenges in the past few decades and the people now are facing the direct impacts of these man-made catastrophes and hence it warrants for urgent climate action. The main aim of this research work to examine whether this climate change discussion is only limited to the people of some developed nations and a certain section of societies or it is equally discussed globally. It is clearly inferred from the results that not only the developed nations like Sweden, France, Germany, England, United Stated, Norway and Canada are working towards desired climate action; even the developing nations like India, Malaysia, African countries are equally participating. People from all over the world and from different backgrounds have become quite aware of the issues arising due to climate change and are raising their voices for resolving their concerns. There has been a constant debate and dialogue among nations regarding the climate problems that are been currently faced and will continue to face due to climate change; however, we have a long way to go before we have this issue well under control. Moreover, the accomplishment of various other sustainable development goals largely depends on climate action. Innovative solutions, national strategies, global cooperation among nations, stringent rules, awareness-drives, capacity-building are a few preliminary measures need to be implemented to achieve the set targets. The governments are shifting from use of fossil fuels to greener means like electric vehicle to cut down carbon emission and earn more carbon credits. In addition to these, the role of ICT is indispensable as we progress towards sustainability. Inclusion of technologies like internet of things and artificial intelligence can prove highly beneficial in achieving these goals in long run.

References

Rana, N.P., Luthra, S., Mangla, S.K., Islam, R., Roderick, S., Dwivedi, Y.K.: Barriers to the development of smart cities in Indian context. Inf. Syst. Front. **21**(3), 503–525 (2019)

Fathi, S., Srinivasan, R.S., Kibert, C.J., Steiner, R.L., Demirezen, E.: AI-based campus energy use prediction for assessing the effects of climate change. Sustainability **12**(8), 3223 (2020)

Sinha, A., Kumar, P., Rana, N.P., Islam, R., Dwivedi, Y.K.: Impact of internet of things (IoT) in disaster management: a task-technology fit perspective. Ann. Oper. Res. **283**(1–2), 759–794 (2017). https://doi.org/10.1007/s10479-017-2658-1

Kar, A.K., Dwivedi, Y.K.: Theory building with big data-driven research–Moving away from the "What" towards the "Why". Int. J. Inf. Manage. **54**, 102205 (2020)

Aladwani, A.M., Dwivedi, Y.K.: Towards a theory of SocioCitizenry: quality anticipation, trust configuration, and approved adaptation of governmental social media. Int. J. Inf. Manage. **43**, 261–272 (2018)

Alryalat, M.A.A., Rana, N.P., Sahu, G.P., Dwivedi, Y.K., Tajvidi, M.: Use of social media in citizen-centric electronic government services: a literature analysis. Int. J. Electron. Gov. Res. (IJEGR) **13**(3), 55–79 (2017)

Burnap, P., et al.: Detecting tension in online communities with computational Twitter analysis. Technol. Forecast. Soc. Chang. **95**, 96–108 (2015)

Chatfield, A.T., Scholl, H.J.J., Brajawidagda, U.: Tsunami early warnings via Twitter in government: net-savvy citizens' co-production of time-critical public information services. Gov. Inf. Quart. **30**(4), 377–386 (2013)

Climate-Change-News (2019). https://www.climatechangenews.com/2019/06/14/countriesnet-zero-climate-goal/

Cody, E.M., Reagan, A.J., Mitchell, L., Dodds, P.S., Danforth, C.M.: Climate change sentiment on Twitter: an unsolicited public opinion poll. PLoS ONE **10**(8), e0136092 (2015)

Grover, P., Kar, A.K., Dwivedi, Y.K., Janssen, M.: Polarization and acculturation in US Election 2016 outcomes–can twitter analytics predict changes in voting preferences. Technol. Forecast. Soc. Chang. **145**, 438–460 (2019)

Harris, J.K., Moreland-Russell, S., Choucair, B., Mansour, R., Staub, M., Simmons, K.: Tweeting for and against public health policy: response to the Chicago Department of Public Health's electronic cigarette Twitter campaign. J. Med. Internet Res. **16**(10), e238 (2014)

IAEA (2021). https://www.iaea.org/about/overview/sustainable-development-goals/goal-13-climate-action

IISD (2021). https://sdg.iisd.org/commentary/guest-articles/climate-action-and-sustainable-development-are-inseparable/

Kapoor, K.K., Tamilmani, K., Rana, N.P., Patil, P., Dwivedi, Y.K., Nerur, S.: Advances in social media research: past, present and future. Inf. Syst. Front. **20**(3), 531–558 (2018)

La, V.P., et al.: Policy response, social media and science journalism for the sustainability of the public health system amid the COVID-19 outbreak: the Vietnam lessons. Sustainability **12**(7), 2931 (2020)

Naseem, U., Razzak, I., Eklund, P.W.: A survey of pre-processing techniques to improve short-text quality: a case study on hate speech detection on twitter. Multimedia Tools Appl. 1–28 (2020)

Parson, E.A., Haas, P.M., Levy, M.A.: A summary of the major documents signed at the Earth Summit and the Global Forum. Environ. Sci. Policy Sustain. Dev. **34**(8), 12–36 (1992)

Pearce, W., Niederer, S., Özkula, S. M., Sánchez Querubín, N.: The social media life of climate change: Platforms, publics, and future imaginaries. Wiley Interdiscipl. Rev. Climate Change **10**(2), e569 (2019)

Robert, K.W., Parris, T.M., Leiserowitz, A.A.: What is sustainable development? Goals, indicators, values, and practice. Environ. Sci. Policy Sustain. Dev. **47**(3), 8–21 (2005)

Singh, J.P., Dwivedi, Y.K., Rana, N.P., Kumar, A., Kapoor, K.K.: Event classification and location prediction from tweets during disasters. Ann. Oper. Res. **283**(1–2), 737–757 (2017a). https://doi.org/10.1007/s10479-017-2522-3

Singh, P., Dwivedi, Y.K., Kahlon, K.S., Pathania, A., Sawhney, R.S.: Can twitter analytics predict election outcome? An insight from 2017 Punjab assembly elections. Gov. Inf. Quart. **37**(2), 101444 (2020a)

Singh, P., Dwivedi, Y.K., Kahlon, K.S., Sawhney, R.S., Alalwan, A.A., Rana, N.P.: Smart monitoring and controlling of government policies using social media and cloud computing. Inf. Syst. Front. **22**(2), 315–337 (2020b)

Singh, P., Kahlon, K.S., Sawhney, R.S., Vohra, R., Kaur, S.: Social media buzz created by# nanotechnology: insights from Twitter analytics. Nanotechnol. Rev. **7**(6), 521–528 (2018a)

Singh, P., Sawhney, R.S., Kahlon, K.S.: Predicting the outcome of Spanish general elections 2016 using Twitter as a tool. In: Singh, D., Raman, B., Luhach, A.K., Lingras, P. (eds.) Advanced Informatics for Computing Research. CCIS, vol. 712, pp. 73–83. Springer, Singapore (2017b). https://doi.org/10.1007/978-981-10-5780-9_7

Singh, P., Sawhney, R.S., Kahlon, K.S.: Sentiment analysis of demonetization of 500 & 1000 rupee banknotes by Indian government. ICT Express **4**(3), 124–129 (2018b)

Singh, P., Singh, S., Sohal, M., Dwivedi, Y.K., Kahlon, K.S., Sawhney, R.S.: Psychological fear and anxiety caused by COVID-19: insights from Twitter analytics. Asian J. Psychiatry **54**, 102280 (2020c)

UN (2021). https://www.un.org/sustainabledevelopment/climate-change/

UNDP (2021). https://www.undp.org/content/undp/en/home/sustainable-development-goals.html

UNEP (2021). https://www.unep.org/explore-topics/sustainable-development-goals/why-do-sustainable-development-goals-matter/goal-13

UNFCCC (2021). https://unfccc.int/topics/action-on-climate-and-sdgs/action-on-climate-and-sdgs

United Nations (2021). https://www.un.org/development/desa/dpad/wp-content/uploads/sites/45/Note-SDGs-VNRs.pdf

United Nations India (2021). https://in.one.un.org/page/sustainable-development-goals/sdg-13/

Williams, H.T., McMurray, J.R., Kurz, T., Lambert, F.H.: Network analysis reveals open forums and echo chambers in social media discussions of climate change. Global Environ. Change **32**, 126–138 (2015)

Teaching and Learning

A Multi-level Analysis of Mistrust/Trust Formation in Algorithmic Grading

Stephen Jackson[1(✉)] and Niki Panteli[2,3]

[1] Ontario Tech University, Oshawa, ON L1G 0C5, Canada
stephen.jackson@uoit.ca
[2] Royal Holloway, Egham TW20 0EX, Surrey, UK
niki.panteli@rhul.ac.uk
[3] Norwegian University of Science and Technology, Trondheim, Norway

Abstract. While the concept of trust continues to grow in importance among information systems (IS) researchers and practitioners, an investigation of mistrust/trust for- mation in algorithmic grading across multiple levels of analysis has so far been under researched. This paper proposes a multi-level model for analyzing the for- mation of mistrust/trust in algorithmic grading. More specifically, the model ex- amines multiple levels at play by considering how top-down forces may stimulate mistrust/trust at lower levels, but also how lower-level activity can influence mis- trust/trust formation at higher levels. We briefly illustrate how the model can be applied by drawing on the case of the Advanced Level student fiasco in the United Kingdom (UK) that came to head during August 2020, whereby an algorithm was used to determine student grades. Although the paper positions trust as a multifaceted concept, it also acknowledges the importance of researchers to be mindful of issues pertaining to emergence, duality, context, and time.

Keywords: Trust · Mistrust · Algorithmic grading · Multi-level analysis · Multi-level theory

1 Introduction

There has been growing interest in the development and use of computerized algorithmic grading within the educational sector [1]. Put simply, algorithmic grading can be defined as a set of rules or procedures undertaken by computerized systems that can be used to perform calculations or problem solving to assist with student grade prediction. Proponents have acknowledged the potential benefits of artificial intelligence (AI) and algorithms in education for speeding up marking, standardizing the grading process, driving through improvements in efficiencies and forecasting, as well as freeing up instructors marking time to concentrate on other value-added activities [2, 3].

On the other hand, concerns have also been raised. By placing increased control in a set of computerized rules and norms may lead to tutors doubting their own professional expertise, judg- ments and opinions, as well as feeling somehow negatively constrained,

Published by Springer Nature Switzerland AG 2021
D. Dennehy et al. (Eds.): I3E 2021, LNCS 12896, pp. 737–743, 2021.
https://doi.org/10.1007/978-3-030-85447-8_61

if not alienated [4, 5]. As algorithmic grading develops through time, particularly with advances in AI, this may shape and, in cases, raise the expectations of tutors into believing that these new breeds of applications can provide a more reliable, accurate and fairer tool for marking over traditional methods.

Additionally, the increased reliance on computerized grading tools may ignore or downplay other important contextual factors that can influence student performance at particular points in time. Concerns have also been raised in relation to the overall effectiveness of AI-based grading algorithms in the electronic age. Parsons [6], for instance, reported how US students were able to outwit the AI algorithm used to assign assessment grades. Realizing that the algorithm was merely scanning a series of keywords based on the topic of the assessment, students were able to "game the system" by inserting keywords, rather than provide a detailed and comprehensive answer.

While the use of algorithms has the potential to bring educational benefits, the extent to which the educational sector can truly harness AI and algorithms for marking and other educational purposes is still not clear and evolving [7, 8]. One important issue that lies at the very heart of computerized applications, affecting how they are successfully used and deployed, is trust. Li *et al.* [9], based on the work of Mayer *et al.* [10], define trust as the "willingness of a party to be vulnerable to the actions of another party based on the expectation that the other will perform a particular action important to the trustor, irrespective of the ability to monitor or control that other party". Siau and Wang [11] acknowl edged that trust is an essential element in building relations and for nurturing user acceptance. The authors stress that in the case of AI "both initial trust formation and continuous trust development deserve special attention". In a similar vein, Gille *et al.* [12] note "trust is a critical determinant of the successful adoption of AI".

Although the physical aspects of AI-based technologies, including how it performs and func- tions, can affect trust formation [13], what must also be considered is how those responsible for developing and deploying AI can influence the trust creation process [11]. A high degree of trust, as a confident and optimistic anticipation in the actions and behavior of another stakeholder, can facilitate integrity and transparency. In conditions of vagueness or when operating under a situation of incomplete information and knowledge, the establishment of trust between stakeholders becomes an ever-important element for reducing complexity and nurturing openness [14–17]. The importance of trust is further accentuated by its absence and its replacement with mistrust which weakens and jeopardizes relationships [18]. Mistrust can have an unconstructive impact on building a culture conducive to AI use, promoting values of suspicion and protectiveness [19]. Furthermore, it has been acknowledged that if trust is not evident, this can make the use and adoption of technology more difficult to attain [20–23].

Regardless of the importance of trust in the adoption and use of AI and technology in general, our understanding of mistrust/trust in relation to the study of algorithmic grading from a multi- level analysis has been limited. It is our position that with the increasing popularity of AI for educational purposes, this issue requires further attention. This paper acknowledges that in order for researchers to understand how mistrust/trust influences algorithmic grading uptake and use, among other forms of AI, the focus of attention needs to shift from solely concentrating on just one level to also understanding the multi-faceted and dynamic nature of trust across multiple levels.

In what follows, we present the case of the Advanced (A) Level AI application to determine student grades in August 2020 in the United Kingdom. Drawing on this case, we introduce a model based on multi-level theory.

2 The Case of the A-Level Exam Algorithm

In the year 2020, the COVID-19 pandemic caused an unprecedented disruption to the educational sector worldwide, contributing to the redesign of learning and assessment systems [24]. Faced with a tough decision, The Office of Qualifications and Examinations Regulation (Ofqual) in the UK had to decide how best to predict student A-Level grades due to the problems caused by the COVID-19 pandemic that prevented students from physically sitting their exams [25].

A-Level grades play a major part in determining university admissions, as well as direct routes into employment and apprenticeships. As the reliance on student grade predictions by teachers may have run the risk of grade inflation, it was decided to use an algorithm to calculate grades. According to the BBC [26] "Teachers were asked to supply for each pupil for every subject: an estimated grade and a ranking compared with every other pupil at the school within that same estimated grade. These were put through an algorithm, which also factored in the school's per- formances in each subject over the previous three years. The idea was that the grades this year - even without exams - would be consistent with how schools had done in the past".

However, the algorithm wreaked havoc in that it downgraded tens of thousands of students. When the results were announced in August 2020, almost 40% of grades in Wales, Northern Ireland and England were lower than the predictions provided by teachers. What became apparent was that the algorithm affected students from state schools more than those from private schools. In other words, students from poorer backgrounds were more likely to receive lower grades than those from areas that are more affluent. A major reason for this was that the algorithm took into consideration the historical performance of the school. However, as put by Elbanna and Engesmo [27] "...data about the past doesn't necessarily help you make adequate decisions about the present or the future. It blocks any chances of change and development – like when a school improves its teaching or one year group of students performs better than their peers in previous years". Therefore, a good student who was from a school that underachieved may likely have his/her grades downgraded. Even though the UK government initially presented the AI system as "robust", within a few days and following public uproar, it made a u-turn and abolished the system reversing to teacher assessment instead [26].

3 Conceptual Multi-level Model and Application

The proposed model is based on multi-level theory [28–30]. The model was formulated out of the concern that researchers tend to study one level, rather than accounting for multiple levels. A key assumption is that considering the phenomena of interest from just one level, can potentially, although not always, lead to a restrictive view. As trust is fundamentally about interrelated social relations, it is difficult not to consider trust as consisting of social relations influenced by other social relations (levels).

For this reason, a multi-level model which considers government, organizational, group and individual factors across different stages of AI development and use, is useful as it can be applied to understand the multi-faceted nature of mistrust/trust, particularly the dynamic interplay be- tween macro and micro levels. The government level of analysis considers the structure and na- ture of the political/government system and how this can influence the AI trust enactment pro- cess. At the organizational level, the focus is on the way company size, culture, values and prac- tices foster trust or mistrust in AI. At the group level, individuals may group together to share common values, beliefs and assumptions regarding trust and AI. Trust at the individual layer reflects the values of oneself. This may include the personal values, beliefs, attitudes and preju- dices which users have towards AI. An overview of the proposed model is shown in Fig. 1.

Fig. 1. Conceptual model

Higher-level activity can shape and influence trust formation at lower levels, but lower levels may in turn influence trust development at higher levels. The influence at various levels is best considered as dynamic and changing. Not only does the proposed model bridge macro and micro levels, but also the situational context that gives rise to trust/mistrust should not be neglected. Our position is that these influences should take place as part of a co-creative effort rather than at separate stages as it was the case with the A-level AI example.

Drawing on Fig. 1, top-down forces at play e.g., government policies, procedures and prac- tices can influence the formation of mistrust/trust among lower-level activity, enabling or con- straining the actions of groups and individuals. In the case of the A-Level grading controversy, the use of the Ofqual algorithm to predict grades, the inclusion of the schools past performance over 3 years, as well as not basing grades solely on teacher predicted grades, reinforced a con- straining environment at lower levels [31, 32]. Many students, because of their grades being downgraded, lost their university place and blamed the government for playing with their future. Students, teachers, parents and politicians united in opposition, as exemplified through protests and gatherings, raising fundamental concerns about the fairness, bias and accuracy surrounding the algorithm. The situation that emerged within a very short period of time, at both the group and individual levels, was one of uncertainty and mistrust [31].

The model also captures how emergent forms of action and behavior from lower levels can shape and influence changes at the higher level, including trust development processes. While the government initially defended its use of an algorithm to determine grades as being dependable and accurate, in the face of increased scrutiny, it was announced that the algorithm had short- comings and was not as reliable as first envisioned. Indeed, the Prime Minister Boris Johnston later referred to it as a "mutant algorithm" [33]. As opposition to the flawed algorithm grew, the government decided to make a u-turn and it was revealed that grades would be awarded based on teachers' recommendations [34]. Although awarding student grades based solely on teacher grade predictions was initially disregarded by Ofqual on the basis of being unfair, lower-level activity reinforced a reversal of norms and policies, as well as readjustment of trust development processes and procedures at the upper-level. More explicitly, rather than placing unbridled trust in the use of algorithms for grade predictions, trust was now placed in the hands of humans (teachers) – a practice which the government would continue to enact the following year. As Education Secretary Gavin Williamson noted in January 2021 "this year we're going to put our trust in teachers rather than algorithms" [35].

4 Concluding Thoughts

This short paper set out to investigate mistrust/trust formation in the context of algorithmic grad- ing by drawing briefly on the UK A-Level grades debacle in summer 2020. While the study of trust and computerized applications represents a growing and important area of inquiry, research on algorithmic grading and issues pertaining to mistrust/trust are still at a nascent stage and much remains to explore these issues in greater depth. Comprehending how these two areas fuse to- gether is an important endeavor and may reveal unique insights not previously known or ex- plored. As a way of advancing our understanding of trust in relation to the adoption of algorithms, as well as other forms of AI, Robotics and Machine Learning, there is increased need for studies to investigate further its dynamic and multi-faceted nature, how trust emerges across multiple levels, as well as remaining sensitive to emergence, context, dynamism, and change.

References

1. Kabudi, T., Pappas, I., Olsen, D.H.: AI-enabled adaptive learning systems: a systematic mapping of the literature. Comput. Educ. Artif. Intell. **2**, 1–12 (2021)
2. Goel, A.K., Joyner, D.A.: Using AI to teach AI: lessons from an online AI class. AI. Mag. **38**(2), 48–59 (2017)
3. Khare, K., Stewart, B., Khare, A.: Artificial intelligence and the student experience: an institutional perspective. IAFOR. J. Educ. **6**(3), 63–78 (2018)
4. Guskey, T.R., Jung, L.A.: Grading: Why you should trust your judgment. Educ. Leadersh. **73**(7), 50 (2016)
5. Kolchenko, V.: Can modern AI replace teachers? Not so fast! Artificial intelligence and adaptive learning: personalized education in the AI age. HAPS. Educ. **22**(3), 249–252 (2018)

6. Parsons, J.: Students figure out how to cheat AI grading algorithm (2021). https://metro.co.uk/2020/09/04/students-figure-out-how-to-cheat-ai-grading-algorithm-13222401/. Accessed 05 May 2021
7. Popenici, S.A.D., Kerr, S.: Exploring the impact of artificial intelligence on teaching and learning in higher education. Res. Pract. Technol. Enhanced Learn. **12**(1), 1–13 (2017). https://doi.org/10.1186/s41039-017-0062-8
8. Schiff, D.: Out of the laboratory and into the classroom: the future of artificial intelligence in education. AI Soc. **36**(1), 331–348 (2020). https://doi.org/10.1007/s00146-020-01033-8
9. Li, X., Hess, T.J., Valacich, J.S.: Why do we trust new technology? A study of initial trust formation with organizational information systems. J. Strateg. Inf. Syst. **17**(1), 39–71 (2008)
10. Mayer, R., Davis, J., Schorman, F.: An integrative model of organizational trust. Acad. Manage. J. **20**(3), 709–734 (1995)
11. Siau, K., Wang, W.: Building trust in artificial intelligence, machine learning and robotics. Cut. IT. J. **31**(2), 47–53 (2018)
12. Gille, F., Jobin, A., Ienca, M.: What we talk about when we talk about trust: theory of trust for AI in healthcare. Artif. Intell. Med. **1**, 1–3 (2020)
13. Sethumadhavan, A.: Trust in artificial intelligence. Ergon. Des. **27**(2), 34 (2019)
14. Adler, P.: Market, hierarchy and trust: the knowledge economy and the future of capitalism. Organ. Sci. **12**(2), 215–234 (2001)
15. Currall, S., Judge, T.: Measuring trust between organization boundary role persons. Organ. Behav. Hum. Decis. Process. **64**(2), 151–170 (1995)
16. Fukuyama, F.: Trust: The Social Virtues and the Creation of Prosperity. Penguin, London (1996)
17. Inkpen, A.: Creating Knowledge through Collaboration. Calif. Manage. Rev. **39**(1), 123–140 (1996)
18. Luhmann, N.: Trust and Power. John Wiley and Sons, London (1979)
19. Jackson, S., Panteli, N.: Trust in the era of artificial intelligence: a multi-layer analysis. In: Proceedings of the 34th Annual British Academy of Management Conference, pp. 1–6 (2020)
20. Jackson, S.: Organizational culture and information systems adoption: a three-perspective approach. Inf. Organ. **21**(2), 57–83 (2011)
21. Mohr, H., Walter, Z.: Formation of consumers' perceived information security: examining the transfer of trust in online retailers. Inf. Syst. Front. **21**, 1231–1250 (2019)
22. Sharma, S., Sharma, M.: Examining the role of trust and quality dimensions in the actual usage of mobile banking services: an empirical investigation. Int. J. Inf. Manage. **44**, 65–75 (2019)
23. Wagner, E., Newell, S.: Repairing ERP: producing social order to create a working information system. J. Appl. Behav. Anal. **42**(1), 40–57 (2006)
24. Pappas, I.O., Giannakos, M.N.: Rethinking learning design in IT education during a pandemic. Front. Educ. **6**, 103 (2021)
25. An algorithm determined UK students' grades. Chaos ensued (2020). https://www.wired.com/story/an-algorithm-determined-uk-students-grades-chaos-ensued/. Accessed 08 May 2021
26. A-levels and GCSEs: How did the exam algorithm work? (2020). https://www.bbc.co.uk/news/explainers-53807730. Accessed 08 May 2021
27. A-level results: why algorithms get things so wrong – and what we can do to fix them (2020). https://theconversation.com/a-level-results-why-algorithms-get-things-so-wrong-and-what-we-can-do-to-fix-them-142879. Accessed 08 May 2021
28. Erez, M., Gati, E.: A dynamic, multi-level model of culture: from the micro level of the individual to the macro level of a global culture. Appl. Psychol. **53**(4), 583–598 (2004)
29. Klein, K., Kozlowski, S.: Multilevel Theory, Research, and Methods in Organizations: Foundations. Extensions and New Directions, San Francisco (2000)

30. Lumineau, F., Schilke, O.: Trust development across levels of analysis: an embedded-agency perspective. J. Trust. Res. **8**(2), 238–248 (2018)
31. Why did the A-level algorithm say no? (2020). https://www.bbc.com/news/education-53787203. Accessed 07 May 2021
32. "F**k the algorithm"? What the world can learn from the UK's A-level grading fiasco (2020). https://blogs.lse.ac.uk/impactofsocialsciences/2020/08/26/fk-the-algorithm-what-the-world-can-learn-from-the-uks-a-level-grading-fiasco/#comments. Accessed 08 May 2021
33. 'Mutant algorithm': boring B-movie or another excuse from Boris Johnson? (2020). https://www.theguard-ian.com/books/2020/sep/03/mutant-algorithm-boring-b-movie-or-another-excuse-from-boris-johnson. Accessed 08 May 2021
34. UK government makes dramatic exam results U-turn after national outcry (2020). https://www.cnn.com/2020/08/17/europe/uk-school-exams-coronavirus-gbr-intl/index.html. Accessed 08 May 2021
35. Exams in England will be replaced by school-based assessments, says Gavin Williamson (2021). https://www.standard.co.uk/news/education/gavin-williamson-a-levels-gsces-remote-learning-b719481.html. Accessed 08 May 2021

Computational Numeracy (CN) for Under-Prepared, Novice Programming Students

Carla Coetzee(✉) and Machdel Matthee

Department of Informatics, University of Pretoria, Pretoria, South Africa
CoetzeeC@tut.ac.za, machdel.matthee@up.ac.za

Abstract. Numeracy has become a critically important skill in data rich environments. A large number of first-year ICT students entering HEIs in South Africa lack computational thinking and problem-solving skills and consequently they are not prepared for programming. Many of these students are not proficient enough in numeracy to solve programming problems that require knowledge and understanding of numeracy concepts. A new concept, Computational Numeracy (CN) for under-prepared, novice programming students, is presented in this article. The purpose of this conceptual article is to show how the components of Computational Numeracy were developed by exploring and reviewing its basic building blocks: computational thinking and numeracy. A critical synthesis of published research related to numeracy and computational thinking related to programming skills to define Computational Numeracy for under-prepared, novice programming students, is presented. Six components of computational thinking were selected and mapped to numeracy in a typical programming problem to demonstrate the links between computational thinking and numeracy and how it can be seen as CN. Future research includes the development of a framework to guide lecturers at HEIs on how to teach CN to under-prepared, novice program ming students.

Keywords: Numeracy · Computational thinking · Programming · Computational numeracy · Under-prepared ICT students

1 Introduction

To interpret numbers, graphs and other statistical data, numeracy skills are becoming increasingly important in the 21st century economy. In adults' daily lives, essential tasks such as shopping for groceries, using recipes, balancing budgets, and doing home improvements, the importance of numeracy skills cannot be underestimated. One of the more frequently used, concise definitions of numeracy states that numeracy is the *"ability to access, use, interpret and communicate quantitative information and ideas, in order to engage in and manage the quantitative demands of a range of situations in adult life"* [1:48]. Therefore, it can be concluded that adults are dependent on basic numeracy.

Published by Springer Nature Switzerland AG 2021
D. Dennehy et al. (Eds.): I3E 2021, LNCS 12896, pp. 744–756, 2021.
https://doi.org/10.1007/978-3-030-85447-8_62

In Steen's seminal publication about quantitative literacy (numeracy), they distinguish between numeracy and mathematics and argued that *"Numeracy is not the same as mathematics, nor is it an alternative to mathematics. Mathematics is abstract and Platonic, offering absolute truths about relations among ideal objects. Numeracy is concrete and contextual, offering contingent solutions to problems about real situations. Whereas mathematics asks students to rise above context, quantitative literacy is anchored in the messy contexts of real life. Truly, today's students need both mathemat ics and numeracy."* [2:1].

It is widely believed that mathematics is the most appropriate subject for developing problem-solving and numeracy skills, even though this is usually not the case [3–5]. Traditional mathematics taught in schools, inadequately prepare students for the quantitative nature of life in the twenty-first century [2]. As far back as 1990, it was recommended that mathematics at school level should develop students' numeracy skills, also referred to as quantitative reasoning, to understand the relationships between mathematics and "real-life situations" [6].

Competencies in basic numeracy and mathematics are regarded as essential for computer science students [7]. Learners often leave school, lacking the basic mathematical and numeracy skills that are required in tertiary programming modules forming part of ICT courses [8]. A significant percentage of South African learners lack the mathematical proficiency needed for tertiary studies [9]. It could be argued that the lack of mathematics proficiency ultimately influences students' numeracy skills. The poor quality of mathematics education in South African schools potentially restrict learners' prospects in terms of further education and training, and more specifically, their access to ICT qualifications which includes programming subjects [10, 11]. More importantly, researchers predict that the cognitive strategies or problem-solving skills underlying programming, also called computational thinking, will become pervasive in all disciplines and walks of life [12].

There is a strong relationship between the problem-solving skills needed for programming and computational thinking skills. Problem-solving skills, which include computational thinking skills, are essential for programming students [13]. One of the definitions of computational thinking which is frequently quoted is the following: *"Computational Thinking is the process of formulating problems and transforming them into computational steps and algorithms."* [14:832].

The layout of the paper is as follows: Section two provides the research objective followed by an overview of the concept Computational thinking (section three) and Numeracy (Sect. 4). In section five, the concept CN is developed followed by an illustration of it in Sect. 6. The paper concludes by suggesting further research to be undertaken including the development of a CN teaching framework to empower lecturers to incorporate the concepts in their teaching.

2 Research Objective

This article addresses the following research question: What is meant by CN for under-prepared, novice programming students? A literature review was conducted to answer the research question and to provide a critical synthesis of published research related to numeracy and computational thinking related to programming skills. The definition of Computational Numeracy for under-prepared, novice programming students, is presented in Sect. 4.

3 Computational Thinking

Research in the field of Computational Thinking (CT) is most often aligned with Computing Education Research (CER), including programming education [15]. The development of CT as a research topic spans several decades, beginning in the 1960s and extending to the present, but in a seminal article, published in 2006, the author reimagined the older definitions of the concept [16]. The majority of CT publications and research originated in the US and were published in two waves over the years between 2006 and 2012 followed by the second wave which started in 2013 [15].

The well-known author, Wing, believes computational thinking is not just for computer scientists but for everyone, and she believes it should be taught at the same level of importance as reading, writing, and doing arithmetic [16].

A group of authors identified 59 definitions for CT and reasons that CT is a 21st century skill which enables individuals to solve problems in their daily lives [17]. One of the definitions in literature states that CT is *"essentially a framework for defining a set of critical reasoning and problem-solving skills"* [18]. Some authors concur that and define CT as the path followed from the original problem description, the development of an algorithm and finally the final stages of finding and evaluating a solution [18, 19].

The components, strategies, or stages, of CT vary in the literature and include the following: Abstraction; Algorithmic Thinking or Algorithms; Automation; Decompositions or Problem Decomposition; Pattern Recognition; Parallelisation; Simulation; Analysis; Debugging; Evaluation; and Generalisation [12, 16, 20–27]. We must add that CT requires us to use critical thinking and is embedded in the fundamental principles of computer science (programming) that can be applied in a range of subject areas [28, 29]. Some, or all, of the above components of computational thinking could be included in the final operational definition of CN.

4 Numeracy

The main objective of numeracy, also referred to as quantitative literacy, adult numeracy and even quantitative reasoning, is to be able to understand (basic) mathematics in real-life contexts [30]. Furthermore, it can be said that school mathematics competencies should include numeracy concepts to prepare learners for a variety of quantitative contexts in real-life [31].

In South Africa, the NBT Quantitative Literacy (NBT QL) test is written by school-leavers to determine the level of numeracy and to provide HEIs with supplementary information that could be used for selection and placement of students as well as academic support to newcomer students [32]. The tests assess school-leaving higher education applicants with the objective to address the following question: *"What is the academic literacy, quantitative literacy [numeracy] and mathematics levels of proficiencies of the school-leaving population, who wish to continue with higher education, at the point prior to their entry into higher education at which they could realistically be expected to cope with the demands of higher education study?"* [32:2].

Each one of the three tests were developed, based on constructs relevant to the specific domain, to address the above question with levels of proficiency as the primary focus. The NBT QL test assesses candidates' ability to solve problems in a real context that is relevant to higher education study while using basic quantitative information, the information could be represented verbally, graphically, in tables or by symbols.

The need for numeracy intervention is evident when the NBT QL results in 2020 of 511 first-year ICT (diploma) students, at a South African University of Technology (from now on referred to as University X), are considered. Only one of the 511 students was considered proficient whereas 96% of the students were in the basic (results less than 34%) and lower intermediate bands (results from 34% to 49%). Students in the Lower Intermediate band will not cope if not placed in extended programmes. Students in the Basic band have serious learning challenges and should be discouraged to enroll at universities (testing was done by Centre for Educational Testing for Access and Placement in February 2020). The results of the NBT QL tests, mentioned above, as well as national results, are indicative of the fact that South African HEIs need to address newcomers' lack of numeracy as a matter of urgency.

"Numeracy, not calculus, is the key to understanding our data-drenched society" [33:2]. The Programme for International Assessment of Adult Competencies (PIAAC) refers to numeracy as the "ability to access, use, interpret and communicate mathematical information and ideas, in order to engage in and manage the mathematical demands of a range of situations in adult life" [34, 35]. The PIAAC further refers to numerate behaviour as dealing with problem-solving in real-world contexts where problems are numerical in nature, containing mathematical content that could be represented in mul tiple ways.

Numeracy skills further include the ability to demonstrate numerate behaviour as described by some, or all, of the following processes [35, 36]:

- Conceptual understanding of mathematics and the relevant mathematical knowledge: In order to reach this point of conceptual understanding in mathematics, called mathematical proficiency, students need to be guided (taught) through relevant mathematical and numeracy concepts [37, 38].

- Adaptive reasoning and problem-solving skills:
  - Adaptive reasoning is the ability to think in a logical way and to understand the relationships between concepts and contexts [38].
  - Problem-solving requires the ability to reason about the appropriate solutions and finding alternative solutions to problems [38].
- Literacy skills (ability to read, write and talk).
- Knowledge of the context of the problem.
- Prior numeracy-related experiences.

In a workshop hosted by the Higher Education Quality Control Council of Ontario (HEQCC), the improvement of numeracy skills of students in postsecondary (higher) education, was explored. The six principles that emerged from the workshop concur with the concept of numerate behaviour as described above [35–39]. The principles should therefore be taken into consideration when addressing the improvement of numeracy skills of students enrolled at higher education institutions:

- The need for numeracy skills is evident in all aspects of our lives;
- Numeracy does not require advanced mathematical skills;
- Numeracy skills are developed through all life-stages, and the development thereof is an ongoing process;
- To be numerate, one must be able to engage with quantitative information represented in different ways, for example, graphs, text, diagrams, maps, and tables;
- Basic number sense (numeracy skills) is essential to make informed decisions when faced with quantitative data or information [40].

The view that mathematics and numeracy are inseparable has probably contributed to the fact that numeracy has received less attention in higher education institutions. To enable programming students with the necessary numeracy skills to solve programming problems, academics at University X, where the first author is a lecturer, created a curriculum for a module called Computational Mathematics (CM). The students are studying towards a National Diploma in Informatics and mostly come from rural, resource-deprived schools. Most of the cohort is registered for the extended course due to poor grade 12 results. The objective of this module is to improve students' computational thinking and problem-solving skills, while preparing them for the quantitative nature of programming problems. The theoretical knowledge obtained from this extended module (CM) is expected to enable students to solve problems of a quantitative nature when programming while contributing to the development of students' reasoning and problem-solving skills.

Based on the six principles mentioned above [40], the concept of numerate behaviour [31, 33, 35, 36, 40, 41] the topics of the NBT QL test, as well as personal experience, numeracy concepts included in the Computational Mathematics module at University X, are: Number Sense, Number System, Fractions and Percentages, Ratios, Rates and Proportions, Basic Algebra, Measurements and Elementary Statistics.

First-year (novice) programming students must be able to solve problems, reason about solutions and then write algorithms to solve the problems. Real-world, quantitative problems must be solved in the known context from where these are translated into a program or a programming concept that can be applied in a real-world problem-solving scenario [42].

It is critical to understand that programming activities do not solely include the syntax and semantics of a programming language, it also requires several other skills and competencies, including computational thinking and numeracy [43]. Therefore, students who study programming must be able to solve and apply problems of a numerical nature.

5 Towards Defining Computational Numeracy

The focus of this article is to identify the components of CT and Numeracy relevant to CN, specifically for under-prepared, novice programming students, by exploring and reviewing both computational thinking and numeracy. The only reference to the term "Computational Numeracy" in literature, was found in a conference paper in the year 2000 where the term computational numeracy was used to refer to computational fluency [44]. This author regards a student as computationally fluent when he/she is fluent in the basic facts of addition, subtraction, multiplication, and division. Computational fluency is regarded as a goal for mathematics education to enable learners (students) to cope with the cognitive demand of more challenging mathematical problems [44].

The term Computational Numeracy will be used to underpin the computational thinking and numeracy skills that novice programming students need to successfully solve programming problems. Due to the nature of both numeracy and programming, six concepts of computational thinking were selected from literature to define CN for under-prepared, novice programming students (see Table 1). Referring to the PIAAC assessment domains of the Survey of Adult Skills, CT skills can be considered as cognitive strategies [45]. The cognitive strategies need to be applied to specific content, within a specific context, therefore the inclusion of Numeracy Content and Students' Profile, also referred to as the Context [45].

The majority of the first-year ICT students at the said University X are from disadvantaged backgrounds and had little or no exposure to computers and/or programming. The challenge is to teach the students computational thinking skills which includes reasoning and problem-solving skills. Applying the concepts of CN in the modules, Computational Mathematics and Principles of Programming at University X, is expected to contribute to the development of students' reasoning and problem-solving skills which in turn will enable them to solve problems of a quantitative nature when programming. The developers of the modules are constantly integrating the concepts of numeracy and programming

Table 1. The domains of computational numeracy (headings adapted from [45])

Content (Numeracy)	CT Skills (Cognitive strategies)	Context (Students' Profile)
Number Sense; Number Systems; Fractions, Percentages; Ratios, Rates and Proportions; Basic Algebra; Measurements; and Elementary Statistics.	Problem Decomposition; Pattern Recognition; Abstraction; Algorithmic Thinking; Evaluation; Generalisation.	Poor quality schooling; Lack of mathematical and numeracy proficiency; In need of extensive support, preferably in extended courses.

in both modules trying to prevent working in silos. Students are made aware of the links between the Computational Mathematics and Principles of Programming modules, and of the fact that they need the problem-solving skills they acquire in both modules to succeed in the rest of their ICT careers.

A typical, basic problem which is used in both the Computational Mathematics and Programming Principles modules at University X, will now be discussed to further explain the relevancy of CN for under-prepared, novice programming students.

6 Computational Numeracy Illustrated

During lectures of the module Programming Principles, the principles of programming are first demonstrated by using Scratch 3.0 (block-based visual programming language) after which Java (class-based, object-oriented programming language) is introduced. *"Scratch software appeared to be an engaging and relatively easy to use space for problem solving…Scratch provided a worthwhile and motivating programming environment to explore some mathematical ideas"* [46:55].

By the time students are expected to start using Java, they are familiar with planning their programs, using input-processing-output (IPO) charts, and writing algorithms in pseudocode. The students must write a very basic Java program as one of their first programming assignments; a similar problem is presented to students during their Computational Mathematics classes to reinforce the numeracy concepts of volume and surface area, see Table 2.

Table 2. Computational numeracy applied

Numeracy question *(Module: Computational Mathematics)*	**Programming question** *(Module: Programming Principles)*
A local gym built a new indoor swimming pool. The dimensions of the pool are as follows: The length 25 m and the width of 15 m. • Calculate the number of litres that will be needed to fill the pool for the first time if the pool is 1.8 metres deep. • The inside of the pool needs to be waterproofed. 1 litre of waterproofing paint covers 7.75 m^2. Calculate how many 5 litre containers of paint will be needed for 2 coats. Only full tins of paint can be bought.	A fish farmer built a new dam on his farm. The known dimensions of the dam are: Length is 15 metres and width is 10 metres. Open the file called FishDam.java that you downloaded from the LMS. Add code to create a Java program to calculate and display the following: • The number of litres that will be needed to fill the dam for the first time if the dam is a certain depth. Tip: $1m^3$ = 1000 litres • The inside of the dam needs to be waterproofed. 1 litre of paint covers $5.5m^2$. • The program should ask the user how many coats of paint should be applied. • Then calculate and display the numbers of tins of paint to be bought. Only full tins of paint can be bought. • Format the number of litres using a thousand separator. • Use constant values where possible.
What are the main differences between the above problem statements?	
• The specific values are given. • The students use known formulae to calculate the results, using given values. • Calculations are done on a calculator (or on paper).	• The students must understand and apply the concept of variables. • The user decides which values must be used. • The formulae are incorporated in the algorithm (processing).
What are the similarities between the above problem statements?	
Selection of the "appropriate arithmetic operation", correct use and execution of the formulae in numeracy and programming could be considered as a computational skill [47], also described as algorithmic thinking. Students must understand numeracy concepts to apply formulae correctly. The numeracy concepts could include the arithmetic operations (addition, subtraction, multiplication, division) and the relevant rules, for example, order of operations.	

(*continued*)

Table 2. (*continued*)

Following a problem-solving process* [48] *the components of CN can be linked to the above problem statements:

Identify the Problem:

Problem Decomposition: Programming requires complex problems to be broken down into smaller, more manageable problems, it is also referred to as "divide and conquer" [22]. Similar skills are needed for solving numeracy problems. The student must break up the problem in smaller sections:

- To calculate the number of litres (of water), the students must identify that volume must be calculated first. To calculate how much paint is needed, the students must identify that total surface area must be calculated first.

Abstraction: Abstraction is a process of identifying and removing redundant information from a problem, resulting in a problem without unnecessary detail [23]. What is the redundant information in the above problem statements?

- "A fish farmer built a new dam on his farm" and "A local gym built a new indoor swimming pool".

It is only necessary for students to know that it is a dam or a pool and what a dam or a pool is (dams and pools are usually filled with water and has certain measurements called dimensions).

Gather data:

Pattern Recognition: When solving a problem, it is valuable to look for patterns and/or trends within the problem, or patterns previously recognised in other problems [23].Students are (supposed to be) familiar with the concepts of volume and total surface area from school mathematics and the Computational Mathematics course. They should recognize the similarities and apply their numeracy skills in this programming context.

Plan the Solution:

Algorithmic Thinking: When expressing the problem in sequential steps, it becomes an algorithm. Understanding and writing calculations in steps, is algorithmic thinking, whether in pseudo code, or in terms of numbers and mathematical operations. Following an algorithmic thinking approach, simplifies problem-solving [22]. When writing the pseudocode, numeracy principles are incorporated, values are unknown, and the user should provide values:

- To calculate the volume and the total surface area, the length, width, and depth is needed. The depth is unknown and therefore the student must understand that the user must provide the depth for the program to produce the correct solution (output). The user may also decide (and capture) how many coats of paint he/she wants to paint.

Implement and Assess the Solution:

(*continued*)

Table 2. *(continued)*

Evaluation: It is crucial to judge (test) whether a solution is effective or correct, an effective solution could also be generalised [18], [19]. Students are encouraged to reflect whether the output of their programs correlate with the calculations done with a calculator. They must experiment and try with different values as well as with null values to test possible logical errors.

Generalisation: Students may recognise similarities with problems they previously solved and then apply their prior knowledge to solve a new problem [26]. In the "Report of a Workshop of Pedagogical Aspects of Computational Thinking", Kolodner emphasised that when a student is able to reflect on a problem and its solution, and then teach a peer how to solve the problem, the student demonstrates computational thinking [49]. Students should recognise the similarities of exercises done in the Computational Mathematics class and apply it to the given scenario in programming.

7 Conclusion

First-year ICT students at University X are under-prepared for tertiary studies, and even more so under-prepared for the problem-solving nature of programming. Students qualify for entrance to the extended ICT diplomas with an average mark of 50% to 59% for Grade 12 Mathematics or 80% to 89% for Grade 12 Mathematical Literacy. Unfortunately, most of the numeracy concepts are only taught in primary school (Grades 1 to 7) and by the time learners reach Grade 12, most of it has been forgotten. The students' knowledge of basic numeracy has therefore proven to be inadequate for solving programming problems of a quantitative nature. Therefore, students find ICT studies challenging without adequate numeracy skills. Numeracy is commonly rooted in real life scenarios, which is reflected in programming in a wide variety of contexts.

This paper presented Computational Numeracy as a new concept to be used in the teaching of under-prepared programming students. An initial definition of the concept includes different components: content (numeracy), cognitive strategies (computational thinking) and context (students with low numeracy skills levels due to different environmental factors). Computational Numeracy teaching strategies need to take these three components into account. The concept was illustrated by showing how these components are used in the teaching of numeracy and programming to students at a university of technology in South Africa.

Although ICT lecturers in South Africa are well-qualified in their field of study, most of the ICT lecturers at University X do not have teaching qualifications and are therefore not well equipped to teach under-prepared students. Teaching under-prepared, novice students to program is challenging, especially if a lecturer is a seasoned programmer.

Going back to basics and teaching students problem-solving, numeracy and com putational thinking skills, while teaching programming, is a challenge, and a skill. As part of a larger study, a framework will be developed, providing guidance to lecturers to assist novice, under-prepared programming students in developing a solid foundation for their ICT studies.

References

1. OECD: Skills Matter. OECD (2016). https://doi.org/10.1787/9789264258051-en
2. Steen, L.A.: Mathematics and numeracy: two literacies, one language. Math. Educ. **6**(1), 10–16 (2001)
3. Heymann, H.W.: Why Teach Mathematics? A Focus on General Education. Kluwer Academic, Dordrecht (2010)
4. Resnick, L.B.: Nested learning systems for the thinking curriculum. Educ. Res. **39**, 183–197 (2010). https://doi.org/10.3102/0013189X10364671
5. Spaull, N., Taylor, S.: Access to what? Creating a composite measure of educational quantity and educational quality for 11 African countries. Comp. Educ. Rev. **59**, 133–165 (2015). https://doi.org/10.1086/679295
6. Steen, L.A.: National Research Council (U.S.). Mathematical Sciences Education Board: On the shoulders of giants: new approaches to numeracy. National Academy Press (1990)
7. Oddie, A., Hazlewood, P., Blakeway, S., Whitfield, A.: Introductory problem solving and programming: robotics versus traditional approaches. Innov. Teach. Learn. Inf. Comput. Sci. **9**, 1–11 (2010). https://doi.org/10.11120/ital.2010.09020011
8. Barlow-Jones, G., Chetty, J.: The Effects of a Social Constructivist Pedagogy on At-risk Students Completing a Computer Programming Course at a Post-Secondary Institution (2012)
9. Spaull, N., Kotze, J.: Starting behind and staying behind in South Africa. The case of insurmountable learning deficits in mathematics. Int. J. Educ. Dev. **41**, 13–24 (2015). https://doi.org/10.1016/j.ijedudev.2015.01.002
10. Marnewick, C.: The mystery of student selection: are there any selection criteria? Educ. Stud. **38**, 123–137 (2012). https://doi.org/10.1080/03055698.2011.567041
11. Barlow-Jones, G.: High school mathematics marks as an admission criterion for entry into programming courses at a South African university (2015)
12. Wing, J.M.: Computational thinking and thinking about computing. Philos. Trans. R. Soc. A: Math. Phys. Eng. Sci. **366**, 3717–3725 (2008). https://doi.org/10.1098/rsta.2008.0118
13. de Jong, I.: Teaching computational thinking with interventions adapted to undergraduate students' proficiency levels. In: Annual Conference on Innovation and Technology in Computer Science Education, ITiCSE, pp. 571–572. Association for Computing Machinery (2020). https://doi.org/10.1145/3341525.3394001
14. Aho, A.V.: Computation and computational thinking. Comput. J. **55**, 833–835 (2012). https://doi.org/10.1093/comjnl/bxs074
15. Saqr, M., Ng, K., Oyelere, S.S., Tedre, M.: People, ideas, milestones: a scientometric study of computational thinking. ACM Trans. Comput. Educ. **21**, 1–17 (2021). https://doi.org/10.1145/3445984
16. Wing, J.M.: Computational thinking. Commun. ACM **49**, 33–35 (2006)
17. Haseski, H.I., Ilic, U., Tugtekin, U.: Defining a new 21st century skill-computational thinking: concepts and trends. Int. Educ. Stud. **11**, 29 (2018). https://doi.org/10.5539/ies.v11n4p29
18. Hunsaker, E.: Computational thinking (2018)
19. Sethi, R.J.: Essential Computational Thinking Computer Vision-Group Analyis in Video View project Scientific Workflows for Visual Stylometry: Digital Tools for Exploring the Nature of Artistic Style in the Visual Arts View project

20. Angeli, C., Voogt, J., Fluck, A.: A K-6 computational thinking curriculum framework: implications for teacher knowledge (2016)
21. Barr, V., Stephenson, C.: Bringing computational thinking to K-12: what is involved and what is the role of the computer science education community? ACM Inroads **2**, 48–54 (2011). https://doi.org/10.1145/1929887.1929905
22. Cansu, F.K., Cansu, S.K.: An overview of computational thinking. Int. J. Comput. Sci. Educ. Sch. **3**, 17–30 (2019). https://doi.org/10.21585/ijcses.v3i1.53
23. Csizmadia, A., Curzon, P., Humphreys, S., Ng, T., Selby, C., Woollard, J.: Computational Thinking - A Guide for Teachers (2015)
24. Lee, I., et al.: Computational thinking for youth in practice. ACM Inroads **2**, 32–37 (2011). https://doi.org/10.1145/1929887.1929902
25. Hello World issue 4—Hello World. https://helloworld.raspberrypi.org/issues/4. Accessed 10 May 2021
26. Selby, C.C., Woollard, J.: Computational thinking: the developing definition (2010)
27. Wing, J.M.: Computational thinking: what and why? (2010)
28. Weintrop, D., et al.: Defining computational thinking for mathematics and science classrooms. J. Sci. Educ. Technol. **25**(1), 127–147 (2015). https://doi.org/10.1007/s10956-015-9581-5
29. Yadav, A., Hong, H., Stephenson, C.: Computational thinking for all: pedagogical approaches to embedding 21st century problem solving in K-12 classrooms. TechTrends **60**, 565–568 (2016). https://doi.org/10.1007/s11528016-0087-7
30. van Peursem, D., Keller, C., Pietrzak, D., Wagner, C., Bennett, C.: A Comparison of performance and attitudes between students enrolled in college algebra vs. quantitative literacy. Math. Comput. Educ. **46**, 107 (2012)
31. Jablonka, E.: The evolvement of numeracy and mathematical literacy curricula and the construction of hierarchies of numerate or mathematically literate subjects. ZDM Math. Educ. **47**(4), 599–609 (2015). https://doi.org/10.1007/s11858-015-0691-6
32. Centre for Educational Testing for Access and Placement: The National Benchmark Tests National Report 2018 Intake Cycle (2018)
33. Steen, L.A.: Numeracy: the new literacy for a data-drenched society. Educ. Leadersh. **57**, 8–13 (1999)
34. OECD: Literacy, Numeracy and Problem Solving in Technology-Rich Environments: Framework for the OECD Survey of Adult Skills (2012)
35. Alatorre, S., Close, S., Evans, J., Kingdom, U., Johansen, L., Maguire, T.: PIAAC Numeracy: a Conceptual Framework. Education (2009)
36. Curry, D., Soroui, J.: Using the PIAAC numeracy framework to guide instruction: an introduction for adult educators (2017)
37. Pei, C. (Yu), Weintrop, D., Wilensky, U.: Cultivating computational thinking practices and mathematical habits of mind in lattice land. Math. Think. Learn. **20**, 75–89 (2018). https://doi.org/10.1080/10986065.2018.1403543
38. Kilpatrick, J., Swafford, J., Findell, B.: Adding it up: helping children learn mathematics Jeremy. Society. II (2001)
39. OECD: Literacy, Numeracy and Problem Solving in Technology-Rich Environments. OECD Publishing, Paris (2012). https://doi.org/10.1787/9789264128859-en
40. Brumwell, S., Macfarlane, A.: Improving Numeracy Skills of Postsecondary Students: What is the Way Forward? The Higher Education Quality Council of Ontario (2020)
41. Peursem, V.: A comparison of performance and attitudes between students enrolled in college algebra vs. quantitative literacy. Math. Comput. Educ. **46**(2), 107–118 (2012)
42. Rogalski, J., Samurçay, R.: Acquisition of programming knowledge and skills. In: Psychology of Programming, pp. 157–174. Elsevier (1990). https://doi.org/10.1016/b978-0-12-350772-3.50015-x

43. Attallah, B., Ilagure, Z., Chang, Y.K.: The impact of competencies in mathematics and beyond on learning computer programming in higher education. In: ITT 2018 - Information Technology Trends: Emerging Technologies for Artificial Intelligence, pp. 77–81. Institute of Electrical and Electronics Engineers Inc. (2019). https://doi.org/10.1109/CTIT.2018.8649527
44. Australian Council for Educational Research (ACER): Australian Council for Educational Research (ACER). Research Conference (2000: Brisbane): Improving Numeracy Learning: Research Conference 2000, Proceedings (2000)
45. OECD Skills Outlook 2013. OECD (2013). https://doi.org/10.1787/9789264204256-en
46. Calder, N.: Using scratch to facilitate mathematical thinking. Waikato J. Educ. **23**, 43–58 (2018)
47. Millians, M.: Computational skills. In: Encyclopedia of Child Behavior and Development (2011). https://doi.org/10.1007/978-0-387-79061-9
48. Kalelioğlu, F., Gülbahar, Y., Kukul, V.: A framework for computational thinking based on a systematic research review (2016)
49. Report of a Workshop on the Pedagogical Aspects of Computational Thinking. National Academies Press (2011). https://doi.org/10.17226/13170

Using Data Analytics to Detect Possible Collusion in a Multiple Choice Quiz Test

Michael Lang(✉)

School of Business and Economics, NUI Galway, Galway, Ireland
michael.lang@nuigalway.ie

Abstract. This paper reports on the experiences of using an on-line MCQ test to assess students' knowledge for a postgraduate module. Because of the COVID-19 pandemic, the test was taken in a remote non-proctored environment. Although it was executed under timed conditions with students seeing questions in a randomised order, algorithmic analysis of the response patterns suggests that collusion occurred during the test. Practical implications for assessment design and administration are discussed.

Keywords: IS education · MCQ tests · Academic integrity · Data analytics

1 Introduction and Background

Assuring academic integrity on computer programming assessments is a perennial challenge for university educators [1], and has been further exacerbated by the extraordinary unplanned constraints imposed by the COVID-19 pandemic [2, 3]. Information systems programmes across Europe have seen major increases in intake in recent years, many of these additional students coming from outside the EU. These larger, culturally diverse classrooms have already forced lecturers to rethink their learning design. On top of this, teaching staff have now been catapulted (by the ongoing pandemic) into an on-line environment that for many is a first-time venture into terra incognito.

Prior literature on academic integrity in computing and information systems has indicated that there may be behavioural differences across gender, national culture, maturity and English language proficiency [4, 5]. The latter is not so much of an issue in programming modules. There are several other factors that can contribute to plagiarism and academic dishonesty, including time pressure, required effort, social norms, low self-efficacy, personal morals and conscientiousness, awareness of rules, awareness of detection techniques, and perceived risk of detection [6]. Interestingly, Harris et al. [7] found no differences in self-reported behaviour of students within on-line learning environments and those in traditional environments, as reported in previous studies [8].

This paper reflects on the experiences of assessing a postgraduate Database Systems module at an Irish university in the 2020/2021 academic year. The method of assessment was a Multiple Choice Quiz (MCQ) test which was administered on-line in a timed examination. The research questions were:

Published by Springer Nature Switzerland AG 2021
D. Dennehy et al. (Eds.): I3E 2021, LNCS 12896, pp. 757–762, 2021.
https://doi.org/10.1007/978-3-030-85447-8_63

- Does nationality affect a student's tendency to cheat in an on-line non-proctored examination?
- Does gender affect a student's tendency to cheat in an on-line non-proctored examination?
- Does age affect a student's tendency to cheat in an on-line non-proctored examination?
- Does peer network affect a student's tendency to cheat in an on-line non-proctored examination?

The structure of this paper is as follows: Sect. 2 describes the teaching and assessment case study environment, Sect. 3 analyses and discusses the findings, and Sect. 4 presents conclusions and implications for teaching practice.

2 Description of Case Study

"Database Systems Development" was taken by 167 students spread across three separate programmes. The class was 36% female and 64% male, made up of 12 different nationalities, of which Ireland (38%), India (44%) and China (11%) were the biggest cohorts, with the remainder (7%) coming from Nigeria, Cameroon, USA, Mexico, Brazil, France, Ukraine, Pakistan and Indonesia. The median age was 25.4 years. The majority of the international students arrived in Ireland prior to semester but a few remained in their home countries. Under normal circumstances, this module would have been taught in a lecture hall. However, because of the COVID-19 pandemic, it was taught on-line across 11 weeks with a regular scheduled slot on Microsoft Teams each week. In previous years, the end-of-semester examination was in the form of an invigilated Multiple Choice Quiz (MCQ) test, taken in an examination centre. For the 2020/2021 academic year, this was replaced by an on-line MCQ test taken in the student's place of residence.

It was initially proposed that the examination would be subject to remote proctoring. However, in view of legitimate concerns raised by students about privacy, unreliable internet connectivity, possible power outages or other technical difficulties, and additional stress at an already difficult time, it was decided not to proceed with remote proctoring. Instead, following Nguyen et al. [10], candidates were required to declare in advance of the test that they had read the rules "and pledge, on my honour, to fully abide by them". To allow for possible connectivity problems, students were assured that there would be a degree of leniency with the examination duration, with a 30 min grace period before shut down. This was also intended to offset time pressure issues, a factor that has shown up in prior studies as a major contributing factor in cheating [6].

All students were issued an email one week in advance of the examination, clearly setting out the format and rules that would apply. This included a notice that algorithms would be used to detect suspicious activity and a strict warning was served not to communicate or collude with others during the test. Again, this was intended to mitigate contributory factors identified by Moss et al. [6].

2.1 Format of Examination

The test consisted of 50 multiple choice quiz (MCQ) questions, each with four possible options of which one and only one was correct. MCQ tests are prone to cheating, and indeed this had been previously experienced in this module, with students using pre-devised signals to communicate to each other in examination halls. Problems when going on-line were therefore anticipated, especially with no proctoring and students living together or connected virtually. It was assumed, given the absence of remote proctoring, that students would use their notes, even if asked not to do so. The test was therefore designed on this basis and students were told that it would be "open book". However, so that they would be under no illusions, they were advised that the questions would be "set in such a way that you need to understand concepts and apply your knowledge, not merely memorise material". As such, given the time constraint of the examination (2 h), if students had to resort to consulting their notes frequently, they would place themselves under pressure and this was made known to them.

The first half of the test examined knowledge of database design concepts. Most of these questions put forward four assertions and the candidate was required to use his/her understanding of the theory to decide which assertion was true or false. A few other questions in this section presented data modelling scenarios with four possible choices, again requiring the candidate to consider options and make a decision, thus requiring higher order thinking skills at the Analyse → Synthesise → Evaluate end of the Bloom et al. [9] taxonomy. Such higher order MCQ questions have been found to be effective in science education [10].

The second half of the test was based on knowledge of the Structured Query Language (SQL). The questions used a database schema that students were given in advance and asked to print out. The lectures and course exercises also used this same database so students were familiar with it and were expected to have practiced upon it. Instead of being asked to write SQL code from scratch, students' knowledge was assessed by other means: (1) "fill in the blanks" questions that required them to complete an SQL query by inserting the correct missing words in the correct order, (2) being asked to evaluate four different ways of solving a problem and selecting which of these ways is valid or not valid, (3) inspecting code snippets and being asked to detect which line(s) contain errors, if any, and (4) inspecting code and being asked what output it would generate.

The quiz was administered using Microsoft Forms, which required users to authenticate themselves using their university Office365 account credentials. Several days in advance, they were given a "mock" test with 10 sample questions and the precise rules and instructions that would apply.

2.2 Student Performance

In advance of the test, there was quite a degree of trepidation amongst students about it being MCQ format and being a timed examination (all their other modules, with just one exception, used take-home assignments). After the test, the feeling was much more positive. One student said that *"My overall experience with the exam was really nice, I enjoyed each and every question asked, they were certainly tricky but it's just required to use a bit of brain and knowledge. I would say that if a student has gone through your class notes that you've shared all along and did the exercise queries, they can achieve an excellent score in it"*. The performance scores on questions were very strong, with just 8 of the 50 having less than 50% correct. The median across the test was 79% correct, ranging from 10% on a question that only a very few students got right up to 100% on one question that they all answered correctly. Although this level of performance might suggest that the test was easy with a low level of discrimination amongst the possible answers, it can be alternatively explained by the fact that many of the students had some prior knowledge of databases and had obtained first class honours undergraduate degrees.

3 Analysis and Discussion

With a MCQ test in a class of high performers, it can be difficult to detect collusion because the majority of students will consistently pick the correct answers. Instead, it can be revealing to compare patterns of incorrect responses [11]. In theory, the probability of two students randomly picking the same incorrect answer from two four-option questions is (3 matching pairs)/(9 possible combinations) = 0.33. Therefore, if students have five matching incorrect answers, the probability is 0.33^5 which is less than a 1 in 250 chance. However, this is not a random process; incorrect answers do not have equal probability of being chosen because some may be easier to eliminate than others. For the purposes of this exercise, it was therefore assumed that a threshold of 8 similar incorrect responses would be used.

The MCQ test responses were exported from Microsoft Forms into a MySQL database, where they were transposed and a paired-list of possible collusion suspects was generated. Additionally, data on age, nationality and gender were linked to the responses. It was assumed that students took the test at their registered addresses so those details were converted into latitude and longitude coordinates using Google Maps and also imported.

The highest number of shared incorrect responses was 16. The statistical probability of this occurring (based on equal weighting for each option) is 1 in 50 million so, if going just by mathematics, it would be an absolute certainty that this pair of students colluded. However, these two students were in two different Masters programmes, live thousands of kilometres apart and, to the best of the examiner's knowledge, have never communicated with each other. Both students failed the test and had several other incorrect responses.

Out of a class of 167 students, 70 (42%) had eight or more similar incorrect answers to other students. Of those 70, several had eight or more similar incorrect answers in common with more than one student. The results of the similarity analysis were then exported from MySQL and imported into a Neo4J database, where graph queries were executed to detect suspicious clusters. This revealed several mini-networks of students who had numerous identical incorrect responses (see Fig. 1).

Not surprisingly, six clusters were found amongst cohabiting students, including one group of four and another of three. Amongst students that were geographically distributed, several clusters of four or more students with similar answer patterns were also identified. Interestingly, these clusters were mostly of the same nationality, with Irish students and Indian students not mixing but rather forming their own groups. Chinese students barely featured at all, seemingly keeping to themselves (which might be because most of them were not in Ireland). Overall, 63% of Irish students and 31% of Indians were found to have suspicious response patterns. On the face of it, this seems to suggest that nationality does make a difference. However, self-efficacy may be a moderating

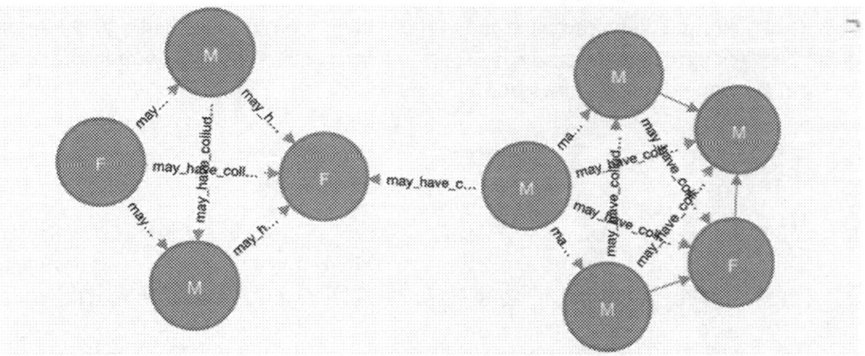

Fig. 1. Examples of mini-networks of collusion suspects detected by Neo4J graph query.

factor here because many of the Indian students had substantial prior experience in database design and development. For other nationalities, the numbers are too small to be statistically meaningful.

While the presence of these clusters cannot be taken as absolute proof that collusion took place during the test, and perhaps the excuses of "I and my friend both got it wrong because we studied together" or "we both picked the second most likely options" can explain some of the similarity, it does seem quite likely that, even though students were seeing the questions in a different random order, some of them were in communication with each other during the test and comparing responses.

As regards gender and age, no differences were observed; males and females were just as likely to engage in this behaviour, as were younger students and mature students.

4 Conclusions and Implications

This work-in-progress paper set out to explore if the factors of nationality, gender, age and peer network affected a student's tendency to cheat in an on-line non-proctored MCQ examination situation. Gender and age were found not to have any impact, but nationality and peer networks did appear to be at play with several cases of suspected collusion. Because the evidential base was quite weak and the cost of investigating suspicious cases is high, none of these cases were brought forward for further action.

The lessons learned from implementing an on-line MCQ test with randomised order suggest that this could work effectively if administered in an invigilated examination centre. It could also function well if the on-line class were geographically distributed, unlike the very unusual situation that occurred during COVID-19 where international students travelled abroad, only to become engaged in distance education while actually living on or near campus with other international classmates. However, if students are permitted to take tests on-line in non-proctored environments, it seems likely based on the experiences reported herein that many of them will engage in behaviour to cheat the test. The use of constraints such as tighter time limits, no facility to navigate back to review answers, and screen-at-a-time design have all been suggested in the literature, but these could just drive students towards more innovative ways of beating the system.

Further study is required on the phenomenon of "classroom culture", and how students from diverse backgrounds coalesce to form on-line peer learning communities with shared social norms, ethical values and honour codes.

References

1. Sheard, J., Butler, M., Falkner, K., Morgan, M., Weerasinghe, A.: Strategies for maintaining academic integrity in first-year computing courses. In: Proceedings of the ACM Conference on Innovation and Technology in Computer Science Education, Bologna, Italy, pp. 244–249 (2017)
2. Senel, S., Senel, H.C.: Remote assessment in higher education during COVID-19 pandemic. Int. J. Assessm. Tools Educ. **8**(2), 181–199 (2021)
3. Pappas, I.O., Giannakos, M.N.: Rethinking learning design in IT education during a pandemic. Front. Educ. **6**, 652856 (2021). https://doi.org/10.3389/feduc.2021.652856
4. Adair, J.H., Linderman, J.L.: Computer ethics and academic honesty: developing a survey instrument. ACM SIGCSE Bull. **17**(1), 93–98 (1985)
5. Atkinson, D., Nau, S.Z., Symons, C.: Ten years in the academic integrity trenches: experiences and issues. J. Inf. Syst. Educ. **27**(3), 197–208 (2016)
6. Moss, S.A., White, B., Lee, J.: A systematic review into the psychological causes and correlates of plagiarism. Ethics Behav. **28**(4), 261–283 (2018)
7. Harris, L., Harrison, D., McNally, D., Ford, C.: Academic integrity in an online culture: do McCabe's findings hold true for online, adult learners? J. Acad. Ethics **18**(4), 419–434 (2019)
8. McCabe, D.L., Treviño, L.K., Butterfield, K.D.: Cheating in academic institutions: a decade of research. Ethics Behav. **11**(3), 219–232 (2001)
9. Bloom, B.S., Engelhart, M.D., Furst, E.J., Hill, W.H., Krathwohl, D.R.: Taxonomy of educational objectives: the classification of educational goals. In: Handbook 1: Cognitive Domain. David McKay, New York (1956)
10. Nguyen, J.G., Keuseman, K.J., Humston, J.J.: Minimize online cheating for online assessments during COVID-19 pandemic. J. Chem. Educ. **97**(9), 3429–3435 (2020)
11. Ercole, A., Whittlestone, K.D., Melvin, D.G., Rashbass, J.: Collusion detection in multiple choice examinations. Med. Educ. **36**(2), 166–172 (2002)

Perceptions of Students for a Gamification Approach: Cities Skylines as a Pedagogical Tool in Urban Planning Education

Tayyeb Ahmed Khan and Xin Zhao(✉)

University of Sheffield, Sheffield, UK
Xin.Zhao@Sheffield.ac.uk

Abstract. Gamification, the use of game elements in non-game contexts, has been widely adopted for pedagogic purposes, allowing a synchronism in student's engagement, motivation and learning. This research aims to evaluate the effectiveness of the simulation game Cities Skylines for teaching the Urban Planning discipline from the perspectives of students. Eight in-depth semi-structured interviews were thematically analysed. The findings of the study indicate that visual elements of the game allowed students to develop a conceptual understanding. Although the game fosters critical thinking and problem-solving skills, its internal limitations hinder students from confidently applying knowledge in the real world. The study also demonstrates the importance of the instructor's role to retrieve the maximum pedagogic benefits from the game.

Keywords: Gamification · Simulation games · Student learning · Urban planning education

1 Introduction

Education institutions realise the value of games as a pedagogical tool, considering their increasing sophistication in terms of technology, game mechanics, visual imagery and communicative elements. According to the literature, pedagogic games can harness students' motivation, engagement and persistence, teaching complex disciplinary concepts that can be retained in memory for a longer period of time [1, 2]. Recent studies also highlight the educational value of simulation games for student learning, arguing that such games could provide students with practice grounds that are related to real-world contexts [3].

This study examines the use and pedagogical potential of *Cities Skyline* in an Urban Planning module. City Skylines is an open-world city building simulation game where players are involved in urban planning and governance. Players are tasked with developing small to functional mega-cities by developing roads and infrastructure, zoning districts, utility management, public transport, taxation and implementing civil policies. Amongst others, players are also involved in the management of the city's economic performance and control elements of health & safety, education, employment levels,

Published by Springer Nature Switzerland AG 2021
D. Dennehy et al. (Eds.): I3E 2021, LNCS 12896, pp. 763–773, 2021.
https://doi.org/10.1007/978-3-030-85447-8_64

pollution and sustainable growth. Additionally, the game provides enormous creative freedom in its sandbox mode and has several mods/expansion packs to augment the development of superior cities.

Research has investigated the potential of Cities Skyline as an educational tool in a wide range of fields, such as real estate studies [4], environmental sciences [5] and journalism [6]. However, an insufficient number of empirical studies regarding the educational benefits of Cities Skylines in urban planning education remain; specifically, there is an apparent lack of studies that evaluate the benefits of Cities Skylines from the critical lens of learning theories.

Informed by Kolb's Experiential Learning model [7], this paper aims to evaluate the effectiveness of the simulation game Cities Skylines for teaching Urban Planning discipline from the perspective of students. It focuses on the lens of learning outcomes, namely, cognitive, behavioural and affective outcomes.

2 Literature Review

2.1 Games in Education

Games allow users a constant form of "interactivity" that feeds their gaming experience when they receive valuable feedback corresponding to their actions as the gaming narrative unfolds. The ability to control their environment and characters enables users to utilise control mechanisms to overcome challenges they may face. It also allows profound associations and sensitivities with the characters that fuel their identity as players. Most importantly, games allow players a form of immersion and integration within the game; being present in a make-belief world encircled by challenges is arguably the highest pleasurable gaming aspect [8, 9]. Educational games connect these elements into an alternative universe and disciplinary scenarios enabling users to relate to the character's circumstances within the game. Developers then provide all the necessary tools to players that are required for them to comprehend their distinctive situation and their connections in real-life situations [10]. Various disciplines have made profound use of this teaching method to validate its use in pedagogy [3, 11–13].

2.2 Effective Features of Educational Games

There are certain features of critical importance in games to be considered as useful tools for learning. These features are the main component for learning requiring "deliberate intertwining with pedagogical content to ensure successful learning" [14, p. 31]. These were identified as the Back Story & Production, Environment & Realism, Adaptivity and Interactivity & Debriefing [14, 15].

Backstory and Production. The narrative structure, which is regarded as the "sticky element", is closely associated with the immersiveness of computer games; players' interests remain consistently high while exploring in-game complexities. The "narrative-pedagogical mechanism" is the first contact between the game and the wider world, allowing players to interact with gameplay, in-game elements and fellow players [16].

Moreover, learning and knowledge, which ought to be carefully considered, is embedded within the games [17]. The immersive function, however, is not a promising element for learning, where irrelevant material or over-doing narrative can be counter-productive to learning processes [18].

Environment and Realism. An environment of realism is directly proportional to the skill level of students and their experiences; the higher the fidelity (realism) and complexity the game reaches, the greater learning opportunities there are for experienced players. Notably, with a high learning curve in realism, players feel more challenged and motivated [19]. For mature students, realism is a persuasive feature for learning-simulations at tertiary education, thereby giving it greater approval for learning [14].

Adaptivity and Interactivity. Fundamentally, the knowledge tool must adapt to the learner's abilities and preferences for effective learning given the individual differences in learning capabilities [20]. Researchers have identified several adaptive features for in-game systems, including catering to one's preferred presentation and format of the information, enabling them to see "different page content of the same knowledge point" [21, p. 163]. Specifically, researchers argue that game systems should monitor players' learning progress, i.e., areas mastered in the form of a "knowledge tree", provide relevant links to areas from where the learner can acquire related information/fundamentals subject to accomplish tasks. The interactive function of feedback and engagement with the game systems is central to transferring knowledge between the game and the learner. Research suggests that interactivity features could bring out positive effects on a student's feelings of social presence [22].

Debriefing. As part of the evaluation framework, debriefing covers the knowledge sharing practices between students based on their experiences in the game. Debriefing enables knowledge sharing practices to accomplish tasks and increases gaming engagement levels. These happen through progress tracking, animated agents, discussion forums, live-chats. Crookall emphasises this point, stating "learning comes from the debriefing, not from the game" [23, p. 907].

2.3 Experiential Learning

Experiential learning is defined as learning which "exists when a personally responsible participant cognitively, affectively, and behaviourally processes knowledge, skills, and/or attitudes in a learning situation, characterised by a high level of active involvement" [7, 24]. Previous research demonstrates that experiential learning can bring out better conceptual understanding, critical thinking and problem-solving skills, increased enthusiasm, better performance, a higher level of self-confidence and learning enhancement [25].

Experiential learning fosters several learning outcomes that could guide researchers in measuring effectiveness in educational games. Ranchhod identifies them as: Cognitive Development (conceptual understanding): where students internalise concepts, terminologies and core principles of the discipline. Behavioural Development (skill development): The realistic representation of the world enables students to transfer their acquired skills to real-world situations. Affective Development (Evaluation): "Skills development has a positive impact on students' affective evaluation of the simulation game exercise", enhancing students' engagement and satisfaction and improving their attitudes towards the discipline [25].

3 Methodology

This research adopts a qualitative approach based on the research philosophy of interpretivism, in which "interpretive researchers assume that access to reality is only through social constructions such as language, consciousness, shared meanings, and instruments" [29, p. 38]. The semi-structured interview method was used to gather data from a sample size of eight participants. Each interview was 45 min in duration.

3.1 Participants and Contextual Background

Participants were post-graduate students (ages 22–27 years). Seven of them were part of an Urban & Regional Planning program, while one was studying at a Real Estate program at a British University. They had taken the *Sustainable Development* module, in which they were introduced to the *Cities: Skyline* game. Three participants had completed undergraduate degrees in Geography, while the remaining undergraduate participants (five) had one to five years of work experience and studied in one of the following disciplines: Architecture, Electrical Engineering, Biosciences, Urban Planning, and Business Management. The students were not notified of the game being introduced as a teaching tool in the module, so it did not influence their decision to take the module.

The students were taught about the concept of sustainable development, which is complex and difficult to comprehend. To address this, each student was required to explore sustainability by developing their virtual cities according to concepts learnt in class, but using real-world policies as a basis. They were then encouraged to broadly analyze their concept with another student. This allowed the students to form a balanced understanding of the otherwise ambiguous concept of urban sustainability.

The learning goal of the module was to prepare students to write sustainable development policy papers as their final assignment. The game on its own does not have any direct link to writing policy papers. It merely serves as "a backdrop to things learnt" (Respondent 3) and provides a learning/supporting environment for the implementation of key concepts to be reflected on. Based on these reflections, policy papers are written.

Cities: Skyline is a single-player, off-the-shelf game and, therefore, restricts collaborative learning due to the absence of networking. To overcome this constraint, the class instructor grouped students into pairs to enable knowledge sharing before further guiding them on the practical implementations of their learnings within real-life contexts.

Two classroom sessions were dedicated to training students for setting up and installing the game. The instructor played a pivotal role in familiarizing students with the game interface and teaching them the in-game tools. Students were introduced to the five different build-types/zones: commercial, residential, industrial, municipal, and office. The students were divided into pairs and tasked to use the game as a "canvas" for building cities according to the sustainable development concepts and theories learnt in class.

Students learnt sustainable-development concepts in class and gameplay took place both in and outside of lecture sessions. There was no time limitation on students playing the game; however, to reduce the learning curve and keep the game interface simple, the vanilla version (original game with no expansion packs) was utilized. While playing, students simply monitored how the population in their cities evolved and responded to their city building policies as their cities grew over time. Based on this information and the in-game restrictions (what the player wanted to do versus what the game allowed them to do), students reflected on what they learnt and their overall experiences in the following in-class Q&A session.

Students discussed their experiences with the instructor to deepen their understanding of concepts, which included discussing in-game limitations to find alternative approaches. The instructor played a key role in instigating debate and discussion among learners to critically reflect on their solutions and ideas of what they may do in realistic situations. Students would also consider improved methods of achieving sustainability and, under the guidance of the instructor, debate on why certain policies are effective in specific real-life scenarios.

3.2 Semi-structured Interviews

Data Semi-structured interviews were conducted in a conversational manner [30]. This method was undertaken to ensure the interviewees were relaxed and able to share as much as possible from their experience. These conversations were intended to open up new subject areas and help reveal valuable information leading to high value data [31]. The researcher had no experience with the game nor did they have any relations to the participants. The interviews were audio-recorded and later transcribed. This research has received ethics approval and informed consent was collected prior to all interviews. When recording the interviews, respondents were assigned alias names.

The questions used to structure the interviews were devised through "inventory of learning goals" categories, which were previously used for a marketing strategy simulation game [25]. The current paper uses the same categories to devise questions related to the experimental learning of Cities: Skyline. The four categories of the interview questions are as follows:

Within the Learner's Background category, questions were geared to identify each learner's specifications, which includes the learner's age, previous education, and work experience. Questions in the Cognitive category were geared towards conceptual understanding, which included understanding sustainable-development theories, core concepts, and terminologies. (Example Question: "How has the game assisted you in learning core Urban Planning concepts and principles? Please name a few.") Questions within the Behavior Implications category were aimed to find out about the game's influence on fostering skill development. (Example Question: "Has the game facilitated in you Urban Planning creativity? If yes, give some examples.") And lastly, questions within the Affective Evaluation category were aimed to identify the game's influence on emotional aspects as an effective learning tool. For example, whether learners did or did not feel highly involved and engaged in their learning experiences. (Example Questions:

"How has the game contributed to your interest in the Urban Planning field; how has it influenced your motivation and engagement level (if it has) in the learning process?).

A pilot study of the interviews was conducted to allow the interviewer to familiarize oneself with the script flow and understand how the conversational style of the interview would allow for further questioning [32]. This also helped the interviewer determine the interview duration, so that it would remain within the timeframe noted on the consent form. The test also helped identify the relevance of the questions and helped the interviewer determine which questions could benefit from an explanation or an example to provide clearer understanding to the interviewee.

3.3 Data Analysis

The data was analyzed iteratively by researcher through the inductive approach by using a Thematic Analysis approach [26]. This involved finding commonalities and repetitions which are identified by comparisons of interviews and themes are identified. This method is useful as it provides flexibility and is suitable for new research interviewers. It is appropriate for analysing and summarising masses of in-depth raw-data and is convenient for highlighting similarities and differences between them. It is popular for psychological interpretations/analysis of raw-data and allows generation of unanticipated findings.

Thematic Analysis was done in the following stages:

1. Familiarization with research data.
2. Insertion of line numbers to function as markers.
3. Categories (Cognitive, Behavioral, Affective) assigned a distinct colour code.
4. Coloured coding applied to data, where it was felt that respondent touched upon a subject directly or indirectly relating to a specific category in his/her responses.
5. Data was then inserted under the similar color-coded Category Tables.
6. Themes were identified and marked as Dominant Theme or Sub-theme accordingly.
7. Data was re-analysed, and similar themes were extracted and inserted into Themes Tables.

4 Results and Discussions

The results focus on key areas of student learning experiences. Following the experiential learning model, the results are presented through three lenses: Cognitive, Behavioral, and Affective learning outcomes.

4.1 Cognitive Development (Conceptual Understanding)

Analysis of data suggests that although Cities Skylines could enhance student conceptual knowledge on sustainable development, it lacks subject related terminologies and guidance from the teacher. Research indicates that simulation games allowed users to implement and test several geographical concepts that assisted in their understandings [3, 7]. This research acts as an extension to that research, where students took the opportunity to implement an array of sustainability concepts in Cities Skylines. This augmented their conceptual-understanding, as the game helped them visualise and monitor its effects in a simulated-world. Consequences encountered based on learner's decisions and designs in the game also complimented student learning outcome.

> The theory comes hand in hand with the implementation of the game (…) It is a tool to give me more insight about the concept that is delivered (…) This game gives you an understanding about sustainable development [Participant 1].

Learning new terminologies from the simulation is an essential indicator of pedagogic effectiveness [25]. Cities Skylines did not provide convincing results for introducing new urban-planning/sustainable-development terminologies. It used simple English terms to help students to develop a general understanding of those terms.

> When I was making green cities, Green is a term that is not new for me, so when you put it into a working city, it is a whole different thing [Participant 1].

Our data suggest that the instructor's role becomes central, as students who failed to recognise this method for learning, had a negative experience of using the game. This is consistent with the literature [27, 28], suggesting the instructor needs to play a vital role as a facilitator in the learning process to draw out the maximum pedagogic potential of games. This highlights the importance of the instructor in providing a debriefing on how learning would take place and keeping close attention to student's learning process.

> The game does not connect to the concept because of its own set of principles (…) The game has set existing policies that have to be used – if I disapprove anything within the game, I have to go along with it [Participant 2].

A real challenge for students was to accurately reflect on the connections they could make with the game and its application in real life. The game, however, does not prepare students for its applicability in real-life situations due to its built-in limitations. For example, participant 6 stated that they wanted to implement car-free zones, but it was simply not achievable in the game. Here, the course instructor role's remains central in instigating debate and discussions amongst students to critically reflect on their ideas of what they ought to do in realistic situations.

> The critical process of having an idea of what you want to do with your city and not being able to do it, allows you to analyse what you might do in real life situation (…) It allows you to understand and apply the concepts however in real life on a lot of complex and wider scale [Participant 3].

In general, the game functions as a "canvas" for testing taught concepts. It is not a self-autonomised tool for learning concepts and terminologies, though it does demonstrate the profound potential for further development. This tool requires close facilitation by the instructor to ward off impacts of limitations, to achieve maximum pedagogic benefits. Therefore, it has been relatively successful in delivering conceptual understanding. It is instrumental for knowledge retention; however, it cannot replace training for real-life situations. Majority of participants advocated its use as having helped them to feel confident about their learning.

4.2 Behavioural Development (Skill Development)

Data analysis suggests that students value Cities Skylines for enhancing their critical thinking and problem-solving skills. Although creativity was also frequently mentioned by students, it could not be easily transferred into real-life contexts. In addition, students felt the built-in limitations of the game does not encourage collaborative learning.

Students identified certain knowledge-gaps that the game had helped them fill as they pursued their sustainable-development goals. Countering traffic problems was one of the significant challenges for some students. They had learnt how to critically evaluate the situation and design practical solutions, notably paying close attention to the order of functioning of traffic lights and the need to consider quality-of-roads, weather, residents nearby as opposed to emphasising widening roads to counter traffic issues. This is consistent with the literature which suggests that simulation games could promote student critical thinking skills [33].

> In case of traffic congestion, you need to critically think on how to solve the traffic problem in the area. When you build new settlements or residential areas you are thinking what the implication is it would have on my transport, am I going to need more schools, healthcare facilities, more services. So, it's a critical process [Participant 3]

According to students, the game provided them with a risk-free zone to be creative in designing urban cities. Nevertheless, they were not sure how these creative solutions could be transferred into real-life contexts.

> Planning cannot happen without inclusion of stakeholders (…) community would create like an action group against my development or vote against my development. You can't just make a road or a school; you actually have to go through the political process, get planning permission and go through public engagement, whereas there is none of that in the game [Participant 3].

As Cities-Skylines was a single-player game, students revealed the need for improved collaboration elements, such as multiplayer, forums, discussion groups, video display and voice chats.

> I'm not sure if it has chatrooms on it but I didn't see anything multiplayer or anything Because I think we just go guided on a solo play environment and I never played the game before and you had one account and you had to do a new game from there [Participant 8]

Overall, Cities Skylines generates specific skills for students; major ones include critical thinking and problem-solving skills. It also delivers in fulfilling certain knowledge-gaps in specific areas, where students experience unexpected consequences based on their decisions within the game. The game also addresses key matters related to districts, zoning and public services. Students highly approve of its skill generation, but they find an immense gap as a medium for applying acquired skills in real-life contexts.

4.3 Affective Development (Evaluation)

In this category, results showed that most students were highly motivated and engaged as they encountered the course material through the game. This is consistent with the existing research which reveals that simulation learning enhances trainees' affective and cognitive processes [1, 33].

However, improvements are needed to align student game experience with their learning objectives. Several participants reflected on a change of perception of learning, with increased interest, demonstrated that Cities Skylines is a valuable tool to aid traditional learning methods. This resulted in most students demonstrating immense satisfaction derived from the learning process.

> This is the first time I have experienced being taught theory using a game, I think this is a very interesting approach and a good way to do it. For motivation I will give it an 8/10. The game is very engaging; I would give a 9 or 9.5/10. It is a very demanding game [Participant 1]

However, the absence of a back story (debriefing) limited students' ability to connect game experience with real-life contexts. This shifted enormous responsibility on the instructor to stir the game experience and structure the lesson to bridge this gap.

> But I didn't know how this game was going to relate to the module [Participant 2]

Contrary to the results of existing research, which emphasize the role of computer-aided instructions (CAI) in the learning process [34, 35], our research suggests that CAI is not adequate as a sole instructional tool. The role of the instructor is of paramount importance to extract the pedagogic benefits and fend off in-game restrictions.

> There is a tug-of-war of interests there because, if I do not comply with the notification (instructions) of the game, something will happen to your residents ... they will leave your city [Participant 1]

In summary, positive developments were identified in terms of students' conceptual understanding, skill development, motivation, and satisfaction, which also effected their attitudes toward the subject. Nevertheless, the instructor's role is of paramount importance to keep the game in check, to prevent students from veering away from the learning objectives, and to extract maximum learning outcomes from the game.

5 Conclusion and Recommendations

This study reveals the pedagogical and phenomenological aspects of the simulation game, *Cities: Skylines*, for the urban-planning discipline. Eight in-depth interviews were conducted with postgraduate students from the sustainable development module to explore their views on the effectiveness of the game. The findings provide empirical evidence that *Cities: Skylines* can be an effective pedagogical tool for enhancing students' conceptual knowledge, while increasing motivation and satisfaction regarding the learning process. The research results suggest that elements of the game could help develop specific skills relevant to urban planning disciplines, including critical thinking, problem solving, and creative thinking. To be considered an effective educational tool, knowledge sharing and interactivity are of critical importance. Hence, it is recommended that game developers design educational games with a multiplayer option in order to enhance networked interactivity. Research limitations revealed gaps in the development of subject-related terminologies and the transferability of knowledge to real-life contexts. Thus, this research highlights the need for aligning game experience with the learning objectives of the module. This research also acknowledges the essential role of the instructor in bridging the gap between knowledge and skills acquired within the game and in real-life contexts. Future research would benefit from a larger sample size or a mixed-methods approach. Future research could also involve testing using the game *Cities: Skylines - Green Cities*, which is a recent expansion showing promising predisposition for teaching subjects related to sustainable development.

References

1. Sitzmann, T.: A meta-analytic examination of the instructional effectiveness of computer-based simulation games. Pers. Psychol. **64**(2), 489–528 (2011)
2. Owston, R.D.: Computer games and the quest to find their affordances for learning. Educ. Res. **41**(3), 105–106 (2012)
3. Kim, M., Shin, J.: The pedagogical benefits of SimCity in urban geography education. J. Geogr. **115**(2), 39–50 (2016)
4. Haahtela, P.: Gamification of education: cities skylines as an educational tool for real estate and land use planning studies (2015)
5. Fernández, P., Ceacero-Moreno, M.: Study of the training of environmentalists through gamification as a university course. Sustainability **13**, 2323 (2021)
6. Sergeyeva, O., Bogomiagkova, E., Orekh, E., Kolesnik, N.: Gamification as a trend in the development of civic and political participation. In: Chugunov, A., Khodachek, I., Misnikov, Y., Trutnev, D. (eds.) EGOSE 2019. CCIS, vol. 1135, pp. 125–137. Springer, Cham (2020). https://doi.org/10.1007/978-3-030-39296-3_10
7. Kolb, D.A.: Experiential Learning: Experience as the Source of Learning and Development. FT Press, New Jersey (2014)
8. Jin, S.A.A.: Avatars mirroring the actual self-versus projecting the ideal self: the effects of self-priming on interactivity and immersion in an exergame, Wii Fit. CyberPsychol. Behav. **12**(6), 761–765 (2009)
9. Blumberg, F.C., Pagnotta, J.N.: Gameplay and educational outcomes: reminders for educational game development. Games Health Res. Dev. Clin. Appl. **3**(2), 115–116 (2014)
10. Matuozzi, R.N.: Building Imaginary Worlds: The Theory and History of Subcreation. Mark JP Wolf, Routledge, New York (2014)
11. Guo, J., Singer, N., Bastide, R.: Design of a serious game in training non-clinical skills for professionals in health care area. In: IEEE 3rd International Conference on Serious Games and Applications for Health (SeGAH), Rio de Janeiro, Brazil, pp. 1–6 (2014)
12. Dunne, J.R., McDonald, C.L.: Pulse!!: a model for research and development of virtual-reality learning in military medical education and training. Mil. Med. **175**(7), 25–27 (2010)
13. Joubert, P., Roodt, S.: The relationship between prior game experience and digital game-based learning: an INNOV8 case-study. In: AIS Special Interest Group for Education (SIGEd 2010) Conference (2010)
14. Ravyse, W.S., Seugnet Blignaut, A., Leendertz, V., Woolner, A.: Success factors for serious games to enhance learning: a systematic review. Virtual Real. **21**(1), 31–58 (2016). https://doi.org/10.1007/s10055-016-0298-4

15. Ismailović, D., Haladjian, J., Köhler, B., Pagano, D., Brügge, B.: Adaptive serious game development. In: Proceedings of the Second International Workshop on Games and Software Engineering: Realising User Engagement with Game Engineering Techniques, Zurich, pp. 23–26. IEEE Press (2012)
16. Lim, T., et al.: Narrative Serious Game Mechanics (NSGM) – insights into the narrative-pedagogical mechanism. In: Göbel, S., Wiemeyer, J. (eds.) GameDays 2014. LNCS, vol. 8395, pp. 23–34. Springer, Cham (2014). https://doi.org/10.1007/978-3-319-05972-3_4
17. Marlow, C.M.: Games and learning in landscape architecture. In: Report on the Conference Digital Landscape Architecture, pp. 236–243 (2009)
18. Adams, D.M., Mayer, R.E., MacNamara, A., Koenig, A., Wainess, R.: Narrative games for learning: testing the discovery and narrative hypotheses. J. Educ. Psychol. **104**(1), 235 (2012)
19. Tashiro, J.S., Dunlap, D.: The impact of realism on learning engagement in educational games. In: Proceedings of the 2007 Conference on Future Play, Toronto, pp. 113–120. ACM (2007)
20. Andersen, E.: Optimising adaptivity in educational games. In: Proceedings of the International Conference on the Foundations of Digital Games, North Carolina, pp. 279–281. ACM (2012)
21. Zhang, X., Zhong, S., Pan, Z., Wong, K., Yun, R. (eds.): Edutainment 2010. LNCS, vol. 6249. Springer, Heidelberg (2010). https://doi.org/10.1007/978-3-642-14533-9
22. Lee, K.M., Jeong, E.J., Park, N., Ryu, S.: Effects of interactivity in educational games: a mediating role of social presence on learning outcomes. Int. J. Hum. Comput. Interact. **27**(7), 620–633 (2011)
23. Crookall, D.: Serious games, debriefing, and simulation/gaming as a discipline. Simul. Gaming **41**(6), 898–920 (2010)
24. Hoover, J.D., Carlton J.W.: An experiential-cognitive methodology in the first course in management: some preliminary results. In: Proceedings of the Annual ABSEL Conference (1975)
25. Ranchhod, A., Gurău, C., Loukis, E., Trivedi, R.: Evaluating the educational effectiveness of simulation games: a value generation model. Inf. Sci. **264**, 75–90 (2014)
26. Braun, V., Clarke, V.: Using thematic analysis in psychology. Qual. Res. Psychol. **3**(2), 77–101 (2006)
27. Charsky, D., Mims, C.: Integrating commercial off-the-shelf video games into school curriculums. TechTrends **52**(5), 38–44 (2008)
28. Dyson, B., Griffin, L.L., Hastie, P.: Sport education, tactical games, and cooperative learning: theoretical and pedagogical considerations. Quest **56**(2), 226–240 (2004)
29. Myers, M.D.: Qualitative Research in Business and Management. Sage, London (2019)
30. Raworth, K., Sweetman, C., Narayan, S., Rowlands, J., Hopkins, A.: Conducting Semi-Structured Interviews. Oxfam, Nairobi (2012)
31. Abildgaard, J.S., Saksvik, P.Ø., Nielsen, K.: How to measure the intervention process? An assessment of qualitative and quantitative approaches to data collection in the process evaluation of organizational interventions. Front. Psychol. **7**, 13 (2016)
32. Turner, D.W., III.: Qualitative interview design: a practical guide for novice investigators. Qual. Rep. **15**(3), 754 (2010)
33. Ibrahim, R., Yusoff, R.C.M., Mohamed-Omar, H., Jaafar, A.: Students perceptions of using educational games to learn introductory programming. Comput. Inf. Sci. **4**(1), 205 (2011)
34. Usman, Y.D., Madudili, G.C.: Assessment of the impact of computer assisted instruction on teaching and learning in Nigeria: a theoretical viewpoint. Int. J. Educ. Dev. Inf. Commun. Technol. **16**(2), 259–271 (2020)
35. Vogel, J.J., Vogel, D.S., Cannon-Bowers, J., Bowers, C.A., Muse, K., Wright, M.: Computer gaming and interactive simulations for learning: a meta-analysis. J. Educ. Comput. Res. **34**(3), 229–243 (2006)

Social Exclusion in Gamified Information Systems

Arthur E. van der Poll[1(✉)], Izak van Zyl[2], and Jan H. Kroeze[1]

[1] School of Computing, University of South Africa, Science Campus, Roodepoort, South Africa
39475964@mylife.unisa.ac.za, kroezjh@unisa.ac.za

[2] Centre for Communication Studies, Faculty of Informatics and Design, Cape Peninsula University of Technology, Cape Town, South Africa
VanZylIz@cput.ac.za

Abstract. Gamification is broadly defined as the use of game-related features and practices (e.g., points, rewards, and competition) in environments that are not related to entertainment. In Information Systems learning, gamification can be considered to improve students' interpersonal skills and to develop their digital literacy. This study highlights that gamification can have the opposite effect; we argue that gamification's technical systems often have oppressive qualities that socially exclude students. We recommend that educational software designers and vendors include students as co-designers of technical systems, thereby allowing for participatory and representative Information Systems learning.

Keywords: Gamification · Information systems · Digital exclusion · Social exclusion · Africanisation · Decolonisation

1 Introduction

The theme of the i3e2021 conference is *"Responsible AI and Analytics for an Ethical and Inclusive Digitised Society"*. In this paper, we depart from the assumption that Artificial Intelligence (AI), analytics, and information systems create positive opportunities. It also has negative consequences for individuals and societies [cf. 1, 2]. Despite the social and economic benefits of information systems in the domain of AI, its ethical concerns, including social exclusion, must be understood.

In this paper, we explore some of the negative aspects that emerge from using gamified information systems, and particularly for higher education students from resource-limited backgrounds in South Africa. In what follows, we report on some of the experiences of students enrolled in an Information Systems (IS) undergraduate course that was gamified to encourage learner motivation. We argue that gamification software (technical systems) may have oppressive qualities that stifle engagement and autonomy. Additionally, we shed light on the possibility of Africanising gamification through reflection from both inside and outside Western epistemology.

In the next section, we describe gamification in the context of information systems and AI. Thereafter, we describe the concept of a gamified information system. We present

Published by Springer Nature Switzerland AG 2021
D. Dennehy et al. (Eds.): I3E 2021, LNCS 12896, pp. 774–786, 2021.
https://doi.org/10.1007/978-3-030-85447-8_65

Social Cognitive Theory as the theoretical basis of our research and give an overview of the study's research method. Supported by empirical data, we then explore how students are unintentionally excluded through gamification. We conclude with recommendations that promote social inclusion of students/players in gamified information systems.

2 Gamification and AI

Gamification is broadly defined as the use of game-related features and practices (e.g., points, rewards, and competition) in environments that are not related to entertainment [3]. A systematic literature review by Khakpour and Colomo-Palacios [4] indicates that gamification and Artificial Intelligence – machine learning (ML) in particular – are used in a cooperative manner to augment the effect of one another towards a predefined task. AI is defined as the use of machines and computers to simulate the decision-making abilities of human intelligence [5]. ML (a branch of AI) refers to applications that learn from data and enhance predictive accuracy over time without being programmed to do so [6]. López and Tucker [7] applied ML for affect state (i.e., emotion) recognition to predict student performance on a gamified learning task. The authors used a multimodal infrared Kinect sensor to record facial keypoint data while students engaged in obstacle avoidance. Students performed a series of body motions (e.g., jump, bend) to pass through sets of obstacles without making physical contact. A gamified application – on a data projector screen – displayed, for example, points awarded to the player for successfully passing through an obstacle or win states, indicating whether they lost or won.

2.1 Gamification and Social Inclusion in IS Learning

Social inclusion is broadly defined as having a sense of being part of a group [8]. Vygotsky [9] argues that a learner cannot comprehend a new concept or idea without the support of a peer or teacher. In a meta-analysis, Yiping, Abrami and D'Apollonia [10] find that small cooperative groups achieved improved learning with computer technology compared to individuals. Indeed, students in groups tend to acquire more individual knowledge than students learning with computer technology individually [10]. In IS usage, individual tasks are often embedded in group tasks or routines. Therefore, some form of collaboration occurs [11]. In addition, the speed of current technological advancements calls for AI interventions in team composition, according to Webber et al. [12]. To adapt to rapid organisational changes, today's teams/groups need fluid membership that changes in accordance with the project's specs and resource needs. AI can learn from such changes and make recommendations to improve team formation [12].

Bilgin and Gul [13] investigate the effect of gamification on group cohesion and academic achievement. Their research sample was pre-service teachers enrolled in an Information Technology course. The authors conducted an experiment which compared a gamified (experimental) group with a traditional (control) group. Game elements such as badges, points, leaderboards, and challenges were introduced in the gamified group while being absent in the traditional group. For example, students in the gamified group received badges on their scores, earning recognition from their teachers and peers.

The comparison revealed that gamified groups indicated higher group cohesion than traditional groups.

Despite the promise of group learning, individual learning should not be dismissed. Social inclusion is also characterised by individuals who pursue personal goals through group interaction, while still making a meaningful contribution to the group – the result is reciprocity [8]. Individual learning has an important role in IS [14] and game-based [15] learning contexts. The ACM and AIS state that IS graduates and professionals should be able to "collaborate with other professionals as well as perform successfully at the individual level" [14]. McFarland [15] argues that individual play gives students more learner autonomy to demonstrate their individual learning progression through gameplay.

2.2 'Intelligent' Information Systems

According to Lee [6], information systems comprise three primary systems: social, technical, and knowledge. The social system includes the people who interact with the technical system; the technical system includes data structures, networks, hardware, and software. The examination of the design, properties and behaviour produced by the mutual transformational exchange is the knowledge system. The "mutually and iteratively transformational interactions" among the three systems result in an information system [6]. Lee [6] argues that the technical system does not have to be digital technology but can also be the coordination of human resources that support the processing of materials into services and products.

Lee [16] criticises conceptions of 'information systems' that emphasise information requirements. The information system is instead the result of reciprocal transformational exchange between the social system and the technical system. The exchange is transformational insofar as the technical system is changed (i.e., transformed) when the social system fulfils requirements the technical system poses to it. This change triggers different and new requirements for the social system to satisfy.

We argue that Lee's notion of a social system is not workable in Artificial General Intelligence (AGI). AGI is also known as 'strong AI' and the term derives from the idea that human intelligence is a general phenomenon that can be replicated by a computer. Although AGI can emulate many human-like properties, it is often still conceived as artificial narrow intelligence (ANI). ANI, also known as 'weak AI', is restricted to specific tasks. An example is Deep Blue, which was designed to outplay humans in chess. In 1997, Deep Blue defeated Garry Kasparov, a world champion of chess. Although emulation of intelligence is impressive, one can hardly claim that it has gained human intelligence [17, 18].

Descartes's Cartesian dualism [19] rejects the hypothesis of a machine that is phenomenologically indistinguishable from man. Cartesian dualism is the belief that the mind is non-physical; namely, the mind is separate from the body. Here, the mind is associated with consciousness and distinguishable from the seat of intelligence: the brain. In view of Cartesian dualism, the core idea of AI is problematised, based on theories which maintain that brain processes and mental processes are the same [20].

In Cartesian dualism, subjectivism (i.e., thought) is inseparable from a 'thing that thinks'. The thing that thinks is 'I'. I am "a thing that thinks; that is, I am mind, or intelligence, or intellect, or reason" [19].

Therefore, as a thinking thing, 'I' have a subjective experience of the world. By implication, the subjective mind cannot be mapped digitally onto a computational system. As Fjelland [17] points out, humans are subjective, social beings who function in a social world. Furthermore, AI – in a strict sense – is not part of our social world – AI is an assembly of algorithms and numbers. Fjelland concludes that learning about another person does not warrant scrutiny into the chemistry of their brain, but instead requires engaging with their subjective lifeworld.

2.3 Gamified Technical Systems

The gamified technical system used for this study is Quizlet Live, an online game-based learning platform [21]. Of particular interest to the authors is its 'progress-reset' feature. In a Quizlet Live game, students take a quiz – based on their learning content – on a digital device (i.e., PC, tablet, smart phone). While students play, the instructor displays their progress as a race via an interactive leaderboard. If a question is answered incorrectly, the system resets players' progress to zero; they must start again. In addition, the incorrectly answered question will reappear later in the game [21].

We regard Quizlet's progress-reset feature as ANI. Aside from ANI's focus on single tasks with accurate precision, it is also bound by predefined algorithmic rules. One of ANI's primary benefits is the rapid automation of time-consuming tasks [17, 18]. It is conceivable that an instructor can emulate Quizlet Live's progress-reset functionality in a non-computerised setting. However, they will not be able to assess wrong/correct answers and progress-reset as quickly and effectively as the technical system. The progress-reset feature as an ANI is consistent with Rich's [22] definition of AI: "the study of how to make computers do things that people are better at". Indeed, computers outperform humans in the rapid execution of most computations.

Quizlet's progress-reset feature is an example of a 'replay' game element. When players replay a part of a game, they typically do so to master their gameplay skills [15]. In a pedagogical context, McFarland defines replay as the redoing or relearning of skills and concepts to master [11]. We observe a connection between replay and the Depth of Knowledge Metric in the ACM and AIS curriculum guide. The metric entails learning by repetition to help students master conceptual and technical skills of which they have insufficient knowledge [14].

In some gaming contexts, replay has a negative social connotation. For example, in violent video games, aggressive actions are incentivised – i.e., players who defeat their enemies are rewarded with praise by other players or with badges by the game designers. Moreover, game designers often do not make visible in video games the consequences of aggressive behaviour [23]. Similarly, we seek to highlight the implicit and often hidden negative social implications of replay in an IS learning context.

3 The Alienated Gamified Social System

In this section, we focus on the role of gamified technical systems in alienating the social system. Technical systems can potentially alienate social systems as its end-users are not able to change the software's source code. Software vendors establish control by employing copyright restrictions on the executable code and treating it as a trade secret. Hall and Pesenti [24] highlight a lack of access to data in AI development; top AI organisations keep data confined to their own design initiatives. These measures are taken to safeguard profit imperatives and serve as technical barriers to competing software vendors [25]. Glass [25] argues that such capitalist commitments misrepresent users' interests and needs. Consequently, the social system is deprived of opportunities to change the source code for its emerging and diverse needs. Likewise, Sonnenburg et al. [26] observe that "few machine learning researchers currently publish the software and/or source code."

Berry [27] argues that software design is entrenched in neoliberal principles. Neoliberalism is part of the broader capitalist system and linked to Western ideas of wealth accrual. Therefore, digital technology is used as a capitalist tool through which a certain type of dominant knowledge can be sustained. A further consequence is that endeavours to develop indigenous knowledge with the aid of digital technology are stifled. In similar vein, Hagerty and Rubinov observe that people from low-income countries are "underrepresented in the datasets central to developing AI systems" [28].

The free and open-source software (FOSS) and decolonisation movements counteract the social exclusion that stems from proprietary software. As opposed to proprietary software, FOSS permits users to examine the code that they use, to change it if they prefer, and to communicate the changes to the inventor for implementation in future versions of the software. The outcome is that autonomy is sustained among software users [29]. Sonnenburg et al. [26], however, point out that open source software (or 'open science' in the context of scientific research) is never truly free or open. Although small in number, open data sets including Caltech 101, the Delph repository, and the UCT Machine Learning Repository have made significant contributions to progress in ML [26].

Geyser [30] calls for decolonising and diversifying game design courses and uses an example of a first-year game design course she offers at a South African university. She distinguishes between two types of students in the game design course: experienced players and novices. In contrast to novices, skilled players have extensive gameplay experience, attended wealthier schools, and were taught in the subjects Information Technology and Visual Arts. Conversely, novices are mostly black students from resource-poor backgrounds, and with little or no technical knowledge or access to computer infrastructure. Novices tend to be second-language English speakers, which disadvantages them, as a good command of English is a central requirement for the course.

The challenge these second-language users face is their unfamiliarity with gaming registers [30]. Registers are defined by Gee [31] as a vernacular used for a specific purpose, e.g., the language of video game players. Therefore, the Western tradition of thought and action, entrenched in digital games, is not (always) easily understood by students who are not prolific game players. Geyser recommends that curriculum developers draw from students' local social and cultural backgrounds (e.g., language) and metaphors to decolonise game design curricula. Geyser further recommends that practitioners and curriculum developers draw from a rich tradition of precolonial games to decolonise game courses. Indeed, Nxumalo and Mncube advocate the play of indigenous games in schools to decolonise curricula [32].

4 The Knowledge System: Social Cognitive Theory

We use Bandura's [33] Social Cognitive Theory (SCT) as a theoretical framework to understand social inclusion and exclusion in gamification. The SCT concept – collective efficacy [34] – will frame our discussion about group cohesion. Collective efficacy refers to the shared belief of a group to achieve a desired result. To analyse the concept of oppressive, intelligent gamified technical systems that alienate the social system, we use SCT's triadic causation model (TCM) [33]. TCM is based on reciprocal determinism, which is the idea that human agency and learning function within an interactive social environment. TCM includes *personal (p)*, *environmental (e)*, and *behavioural (b)* determinants exerting influence on each other – see Fig. 1[1].

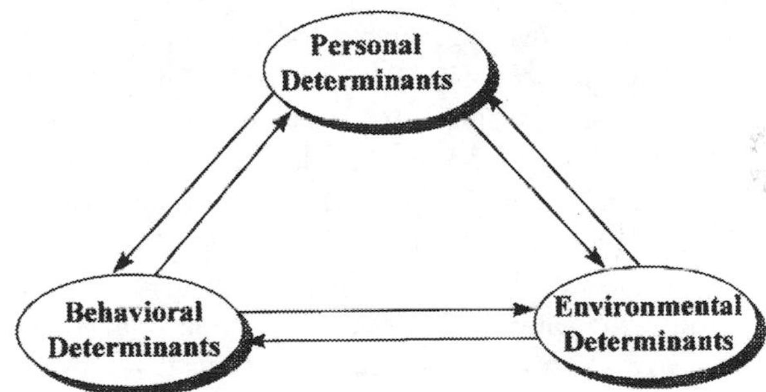

Fig. 1. The triadic causation model of Social Cognitive Theory [20].

Bandura describes the three components and the relationship between them as follows [33]:

Behavioural Determinants ⇔ Environmental Determinants. A person's behaviour exerts influence on environmental conditions. Likewise, a person's behaviour is partially influenced by environmental conditions. In the context of this study, unless students engage with gamification imparted with some form of AI, they do not praise or question its effectiveness.

Personal Determinants ⇔ Behavioural Determinants. A person's expectations affect the behaviour and the motives behind their actions. In turn, a person's actions affect their personal perceptions of phenomena. In the context this study, the extent to which a student is receptive to AI-based gamification depends on whether it meets with their personal learning experience.

[1] From "Social cognitive theory of mass communication" by A. Bandura, 2001, *Media Psychology, 3,* p. 266. Copyright [2001] by Taylor & Francis Ltd (http://www.tandfonline.com). Reprinted with permission.

Environmental Determinants ⇔ Personal Determinants. Observable personal traits affect how people perceive different social environments. In the context of this study, information systems and AI present different meanings to different individuals.

5 Method

The empirical data presented in this paper was collected as part of a larger gamification study that was conducted by the first author. The research sample was first-year IS students at a South African University of Technology. SCT was deployed as a theoretical framework and Action Research (AR) as a research strategy. Data was gathered via semi-structured interviews, focus groups and participant observation across two Action Research cycles. The established Action Research model by Lewin [35] – the founder of Action Research – guided data collection. Lewin's Action Research model diagnoses a problem, plans actions, implements planned actions, and assesses those actions to resolve problems [35].

In the first AR cycle, teams were selected randomly. The first author observed that there was a lack of interaction between group members during the gamification sessions. He attributed this to the participants not knowing each other, despite being grouped in the same lessons and roster. To address this issue, the first author asked students to choose their own teammates for the second AR cycle. The rationale that underpins this team formation strategy is the notion that group interaction will improve if students engage in gameplay with friends, whom they trust.

The first finding – social alienation – that emanated from team formation was captured in response to the following interview question: In cycle one, I randomly assigned participants to a team; in cycle two, I informed participants that they can choose whom they want to be with on a team. Which of these two ways of forming a team do you prefer and why? The second finding – language – stems from participant observation (discussed in more depth in the next section).

6 Findings

Aligned with the aim of illuminating the oppressive qualities of 'intelligent' technical systems, the results focus on Quizlet's 'progress-reset' function (discussed in Sect. 2.2). In the present study, students who disliked progress reset were observed to be withdrawn or had a poor grasp of the English language. In addition, these students were observed to contribute little to group interaction or struggled to form relationships with the prospect of effective group work.

6.1 Social Alienation

Withdrawn students struggled to establish strong social bonds; therefore, choosing team members to play Quizlet Live was difficult. The result was a lack of cooperation between members, causing many progress-resets. This reflects in students' remarks about team formation and communication: "some people… they do know some of the people that were in class, which doesn't bode well for others who don't know people that they trust... It wasn't really fair for people who did not have information about their classmates" [Student 7]; "[t]he other people, they know each other. And me, I'm not talking too much in the classroom. I know Student 12 but we don't talk a lot" [Student 11]; "[w]e had a third person, I don't remember him, he was there" [Student 15].

We link the issue of withdrawn students to Quizlet Live being available only in team play mode at the time the empirical research was conducted. Shortly after the research concluded, Quizlet added single-player mode to the technical system. As we mentioned earlier, individual play should not be dismissed. Student 11 states, "I play with other people like friends, but I'm not really a player of a group"; Student 3 states, "I think it would be more interesting doing it individually, you are going to be the one writing the exam. So it is good to play the game based on just your knowledge ... you gonna exactly see the level you are on. You only see the level your group is on". Bandura [34] states that a group's united effort towards the desired success is greatly affected by the performance of its individual members.

Since this paper is part of a wider research effort, practitioners might argue that social alienation could be accounted for in the use of a gamification framework, e.g., Octalysis [36]. However, Octalysis' fifth core drive – which would have informed discussion about 'social alienation' – is not a game element, but a persuasive learning element [see 37]. This core drive relates to group quests and companionship in gamification, and deploys methods such as mentorship and social prods, among others, to strengthen social interaction in a group [36].

Landers and colleagues argue that "if identical psychological effects can be created without a game, whether regarding persuasion, learning, or any other practical outcome, then the creation of a game is a waste of resources. If gameful design is functionally identical to existing interventions used to change behavior, there is no reason to study gameful design either" [38]. To this end, Webber et al.'s [12] notion of AI intervention (highlighted in Sect. 2.1) to optimise team formation can be valuable as a pre-implementation strategy to improve team collaboration in gamification.

6.2 Language

The language issue was raised when a lecturer participant drew the first author's attention to Student 11 and his teammates who encountered many progress-resets. Student 11 seemed unnerved and contributed little to the deliberations about the correct potential answer to quiz questions. The lecturer said that he struggles with English as his mother tongue is French; she explained that he reads slowly to understand the proper context of what he reads. In his individual interview, Student 11 gave the following answer to a question about the most difficult challenge that he faced in the IS course, "it's my language, because I used to speak French...you know changing the language, changing all of the stuff".

However, unless students speak the same language, changing Quizlet's [10] language setting – for example, to French – is impractical. Besides, the primary medium of instruction of this IS course is English. Moreover, non-fluent English-speaking students generally embrace English as an instruction medium [39]. This is linked to the perception that English proficiency (and computing registers embedded in English) is essential to perform in a hyperconnected, globalised information and communication society [27]. Also, there is a paucity of indigenous languages in the computing field, which compromises attempts to Africanise computing curricula. Therefore, it is not easy to translate computing registers to meaningful, relatable indigenous terms. In English, for example, the meaning of a graphical user interface 'menu' and 'list' is different; in isiXhosa, the term 'uludwe' refers to both a menu and list [40].

The following responses reflect the statements above: "Isn't it like Java or something where if you are in a medical area, you say medical words and another person won't understand… and if you translate it, it doesn't make sense" [Student 6]; "Me personally, I prefer learning in English because that is what most of the subjects are in. For the person[2] in question who is Xhosa, I think it will be better than to discuss the subject in English. Regarding the subject, there is no Xhosa in Java so…" [Student 10]; "programming is more easy if you are English speaker when you do programming because there is no other term, you cannot translate it to French. … Programming is a programming language, but it is in English also. So I think it is better to do Programming in English to try to learn English and to do Programming" [Student 11].

Beliefs of English as the *de facto* language should not instil the notion that it is not necessary to develop IS content in other languages. Gamification can offer solutions; an example is Von Holy et al. [41] who created a web-based digital repository – called BantuWeb – as an instrument to motivate users to add 'resource scarce languages'. An instance of gamified features includes users earning points for contributing content on the website. The points are listed on a leaderboard with the aim of promoting competition between users to add content and compete for a higher rank.

This finding illustrates the 'narrowness' of progress-reset as an ANI. That is, it cannot account for all social factors – in this instance, language – in the process of managing progress. This relationship between ANI and gamification remains valuable in the narrow context of language acquisition. For example, to assist students in learning the vocabulary of a new language, Lungu [42] presents an AI ecosystem which monitors reader applications to track learners' reading activities. The AI constructs a model of learners' developing knowledge to recommend tailored reading sessions to them. The service interface includes a *Motivator* agent that deploys gamification strategies as a feedback mechanism to keep learners motivated.

7 Discussion and Potential Solutions

In Sect. 3, we argue that neoliberal elements in the design of intelligent technical systems could be oppressive. Consequently, users' choices in the direction of their technological experience could be prohibited. A major assumption we highlighted is that the designers of technical systems/AI presuppose the social requirements of their users or their own social background. This bias is further compounded by technical systems designed according to Western standards, given that digital technology and AI are predominantly produced and consumed in the West [43]. Subsequently, context-bound experiences of users in non-Western settings are mostly ignored. Consistent with SCT, personal (p)

[2] Student 10 (a non-Xhosa speaking student) is referring to a Xhosa speaking student.

determinants – i.e., weak sociality and insufficient English skills – negatively affect student behaviour (b) and the information systems environment (e) when engaging gamified technical systems:

Personal Determinants ⇔ Behavioural Determinants. Introverted and second-language English speaking students struggle to perform in gamified information systems. We anticipate that introverted students will perform better in both individual gameplay and group gameplay following exposure to individual play. We anticipate that second-language English speaking students will perform better if they partake in translating computing registers to relatable local languages, by participating in Africanisation research projects.

Personal Determinants ⇔ Environmental Determinants. For introverted students, little knowledge acquisition occurs through gamified information systems because of a strong emphasis on group work. Little knowledge acquisition also occurs for second-language English speaking students because gamified information systems are (typically) embedded in Western epistemology, which in turn, is communicated in English. But we expect students with personal goals to improve their English or to take part in attempts to Africanise game design courses/research projects that will enable them to cope in a gamified information systems environment. And individual efficacy, which we expect to increase through individual gameplay, is valuable in IS environments focused on group work.

Behavioural Determinants ⇔ Environmental Determinants. If introverted students' performance improves through individual gameplay, we expect them to improve in group gameplay environments. We anticipate that second-language English speaking students will perform better as gamification information systems gradually become decolonised. We also expect that second-language English speaking students' performance will gradually improve in English-dominated gamified information systems environments as a direct implication of improved English abilities achieved via personal goals.

To Africanise the design process in a gamified technical system, we advance the deployment of a player-centred Design Science research strategy. Our ideation of design science research involves more than students evaluating 'smart' gamified technical systems in the post-implementation phase; students should be able to collaborate with game programmers and AI designers to plan, study, implement and change the source code [26]. Indeed, Yordanova [44] highlights the lack of skills for designing AI and recommends that more institutions introduce Bachelors, Master, and PhD programmes in AI design. From a programmer's point of view, we recognise that student participation in the design of AI infused gamified applications may not offer significant value to system design and maintenance. This is because students or gamers might not possess advanced programming skills. Yet, at the very least, IS departments and game designers should facilitate a process where students integrate cultural and indigenous knowledge and constructs into game design.

8 Concluding Remarks

This paper discusses how 'intelligent' gamified information systems exclude students based on their background. We highlighted how the technical system often oppresses the social system, whereby it does not fulfil the requirements of the social system. Oppressive qualities in technical systems are a manifestation of the interests of its designers, embodied in source code not accessible to be viewed or changed by users. The result is that the complexities of the social system – e.g., non-English language and social alienation – are not considered. To democratise gamified information systems, we call on software designers, vendors, and academic institutions to collaborate with students when designing systems. Such endeavours could make significant contributions to the indigenisation and specifically the Africanisation of the IS discipline.

References

1. Ransbotham, S., Fichman, R.G., Gopal, R., Gupta, A.: Ubiquitous IT and digital vulnerabilities. Inf. Syst. Res. **27**(4), 834–847 (2016)
2. Majchrzak, A., Markus, L.M., Wareham, J.: Designing for digital transformation: lessons for information systems research from the study of ICT and societal challenges. MIS Q. **40**(2), 1187–1200 (2016)
3. Deterding, S., Dixon, D., Khaled, R., Nacke, L.: From game design elements to gamefulness: defining gamification. In: Proceedings of the 15th International Academic MindTrek Conference on Envisioning Future Media Environments - MindTrek 2011, Tampere, Finland (2011)
4. Khakpour, A., Colomo-Palacios, R.: Convergence of gamification and machine learning: a systematic literature review. Technol. Knowl. Learn. **26**(3), 597–636 (2020). https://doi.org/10.1007/s10758-020-09456-4
5. McCarthy, J.: What is Artificial Intelligence? Stanford University, Stanford (2007)
6. IBM: Machine Learning. https://www.ibm.com/za-en/cloud/learn/machine-learning. Accessed 03 May 2021
7. López, C., Tucker, C.: Toward personalized adaptive gamification: a machine learning model for predicting performance. Inst. Electr. Electron. Eng. Trans. Games **12**(2), 155–168 (2020)
8. Cobigo, V., Ouellette-Kuntz, H., Lysaght, R., Martin, L.: Shifting our conceptualization of social inclusion. Stigma Res. Action **2**(2), 75–84 (2012)
9. Vygotsky, L.: Mind in Society: The Development of Higher Psychological Processes. Harvard University Press, Cambridge (1978)
10. Yiping, L., Abrami, P.C., D'Apollonia, S.: Small group and individual learning with technology: a meta-analysis. Rev. Educ. Res. **71**(3), 449–521 (2001)
11. Polites, G., Karahanna, E.: The embeddedness of information systems habits in organizational and individual level routines: development and disruption. MIS Q. **37**, 221–246 (2013)
12. Webber, S.S., Detjen, J., MacLean, T.L., Thomas, D.: Team challenges: is artificial intelligence the solution? Bus. Horiz. **62**(6), 741–750 (2019)
13. Bilgin, C.U., Gul, A.: Investigating the effectiveness of gamification on group cohesion, attitude, and academic achievement in collaborative learning environments. TechTrends **64**(1), 124–136 (2020)
14. ACM, AIS: IS 2010 Curriculum Guidelines for Undergraduate Degree Programs in Information Systems. ACM and AIS, New York (2010)

15. McFarland, J.: Teacher Perspectives on the Implementation of Gamification. California Lutheran University, Thousand Oaks (2017)
16. Lee, A.S.: Thinking about social theory and philosophy for information systems. In: Mingers, J., Willcocks, L. (eds.) Social Theory and Philosophy for Information Systems. John Wiley & Sons, Ltd., Chichester (2004)
17. Fjelland, R.: Why general artificial intelligence will not be realized. Humanit. Soc. Sci. Commun. **7**(1), 1–9 (2020)
18. Bundy, A.: Preparing for the future of Artificial Intelligence. AI Soc. **32**(2), 285–287 (2017)
19. Descartes, R.: The Philosophical Writings of Descartes. Cambridge University Press, Cambridge (1984)
20. Nath, R.: A Cartesian critique of the artificial intelligence. Philos. Pap. Rev. **2**(2010), 27–33 (2010)
21. Quizlet: How to Play Quizlet Live. YouTube, US (2018). https://www.youtube.com/watch?v=q64qTBfK0iE
22. Rich, E.: Artificial intelligence and the humanities. Comput. Humanit. **19**, 117–122 (1985)
23. Groves, C.L., Anderson, C.A.: Negative effects of video game play. In: Nakatsu, R., Rauterberg, M., Ciancarini, P. (eds.) Handbook of Digital Games and Entertainment Technologies, pp. 1297–1322. Springer, Singapore (2016)
24. Hall, W., Pesenti, J.: Growing the artificial intelligence industry in the UK (2017). https://assets.publishing.service.gov.uk/government/uploads/system/uploads/attachment_data/file/652097/Growing_the_artificial_intelligence_industry_in_the_UK.pdf
25. Glass, E.: Software of the oppressed: reprogramming the invisible discipline (2018). https://academicworks.cuny.edu/gc_etds/2889
26. Sonnenburg, S., et al.: The need for open source software in machine learning. J. Mach. Learn. Res. **8**, 2443–2466 (2007)
27. Berry, M.: Power/knowledge in the information age: the epistemological implications of ICTs and education for all. In: Language & Literacy Graduate Student Conference, pp. 1–10. University of Victoria, Victoria (2008)
28. Hagerty, A., Rubinov, I.: Global AI ethics: a review of the social impacts and ethical implications of artificial intelligence. arXiv:1907.07892v1 (2019)
29. Chopra, S., Dexter, S.: Decoding Liberation: The Promise of Free and Open Source Software. Routledge, New York (2007)
30. Geyser, H.: Decolonising the games curriculum: interventions in an introductory game design course. Open Libr. Humanit. **4**(1) (2018)
31. Gee, J.P.: A sociocultural perspective on opportunity to learn. In: Moss, P., Pullin, D., Gee, J., Haertel, E., Jones Young, L. (eds.) Assessment, Equity and Opportunity to Learn, pp. 76–108. Cambridge University Press, Cambridge (2008)
32. Nxumalo, S.A., Mncube, D.W.: Using indigenous games and knowledge to decolonise the school curriculum: ubuntu perspectives. Perspect. Educ. **36**(2), 103–118 (2018)
33. Bandura, A.: Social cognitive theory of mass communication. Media Psychol. **3**, 265–299 (2001)
34. Bandura, A.: Exercise of human agency through collective efficacy. Curr. Dir. Psychol. Sci. **9**(3), 75–78 (2000)
35. Lewin, K.: Action research and minority problems. J. Soc. Issues **2**(4), 34–46 (1946)
36. Chou, Y.: The 8 core drives of gamification (#5): social influence & relatedness. https://yukaichou.com/gamification-study/8-core-drives-of-gamification-5-social-influence-relatedness/. Accessed 02 May 2021
37. Zulkifli, A.N., Noor, N.M., Bakar, J.A.A., Mat, R.C., Ahmad, M.: A conceptual model of interactive persuasive learning system for elderly to encourage computer-based learning process. In: Proceedings - 2013 International Conference on Informatics and Creative Multimedia, pp. 7–12. IEEE, New York (2013)

38. Landers, R.N., Tondello, G.F., Kappen, D.L., Collmus, A.B., Mekler, E.D., Nacke, L.E.: Defining gameful experience as a psychological state caused by gameplay: replacing the term ‘gamefulness’ with three distinct constructs. Int. J. Hum. Comput. Stud. **127**, 81–94 (2019)
39. Liebenberg, S., Van der Walt, A.: Why Afrikaans doesn’t qualify for special treatment at universities. The Conversation. https://theconversation.com/why-afrikaans-doesnt-qualify-for-special-treatment-at-universities-51916. Accessed 27 May 2018
40. Dalvit, L., Murray, S., Terzoli, A.: The role of indigenous knowledge in computer education in Africa. In: Kendall, M., Samways, B. (eds.) Learning to Live in the Knowledge Society. ITIFIP, vol. 281, pp. 287–294. Springer, Boston (2008). https://doi.org/10.1007/978-0-387-09729-9_43
41. Von Holy, A., Bresler, A., Shuman, O., Chavula, C., Suleman, H.: BantuWeb: a digital library for resource scarce South African languages. In: South African Institute for Computer Scientists and Information Technologists, ACM Digital Library (2017). https://doi.org/10.1145/3129416.3129446
42. Lungu, M.F.: Bootstrapping an ubiquitous monitoring ecosystem for accelerating vocabulary acquisition. In: 10th European Conference on Software Architecture, pp. 1–4. ACM, New York (2016)
43. Muwanga-Zake, J.W.F.: Narrative research across cultures: epistemological concerns in Africa. Curr. Narratives **1**(2), 68–83 (2010)
44. Yordanova, Z.: Gamification as a tool for supporting Artificial Intelligence development – State of Art. In: Botto-Tobar, M., Zambrano Vizuete, M., Torres-Carrión, P., Montes León, S., Pizarro Vásquez, G., Durakovic, B. (eds.) ICAT 2019. CCIS, vol. 1193, pp. 313–324. Springer, Cham (2020). https://doi.org/10.1007/978-3-030-42517-3_24

Correction to: Responsible AI and Analytics for an Ethical and Inclusive Digitized Society

Denis Dennehy, Anastasia Griva, Nancy Pouloudi,
Yogesh K. Dwivedi, Ilias Pappas, and Matti Mäntymäki

Correction to:
D. Dennehy et al. (Eds.): *Responsible AI and Analytics for an Ethical and Inclusive Digitized Society*, LNCS 12896, https://doi.org/10.1007/978-3-030-85447-8

For Chapter 29:
In an older version of this paper, only one of Devinder Thapa's two affiliations was listed. This has been corrected.

For Chapter 34:
In an older version of this paper, the term "adaptive agility" was employed instead of "entrepreneurial agility" in one of the last sentences in Sect. 5.2. This has been corrected.

The updated version of these chapters can be found at
https://doi.org/10.1007/978-3-030-85447-8_29
https://doi.org/10.1007/978-3-030-85447-8_34

Published by Springer Nature Switzerland AG 2021
D. Dennehy et al. (Eds.): I3E 2021, LNCS 12896, p. C1, 2021.
https://doi.org/10.1007/978-3-030-85447-8_66

Author Index

Abbott, Pamela Y. 371
Abedin, Babak 259
Abrams, Nicholas 150
Adhikari, Abhishruti 150
Agbeko, Michael Nartey 60
Agyei-Owusu, Benjamin 441, 481
Ahmad, Iftikhar 622
Ahmad, Muhammad Ovais 622
Al Ariss, Akram 307
Alshahrani, Albandari 71
Amedofu, Mawuli Kobla 481
Apostolou, Dimitris 120
Asamoah, David 441, 481

Baker, Elizabeth White 161
Bargh, Mortaza S. 292
Bawack, Ransome Epie 681
Bick, Markus 532
Birkstedt, Teemu 609
Boateng, Richard 60
Bonhoure, Emilie 681
Bousdekis, Alexandros 120
Boyle, Daire 185

Cadden, Trevor 467
Cao, Guangming 467
Carter, Sarah E. 285
Champagnie, Samantha 94
Choenni, Sunil 292
Chowdhury, Tanay 233
Christonasis, Antonis M. 47
Coetzee, Carla 744

Dennehy, Denis 71, 454, 545, 656
Doran, Patrick 596
Dremel, Chirstian 208
du Plessis, Gustav 318
Dwivedi, Yogesh K. 495, 723

Effah, John 60
Elbanna, Amany 18, 29
Enholm, Ida Merete 208

Fosso-Wamba, Samuel 454

Gao, Shang 383
Gerber, Aurona 580
Giraud, Laurent 307
Gizelis, Christos A. 47
Gkinko, Lorentsa 18, 29
Gogan, Janis L. 94
Griva, Anastasia 545
Grobbelaar, Sara Saartjie 342
Guo, Hong 383
Gupta, Samrat 704

Hattingh, M. J. 567
Heinrich, Kai 245
Herm, Lukas-Valentin 245
Hernandez, Selena 307
Herrera, Lucia Castro 710
Hyrynsalmi, Sami 609

Ichino, Masatsugu 643
Intezari, Ali 109
Islam, A. K. M. Najmul 609
Ismagilova, Elvira 495

Jackson, Stephen 737
Jain, Gaurav 704
Janiesch, Christian 245

Kar, Arpan Kumar 132, 692
Karki, Yashoda 330
Kaur, Surleen 723
Kefalogiannis, Michalis 47
Kennedy, Rónán 198
Khan, Iqra Sadaf 622
Khan, Tayyeb Ahmed 763
Koniakou, Vasiliki 173
Kroeze, Jan H. 774
Krogstie, John 208
Kumar, Abhinav 670
Kumar, Gunjan 670
Kumi, Caleb Amankwaa 441, 481
Kushwaha, Amit Kumar 132

Laato, Samuli 609
Lang, Michael 757

Langley, David 656
Leo, J. 567
Lepenioti, Katerina 120
Li, Jingyue 383
Luzipo, Sikho 580

Majchrzak, Tim A. 710
Manisha 656
Mäntymäki, Matti 71, 220, 609
Marikyan, Davit 555
Marjanovic, Olivera 259
Martins, Jorge Tiago 411
Matope, Stephen 519
Matthee, Machdel 744
Mehra, Vishal 692
Mentzas, Gregoris 120
Merhi, Mohammad I. 40
Mikalef, Patrick 208
Minkkinen, Matti 220
Misargopoulos, Antonios 47
Murawski, Matthias 532
Mygland, Morten Johan 3

Nadeem, Ayesha 259
Namvar, Morteza 109
Netten, Niels 292
Niederman, Fred 161
Nikolopoulos-Gkamatsis, Filippos 47
Noonan, Jean 596

Onofrei, George 467
Oredo, John 233

Palaiogeorgou, Polyxeni 47
Panteli, Niki 737
Papagiannidis, Emmanouil 208
Papagiannidis, Savvas 555
Pappas, Ilias O. 3, 144
Petersen, Candice 506
Pharswan, Ruchika 132

Rana, Nripendra 495
Rana, Omer 555
Ranjan, Rajiv 555
Reidy, Caoimhe 656

Sam, Abraham Kuuku 342
Sarema, Blessed 519
Sarin, Pooja 692
Sawhney, Ravinder Singh 692, 723
Schibbye, Morten 3
Scomparin, Serena 532
Seymour, Lisa F. 506
Sharma, Sandeep 723
Sidaoui, Mouwafac 150
Singh, Jyoti Prakash 670
Singh, Prabhsimran 692, 723
Smite, Darja 383
Smuts, Hanlie 318, 356, 423
Smuts, Stefan 423
Smyth, Conn 454
Soondka, Abdul Qadir 356
Suijker, Arjen 292

Thapa, Devinder 144, 330, 710
Thummadi, Babu Veeresh 629
Tiwari, Amit Anand 704
Towey, Mark 656
Treacy, Raymond 467
Twinomurinzi, Hossana 271

van de Wetering, Rogier 82, 397
van der Merwe, Alta 423
van der Poll, Arthur E. 774
van Zyl, Izak 774
Vasconcelos, Ana Cristina 411
Vassilakopoulou, Polyxeni 3

Wang, Jing 371
Wanner, Jonas 245

Xivuri, Khensani 271

Yang, Ying 467
Yoshikawa, Kento 643
Yoshiura, Hiroshi 643

Zaher, Ali 307
Zamani, Efpraxia D. 371, 411
Zhao, Xin 763
Zhu, Yuzhen 411
Zimmer, Markus Philipp 220

ʻhe United States
ʼaylor Publisher Services